SECURITY ANALYSIS AND PORTFOLIO MANAGEMENT

AF819630

Shalini Talwar

K. J. Somaiya Institute of Management Studies and Research, Mumbai

CENGAGE Learning

Andover • Melbourne • Mexico City • Stamford, CT • Toronto • Hong Kong • New Delhi • Seoul • Singapore • Tokyo

CENGAGE
Learning

Security Analysis and Portfolio Management
Shalini Talwar
Cover Image: © Thinkstock

ISBN-13: 978-81-315-2449-7
ISBN-10: 81-315-2449-3

Cengage Learning India Private Limited
T-303, 3rd Floor
DAV Complex, Plot 3
Mayur Vihar Phase 1
Delhi-110091

Cengage Learning is a leading provider of customized learning solutions with office locations around the globe, including Andover, Melbourne, Mexico City, Stamford (CT), Toronto, Hong Kong, New Delhi, Seoul, Singapore, and Tokyo. Locate your local office at: **www.cengage.com/global**

Cengage Learning products are represented in Canada by Nelson Education, Ltd.

For product information, visit **www.cengage.co.in**

Printed by:
Rajiv Book Binding House
D-1518, DSIIDC Industrial Complex,
Narela, New Delhi 110040

Printed in India
Print Number: 08 Print Year: 2024

To my parents, my husband Manish,
my boys, Nachiket and Samarth and
my sister, Shailja Rathaur.

Contents

Preface

Security Analysis and Portfolio Management (SAPM) is a subject that has intrigued me since my student days. The fascination has grown over the years as I got an opportunity to build up on my repertoire of knowledge about SAPM and share it with my management students year after year for nearly two decades. The thrill of discussing market swings, analysing securities and trying to predict the future returns and volatility has not waned so far and is not likely to happen anywhere in near future.

Analysis of securities that are to be selected for making investment portfolio has been undertaken in some form or the other for more than 150 years. However, the approach that we see today is deeply rooted in the thoughts on investment postulated and published by luminaries like Markowitz, Sharpe, Lintner and Mossin, among others. In fact, our approach to modern investment, as we see it today, started evolving after Harry Markowitz, who I would not hesitate to call Father of Modern Investment, published his path breaking theory, "Modern Portfolio Theory" in early nineteen fifties with its undeniable logic of relevance of interactive risk among securities and the visual appeal of efficient frontier. Rest, as they say, is history.

We have witnessed exciting times in financial markets during past three decades. The swings have been spectacular with unprecedented creation as well as erosion of market capitalization, particularly in the equities market. In addition to market swings, another notable feature is the rising awareness about financial markets at the retail and grassroots levels. This growing interest in equity markets in our country has motivated me to make an attempt at writing on a subject that is an integral part of my thinking. This is my first attempt at writing a book on SAPM and I hope I have been able to present the body of knowledge on the subject in such a way that all readers, beginners as well as experienced analysts, will find some meaningful takeaway in it. The book has definitely been written keeping in mind a wide range of audience, spanning students of finance, market participants, professionals and investment advisors.

I have consciously not divided the book into parts and have tried to follow a sequence that helps build up the knowledge and information in a contextual manner. The focus of all cases, problems and text is the Indian financial market.

Chapters 1 and 2 are introductory chapters, intending to help the readers understand the various parameters and dimensions of investment. Chapter 2 discusses Indian equity and debt markets in the context of regulatory developments, operational procedures and performance measures. The emphasis is less on theoretical underpinnings and more on the evolving dynamics and key segments and instruments.

Chapter 3 is one of the key chapters of the book and it provides an extensive and in-depth coverage of risk and return analysis in terms of investments, particularly in equity. Considering the need and importance of sound investment approach, risk-return analysis and computation has been discussed comprehensively so that learners are not deprived of details just for the sake of brevity or simplicity or both.

The next three chapters, Chapters 4, 5 and 6, discuss the landmark theories and asset pricing models. Modern portfolio theory, single index model, capital market theory, capital asset pricing model and multi-factor models like arbitrage pricing theory and Fama-French model have been discussed extensively in these chapters. For all three chapters, I have tried to sequence the topics so that the understanding of the length and the breadth of the theories is built up gradually and clutter is avoided.

Asset allocation is a key part of investment decision and the same has been described in Chapter 7 from a practical perspective.

Portfolio performance measures such as M^2, Sortino's ratio and Fama's net selectivity have also been discussed in Chapter 8, in addition to the more common measures of portfolio performance like Sharpe ratio, Treynor ratio, Information ratio and Jensen's alpha. In a way, discussion on portfolio management comes to an end with Chapter 8.

Chapter 9 onward the focus shifts to security analysis. Equity valuation, fundamental analysis, technical analysis, introduction to behavioral finance and efficient market hypothesis have been discoursed in detail in Chapters 9 through 14. Here my effort has been to make details less dreary and more market-oriented.

Chapters 15 and 16 are oriented completely toward debt-related instruments, debt markets and valuation of debt securities. In Chapter 17, an introductory discussion on mutual funds as an alternative investment avenue has been presented. Chapters 18 and 19 elucidate the key features of two derivatives instruments, futures and options, and also expound the operations of derivatives markets in India.

The book ends with Chapter 20, which gives an overview of the issues and advantages associated with international investments.

There are some principles that I have tried to adhere to while writing this book. These principles are comprehensive coverage, use of real-world examples related to Indian markets, application of spread sheets as a way of learning and less emphasis on theoretical discussion.

Shalini Talwar

Acknowledgements

This book is a culmination of my experiences and learning over the past two decades. There are a number of people who have helped me in formulating my ideas and committing them to paper in the form of this textbook on *Security Analysis and Portfolio Management*.

I express my deep gratitude to Dr. Harsh Dwivedi, Professor, R.A. Podar Institute of Management, Faculty of Management Studies, University of Rajasthan, Jaipur and Dr. G.S. Batra, Professor and Head at the School of Management Studies, Punjabi University, Patiala for mentoring me in my professional life.

I would also like to put on record my sincere appreciation for all my management students in Jaipur and Mumbai for their curiosity and persistence to learn which motivated me to read more and share more.

Writing a book as sole author is a tremendous task and I am thankful to Mr. Vispi Rusi Bhathena, CEO, BSE Broker's Forum, Mumbai, Dr. V. Aditya Srinivas, COO & Chief Economist, BSE Broker's Forum, Mumbai, Aparna Bhat, Assistant Professor, Department of Finance, K.J. Somaiya Institute of Management Studies and Research, Mumbai and Nupur Gupta-Bhattacharya, Assistant Professor, Department of Finance, K.J. Somaiya Institute of Management Studies and Research, Mumbai for contributing some chapters/sections for the book.

Last but not the least, I would like to express my admiration for the editorial team at Cengage Learning for their patience, professionalism and commitment.

Shalini Talwar

Key Features

- Optimal mix of theoretical concepts and practical applications.

Capital Asset Pricing Model

Usually referred to as CAPM, this model occupies a central place in Financial Economics. It has played a pivotal role in the advances in quantitative investment management since its introduction in 1960s. The capital asset pricing model is a set of predictions that are related to the equilibrium expected returns on risky assets. It explains why assets are priced the way they are.

The capital asset pricing model states that the expected risk premium on each investment is proportional to its beta. This means that each investment should lie on the sloping security market line connecting Treasury bills and the market portfolio.

The model gives a precise quantification of the relationship that is observable between required or expected return and risk of any asset. Such a quantification of fair value provides benchmark rate for evaluation of investment alternatives by comparing the expected return forecast by us with the fair value as given by CAPM. A comparison of estimated return with the return computed using CAPM helps to determine whether the asset is under-valued, over-valued or fairly priced in the market.

Figure 6.11 How CAPM is used?

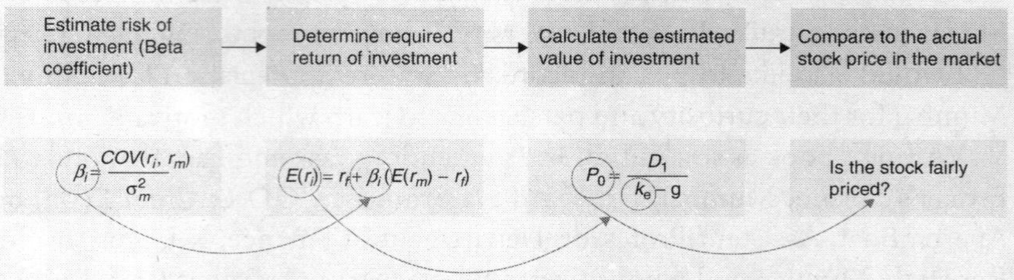

- Emphasis on Indian markets and Indian examples.

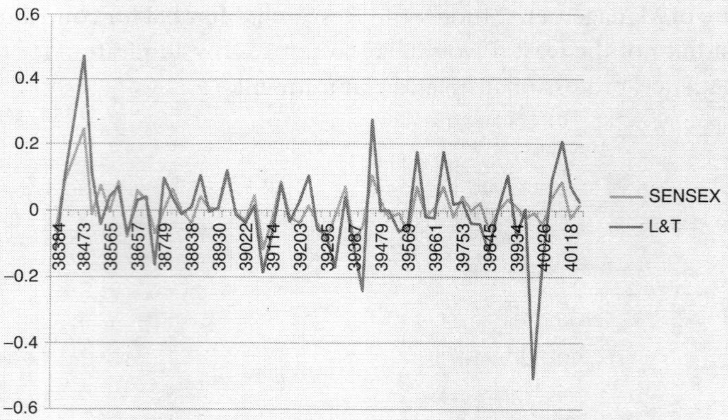

- Illustrative numerical examples within text.

Numerical Example 8

Penwood, an Indian home appliance firm, paid dividend of ₹0.75 per share on earnings per share of ₹1.25 in 2010. The payout ratio is expected to remain unchanged. The growth rate of earnings per share has been 12% over the past 5 years but it is expected to decline linearly over the next 10 years to 5%. The beta for the stock is 0.9, the market risk premium is 6% and the risk-free rate is 5%. Calculate the current value of equity using the H-model.

Solution:

The value of firm's share can be calculated using H-model.

- Extensive spreadsheet applications illustrated lucidly. Emphasis has been laid on portfolio construction through the use of MS Excel applications and Solver.

Spreadsheet Application 2 *Constructing Minimum Variance Portfolio using Solver in MS Excel.*

Use following information to generate a minimum variance portfolio:

1. **Risk and Return of Securities:**

	A	B	C
1			
2	Scrips	Std Deviation	Expected Return
3	BHEL	0.809	-0.409
4	CIPLA	0.233	0.150
5	DR REDDYS LABS	0.255	0.351
6	HERO MOTOCORP	0.287	0.175
7	HUL	0.236	0.159
8	INFOSYS	0.293	0.200

- End of the chapter practice numericals, situation analysis caselets and concept questions.

CASE STUDY

The sectoral report of Indian automobile industry available at http://www.ibef.org/ is given below. The industry as a whole seems to be doing very well. Analyze the industry using porter's model.

The Indian automobile sector is one of India's most vibrant industries. The industry accounts for 22% of the country's manufacturing gross domestic product (GDP). It comprises passenger cars, two-wheelers, three-wheelers and commercial vehicles and is currently the seventh-largest in the world with an average annual production of 17.5 million vehicles, of which 2.3 million are exported. The Indian auto market has the potential to dominate the global auto industry, provided a conducive environment is created for potential innovators to come up with new pilot projects.

- Text boxes titled **Marketview** to share the information on latest developments.

Marketview 11.1 Corporate Governance Issues at Maruti Suzuki

Suzuki Motor Corporation (SMC) had come up with a proposal to set up a wholly owned subsidiary in India that seemed to adversely affect the interests of the minority shareholders of its existing partly owned subsidiary, Maruti Suzuki India Ltd. Markets and all classes of investors reacted quite adversely to the proposal, causing SMC to water it down and seek the consent of the minority shareholders of Maruti in accordance with the provisions of Section 188 of the new Companies Act. It also issued several clarifications regarding the funding and transfer of the plant to Maruti.

This entire drama at SMC has raised certain corporate governance issues for the company, namely:

- Text boxes titled **Beyond the Basics** to share advanced applications with the readers without breaking the continuity of the text.

Beyond the Basics 9.2 Residual Income Method for Equity Valuation

As discussed above, a company can be valued using different methods. An analyst can choose to use relative valuation approach and compare multiples of a firm with other firms within its industry or he can opt to use an absolute valuation model such as dividend discount method to calculate the intrinsic value of the firm. Apart from DDM and other DCF variants, there is one more method of absolute valuation that is very popular amongst analysts, though not commonly known. This method is called the residual income method of equity valuation.

1 Introduction: Dimensions and Attributes of Investments

CHAPTER OBJECTIVES

- ❒ Understanding the concept of savings and investment
- ❒ Distinguishing between investments, speculation and gambling
- ❒ Describing key investment avenues
- ❒ Discussing the process of portfolio management in detail

The concept of savings is as old as mankind. Since times immemorial, human beings have had the tendency to put a part of their current income aside for some future purpose. The current income of a person is broadly divided into two parts, current consumption and deferred consumption. Savings from the current income can be treated as income put away for future consumption. Thus savings entail a sacrifice of present consumption to provide for some future need. These savings are invested through the financial system to earn returns. Investment of savings wisely is the key to economic well-being in the long run. Therefore, the decision of when to invest and where to invest should be taken after a lot of deliberation and careful consideration.

There are a number of instruments available for investment of savings such as bank deposits, bonds, stocks, mutual funds, real assets and so on. Each instrument differs from the other in some way or the other. The investors in any economy need to understand the characteristics of each instrument to ascertain which one would best suit their needs. Each investment avenue or instrument has its own risk and return. Further, the investors also need to understand the fact that they should invest in more than one instrument. This means that they should spread their savings across a variety of investment instruments that have different risk-return characteristics. In investment management, such a collection of securities is called a portfolio.

This book discusses various aspects of investments in detail. The main concepts discussed in this book include the concept of risk and return in investment, security analysis, portfolio construction and management techniques, portfolio performance measurement and portfolio revision.

Investment

Savings or deferred consumption become investment only when they enter the financial system. Thus savings and investments are two different concepts. An investment is a sacrifice of current consumption to generate future benefits. Investment can be best described as deployment of funds in various instruments to earn returns.

TABLE 1.1 Gross domestic savings and investment in India

S.No.	Item	(Amount in ₹crore)				(Percent of GDP at market prices)			
		2009–10	2010–11 (3rd RE)	2011–12 (2nd RE)	2012–13 (1st RE)	2009–10	2010–11 (3rd RE)	2011–12 (2nd RE)	2012–13 (1st RE)
	1	2	3	4	5	6	7	8	9
1	Household saving of which:	16,30,799	18,00,174	20,54,737	22,12,414	25.2	23.1	22.8	21.9
	(a) Financial assets	7,74,753	7,73,859	6,32,196	7,17,131	12.0	9.9	7.0	7.1
	(b) Physical assets	8,56,046	10,26,315	14,22,541	14,95,283	13.2	13.2	15.8	14.8
2	Private corporate saving	5,40,955	6,20,300	6,58,428	7,13,141	8.4	8.0	7.3	7.1
3	Public sector saving	10,585	2,01,268	1,11,295	1,17,919	0.2	2.6	1.2	1.2
4	Gross domestic saving	21,82,338	26,21,742	28,24,459	30,43,474	33.7	33.7	31.3	30.1
5	Net capital inflow	1,80,794	2,19,715	3,76,174	4,77,925	2.8	2.8	4.2	4.7
6	Gross domestic capital formation	23,63,132	28,41,457	32,00,633	35,21,399	36.5	36.5	35.5	34.8
7	Total consumption expenditure $(a + b)$	44,78,717	52,50,459	61,67,791	69,61,191	69.1	67.5	68.5	68.8
	(a) Private final consumption expenditure	37,07,566	43,60,323	51,41,896	57,72,059	57.2	56.0	57.1	57.1
	(b) Goverment final consumption expenditure	7,71,151	8,90,136	10,25,895	11,89,132	11.9	11.4	11.4	11.8
Memo items									
Saving-investment balance (4–6)		−1,80,794	−2,19,715	−3,76,174	−4,77,925	−2.8	−2.8	−4.2	−4.7
Public sector balance#		−5,82,203	−4,55,180	−5,84,540	−7,04,043	−9.0	−5.8	−6.5	−7.0
Private sector balance#		5,29,599	3,96,343	−3,77,342	5,04,791	8.2	5.1	4.2	5.0
(a) Private corporate sector		−2,45,154	−3,77,516	−2,54,854	−2,12,340	−3.8	−4.8	−2.8	−2.1
(b) Household sector		7,74,753	7,73,859	6,32,196	7,17,131	12.0	9.9	7.0	7.1

RE: Revised Estimate

Investment figures are not adjusted for errors and omissions.

Source: Central Statistical Office, accessed on December 17, 2014.

The returns may be in the form of current income and or capital appreciation. Table 1.1 exhibits gross domestic savings and investment in India.

There are a few general characteristics of investments. Investments imply parting with funds, waiting for the returns to come and facing the fear that the returns might not be as anticipated. In the language of finance, these characteristics of investment can be summed up in two dimensions: time and risk. The sacrifice of funds takes place immediately in the present. The benefit or the return is expected in the future and is uncertain for most investments. There are few instruments like government securities in which the returns are certain and it is only the time element that is taken into consideration. In other investments like stocks and bonds, the uncertainty of return or risk as well as time are dominant considerations.

Investments can be discussed further from two points of view: financial investments and economic investments. In the financial sense, investment implies deploying funds in investment avenues to generate income in the form of interest, dividend, bonus, retirement benefits or appreciation in the value of the original investment. Instruments like shares, bonds, insurance policies, bank deposits, etc. are the avenues for financial investments. Financial investments generate financial assets.

Investments in economic sense imply net additions to the economy's capital stocks as represented by goods and services used in the production of other goods and services. Economic investment is an investment for the formation of new and productive capital in the form of new plant, machinery, inventories and other facilities and inputs required for the production of goods and services.

To summarize, investment in financial sense leads to the creation of financial assets and the investment in economic sense leads to the creation of physical or real assets. The types of investment are inter-related and inter-dependent. The money invested in financial assets flows in the form of capital to the physical assets. Some part of income generated by using physical assets flows as savings into financial assets and the cycle continues. The bottom line is that all investments result in creation of assets, either financial or real.

Investment, Speculation and Gambling

Two terms, speculation and gambling often come up in the discussion about investments.

Speculation may be described as a short-term investment undertaken with the sole purpose of generating high returns. Speculative investments are inherently risky.

An investment differs from speculation in the sense that it is a decision based on analysis and careful consideration. Further, it offers safety of the original amount and some reasonable returns.

The differences between investment and speculation may be listed as follows:

1. **Time Period:** Investment is usually long-term in nature and speculation is short-term. The planning horizon or the holding period of an investor is relatively longer (usually at least one year). An investor is willing to commit his funds for a longer period and wait for returns whereas the speculator is interested in quick gains from short-term trades. A typical speculator's holding period varies from a few days to a few months.
2. **Risk Characteristics:** Risk refers to the possibility that the return from an investment may not be as expected. An investor is usually unwilling to assume more than a moderate level of risk. Conversely, a speculator is usually ready to assume significantly high level of risk.
3. **Return Requirements:** An investor is usually ready to settle for a modest rate of return that is commensurate with the amount of risk he is ready to accept. In other words, investor trades-off higher return, as he is comfortable with a lower level of risk. On the other hand, a speculator is inherently chasing higher returns to compensate the high level of risk borne by him.

4. **Capital Appreciation:** An investor purchases a security or an asset with a view to earning a current income and/or capital appreciation in the value of the investment. On the other hand, a speculator's sole motive is to benefit from price changes in near-term. He is not interested in current income, rather he benefits from appreciation in the price of the asset.
5. **Basis of Investment Decision:** An investor typically uses formal tools of investment analysis to evaluate broad fundamental factors and the prospects of the firm in which he is investing his money. Conversely, a speculator relies more on rumors, chart patterns, price trends and market sentiments to buy an asset.
6. **Investible Funds:** An investor primarily searches investment avenues for his own money that he has saved by deferring current consumption. Usually, he does not borrow money from other sources to make investments. However, a speculator is in the market with the sole aim of making profit from some opportunity that has come up in the market and he is willing to borrow funds from other sources to invest and earn more returns.

Though there are differences between investment and speculation, ultimately both involve parting with money to generate returns.

Coming to gambling, it is fundamentally different from both speculation and investment. Gambling usually involves putting money in horse races, casinos, lotteries, card games, etc. It is undertaken not only for returns but for thrill and excitement as well. The outcome of gambling is known immediately. It is completely unplanned, artificial and involves taking unnecessary risks that cannot even be truly assessed. Gambling involves taking unduly high risk without having any basis for commensurate economic returns. The fact is that there is no comparison between gambling and investment because one is undertaken for thrill and fun whereas the other is a completely planned and evaluated economic activity.

Features of Investment

All investments have certain characteristic features. These features form the basis of investment decisions. We are going to refer to these features in many chapters of this book so we should begin with developing a preliminary understanding. As mentioned above, all investments have two key features: risk and return. So we will first discuss these two and then take up two more features of investments viz., safety and liquidity. Key features of investment are illustrated in Figure 1.1.

Risk

Risk implies uncertainty in outcome and it is an inherent part of any investment. The term risk in the context of investment relates to uncertainty about the current income as well as capital appreciation. Risk of investment includes the probability of non-payment of current dues, non-payment of capital, delay in repayment of capital, depreciation in the value of capital and variability of returns. Different investment avenues have different risks associated with them. The risk of any investment instrument depends on its nature, however there are a few general observations about risk that hold true for almost all types of assets. These are:

1. The longer the holding or maturity period, the greater is the risk of investment.
2. The lower the credibility or the credit worthiness of the borrower of funds (issuer of security), the larger is the risk. In this context, the instruments issued by the government are considered to have low or no risk.

Figure 1.1 Features of investment.

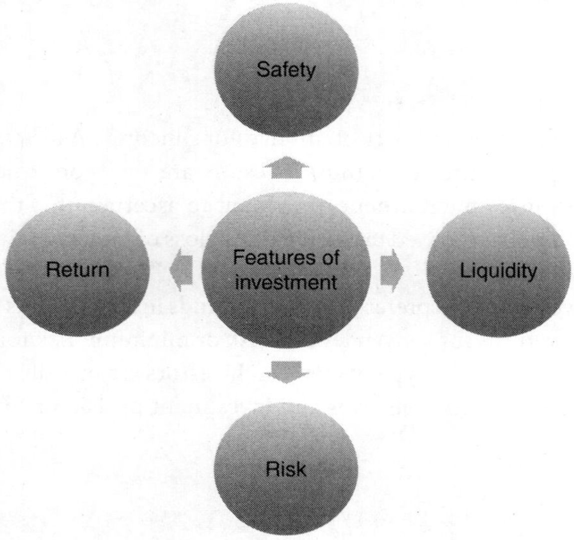

3. Instruments involving ownership like equity shares are more risky as compared to debt instruments.
4. There is also a trade-off between risk and return. High level of risk is invariably accompanied by expectation of higher level of returns.

Returns

Returns are the primary motive behind investments. All investments are made in expectation of earning a reward or return. When investors invest money in any asset, they make a sacrifice by postponing present consumption and they want to be duly rewarded for their sacrifice. The amount of return that is expected from holding an investment asset depends on the level of risk taken, the issuer of the asset, the nature of the investment, the holding or maturity period and a number of other factors. Irrespective of the amount or level of returns expected from holding an asset, most returns comprise of two parts: current income which can be in the form of interest, dividend, etc. and capital appreciation which comes from the difference between the price at which the asset is sold and the price at which it was purchased at the beginning of the holding period. Investment avenues are classified into different types on the basis of different rates of return they are expected to generate.

Liquidity

Another feature of investments that is important to the investors is the speed at which they can be converted into cash, i.e., how liquid they are. Investments that can be sold easily without loss of money and time are said to be liquidity instruments. Liquid instruments are easily marketable. Some investments like deposits with banks, post offices and companies are not marketable. These are deemed to be illiquid instruments. Further, there are some instruments like debentures that are listed and therefore marketable in theory but difficult to sell in practice because there are no buyers in many cases. The liquidity of such instruments is negligible. Equity shares issued by listed companies are considered to be the most liquid instruments as they are easily marketable through the stock exchanges they are listed on.

Safety

Investment is made out of the unconsumed part of an investor's income. As explained above, it represents a sacrifice of the current consumption. Therefore, most investors are very concerned about the safety of their investment. While choosing any investment avenue, they want to ascertain that their principal amount or the original corpus will remain safe and be returned to them without loss of money or time on maturity or at the end of the holding period, as the case may be.

To sum it up, any rational investor would prefer to invest his funds in instruments that are liquid, ensure safety of principal and give maximum returns for a given level of risk or minimum risk for a given level of return. The four parameters also vary depending on the type of investor. Investors are broadly classified into individual and institutional investors. They differ in their objectives and investment decision making as discussed in Beyond the Basics 1.1.

Beyond the Basics 1.1 The Difference between Individual and Institutional Investors

Individual and institutional investors differ from each other in their investment objectives and attributes. Many investment advisors and entities like banks and investment consultants commit the mistake of treating the two diverse kinds of investors in the same manner. Obviously, they fail to satisfy their clients. It is important for such entities to understand the difference between the characteristics of a typical individual and institutional investor. Six notable differences between the two categories may be mentioned as:

1. Most individual investors are likely to discontinue adding more funds to the portfolio after some time.
2. Investment decisions of individual investors are affected by their tax liabilities, as they typically do not have tax-exempt status that some institutional investors have.
3 A typical individual investor gives more importance to the advisory relationship and service rather than the product. However, in case of most institutional investors, it is the product that is important.
4. Most individual investors prefer to take their own investment decisions except in case of major events like sale of business. They are more likely to turn to brokers for investment ideas and not hire professional advisors or consultants.
5. Due to their low bargaining power and 'bundling' of fees, individual investors end up paying more for the same investment services as compared to institutional investors of comparable size.
6. Most individual investors are not encumbered with regulatory oversight and the pressure of following 'prudent practices' that may affect their investment decision-making. Institutional investors have to keep in mind many regulatory provisions while taking investment decisions.

Source: Based on inputs from http://jimlorenzen.wordpress.com/, accessed on November 21, 2014.

Investment Avenues

Investment avenues refer to the alternative instruments in which their savings can be deployed by the investors. The choice of instruments available for investment is very large and all differ from one another in some way or the other. The broadest distinction that can be made between the investment avenues is by classifying them into two groups viz., financial assets and real assets.

Financial assets or instruments represent the claims on the issuer recorded in paper or electronic form. The main financial assets or instruments are equity shares, corporate bonds, government securities, bank fixed deposits, insurance policies, mutual fund units and derivative instruments.

Real assets represent the tangible or the fixed assets like residential, agricultural and commercial properties, art objects, precious metals like gold and silver and precious stones.

The investment avenues can be broadly categorized under the following heads:

1. Corporate securities
2. Deposits
3. Mutual fund schemes
4. Derivative securities
5. Insurance products
6. Retirement products
7. Government securities
8. Money market instruments
9. Real estate
10. Art objects
11. Precious metals and stones
12. Commodities

Key investment avenues are exhibited in Figure 1.2.

Figure 1.2 Key financial and real assets.

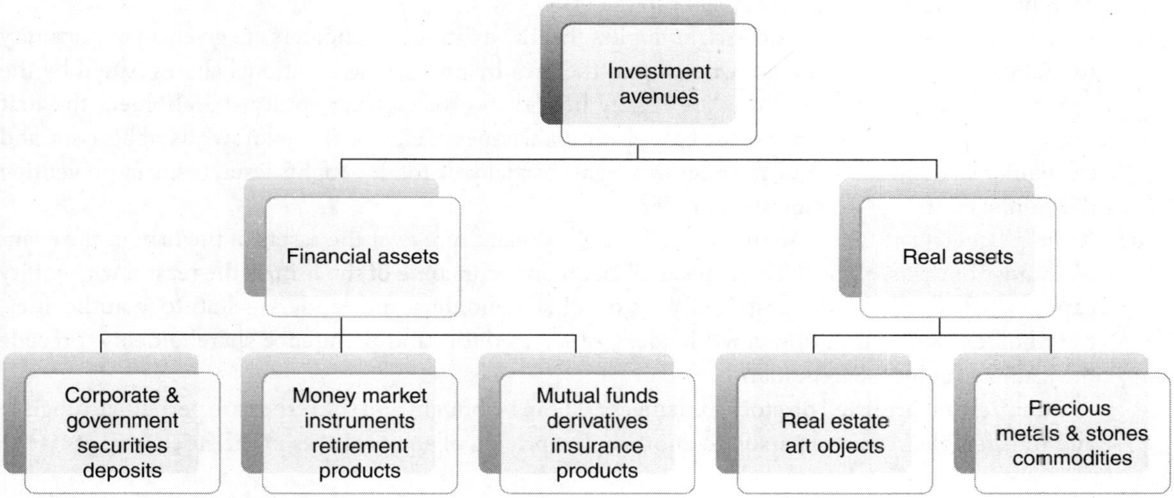

To invest wisely, the investors need to understand all the investment avenues at their disposal. Let us understand the key features of some of the important investment avenues mentioned above.

Corporate Securities

Corporate securities is an umbrella term used to refer to the securities issued by joint stock companies in the private sector. These securities include equity shares or common stock, preference shares or preferred stock and debentures. Shares and bonds are the key instruments on which most of our discussion throughout the book will be focused. The key features of these instruments are discussed below:

1. **Equity Shares:** Equity shares represent ownership capital of a firm as the equity shareholders are collectively the owners of the company whose equity shares they hold. They enjoy the rewards of ownership and bear the risks associated with it. Equity shares do not have fixed dividend and hence belong to the high risk–high return category of instruments. The liability of each equity share is limited to its capital contribution. The rights enjoyed by the equity shareholders are:
   (a) *Right to income (dividend)*: Equity shareholders are entitled to receive a return for their contribution to capital. They have a residual claim on the net profit of the firm. The term residual income represents the part of profits left after satisfying the claims of all other classes of investors. This income is simply equal to net profit or profit after tax (PAT) minus the preference dividend, if any.

   It should be noted here that equity shareholders are entitled to receive the dividend as declared by the board of directors at its discretion. The board of directors is not legally bound to declare dividends. The dividend decision is their right and they may choose to retain whole or a part of the income of equity shareholders.

   (b) *Right to control:* As the owners of the firm, equity shareholders have the right to vote on all resolutions tabled before the company. They also have the right to elect the board of directors and they, in turn, select the management that controls the working of the firm. This implies that equity shareholders exercise control over the operations of the firm indirectly. However, this is only theoretically correct. In practice, the shareholders are unorganized and unable to exercise any effective indirect control over the firm's operations. Most shareholders never attend any meeting or cast their votes. Usually, the management of the firm is able to hold the control of the company with the help of a small number of shareholders representing the key stake in the firm.

   (c) *Pre-emptive right:* The pre-emptive right implies that the existing shareholders are given an opportunity to maintain their proportional ownership in the firm by purchasing additional shares issued by the firm to raise more capital. Firms are legally bound to give existing equity shareholders the first opportunity to purchase, on pro rata basis, additional issues of equity. This is known as rights issue and the equity shareholders can surrender this right, partially or totally. Rights issue helps in preventing dilution of control of existing shareholders.

   (d) *Right in liquidation:* Equity shareholders have a residual claim over the assets of the firm in the event of liquidation. This, along with the residual claim on the income of the firm, is the reason why equity capital is also called risk capital. Claims of all stakeholders and lenders—statutory authorities, bondholders, secured & unsecured lenders, other creditors and preference shareholders—precede the claims of equity shareholders.

   Equity shares are listed on stock exchanges and can be bought and sold. They are perpetual, fungible and transferable from one person to another. The pricing of equity shares in the stock markets is the key concern of investment management and we will discuss all the aspects related to investment in equity in detail in the subsequent chapters of the book. Exhibit 1.1 represents the amount of funds raised in India through new issue of equity since 2003.

Exhibit 1.1 Amount of Funds Raised in India Through New Issue of Equity since 2003

Year	No. of issues	Amount raised (₹ crore)
2003	12	1,699.80
2004	25	13,121.47
2005	53	9,989.52
2006	73	19,852.46
2007	100	34,179.11
2008	37	16,904.42
2009	20	19,544.00
2010	64	37,534.65
2011	37	5,966.28
2012	25	6,937.93
2013*	35	1,601.75

*Till November 2013

Source: Prime database, accessed on November 17, 2014.

2. **Preference Shares:** Preference capital represents a hybrid form of financing—it takes some characteristics of equity capital and some of debentures. It resembles equity in the following ways: (i) Dividend is payable on preference shares (ii) Dividend is payable only out of distributable profits (net profit after tax); and (iii) preference dividend is paid out of post-tax income and like equity dividend it is not a tax-deductible payment.

Preference capital resembles debt capital in following ways: (i) Like debentures have a specified rate of interest, similarly, the dividend rate of preference capital is usually fixed; (ii) like debenture holders, the claim of preference shareholders gets a priority over the claim of equity shareholders; and (iii) preference shareholders do not enjoy the right to vote in normal circumstances. However, there is a provision of granting voting rights to preference shareholders under certain circumstances, if preference dividend is skipped by the company.

Preference shares in India usually carry a cumulative feature with respect to dividends. This implies that unpaid dividends of any year are carried forward and are payable in future. Further, a company that has preference capital cannot declare equity dividends unless preference dividends are paid with arrears, if any. Unlike equity shares that are perpetual in existence, preference shares have a fixed maturity and are usually redeemable after three to fifteen years. Owing to fixed rate of dividend and precedence over equity in case of residual claims on income, preference capital is considered to be less risky than equity capital. Preference shares have not been very popular among Indian companies but a surge in the issuance of preference shares has been observed in the recent times with many companies opting to use preference shares in their efforts to undertake debt restructuring. Exhibit 1.2 displays the amount of preference capital raised in India between 2007–2012.

Exhibit 1.2 Amount of Preference Capital Raised in India between 2007–2012

	No of isues	Size (₹ crore)
2012	17	1,409
2011	39	8,438
2010	26	2,830
2009	25	3,304
2008	9	464
2007	12	2,033

Source: ETIG & CAPITALINE Database, accessed on December 31, 2014.

3. **Debentures:** Debentures are financial instruments for raising long-term debt capital. Debenture holders are the creditors of the company and the company is liable to pay them interest and repay the capital at specified intervals of time. Interest payment on debenture is a legal obligation of the firm, unlike payment of dividends on equity shares. Interest paid on debentures is a tax-deductible expense. Debentures may carry a fixed, floating or zero rate of interest.

   They have to be redeemed as per the terms of the issue, whereas equity share capital is perpetual, it need not be redeemed. Debenture holders are not entitled to vote, however debentures provide more flexibility than term loans. Debentures offer many choices to issuers with respect to maturity, interest rate, security, repayment and special features. Debentures may carry a 'call' feature that provides the issuing company the option to redeem it at a pre-specified price before the maturity period. Debentures may also carry a 'put' feature which gives the holder the right to redeem the debenture at specified times at predetermined prices.

   Debentures are usually secured by a charge on the immovable properties of the company. The interests of the debenture holders are represented by a trustee, which is usually an insurance company, a bank or a firm of attorneys. The trustee is responsible for ensuring that the issuing company fulfills all its contractual obligations towards the debenture holders.

   On the basis of convertibility, debentures can be classified into:

   (a) *Non convertible debentures (NCDs):* These debentures cannot be converted into equity shares and will be redeemed at the end of the maturity period.

   (b) *Fully convertible debentures (FCDs):* These debentures will be converted into equity shares after a specified period of time at one stroke or in installments. These debentures may or may not carry interest till the date of conversion.

   (c) *Partly convertible debentures (PCDs):* These are debentures, a portion of which will be converted into equity share capital after a specified period, whereas the non-convertible (NCD) portion of the PCD will be redeemed as per the terms of the issue after the maturity period.

Deposits

A large portion of the savings in India is invested in deposit schemes of banks, post office and companies. The deposits with bank are either in the form of saving accounts or fixed deposits (FDs). Saving deposits can be withdrawn without penalty at any point in time and have low interest rates. Fixed deposits have pre-specified maturities of varying durations and are usually held till the maturity date because premature withdrawal attracts penalties. Fixed deposits carry higher interest rates as compared to saving accounts. Interest is payable quarterly, half-yearly or annually. FDs may also be recurring deposits wherein a fixed amount is invested at regular intervals. Many FDs have the option of reinvestment of interest as it gets accrued. In such a case, both the principal and accumulated interest are paid on maturity.

In addition to banks, post offices in India also have many saving accounts, time deposits and monthly income schemes. Bank and post office deposit schemes are considered to be very safe and offer lower rates of interest as compared to the company deposit schemes of joint stock companies that also accept fixed deposits from the public. The maturity period of company fixed deposits varies from three to five years.

In addition to deposits, the Government of India also offers many small savings scheme to individual investors through select banks and post offices. These schemes include public provident fund schemes (PPF), National Saving Certificate Scheme, etc.

Mutual Fund Schemes

Mutual funds are collective investment schemes that invest in debt, equity or a mix of the two. The first mutual fund of India was offered for investment by UTI. Thereafter a number of private sector mutual funds have come up in India and as a result, the mutual funds market in India has become quite large in the past few years. Mutual funds have been discussed in detail in Chapter 17 of this book.

Derivative Securities

Financial derivatives are securities that take their value from underlying assets. Derivatives are innovative instruments that have become very popular in the recent years. They are mainly used to hedge risk of investing in financial assets. There are four main types of financial derivatives viz., options, futures, swaps and forwards. Derivatives have been discussed in detail in Chapters 18 and 19 of this book.

Insurance Products

Insurance products available in India have been designed to meet both the protection and savings need of the investors. The Indian insurance market has come a long way from the days of government owned Life Insurance Corporation Ltd. The number and variety of policy options available in India vary from term assurance plans, investment-oriented plans, tax saving plans, money back plans to unit linked insurance plans. The presence of private players in insurance sector has increased since economic liberalization and many foreign companies have also entered the sector through joint ventures.

Retirement Products

Retirement related saving products have received a lot of attention of regulators in India. The retirement-related investment products available in India are broadly divided into two types: mandatory retirement schemes like

Employees Provident Fund (EPF) Scheme, 1952, Employees Pension Scheme (EPS), 1995 and New Pension Scheme and voluntary retirement schemes that include pension plans offered by insurance companies and mutual funds.

Government Securities

The Government of India, state governments and semi-government bodies like the public sector undertakings issue debt related securities viz., government securities and public sector bonds to borrow money from the investing public. The government securities are also called gilt-edged securities since they are very safe avenues of investment because of the credibility of the issuing government.

Money Market Instruments

Debt instruments that have short-term maturity (less than one year) are called money market instruments. These instruments offer high liquidity and very low risk. The money market in India is dominated by institutional participants like banks, government, financial institutions and corporates. The key instruments traded in the money market are treasury bills, certificates of deposit, commercial papers, repos and reverse repos and collateralized borrowing and lending obligations (CBLOs).

Real Assets

Real estate, art objects, precious metals and stones and commodities constitute real assets. Traditionally, Indians have always been fond of investing in gold and real estate. In the recent years, investment in art objects has also increased. Paintings by Indian artists have been sold recently for crore of rupees per painting.

The commodities market in India is still in nascent stage. Both forward and spot commodities markets had started to take-off in India with the setting up of MCX, NCDEX, etc. but the NSEL scam that surfaced in July–August 2013, has dealt with a severe blow to the growth of commodities market in India.

The Process of Investment

Investors want to invest their savings in stocks and bonds to earn good returns. But investing in these instruments is not a simple or easy task. It is well-known that investing in financial securities is very rewarding but it can prove to be very risky as well. There are a large number of stocks and bonds available. A lot of skill and knowledge is required to select the right assets that would not expose the investors to undue risks.

The investors endeavor to reduce the risk of investment in stocks and bonds not only by choosing the correct assets but also by spreading their investible funds across a number of investments, i.e., by creating a collection of assets. This collection of assets is called portfolio.

The process of investment is actually the process of portfolio management that comprises two broad phases namely, framing of investment policy and strategy and implementation and review of investment decision. These two phases are further divided into four sub-phases each.

The first phase, framing of investment policy and strategy, comprises four sub-phases namely:

1. Specification of objectives and constraints of investment

2. Quantification of capital market expectations
3. Asset allocation
4. Formulation of bond and equity portfolio management strategies

The second phase, implementation and review of investment decision, comprises four sub-phases namely:

1. Choice of securities
2. Execution of portfolio decision
3. Portfolio revision and rebalancing
4. Portfolio performance management

The entire process of portfolio management along with its phases and sub-phases is illustrated in Figure 1.3.

Figure 1.3 Phases of portfolio management.

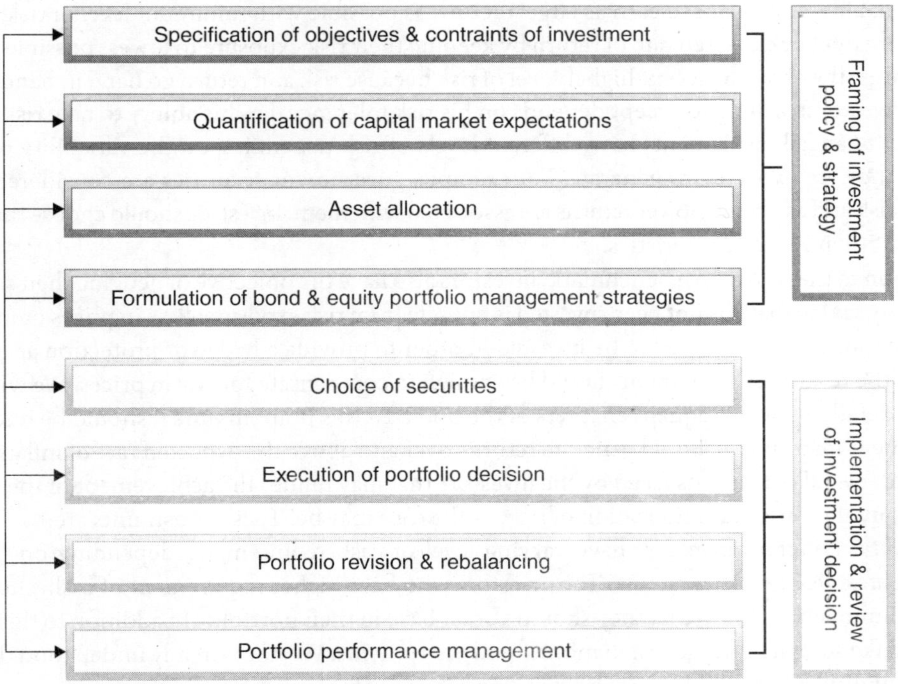

The process of portfolio management or investment management is very complex and the phases that constitute it are interrelated and dynamic. However, we will discuss them in a sequential order for the ease of understanding.

Let us discuss all the phases of portfolio management now.

Framing of Investment Policy and Strategy

In the first step towards portfolio management, the investment policy and the strategy for management of the portfolio need to be formulated. As mentioned above, this phase comprises of four sub-phases.

1. **Specification of Objectives and Constraints of Investment:** The investors need to begin with specification of their objectives in investment, the constraints they face and their preferences.

   A typical investor would have one or more of the following investment objectives:

   (a) *Income:* Investors part with their money in the hope of generating a steady stream of income for the duration of the investment. This income can be in the form of dividend or interest.

   (b) *Growth:* In addition to a steady stream of income, investors may also hope to benefit from the appreciation in the value of security.

   (c) *Stability:* In addition to growth and income, the investors want to protect their principal amount or the funds invested from depreciation and/or complete loss.

   The above stated objectives of investors represent the risk and return aspects of investment. Therefore, from the perspective of investment management or portfolio management, it can be said that the objective of investment is the maximization of returns for a given level of risk or minimization of risk for a given level of return.

   All rational investors want to earn as large a return as possible with minimum level of risk. Investors try to earn their target or expected rate of return by keeping their risk exposure to lowest possible level. To earn higher returns, they have to accept higher level of risk because risk and return go hand in hand. The amount of risk an investor is willing to accept depends on his risk tolerance, i.e., his ability to take risk.

   Different financial instruments have different levels of risk depending on the variability or volatility of the return they are expected to generate. For example, government securities are considered safe so they have lower risk and as a result, lower returns are associated with them. Investors should choose the instruments that best suit their risk characteristics.

   In addition to the risk-return benchmark, investors also have the objective of hedging their savings against inflation. Any saving that has not been invested is not safe from risk exposure. Rise in prices or inflation erode the value of money. Savings need to be invested in order to provide a hedge or protection against inflation. Obviously, the return on investment should be enough to compensate for rise in prices. We will discuss this concept in detail in the subsequent chapters of the book. At this point in time it should be understood that any investment instrument should generate returns over and above the expected rate of inflation.

   There are several constraints faced by the investors that may hinder the achievement of the stated goal of maximization of return or minimization of risk, as the case may be. These constraints are:

   (a) *Liquidity:* Different investors have varying level of cash requirement, depending on their lifecycle stage, lifestyle and other factors. The investors who have higher requirement of cash, should establish a minimum level of cash that they should always have in their portfolio. In addition to this, they should also make sure that they invest in more liquid instruments. We have already understood the concept of the liquidity of investments in the preceding sections of this chapter.

   (b) *Income:* The level of income that investors have influences how much they are able to save for investment. Therefore, current income acts as a constraint in pursuit of investment objectives by any investor.

   (c) *Investment horizon:* Investors invest their savings for some future use. Accordingly, they have to choose the assets whose maturities coincide with the time when they need their funds in the future. Thus, the duration for which the investors want to invest their funds also acts as a constraint in the choice of investment instruments.

(d) *Tax liability:* The return on most investments is treated as a part of investors' income and taxed at a certain rate. Therefore, the tax bracket the investor is in also influences his choice of investment avenues. Naturally, investors with high tax liability would try to find avenues of investment that offer tax shelter. In addition, there are several investments that qualify for tax rebates under the provisions of the Income Tax Act in India. Investors trying to reduce their tax liability also seek investments that offer tax savings.

(e) *Regulatory requirements:* The Government also imposes many restrictions on investments, more so in the case of institutional investors. These restrictions act as constraints in the choice of the investment assets.

(f) *Unique circumstances:* Each investor has certain unique circumstances and requirements. Some might need to provide for the future care of a mentally challenged child or ageing parents or any other situation. These specific requirements also act as a constraint in the choice of investment avenues.

The specification of the objectives and constraints of investment help in framing the investment policy statement of an investor that specifies the portfolio policies pertaining to asset allocation, diversification, risk profile, income generation and tax considerations.

2. **Quantification of Capital Market Expectations:** Asset allocation needs to be undertaken on the basis of the investor's expectation of risk and return prospects of various asset classes. The risk and returns associated with the asset classes are influenced by capital market expectations or macro expectations. Therefore, as an input to asset allocation, capital market expectations need to be quantified. For instance, if an investor's investment policy statement specifies and defines seven broad asset classes, then the investor will need to formulate long-term expectations concerning those asset classes as an input for asset allocation.

   The quantification of capital market expectations requires forecasts and estimates pertaining to the aggregate economic output in the economy, distribution of the output among various factors of production and the allocation of income for capital to different asset classes. It is a complex exercise that requires the use of a large amount of historical data and sophisticated forecasting tools.

3. **Asset Allocation:** We have discussed different investment avenues in the preceding sections of this chapter. They represent broad asset classes that an investor can consider for investing. The main asset classes include equity, debt, money market instruments, real estate, precious metal and others. Asset allocation means determination of the mix of assets to be included in the portfolio. It has been discussed in detail in Chapter 7 of this book.

4. **Formulation of Bond and Equity Portfolio Management Strategies:** After the determination of the portfolio mix, appropriate portfolio strategy needs to be formulated for management of the portfolios of asset classes within the overall portfolio. There are two broad portfolio management strategies namely, active and passive, that can be used for the management of bond and equity portfolios.

   Active portfolio management is commonly used by investment professionals and aggressive investors with an objective of striving for superior risk-adjusted returns. The principal vectors of an active strategy are:

   – Market Timing
   – Sector Rotation
   – Security Selection

   On the other hand, a passive portfolio management strategy refers to the practice of creation of well-diversified portfolio at a specified level of risk and holding it relatively unchanged over a certain period of time. A passive portfolio is usually revised only if it becomes inadequately diversified or inconsistent with the investor's risk-return characteristics. These strategies have been explained in detail in subsequent chapters of this book.

Implementation and Review of Investment Decision

The first phase of portfolio management helps us in the determination of portfolio mix in terms of broad asset classes to be included. In the next phase, we need to identify the individual securities representing the asset classes to be included in the portfolio. Thereafter, those securities need to be bought from the market. With this the implementation phase of the portfolio is complete. However, investment management is a dynamic activity and the portfolios once executed need to be revised, rebalanced and measured to ensure that they do not drift away from the investors' investment objectives and constraints. As mentioned above, this phase of portfolio management comprises four sub-phases:

1. **Choice of Securities:** Bonds and stocks (since these are the major asset classes that comprise a portfolio) are selected on the basis of their individual risk return characteristics and their ability to suit the investor's requirements. Bonds are typically selected on the basis of yield to maturity, safety from default risk, liquidity and tax benefits. Equities are selected on the basis of one of the three approaches to security analysis or a mix of them. These approaches are technical analysis, fundamental analysis and efficient market hypothesis. These approaches have been discussed in detail from Chapters 10 to 14 of this book.
2. **Execution of Portfolio Decision:** This phase involves the actual sale or purchase of the selected securities in the decided proportion from the securities market. The details of the operation of securities markets in India, how securities are bought and sold and who are the major players in the market is discussed in detail in Chapter 2.
3. **Portfolio Revision and Rebalancing:** Portfolios need to be revised and the asset allocation needs to be balanced from time to time as the changes in the markets and investment environment may cause the portfolios to move away from the stated investment policy. This topic has been discussed in detail in Chapter 8 of this book.
4. **Portfolio Performance Management:** Portfolios are constructed with the objective of meeting the risk and return objectives of an investor. It is essential to know whether the portfolios formed after much deliberation and effort have succeeded in generating the expected level of returns for the investors. Many tools have been developed to measure the performance of a portfolio in terms of its risk and return profile. These tools have been explained in detail in Chapter 8 of this book.

SUMMARY

☑ Investment of savings wisely is the key to economic well-being in the long run. Therefore, the decision of when to invest and where to invest should be taken after a lot of deliberation and careful consideration.

☑ There are a number of instruments available for investment of savings such as bank deposits, bonds, stocks, mutual funds, real assets and so on. Each investment avenue or instrument has its own risks and returns.

☑ The investors in the economy need to understand the characteristics of each instrument to determine which one would best suit their needs.

- ☑ Investors should spread their savings across a variety of investment instruments that have different risk-return characteristics. In investment management, such a collection of securities is called a portfolio.
- ☑ In the language of finance, the characteristics of investment can be summed up in two dimensions: time and risk.
- ☑ There are few instruments like government securities in which the returns are certain and it is only the time element that is taken into consideration. In other investments like stocks and bonds, the uncertainty of return or risk as well as time are dominant considerations.
- ☑ Instruments like shares, bonds, insurance policies, bank deposits, etc. are the avenues for financial investments. Financial investments generate financial assets.
- ☑ Economic investment is an investment for the formation of new and productive capital in the form of new plant, machinery, inventories and other facilities and inputs required for the production of goods and services.
- ☑ The bottom line is that all investments result in creation of assets either financial or real.
- ☑ Speculation may be described as a short-term investment undertaken with the sole purpose of generating high returns. Speculative investments are inherently risky.
- ☑ Gambling usually involves putting money in horse races, casinos, lotteries, card games, etc. It is undertaken not only for returns but for thrill and excitement as well.
- ☑ Any rational investor would prefer to invest his funds in instruments that are liquid, ensure safety of principal and give maximum returns for a given level of risk or minimum risk for a given level return.
- ☑ Investment avenues refer to the alternative instruments in which their savings can be deployed by the investors. The investment avenues can be broadly categorized under the following heads: corporate securities, deposits, mutual fund schemes, derivative securities, insurance products, retirement products, government securities, money market instruments, real estate, art objects, precious metals and stones and commodities.
- ☑ The process of investment is actually the process of portfolio management that comprises two broad phases, namely, framing of investment policy and strategy and implementation and review of investment decision.

KEY WORDS

CONCEPT QUESTIONS

1. An investor's motives to invest are inherently different from those of a speculator yet both are key to efficient functioning of the market. Explain.
2. A portfolio manager needs to be sensitive to differences between the objectives and constraints of individual and institutional investors. Discuss.
3. A person who acquires equity stock of a company becomes exposed to certain risks and entitled to certain benefits that come with the ownership of a company. Explain the statement.
4. Are preference shares a popular mode of raising capital in India? What do the numbers say?
5. Asset allocation is a key step in the construction of a portfolio. Discuss the key inputs that need to be generated to ensure optimal allocation in an investment portfolio.
6. Financial assets are often referred to as 'securities.' In the recent past there has been a lot of debate on calling instruments that offer uncertain returns 'securities.' What do you understand by uncertain returns? Are you comfortable with the use of the word 'securities' in the context of such investments?
7. Quantification of capital market expectations is the most difficult and elusive part of the portfolio management process. Explain.
8. Fixed income securities and equities are two totally different classes of investment avenues. Discuss.
9. Explain the statement, "All rational investors want to earn as large a return as possible with minimum level of risk."
10. "The bottom line is that all investments result in creation of assets either financial or real." What is the statement referring to? Discuss in detail.

The Investment Environment: Securities Market of India

2

CHAPTER OBJECTIVES

- ❐ Learning about the key segments of the Indian securities market
- ❐ Understanding the role of securities market in India
- ❐ Discussing the growth of equity and fixed income markets of India
- ❐ Highlighting the performance of the major stock indices of Indian stock exchanges
- ❐ Assessing the role of SEBI in the growth of India capital markets

To execute the portfolio decision, the investors need to actually procure the securities from the markets they are sold in. Yes, like any other good or service, securities can also be procured from a market of their own. Securities markets are quite different from the market of physical goods and services. The markets for securities are highly regulated entities with many participants. The selling and buying of securities in these markets is called 'trading.' Trading of financial securities takes place in a completely automated manner through certain intermediaries recognized by the markets.

Everyday, we come across cues emerging from the securities markets. For instance, the news that S&P BSE SENSEX crossed the 25000 mark became a topic for many a deliberations in the country for many days. Issue of corporate bonds and government securities also attract the attention of investors. Another bit of information that never fails to hit the headlines is the announcement by The Reserve Bank of India's announcement about cutting or increasing the key lending rates in the country.

All these bits of information pertain to the equity market, the debt market and the government securities market which together make the securities market in India. In this chapter, we will learn about the main markets for securities, the main participants in these markets and how the securities are traded.

Financial Market in India

Financial markets are the markets for dealing in financial claims and financial assets. Various segments of financial markets in India are illustrated in Figure 2.1. The organized financial markets in India are divided into two broad categories:

1. Money market
2. Capital market

Figure 2.1 Segments of financial markets in India.

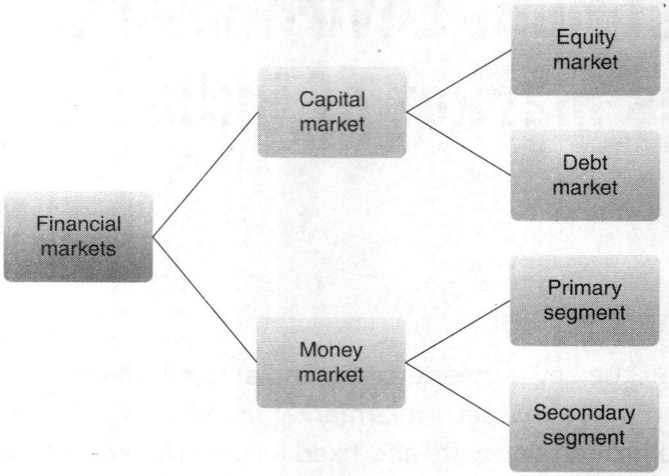

The money market is a market for short-term securities. It is a market for overnight funds as well as instruments having maturities of less than one year. It has no physical location and the transactions in this market take place over telephone. The main participants in this market are the Reserve Bank of India, mutual funds, Discount and Finance House of India, insurance companies, banks, state governments, corporate houses, public sector undertakings, non-resident Indians and other institutional players. The market is driven by the demand and supply of money. The main instruments are t-bills, certificates of deposit, commercial bills, call/notice money market, cash management bills and collateralized borrowing and lending obligation.

The average turnover of Indian money markets is ₹1,00,000 crore daily, representing nearly 2% of the country's GDP. Though the turnover in the Indian money markets is many times larger than that in the capital markets, yet our markets are very small as compared to daily turnovers in the money markets of the developed countries.

The capital market is the market for long-term securities, i.e., the securities having maturities of more than one-year. It is a market for long-term funds, both debt and equity, raised domestically and internationally. Capital market serves as a channel for mobilizing the savings of individuals and institutions. It comprises two segments: primary market and secondary market. Primary market deals with new issues and secondary market deals with existing issues of securities. The secondary market is further divided into two components namely, over-the-counter market and exchange traded market. Since our discussion in this book will mainly focus on debt and equity, we will discuss the markets related to these two instruments in detail now.

Another way of segmenting securities markets, a way more relevant to our discussion, is to divide the securities market into three segments, namely, equity market, debt market and derivatives market. The structure of the securities market in India is shown in Figure 2.2.

Let us discuss the debt and equity markets in detail now. Derivatives market in India has been discussed in Chapters 18 and19 of this book.

Figure 2.2 The structure of the securities market in India.

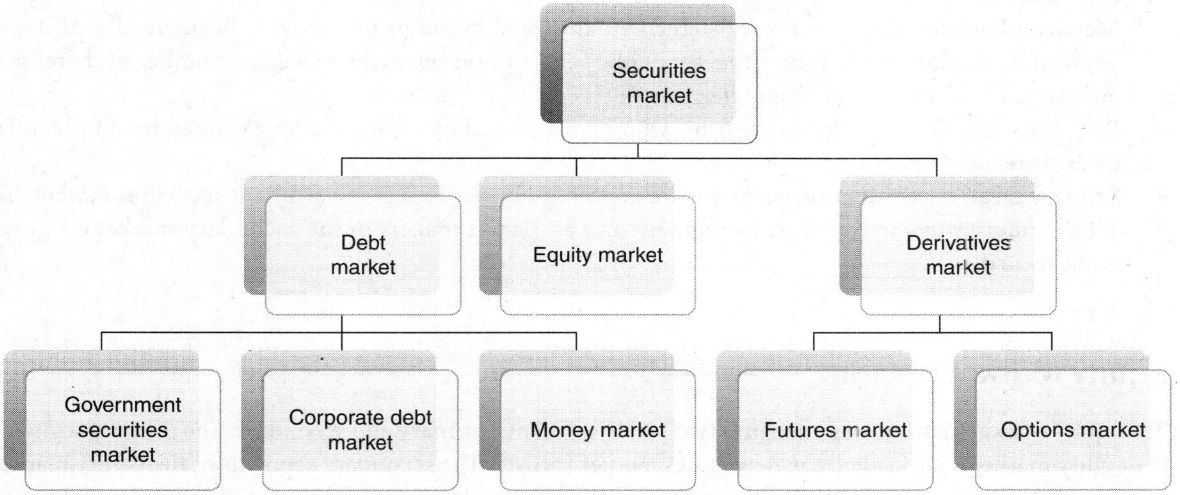

Participants in Securities Markets in India

The Indian securities market comprises a number of intermediaries or participants who act as a channel between the investors and the bodies looking to raise funds. The main participants are:

1. Regulatory bodies like the Company Law Board (CLB) (responsible for administration of the Companies Act, 1956), the Reserve Bank of India (RBI) (responsible for the supervision of banks, money market and government securities market), the Securities and Exchange Board of India (SEBI) (responsible for the regulation of the capital market), the Department of Economic Affairs (DEA) (concerned with the functioning of the financial markets) and the Ministry of Company Affairs (MCA) (responsible for the administration of corporates).
2. Stock exchanges like NSE and BSE where already issued securities are bought and sold. Securities need to be listed to be traded on stock exchanges. About 10,000 securities are listed on all the stock exchanges in India put together.
3. Depositories like the National Securities Depository Limited (NSDL) and the Central Securities Depository Limited (CSDL) which hold securities in dematerialized or paperless form through electronic book entries. By the end of March 2014, there were 130.6 lakh demat accounts at NSDL and 87.8 lakh demat accounts at CDSL. As on March 31, 2014, 12,210 companies had signed up for dematerialization at NSDL and 8,630 at CDSL.[1]
4. Brokers who are intermediaries through whom investors buy and sell shares are registered members of the stock exchanges.

[1] http://www.sebi.gov.in/, accessed on December 31, 2014.

5. Foreign Institutional Investors who are foreign firms registered with the SEBI to undertake transactions in the Indian capital market have become major players in the Indian markets in the past few years.
6. Merchant Bankers who are firms registered with the SEBI specialize in managing the issue of securities.
7. Underwriters who act like guarantors for public subscription subscribe to a given number of shares in the event of under-subscription by public.
8. Registrars and Transfer Agents are firms who are employed by a company or a mutual fund to handle all investor-related services.
9. Primary Dealers are functionaries who are appointed by the RBI in government securities market. They act as underwriters in the primary segment and as market makers in the secondary market for government securities.

Equity Market in India

The equity market in India is divided into two major segments, primary and secondary. The primary segment of the equity market is also called the new issues market (NIM). The secondary segment of the equity market in India comprises the stock exchanges where the issued securities are listed and traded. Bombay Stock Exchange (BSE) and National Stock Exchange (NSE) are the main stock exchanges of the country. Let us discuss the two main types of equity markets in India in detail.

New Issues Market

Primary market in India remained dull and shallow for a long time under the regime of Controller of Capital Issues (CCI). The wave of economic reforms sweeping the country in 1991 benefited the NIM as well. In 1992, CCI was abolished and a new regulatory authority, Securities Exchange Board of India was established and entrusted with the responsibility of developing and regulating the Indian securities market. The primary markets in India have become vibrant on account of the number of reforms and initiatives taken by SEBI. Free pricing of equity and increase in the efficiency of the delivery system through dematerialization of shares are among the key initiatives taken by SEBI since its establishment. A cornerstone of SEBI's role in the Indian capital market has been its extreme emphasis on investor protection. SEBI's commitment to protect the interest of retail investors has increased the participation in the equity market in the country. Year after year, SEBI's role has been expanded and its position strengthened through various ordinances and notifications. The latest ordinance can be read in the Beyond the Basics 2.1.

Beyond the Basics 2.1 Powers Conferred on SEBI vide the Securities Laws (Amendment) Ordinance, 2014

On March 28, 2014, The Securities Laws (Amendment) Ordinance, 2014 was promulgated by the President of India under Article 123 of the Constitution of India. The ordinance was intended to amend the Securities and Exchange Board of India Act, 1992, the Securities Contracts (Regulation) Act, 1956 and the Depositories Act, 1996.

The main provisions of the said Ordinance were related to:

1. **Power to Call for Information:** This provision empowers SEBI to call for information from any person/s in relation to investigation of any transaction associated with the securities markets.
2. **Power to Call for or Furnish Information to Other Authorities:** The Ordinance has expanded SEBI's powers to call for or share information with its regulatory counterparts in other countries. The information may pertain to prevention, detection, enforcement and investigation of violations with respect to securities. However, such sharing of information by SEBI is subject to the proviso that a memorandum of understanding be signed between SEBI and its overseas counterpart with the prior approval of the Central Government.
3. **Collective Investment Scheme (CIS):** The Ordinance has come up with certain clarifications in the definition of CIS and the concept of deemed CIS. It has also granted SEBI the power to define additional parameters that would enable it to bring an activity within the ambit of CIS on a case-to-case basis if it is important from the regulatory point of view.

   The ordinance has also empowered the Central Government to exempt any scheme or arrangement from the ambit of CIS. However, it can do so only in consultation with SEBI.
4. **Explicit Power to Disgorge Ill-gotten Gains and Power to Credit Disgorgement Amount to Investor Protection and Education Fund and Utilization of the Same:** SEBI has been empowered by the Ordinance to disgorge ill-gotten gains and credit the same to the Investor Protection and Education Fund and utilize the said monies as per the laid down provisions.
5. **Power to Conduct Search and Seizure:** The Ordinance permits SEBI officials to conduct search and seizure as required, with the authorization of Chairman, SEBI.
6. **Explicit Powers for Settlement:** The Ordinance has also empowered SEBI to settle administrative and civil proceedings in accordance with the procedures specified in the regulations.
7. **Power of Review of Orders Passed by Adjudicating Officers:** The ordinance has empowered SEBI Board to suo moto review any order passed by the Adjudicating Officer and impose a higher penalty if required.
8. **Attachment and Recovery:** SEBI has now been empowered to attach and sell movable, immovable property and attach bank accounts of the defaulters to recover outstanding penalties.
9. **Special Courts and Deemed Public Prosecutors:** The Ordinance has also facilitated the constitution of Special Courts for prosecution of offenders under securities laws.

Source: http://www.sebi.gov.in/, accessed on January 7, 2015.

Indian companies can raise equity capital from the primary market through three alternative routes:

- Public issue
- Rights issue
- Private placement

These are further classified into different categories as shown in Figure 2.3.

Figure 2.3 Categories of issues.

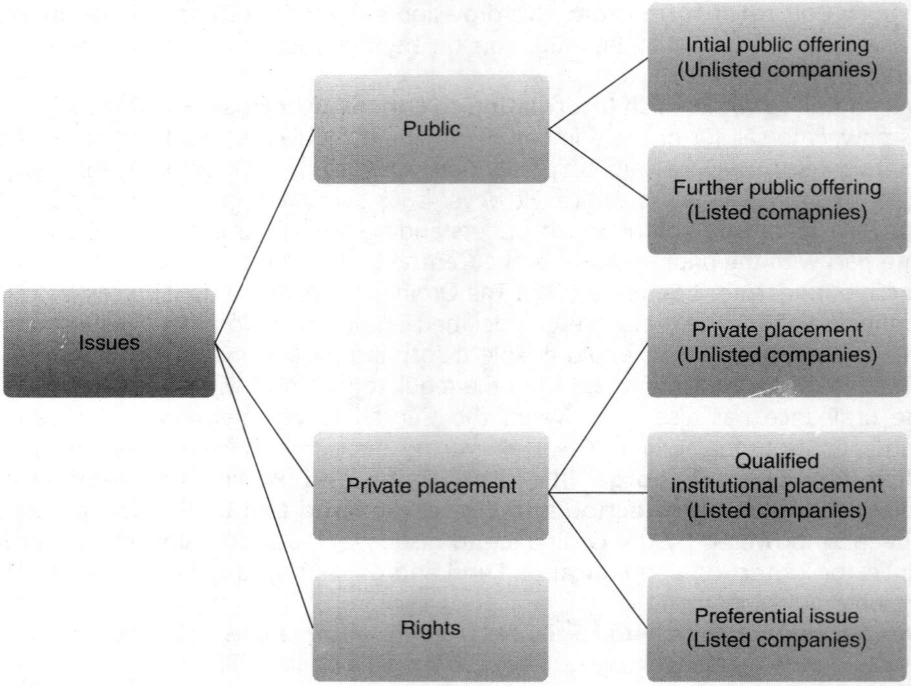

1. **Public Issues:** Public issues are the most important mode of raising equity capital in India. They mean offering shares to the general public for subscription. Public issues are governed by the provisions of the Companies Act 1956, ICDR (Issue of capital and disclosure requirements) regulations, SEBI and the listing requirements of the stock exchanges. The issue of shares to the general public involves a fairly elaborate process that begins with the approval of the board of directors and shareholders of the company. Lead manager manages the issue and the other functionaries involved are co-managers, advisors, underwriters, bankers, registrars and brokers.

   The issue is offered to the general public through a prospectus that needs to be approved by SEBI. In addition, all the companies coming out with public issues need to file for listing on the stock exchanges on which they are to be traded post-issuance.

   When a company offers equity to the general public for subscription for the first time, it is called initial public offering (IPO). Grading of IPOs has been introduced in India, as detailed in Beyond the Basics 2.2. Any subsequent issue is called follow-on public offering (FPO).

   SEBI has also introduced a method of fast-track issue (FTI) on the lines of the seasoned issuer model in US. Under the fast-track mechanism of issuing securities, listed companies will be allowed to raise funds more quickly. Under this mechanism, lead managers can proceed with an issue of a company listed on the NSE or BSE after filing the offer document with SEBI.

   The new mechanism is applicable only for those companies that are listed on the BSE or NSE for at least three years and have had a market capitalization of at least ₹10,000 crore over the last one year.

Beyond the Basics 2.2 What is 'IPO Grading'?

Credit rating of debt instruments has been prevalent for a long time in India. Now, the concept of IPO grading has also come up in which a grade is assigned by a Credit Rating Agency registered with SEBI to the initial public offering (IPO) of equity shares and related securities. The purpose of grading is to make additional information available to the investors in order to facilitate better assessment of equity shares offered through the IPO under consideration.

Each grade represents a relative assessment of the fundamentals of the issue under consideration with respect to the other listed equity securities in India. The grading is generally assigned on a five-point point scale with 5 indicating strong fundamentals. The grades from 1 to 5 are assigned as given below:

IPO grade 1: Poor fundamentals
IPO grade 2: Below-average fundamentals
IPO grade 3: Average fundamentals
IPO grade 4: Above-average fundamentals
IPO grade 5: Strong fundamentals

Source: http://www.sebi.gov.in/, accessed on December 29, 2015.

The new issues market in India has grown by leaps and bounds in the recent past. Resource mobilization through public and rights issues in the past two years is exhibited in Table 2.1 and mega equity issues (issues above ₹300 crore) in 2013–14 are exhibited in Table 2.2.

TABLE 2.1 Resource mobilization through public and rights issues

Particulars	2012–13		2013–14		Percenatage share in total amount	
	No. of issues	Amount (₹ crore)	No. of issues	Amount (₹ crore)	2012–13	2013–14
1	2	3	4	5	6	7
1. **Public issues** (i) + (ii)	**53**	**23,510**	**75**	**51,075**	**72.4**	**91.8**
(i) Public issues						
(*Equity/PCD/FCD*) of which	**33**	**6,528**	**40**	**8,692**	**20.1**	**15.6**
IPOs	33	6,528	38	1,236	20.1	2.2
FPOs	0	0	2	7,457	0	13.4

(*Continued*)

TABLE 2.1 Continued

Particulars	2012–13		2013–14		Percenatage share in total amount	
	No. of issues	Amount (₹ crore)	No. of issues	Amount (₹ crore)	2012–13	2013–14
1	2	3	4	5	6	7
(ii) Public issues (BOnd/NCD)	20	16,982	35	42,383	52.3	76.2
2. Rights issues	**16**	**8,945**	**15**	**4,576**	**27.6**	**8.2**
Total equity issues *(1(i) + 2)*	49	15,473	55	13,269	47.7	23.8
Total equity and bond *(1 + 2)*	**69**	**32,455**	**90**	**55,652**	**100**	**100**
Memo items: Offer for sale	*4*	*1,589*	*4*	*3,096*	*4.9*	*5.6*

Notes: 1) The primary market resource mobilization is inclusive of the amount raised in the SME platform.
2) All offers for sale have been included under the head of IPOs/FPOs

Source: http://www.sebi.gov.in/, accessed on December 29, 2014.

TABLE 2.2 Mega equity issues in 2013–14

No.	Name of the entity	Type of issue	Type of instrument	Date of opening of issue	Offer size (₹ crore)	Percentage share in total amount
1	2	3	4	5	6	7
1	Just Dial Ltd	IPO	Equity	20-May-13	919	1.76
2	Kesoram Industries Ltd	Rights	Equity	3-Jun-13	416	0.80
3	Reliance Mediaworks Ltd	Rights	Equity	6-Aug-13	600	1.15
4	Godrej Properties Ltd	Rights	Equity	28-Aug-13	700	1.34
5	Power Grid Corporation of India Ltd	FPO	Equity	3-Dec-13	6,959	13.35
6	Engineers India Ltd	FPO	Equity	6-Feb-14	498	0.96
7	The Tata Power Company Limited	Rights	Equity	31-Mar-14	1,993	3.83

Source: http://www.sebi.gov.in/, accessed on December 29, 2014.

2. **Rights Issues:** Rights issues refer to offering of additional equity to existing shareholders, as explained in Chapter 1.
3. **Private Placement:** A private placement of equity and convertible debenture is an issue of securities by a listed company to a select, small group of people not exceeding 49. It can be in the form of preferential allotment or qualified institutional placement.
   (a) *Preferential allotment:* Preferential allotment of shares by listed companies is the process of allotment of shares on a preferential basis to a select group of investors in accordance with the provisions of section 81 of the Companies Act, 1956. The select group includes financial institutions, mutual funds and high net worth individuals. Table 2.3 exhibits the resource mobilization through preferential allotment over the past few years.

TABLE 2.3 Resource mobilization through preferential allotment

Year/ month	NSE		BSE		Common		Total	
	No. of issues	Amount (₹ crore)	No. of issues	Amount (₹crore)	No. of issues	Amount (₹ crore)	No. of issues	Amount (₹ crore)
1	2	3	4	5	6	7	8	9
2010–11	**83**	**1,393**	**156**	**12,072**	**134**	**17,046**	**373**	**30,511**
2011–12	**133**	**2,820**	**88**	**4,166**	**90**	**18,723**	**311**	**25,709**
2012–13	**188**	**7,442**	**87**	**12,729**	**145**	**26,768**	**420**	**46,939**
2013–14	**222**	**3,789**	**24**	**1,029**	**165**	**41,645**	**411**	**46,463**
Apr-13	21	659	3	42	13	11,143	37	11,844
May-13	24	403	0	0	32	3,767	56	4,170
Jun-13	20	179	0	0	13	11,699	33	11,878
Jul-13	15	371	2	88	10	1,147	27	1,605
Aug-13	24	178	4	431	7	453	35	1,062
Sep-13	17	323	4	71	11	532	32	926
Oct-13	20	367	4	63	7	2935	31	3366
Nov-13	14	132	1	2	9	622	24	756
Dec-13	10	414	3	17	14	6512	27	6943
Jan-14	16	33	2	316	31	460	49	809
Feb-14	15	152	0	0	6	534	21	686
Mar-14	26	577	1	0	12	1,841	39	2,418

Source: www.bseindia.com and www.nseindia.com, accessed on January 3, 2015.

(b) *Qualified institutional placement (QIP):* Qualified institutional placement (QIP) has been allowed in the Indian securities market in addition to the public and rights issues with a view to easing the process of fund raising in domestic market. In a QIP, a listed Indian company can issue equity shares, fully and partly convertible debentures, or any security other than warrants which are convertible to equity shares by a Qualified Institutional Buyer (QIB) as per the provisions of SEBI (ICDR) regulations. Table 2.4 exhibits resource mobilization through QIP over the past few years.

TABLE 2.4 Resource mobilization through QIP

Year/ month	NSE		BSE		Common		Total	
	No. of issues	Amount (₹ crore)	No. of issues	Amount (₹ crore)	No. of issues	Amount (₹ crore)	No. of issues	Amount (₹ crore)
1	2	3	4	5	6	7	8	9
2010–11	**10**	**2,802**	**3**	**90**	**46**	**22,959**	**59**	**25,850**
2011–12	**1**	**8**	**1**	**40**	**14**	**2,114**	**16**	**2,163**
2012–13	**1**	**950**	**1**	**160**	**43**	**14,885**	**45**	**15,996**
2013–14	**1**	**160**	**0**	**0**	**16**	**13,503**	**17**	**13,633**
Apr-13	1	160	0	0	3	227	4	387
May-13	0	0	0	0	5	2,833	5	2,833
Jun-13	0	0	0	0	2	1,066	2	1,066
Jul-13	0	0	0	0	2	918	2	918
Aug-13	0	0	0	0	0	0	0	0
Sep-13	0	0	0	0	0	0	0	0
Oct-13	0	0	0	0	0	0	0	0
Nov-13	0	0	0	0	0	0	0	0
Dec-13	0	0	0	0	1	280	1	287
Jan-14	0	0	0	0	1	67	1	67
Feb-14	0	0	0	0	2	8,113	2	8,113
Mar-14	0	0	0	0	0	0	0	0

Source: www.bseindia.com and www.nseindia.com, accessed on January 3, 2015.

Beyond the Basics 2.3 Anchor Investors (AIs)

Anchor Investors may be described as investors who are committed and can be relied upon to anchor/support capital issue in the existing market condition, be it adverse or favorable.

The concept of Anchor Investors was introduced in India in June 2009. They were envisaged as investors who would come forward to anchor a transaction in securities. Regulation 2(1)(c) of SEBI (ICDR) Regulations defines 'Anchor Investor' as a qualified institutional buyer who makes an application in a public issue through the book building process and the value of the application is equal to ₹10 crore or more.

Further, the regulation stipulates that the allocation to such investors shall be made on a discretionary basis, subject to a lower limit of at least two AIs for allocation of up to ₹250 crore and 5 AIs for allocation of more than ₹250 crore.

AIs have an important role in the success of any issue in the market. Thus, to increase their share in an issue, SEBI has recently decided to increase the bucket of AIs to 60% from the current level of 30% of the institutional bucket.

Source: http://www.sebi.gov.in/, accessed on January 5, 2015.

Beyond the Basics 2.4 What is Green-Shoe Option?

Green-Shoe option is a term used to indicate an option of allocating shares over and above the shares included in a public issue and operating a price stabilizing mechanism after listing of the issue for a period of not more than 30 days in accordance with the provisions of Chapter VIIIA of DIP Guidelines of SEBI. This option is granted to an issuing company to be put into effect through a stabilizing agent. The upper limit for over-allotment is 15% of the issue size.

An issue with green-shoe option is useful from an investor's perspective as it may increase the probability of getting shares. Further, it may also lead to relatively more stable post-listing prices of the concerned issue as compared to the market as a whole.

Source: http://www.moneycontrol.com/, accessed on January 5, 2015.

Pricing of new issues

Public issues are offered for subscription at predetermined prices, i.e., fixed price issues or at the prices determined through book building. Under book building a price range is offered, so that the investors can determine the right price of the share. Book building is actually a price discovery method. In this method, a particular price point is not fixed for the shares, instead a price range, e.g., ₹180–200 is given. The lowest price (₹180) is known as the floor price and the highest price (₹200) is known as the cap price.

The investors are required to bid for shares. When bidding for the shares, they have to decide the price at which they would like to bid for the shares from the given range, for e.g., ₹180, ₹190 or ₹200.

Once the bidding is over, the lead manager decides the issue price in consultation with the issuer on the basis of demand for shares. Pricing is usually set at such a level that there is latent demand to ensure a post-listing price that is higher than the issue price. The price at which the shares are allotted is known as the cut off price. Normally the issue is kept open for 5 days. If the issue price is less than the cap price, the investors who bid at the cap price receive a refund and those who bid at the floor price are required to pay the additional amount. The issuer and the lead manager also fix the issue size and allotment pattern.

Allotment of new issues

As per the existing provisions, a minimum 25% of the issue is to be allotted to individuals bidding up to 1000 shares, a minimum of 15% of the issue is to be allotted to corporates, high net worth individuals and individual investors bidding more than 1000 shares and a maximum 60% is to be allotted to QIBs. In case of over-subscription, allotment to each category has to be done on a proportionate basis.

Beyond the Basics 2.5 Bought Out Deals

Bought out deal is an equity deal in which an investment bank commits to buy the entire equity offering from the client company. Such a deal eliminates the financing risk for the company but the company usually ends up getting a lower price for its offering because investment bank usually offsets its risk by negotiating a significant discount when buying the offering from the client.

Beyond the Basics 2.6 SEBI's ASBA Facility in Public and Rights Issues

ASBA means "Application Supported by Blocked Amount." It refers to an application for authorizing a bank to block the application money in the bank account, for the purpose of subscribing to an issue. For investors applying through ASBA facility for subscription to an issue, the application money is debited from their bank account only after their application is earmarked for allotment or the issuer withdraws the issue or the issue fails due to certain factors.

Source: http://www.sebi.gov.in/, accessed on January 6, 2015.

Secondary Market

The secondary market for equity shares is represented by the stock exchanges. As per SEBI website, there are 21 stock exchanges in India as of December 2014. The Hyderabad Securities and Enterprises Ltd (erstwhile Hyderabad Stock Exchange), Coimbatore Stock Exchange Ltd, Saurashtra Kutch Stock Exchange Ltd and Mangalore Stock Exchange have been granted exit by a SEBI vide order dated January 25, 2013, April 3, 2013, April 5, 2013 and March 3, 2014, respectively. The list of 21 stock exchanges includes BSE, NSE, MCX Stock Exchange, OTC Exchange of India, United Stock Exchange of India Limited, Inter-Connected Stock Exchange of India Limited and 15 regional stock exchanges.

Bombay Stock Exchange (BSE) and National Stock Exchange (NSE) are the two major stock exchanges of the country. They account for almost 100% turnover in the secondary equity market in the country.

BSE is one of the oldest stock exchanges in the world. It is a corporatized and demutualized entity, with a broad shareholder-base which includes two leading global exchanges, Deutsche Bourse and Singapore Exchange as strategic partners. BSE provides market for trading in equity, debt instruments, derivatives and mutual funds. It also has a platform for trading in equities of small-and-medium enterprises (SME). BSE provides many other services including risk management, clearing, settlement, market data services and education.

Beyond the Basics 2.7 BSE IndoNext

SMEs (small and medium enterprises) are an important part of the Indian economy. In the recent past, concerns have been expressed with regard to the inability of the companies in this segment to tap the capital markets to raise equity and debt to fund their capital expenditure plans.

BSE IndoNext is an alternate national platform created jointly by BSE (Bombay Stock Exchange) and FISE (Federation of Indian Stock Exchanges), which represents 20 RSEs (Regional Stock Exchanges), to benefit small and medium size companies in the country. The platform is intended to help SMEs raise equity and debt through public issue and facilitate trading of the capital in such companies through stock exchanges. BSE IndoNext offers the advantage of creating a unified national trading platform with a large number of member participation that would provide a vibrant and active trading platform for SMEs.

The BSE IndoNext is envisaged to help the investors reach the BSE IndoNext traded scrips not only through the network of BSE but also through the network of nearly 7,000 members of regional stock exchanges with wide geographic reach.

Source: http://www.bseindia.com/, accessed on January 6, 2015.

More than 5000 companies are listed on BSE making it the world's No. 1 exchange in terms of listed members. The companies listed on BSE Ltd commanded a total market capitalization of USD 1.32 trillion as of January 2013. It is also one of the world's leading exchanges (3rd largest in December 2012) for Index options trading.[2]

The trading system used by BSE was based on open outcry but it migrated to BOLT (Bombay Online Trading) in 1995 which is a fully automated and computerized mode of trading. In 1996, SEBI permitted BSE to extend BOLT network outside Mumbai as well. The securities traded on BSE are listed as per its guidelines and are divided into different groups, viz., A, B, S, T, TS and Z on the basis of several factors like market capitalization, trading volumes and numbers, track records, profits, dividends, shareholding patterns, and some qualitative aspects.

BSE has also jointly created an alternate national platform called BSE IndoNext with the Federation of Indian Stock Exchanges.

National Stock Exchange (NSE) was established in 1994 and started trading in the equities segment (Capital Market segment) on November 3, 1994. It is the largest exchange in India in terms of volumes transacted. NSE operates on the 'National Exchange for Automated Trading' (NEAT) system that is a fully automated screen

---

[2] World Federation of Exchanges.

based trading system. It works on the principle of an order driven market. The members of the exchange are connected from their dispersed locations to the main system at the NSE through a high-speed, efficient satellite tele-communication network.

Various products traded on the Capital Market segment of NSE include equity shares, preference shares, warrants, debentures, exchange traded funds, mutual funds (close ended), government securities and Indian depository receipts. For trading purpose, each asset type has been assigned a series.

Trading and settlement

Each stock exchange has certain listed and permitted securities that can be bought and sold by investors through the brokers registered with the exchanges. Investors place orders with the brokers and these orders can be: market orders (to be executed as per the prevailing market rates) and limit orders (to be executed at the price specified by the investor).

Compulsory rolling settlement

All transactions in all groups of securities in the Equity segment listed on BSE and NSE are required to be settled on $T + 2$ basis (w.e.f., April 1, 2003), called the rolling settlement. A $T + 2$ settlement cycle implies that the settlement of transactions done on day T (trade day) takes place on second business day (excluding Saturdays, Sundays, bank and Exchange trading holidays) after the trade day. In case of rolling settlements, pay-in and pay-out of both funds and securities is completed on the same day.

Though transactions in most securities are settled under rolling settlement, yet there are some securities like the "*Z*" group or "*T*" group securities that are settled only on a gross basis.

Circuit breakers

To protect the market from volatility, there is a concept of circuit breaker limits that are set for individual stocks as well as the market as a whole. In case of abnormal price movements, the exchange can suspend trading by applying circuit breakers.

SEBI vide circular number CIR/MRD/DP/25/2013 dated September 3, 2013 has issued revised guidelines for circuit breakers that are given below[3]:

The index-based market-wide circuit breaker system applies at 3 stages of the index movement, either way, viz., at 10%, 15% and 20%. These circuit breakers, when triggered, bring about a coordinated trading halt in all equity and equity derivative markets nationwide. The market-wide circuit breakers are triggered by movement of either the BSE SENSEX or the CNX Nifty, whichever is breached earlier. In this regard the exchange has issued a circular number 85/2013 (Download No-24709) dated October 11, 2013.

After the index based market-wide circuit filter breach, the markets reopen with a pre-open call auction session. The extent of duration of the market halt and pre-open session is as given in Table 2.5.

Stock market indices

A stock market index is a measure of the general movement of the market. An index comprises a selection of stocks and may represent the entire market or some important segments. As the stocks within an index change

[3] http://www.nseindia.com/, accessed on January 3, 2015.

TABLE 2.5 Extent of duration of the market halt and pre-open session

Trigger limit	Trigger time	Market halt duration	Pre-open call auction session post market halt
10%	Before 1:00 pm.	45 Minutes	15 Minutes
	At or after 1:00 pm up to 2.30 pm	15 Minutes	15 Minutes
	At or after 2.30 pm	No halt	Not applicable
15%	Before 1 pm	1 hour 45 minutes	15 Minutes
	At or after 1:00 pm before 2:00 pm	45 Minutes	15 Minutes
	On or after 2:00 pm	Remainder of the day	Not applicable
20%	Any time during market hours	Remainder of the day	Not applicable

in value, the index also changes in value. All stock exchanges have many indices that represent how the market or a particular sector is performing. These indices serve as a benchmark for performance measurement of stocks or portfolios such as mutual fund investments.

The indices can be of three types:

1. **Price-Weighted Index:** It is based on the sum of the prices of the sample stocks on a certain date in relation to a base date.
2. **Equal-Weighted Index:** It is based on the simple arithmetic average of the price relatives of sample stocks on a certain date in relation to a base date.
3. **Value-Weighted Index:** It is based on the aggregate market capitalization of the sample stocks on a certain date in relation to a base date.

Let us understand the calculation of index value for the above three types of indices with the help of a Numerical Example.

Numerical Example 1

Consider the data given below for two days and 10 stocks to calculate the index value of price-weighted, equal-weighted and value-weighted indices on day t if the index value on the base date is 100.

Share	Base date price	t day price	Number of O/S shares (in million)
1	60	80	7
2	50	60	8
3	110	100	10

(*Continued*)

Continued

Share	Base date price	*t* day price	Number of O/S shares (in million)
4	30	80	14
5	25	36	13
6	42	39	5
7	119	145	9
8	75	130	20
9	29	50	15
10	80	100	14

A	B	C	D	E	F	G
Share	Base Date Price	*t* day Price	Price Relative (Columns (C/B)*100	Number of O/S Shares (in million)	Base Date Market Capitalization (₹ in Million) (Columns B*E)	*t* day Market Capitalization (₹ in Million) (Columns C*E)
1	60	80	133	7	420	560
2	50	60	120	8	400	480
3	110	100	91	10	1100	1000
4	30	80	267	14	420	1120
5	25	36	144	13	325	468
6	42	39	93	5	210	195
7	119	145	122	9	1071	1305
8	75	130	173	20	1500	2600
9	29	50	172	15	435	750
10	80	100	125	14	1120	1400
Total	620	820	1440		7001	9878

Solution:

To construct price-weighted, equal-weighted and value-weighted indices comprising of the given 10 stocks, we need to calculate the total price on base date as well as on *t* day.

$$\text{Total price on base date} = 60 + 50 + 110 + 30 + 25 + 42 + 119 + 75 + 29 + 80 = 620$$

Similarly, total price on day $t = 820$

Calculation of price relative and market capitalization:

1. Value of price-weighted index on day t: $(820/620) \times 100 = 132$
2. Value of equal-weighted index on day t: $(1440/1000) \times 100 = 144$
3. Value of value-weighted index on day t: $(9878/7001) \times 100 = 141$

In practice, index value on a given day is calculated on the basis of the index value on the previous day.

Stock Market Indices in India

As mentioned above, the two main stock exchanges in the country are BSE and NSE. Both have many indices based on different stock samples.

BSE stock indices: There are a large number of indices in BSE that track some or the other sector or theme as shown in Exhibit 2.1. However, S&P BSE SENSEX is the most important and most tracked index of BSE. It was launched on January 1, 1986. It is designed to measure the performance of the 30 largest, most liquid and financially sound companies across key sectors of the Indian economy that are listed on BSE Ltd.[4]

Exhibit 2.1 List of Indices on BSE

Close [x]

Broad Indices	Investment Strategy Indices	Sectoral Indices
S&P BSE SENSEX	S&P BSE IPO	S&P BSE AUTO
➤ Sectorwise Market Capitalization	S&P BSE SME IPO	S&P BSE BANKEX
➤ Index Constituents	S&P BSE DOLLEX 30	S&P BSE CAPITAL GOODS
➤ About S&P BSE SENSEX	S&P BSE DOLLEX 100	S&P BSE CONSUMER DURABLES
S&P BSE MID CAP	S&P BSE DOLLEX 200	S&P BSE FMCG
S&P BSE SMALL CAP	S&P BSE SENSEX Futures Index	S&P BSE HEALTHCARE
S&P BSE 100	S&P BSE SENSEX Futures Index (USD)	S&P BSE IT
S&P BSE 200	**Volatility Indices**	S&P BSE METAL
S&P BSE 500	S&P BSE REAL VOL-1MTH	S&P BSE OIL & GAS
	S&P BSE REAL VOL-2MTH	S&P BSE POWER
Thematic Indices	S&P BSE REAL VOL-3MTH	S&P BSE REALITY
S&P BSE PSU	**Sustainability Indices**	S&P BSE TECK
S&P BSE India Infrastructure Index	S&P BSE GREENEX	
S&P BSE CPSE	S&P BSE CARBONEX	
S&P BSE 500 SHARIAH		

Source: http://www.bseindia.com/, accessed on January 3, 2015.

[4] http://www.asiaindex.co.in/, accessed on January 3, 2015.

NSE stock indices: There are a large number of indices in NSE that track some or the other sector or theme as shown in Exhibit 2.2. However, CNX Nifty is its major index. It is a well diversified 50 stock index accounting for 23 sectors of the economy. It is used for a variety of purposes such as benchmarking fund portfolios, index-based derivatives and index funds. The CNX Nifty index represents about 66.85% of the free float market capitalization of the stocks listed on NSE as on June 30, 2014. The total traded value for the last six months ending June 2014 of all index constituents is approximately 50.39% of the traded value of all stocks on the NSE.[5]

Exhibit 2.2 List of Indices on NSE

Broad Market Indices	Sectoral Indices	Thematic Indices	Strategy Indices
CNX Nifty	CNX Auto Index	CNX Commodities Index	CNX 100 Equal Weight
CNX Nifty Junior	CNX Bank Index	CNX Consumption Index	CNX Alpha Index
LIX 15	CNX Energy Index	CPSE Index	CNX Defty
LIX15 Midcap	CNX Finance Index	CNX Infrastructure Index	CNX Dividend Opportunities Index
CNX 100	CNX FMCG Index	CNX MNC Index	CNX High Beta Index
CNX 200	CNX IT Index	CNX PSE Index	CNX Low Volatility Index
CNX 500	CNX Media Index	CNX Service Sector Index	CNX Nifty Dividend
CNX Midcap	CNX Metal Index	CNX Shariah25	NV20 Index
Nifty Midcap 50	CNX Pharma Index	CNX Nifty Shariah / CNX 500 Shariah	NI15 Index
CNX Smallcap Index	CNX PSU Bank Index		Nifty PR 1X Inverse
India Vix	CNX Realty Index		Nifty PR 2X Leverage
	IISL CNX Industry Indices		Nifty TR 2X Leverage
			Nifty TR 1X Inverse

Source: http://www.nseindia.com/, accessed on January 3, 2015.

Performance of Indian Stock Markets

During 2013–14, the benchmark indices BSE SENSEX and CNX Nifty increased by 18.8% and 18.0%, respectively, over March 31, 2013. In the cash segment, while the turnover at BSE declined by 4.9%, the turnover at NSE increased by 3.7% during 2013–14 as compared to a fall of 17.8% and 3.7%, respectively during 2012–13. BSE and NSE together contributed 99.7% of the turnover, of which NSE accounted for 84.1% in the total turnover in cash market whereas BSE accounted for 15.6%.

The market capitalization of BSE has been higher than that of NSE in India reflecting large number of shares being listed in BSE. The market capitalization of BSE rose by 16.1% to ₹74,15,296 crore in 2013–14

[5] http://www.nseindia.com/, accessed on January 3, 2015.

from ₹63,87,887 crore in 2012–13. On the other hand, at NSE the market capitalization increased by 16.6% to ₹72,77,720 crore in 2013–14 from ₹62,39,035 crore in 2012–13.

Few key ratios such as market capitalization to GDP (m-cap ratio), traded value to GDP (traded value ratio) and price to earnings per share (P/E ratio) are monitored to gauge the extent of development of stock market.[6] After declining for three successive years, the market capitalization ratios have improved during 2013–14. The

Figure 2.4 Movements of benchmark stock indices.

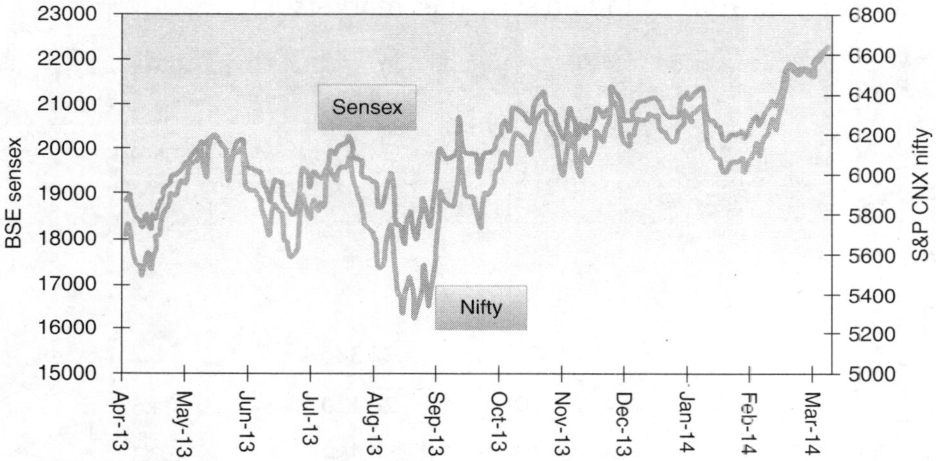

Source: Based on closing price of S&P BSE SENSEX and CNX Nifty extracted from www.bseindia.com and www.nseindia.com, accessed on January 3, 2015.

TABLE 2.6 Major stock indices and their percentage variation

Year/ month	BSE sensex	Percentage variation	BSE 100	Percentage variation	CNX nifty	Percentage variation	CNX 500	Percentage variation	SX40	Percentage variation
1	2	3	4	5	6	7	8	9	10	11
2008–09	9,709	−37.9	2,867	−40	3,021	−36.2	2,295	−40	Na	Na
2009–10	17,528	80.5	5,394	88.2	5,249	73.8	4,313	87.9	Na	Na
2010–11	19,445	10.9	5,856	8.6	5,834	11.1	4,626	7.3	Na	Na
2011–12	17,404	−10.5	5,315	−9.2	5,296	−9.2	4,222	−4.1	Na	Na
2012–13	18,836	8.2	5,679	6.8	5,683	7.3	4,438	5.1	Na	Na
2013–14	22,386	18.8	6,707	18.1	6,704	18.0	5,225	17.7	13,298	Na

Source: Websites of BSE, NSE and MCX-SX, accessed on January 7, 2015.

[6] http://www.sebi.gov.in, accessed on January 7, 2015.

BSE market capitalization to GDP ratio has increased from 63.2% in 2012–13 to 65.3% in 2013–14. Similarly, at NSE also the ratio has increased from 61.7% in 2012–13 to 64.1% in 2013–14. The all-India cash turnover to GDP ratio, however, declined further in 2013–14 to 29.5 percent from 32.2 percent in 2012–13.

Figure 2.4 exhibits the performance of Nifty and SENSEX over the years. Table 2.6 displays **variations in major stock indices** in India. Table 2.7 displays the changes in major indicators of Indian securities markets.

TABLE 2.7 Major indicators of indian securities markets

Item	2012–13	2013–14	Percentage variation over the previous year	
			2012–13	2013–14
1	2	3	4	5
A. Indices				
BSE sensex				
Year-end	18,836	22,386	8.2	18.8
Average	18,202	20,120	4.5	10.5
CNX nifty	5,683	6,704	7.3	18
Year-end	5,520	6,010	5.3	8.9
Average	NA	13,298	NA	NA
SX40	NA	11,960	NA	NA
Year-end				
average				
B. Annualised volatility (percent)				
BSE sensex	12.5	17.5	NA	NA
CNX nifty	12.9	18.1	NA	NA
SX40	NA	16.5	NA	NA
C. Total turnover (₹ crore)				
Cash segment (All-india) of *which*	32,57,086	33,41,337	−6.4	2.6
BSE	5,48,774	5,21,664	−17.8	−4.9
NSE	27,08,279	28,08,488	−3.7	−3.7
MCX-SX	33	11,185	NA	3793*

Recent Developments in Indian Capital Markets

Along with the sweeping reforms on the procedural front, regulators have also introduced a number of risk management initiatives to minimize the market, operational and systemic risk. To protect the investors from risk, SEBI requires the exchanges to have:

1. Individual securities and index-based market-wide circuit breakers
2. Value at Risk (VaR) based margins
3. Mark-to-market margins
4. Time limits for margin payments ($T + 1$ basis)
5. Real-time monitoring of intraday trading limits and gross exposure limits

Beyond the Basics 2.8 NSE VaR for Government Securities

Since the global financial melt-down in 2008, risk management has been a key concern for all financial market regulators and participants across the world. NSE (National Stock Exchange) has also taken various initiatives to make its risk management systems more robust and to develop the market infrastructure further.

A VaR (value at risk) system has been developed by NSE for measuring the market risk related to Government of India (GoI) securities. The NSE-VaR system builds on the daily yield curves available in the NSE database (NSE-ZCYC). NSE-ZCYC is known for its conceptual soundness and empirical performance and is popular amongst market participants seeking fixed income instruments.

The system enables measuring of VaR through five alternative methods—variance-covariance (normal), historical simulation, weighted normal, weighted historical simulation and the extreme value methods.

Source: http://www.nseindia.com, accessed on January 5, 2015.

Debt Market in India[7]

The debt market in India, also called the Indian Fixed Income Market, comprises three main segments viz., the government securities market, the corporate debt market and the money market.

Prior to the economic reforms in India in 1991, the Indian fixed income markets had predominantly functioned in an administered interest rate regime, where debt instruments generated fixed returns. The Government's constant requirement for funds to bridge the gap between its budget and fiscal deficit was met by an automatic monetization practice and by overdraft methods. Contractual savings, postal savings and national saving schemes were the chief debt instruments with fixed risk free returns with a sovereign guarantee from the Government. Banks had high statutory liquidity ratio (SLR) requirements to be met and hence held a large

[7] This section has been contributed by Ms. Nupur Gupta-Bhattacharya, MBA, CFA (India), working as Assistant Professor in Department of Finance at K.J. Somaiya Institute of Management Studies and Research, Mumbai, India.

portion of Government papers as a major part of their investments. In India, the implementation of the Narasimham Committee recommendations on banking sector reforms in 1998, progressively replaced the administered interest rates with market determined interest rates (with a few exceptions). Interest rates underwent a moribund trend during the 2002–2005 due to competition as well as the high liquidity in the system.

Since 2010–2014, interest rates have undergone an increasing trend (refer Figure 2.5), thereby entailing that the Indian economy is slowly falling in line with the interest rate series that are witnessed in the developed countries. Therefore, the players in the fixed income market need to get habituated to this change, and develop relevant instruments to handle this new development.

Figure 2.5 Interest rate scenario in India.

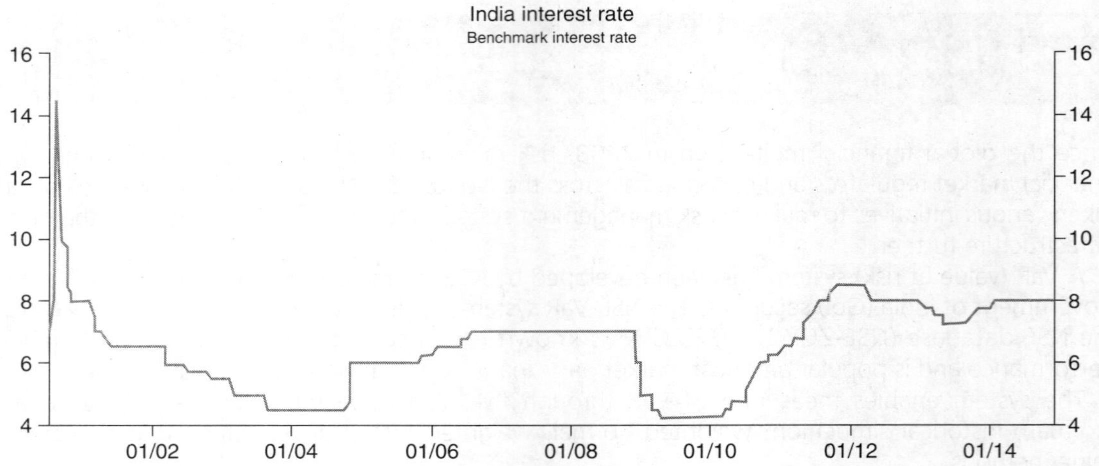

The Indian fixed income markets can be analyzed in terms of the following categories:

1. Government securities markets comprising Central Government Securities (G-Sec) and State Development Loans. This market is regulated by the Reserve Bank of India (RBI).
2. Money markets encompassing call money, term money, the Repo and the Reverse Repo, Collaterized Borrowing and Lending Obligations (CBLO), Treasury Bills, Commercial Papers, Certificates of Deposits, Inter Corporate deposits and Bill Discounting. This market is regulated by the Reserve bank of India (RBI).
3. Corporate debts including PSU Bonds, Corporate Debentures and Bonds of Financial Institutions and Banks. This market is regulated by the Securities Exchange Board of India (SEBI).

Money Market Instruments in India

1. **Treasury Bills:** Treasury Bills are issued by the RBI on behalf of the Government of India, and are thus actually a class of Government Securities.

- Currently, T-Bills are issued for the following maturity periods:
  (a) 91 days
  (b) 182 days
  (c) 364 days

The Market Stabilization Scheme (MSS) was initiated on April 1, 2004 under an MOU between the Government of India and the RBI. Treasury bills and dated securities of the central government are issued as an instrument of stabilization. The tenure, timing of issuances along with the amount is notified by the RBI as a calendar of issuances.

The RBI conducts auctions for 182–day and 364-day t-Bills on a fortnightly basis, whereas for 91-day t-Bills, it holds auctions on a weekly basis. There is a notified value of bills available for the auction for 91-day t-Bills, which is announced 2 days before the auction. There is no specified amount for the auction pertaining to 364-day t-Bills. Thus, at any given point of time, it is possible to buy t-Bills to tailor one's investment requirements.

2. **Commercial Paper (CP):** These are issued by corporate entities in denominations of ₹2.5 million and usually have a maturity period of 90 days. Although CPs can also be issued for maturity periods of 180 days and one year, the most active market is for 90-day CPs. CPs have to be compulsorily rated by a recognized credit rating agency and only those corporate entities who have a minimum credit rating of A3. The funds raised through CPs do not represent fresh borrowings for the corporate issuer, but instead they merely substitute a part of the banking limits available to it.
3. **Certificate of Deposits (CD):** These are issued by banks in denominations of ₹0.5 million, and have a maturity period ranging from 30 days to 3 years. Banks are allowed to issue CDs with a maturity period of less than one year, whereas financial institutions are allowed to issue CDs with a maturity period of at least one year. The fixed income market is most active for the one year maturity bracket; whereas longer dated securities are not much in demand. One of the main reasons for being an active market for CDs is that their issuance does not attract reserve requirements as they are obligations issued by a bank.
4. **Public Sector Undertaking Bonds (PSU bonds):** These are long-term debt instruments issued by Public Sector Undertakings (PSUs). The issuance of these bonds began in a big way in the late eighties when the central Government Stopped/reduced funding to PSUs through the general budget. Their maturity period ranges between 2 and 20 years. Most PSU bonds in India are made on a private placement basis, as they are meant for a targeted investor base at market determined interest rates. These PSU bonds are offered in two ways—with taxable coupons and the other with tax free coupons.
5. **Bonds of Public Financial Institutions (PFIs):** Apart from PSUs, Financial Institutions in India are allowed to issue bonds, in a much higher quantum, and this is done in the following two ways:
   (a) Public issues targeted at retail investors and trusts.
   (b) Private placements to large institutional investors.

   Usually, transfers of the former type of bonds are exempt from stamp duty, whereas only a part of the bonds issued privately have this faculty. On an incremental basis, bonds of PFIs are second only to GOI securities in their value of issuance.
6. **Retail Debt:** With effect from January 2002, the RBI has permitted retail investors to submit non-competitive bids at primary option through any bank or primary dealer. The minimum amount of the bid is ₹10,000 and multiples thereof subject to the condition that a single bid does not exceed ₹1 crore. Table 2.8 highlights the growth trajectory of retail debt segment in the Indian capital markets.

These are long term debt instruments issued by private sector companies with face values of generally ₹1000. They have maturity periods ranging between 1 to 15 years. These debentures are less liquid as compared

TABLE 2.8 RDM business growth in India

Month/Year	No of trades	Traded quantity	Traded value (₹ lakhs)
2014–2015	0	0	0.00
2013–2014	2	50	0.06
2012–2013	5	2,00,030	194.55
2011–2012	3	30	0.03
2010–2011	5	50	0.05
2009–2010	7	70	0.09
2008–2009	1	10	0.01
2007–2008	2	20	0.02
2006–2007	4	12,120	13.69
2005–2006	0	0	0.00
2004–2005	31	1,22,390	149.28
2003–2004	382	1,19,920	154.84
2002–2003	553	2,53,100	309.82

Source: http://www.nseindia.com/products/content/debt/rdm/historical_rdm_businessgrowth.htmCorporateDebentures, accessed on December 8, 2014.

to PSU bonds, and their liquidity is inversely proportional to the residual maturity. A key feature that distinguishes debentures, from bonds is that the former involves stamp duty payment. Debenture stamp duty and the quantum of incidences vary among states. There are two kinds of stamp duties levied on debentures, viz., issuance and transfer. Issuance stamp duty is paid in the state where the principal mortgage deed is registered. Over the years, although issuance stamp duties have been found to be declining, they are reasonably uniform. Stamp duty on transfer is paid to the state in which the registered office of the company is located. Transfer stamp duty remains high in many states, and is probably the biggest deterrent for trading in debentures, resulting in a lack of liquidity.

7. **Pass through Certificates (PTCs):** This is an instrument with cash flows derived from the cash flow of another underlying instrument or loan. They are most commonly issued by foreign banks, such as the Citibank, on the basis of their car loan or mortgage/housing loan portfolio.

Major developments in the Indian corporate bond market are illustrated in Exhibit 2.3.

Since security and credit worthiness are two key factors in debt securities, credit rating plays a very important role. The nearby box illustrates the credit rating practices at CRISIL.

Exhibit 2.4 exhibits the rating scale for long-term instruments by Credit Rating and Information Services of India Limited (CRISIL).

Marketview 2.1 Mobilization of Retail Debt in India

Indian Firms acquired ₹4,000 crore via NCDs as of August 2014 via retail issuance of non-convertible debentures in the ongoing fiscal year (2014–15), primarily to meet working capital requirements. A swelling amount of ₹42,383 crore was garnered through 35 issues of NCDs in the entire fiscal year 2013–14. NCDs are bonds that cannot be converted into stocks and usually offer higher interest rates than convertible debentures. According to the latest data available with the Securities and Exchange Board of India (SEBI), a total of nine companies including Shriram City Union Finance, SREI Infrastructure Finance Ltd and Muthoot Finance Ltd collectively raised ₹3,939 crore via NCDs till during the current fiscal year (till August 4, 2014) 2014–15 through 10 issues. This was more than ₹1,550 crore which was originally targeted. Kosamattam Finance Ltd opted for the NCD route twice to raise funds. Individually, Shriram Transport Finance Company Limited raised ₹1,975 crore against a target of ₹500. Muthoot Finance collected ₹466 crore against a base size of ₹250 crore and ECL Finance garnered ₹400 crore against the target size of ₹200 crore. Besides, Muthoottu Mini Financiers raked in ₹262 crore against a target of ₹125 crore and Muthoot Fincorp mopped up ₹207 crore against a base size of ₹100 crore. During April-August period of 2013–14, only two firms—Shriram Transport Finance Company Ltd and SREI Infrastructure Finance—had raised ₹736 crore and ₹134 crore, respectively, via NCDs.

Source: http://profit.ndtv.com/news/corporates/article-indian-companies-garner-rs-4-000-crore-via-ncds-in-fy15-so-far-656217, accessed on December 8, 2014.

TABLE 2.9 Extract of some listed Indian Bonds on NSE

Company	NSE series	Last price	Change (%)	Face value
ECL Finance	N2	1,099.99	0.59%	1000
ECL Finance	N1	1,027.00	0.39%	1000
Housing and Urban Development Corporation	N2	1,145.98	–0.09%	1000
Housing and Urban Development Corporation	N5	1,088.00	0.69%	1000
India Infoline Finance	N7	1,285.00	–3.02%	1000
India Infoline Finance	N8	1,023.60	–0.23%	1000
India Infoline Finance	N5	1,051.75	0%	1000

Exhibit 2.3 Major Development in the Indian Corporate Bond Market

Year	Reforms	Objectives	Outcomes
December 2006	SEBI permits BSE to set up a reporting platform.	Capturing all trade information about corporate bonds to enable efficient price discovery and reliable clearing and settlement process.	SEBI has been publishing data on trades on the three platforms (BSE, NSE and FIMMDA) on its website from 2007.
January 2007	SEBI will be responsible for the primary market (Public issues and private placement by listed companies) and secondary market. RBI will be responsible for the repo/reverse repo transactions in corporate debt.	Clarity on the agencies responsible for different segments of the corporate debt market.	SEBI has been implementing reforms in the public issues and private placement market. RBI recently introduced guidelines for corporate repos.
January 2007	Corporate Bonds will be traded using existing exchanges at NSE and BSE. There would be no separate trading platforms for different kinds of (retail vs. Institutional) investors.	Efficient use of existing infrastructure.	Functioning well.
April 2007	SEBI allows stock exchanges to provide services for clearing and settlement of corporate bonds.	Develop a transparent and efficient secondary market for corporate bonds.	Became operational (July 2007). Trading is captured and reported by SEBI on its website from August 2007.
April 2007	SEBI permits both BSE and NSE to have in place corporate bond trading platforms.	Capturing all trade information about corporate bonds to enable efficient price discovery and reliable clearing and settlement process.	Progress has been slow as market continues to be dominated by private placements.
April 2007	SEBI reduces tradable lots in corporate bonds.	Encourage participation of retail investors. Provide access to better information about companies issuing debentures.	Expected to improve participation in the corporate bond market.
August 2007	SEBI makes it mandatory that companies issuing debentures should disseminate all information (default to pay interest, revision of ratings, etc.) about the debentures to the investors and general public.	Provide access to better information about companies issuing debentures.	Expected to improve participation in the corporate bond market.
May 2008	Corporate Bonds and Securitization Advisory Committee (CoBoSAC) set up to make recommendations to SEBI.	Advisement on developing market for corporate bonds and securitized debt instruments.	Functioning well. Four meetings have been conducted so far to discuss and advise on the bond market.
May 2009	Simplified listing agreement put in place by SEBI.	Reduction in time and cost of issuance process. (Especially for companies with listed equity who have complied with the detailed disclosure requirements).	Expected to reduce the long and expensive issuance process for corporate debt.

(*Continued*)

Exhibit 2.3 Continued

Year	Reforms	Objectives	Outcomes
August 2009	Mandatory to report inter-scheme transfers of corporate bonds by Mutual funds (on NSE, BSE and FIMMDA).	More detailed information dissemination on trading.	Operational
October 2009	SEBI mandated the clearing and settlement of all trades through National Securities Clearing Corporation (NSCCL) or the Indian Clearing Corporation Limited (ICCL).	Clearing and settlement of trades in this market to follow the International Organization of Security Commissions (IOSCO) standards and the global best practices by way of well-established clearing and settlement procedures through recognized clearing and settlement agencies.	Clearing and settlement commenced through both clearing agencies at BSE and NSE from December 2009.

Source: http://rbi.org.in/scripts/PublicationsView.aspx?id=15725, accessed on December 8, 2014.

Beyond the Basics 2.9 CRISIL's Long-term Ratings

CRISIL's long-term ratings reflect CRISIL's current opinion on the relative safety of timely payment of interest and principal on the rated financial obligations which have an originally contracted maturity of more than one year.

The long-term debt obligations typically rated by CRISIL includes:

1. Non-convertible debentures/Bonds/Preference shares
2. Fixed deposits
3. Loans
4. Structured debt

CRISIL rates a wide range of entities for long-term debt obligations, which includes:

1. Industrial companies
2. Banks
3. Non-banking financial companies (NBFCs)
4. Infrastructure entities
5. Microfinance institutions
6. Insurance companies
7. Mutual funds
8. State governments
9. Urban local bodies

Source: http://www.crisil.com/ratings/credit-ratings-bonds-long-terms.html, accessed on December 13, 2014.

Exhibit 2.4 CRISIL Rating Scale for Long-Term Instruments

CRISIL AAA (Highest Safety)	Instruments with this rating are considered to have the highest degree of safety regarding timely servicing of financial obligations. Such instruments carry lowest credit risk.
CRISIL AA (High Safety)	Instruments with this rating are considered to have high degree of safety regarding timely servicing of financial obligations. Such instruments carry very low credit risk.
CRISIL A (Adequate Safety)	Instruments with this rating are considered to have adequate degree of safety regarding timely servicing of financial obligations. Such instruments carry low credit risk.
CRISIL BBB (Moderate Safety)	Instruments with this rating are considered to have moderate degree of safety regarding timely servicing of financial obligations. Such instruments carry moderate credit risk.
CRISIL BB (Moderate Risk)	Instruments with this rating are considered to have moderate risk of default regarding timely servicing of financial obligations.
CRISIL B (High Risk)	Instruments with this rating are considered to have high risk of default regarding timely servicing of financial obligations.
CRISIL C (Very High Risk)	Instruments with this rating are considered to have very high risk of default regarding timely servicing of financial obligations.
CRISIL D Default	Instruments with this rating are in default or are expected to be in default soon.

Note: *1) CRISIL may apply '+' (plus) or '–' (minus) signs for ratings from 'CRISIL AA' to 'CRISIL C' to reflect comparative standing within the category.*

2) CRISIL may assign rating outlooks for ratings from 'CRISIL AAA' to 'CRISIL B'. Ratings on Rating Watch will not carry outlooks. A rating outlook indicates the direction in which a rating may move over a medium-term horizon of one to two years. A rating outlook can be 'Positive', 'Stable' or 'Negative'. A 'Positive' or 'Negative' rating outlook is not necessarily a precursor of a rating change.

3) A suffix of 'r' indicates investments carrying non-credit risk.The 'r' suffix indicates that payments on the rated instrument have significant risks other than credit risk. The terms of the instrument specify that the payments to investors will not be fixed, and could be linked to one or more external variables such as commodity prices, equity indices, or foreign exchange rates. This could result in variability in payments, including possible material loss of principal, because of adverse movement in value of the external variables. The risk of such adverse movement in price/value is not addressed by the rating.

4) CRISIL may assign a rating of 'NM' (Not Meaningful) to instruments that have factors present in them, which render the outstanding rating meaningless. These include reorganization or liquidation of the issuer, the obligation being under dispute in a court of law or before a statutory authority.

5) A prefix of 'PP-MLD' indicates that the instrument is a principal-protected market-linked debenture. The terms of such instruments indicate that while the issuer promises to pay back the face value/principal of the instrument, the coupon rates of these instruments will not be fixed, and could be linked to one or more external variables such as commodity prices, equity share prices, indices or foreign exchange rates.

Source: http://www.crisil.com/ratings/credit-ratings-bonds-long-terms.html, accessed on December 13, 2014.

SUMMARY

- ☑ The markets for securities are highly regulated entities with many participants. Trading of financial securities takes place in a completely automated manner through certain intermediaries recognized by the markets.

- ☑ The organized financial markets in India are divided into two broad categories:
  1. Money market
  2. Capital market

- ☑ The money market is a market for short-term securities. The main instruments are T-bills, certificates of deposit, commercial bills, call/notice money market, cash management bills and collateralized borrowing and lending obligation.

- ☑ The average turnover of Indian money markets is ₹1,00,000 crore daily, representing nearly 2% of the country's GDP.

- ☑ The capital market is the market for long-term securities, i.e., the securities having maturities of more than one-year. It is a market for long-term funds, both debt and equity, raised domestically and internationally.

- ☑ The equity market in India is divided into two major segments, primary and secondary. The primary segment of the equity market is also called the new issues market (NIM).

- ☑ The secondary segment of the equity market in India comprises of the stock exchanges where the issued securities are listed and traded. Bombay Stock Exchange (BSE) and National Stock Exchange (NSE) are the main stock exchanges in the country.

- ☑ The primary markets in India have become vibrant on account of a number of reforms and initiatives taken by SEBI. Free pricing of equity and increase in efficiency of the delivery system through dematerialization of shares have been amongst the key initiatives taken by SEBI since its establishment.

- ☑ Indian companies can raise equity capital from the primary market through three alternative routes:
  1. Public issue
  2. Rights issue
  3. Private placement

- ☑ Public issues are offered for subscription at predetermined prices, i.e., fixed price issues or at the prices determined through book building.

- ☑ As per the SEBI website, there are 21 stock exchanges in India as of December 2014. Bombay Stock Exchange (BSE) and National Stock Exchange (NSE) are the two major stock exchanges of the country. They account for almost 100% turnover in the secondary equity market in the country.

- ☑ All transactions in all groups of securities in the Equity segment listed on BSE and NSE are required to be settled on T + 2 basis (w.e.f. from April 1, 2003), called the rolling settlement.

☑ The indices can be of three types: Price-weighted, equal-weighted and value-weighted index.

☑ There are a large number of indices in BSE and NSE that track some or the other sector or theme. However, S&P BSE SENSEX and CNX Nifty are the most tracked indices in the country.

☑ The debt market in India, also called the Indian Fixed Income Market, comprises three main segments, viz., the government securities market, the corporate debt market and the money market.

KEY WORDS

CONCEPT QUESTIONS

1. Discuss the efficacy of the ratings of securities granted by various rating agencies in the light of the increased competition among the rating agencies in the country.

2. How has the abolition of the Controller of Capital Issues transformed the landscape of fund raising in the country?

3. Download relevant data from the BSE website and comment on the performance of the realty sector as compared to S&P BSE SENSEX over the past few years.

4. Discuss the initiatives taken by the government to boost the corporate bond market in the country. Why is the market still shallow despite the regulatory efforts to promote it?

5. Consider the data given below for two days and 5 stocks to calculate the index value of price-weighted, equal-weighted and value-weighted indices on day *t* if the index value on the base date is 100.

Share	Base Date Price	*t* Day Price	Number of O/S Shares (in million)
1	75	90	9
2	80	70	10
3	130	150	14
4	40	100	15
5	35	67	11

6. Write a commentary on the growth of Indian securities market.

7. Foreign Institutional Investors have made a major contribution towards the growth of Indian stock market. Do you agree? Why?

8. Discuss the measures taken by SEBI to minimize the market, operational and systemic risk to which investors are exposed to in the India securities market.

9. Government securities market and money markets play a key role in the Indian securities market. Discuss.

10. Explain the role of various intermediaries involved in making a company's initial public offer available to the general public for subscription.

Risk-Return Analysis: The Measurement of Risk and Return

3

CHAPTER OBJECTIVES

- ❒ Understanding the concept of risk and return
- ❒ Evaluating different ex-post measures of return
- ❒ Discussing the concept of probability and expected return
- ❒ Assessing the concept of individual and interactive risk
- ❒ Computing risk measurements like standard deviation, variance, correlation and covariance
- ❒ Exploring the concept of beta

Though the motives to invest may span from income to growth, stability to safety to a host of specific individual objectives, yet the most prominent reason to invest continues to be the pecuniary motive to earn returns. People are very comfortable talking about the returns portion of their investment decision but they tend to overlook or avoid another inherent part of investment decision, i.e., ***risk***. In fact, there seems to be a very obvious abhorrence towards risk on the part of investors. But closing one's eyes would not make the threat go away. Risk and return co-exist, therefore, active pursuit of investment avenues giving high return for low or no risk is as fallacious as believing in a diet pill that would allow one to binge eat and yet lose weight.

Selecting investments solely on the basis of maximization of returns can lead to erroneous results. Universal truth is that risk and return are inexorably tied to one another and investing is nothing but a risk-return trade-off. In fact the concept of 'risk-free asset', often represented by government securities, seems to be challenged by the recent developments in the market such as sovereign debt crisis in Europe and downgrade of US credit rating by Standard and Poor's (S&P)(refer Marketview 3.1).

Acceptance of the fact that risk is a part and parcel of any investment decision and analyzing securities and portfolios in the context of both risk and return leads to better choice of investment mix. A clear understanding of risk and return and what impacts them is the essential building block of the investment parable. To summarize, risk and return are the key determinants of security prices. Performance analysis of any investment requires that the investors measure returns over a given period of time. Return and risk being intricately related, measurement of return automatically helps in understanding the investment risks better.

Any investment decision comprises two major areas:

1. Identification of the assets/securities to be held
2. Proportionate allocation of investible surplus to the assets/securities thus identified

Both the above-mentioned decisions are made through a two-step process, viz.,

1. Security analysis
2. Portfolio analysis and selection

The process of preparing the estimates of return and risk associated with securities available for investment over a given holding period is called security analysis. It provides inputs for the second important decision in investment process, i.e., allocation of funds. Comparison of risk-return profiles thus generated to decide fund allocation constitutes portfolio analysis and selection.

Since security analysis is based on the premise that investors are concerned with the returns, they can expect from holding a security for a finite period and the risk that the returns would be less than expected, therefore risk-return analysis becomes a key area of focus in the investment process.

This chapter aims at providing a deep insight into the attributes of investment risk and return and their measurement.

Marketview 3.1 S&P Downgrades U.S. Credit Rating for the First Time in History

The world was shocked in August 2011 by the downgrade of U.S. credit rating by Standard & Poor's to below AAA. The U.S. credit rating has never been downgraded in the past and this downgrade has become a symbol of changing times. It has been considered by analysts as a huge setback for the American political system.

In its announcement of downgrade, the credit rating company categorically stated that "political brinkmanship" in the context of debate over the debt seems to indicate that the U.S. government's ability to manage its finances is "less stable, less effective and less predictable."

The downgrade of U.S. credit rating to AA + made the world's safest investments, the AAA rated U.S. Treasury bonds, seem riskier for investors. These bonds have enjoyed AAA rating for more than 70 years and have helped US borrow at very cheap rates to fund its government operations.

The sovereign debt crisis in Europe has also raised questions about this so-called 'risk-free rate of return.'

Source: Based on story published on http://www.washingtonpost.com/business/economy/sandp-considering-first-downgrade-of-us-credit-rating/2011/08/05/gIQAqKelxl_print.html, accessed on October 25, 2014.

Security Return

All rational investors seek to maximize possible returns on their investments. The term 'maximum possible return' accommodates the element of risk in the returns that can be earned from investing in available securities. It allows for the possibility that returns may vary from their theoretical maximum level.

Not only is return the ultimate culmination of the investment decision but it is also a key metric in evaluating alternative investment options. Both historical and estimated returns are essential part of investment decisions.

Meaning of Return

Simply put, return is gain or loss that arises from holding a security for a particular period. It is usually quoted in percentage terms. Gain or loss from holding a security for a certain period can be decomposed into two distinct components:

1. Income
2. Capital gain/loss

Income represents the periodic cash receipts during the holding period and it can be called current income. Depending on the type of security, this income can be in the form of either interest or dividend. The term yield is often used in the context of income. It expresses the income component of return relative to the purchase price of the security. To illustrate with an example, the yield on a ₹1000 par value, 7% coupon bond purchased for ₹900 would be 7.78%(70/900). Similarly, the yield on a common stock paying Re. 1 in dividends per year and purchased for ₹40 per share is 2.5%.

Capital gain/loss represents the change in the price of the security during the holding period. The capital gain or loss is computed on the basis of the difference between the acquisition/purchase price of the asset and the price at which it is sold at the end of the holding period. If the purchase price exceeds the price at which the security is sold, the difference is termed as capital loss and if the purchase price is less than the selling price of the security, the difference between the two is termed as capital gain.

Thus conceptually,

$$\text{Total Return} = \text{Income or Yield} + \text{Capital Gain or Loss}$$

In the context of investment decision, we need to distinguish between various terms related to return such as real return, nominal return, realized return, expected return, required return, excess return and risk-free rate of return. These concepts have been explained in the subsequent sections.

Real and Nominal Rate of Return

The nominal rate of return is the contractual rate promised to be paid on a deposit, loan, savings account or other financial contracts over a specified period of time. Once committed, it does not fluctuate with changes in company or market conditions. Effectually, the nominal rate is the money earned on an investment before adjusting it for factors such as inflation. Assuming there is no risk of default, nominal rate of return can be called risk-free rate of return but the same becomes risky when evaluated in terms of the purchasing power because of the uncertainty in the rate of inflation.

The rate of return on an investment that has been adjusted for changes in prices due to inflation or other external effects is called the real rate of return. Thus, while nominal rate of return expresses growth rate of money invested, the real rate of return measures the growth rate of investor's purchasing power. For example, let's assume your bank pays you an interest of 7% per annum on your deposit with it. If the current rate of inflation is 3% per annum, then the real return on your deposit would be 4%. This means that even if the contractual rate of return is 7%, the real value of your savings appreciates by 4% only during one-year period due to the impact of inflation.

Concept of Realized Return and Expected Return

Given the central role of returns in investment decision-making, we need to distinguish between certain types of returns that serve as the basis for choice of security/asset to invest in. Two such concepts are realized return and expected return. Realized return is a post-facto return. It is that return which has already been generated. It is therefore a historical return, something that has occurred in the past. It is the actual amount of return that a security earns during its holding period. To understand the concept of realized return better, let's use a Numerical Example. Suppose an amount of ₹15000 is put under fixed deposit with SBI on January 1, 2013 at a nominal interest rate of 9% for one year. On December 31, 2013, the deposit will amount to ₹16350 (15000 + 1350). The realized return on the FD is 1350/15000 or 9%. In another example, suppose the total annual return on BSE SENSEX for a given year was 11%. This would have been the realized return of the investor who had invested in 30 shares in the index on January 1, of the given year and sold them on December 31, of the same year.

Realized return is used for evaluating how an investment has actually performed in the past and also for making projections and predictions for the future. On the other hand, expected return is an anticipated return, i.e., the return an investor expects to earn over some future period. It is a return that an investor predicts based on a number of factors to decide whether to invest or not. Though it is a forecasted return that may or may not occur, yet it forms the basis for the choice of a particular security for investment. If the expected return has positive value, the investor may go ahead and acquire the security. However, it needs to be understood that the expected return is usually based on historical data and is not absolutely assured. Investors may purchase an asset/security if the expected return is adequate, but they must appreciate the fact that the predicted expected return may or may not be actually realized.

Expected return is computed by assigning probabilities to various possible outcomes/returns. It is the weighted average of all probable returns for that investment. It's the most likely return one can expect to earn from an investment based on its risk. Expected return depends on the expected price of the security and the current price at which the security under consideration is quoting. The exact computation of expected return has been illustrated in the subsequent sections of this chapter.

Required Return, Excess Return and Holding Period Return

Another term related to choice of asset/security to invest in is '***required rate of return*** (RRR).' Required return is the minimum return earned by an investment that will induce an investor to put his money into a particular security/asset. It is the lowest amount that an investor needs to get him to choose an investment. It's an opportunity cost. It is the return that an investor wants as compensation for the risk that he is bearing by parting with his savings. In other words, required rate of return is the incentive needed to make the investor part with his money. RRR serves as a benchmark to help investors decide where to put their money.

So how do investors determine RRR? A logical beginning point would be ***risk free rate of return***, a return that is theoretically available to all the investors without taking any risk. Risk-free rate of return is the return from an investment with zero risk. It represents the return an investor would expect from an absolutely risk-free investment over its holding period. In practice, however, the risk-free rate does not exist as even the safest investments might carry some risk. However, in the study of investment management, risk-free rate is theoretically accepted to exist and the interest rate on Government securities is often used as a proxy for risk-free rate.

Obviously investors would look to be compensated over and above the risk-free rate if they park their money in risky assets. In other words, they expect a reward for taking additional risk and this reward is called 'risk premium' in the language of investing. Thus a rational investor's required rate of return on any security/asset comprises two parts: risk-free rate and risk premium.

Simply put,

$$\text{Required Rate of Return} = \text{Risk free return} + \text{Risk premium}$$

$$\text{Risk Premium} = pr + fr + br + mr + or$$

where

pr = Compensation for bearing purchasing power risk
fr = Compensation for bearing financial risk
br = Compensation for bearing business risk
mr = Compensation for bearing market risk
or = Compensation for bearing other risks.

Required rate of return may also be represented as exhibited in Figure 3.1.

Figure 3.1 Required rate of return.

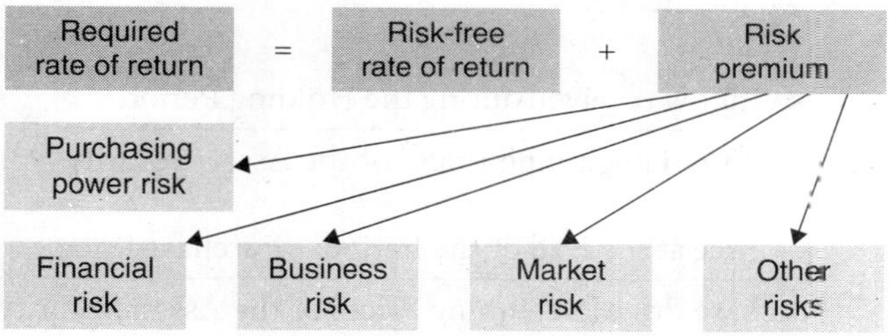

To understand how RRR impacts asset/security choice, assume you require a return of 10% per annum as an inducement to make you invest your money in a share that you believe you can easily sell in the market at the end of a certain period. The risk-free rates is 4%. Your estimation of 10% RRR is based on the reasoning that if you don't earn even 6% risk premium, then you'd be better off putting your money in a risk-free asset. Only the lure of additional 6% can make you consider investing in stocks that are inherently volatile and whose returns are not guaranteed. It is important to note here that RRR will be different for every individual investor depending on his goals, constraints, appetite to take risk and other unique factors.

Another metric used to evaluate the efficacy of investment decision is ***excess return***. It is defined as return rate on an asset/security relative to the risk-free rate of return rate. It is measured as the difference between the actual return on a risky asset and risk-free rate of return during a given period. For example, if the rate of return is 9% and the risk-free rate is 3%, then the investment's excess return is 6%. Excess returns are returns in excess of those required by some asset pricing models that form integral part of the investment theory.

Alternately, excess returns from a security or portfolio are defined as returns that exceed some benchmark or index with a comparable level of risk. In fact, the concept of excess return is widely used as a measure of the predictive ability and value addition by the portfolio manager. It is also called 'alpha' and it measures the manager's ability to "beat the market."

For example, consider a large-cap Indian Mutual Fund that has the same level of risk as the NSE Nifty. If the fund generates a return of 13% in a year when the Nifty has only advanced 9%, the difference of 4% is the excess return, or the alpha generated by the fund manager of that large cap fund. As discussed later in the book, critics of managed portfolios have always contented, with strong empirical evidence, that it is near to impossible to beat the market and generate excess returns on a consistent basis over long-term. The assertion that most fund managers tend to underperform the benchmark index over extended periods has led to the increasing popularity of index funds and exchange-traded funds amongst individual investors.

Yet another term, ***holding period return***, has been used liberally in the preceding text. It represents the rate of return over the period for which the asset/security has been actually held.

Measurement of Ex-post Return and Expected Return

Total return

Total return (holding period return) on an asset/security may be computed as

$$= \frac{\text{Cash Inflow during the Holding Period} + \text{Price Change over the Holding Period}}{\text{Purchase Price (Beginning Price) of the Asset/Security}}$$

The above equation comprises two distinct parts:

$$\text{Current Yield} = \frac{\text{Cash Inflow received during the Holding Period}}{\text{Purchase Price (Beginning Price) of the Asset/Security}}$$

$$\text{Capital Gain/Loss} = \frac{\text{Price at the End of the Period} - \text{Purchase Price}}{\text{Purchase Price (Beginning Price) of the Asset/Security}}$$

Numerical Example 1

Consider the following information for an equity share to calculate its total returns:

Price at the beginning of the year = ₹50
Dividend paid at the end of the year = ₹1.2
Selling price at the end of the year = ₹60

Solution:

$$\text{Total return} = \frac{1.2 + (60 - 50)}{50} = 0.224 \text{ or } 22.4\%$$

This can be decomposed into current yield and capital gains

$$\text{Total return} = \frac{1.2}{50} + \frac{(60-50)}{50} = 0.224 \text{ or } 22.4\%$$

Since total return includes both yield and price change and measures return on original investment, it can be used for comparative analysis of returns over a given period of time.

Calculation of total return for CNX Nifty is illustrated in Beyond the Basics 3.1.

In the case of fixed income securities, the computation of holding period return is slightly more complicated, especially when one needs to compare bonds/securities of differing maturities. In such situation, total return needs to be re-expressed as the rate of return for a common period for all the securities under consideration. Typically all such investment returns are expressed as an effective annual rate (EAR), which is nothing but % increment in the funds invested over a single year horizon. EAR can be computed through following equation:

$$1 + \text{EAR} = [1 + r_f(T)]^{1/T}$$

where $r_f(T)$ is the total return over a holding period of length T and it is calculated as:

$$r_f(T) = \frac{\text{Par Value}}{\text{Price at Time } T} - 1$$

Beyond the Basics 3.1 The CNX Nifty

The CNX Nifty is a 50 stock index accounting for 22 sectors of the economy. It represents about 70.14% of the free float market capitalization of the stocks listed on NSE as on March 31, 2014.

The total traded value for the last six months ending March 2014 of all index constituents is approximately 55.67% of the traded value of all stocks on the NSE.

Impact cost of the CNX Nifty for a portfolio size of ₹50 lakh is 0.06% for the month of March 2014.

CNX Nifty is professionally maintained and is ideal for derivatives trading.

Total returns index

CNX Nifty reflects the return one would get if investment is made in the index portfolios. As Nifty is computed in real-time, it takes into account only the price movements. However, the price indices do not consider the return from dividend payments of index constituent stocks. Only the capital gains due to price movement is measured by the price index. In order to get a true picture of returns, the dividends received from the index constituent stocks also need to be included in the index movement. Such an index, which includes the dividends received, is called the total returns index.

The total returns Index is an index to reflect the returns on the index from index gain/loss plus dividend payments by constituent index stocks.

Total returns index - methodology

Index information on the following are the prerequisites for calculation of total returns (TR) index:

1. Price index close
2. Price index returns
3. Dividend payouts in rupees
4. Index base capitalization on ex-dividend date

Dividend payouts as they occur are indexed on ex-date.

$$\text{Indexed Dividend} = \frac{\{\text{Dividend payout (₹)} \times 1000\}}{\text{Base cap of index (₹)}}$$

Indexed dividends are then reinvested in the index to give TR index.

$$\text{TR Index} = [\text{Prev. TR Index} + (\text{Prev. TR Index} \times \text{Index Returns})] + [\text{Indexed Dividends} + (\text{Indexed Dividends} \times \text{Index Returns})]$$

Base for both the Close index and TR index close will be the same.

Example:

Base index for both the Index and TR index is 1000.

$$\text{Index Return} = (\text{Current Index} - \text{Prev. Index})/\text{Prev. Index}.$$

$$* = [948.82 + (948.82 \times -0.03326)] + [0.096774 + (0.096774 \times -0.03326)]$$

$$= 948.82 + (-31.5577532) + 0.096774 + (-0.00321870324)$$

$$= 917.2622468 + 0.09355529676$$

$$= 917.3536 \text{ (rounding)}$$

$$** = [913.3031 + (913.3031 \times -0.01)] + [0.139905 + (0.139905 \times -0.01)]$$

$$= 913.3031 + (-9.133031) + 0.139905 + (-0.00139905)$$

$$= 904.170069 + 0.13850595$$

$$= 904.3107 \text{ (rounding)}$$

Note: The indexed dividend on Day 7 will participate in the TR index from Day 7 and the indexed dividend on Day 10 will participate from Day 10.

Source: Quoted from http://www.nseindia.com/products/content/equities/indices/cnx_nifty.htm#, accessed on October 31, 2014.

Rates on short-term investments having duration of less than one year are often annualized using simple interest. These are called APR (Annual Percentage Rates).

The relationship between APR, EAR and compounding period is expressed as:

$$\text{APR}^{1} = \frac{(1+\text{EAR})^{T}-1}{T}$$

where $r_f(T) = T \times \text{APR}$

Real rate of return

The concept of real return was introduced earlier in this chapter. Let's see how it is computed.

$$\text{Real Rate of Return} = \frac{1+\text{Nominal Return}}{1+\text{Inflation Rate}} - 1$$

The same formula is applicable to returns of individual years as well as average total returns.

Numerical Example 2

Given an inflation rate of 4% and total return of 17% on an equity share over one year horizon, calculate the inflation adjusted real return.

Solution:

$$\text{Real Rate of Return} = \frac{1+0.17}{1+0.04} - 1 = 0.125 \text{ or } 12.5\%$$

Statistical measures of return

In investment management we need statistical tools to make certain computations using a series of total returns. The two most common tools are:

1. Arithmetic Mean (AM)
2. Geometric Mean (GM)

Arithmetic mean or simply mean of a series of total returns is computed as:

$$\bar{R} = \frac{\sum_{i=1}^{n} R_i}{n}$$

[1] This equation is derived by substituting $r_f(T) = T \times \text{APR}$ in $1 + \text{EAR} = [1 + r_f(T)]^{1/T}$

where

$\bar{R}$ = Arithmetic mean of total returns

R_i = ith value of the total return ($i = 1, 2, 3 \ldots n$)

n = Number of total returns

Numerical Example 3

Use the annual returns of an index over a ten-year period given in Table 3.1 to calculate the mean of returns.

TABLE 3.1 Annual returns (%)

Year	Annual Returns (%)*
2001	−16.2
2002	3.3
2003	71.9
2004	10.7
2005	36.3
2006	39.8
2007	54.8
2008	−51.8
2009	75.8
2010	17.9

Solution:

$$\bar{R} = \frac{(-16.2 + 3.3 + 71.9 + 10.7 + 36.3 + 39.8 + 54.8 - 51.8 + 75.8 + 17.9)}{10}$$

$$= 24.25$$

Spreadsheet Application 1 Consider a security that was bought at a price of ₹6000. At the end of the year 1, its price became ₹6550. At the end of the second year, its price reached a level of ₹ 6990 and at the end of third year, its price rose to ₹7458. The investor sold the security at the end of fourth year when its price was ₹7760. Calculate his average returns.

Solution:

Here, first the holding period return for each year needs to be computed using the following formula.

$$\text{Holding Period Return}^* = \frac{\text{Price at the End of the Period} - \text{Purchase Price}}{\text{Purchase Price (Beginning Price) of the Asset/Security}}$$

* Since there is no dividend.

Here, we need to calculate holding period return for each year, assuming that security was held for only one year at a time.

	A	B	C	D	E
1	Year	Price at the beginning of the holding period	Pice at the end of the holding period	HPR	
2	1	6000	6550	=(C2-B2)/B2	
3	2	6550	6990	0.067176	
4	3	6990	7458	0.066953	
5	4	7458	7760	0.040493	

	A	B	C	D
1	Year	Price at the beginning of the holding period	Pice at the end of the holding period	HPR
2	1	6000	6550	0.091667
3	2	6550	6990	0.067176
4	3	6990	7458	0.066953
5	4	7458	7760	0.040493
			Average Return	**6.657211**

Investor's average return is the average of the HPR earned by him every year. It can be calculated using AVERAGE Function in MS Excel.

	A	B	C	D	E
1	Year	Price at the beginning of the holding period	Pice at the end of the holding period	HPR	
2	1	6000	6550	0.091667	
3	2	6550	6990	0.067176	
4	3	6990	7458	0.066953	
5	4	7458	7760	0.040493	
6			**Average Return**	=AVERAGE(D2:D5)	

	A	B	C	D
1	Year	Price at the beginning of the holding period	Price at the end of the holding period	HPR
2	1	6000	6550	0.091667
3	2	6550	6990	0.067176
4	3	6990	7458	0.066953
5	4	7458	7760	0.040493
6			Average Return	0.066572

Thus, the average return earned by the investor who held the security till the end of the fourth year is 6.66%.

Spreadsheet Application 2 Numerical Example 1 can be solved in MS Excel as follows:

	A	B
1	Year	Annual Returns (%)*
2	2001	-16.2
3	2002	3.3
4	2003	71.9
5	2004	10.7
6	2005	36.3
7	2006	39.8
8	2007	54.8
9	2008	-51.8
10	2009	75.8
11	2010	17.9
12	Average Return	= AVERAGE(B2:B11)

	A	B
1	Year	Annual Returns (%)*
2	2001	-16.2
3	2002	3.3
4	2003	71.9
5	2004	10.7
6	2005	36.3
7	2006	39.8
8	2007	54.8
9	2008	-51.8
10	2009	75.8
11	2010	17.9
12	Average Return	24.25

The average return is 24.25%

Arithmetic mean is the most suitable measure of a series of return calculated for a certain period. However, in case of percentage changes in value over time, it may lead to incorrect results. For example, suppose an investor purchased a stock in year 1 for ₹60 and it rose to ₹120 by year-end. The return at the end of first year is 100% $[(120-60)/60]$. In the second year the stock falls from ₹120 to ₹60 at the end of the year. The return in year 2 is –50% $[(60-120)/120]$. We can summarize following information about the stock:

Year	Total Returns (%)
1	100
2	–50

Therefore, arithmetic mean of the return on the stock would be:

$$= \frac{[100 + (-50)]}{2}$$

$$= 25\%$$

This is an incorrect representation of the actual return earned by an investor who has held the stock for two years. Using the formula to calculate HPR (assuming no dividends), the return works out to be (60 – 60)/60. The investor has earned no return because the price at the end of his holding period is same as the price at which he had acquired the stock.

Clearly, arithmetic mean is not the right statistical measure in such cases. We need to consider another average that describes true returns over multiple periods more accurately. Such a measure is **geometric average return** as it is more suited to show the realized changes in wealth over multiple periods. Geometric mean is considered a better measure of long-term mean return as it measures the compound annual rate of return taking the beginning and end of period values into consideration.

Mathematically,

$$G = [(1 + R_1)\ (1 + R_2) \ldots\ (1 + R_n)]^{1/n} - 1$$

where
R = Total return
n = Number of periods
$1 + R$ = Return relative

The return relative used in calculating geometric mean irons out the negative total returns which cannot be used in mathematics. Going back to our example of stock purchased for ₹60, rising to ₹120 and then falling back to ₹60 over a two-year horizon, geometric return would be:

Year 1 Return Relative = $1 + R = 1 + 100\%$ or $1 + 1 = 2$

Year 2 Return Relative = $1 + R = 1 + (-50\%)$ or $1 - 0.5 = 0.5$

Substituting the above values in the equation for geometric mean, we get

$$G = [(1 + R_1)\ (1 + R_2)]^{1/2} - 1$$

$$= 0$$

Arithmetic mean is a good measure of expected rate of return for a single holding period but it gives biased result in case of multiple holding periods, particularly in the case of volatile securities. AM values tend to be equal to

GM values if the rate of return across multiple holding periods is same. If the rates are not same, AM will tend to be higher than GM. The greater the volatility of returns, the higher the difference.

Numerical Example 4

Calculate geometric mean using data given in Table 3.1.

Solution:

$$G = [\{1 + (-0.162)\}\{1 + 0.033\}\{1 + 0.719\}\{1 + 0.107\}\{1 + 0.363\}\{1 + 0.398\}\{1 + 0.548\}$$

$$\{1 + (-0.518)\}\{1 + 0.758\}\{1 + 0.179\}]^{1/10} - 1$$

$$= (4.854)^{1/10} - 1$$

$$= 1.17 - 1$$

$$= 0.1711 \text{ or } 17.11\%$$

Spreadsheet Application 3 Numerical Example 4 can be solved using MS Excel as follows:

First, annual returns need to be converted into decimals and return relative needs to be computed as shown in the window below.

	A	B	C	D
1	Year	Annual Returns (%)*	Annual Returns	Return Relative
2	2001	-16.2	-0.162	=1+C2
3	2002	3.3	0.033	1.033
4	2003	71.9	0.719	1.719
5	2004	10.7	0.107	1.107
6	2005	36.3	0.363	1.363
7	2006	39.8	0.398	1.398
8	2007	54.8	0.548	1.548
9	2008	-51.8	-0.518	0.482
10	2009	75.8	0.758	1.758
11	2010	17.9	0.179	1.179

Now, geometric average returns can be calculated using the GEOMEAN Function of MS Excel. Finally, subtract 1 from the output.

	A	B	C	D	E
1	**Year**	**Annual Returns (%)***	Annual Returns	Return Relative	
2	2001	-16.2	-0.162	0.838	
3	2002	3.3	0.033	1.033	
4	2003	71.9	0.719	1.719	
5	2004	10.7	0.107	1.107	
6	2005	36.3	0.363	1.363	
7	2006	39.8	0.398	1.398	
8	2007	54.8	0.548	1.548	
9	2008	-51.8	-0.518	0.482	
10	2009	75.8	0.758	1.758	
11	2010	17.9	0.179	1.179	
12	**Geometric Average Return**			=GEOMEAN(D2:D11)-1	

The answer may be given as:

	A	B	C	D
1	**Year**	**Annual Returns (%)***	Annual Returns	Return Relative
2	2001	-16.2	-0.162	0.838
3	2002	3.3	0.033	1.033
4	2003	71.9	0.719	1.719
5	2004	10.7	0.107	1.107
6	2005	36.3	0.363	1.363
7	2006	39.8	0.398	1.398
8	2007	54.8	0.548	1.548
9	2008	-51.8	-0.518	0.482
10	2009	75.8	0.758	1.758
11	2010	17.9	0.179	1.179
12	**Geometric Average Return**			0.171149

The geometric average return is 17.11%.

Expected returns

Security analysts and investors operate in an environment of uncertainty where predicting future returns to serve as indicator for asset/security selection becomes very challenging. In the context of common stock, various forces including macroeconomic, socio-political and company-specific factors impact the improbability surrounding the share prices and dividends in future. When an analyst/investor assesses an investment choice, he anticipates the asset/security to earn a certain return, say 12%. But this is actually an analyst's/investor's most likely estimate, called a point estimate. But one needs to acknowledge rationally and logically that such a point estimate is highly uncertain to occur in future as there is a possibility that under uncertain conditions, the return might actually go very low or reach a very high level. Analysts try to overcome this uncertainty surrounding the point estimate of return by specifying a larger range of possible returns from an investment.

In an attempt to develop a clearer picture of the future, analysts strive not only to generate reasonable estimates of return but also try to quantify the degree of uncertainty by assigning probabilities to each possible outcome or return. By doing so, analysts express the degree of confidence they have in their estimates. The probability values range from 0 to 1, wherein zero means no chance of return and one implies complete certainty that the specified return will occur. While undertaking security analysis, an analyst has to come up with different estimates of probable returns and assign probability to each subjectively as well as intuitively after studying economic, industry and company related factors. The probabilities so generated reflect the chances of occurrence of different estimates of return with changes in market conditions.

How to generate these probabilities is a question that needs to be addressed with careful consideration. While a lot of judgment and experience of the analyst goes into assigning probabilities to possible outcomes, the best way to go about assigning these probabilities is to base them on the data of the historical performance of the asset under consideration or similar asset modified by the analyst's expectations for the future. For example, an analyst may know that about 30% of the time, the return rate on asset under consideration was 10%. He can use this information along with forecasts regarding the economy to derive a better estimate of what is most likely to happen in the future.

Probabilities and many estimates of probable outcomes help the analysts predict the most likely return that a security may earn, given the fluctuations and changes in the market conditions in response to the changes in economy, industry and the related firm.

Such estimates of probable outcomes are weighted by their probabilities to give us a key metric in investment decision, namely, expected return.

Expected return is nothing but a sum of the weighted average of probable returns that can be expected to be earned from holding a security. In other words, expected return is the sum of the products of possible returns with their respective probabilities

To elaborate, various estimates of possible returns that can be earned from a security are multiplied with their respective probability of occurrence and the results are added together to yield weighted average return or expected return. This is considered as the most likely return that can be earned from holding a security for a specified period.

Mathematically,

$$\text{Expected Return} = \sum_{i=1}^{n} (\text{Probability of return}) \times (\text{Possible return})$$

$$E(R_i) = (P_1)(R_1) + (P_2)(R_2) + (P_3)(R_3) + \cdots (P_n)(R_n)$$

Let us understand the concept with the help of a Numerical Example.

Numerical Example 5

Table 3.2 below provides a probability distribution for the returns on stocks *A* and *B* under varying economic conditions as expressed by states 1, 2, 3 and 4. For example, state 1 can represent boom, state 2 recession, state 3 normal growth and so on. The probabilities reflect the likelihood of occurrence of each respective state. Use this information to calculate expected returns of stocks *A* and *B*.

TABLE 3.2 Probability distribution for the returns on stocks *A* and *B*

State	Probability	Return on stock *A*	Return on stock *B*
1	20%	5%	50%
2	30%	10%	20%
3	20%	20%	−10%
4	30%	15%	10%

Solution:

In this example, the expected return for stock A and stock B would be calculated as follows:

$$E[R]_A = .2(5\%) + .3(10\%) + .2(20\%) + .3(15\%) + = 12.5\%$$

$$E[R]_B = .2(50\%) + .3(20\%) + .2(-10\%) + .3(10\%) = 17\%$$

Spreadsheet Application 4 *Expected return can be calculated using SUMPRODUCT Function of MS Excel.*
Return on Stock A (using data from Numerical Example 5) can be calculated using MS Excel as:

	A	B	C	D	E
1	State	Probability	Return On Stock A		
2	1	20%	5%		
3	2	30%	10%		
4	3	20%	20%		
5	4	30%	15%		
6		Expected Return	=SUMPRODUCT(B2:B5,C2:C5)		

	A	B	C
1	State	Probability	Return On Stock A
2	1	20%	5%
3	2	30%	10%
4	3	20%	20%
5	4	30%	15%
6		Expected Return	0.125

The expected return of security A is 12.5%.

To better understand the computation of expected return of a stock under the condition of uncertainty, let us examine the following scenarios:

1. **Perfect Certainty in Economic Environment:** Perfect certainty is a situation where future returns can be forecasted with great degree of accuracy. Such a situation allows only one possible/probable return; say 5% that can be said to have a probability of 100% or 1. In this case, expected return may be computed as:

   $$E(R_i) = (1.0)(0.05) = 0.05$$

   It may be illustrated graphically (Figure 3.2) as follows:

Figure 3.2 Perfect certainty in economic environment.

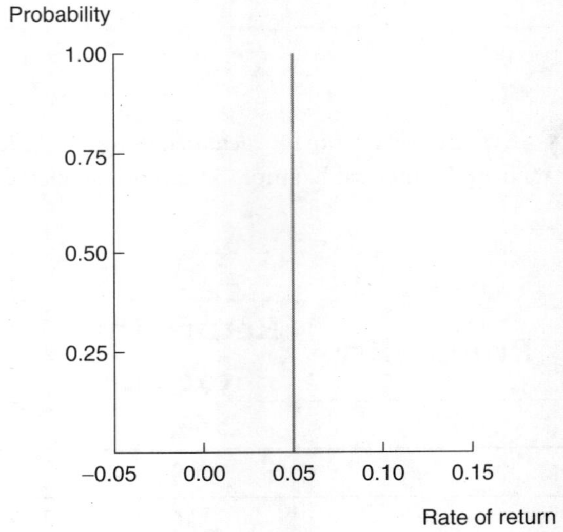

2. **Uncertainty in Economic Environment:** In this scenario, investor is faced with different probable returns resulting from different possible economic conditions. Depending on the expected economic scenario, an analyst may map his expectations for returns and their probabilities as exhibited in Figure 3.3:

Figure 3.3 Uncertainty in economic environment.

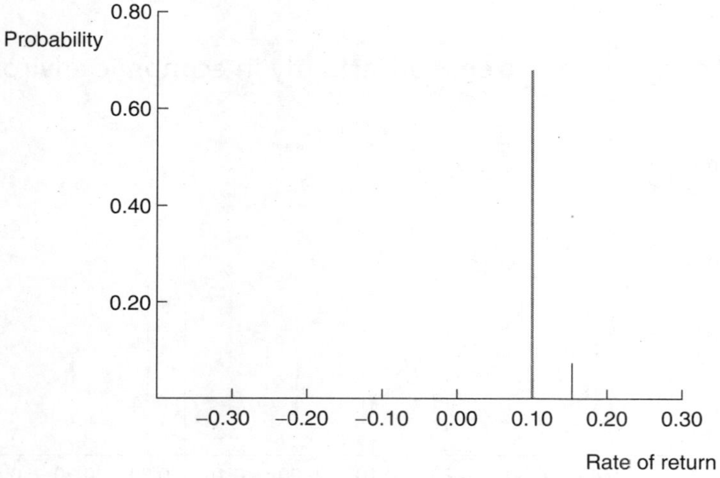

Numerical Example 6

Calculate expected return using information exhibited in Table 3.3.

TABLE 3.3 Expectations for returns and their probabilities under uncertainty

Economic conditions	Probability	Rate of return
Strong and booming economy, low or no inflation	0.15	0.15
Weak and recessionary economy, above-average inflation	0.15	−0.20
Stable economy with no major changes	0.70	0.10

Solution:

Computation of expected rate of return:

$$E(R_i) = [(0.15)(0.15)] + [(0.15)(-0.20)] + [(0.70)(0.10)]$$

$$= 0.0625$$

3. **Condition of Extreme Uncertainty in Economic Environment:** Condition of extreme uncertainty occurs when a large number of outcomes are possible but each has a low probability. Under such condition, the analysts come out with numerous outcomes from a wide range of possibilities. Let us consider an analyst who expects 10 probable outcomes ranging from −40% to 50% with the same probability for each rate of

return. Clearly such asset/security can be considered to be extremely risky. Graphically, the condition of extreme uncertainty in economic environment may be illustrated as given in Figure 3.4.

Figure 3.4 Condition of extreme uncertainty in economic environment.

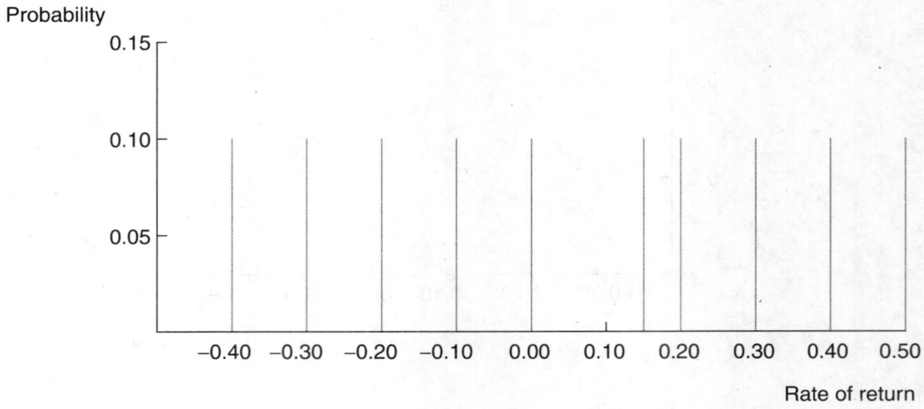

Numerical Example 7

Calculate expected return using date given in Table 3.4.

TABLE 3.4 Expectations of returns and their probabilities under extreme uncertainty

Probability	Rate of Return
0.10	−0.40
0.10	−0.30
0.10	−0.20
0.10	−0.10
0.10	0.00
0.10	0.15
0.10	0.20
0.10	0.30
0.10	0.40
0.10	0.50

Solution:

Computation of expected rate of return:

$$E(R_i) = [(0.10)(-0.40)] + [(0.10)(-0.30)] + [(0.10)(-0.20)] + [(0.10)(-0.10)]$$

$$+ [(0.10)(0.00)] + [(0.10)(0.15)] + [(0.10)(0.20)] + [(0.10)(0.30)]$$

$$+ [(0.10)(0.40)] + [(0.10)(0.50)]$$

$$= 0.055$$

The expected rate of return of this asset is 5.5% which is nearly the same as the return on asset having perfect certainty of return (probability = 1). The asset that has unit probability of occurrence of a return is said to be risk-free asset. For example, the asset discussed under the condition of perfect certainty in economic environment can be called risk-free asset which will definitely yield 5% return.

A rational investor might settle for investing in a risk-free asset with guaranteed return instead of exposing himself to high volatility characterizing the situation of extreme uncertainty.

Continuous Probability Distribution

The probability distribution of rates of returns explained above is known as discrete distribution because probabilities have been assigned to a limited number of specific values. In finance, however, probability distributions are not regarded to be discrete. Instead, they are generally regarded as continuous, even though they might actually be discrete. Under continuous probability distribution, probabilities are assigned to intervals between two points and not specific points as done in the discrete distribution. So in place of giving probabilities like 'there is a probability of 0.40 that 20% return will accrue,' in continuous probability distribution, it is stated that there is a probability of 0.40 that the return will fall between 1 and 20%.

The normal distribution: The most commonly used probability distribution in finance is the normal distribution that is a continuous probability distribution. It is also called the Gaussian distribution and it is represented by the bell curve. In a normal distribution, things tend towards the mean. All values are plotted in a symmetrical fashion in this curve with most results clustered around the probability's mean. But not all values plot near the mean. They are equally likely to plot above or below the mean value. The values tail off symmetrically away from the mean though grouping generally takes place at values close to the mean.

The normal distribution is very frequently used in stock market analysis. Given an adequate number of observations within a sample size, it can be assumed that returns follow a normal distribution. As in case of any distribution, the mean, skewness and kurtosis coefficients of the distribution should be calculated to ascertain the type of distribution.

Graphically (Figure 3.5), the normal distribution may be exhibited as:

Figure 3.5 The bell curve.

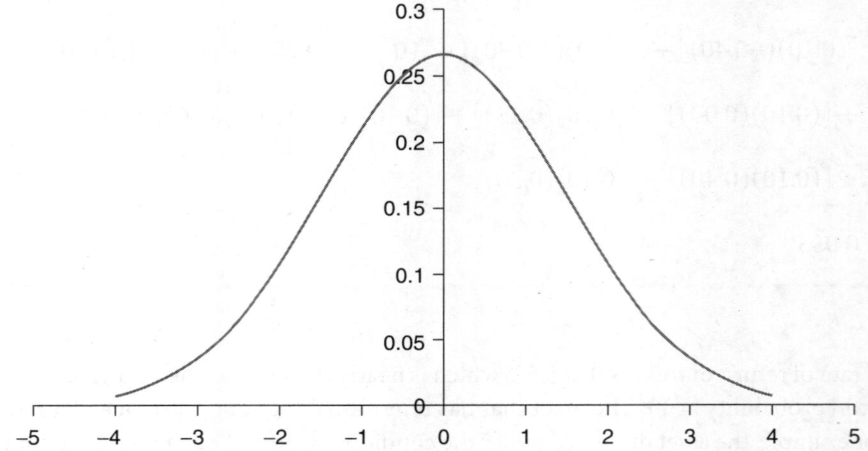

Asset returns are generally identified by their long-term projections based on historical returns and future expectations of the analysts. If the stock market returns follow a normal distribution, the bell curve is a great tool to evaluate the risk of investing and predicting returns. To understand the concept, let's consider standard normal distribution where the arithmetic average is plotted in the middle and standard deviations[2] are plotted on either side of the mean. Assume a mean value of zero and a standard deviation of 1%. If we apply assets/securities to this curve, then 68% of the returns will fall within one standard deviation of the mean (−1% and 1%), 95.5% of the returns will fall within two standard deviations of the mean (−2% and 2%) and 99.7% of the returns (with the tails included) will fall between three standard deviation of mean (−3% and 3%).

Modern Portfolio Theory (a key theory in portfolio management) uses the normal distribution to describe portfolio returns. As stated above, normal distribution is useful in making stock market predictions. Bell curve can be used to estimate how large market movements can be expected, assuming that returns are normally distributed. For example, given 6.6% as the daily standard deviation (discussed in the next section) for a stock, we would expect its returns to fluctuate between +6.6% and −6.6% with 68% of confidence. It goes without saying that if an analyst is in a position to assume with a 95 percent probability where the stock return will be in future; he can take a better investment decision.

In the past it was assumed and often observed as well, that most stock markets tend to fall into normal distribution patterns. In such situations, bell curve has good predictive qualities but when stock return tend to break away from a normal distribution, bell curve may or may not be useful as a predictive tool. Latest research has started to uncover the fact that actual stock return distributions are neither normal nor symmetrical. Rather they appear to be elliptical, hyperbolic and asymmetrical at times in some cases, and even completely indefinable in other situations. So one needs to be aware of the fact that stocks are inherently risky and it is difficult to make forecast with significant degree of confidence using normal probability distribution predictive tools over shorter time span[3].

---

[2] It is measure of risk. It has been discussed in detail in the upcoming sections of the chapter.

[3] The increasing realization that stock market returns may not be quite normally distributed has led to the use of three methods to make risk measurement more robust. These are Value at Risk (VaR), Conditional Tail Expectations (CTE) and Lower Partial Standard Deviation (LPSD).

The normal distribution also suffers from a lack of relevance to investors' choices, as it treats both upside potential and downside uncertainty symmetrically in calculating the variance of a portfolio. This is contrary to investors' thinking, as has been explained in the upcoming sections of the chapter.

In the recent times, another aspect of investor behavior that has served as the basis to criticize normal distribution is its inability to capture the 'herd's instinct.'[4]

Many analysts have proposed the use of fat-tailed[5] distributions to overcome some of the challenges of normal distribution. Fat tails (Figure 3.6) allow higher frequencies for extreme values of returns, since in the stock market, investor psyche often tends to push the market to extremes more frequently than the normal distribution would predict.

Deviation from normality can be assessed through a measure of asymmetry called skewness. Positive value of skewness indicates distribution skewed to the right and negative value of skewness indicates distribution skewed toward left. Another indication of deviation from normality is fat tails and slender shoulders, indicating less probability clustered at this center. The degree of fat tails is measured by kurtosis.

Figure 3.6 Derivations from normality.

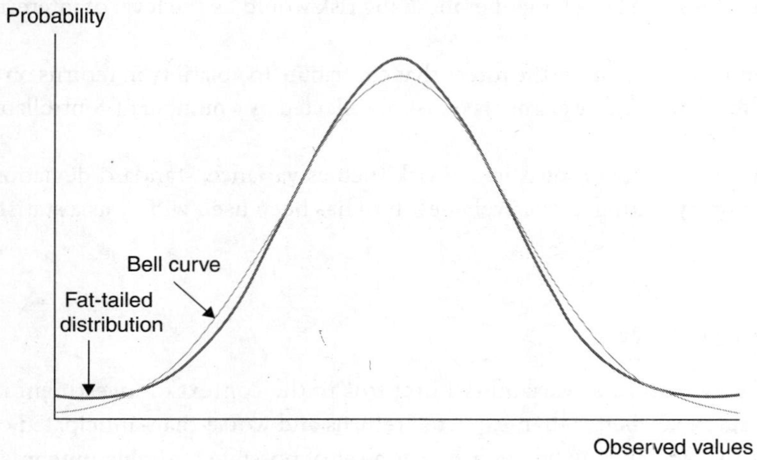

Risk

In layman's words, risk is an unwelcome and unsolicited event that may or may not occur to cause some kind of damage or loss. In the context of investment management, risk represents a possibility of loss from putting one's money in assets/securities. In the preceding sections of the chapter, we have discussed investment returns in detail. It needs to be understood that except for the returns in case of risk-free asset, none of the risky assets offer

[4] A tendency of investors to act as part of prevailing trend, i.e., if everyone else is selling, an investor is more likely to choose to sell and if everyone is buying, he may end up doing the same.

[5] Distribution where the extreme left and right parts of the curve for stock price would more often than not plot slightly higher than would normally be expected.

assured returns. So it is imperative for the investors and analysts to not only forecast future returns with great care but also analyze and measure the risk of non-occurrence of the expected returns thus estimated.

Defining Risk

Risk in the context of investments accommodates the possibility that the realized or actual outcome of an investment decision in terms of return may vary substantially from the expected outcome. Risk may be defined as the unexpected variability or volatility of returns on an investment. It is an indicator of the uncertainty of getting the expected outcome/result in the future.

From the point of view of common stock, the risk associated with equity investment comes from two elements:

1. Possibility that dividends declared by the company may not turn out to be as expected.
2. Possibility that the share price may not rise as anticipated.

The first possibility would adversely impact the current yield of the concerned share and the second possibility could lead to lower capital gains or even result in some capital loss.

In case of debt securities, the key element embodying risk would be the level of interest rates and possibility of default.

Thus price, dividend and interest are the forces that contribute to volatility in returns on assets/securities and these are called elements of risk. These elements of risk are affected by a number of controllable and uncontrollable factors.

The literature offers a number of measures of risk such as variance, standard deviation, semi variance and range. In the contemporary setting, a relatively new tool has been used widely as a statistical measure of risk. It is called Beta (β).

Upside and Downside Risk

It should be noted that volatility or variability of returns in the context of investment in securities signifies fluctuations on both sides, i.e., better-than-expected returns and worse-than-anticipated outcomes. The first is referred to as 'upside risk' which may be described as a set of possible desirable outcomes in a situation characterized by uncertainty. Upside risk represents the potential, or the likelihood that an asset/security will see an unanticipated increase in its value. From a practical point of view, investors will obviously not dislike upside volatility; they only have aversion for downside volatility.

Since no rational investor would mind an upside risk that indicates a possibility of higher than anticipated returns, therefore the risk that the analysts and investors try to measure and mitigate actively is actually the risk of garnering worse-than-anticipated outcomes, formally called the downside risk. Downside risk represents a worst-case scenario, embodying in itself a possibility that the realized return may turn out to be much less than the expected one. Downside risk is an estimation of an investment's potential to depreciate in value with unfavorable change in market conditions. It has been observed that many securities that have high probability of downside risk also offer a higher opportunity for upside rewards/gains.

Analysts often compare the downside risk associated with investments to their possible upside while selecting securities for investment.

Risks in Investment: Systematic and Unsystematic Risk

As mentioned above, the elements of risk, viz., dividend/interest and price of security are affected by a host of controllable and uncontrollable factors. These factors serve as the basis for identifying two main types of risks associated with securities, viz.,

1. Systematic risk
2. Unsystematic risk

Systematic risk results from many external and uncontrollable factors that have a wide effect and are broad in scope. Unsystematic risk is the outcome of numerous internal and controllable factors that are atypical of a single firm or to some extent, industry.

Systematic risk

Systematic risk is also called the non-diversifiable risk in the contemporary financial literature. It represents that portion of variability in return which is inherent to the entire market and is caused by general economic, political and social factors (Figure 3.7). As the name non-diversifiable suggests, systematic risk is that portion of security risk which has to be accepted, as it cannot be mitigated.

Figure 3.7 Systematic risk.

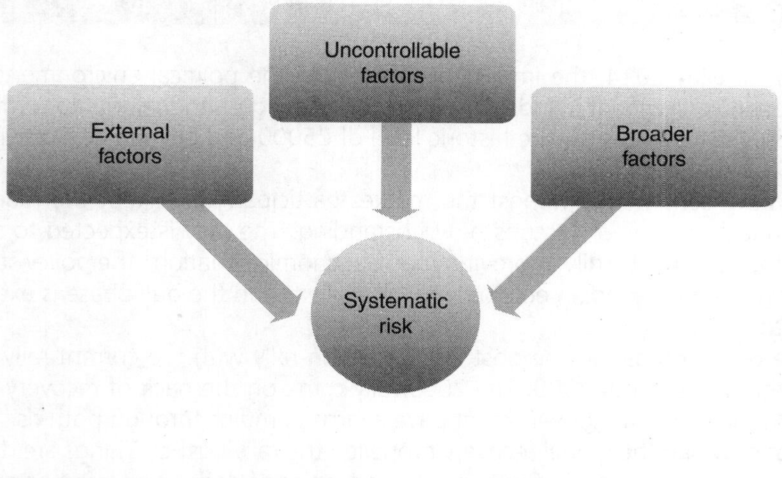

Risks that may be categorized as systematic are:

1. **Market Risk:** Downside movement in stock price even when the concerned company is recording a rise in earnings is a very common occurrence in stock markets. Such variations that belie the underlying fundamentals can be attributed largely to investor attitude and behavior. This kind of variation in price of a share even when the company's earnings are stable or even rising is called market risk and it is caused mainly

by the changes in investors' attitude towards and expectations from equity markets in general or a few stocks in particular.

In other words, a fall in stock price from time to time without any significant variation in the company's fundamentals is referred to as market risk. It is so broad that no firm can have any control over it. Investors' attitude is triggered by a host of tangible and intangible factors. The tangible factors are changes in economic environment, macroeconomic policy variations, etc. These include events like fall of government, elections, war, major readjustment in monetary policy, cross-border relations, regional issues, uprisings, ideological changes, changes in political regime, etc. A downturn in economy may affect all the firms in the economy and cause share prices to plummet.

The excerpt reproduced in Marketview 3.2 is a classic example of impact of political and macro-economic factors on Indian stock price behavior.

Intangible factors include herd's instinct, fear of loss, market psychology, rumors, etc. Investors, particularly individuals, tend to be affected by the rumors that are generally floated by the interested parties to mislead the market. Any non-market news such as spread of flu or assassination or death of a prominent personality or some other factor may cause fear of loss in the minds of investors and they may start selling their shares despite no change in company fundamentals and such selling spree often becomes contagious, causing a large-scale selling that pushes the prices down.

2. **Interest Rate Risk:** Interest rate risk may be defined as the possibility of fall in the value of a security, especially a bond, resulting from a rise in interest rates in the market. It is the risk of change in value of a fixed income security on account of changes in the level of interest rates.

Marketview 3.2 Indian Equity Markets' Response to Change in Political Leadership

Since the month of May 2014, the impact of changes in the political environment on the market movement has been very evident in India. With a single party getting majority to form government at the center, the SENSEX galloped to the historic level of 25000 and beyond at a dream pace. The rise has been called as "the hope rally."

Extremely positive sentiment amongst the market participants has kept the markets in the bull mood since the elections, minor hiccups notwithstanding. The rally is expected to sustain as it has come riding on the back of steadily improving macroeconomic situation. The policy steps taken in the previous year have made the Indian economy more resilient and the bull phase is expected to prevail for a long time to come.

Analysts have been comparing the post 2009-election rally with the current rally. But it needs to be understood that 2014 is not 2009. The 2009 rally came on the back of recovery from the global financial crisis. At that time, the government gave a large stimulus through both fiscal and monetary policy to the economy and the global recovery propelled the rally further. Things are different in 2014. Prolonged economic slow-down, sluggish growth and issues of deficit and inflation are likely to make recovery and revival slower than before. Biggest concern is the mounting debt of companies in the infrastructure sector, which is being considered as an impediment to their ability to raise funds and undertake projects.

Source: Based on story published on http://www.business-standard.com/article/markets/equity-outlook-be-patient-to-benefit-from-rally-114041400031_1.html, accessed on November 1, 2014.

Interest rate risk impacts the value of bonds more directly than common stock, and it is a major risk for bondholders[6]. To put it briefly, the prices of bonds fall with the rise in interest rates in the market and rise with the fall in interest rates in the market. The rationale behind such a behavior is that as interest rates rise, the opportunity cost of holding a bond decreases because the investors are in a position to earn greater returns by moving to investments offering the higher interest rate. For example, a 7% bond is worth more if interest rates decrease to 6% since the bondholder continues to receive a fixed return which is higher than the return currently offered by the market as a consequence of the decrease in rates.

Changes in interest rates indirectly affect the stock prices by affecting the cost of borrowing. This impact is significant because a rise in interest rates makes margin buying expensive. Further, the profits of corporations are also affected by rising interest rates as most of them employ debt in their capital structure. Both the above factors can potentially push stock prices down.

3. **Purchasing Power Risk:** Unconsumed part of income gets channelized into investment when an investor decides to park his funds in some asset/security. Thus, any investment effectively represents deferred consumption, i.e., a forgone opportunity to buy some goods or services in the present time. If the prices of the goods or services rise during the holding period of the security over and above those prevailing at the time of investment, the investor has in fact, lost some purchasing power. He will now have to shell out more money for the same set of goods and services. This erosion of purchasing power on account of inflation negatively affects the expectations and psychology of investors and adversely impacts the prices of securities.

Unsystematic risk

Unsystematic Risk is also known as "specific or unique risk" or "diversifiable risk." This risk is specific to individual shares and it represents that component of a stock's return which is uncorrelated to general market conditions. It is the company or industry specific risk that is inherent in each investment. It affects a very specific group of securities or an individual security through changes in factors such as operating conditions, operational efficiency, cost of capital, extent of borrowed funds, attitude of management, etc. (Figure 3.8). It is called

Figure 3.8 Unsystematic risk.

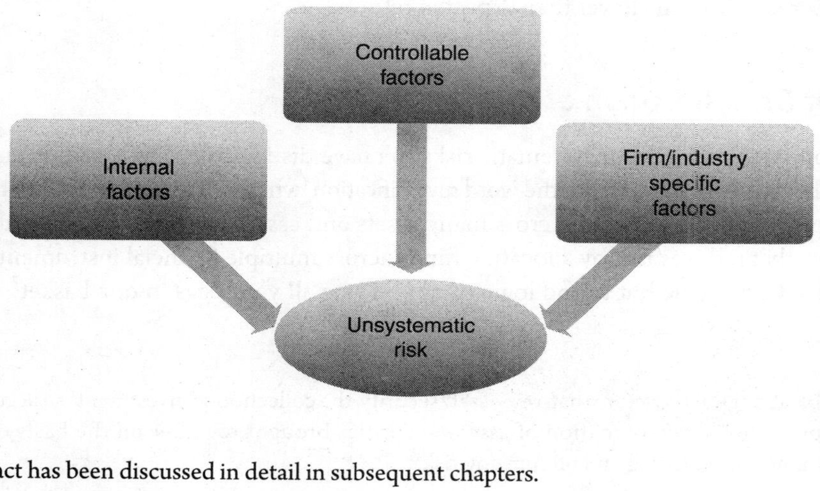

[6] The extent of impact has been discussed in detail in subsequent chapters.

"diversifiable risk" because it can be mitigated or diversified away by increasing the number and variety of stocks on which you allocate your funds.

For example, news that is specific to a small number of stocks, such as a sudden strike by the employees of a company you have shares in, is considered to be unsystematic risk. A news or event that affects all the firms in an industry may also be considered a source of unsystematic risk. To illustrate, the controversy and the policy paralysis related to allowing FDI in retail sector in India has negatively affected most companies in that space.

The two main components of unsystematic risk are:

1. **Business Risk:** Business risk is the probability of loss that is intrinsic part of the operating conditions of an organization. Business risk is associated with the efficiency and effectiveness of a firm's operations within the operating milieu that is imposed on it. It expresses the possibility of a company making less than anticipated profits or even making a loss. The criticality of this type of risk is highlighted by the fact that it can impair a firm's ability to generate returns on its investments and cause variations in its operating income and dividends.

   Business risk faced by a firm is reflected in its operating cost that can be split into two parts, fixed and variable. It is the fixed cost component that increases the business risk. If revenues decline due to some reason, the profits would go down because of the high fixed cost component. In fact, in financial literature, business risk is defined as the variability of EBIT due to high proportion of fixed cost in the firm, amongst other things. It is measured by degree of operating leverage (DOL).

   Business risk is influenced by a number of factors including sales/demand variability, fluctuations in per-unit price, input price variability, increase in competition, prevailing economic climate and government regulations.
2. **Financial Risk:** Financial risk is associated with the way a firm finances itself. It depends on the type of securities issued: the higher the debt, the greater the financial risk.

   It is the risk that arises from the employment of borrowed funds in the capital structure of the firm. Existence of debt creates a fixed liability in the form of periodic interest payment. Higher the interest burden, the lower is the amount available for dividends on share.

   Financial risk is defined as the variability of EPS of a firm due to the presence of debt and it is measured by degree of financial leverage (DFL). Debt financing or financial leverage affects the share prices by increasing the possibility of fluctuation in return on common stock. It affects the expectations of equity investors by enhancing their risk of earning lower than expected returns.

The Concept of Diversification of Risk

In our discussion on systematic and unsystematic risks, we have distinguished between diversifiable and non-diversifiable risks. The terms are drawn from the word diversification, which when used in the context of investment implies spreading one's investible surplus across many assets and asset classes. In other words, diversification refers to a technique that reduces risk by allocating funds across multiple financial instruments, industries and other categories based on simple but sound logic of not putting all your eggs in one basket[7]. It is achieved by

---

[7] The moment one talks about holding more than one asset/security, the collection of investments so accumulated becomes a PORTFOLIO. A portfolio is a combination of assets/securities brought together on the basis of the principle of diversification that is aimed at spreading and minimizing risk.

investing money in different areas that would each react differently to the same event/factor. Diversification aims to maximize returns while mitigating or minimizing risks. Though diversification does not guarantee against loss, it certainly is the most important element of reaching long-term investment goals.

The concept of diversification emphasizes holding different asset classes. The reason is that different assets—such as bonds and stocks—will react differently to adverse events and a combination of such asset classes will insulate the portfolio from excessive market swings and volatility. For example, holding a mix of bond and equity might be a good idea because generally, the two move in opposite directions. A portfolio diversified across both areas will be protected from adverse result of one because of the balancing effect of the positive returns from another.

But diversification cannot eliminate the risk of investing completely. One can eliminate unsystematic risk caused by company specific factors through diversification but systematic risk that affects the entire market cannot be avoided through it. The fact is that even a portfolio of well-diversified assets/securities will have some risk associated with it.

Measures of Risk: Variance, Standard Deviation, Semi-variance and Range

The preceding discussion clearly highlights the fact that an investor needs to understand and measure risks associated with the returns he expects from investment in any asset/security. There are many measures of risk that are available at the disposal of analysts and investors. The main measures include:

1. Variance
2. Standard Deviation
3. Semi-variance and
4. Range

Since risk expresses the probability of adverse outcome, any method for quantification of risk should provide for a measurement of dispersion of returns around the expected return. Variance and standard deviation of expected returns are two such statistical measures of dispersion where larger variance or standard deviation is an indicator of greater dispersion. The more dispersed the expected returns, the greater the uncertainty associated with them.

Variance is widely used in finance but at the same time it is also criticized because it considers all dispersions, positive as well as negative. Critics of the use of variance as a measure of risk claim that positive deviations (upside risk) are appreciated by investors so a true measure of risk should consider only negative deviations (downside risk). Harry Markowitz[8], a passionate supporter of variance as the measure of risk, recognized the importance of this idea. He realized that investors are interested in minimizing downside risk for two reasons:

1. Only downside risk or safety first is relevant to an investor and
2. Security returns may not be normally distributed.

Therefore a downside risk measure would help investors make proper decisions when faced with non-normal security return distributions. Markowitz has shown that when distributions are normally distributed, both the downside risk measure and the variance provide the correct answer. However, if the distributions are not

[8] Proponent of Modern Portfolio Theory (discussed in detail in subsequent chapters).

normally distributed then only the downside risk measure provides a correct answer. Markowitz suggested two measures for capturing downside risk: a semi-variance computed from the mean return or below-mean semi variance and a semi-variance computed from a target return or below-target semi-variance.

The semi-variance seems to be a better measure of downside risk as it is backed by theoretical, empirical and practical considerations. As stated above, Harry Markowitz himself admitted this. While receiving his Nobel Prize, Markowitz (1991) stated that "... it can further help evaluate the adequacy of mean and variance, or alternate practical measures, as criteria." In addition, he stated that "perhaps ... some other measure of portfolio risk will serve in a two parameter analysis ... Semi variance seems more plausible than variance as a measure of risk, since it is concerned only with adverse deviations."[9]

After proposing the semi variance measure, Markowitz stayed with the variance measure because it was computationally simpler. The semi-variance optimization models using a co-semi variance matrix require twice the number of data inputs than the variance model. Further continued use of variance by Markowitz has been defended on the grounds that historical returns of stock have been approximately symmetrical. For symmetrically distributed returns, it doesn't make any difference whether variance is used or semi-variance is applied. Skewness needs to be considered only when returns are not distributed symmetrically.

The same debate has persisted with standard deviation, the square root of variance. Although standard deviation of returns is a very popular measure of risk, there are several issues that limit its usefulness. Like variance, it is an appropriate measure of risk only when the distribution of returns is symmetric. Further, it can be applied only when the distribution of returns is normal. Existence of these two conditions, symmetry and normality, have been challenged by empirical evidence refuting them in the context of stock market returns. Another problem with standard deviation is that one doesn't know the value of the returns in the very low probability areas on left and right extremes of the curve, called the tails. These so-called 'tails' pose a real challenge in the use of normal distribution. To elaborate, though you might have only a 5% chance of a tail return, its value could be negative 15% in one day. However, this kind of quantification of the magnitude of the returns in the distant tails is not possible.

The concept of semi-deviation has also been proposed in this context. Semi-deviation or downside standard deviation of returns has received a lot of support as an alternative measure of risk from both practitioners and theorists.

There is another measure of risk that finds a mention in the literature. It is called '*range of returns*.' It is an indicator of the limits between which variation is possible and is measured as the difference between lowest and highest expected return. The larger the range of expected return, the greater the uncertainty surrounding the future expected returns.

Despite the availability of many measures of risk, henceforth we will use only variance and/or standard deviation because these measures are intuitively appealing, widely accepted and applied in asset pricing models that form the backbone of modern portfolio management.

Measurement of Risk of Individual Security

As stated above, variance and standard deviation of returns are most commonly used measures of risk in financial literature. Let us understand how they are computed for individual security.

---

[9] Mean-Semi Variance Behavior: An Alternative Behavioral Model, Javier Estrada IESE Business School (Barcelona, Spain) Department of Finance, February, 2002, http://www.fep.up.pt/investigacao/cempre/actividades/sem_fin/sem_fin_01/papers_pdf/paper_sem_fin_12abr02_i.pdf, accessed on October 16, 2014.

Variance may be computed as expected value of squared deviations:

$$\sigma^2 = \sum_{i=1}^{n} (\text{Probaility}) \times (\text{Possible Return} - \text{Expected Return})^2$$

$$\sum_{i=1}^{n} (P_i)[R_i - E(R_i)]^2$$

Standard deviation is calculated as:

$$\text{Standard Deviation} = \sqrt{\text{Variance}}$$

Numerical Example 8

Calculate variance and standard deviation of returns for a stock using the following probability distribution of returns given in Table 3.5.

TABLE 3.5 Possible returns and probability distribution of returns

Possible Returns	Probability
30	0.1
40	0.3
50	0.4
70	0.1
80	0.1

Solution:

$$\text{Expected Return} = 30 \times 0.1 + 40 \times 0.3 + 50 \times 0.4 + 70 \times 0.1 + 80 \times 0.1 = 50\%$$

$$\text{Variance} = 40 + 30 + 0 + 40 + 90$$

$$= 200$$

$$\text{Standard Deviation} = \sqrt{200}$$

$$= 14.142$$

Solution may be presented in tabular form as displayed in Table 3.6.

TABLE 3.6 Calculations

Possible Returns	Probability	Deviation from $E(R) = \{R_i - E(R)\}$	$\{R_i - E(R)\}^2$	Probability × $\{R_i - E(R)\}^2$
30	0.1	−20	400	40
40	0.3	−10	100	30
50	0.4	0	0	0
70	0.1	20	400	40
80	0.1	30	900	90

Spreadsheet Application 5 We can solve Numerical Example 8 using spreadsheet in the following manner.

	A	B	C	D
1	Possible Returns	Probability		
2	30	0.1		
3	40	0.3		
4	50	0.4		
5	70	0.1		
6	80	0.1		
7				
8	Expected Return	=SUMPRODUCT(A2:A6, B2:B6)		

7				
8	Expected Return	50		
9				
10	Possible Returns	Deviation from Expected Return	Squared Deviation from Expected Return	Probability
11	30	=A11-$B$8	400	0.1
12	40	-10	100	0.3
13	50	0	0	0.4
14	70	20	400	0.1
15	80	30	900	0.1

10	Possible Returns	Deviation from Expected Return	Squared Deviation from Expected Return	Probability		
11	30	-20	400	0.1		
12	40	-10	100	0.3		
13	50	0	0	0.4		
14	70	20	400	0.1		
15	80	30	900	0.1		
16			Variance	=SUMPRODUCT(C11:C15,D11:D15)		
17			Standard Deviation	14.142136		

Variance and standard deviation may be calculated as:

	A	B	C	D
1	Possible Returns	Probability		
2	30	0.1		
3	40	0.3		
4	50	0.4		
5	70	0.1		
6	80	0.1		
7				
8	Expected Return	50		
9				
10	Possible Returns	Deviation from Expected Return	Squared Deviation from Expected Return	Probability
11	30	-20	400	0.1
12	40	-10	100	0.3
13	50	0	0	0.4
14	70	20	400	0.1
15	80	30	900	0.1
16			Variance	200
17			Standard Deviation	14.1421356

A summary of the above steps in calculation may be presented as:

	A	B	C
1	Possible Returns	Probabilty	Squared Deviations from Expected Return
2	30	0.1	400
3	40	0.3	100
4	50	0.4	0
5	70	0.1	400
6	80	0.1	900
7	Expected Return SUMPRODUCT(A2:A6 , B2:B6) = 50		
8	Standard Deviation SUMPRODUCT(B2:B6 , C2:C6)^.5 =14.142		

Variance and standard deviation of a series of historical returns may also be computed as[10]:

$$\sigma^2 = \left[\frac{\sum_{i=1}^{n}(R_i - \bar{R})^2}{n-1}\right]$$

$$\sigma = \sqrt{\sigma^2}$$

where
σ^2 = Variance of return
σ = Standard deviation of return
R_i = Return for the stock during period i (i = 1, 2, 3 ..., n)
n = Number of periods
$\bar{R}$ = Arithmetic average return

Numerical Example 9

Consider the returns over a period of 6 years given in Table 3.7.

TABLE 3.7 Returns over a period of 6 years

Period	Return
1	10
2	12
3	20
4	−10
5	14
6	9

Calculate variance and standard deviation.

Solution:

The solution is given in tabular form in Table 3.8.

[10] Note $n - 1$ in the denominator of this formula for calculation of variance. Some authors also use 'n.' When only 'n' is used, there is a downward bias as we are using deviation from sample's arithmetic mean instead of expected return. This introduces an estimation error, sometimes called *degree of freedom bias*. To eliminate this bias, the arithmetic average of squared deviations is multiplied by factor $n/(n - 1)$, resulting in the formula stated above.

TABLE 3.8 Calculations

Period	Return	$(R_i - \bar{R})$	$(R_i - \bar{R})^2$
1	10	4.5	20.25
2	12	6.5	42.25
3	20	14.5	210.25
4	−10	−15.5	240.25
5	14	8.5	72.25
6	9	3.5	12.25

Variance

$$\sigma^2 = \left[\frac{\sum_{i=1}^{n}(R_i - \bar{R})^2}{n-1}\right]$$

$$= \frac{(20.25 + 42.25 + 210.25 + 240.25 + 72.25 + 12.25)}{(6-1)}$$

$$= \frac{597.5}{5}$$

$$= 119.5$$

Standard Deviation

$$\sigma = \sqrt{\sigma^2}$$

$$= \sqrt{119.5}$$

$$= 10.931$$

Spreadsheet Application 6 *Calculating annual returns and standard deviation for stock market data using MS Excel.*

Calculate annual returns and annual standard deviation of Reliance Industries for a period from January 2009 through December 2013.

Solution:

Monthly average returns and their standard deviation can be calculated in MS Excel using Excel functions for the same. To calculate annualized average returns, multiply the monthly mean returns with 12 (since the closing price data is monthly. If the closing price data is daily, then 300 trading days can be assumed. Internationally 252 days are used). Calculate annualized standard deviation by multiplying the standard deviation with square root 12 ($\sqrt{12}$).

	A	B
43	Jun-12	4.3583
44	Jul-12	0.7296
45	Aug-12	3.8426
46	Sep-12	8.0546
47	Oct-12	-3.8313
48	Nov-12	-1.4195
49	Dec-12	5.5372
50	Jan-13	5.5008
51	Feb-13	-8.4579
52	Mar-13	-5.1574
53	Apr-13	1.8504
54	May-13	2.1899
55	Jun-13	6.7494
56	Jul-13	1.1249
57	Aug-13	-2.3272
58	Sep-13	-3.4892
59	Oct-13	10.3858
60	Nov-13	-6.7147
61	Dec-13	4.7723
62	**Average Returns**	-0.6656
63	**Annualized Average Returns**	=B62*12

The annualized average return of Reliance Industries for the given period is –7.99%.

	A	B	C
43	Jun-12	4.3583	
44	Jul-12	0.7296	
45	Aug-12	3.8426	
46	Sep-12	8.0546	
47	Oct-12	-3.8313	
48	Nov-12	-1.4195	
49	Dec-12	5.5372	
50	Jan-13	5.5008	
51	Feb-13	-8.4579	
52	Mar-13	-5.1574	
53	Apr-13	1.8504	
54	May-13	2.1899	
55	Jun-13	6.7494	
56	Jul-13	1.1249	
57	Aug-13	-2.3272	
58	Sep-13	-3.4892	
59	Oct-13	10.3858	
60	Nov-13	-6.7147	
61	Dec-13	4.7723	
62	**Average Returns**	-0.6656	
63	**Annualized Average Returns**	-7.987	
64	**Standard Deviation**	11.401	
65	**Annualized Standard Deviation**	=B64*SQRT(12)	

The annualized standard deviation of Reliance Industries for the given period is 39.49%.

Beta as a Measure of Risk

Beta or beta coefficient, as it is sometimes called, is a statistic that is a key measure of risk in contemporary financial theory. It may be defined as a measure of the systematic risk of a security in comparison to the market as a whole, generally represented by some index. It captures that part of investment risk, which cannot be eliminated by diversification. Beta is a handy tool for ex-post evaluation of the extent of risk taken in diversified portfolio management and judging the efficacy of the investment manager in achieving the desirable risk-return profile. It is used in the capital asset pricing model (CAPM), a model that occupies the central position in modern portfolio theory.

By definition, the beta of market is 1.0 and beta of individual stock is a measure of how much it deviates vis -a-vis the market. A beta of above 1.0 indicates that the concerned share swings more than the market over a period of time. For example, if a stock has a beta of 1.2, it is theoretically 20% more volatile than the market as a whole. To illustrate the concept further, consider a stock that has a beta of 2; this implies that if the market is expected to provide a return of 15%, we can expect this stock to generate a return of 30%. On the flip side, if we expect the market to give a loss of 10%, we can expect our stock to give us a loss of 20% (−20% return).

A beta of less than 1 indicates that the stock moves less than the market. A beta of 1 indicates that the stock would move proportionately to the market. High-beta stocks have more potential for higher returns as they are supposed to be riskier. Low beta stocks, on the other hand, have lower returns, as they are perceived to be less risky.

Actually, assets can be broken down into two categories based on their betas, pro-cyclical and counter-cyclical. Pro-cyclical assets are described as aggressive, high-beta securities with exposure to higher market volatility. They generate most of their returns from economic growth. Counter-cyclical assets are described as defensive, low-beta securities with little exposure to market volatility. They generate most of their returns from income.

Betas of defensive stocks are less than one. Many utilities, pharmaceuticals and fast-moving consumer goods stocks have a beta of less than 1. Conversely, stocks of companies in sectors such as capital goods, banking and real estate have high beta. A beta of less than zero, i.e., a negative beta is also possible though highly unlikely. Such stock would have an inverse relation with the market return. Many gold-related stocks have been observed

TABLE 3.9 Betas of selected indian stocks

Company	Beta
Axis Bank Ltd	1.68
Bharti Airtel Ltd	0.97
Dr. Reddy's Laboratories Ltd	0.47
Housing Development Finance Corporation Ltd HDFC	0.92
Hindalco Industries Ltd	1.42
Hindustan Unilever Ltd	0.35
ICICI Bank Ltd	1.76
Infosys Ltd	0.73
ITC Ltd	0.6
Reliance Industries Ltd	1.07

Source: http://in.reuters.com/finance/stocks-quotes

to have a negative beta. Beta of 0 can also exist. One good example of zero-beta is cash whose value remains unchanged regardless of the market movement, given no inflation. Another example of zero beta asset is treasury bonds. It is important to note here that zero value of beta doesn't mean risk-free asset. It simply implies that its correlation (explained in the next section) with the market is zero.

Further, beta has no upper or lower limit, and betas as large as 3 or 4, though rare, can occur for highly volatile stocks.

Calculation of beta

Two statistical measures, correlation method and regression method, are used to calculate beta using historical data of returns of a security as well as the market represented by some index of performance like BSE SENSEX, CNX Nifty, etc.

1. **Correlation Method:**

$$\beta_i = \frac{r_{\text{im}}\sigma_i\sigma_m}{\sigma_m^2}$$

where

r_{im} = Correlation coefficient between the returns of stock *i* and the returns of the market index

σ_i = Standard deviation of returns of stock *i*

σ_m = Standard deviation of returns of the market index

σ_m^2 = Variance of the market returns

The correlation coefficient can be statistically computed as:

$$r = \frac{n\Sigma XY - (\Sigma X)(\Sigma Y)}{\sqrt{n\Sigma X^2 - (\Sigma X)^2}\sqrt{n\Sigma Y^2 - (\Sigma Y)^2}}$$

where X and Y represent the market and security i, respectively.

Numerical Example 10

Use the monthly return data for stock A and a market index for a 12-month period given in Table 3.10 to calculate beta using correlation method.

TABLE 3.10 Monthly return data (%) for stock A and market index

Month	Stock A	Market Index
1	9.43	7.41
2	0.00	−5.33

(Continued)

TABLE 3.10 Continued

Month	Stock A	Market Index
3	−4.31	−7.35
4	−18.92	−14.64
5	−6.65	1.58
6	26.57	15.19
7	20.00	5.11
8	2.93	0.76
9	5.20	−0.97
10	20.00	10.44
11	21.00	17.47
12	30.00	20.15

Solution:

The correlation coefficient can be statistically computed as:

$$r = \frac{n\Sigma XY - (\Sigma X)(\Sigma Y)}{\sqrt{n\Sigma X^2 - (\Sigma X)^2}\sqrt{n\Sigma Y^2 - (\Sigma Y)^2}}$$

where market index is the variable X and stock A is variable Y.

And beta can be computed using:

$$\beta_i = \frac{r_{\text{im}}\sigma_i\sigma_m}{\sigma_m^2}$$

To apply this formula, we need to know r_{im}, σ_i, σ_m and σ_m^2.

Solution may be tabulated as given in Table 3.11.

TABLE 3.11 Calculations

Month	Stock $A(Y)(R_i)$	Market Index $(X)(R_m)$	Y^2	X^2	XY
1	9.43	7.41	88.9249	54.9081	69.8763
2	0.00	−5.33	0.0000	28.4089	0

(*Continued*)

TABLE 3.11 Continued

Month	Stock $A(Y)(R_i)$	Market Index $(X)(R_m)$	Y^2	X^2	XY
3	−4.31	−7.35	18.5761	54.0225	31.6785
4	−18.92	−14.64	357.9664	214.3296	276.9888
5	−6.65	1.58	44.2225	2.4964	−10.507
6	26.57	15.19	705.9649	230.7361	403.5983
7	20.00	5.11	400.0000	26.1121	102.2
8	2.93	0.76	8.5849	0.5776	2.2268
9	5.20	−0.97	27.0400	0.9409	−5.044
10	20.00	10.44	400.0000	108.9936	208.8
11	21.00	17.47	441.0000	305.2009	366.87
12	30.00	20.15	900.0000	406.0225	604.5

ΣY or $\Sigma R_i = 105.25$

Mean = 8.77

ΣX or $\Sigma R_m = 49.82$

Mean = 4.15

$\Sigma Y^2 = 3392.28$

$\Sigma X^2 = 1432.75$

$\Sigma XY = 2051.19$

$$r_{\text{im}} = \frac{\{(12 \times 2051.17) - (49.82 \times 105.25)\}}{\sqrt{\{(12 \times 1432.750) - (49.82)^2\}} - \sqrt{\{(12 \times 3392.28)(105.25)^2\}}}$$

$$= 0.928$$

Variance and standard deviation can be calculated using the following formula:

$$\sigma^2 = \left[\frac{\sum_{i=1}^{n}(R_i - \bar{R})^2}{n-1}\right]$$

$$\sigma = \sqrt{\sigma^2}$$

Variance and standard deviation of Stock A may be calculated as tabulated in Table 3.12.

TABLE 3.12 Calculations

Month	Stock $A(Y)(R_i)$	$(R_i - \bar{\bar{R}})$	$(R_i - \bar{\bar{R}})^2$
1	9.43	0.66	0.4356
2	0.00	−8.77	76.9129
3	−4.31	−13.08	171.0864
4	−18.92	−27.69	766.7361
5	−6.65	−15.42	237.7764
6	26.57	17.80	316.8400
7	20.00	11.23	126.1129
8	2.93	−5.84	34.1056
9	5.20	−3.57	12.7449
10	20.00	11.23	126.1129
11	21.00	12.23	149.5729
12	30.00	21.23	450.7129

$$\Sigma(R_i - \bar{R})^2 = 2469.15, N = 12$$

Substituting the values in the formula of variance, we get

$$\sigma_A^2 = \frac{2469.15}{(12-1)}$$

$$= 224.4681$$

$$\sigma_A = \sqrt{224.4681}$$

$$= 14.98$$

Variance and standard deviation of market index may be calculated as tabulated in Table 3.13.

TABLE 3.13 Calculations

Month	Market Index $(X)(R_m)$	$\{R_i - R)\}$	$\{R_i - R)\}^2$
1	7.41	3.26	10.6276
2	−5.33	−9.48	89.8704
3	−7.35	−11.5	132.2500
4	−14.64	−18.79	353.0641
5	1.58	−2.57	6.6049
6	15.19	11.04	121.8816
7	5.11	0.96	0.9216
8	0.76	−3.39	11.4921
9	−0.97	−5.12	26.2144
10	10.44	6.29	39.5641
11	17.47	13.32	177.4224
12	20.15	16	256.0000

$$\sigma_m^2 = \frac{1225.9132}{(12-1)}$$

$$= 111.4467$$

$$\sigma_m = \sqrt{111.4467}$$

$$= 10.557$$

Substituting the values calculated above in the formula for calculation of beta, we get

$$\text{Beta} = \frac{(0.928 \times 14.98 \times 10.557)}{111.4467}$$

$$= 1.317$$

2. **Regression Method:** The regression model[11] is represented by a linear relationship between a dependent variable, the returns of a security and an independent variable, the returns of a market. Beta is the slope of the following regression relationship:

$$R_i = \alpha + \beta R_m$$

where
R_i = Return of individual security
R_m = Return of market index
α = Estimated return of individual security when the market is not moving

Numerical Example 11

Calculate beta and alpha by the regression method using the data given in the numerical illustration for beta calculation using the correlation method.

Here dependent variable is Stock *A*
Independent Variable is market index

Solution:

As per the given data, we will apply the following formula to calculate beta:

$$Y = \alpha + \beta X$$

$$\alpha = \overline{Y} - \beta\overline{X}$$

$$\beta = \frac{n\Sigma XY - (\Sigma X)(\Sigma Y)}{n\Sigma X^2 - (\Sigma X)^2}$$

---

[11] Statistically, β may be calculated as:

$$Y = \alpha + \beta X$$

$$\alpha = \overline{Y} - \beta\overline{X}$$

$$\beta = \frac{n\Sigma XY - (\Sigma X)(\Sigma Y)}{n\Sigma X^2 - (\Sigma X)^2}$$

where
n = Number of items
X = Independent variable scores
Y = Dependent variable scores
$\overline{X}$ = Mean value of independent variable scores
$\overline{Y}$ = Mean value of dependent vaiable scores

The following values have already been calculated in the above example:

ΣY or $\Sigma R_i = 105.25$

ΣX or $\Sigma R_m = 49.82$

$\Sigma X^2 = 1432.75$

$\Sigma XY = 2051.19$

$n = 12$

Mean of $Y = 8.77$

Mean of $X = 4.15$

Substituting the value in the formula for beta and alpha, we get

$$\beta = \frac{\{(12 \times 2051.19) - (49.82 \times 105.25)\}}{\{(12 \times 1432.75) - (49.82)^2\}}$$

$$= 1.317$$

$$\alpha = 8.77 - (1.317)(4.15)$$

$$= 3.304$$

A common measure of beta of security *i* is:

$$\beta_i = \frac{\sigma_{im}}{\sigma_m^2}$$

where
β_i = Slope of regression line
σ_{im} = Covariance[12] between returns of security *i* and the market
σ_m^2 = Variance of the return on market portfolio

The above formula is used to calculate beta using spreadsheet. Reliability of this risk measure is determined by calculating its *r*-squared or coefficient of determination. *R*-squared is the square of correlation coefficient and it is a measure of how closely fitted the data points are to the line of best fit. The squared correlation coefficient (r^2) is the proportion of variance in security *i* that can be accounted for by knowing market, the independent variable. It is one of the best means for evaluating the strength of a relationship.

[12] Discussed in the next section.

Spreadsheet Application 7 *Calculation of beta and r-squared using MS Excel.*

Solution:

	A	B	C	D
1	Month	Stock A	Market Index	
2	1	-0.75	-0.35	
3	2	4.45	-0.59	
4	3	-3.05	-1.03	
5	4	3.41	1.64	
6	5	10.13	7.67	
7	6	2.36	1.13	
8	7	-0.42	0.72	
9	8	5.51	0.84	
10	9	7.8	5.05	
11	10	2.6	1.21	
12	11	-4.81	0.39	
13	12	-1.91	-1.96	
14	Covariance of Stock A and the market index COVAR(B2:B13,C2:C13) =8.7			
15	Variance of the market index VAR(C2:C13) = 7.13			
16	Beta= COVAR(B2:B13,C2:C13)/VAR(C2:C13) =1.22			
17	Coefficient of determination RSQ(B2:B13,C2:C13) = 0.629			

Spreadsheet Application 8 *Beta of a security can be calculated using MS Excel by regressing the returns of stock on market index. Calculate beta of Reliance Industries on S&P BSE SENSEX for a period from January 2009 through December 2013.*

Solution:

To begin with, calculate lognormal returns in MS Excel (using the function LN) for the closing levels of both time series using the following formula:

$$r = \ln\left(\frac{P_t}{P_{t-1}}\right) \times 100$$

where r = Return, P_t = Price of the day, P_{t-1} = Price of the previous day

	A	B	C	D	E
1	Month	Reliance Close Price	SENSEX Closing Price	Reliance LN Returns	SENSEX LN Returns
2	Jan-09	1325.2	9424.24		
3	Feb-09	1265.05	8891.61	=LN(B3/B2)*100	
4	Mar-09	1523.2	9708.5	18.57017	8.789365
5	Apr-09	1802.7	11403.25	16.84722	16.08966
6	May-09	2277.5	14625.25	23.37928	24.88511
7	Jun-09	2023.35	14493.84	-11.8324	-0.90258

Thereafter, regress the series using Data Analysis in MS Excel.

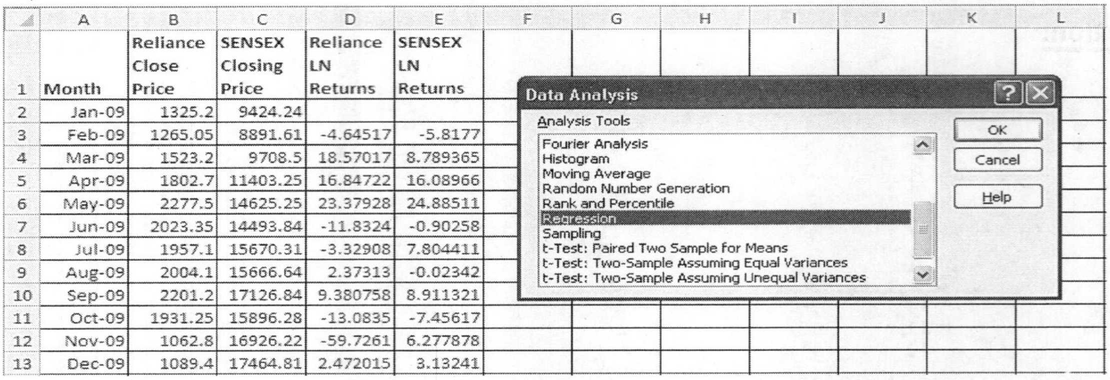

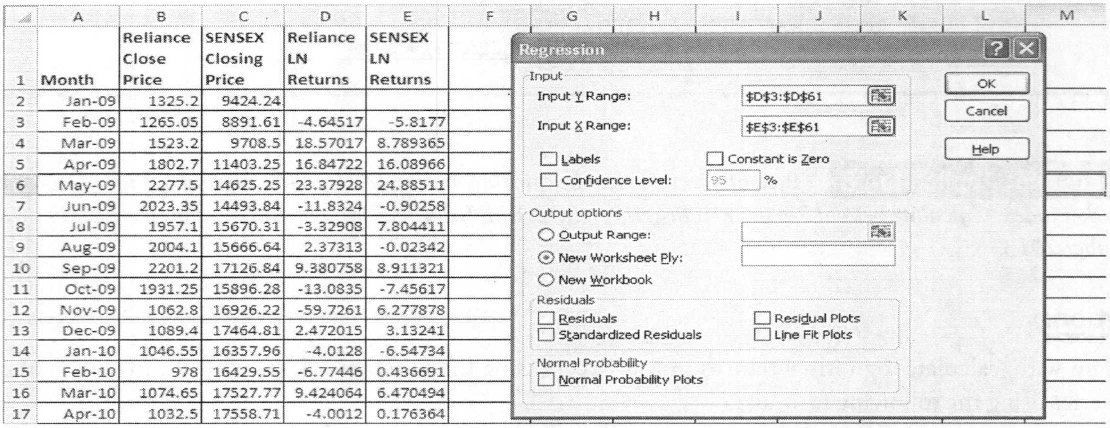

SUMMARY OUTPUT

Regression Statistics	
Multiple R	0.506365437
R Square	0.256405956
Adjusted R Square	0.243360446
Standard Error	9.917024079
Observations	59

ANOVA

	df	*SS*	*MS*	*F*	*Significance F*
Regression	1	1932.990843	1932.991	19.6543	4.27999E-05
Residual	57	5605.799895	98.3477		
Total	58	7538.790739			

	Coefficients	*Standard Error*	*t Stat*	*P-value*	*Lower 95%*	*Upper 95%*	*Lower 95.0%*	*Upper 95.0%*
Intercept	-1.912524988	1.321366025	-1.44738	0.153267	-4.558514813	0.733464836	-4.558514813	0.733464836
X Variable 1	0.908985683	0.20503288	4.433365	4.28E-05	0.498414422	1.319556943	0.498414422	1.319556943

The value of beta is highlighted. It is 0.909.

Challenges in use of beta as a proxy of risk

Using beta as a measure of systematic risk has its own limitations. Problem lies with the fact that most analysts consider only the magnitude of beta without considering its statistical significance (r-square value of the regression line). Beta, being a statistical variable, should be considered in the context of its statistical significance. Higher r-square value indicates higher correlation and a stronger relationship between returns of the asset and the market.

Though beta is an intuitively appealing and easily quantifiable measure, some critics contend that beta calculation, as it exists, doesn't incorporate new information. Betas are based on past price behavior that is considered by many analysts to be a very poor predictor of the future. Moreover, stocks that are relatively new to the market might not have sufficient past price data to establish a reliable beta. Furthermore, the beta of a single stock may change over time with changes in its price, which makes it unreliable for investors with long-term horizons. However, this kind of beta is a good risk metric for traders who buy and sell stocks within short time periods.

For many investors, it doesn't make much sense to use beta as a proxy for risk because it doesn't distinguish between upside and downside price changes. For most investors, downside movements are a possibility of suffering a loss but upside ones mean an opportunity of earning more.

Many approaches have been proposed to overcome the problems in use of historical beta. One approach involves adjustment of historical beta. Betas that are calculated solely on the basis of historical price data are called unadjusted betas. However, such beta estimate is largely rear-looking and is not considered a good indicator of the future. Since beta is a key metric in portfolio management, many analysts use what is known as adjusted beta by applying certain models. Adjusted beta is an estimate of security's future beta and its calculation is based on the statistical observation that over time, betas tend to demonstrate mean reverting properties, i.e., they show a tendency to move toward the average beta for the market (beta = 1). Thus, over an extended period of time, betas significantly above 1 may decline and betas below 1 may rise up towards 1.

A procedure that is frequently used for calculating adjusted beta is to take weighted average of two parameters: the historical beta and the value of the market beta. The weights assigned depend on the errors in historical estimation and dispersion of individual stocks around the market. If estimation errors are large, weight assigned to historical beta should be small and vice versa. If the dispersion of individual stocks around the market average is large, the weight assigned to market beta should be small. For example, Merill Lynch, in its prediction of beta, assigns a weight of 0.66 to historical beta and a weight of 0.34 to the market average.[13]

Predicting beta becomes a very crucial exercise because the beta calculated from historical data cannot be assumed to be constant or stable. While the beta calculted from the past data is handy in interpreting past performance, forward-looking betas need to be predicted for future-oriented risk analysis. One needs to understand the fact that beta is not a representation of causal relationship between market and security return, rather it is a reflection of the fact that both security and market returns are driven by a third variable—the economy. So a more effective way of forecasting beta would be to quantify the relationship between the market, the security returns and economy related factors. These factors could be inflation, GDP and fiscal deficit, to name a few. A beta forecasted through this approach of analyzing the fundamentals of the economy may be called a 'fundamental beta.'

---

[13] Merill Lynch's booklet titled *Security Risk Evaluation Service.*

Concept and Measurement of Interactive Risk

The concept of portfolio and combination of securities has already been introduced. So far, we have learnt how to compute return and risk for individual securities. Let us now learn how to calculate the risk of a group of securities comprising a portfolio. The risk that is relevant in case of portfolio is called interactive risk and it is measured in terms of co-movement and co-variation.

Co-movement describes the event of an asset's return 'moving with' returns of another asset. It is the tendency of two variables, the returns from two assets/securities in our case, to move in parallel manner. It can be measured using:

1. The correlation coefficient
2. The covariance

The correlation coefficient

It is a relative measure of co-movement of asset returns that places assets on a scale of −1 to + 1. Where returns move exactly in unison, perfect correlation is said to exist and its value is equal to +1, and where the exactly opposite movements happen, perfect negative correlation exists and its value is equal to −1. Most investments generally have a positive correlation of (0 and +1) but in portfolio analysis, as we will discuss later, assets having negative correlation are much sought after.

Measurement of correlation Covariance and correlation are conceptually the same because both of them reflect the degree of co-movement or co-variation between returns of two assets. Mathematically, the two terms are related as follows:

$$\text{Cor}(R_i, R_j) = \frac{\text{Cov}(R_i, R_j)}{\sigma(R_i)\sigma(R_j)}$$

where

$\text{Cor}(R_i, R_j)$ = Correlation coefficient between the returns on assets *i* and *j*

$\text{Cov}(R_i, R_j)$ = Covariance between the returns on assets *i* and *j*

$\sigma(R_i)\,\sigma(R_j)$ = Standard deviation of the returns on assets *i* and *j*

Figure 3.9 Graphical illustration of correlations (+1, 0 & −1).

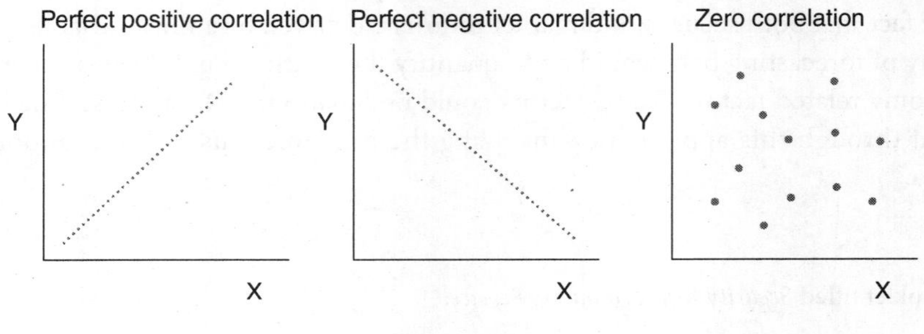

Thus, the correlation coefficient is simply the covariance of two assets divided by the product of their standard deviations. It indicates how much i and j vary together as a proportion of their combined individual variations/deviations. Thus, correlation between securities/assets depends on:

1. The covariance between them and
2. The standard deviation of each.

Correlation coefficient are illustrated graphically in Figures 3.9 and 3.10.

Figure 3.10 Graphical illustration of degree of correlation between X and Y lying between +1 and −1.

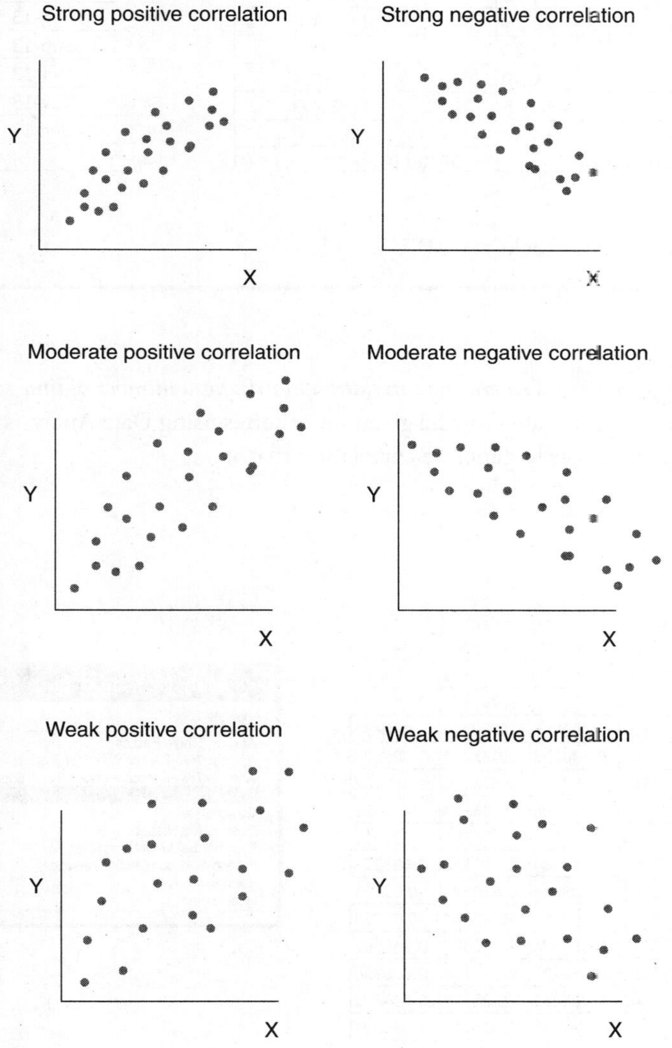

Spreadsheet Application 9 *Calculating correlation between two series or returns using MS Excel.*

Use returns on two scrips, Mahindra & Mahindra (M&M) and Bharti Airtel to calculate correlation between them for a period from January 2009 through December 2013.

Solution:

Correlation can be calculated using the Excel Function CORREL.

	A	B	C
51	Mar-13	-1.143	-10.329
52	Apr-13	6.936	8.834
53	May-13	4.481	-5.879
54	Jun-13	0.129	-3.092
55	Jul-13	-5.793	16.856
56	Aug-13	-15.523	-14.432
57	Sep-13	5.820	6.390
58	Oct-13	7.059	13.610
59	Nov-13	6.245	-10.837
60	Dec-13	-0.222	0.988
61		Correlation	=CORREL(B2:B60,C2:C60)

	A	B	C
51	Mar-13	-1.143	-10.329
52	Apr-13	6.936	8.834
53	May-13	4.481	-5.879
54	Jun-13	0.129	-3.092
55	Jul-13	-5.793	16.856
56	Aug-13	-15.523	-14.432
57	Sep-13	5.820	6.390
58	Oct-13	7.059	13.610
59	Nov-13	6.245	-10.837
60	Dec-13	-0.222	0.988
61		Correlation	-0.0733

The correlation between the two stocks is –0.0733.

Spreadsheet Application 10 *Generating correlation matrix for a number of time series.*

Correlation matrix can be generated for the given set of series using Data Analysis in MS Excel.
Use the time series given below to generate correlation matrix,

Solution:

	A	B	C	D	E	F
1	Series 1	Series 2	Series 3	Series 4	Series 5	Series 6
2	-0.00023	-0.04215	0.02195	-0.02525	-0.03622	0.04581
3	0.089113	0.060543	0.049805	0.030264	0.095393	0.093214
4	-0.07456	0.037356	-0.05684	-0.00805	-0.02278	-0.0454
5	0.062779	0.00315	-0.016	0.030092	0.032455	0.005574
6	0.031324	0.002334	0.07858	0.058812	0.076878	0.063902
7	-0.06547	-0.08342	-0.04892	-0.05398	-0.06923	-0.0531
8	0.004367	0.0239	-0.00491	0.002005	-0.02711	0.035013
9	0.064705	0.030142	0.059803	0.048464	0.063052	0.088321
10	0.001764	-0.00618	0.028368	0.029736	0.010574	-0.03155
11	-0.0356	-0.06576	-0.05932	-0.07757	-0.08202	-0.01728
12	0.043665	0.018239	0.034164	0.029676	-0.00607	0.060597
13	0.009412	0.04378	0.035311	0.052282	0.057174	0.070828
14	0.005738	-0.02374	-0.00947	-0.01259	-0.01878	0.064872
15	0.110416	0.084988	0.071976	0.04872	0.078443	0.065801

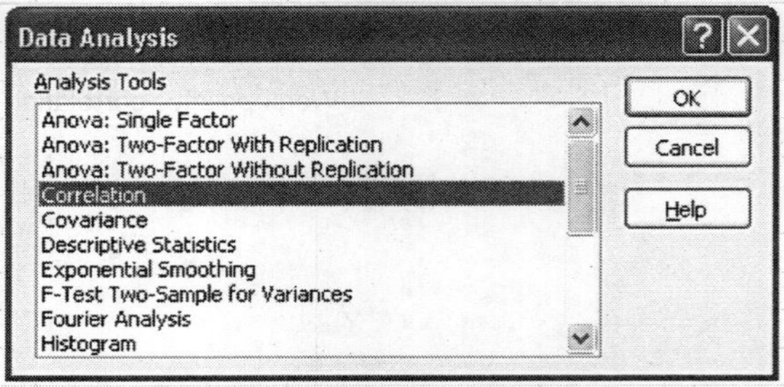

	A	B	C	D	E	F
1	Series 1	Series 2	Series 3	Series 4	Series 5	Series 6
2	-0.00023	-0.04215	0.02195	-0.02525	-0.03622	0.04581
3	0.089113	0.060543	0.049805	0.030264	0.095393	0.093214
4	-0.07456	0.037356	-0.05684	-0.00805	-0.02278	-0.0454
5	0.062779	0.00315	-0.016	0.030092	0.032455	0.005574
6	0.031324	0.002334	0.07858	0.058812	0.076878	0.063902
7	-0.06547	-0.08342	-0.04892	-0.05398	-0.06923	-0.0531
8	0.004367	0.0239	-0.00491	0.002005	-0.02711	0.035013
9	0.064705	0.030142	0.059803	0.048464	0.063052	0.088321
10	0.001764	-0.00618	0.028368	0.029736	0.010574	-0.03155
11	-0.0356	-0.06576	-0.05932	-0.07757	-0.08202	-0.01728
12	0.043665	0.018239	0.034164	0.029676	-0.00607	0.060597
13	0.009412	0.04378	0.035311	0.052282	0.057174	0.070828
14	0.005738	-0.02374	-0.00947	-0.01259	-0.01878	0.064872

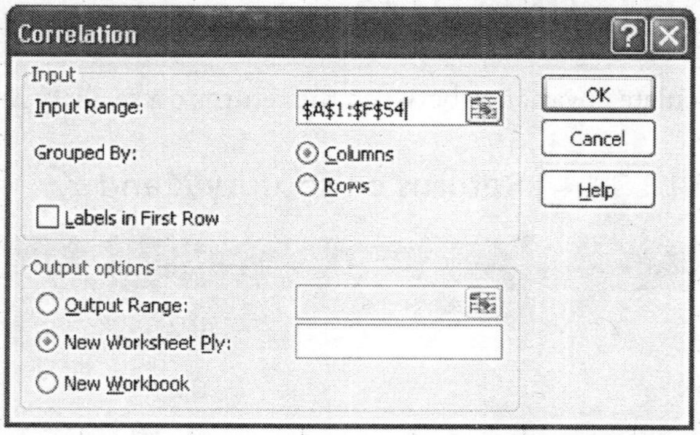

The correlation matrix thus generated is exhibited below:

	A	B	C	D	E	F	G
1		*Series 1*	*Series 2*	*Series 3*	*Series 4*	*Series 5*	*Series 6*
2	Series 1	1					
3	Series 2	0.584	1.000				
4	Series 3	0.659	0.654	1.000			
5	Series 4	0.688	0.792	0.805	1.000		
6	Series 5	0.661	0.664	0.796	0.772	1.000	
7	Series 6	0.554	0.610	0.644	0.689	0.528	1.000

The covariance

It is an absolute measure of interactive risk with no upper or lower limits and it can be positive or negative.

Measurement of covariance Covariance is a measure of the degree to which the returns of two assets vary or change together. A positive covariance signifies that the said returns move in the same direction whereas negative covariance implies that the returns move in opposite directions. If the returns of two assets are independent of each other, the covariance is zero. The covariance between two assets/security say i and j, is calculated as follows:

$$\text{Cov}(R_x, R_y) = p_1[R_{x1} - E(R_x)][R_{y1} - E(R_y)] + p_2[R_{x2} - E(R_x)][R_{y2} - E(R_y)] + \cdots + p_n[R_{xn} - E(R_x)][R_{yn} - E(R_y)]$$

where

$p_1, p_2 \ldots p_n$ = Probabilities associated with states 1, ... n
$R_{i1}, \ldots R_{in}$ = Return on assets i in states 1, ... n
$R_{j1}, \ldots R_{jn}$ = Return on assets j in states 1, ... n
$E(R_i), E(R_j)$ = Expected return on as sets i and j

Numerical Example 12

Calculate covariance between the returns on security *X* and *Y* using following information (Table 3.14):

TABLE 3.14 Returns on security *X* and *Y*

Situation	Probability	Security *X* (return %)	Security *Y* (return %)
1	0.2	7	0
2	0.2	13	9
3	0.5	15	18
4	0.1	23	24

Solution:

Here, covariance between the returns on security *X* and *Y* can be calculated using the following formula:

$$\text{Cov}(R_x, R_y) = p_1[R_{x1} - E(R_x)][R_{y1} - E(R_y)] + p_2[R_{x2} - E(R_x)][R_{y2} - E(R_y)] + \cdots$$
$$+ p_n[R_{xn} - E(R_x)][R_{yn} - E(R_y)]$$

Expected Return of *X* and *Y* may be calculated using the following formula:

$$\text{Expected Return} = \sum_{i=1}^{n} (\text{Probability of return}) \times (\text{Possible return})$$
$$E(R_i) = (P_1)(R_1) + (P_2)(R_2) + (P_3)(R_3) + \cdots (P_n)(R_n)$$

$E(R_x) = 13.8$

$E(R_y) = 13.2$

$$\text{Covariance} = 0.2 \times (7 - 13.8) \times (0 - 13.2) + 0.2 \times (13 - 13.8) \times (9 - 13.2) + 0.5 \times (15 - 13.8)$$
$$\times (18 - 13.2) + 0.1 \times (23 - 13.8) \times (24\text{-}13.2)$$
$$= 31.44$$

Covariance may also be calculated as:

$$\text{Cov}(R_i, R_j) = \frac{\sum^{n} [R_i - \bar{R}_i][R_j - \bar{R}_j]}{N}$$

where
$\text{Cov}(R_i, R_j)$ = Covariance between i and j
R_i = Return on security i
R_j = Return on security j
N = Number of observations
$\overline{R}_j$ = Expected Return on security i
$\overline{R}_i$ = Expected Return on security j

Numerical Example 13

The historical rates of return of two securities over the past 5 years are given in Table 3.15. Calculate the covariance of the two securities.

TABLE 3.15 Historical rates of return of two securities

Years	Security 1 (return %)	Security 2 (return %)
1	12	20
2	8	24
3	7	25
4	14	22
5	16	20

Solution:

The formula to be used for calculation of covariance is:

$$\text{Cov}(R_i, R_j) = \frac{\sum^{n}[R_i - \overline{R}_i][R_j - \overline{R}_j]}{N}$$

$$\text{Mean return of security 1} = \frac{(12+8+7+14+16)}{5} = 11.4$$

$$\text{Mean return of security 2} = \frac{(20+24+25+22+20)}{5} = 22.2$$

$$\text{Covariance} = \frac{\begin{aligned}\{(12-11.4)\times(20-22.2)+(8-11.4)\times(24-22.2)+(7-11.4)\times(25-22.2)\\ +(14-11.4)\times(22-22.2)+(16-11.4)\times(20-22.2)\}\end{aligned}}{5}$$

$$= -6.08$$

Spreadsheet Application 11 *Covariance can be calculated using COVARIANCE.P function of MS Excel.*

Covariance between returns on Security 1and Security 2 (using data from Numerical Example 14) can be calculated using MS Excel as:

	A	B	C	D	E
1	Years	Security 1(return %)	Security 2(return %)		
2	1	12	20		
3	2	8	24		
4	3	7	25		
5	4	14	22		
6	5	16	20		
7		Covariance	=COVARIANCE.P(B2:B6, C2:C6)		

	A	B	C
1	Years	Security 1(return %)	Security 2(return %)
2	1	12	20
3	2	8	24
4	3	7	25
5	4	14	22
6	5	16	20
7		**Covariance**	**-6.08**

Covariance between returns on Security 1 and Security 2 is –6.08.

* It is better to generate covariance matrix by using the formula Cov = $r_{xy}\sigma_x\sigma_y$.

Investor Risk Profile and Indifference Curve Analysis

Investment is the commitment of investible surplus to the purchase of financial instruments or other assets. The primary motive of investing is to earn a reasonable positive return in the form of interest/dividend, other income and appreciation in the value of the instrument.

Investors have a plethora of financial instruments such as bonds, stock, preference shares, fixed deposits, government securities, provident fund schemes, national savings schemes, mutual fund, life insurance as well as a number of alternative investments like real estate, precious metals, derivatives, etc. to choose from while making investment decision. We also know that investors are guided by objectives like safety, income, capital appreciation, tax planning, retirement planning, marketability/liquidity, etc. while making their asset choice. At the same time, the investors are constrained by factors such as income, life cycle stage, time horizon, liquidity and risk aversion while taking a decision to invest. Of all the constraints, risk aversion is one factor that takes precedence above all others. An investor might have liquidity but might not invest anywhere if he is uncomfortable with the level of risk. How and why people invest depends mainly on their risk-taking behavior. In fact, in final analysis, all investment decisions boil down to risk-return trade-off.

Risk-return trade off

Risk-Return trade off begins with a decision about the amount of risk an investor can take while remaining comfortable with his investments. It represents the balance between the desire for minimum possible risk and maximum possible return. As a rule, low risk (low standard deviation) is an indicator of low potential returns and high risk (high standard deviation) is associated with high potential returns. The term potential implies that taking high risk doesn't mean that high returns are guaranteed. They may or may not happen in future. The risk-return trade off illustrated graphically in Figure 3.11, signifies that the higher risk gives rise to the possibility of higher returns.

At the same time, it should be understood that high risk also indicates higher potential for losses. In other words, risk-return trade off implies that an investor seeking higher possible returns has to accept the higher level

Figure 3.11 Risk/return trade-off.

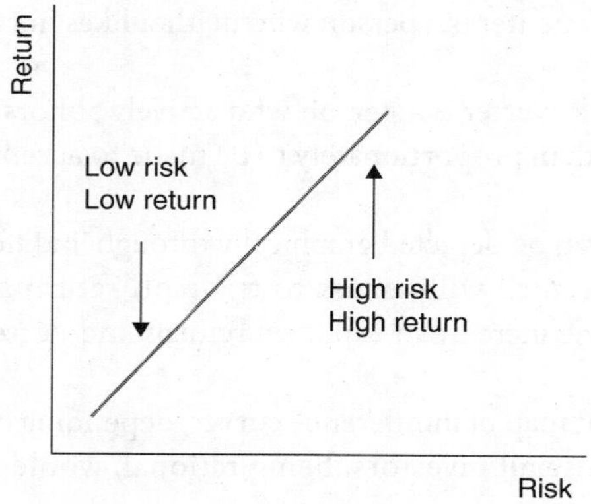

of risk that would characterize such a return. This leads us to another term called risk-reward concept, which means higher return may be looked at as reward that compensate an investor for bearing a higher level of risk.

The most important thing that drives risk-return trade off is the attitude of investors towards risk. Investors differ in their willingness to take a higher level or as a matter of fact, any risk at all. It is, therefore, pertinent to discuss the terms that are related to the risk profile of an investor. These include risk preference, risk tolerance and risk aversion.

1. **Risk Preference:** Risk preference is an indicator of the amount of risk an investor can handle and it differs for each individual. Risk preference of an investor is dependent on two things, liquidity (the amount of money in the hands of the investor) and the time horizon of investment. Risk preference is driven by risk tolerance of an investor.
2. **Risk Tolerance:** Risk tolerance of an investor is the function of his psychological make-up. It is conditioned by investment constraints such as life cycle stage, income, etc. On the basis of their willingness to take risk, investors may be classified as conservative or aggressive, with the word conservative implying a preference for low risk and aggressive implying a willingness to take higher risk. To put it differently, an investor is considered aggressive or conservative on the basis of his mental make-up or risk tolerance.
3. **Risk Aversion:** Risk aversion or risk avoidance, as it is sometimes called, is a concept in finance that has been borrowed from psychology. In the context of finance, it is based on the behavior of investors when they are faced with uncertainty. Risk aversion expresses the unwillingness of a person to forego a lower but more certain pay-off for a higher but more uncertain payoff. For instance, a risk-averse investor might choose to put his money into a bank fixed deposit with a low but guaranteed interest rate, rather than into a share that may earn high returns, but also has a possibility of giving a loss. Risk aversion also implies that investors inherently pursue low risk. Out of any two investments offering same expected returns but different risks, investors will invariably pick the one with lower risk.

Risk aversion may also be described as the tendency of investors to avoid unnecessary risk that characterizes risky investments. Though it is universally accepted that for risk averse investors, higher risk investments must offer higher expected returns yet how high these returns should be is subjective and differs from investor to investor. Depending on the extent to which they need to be compensated with higher return for accepting a higher level of risk, investors can be called:

(a) *Risk lovers*: Risk lovers are investors who are willing to accept higher level of risk for even a low increase in returns. A risk lover is ready to take a higher risk without a proportionate increase in the expected returns.

(b) *Risk neutral or neuters*:Risk neuter is a person who neither likes nor dislikes taking risk. In reality, such a person may not exist.

(c) *Risk averse or averters*: Risk averter is a person who actively abhors risk and avoids it. He would need to be compensated more than proportionately to be made to accept a higher level of risk.

The risk preference of investors can be depicted graphically through 'indifference curves' or 'utility functions.' Indifference curve represents investor's willingness to trade off return and risk. Utility, as presented by indifference curve, increases with the increase in expected returns and decreases with the increase in risk and risk-aversion.

Each investor will have a different map of indifference curves, depending on his risk preference. In difference curves have a positive slope because all investors, being rational, would seek higher return for accepting higher risk.

Graphically, a typical indifference curve may be illustrated as given in Figure 3.12.

Figure 3.12 A typical indifference curve.

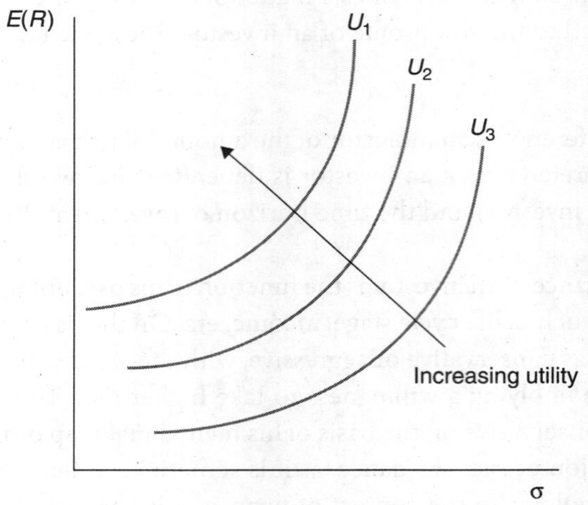

E(*R*) represents expected return and σ represents risk.

The above graph shows three indifference curves for the same investor. These represent different levels of utility for him. However, the utility is the same anywhere on the same curve. This happens because when the risk increases, the investor demands more return in accordance with his utility function and this keeps the level of utility the same along the curve. Further, given a choice, the investor can increase his utility by moving to a higher indifference curve that would offer lower risk for same level of return. Generally speaking, the utility of risk-averse investors rises as we move leftward on the graph.

The degree of slope of these curves will indicate the extent of risk aversion of an investor. The slope of the indifference curve of a conservative (risk-fearing) investor requiring more than proportionate increase in return for accepting small increase in risk would be different from the slope of the indifference curve of a more aggressive investor (risk lover) who would be willing to accept less than proportionate increase in return for assuming higher risk. This implies that although both types of investors dislike risk yet their risk-return trade off varies in degrees.

Utility curve of risk averse investor is illustrated in Figure 3.13.

Figure 3.13 Utility curve of risk averse investor.

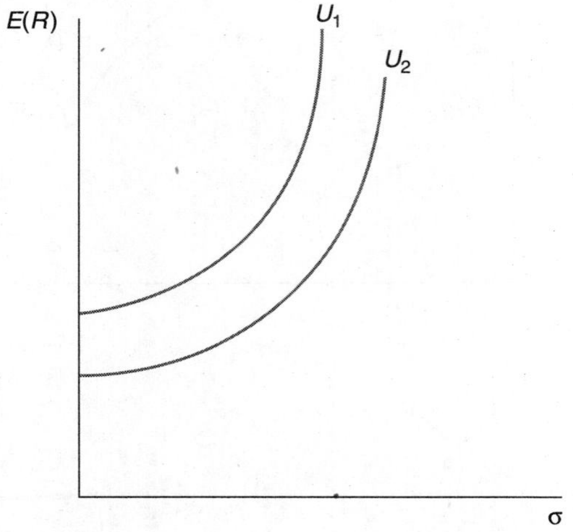

Utility curve of risk neutral investor is illustrated in Figure 3.14.

Figure 3.14 Utility curve of risk neutral investor.

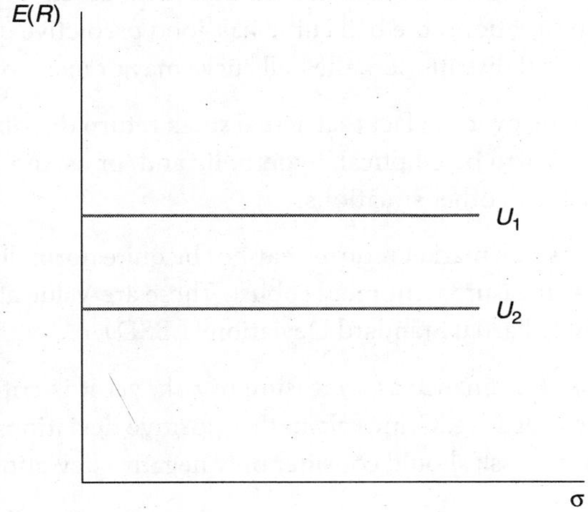

Utility curve of risk-seeking (risk lover) investor is illustrated in Figure 3.15.

Figure 3.15 Utility curve of risk-seeking investor.

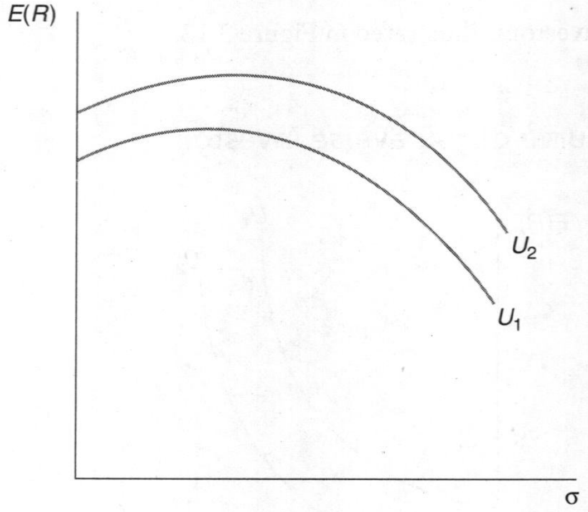

SUMMARY

☑ Any investment decision comprises two major areas:
(a) Identification of the assets/securities to be held.
(b) Proportionate allocation of investible surplus to the assets/securities thus identified.

☑ Expected return is an anticipated return, i.e., a return an investor expects to earn over some future period. It is a return that an investor predicts based on a number of factors to decide whether to invest or not.

☑ In the past it was assumed and often observed as well that most stock markets tend to fall into normal distribution patterns. In such situations, the bell curve has good predictive qualities but when stock return tend to break away from a normal distribution, the bell curve may or may not be useful as a predictive tool.

☑ Latest research has started to uncover the fact that actual stock return distributions are neither normal nor symmetrical. Rather they appear to be elliptical, hyperbolic and/or asymmetrical at times in some cases, and even completely indefinable in other situations.

☑ The increasing realization that stock market returns may not be quite normally distributed has led to the use of three methods to make risk measurement more robust. These are Value at Risk (VaR), Conditional Tail Expectations (CTE) and Lower Partial Standard Deviation (LPSD).

☑ Though variance is widely used in finance as a measure of risk, yet it is criticized because it considers all dispersions, positive as well as negative. Critics claim that positive deviations (upside risk) are appreciated by investors, so a true measure of risk should consider only negative deviations (downside risk).

- ☑ Markowitz suggested two measures for measuring downside risk, a semi variance computed from the mean return or below-mean semi variance and a semi-variance computed from a target return or below-target semi variance.
- ☑ Semi deviation or downside standard deviation of returns has also received a lot of support as an alternative measure of risk from both practitioners and theorists.
- ☑ Though beta is an intuitively appealing and easily quantifiable measure, some critics contend that beta calculation, as it exists, doesn't incorporate new information. Betas are based on past price behavior that is considered by many analysts to be a very poor predictor of the future.
- ☑ As a rule, low risk is an indicator of low potential returns and high risk is associated with high potential returns. The term potential implies that taking high risk doesn't mean that high returns are guaranteed.
- ☑ The most important thing that drives risk return trade-off is the attitude of investors towards risk. Investors differ in their willingness to take a higher level, or as a matter of fact, any risk at all.
- ☑ Utility, as presented by indifference curve, increases with the increase in expected returns and decreases with the increase in risk and risk-aversion.
- ☑ Each investor will have a different map of indifference curves, depending on his risk preference. Indifference curves have a positive slope because all investors, being rational, would seek higher return for accepting higher risk.
- ☑ The degree of slope of these curves will indicate the extent of risk aversion of an investor.

KEY WORDS

Adjusted beta 97
Beta 74
Correlation coefficient 98
Covariance 101
Diversification of risk 78
Effective annual rate 57
Excess return 54
Expected return 54
Fat tails 73
Fundamental beta 97
Holding period return 54
Indifference curve 104
Interactive risk 97
Nominal return 53
Normal distribution 71
Portfolio 52
R-squared 94
Range 79
Real return 53
Realized return 54
Required return 54
Risk aversion 105
Risk preference 105
Risk premium 55
Risk tolerance 105
Risk-free return 52
Risk-return trade off 104
Risk-reward concept 105
Semi variance 79
Standard deviation 79
Systematic & unsystematic risk 75
Upside & downside risk 74
Variance 79

CONCEPT QUESTIONS

1. What do you understand by the 'the slope of an investor's indifference curve'?
Describe how a typical risk-averse investor's risk-return trade off will change at different points along any one of his indifference curves.

2. "The much-used metric in investment theory: 'risk-free rate' seems to be more mythical and unreal in the modern times." Analyze the statement.

3. Variance as a measure of risk suffers from a severe drawback that makes it less appealing to practitioners though it continues to enchant the academicians. What is the drawback and how has it been proposed to be overcome?

4. In the new world with newer nuances of risk and return, security returns follow a more asymmetrical pattern more often than not. This makes computation of risk challenging. Explain in detail.

5. Many analysts have proposed the use of fat-tailed distributions to overcome some of the challenges of normal distribution. Discuss.

6. While investing, the investors cannot just expect returns without incurring any risk. However, they can diversify certain investment risks. Elaborate.

7. Risk return trade off forms the basis of an individual's investment decision. How?

8. What is beta? Discuss its relevance in investment risk-return analysis.

9. "Individual security risk is not relevant in portfolio diversification." Then what is? Discuss.

10. "Risk is defined as the unexpected variability or volatility of returns on an investment." What are the main types of risks that you need to understand and manage as an investment adviser?

PRACTICE PROBLEMS

1. Using data from the table given below, calculate arithmetic average and geometric mean of returns for the entire period given in the table. Comment on the outcome with a view to highlighting the difference in results of arithmetic-geometric mean

CNX NIFTY Index*				
Year	**Open**	**High**	**Low**	**Close**
1996–97	988.33	1203.11	775.43	968.30
1997–98	931.95	1297.10	929.05	1116.90
1998–99	1117.15	1247.15	800.10	1078.05
1999–00	1082.55	1818.15	916.00	1528.45
2000–01	1528.70	1636.95	1098.75	1148.20
2001–02	1148.10	1207.00	849.95	1129.55
2002–03	1129.85	1153.30	920.10	978.20

(*Continued*)

Continued

CNX NIFTY Index*				
Year	Open	High	Low	Close
2003–04	977.40	2014.65	920.00	1771.90
2004–05	1771.45	2183.45	1292.20	2035.65
2005–06	2035.90	3433.85	1896.30	3402.55
2006–07	3403.15	4245.30	2595.65	3821.55
2007–08	3820.00	6357.10	3617.00	4734.50
2008–09	4735.65	5298.85	2252.75	3020.95
2009–10	3023.85	5329.55	2965.70	5249.10
2010–11	5249.20	6338.50	4786.45	5833.75
2011–12	5835.00	5944.45	4531.15	5295.55
2012–13	5296.35	6111.80	4770.35	5682.55

*CNX Nifty commenced from November 3, 1995

2. Use the following daily price movement of ICICI Bank scrip on Bombay Stock Exchange to calculate its return for the month of April 2014.

Date	Close Price
01-Apr-14	1223.8
02-Apr-14	1242.55
03-Apr-14	1235.2
04-Apr-14	1230.35
07-Apr-14	1209.05
09-Apr-14	1259.55
10-Apr-14	1246.15
11-Apr-14	1235.5
15-Apr-14	1218.05
16-Apr-14	1222.3
17-Apr-14	1262

(Continued)

Continued

Date	Close Price
21-Apr-14	1281.55
22-Apr-14	1287.9
23-Apr-14	1299.05
25-Apr-14	1269.3
28-Apr-14	1273.85
29-Apr-14	1262.05
30-Apr-14	1244.8

3. Calculate variance of returns of HDFC over a period extending from 2004 to 2013, assuming a dividend of ₹3 per share paid at the end of 2006 and a dividend of ₹2 per share paid at the end of 2011.

HDFC BSE: 500010	NSE: HDFC	ISIN: INE0		
Historic Data for the Period on BSE				
Period High: 933.00	Period Low: 94.60	Change in market-cap: 581.42%		
Date	Open	High	Low	Close
2004	129.7	161.6	94.6	153.22
2005	153.8	260.7	135.84	241.07
2006	242.4	340.2	192.4	324.91
2007	323	639	279.42	574.49
2008	585	651.4	240.4	297.51
2009	299	575	223.22	535.57
2010	536.2	780.05	460	727.95
2011	731	738.45	582.25	649.45
2012	648.15	882	610.7	828.1
2013	829	931	632.2	796.3

4. Assume that there are 2 stocks and 5 states of the world. Each state can occur with equal probability. Given the returns of the two in the following table, calculate expected return and variance of each stock and the covariance between the returns of the two.

	State 1	State 2	State 3	State 4	State 5
Sun Industries Ltd. Possible returns	5	7	1	9	3
Zenith Solutions Possible returns	9	6	5	4	8

5. Use correlation method to calculate beta of TCS scrip from following monthly return data for the scrip as well as BSE SENSEX for a 12-month period:

Month	BSE SENSEX	TCS
Jan-13	−5.19	12.81
Feb-13	−0.14	3.77
Mar-13	3.55	−12.44
Apr-13	1.31	8.96
May-13	−1.84	1.25
Jun-13	−0.26	19.54
Jul-13	−3.75	11.46
Aug-13	4.08	−4.77
Sep-13	9.21	9.42
Oct-13	−1.76	−4.92
Nov-13	1.82	8.30
Dec-13	−3.10	3.01

Comment on the result and explain the behavior of TCS scrip vis-à-vis the market.

6. Compute beta and alpha of Ambuja Stock from following monthly return data for the stock as well as CNX Nifty for a 12-month period:

Month	CNX Nifty	Ambuja
Jan-13	0.81	−1.49
Feb-13	−4.65	−3.14
Mar-13	−0.27	−9.50
Apr-13	5.17	9.07
May-13	−1.00	−6.18

(*Continued*)

Continued

Month	CNX Nifty	Ambuja
Jun-13	−0.68	6.03
Jul-13	−2.90	−11.43
Aug-13	−3.09	1.58
Sep-13	4.13	5.82
Oct-13	9.12	4.56
Nov-13	−1.42	−1.73
Dec-13	1.35	−0.70

7. ABBL Corp. Ltd.'s scrip costing ₹130 is expected to pay a dividend of ₹3 at the end of the year. The possible prices that the stock might sell for at the end of the year with respective probabilities is as follows:

Price (₹)	Probability
125	0.1
130	0.1
135	0.2
140	0.3
145	0.2
150	0.1

Calculate expected return and standard deviation of returns of the stock.

8. Calculate expected return of each security and their covariance for the given forecast:

Economic Condition	Probability	BPC Ltd. (return %)	MKM United (return %)
Booming	0.4	20	16
Stable	0.2	10	11
Recessionary	0.4	−8	4

9. Based on the data given below, calculate the real rate of return on T-bills for each individual year given in the table. Comment on the results.

Year	Inflation rate (%)	T-Bill rate (%)
1996–97	4.61	11.35
1997–98	4.40	9.29
1998–99	5.95	9.95
1999–00	3.27	10.05
2000–01	7.16	9.73
2001–02	3.60	7.12
2002–03	3.41	5.88
2003–04	5.46	4.55
2004–05	6.48	5.11
2005–06	4.38	5.90
2006–07	5.42	7.09
2007–08	4.75	7.40

10. An analyst is considering the purchase of three securities: BHEL(B), HCL(H) and IPCA(I) for the next year. The returns of the securities depend on next year's state of the stock market. He has forecasted estimated rates of return and assigned probabilities to them as shown in the table given below:

State of market	Probability of occurrence	Rates of return of securities		
		B	H	I
Recession	0.25	10%	9%	14%
Average	0.25	14%	13%	12%
Boom	0.50	16%	18%	10%

a. Find each stock's expected rate of return, variance and standard deviation.
b. What are the covariances between security A and B, B and C and A and C?

CASELET

Assume you are a portfolio manager. Your neighbor, Mr. Wiley approaches you to help select two securities for him out of the five that his investment adviser has identified for him. His investment adviser has also sent him a brief analysis of the market related information. According to that report, everyone in the market is anticipating an investor-friendly budget to be announced soon. In addition, Mr. Wiley's investment adviser has also given him the following information regarding the stock:

Stock	Beta	R^2	Volatility	Monthly return
MMM Ltd.	0.78	0.29	3.568	23.24
Jetlink Ltd.	1.05	0.19	2.875	9.72
Carbonplus Ltd.	1.38	0.49	4.823	29.78
Swan Ltd.	1.22	0.37	4.388	32.75
Kare India Ltd.	0.45	0.24	3.421	31.68

* Beta and R^2 value are for one year. Standard deviation of daily returns is also for the same period.

Use the above information to choose two securities that are likely to give best returns to Mr. Wiley and explain the reason behind your selection.

REFERENCES

B. Rosenberg, "Prediction of Common Stock Betas." *Journal of Portfolio Management* Winter 1985.
James B. Wiggins, "Betas in Up and Down Markets." *Financial Review*, February 1992.
R.A. Brealey, *An Introduction to Risk and Return on Common Stocks.* Cambridge, Mass: M.I.T. Press, 1969.
Robert A. Olsen, "Investment Risk: The Experts' Perspective," *Financial Analysts Journal*, 53, no. 2, March/April 1997: 62–66.

Portfolio Analysis: The Mechanics of Investment

4

CHAPTER OBJECTIVES

- ❒ Understanding the main tenets of Modern Portfolio Theory
- ❒ Calculating portfolio risk and return
- ❒ Discussing the concept of efficient frontier
- ❒ Exploring the concept of adequate diversification
- ❒ Constructing optimal portfolio using MPT

By now we know that most assets/securities at the disposal of investors are risky and an investor is in a state of perpetual confusion over which security to invest in. We also know that an investor's collection of securities to which he allocates his funds is formally called a portfolio. The challenge lies in creating that portfolio. Investors need to identify and choose securities that meet their requirements of risk and return. Further, such securities need to be identified taking into consideration a number of factors. The problem of choice of securities/assets in reality is not limited to choosing each security in isolation; rather it is a process of selecting an entire bunch of them out of a large set of possible combinations that make up probable portfolios. Such situation is referred to as portfolio selection problem and the modern solution to it was offered in 1952 by Harry Markowitz, whose extensive work in quantification of portfolio risk and return continues to be the cornerstone of modern approach to investing in portfolios.

His path breaking approach was in direct contrast to the then prevailing approach to investing: the 'traditional portfolio theory (TPT),' as we may be tempted to call it. It was a simplistic approach to investment that was also rooted in risk-return analysis. But its basic idea was combining a number of unique securities with desirable risk-return profiles to form a portfolio. Typically, the process of formation of portfolio under the auspices of traditional approach comprised of consideration of risk of an asset in its totality and selection of each security on the basis of its ability to provide a reasonable return for a given level of risk. Diversification, under this approach, was done through spreading the funds across different asset classes such as stocks, bonds, etc. and different industries. Thus, the criteria for selection of each security was the matching of risk and return, which could vary for each individual, making it subjective, as it relied more on the intuition of the concerned investor. Under TPT, the standard investment advice was to select the securities offering the best opportunities for return with the least risk and then construct a portfolio from these. An investor following this advice might end up holding a portfolio comprising stocks of many firms of the same industry, for example, banking, if they all offered good risk-reward characteristics. Clearly it could spell serious trouble for the portfolio if the banking industry started facing tough time during the holding period. Intuitively, this is unappealing. The greater issue in the use of this approach was that no thought was spared to the interplay of risk between the handpicked individual assets/securities, and if it was considered, then it can be safely said that it was not clearly articulated and spelled.

Through his theory, introduced with his paper "Portfolio Selection," which appeared in the 1952 *Journal of Finance*[1], Markowitz tried to address this intuitively incorrect behavior. He proposed that the selection of portfolios should be guided by their overall risk-reward characteristics instead of focusing on individual securities and bundling the best ones (in terms of risk-return profile) together to make a portfolio. MPT successfully dealt with the issue of interactive risk between the component securities of a portfolio to offer a better explanation of portfolio risk and return.

To summarize, at a time when investors were selecting securities to form a portfolio in accordance with the behavior proposed by the traditional portfolio theory, MPT (modern portfolio theory) was the first theory to formally recognize the fact that portfolio creation was not simply amassing of individual securities with fantastic risk-return profiles. The new theory stated that the objectives of a portfolio can be truly realized only after it has been created by considering the interplay of risk between the component securities.

Modern Portfolio Theory (MPT): Conceptual Framework

MPT or single period mean variance optimization (MVO) was first formulated by Markowitz. Markowitz's single period model solves the problem of portfolio analysis using the following inputs:

- the expected return for each asset/security
- the standard deviation/variance of each asset/security
- the correlation/covariance between these assets/securities

To generate the following output:

The efficient frontier, i.e., the set of portfolios that offer expected returns greater than any other portfolio with the same risk, and lesser risk than any other portfolio with the same return.

MPT postulates that a rational investor will always seek to maximize returns from his set of assets (portfolio) for a given level of risk or minimize risk of his portfolio for a given level of return. To explain further, in the mean-variance world of Markowitz, rational investors, given a choice between two investments with the same expected returns but different risk, will always choose the one with the lower risk for the same level of return or higher return for the same level of risk. Consider Figure 4.1. There are two portfolios, A and B. In instance 1, portfolio A gives higher return for the same level of risk as compared to portfolio B. A rational investor would always select A. In instance 2, portfolio A gives lower risk for same level of return as compared to portfolio B. Again, a rational investor would always select A.

The theory proposes how rational investors seeking to maximize (or more correctly optimize) expected return based on a certain level of risk, need to make their portfolios. Clearly the emphasis is on the fact that acceptance of a higher level of risk is an inherent part of seeking higher reward. The aim is to identify an investor's acceptable level of risk tolerance, and then make a portfolio that can offer maximum expected return

[1] Also called Mean Variance Theory or Portfolio Theory or Portfolio Management Theory. The theory was proposed by Harry Markowitz in this paper published in 1952. {Raj: Markowitz, H. (1952). Portfolio selection. *Journal of Finance*, 7, 77–91.}

Figure 4.1 Portfolio selection.

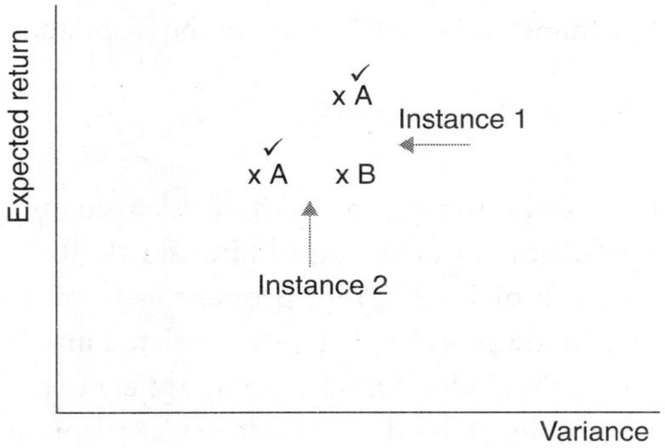

for that level of risk. The fundamental concept of MPT is that the securities/assets comprising an investment portfolio should not be identified on the basis of their individual merit, rather each asset/security should be evaluated in terms of how its price changes relative to the changes in returns on other assets/securities in the portfolio. According to the theory, it is possible for an investor to construct an "efficient frontier" that is the locus of all efficient portfolios.[2] The fundamental concept of MPT is illustrated in Figure 4.2.

Figure 4.2 The fundamental concept of MPT.

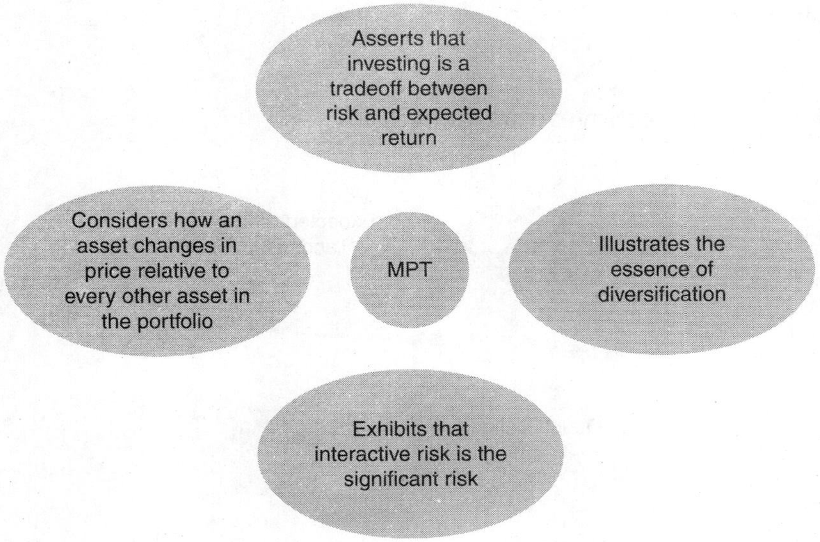

[2] It should be understood that the creation of a portfolio is not limited to identification of securities to be held. It also includes decisions regarding the proportion of funds to be allocated to each asset/security thus identified. MPT helps us address both these issues.

Modern Portfolio Theory: The Basic Assumptions

There are certain basic assumptions that underlie the behavior of an investor who constructs his portfolio in accordance with this theory. The conceptual framework of MPT rests on the foundation of following fundamental tenets:

Risk aversion

The theory assumes that all investors exhibit the rational trait of risk aversion, i.e., a natural inclination towards lower level as risk and seeking compensation for incurring additional risk. Risk aversion-preference is a complex phenomenon where each individual exhibits a different propensity to take risk. This means each individual investor has a different level of tolerance towards risk that gets translated into his expectation of return from his investment. Further, it has been noticed that individuals who may appear to be risk-seekers when small amounts are involved (such as in lotteries or gambling), tend to exhibit risk aversion in case of allocation of large funds to a portfolio (for example, risk-seekers buy insurance products to shield themselves in case of large losses such as damage of property or accident, exhibiting risk aversion when stakes are high). Thus, it can be safely accepted that all investors would exhibit some extent of risk aversion in portfolio investment. This indicates a positive relationship between risk and expected return, a fact that has also been supported by the analysis of historical investment records.

Investment decision is driven by two sole considerations: risk and return

An investor behaving in accordance with MPT would always measure risk in terms of variability of expected returns and choose a portfolio solely on the basis of risk-return analysis. Thus the utility curves of such investor would be a function of only two parameters: holding period expected return and risk. Figure 4.3 illustrates the criteria for in investment decision.

Figure 4.3 Criteria for investment decision.

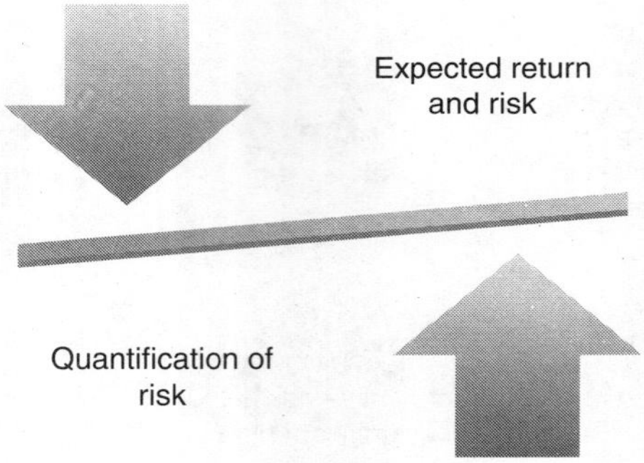

Finite holding period

This assumption explains the investor's behavior when he is investing in accordance with the provisions of MPT. Herein an investor holding '*X*' amount of money would evaluate alternative securities in the context of a single holding period. As the risk and return of securities under consideration are uncertain for this future period, the investor generates an array of possible holding period returns and assigns probabilities to them[3] to calculate the most likely or the expected holding period return. Here an investor is guided by the consideration of beginning of the period wealth (funds in hand before investing) and end of the holding period (terminal) wealth.

Maximization of expected returns or single period expected utility

This assumption can be explained through basic economic fundamental of insatiation which implies that investors always prefer higher levels of terminal wealth (initial investment + holding period returns) to lower levels of the same. This justifies MPT statement that the investors always seek to maximize expected returns of portfolio for a given level of risk.

The assumption of insatiation requires that the utility curve of a risk averse investor is upward sloping and convex. Further, a risk-averse investor has diminishing marginal utility of wealth, i.e., each additional unit of wealth provides the investor extra amount of wealth but smaller utility or satisfaction. Thus a risk averse investor needs to be compensated more than proportionately for bearing additional risk.

To summarize the impact of the above assumptions on investor behavior, we can state that a risk averse investor evaluates portfolios in terms of the probability distribution of their expected returns over some finite holding period. Further, he measures the risk of the portfolios in terms of the variability of expected returns and seeks to maximize his one-period utility.

The assumptions discussed in the preceding part of the chapter lead us to a key term in Markowitz theory: efficient portfolio. An efficient portfolio may be described as such a composition of assets/securities that offers higher expected return than any other combination of the these assets or lower risk than any other combination of such assets.

In other words, an efficient portfolio offers maximum possible expected return for a given level of risk or lowest possible risk for a given level of return.

Markowitz Risk-Return Optimization: The Mathematical Model

In the preceding sections, we have discussed the problem of portfolio selection faced by every investor. MPT guides the investor in his investment decision by stating that an investor should aim to maximize return for a given level of risk or minimize risk for a given level of return. Clearly, to make a portfolio in this context, investors/analysts need to quantify risk and return. MPT quantifies diversification by providing us with formulas to measure portfolio risk and expected return. It proposes the use of standard deviation or variance as a proxy for quantification of portfolio risk and the use of expected return of individual securities for the quantification of portfolio returns. Different components of the mathematical model of MPT are highlighted in Figure 4.4.

Thus to measure portfolio risk and return, the model uses:

1. Expected returns of individual securities comprising the portfolio
2. Variance or standard deviation of individual securities comprising the portfolio
3. Interactive risk of each pair of securities comprising the portfolio.

---

[3] As explained in detail in Chapter 3.

Figure 4.4 The mathematical model of MPT.

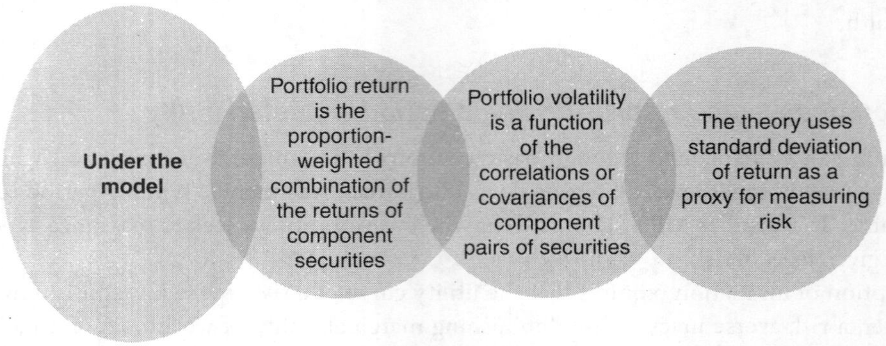

The concept of interactive risk is the key contribution of MPT that has brought forth the need to consider securities for portfolios not only in terms of their individual risk-return but also in terms of the risk of each security of the portfolio vis-a-vis the risk of every other security in the portfolio.

We have already learnt the concept of interactive risk measured by covariance and/or correlation between the returns of two securities. The same measures are used here. In the context of MPT, covariance of returns needs to be calculated for each pair of securities in the portfolio. Let's illustrate the concept with the help of a hypothetical portfolio comprising of RIL, Wipro and Lupin.

To create various portfolios using these three scrips, an investor will be ıequired to compute expected return of RIL, Wipro and Lupin individually by generating a number of possible returns and assigning probabilities to them. You may recall, expected return is computed as

$$\text{Expected return} = \sum_{i=1}^{n} (\text{Probability of return}) \times (\text{Possible return})$$

$$E(R_i) = (P_1)(R_1) + (P_2)(R_2) + (P_3)(R_3) + \cdots (P_n)(R_n)$$

He would then be required to compute variance of returns of each individual scrip (RIL, Wipro and Lupin) using the probability distribution and expected returns. It is computed using the following formula:

Variance

$$\sigma^2 = \sum_{i=1}^{n} (\text{Probability}) \times (\text{Possible return} - \text{Expected return})^2$$

$$= \frac{\sum_{i=1}^{n} [R_i - \overline{R}]^2}{n-1}$$

Thereafter, he would be required to compute the interactive risk of each pair of security (RIL-Wipro, Wipro-Lupin and RIL-Lupin) by quantifying their covariance/correlation using the formula explained in Chapter 3.

Covariance

$$\text{Cov}(R_x, R_y) = p_1[R_{x1} - E(R_x)][R_{y1} - E(R_y)] + p_2[R_{x2} - E(R_x)][R_{y2} - E(R_y)] + p_n[R_{xn} - E(R_x)][R_{yn} - E(R_y)]$$

$$\text{Cov}(R_x, R_y) = \frac{\sum^{n}[R_x - \bar{R}_x][R_y - \bar{R}_y]}{N}$$

Correlation

$$\text{Cov}(R_i, R_j) = \frac{\text{Cov}(R_i, R_j)}{\sigma(R_i)\sigma(R_j)}$$

Armed with these estimates of expected returns, variances and covariances, the investor would then allocate his investible surplus (say X) to these scrips. N different portfolios can be created from the same three scrips by allocating varying proportion of funds to RIL, Wipro and Lupin. For example, the proportions could be 25%, 35% and 40% or 30%, 40% and 30% or 50%, 25% and 25% or any other such combination. Of all the portfolios that can be made in this manner using the three scrips in our example, a rational investor would be interested only in the portfolio that is efficient, meaning a portfolio that gives maximum return for a given level of risk or lowest risk for a given level of return. Once the allocation has been decided, the investor can quantify portfolio risk and return.

Quantification of Portfolio Return

The expected rate of return for a portfolio of assets/securities is nothing but a weighted average of the expected returns of the component securities. The weights are in the proportion of the total funds allocated to each.

Symbolically,

$$R_p = \sum_{i=1}^{N}(X_i)(R_i)$$

where

R_p = Expected return to portfolio
X_i = Proportion of total portfolio invested in security i
R_i = Expected return to security i
N = Total number of securities in the portfolio

Numerical Example 1

Computation of Portfolio Return

Consider the following two securities:

Zee Telefilms
Expected Return $E(R) = 12\%$
Standard Deviation $(\sigma) = 0.10$

Vardhman Special Steels Ltd.
Expected Return $E(R) = 17\%$
Standard Deviation $(\sigma) = 0.15$

Compute portfolio return if 75% of the portfolio funds are in Zee Telefilms and 25% in Vardhman Special Steels Ltd.

Solution:

$$R_p = \sum_{i=1}^{N} (X_i)(R_i)$$

$$R_p = (0.75)(12) + (0.25)(17)$$
$$= 9 + 4.25$$
$$= 13.25\%$$

An expected return vector can be used to calculate expected return of a portfolio comprising 'n' securities. The vector comprises a single column, each row of which represents the expected return of the individual securities, i.e., row 1 represents security 1's expected return. Going back to our example of RIL, Wipro and Lupin, the expected return vector may be expressed as:

$$\begin{matrix} R_1 \\ R_2 \\ R_3 \end{matrix} \begin{bmatrix} E(R)_{RIL} \\ E(R)_W \\ E(R)_L \end{bmatrix}$$

Quantification of Portfolio Risk

An acceptable measure of portfolio risk is one that is able to quantify the magnitude of bad outcomes by taking into account the probability of such occurrences. A measure of risk that estimates the extent of divergence of the actual outcome from the anticipated one is the ideal metric for measuring portfolio risk. Standard deviation/variance is one such metric that is used to compute portfolio risk in MPT. We have already discussed in detail the pros and cons of using these measures of risk in Chapter 3.

Markowitz model takes into consideration not only individual standard deviation of component securities/assets but also their interactive risk as measured by covariance and correlation. This emphasis on interactive risk makes portfolio risk computation somewhat contorted. It cannot be a simple weighted average of individual security risk as in the case of portfolio expected returns.

Symbolically,

$$\sigma_p^2 = \sum_{i=1}^{N} \sum_{j=1}^{N} X_i X_j r_{i,j} \sigma_i \sigma_j$$

where
$\sigma_p^{\,2}$ = Expected portfolio variance
σ_p = Portfolio standard deviation
X_i = Proportion of total portfolio invested in security i
X_j = Proportion of total portfolio invested in security j
r_{ij} = Coefficient of correlation between securities i and j
σ_i = Standard deviation of security i
σ_j = Standard deviation of security j
N = Total number of securities in the portfolio

You may recall, $r_{ij}\,\sigma_i\,\sigma_j$ = covariance of the two securities

Double summation signifies the products of weights for pair of security X_i and X_j and their covariances. It involves both variance and covariances.

To understand the formula more clearly, let's see the formula if $N = 2$, i.e., two-security case. It can be written as:

$$\sigma_p^2 = X_1\,X_1\,r_{1.1}\,\sigma_1\,\sigma_1 + X_2\,X_2\,r_{2.2}\,\sigma_2\,\sigma_2 + X_1\,X_2\,r_{1.2}\,\sigma_1\,\sigma_2 + X_1\,X_2\,r_{2.1}\,\sigma_2\,\sigma_1$$

Each security has a perfect positive correlation with itself, therefore, in term 1 and 2, $r_{1.1}$ and $r_{2.2} = 1$. Therefore, we are left with $X_1^2\,\sigma_1^2$ and $X_2^2\,\sigma_2^2$. Terms 3 and 4 are mathematically the same because $r_{1.2} = r_{2.1}$. They can be written as $2\,X_1\,X_2\,r_{1.2}\,\sigma_1\sigma_2$.

We already know $r_{1.2}\,\sigma_1\,\sigma_2 = \text{cov}_{12}$, so the third term can also be written as:

$$2\,X_1\,X_2\,\text{cov}_{1.2}$$

Therefore, portfolio risk in 2-security case is measured by:

$$\sigma_p^2 = X_1^2\,\sigma_1^2 + X_2^2\,\sigma_2^2 + 2\,X_1\,X_2\,\text{cov}_{1.2}$$

where
σ_p = Portfolio standard deviation
X_1 = % of total portfolio value in stock 1
X_2 = % of total portfolio value in stock 2
σ_1 = Standard deviation of stock 1
σ_2 = Standard deviation of stock 2
r_{12} = Correlation coefficient of 1 and 2
cov_{12} = Covariance of 1 and 2

Numerical Example 2

Computation of Portfolio Risk in 2-Security Case

Consider the following two securities:

Zee Telefilms
Expected Return $E(R) = 12\%$
Standard Deviation $(\sigma) = 0.10$

Vardhman Special Steels Ltd.
Expected Return $E(R) = 17\%$
Standard Deviation $(\sigma) = 0.15$

Compute portfolio risk if 75% of the portfolio funds are in Zee Telefilms and 25% in Vardhman Special Steels Ltd and the coefficient of correlation is +0.50.

Solution:

$$\sigma_p^2 = X_1^2\sigma_1^2 + X_2^2\sigma_2^2 + 2X_1X_2r_{1.2}\sigma_1\sigma_2$$

$$= (0.75)^2(0.10)^2 + (0.25)^2(0.15)^2 + 2(0.75)(0.25)(0.5)(0.10)(0.15)$$

$$= 0.005625 + 0.00140625 + 0.0028125$$

$$= 0.00984375$$

$$\text{Standard deviation} = \sqrt{0.00984375}$$

$$= 0.0992$$

Now let's consider a 3-security case. The portfolio risk may be computed as

$$\sigma_p^2 = \sum_{i=1}^{3}\sum_{j=1}^{3} X_i X_j r_{i.j}\sigma_i\sigma_j$$

or

$$\sigma_p^2 = X_1^2\sigma_1^2 + X_2^2\sigma_2^2 + X_3^2\sigma_3^2 + 2X_1X_2\text{cov}_{1.2} + 2X_1X_3\text{cov}_{1.3} + 2X_2X_3\text{cov}_{2.3}$$

Numerical Example 3

Computation of Portfolio Return and Risk in a 3-Security Case

Consider the following 3 securities and the relevant data on each:

	ABB	JKC	HCL
Expected Return	10	11	7
Std. Deviation	10	15	5
Correlation Coefficients			

(Continued)

Continued

	ABB	JKC	HCL
Stocks 1, 2	0.3		
Stocks 2, 3	0.4		
Stocks 1, 3	0.5		

Compute portfolio risk and return if the following proportions are assigned to each stock: ABB = 0.2, JKC = 0.4 and HCL = 0.4.

Solution:

Portfolio return:

$$R_p = \sum_{i=1}^{N} (X_i)(R_i)$$

$$R_p = (0.2)(10) + (0.4)(11) + (0.40)(7)$$

$$= 9.2\%$$

Portfolio risk

$$\sigma_p^2 = X_1^2\sigma_1^2 + X_2^2\sigma_2^2 + X_3^2\sigma_3^2 + 2\,X_1\,X_2\,\text{cov}_{1.2} + 2\,X_1\,X_3\,\text{cov}_{1.3} + 2\,X_2\,X_3\,\text{cov}_{2.3}$$

$$\sigma_p^2 = (0.2)^2(10)^2 + (0.4)^2(15)^2 + (0.4)^2(5)^2 + 2(0.2)(0.4)(0.3)(10)(15)$$

$$+ 2(0.4)(0.4)(0.4)(15)(5) + 2(0.2)(0.4)(0.5)(10)(5)$$

$$= 4 + 36 + 4 + 7.20 + 9.6 + 4 = 64.8$$

$$\text{Standard deviation} = \sqrt{64.8}$$

$$= 8.0$$

The variance-covariance matrix

$$\begin{array}{c} \\ R_1 \\ R_2 \\ R_3 \end{array} \begin{array}{c} \begin{array}{ccc} C_1 & C_2 & C_3 \end{array} \\ \begin{bmatrix} \sigma_1^2 & \text{cov}_{1.2} & \text{cov}_{1.3} \\ \text{cov}_{2.1} & \sigma_2^2 & \text{cov}_{2.3} \\ \text{cov}_{3.1} & \text{cov}_{3.2} & \sigma_3^2 \end{bmatrix} \end{array}$$

In a matrix, total number of rows and columns are equal, therefore total number of cells in the matrix of n securities is n^2. The variance of each individual security appears diagonally, extending from cell 1 in row 1 to cell 2 in row 2 to cell 3 in row 3. Further, the matrix is symmetric, i.e., number appearing in row 1, column 2 also appears in row 2, column 1. It is so because covariance doesn't depend on order of securities, i.e., whether it is $cov_{1.2}$ or $cov_{2.1}$, it is the same thing.

Numerical Example 4

Use the given information to compute the expected return of a portfolio comprising RIL, Wipro and Lupin.

Security	Number of Shares in Portfolio	Initial Market Price Per Share (₹)	Expected End-of-period Price Per Share (₹)
RIL	100	1000	1100
Wipro	200	500	600
Lupin	100	900	1000

Solution:

1. Proportion of each security in the portfolio

Security	Number of Shares in the Portfolio	Initial Market Price Per Share (₹)	Total Investment in Each Security	Proportion of Initial Market Value of Portfolio (Total Investment in Each Security/ Initial Market Value of Portfolio)
RIL	100	1000	100000	0.344827586
Wipro	200	500	100000	0.344827586
Lupin	100	900	90000	0.310344828
		Initial Market value of portfolio = 290000		Sum of proportions = 1

2. Expected return of each security

Security	Initial Market Price Per Share (₹)	Expected End-of-period Price Per Share (₹)	Expected Return of Security (%) [(End Price – Beginning Price)/ Beginning Price]
RIL	1000	1100	10
Wipro	500	600	20
Lupin	900	1000	11.11

3. Expected return of portfolio (using individual expected returns and proportion of each security in the portfolio)

Security	Expected Return of Security (%)	Proportion of Initial Market Value of Portfolio	Weighted Returns of Each Security
RIL	10	0.344827586	3.44827586
Wipro	20	0.344827586	6.89655172
Lupin	11.11	0.310344828	3.447931039
		Portfolio expected return = 13.79%	

4. Expected return of portfolio (using expected end of period price of each security in the portfolio)

Security	Number of Shares in Portfolio	Expected End-of-period Price Per Share (₹)	Aggregate Expected End-of-Period Value of Each Security
RIL	100	1100	110000
Wipro	200	600	120000
Lupin	100	1000	100000
		Expected end-of-period value of the portfolio = 330000	

$$\text{Portfolio Expected Return} = \frac{\text{Exp. End-of-period Value of Portfolio} - \text{Initial Market Value of Portfolio}}{\text{Initial Market Value of Portfolio}}$$

$$= \frac{330000 - 290000}{290000}$$

$$= 13.79\%$$

Effect of Combining Securities in a Portfolio

Based on the principle of diversification, it can be said that holding at least two securities is probably less risky than holding a portfolio comprising entirely of anyone of the two. Is it always true? Is portfolio risk invariably reduced when you include more securities in it? Obviously, the answer is: not always. So when does the portfolio risk reduce as securities are added to it? In other words, is there a way to combine two risky assets in such a way that a portfolio with some proportion of the two is less risky than an exclusive portfolio of the less risky asset?

Yes indeed. There is a way given in the MPT to achieve the same and it is dependent on the degree of covariance or correlation between the assets under consideration. For the ease of understanding, we will confine our discussion to a portfolio of two securities to assess the impact of the degree of correlation on the risk of the portfolio. Let's consider the following situations:

1. **Combining Securities with the Same Individual Expected Return and Risk but Changing Correlations:** Let's illustrate the impact of changing interactive risk on the portfolio risk through the following example:

   Assume there are two securities that are chosen by an investor to make a portfolio. Both securities have same expected returns, i.e., $E(R_1) = E(R_2) = 0.30$. Incidentally, the two have same standard deviations as well, i.e., $\sigma_1 = \sigma_2 = 0.10$. Further, for ease of calculation, let's assume that 50% of the funds are allocated to security 1 and the balance 50% are allocated to security 2. Now we need to compute the portfolio risk.

   $$\text{Portfolio expected return} = E(R_p) = (0.5)(0.30) + (0.5)(0.30) = 0.30$$

   Let's assume different values of correlation between these two securities and compute portfolio risk.

   $$r_{1.2} = +1.00$$

   $$r_{1.2} = +0.40$$

   $$r_{1.2} = 0.00$$

   $$r_{1.2} = -0.40$$

   $$r_{1.2} = -1.00$$

   We know, covariance $= r_{1.2}\, \sigma_1\, \sigma_2$

   Therefore the value of covariance for each the above values of correlation may be computed as:

   $$\text{cov}_{1.2} = 1(0.1)(0.1) = +0.01$$

   $$\text{cov}_{1.2} = 0.4(0.1)(0.1) = +0.004$$

   $$\text{cov}_{1.2} = 0(0.1)(0.1) = 0$$

   $$\text{cov}_{1.2} = -0.4(0.1)(0.1) = -0.004$$

   $$\text{cov}_{1.2} = -1(0.1)(0.1) = -0.01$$

   Let's compute portfolio variance for each value of covariance.

   (a) $r_{1.2} = +1.00$

   $$\sigma_p^2 = (0.5)^2(0.1)^2 + (0.5)^2(0.1)^2 + 2(0.5)(0.5)(0.01) = 0.01$$

   The portfolio risk of the portfolio resulting from combining two securities here is same as the risk of any of the individual security included in the portfolio. We can see that when the correlation is perfectly positive, we do not benefit from combining such securities because there is no reduction in risk. In such a situation, it would be better to hold any one asset in the portfolio since the two are identical.

(b) $r_{1.2} = +0.40$

$$\sigma_p^2 = (0.5)^2(0.1)^2 + (0.5)^2(0.1)^2 + 2(0.5)(0.5)(0.004) = 0.007$$

The portfolio risk of the portfolio resulting from combining two securities here is little less than the risk of any of the individual securities included in the portfolio. We can see that while keeping everything else the same and decreasing the correlation to 0.40, we have been able to reduce the portfolio variance to a level less than the variance of either of the component securities without sacrificing portfolio returns. Thus we can say that less than perfect positive correlation between component securities of a portfolio can have the effect of reducing the portfolio risk to a level lower than the risk of either of the component securities.

(c) $r_{1.2} = 0.00$

$$\sigma_p^2 = (0.5)^2(0.1)^2 + (0.5)^2(0.1)^2 + 2(0.5)(0.5)(0.00) = 0.005$$

The portfolio risk of the portfolio resulting from combining two securities is decreased significantly in this instance. We can see that while keeping everything else the same and decreasing the correlation to = 0.00, we have been able to reduce the portfolio variance further to a level much less than the variance of either of the component securities without sacrificing portfolio returns. Thus, we can say that no correlation between component securities of a portfolio can have a much better effect on the portfolio risk than any level of positive correlation.

Similarly,

(d) $r_{1.2} = -0.40$

$$\sigma_p^2 = (0.5)^2(0.1)^2 + (0.5)^2(0.1)^2 + 2(0.5)(0.5)(-0.004) = 0.003$$

(e) $r_{1.2} = -1.00$

$$\sigma_p^2 = (0.5)^2(0.1)^2 + (0.5)^2(0.1)^2 + 2(0.5)(0.5)(-0.01) = 0.00$$

In case of negative correlation between the securities in our example, the portfolio risk is substantially reduced by changing no other parameter except for the correlation. In the case where the correlation is perfectly negative, the portfolio risk drops to zero. Thus just by decreasing the correlation between the two securities, while keeping the proportions, expected return and risk of individual securities the same, we have been able to reduce the risk of portfolio consisting of the two risky securities.

This possibility of combining two or more risky securities that are less than perfectly positively correlated to form a portfolio that has a level of risk which is lower than any of the component securities is called portfolio effect. The benefit of this kind of diversification is maximum in case of perfectly negatively correlated securities.

2. **Combining Securities Having Different Individual Expected Return and Risk and Changing their Correlations:** Let's illustrate the impact of changing interactive risk on the portfolio risk through the following example:

Assume there are two securities that are chosen by an investor to make a portfolio. The expected return of security 1, i.e., $E(R_1) = 0.10$ and expected return of security 2, i.e., $E(R_2) = 0.20$. The standard deviation of security 1, i.e., $\sigma_1 = 0.06$ and standard deviation of security 2, i.e., $\sigma_2 = 0.11$. Further, for the ease of calculation, let's assume that 50% of the funds are allocated to security 1 and the balance 50% are allocated to the security 2. Now we need to compute the portfolio risk.

$$\text{Portfolio expected return} = E(R_p) = (0.5)(0.10) + (0.5)(0.20) = 0.15$$

Let's assume different values of correlation between these two securities and compute the portfolio risk.

$$r_{1.2} = +1.00$$

$$r_{1.2} = +0.40$$

$$r_{1.2} = 0.00$$

$$r_{1.2} = -0.40$$

$$r_{1.2} = -1.00$$

We know, covariance $= r_{1.2}\,\sigma_1\,\sigma_2$

Therefore the value of covariance for each of the above values of correlation may be computed as:

$$\text{cov}_{1.2} = 1(0.06)(0.11) = +0.0066$$

$$\text{cov}_{1.2} = 0.4(0.06)(0.11) = +0.00264$$

$$\text{cov}_{1.2} = 0(0.06)(0.11) = 0$$

$$\text{cov}_{1.2} = -0.4(0.06)(0.11) = -0.00264$$

$$\text{cov}_{1.2} = -1(0.06)(0.11) = -0.0066$$

Let's compute portfolio variance for each value of covariance.

(a) $r_{1.2} = +1.00$

$$\sigma_p^2 = (0.5)^2(0.06)^2 + (0.5)^2(0.11)^2 + 2(0.5)(0.5)(0.0066) = 0.007225$$

If we calculate a simple weighted average of the individual standard deviations of the securities under consideration, we get:

$$(0.5)(0.06) + (0.5)(0.11) = 0.085$$

or variance = 0.007225

Thus, we can say that if we combine perfectly positively correlated securities to make a portfolio, then the standard deviation of the resultant portfolio will be equal to the weighted average of the standard deviations of the two securities (weights represent the proportion of funds allocated to each). In other words, the standard deviation of the portfolio in such a case will vary in a linear manner to the changes in the proportion of funds allocated to each.

The calculations given below illustrate that as the correlation between the two securities decreases, the portfolio risk becomes less than the weighted sum of the risk of the two securities.

(b) $r_{1.2} = +0.40$

$$\sigma_p^2 = (0.5)^2(0.06)^2 + (0.5)^2(0.11)^2 + 2(0.5)(0.5)(0.00264) = 0.005245$$

(c) $r_{1.2} = 0.00$

$$\sigma_p^2 = (0.5)^2(0.06)^2 + (0.5)^2(0.11)^2 + 2(0.5)(0.5)(0.00) = 0.003925$$

(d) $r_{1.2} = -0.40$

$$\sigma_p^2 = (0.5)^2(0.06)^2 + (0.5)^2(0.11)^2 + 2(0.5)(0.5)(-0.00264) = 0.002605$$

(e) $r_{1.2} = -1.00$

$$\sigma_p^2 = (0.5)^2(0.06)^2 + (0.5)^2(0.11)^2 + 2(0.5)(0.5)(-0.0066) = 0.000625$$

Though the portfolio standard deviation/variance is decreased, as correlation between the securities decreases, in this instance, we see it doesn't become zero for perfect negative correlation as it happened in scenario A. This shows that apart from correlations there are other factors such as proportion of funds allocated to each security that also influence the portfolio standard deviation. To understand this, let us consider scenario C.

3. **Combining Securities Having Different Individual Expected Return and Risk and Changing their Proportions While Keeping Correlation Constant:** Let's illustrate the impact of changing proportions on the portfolio risk in this case through the following example:

Assume there are two securities that are chosen by an investor to make a portfolio. The expected return of security 1, i.e., $E(R_1) = 0.10$ and expected return of security 2, i.e., $E(R_2) = 0.20$. The standard deviation of security 1, i.e., $\sigma_1 = 0.06$ and standard deviation of security 2, i.e., $\sigma_2 = 0.11$. Further, for the ease of calculation, let's assume that their correlation coefficient is equal to 0. The changing proportions are:

Security 1(W_1)	Security 2(W_2)
1.00	0.00
0.80	0.20

(*Continued*)

Continued

Security 1(W_1)	Security 2(W_2)
0.60	0.40
0.50	0.50
0.30	0.70
0.20	0.80
0.00	1.00

Here we begin with a portfolio consisting of hundred percent of funds allocated to security 1 and no funds in security 2, i.e., the portfolio comprises only security 1. Thereafter we have allocated 80% of the funds to security 1 and 20% to security 2 and ended with a portfolio comprising only security 2.

In the preceding scenarios (A and B), the expected return had not changed for different hypothetical values, but here this will not be the case because the proportions are changing. Therefore, let's begin with computing the expected return of the portfolio for varying proportions.

Portfolio Expected return:

(a) $W_1 = 1, W_2 = 0$

$$E(R_p) = (1)(0.10) + (0.0)(0.20) = 0.1$$

(b) $W_1 = 0.80, W_2 = 0.20$

$$E(R_p) = (0.80)(0.10) + (0.20)(0.20) = 0.12$$

(c) $W_1 = 0.60, W_2 = 0.40$

$$E(R_p) = (0.60)(0.10) + (0.40)(0.20) = 0.14$$

(d) $W_1 = 0.50, W_2 = 0.50$

$$E(R_p) = (0.5)(0.10) + (0.5)(0.20) = 0.15$$

(e) $W_1 = 0.30, W_2 = 0.70$

$$E(R_p) = (0.30)(0.10) + (0.70)(0.20) = 0.17$$

(f) $W_1 = 0.20, W_2 = 0.80$

$$E(R_p) = (0.20)(0.10) + (0.80)(0.20) = 0.18$$

(g) $W_1 = 0, W_2 = 1$

$$E(R_p) = (0.00)(0.10) + (1.0)(0.20) = 0.2$$

Now we need to compute the portfolio risk.

(a) $W_1 = 1, W_2 = 0, r_{1.2} = 0.00\ (\text{cov}_{1.2} = 0)$

$$\sigma_p^2 = (1.0)^2(0.06)^2 + (0.0)^2(0.11)^2 + 2(1.0)(0.0)(0.00) = 0.0036$$

(b) $W_1 = 0.80, W_2 = 0.20, r_{1.2} = 0.00, (\text{cov}_{1.2} = 0)$

$$\sigma_p^2 = (0.8)^2(0.06)^2 + (0.2)^2(0.11)^2 + 2(0.8)(0.2)(0.00) = 0.002788$$

(c) $W_1 = 0.60, W_2 = 0.40, r_{1.2} = 0.00, (\text{cov}_{1.2} = 0)$

$$\sigma_p^2 = (0.6)^2(0.06)^2 + (0.4)^2(0.11)^2 + 2(0.6)(0.4)(0.00) = 0.003232$$

(d) $W_1 = 0.50, W_2 = 0.50, r_{1.2} = 0.00, (\text{cov}_{1.2} = 0)$

$$\sigma_p^2 = (0.5)^2(0.06)^2 + (0.5)^2(0.11)^2 + 2(0.5)(0.5)(0.00) = 0.003925$$

(e) $W_1 = 0.30, W_2 = 0.70, r_{1.2} = 0.00, (\text{cov}_{1.2} = 0)$

$$\sigma_p^2 = (0.3)^2(0.06)^2 + (0.7)^2(0.11)^2 + 2(0.3)(0.7)(0.00) = 0.006253$$

(f) $W_1 = 0.20, W_2 = 0.80, r_{1.2} = 0.00, (\text{cov}_{1.2} = 0)$

$$\sigma_p^2 = (0.2)^2(0.06)^2 + (0.8)^2(0.11)^2 + 2(0.2)(0.8)(0.00) = 0.007888$$

(g) $W_1 = 0, W_2 = 1, r_{1.2} = 0.00, (\text{cov}_{1.2} = 0)$

$$\sigma_p^2 = (0.0)^2(0.06)^2 + (1.0)^2(0.11)^2 + 2(1.0)(0.0)(0.00) = 0.0121$$

All the above computations may be presented in tabular form as:

Case	Security 1(W_1)	Security 2(W_2)	$E(R_p)$	σ_p^2
1	1.00	0.00	0.1	0.0036
2	0.80	0.20	0.12	0.002788
3	0.60	0.40	0.14	0.003232
4	0.50	0.50	0.15	0.003925
5	0.30	0.70	0.17	0.006253
6	0.20	0.80	0.18	0.007888
7	0.00	1.00	0.2	0.0121

We can see from the above data that certain proportions yield lower portfolio risk as compared with the others when all other parameters are the same.

MS Excel-based models can be used to calculate portfolio risk and return for given securities by automatically varying the proportions to generate many possible portfolios.

Our computations using scenarios 1, 2 and 3 show that portfolio standard deviation/variance is sensitive to:

1. The proportion of funds allocated to each security
2. The standard deviation of each individual security
3. The covariance/correlation between the two securities.

The computations given above show that there can be large number of possible portfolios that an investor can generate by varying the proportions and keeping other parameters such as expected returns, standard deviations and covariance constant. The problem of computations becomes more challenging when we accept the fact that in the real world, a large number of assets/securities available for investment, further magnify the problem of choice of portfolio.

Computation of Proportions for Minimum Variance Portfolio

By now we know that diversification is most effective when the correlation between a pair of assets/securities is −1 and it is least effective when the correlation coefficient is +1. As a result, investors desiring to reduce the risk of their portfolio as much as possible, need to find pairs of assets/securities that have a correlation close to −1. The essence of diversification is that it is possible to make a portfolio with risk less than the risk of individual securities taken separately if they are combined in a certain proportion and have a certain degree of less than perfect positive correlation.

As explained above, securities can be combined in such a proportion that the combination yields the minimum variance portfolio, i.e., a portfolio that has a variance less than the variance of any of the component securities taken individually. Combining perfectly positive correlated securities does not yield the benefits of diversification. However, diversification benefits can be achieved by combining securities with less than perfect positive correlation as well as negative correlation in certain proportion. Let us determine the proportion of funds to be invested in each security such that the portfolio risk becomes zero.

1. **Combining Perfectly Negatively Correlated Securities:** The portfolio variance can be calculated as:

$$\sigma_p^2 = X_1^2\sigma_1^2 + X_2^2\sigma_2^2 + 2X_1X_2r_{1.2}\sigma_1\sigma_2$$

For $r_{1.2} = -1$, the above equation can be rewritten as:

$$\sigma_p^2 = X_1^2\sigma_1^2 + X_2^2\sigma_2^2 - 2X_1X_2\sigma_1\sigma_2 \text{ or } (X_1\sigma_1 - X_2\sigma_2)^2$$

So, $\sigma_p = X_1\sigma_1 - X_2\sigma_2$

Since, we are considering a two security case, $X_2 = 1 - X_1$

Substituting this value of X_2 in the above equation, we get

$$\sigma_p = X_1\sigma_1 - (1 - X_1)\sigma_2 = X_1(\sigma_1 + \sigma_2) - \sigma_2$$

σ_p can be made zero by setting

$$X_1 = \frac{\sigma_2}{(\sigma_1 + \sigma_2)}$$

2. **Combining Positively and Negatively Correlated Securities (Other than Perfect Positive or Negative Correlation):** Most investors generally invest in two main categories of securities, stocks and bonds. We need to determine what are the exact proportions they need to be combined in (given their correlations) to construct minimum variance portfolio.

   The variance of a portfolio consisting of bond and equity can be given by:

$$\sigma_p^2 = X_D^2\sigma_D^2 + X_E^2\sigma_E^2 + 2X_D X_E r_{D.E}\sigma_D\sigma_E$$

where subscript D stands for bonds and E stands for equity. X_D represents the amount of portfolio funds in bond and X_E represents the amount of portfolio funds in equity, such that

$$X_E = 1 - X_D$$

The value of X_D that minimizes portfolio variance is

$$X_D(\min)^4 = \frac{\sigma_E^2 - r_{D.E}\sigma_D\sigma_E}{\sigma_D^2 + \sigma_E^2 - 2r_{D.E}\sigma_D\sigma_E}$$

Since $r_{D.E}\sigma_D\sigma_E = \text{Cov}_{(D,E)}$

---

[4] This formula may be derived as

$$\sigma_p^2 = X_D^2\sigma_D^2 + X_E^2\sigma_E^2 + 2X_D X_E r_{D.E}\sigma_D\sigma_E$$

Since, $X_E = 1 - X_D$, the above equation may be rewritten as:

$$\sigma_p^2 = X_D^2\sigma_D^2 + (1 - X_D)^2\sigma_E^2 + 2X_D(1 - X_D)r_{D.E}\sigma_D\sigma_E$$

The first derivative of σ_p^2 with respect to X_D is:

$$\frac{d\sigma_p^2}{dX_D} = 2X_D\sigma_D^2 + 2(1 - X_D)\times(-1)\times\sigma_E^2 + 2(1 - X_D)r_{D.E}\sigma_D\sigma_E - 2X_D r_{D.E}\sigma_D\sigma_E$$

Setting the first derivative of σ_p^2 with respect to X_D equal to zero and solving it for X_D, we get

$$X_D(\min) = \frac{\sigma_E^2 - r_{D.E}\sigma_D\sigma_E}{\sigma_D^2 + \sigma_E^2 - 2r_{D.E}\sigma_D\sigma_E}$$

Therefore,

$$X_D(\min)^4 = \frac{\sigma_E^2 - \text{Cov}_{(D,E)}}{\sigma_D^2 + \sigma_E^2 - 2\,\text{Cov}_{(D,E)}}$$

Graphical Illustration of Portfolio Effect in Two-Security Case

Let's once again consider scenario A, B and C that we discussed in the preceding section. The scenarios were:

1. **Combining Securities with the Same Individual Expected Return and Risk but Changing Correlations:** Assume there are two securities that are chosen by an investor to make a portfolio. Both securities have the same expected returns, i.e., $E(R_1) = E(R_2) = 0.30$. Incidentally, the two have same standard deviations as well, i.e., $\sigma_1 = \sigma_2 = 0.10$. Further, for the ease of calculation, let's assume that 50% of the funds are allocated to security 1 and the balance 50% are allocated to the security 2. For the purpose of graphical illustration let us consider $r_{1.2} = -1.00$.

   Figure 4.5 exhibits time patterns of returns of security 1 and 2 that are combined in the given proportion to make this portfolio. Since the correlation coefficient between security 1 and 2 is –1, they move in the exact opposite direction, i.e., when the return of security 1 will go up, the return of security 2 will go down by the exact same amount; and vice versa. Thus, when security 2 is going through bad times, the security 1 would be going through good times and the portfolio returns would remain protected.

Figure 4.5 Time patterns of returns of security 1 and 2.

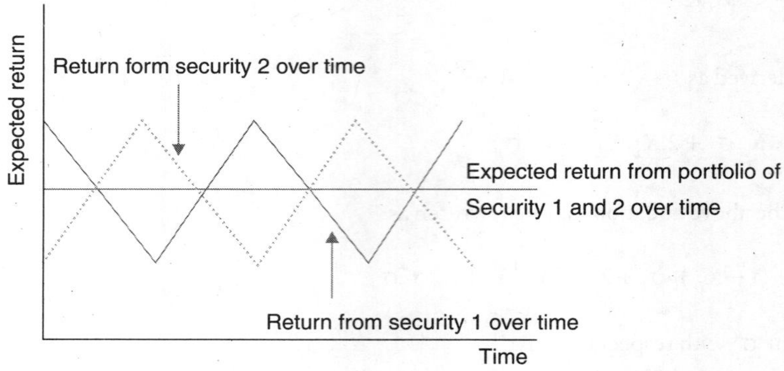

In the portfolio under consideration, the investor has split the funds equally between the two securities, and the volatility of the two balances one another completely in such a way that portfolio has no volatility at all. We can say that in this particular case diversification has been perfect.

Now for the same set of parameters, let's consider a portfolio of security 1 and 2 when they have a perfect positive correlation ($r_{1.2} = +1.00$). In such a situation, the returns of the two securities move in perfect tandem over time and the portfolio returns follow the same path. In the portfolio under consideration, the

Figure 4.6 Time patterns of returns of security 1 and 2.

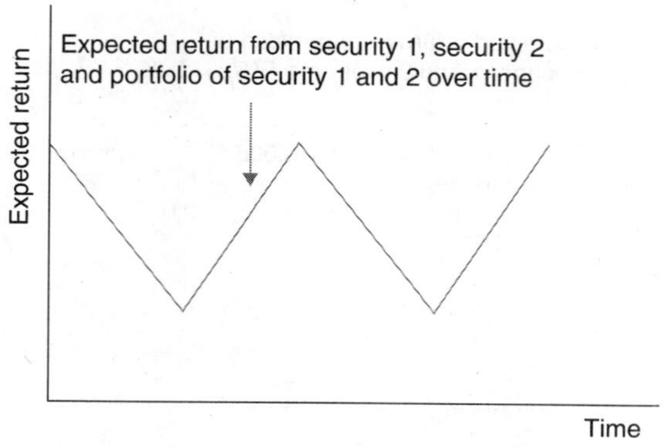

investor has split the funds equally between the two securities, so the return of the portfolio imitates that of the two securities, as shown in Figure 4.6. As a result, the portfolio has the same amount of volatility as those of securities 1 and 2, which means that diversification has not been effective at all.

To plot the portfolio standard deviations and returns, we will use the following data computed above:

$$\text{Portfolio expected return} = E(R_p) = (0.5)(0.30) + (0.5)(0.30) = 0.30$$

Since in our example, we are keeping the proportion constant and changing only the correlation coefficients, $E(R_p) = 0.30$ will remain the same for different values of portfolio risk computed by changing $r_{1.2}$. So we have

(a) $\sigma_p^2 = 0.01$

(b) $\sigma_p^2 = 0.007$

(c) $\sigma_p^2 = 0.005$

(d) $\sigma_p^2 = 0.003$

(e) $\sigma_p^2 = 0.00$

This may be graphically represented as in Figure 4.7.

2. **Combining Securities Having Different Individual Expected Return and Risk and Changing their Correlations:** Assume there are two securities that are chosen by an investor to make a portfolio. The expected return of security 1, i.e., $E(R_1) = 0.10$ and expected return of security 2, i.e., $E(R_2) = 0.20$. The standard deviation of security 1, i.e., $\sigma_1 = 0.06$ and standard deviation of security 2, i.e., $\sigma_2 = 0.11$. Further, for the ease of calculation, let's assume that 50% of the funds are allocated to security 1 and the balance 50% are allocated to the security 2.

   To plot the portfolio standard deviations and returns, we will use the following data computed above:

$$\text{Portfolio expected return} = E(R_p) = (0.5)(0.10) + (0.5)(0.20) = 0.15$$

Figure 4.7 Expected return and risk of portfolio.

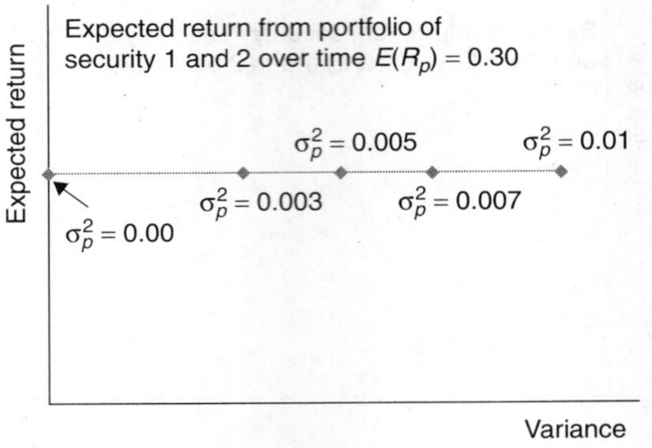

Since in our example, we are keeping the proportion constant and changing only the correlation coefficients, $E(R_p) = 0.15$ will remain the same for different values of portfolio risk computed by changing $r_{1.2}$. So we have

(a) $\sigma_p^2 = 0.007225$

(b) $\sigma_p^2 = 0.005245$

(c) $\sigma_p^2 = 0.003925$

(d) $\sigma_p^2 = 0.002605$

(e) $\sigma_p^2 = 0.000625$

This may be graphically represented as in Figure 4.8.

Figure 4.8 Expected return and risk of portfolio.

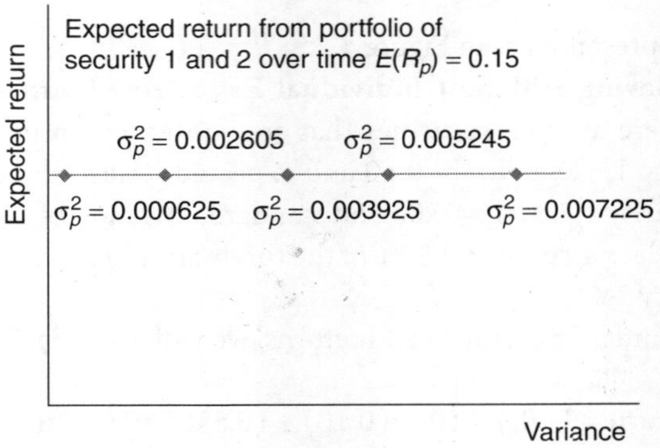

3. **Combining Securities Having Different Individual Expected Return and Risk and Changing Their Proportions While Keeping Correlation Constant:** Assume there are two securities that are chosen by an investor to make a portfolio. The expected return of security 1, i.e., $E(R_1) = 0.10$ and expected return of security 2, i.e., $E(R_2) = 0.20$. The standard deviation of security 1, i.e., $\sigma_1 = 0.06$ and standard deviation of security 2, i.e., $\sigma_2 = 0.11$. Further, for the ease of calculation, let's assume that their correlation coefficient is equal to 0. The changing proportions are:

Security 1(W_1)	Security 2(W_2)
1.00	0.00
0.80	0.20
0.60	0.40
0.50	0.50
0.30	0.70
0.20	0.80
0.00	1.00

Different variables as computed in the preceding section of the chapter:

Case	Security 1(W_1)	Security 2(W_2)	$E(R_p)$	σ_p^2
1	1.00	0.00	0.1	0.0036
2	0.80	0.20	0.12	0.002788
3	0.60	0.40	0.14	0.003232
4	0.50	0.50	0.15	0.003925
5	0.30	0.70	0.17	0.006253
6	0.20	0.80	0.18	0.007888
7	0.00	1.00	0.2	0.0121

A complete curve can be derived by varying the proportions by small increments and the above table may be graphically represented as in Figure 4.9.

The curve depicted in Figure 4.9 represents different portfolios comprising security 1 and 2 that are attainable by an investor. Along the curve, the volatility of the portfolio changes as its composition changes. The upper end of the curve represents the case wherein the entire fund is allocated to the riskier security 2. As the composition of the portfolio shifts from only riskier to more and more of less risky security 1, the risk level of the portfolio falls because lower risk security is a safer investment.

Figure 4.9 Different portfolios comprising security 1 and 2.

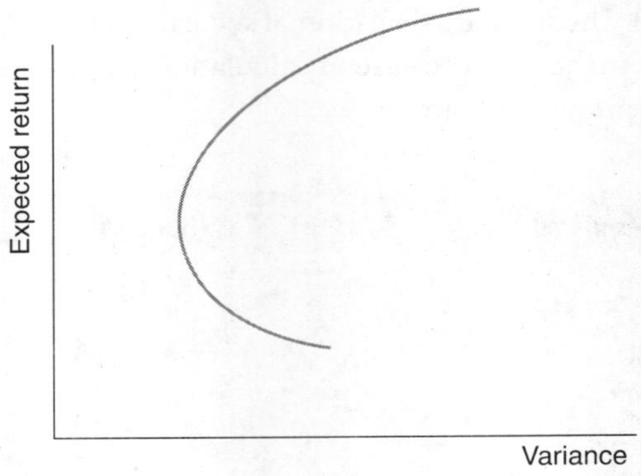

However, after falling to a certain level, the variance of the portfolio "bottoms out" at a certain proportion of 1 and 2. This particular portfolio that has minimum level of risk for the two given securities having a given correlation coefficient is known as the minimum variance portfolio. It is not possible to lower the volatility of the portfolio any further in this situation. Increasing the proportion of lower-risk security further will only lead to rise in risk level of the portfolio so constituted. It is this mean-variance portfolio that interests a rational investor. As mentioned above, it can be arrived at when the coefficient of correlation between the two securities is less than the ratio of the smaller standard deviation to the larger standard deviation and the % of the portfolio in less risky stock is equal to the standard deviation of more risky security divided by the sum of the standard deviations of both securities.

The power of diversification proposed by MPT allows an investor to lower the portfolio variance beyond the individual variances of the assets/securities it contains. The minimum variance portfolio depicted in Figure 4.10 is the one that achieves the maximum effect of diversification for a rational investor.

Figure 4.10 Minimum variance portfolio.

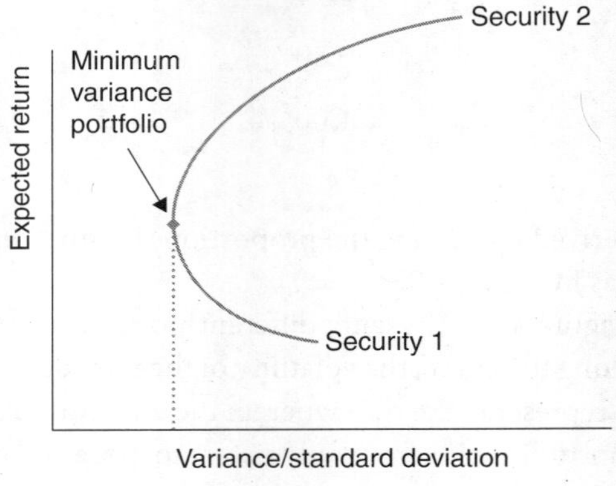

You may recall that we had made the above computations keeping $r_{1.2} = 0.00$ ($cov_{1.2} = 0$). If we change the values of $r_{1.2}$ between +1.00 to −1.00 and make computations of expected portfolio risk and return and plot them, then the two-security case with varying correlations and proportions can be exhibited as shown in Figure 4.11.

Figure 4.11 Graphical illustration of two-security case.

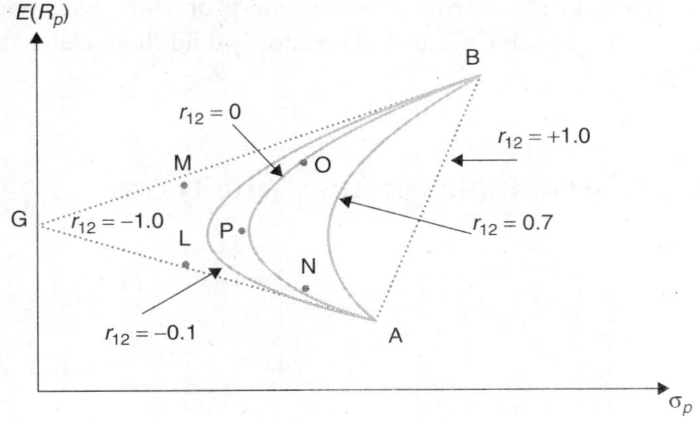

Various cases where the correlation between two securities 1 and 2 ranging from −1.0 to + 1.0 are shown in Figure 4.11. Points A and B represent pure holdings (100%) of securities 1 and 2, respectively. The intermediate points along the line segment AB represent portfolios containing various combinations of the two securities formed by varying their respective proportions. The line segment, AB, is a straight line representing $r_{12} = +1.0$. This line shows the inability of a portfolio of perfectly positively correlated securities to serve as a means to reduce volatility. Point A on the line segment has no point to its left; i.e., there is no combination of 1 and 2 that has a lower variance than that of 1. Neither 1 nor 2 can help offset the risk of the other, so in this situation, a rational investor who wishes to minimize risk would invest in security 1 only.

The curved parts in the figure represent values of r_{12} lying between −1.0 and + 1.0. The curve with points O, P and N represents $r_{12} = 0$. Its left most will never touch the vertical axis, i.e., there is no point where $\sigma_p = 0$.

The line segment, AGB, represents $r_{12} = -1.0$. This line shows that with perfect negative correlation, portfolio risk can be reduced to zero (point G). Both, points M and L on line segment AGB, have the same level of risk but M gives higher return than L, so we can say M is a better portfolio then L or L is inferior to M. Yet another way to put it is that M is a dominant or superior portfolio. Going by the same logic, all portfolios lying along AG are inferior to all portfolios lying along GB, though both segments represent portfolios consisting of varying proportions of securities 1 and 2 when they are perfectly negatively correlated. Obviously, no rational investor would like to hold an inferior portfolio.

Similarly, along the curve representing $r_{12} = 0$, segment BOP contains portfolios that are superior to the portfolios along the line segment PNA, despite the correlation coefficient being same. This way we can identify many portfolios that are inferior to some other portfolios, though all are giving some benefit of diversification.

Figure 4.12 exhibits the risk-return relationship of a three-security portfolio for a certain level of correlation. In this case, the interactive risk between AB, BC and AC is to be considered. Needless to say, the analysis here will be more complicated than in the case of two-security illustration.

The above discussion highlights the fact that it is possible to generate many portfolios that give the benefit of diversification as per MPT. In our graphical illustration, many portfolios lying along the line segments and elliptical curve are such portfolios. These portfolios are called 'feasible portfolios.' A feasible portfolio is a portfolio that an investor can construct, given the assets available[5]. In other words, feasible portfolios are portfolios that can be superior or inferior. As we have already seen, the superior portfolios give higher return for the same level of risk or lower risk for the same level of return. Such portfolios are called 'efficient portfolios' in MPT. According to MPT, all rational investors would choose efficient portfolios within the set of all feasible portfolios.

Figure 4.12 Graphical illustration of three-security case.

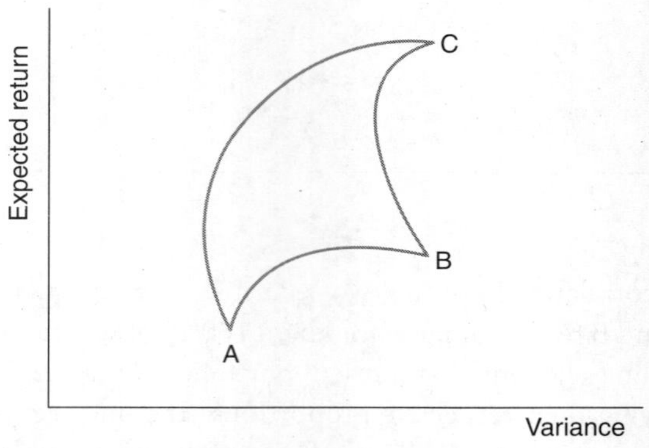

The Efficient Frontier

A Markowitz efficient portfolio may be defined as a portfolio where no added diversification can lower the portfolio's risk for a given level of return expectation.

An envelope curve that is the locus of all the superior or dominating or efficient portfolios is called the efficient frontier. The efficient frontier is a collection of all efficient portfolios. There are no other portfolios that offer a better risk-return profile than those on the efficient frontier. It is a graphical representation of the Markowitz efficient set of portfolios.

The efficient frontier is conventionally plotted on a graph, as exhibited in Figure 4.13, with the standard deviation (risk) on the horizontal axis (x axis), and the expected return on the vertical axis (y axis).

Let us understand how the efficient frontier is generated. We have seen in the two and three-security cases discussed above, that it is possible to generate a large number of feasible portfolios. Faced with a large number of such portfolios, an investor might get confused and unable to make a choice. In MPT, the investor is helped in making this choice by distinguishing between superior and inferior portfolios. To save the investors from the

[5] http://www.nasdaq.com/investing/glossary/f/feasible-portfolio, accessed on January 10, 2015.

Figure 4.13 Efficient frontier.

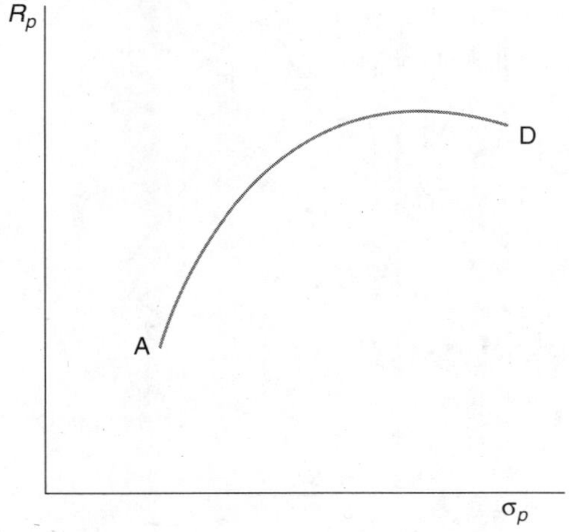

tedious task of generating all feasible portfolios and isolating the efficient ones while dropping the inefficient ones, Markowitz devised a computational model based on quadratic programming[6]. This computational model enables investors to completely ignore the inferior portfolios and only focus on efficient portfolios that lie along the efficient frontier traced by the model.

The main significance of this model is that it makes it possible for an investor to go beyond two- and three-securities portfolios and consider *n* number of securities for inclusion in their portfolios, as is the case in most real-world portfolio analysis problems.

The model uses the expected return and variance for each security (two, three or more) and covariances/correlation coefficients for each pair of securities under consideration to calculate risk and return for a portfolio comprising of some or all of these securities in some proportion. The usefulness of the model lies in its ability to identify the least risk portfolio for a given level of return. The procedure is repeated with different levels of expected returns to yield the minimum-risk portfolios for each. Effectively, the quadratic programming approach manipulates the portfolio proportions to arrive at the minimum variance portfolio. Alternatively, the efficient portfolios can be identified by specifying various levels of portfolio standard deviations and picking the portfolios that offer the highest expected return for a given level of portfolio variance. Either way, the model ends up giving all efficient portfolios and rejecting all dominated ones so that the investors need not tangle with a large universe of feasible but rationally unacceptable portfolios.

Figure 4.14 depicts the process described above. For return level R_1, the programming calculation indicates that point A is the least-risk portfolio and automatically rejects point *X* that gives same return for a higher level of risk. The model automatically rejects all such inefficient portfolios. Since there is no portfolio to the left of A, it is the most efficient portfolio at that level of return. Conversely, for risk level σ_2, portfolio B gives higher return than *X*. The model rejects all such portfolios that give lower return for a given level of risk. Further, there is no point directly above or to the left of B for the given level of risk, so it is the most efficient portfolio for the

[6] J.F. Weston and W. Berneck, "Programming Investment Portfolio Construction," *Analysts Journal*, May 1955, 51–55. It gives a graphic approach to the solution of the efficient frontier.

Figure 4.14 Efficient and inferior portfolios.

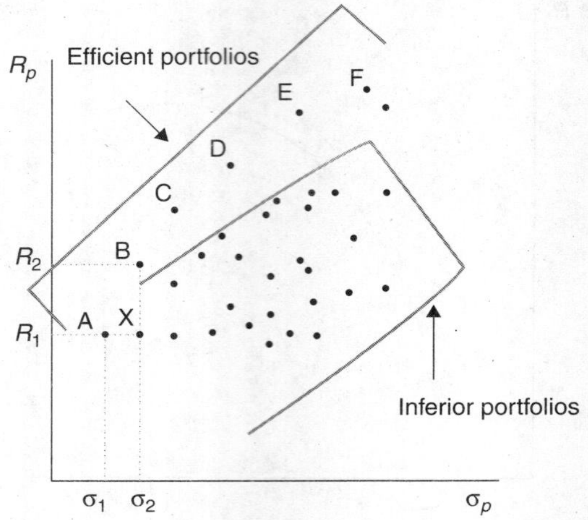

return level R_2. All points from A to F are generated in this manner. The locus of points from A to F including all intermediate points is the result of tracing process that gives us our efficient frontier.

In Figure 4.15, we see an efficient frontier AB. The line AB divides the space between portfolios that are possible and those that cannot be attained ("impossible"). MPT provides for identification of all possible portfolios and rejecting all inferior ones from this set of possibilities. All the accepted ones are then called the efficient portfolios and they lie along a curve called the efficient frontier.

Figure 4.15 Efficient frontier.

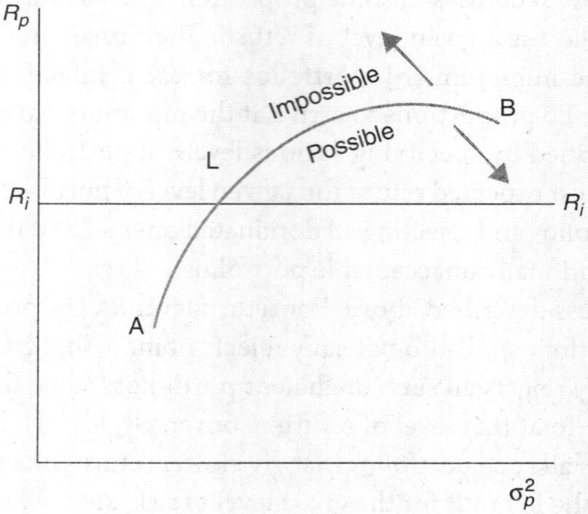

Spreadsheet Application 1 *Formation of two-security portfolios and tracing efficient frontier using MS Excel.*
Consider following securities and the given parameters:

	Exp return	Std deviation
Security A	15%	21%
Security B	18%	29%
Correlation Coefficient	0.3	

Let us first compute the portfolio risk and return (using MPT formula described in the preceding sections of the chapter) when they are combined in such a proportion that A constitutes 10% and B constitutes 90% of the portfolio.

	A	B	C	D	E
1		Exp return	Std deviatio	weight	
2	Security A	15%	21%	0.1	
3	Security B	18%	29%	0.9	
4	Correlation Coefficie	0.3			
5					
6	Portfolio Return	=D2*B2+D3*B3			

	A	B	C	D	E
1		Exp return	Std deviatio	weight	
2	Security A	15%	21%	0.1	
3	Security B	18%	29%	0.9	
4	Correlation Coefficie	0.3			
5					
6	Portfolio Return	0.177			
7	Portfolio Risk	=SQRT(D2*D2*C2*C2+D3*D3*C3*C3+2*D2*D3*C2*C3*B4)			

Similarly, alternative portfolios can be generated by varying the weights of the two securities. The risk/return profile of different combinations is exhibited below:

	A	B	C	D
1		Exp return	Std deviatio	weight
2	Security A	15%	21%	0.1
3	Security B	18%	29%	0.9
4	Correlation Coefficie	0.3		
5				
6	Portfolio Return	0.177		
7	Portfolio Risk	0.268		
8				
9		Risk	Return	
10	Weight of Security A	0.268049622	0.177	
11	0	0.29	0.18	
12	0.1	=TABLE(,D2)	0.177	
13	0.2	0.247859638	0.174	
14	0.3	0.229894324	0.171	
15	0.4	0.214712831	0.168	
16	0.5	0.202940878	0.165	
17	0.6	0.195196311	0.162	
18	0.7	0.191967185	0.159	
19	0.8	0.193479715	0.156	
20	0.9	0.199626151	0.153	
21	1	0.21	0.15	

We can see that the minimum variance portfolio of these two securities has 70% of the portfolio funds invested in security A. The standard deviation of this portfolio is 0.192, which is less than the standard deviation of either of the two securities.

Use Scatter plot to plot the efficient frontier with standard deviation on x-axis and expected return on y-axis.

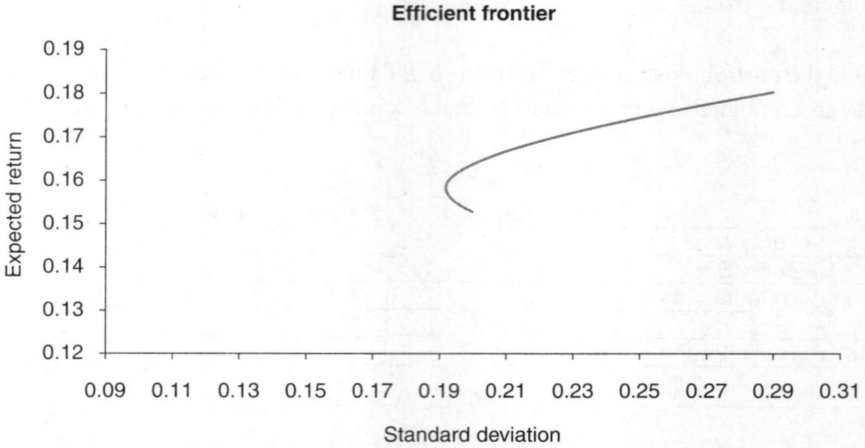

Spreadsheet Application 2 *Constructing Minimum Variance Portfolio using Solver in MS Excel.*
Use following information to generate a minimum variance portfolio:

1. **Risk and Return of Securities:**

	A	B	C
1			
2	Scrips	Std Deviation	Expected Return
3	BHEL	0.809	-0.409
4	CIPLA	0.233	0.150
5	DR REDDYS LABS	0.255	0.351
6	HERO MOTOCORP	0.287	0.175
7	HUL	0.236	0.159
8	INFOSYS	0.293	0.200

2. **Covariance Matrix:**

	BHEL	CIPLA	DR REDDYS LABS	HERO MOTOCORP	HUL	INFOSYS
BHEL	0.6544					
CIPLA	-0.0036	0.0542				
DR REDDYS LABS	-0.0156	0.0227	0.0648			
HERO MOTOCORP	-0.0085	0.0149	0.0309	0.0825		
HUL	-0.0317	0.0187	0.0089	0.0171	0.0556	
INFOSYS	-0.0177	0.0150	0.0174	0.0172	-0.0013	0.0859

Solution:

The following steps need to be taken to generate the minimum variance portfolio:

Begin with assigning equal weights to each security and calculate the portfolio expected return and standard deviation using MMULT function in MS Excel.

	A	B	C	D	E	F	G	H
1								
2	Scrips	Std Deviation	Expected Return					
3	BHEL	0.809	-0.409					
4	CIPLA	0.233	0.150					
5	DR REDDYS LABS	0.255	0.351					
6	HERO MOTOCORP	0.287	0.175					
7	HUL	0.236	0.159					
8	INFOSYS	0.293	0.200					
9								
10								
11	**Weights**	Scrips						
12			BHEL	CIPLA	DR REDDYS LABS	HERO MOTOCORP	HUL	INFOSYS
13	0.062	BHEL	0.6544	-0.0036	-0.0156	-0.0085	-0.0317	-0.0177
14	0.151	CIPLA	-0.0036	0.0542	0.0227	0.0149	0.0187	0.0150
15	0.171	DR REDDYS LABS	-0.0156	0.0227	0.0648	0.0309	0.0089	0.0174
16	0.073	HERO MOTOCORP	-0.0085	0.0149	0.0309	0.0825	0.0171	0.0172
17	0.341	HUL	-0.0317	0.0187	0.0089	0.0171	0.0556	-0.0013
18	0.202	INFOSYS	-0.0177	0.0150	0.0174	0.0172	-0.0013	0.0859
19	1							
20	=MMULT(TRANSPOSE(A13:	Portfolio Expected Return						
21	A18),C3:C8)	Portfolio Std. Dev						

	A	B	C	D	E	F	G	H
1								
2	Scrips	Std Deviation	Expected Return					
3	BHEL	0.809	-0.409					
4	CIPLA	0.233	0.150					
5	DR REDDYS LABS	0.255	0.351					
6	HERO MOTOCORP	0.287	0.175					
7	HUL	0.236	0.159					
8	INFOSYS	0.293	0.200					
9								
10								
11	**Weights**	Scrips						
12			BHEL	CIPLA	DR REDDYS LABS	HERO MOTOCORP	HUL	INFOSYS
13	0.167	BHEL	0.6544	-0.0036	-0.0156	-0.0085	-0.0317	-0.0177
14	0.167	CIPLA	-0.0036	0.0542	0.0227	0.0149	0.0187	0.0150
15	0.167	DR REDDYS LABS	-0.0156	0.0227	0.0648	0.0309	0.0089	0.0174
16	0.167	HERO MOTOCORP	-0.0085	0.0149	0.0309	0.0825	0.0171	0.0172
17	0.167	HUL	-0.0317	0.0187	0.0089	0.0171	0.0556	-0.0013
18	0.167	INFOSYS	-0.0177	0.0150	0.0174	0.0172	-0.0013	0.0859
19	1							
20	#VALUE!	Portfolio Expected Return						
21	=SQRT(MMULT(	Portfolio Std. Dev						
22	TRANSPOSE(A13:							
23	A18),MMULT(C13:	Minimum Var						
24	H18,A13:A18)))	0.164587067						

Remember, after inputting the MMULT function, always press shift+control+enter.

Thereafter set up the solver. As can be seen in the exhibit, the 'Objective' is to minimize portfolio standard deviation and the constraint is that the portfolio weight should not exceed 1. We have included another constraint related to shorting. We have prevented shorting by putting the constraint that the weight of any of the stock should not go below zero. The solver window and the output minimum variance portfolio are exhibited below:

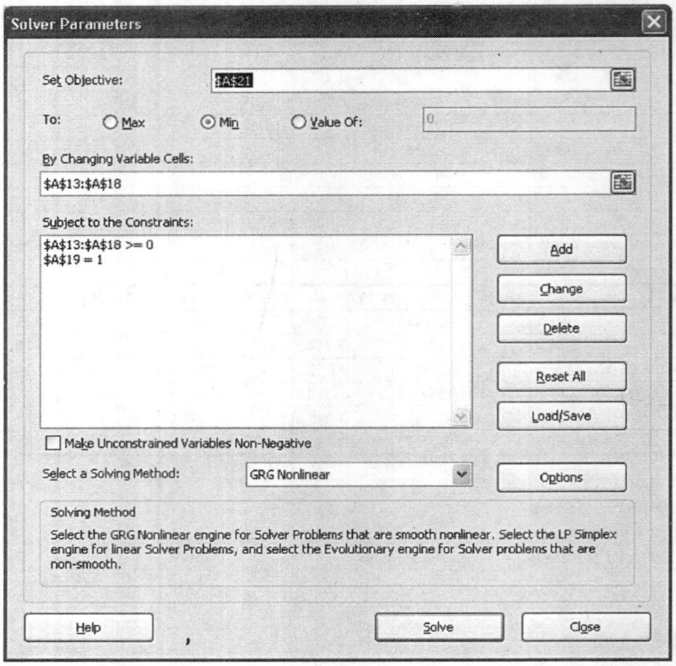

	A	B	C	D	E	F	G	H
1								
2	Scrips	Std Deviation	Expected Return					
3	BHEL	0.809	-0.409					
4	CIPLA	0.233	0.150					
5	DR REDDYS LABS	0.255	0.351					
6	HERO MOTOCORP	0.287	0.175					
7	HUL	0.236	0.159					
8	INFOSYS	0.293	0.200					
9								
10								
11	Weights	Scrips						
12			BHEL	CIPLA	DR REDDYS LABS	HERO MOTOCORP	HUL	INFOSYS
13	0.062	BHEL	0.6544	-0.0036	-0.0156	-0.0085	-0.0317	-0.0177
14	0.151	CIPLA	-0.0036	0.0542	0.0227	0.0149	0.0187	0.0150
15	0.171	DR REDDYS LABS	-0.0156	0.0227	0.0648	0.0309	0.0089	0.0174
16	0.073	HERO MOTOCORP	-0.0085	0.0149	0.0309	0.0825	0.0171	0.0172
17	0.341	HUL	-0.0317	0.0187	0.0089	0.0171	0.0556	-0.0013
18	0.202	INFOSYS	-0.0177	0.0150	0.0174	0.0172	-0.0013	0.0859
19	1							
20	0.1646	Portfolio Expected Return						
21	0.1494	Portfolio Std. Dev						

We can see that the portfolio standard deviation is less than the standard deviation of any of scrips taken individually when the six scrips are combined in the following proportion/weights:

BHEL	0.062
CIPLA	0.151
DR REDDYS LABS	0.171
HERO MOTOCORP	0.073
HUL	0.341
INFOSYS	0.202

Spreadsheet Application 3 *Calculating portfolios as per key statements of MPT:*

1. Maximizing portfolio expected return for a given level of risk
2. Minimizing portfolio standard deviation for a given level of return

Let us use the data from spreadsheet application 2 and calculate the two portfolios as described by MPT to show the power of diversification.

1. **Maximizing Portfolio Expected Return for a Given Level of Risk:** We can see in the window below that the lowest standard deviation is 0.233 (Cipla).

	A	B	C
1			
2	Scrips	Std Deviation	Expected Return
3	BHEL	0.809	-0.409
4	CIPLA	0.233	0.150
5	DR REDDYS LABS	0.255	0.351
6	HERO MOTOCORP	0.287	0.175
7	HUL	0.236	0.159
8	INFOSYS	0.293	0.200

We need to set up the solver to accommodate the new constraint. As can be seen in the exhibit, the 'Objective' is to maximize portfolio expected return for given level of standard deviation. First constraint is that the portfolio weight should not exceed 1. We have included another constraint related to shorting. We have prevented shorting by putting the constraint that the weight of any of the stock should not go below zero. To generate portfolio with maximum return for a given level of risk, we have added another constraint which states that the portfolio standard deviation should be less than equal to 0.233. The solver window is exhibited below:

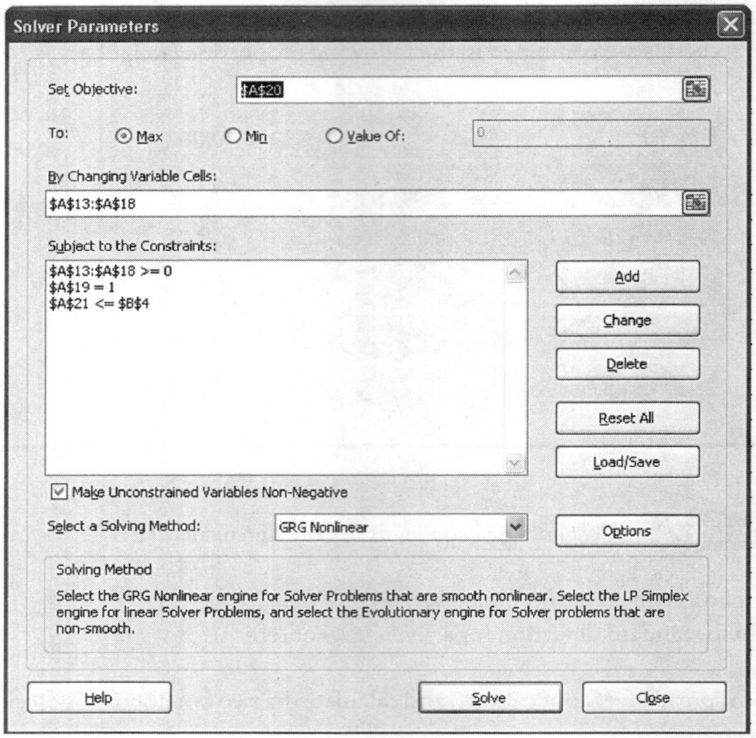

The output of solver window and the output minimum variance portfolio are exhibited below:

	A	B	C	D	E	F	G	H
2	Scrips	Std Deviation	Expected Return					
3	BHEL	0.809	-0.409					
4	CIPLA	0.233	0.150					
5	DR REDDYS LABS	0.255	0.351					
6	HERO MOTOCORP	0.287	0.175					
7	HUL	0.236	0.159					
8	INFOSYS	0.293	0.200					
9								
10								
11	Weights	Scrips						
12			BHEL	CIPLA	DR REDDYS LABS	HERO MOTOCORP	HUL	INFOSYS
13	0.000	BHEL	0.654418533	-0.00363974	-0.015558808	-0.008526821	-0.03166327	-0.01774188
14	0.000	CIPLA	-0.003639742	0.0541689	0.022688923	0.0148877	0.01874199	0.01502644
15	0.887	DR REDDYS LABS	-0.015558808	0.02268892	0.06478015	0.030939741	0.00892021	0.01735732
16	0.000	HERO MOTOCORP	-0.008526821	0.0148877	0.030939741	0.08248539	0.01711634	0.01722844
17	0.050	HUL	-0.031663271	0.01874199	0.008920205	0.017116336	0.05556343	-0.00132894
18	0.063	INFOSYS	-0.017741875	0.01502644	0.017357318	0.017228437	-0.00132894	0.08594928
19	1							
20	0.332	Portfolio Expected Return						
21	0.2327	Portfolio Std. Dev						

We can see that a portfolio consisting of following proportions of the given securities can reduce the portfolio standard deviation to a level that is less than the standard deviation of any of the component securities:

BHEL	0.000
CIPLA	0.000
DR REDDYS LABS	0.887
HERO MOTOCORP	0.000
HUL	0.050
INFOSYS	0.063

2. **Minimizing Portfolio Standard Deviation for a Given Level of Return:** Similarly, we can identify a portfolio that minimizes risk for a target level of return, say 0.15. We need to set up the solver to accommodate the new constraint. As can be seen in the exhibit, the 'Objective' is to minimize portfolio standard deviation for a given level of return. To generate portfolio with minimum portfolio standard for a given level of return, we have added another constraint which states that the portfolio expected return and should be greater than equal to 0.15. The solver window is exhibited below:

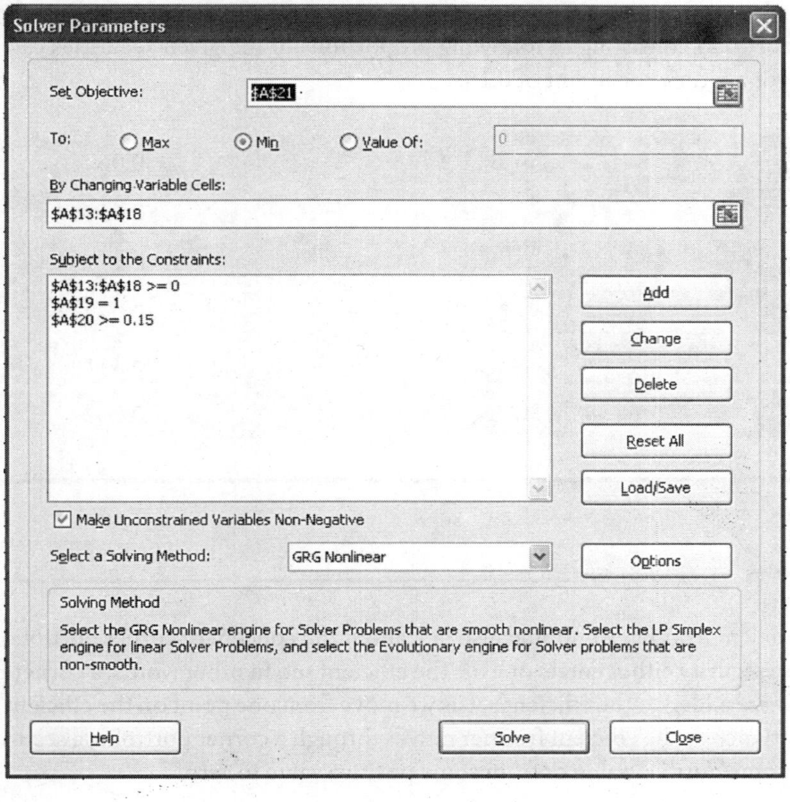

The portfolio risk, return and weights for the portfolio generated using the above two constraints are exhibited in the window below:

	A	B	C	D	E	F	G	H
1								
2	Scrips	Std Deviation	Expected Return					
3	BHEL	0.809	-0.409					
4	CIPLA	0.233	0.150					
5	DR REDDYS LABS	0.255	0.351					
6	HERO MOTOCORP	0.287	0.175					
7	HUL	0.236	0.159					
8	INFOSYS	0.293	0.200					
9								
10								
11	**Weights**	Scrips						
12			BHEL	CIPLA	DR REDDYS LABS	HERO MOTOCORP	HUL	INFOSYS
13	0.062	BHEL	0.654418533	-0.00363974	-0.015558808	-0.008526821	-0.03166327	-0.01774188
14	0.151	CIPLA	-0.003639742	0.0541689	0.022688923	0.0148877	0.01874199	0.01502644
15	0.171	DR REDDYS LABS	-0.015558808	0.02268892	0.06478015	0.030939741	0.00892021	0.01735732
16	0.073	HERO MOTOCORP	-0.008526821	0.0148877	0.030939741	0.08248539	0.01711634	0.01722844
17	0.341	HUL	-0.031663271	0.01874199	0.008920205	0.017116336	0.05556343	-0.00132894
18	0.202	INFOSYS	-0.017741875	0.01502644	0.017357318	0.017228437	-0.00132894	0.08594928
19	1							
20	0.165	Portfolio Expected Return						
21	0.1494	Portfolio Std. Dev						

We can see that a portfolio consisting of following proportions of the given securities can minimize portfolio standard deviation for a return constraint of 0.15:

BHEL	0.062
CIPLA	0.151
DR REDDYS LABS	0.171
HERO MOTOCORP	0.073
HUL	0.341
INFOSYS	0.202

Corner Portfolio

While discussing efficient frontier, we should also talk about the concept of corner portfolio. A corner portfolio is a portfolio where a security either enters or exits the efficient set. In other words, a corner portfolio comprises all the securities that are added to the efficient set as we move from one point on the efficient frontier to another. As the minimum-variance or the efficient frontier moves through a corner portfolio, a security's weight changes either from zero to some positive value or from some positive value to zero.

Portfolio Selection: What Next After Generating the Efficient Frontier?

Through the above analysis, we have identified a curve called 'Efficient Frontier' by eliminating a large number of feasible portfolios. We know that efficient frontier is the locus of all efficient or dominant portfolios. An obvious question now is what next? What should an investor do once the frontier is generated?

Clearly, the investor will now choose a portfolio. Which portfolio will be chosen out of all the efficient ones that lie along the efficient frontier will depend on each individual investor's characteristics. Being rational, each investor will choose a portfolio that is best for him according to his risk preference or risk tolerance[7]. A portfolio selected by an investor according to his propensity to take risk is known as the optimal portfolio and it has the following characteristics:

- Lies on the efficient frontier.
- Possesses only so much volatility as the investor is willing to assume.
- Gives maximum possible expected return for that level of risk.

Harry Markowitz used the concept of optimal portfolio in 1952 and thus this concept is also a part of the modern portfolio theory. You may recall that this theory assumes that an investor is rational and risk averse. Therefore, he always tries to minimize risk while striving for the highest return possible. While investing in accordance with the provisions of MPT, an investor has to decide how much risk he can handle and then allocate his funds to that efficient portfolio that gives him an acceptable level of risk.

We can understand the entire process of how the optimal portfolio works by going back to the concept of utility and indifference curves of an investor. To determine the optimal portfolio on the efficient frontier, the investor's risk-return tradeoff must be known.

The slope of the efficient frontier at any point measures the additional expected return that can be obtained by taking incremental risk. This represents the return-risk tradeoff of portfolios. The slope of the efficient frontier decreases as we move upward toward the point that has no point to its right or above. Further, this slope implies that additional unit of risk is rewarded with diminishing increment in returns. Mathematically, the slope of efficient frontier may be measured as:

$$\frac{\Delta E(R_p)}{\Delta E(\sigma_p)}$$

where

$E(R_p)$ = Portfolio expected return

$E(\sigma_p)$ = Portfolio expected standard deviation

From investor's point of view, the amount of satisfaction or utility that he gets from his investment can be depicted through 'indifference or utility curves.' These curves represent an individual's risk preference and each investor has a different map of indifference curves, depending on his ability to take risk. As we have discussed in Chapter 3, the indifference curves of an investor represent the tradeoff he is willing to make between expected risk and return.

---

[7] We have already understood these concepts in Chapter 3 of this book.

The efficient frontier, a measure of portfolio's risk-return tradeoff, and utility curve, a measure of an individual investor's risk-return tradeoff, are then used in conjunction to determine the optimal portfolio. Each investor will end up choosing a particular portfolio that suits his risk profile and any two investors will select the same portfolio only when they have the same set of indifference curves. Such a portfolio will be the portfolio at which one of the investor's indifference curves is tangential to the efficient frontier. This portfolio is called the optimal portfolio of that investor as it gives him the highest utility. The point of tangency occurs where the investor's risk-aversion equals the slope of the efficient frontier. The more risk-averse an investor, the lower the position of the optimal portfolio on the efficient frontier.

Figure 4.16 gives an indifference map for two hypothetical investors, one of them is strongly risk averse and the other is less risk averse. The curves labeled U_{11}, U_{22} and U_{33} represent the utility curves of a strongly risk averse investor and the curves labeled U_1, U_2 and U_3 represent the utility curves of a less risk averse investor.

Figure 4.16 Portfolio selection.

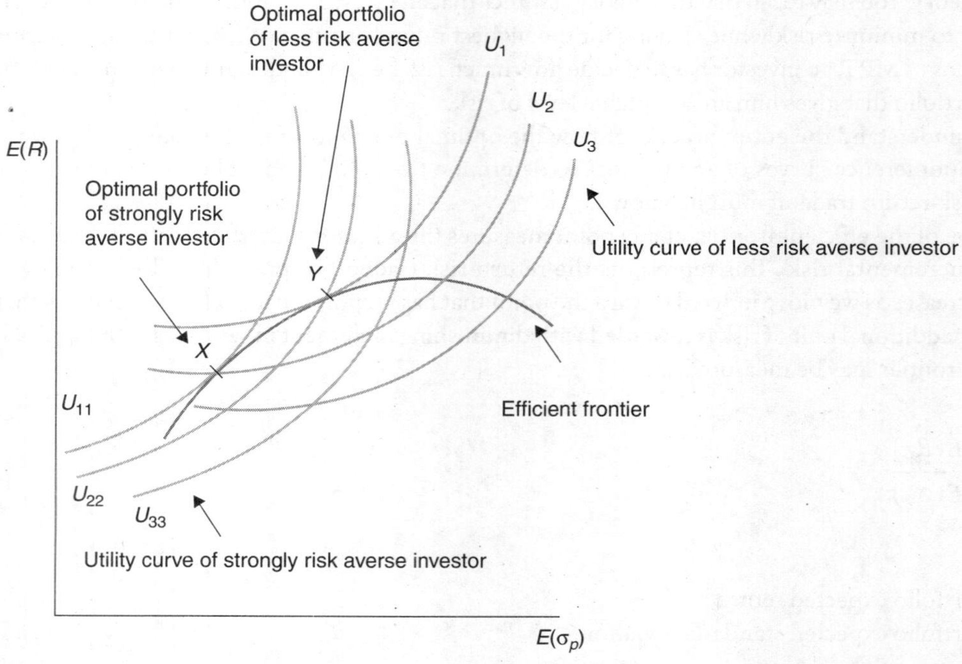

Point X is the point of tangency of U_{11} to the efficient frontier and the portfolio lying on this point is this investor's optimal portfolio. He should invest his funds in this portfolio, as his utility is highest at this point.

Point Y is the point of tangency of U_1 to the efficient frontier and the portfolio lying on this point is this investor's optimal portfolio. He should invest his funds in this portfolio, as his utility is highest at this point.

You may notice that point X lies below Y, showing that more risk averse the investor, the lower his optimal portfolio on the efficient frontier.

Markowitz Portfolio Optimization[8]

The concept of risk-adjusted return can be used as an effective decision rule for selecting an optimal portfolio for an investor. This risk-adjusted return takes both risk and return into account and it can be termed as the utility of the portfolio for an investor. The utility of a portfolio to an investor is measured as the difference between the expected return of the portfolio and the risk penalty. This risk penalty depends on portfolio volatility and investor's risk preference or tolerance.

We have learnt in our discussion on indifference curves in Chapter 3 that with an increase in the level of risk, each additional unit of risk is more undesirable. As a simple quantification, it has been suggested in financial theory that twice the risk is four times as undesirable. Mathematically, risk penalty may be computed as follows:

$$\text{Risk penalty} = \frac{\text{Risk squared}}{(\text{Risk tolerance})}$$

Risk squared is the variance of return of the portfolio. Risk tolerance can take any value from 0 through 100. To put it in words, risk tolerance is a measure of an investor's willingness to bear additional risk. The lower this number, the more risk averse the investor and the higher the risk penalty.

Once risk penalty is computed, the investor in question can calculate his utility using the following formula:

$$\text{Utility} = E(R_p) - \text{Risk penalty}$$

The optimal portfolio for an investor would be the one from the efficient set that maximizes his utility.

Numerical Example 5

Calculation of Utility

Use the following information on the risk-return profile of five portfolios and risk tolerance of an investor to calculate the utility of each portfolio and identify the optimal portfolio for this investor.

	Portfolio Parameters				
	Portfolio 1	Portfolio 2	Portfolio 3	Portfolio 4	Portfolio 5
Expected Return (%)	10	7	9	11	8
Standard deviation (%)	8	5	7	9	6
Risk tolerance (%)	40	40	40	40	40

[8] Based on William Sharpe, "Practical Aspects of Portfolio Optimization," in *Improving the Investment Decision Process* (Charlottesville. V A.: Institute of Chartered Financial Analysts/Dow Jones-Irwin. 1984).

Solution:

Utility can be calculated by using the following formula:

$$\text{Utility} = E(R_p) - \text{Risk penalty}$$

Expected return is already given, so we need to compute risk penalty to compute utility.

1. **Calculation of Risk Penalty:**

$$\text{Risk penalty} = \frac{\text{Risk squared}}{(\text{Risk tolerance})}$$

Portfolio 1

$$\text{Risk penalty} = \frac{8 \times 8}{40}$$
$$= 1.6\%$$

Portfolio 2

$$\text{Risk penalty} = \frac{5 \times 5}{40}$$
$$= 0.625\%$$

Portfolio 3

$$\text{Risk penalty} = \frac{7 \times 7}{40}$$
$$= 1.225\%$$

Portfolio 4

$$\text{Risk penalty} = \frac{9 \times 9}{40}$$
$$= 2.025\%$$

Portfolio 5

$$\text{Risk penalty} = \frac{6 \times 6}{40}$$
$$= 0.9\%$$

2. **Calculation of Utility:** Utility $= E(R_p) -$ Risk Penalty

Portfolio 1

$$\text{Utility} = 10 - 1.6$$
$$= 8.4\ \%$$

Portfolio 2

$$\text{Utility} = 7 - 0.625$$
$$= 6.375\ \%$$

Portfolio 3

$$\text{Utility} = 9 - 1.225$$
$$= 7.775\ \%$$

Portfolio 4

$$\text{Utility} = 11 - 2.025$$
$$= 8.975\ \%$$

Portfolio 5

$$\text{Utility} = 8 - 0.9$$
$$= 7.1\ \%$$

Since portfolio 4 gives the highest utility, it is the optimal portfolio for the investor under consideration.

Alternative Method for Computing Utility

The concept of utility curves or indifference curves serves as a key factor in portfolio selection. We already know that the investors who are more risk averse need to be compensated more than proportionately for accepting small increments in risk. In other words, they penalize the riskier investments by desiring a much higher expected return from such investments. The greater the risk, the higher the penalty (also reflected in the concept of risk penalty in Markowitz' optimization).

To fully understand the role of risk aversion in portfolio selection, let's consider the following example:

Suppose the risk-free rate of return is 4% and there are 3 options of risky portfolios to choose from. These portfolios have the following characteristics:

Portfolio	Expected Return (%)	Standard Deviation (%)	Risk Premium (%)
Low risk	6	5	2
Moderate/Intermediate risk	8	9	4
High risk	12	18	7

An investor taking a decision to invest solely on the basis of expected return would find it easy to choose the portfolio offering the highest expected return, i.e., portfolio offering expected return of 12%. But when risk aversion enters the mix, the portfolio offering highest expected return might not actually be an obvious choice.

The above matrix clearly shows that a higher level of risk is being compensated with a higher risk premium. Whether such a compensation will be acceptable to investors will depend on how much return each investor is willing to tradeoff against risk. Thus we need to quantify the rate at which an investor would be willing to tradeoff return against risk.

Such quantification happens by assigning utility to the alternative portfolio choices on the basis of their risk-return characteristics. In doing so, higher utility values are assigned to more attractive risk-return profile. Each investor will then select a portfolio that offers the highest utility to him.

One of the formulas used by financial theorists for quantifying utility is

$$U = E(R)^* - \frac{1}{2} A\sigma^2$$

where
U = Utility value
$E(R)^*$ = Return (must be expressed as decimal rather than %)
A = Index or measure of risk aversion of an individual investor
σ^2 = Variance

½ is a scaling convention.

The formula clearly shows that the expected return increases the utility value and risk decreases it to the extent of an investor's risk aversion as measured by A. Obviously, the portfolio giving highest utility will be selected.

In case of risk-free portfolio, the second half of the formula would be zero. Therefore its utility would be same for all the investors. In our example it is 0.04.

For risky portfolios, the estimate of U will depend on A. In case of risk neutral investors, $A = 0$ and the selection of portfolio is solely driven by the level of expected return because for such investors the level of risk is irrelevant.

For a risk seeker, A is < 0. Such investor may not exhibit utility maximizing behavior because he does not penalize higher risk with more than proportionate compensation in the form of return. For him riskiness of investment offers a great degree of 'fun' that makes him accept higher risk with substantially lower increase in returns.

Obviously, risk averse investors will have a higher value of A as they penalize risk more.

To understand the concept clearly, let's consider three investors who have varying extent of risk aversion:

For Mr. X, $A = 2$

Mr. Y, $A = 3$

Mr. Z, $A = 4$

Continuing with the same risk-return characteristics as given in the table above, we can compute utility of each portfolio for Mr. X, Mr. Y and Mr. Z.

We can compute the utility for each portfolio by substituting the values from the above table in the following formula:

$$U = E(R)^* - \frac{1}{2} A\sigma^2$$

For example, for Mr. X, utility score for portfolio L can be computed as:

$$U = 0.06 - \frac{1}{2}(2)(0.05)^2 = 0.06 - 0.0025 = 0.0575$$

The following values have been computed by substituting the relevant information in the same formula.

Investor	Utility Score for L	Utility Score for M	Utility Score for H
Mr. X ($A = 2$)	0.0575	0.0719	**0.0876**
Mr. Y ($A = 3$)	0.05625	0.06785	**0.0714**
Mr. Z ($A = 4$)	0.055	**0.0638**	0.0552

The values highlighted in the above table indicate the portfolio that offers the highest utility to the concerned investor. We observe at for $A = 4$, Mr. Z is more risk averse, so the medium risk portfolio offers him higher utility. Thus, the higher the value of A, the higher the utility score of less risky portfolio. The utility score of the risk-free portfolio is 0.04, which is less than the utility scores of more risky portfolios, so no investor will select it. Thus, the choice of optimal portfolio is driven solely by the utility score.

Extension of Modern Portfolio Theory: Capital Market Line

James Tobin[9] (1958) expanded on Markowitz's work by adding a risk-free asset to the analysis. This led to the notion of a super-efficient portfolio and the capital market line.

It was suggested that by combining a risk-free asset with a portfolio on the efficient frontier, it is possible to generate a new efficient frontier that is the locus of portfolios whose risk-return profiles are superior to those of portfolios on the old efficient frontier.

[9] James Tobin, Liquidity preference as behavior towards risk, *The Review of Economic Studies*, 1958, 25, 65–68.

When risk-free borrowing and lending is introduced into the mix, some significant changes are witnessed. Risk free borrowing and lending means borrowing and lending at r_f (risk- free rate). Risk-free lending implies an investment in riskless assets such as a T-bill. Risk-free borrowing implies taking a loan at risk-free rate of interest to invest in portfolio of risky assets/securities. Since risk-free asset has no correlation with any risky portfolio in the feasible portfolio space, a combination of risk-free asset with any risky portfolio in the zone of feasibility is represented by a straight line. Thus, risk-free borrowing and lending options transform the efficient frontier into a straight line. This straight line is referred to as capital market line and it is tangential to the old efficient frontier as shown in Figure 4.17.[10]

Figure 4.17 Capital market line.

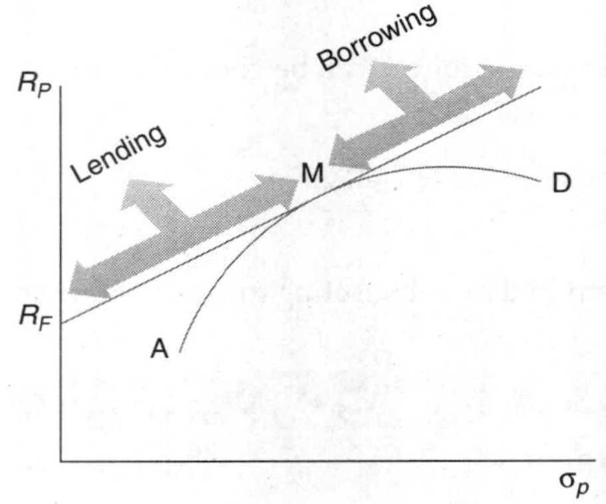

Limitations of Modern Portfolio Theory

The dynamics of a portfolio constructed using MPT becomes quite complex as the number of assets/securities increases. We have illustrated the portfolio risk and return computations in the preceding part of this chapter. Readers can see how the number of computations increase as we move from 2 to 3 security case. In real world situation, there will be many more securities to be considered in making an investment portfolio. As more and more securities are inducted in the portfolio, the computations increase manifold and become too difficult for investor to handle manually. Mathematical analysis through the use of Markowitz algorithm solves the computational problem to a large extent for an *n*-security portfolio, but the real challenge for the model comes from the need to generate large number of input data required for applying this theory to portfolio analysis.

For *n*-security portfolio, the inputs required are:

1. $E(R)$ of each security, i.e., N number of inputs.
2. Variance of returns of each security, i.e., N number of inputs.
3. Covariances of each pair of securities, i.e., $(N^2 - N)/2$ number of inputs.

[10] Capital Market Line has been discussed in detail in the subsequent chapters of this book.

Thus, the total number of inputs required to apply MPT to portfolio analysis of n-security portfolio are:

$$\frac{N(N+3)}{2}$$

So for $n = 50$, i.e., for a 50-security portfolio, inputs required are:

$$\frac{50(50+3)}{2}$$

$$= 1325$$

Markowitz model is, thus, extremely complicated in its data requirement and it imposes excessive demands on analysts[11].

In the real world, analysts tend to specialize in sectors/industries. So an analyst specializing in pharma sector would know about and forecast expected returns and risks of individual stocks like Lupin, Ipca, Dr Reddys Labs, Cipla, and Aurobindo Pharm amongst others. In fact, there are 121 pharma companies listed on BSE (Exhibit 4.1). So an analyst specializing in this sector would have to be familiar with most of these firms.

Exhibit 4.1 Pharma companies listed on BSE

Dr Reddys Labs	Pfizer	Shilpa	Ortin Labs
Cipla	Unichem Labs	Morepen Lab	Roselabs
Lupin	Novartis India	Albert David	Jenburkt Pharma
Aurobindo Pharmw	Ajanta Pharma	Suven Life Sci	Hester Bio
Cadila Health	Aarti Drugs	Kopran	Medicamen Bio
Jubilant Life	JB Chemicals	Anuh Pharma	Makers Labs
Ipca Labs	Merck	SMS Pharma	Alpa Labs
Torrent Pharma	Shasun Pharma	RPG Life	NGL Fine Chem
GlaxoSmithKline	Parabolic Drugs	Lincoln Pharma	Natural Capsule
Wockhardt	FDC	Parenteral Drug	Lactose Ind a
Sun Pharma	Granules India	Elder Healthcare	Auro Labs
Divis Labs	Wyeth	Smruthi Organic	Coral Labs

(Continued)

[11] Solution to this problem of large number of input data was offered by William Sharpe in the form of his model called Single Index Model. It has been discussed in detail in the next chapter.

EXHIBIT 4.1 Continued

Dr Reddys Labs	Pfizer	Shilpa	Ortin Labs
Glenmark	Arvind Remedies	Alembic	BDH Industries
Orchid Chemical	Hikal	Bharat Immuno	Nutraplus Prod
Sanofi India	Indoco Remedies	Aarey Drugs	Vikram Thermo
Nectar Life	Panacea Biotec	Bafna Pharma	Advik Labors
Alembic Pharma	Natco Pharma	Astec Life	Sandu Pharma
Piramal Enter	Dishman Pharma	Sanjivani Paren	Kilitch Drugs
Elder Pharma	Neuland Lab	Themis Medicare	Gennex Labs
Ind-Swift Labs	Vivimed Labs	Bal Pharma	Guj Themis
Sharon Bio Medi	Wanbury	Amrutanjan Heal	Hiran Orgochem
Patidar Build	AstraZeneca	Caplin Labs	Wintac
Biofil Chem	TTK Healthcare	Syncom Formula	DIL
Trimurthi Drugs	Mahavir Advance	Ahlcon Parent	Ambalal Sarabha
Piramal Phytoca	Toheal Pharm	Gufic Bio	Beryl Drugs
Unjha Formula	Rekvina Labs	Lyka Labs	Ishita Drugs
Venmax Drugs	Welcure Drugs	Sun Pharma Adv	Zyden Gentec
Zenith Health	Rubra Medicamen	Brooks Labs	Vista Pharma
Zenotech Labs	Transchem	Fervent Synergi	Pharmasia
Saamya Biotech	Combat Drugs	Pharmaids Pharm	Colinz Labs
			Country Condos

So, being a specialist in the sector, even if he limits himself to domestic pharma companies, he will already be handling a large number of input variables. Now if he were to follow MPT in word and deed, then he would be required to track the variances of each pair of securities within the industry as well as their covariances with many other shares in many other sectors. There are 112 sectors (Exhibit 4.2) that have scrips listed under them on BSE. The number of data inputs already boggles the mind and the number of scrips listed under each sector have not even been mentioned yet.

Further the discussion is limited to equity only so far. A really diversified portfolio would consist of many asset classes such as domestic and non-domestic equity, domestic and non-domestic fixed income securities, alternative investments[12] and cash and cash equivalents. The scenario becomes bleaker for the

[12] Alternative investments include real estate, private equity, natural resources, commodities, etc.

Exhibit 4.2 Sectors under which scrips are listed on BSE

Abrasives	Electric Equipment	Plastics
Aluminum	Electricals	Power – Generation/Distribution
Aquaculture	Electrodes/Graphite	Power – Transmission/Equipment
Auto – 2 & 3 Wheelers	Engineering	Printing & Stationery
Auto – Cars & Jeeps	Engineering – Heavy	Pumps
Auto – LCVs/HCVs	Engines	Refineries
Auto – Tractors	Fasteners	Retail
Auto Ancillaries	Fertilizers	Rubber
Banks – Private Sector	Finance – General	Shipping
Banks – Public Sector	Finance – Housing	Steel – CR/HR Strips
Bearings	Finance – Investments	Steel – GP/GC Sheets
Breweries & Distilleries	Finance – Leasing & Hire Purchase	Steel – Large
Cables – Power/Others	Finance – Term Lending Institutions	Steel – Medium / Small
Cables – Telephone	Food Processing	Steel – Pig Iron
Castings & Forgings	Glass & Glass Products	Steel – Rolling
Cement – Major	Hospitals & Medical Services	Steel – Sponge Iron
Cement – Mini	Hotels	Steel – Tubes/Pipes
Cement – Products/Building Materials	Infrastructure – General	Sugar
Ceramics/Granite	Leather Products	Telecommunications – Equipment
Chemicals	Lubricants	Telecommunications – Service
Cigarettes	Machine Tools	Textiles – Composite Mills
Compressors	Media & Entertainment	Textiles – Cotton Blended
Computers – Hardware	Metals – Non Ferrous	Textiles – Denim
Computers – Software	Mining/Minerals	Textiles – General

(*Continued*)

EXHIBIT 4.2 Continued

Abrasives	Electric Equipment	Plastics
Computers – Software – Training	Miscellaneous	Textiles – Hosiery/Knitwear
Computers – Software Medium/Small	Oil Drilling And Exploration	Textiles – Machinery
Construction & Contracting – Civil	Packaging	Textiles – Manmade
Construction & Contracting – Housing	Paints/Varnishes	Textiles – Processing
Construction & Contracting – Real Estate	Paper	Textiles – Readymade Apparels
Consumer Goods – Electronic	Personal Care	Textiles – Spinning – Cotton Blended
Consumer Goods – White Goods	Pesticides/Agro Chemicals	Textiles – Spinning – Synthetic Blended
Couriers	Petrochemicals	Textiles – Synthetic/Silk
Detergents	Pharmaceuticals	Textiles – Terry Towels
Diamond Cutting/Precious Metals/Jewelry	Plantations – Tea & Coffee	Textiles – Weaving
Diversified	Dyes & Pigments	Textiles – Woolen/Worsted
Domestic Appliances	Edible Oils & Solvent Extraction	Trading
Dry Cells	Vanaspati/Oils	Transport & Logistics
		Tyres

practical applicability of MPT. This is not how the investment world can function smoothly. However, MPT continues to be the cornerstone of modern portfolio approach and it serves as the guideline for portfolio analysis.[13]

Ben Graham (author of the book the intelligent investor) has suggested that adequate diversification can be achieved by holding 10 to 30 assets in a portfolio. Evans and Archer[14] found that portfolios comprising of as low as 10 securities, had standard deviation almost the same as the market. There are others who pay even 200 is pecunities are not enough for adequate diversification. The debate cntinues.

Though there is no consensus in the literature on any one number but it is universally accepted that increasing the number of assets/securities beyond a certain point might become so expensive that it might not be profitable enough to expand the portfolio any further. An extract (Market Reality 4.2) from an article on Internet makes for an interesting and informative reading from Indian perspective.

---

[13] Some thoughts on modern-day applicability of MPT have been presented at the end of the chapter.

[14] J.L. Evans and S.H. Archer, "Diversification and the reduction of dispersion: An emperical analysis," *The Journal of Finance*, 1968, 23, 761–767.

Market Reality 4.1 What Value Should n Take for a Well-Diversified Portfolio?

What Value Should n Take for a Well-Diversified Portfolio?

As an investor, the main question that comes to one's mind is how many assets/securities should be held in a portfolio to make it well-diversified. In other words, what is the adequate number of assets/securities that should comprise a portfolio? Traditionally, the approach was: the more the merrier, i.e., larger the number of securities held, the better it is. However, MPT has steered the thought away from quantity to quality, i.e., inclusion of the right kind of security (right kind being those that have less than perfect positive correlation with other securities in the portfolio). The challenge comes from the fact that most assets and most asset classes tend to exhibit positive correlation, making the existence of zero-risk portfolio a myth.

Coming to the question of how many of the right kind of securities, one tends to find different numbers being bandied around from 15 to 20 to 30. There are many interesting views related to "adequate diversification."

Market Reality 4.2 Rakesh Jhunjhunwala's Portfolio

Rakesh Jhunjhunwala is known in the investment community as a typical buy-and-hold investor. Once he is convinced about the prospects of a stock, he prefers to hold it, irrespective of the short-term market movements. He is not only a buy and hold investor but also a concentrated investor. As can be seen in the image below, 65% of the value of his portfolio comes from only 3 stocks.

Jhunjhunwala's Top Bets

Company	Titan industries	Crisil	Lupin
Stake	7.51%	7.85%	1.87%
Value*	1532	575	464

* ₹crore

Source: Business Standard.

Business Standard reported sometime back that at a meeting conducted by a forum in 2012, Jhunjhunwala stated that he intended to reduce the variety of stocks in his portfolio to about one third of his then holding.

He also made it clear that many listed stocks were very attractive investment options and that he was not interested in private equity.

Source: http://rakesh-jhunjhunwala.in/index.php/2012/04/27/rakesh-jhunjhunwalas-portfolio-in-2013, accessed on November 7, 2014.

SUMMARY

☑ The problem of choice of securities/assets in reality is not limited to choosing each security in isolation; rather it is a process of selecting an entire bunch of them out of a large set of possible combinations that make up probable portfolios. Such situation is referred to as portfolio selection problem and the modern solution to it was offered in 1952 by Harry Markowitz, whose extensive work in quantification of portfolio risk and return continues to be the cornerstone of modern approach to investing in portfolios.

☑ At a time when investors were selecting securities to form a portfolio in accordance with the behavior proposed by traditional portfolio theory, MPT (modern portfolio theory) was the first theory to formally recognize the fact that portfolio creation was not simply amassing of individual securities with fantastic risk-return profiles. The new theory stated that objectives of a portfolio could be truly realized only after it has been created by considering the interplay of risk between the component securities.

☑ MPT postulates that a rational investor will always seek to maximize returns from his set of assets (portfolio) for a given level of risk or minimize risk of his portfolio for a given level of return. It quantifies diversification by providing us with formulas to measure portfolio risk and expected return.

☑ The fundamental concept of MPT is that the securities/assets comprising an investment portfolio should not be identified on the basis of their individual merit; rather, each asset/security should be evaluated in terms of how its price changes relative to the changes in returns on other assets/securities in the portfolio.

☑ Risk averse investors evaluate portfolios in terms of the probability distribution of their expected returns over some holding period. Further, they measure the risk of the portfolios in terms of the variability of expected returns and seeks to maximize their one-period utility.

☑ The possibility of combining two or more risky securities that are less than perfectly positively correlated to form a portfolio that has a level of risk which is lower than any of the component securities is called portfolio effect. The benefit of this kind of diversification is maximum in case of perfectly negatively correlated securities.

☑ Portfolio standard deviation/variance is sensitive to:
(a) The proportion of funds allocated to each security.
(b) The standard deviation of each individual security.
(c) The covariance/correlation between two securities.

☑ Superior portfolios give higher return for the same level of risk or lower risk for the same level of return. Such portfolios are called 'efficient portfolios' in MPT. According to MPT, all rational investors would choose efficient portfolios within the set of all feasible portfolios.

☑ An envelope curve that is the locus of all the superior or dominating or efficient portfolios is called the efficient frontier. There are no other portfolios that offer a better risk-return profile than those on the efficient frontier.

☑ While investing in accordance with the provisions of MPT, an investor has to decide how much risk he can handle and then allocate his funds to that efficient portfolio that gives him an acceptable level of risk.

☑ The efficient frontier, a measure of portfolio's risk-return tradeoff, and utility curve, a measure of an individual investor's risk-return tradeoff, are used in conjunction to determine the optimal portfolio.

☑ James Tobin (1958) expanded on Markowitz's work by adding a risk-free asset to the analysis. This lead to the notion of a super-efficient portfolio and the capital market line.

☑ Though there is no consensus in the literature on any one number but it is universally accepted that increasing the number of assets/securities beyond a certain point might become so expensive that it might not be profitable enough to expand the portfolio any further.

KEY WORDS

Adequate diversification **167**
Capital market line **161**
Diversification **167**
Efficient frontier **144**
Efficient portfolio **146**
Expected utility **121**
Feasible portfolios **144**
Insatiation **121**
Mean variance optimization **118**
Minimum variance portfolio **136**
Modern portfolio theory **161**
Optimal portfolio **156**
Portfolio analysis **117**
Portfolio effect **138**
Portfolio optimization **157**
Portfolio return **123**
Portfolio risk **124**
Portfolio selection **155**
Risk aversion **120**
Risk penalty **157**
Risk tolerance **157**
Terminal wealth **121**
Traditional portfolio theory **117**
Utility **157**

CONCEPT QUESTIONS

1. In real world, an investor has to typically consider many asset classes to identify his optimal portfolio. Applying MPT to equity is challenging enough but extending its use to other asset classes, particularly alternative investments, seems almost impossible. In your opinion, what are the challenges an investor is likely to face if he tries to generate expected returns, standard deviations and correlation data for asset classes other than equity?

2. "Risk free lending and borrowing change the shape of the efficient frontier to a straight line." Explain the statement and describe MPT in brief.

3. Explain why and how the concepts of diversification and covariance are closely related.
4. Write out the Markowitz expressions for expected return and standard deviation for a portfolio comprising 6 securities. Comment on the formula thus generated.
5. Stock A has standard deviation equal to 0.17 and stock B has a standard deviation equal to 0.22. Is it possible to combine these two stocks to form a portfolio that has lower volatility then either of the two stocks. If yes, why? If no, why?
6. According to MPT, all rational investors will choose a portfolio lying on the efficient Frontier. How would they choose it and why could the choice of each investor be different from the others?
7. As new securities are added to the portfolio, the significance of each individual security decreases whereas the importance of their interactive risk increases. Explain the statement.
8. Express your views on the number of securities that are required to be inducted in a portfolio to ensure adequate diversification.

PRACTICE PROBLEMS

1. Consider the following price data for 5 scrips: Bajaj Auto, Reliance, NTPC, M&M and Lupin Ltd. on BSE for a period extending from May 2013 to April 2014:

Bajaj Auto		Reliance		NTPC		M&M		Lupin Ltd	
Month	**Close**	**Month**	**Close**	**Month**	**Close**	**Month**	**Close**	**Month**	**Close**
13-May	1,822.65	13-May	805.6	13-May	154.4	13-May	965.3	13-May	740.15
13-Jun	1,917.45	13-Jun	861.85	13-Jun	143.7	13-Jun	966.55	13-Jun	779.6
13-Jul	1,935.70	13-Jul	871.6	13-Jul	130.6	13-Jul	912.15	13-Jul	871.45
13-Aug	1,839.50	13-Aug	851.55	13-Aug	130.75	13-Aug	781	13-Aug	800.2
13-Sep	1,988.20	13-Sep	822.35	13-Sep	148.2	13-Sep	827.8	13-Sep	854.7
13-Oct	2,129.00	13-Oct	912.35	13-Oct	148.7	13-Oct	888.35	13-Oct	887.15
13-Nov	1,974.75	13-Nov	853.1	13-Nov	147.35	13-Nov	945.6	13-Nov	855.45
13-Dec	1,910.55	13-Dec	894.8	13-Dec	136.8	13-Dec	943.5	13-Dec	908.6
14-Jan	1,902.80	14-Jan	830.85	14-Jan	126.4	14-Jan	890.45	14-Jan	882.05
14-Feb	1,942.70	14-Feb	799.25	14-Feb	112.6	14-Feb	973.45	14-Feb	993.45
14-Mar	2,078.30	14-Mar	929.5	14-Mar	119.95	14-Mar	980.65	14-Mar	935.9
14-Apr	1,913.45	14-Apr	935.3	14-Apr	116.25	14-Apr	1,072.15	14-Apr	989.9

Calculate portfolio risk and return for the following portfolios:

a. Portfolio 1 comprising Reliance scrip only.
b. Portfolio 2 comprising Reliance and Bajaj Auto scrips.
c. Portfolio 3 comprising Reliance, Bajaj Auto and Lupin scrips.
d. Portfolio 4 comprising Reliance, Bajaj Auto, M&M and NTPC scrips.

Assume:

1. No dividends have been paid on any of the given scrips for the period under consideration.
2. The portfolio funds are divided equally amongst all component scrips.
3. The correlation between each pair of security is +0.5.

2. A portfolio is constituted with four securities having the following characteristics:

Stock	Expected Return (%)	Proportion of Funds
Axis Bank	18.5	0.20
ACC	24.3	0.15
Pidilite Ind	16.4	0.40
Trent	21.2	0.25

Calculate the expected return of the portfolio.

3. Consider the following standard deviations and correlation coefficients for three stocks viz., TCS, Provogue and SKF India.

		Correlation with Stock		
Stock	Std. Deviation	TCS	Provogue	SKF India
TCS	9	1	0.70	−0.5
Provogue	6	0.70	1	0.2
SKF India	10	−0.5	0.2	1

Calculate:

a. Standard deviation of a portfolio composed of equal proportion of TCS and SKF India.
b. Standard deviation of a portfolio composed of 20% of TCS, 50% of Provogue and 30% of SKF India.

4. Given below is the variance-covariance matrix for three securities, calculate variance of a portfolio with proportional investments in the assets $X_A = 0.3$, $X_B = 0.4$ and $X_C = 0.3$.

	Security A	Security B	Security C
Security A	24	12	10
Security B	12	32	−8
Security C	10	−8	48

5. Compute expected return of a portfolio comprising of these three securities using the following information:

Security	Number of Shares in Portfolio	Initial Market Price Per Share (₹)	Expected End-of-period Price Per Share (₹)
Elder Health Care Ltd.	150	47.90	64.05
Som Distilleries & Breweries Ltd.	200	282.20	217.00
Ingersoll-Rand (India) Ltd.	100	407.10	481.80

6. Given is the risk-return profile of 7 portfolios that an investor is considering for investing. Which of these portfolios is his optimal portfolio if his risk tolerance is 30%. Interpret the outcome.

	Portfolio Parameters						
	Portfolio 1	Portfolio 2	Portfolio 3	Portfolio 4	Portfolio 5	Portfolio 6	Portfolio 7
Expected Return (%)	14	8	11	12	8	10	9
Std. deviation (%)	10	5	7	9	6	8	9

7. Suppose an analyst has provided you the following estimates in respect of equity shares of Motherson Sumi, Hipolin, VST Tillers and Thermax.

Stock	Expected Return (%)	Std. Deviation (%)	Proportion of Funds
Motherson Sumi	17	7.4	0.25
Hipolin	23	8.2	0.15
VST Tillers	15	6.7	0.35
Thermax	20	9.1	0.25

Correlation coefficient of returns between:

Motherson Sumi & Hipolin = 0.4

VST Tillers & Thermax = 0.6

Motherson Sumi & VST Tillers = 0.3

Hipolin & VST Tillers = 0.5

Motherson Sumi & Thermax = 0.4

Hipolin & Thermax = 0.8

Estimate the portfolio's mean return and variance.

8. There are four investors (Sam, Sagar, Amit and Rahul) who want to identify their optimal portfolio from the given set of portfolios.

For Mr. Sam, $A = 3$

Mr. Sagar, $A = 4$

Mr. Amit, $A = 5$

Mr. Rahul, $A = 6$

The risk-free rate of return is 5% and the risk-return characteristics of the portfolios are:

Portfolio	Expected Return (₹)	Standard Deviation (₹)	Risk Premium (₹)
Low risk	8	6	3
Moderate/ Intermediate risk	11	10	5
High risk	14	18	8

Which portfolio is the optimal portfolio of each of the investor? Explain the outcome.

9. **Case:** Suppose security analysts forecasting the anticipated returns in the stock market in India are basing their expectations of future largely on the state of the global economy that is still in a recessionary mode and the threat of escalation of political tension in Central Europe and Middle East. They anticipate that there is a 25% chance that these factors can bring about a downtrend and recession in the market. However, the Indian economy seems to be recovering and the analysts feel that if the macroeconomic fundamentals continue to improve, there is a 50% chance that the market would continue to be stable and grow normally. Further, with Standard and Poor's raised outlook for India's from "BBB-minus" rating to "stable," the analysts feel that there is a 25% chance of boom in the stock market.

Mr. Lee has decided to invest in three stocks: Vespro Ltd. and Microsim Ltd. in the IT sector and Goodlife Ltd. from the consumer goods segment. The rate of return on the three stocks in case of recession is: 10% for Vespro Ltd., 14% for Microsim Ltd. and 9% for Goodlife Ltd. In case of normal performance, the rate of return on the three stocks is: 14% for Vespro Ltd., 12% for Microsim Ltd. and 13% for Goodlife Ltd. If boom conditions prevail in the market, the rate of return on the three stocks is: 16% for Vespro Ltd., 10% for Microsim Ltd. and 18% for Goodlife Ltd.

If Mr. Lee invests one-third of his funds in each security to construct a portfolio, what will be his portfolio risk and return?

APPENDIX

Measuring Portfolio Risk[1]

How can we measure portfolio risk? Value-at-Risk (VaR) is a statistical tool for measuring possible loss over a defined time horizon and a defined confidence level. For instance, a 6% VaR on a portfolio of ₹1 crore at a confidence level of 99% and a holding period of one day implies that the portfolio could possibly lose up to ₹6 lakh on a given trading day but the losses are expected to exceed this number only 1% of the time or roughly 3 days (assuming 252 trading days in a year). The VaR number thus answers the question – "What level of loss is such that it will be exceeded only x% of the time over n trading days?" Here x% represents the significance level while $1 - x$% represents the confidence level. A confidence level of 99% translates to a significance level of 1%. The significance level is the probability that the actual loss may exceed the VaR estimate. The holding period and the confidence level are critical for the computation of the VaR. Higher the confidence level required, higher would be the VaR number. Similarly, the VaR number will be higher for a longer holding period.

There are three well-known methods of computing VaR: the variance-covariance or delta-normal method, historical simulation and Monte Carlo simulation. The variance-covariance method is most appropriate for portfolios with linear positions such as stock and bond portfolios. VaR estimation for portfolios with non-linear or option-like features requires the use of the other two methods.

We will focus here on the variance-covariance method of estimating VaR. The variance-covariance method assumes that portfolio returns follow a normal distribution. Since the VaR is an estimate of loss or downside risk we are interested only in the 'left tail' of the distribution. For a given confidence level α we would like to identify a number such that the probability mass below this number is 100 minus α. This number is known as the quantile of the standard normal distribution. Now since the variance-covariance method assumes that the portfolio returns are distributed normally, we can easily determine the quantile corresponding to the required confidence level. For instance, under a bell-shaped curve we can be certain that 95% of the observations will lie within 1.645 standard deviations from the mean. The number 1.645 represents that quantile of the standard normal distribution below which only 5% of the observations will lie. Hence the VaR estimate at the 95% confidence level is simply the portfolio loss times 1.645.

The computation of VaR for a pure stock portfolio using the variance-covariance method is illustrated below. Let us suppose that a fund manager with a stock portfolio of ₹10 crore has a holding period of 10 days and the required confidence level is 99%. He wants to know the level of portfolio loss that will not be exceeded over his holding period with a 99% probability. The first step is to estimate the portfolio volatility. This would require estimates of the volatilitiesfor each stock in the portfolio and the pair-wise correlations between the individual stock returns. Usually such estimates are based on historical weekly or monthly returns. This example has used monthly stock returns to estimate the volatilities and correlations. The monthly volatilities of each stock are annualized by multiplying by the square root of 12. Assuming that the portfolio is equally-weighted we arrive at an annualized volatility of 16.32% for the portfolio. The required confidence level of 99%translates to a quantile of 2.3263 for the standard normal distribution. The annualized VaR is therefore 16.32% *2.3263 which is 37.97%. However we are interested in the VaR estimate for a 10-day holding period. Hence the annualized VaR estimate is converted to a 10-day estimate by multiplying by $\sqrt{10/252}$ where 252 represents the number of trading days in a year. Thus the 10-day VaR is estimated at 7.56% of the portfolio value or ₹75.64 lakh.

[1] Contributed by Ms. Aparna Bhat, FCA, FRM, working as Assistant Professor in Department of Finance at K.J. Somaiya Institute of Management Studies and Research, Mumbai, India.

TABLE A.1 The covariance matrix for a five-stock portfolio

	CIPLA	DRREDDY	HERO	HUL	INFY	Weights
CIPLA	0.054169	0.022689	0.014888	0.018742	0.015026	**0.20**
DRREDDY	0.022689	0.06478	0.03094	0.00892	0.017357	**0.20**
HERO	0.014888	0.03094	0.082485	0.017116	0.017228	**0.20**
HUL	0.018742	0.00892	0.017116	0.055563	−0.00133	**0.20**
INFY	0.015026	0.017357	0.017228	−0.00133	0.085949	**0.20**
Weights	**0.20**	**0.20**	**0.20**	**0.20**	**0.20**	**1.00**

VaR calculation using MS Excel:

Step 1: Compute the volatilities for each stock and the pair-wise correlations.

	A	B	C	D	E	F	G	H	I	J	K
1											
2	Stock	AnnVol									
3	BHEL ret	0.335194991									
4	CIPLAret	0.23274214				CIPLA	DRREDDY	HERO	HUL	INFY	Weights
5	DRReddyret	0.25451945			CIPLA	0.054169	0.022688923	0.014888	0.018742	0.015026	0.20
6	Heromotoret	0.287202699			DRREDDY	0.022689	0.06478015	0.03094	0.00892	0.017357	0.20
7	HULret	0.235718971			HERO	0.014888	0.030939741	0.082485	0.017116	0.017228	0.20
8	Infyret	0.293171076			HUL	0.018742	0.008920205	0.017116	0.055563	-0.001329	0.20
9					INFY	0.015026	0.017357318	0.017228	-0.001329	0.085949	0.20
10					Weights	0.20	0.20	0.20	0.20	0.20	1.00
11											
12				Annualized volatility	16.32%						
13											
14				Confidence level	0.99						
15		Correlations		Holding period	10	days					
16	Cipla-Drreddy	=CORREL(Returns!L3:L61,Returns!M3:M61)									
17	Cipla-Hero	0.222722484		VaR (%)	7.56%						
18	Cipla-HUL	0.341622156		Portfolio value (Rs.)	10	crore					
19	Cipla-Infy	0.22022159		VaR (Rs.)	7564412.80						
20	Drreddy-Hero	0.423259953									
21	Drreddy-HUL	0.148682326									
22	DrReddy-Infy	0.232616509									
23	Hero_HUL	0.252829495									
24	Hero-Infy	0.204614423									
25	HUL_Infy	-0.019230503									

	A	B	C	D	E	F	G	H	I	J	K
1											
2	Stock	AnnVol									
3	BHEL ret	0.335194991									
4	CIPLAret	0.23274214				CIPLA	DRREDDY	HERO	HUL	INFY	Weights
5	DRReddyret	0.25451945			CIPLA	0.054169	0.022688923	0.014888	0.018742	0.015026	0.20
6	Heromotoret	0.287202699			DRREDDY	0.022689	0.06478015	0.03094	0.00892	0.017357	0.20
7	HULret	0.235718971			HERO	0.014888	0.030939741	0.082485	0.017116	0.017228	0.20
8	Infyret	0.293171076			HUL	0.018742	0.008920205	0.017116	0.055563	-0.00133	0.20
9					INFY	0.015026	0.017357318	0.017228	-0.00133	0.085949	0.20
10					Weights	0.20	0.20	0.20	0.20	0.20	1.00
11											
12				Annualized volatility	=SQRT(MMULT(F10:J10,MMULT(F5:J9,K5:K9)))						
13											
14				Confidence level	0.99						
15		Correlations		Holding period	10	days					
16	Cipla-Drreddy	0.383016847									
17	Cipla-Hero	0.222722484		VaR (%)	7.56%						
18	Cipla-HUL	0.341622156		Portfolio value (Rs.)	10	crore					
19	Cipla-Infy	0.22022159		VaR (Rs.)	7564412.80						
20	Drreddy-Hero	0.423259953									
21	Drreddy-HUL	0.148682326									
22	DrReddy-Infy	0.232616509									
23	Hero_HUL	0.252829495									
24	Hero-Infy	0.204614423									
25	HUL_Infy	-0.019230503									
26											

Step 2: Build the variance-covariance matrix for the portfolio and compute the annualized portfolio volatility.

Step 3: Compute the quantile corresponding to the confidence level α using the Excel function NORMSINV and multiply this by the portfolio percentage volatility to get the percentage VaR on an annual basis. Multiply this number by a factor of $\sqrt{10/252}$ in order to get the percentage VaR for a holding period of 10 days.

Step 4: The percentage VaR computed in step 3 is multiplied by the value of the portfolio to get the VaR in rupees.

	A	B	C	D	E	F	G	H	I	J	K
1											
2	Stock	AnnVol									
3	BHEL ret	0.335194991									
4	CIPLAret	0.23274214				CIPLA	DRREDDY	HERO	HUL	INFY	Weights
5	DRReddyret	0.25451945			CIPLA	0.054169	0.022688923	0.014888	0.018742	0.015026	0.20
6	Heromotoret	0.287202699			DRREDDY	0.022689	0.06478015	0.03094	0.00892	0.017357	0.20
7	HULret	0.235718971			HERO	0.014888	0.030939741	0.082485	0.017116	0.017228	0.20
8	Infyret	0.293171076			HUL	0.018742	0.008920205	0.017116	0.055563	-0.00133	0.20
9					INFY	0.015026	0.017357318	0.017228	-0.00133	0.085949	0.20
10					Weights	0.20	0.20	0.20	0.20	0.20	1.00
11											
12				Annualized volatility	16.32%						
13											
14				Confidence level	0.99						
15		Correlations		Holding period	10	days					
16	Cipla-Drreddy	0.383016847									
17	Cipla-Hero	0.222722484		VaR (%)	=NORMSINV(E14)*E12*SQRT(E15/252)						
18	Cipla-HUL	0.341622156		Portfolio value (Rs.)	10	crore					
19	Cipla-Infy	0.22022159		VaR (Rs.)	7564412.80						
20	Drreddy-Hero	0.423259953									
21	Drreddy-HUL	0.148682326									
22	DrReddy-Infy	0.232616509									
23	Hero_HUL	0.252829495									
24	Hero-Infy	0.204614423									
25	HUL_Infy	-0.019230503									
26											

	A	B	C	D	E	F	G	H	I	J	K	L
1												
2	Stock	AnnVol										
3	BHEL ret	0.335194991										
4	CIPLAret	0.23274214				CIPLA	DRREDDY	HERO	HUL	INFY	Weights	
5	DRReddyret	0.25451945			CIPLA	0.054169	0.022688923	0.014888	0.018742	0.015026	0.20	
6	Heromotoret	0.287202699			DRREDDY	0.022689	0.06478015	0.03094	0.00892	0.017357	0.20	
7	HULret	0.235718971			HERO	0.014888	0.030939741	0.082485	0.017116	0.017228	0.20	
8	Infyret	0.293171076			HUL	0.018742	0.008920205	0.017116	0.055563	-0.00133	0.20	
9					INFY	0.015026	0.017357318	0.017228	-0.00133	0.085949	0.20	
10					Weights	0.20	0.20	0.20	0.20	0.20	1.00	
11												
12				Annualized volatility	16.32%							
13												
14				Confidence level	0.99							
15		Correlations		Holding period	10	days						
16	Cipla-Drreddy	0.383016847										
17	Cipla-Hero	0.222722484		VaR (%)	7.56%							
18	Cipla-HUL	0.341622156		Portfolio value (Rs.)	10	crore						
19	Cipla-Infy	0.22022159		VaR (Rs.)	7564412.80							
20	Drreddy-Hero	0.423259953										
21	Drreddy-HUL	0.148682326										
22	DrReddy-Infy	0.232616509										
23	Hero_HUL	0.252829495										
24	Hero-Infy	0.204614423										
25	HUL_Infy	-0.019230503										
26												

Closer Look at Security Risk Premiums: Sharpe's Single Index Model

5

CHAPTER OBJECTIVES

- Discussing the basic tenets of the single index model
- Assessing systematic and unsystematic risk of individual securities and portfolio
- Evaluating beta-excess return relationship
- Constructing optimal risky using single index model

Markowitz Portfolio optimization, introduced in the previous chapter, suffers from some serious drawbacks. The key issue with MPT is that it is highly information intensive and the number of inputs required for making portfolios comprising large number of assets severely hinders its operationality.

The solution to this problem of MPT was put forth by William Sharpe[1] who took a cue from Markowitz' seminal contribution in which he had suggested the use of an index for generating the required covariances. Sharpe developed a single index model that simplified computations and brought down the number of inputs for portfolio analysis to $3N+2$ from $N(N+3)/2$ required by Markowitz Model.

Single Index Model

Sharpe used a broad index of securities (like S&P BSE SENSEX or S&P 500 or STI) as a proxy for measuring the change in expected return of a security due to macroeconomic factors. Sharpe's model is also called market model as it assumes that the co-movement between two stocks is due to their movement with the index representing the market as a whole. The model implies that the rates of returns of securities are correlated on account of their individual relationship with some basic underlying factors. The sensitivity of a stock to the movement in the market index is measured by beta. Sharpe's model or the single index model is symbolically expressed as:

$$r_i = \alpha_i + \beta_i r_m + e_i \tag{1}$$

[1] William F. Sharpe, "A Simplified Model of Portfolio Analysis," *Management Science*, January 1963.

where

r_i = Return on security i

r_m = Return on market

α_i = Intercept giving constant return

β_i = Measure of the sensitivity of security's return to that of the market index

e_i = Error term

Equation (1) represents the equation for calculation of return on individual security. Since the index model is linear, α_i (intercept) and β_i (slope) can be estimated on the index using a single-variable linear regression.[2]

To estimate the regression, historical data of paired observation $R_i(t)$ and $R_m(t)$ are obtained. t denotes the date of the observation. The regression equation may be expressed as:

$$r_i(t) = \alpha_i + \beta_i r_m(t) + e_i(t) \tag{2}$$

where α_i is that value of security's expected excess return when the excess return of the market is zero. β_i is the slope of the regression equation and it measures the amount by which a security's return increases or decreases in response to 1% increase or decrease in return on the index. e_i is the firm-specific surprise factor in the security's return. It is called residual. It captures the difference between the actual return and the expected return, given a market index return.

The single index model is based on certain assumptions:

1. The error term (e_i) is a zero mean term with finite variance. Its covariance with the market portfolio is zero.
2. Securities have no other relationship except the one expressed through their common response to the return on market index. Thus, the error term of one security has no connection with the error term of another security.

$$\text{Cov}\,(e_i, e_j) = 0$$

3. The expected value of error term is zero.

$$E(e_i) = 0$$

Risk Return Relationship in Single Index Model

It is known that the return parameter to be used in the context of an individual security or a portfolio is called expected return. Sharpe's model also gives an equation or formula for the computation of the expected return of a security.

Further, the risk calculations of Sharpe's model differ from MPT. In addition to the use of variance, beta is also used as a measure of risk. Let us understand the risk-return calculations using the single index model.

[2] Some practitioners regress excess return of a security $r_i - r_f$ on excess return of the market, while others use total returns. This is done usually when daily data is used. In such cases, the value of r_f is so small that there is barely any difference between total and excess returns.

Beta – Expected Return Relationship

Since $E(e_i) = 0$, we can rewrite equation (1) to obtain the relationship between expected return of a security and its beta.

$$E(r_i) = \alpha_i + \beta_i E(r_m) \tag{3}$$

Thus, the single index model divides the return on a security into two components:

1. a unique part, α_i
2. a market-related part, β_i

The unique part is related to a micro event, affecting an individual company and the market related part is a macro event that is broad-based and affects all (or most) of the firms.

The first term of the equation, α_i is a measure of non-market premium. If a security is under-priced, the alpha value may be large and it may offer an attractive expected return. When security prices are in equilibrium, i.e., all securities are fairly priced, value of α is driven to zero. However, for our purpose, let us assume that security analysts come up with their own estimate of alpha. Managers forecast alpha on the basis of the confidence that they can find stocks with non-zero alpha through superior security analysis.

Variance, Covariance and Correlation as Measures of Risk

Both, the variances of individual securities and the covariance between any pair of security under this model are determined by the security betas and the properties of the chosen market index.

1. **Variance:** According to this model, for any security

   Total risk = Systematic risk + Unique or firm specific risk

   Symbolically,

$$\sigma_i^2 = \beta_i^2 \sigma_m^2 + \sigma^2(e_i) \tag{4}$$

   $\beta_i^2 \sigma_m^2$ is the variance due to the uncertainty of the market index and it is called the systematic risk of the security. $\sigma^2(e_i)$ is the variance due to firm-specific uncertainty. It is also called residual variance. According to Sharpe, systematic risk is the risk explained by the index and unsystematic risk is the risk that is not explained by the index. The coefficient of determination (R^2) tells us the percentage of the variance of a security's return that is explained by the variation of return on the index (or market).
2. **Covariance:** Covariance between any pair of securities is computed in this model as product of the respective betas and the variance of the market.[3]

   Cov (r_i, r_j) = Product of betas × Variance of market index

$$\text{Cov}(r_i, r_j) = \beta_i \beta_j (\sigma_m^2) \tag{5}$$

[3] α_i can be dropped from the covariance terms because it is a constant and thus has zero covariance with all variables.

The value of covariance is equal to 0, if beta of either security is zero, i.e., either security is not impacted by market news. Covariance is > 0, if both securities have positive beta or both have negative beta, i.e., their returns move in the same direction and covariance is < 0, if one security has positive beta and the other has negative beta, i.e., returns of both move in opposite direction.

The covariance between the return on stock *i* and the market index is given as:

$$\text{Cov}\,(r_i, r_m) = \beta_i\,(\sigma_m^2) \tag{6}$$

The error term has no covariance with the market as it is firm-specific or non-systematic component and is independent of the market wide or systematic component. Therefore, $\text{Cov}\,(e_i, r_m) = 0$.

3. **Correlation:** Correlation between two securities, *i* and *j* may be given as the product of correlations of *i* and *j* with the market.

We know,

$$\text{Corr}\,(r_i, r_j) = \frac{\text{Cov}\,(r_i, r_j)}{\sigma_i \sigma_j}$$

Substituting the value of covariance from equation (5), we get

$$\text{Corr}\,(r_i, r_j) = \frac{\beta_i \beta_j (\sigma_m^2)}{\sigma_i \sigma_j}$$

Multiplying and dividing the above equation by σ_m^2, we get

$$\text{Corr}\,(r_i, r_j) = \frac{(\beta_i \sigma_m^2)(\beta_j \sigma_m^2)}{(\sigma_i \sigma_m)(\sigma_j \sigma_m)} \tag{7}$$

or

$$\text{Corr}\,(r_i, r_j) = \text{Corr}\,(r_i, r_m) \times \text{Corr}\,(r_j, r_m)$$

i.e., correlation of two securities, *i* and *j*, is a product of the correlation of each with the market.

Equations (3) and (4) indicate that the single index model can be computed through estimation of three parameters viz., α, β and $\sigma(e)$ for individual securities in addition to the market index risk premium and variance, which is same for all securities. All these values can be estimated through ex-post analysis and/or judgmental evaluation. Let us understand the model with the help of Numerical Examples.

Numerical Example 1

Use the information given below to compute the following for Biz Tech Ltd.:

1. Total variance
2. Variance explained by the index

Year	Biz Tech Ltd	Market index
1	5	40
2	10	30
3	6	20
Average	7	30
Variance	4.7	66.7
Beta	−0.04	
Coefficient of Determination	0.036	

Solution:

1. **Total Variance:** The total risk of a security may be calculated as:

$$\sigma_i^2 = \beta_i^2 \sigma_m^2 + \sigma^2(e_i)$$

$\beta_i^2 \sigma_m^2$ represents the systematic risk and may be computed for Biz Tech as:

$$= (-0.04)^2 + (66.7)$$

$$= 0.17$$

Unsystematic risk of Biz Tech may be calculated as:

Total variance – Systematic risk

$$= 4.7 - 0.17$$

$$= 4.53$$

Alternately, unsystematic risk of Biz Tech may be calculated as:

Total variance (1-coefficient of determination)

$$= 4.7\ (1 - 0.036)$$

$$= 4.53$$

2. **Variance Explained by the Index:** Variance explained by the index is systematic risk. We have calculated it above. It is equal to 0.17.

Alternately, variance explained by index = Total variance × Coefficient of determination

$$= 4.7 \times 0.036$$

$$= 0.17$$

Numerical Example 2

Three stocks, Aura Atomsphere Ltd. Luxury Lifestyle Ltd. and Indoor Solutions Ltd. comprise the financial market and satisfy single-index model. Following information is available about them:

Stock	Capitalization (₹ in million)	Beta	Mean excess Return (%)	Standard Deviation (%)
Aura Atomsphere Ltd.	3000	1	11	40
Luxury Lifestyle Ltd.	2000	0.3	3	29
Indoor Solutions Ltd.	1500	1.6	16	51
Market Index				25

Compute the following on the basis of the information given above:

1. The mean excess return of the index
2. Variance of Luxury Lifestyle Ltd., split into the two components
3. Covariance between Luxury Lifestyle Ltd. and the index
4. Covariance between Luxury Lifestyle Ltd. and Aura Atmosphere Ltd.

Solution:

Since the market comprises only three stocks, the total market capitalization = 3000 + 2000 + 1500 = 6500.

1. **The Mean Excess Return of the Index:**

$$= \frac{3000}{6500} \times 11 + \frac{2000}{6500} \times 3 + \frac{1500}{6500} \times 16$$

$$= 9.69\%$$

2. **Variance of Luxury Lifestyle Ltd., Split into the Two Components:**
We know, variance of a stock using single index model is computed as:

$$\sigma_i^2 = \beta_i^2 \sigma_m^2 + \sigma^2(e_i)$$

Systematic risk ($\beta_i^2 \sigma_m^2$) of Luxury Lifestyle Ltd.

$$= (0.3)^2 \times (.25)^2$$

$$= 0.005625$$

Firm specific risk ($\sigma^2(e_i)$) of Luxury Lifestyle Ltd.

$$= \sigma_i^2 - \beta_i^2 \sigma_m^2$$

$$= (0.29)^2 - (0.3)^2 \times (.25)^2$$

$$= 0.078475$$

3. **Covariance Between Luxury Lifestyle Ltd. and the Index:**
We know, covariance between a stock and the index is computed as

$$\text{Cov}(r_i, r_m) = \beta_i (\sigma_m^2)$$

$$= 0.3 \times (.25)^2$$

$$= 0.01875$$

4. **Covariance Between Luxury Lifestyle Ltd. and Aura Atomsphere Ltd.:**
We know, covariance between two stocks is computed as:

$$\text{Cov}(r_i, r_j) = \beta_i \beta_j (\sigma_m^2)$$

$$= 0.3 \times 1 \times (.25)^2$$

$$= 0.01875$$

Security Characteristic Line

Sharpe's single index model is represented by the equation:

$$r_i = \alpha_i + \beta_i r_m + e_i$$

It is the equation for calculation of return on individual security. Since the index model is linear, α_i (intercept) and β_i (slope) can be estimated on the index using a single-variable linear regression. The regression equation, as illustrated in the beginning of the chapter, may be expressed as:

$$r_i(t) = \alpha_i + \beta_i r_m(t) + e_i(t)$$

Security characteristic line (SCL) is the graphical illustration of the above equation. SCL is a regression line that represents the relationship between the returns on the stock and the returns on the market over a period of time in the past (It can be used to forecast the future, assuming the future will be similar to the past).

Some authors plot excess returns (returns net of risk-free rate) of the market index and the security, while others use total returns.

In practice also, alpha and beta are actually calculated by taking total returns[4] (as we will do later in the chapter while discussing spreadsheet application of the model) and not the excess return. The reason is that changes in $r_f(1-\beta)$ on monthly basis are so small that its impact is swamped by the actual stock return volatility. This kind of computation leads to a different value of alpha from the one which is computed using the following regression equation: $r - r_f = \alpha + \beta(r_m - r_f) + e$ which represents the original Sharpe's model.

The slope of the characteristic line is the Beta Coefficient. The degree to which the characteristic line explains the variability in returns on the stock (the dependent variable) is measured by the coefficient of determination or *r*-squared.

If the coefficient of determination is equal to 1.00, it would imply that all the points of observation would lie on SCL. This would mean that the characteristic line explains 100% of the variability of the dependent variable (the stock returns).

Figure 5.1 Security characteristic line.

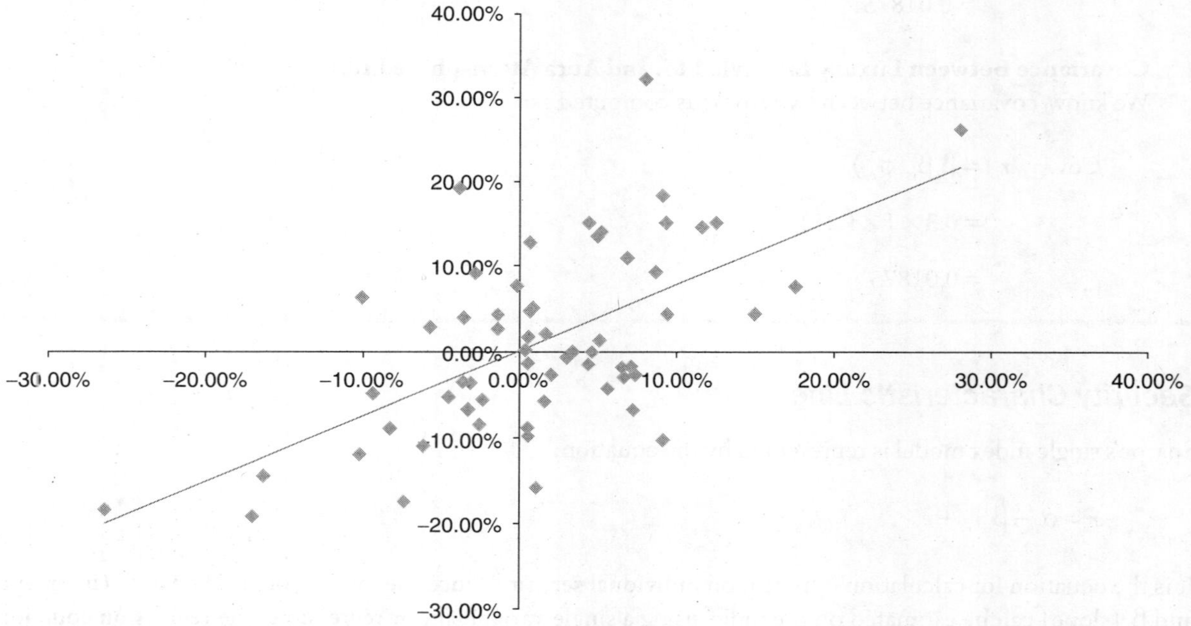

The alpha is the vertical intercept of the characteristic line. Many analysts and portfolio managers search out stocks with high alphas. Figure 5.1 exhibits SCL with alpha equal to zero.

[4] Merill Lynch also uses total returns in computation of regression output.

Spreadsheet Application 1 *Generating security characteristic line using MS Excel.*

Use L&T Ltd's monthly return data with the data of S&P BSE SENSEX for a period from January 2009 through December 2013 to generate its security characteristic line (SCL).

Solution:

We need to calculate α and β of L&T to generate its SCL.

Alpha and beta values of L&T are obtained by regressing its returns on those of SENSEX.

Spreadsheet exhibited below shows the regression statistics. Beta of L&T = 1.5895 and Alpha = −0.141. *R* Square value of 0.5383 indicates that 53.83 % of the variance in L&T's returns is explained by the index.

Let us understand the output of regression analysis in detail. The value of multiple *R* equal to 0.7383 is quite high, indicating that L&T follows the movement in SENSEX quite closely. The second statistic, *R* square (0.5451), indicates that 54.51% of variance in returns of L&T is attributable to the variation in the returns of SENSEX. The third statistic, adjusted *R* square, is 0.5371 (slightly less than R^2) as it corrects for an upward bias in the value of R^2 coming from the use of the fitted values of α and β. With the number of observations we have used, this bias is quite small. Next statistic is standard error, which we will discuss a little later.

Moving to analysis of variance, SS represents sum of squares (0.5941). It indicates the portion of the variance of L&T that is explained by SENSEX, the independent variable. (It is measured as $\beta_i^2\sigma_m^2$). The residual value in MS column (0.0087) represents the portion of returns of L&T that is independent of SENSEX. Standard error, mentioned earlier, is nothing but square root of this value of MS. Standard error of regression is nothing but standard deviation of residuals. In the end, we have the α value of −0.0144 which is statistically insignificant and the null hypothesis of the true value of alpha being zero cannot be rejected. Even if alpha is economically and statistically significant, its value cannot be used for future forecast.

This is the reason why security analysis is so challenging. The last and the most important statistic is beta. Here the beta value is 1.5935 with standard error of 0.1928. It is statistically significant, thereby rejecting the null hypothesis that L&T's true beta is zero.

SUMMARY OUTPUT								
Regression Statistics								
Multiple R	0.73832417							
R Square	0.54512259							
Adjusted R Square	0.53714228							
Standard Error	0.09325663							
Observations	59							
ANOVA								
	df	*SS*	*MS*	*F*	*Significance F*			
Regression	1	0.594065144	0.59406514	68.3084862	2.49974E-11			
Residual	57	0.495717517	0.0086968					
Total	58	1.089782661						
	Coefficients	*Standard Error*	*t Stat*	*P-value*	*Lower 95%*	*Upper 95%*	*Lower 95.0%*	*Upper 95.0%*
Intercept	-0.0144051	0.012425717	-1.1592999	0.25116745	-0.039287204	0.01047694	-0.0392872	0.010476936
X Variable 1	1.5935261	0.192806579	8.26489481	2.4997E-11	1.207437581	1.97961461	1.207437581	1.979614611

Since beta is positive, L&T's returns should move in the same direction as the market. Plot of L&T's returns, exhibited below, confirms L&T's movement in the same direction as the market. However, the volatility of L&T's returns is higher. This is due to beta value of more than 1.

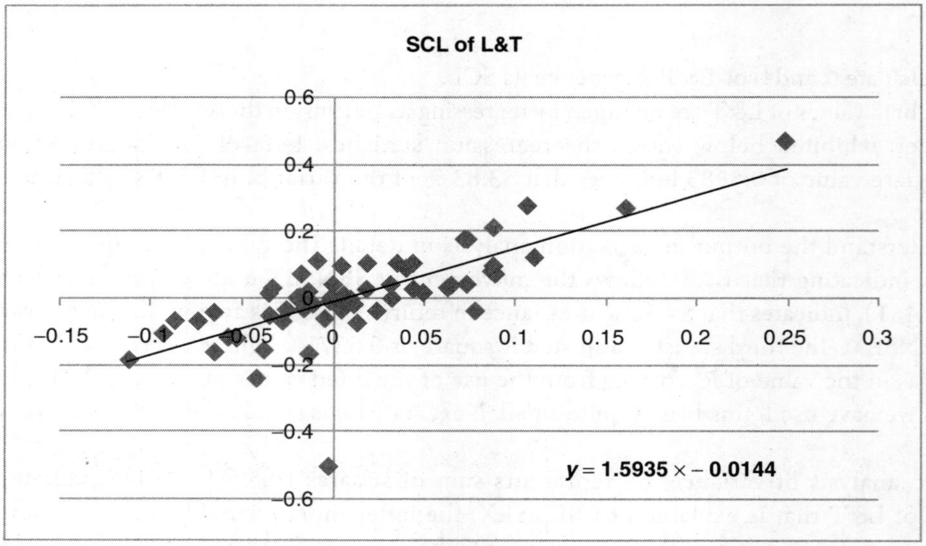

Since Beta of L&T = 1.5935 and Alpha = −0.0144, the equation of the regression line may be given as:

$$y = 1.5935 \times -0.0144.$$

This regression line is SCL and it is plotted as given below:

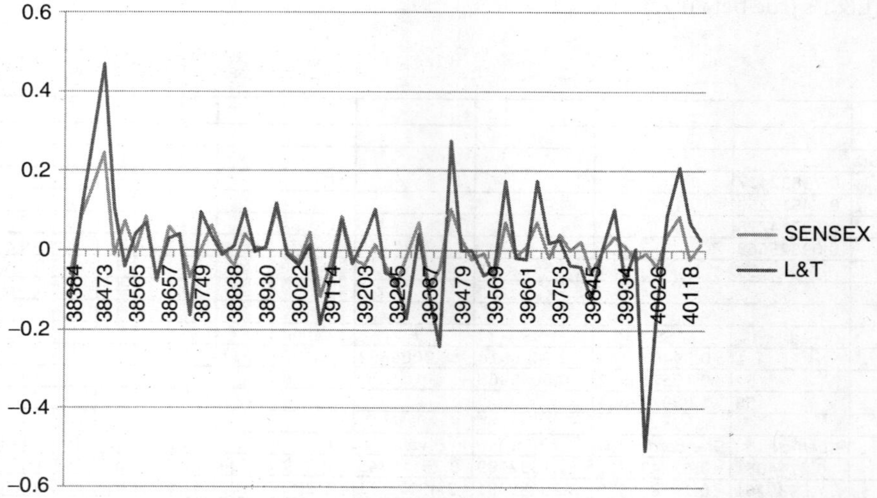

Application of the single index model for diversification

So far we have discussed the single index model in the context of individual stocks. The single index model and its risk-return computation can also be used for diversification, i.e., for construction of a portfolio.[5] For portfolio, equation (1) can be rewritten as:

$$R_p = \alpha_p + \beta_p r_m + e_p \tag{8}$$

where
R_p = Return on portfolio
r_m = Return on market
α_p = Intercept giving constant return
β_p = Measure of the sensitivity of portfolio's return to that of the market index
e_p = Error term

It is observed that as the number of stocks in the portfolio increases, the portfolio risk coming from non-market factors becomes smaller and smaller and appropriate number of securities diversify it completely. The market risk continues to be there regardless of the number of shares in the portfolio.

Let us investigate these results for an equally-weighted portfolio of 'n' securities where weight of each security is equal to $1/n$.

The ***return of the portfolio*** may be computed as:

$$r_p = \sum_{i=1}^{n} (w_i)(r_i)$$

or

$$r_p = \frac{1}{n}\sum_{i=1}^{n} (r_i)$$

or

$$r_p = \frac{1}{n}\sum_{i=1}^{n} \alpha_i + \beta_i r_m + e_i$$

or

$$r_p = \frac{1}{n}\sum_{i=1}^{n} \alpha_i + \left(\frac{1}{n}\sum_{i=1}^{n} \beta_i\right) r_m + \frac{1}{n}\sum_{i=1}^{n} e_i \tag{9}$$

[5] Based on an optimizing model for managers seeking superior returns through security analysis. The model was proposed by Treynor and Black. Jack Treynor and Fischer Black, "How to use security analysis to improve portfolio selection," *Journal of Business*, January 1973.

From equation (8), we know portfolio's sensitivity to market is given by β_p. Since Beta of portfolio is a summation of the weighted average of the betas of the component securities of the portfolio, β_p may be measured here as:

$$\beta_p = \frac{1}{n}\sum_{i=1}^{n}\beta_i$$

The non-market component of the portfolio, return α_p in equation (8) can be measured as shown in equation (9), i.e., average of alphas of component securities.

$$\alpha_p = \frac{1}{n}\sum_{i=1}^{n}\alpha_i$$

The second non-market component e_p in equation (8) is measured as shown in equation (9), i.e., average of firm-specific random terms of component securities.

$$e_p = \frac{1}{n}\sum_{i=1}^{n}e_i$$

The ***risk of the portfolio*** may be computed as:

To generate portfolio variance, equation (4) can be rewritten as follows:

$$\sigma_p^2 = \beta_p^2\sigma_m^2 + \sigma^2(e_p) \tag{10}$$

Equation (10) represents the total risk of the portfolio. The first part, $\beta_p^2\sigma_m^2$ represents the systematic risk, which depends on market-wide movements and this risk persists irrespective of the number of stocks in the portfolio as shown in Figure 5.2:

Figure 5.2 Portfolio risk and diversification.

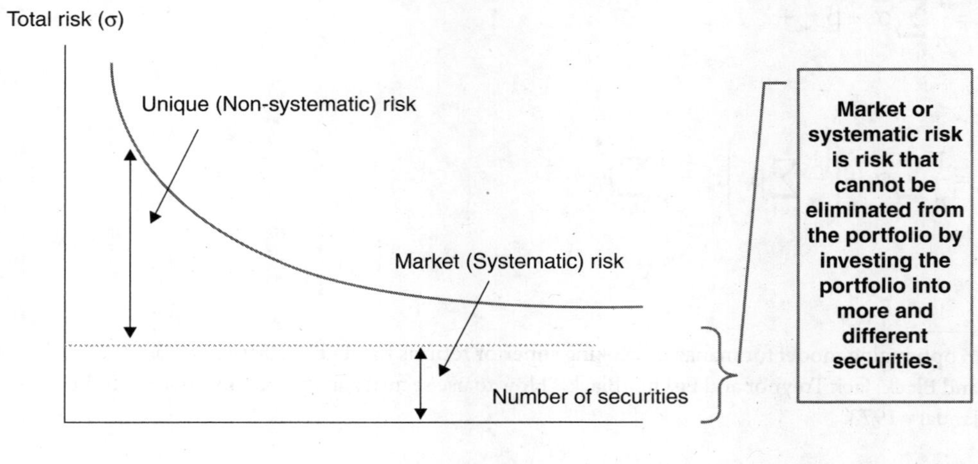

It can be argued that a zero systematic risk portfolio can be computed by including appropriate number of negative and positive beta assets in the portfolio. However, this is more of a theoretical argument than a market reality because negative beta assets are few and far between.

The second part of equation (10), $\sigma^2(e_p)$ represents the non-systematic risk of the portfolio, which is attributable to firm-specific factor, e_p. As the value of e_i for each security is independent of the other securities and all have zero expected values, the law of averages can be taken to deduce that as the number of stocks in the portfolio are increased, e_i components will tend to cancel out, making non-market risk of the portfolio negligible. Thus, the non-market risk is also called the diversifiable risk. As diversification increases, the total variance of the portfolio becomes equal to its systematic risk ($\beta_p^2 \sigma_m^2$).

Thus, the total risk of an equally weighted portfolio of 'n' securities is given by:

$$\sigma_p^2 = \sigma_m^2 \left(\sum_{i=1}^{n} \frac{1}{n} \beta_i \right)^2 + \sum_{i=1}^{n} \left(\frac{1}{n} \right)^2 \sigma^2(e_i) \tag{11}$$

Assuming that the entire diversifiable risk has been eliminated, as explained above, the portfolio risk may be measured as:

$$\sigma_p^2 = \sigma_m^2 \left(\sum_{i=1}^{n} \frac{1}{n} \beta_i \right)^2 \tag{12}$$

Generation of Optimal Risky Portfolio Using Treynor Black Model and Index Model

Generation of optimal risky portfolio requires computation of following inputs:

1. **Risk Premium and Risk of the Market Index:** These inputs are generated through macroeconomic analysis.
2. **Beta and Residual Variances $\sigma^2(e_i)$ of all Securities Under Consideration:** These inputs are generated statistically by regressing the returns of the securities to the returns of the index, say S&P BSE SENSEX.
3. **Expected Return on Individual Securities:** It is calculated using security beta and risk premium of the market index.
4. **Security Alphas:** This input is generated on the basis of the forecast of expected return using fundamental analysis and valuation models.

Comprehensive and separate macroeconomic and security-specific analysis should be undertaken to ensure consistency and accuracy in estimates.

Before we take optimal risky portfolio construction further, let us understand certain nuances of the same. Investors seeking only diversification would hold index funds which replicate the market index. However, security analysis gives investors an opportunity to identify securities with non-zero alphas and take a differential position in them. The cost of such position is departure from efficient diversification[6] and assumption of

[6] Investment in a portfolio that will give either the highest return for a given level of risk, or the lowest risk for a given level of return.

additional firm specific risk. Thus, the model shows us that optimal risky portfolio trades off search for alpha against deviation from efficient diversification.

Optimal Risky Portfolio under the model comprises active portfolio including 'n' number of actively analyzed and researched securities and a passive portfolio representing the market index, say SENSEX, which would be the $n + 1$th asset in the portfolio. As mentioned above, inputs in the form of risk premium, standard deviation, beta coefficients, alpha values and residual variances would have to be generated for making optimal risky portfolio.

The risk-return trade-off of the optimal risky portfolio comes from holding the passive portfolio that enables diversification without incurring firm-specific risk. The investment in active portfolio increases the returns of the optimal portfolio by focusing on securities with positive alpha. However, this return comes from taking additional firm-specific risk. Thus, the optimal risky portfolio trades off the search for positive alphas against deviation from the efficient diversification.

Inclusion of market index ($n + 1$th security in the portfolio) solves the problem of inadequate diversification as it might not be possible to include large number of risky securities, i.e., the investable universe of securities may be limited (either on account of resources or conditions imposed by investors).

The portfolio parameters can be estimated as:

1. **Portfolio Alpha:**

$$\alpha_p = \sum_{i=1}^{n+1} w_i \alpha_i \tag{13}$$

For index, $\alpha_{n+1} = \alpha_m = 0$

2. **Portfolio Beta:**

$$\beta_p = \sum_{i=1}^{n+1} w_i \beta_i \tag{14}$$

For index, $\beta_{n+1} = \beta_m = 1$

3. **Portfolio Residual Variance:**

$$\sigma^2(e_p) = \sum_{i=1}^{n+1} w_i^2 \sigma^2(e_i) \tag{15}$$

For Index, $\sigma^2(e_{n+1}) = \sigma^2(e_m) = 0$

4. **Portfolio Expected Return:**

$$E(r_p) = \sum_{i=1}^{n+1} w_i \alpha_i + E(r_m) \sum_{i=1}^{n+1} w_i \beta_i \tag{16}$$

It may be noted here that we have used excess return. Excess return is measured as the difference between the expected return and the prevailing t-bill rate (proxy for risk-free rate).

As explained in our section SCL, practitioners prefer to use total rather than excess returns (deviations from T-bill rates).

5. **Portfolio Risk:**

$$\sigma_p^2 = \sigma_m^2 \left\{ \sum_{i=1}^{n+1} (w_i \beta_i) \right\}^2 + \sum_{i=1}^{n+1} w_i^2 \sigma^2(e_i) \tag{17}$$

The objective of optimization process is to maximize Sharpe ratio of the portfolio by varying portfolio weights invested in the securities in the active portfolio and the index.

$$\text{Sharpe ratio} = \frac{(r_p - r_f)}{\sigma_p} \quad \text{or} \quad \frac{E(r_p)}{\sigma_p} \tag{18}$$

To take our portfolio construction further, we need to identify optimal weights of 'n' assets in the active portfolio. For generating the weights, assume active portfolio (A) has a beta of 1. In such case, the optimal weight in the active portfolio would be proportional to the ratio

$$\frac{\alpha_A}{\sigma^2(e_A)} \tag{19}$$

The ratio balances the contribution of the active portfolio to returns as measured by its alpha against its contribution to portfolio variance (residual variance).

For index or passive portfolio, this proportion is equal to the ratio of the excess return on the index and the variance of the index. Symbolically,

$$\frac{E(r_m)}{\sigma_m^2}$$

Hence, given that its beta is 1, the initial weight of active portfolio may be computed as

$$w_A' = \frac{((\alpha_A/\sigma^2(e_A))}{(E(r_m)/\sigma_m^2)} \tag{20}$$

As beta of active portfolio increases, the correlation between the active and passive (market index) portfolio also increases. This leads to increased weight of active portfolio and consequently decrease in passive portfolio weight. The new weight may be given as

$$w_A = \frac{w_A'}{(1 + (1 - \beta_A) w_A')} \tag{21}$$

When beta $= 1$, $w_A = w_A'$

Since the overall portfolio (comprising active and passive portfolios) weight is 1, the weight of passive portfolio in $1 - w_A$.

We now have active portfolio's alpha, beta and residual variance and the respective weight of the two portfolios. We can use these to compute portfolio's expected return, variance and Sharpe ratio.

The Sharpe ratio of an optimally constructed risky portfolio (A) will exceed the Sharpe ratio of the index portfolio (the passive strategy). The relationship may be expressed symbolically as:

$$S_p^2 = S_m^2 + \left(\frac{\alpha_A}{\sigma(e_A)}\right)^2 \tag{22}$$

Thus, Sharpe ratio of the overall portfolio (S_p) is equal to the sum of the Sharpe ratio of the index (S_m) plus $\alpha_A/\sigma(e_A)$.

The term $\alpha_A/\sigma(e_A)$ represents contribution of the active portfolio to the Sharpe ratio of the overall risky portfolio when the weight of the active portfolio is optimal (w_A). This ratio is called the ***information ratio*** and it measures the extra returns an investor can earn by finding non-zero alpha securities through security analysis vis-a-vis the additional firm specific risk (incurred by investor when he over-weighs or under-weighs securities relative to market index). The quantitative implication of equation (22) is that Sharpe ratio of the overall portfolio can be maximized by maximizing the information ratio of portfolio A.

For computing weights of individual securities in active portfolio, the decision rule is that the Sharpe ratio of active portfolio becomes maximized when the weight of each security is in the proportion of $\alpha_i/\sigma^2(e_i)$ (ratio of security's alpha and its residual variance) and total active portfolio weight is equal to w_A.

$$w_i = w_A \frac{\alpha_i/\sigma^2(e_i)}{\sum_{i=1}^{n} \alpha_i/\sigma^2(e_i)} \tag{23}$$

Further, we see that contribution of each security to the active portfolio's information ratio depends on its own information ratio, i.e.

$$\left(\frac{\alpha_A}{\sigma(e_A)}\right)^2 = \sum_{i=1}^{n}\left(\frac{\sigma_i}{\sigma(e_i)}\right)^2 \tag{24}$$

The model reveals the significance of information ratio in taking advantage of superior security analysis, whereby an analyst is able to find securities with positive risk premium for non-market risk (α). Of course, he will have to accept the increase in portfolio variance due to the increase in firm specific risk (residual variance).

We can observe from equation (23) that a security will have short position in optimal risky portfolio if its alpha is negative. If shorting is not allowed, such a security will have to be taken out of the active portfolio. It can also be stated that as the number of securities with positive non-zero alphas increase (if short position are prohibited), the active portfolio becomes better diversified and its weight in overall portfolio (active + passive) increases, causing a decrease in the weight of the passive portfolio.

The optimization procedure detailed above may be summarized as:

1. Determine initial weight of each security in the portfolio as:

$$w_i' = \frac{\alpha_i}{\sigma^2(e_i)}$$

2. Scale the initial weights determined above to make portfolio weights to sum to 1.

$$w_i = \frac{w_i'}{\sum_{i=1}^{n} w'}$$

3. Compute non-market risk premiums or alphas of the active portfolio.

$$\alpha_A = \sum_{i=1}^{n} w_i \alpha_i$$

4. Compute the residual variance of the active portfolio.

$$\sigma^2(e_A) = \sum_{i=1}^{n} w_i^2 \sigma^2(e_i)$$

5. Calculate the initial position of portfolio A, assuming beta = 1.

$$w_A' = \frac{(\alpha_A/\sigma^2(e_A))}{(E(r_m)/\sigma_m^2)}$$

6. Compute the beta of the active portfolio.

$$\beta_A = \sum_{i=1}^{n} w_i \beta_i$$

7. Adjust or scale the initial weight/position in active portfolio.

$$w_A = \frac{w_A'}{(1+(1-\beta_A)w_A')}$$

Weight of passive portfolio (w_m) in optimal risky portfolio $= 1 - w_A$
Weight of each security in the active portfolio $= w_A w_i$

8. Risk premium of the optimal risky portfolio.

$$E(r_p) = w_A \alpha_A + (w_m \beta_m + w_A \beta_A)\, E(r_m)$$

Since $\beta_m = 1$,

$$E(r_p) = w_A\alpha_A + (w_m + w_A\beta_A)\,E(r_m)$$

9. Compute the variance of the overall portfolio.

$$\sigma_p^2 = (w_m\beta_m + w_A\beta_A)^2\sigma_m^2 + (w_A\sigma(e_A))^2$$

Since $\beta_m = 1$,

$$\sigma_p^2 = (w_m + w_A\beta_A)^2\sigma_m^2 + (w_A\sigma(e_A))^2$$

Spreadsheet Application 2 *Implementing Sharpe's single index model using MS Excel.*
Generate optimal risky portfolio using ITC, Reliance Industries, NTPC, L&T and ICICI Bank as component securities and S&P BSE SENSEX as the market index.

Solution:

The Treynor Black model allows us to generate optimal risky portfolios. Just like MPT, it is easy to setup the optimization process to trace the efficient frontier in this model. Assuming that the expected value of e_i is zero, the return on individual security can be computed as:

$$r_i = \alpha_i + \beta_i\, r_m$$

The above equation can be used to generate $n + 1$ expected returns if we have the estimates of α_i, β_i and risk premium of the market portfolio.

The equation for calculation of covariance between each pair of security,

$$\text{Cov}\,(r_i, r_j) = \beta_i\beta_j\,(\sigma_m^2)$$

can be used to generate covariance matrix if we have the estimates of beta coefficient and residual variances along with variance of the market index. Once risk premium and covariances are generated, optimization programme can be run just as in MPT.

Let us use the steps illustrated above to construct risky portfolio in a spreadsheet.

Standard derivation of total returns have been computed by taking the returns of the securities and the index from January 2009 through December 2013.

The beta values have been computed by regressing the returns of each stock on SENSEX using the data from January 2009 through December 2013.

All inputs including correlation with the SENSEX have been computed using MS Excel functions as explained in the previous chapter.

The systematic and the residual components have been computed using the equation $\sigma_i^2 = \beta_i^2\sigma_m^2 + \sigma^2(e_i)$. The computations are exhibited below.

	A	B	C	D	E	F	G
1	SD of Sensex	Variance of Sensex					
2	0.22	0.0484					
3							
4	Systematic & Residual Variance						
5		Beta	Beta sq	Systematic Variance	STD dev	Variance	Residual Variance
6	ITC	0.32	0.102	=C6*$B$2	0.3667	0.1345	0.1295
7	Maruti Suzuki	1.22	1.479	0.0716	0.3908	0.1527	0.0812
8	Reliance Industries	0.91	0.826	0.0400	0.3949	0.1560	0.1160
9	NTPC	0.70	0.486	0.0235	0.2326	0.0541	0.0306
10	L&T	1.59	2.539	0.1229	0.4748	0.2255	0.1026
11	ICICI Bank	1.77	3.119	0.1510	0.4342	0.1885	0.0376

High value of residual standard deviations (column E) for all six stocks show a need for diversification (You may recall that diversification is undertaken to eliminate the residual of the firm specific risk).

Risk Profile of S&P BSE SENSEX and Six Stocks may be illustrated as:

3	Table 1: Risk Profile of S&P BSE SENSEX and Six Stocks					
4						
5		Std. Dev of Total Returns	Beta	Variance of Systematic Component	Residual Variance	Correlation with the SENSEX
6	S&P BSE SENSEX	0.22	1.00	0.0484	0	1
7	ITC	0.367	0.32	0.0049	0.1295	0.19
8	Maruti Suzuki	0.391	1.22	0.0716	0.0812	0.68
9	Reliance Industries	0.395	0.91	0.0400	0.1160	0.51
10	NTPC	0.233	0.70	0.0235	0.0306	0.66
11	L&T	0.475	1.59	0.1229	0.1026	0.74
12	ICICI Bank	0.434	1.77	0.1510	0.0376	0.89

The spreadsheet window given below exhibits the covariance matrix. Variance for SENSEX and all the stocks have been computed using MS Excel. The covariance of each pair is computed using the formula $\beta_i\beta_j\,(\sigma_m^2)$.

The covariance matrix

14	Table 2: The Covariance Matrix								
15									
16			S&P BSE SENSEX	ITC	Maruti Suzuki	Reliance Industries	NTPC	L&T	ICICI Bank
17		Beta	1.00	0.32	1.22	0.91	0.70	1.59	1.77
18	S&P BSE SENSEX	1.00	0.0484						
19	ITC	0.32	0.0155	0.1345					
20	Maruti Suzuki	1.22	0.0589	0.0188	0.1527				
21	Reliance Industries	0.91	0.0440	0.0141	0.0535	0.1560			
22	NTPC	0.70	0.0337	0.0108	0.0410	0.0307	0.0541		
23	L&T	1.59	0.0771	0.0246	0.0938	0.0701	0.0538	0.2255	
24	ICICI Bank	1.77	0.0855	0.0273	0.1039	0.0777	0.0596	0.1362	0.1885

13	Risk Premiums		
14	Sensex Returns		
15	0.165		
16		Beta	Risk premium
17	ITC	0.32	=B17*$A$15
18	Maruti Suzuki	1.22	0.200
19	Reliance Industries	0.91	0.150
20	NTPC	0.70	0.115
21	L&T	1.59	0.262
22	ICICI Bank	1.77	0.291

The risk premiums are computed as $\beta_i\ E(r_m)$ (assuming no macroeconomic analysis for predicting risk premium and using total returns). In real market setting, the analysts forecast risk premium using macroeconomic analysis. This means that for the current example, the risk premium of the chosen securities is assumed to be derived solely from each security's co-movement with the market.

Alpha values have been assigned hypothetically. However, in real market setting alpha value is estimated by analysts through security analysis. Here, we should understand the importance of alpha. All firms with identical beta will have identical systematic components of their risk premiums but they will differ in their alpha components. Thus, alpha helps in distinguishing whether a security is a good buy or not. Higher the positive value of alpha, the better the security as it provides premium over and above the premium it derives from the sensitivity of its returns to the market.

Risk premium and alpha values

26	**Table 3: Risk Premium & Alpha Values**							
27								
28								
29		**S&P BSE SENSEX**	**ITC**	**Maruti Suzuki**	**Reliance Industries**	**NTPC**	**L&T**	**ICICI Bank**
30	**Alpha**	0	0.0160	0.0130	-0.0110	0.0032	-0.0060	0.0080
31	**Risk premium**	0.1646	0.0526	0.2002	0.1496	0.1147	0.2623	0.2907

Thus, a positive alpha security should be over-weighted in the overall portfolio instead of the passive alternative of using market index portfolio as a risky vehicle. Conversely, a negative alpha security is over-priced and its weight should be reduced in the portfolio. In extreme cases, a short position (if permitted) can be created by making the weight negative.

The spreadsheet window given below exhibits all the portfolio inputs described in points 1 to 9.

33	**Table 4: Optimal Risky Portfolio Parameters**									
34										
35		**S&P BSE SENSEX**	**Active Portfolio (A)**		**ITC**	**Maruti Suzuki**	**Reliance Industries**	**NTPC**	**L&T**	**ICICI Bank**
36				$\sigma^2(e)$	0.1295	0.0812	0.1160	0.0306	0.1026	0.0376
37			0.4479	$\alpha / \sigma^2(e)$	0.1235	0.1601	-0.0948	0.1045	-0.0585	0.2130
38			1.0000	$W_0(i)$	0.2758	0.3575	-0.2117	0.2334	-0.1306	0.4756
39				$[W_0(i)]^2$	0.0761	0.1278	0.0448	0.0545	0.0171	0.2262
40	α_A		0.0167							
41	$\sigma^2(e_A)$		0.0373							
42	W'_A		0.1317	**Overall**						
43	W_A	0.8661	0.1339	**Portfolio**	0.0369	0.0479	-0.0284	0.0313	-0.0175	0.0637
44	Beta	1	1.1249	1.0167	0.32	1.22	0.91	0.70	1.59	1.77
45	Risk premium	0.1646	0.2019	0.1696	0.0526	0.2002	0.1496	0.1147	0.2623	0.2907
46	Standard Deviation	0.2200	0.3140	0.2252						
47	Sharpe Ratio	0.75	0.64	0.7532						

The consolidated output of the model's portfolio optimization is given below.

	A	B	C	D	E	F	G	H	I	J
1	**Impementing Index Model with S&P BSE SENSEX and Six Stocks**									
2										
3	**Table 1: Risk Profile of S&P BSE SENSEX and Six Stocks**									
4										
5		Std. Dev of Total Returns	Beta	Variance of Systematic Component	Residual Variance	Correlation with the SENSEX				
6	**S&P BSE SENSEX**	0.22	1.00	0.0484	0	1				
7	**ITC**	0.367	0.32	0.0049	0.1295	0.19				
8	**Maruti Suzuki**	0.391	1.22	0.0716	0.0812	0.68				
9	**Reliance Industries**	0.395	0.91	0.0400	0.1160	0.51				
10	**NTPC**	0.233	0.70	0.0235	0.0306	0.66				
11	**L&T**	0.475	1.59	0.1229	0.1026	0.74				
12	**ICICI Bank**	0.434	1.77	0.1510	0.0376	0.89				
13										
14	**Table 2: The Covariance Matrix**									
15										
16			S&P BSE SENSEX	ITC	Maruti Suzuki	Reliance Industries	NTPC	L&T	ICICI Bank	
17		Beta	1.00	0.32	1.22	0.91	0.70	1.59	1.77	
18	**S&P BSE SENSEX**	1.00	0.0484							Cel C18 =B6^2
19	**ITC**	0.32	0.0155	0.1345						Cel C19 ==C$17*$B19*$B$6^2
20	**Maruti Suzuki**	1.22	0.0589	0.0188	0.1527					
21	**Reliance Industries**	0.91	0.0440	0.0141	0.0535	0.1560				
22	**NTPC**	0.70	0.0337	0.0108	0.0410	0.0307	0.0541			
23	**L&T**	1.59	0.0771	0.0246	0.0938	0.0701	0.0538	0.2255		
24	**ICICI Bank**	1.77	0.0855	0.0273	0.1039	0.0777	0.0596	0.1362	0.1885	
25										
26	**Table 3: Risk Premium & Alpha Values**									
27										
28										
29		S&P BSE SENSEX	ITC	Maruti Suzuki	Reliance Industries	NTPC	L&T	ICICI Bank		
30	**Alpha**	0	0.0160	0.0130	-0.0110	0.0032	-0.0060	0.0080		
31	**Risk premium**	0.1646	0.0526	0.2002	0.1496	0.1147	0.2623	0.2907		
32										
33	**Table 4: Optimal Risky Portfolio Parameters**									
34										
35		S&P BSE SENSEX	Active Portfolio (A)		ITC	Maruti Suzuki	Reliance Industries	NTPC	L&T	ICICI Bank
36				$\sigma^2(e)$	0.1295	0.0812	0.1160	0.0306	0.1026	0.0376
37			0.4479	$\alpha / \sigma^2(e)$	0.1235	0.1601	-0.0948	0.1045	-0.0585	0.2130
38			1.0000	$W_0(i)$	0.2758	0.3575	-0.2117	0.2334	-0.1306	0.4756
39				$[W_0(i)]^2$	0.0761	0.1278	0.0448	0.0545	0.0171	0.2262
40	α_A		0.0167							
41	$\sigma^2(e_A)$		0.0373							
42	W'_A		0.1317	**Overall**						
43	W_A	0.8661	0.1339	**Portfolio**	0.0369	0.0479	-0.0284	0.0313	-0.0175	0.0637
44	Beta	1	1.1249	1.0167	0.32	1.22	0.91	0.70	1.59	1.77
45	Risk premium	0.1646	0.2019	0.1696	0.0526	0.2002	0.1496	0.1147	0.2623	0.2907
46	Standard Deviation	0.2200	0.3140	0.2252						
47	Sharpe Ratio	0.75	0.64	0.7532						

The table given above illustrates the calculations for optimal risky portfolio. It essentially summarizes and captures information from four tables or panels above it. You may recall that while forming portfolio using MPT, we had disallowed short sales. However, in the current calculations, we are considering short sales as well. The negative signs in column G and I and row 38 show short sales for Reliance Industries and L&T. ICICI Bank constitutes nearly 48% of the total weight, showing that the portfolio formed here is relatively aggressive. Further, you may notice that securities with negative weights (short sale) also have negative α value (Table 3). The α value of active portfolio constituted here is 1.67% which is greater than α values of any of the individual α forecasts of the constituent stocks. The residual variance $(\sigma^2(e_A))$ of the active portfolio is 0.0373. Thus the weight in the active portfolio is scaled down to 0.1339 and the passive portfolio (Index portfolio of S&P BSE

SENSEX) is weighted at 0.8661. The Beta of optimal risky portfolio is 1.0167, its risk premium is 16.96% with a standard deviation of 22.52%.

There is a marginal improvement in Sharpe ratio of overall portfolio (0.7532) over the Sharpe ratio of index portfolio (0.75).

Critique of Sharpe's Single Index Model

The single index model scores over Markowitz' MPT in that it reduces the computational requirements tremendously. For example, if 100 securities are being considered for a portfolio, single index model would require only 302 inputs ($3N+2$) whereas as the inputs for Markowitz model will be 5150 ($N(N+3)/2$).

Table 5.1 exhibits the difference in computational requirements of MPT and Sharpe's single index model.

The single index model not only reduces the computational complexity but also performs well as compared to Markowitz model.

TABLE 5.1 Computational requirements of MPT and Sharpe's model

Number of Securities	Markowitz Convariances	Sharpe Index Coefficients
10	45	10
50	1,225	50
100	4,950	100
1,000	499,500	1,000
2,000	1,999,000	2,000

In his study, William Sharpe noted a lot of similarities between the efficient portfolios generated by his model and Markowitz optimization. Many other studies have also proven the same.

There is one more important advantage offered by the single index model which is crucial for specialization of effort in security analysis. Because the covariances are calculated with respect to market, the analysts can specialize in sectors without having to worry about finding common ground for calculating covariances of their sector's securities with that of the other sectors.

However, Sharpe's model suffers from limitation of being over simplistic in its assumptions about real-world uncertainty.

The simple split between systematic and firm-specific risk tends to overlook many sources of dependence in stock return, particularly those coming from industry events; happenings that affect all or many firms in an industry without affecting the market. Such an impact will not give accurate measure of return because it will ignore the fact that the residuals of the two stocks from the same industry (say Infosys and Wipro) are co-related. Sharpe's model will assume this correlation to be zero whereas Markowitz model will capture this correlation because it is based on computing covariances between each pair of securities. The Markowitz optimizer will automatically place smaller weight on both Infosys and Wipro because their higher correlation reduces their diversification value. So Markowitz model will automatically generate a portfolio with lower variance making it superior to the optimal portfolio of same stock generated using Sharpe's model.

Computation of beta values for securities has also raised many questions. You may recall, we have discussed the computation of beta and challenges in the use of beta as a proxy of systematic risk in detail in our chapter on risk and return analysis.

Despite the theoretical superiority of MPT, single index model scores due to its practicality. The 'inprinciple' edge of MPT over Sharpe's model becomes compromised because of the long number of computations that have the effect of cumulation of estimation errors, causing MPT portfolio to be inferior.

Industry practitioners are lured by the Sharpe's optimization because it provides a convenient benchmark for security analysis in the form of non-zero alpha securities.

SUMMARY

- ☑ Sharpe developed a single index model that simplified computations and brought down the number of portfolio inputs to $3N+2$ from $N(N+3)/2$ required by Markowitz Model.
- ☑ Sharpe used a broad index of securities as a proxy for measuring the change in expected return from a security due to macroeconomic factors.
- ☑ Also called the market model, Sharpe's model assumes that co-movement between stocks is due to movement in the index and the rates of return on securities are related only through their common relationships with some basic underlying factor.
- ☑ The single index model divides return into two components, a unique part, α_i and a market-related part, β_i.
- ☑ The unique part is a micro event, affecting an individual company and the market related part is a macro event that is broad-based and affects all (or most) of the firms.
- ☑ α_i is a measure of non-market premium. If a security is under-priced, the alpha value may be large and it may offer an attractive expected return.
- ☑ Managers forecast alpha on the basis of the confidence that they can find stocks with non-zero alpha through superior security analysis.
- ☑ The variances of individual securities and the covariance between any pair of security under Sharpe's model are determined by the security betas and the properties of the chosen market index.
- ☑ The model divides the total risk of investment into two parts, systematic risk and unique or firm specific risk.
- ☑ According to Sharpe, systematic risk is the risk explained by the index and unsystematic risk is the risk that is not explained by the index.
- ☑ The coefficient of determination (r_2) tells us the percentage of the variance of the security's return that is explained by the variation of return on the index (or market).
- ☑ Covariance between any pair of securities is computed in this model as product of the respective betas and the variance of the market.

- ☑ The error term has no covariance with the market as it is firm-specific or non-systematic component and is independent of the market wide or systematic component. Therefore, Cov $(e_i, r_m) = 0$.
- ☑ Correlation between two securities, *i* and *j* may be given as the product of correlations of *i* and *j* with the market.
- ☑ The model proposed by Sharpe can be used for diversification, i.e., for construction of a portfolio.
- ☑ SCL is a regression line that represents the relationship between the returns on the stock and the returns on the market over a period of time in the past.
- ☑ The slope of the characteristic line is the beta coefficient. The degree to which the characteristic line explains the variability in returns on the stock (the dependent variable) is measured by the coefficient of determination or *r*-squared.
- ☑ The alpha is the vertical intercept of the characteristic line. Many analysts and portfolio managers search out stocks with high alphas.
- ☑ Sharpe's model suffers from the limitation of being over simplistic in its assumptions about real-world uncertainty. The simple split between the systematic and firm-specific risk tends to overlook many sources of dependence in stock return.
- ☑ Despite the theoretical superiority of MPT, single index model scores due to its practicality. The 'inprinciple' edge of MPT over Sharpe's model becomes compromised because of the long number of computations that have the effect of cumulation of estimation errors, causing MPT portfolio to be inferior.
- ☑ Industry practitioners are lured by Sharpe's optimization because it provides convenient benchmark for security analysis in the form of non-zero alpha securities.

KEY WORDS

CONCEPT QUESTIONS

1. An investor planning to shift his funds from pure passive investing to actively managed portfolios has to understand certain trade-offs that he will need to make. Discuss.
2. Comparatively analyze Sharpe's single index model and MPT. Which one would you prefer to use as a practitioner? Why?

3. Discuss the term 'seeking alpha.' Bring out the nuances associated with the word 'alpha' in the context of Sharpe's single index model.
4. In what situations does the MPT prove to be superior to Sharpe's single index model?
5. The two Greek letters, alpha and beta form the cornerstones of Sharpe's market model. Discuss the difficulties that a manager could face in estimating the two parameters.
6. Practitioners usually estimate the index model using total rather than excess rates of return. Explain the statement.
7. Two ratios: Sharpe ratio and information ratio are used in Sharpe's optimization as key variables. Evaluate their role in the process of construction of optimal risky portfolio using Sharpe's Model.

PRACTICE PROBLEMS

1. Consider the stocks of WKC Ltd. and ZKH Ltd. The Index model of the two is represented as:

$$r_{\text{WKC}} = 1.1\% + 0.9r_m + e_{\text{WKC}}$$

$$r_{\text{ZKH}} = -2.1\% + 1.2r_m + e_{\text{ZKH}}$$

The standard deviation of the market index is 21% and the firm specific risk of WKC Ltd. is 841 and ZKH Ltd. is 121.

Compute the following:

a. Standard deviation of each stock.
b. Covariance between the two stocks.
c. Non-systematic standard deviation of a portfolio comprising 50% of WKC and ZKH each.

2. Compute the number of inputs required for a portfolio analysis involving 80 securities in the Markowitz and Sharpe's models. Comment on the results.
3. Use the information given below to calculate portfolio variance and returns of a portfolio spread equally across the given four stocks.

Stock	Alpha	Beta	Residual variance
SL Personal Care Ltd.	0.16	0.91	44.25
HS Broadband Ltd.	2.56	1.39	135.52
TMC Publishers Ltd.	1.45	1.76	195.68
Marer & Marer	2.56	1.19	52.02
Market Return	12%		
Market Variance	29		

4. Use the information given below to compute variance explained by the index for South Asian Paints Ltd.

Year	South Asian Paints Ltd.	Market index
Returns	9	33
Variance	5.2	68.9
Beta	–0.08	
Coefficient of determination	0.039	

5. Which stock should be preferred by a rational investor on the basis of the risk return characteristics given below?

Stock	Return	Total risk
A	0.378	0.657
B	0.257	0.195
C	0.259	0.394
D	0.564	0.499
E	0.234	0.211

6. Four stocks, Moon Cruise Liners Ltd., Adventure Travels Ltd., High Air Ltd. and Jet Motors Ltd. are the only constituents of the capital market. All four satisfy Sharpe's market model.

Stock	Capitalization (₹ in million)	Beta	Mean excess return (%)	Standard deviation (%)
Moon Cruise Liners Ltd.	5000	1.3	12	38
Adventure Travels Ltd.	3500	0.4	4	28
High Air Ltd.	2300	1.5	17	53
Jet Motors Ltd.	6800	0.95	13	47
Market Index	17600			29

Compute the following on the basis of the information given above:

a. The mean excess return of the index.
b. Variances of all four stocks split into the two components.
c. Covariance between High Air Ltd. and the index.
d. Covariance between Moon Cruise Liners Ltd. and Adventure Travels Ltd.

7. Consider following information about two stocks, ABT and VCT.

Stock	$E(r)$	Beta	Residual SD
ABT	14%	0.85	32%
VCT	19%	1.3	41%
Market Index Standard Deviation: 25%			
Risk-free rate: 7%			

Calculate the following:

a. Total risk of the two stocks.

b. Beta, standard deviation, expected return and non-systematic risk of the portfolio comprising 35% in ABT, 40% in VCT and 25% in T-bills.

8. A portfolio manager generates the following inputs from macro and micro forecasts:

Stock	$E(r)(\%)$	Beta	Res SD(%)
A	21	1.35	56
B	19	1.7	70
C	16	0.8	59
D	13	1	54

The current T-bills yield is 7%. The expected return of passive portfolio is 17% with a standard deviation of 25%. Compute expected excess returns, alphas and residual variances for the above stocks.

9. Consider two stocks A and B. Following equations represent the index model estimated from excess returns for the two stocks:

$$R_A = 4\% + 0.6\, R_M + e_A$$

$$R_B = 3\% + 1.3\, R_M + e_B$$

The standard deviation of the market index is 22%, RSQ of stock A is 0.22 and the RSQ of stock B is 0.14.

Calculate the following for A and B:

a. Standard deviation

b. Systematic and firm-specific components

10. **Case:** Regress Lupin Ltd. on S&P BSE SENSEX and plot a scatter of their total returns. Following monthly return data may be used for the same:

Month	SENSEX	Lupin Ltd.
Jan-13	19894.98	604.45
Feb-13	18861.54	585.2
Mar-13	18835.77	629.05
Apr-13	19504.18	701.7
May-13	19760.3	740.15
Jun-13	19395.81	779.6
Jul-13	19345.7	871.45
Aug-13	18619.72	800.2
Sep-13	19379.77	854.7
Oct-13	21164.52	887.15
Nov-13	20791.93	855.45
Dec-13	21170.68	908.6
Jan-14	20513.85	882.05
Feb-14	21120.12	993.45
Mar-14	22386.27	935.9
Apr-14	22417.8	989.9
May-14	24217.34	936.1
Jun-14	25413.78	1048.65
Jul-14	25894.97	1182.05
Aug-14	26638.11	1287
Sep-14	26630.51	1394.95
Oct-14	27865.83	1369.1

CASELET

Anaya, a successful young entrepreneur, is contemplating to reinvest her savings which she has kept in bank fixed deposits so far. She wants to generate higher returns than those given to her by the FDs. She has been reading that equity markets have on an average given a return of 14–15% and she is tempted to invest in equity. On the basis of her research and help of a management student, Sam, living in her apartment block, she decides to choose three stocks out of the stocks that comprise S&P BSE SENSEX. Randomly she chooses Maruti Suzuki Limited, Hero Motocorp and HUL and decides to spread her funds equally across them. Sam has downloaded data related to these three stocks and SENSEX for a period from January 2009 through December 2013. He comes up with the following information about the three stocks and SENSEX:

	Maruti Suzuki Limited	Hero Motocorp	HUL	SENSEX
Returns	26.9%	17.5%	15.9%	16.5%
Unsystematic Risk ($\sigma^2(e_i)$)	0.080	0.062	0.057	Standard Deviation: 22%
Correlation with SENSEX	0.679	0.516	0.116	
Beta	1.22	0.67	0.12	
Alpha	0.0024	0.0054	0.0116	

Use Sharpe's Single Index model to analyze the outcome of Anaya's choice.

Building up on Modern Portfolio Theory: Capital Market Theory and Factor Models

6

CHAPTER OBJECTIVES

- ❒ Analyzing the implications of risk-free borrowing and lending
- ❒ Evaluating CAPM and its implication for portfolio managers
- ❒ Understanding the role of multifactor models in asset pricing
- ❒ Discussing arbitrage portfolio and its implications

The portfolio theory introduced in Chapter 4 was the first formal attempt in the financial literature to quantify the risk and return of a portfolio. The theory discusses how investors can construct an optimal portfolio to suit their risk profile with the help of efficient diversification. Many theories to quantify portfolio risk and return and value risky assets were put forth after the pioneering work of Markowitz.

We had closed our discussion in Chapter 4 with the conversion of the curved efficient frontier of Markowitz into a straight line that is tangential to the original frontier. This was achieved by introducing risk-free assets into the portfolio of risky assets. In this chapter, we will build up on where we closed the discussion in MPT. Through our deliberations in this chapter, we will increase our understanding of optimal risky portfolios and their construction.

In addition to the above, we will draw upon Sharpe's single index model, discussed in the preceding chapter, to understand the most feted asset pricing model in financial theory namely, Capital Asset Pricing Model (CAPM).

As a result of the introduction of risk-free assets, the process of portfolio construction using MPT can be viewed to have two distinct parts:

1. Selecting of risky assets such as equity and long-term bonds, and
2. Deciding how to split the investible surplus between the risky portfolio and a risk-free asset such as a short-term Treasury bill.

Obviously, such a decision cannot be undertaken without knowing expected return-risk profile of the resultant portfolio. This chapter elaborates upon this fundamental part of the asset allocation problem. The discussion concerns Capital Market Theory (CMT) and Capital Asset Pricing Model (CAPM) that was developed by

Sharpe, Lintner and Mossin. The chapter also describes the multi-factor models developed in response to criticism of CAPM by many financial theorists.

Capital Market Theory

As mentioned above, Capital Market Theory builds on Modern Portfolio Theory. It is expected that the readers have already examined the risk-return calculations for portfolio of risky assets and derived the aggregate efficient frontier. It is important to remember that all the rational investors making their investment decision using MPT would look to maximize their utility in terms of risk and return by choosing a portfolio from efficient frontier at points where their utility curves are tangential to efficient frontier.

Capital Market Theory extends MPT to develop a model for pricing of all risky assets and culminates into CAPM that allows us to determine the required rate of return for risky assets.

Since the Capital Market Theory builds up on MPT, it shares many underlying assumptions with Markowitz' theory. The main assumptions of CMT may be listed as:

1. All investors are Markowitz' efficient investors who choose a portfolio of risky assets from the efficient frontier based on their utility function.
2. It is possible for the investors to lend or borrow any amount of money at risk-free rate of return.
3. All investors are rational and have homogeneous expectations, i.e., their probability distributions for future rates of return are identical.
4. All investors have the same single period investment horizon.
5. The investments are infinitely divisible, i.e., it is possible to buy or sell fractional shares of any asset.
6. There are no transaction costs or taxes involved in buying or selling assets.
7. There is no inflation or changes in inflation are fully anticipated. Likewise changes in interest rates are also fully anticipated.
8. The theory operates in a capital market in equilibrium where all investments are correctly priced according to their risk levels.

Many of the above assumptions seem unrealistic and cast a shadow on the usefulness of the theory. It is important to note here that these assumptions do not make the theory invalid as it has been observed that relaxing many of these assumptions such as risk-free borrowing rate, homogeneous expectations, no transaction cost and taxes, etc. does not alter the basic thrust of the theory. The usefulness of the theory in explaining the rate of return on risky assets implies that some of the unrealistic assumptions must not be significant to the basic objective of the model.

Optimal Risky Portfolio

Since capital market theory expands MPT by introducing risk-free asset in the portfolio generation process, we will begin our discuss about CMT by constructing an optimal risky portfolio. Thereafter, the impact of introduction of risk-free asset will be evaluated.

The basic aim of constructing a portfolio is to achieve the objective of maximization of returns for a given level of risk or minimization of risk for a given level of return. A portfolio of risky assets that helps us achieve this objective is called optimal risky portfolio. It is a portfolio that dominates all other portfolios. Optimal risky portfolio combines the risky assets in certain specific proportions. In investment management, a portfolio of risky assets is considered optimal when the asset proportions are such that a measure called Sharpe's ratio (we will discuss it in detail later in the chapter) is maximized.

Spreadsheet Application 1 **Calculating Optimal Risky Portfolio using MS Excel:**

Soultion:

The main steps for generating portfolio parameters are the same as described in preceding chapters. Let us begin with six securities that have standard deviation and expected returns as exhibited below:

	A	B	C
1			
2	**Scrip name**	**Std. Dev**	**Expected Returns**
3	**HERO MOTOCORP**	0.287	0.175
4	**HINDALCO**	0.433	0.186
5	**HUL**	0.236	0.159
6	**ICICI BANK**	0.434	0.197
7	**INFOSYS**	0.293	0.200
8	**ITC**	0.367	0.188

The variance-covariance matrix has been computed as exhibited below:

	HERO MOTOCORP	**HINDALCO**	**HUL**	**ICICI BANK**	**INFOSYS**	**ITC**
HERO MOTOCORP	1.000	0.408	0.253	0.357	0.205	0.215
HINDALCO	0.408	1.000	-0.066	0.669	0.264	-0.038
HUL	0.253	-0.066	1.000	0.008	-0.019	0.204
ICICI BANK	0.357	0.669	0.008	1.000	0.282	0.056
INFOSYS	0.205	0.264	-0.019	0.282	1.000	0.150
ITC	0.215	-0.038	0.204	0.056	0.150	1.000

As explained above, an optimal risky portfolio is one that maximizes the Sharpe ratio which is calculated as: $(E(r_p) - r_f)/\sigma_p$.

Portfolio expected return and risk have been computed using the MMULT function as described in Chapter 4. For calculating Sharpe ratio, risk-free rate is assumed to be 8.7%.

Set up the solver. As can be seen in the exhibit, the 'Objective' is to maximize Sharpe ratio and the constraint is that the portfolio weight should not exceed 1. We have included another constraint related to shorting. We have prevented shorting by putting the constraint that the weight of any of the stock should not go below zero. The solver window and the output optimal risky portfolio are exhibited below:

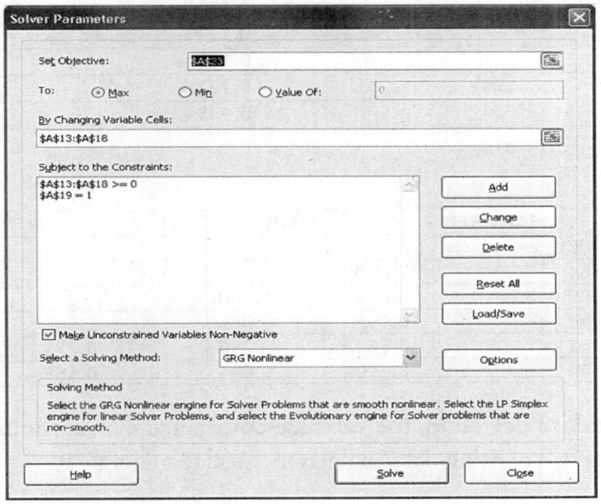

	A	B	C	D	E	F	G	H
1								
2	Scrip name	Std. Dev	Expected Returns					
3	HERO MOTOCORP	0.287	0.175					
4	HINDALCO	0.433	0.186					
5	HUL	0.236	0.159					
6	ICICI BANK	0.434	0.197					
7	INFOSYS	0.293	0.200					
8	ITC	0.367	0.188					
9								
10	Weights	Scripts						
11			HERO MOTOCORP	HINDALCO	HUL	ICICI BANK	INFOSYS	ITC
12	0.052	HERO MOTOCORP	1.000	0.408	0.253	0.357	0.205	0.215
13	0.177	HINDALCO	0.408	1.000	-0.066	0.669	0.264	-0.038
14	0.268	HUL	0.253	-0.066	1.000	0.008	-0.019	0.204
15	0.141	ICICI BANK	0.357	0.669	0.008	1.000	0.282	0.056
16	0.253	INFOSYS	0.205	0.264	-0.019	0.282	1.000	0.150
17	0.110	ITC	0.215	-0.038	0.204	0.056	0.150	1.000
18	1							
19	0.1758	Portfolio Expected Return						
20	0.0870	Risk-free rate						
21	0.3182	Portfolio Std. Dev						
22	0.279	Sharpe Ratio						

Cells A13 to A 18 exhibit the weights at which the Sharpe's ratio is maximized for the given portfolio.

Spreadsheet Application 2 **Generating efficient frontier for portfolio of risky assets using MS Excel:**

Soultion:

The main steps for generating portfolio parameters are the same as described in preceding chapters. Let us consider closing values of six indices representing equity market of six countries namely, BSE SENSEX (India), HANG SENG (Hong Kong), STI (Singapore), TSEC (Taiwan), SET (Thailand), and KOSPI (South Korea) for a period from January 2009 through December 2013. The six indices have standard deviation and expected returns as exhibited below:

	A	B	C
1		Annualized Standard Deviation	Annualized Avg. Deviation
2	SENSEX	0.179	0.068
3	HANGSENG	0.186	0.028
4	KOSPI	0.154	0.058
5	STI	0.140	0.040
6	TSEC	0.162	0.044
7	SET	0.183	0.166

Correlation Matrix

	SENSEX	HANGSENG	KOSPI	STI	TSEC	SET
SENSEX	1.000					
HANGSENG	0.584	1.000				
KOSPI	0.659	0.654	1.000			
STI	0.688	0.792	0.805	1.000		
TSEC	0.661	0.664	0.796	0.772	1.000	
SET	0.554	0.610	0.644	0.689	0.528	1.000

While using annualized standard deviation, the variance-covariance matrix should ideally be generated using the formula $\text{Cov} = r_{xy}\sigma_y\sigma_y$ instead of using data analysis in Excel to generate it.

Covariance Matrix

	SENSEX	HANGSENG	KOSPI	STI	TSEC	SET
SENSEX	0.0319	0.0194	0.0181	0.0171	0.0191	0.0182
HANGSENG	0.0194	0.0347	0.0188	0.0206	0.0200	0.0208
KOSPI	0.0181	0.0188	0.0237	0.0173	0.0198	0.0182
STI	0.0171	0.0206	0.0173	0.0195	0.0174	0.0176
TSEC	0.0191	0.0200	0.0198	0.0174	0.0261	0.0157
SET	0.0182	0.0208	0.0182	0.0176	0.0157	0.0336

As explained above, an optimal risky portfolio is one that maximizes the Sharpe ratio which is calculated as: $(E(r_p) - r_f)/\sigma_p$.

Portfolio expected return and risk have been computed using the MMULT function as described in Chapter 4.

For calculating Sharpe ratio, expected portfolio return is divided directly by portfolio standard deviation instead of using a hypothetical risk-free rate.

Set up the solver. As described in Chapter 4, the 'Objective' is to minimize portfolio standard deviation and the constraint is that the portfolio weight should not exceed 1. We have included another constraint related to shorting. We have prevented shorting by putting the constraint that the weight of any of the stock should not go below zero. This gives the minimum variance portfolio.

Thereafter, the 'Objective' is to maximize Sharpe ratio and the constraint is that the portfolio weight should not exceed 1. We have again included another constraint related to shorting. We have also prevented shorting by putting the constraint that the weight of any of the stock should not go below zero. This gives the optimal risky portfolio.

We need more portfolios to chart the efficient frontier. For this purpose in addition to the constraint on portfolio weight and short selling, another constraint has been added by setting the portfolio expected return equal to certain randomly specified values of return (obviously, the random values lie between the returns on the minimum variance portfolio and the optimal risky portfolio). The solver window with additional constraint is displayed below:

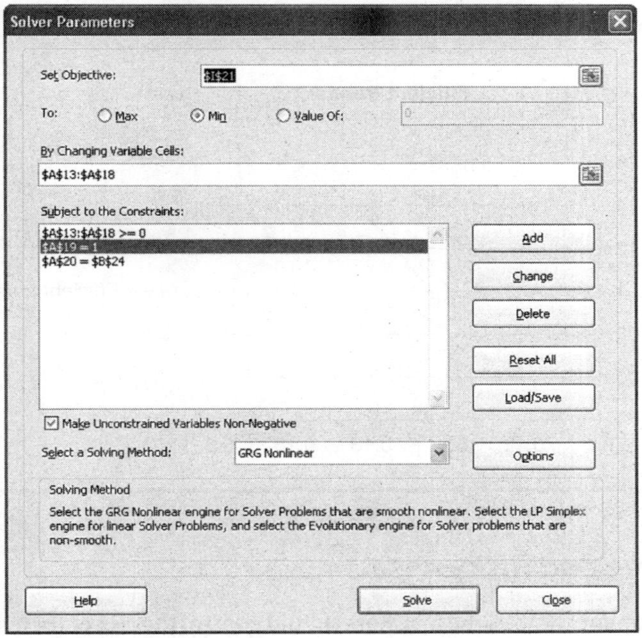

The expected return of the minimum variance portfolio is 5.35% and that of the optimal risky portfolio is 16.6%. We have used returns equal to 8%, 10%, 12%, 14% and 16% to compute other portfolios for tracing the efficient frontier. The portfolios thus generated are exhibited below:

25		Minimum Variance Portfolio	Portfolio Mean Return = .08	Portfolio Mean Return = .10	Portfolio Mean Return = 0.12	Portfolio Mean Return = 0.14	Portfolio Mean Return = 0.16	Optimal Risky Portfolio
26	**Expected return**	0.0535	0.080	0.1	0.12	0.14	0.160	0.166
27	**SD**	0.1365	0.1394	0.1450	0.1534	0.1644	0.1785	0.1834
28	**Sharpe's Ratio**	0.392	0.5741	0.689	0.782	0.852	0.8966	0.9051
29	**Weights**							
30	SENSEX	0.062	0.088	0.098	0.110	0.100	0.061	0.000
31	HANGSENG	0.000	0.000	0.000	0.000	0.000	0.000	0.000
32	KOSPI	0.151	0.135	0.123	0.112	0.041	0.000	0.000
33	STI	0.613	0.389	0.223	0.058	0.000	0.000	0.000
34	TSEC	0.103	0.112	0.122	0.130	0.096	0.000	0.000
35	SET	0.070	0.276	0.433	0.590	0.762	0.939	1.000

The above generated portfolios have been used to trace the efficient frontier using the scatter plot. The parameters specified for generating the plot are:

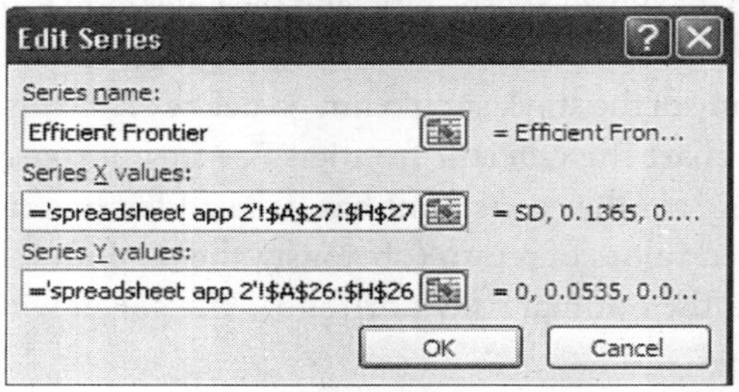

The efficient frontier generated is exhibited below:

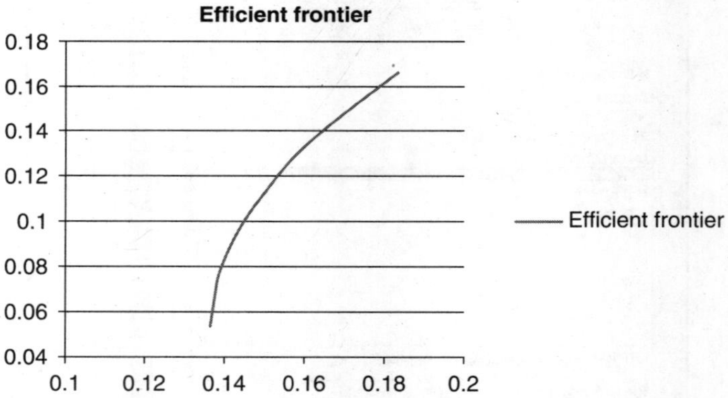

Portfolio of Risk-Free and Risky Assets

While making their investment choices, the investors should control the risk of their investment by constructing portfolios using securities from different asset classes. Some assets like stocks and bonds are risky where as other

assets like t-bills are risk-free. The simplest way to control the risk of an investment portfolio is to include some low risk security like t-bill along with a set of risky assets. Such capital allocation decision is an asset allocation decision since it implies choosing broad asset classes and not specific securities within each class. The most basic asset allocation decision is to choose how much of the portfolio fund to place in risky assets versus the risk-free instruments.

In this section, we will consider a portfolio comprising a risk-free asset and risky asset. Risk-free assets have zero standard deviation of expected returns because the expected returns are entirely certain. Since the standard deviation of risk-free assets is zero, the covariance of the returns of such assets with any other asset will always be zero. You may recall, covariance between securities is an important metric for inclusion of securities in Markowitz' portfolio.

The fact that risk-free asset has zero standard deviation simplifies the portfolio risk computations using MPT. Suppose an investor has already decided the risky portfolio he is going to invest in. The amount he allocates to this portfolio is 'x' and the expected return of this portfolio is $E(r_i)$. If such an investor decides to include risk-free asset in his portfolio, the amount that he will invest in the risk-free asset will be $(1 - x)$, i.e., total portfolio funds minus the funds allocated to the risky portfolio. Such investment in risk-free asset may be called risk-free lending. Assume that the return on risk-free asset is represented by r_f. Let us see what happens to the returns and standard deviation of the portfolio thus formed.

Expected return of the portfolio ($E(r_{port})$): We already know from Markowitz' theory that the expected return of a portfolio is equal to the sum of the expected returns of the component securities weighted by their respective share in portfolio funds.

Symbolically,

$$E(r_{port}) = xE(r_i) + (1 - x)\, r_f$$

or

$$E(r_{port}) = r_f + x(E(r_i) - r_f) \tag{1}$$

where $(E(r_i) - r_f)$ is the risk premium on the risky asset.

The result is quite easy to understand. Any portfolio's minimum/base return is equal to risk-free rate. Inclusion of risky assets makes the portfolio more risky for the investors, who being rational and risk averse, require a positive risk premium to take on a risky position. This risk premium depends on the difference between the expected return on risky portfolio and risk-free rate of return $(E(r_p) - r_f)$ and the funds allocated to risky portfolio (x).

Portfolio standard deviation: You may recall that in MPT, calculation of portfolio risk is more complex than the computation of portfolio expected returns because we need to take into consideration not only the individual standard deviation of the component securities but also their interactive risk as measured by the covariance between the returns of two securities. As we know, covariance is computed as $r_{xy}\sigma_x\sigma_y$.

As mentioned above, standard deviation of risk-free asset is zero, therefore its covariance with any other asset, risky or risk-free is zero. With the result, that the standard deviation of a portfolio comprising a risky and a risk-free asset is simply the standard deviation of the portfolio of risky asset multiplied with its proportion of funds. Variance of the portfolio of risky and risk-free assets can be calculated as:

$$\sigma^2_{port} = x^2\sigma^2_p + (1-x)^2\,\sigma_{rf} + 2\,r_{prf}\,\sigma_p\,\sigma_{rf}x(1-x) \tag{2}$$

where
r_{prf} = Correlation between the returns of risky and risk-free assets
σ_{rf} = Standard deviation of risk-free asset = 0
σ_p = Standard deviation of risky asset
x = Proportion of portfolio in risky asset
$1 - x$ = Proportion of portfolio in risk-free asset

Since $\sigma_{rf} = 0$, equation (2) can be written as

$$\sigma^2_{\text{port}} = x^2\sigma^2_p + 0 + 0$$

or

$$\sigma_{\text{port}} = x\sigma_p \tag{3}$$

Thus, the standard deviation of a portfolio that consists of a combination of risk-free and risky-assets is the linear proportion of the standard deviation of the risky asset portfolio. Several combinations of expected return-standard deviation can be obtained by creating such portfolios. The line joining all such combinations is called the Capital Allocation Line (CAL).

Capital Allocation Line

CAL is the outcome of the plotting of risk and return of the portfolio comprising risk-free asset and risky assets illustrated above. It is obtained by plotting the different combinations of expected return and standard deviation available to an investor who combines his optimal risky portfolio with a risk-free asset in the expected return-standard deviation plane. The same is exhibited in Figure 6.1.

Figure 6.1 Investment opportunity set for a portfolio of risky and risk-free assets.

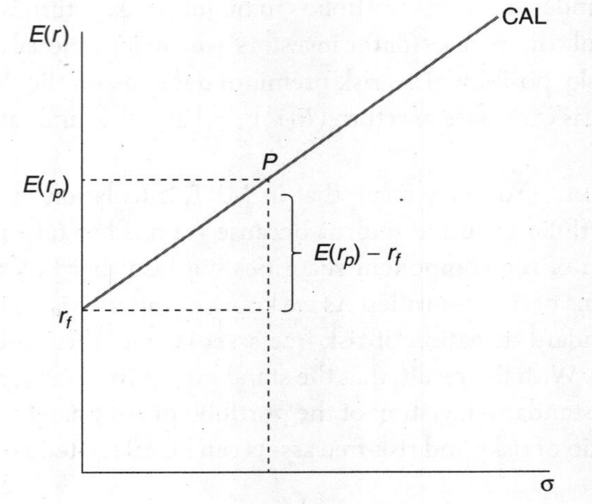

The CAL describes the expected results of an individual investor's decision on how to split his capital among risk-free and risky assets. CAL has been plotted in the expected return-standard deviation space and expresses a linear relationship between the two. The linearity of CAL implies that as the fraction of funds in the risky portfolio increase, the expected return and standard derivation also increases.

We can derive the equation of straight line connecting r_f and P by rearranging equations (1) and (3).

We know from equation (1)

$$E(r_{\text{port}}) = r_f + x(E(r_i) - r_f)$$

From equation 3 we know

$$\sigma_{\text{port}} = x\sigma_p$$

or

$$x = \frac{\sigma_{\text{port}}}{\sigma_p} \tag{4}$$

Substituting the value of x from equation (4), equation (1) can be rewritten as

$$E(r_{\text{port}}) = r_f + \left(\frac{\sigma_{\text{port}}}{\sigma_p}\right)(E(r_p) - r_f) \tag{5}$$

Thus the expected return of a portfolio of risky and risky-free assets as a function of its standard deviation is a straight line with intercept r_f and slope, S, which is measured as:

$$S = \frac{(E(r_p) - r_f)}{\sigma_p} \tag{6}$$

All points along CAL represent investment opportunity set which is a collection of feasible combinations of portfolios of risky and risk-free assets obtained by changing the value of x. This means that the different portfolios obtained by changing the amount of funds invested in the risky assets lie along the capital allocation line. An investor who wants to hold an optimal combination of risk-free and risky asset can choose a portfolio from CAL depending upon his risk tolerance. CAL offers the best risk-return trade-off achievable, given our expectations.

The slope of CAL measures the incremental return for incremental risk, i.e., increase in expected return per unit rise in standard deviation. For this reason it is called ***reward to volatility ratio or Sharpe's ratio***. Equation (5) represents the best possible risk-return trade-off, given the expectations of the investor. It is a measure of the additional return an investor demands to be induced to take an extra unit of risk. Different combinations of risk-free assets with risky portfolio along the efficient frontier can yield many capital allocation lines (CAL) as exhibited in Figure 6.2.

The CAL with highest feasible reward-to-volatility ratio is the best feasible CAL. The reward-to-volatility ratio of the best feasible CAL is given by the Sharpe's ratio of the Optimal Risky portfolio.

Figure 6.2

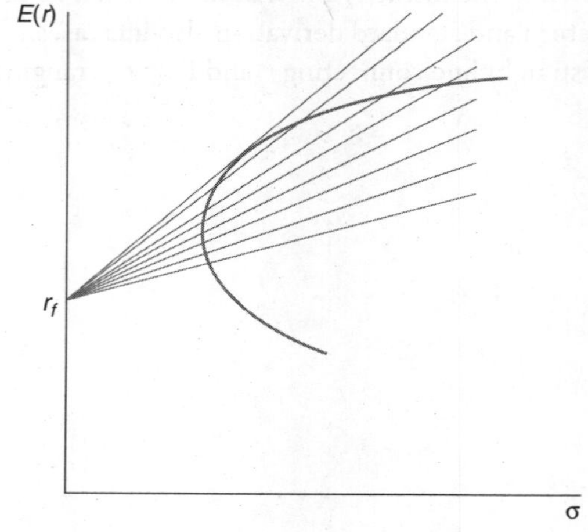

If a portfolio lies on best feasible CAL, its Sharpe's ratio is equal to the Sharpe's ratio of the optimal risky portfolio. We will discuss this concept in detail in the subsequent sections of this chapter. Before discussing CAL any further, we should explore the impact of combining risky and risk-free assets to form optimal risky portfolio.

Constructing the Optimal Risky Portfolio with Two Risky and One Risk-Free Asset

Let us assume that our optimal risky portfolio comprises only two risky assets (say stock and long-term bonds) and a risk-free asset (say *t*-bills). To compute the expected return and the standard deviation of the returns of the optimal risky portfolio comprising the three securities, we will need to first determine the optimal combination of the two risky assets that will then be mixed with the risk-free asset. Thus, we need to compute the respective proportion of each of the risky asset in the portfolio on CAL that would then be combined with the risk-free asset in certain proportion.

Our aim is to find weights that will result in the risky portfolio with the highest Sharpe's ratio (i.e., highest slope of the CAL). Thus, our objective is to maximize the slope of the CAL (refer to equation 6 for slope of CAL) for a portfolio. This means we need to maximize our objective function.

$$S = \frac{(E(r_p) - r_f)}{\sigma_p}$$

Since we want to maximize the objective function, S, we should satisfy the constraint that the portfolio weights of the two risky assets should be equal to 1.0 (100%). (In this case the weight of stock portfolio and the weight of the bond portfolio should be equal to 1).

Using standard tools of calculus, we can arrive at the weights of the two risky assets. Weight of bond portfolio in the risky portfolio comprising two assets only (stock and bond) may be computed using the following equation:

$$W_B = \frac{\{(E(r_B)-r_f)(\sigma_E^2) - \{(E(r_E)-r_f)\text{Cov}(r_B, r_E)\}}{\{(E(r_B)-r_f)(\sigma_E^2) + (E(r_E)-r_f)(\sigma_D^2) - ((E(r_B)-r_f) + (E(r_E)-r_f))\text{Cov}(r_B, r_E)\}} \quad (7)$$

Numerical Examples 1 and 2 illustrate the construction of optimal risky portfolio using risky as well as risk-free asset.

Numerical Example 1

Use the given information to compute the weights of portfolio of large cap stocks and portfolio of corporate bonds combined to form a risky portfolio to be mixed with a risk-free asset giving a rate of return equal to 5%.

	Large Cap Stocks	Corporate Bonds
Expected Return	14%	9%
Variance	225	100
Standard Deviation	15%	10%
Correlation(r_{DE})	0.5	

Solution:

The required weights can be computed using the following equation:

$$W_B = \frac{\{(E(r_B)-r_f)(\sigma_E^2) - \{(E(r_E)-r_f)\text{Cov}(r_B, r_E)\}}{\{(E(r_B)-r_f)(\sigma_E^2) + (E(r_E)-r_f)(\sigma_D^2) - ((E(r_B)-r_f) + (E(r_E)-r_f))\text{Cov}(r_B, r_E)\}}$$

Given: $E(r_B) = 9\%, E(r_E) = 14\%, r_f = 5\%, \sigma_D^2 = 100, \sigma_E^2 = 225$

All variables other than covariance are given. We know

$$\text{Covariance} = \sigma_D \, \sigma_E \, r_{DE} = 10 \times 15 \times 0.5 = 75$$

Substituting the values, we get

$$W_B = \frac{\{(9-5)(225) - \{(14-5)(75)\}}{\{(9-5)(225) + (14-5)(100) - (9-5+14-5)(75)}$$

$$= \frac{225}{825}$$

$$= 0.27$$

The weight of large cap portfolio $= 1 - 0.27 = 0.73$

Numerical Example 2

Compute the expected return and risk of the portfolio formed by combining a risk-free asset with the securities given below:

1. Large cap stock
2. Corporate bond

The key metrics are given as:

	Large Cap Stocks (A)	Corporate Bond (B)	Risk-free Asset (C)
Expected Return	16%	7%	5%
Variance	225	100	0
Standard Deviation	15%	10%	0
Correlations			
A & B	0.7		
A & C	0		
B & C	0		

Tabulate and trace the opportunity set of portfolios for both cases.

Solution:

1. Let us consider a portfolio comprising risk-free asset and large cap stock in varying proportions (x (amount invested in large cap stock) = 0, 20, 40, 60 & 100).
   The expected return of the portfolio can be calculated using the equation

$$E(r_{\text{port}}) = xE(r_i) + (1 - x)\, r_f$$

Substituting the given values, the above equation can be rewritten as:

$$E(r_{\text{port}}) = x(0.16) + (1 - x)\ (0.05)$$

The expected return of the portfolio can be calculated using the equation

$$\sigma^2_{\text{port}} = x^2\sigma^2_p + (1-x)^2\sigma_{\text{rf}} + 2\, r_{\text{prf}}\, \sigma_p\, \sigma_{\text{rf}} x(1-x)$$

Substituting the given values, the above equation can be rewritten as:

$$\sigma^2_{port} = x^2(0.15)^2 + (1-x)^2(0) + 2(0)(0.15)(0)x(1-x)$$

Varying the value of x, we get the following values of $E(r_{port})$ and σ_{port}

Large Cap Stock	Risk-free Asset	$E(r)$	σ_{port}
0	100	5.00	0.00
20	80	7.20	3.00
40	60	9.40	6.00
60	40	11.60	9.00
80	20	13.80	12.00
100	0	16.00	15.00

CAL can be traced by plotting the computed values in the expected return-standard deviation space. It is the locus of the portfolios with maximum expected return for a given level of risk. So an investor who wants to hold an optimal combination of risk-free and this large cap stock can choose a portfolio from CAL depending on his risk tolerance.

Capital allocation line for portfolio of large cap stock and risk-free asset may be exhibited as:

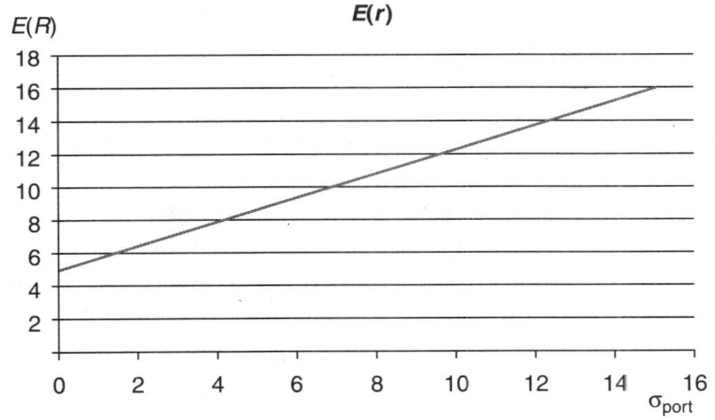

2. Let us consider a portfolio comprising risk-free asset and corporate bond in varying proportions (x (amount invested in large cap stock) = 0, 20, 40, 60 & 100).
The portfolio risk and return may be computed as:

$$E(r_{port}) = x(0.07) + (1-x)(0.05)$$

$$\sigma^2_{port} = x^2(0.10)^2 + (1-x)^2(0) + 2(0)(0.10)(0)x(1-x)$$

Varying the value of x, we get following values of $E(r_{port})$ and σ_{port}

Corporate Bond	Risk-free Asset	$E(r)$	σ_{port}
0	100	5.00	0.00
20	80	5.40	2.00
40	60	5.80	4.00
60	40	6.20	6.00
80	20	6.60	8.00
100	0	7.00	10.00

Capital Allocation Line for portfolio of corporate bond and risk-free asset may be exhibited as:

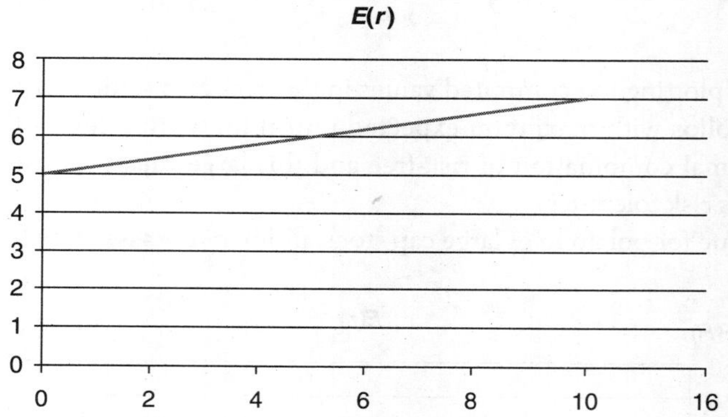

The preceding discussion mainly focuses on portfolio of risky and risk-free assets. This is called as risk-free lending. Risk-free lending implies investment in an asset that gives risk-free rate of return. To put it differently, risk-free lending means including a risk-free asset in the portfolio. In Figure 6.1, risk-free lending is represented by line segment $r_f P$.

Now let us consider the line segment above point *P* in Figure 6.1. It is obtained by introducing risk-free borrowing or leverage in the portfolio of risky assets.

If investors can borrow at risk-free rate and invest more funds in the risky portfolio, then we can obtain the line segment beyond point P in Figure 6.1. Such an increased investment in risky portfolio by borrowing funds at risk-free rate of return enables the investors to attain higher level of expected return in exchange for accepting higher level of risk.

In such a situation, the investors will earn some return on amount x already invested in the risky portfolio plus additional return on amount 'y' invested in risky portfolio by borrowing at risk-free rate. However, the investors will need to pay an interest on their borrowings at risk-free rate return and this would decrease the portfolio returns by an amount equal to yr_f.

Symbolically,

$$E(r_{\text{port}}) = (x+y)\,E(r_p) - yr_f \tag{8}$$

Portfolio risk may be computed as

$$\sigma_{\text{port}} = (x+y)\sigma_p \tag{9}$$

Risk-free lending and borrowing transform the curved efficient frontier into a straight line as illustrate in Figures 6.3 and 6.4.

To derive equation for CML, consider equation (5) representing CAL

Figure 6.3 Risk-free lending.

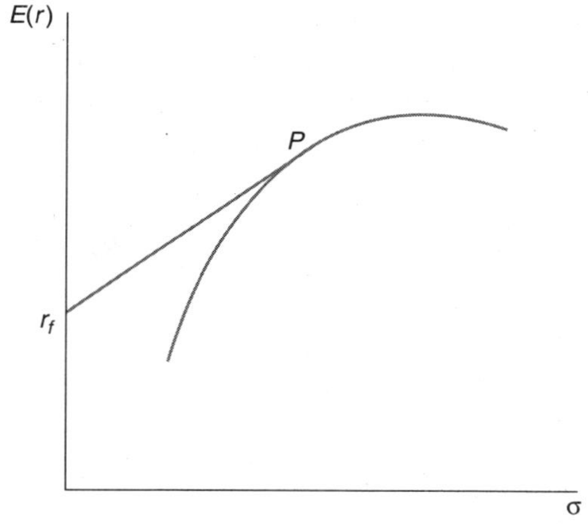

Figure 6.4 Risk-free borrowing.

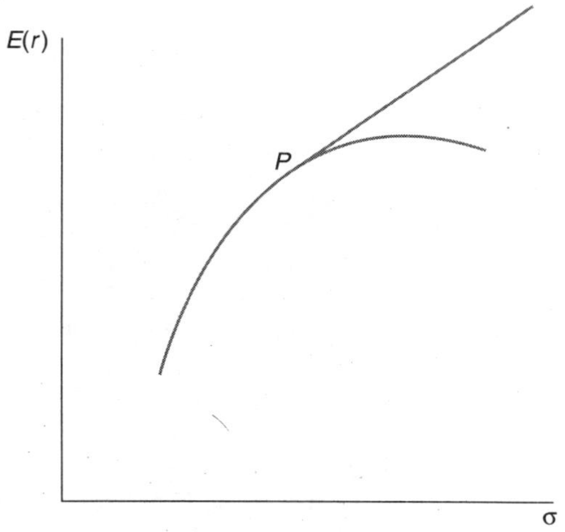

$$E(r_{\text{port}}) = r_f + \left(\frac{\sigma_{\text{port}}}{\sigma_p}\right)(E(r_p) - r_f)$$

It may be rewritten as follows to make it an equation for CML

$$E(r_p) = r_f + (\sigma_p)\left(\frac{(E(r_m) - r_f)}{\sigma_m}\right) \tag{10}$$

where
$E(r_p)$ = Expected return on a portfolio '*P*' located on CML
$E(r_m)$ = Expected return on the market portfolio '*M*'
r_f = Risk-free rate
σ_p = Standard deviation of return on portfolio '*P*'
σ_{m} = Standard deviation of return on the market portfolio '*M*'

Conceptually, the CML equation is:

Expected Return on Portfolio = Price of Time + (Price of Risk) (Amount of Risk)

The slope of CML as measured by

$$\frac{(E(r_m) - r_f)}{\sigma_m} \tag{11}$$

is called the market price of risk because it indicates the premium per unit of market risk.

Let us understand the effect of both risk-free lending and borrowing on portfolio return and risk with the help of a Numerical Example.

Numerical Example 3

Consider a risk-free asset and a portfolio of risky assets with the following risk-return characteristics:

	Risky Portfolio (A)	Risk-free Asset (B)
Expected Return	11%	5%
Variance	49	0
Standard Deviation	7%	0
Correlations		
A & B	0	

An investor originally holds a portfolio of risky assets only and he has invested all is funds in this portfolio. Compute the risk and return of the new portfolio if the investor holding this risky portfolio decides to:

1. Invest 50% of his funds in risk-free assets (This implies risk-free lending).
2. Increase his investment in risky portfolio by borrowing an amount equal to 25% of his original investment (This implies risk-free borrowing).

Solution:

1. **Risk-Free Lending:** New portfolio of the investor comprises 50% investment in risky assets and 50% investment in risk-free assets. The risk and return of the new portfolio may be computed as:

$$E(r_{\text{port}}) = 0.5\ (0.11) + 0.5\ (0.05) = 8\%$$

$$\sigma^2_{\text{port}} = (0.5)^2(0.07)^2 = 12.25\%$$

$$\sigma_{\text{port}} = 3.5\%$$

The results show that both return and risk of the investor have reduced.

2. **Risk-Free Borrowing:** New portfolio of the investor comprises 125% investment in risky assets, where investor had already invested 100% of his funds in the portfolio of risky assets and he has borrowed 25% of his original investment to invest more in the risky portfolio. The rate at which the additional funds have been borrowed is equal to 5% (risk-free rate). The risk and return of the new, leveraged portfolio may be computed as:

$$E(r_{\text{port}}) = (x + y)\ E(r_p) - yr_f$$

$$x = 1, y = 0.25$$

$$E(r_{\text{port}}) = (1 + 0.25)\ (0.11) - (0.25)(0.05) = 0.125 \quad \text{or} \quad 12.5\%$$

$$\sigma_{\text{port}} = (x + y)\sigma_p$$

$$\sigma_{\text{port}} = (1 + 0.25)(0.07)^2 = 8.75\%$$

The results show that both return and risk of the investor have increased.

Marketview 6.1 Buying on Margin

In market, investors can invest in risky portfolios by borrowing quite easily if they have a margin account with a broker. All they need to do is instruct the broker to buy on margin.

Numerical Example 4

Consider an investor whose tangency portfolio has an expected return of 16% and the standard deviation of 25%. The rate of return on risk-free asset is 5%. Answer the following on the basis of the given information:

1. If the investor decides to shift a part of his portfolio funds to the risk-free asset to lower the portfolio risk to 11%, how much amount should he shift to the risk-free asset? Compute the expected return of the resultant portfolio.
2. If the investor wants an expected return of 20%, what should be the proportion of funds in the tangency portfolio?
3. What is the additional return that this investor demands for taking extra unit of risk?

Solution:

1. We know $\sigma_{\text{port}} = x\sigma_p$

   Therefore, $x = \text{proportion of funds in risky portfolio} = \dfrac{\sigma_{\text{port}}}{\sigma_p}$

   We want a portfolio standard deviation (σ_{port}) of 11%, σ_p is given = 25%

   Substituting the values, $x = \dfrac{0.11}{0.25} = 0.44 = 44\%$

   Thus, the investor should shift 56% of the portfolio funds to risk-free asset. The expected return of the new portfolio may be computed as:

   $$E(r_{\text{port}}) = xE(r_i) + (1 - x)\, r_f$$

   Substituting the given values, the above equation can be rewritten as:

   $$E(r_{\text{port}}) = (0.44)\,(0.16) + (0.56)\,(0.05) = 9.84\%$$

2. The expected return of the new portfolio may be computed as:

   $$E(r_{\text{port}}) = x\,E(r_i) + (1 - x)\, r_f$$

   The given values are:

   $$E(r_{\text{port}}) = 20\%,\ E(r_i) = 16\%,\ r_f = 5\%$$

   Substituting the given values in the above equation, we can compute the value of x, which represents the proportion of funds in the tangency portfolio.

   $$0.20 = x\,(0.16) + (1 - x)(0.05)$$

$$0.20 = 0.05 + 0.11x$$

$$x = 1.36$$

Here, the proportion of the funds to be invested in tangency portfolio is coming to 1.36. This implies that the investor needs to undertake risk-free borrowing at the risk-free rate to generate an expected return of 20%. Therefore, he needs to borrow an amount equal to 36% of his original investment.

3. We know that the slope of CAL is a measure of the additional returns that an investor requires to be induced to take on one extra unit of risk. Symbolically,

$$S = \frac{(E(r_p) - r_f)}{\sigma_p}$$

Given,

$$E(r_p) = 16\%, r_f = 5\% \text{ and } \sigma_p = 25\%.$$

Substituting the given values in the above equation,

$$= \frac{(0.16 - 0.05)}{0.25}$$

$$= 0.44.$$

Thus, this investor demands an additional 44 basis points of expected return for every 1% increase in portfolio risk.

Capital Market Line: Passive Investment Strategy

In the preceding section of the chapter, we discussed the derivation of the capital allocation line (CAL) using risk-free asset and risky portfolio. The risky portfolio used in the derivation of CAL may be determined from an active or a passive strategy. Suppose an investor wants to avoid a strategy that involves any direct or indirect security analysis, i.e., he is keen to follow a passive strategy that does not require security analysis. He might be tempted to choose a passive strategy because active strategy is quite expensive and time consuming. Further, there is a school of thought that believes that most securities are likely to be fairly priced in the market and it is difficult to locate undervalued or overvalued securities (Efficient Market Hypothesis which is discussed in chapter 14). In such a case, his optimal strategy would be to allocate his funds between a risk-free asset and a broad diversified portfolio, called market portfolio and achieve his desired risk level through the use of risk-free asset. The capital allocation line that represents varying combinations of a broad diversified portfolio and risk-free asset is called the capital market line (CML) as illustrated in Figure 6.5.

CML is tangential to the efficient frontier, which is the locus of all optimal risky portfolios. Further, of all the lines that can be drawn from the risk-free rate to the efficient frontier, the tangential line has the maximum slope and the best risk-return trade-off (the best feasible CAL referred to in the preceding discussion). CML has the steepest slope, as exhibited in Figure 6.6.

Figure 6.5 Capital market line.

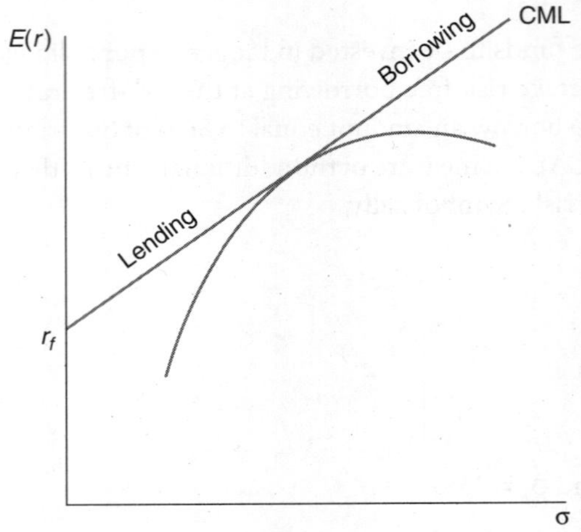

Figure 6.6 Best feasible CAL.

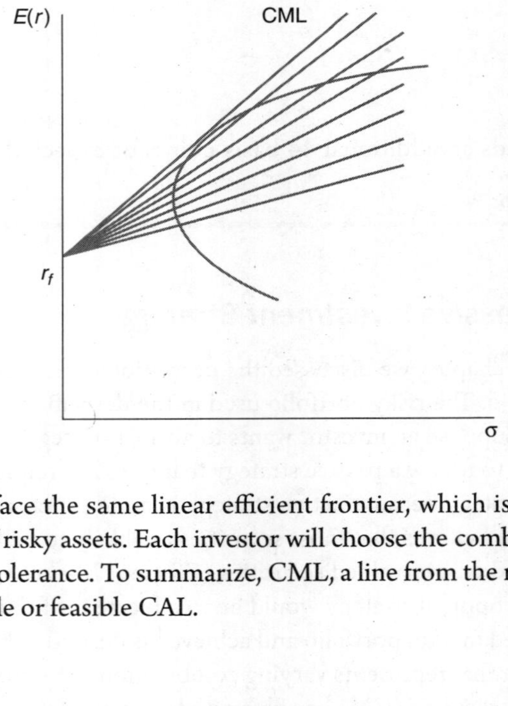

Thus, all rational investors face the same linear efficient frontier, which is an outcome of the addition of risk-free asset to the portfolio of risky assets. Each investor will choose the combination of the risky and risk-free asset as determined by his risk tolerance. To summarize, CML, a line from the risk-free rate through the market portfolio M, is the best attainable or feasible CAL.

Market portfolio

Let us discuss CML and tangency portfolio a little bit more. We know from our discussion on portfolio theory that all possible portfolios comprising two perfectly correlated assets lie along a straight line. CML, being a straight line, all portfolios along it are perfectly positively correlated and all the variability of each portfolio comes from the tangency portfolio, M. In other words, all the portfolios along CML represent varying combinations of risky portfolio, M and risk-free asset.

The tangency portfolio M has the highest portfolio possibility line.All investors hold the tangency portfolio and achieve their risk preference by borrowing or lending at risk-free rate to lie somewhere on CML.

Therefore M must include all possible risky assets that are available for investing. Since the theory assumes market equilibrium, this portfolio M would necessarily comprise all risky assets in the proportion of their market value. Since this portfolio includes all risky assets in proportion of their market value, it is called market portfolio.

To understand the concept of market portfolio better, let's assume that the entire world financial market consists of three stocks: those of Company A, Company B and Company C.

Company A's market capitalization is ₹1 billion
Company B's market capitalization is ₹2 billion
Company C's market capitalization is ₹3 billion

The total market portfolio would then consist of the following:

17% Company A stock (1 billion/6 billion)
33% Company B stock (2 billion/6 billion)
50% Company C stock (3 billion/6 billion)

Market portfolio includes all stocks, bonds, alternative investments, art and all other conceivable forms of risky assets. It is, thus, logical to call such a portfolio a completely diversified portfolio, i.e., all the unique risk has been eliminated, leaving behind only the non-diversifiable risk or the systematic risk. In theory, all traded assets in the world are included in the market portfolio. In practice, this seems to be impossible, so the market portfolio is taken to be represented by some or the other index of market activity like CNX Nifty.

Numerical Example 5

Mr. Ken has invested in a portfolio that has no unsystematic risk, i.e., it is a well-diversified portfolio comprising risky and risk-free assets. His portfolio is located on the CML, consistent with his risk aversion. Calculate the expected return on Mr. Ken's portfolio if the standard deviation of the market portfolio is 25% and the expected return is 16%. The standard deviation of Mr. Ken's portfolio is 21%. The risk-free rate is 5%.

Solution:

Since Mr. Ken is a mean variance optimizer, as indicated by his choice of portfolio from CML, the return on his portfolio may be computed by the equation of CML.

$$E(r_p)=r_f+(\sigma_p)\left(\frac{(E(r_m)-r_f)}{\sigma_m}\right)$$

Given

$$r_f=5\%,\ \sigma_p=21\%,\ E(r_m)=16\% \text{ and } \sigma_m=25\%$$

Substituting the given values in the CML equation, we get

$$E(r_p) = 0.05 + (0.21)((0.16 - 0.05)/0.25) = 14.24\%$$

Spreadsheet Application 3 **Plotting CML and Efficient frontier for a portfolio comprising risky and risk-free assets.**

Solution:

Let us assume that there are two securities, A and B. The expected return, standard deviation, correlation and covariance related to the two securities are as exhibited below:

30	**Security A**			
31	Exp Return			**13.00%**
32	Std Deviation			**19.00%**
33	Variance			**0.0361**
34				
35	**Security B**			
36	Exp Return			**15.00%**
37	Std Deviation			**30.00%**
38	Variance			**0.0900**
39				
40	**A,B**			
41	Correlation (A,B)			**30.00%**
42	Covariance (A,B)			0.01710

To begin with, let us construct alternate portfolios of the above two risky securities by varying their weights. Assuming a risk-free rate of 7%, we will also calculate the Sharpe ratio. The possible portfolios formed by varying the weight of security A from 0 to 1, in increments of 0.1, are exhibited below:

% in Security A	% in Security B	Portfolio Expected Return	Standard Deviation	Sharpe Ratio
0%	100%	15.0%	30.0%	26.7%
10%	90%	14.8%	27.6%	28.2%
20%	80%	14.6%	25.4%	29.9%
30%	70%	14.4%	23.4%	31.7%
40%	60%	14.2%	21.5%	33.4%
50%	50%	14.0%	20.0%	35.0%
60%	40%	13.8%	18.9%	36.0%
70%	**30%**	**13.6%**	**18.2%**	**36.3%**
80%	20%	13.4%	17.9%	35.7%
90%	10%	13.2%	18.2%	34.0%
100%	0%	13.0%	19.0%	31.6%

Charting the above values will give us the efficient frontier. The portfolio with highest Sharpe ratio is the Market portfolio.

To plot CML, consider the market portfolio generated above. It may be represented as:

Maximum Sharpe Ratio (market portfolio)				
70.0%	30.0%	13.6%	18.2%	**36.3%**

Now, we need to combine the above portfolio of risky assets with the risk-free asset (having a return of 7%). The possible portfolios formed by varying the weights of risk-free asset are exhibited below. The positive weights of risk-free assets represent risk-free lending and the negative weights of risk-free assets represent risk-free borrowing.

	A	B	C	D	E	F	G	H
1								
2	**Riskless rate**		**7.00%**					
3								
4								
5	**Market Portfolio (M)**		**Percent**		**% in Risk-free Asset**	**% in Market Portfolio**	**Expected Return CML**	**Std. Deviation**
6	**Security A**		70.0%		100%	0%	**7.00%**	0.00%
7	**Security B**		30.0%		90%	10%	**7.66%**	1.82%
8	**Exp return of Market Portfolio**		13.60%		80%	20%	**8.32%**	3.63%
9	**Std. Deviation of Market Portfolio**		18.16%		70%	30%	**8.98%**	5.45%
10					60%	40%	**9.64%**	7.26%
11					50%	50%	**10.30%**	9.08%
12					40%	60%	**10.96%**	10.90%
13					30%	70%	**11.62%**	12.71%
14					20%	80%	**12.28%**	14.53%
15					10%	90%	**12.94%**	16.34%
16					0%	100%	**13.60%**	18.16%
17					-10%	110%	**14.26%**	19.98%
18					-20%	120%	**14.92%**	21.79%
19					-30%	130%	**15.58%**	23.61%
20					-40%	140%	**16.24%**	25.42%
21					-50%	150%	**16.90%**	27.24%
22					-60%	160%	**17.56%**	29.06%
23					-70%	170%	**18.22%**	30.87%

To generate a plot of CML and efficient, frontier together, insert chart for two series: CML and Efficient frontier. The plot is exhibited below:

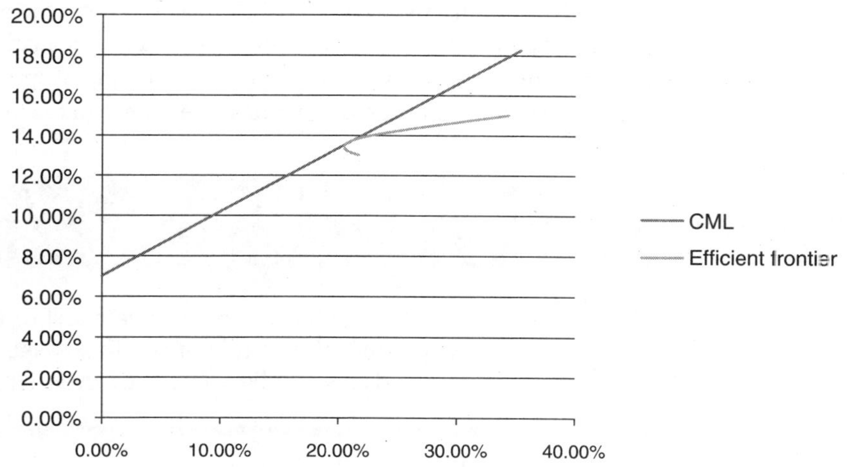

To summarize, the main implication of the capital market line is that all the rational mean-variance investors, whatever the level of their risk aversion, will invest in a combination of risk-free asset and market portfolio. As described in the chapter on modern portfolio theory, each investor will choose a point on CML at which his indifference curve is tangential to the CML as this would maximize his utility.

Why do all investors hold the market portfolio? If all the investors use mean variance analysis for the same universe of securities for the same holding period and have homogeneous expectations about risk and returns, logically all of them will arrive at the identical determination of the optimal risky portfolio, the market portfolio, that lies on the efficient frontier.

The Separation Theorem

James Tobin (1958)[1] expanded on Markowitz's work by adding a risk-free asset to the analysis, as explained above. The effect of adding risk-free asset to Markowitz' efficient portfolios has been described above. We know that the straight line obtained by adding risk-free asset to a portfolio of risky assets is called CML. It has also been called "enhanced efficient frontier" by some authors.

As discussed above, the main implication of CML for investors is that regardless of the level of their risk-aversion, all rational investors will hold only two securities:

1. The market portfolio
2. The risk-free asset

Conservative or risk averse investors will choose a point near the lower left of the CML whereas growth-oriented investors who have lower risk aversion will choose to be higher up on CML.

This implication of CML has been formalized into a theorem, called the separation theorem by James Tobin. According to Tobin, the investment process of a rational investor using mean variance criterion for investing can be separated into two distinct steps:

1. The construction of an efficient portfolio as described by MPT (INVESTMENT DECISION). This is a purely technical exercise for determination of the optimal risky portfolio. As explained above, the best risky portfolio is same for all the investors, regardless of their risk aversion. This portfolio is called the market portfolio.
2. The decision to combine this efficient portfolio with a riskless investment as proposed by Tobin (FINANCING DECISION). This decision depends on the personal preference of the investor.

Marketview 6.2 Do all Investors Invest in the same Optimal Risky Portfolio?

The chief implication of Capital Market Theory is that all portfolio managers will offer the market portfolio to all their clients regardless of their degree of risk tolerance. This makes professional portfolio management more efficient, less costly and less cumbersome. However, we know that in

[1] James Tobin, "Liquidity Preferences as Behavior Towards Risk," *The Review of Economic Studies*, February 1958.

practice different portfolio managers derive different efficient frontiers based on their inputs and offer different optimal risky portfolios to their investors. The disparity in inputs and optimal risky portfolios comes due to security analysis and specific needs of the clients.

The quality of security analysis is crucial to the success of active portfolio management. A passive investment strategy can result in a better CAL if the security analysis undertaken for active portfolio management is inferior and fails to tilt the portfolio proportions towards mispriced securities. However, capital market theory gives us a sound theoretical basis for the mutual fund industry by way of implying that a limited number of risky portfolios may be sufficient to serve the demands of a wide range of investors.

In our discussion so far, we have presented a mean variance theory that describes the expected return of only efficient portfolios but now we will move to an asset pricing theory that describes expected returns of all portfolios, efficient as well as inefficient. We will expand our discussion to learn how expected returns are determined in competitive markets for securities.

Capital Asset Pricing Model

Usually referred to as CAPM, this model occupies a central place in Financial Economics. It has played a pivotal role in the advances in quantitative investment management since its introduction in 1960s. The capital asset pricing model is a set of predictions that are related to the equilibrium expected returns on risky assets. It explains why assets are priced the way they are.

The capital asset pricing model states that the expected risk premium on each investment is proportional to its beta. This means that each investment should lie on the sloping security market line connecting Treasury bills and the market portfolio.

The model gives a precise quantification of the relationship that is observable between required or expected return and risk of any asset. Such a quantification of fair value provides benchmark rate for evaluation of investment alternatives by comparing the expected return forecast by us with the fair value as given by CAPM. A comparison of estimated return with the return computed using CAPM helps to determine whether the asset is under-valued, over-valued or fairly priced in the market.

It also helps in valuing an asset by providing an appropriate discount rate to use in valuation models. The model is also handy in determining an estimate of the expected return of assets that are yet to be traded such as the new issue of shares. Due to its extreme usefulness and acceptable accuracy, CAPM is widely used despite failing to withstand many empirical tests.

CAPM was developed twelve years after the introduction of MPT by Markowitz in 1952. It was developed by William Sharpe,[2] John Lintner[3] and Jan Mossin.[4]

As is true with all models, CAPM also makes certain assumptions. The main ones may be listed as:

[2] William Sharpe, "Capital Asset Prices: A Theory of Market Equilibrium," *Journal of Finance*, September 1964.
[3] John Lintner, "The Valuation of Risk Assets and the Selection of Risky Investments in Stock Portfolios and Capital Budgets," *Review of Economics and Statistics*, February 1965.
[4] Jan Mossin, "Equilibrium in a Capital Asset Market," *Econometrica*, October 1966.

1. No taxes on returns or transaction costs on trades.
2. Investors can borrow and lend at risk-free rate without any limitation and they are free to short sell any asset in any quantity.
3. Investors have homogeneous expectations regarding mean returns, correlations and variances of risky assets.
4. All assets are tradable and can be bought and sold in any quantity without impacting prices.
5. The model continues with the main assumptions of mean variance theory that all investors need to know only covariances, variances and expected returns to determine their optimal portfolios.

Later on in the chapter we will assess how CAPM is affected when some of the above assumptions are relaxed.

The assumptions of CAPM imply that all investors are price-takers with identical single holding period. They are rational mean variance optimizers who use MPT for portfolio selection.

Let us understand the implications of CAPM in perspective of what we have learnt so far.

1. Since all investors use MPT, they all hold market portfolio of risky assets as their optimal risky portfolio and differ only in the amount they put in risk-free asset.
2. Since market portfolio comprises all risky assets, it should offer risk premium that can be quantified in terms of degree of risk aversion.

   Mathematically, $E(r_m) - r_f = \bar{A}\sigma_m^2$ (12)

   where
   σ_m^2 = Variance of market portfolio
   $\bar{A}$ = Average degree of risk aversion across investors
   $E(r_m)$ = Expected return on market portfolio
   r_f = Risk-free rate of return

   Since market portfolio is a completely diversified portfolio, σ_m^2 represents systematic risk of the universe of investment.

Numerical Example 6

Suppose the S&P BSE SENSEX has given an average excess return equal to 12% in the past 10 years and its standard deviation is 21%. What should be the average degree of risk aversion across investors?

Solution:

We know

$$E(r_m) - r_f = \bar{A}\sigma_m^2 \text{ or}$$

$$\bar{A} = \frac{(E(r_m) - r_f)}{\sigma_m^2}$$

Given

$$E(r_m) - r_f) = 12\%, \sigma_m^2 = 0.0441$$

Therefore, average degree of risk aversion across investors (Ā) is:

$$\bar{A} = \frac{0.12}{0.0441}$$

$$= 2.72.$$

3. The risk premium of individual assets depends on the risk premium of the market portfolio and beta coefficient, which measures the extent to which the returns of an asset move with the market. We have discussed the concept of beta in Chapter 3.
4. In the world of CAPM assumptions, CML represents the linear efficient frontier and the investors invest in a combination of risk-free asset and market portfolio M, which is the point of tangency of CML to Markowitz' efficient frontier.

   Under CAPM, expected returns of all assets and portfolio whether efficient or not, can be described through the following equation

$$E(r_i) = r_f + \beta_i (E(r_m) - r_f) \tag{13}$$

where
$E(r_i)$ = Expected return of individual security
r_f = Risk-free rate of return
β_i = Systematic risk of individual security
$E(r_m) - r_f$ = Market risk premium

Equation (13) is the mathematical expression of CAPM. It describes an asset's expected returns as a linear function of its beta, which measures the asset's sensitivity to market movements. The equation of the model splits the expected or required return of an asset into two parts:

(a) First, the risk-free return and
(b) Second, the extra return $\beta_i(E(r_m) - r_f)$ represents the expected excess return on the market and is called market risk premium. This market risk premium when multiplied with the beta of a security gives the risk premium for that security.

Numerical Example 7

Consider two stocks, TMK Ltd. and CBK Ltd.

	TMK Ltd.	CBK Ltd.
Expected Return	9%	13%
Beta	0.70	1.30

The two stocks are correctly priced as per CAPM. Calculate the return of the market portfolio and the risk-free asset.

Solution:

The CAPM equation is:

$$E(r_i) = r_f + \beta_i\,(E(r_m) - r_f)$$

The equation for TMK Ltd is:

$$9 = r_f + 0.7(E(r_m) - r_f)$$

$$9 = 0.3r_f + 0.7E(r_m) \quad \text{(a)}$$

The equation for CBK Ltd is:

$$13 = r_f + 1.30(E(r_m) - r_f)$$

$$13 = -0.30\,r_f + 1.30E(r_m) \quad \text{(b)}$$

Adding equation (a) and (b), we get

$$22 = 2E(r_m)$$

Therefore, return on market portfolio $(E(r_m)) = \dfrac{22}{2} = 11\%$

Substituting the value of $E(r_m)$ in equation (a), we get

$$9 = 0.3r_f + 0.7(11)$$

$$1.3 = 0.3r_f$$

or

$$r_f = 4.33\%$$

All the implications of CAPM can be demonstrated graphically through Security Market Line (SML), which is a visual presentation of the relationship between expected rate of return and risk of an asset. It is a graphical expression of the CAPM equation. The equation of SML can be used to generate expected or required rate of return for any asset using its beta. The rate so obtained can be compared with investor's estimated rate of return to determine whether the asset is under-valued, fairly-valued or over-valued.

Beyond the Basics 6.1 Mutual Fund Theorem

The mutual fund theorem is another manifestation of the separation theorem discussed in the preceding part of the chapter. The mutual fund theorem is an investing theory postulated by James Tobin, which states that all rational investors should invest in identical portfolio of "risky assets" (the market portfolio) combined with some percentage of risk-free assets. A risk-averse investor would hold a higher percentage of risk-free asset, but would hold the same portfolio of risky investments as an investor with low risk-aversion.

In practical terms, the implication of mutual fund theorem is that the investors behaving within the mean-variance framework will invest their entire risky portfolio in a market-index or a mutual fund. The viability of the mutual fund theorem has been questioned as it rests on several assumptions that are not found in the real market.

Nonetheless, the mutual fund theorem does help the passive investor by implying that the market index may be seen as a reasonable approximation to an optimal risky portfolio.

Numerical Example 8

Mr. Vij is evaluating his options as he wants to invest in equity shares. He has short-listed the share of SJB InfoTech Ltd. He expects the stock to earn a return of 16%. The risk-free rate of return is 7% and the return on the market is 14%. He has checked various websites for the value of beta of this stock. He has got two values:

1. Beta = 1.4
2. Beta = 1.20

Should he buy the stock? Does the value of beta affect his buying decision in any way?

Solution:

A decision about whether or not to buy the stock can be taken on the basis of CAPM. If the expected return of the stock (16% in our example) exceeds the equilibrium return given by CAPM, Mr. Vij should buy the stock. Let us compute CAPM return for the stock using both values of beta.

1. Beta = 1.4

$$E(r_i) = r_f + \beta_i \, (E(r_m) - r_f)$$

$$E(r_i) = 7 + 1.4\,(14 - 7)$$

$$E(r_i) = 16.8\%$$

The expected return of the security is 16% and it is less than the CAPM returns, so Mr. Vij should not buy the stock.

2. Beta = 1.20

$$E(r_i) = r_f + \beta_i\,(E(r_m) - r_f)$$

$$E(r_i) = 7 + 1.2\,(14 - 7)$$

$$E(r_i) = 15.4\%$$

The expected return of security is 16% and it is more than the CAPM returns, so Mr. Vij should buy the stock.

The value of beta has impacted the buying decision for the share so Mr. Vij should ascertain the correct value of beta before taking the decision to buy the share.

Numerical Example 9

Calculate the beta of the portfolio comprising IBM, GM and Walmart. The amounts invested and betas are given below:

Stock	Amount invested (₹)	Beta
IBM	60,000	0.9
GM	40,000	1.1
Walmart	20,000	1.3

Solution:

Portfolio beta is calculated as weighted average of betas of the component stocks

$$\beta_p = \Sigma\, w_i \beta_i$$

Stock	Amount invested (₹)	Portfolio weights	Beta	Portfolio Beta
IBM	60,000	50%	0.9	0.45
GM	40,000	33%	1.1	0.37
Walmart	20,000	17%	1.3	0.22
Portfolio	120,000	100%		1.03

Thus, the portfolio beta is 1.03.

Security Market Line (SML)

All efficient portfolios lie along CML but the issue is that where will the inefficient portfolios and individual securities lie in terms of the risk-return space? Typically, they would lie below CML on account of inefficiency or lack of risk diversification. They may also be expected to lie scattered in the feasible region. However, CAPM postulates that all individual assets and inefficient portfolios display a linear relationship between their expected returns and their covariance with the market portfolio. This relationship is represented graphically through SML. It represents a reward-risk relationship that is symbolically expressed through equation (13).

$$E(r_i) = r_f + \beta_i(E(r_m) - r_f)$$

Substituting value of $\beta_i = \mathrm{Cov}(r_i, r_m)/\sigma_m^2$, equation (13) can be written as:

$$E(r_i) = r_f + \left\{\frac{(E(r_m) - r_f)}{\sigma_m^2}\right\}\mathrm{cov}(r_i, r_m) \tag{14}$$

In the above equation, $\{(E(r_m) - r_f)/\sigma_m^2\}$ is called price per unit of risk.

To take the discussion further, SML can be taken to reflect the risk-reward ratio for an individual security. It assumes that the security is held in a well-diversified portfolio and beta of the security is a measure of the risk that the security contributes to the optimal risky portfolio/diversified portfolio.

The reward-to-risk ratio of individual security *i* is given by

$$\frac{(E(r_i) - r_f)}{\mathrm{cov}(r_i, r_m)} \tag{15}$$

Reward-to-risk ratio of the market portfolio M is given by

$$\frac{(E(r_m) - r_f)}{\sigma_m^2} \tag{16}$$

The fundamental implication of SML is that in equilibrium, all assets and portfolios should have the same reward-to-risk ratio and it must be equal to the reward-to-risk ratio for the market. Therefore,

$$\frac{(E(r_i) - r_f)}{\mathrm{cov}(r_i, r_m)} = \frac{(E(r_m) - r_f)}{\sigma_m^2} \tag{17}$$

or

$$(E(r_i) - r_f) = (\mathrm{cov}(r_i, r_m))\left(\frac{(E(r_m) - r_f)}{\sigma_m^2}\right) \tag{18}$$

Since, $\dfrac{\text{cov}(r_i, r_m)}{\sigma_m^2} = \beta_i$

Equation (18) can be rewritten to get equation (13), the original CAPM equation.

Conceptually, β is the slope of the linear regression line in which the returns of a security are regressed on the returns of the market. As the beta of the market is 1, the slope of SML is the risk premium of the market portfolio and it represents the reward for bearing an average amount of systematic risk.

SML is exhibited in Figure 6.7. The graph depicts $E(r)$ on Y-axis and β on X-axis. The SML uses the beta coefficient as the measure of relevant risk. It illustrates the linear relationship between return of security i and its systematic risk denoted by β.

Figure 6.7 Security market line.

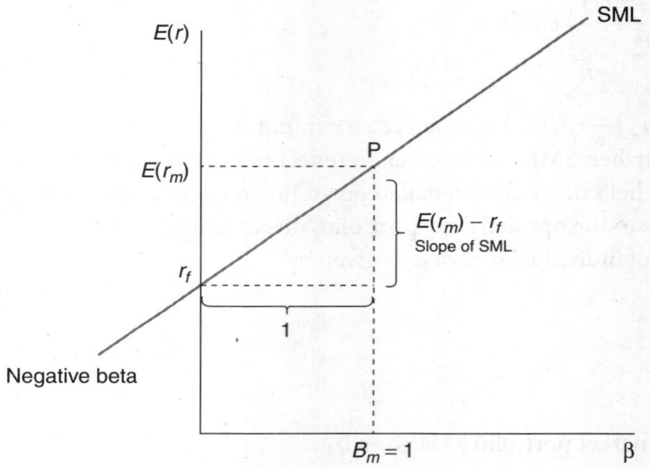

The SML and Undervalued and Overvalued Assets

The security market line provides a benchmark for the evaluation of investment performance. Given the risk of an investment, as measured by its beta, the SML provides the required rate of return necessary to compensate investors for both risk as well as the time value of money. In equilibrium, all assets are so priced that their estimated rates of return are consistent with their level of systematic risk. In such a situation, all assets and portfolios (efficient or inefficient) will lie along SML.

If any asset's estimated rate of return plots above the SML, it is considered to be underpriced because it implies that the investor's estimated rate of return for that asset is above the CAPM required rate of return, based on its systematic risk.

On the other hand, assets with estimated returns plotting below SML are considered to be overpriced. The plotting of returns below SML indicates that investor's estimated return are less than the CAPM required returns based on the asset's systematic risk.

The above discussion can be summarized as:

A security is undervalued if its estimated return > required or expected return. Hence it will plot above the SML.
A security is overvalued if its estimated return < required or expected return. Hence it will plot below the SML.
A security is fairly priced if its estimated return = required or expected return. Hence it will plot on SML.

Spreadsheet Application 4 **Plotting SML using MS Excel.**

Solution:

We will use the data from spreadsheet application 3 to plot SML using Excel. We need to go through the same steps to arrive at market portfolio and calculate possible portfolios by combining varying proportions of A and B.

SML is plotted in the Beta and return space. Therefore, to plot SML, we need to calculate CAPM returns and to identify over-valued and under-valued securities, we need to calculate estimated returns as well.

Here, we will use the following formula for computation of beta:

$$\beta_i = \frac{\text{cov}(r_i, r_m)}{\sigma_m^2}$$

Before calculating beta, covariance and variance of market needs to be calculated. Variance of the market can be calculated as illustrated in spreadsheet application 3 of this chapter. Covariance can be calculated as:

	B	C	D	E	F	G	H	I	J
1	Riskless rate	7.00%							
2									
3	Security A								
4	Exp Return	13.00%							
5	Std Deviation	19.00%							
6	Variance	0.0361							
7									
8	Security B								
9	Exp Return	15.00%							
10	Std Deviation	30.00%							
11	Variance	0.0900							
12									
13	Correlation	30.00%							
14	Covariance	0.01710							
15									
16	Market Portfolio (M)								
17	Security A	70.0%							
18	Security B	30.0%							
19	Exp return of Market Portfolio	13.60%							
20	Std. Deviation of Market Portfolio	18.16%							
21	$R_m - r_f$	6.60%							
22									
23	For Plotting SML								
24	Security A	150%	100%	50%	70%	0%	-50%	-100%	
25	Security B	-50%	0%	50%	30%	100%	150%	200%	
26									
27	Covariance (Port, Market)	=C24*$C$17*$C$6+C25*$C$18*$C$11+(C24*$C$18+C25*$C$17)*$C$14							

Using the variance of the market and covariance of market and portfolios formed by combining A & B, beta can be calculated for each portfolio as follows:

	B	C	D	E	F	G	H	I
1	Riskless rate	7.00%						
2								
3	Security A							
4	Exp Return	13.00%						
5	Std Deviation	19.00%						
6	Variance	0.0361						
7								
8	Security B							
9	Exp Return	15.00%						
10	Std Deviation	30.00%						
11	Variance	0.0900						
12								
13	Correlation	30.00%						
14	Covariance	0.01710						
15								
16	Market Portfolio (M)							
17	Security A	70.0%						
18	Security B	30.0%						
19	Exp return of Market Portfolio	13.60%						
20	Std. Deviation of Market Portfolio	18.16%						
21	$R_m - r_f$	6.60%						
22								
23	For Plotting SML							
24	Security A	150%	100%	50%	70%	0%	-50%	-100%
25	Security B	-50%	0%	50%	30%	100%	150%	200%
26								
27	Covariance (Port, Market)	0.026	0.030	0.035	0.033	0.039	0.043	0.048
28	Beta	=C27/$C$20^2		1.052	1.000	1.182	1.312	1.442

CAPM return may be calculated using following formula:

$$E(r_i) = r_f + \beta_i \left(E(r_m) - r_f\right)$$

	B	C	D	E	F	G	H	I
1	Riskless rate	7.00%						
2								
3	Security A							
4	Exp Return	13.00%						
5	Std Deviation	19.00%						
6	Variance	0.0361						
7								
8	Security B							
9	Exp Return	15.00%						
10	Std Deviation	30.00%						
11	Variance	0.0900						
12								
13	Correlation	30.00%						
14	Covariance	0.01710						
15								
16	Market Portfolio (M)							
17	Security A	70.0%						
18	Security B	30.0%						
19	Exp return of Market Portfolio	13.60%						
20	Std. Deviation of Market Portfolio	18.16%						
21	$R_m - r_f$	6.60%						
22								
23	For Plotting SML							
24	Security A	150%	100%	50%	70%	0%	-50%	-100%
25	Security B	-50%	0%	50%	30%	100%	150%	200%
26								
27	Covariance (Port, Market)	0.026	0.030	0.035	0.033	0.039	0.043	0.048
28	Beta	0.792	0.922	1.052	1.000	1.182	1.312	1.442
29	CAPM Return	=$C$1+C28*$C$21		13.9%	13.6%	14.8%	15.7%	16.5%

The expected (estimated) return may be calculated using the following MPT portfolio expected return formula:

$$R_p = \sum_{i=1}^{N} (X_i)(R_i)$$

	B	C	D	E	F	G	H	I
1	Riskless rate	7.00%						
2								
3	Security A							
4	Exp Return	13.00%						
5	Std Deviation	19.00%						
6	Variance	0.0361						
7								
8	Security B							
9	Exp Return	15.00%						
10	Std Deviation	30.00%						
11	Variance	0.0900						
12								
13	Correlation	30.00%						
14	Covariance	0.01710						
15								
16	Market Portfolio (M)							
17	Security A	70.0%						
18	Security B	30.0%						
19	Exp return of Market Portfolio	13.60%						
20	Std. Deviation of Market Portfolio	18.16%						
21	$R_m - r_f$	6.60%						
22								
23	For Plotting SML							
24	Security A	150%	100%	50%	70%	0%	-50%	-100%
25	Security B	-50%	0%	50%	30%	100%	150%	200%
26								
27	Covariance (Port, Market)	0.026	0.030	0.035	0.033	0.039	0.043	0.048
28	Beta	0.792	0.922	1.052	1.000	1.182	1.312	1.442
29	CAPM Return	12.2%	13.1%	13.9%	13.6%	14.8%	15.7%	16.5%
30	Estimated Return	=C24*$C$4+C25*$C$9			13.6%	15.0%	16.0%	17.0%

The complete output of the above calculation is exhibited below:

	B	C	D	E	F	G	H	I
1	Riskless rate	7.00%						
2								
3	Security A							
4	Exp Return	13.00%						
5	Std Deviation	19.00%						
6	Variance	0.0361						
7								
8	Security B							
9	Exp Return	15.00%						
10	Std Deviation	30.00%						
11	Variance	0.0900						
12								
13	Correlation	30.00%						
14	Covariance	0.01710						
15								
16	Market Portfolio (M)							
17	Security A	70.0%						
18	Security B	30.0%						
19	Exp return of Market Portfolio	13.60%						
20	Std. Deviation of Market Portfolio	18.16%						
21	$R_m - r_f$	6.60%						
22								
23	For Plotting SML							
24	Security A	150%	100%	50%	70%	0%	-50%	-100%
25	Security B	-50%	0%	50%	30%	100%	150%	200%
26								
27	Covariance (Port, Market)	0.026	0.030	0.035	0.033	0.039	0.043	0.048
28	Beta	0.792	0.922	1.052	1.000	1.182	1.312	1.442
29	CAPM Return	12.2%	13.1%	13.9%	13.6%	14.8%	15.7%	16.5%
30	Estimated Return	12.0%	13.0%	14.0%	13.6%	15.0%	16.0%	17.0%

To plot SML, we need beta, CAPM returns and risk-free rate of return.

	Beta	CAPM Return
	0.7919	0.122263956
	0.9218	0.130839527
	1.0517	0.139415099
	0.9998	0.13598487
	1.1817	0.14799067
	1.3116	0.156566242
	1.4415	0.165141813
Risk-free Asset	0	0.07

SML is plotted with beta on *x*-axis and returns on *y*-axis.

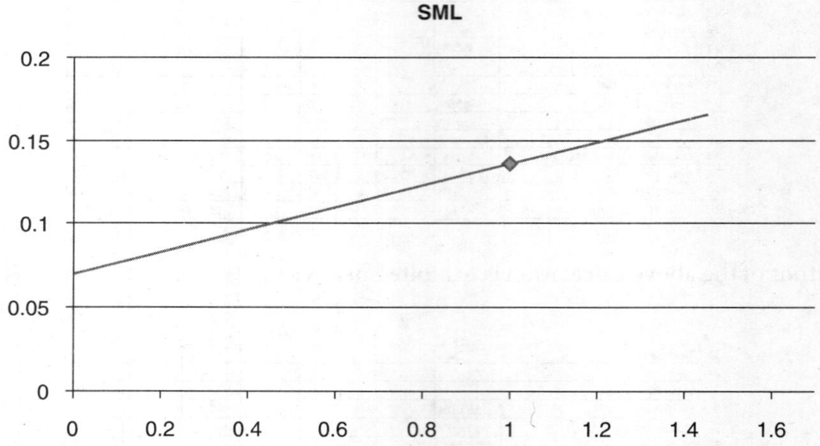

Required or Expected Returns

The expected or required rate of return for a risky asset is determined by CAPM. It comprises risk-free rate of return and a risk premium depending on the systematic risk or beta of the security. Let us understand the calculation of required returns for different securities with the help of Numerical Example 10.

Numerical Example 10

Consider following stocks and their betas. Compute their required rate of return or expected return if the risk-free rate is 6% and the return on the market portfolio is 9%.

Stock	Beta
TWT Ltd.	0.8
KBG Ltd.	1
CWR Ltd.	1.2
DRT Ltd.	1.38
WEW Ltd.	−0.35

Solution:

We can compute the expected or the required return of a security by using the equation of SML

$$E(r_i) = r_f + \beta_i(E(r_m) - r_f)$$

Substituting the given values in the above equation, we get

TWT Ltd. $E(r_i) = 0.06 + 0.80\ (0.09 - 0.06) = 8\%$

KBG Ltd. $E(r_i) = 0.06 + 1.00\ (0.09 - 0.06) = 9\%$

CWR Ltd. $E(r_i) = 0.06 + 1.2\ (0.09 - 0.06) = 10\ \%$

DRT Ltd. $E(r_i) = 0.06 + 1.38\ (0.09 - 0.06) = 10\%$

WEW Ltd. $E(r_i) = 0.06 + (-0.35)\ (0.09 - 0.06) = 5\%$

The returns calculated above are the expected (required) rates of return that these stocks should generate as determined by their systematic risks. TWT Ltd: has lower beta than the market, therefore its expected (required) return is less than the return on the market portfolio of risky assets. KBG Ltd. has a beta equal to the beta of the market, so its required rate of return is also equal to the expected market return of 9%. CWR Ltd. and DRT Ltd. have betas more than that of the market, so their required returns are higher than the market. WEW Ltd. has a negative beta so its required rate of return is expected to be below the risk-free rate of 6%. Negative beta stocks are hard to come by.

Estimated Returns

Estimated returns are calculated on the basis of forecasts made by security analysts about the price and dividends of a security. Analysts base their forecasts on extensive fundamental analysis for a given holding period.

These returns are calculated using the equity valuation models discussed in Chapter 9. These are the returns that make investors take a buy/sell decision. Let us understand the calculation of required returns for different securities with the help of Numerical Example 11.

Numerical Example 11

Consider the stocks discussed in Numerical Example 9 again. Use the given information to calculate the estimated returns of each stock (for single holding period).

Stock	Current Price (P_t)(₹)	Expected Price (P_{t+1})(₹)	Expected Dividend (D_{t+1})(₹)
TWT Ltd.	26	27	1.1
KBG Ltd.	41	43	0.5
CWR Ltd.	34	38	1.3
DRT Ltd.	65	67	1.12
WEW Ltd.	49	52	—

Solution:

The estimated returns on each stock can be calculated using the single holding period formula:

$$r_i = \frac{(D_{t+1} + P_{t+1} - P_t)}{P_t}$$

Substituting the given values in the above equation, we get

$$\text{TWT Ltd. } r_i = \frac{(1.1 + (27 - 26))}{26} = 8\%$$

$$\text{KBG Ltd. } r_i = \frac{(0.5 + (43 - 41))}{41} = 6\%$$

$$\text{CWR Ltd. } r_i = \frac{(1.3 + (38 - 34))}{34} = 15.6\%$$

$$\text{DRT Ltd. } r_i = \frac{(1.12 + (67 - 65))}{65} = 40.80\%$$

$$\text{WEW Ltd. } r_i = \frac{(0 + (52 - 49))}{49} = 6.1\%$$

Numerical Example 12

Consider the required and estimated return calculated in Numerical Examples 9 and 10 to determine which securities are overvalued, undervalued or fairly valued. Given:

Stock	Required Rate (%)	Estimated Future Rate of Return (%)
TWT Ltd.	8	8
KBG Ltd.	9	6
CWR Ltd.	10	15.6
DRT Ltd.	10	4.8
WEW Ltd.	5	6.12

Solution:

By comparing the estimated and the required rate of return, we can determine whether the security is overvalued, undervalued or fairly valued. The decision rule is:

A security is undervalued if its estimated return > required or expected return. Hence it will plot above the SML.
A security is overvalued if its estimated return < required or expected return. Hence it will plot below the SML.
A security is fairly priced if its estimated return = required or expected return. Hence it will plot on SML.

Based on the above rule, the given securities are valued as:

Stock	Required Rate (%)	Estimated Future Rate of Return (%)	Evaluation
TWT Ltd	8	8	Fairly Priced
KBG Ltd.	9	6	Overvalued
CWR Ltd.	10	15.6	Undervalued
DRT Ltd.	10	4.8	Overvalued
WEW Ltd.	5	6.12	Undervalued

We know that in equilibrium, all securities should plot on the SML. In our Numerical Example only TWT Ltd. will plot on SML. CWR Ltd. and WEW Ltd. are undervalued, therefore they will plot above SML. KBG Ltd. and DRT Ltd. are overvalued, therefore they will plot below SML.

The under, over and fairly valued securities and their plotting on SML is exhibited in Figure 6.8.

Figure 6.8 Overvalued and undervalued stocks.

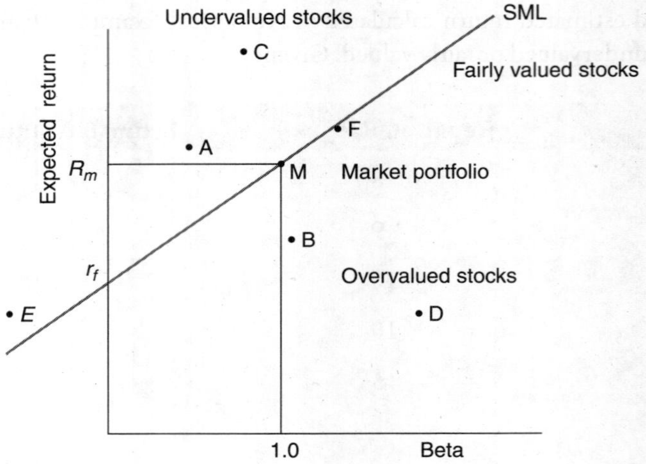

Using SML to Buy/Sell Securities

In equilibrium, all assets and portfolios of assets should be priced so that their required returns are equal to their estimated returns for the actual holding period.

Any security that plots above the SML would be considered underpriced because it implies that the returns estimated to be received are more than the returns consistent with the systematic risk of the security. This kind of security is an attractive investment target. Obviously, investors will rush in to buy the security but the buying pressure will cause the market price to rise, thereby causing the estimated return to fall until it equals the required return. Thus, the security will move towards its equilibrium value and plot on SML as shown in Figure 6.9.

Figure 6.9 Overvalued and undervalued stocks.

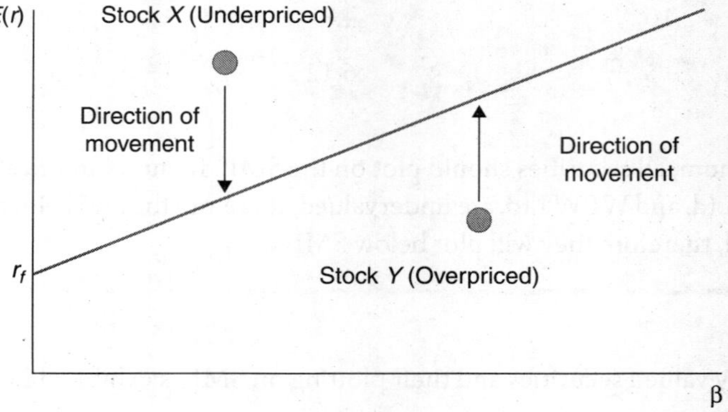

Any security that plots below the SML would be considered overpriced because it implies that the returns estimated to be received are less than the returns consistent with the systematic risk of the security. Obviously, investors will rush in to sell the security but the selling pressure will cause the market price to fall, thereby causing the estimated return to rise until it equals the required return. Thus, the security will move towards its equilibrium value and plot on SML.

Consider Figure 6.8. Assuming that the investor trusted the security analyst who has forecasted the relevant data for calculation of estimated returns, he will take no action regarding Stock F, but he will buy Stocks C and E and sell Stocks B and D. An aggressive investor might even look to short sell stocks B and D, short as the prices are expected to come down in future.

Alpha: The overvaluation or undervaluation of a security is judged on the basis of the difference between the estimated and the required returns of a security. This difference between estimated return and expected or required return is sometimes referred to as a stock's alpha or its excess return. Alpha can be positive (if the stock is undervalued) or negative (if the stock is overvalued). Alpha equal to zero indicates that the stock is located on the SML and is fairly valued in line with its systematic risk. The alphas of two stocks *A* and *B* are exhibited in Figure 6.10.

Figure 6.10 The alphas of two stocks *A* and *B*.

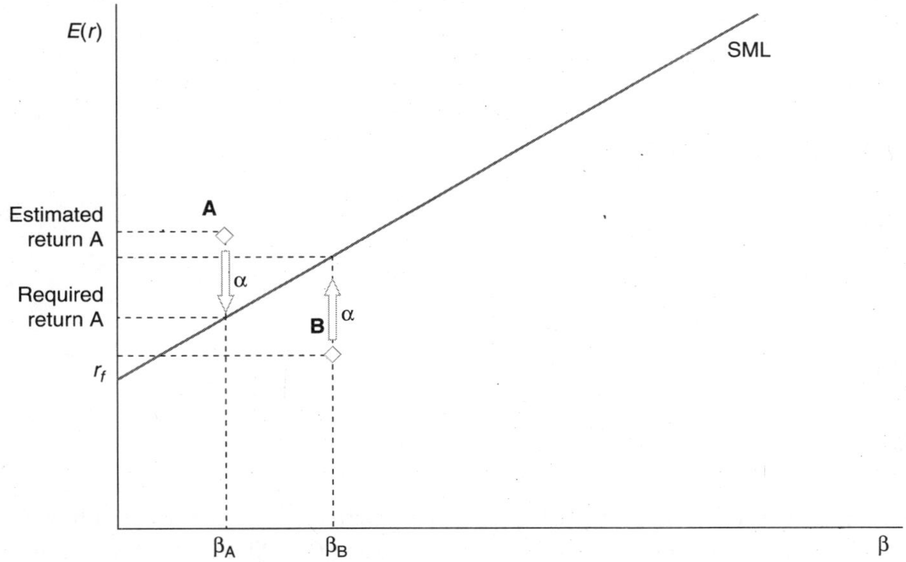

Numerical Example 13

Consider the given information to answer the questions given below. Risk-free rate of return = 5%

1. Which is the better stock to buy?

2. Calculate the required rate of return of a project with expected beta of 1.2, if the risk-free rate of return is 7% and expected return of market is 15%.
3. If the IRR of the above referred project is 20%, should the project be accepted?

	Estimated Return (%)	Beta
Market	11	1
KP Systems	13	1
VD Suppliers	14	1.5

Solution:

1. The better stock to buy would be the one that has higher alpha as per CAPM

$$E(r_i) = r_f + \beta_i(E(r_m) - r_f)$$

KP Systems

$$E(r_i) = 0.05 + 1\ (0.11 - 0.05) = 11\%$$

VD Suppliers

$$E(r_i) = 0.05 + (1.5)\ (0.11 - 0.05) = 14\%$$

KP Systems

$$\text{Alpha} = 13 - 11 = 2\%$$

VD Suppliers

$$\text{Alpha} = 14 - 14 = 0$$

VD Suppliers is fairly priced. However, KP Systems has positive alpha and is a better buy.

2. Required rate of return of the project may be computed using CAPM. Substituting the given values in the CAPM equation, we get

$$E(r_i) = 0.07 + (1.2)\ (0.15 - 0.07) = 16.6\%$$

This is the project hurdle rate.

3. The project is desirable as its IRR of 20% is higher than the hurdle rate of 16.6%.

Relationship Between SML and CML

The CML traces the risk premiums of efficient portfolios (portfolios composed of the risky market portfolio and the risk-free asset) as a function of portfolio standard deviation. The SML, on the other hand, exhibits individual asset risk premiums as a function of asset risk as measured by beta. The SML is valid for both, efficient portfolios and individual assets. The fact is that capital market line, generated by adding risk-free borrowing and lending to Markowitz efficient frontier of risky securities is nothing but a special case of SML. This can be shown as below.

SML equation can be given from equation (14) as:

$$E(r_i) = r_f + \left\{ \frac{E(r_m) - r_f}{\sigma_m^2} \right\} \{\text{cov}(r_i, r_m)\}$$

where

$$\text{cov}(r_i, r_m) = r_{i,m} \sigma_i \sigma_m$$

So SML may be re written as:

$$E(r_i) = r_f + \left\{ \frac{E(r_m) - r_f}{\sigma_m} \right\} (r_{i,m} \sigma_i)$$

Remember that efficient portfolios (portfolios that lie on CML) have perfect positive correlation (+1) on returns of *i* and *M*. So for efficient portfolios, SML can be written as:

$$E(r_e) = r_f + \left\{ \frac{(E(r_m) - r_f)}{\sigma_m} \right\} \sigma_e \qquad (19)$$

Subscript e represents efficient portfolio.

Equation (19) is same as equation (10), the equation of CML. Thus CML is just a special case of SML.

CAPM: A Quick Look Back

CAPM is a key model of financial theory and is used for calculation of project hurdle rate, required rate of return on investment, systematic risk of investment and determination of excess return on investment. Figure 6.11 illustrates how CAPM is used.

Analysts can make estimates or forecasts about the risk and return on stock and the market portfolio. These forecasts are used to generate inputs to calculate the beta coefficient for the stock. Thereafter, the required return on a stock can be computed using the stock's beta coefficient, the expected return on the market portfolio and the risk-free rate of return. The required return so calculated is then used in dividend discount models (discussed later in the book) to estimate the 'intrinsic value' of the stock. The intrinsic value generated using the dividend discount model is compared with the actual stock price in the market to judge if the stock is fairly priced or mispriced in the market.

Figure 6.11 How CAPM is used?

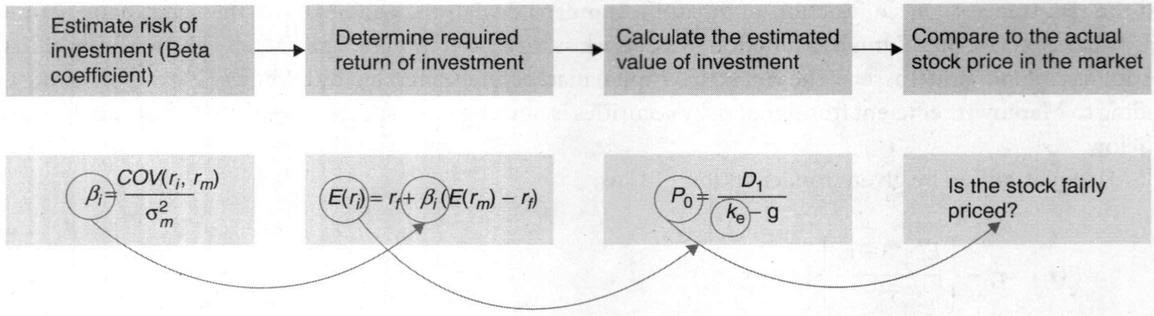

Most importantly, CAPM describes the equilibrium in financial market where all undervalued and overvalued assets move towards SML due to the operation of market forces that restore equilibrium. If a stock has estimated returns that are higher than CAPM returns, it will be demanded by more investors, pushing its price up and lowering its expected returns. Thus, the equilibrium is restored.

Completely diversified, all-inclusive market portfolio as described by CAPM, is a theoretical possibility that is unobservable in the markets. In practice, this market portfolio is actually some broad-based index. Since CAPM is mainly used for valuing equity, the indices that are generally chosen are broad based value-weighted indices S&P BSE SENSEX or S&P 500.

Spreadsheet Application 5 **Application of CAPM for estimation of cost of equity can be demonstrated through MS Excel.**

Solution:

Let us estimate the cost of equity for HUL using CAPM. For this purpose, we need to regress the LN returns of HUL (2009 to 2013) on LN returns of SENSEX (2009 to 2013). (Explained in Chapter 4). Assume the following information:

30 year *T* Bond rate = 8.72%

Market risk premium = 10%

According to CAPM, the expected return from the investor's perspective or cost of equity from the company's perspective is:

$$r_f + \beta \times \text{Market risk premium}$$

Beta can be calculated by regression. Risk-free rate is often proxied by the Treasury bill or Treasury bond rate. There has been some debate around whether to use long-term bond rate or short-term bond rate as risk-free rate. Some analysts argue that the choice of the duration of the treasury instrument should be linked to the investment horizon of the investor. This implies that the investors with long term horizon should use long-term T-Bond rates (10 year or 30 Year) and those with short-term horizon should use t-bill rate (short-term).

However, its is advisable for the investors with short-term horizon also to use long-term rates as they get much of their value from the terminal value, which by definition, runs to infinity.

Beta: The value of beta is 0.124.

Using the computed value of beta and the given values of market risk premium as 10% and the 30 year *T* Bond rate as 8.72%, CAPM yields the cost of equity as:

$$\mathbf{8.72\% + 0.124 \times 10\% = 9.96\%}$$

	A	B	C	D	E	F	G	H	I
1	SUMMARY OUTPUT								
2									
3	*Regression Statistics*								
4	Multiple R	0.115807457							
5	R Square	0.013411367							
6	Adjusted R Square	-0.003897205							
7	Standard Error	0.068178672							
8	Observations	59							
9									
10	ANOVA								
11		*df*	*SS*	*MS*	*F*	*Significance F*			
12	Regression	1	0.003601711	0.003601711	0.774839587	0.382420382			
13	Residual	57	0.264954882	0.004648331					
14	Total	58	0.268556593						
15									
16		*Coefficients*	*Standard Error*	*t Stat*	*P-value*	*Lower 95%*	*Upper 95%*	*Lower 95.0%*	*Upper 95.0%*
17	Intercept	0.011552449	0.009084276	1.27169737	0.208645053	-0.006638499	0.029743398	-0.006638499	0.029743398
18	X Variable 1	0.124078513	0.140958309	0.88024973	0.382420382	-0.158185631	0.406342657	-0.158185631	0.406342657

Relaxing CAPM Assumptions

We began our discussion about CAPM by presenting certain assumptions that create a make-believe world for CAPM to hold true. These assumptions have been criticized on the ground that they are far from the market reality. Further, critics say that the applicability of CAPM is questionable without these assumptions. Let us now see what happens when we relax some of the assumptions, i.e., introduce a touch of reality in CAPM's make believe world.

The assumptions that we will relax to see the impact of CML and SML are:

1. Differential Borrowing and Lending
2. Zero-Beta Portfolio
3. Transaction Costs
4. Heterogeneous Expectations and Planning Periods
5. Taxes

Differential borrowing and lending rates

One of the CAPM's assumption is that the investors can borrow or lend money at the same risk-free rate of return. It is easy to accept that investors can lend as much as they want at risk-free rate of return by buying government securities (e.g., t-bills).

However, individual investors cannot borrow at risk-free rate because they cannot guarantee against default risk. No lender would be willing to lend to individuals at such a low rate. In such situation they have to borrow at a rate that is higher than the risk-free rate. As a result of this, the slope of CAL beyond point P in Figure 6.1 becomes

$$\frac{E(r_p) - r_f'}{\sigma_p}$$

This makes CAL kinked above point $P(x > 1)$ compared to the line segment below point $P(x < 1)$, as illustrated in Figure 6.12.

Figure 6.12 Investment opportunity set for differential borrowing and lending rate.

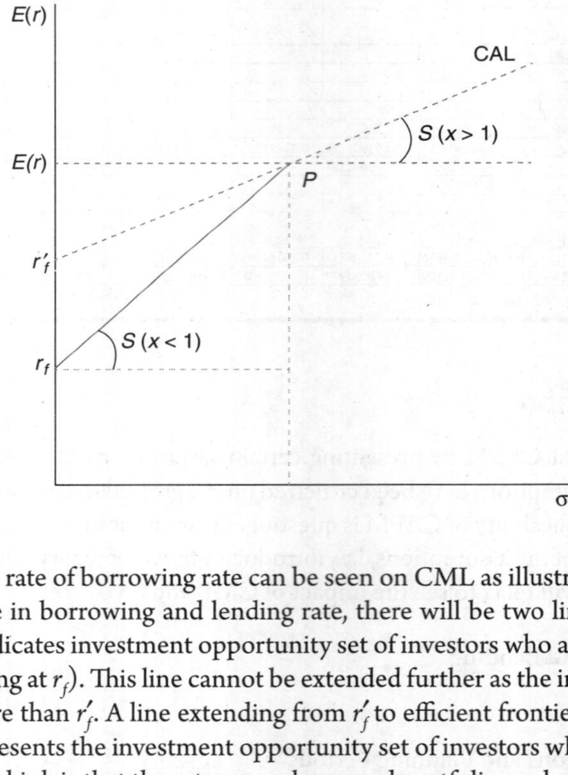

The impact of differential rate of borrowing rate can be seen on CML as illustrated in Figure 6.13.

Because of the difference in borrowing and lending rate, there will be two lines, tangential to the efficient frontier. The segment $r_f F$ indicates investment opportunity set of investors who add risk-free asset to their risky portfolio (i.e., risk-free lending at r_f). This line cannot be extended further as the investors, in reality, can borrow only at a rate r_f' which is more than r_f'. A line extending from r_f' to efficient frontier is tangential to it at point K. So the line segment KG represents the investment opportunity set of investors who borrow money to buy risky asset. The implication of this kink is that the returns on leveraged portfolio are less than as originally indicated.

Impact of zero-beta model

Black (1972) derived an alternative model of CAPM that did not require risk-free rate. The model is based on the fact that there are many portfolios in the feasible set whose returns are completely uncorrelated to the market. Such portfolio can be said to have zero-beta, i.e., no systematic risk and their variance comes from their

Figure 6.13 Kinked CML.

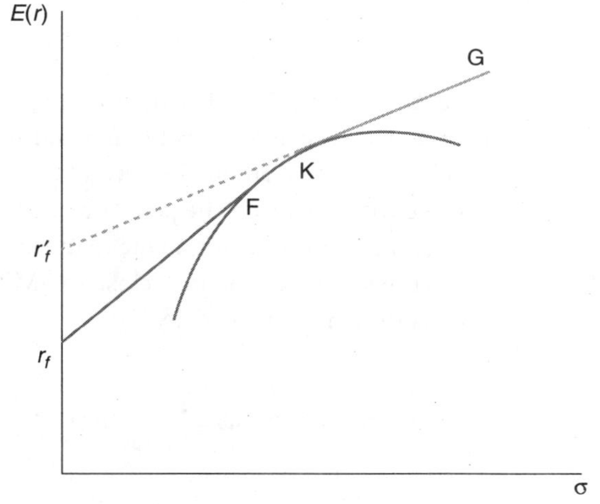

unsystematic risk. Out of these several zero-beta portfolios, investors select the one that has minimum variance. The availability of zero beta portfolio allows construction of linear SML, however it does not impact CML.

Adding zero-beta portfolio to the portfolio of risky assets gives a linear SML that is flatter than the original SML because the market risk premium would be smaller as exhibited in Figure 6.14. The equation of new zero-beta CAPM is given as:

$$E(r_i) = E(r_z) + \beta_i(E(r_m) - E(r_z)) \tag{20}$$

where $E(r_z)$ is the expected return on the zero-beta portfolio.

Figure 6.14 Security market line with a zero-beta portfolio.

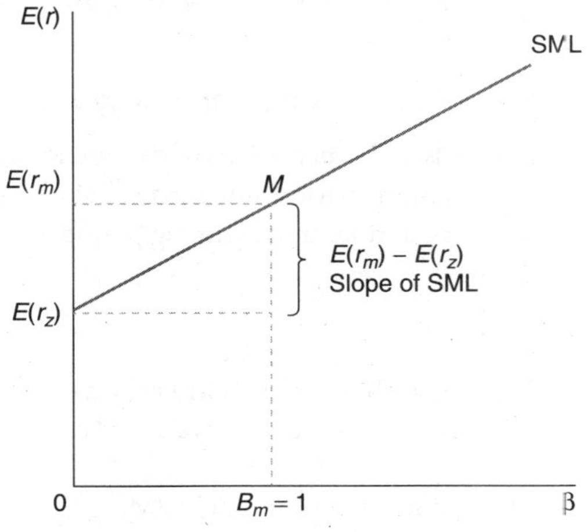

Subsequent to its introduction, many studies have tested the zero-beta model and the results have been conflicting.

Impact of transaction costs

The existence of transaction costs impacts the assumption that the investors will buy or sell the mispriced securities, i.e., the undervalued or the overvalued securities. This buying and selling of mispriced securities is expected to restore the equilibrium in the market, so that all the securities lie on SML. If transaction costs exist, investors may not buy or sell all mispriced securities because the potential excess returns may be wiped out by the transaction costs incurred in buying or selling those securities. Due to the impact of transaction costs on the buying and selling behavior of the investors, the securities will plot close to SML but not on it. Thus, there will be a band of SML instead of one single line as shown in Figure 6.15.

Figure 6.15 Security market line with transaction costs.

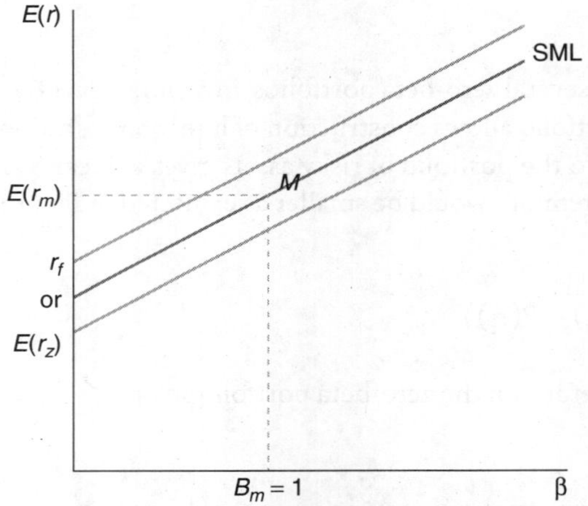

The width of this band is a function of the amount of transaction cost.

Impact of heterogeneous expectations and planning periods

If the investors differ in their holding periods and expectations of risk and return, each would have a unique SML and/or CML. Different expectations and planning period will also lead to a band of SML and/or CML, width of which will depend on the divergence in expectations and planning periods.

Impact of taxes

CAPM assumes that all the returns are tax-free but in real world returns are taxed, that too at differential rates for individuals and institutions. As many investors have heavy tax burdens, this could cause differences in SML and CML among investors.

Thus, relaxation of assumptions has significant impact on CAPM.

Empirical Tests of CAPM

CAPM has been subjected to many empirical tests, some of which have supported the existence of a positive linear relationship between returns and systematic risk while others have criticized not only the model but the tests supporting it as well.

While reviewing the empirical evidence for CAPM, two major issues have to be kept in mind: one is that the studies use historical returns as proxies for expected returns based on the assumption that there will be no divergence between expected and realized returns and the second is that most studies use some market index as proxy for market portfolio, which has been challenged by many academicians.

Empirical tests for CAPM try to answer two major questions:

1. How stable is beta?
2. Does the positive linear relationship between beta and returns on risky assets as hypothesized by CAPM actually exist?

Since beta is used as a principal measure of systematic risk in CAPM, we need to know whether historical betas can be used as estimates of future betas. We also need to understand the implications of the alternative values of beta published by different sources. Studies undertaken to examine the stability of beta have found that it was not stable for individual stocks but the beta for portfolios of stocks was found to be quite stable. Betas published by different sources differ on account of the differences in data used.

The existence of a positive relationship between returns and risk has been confirmed by many studies but the relationship is not completely linear. The outcome of latest studies are mixed. Some studies have found a significant relationship between beta and rates of returns while others have shown that the univariate beta model needs to be supplemented with variables like P/E ratio, skewness, firm size, book-to-market value and leverage.

Researchers like Richard Roll[5] have also raised the issue that it is not possible to derive or measure the true market portfolio as described by CAPM, so it is not possible to test the model or to use it to evaluate the performance of a portfolio.

A major challenge to CAPM came from the following studies: Banz[6] found that small cap stocks outperformed large cap stocks on a risk-adjusted basis. Basu[7] found that low P/E stocks outperformed high P/E stocks, after adjustment for risk. Fama and French[8] showed that "value stocks" (stocks with high book-to-market price ratios) generated larger returns than "growth stocks" (stocks with low book-to-market price ratios) on a risk-adjusted basis.

Current Status of CAPM

CAPM is a powerful and appealing model at the conceptual level as it provides a very useful way to think about risk and return and their relationship. Empirical test data does not support CAPM and its assumptions fully but it continues to be used widely as it is simple, logical and easy to use. Analysts use CAPM to determine required rate of return for a security, identify undervalued and overvalued securities and calculate the hurdle rate for

---

[5] Richard Roll, "A Critique of Asset Pricing Theory's Tests," *Journal of Financial Economics*, March 1977.

[6] R.W. Banz, "The Relationship between Return and Market value of Common Stocks," *Journal of Financial Economics*, March 1981.

[7] S. Basu, "Investment Performance of Common Stocks in Relation to Their Price-earnings Ratios: A Test of Efficient Market Hypothesis," *Journal of Finance*, June 1977.

[8] Eugene F. Fama and Kenneth French, "The Cross Section of Expected Stock Returns," *Journal of Finance*, June 1992.

capital budgeting decisions. Despite all criticism, CAPM has been accepted by the corporate and academic world due to the following reasons:

1. It provides an objective measure of risk premium.
2. It is simple and intuitively appealing model that focuses on diversifiable risk, a risk that has to be accepted.
3. No consensus on substitute of β has emerged in the financial theory.

CAPM is definitely not a perfect model. But the logic of the model is convincing as it provides a useful framework for thinking about risk-return relationship.

However, given the debate that prevails over its empirical validity, CAPM should be used with caution.

The mixed results of the empirical tests of CAPM and the difficulties with the market portfolio as described by CAPM, has led the academic community to put forth many alternative asset pricing models that we will discuss in the next section. Two multifactor models: Arbitrage Pricing Theory (APT) and Fama-French (FF) model have found some support in the academic community.

Multifactor Models

So far we have discussed CAPM, a single factor model which assumes that all variation in asset returns are attributable to a single factor, the market return. Research has shown that asset returns are related to many more factors such as inflation, interest rate movements or many industry-specific factors. This knowledge has led professionals to use multi-factor models in portfolio management.

Further, at a more technical level, the market equilibrium assumption of CAPM rules out arbitrage (use of security mispricing to earn risk-free profits by exploiting their price differential). We know that in real market conditions, arbitrage exists. Over the years, many multi-factor models that take arbitrage opportunity into consideration have been proposed in financial theory.

Multifactor models rest on the premise that the risk-return relationship is more complex then the simplification offered by CAPM. These models of security return provide a way for measurement and management of the exposure of security returns to many economy-wide factors such as interest-rate risk, business cycle risk, etc. The models derive a multi-factor version of SML in which risk premium from exposure to multiple sources of risk can be computed. The no-arbitrage condition is addressed in APT, a well-known multifactor model.

Multifactor models are finding increasing acceptance because they explain asset returns better than the market model and provide for a more detailed analysis of risk. The comprehensive risk analysis is useful in both active and passive portfolio management. In active portfolio management, multifactor models are used by many quantitative investment managers to predict alpha (excess risk-adjusted return) or relative return (return of an asset class vis-à-vis another). In passive portfolio management, analysts use multifactor models to match the factor exposure of the index fund and the index tracked.

Before we discuss few multifactor models in detail, let us understand factors and the basic principles underlying factor models.

Factors and Factor Models

A factor may be described as an underlying element with which many variables are correlated. These factors affect the average return of an asset and represent the 'priced risk' for which investors require additional returns. Such factors are usually called systematic factors.

Multifactor models can be categorized into different categories on the basis of the underlying factors they use. The main multifactor models may be:

1. **Macro-Economic Factor Models** that represent 'factors' or 'surprises' in macroeconomic parameters that impact asset returns.
2. **Statistical Factor Models** that are based on ex-post analysis of returns to explain and reproduce covariances of historical returns.
3. **Fundamental Factor Models** that are based on market related factors such as P/E ratio, market capitalization, book-value-to-price ratio, etc.

It may be noted here that the real world factor models may be more on the lines of mixed factor models and not conform to any single type mentioned above.

Factor Models for Security Return Volatility

We have already discussed Sharpe's model in the preceding chapter. The model recognizes that a part of the risk of a security comes from the market factor and rest of it comes from factors unique to the security.

The model is compelling in its ability to decompose the risk into systematic and firm-specific risk but it falters by confining systematic risk to a single factor, the market return, which in turn is affected by factors such as interest rates, inflation, etc. The fact is that each security may have different sensitivities to interest rates and other such factors and bundling them together into a single variable such as return on some market index seems over simplistic and incorrect. Thus, the practitioners turn to multifactor models for a better decomposition of systematic risk and the sensitivity of securities to this risk.

To build up our understanding of multifactor models, let us begin with a two-factor model based on macroeconomic variables: gross domestic product (GDP) and interest rates. The factor models constituted using these two factors provide a way of measuring changes in the security returns to unanticipated changes in these factors. These unanticipated changes are called '*surprises*.' The equation of the model may be presented as:

$$r_i = E(r_i) + b_{i\text{GDP}}\text{GDP} + b_{i\text{IR}}\text{IR} + e_i \tag{21}$$

where
r_i = Security return
$E(r_i)$ = Expected return
$b_{i\text{GDP}}$ = A coefficient that measures the sensitivity of the security's return to GDP changes
$b_{i\text{IR}}$ = A coefficient that measures the sensitivity of the security's return to changes in interest rates

These coefficients may be called as factor betas or factor loadings or factor sensitivities. The same logic can be extended to 'n' number of factors.

Let us try to understand the 'surprise' or unanticipated changes in a factor. The 'surprise' is a measure of the deviation of actual value of variables such as GDP, inflation, etc., from their predicted value. For example, an economic forecast predicts at the beginning of the month that the inflation will be 0.6% during the month. At the end of the month, the actual inflation is measured as 0.7%. This difference of 0.1% is the surprise inflation.

It is important to understand that the predicted values are already reflected in the stock prices and thereby in their expected return. It is only the surprise that is not reflected in the prices and is something that will impact the returns of security.

We can say that any multifactor model would comprise of three parts: the security's expected return, its unexpected return due to surprises and an error term, where the error term explains the return that is not explained by the first two terms. Clearly, it should represent only the asset-specific risks because common risks are already reflected in the first two terms. For an equity share, the error term may represent the return from unanticipated company-specific factors.

As we are now familiar with the basics of factor models, let us move to two main multifactor models of security returns: Arbitrage pricing theory (APT) and Fama-French Model three-factor model (FFM).

Arbitrage Pricing Theory

APT was proposed by Stephen Ross[9] in his article entitled 'The Arbitrage Theory of Capital Asset Pricing,' which appeared in the Journal of Economic Theory in December 1976. It is an asset-pricing model that rests on the assumption that a security's return is influenced by several independent factors.

APT also predicts SML like CAPM but it explains the security returns in a manner different from CAPM. It is offered as an alternative to CAPM and describes expected returns on a security or a portfolio as a linear function of the risk of security or portfolio with respect to a number of factors.

Though APT begins with the assumption of financial market equilibrium, like CAPM, it makes less strong assumptions than CAPM, keeping itself close to real world setting. These assumptions of APT are:

1. The capital markets are perfectly competitive.
2. Investors tend to prefer more wealth to less wealth with certainty.
3. The return on a security is linearly related to risk factors
4. A factor model can describe security returns
5. A large number of assets are available to investors to help them diversify asset-specific or idiosyncratic risk.
6. Arbitrage opportunities do not exist among well-diversified portfolios and if they do come up then the security markets do not allow them to persist.

On the basis of the above assumptions, APT equation may be given as:

$$r_i = E(r_i) + b_{i1}I_1 + b_{i2}I_2 + \cdots + b_{iK}I_K + e_i \qquad (22)$$

where
r_i = Actual return on asset during a given time period.
$E(r_i)$ = Expected return of asset i when all other risk factors have no changes.
b_i = The sensitivity of the security's return to the common risk factor.
I = Is the surprise in the factor.
e_i = The error term that is random and unique to the security.

APT does not specify the factors I_1, I_2, …, etc. that impact asset returns. It merely establishes a linear relationship between the security return and a small number of factors of systematic risk. Empirical work has suggested that a three or four-factor model is sufficient to capture the effect of systematic factors on security returns. Research

[9] Stephen A. Ross, "Return, Risk and Arbitrage," in I. Friend and J. Bicksler, eds., *Risk and Return in Finance*, Cambridge, Mass.: Ballinger, 1976.

further shows that the key factors are unanticipated shifts in term structure of interest rates, inflation, industrial production, risk premiums, etc.

Ross and others researchers have identified the following macro-economic factors as key factors in explaining the return on a security:

1. Inflation
2. GNP or Gross National Product
3. Confidence
4. Shifts in the Yield Curve

The biggest issue with APT is that it gives no guidance about the factors or their risk premium. A hint about factors can be seen in the work of Chen, Roll, and Ross[10], who used the following set of factors:

IP = % Change in industrial production

EI = % Change in expected inflation

UI = % Change in unanticipated inflation

CG = Excess return of long-term corporate bonds over long-term government bonds

GB = Excess return of long-term government bonds over *T*-bills

The above set of broad factors is obviously one of many possible combinations that can be and have been considered by researchers. There is no strong research evidence to indicate how long a list of factors should be used to represent systematic risk.

Let us take a closer look at a few assumptions and discuss the implications of APT.

The assumption that the security prices can be described by the factor model is fair enough but APT has not specified the number of factors. It states that each stock's return depend partly on certain systematic risk factors like macroeconomic factors and partly on noise—events that are unique to that company. In other words, APT states that the returns on a stock depend on a number of anticipated and unanticipated events. The anticipated events are incorporated by the investors into their expectations of returns and thereby get reflected in the market prices. However, more often than not, some part of the return actually realized might result from these unanticipated events. Even though the unanticipated events are expected to occur, it is difficult to know their direction or magnitude. APT uses the sensitivity of returns on a stock to these events. Factor sensitivity measures the response of return of a security to one unit of increase in a factor, holding all other factors constant. Some securities will be more sensitive to a particular factor than others.

The assumption about the availability of a large number of securities is useful in the formation of a well-diversified portfolio to eliminate asset-specific risk. Empirical evidence has supported this assumption as being a reasonable one as it has been observed that when a portfolio contains many stocks, the variance of its returns is not impacted much by the unsystematic risk of the component assets.

Coming to the no arbitrage assumption or the assumption that arbitrageurs will move to enforce law of one price by buying stock at lower rate and selling it at a higher rate is the most fundamental concept of capital market theory and any violation of this assumption would be an almost unacceptable form of market irrationality.

Let us understand the arbitrage portfolio with the help of a Numerical Example 14.

[10] N. Chen, R. Roll and S. Ross, "Economic Forces and the Stock Market," *Journal of Business* 59, 1986, 383–403.

Numerical Example 14

Consider four securities that have following expected returns and factor sensitivities (b_i) (we are considering a two-factor case):

Stock	Expected Return (%)	b_{i1}	b_{i2}
1	14	0.8	2.0
2	20	3.5	1.7
3	12	1.8	0.7
4	9	2.0	3.3

There is an investor, Jay, who has committed ₹5 lakh to each stock. Thus his initial wealth is ₹20 lakh. Determine if these securities are priced in equilibrium.

Solution:

We can answer the above question by exploring the possibility of the formation of an arbitrage portfolio. An arbitrage portfolio should have weights that satisfy following equations (based on the data given above).

$$Y_1 + Y_2 + Y_3 + Y_4 = 0 \quad (1)$$

$$0.8Y_1 + 3.5Y_2 + 1.8Y_3 + 2.0Y_4 = 0 \quad (2)$$

$$2.0Y_1 + 1.7Y_2 + 0.7Y_3 + 3.3Y_4 = 0 \quad (3)$$

The above equations imply that an arbitrage portfolio must not involve additional commitment of funds and must have żero sensitivity to each factor. Each of the above three equations comprising four unknown variables needs to be satisfied for the formation of an arbitrage portfolio. Mathematically, there are infinite number of solutions as there are more unknowns than equations. We can arrive at a possible solution by arbitrarily choosing a weight for any one of the stock and calculating the same for others. Suppose, we set $Y_1 = 0.1$.

By solving the above equation for $Y_1 = 0.1$, we get $Y_2 = 0.07$, $Y_3 = -0.09$ and $Y_4 = -0.08$.

These proportions represent a potential arbitrage portfolio. Let us see if it gives positive returns.

$$= (0.1 \times 14) + (0.07 \times 20) + (-0.09 \times 12) + (-.08 \times 9) = 1\%.$$

Hence an arbitrage portfolio, based on the purchase of stock 1 and 2 funded by selling 3 and 4, has been identified. Purchase of stock 1 and 2 by investors will push their prices up and consequently bring their expected returns down. On the other hand, sale of stock 3 and 4 will bring their prices down and push their returns up to the equilibrium level. Investors will continue to invest in such arbitrage portfolios until equilibrium is reached.

Here, a distinction between CAPM and APT should be noted. CAPM assumes that all investors tilt their portfolios towards under-priced shares or away from the over-priced shares, as the case may be. The impact of each investor on equilibrium prices is small and it's the aggregate impact which is important. On the other hand, in APT, as a result of no arbitrage condition, only a few investors, who are able to spot the arbitrage opportunity, mobilize large amounts and restore equilibrium.

The Equilibrium Risk-Return Relationship of APT

Equation (22) given below as

$$r_i = E(r_i) + b_{i1}I_1 + b_{i2}I_2 + \cdots + b_{iK}I_K + e_i$$

represents the APT equation for measuring returns. On the basis of this equation, APT establishes an equilibrium relation for risk and return which is as follows:

$$E(r_i) = r_f + b_{i1}\lambda_1 + b_{i2}\lambda_2 + \cdots + b_{iK}\lambda_K \quad (23)$$

$E(r_i)$ = Expected return on security or portfolio
r_f = The risk-free return
λ_j = Risk premium for factor
$b_{i,j}$ = The sensitivity of security or portfolio to factor j
K = Number of factors considered

Same equation is valid for both portfolios and individual assets.

Let us talk about factor risk premium, also called factor price (represented by λ_j). It is a measure of the expected return over and above r_f for a portfolio that has sensitivity of 1 to factor j and a sensitivity of zero to any other factor. A portfolio with sensitivity of 1 to factor j and zero to all other factors can be called as 'pure factor portfolio' for factor j. Such a portfolio can be called 'tracking portfolio' as it follows a particular source of macroeconomic risk that can serve as benchmark portfolio in investment decision. The return on such a portfolio may be computed as:

$$E(r_{pj}) = r_f + \lambda_{pj} \times 1 \quad (24)$$

Therefore,

$$\lambda_{pj} = E(r_{pj}) - r_f \quad (25)$$

To use APT, we need to identify the factors and estimate its parameters like r_f and risk-premiums which would be common for all assets and factor sensitivities which are specific to each asset. Let us understand the risk-return computations using APT with the help of the Numerical Examples.

Numerical Example 15

Consider two factors, *A* and *B*. The expected return on *A* is 11% and that on *B* is 12%. The risk-free rate is 5%. Consider a well-diversified portfolio, *XYZ* that has sensitivity $(b_{i1}) = 0.4$ to factor *A* and sensitivity $(b_{i2}) = 0.6$ to factor *B*. Calculate the risk premiums (λ) on account of the two factors and the total expected return on the portfolio.

Solution:

We know that the expected return of a portfolio that is sensitive to two factors can be calculated using the APT equation:

$$E(r_i) = r_f + b_{i1}\lambda_1 + b_{i2}\lambda_2 + \cdots + b_{iK}\lambda_K$$

Since there are only two factors under consideration, the above equation can be written as:

$$E(r_i) = r_f + b_{i1}\lambda_1 + b_{i2}\lambda_2$$

Given, $r_f = 5\%$, $b_{i1} = 0.4$, $b_{i2} = 0.6$, expected return on *A* is 11% and that of *B* is 12%
We need to calculate λ

We know, $\lambda_{pj} = E(r_{pj}) - r_f$

For factor 1,

$$\lambda = 11 - 4 = 7\%$$

For factor 2,

$$\lambda = 12 - 4 = 8\%$$

Risk premium due to factor $1 = b_{i1}\lambda_1 = 0.4 \times 7 = 2.8$

Risk premium due to factor $2 = b_{i1}\lambda_1 = 0.6 \times 8 = 4.8$

Substituting the values in $E(r_i) = r_f + b_{i1}\lambda_1 + b_{i2}\lambda_2$

$$E(r_i) = 5 + 2.8 + 4.8 = 12.6\%$$

Numerical Example 16

Suppose there are three well-diversified portfolios that are each sensitive to a common factor, *F*. Use the following information to detect arbitrage opportunity:

Portfolio	$E(r)$	Sensitivity to factor F
A	0.07	0.6
B	0.16	2
C	0.0556	0.4

Solution:

According to APT, the returns of a well-diversified portfolio (asset-specific risk has been eliminated) may be given as:

$$E(r_i) = r_f + b_{i1}\lambda_1 + b_{i2}\lambda_2 + \cdots + b_{iK}\lambda_K$$

Since, we are considering a single-factor case, the above equation can be rewritten as:

$$E(r_i) = r_f + b_{i1}\lambda_1$$

One of the APT assumption is that there is a linear relationship between return and risk factors. Two points can define a straight line. So to compute the unknown variables, we need two equations. Let us consider portfolio *A* and *B* to generate two APT equations:

$$E(r_A) = 0.07 = r_f + 0.6\,\lambda_1$$

$$E(r_B) = 0.16 = r_f + 2\,\lambda_1$$

From equation: $0.07 = r_f + 0.6\,\lambda_1$, we get

$$r_f = 0.07 - 0.6\,\lambda_1$$

Substituting this value of r_f in equation: $0.16 = r_f + 2\lambda_1$, we get

$$0.16 = 0.07 - 0.6\lambda_1 + 2\lambda_1$$

$$\lambda_1 = \frac{0.09}{1.4} = 0.064.$$

Therefore, value of r_f may be calculated from:

$$0.07 = r_f + 0.6\,\lambda_1$$

$$r_f = 0.07 - 0.6(0.064) = 0.03\%$$

Thus the APT equation can be written as:

$$E(r_i) = 0.03 + b_{i1}(0.064)$$

If the returns of the portfolios conform to the above equation then we can say that no arbitrage condition exists for those portfolios. We started with the assumption that portfolios *A* and *B* are priced as per APT. Let us check portfolio *C* now. The expected return of *C* as per APT

$$E(r_i) = 0.03 + (0.4)(0.064) = 0.0556$$

This is same as the given expected return for portfolio C. Thus no arbitrage opportunity exists.

Numerical Example 17

Suppose we add another portfolio D to the above set of the portfolios. In addition to this we also construct a portfolio comprising 50% *A* and 50% *C*. Use the following information to detect arbitrage opportunity.

Portfolio	$E(r)$%	Sensitivity to factor *F*
A	0.07	0.6
B	0.16	2
C	0.0556	0.4
D	0.08	0.5
$0.5A + 0.5C$	0.062	0.5

How will arbitrage activity restore equilibrium in the market as per APT?

Solution:

The return and factor sensitivity for the portfolio $0.5A + 0.5B$ is weighted average of the return and factor sensitivity of portfolio *A* and C.

We know portfolios *A*, *B* and C offer no arbitrage opportunity (as seen in example 15). Let us use the APT equation generated above to check if the two new portfolios satisfy the same condition.

$$E(r_i) = 0.03 + b_{i1}(0.064)$$

Portfolio *D*:

$$E(r_i) = 0.03 + (0.5)(0.064) = 0.062$$

This return is different from the given return. Therefore arbitrage opportunity exists.

Given expected return on *D* is 8%. Thus, *D* is undervalued relative to its factor risk. The investor can go long in the portfolio that exploits the arbitrage opportunity (arbitrage portfolio) in *D*. As explained above, for arbitrage portfolio, the overall investment remains the same. So to go long in D, the investor needs to go short in a portfolio that has the same factor sensitivity. We see that our new portfolio, $0.5A + 0.5C$ has the same sensitivity as D. So the investor will go short in this portfolio.

Suppose, the investment in portfolio D is ₹10000. This amount will come from selling short $0.5A + 0.5C$. The net cash flow to arbitrage portfolio is:

	Initial cash flow	Factor sensitivity	Final cash flow
Portfolio D	10000	0.5	10800
Portfolio 0.5A + 0.5C	−10000	−0.5	−10620
Total	0	0	180

The above table shows that, the initial net cash flow is zero. The factor sensitivity of the arbitrage portfolio is also zero. The expected value of the long position in D is $= 10000(1 + 0.08) = 10800$. The expected value of short position in $0.5A + 0.5C$ is $= - 10000(1 + 0.062) = - 10620$. Thus the final expected cash flow from the two positions is ₹180.

Because of the existence of arbitrage, A, C and D cannot be consistent with the equilibrium expressed by equation:

$$E(r_i) = 0.03 + b_{i1}(0.064).$$

If D actually has 8% returns, investors will buy it and raise its price until the arbitrage opportunity vanishes and the expected returns come down to the equilibrium level. Thus arbitrage activity restores equilibrium under APT.

Empirical Evidence of APT

APT does not specify the factors that constitute its equation. So any test of this theory has to begin with identification of specific factors through multivariate techniques before application of APT. The empirical studies conducted so far suggest that there is lack of consensus in the number, type and interpretation of these factors.

APT and CAPM

APT and CAPM are two means to the same end: measurement of asset/portfolio returns. Like CAPM, APT also gives us a benchmark rate that can be used for investment performance evaluation or as a discount rate in capital budgeting and security valuation.

APT's appeal lies in the fact that it draws upon a number of systematic factors to estimate returns as against CAPM that uses only an inherently unobservable and quite mysterious entity- the market portfolio. APT's no-arbitrage condition is satisfied by the rational behavior of few investors who identify this disequilibrium and take advantage of it. CAPM, on the other hand depends on the rationality of all the investors in identifying mispriced securities and pushing them to equilibrium through buying and selling. Despite this weakness, CAPM and its market model continue to dominate APT on grounds of less ambiguity and more universality.

The Fama-French Three-factor Model

Fama-French[11] have proposed an alternative approach for the use of specific macroeconomic factors as required by APT. They have used empirical research output to identify relevant sources of systematic risk related to characteristics of a firm. The Fama French model, that has come to dominate research and industry application is based on certain micro, market-related factors as a source of systematic risk. The Fama-French model uses firm characteristics that empirically seem to proxy for exposure to systematic risk. The factors chosen by Fama-French are the ones which on the basis of the past evidence seem to predict some part of the security return. The model may be mathematically presented as:

$$r_{it} - r_f = \alpha + \beta_{im}(r_{mt} - r_f) + \beta_{iSMB}\text{SMB}_t + \beta_{iHML}\text{HML}_t + e_{it} \tag{26}$$

where
r_{it} = Return on stock i in time t
r_{mt} = Return on the market in time t
β = Sensitivity of the stock to each factor
SMB = Small minus big, i.e., excess of return of portfolio of small stocks over portfolio of large stocks.
HML = High minus low, i.e., excess of return of portfolio of high book-to-market ratio over portfolio of stocks of low book-to-market ratio.

Clearly, the Fama-French model expands CAPM by adding size and value factors to the t market risk factor for explaining the security returns. This model takes into consideration the fact that value and small cap stocks tend to outperform markets on a regular basis. The model adjusts for the outperformance tendency of the value and small cap stocks. This model is used by a number of finance professionals to explain the risk and return of equity portfolios.

After testing CAPM on a large number of portfolios, Fama and French found that on an average, a portfolio's beta explains about 70% of its actual returns. For example, if a portfolio was up 12%, the upward movement of all stocks would explain nearly 70% of the return while the rest 30% is due to other factors not related to beta.

Fama and French proposed the three Factor model to explain this 30% risk. Beta continues to be an important part of their model as it accounts for 70% of the typical diversified portfolio return. However, the size of the stocks in a portfolio and the book-to-market value of the stocks make significant differences captured by the remaining 30%.

---

[11] Eugene F. Fama and Kenneth R. French, "Multifactor Explanations of Asset Pricing Anomalies," *Journal of Finance* 51, 1996, 55–84.

Numerical Example 18

Calculate the expected return on stock i, if $\beta_{im} = 0.9$, $r_f = 6.5\%$, the market risk premium is 6.3%, $\beta_{iSMB} = -0.5$, the expected value for the size factor is 4%, $\beta_{iHML} = -0.3$, and the expected value for the book-to-market factor is 5%.

Solution:

Assuming that the returns of stock i depend on the given factors only, the expected return of stock i may be computed as:

$$E(r_{it}) = r_f + \beta_{im}(r_{mt} - r_f) + \beta_{iSMB}\text{SMB}_t + \beta_{iHML}\text{HML}_t$$

Given

$$r_f = 6.5\%,\ r_{mt} - r_f = 6.3\%,\ \beta_{im} = 0.9,\ \text{SMB}_t = 4\%,\ \beta_{iSMB} = -0.5,\ \text{HML}_t = 5\%,\ \beta_{iHML} = -0.3$$

$$E(r_{it}) = 6.5 + (0.9)(6.3) + (-0.5)(4) + (-0.3)(5) = 8.67\%$$

In 2013, Fama and French introduced a five-factor asset pricing model, adding profitability and investment factors to augment the three-factor model.[12]

Critique of Fama-French Model

In FFM model, market index plays a role in capturing risk premium due to systematic risk coming from macroeconomic factors. To that extent it is aligned with CAPM. The other two factors, SMB and HML have been chosen by Fama-French on the basis of historical data showing that firm size and book-to-market ratios do predict variations in stock returns from CAPM levels. The justification for choosing these two factors is that these factors seem to proxy for yet unknown more-fundamental variables. For example, Fama-French point out that firms that have high book-to-market ratios are more likely to be in financial distress and that the firms with lower capitalization (small stocks) may be more sensitive to fluctuations in business conditions. The problem, with such empirical approach is that it may lead to unnecessary data snooping. Black[13] points out that when researchers scan and rescan the database of returns, many patterns maybe uncovered by pure chance and may not really be consistent for future inferences.

---

[12] Eugene F. Fama and Kenneth R. French, "A Five-Factor Asset Pricing Model", *Fama-Miller Working Paper*, November 2013.

[13] Fischer Black, "Beta and Return," *Journal of Portfolio Management* 20, 1993, 8–18.

SUMMARY

- ☑ Capital Market Theory extends MPT to develop a model for pricing of all risky assets and culminates into CAPM that allows it to determine the required rate of return for risky assets.
- ☑ Since the Capital Market Theory builds up on MPT, it shares many underlying assumptions with Markowitz' theory.
- ☑ The most basic asset allocation decision is to choose how much of the portfolio fund to place in risky assets versus the risk-free instruments.
- ☑ Risk-free asset may be defined as an asset that offers expected returns with certainty. The rate of return earned on such assets is called risk-free rate of return. Theoretically, risk-free rate of return should be equal to the expected long-term growth rate of economy after adjusting it for short-term liquidity.
- ☑ Risk-free assets have zero standard deviation of expected returns because the expected returns are entirely certain. Since the standard deviation of risk-free assets is zero, the covariance of the returns of such assets with any other asset will always be zero.
- ☑ The standard deviation of a portfolio that consists of a combination of risk-free and a risky-asset is the linear proportion of the standard deviation of the risky asset portfolio.
- ☑ CAL is obtained by plotting the different combinations of expected return and standard deviation available to an investor who combines his optimal risky portfolio with risk-free asset in the expected return-standard deviation plane.
- ☑ The slope of CAL measures the incremental return for incremental risk, i.e., increase in expected return per unit rise in standard deviation. For this reason it is called **reward to volatility ratio or Sharpe ratio.**
- ☑ The CAL with highest feasible reward-to-volatility ratio is best feasible CAL. The reward-to-volatility ratio of the best feasible CAL is given by the Sharpe ratio of the optimal risky portfolio.
- ☑ Risk-free lending implies investment in an asset that gives risk-free rate of return. To put it differently, risk-free lending means including a risk-free asset in the portfolio.
- ☑ An increase in investment in risky portfolio by borrowing funds at risk-free rate of return enables the investors to attain higher level of expected return in exchange for accepting higher level of risk.
- ☑ CML is a line from the risk-free rate through the market portfolio M and it is the best attainable or feasible CAL.
- ☑ Market portfolio includes all stocks, bonds, alternative investments, art and all other conceivable forms of risky assets. In practice, it is very difficult to include all the assets, so only equity stocks are included in the market portfolio.
- ☑ The main implication of CML for investors is that regardless of the level of their risk-aversion, all rational investors will hold only two securities: the market portfolio and the risk-free asset.

☑ Conservative or risk averse investors will choose a point near the lower left of the CML whereas growth-oriented investors who have lower risk aversion will choose to be higher up on CML.

☑ The implication of CML has been formalized into a theorem, called the Separation Theorem by James Tobin. According to Tobin, the investment process of a rational investor using mean variance criterion for investing can be separated into two distinct steps: Investment decision and financing decision.

☑ The capital asset pricing model is a set of predictions that are related to equilibrium expected returns on risky assets. It explains why capital assets are priced the way they are.

☑ A comparison of estimated return with the return computed using CAPM helps to determine whether the asset is under-valued, over-valued or fairly priced in the market.

☑ CAPM also helps in valuing an asset by providing an appropriate discount rate to use in valuation models.

☑ Due to its extreme usefulness and acceptable accuracy, CAPM is widely used despite failing to withstand many empirical tests.

☑ SML is a graphical expression of the CAPM equation.

☑ The equation of SML can be used to generate expected or required rate of return for any asset using its beta. The rate so obtained can be compared with investor's estimated rate of return to determine whether the asset is under-valued, fairly-valued or over-valued.

☑ A security is undervalued if its estimated return > required or expected return. Hence it will plot above the SML

☑ A security is overvalued if its estimated return < required or expected return. Hence it will plot below the SML

☑ A security is fairly priced if its estimated return = required or expected return. Hence it will plot on SML

☑ The difference between estimated return and expected or required return is sometimes referred to as a stock's alpha or its excess return. Alpha can be positive (if the stock is undervalued) or negative (if the stock is overvalued). Alpha equal to zero indicates that the stock is located on the SML and is fairly valued in line with its systematic risk.

☑ Empirical test data does not support CAPM and its assumptions fully but it continues to be used widely as it is simple, logical and easy to use.

☑ The mixed results of the empirical tests of CAPM and the difficulties with the market portfolio as described by CAPM has led the academic community to put forth many alternative asset pricing models.

☑ APT and CAPM are two means to the same end: measurement of asset/portfolio returns. Like CAPM, APT also gives us a benchmark rate that can be used for investment performance evaluation or as a discount rate in capital budgeting and security valuation.

☑ APT's appeal lies in the fact that it draws upon a number of systematic factors to estimate returns as against CAPM that uses only an inherently unobservable and quite mysterious entity – the market portfolio.

☑ Fama and French found that on an average, a portfolio's beta explains about 70% of its actual returns. They proposed the Three Factor model to explain the balance 30% risk.

KEY WORDS

Alpha **247**
Beta **251**
Capital market line (CML) **227**
Diversifiable risk **256**
Efficient frontier of risky assets **249**
Expected return **215**
Homogeneous expectations **232**
Market portfolio **227**
Market price of risk **229**
Minimum-variance portfolio **273**
Mutual fund theorem **237**
Optimal risky portfolio **210**
Overvalued **240**
Portfolio opportunity set **217**
Reward-to-variability ratio **274**
Security market line (SML) **239**
Separation theorem **232**
Undervalued **240**
Unsystematic risk **252**
Zero-beta portfolio **253**

CONCEPT QUESTIONS

1. The assumptions that create a make-believe world for CAPM to hold true are far removed from market reality. Do you agree or not?
2. The covariance between a risk-free asset and a risky asset is zero. Demonstrate the case mathematically and explain why it is so.
3. Is capital market line a special case of security market line? Discuss.
4. How do risk-free borrowing and lending transform Markowitz' efficient set?
5. According to capital market theory, even the most risk-averse investors would hold the same risky portfolio. Why? How would they incorporate their risk preference in their investment decision?
6. The enhanced efficient frontier has only one portfolio in common with Markowitz' efficient set. Which is that portfolio and what is the debate surrounding its existence? Why do all other points on old efficient frontier become undesirable?
7. What are the problems associated with the construction of true market portfolio? How can these problems be circumvented?
8. Discuss the implication of the slope of SML. Does the slope of SML change over time? Why?
9. What does SML describe? What would an investor do with the securities that do not plot on SML? Would his decision be impacted by transaction costs?
10. Discuss the implications of Mutual fund theorem for investors using a passive investment strategy?
11. Explain the working of an arbitrage portfolio with the help of a Numerical Example.
12. Fama-French model seems to do a better job of explaining the expected returns of a stock. Do you agree?

PRACTICE PROBLEMS

1. Divya is a typical mean variance optimizer. She holds a well-diversified portfolio that has a standard deviation equal to 22%. Calculate the expected return on her portfolio if the standard deviation of the market portfolio is 27% and the expected return is 18%. The risk-free rate is 7%.

2. Consider two stocks, SH Petrochem and MS Cosmetics. The following table gives an analyst's expected return on two stocks for market returns under two states of economy, good and bad.

States	Market return (%)	SH Petrochem (%)	MS Cosmetics (%)
Bad	7	9	16
Good	21	48	0.25

Answer the following on the basis of the above information.

a. What are the betas of the SH Petrochem stock and MS Cosmetics stock?
b. What is the expected return of each stock if the two states have equal probabilities of occurrence?
c. Give the equation for SML if the two states have equal probabilities of occurrence. The risk-free rate of return is 7%.
d. What is the alpha of the two stocks?

3. Assume that the risk-free rate of return in the economy is 5% and the return on market portfolio is 10%. What is the market risk premium? Calculate return for given stocks if the beta for each is:

Stock	Beta
A	0.75
B	1.06
C	1.13
D	1.34
E	−0.20

4. Consider a risk-free asset and a portfolio of risky assets with following risk-return characteristics:

	Risky portfolio	Risk-free asset
Expected Return	15%	7%
Variance	81	0
Standard Deviation	9%	0

Compute the risk and return of a portfolio if an investor holding it decides to:

a. Invest 40% of his funds in risk-free assets.
b. Increase his investment in risky portfolio by borrowing an amount equal to 30% of his original investment.

5. Suppose the S&P CNX Nifty has given an average excess return equal to 14% in the past 12 years, its standard deviation is 23%.
   a. What should be the average degree of risk aversion across investors?
   b. If the average degree of risk aversion across investors is actually found to be 3.75, calculate the level of excess return that S&P CNX Nifty should have yielded, given its standard deviation.

6. Use the following information to compute the portfolio beta.

Security	Amount invested (₹)	Beta
CNJ Ltd.	1000	0.85
ZKC Ltd.	2500	0.95
DRH Ltd.	3500	1.2
SKK Ltd.	1000	1.1

7. Calculate the risk premium on a portfolio comprising of 30% investment in HCL and 70% in RIL. The beta of HCL is 0.37 and the beta of RIL is 1.08. Given the risk premium of the market portfolio at 9% with a standard deviation of 25%.

8. An analyst gathered following information for three stocks. Assume a risk-free rate of 7% and a market return of 16%. Compute the estimated/forecasted return and required return on each stock, determine whether each stock is undervalued, overvalued or properly valued, and outline an appropriate trading strategy (buy, sell or hold). Exhibit the analysis graphically.

   Forecast Data

Stock	Price today (₹)	Expected price in 1 year (₹)	Expected dividend in 1 year (₹)	Beta
True Worth Ltd.	25	27	1.00	1.0
DSM Enterprises	41	45	2.00	0.8
Crem Tech Ltd.	15	17	0.50	1.2

9. Calculate the expected required rate of return of Google from the following information: *T*-bill rate is 2.75%, the market risk premium is 5.5%, and the forecasted return on the SMB and HML portfolios are 2.5% and 4%. Google's market beta is 1.51, SMB beta is –0.20 and HML beta is –1.33.

10. Suppose two common factors, surprises in industrial production and interest rates affect returns of two stocks MMC Ltd. and MML Ltd. A portfolio manager wants to constitute a portfolio comprising 25% of MMC Ltd. and 75% MML Ltd. The relevant multifactor equation for the two stocks is:

$$r_{MMC} = 0.08 - (1.1)I_{IP} + (1.2)\, I_{INT} + e_{MMC}$$

$$r_{MML} = 0.12 + (2)I_{IP} + (3.8)\, I_{INT} + e_{MML}$$

Answer the following:

a. What is the expression for the return on the portfolio thus formed?

b. Calculate the return on the portfolio, given that the surprises in industrial production and interest rates are 1.5 percent and 0 percent, respectively. Further, the error terms for both stocks is equal to 0.5%.

CASELET

A portfolio manager is considering three portfolios for his client. The first is a mid-cap stock portfolio, the second is a long-term government and corporate bond portfolio, and the third is a pure risk-free asset portfolio comprising t-bills that yield a rate of 7%. The risk-return characteristics of the risky portfolios are:

	Expected return	Std Dev
Stock Portfolio	20%	28%
Bond Portfolio	11%	15%

The correlation between the returns of the two risky portfolios is 0.10.

1. Compute the weights/proportions of the stock and equity portfolios in the minimum-variance portfolio formed by combining the two risky portfolios. What is the expected return and standard deviation of return of the minimum-variance portfolio?
2. Tabulate and trace the investment opportunity set of the portfolio comprising the two risky portfolios by varying the investment proportions for the stock portfolio from zero to 100% in increments of 20%.
3. Determine the weights/proportion of each asset and the expected return and standard deviation of the optimal risky portfolio.
4. Compute the reward-to-variability ratio of the best feasible CAL?
5. The client requires that his portfolio should yield an expected return of 15%, and that his portfolio should lie along the best feasible CAL. Compute the weights/proportion of funds invested in the t-bills and the two risky portfolios that together comprise the optimal risky portfolio. What is the standard deviation of this portfolio?

Financial Wizardry through Strategic Jugglery: Asset Allocation

7

CHAPTER OBJECTIVES

- ❒ Understanding the basics of asset allocation
- ❒ Describing different phases of asset allocation
- ❒ Analyzing types of asset allocation
- ❒ Examining the impact of changes in market level on asset allocation
- ❒ Assessing various asset allocation approaches
- ❒ Learning to formulate bond and equity portfolio management strategies

In the preceding chapters of this book, we have discussed phases of portfolio management and various models and techniques for construction of a portfolio. Let us look at them once again.

Portfolio management begins with the specification of investment policy and strategy. Herein, the investment objectives like income, growth and/or stability are identified and investor risk tolerance/preference is mapped in terms of indifference curves. So basically investment objectives spell out the return requirement and risk characteristics of an individual. The flip side of investment objectives is represented by investment constraints that relate to taxes, regulatory requirement, investment horizon, liquidity and the unique circumstances of individual investor.

The mapping of investment objectives and constraints of individual investor leads to the next phase in the formulation of investment strategy. Quantification of the capital market expectation is a challenging task and it requires intensive research and use of sophisticated forecasting method to specify the time horizon of investment, returns of the asset class under consideration and the risk assessment of the same. The rest of the phases of portfolio management follow thereafter.

A key part of portfolio management is asset allocation. It is a major decision for all investors as selection of asset to invest in and allocating funds to them is critical to the success of investment strategy. Once the portfolio has been executed by identification and acquisition of the specific securities in different asset classes, the portfolio needs to be evaluated, revised and rebalanced. Let us begin our discussion on asset allocation which comprises the most critical phase in portfolio management.

What is the Meaning of Asset Allocation?

Asset allocation broadly refers to the split of funds across different asset classes. It may be defined in simple terms as a plan of how invested funds are divided among different asset classes, such as cash, stocks, bonds, real estate, mutual funds, derivatives and so on. In a more complex sense, asset allocation refers to an investment strategy where one spreads one's investible surplus across different asset classes to reduce risk through diversification. Asset allocation means different things to investors in different context, but broadly speaking, asset allocation can be said to comprise the following steps:

1. **Specification of Asset Classes to be Included in the Portfolio:** As already discussed, broad asset classes available for investment are stocks, fixed income securities, real estate, precious metals, derivatives, commodities, art objects and others. Institutional investors usually limit themselves to bonds, stocks and real estate.
2. **Quantification of Capital Market Expectation:** In this step of asset allocation, analysts and investors use historical data and economic analysis to quantify expected future return over the holding period under consideration for the assets selected for inclusion in the portfolio.
3. **Portfolio Optimization:** Under this step, the portfolio choices need to be optimized. For example, if mean-variance approach is to be used then efficient frontier is to be derived.
4. **Choosing the Optimal Mix of Assets**, i.e., selecting that portfolio from the efficient frontier that best fits the investment objectives and satisfies the investment constraints of the investor.

Let us now examine the intricacies of asset allocation. There are several types or versions of asset allocation that can be found mentioned in various books. These are:

1. Strategic asset allocation
2. Tactical asset allocation
3. Balanced asset allocation
4. Drifting asset allocation
5. Dynamic asset allocation

Of all the above, strategic and tactical asset allocations are the two major types of asset allocation. Let us discuss each in detail.

Strategic Asset Allocation

Strategic asset allocation is the first key element of portfolio management process that focuses on selection of investments. Strategic asset allocation integrates the investors' risk-return profile and investment constraints with the long-run capital market expectations with a view to determining the level of exposure to different asset classes. Strategic allocation represents the execution stage of a portfolio but in the context of broad asset classes. It is actually the initiation of the portfolio construction phase of portfolio management.

Strategic asset allocation commands a lot of attention of professionals because it specifies the investor's accepted exposure to systematic risk. Thus, the significance of strategic asset allocation stems from the fact that distinct and heterogeneous asset classes have different exposures to certain set of systematic or uncontrollable factors. Using strategic asset allocation enables the investors to control systematic risk exposure by diversifying across distinct asset classes as opposed to homogenous set of assets.

The main approaches to strategic asset allocation may be described as:

1. **Asset/Liability Management (ALM) Approach to Strategic Asset Allocation:** Investors whose key objective is to control investment risk take asset/liability management (ALM) approach to strategic asset allocation. In ALM approach to strategic asset allocation, liabilities or financial obligation are modeled and optimal asset allocation is determined with the objective of funding these liabilities. ALM approach can also be used by investors without significant future liabilities by treating future needs such as income as liabilities.
2. **Asset Only (AO) Approach to Strategic Asset Allocation:** As an alternative to ALM approach, investors may also use the asset only approach to strategic asset allocation. Under this approach, liabilities are not modeled explicitly; rather they impact the portfolio selection indirectly. Asset only approach affords less precision in controlling liabilities funding related risks as compared to the ALM approach. Black-Litterman model is an example of AO approach to strategic asset allocation.

   Going back to ALM approach, we can identify it to be dynamic or static. The ALM strategies vary from those that aim to minimize the risk with respect to asset-liabilities to those that seek higher risk for higher expected excess of assets over liabilities.

   Two risk-minimizing ALM strategizes are cash flow matching or exact matching and duration matching or immunization.

   The cash flow matching approach recommends investments in bonds to match future liabilities to minimize risk relative to funding those liabilities. The duration matching approach recommends investments in bonds to match the liabilities in terms of their weighted-average duration. The investments in bond should also have the same present value as those of the future liabilities that the portfolio seeks to immunize.

   The dynamic approach to ALM linked strategic asset allocation recognizes that asset allocation and the returns and liabilities in a given investment period have an impact on the optimal investment decision available for all future time periods. The static approach does not take into consideration the link between optimal investment decisions at different time periods, rather treats optimal decision of each period in isolation. The static approach in simple can be applied to both, AO and ALM approaches but dynamic approach, with all its complexities and costs is more frequently chosen by investors who have significant future liabilities. The choice between AO and ALM approach depends on the needs and circumstances of the investors. ALM approach results in more allocation to fixed-income assets and it is used mainly by investors who have below average risk tolerance. Strategic asset allocation decisions and the basic optimization principles do not differ with the type of investors. Rather, the characteristics of investors are the key basis for the same. Strategic asset allocation becomes relevant only when the models and inputs are chosen on the basis of investors' key characteristics and concerns, whether they are individuals or institutional.

Beyond the Basics 7.1 Black Litterman Model

The Black-Litterman model was developed by Fischer Black and Robert Litterman in 1990 at Goldman Sachs. The model was developed to overcome the challenges and problems in using Markowitz' mean variance theory for portfolio optimization. The Black-Litterman model is a mathematical asset allocation model for unconstrained portfolio optimization which is based on equilibrium assumption that the initial asset allocation by a fund manager for every client should be in the proportion of the market values of the assets to be included in the portfolio. Thereafter, the general allocation so made should be modified to suit the investment objectives and the specific views of the concerned client.

Modern portfolio theory provides solution for the problem of asset allocation once the expected returns, correlations and covariances between the pairs of assets are known. The challenge in applying modern portfolio theory is that even though the covariances of a few assets might be adequately ascertained, it is quite difficult to come up with reasonably accurate estimates of expected returns. Black–Litterman model overcomes this problem by doing away with the need to input estimated expected return for proceeding with asset allocation. It begins by assuming that the initial expected returns are at such a level that the equilibrium asset allocation is same as what is observed in the financial markets. The person seeking to optimize his asset allocation through the Black-Litterman model is required to state how his assumptions/expectations about expected returns differ from those of the market. Further, he is also required to specify the degree of confidence he has in the alternative assumptions. This input is sufficient for the Black–Litterman method to compute the preferred (mean-variance efficient) asset allocation. This process sounds simple, but it is not. To use this model, first, the investors need to delineate their investable universe and then find the market capitalization of asset classes thus identified. After finding the market capitalization, they need to obtain a time series of returns for each asset class to compute a covariance matrix. As a next step towards asset allocation, the investors need to quantify their views regarding expected returns so that they can be applied to compute new estimates of return. Finally, the outputs generated from the model are fed into a portfolio optimizer to generate the efficient frontier and select an efficient portfolio best suited to the investor.

This model is intuitively superior to MPT but there are many difficulties in obtaining the inputs required. Many assets like private equity and real estate are illiquid and it becomes quite difficult for the investors to obtain information about their market capitalization. Further, to obtain time series of returns, investors are often required to use proxy for a given asset class. The proxy could be a market index. Determining the correct proxy could prove to be quite challenging.

It can be said that though the Black Litterman model for asset allocation leads to more stable and diversified portfolios, yet it is difficult to apply because it requires a large amount of data that is not always easy to procure.

Based on information accessed at:

http://www.cis.upenn.edu/~mkearns/finread/intuition.pdf
and http://www.master272.com/finance/BL/JWalters_Black-Litterman.pdf on December 26, 2014.

To summarize, strategic asset allocation can be looked at from the objectives of return and risk. An investor may have both qualitative and quantitative return objectives, but asset allocation becomes more successful by formulating quantitative objectives to capture return and risk levels perceived to be commensurate for achieving qualitative objectives. Further, since strategic asset allocation pertains to long-term needs of investors, quantified return objectives should also take into account the effect of compounding for multiple holding periods.

In case of risk also, both quantitative and qualitative risk objectives are important in the context of strategic asset allocation. Qualitatively, an investor may have a below average or above average risk tolerance. Quantitatively, risk tolerance may be measured in terms of risk aversion (discussed in detail in the Chapter 4).

Risk tolerance may also be quantified in terms of acceptable level of volatility for an investor. This is measured by standard deviation or variance of returns. Another measure for quantification of risk is called shortfall risk

Beyond the Basics 7.2 Shortfall Risk

Investors can also quantify risk in terms of shortfall risk. It may be defined as the risk that the value of the portfolio will remain below some minimum pre-specified level during a pre-specified timeframe. Shortfall risk can be considered to be a subset of the larger concept of downside risk.

Roy's safety-first criterion (Arthur Roy, Safety First and the Holding of Assets, Econometrica 1952 July, 431–450) is the oldest shortfall risk criterion. The shortfall risk criterion refers to the control an investor has over his investment. According to this criterion, an investor exercises control over his investment by ensuring that a certain amount of his invested principal is preserved or kept safe. By doing so, the investor tries to minimize the probability that the return his investment realizes is less than or equal to a specified threshold, *t*.

Roy's safety-first criterion may be called a risk management technique that enables an investor to choose one portfolio over another. The choice is based on the criterion that the probability of decline of returns generated from a portfolio below a minimum desired threshold is minimized.

For example, suppose an investor faces two possible investment options represented by portfolio A and portfolio B. Assuming that the investor's threshold return level is –1%, he will choose the portfolio that can be expected to provide the maximum probability of the return being at least as high as –1%.

Based on information accessed at:

http://www.quantatrisk.com/2014/03/30/roys-safety-first-criterion-in-portfolio-optimization-problem/ and http://www.cyclopaedia.info/wiki/Roy,-s-safety-first-criterion on December 26, 2014.

that captures the possibility that portfolios' value may fall below certain minimum acceptable level during a given holding period. Shortfall risk is the main focus of the ALM approach to strategic asset allocation and it can also be incorporated in the AO approach in many ways.

Phases in strategic asset allocation

For undertaking strategic asset allocation, investment manager needs to specify asset-classes with the weights that would comprise the portfolio to be constructed to meet the investment objectives and satisfy the investment constraints of an investor. The process of strategic asset allocation in the context of ALM approach can be looked as comprising two separate aspects pertaining to capital markets on one hand and investor on the other. These two aspects culminate into inputs for optimization and subsequent portfolio formation.

On the investor's side, factors determining investor's risk tolerance need to be specified. Here, investor's assets, liabilities and net worth need to be quantified and his attitude toward risk needs to be ascertained. A risk tolerance function can be used to portray the relationship between the investor's current risk tolerance and his circumstances (net worth etc.). This risk tolerance function provides a measure of the investor's risk tolerance/aversion at varying levels of outcomes of a portfolio.

On the capital market side, investment manager needs to ascertain the existing state of capital markets on the basis of present and past asset prices, projected and historical asset cash flows and yield curve. The current state of capital markets provides the basis for predicting expected returns of various asset classes and risks associated with these returns. Correlations among returns of various asset classes can also be ascertained here. Choice of prediction models is key at this stage and the investment manager needs to choose ones that help translate the prevailing capital market condition into future expectation with reasonable certainty.

The inputs from the capital market predictions and investor's risk tolerance or aversion can be used as basis for optimization. At this stage, the investment manager needs to use an optimizer to determine the most appropriate mix of assets for the investor.

The choice of optimizers and procedures for asset-mix determinants has received a lot of attention of researchers. There are many objective quantitative tools that are available. However, many investment managers, particularly those dealing with individuals, tend to use qualitative approach to asset-mix determination based on their experience. The quantitative approaches that are popular are mean-variance approach, the Black-Litterman approach and the Monte Carlo simulation. Though the quantitative approaches are the mainstay of strategic asset allocation, traditionally used thumb rules and conventional wisdom is also applied by investment managers, particularly while undertaking strategic asset allocation for individual investors. The following things should be kept in mind while undertaking strategic asset allocation:

1. Investor's risk tolerance should be used as indicators for choice of stock/bonds. Investors having high-risk aversion should tilt their portfolio in favor of bonds whereas investors with low risk aversion should hold more stocks in their portfolio (since equity is riskier then debt). Being risky, equities have returned more than bonds across the globe. This phenomenon has been witnessed in equity markets in India as well where the stock markets have witnessed a CAGR of 14% to 15% in the long run.
2. Many investment managers consider a 60/40 stock/bond allocation as an appropriate starting point for an average investor's strategic asset allocation as such an allocation is considered to be neutral. It is neither too conservative nor too aggressive and in perfect alignment with an average investor's profile.

   In such an allocation, equities bring long-term growth and bonds bring the risk reduction benefits. Diversification within each asset class (stock and bond) ensures an overall well-diversified portfolio.
3. Investment in bonds should increase with decrease in risk tolerance.
4. There is another thumb rule that says that the allocation to stock should be equal to 100 minus the age of investor. This implies that younger investors should have more aggressive asset allocation in terms of inclusion of the riskier asset, namely, equity.

   This approach makes sense because theoretically speaking, young people have longer time frame of investment to make up for the losses they incur on account of market fluctuations. They have longer time-period of relatively low risk earning from employment that is uncorrelated to stock market returns.
5. As a corollary to the thumb rule described above, investors with longer time horizons should allocate larger part of their funds to stocks. The idea behind this is that historically equities have been observed to be less risky to hold in long run as compared to short-run. This has been called 'time diversification' in the investment parlance.

   To be successful, an investment manager needs to understand strategic asset allocation in its entirety with all its quantitative and qualitative aspects.

Applying strategic asset allocation

We are now familiar with the approaches to strategic asset allocation and the steps involved in using it. Two specific issues, namely, selecting the asset classes and implementing strategic asset allocation, need to be looked at in a little detail before we can claim to have a complete understanding of strategic asset allocation. They are discussed here:

1. **Selection of Asset Classes:** Asset class refers to a group of instruments that are relatively homogeneous and have the same attributes. The choice of asset class for the asset mix decision is an important part of the strategic asset allocation and it has long-term impact on the risk and return of the portfolio being constructed. To be able to select asset class effectively, investment manager should be able to specify asset classes based on certain basic criteria like homogeneity, similarity of attributes, mutual exclusivity, i.e., no overlap between different classes and existence of opportunity for diversification, i.e., low correlations with other asset classes. The chosen asset classes should also provide adequate liquidity and opportunity to rebalance without adversely impacting asset class prices or resulting in high transaction cost. We already know the following asset classes:
   (a) *Domestic stock or equity:* It represents the equity shares available for investment within the country of the investor and it is often sub-categorized into large, mid and small cap on the basis of market capitalization.
   (b) *Domestic fixed income securities:* These comprise bonds of varying maturities and are classified on the basis of issuer. Government securities and corporate bonds are the key avenues for investments in fixed income assets. Sometimes, fixed income securities are classified into two types, namely, intermediate-term and long-term domestic bonds.
   (c) *Foreign stock or equity:* This asset class refers to the common stocks listed outside the geographical boundaries of the investor's country. Sometimes an asset class within foreign equity may be classified into two types namely, emerging market and developed market equity.
   (d) *Foreign fixed market securities:* This asset class refers to the investment in instruments with fixed income issued by countries other than the country of the investor. Like equity, this asset class is also categorized into two types, namely, developed market and emerging market fixed income securities.
   (e) *Alternative investments:* All the assets which are not included in the above four categories can be put under the umbrella of alternative investments. These include private equity, commodities, real estate, natural resources, precious metals and stones, to name a few. However, such common categorization is incorrect as there is hardly any homogeneity between real estate and private equity or any other pair.
   (f) *Cash and cash equivalents:* A part of portfolio may also be maintained in the form of cash and cash equivalents for contingency requirement or to take advantage of sudden investment opportunities. The amount of cash and equivalents in any portfolio depend on the amount of liquidity and safety the investor wants. Ideally, 5 to 15% of the portfolio is recommended to be maintained in the form of cash and equivalents.

   Investors are constrained by a number of factors while choosing their asset mix. These include regulatory constraints, tax concerns, high investment requirement (as in the case of private equity), currency and other risk of investing across border, lack of resources, high transaction costs and related expenses associated with investment in certain asset classes and inability to research investment avenues, as in the case of alternative investments where information is not available as widely as in the case of bonds and stock.

   We also need to consider various factors while selecting securities to invest our funds in. The selection of equity is done on the basis of three approaches to security analysis described in the chapters on technical analysis, fundamental analysis and random selection of stock as per efficient market theory. Technical analysis is based on the tools that use price and volume data to decide the direction of the price movement in the future. Technical analysis works best in the markets that are inefficient, i.e., the markets that do not conform to random walk hypothesis.

   Fundamental analysis focuses on E-I-C indicators to determine the intrinsic value of a share. The value so computed is compared with the prevailing market price to decide the buy, sell or hold strategy for a share.

It works best when markets exhibit weak form of efficiency, i.e., they reflect all the past information in the prices of shares. It is also fairly effective in semi-strong efficient markets.

The random selection approach is an off-shoot of efficient market hypothesis and is based on the belief that all securities are properly priced in the market. Nobody can beat the market through specific stock selection. It is a very effective approach when the markets are strongly efficient.

While selecting fixed income securities, we need to consider the following factors:

- The risk of default, i.e., the possibility of non-payment of interest and/or principal by the borrower. Here credit rating plays an important role. If no ratings are available, credit worthiness of borrowers may be assessed through analysis of their financial statements and a study of the industry to which the firm belongs.
- Tax benefit: Investors should look for avenues that give tax advantage in some form so as to reduce their tax burden and preserve their wealth.
- Liquidity: Fixed income securities that are listed in secondary market are easy to sell and convert into cash at a short notice. Such securities should ideally be preferred over the unlisted securities.

2. **Implementing Strategic Asset Allocation:** Apart from choosing the asset-mix, the investors also need to decide their investment approach which could be:
   (a) Passive
   (b) Active
   (c) Enhanced indexing or semi-active
   (d) A combination of some of the above

   They also need to decide how they would execute the investment approach chosen from the above listed options.

   A passive investment option can be implemented through setting a benchmark or a tracking portfolio constructed to replicate the returns to some broad index representing the asset class under consideration.

   Passive position can also be implemented through a derivative-based portfolio comprising cash and long position in (a) swap with underlying asset being the index representing that asset class and (b) index futures for that asset class.

   Active investment option can be exercised without any tracking portfolio, merely by creating a portfolio of cash market securities that represents investors' skills and insights.

   Semi-active investment option can be exercised through a tracking portfolio comprising cash market securities that allow scope for some under/over weight securities relative to index representing the asset class under consideration (with controlled tracking risk). A derivative based portfolio can also be used for semi-active investing.

Other Types of Asset Allocation

This section discusses other type of asset allocations. As stated above, strategic asset allocation has a long-term perspective but investors need to respond to changing market conditions with adjustments in the portfolios. The asset allocation approaches that are used in response to changing market conditions are:

1. Tactical asset allocation
2. Drifting asset allocation
3. Balanced asset allocation
4. Dynamic or insured asset allocation

Let us discuss each briefly.

Tactical asset allocation

It involves making short-term changes/adjustment in asset-mix or asset class proportions on the basis of short-run predictions regarding an asset class performance. By undertaking tactical asset allocation, portfolio manager takes active risk in the hope of earning positive returns, over and above the expenses incurred, using portfolio invested in passively managed index (for a given asset class) as benchmark. Active risk refers to the volatility of active returns, i.e., portfolio return minus the return on the benchmark. Thus, tactical asset allocation is an active strategy of investment at asset class level.

Tactical asset allocation is also referred to as market timing. It involves a departure from strategic asset allocation mix by purposefully over/under weighing asset classes vis-à-vis their proportion in the original allocation. The changes reflect the assessment of the manager in terms of near-term market expectations and perceived disequilibrium/mispricing. In other words, tactical asset allocation is a follow-up of strategic asset allocation and pertains to management of money within the asset class.

Tactical asset allocation tries to exploit the divergence between an investor's short-term views and long-term views (as captured in strategic asset allocation). In economic terms, tactical asset allocation seeks to benefit the investor by using transitory deviation of the values of asset classes from their expected long-term levels.

For example, suppose the total investible surplus is ₹100 and it has been split into a stock-bond mix of 60:40 over long-run. If the investor perceives that the stocks are going to outperform bonds on a risk-adjusted basis in the short-run, then he can step-up the stock component to say 70, thereby raising the beta of the portfolio. If, on the contrary, the investor expects bonds to fare better in the short-run, he can raise the bond component of the portfolio to say 50, and bring the beta down.

Tactical asset allocation is based certain characteristics of the market:

1. Markets are rational.
2. Relative expected returns capture the relative risk perception.
3. Markets are mean reverting, i.e., any deviations/departures from equilibrium are temporary and markets always revert to equilibrium.
4. Investors have objective idea about available returns at least in the context of certain assets and educated forecast can be made for others.

   Deviations from fair value, i.e., market timing can be identified through a variety of analytical tools making forecast about general market conditions. These tools include econometric models, advance-decline analysis, moving average analysis and economic analysis, to name a few. The changes in equilibrium could be brought about by a number of factors.

   Following distinctive features of tactical asset allocation need to be kept in mind:

   (a) Theoretically, market-timing sound like good opportunity but empirical studies show that it does not succeed so frequently when costs of error and transactions are factored in.
   (b) Tactical asset allocation requires expertise and skill. To be really effective as a strategy to generate profits, tactical asset allocation needs to generate returns over and above the transaction costs.
   (c) Tactical asset allocation is contrarian in nature as it indicates buying after market decline and selling after the rise in the market.
   (d) The deviations from fair value which are there for short-term may actually persist beyond the short horizon if the underlying factors change. These factors could be movement along business cycle, central bank policy changes, changes in expected inflation and changes in the risk attributes of assets.
   (e) Investors/managers who want to undertake tactical asset allocation need to be guided by prospective value measures such as yields. Thus, tactical asset allocation is value-oriented.

Drifting asset allocation

Drifting asset allocation policy advocates that no tampering may be done with the initial allocations. It is a typical 'buy and hold' strategy and recommends no rebalancing, irrespective of fluctuations in relative values. For example, consider a portfolio with 60:40 allocation across stock and bond. The payoffs are exhibited in Figure 7.1.

Figure 7.1 Payoff for buy and hold policy.

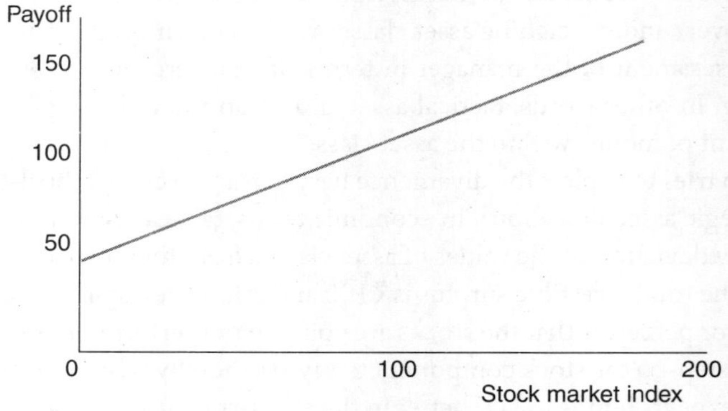

The value of the portfolio varies linearly with the stock market However, the value of the portfolio does not fall below initial investment in bonds and the potential for an upside is limitless. Thus, the policy provides a downside protection. A buy and hold strategy with higher percentage in stocks works wonderfully when stocks outperform bonds. But when bonds out-do stocks, the buy-hold policy for high initial investment in stocks fares really badly.

Balanced asset allocation

Balanced asset allocation policy implies periodical rebalancing of the original portfolio constructed by strategic asset allocation. The rebalancing is undertaken to ensure that the stock-bond mix remains aligned with the

Figure 7.2 Payoff of constant mix policy.

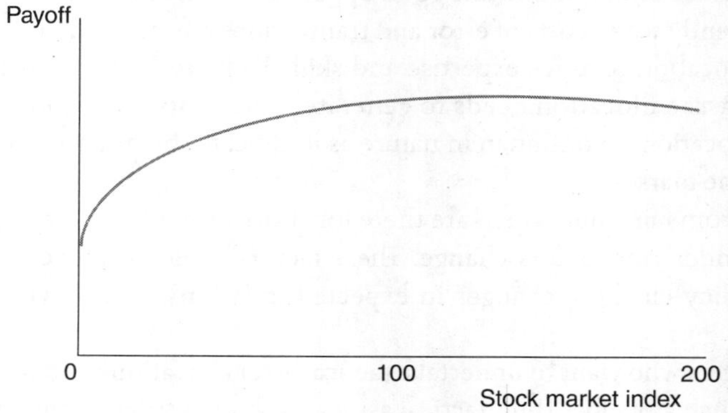

overall long-term asset mix. The aim of balanced asset allocation is to maintain exposure in stocks at a constant proportion of the portfolio. Rebalancing needs to be done whenever the relative value of the components changes. Target proportions are maintained at all times by rebalancing. The payoffs are exhibited in Figure 7.2.

This approach is also called constant mix policy. Let us understand the working of constant mix policy with the help of a Numerical Example.

Numerical Example 1

The initial stock/bond ratio is 50:50 at the stock market level of 100. Constant mix policy implies that the proportion of stocks is always to be maintained at 50% of the portfolio value. Suppose the stock market falls to 80 and the value of portfolio becomes 90 (stock = 40 and bond = 50). Now, in line with the constant mix policy, stock should be 45 (50% of portfolio value). So the investor will switch an amount of 5 from bonds to stock.

Thus, constant mix policy implies buying stocks as they fall and selling when they rise.

Dynamic or insured asset allocation

Dynamic asset allocation is an approach to asset allocation that involves shifting the asset mix in response to changes in conditions in the market. This shifting happens rather mechanistically. A common dynamic asset allocation approach, called constant proportion portfolio insurance (CPPI) policy, is used frequently. Mathematically, this policy may be expressed as:

$$\text{Investment in shares} = m\ (\text{portfolio value-floor}) \qquad (1)$$

where $m > 1$ and it is a multiplier

Constant proportion portfolio insurance policy is a policy of asset allocation that implies buying stocks as they rise and selling stocks as they fall. Clearly, it is opposite of the constant mix policy and the payoff curve in this case is convex (one that rises at an increasing rate as the stock market index moves upwards) as exhibited in Figure 7.3.

Let us understand the working of this policy with a Numerical Example.

Figure 7.3 Payoff of constant proportion portfolio insurance policy.

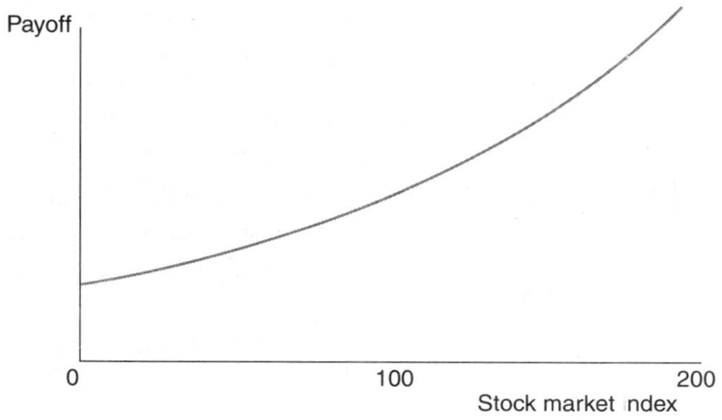

Numerical Example 2

Suppose portfolio value is 100000 and the floor is 75000 and m (multiplier) = 2.

$$\text{Therefore, investment in stock as per equation (1)} = 2\,(100000 - 75000) = 50000$$

If the initial policy is 50:50 in stock and bond, then 50000 is the investment in stocks and 50000 is the investment in bonds.

Suppose the stock market falls by 20%, i.e., from 100 to 80, the value of stock also falls by 20% from 50000 to 40000 and the value of portfolio falls to 40000 + 50000 = 90000.

As per constant proportion portfolio insurance policy, investment in stock for this portfolio value may be computed as:

$$= 2\,(90000 - 75000) = 30000$$

Thus, the investor needs to sell 10000 of stocks and invest the proceeds in bonds. Thus constant proportion portfolio insurance policy implies sell the stock when it is declining.

To consider the situation when the stock market rises, let us assume that the market rises by 50%, from 100 to 150.

In this case the value of stock would rise to 75000 and the value of portfolio would become 75000 + 50000 = 125000.

As per constant proportion portfolio insurance policy, the investment in stock should be:

$$= 2\,(125000 - 75000) = 100000$$

Since the investment in stock is at 75000 only, the investor needs to sell bonds worth 25000 to buy equity. If the stocks rise more, more equity needs to be bought.

A Comparative Assessment of Asset Allocation Approaches

Tactical asset allocation pertains to timing the market and calls for discretionary shifts to take advantage of short-run movements predicted in the market conditions. The other three, drifting, balanced and dynamic asset allocation approaches involve changes in asset-mix on the basis of fixed rules.

Constant proportion portfolio insurance policy does not try to time the market like tactical asset allocation; rather it seeks to align the long-term outcomes of portfolio to investor's objectives without anticipating or timing the market. Tactical asset allocation is, therefore, a different ball game altogether. Let us compare the other three to see which one to use and when.

Let us illustrate the outcome of the three strategies: drifting, balanced and dynamic, with the help of a simple Numerical Example.

Numerical Example 3

Suppose the market is at a level of 100 and the policy pursued is 50:50 allocation to stock and bond with initial portfolio value of 100000. The effect of changes in the market level on a portfolio constructed using the three approaches is exhibited in Table 7.1.

TABLE 7.1 Effect of changes in the market level on a portfolio constructed using drifting, balanced and dynamic asset allocation strategies

Drifting asset allocation (buy and hold)			
	Stock	**Bond**	**Portfolio value**
Initial market level at 100	50000	50000	100000
Market falls to 80 (before rebalancing)	40000	50000	90000
Market falls to 80 (after rebalancing)	40000	50000	90000
Market rises to 100 (before rebalancing)	50000	50000	100000
Market rises to 100 (after rebalancing)	50000	50000	100000

Balance asset allocation (constant mix)			
	Stock	**Bond**	**Portfolio value**
Initial market level at 100	50000	50000	100000
Market falls to 80 (before rebalancing)	40000	50000	90000
Market falls to 80 (after rebalancing)	45000	45000	90000
Market rises to 100 (before rebalancing)	56250	45000	101250
Market rises to 100 (after rebalancing)	50625	50625	101250

Dynamic asset allocation (constant proportion portfolio insurance policy)			
	Stock	**Bond**	**Portfolio value**
Initial market level at 100	50000	50000	100000
Market falls to 80 (before rebalancing)	40000	50000	90000
Market falls to 80 (after rebalancing)*	30000	60000	90000
Market rises to 100 (before rebalancing)	37500	60000	97500
Market rises to 100 (after rebalancing)	45000	52500	97500

* assuming floor = 75000, $M = 2$

The question now arises 'which approach should be used?' Typically, the asset allocation approach depends upon the investors and their response to the market changes. Going by the 'utility theory,' the investors' wealth increases with the rise in market but their prospective returns diminish and vice-versa. Investors' response to this behavior of returns and wealth depends on their characteristics as described below:

1. Long-terms investors are not affected by fluctuation in their wealth and their risk tolerance remains fairly stable. When prospective returns on stocks decrease due to rise in market, they increase their exposure to bonds and when market declines, they increase their exposure to equity. Tactical asset allocation is best suited to such investors.
2. Some investors are affected by fluctuations in wealth in a very limited manner because their risk tolerance fluctuates with their wealth. If their wealth increases with the rise in market, their risk tolerance also rises slightly. Similarly, when their wealth decreases, their risk tolerance decreases slightly. For such investors, balanced asset allocation is best suited.
3. The third group of investors comprises of people who respond like the second group but the degree of responses is stronger. They show more sensitivity to changes in wealth. Their risk tolerance rises as their wealth rises due to advancement of the market. On account of the rise in the risk tolerance, they do not feel the need to lower their exposure in stocks despite the diminishing prospective returns. Similarly, their risk tolerance decreases with the fall in the market and they do not move to reduce their exposure in stocks. Drifting asset allocation is best suited to such investors.
4. The last group of investors is also like the second and third group but their sensitivity to market fluctuation is the strongest. Their risk tolerance rises sharply with the market and they move to increase their exposure to stocks, irrespective of the diminishing returns prospect. Conversely, their risk tolerance decreases sharply with the decrease in the market and they move to reduce their exposure to stocks. Dynamic asset allocation is best suited to these investors.

Equity Portfolio Allocation/Revision Strategies

So far we have discussed asset allocation in the context of the overall portfolio. Now we will move to the portfolio allocation strategies within the equity portfolio. An equity portfolio comprises a number of individual stocks depending on investor's characteristics and risk profile. While constructing and rebalancing equity portfolios, portfolio managers generally use one of the following two strategies:

Constant Proportion Strategy

A manager using the constant proportion policy for asset allocation within equity portfolio constructs the portfolio initially by assigning equal weight to all the component stocks and targets to maintain the proportions at equal level by revising the portfolio at various intervals. Let us understand the working of this strategy with the help of a Numerical Example.

Numerical Example 4

Suppose a fund creates a pure equity portfolio with a corpus of ₹14000000. The portfolio comprises 7 stocks (A, B, C, D, E, F and G) with the proportion of each being equal to 14.29%, i.e., ₹2000000. The initial purchase price and the number of stocks are exhibited in the window given below*:

	A	B	C	D	E
1	Stock	Price Per Share	Funds Allocated	Number of Shares Acquired	Porportion of each Stock
2	A	1250	2000000	1600	14.29
3	B	540	2000000	3704	14.29
4	C	78	2000000	25641	14.29
5	D	1361	2000000	1470	14.29
6	E	363	2000000	5510	14.29
7	F	214	2000000	9346	14.29
8	G	722	2000000	2770	14.29
9			14000000		100.00

Rounding off has been done where required. The proportions have been kept up to two decimal points to capture very small change in value as well.

Suppose, the fund manager chooses to follow a constant proportion strategy to manage the portfolio. Accordingly, he decides to revise the portfolio to restore constant proportion after an interval of two months.

After two months, it is observed that the prices of all shares have changed, resulting in change in the proportion of each stock in the portfolio. The changed position after two months is exhibited in the window given below:

11	After 2 Months				
12	Stock	Price Per Share After Two Months	Number of Shares Held	Funds in Each Security After Two Months	New Proportion
13	A	1334	1600	2134400	13.43
14	B	675	3704	2500000	15.73
15	C	88	25641	2256410	14.20
16	D	1433	1470	2105805	13.25
17	E	401	5510	2209366	13.91
18	F	279	9346	2607477	16.41
19	G	749	2770	2074792	13.06
20				15888250	100.00

As can be seen in the above exhibit, the total value of portfolio has appreciated to ₹15888250. The proportions have also drifted away from the initial equal proportion for ₹2000000. Since, the manager is following constant proportion policy, he will move to buy/sell stocks constituting the portfolio to restore the equal proportion in the light of the changed portfolio value.

To do so, he will buy the stocks that have proportion lower than the target proportion of 14.29% and sell the shares that have proportion higher than the target proportion of 14.29%. The number of stocks bought and sold to restore proportions are exhibited below:

21	Portfolio After Revision to Restore Proportion							
22	Stock	Price Per Share After Two Months	New Proportio	Funds in Each Security After Two Months	Initial/Targe t Porportion of each Stock	Funds in Each Security After Two Months(Post Revision)	Number of Shares Held Post Revision	Number of Shares Bought/Sold to Restore Proportions
23	A	1334	13.43	2134400	14.29	2269750	1701	101
24	B	675	15.73	2500000	14.29	2269750	3363	-341
25	C	88	14.20	2256410	14.29	2269750	25793	152
26	D	1433	13.25	2105805	14.29	2269750	1584	114
27	E	401	13.91	2209366	14.29	2269750	5660	151
28	F	279	16.41	2607477	14.29	2269750	8135	-1210
29	G	749	13.06	2074792	14.29	2269750	3030	260
30				15888250		15888250		

It is clear from the above exhibit that the stocks that have fallen below the target proportion have been bought to increase their share to the target level. A, C, D, E and G are such stocks. Similarly, the stocks that have risen above the target proportion have been sold to decrease their share to the target level. B and F are such stocks.

Complete computations may be presented as given below:

	A	B	C	D	E	F	G	H
1	Stock	Price Per Share	Funds Allocated	Number of Shares Acquired	Porportion of each Stock			
2	A	1250	2000000	1600	14.29			
3	B	540	2000000	3704	14.29			
4	C	78	2000000	25641	14.29			
5	D	1361	2000000	1470	14.29			
6	E	363	2000000	5510	14.29			
7	F	214	2000000	9346	14.29			
8	G	722	2000000	2770	14.29			
9			14000000		100.00			
10								
11	After 2 Months							
12	Stock	Price Per Share After Two Months	Number of Shares Held	Funds in Each Security After Two Months	New Proportion			
13	A	1334	1600	2134400	13.43			
14	B	675	3704	2500000	15.73			
15	C	88	25641	2256410	14.20			
16	D	1433	1470	2105805	13.25			
17	E	401	5510	2209366	13.91			
18	F	279	9346	2607477	16.41			
19	G	749	2770	2074792	13.06			
20				15888250	100.00			
21	Portfolio After Revision to Restore Proportion							
22	Stock	Price Per Share After Two Months	New Proportior	Funds in Each Security After Two Months	Initial/Targe t Porportion of each Stock	Funds in Each Security After Two Months(Post Revision)	Number of Shares Held Post Revision	Number of Shares Bought/Sold to Restore Proportions
23	A	1334	13.43	2134400	14.29	2269750	1701	101
24	B	675	15.73	2500000	14.29	2269750	3363	-341
25	C	88	14.20	2256410	14.29	2269750	25793	152
26	D	1433	13.25	2105805	14.29	2269750	1584	114
27	E	401	13.91	2209366	14.29	2269750	5660	151
28	F	279	16.41	2607477	14.29	2269750	8135	-1210
29	G	749	13.06	2074792	14.29	2269750	3030	260
30				15888250		15888250		

Constant Beta Portfolio Strategy

Managers using constant beta portfolio strategy aim to maintain the same portfolio beta throughout. They start with setting the desired beta and construct the initial portfolio accordingly. Portfolio beta is weighted average of the betas of the component stocks. The weights are determined on the basis of the proportion of the stock in the portfolio. With change in market conditions, the portfolio beta may become higher or lower than the desired beta. To restore the portfolio beta to the desired level, the managers revise the portfolio.

Let us understand the concept of constant portfolio beta with the help of a Numerical Example.

Numerical Example 5

A fund manager has constructed a portfolio with a corpus of ₹10000000. It is a pure equity portfolio that comprises 5 stocks. The fund manager intends to follow a constant beta policy for managing this portfolio. His desired level of portfolio beta is pegged between 1.14 and 1.19.

The initial portfolio parameters are as exhibited in the window below:

	A	B	C	D
1	Stock	Beta	Funds Allocated	Porportion of each Stock
2	A	1.8	1200000	0.12
3	B	0.85	2200000	0.22
4	C	0.99	3100000	0.31
5	D	1.22	2000000	0.20
6	E	1.32	1500000	0.15
7			10000000	1.00
8		Portfolio Beta	1.152	

The initial proportion of the corpus in each stock is pegged as given in the exhibit. The portfolio beta has been calculated using the SUMPRODUCT function of Excel. The portfolio beta thus computed is equal to 1.152. Under this strategy, the proportion of funds in individual securities is a matter of personal choice. The only key constraint is the level of portfolio beta.

Suppose, after two months the portfolio beta shifts to 1.206 due to change in market conditions. It is higher than the desired level of beta. The portfolio with changes in market value of component stocks is exhibited below:

10	After 2 Months			
11	Stock	Beta	Market Value of the Fund	Porportion of each Stock
12	A	1.8	1800000	0.16
13	B	0.85	1900000	0.17
14	C	0.99	2925000	0.27
15	D	1.22	2535000	0.23
16	E	1.32	1800000	0.16
17			10960000	1.00
18		Portfolio Beta	1.206	

To bring beta back in the desired range, the manager will sell the high beta stocks (A, D and E) and buy low beta stocks (B and C). The changes in the portfolio proportions and beta after revision are given below:

20	Portfolio After Revision to Restore Proportion						
21	Stock	Beta	Market Value of the Fund	Porportion of each Stock	Buying/Selling to reach Desired Beta	Market Value After Revision	Proportion After Revision
22	A	1.8	1800000	0.16	-100000	1700000	0.16
23	B	0.85	1900000	0.17	310000	2210000	0.20
24	C	0.99	2925000	0.27	575000	3500000	0.32
25	D	1.22	2535000	0.23	-435000	2100000	0.19
26	E	1.32	1800000	0.16	-350000	1450000	0.13
27			10960000	1.00		10960000	1.00
28		Portfolio Beta	1.206			1.175	

It may be noted here that there is no hard and fast rule with regards to the exact proportion of buying and selling. The amounts of stocks to be bought or sold are determined as per personal preference; the only key consideration is to bring the beta back in the desired zone. Obviously, there can be more than one solution to this problem.

Complete computations may be presented as given below:

	A	B	C	D	E	F	G
1	Stock	Beta	Funds Allocated	Porportion of each Stock			
2	A	1.8	1200000	0.12			
3	B	0.85	2200000	0.22			
4	C	0.99	3100000	0.31			
5	D	1.22	2000000	0.20			
6	E	1.32	1500000	0.15			
7			10000000	1.00			
8		Portfolio Beta	1.152				
9							
10	After 2 Months						
11	Stock	Beta	Market Value of the Fund	Porportion of each Stock			
12	A	1.8	1800000	0.16			
13	B	0.85	1900000	0.17			
14	C	0.99	2925000	0.27			
15	D	1.22	2535000	0.23			
16	E	1.32	1800000	0.16			
17			10960000	1.00			
18		Portfolio Beta	1.206				
19							
20	Portfolio After Revision to Restore Proportion						
21	Stock	Beta	Market Value of the Fund	Porportion of each Stock	Buying/Selling to reach Desired Beta	Market Value After Revision	Proportion After Revision
22	A	1.8	1800000	0.16	-100000	1700000	0.16
23	B	0.85	1900000	0.17	310000	2210000	0.20
24	C	0.99	2925000	0.27	575000	3500000	0.32
25	D	1.22	2535000	0.23	-435000	2100000	0.19
26	E	1.32	1800000	0.16	-350000	1450000	0.13
27			10960000	1.00		10960000	1.00
28		Portfolio Beta	1.206			1.175	

What Next After Asset Allocation?

Once the overall asset mix is determined, investors have to shift their attention to the formulation of an appropriate strategy for each of the two broad components, stocks and bonds. Thus, after asset allocation, one needs to formulate bond and equity portfolio management strategies. Let us discuss them in brief:

Bond Portfolio Management Strategies

Bond portfolio managers can pursue two distinct bond management strategies, active and passive portfolio management strategy. There is also a third strategy, called immunization, which is actually a special case of passive portfolio management. Each of these may be described as follows:

1. **Active Bond Management Strategy:** This strategy is pursued by managers who aspire to achieve higher returns than those commensurate with the level of risk borne in the investment. They seek to earn higher profits by predicting changes in interest rates or by trying to exploit relative mispricing among the bonds available. Thus, active strategy may take two distinct paths, one in which the managers buy bonds when they expect a fall in interest rates or sell bonds when they expect a rise in interest rates (based on the fact that the interest rates and bond prices are inversely related); second in which managers exploit temporary

mispricing by doing bond swaps-sale and purchase of bonds with a view to enhance returns. A number of swaps have been recommended by researchers, the popular ones being tax swaps, substitution swaps, rate anticipation swaps, pure yield swaps and inter-market spread swaps.

2. **Passive Bond Management Strategy:** Passive bond management strategy is pursued by managers who aspire to earn returns commensurate with the level of risk taken. They do not attempt to beat the market, rather they try to maintain an acceptable risk-return level in alignment with the prevailing market conditions. Passive bond managers accept that the bond prices are fairly set and they try to control only the risk aspect of their portfolios. Managers pursuing passive bond portfolio management strategy can opt for one of the two approaches: indexing or buy and hold.

   Under the indexing strategy, the bond managers try to build a portfolio that replicates the performance of some well-known bond index. Such bond-index portfolio will exhibit the same risk-return characteristics as the bond market index it is constructed to mirror.

   A 'buy and hold' strategy is as simple as it sounds. The managers following this strategy simply stick to their initial choices in making the bond portfolios.

3. **Immunization Strategies:** Immunization strategies are basically designed to protect the financial position of the investor against fluctuations in interest rates. Immunization techniques are very popular among institutional investors like pension funds and insurance companies. To implement an immunization strategy, managers create a bond portfolio whose duration matches the duration of the liabilities that need to be met from the portfolio earnings/proceeds. It should be noted that an immunization portfolio cannot be a buy and hold portfolio as periodic rebalancing in response to interest rate variation is required to be continued to maintain the immunized position.

   Dedication strategy is an alternative form of immunization that is more direct. It involves cash flow matching on multi-period basis. This strategy makes rebalancing unnecessary by matching cash flow of portfolio with projected liabilities. To execute dedication strategy, bond portfolio managers buy many zero coupon bonds that match the future obligation requirements.

Equity Portfolio Management Strategies

Equities make up a significant part of a large number of investment portfolios' value. Equity portfolio investors have many strategies at their disposal. The main ones are active, semi-active and passive portfolio management strategy. These may be described as follows:

Active equity portfolio strategy

An active portfolio manager's role is to ensure best possible performance of his portfolio vis-à-vis a pre-specified benchmark, within the parameters of investors' risk and other constraints. The outperformance has to be positive, net of transaction costs. To achieve positive risk-adjusted returns, superior to the benchmark, active portfolio managers need to be skilled in analyzing information, applying investment tools and understanding investment insights. They can use a variety of equity valuation tools and approaches to beat the benchmark, net of incidental costs. The two key equity analysis approaches that the equity portfolio managers can use are technical analysis and fundamental analysis.

1. **Technical Approach:** We will discuss technical analysis in detail in Chapters 12 and 13. Here we will summarize the two mainstays of technical analysis, momentum strategy and contrarian strategy. As the

name suggests, momentum strategy implies persistence of existing trend in prices, i.e., rising stocks can be expected to continue to rise and falling stocks can be expected to continue to fall. The basic logic behind persistence of current trend is market's inertia, i.e., its gradual adjustment or reaction to any new news, good or bad.

Contrarian strategy implies behaving in a contrarian manner, i.e., in a manner opposite to how majority is behaving; buying when others are bearish and selling stock when other are buying it. The logic underlying this strategy is that stock returns are mean-reverting over a period of time.

2. **Fundamental Approach:** We will discuss fundamental analysis in detail in Chapters 10 and 11. Here we will summarize some key aspects of fundamental analysis in the context of equity portfolio management. Fundamental approach to portfolio management is largely based upon picking stocks that are under-valued and making them over-weighted in the equity portfolio vis-à-vis their weight in the market portfolio. Obviously, the approach emphasizes being under-weight in over-valued stock vis-à-vis their weight in the market portfolio. In this context, calculation of intrinsic or fair-value plays a key role because stocks are identified as under or over-valued on the basis of the comparison of their intrinsic value with the current market price.

   Another key feature of fundamental analysis is emphasis on changes in sectoral weights, i.e., shifting portfolio funds from one sector/industry to another based on the predicted outlook or assessment. Many researchers have recommended a specialized investment concept where analysts are required to develop deep insight in a particular sector or industry, become sort of specialists in their chosen sector and exploit their expertise to earn superior returns. Some specialized groups of stocks/companies on which managers have focused upon in the recent times are technology stocks, cyclical stocks, value stocks and growth stocks. Such a compartmentalization has its advantages and disadvantages.

3. **Equity or Investment Styles:** Equity or investment styles: A discussion of active portfolio management is incomplete without talking about varied equity styles. The main equity or investment styles are:
   (a) Growth investment style
   (b) Value investment style
   (c) Market-oriented investment style

Let us discuss them briefly.

Growth investment style is a popular style of investing in which investors are concerned with earnings. They favor stocks that have currently reported high rates of earning growth and are expected to continue to enjoy high growth rates of earning in the future. Growth investors buy 'glamour stocks' that have high P/E ratios, high sales growth relative to overall market trend, high price-to-book-value ratios, low dividend yield and above-average earnings growth rate. In terms of risk, such stocks tend to have beta of more than one. The major risk associated with growth investing is that the forecasted EPS growth might not materialize and P/E multiples may also contract, amplifying the losses. The growth investment style can take two forms: Earnings momentum (high year-on-year quarterly growth in earnings) and consistent growth (high unit-sales growth, profitability and more predictable earnings history).

Value investment style is one in which investors are interested in buying a stock that is relatively cheap in the sense that it has a low P/E ratio. Value stocks typically have low price-to-book ratio, low earnings growth per share, high dividend yield and betas less than one. Since they favor such 'out-of-favor' stocks, managers following value investment style are called contrarian managers.

Market-oriented investment style is favorite of investors who do not restrict themselves to value or growth silos. Such investors adopt a market oriented style of investment under which their primary targets are stocks valued below their perceived intrinsic value, without worrying about where the stocks fall on the growth-value spectrum. They use a variety of valuation tools to value the stocks and invest in a stock at high P/E provided the price is justified by future growth potential in EPS. On the other hand, they are also ready to buy depressed cyclical stocks if they anticipate some recovery.

Passive equity portfolio management

In passive management, the investor does not try to exhibit his investment objectives through changing the stocks held. The passive strategy accepts the efficient market hypothesis (EMH) that the capital markets are efficient and prices reflect all the available information. Thus, the managers following passive management style do not expend effort on generating superior risk-adjusted returns vis-à-vis a benchmark.

The most popular passive investing approach is indexing which implies investing in a portfolio that is designed to match the performance of a specific index.

Marketview 7.1 Index Funds in India

Sr. no.	Index fund	Index	Launched	Issuer
1	Principal index fund	CNX nifty	Jul 1999	Principal PNB AMC private Ltd.
2	UTI nifty index fund	CNX nifty	Mar 2000	UTI AMC private Ltd.
3	Franklin india index fund	CNX nifty	Jun 2000	Franklin templeton AMC (india) private Ltd.
4	SBI nifty index fund	CNX nifty	Dec 2001	SBI funds management Ltd.
5	ICICI prudential index fund	CNX nifty	Feb 2002	ICICI prudential AMC Ltd.
6	HDFC index fund-nifty plan	CNX nifty	Jul 2002	HDFC AMC Ltd.
7	Birla sun life index fund	CNX nifty	Sep 2002	Birla sun life AMC Ltd.
8	LIC NOMURA MF index fund-nifty plan	CNX nifty	Nov 2002	LIC nomura mutual fund AMC Ltd.
9	Tata index fund-nifty plan	CNX nifty	Feb 2003	Tata AMC private Ltd.
10	Canara robeco nifty index fund	CNX nifty	Sep 2004	Canara robeco AMC Ltd.
11	IDFC nifty fund	CNX nifty	May 2010	IDFC AMC Ltd.
12	Taurus nifty index fund	CNX nifty	Jun 2010	Taurus AMC Ltd.
13	IDBI nifty index fund	CNX nifty	Jun 2010	IDBI asset management Ltd.
14	Reliance index fund-nifty plan	CNX nifty	Sep 2010	Reliance capital asset management Ltd.

(Continued)

Continued

Sr. no.	Index fund	Index	Launched	Issuer
15	Goldman sachs CNX 500 fund	CNX 500	Nov 2008	Goldman sachs asset management (india) private ltd.
16	ICICI prudential nifty junior index fund	CNX nifty junior	Jun 2010	ICICI prudential AMC Ltd.
17	IDBI nifty junior index fund	CNX nifty junior	Sep 2010	IDBI asset management Ltd.
18	IIFL dividend opportunities index fund	CNX dividend opportunities	Jun 2012	India infoline AMC Ltd.

Source: http://www.nseindia.com/ accessed on December 1, 2014.

Wells Fargo launched the world's first index portfolio in the US in the year 1971. Although indexing is passive and does not incorporate investor's expectations concerning stocks, indexed portfolios are not at all passive in implementation. The portfolios get adjusted every time a stock is added to or dropped from the index or weights of stocks in index changes due to buyback, follow on public offer (FPO) or other corporate action.

In the past few years, indexed portfolios have become a key part of overall equity allocation. The main categories of indexed portfolios are:

1. ETFs (exchange traded funds that are based on benchmark index)
2. Index mutual funds
3. Pooled accounts (mainly for institutional investors designed to follow a specific index)
4. Equity index futures
5. Equity total return swaps

ETFs can be bought and sold anytime in the secondary market during the trading hours whereas index mutual funds can be bought or sold at NAV (net assets value) declared once a day, at the close of the market. ETFs offer many structural advantages over index mutual funds and also allow short positions. The lure of index mutual funds is in the fact that they are widely accessible and offer considerable range of cost structures. Pooled accounts are very low cost indexed institutional portfolios. Equity index futures also provide a low cost method for obtaining exposure in equity market. Long-term equity exposure in passive form can be obtained through equity total return swaps. The ETRS are relatively low cost and may offer tax advantage as well.

Methods of indexation: There are two main methods for index portfolio construction:

1. **Full Replication:** Under this method, each constituent security of specific index is held in approximately the same proportion as it is in the index. While this approach provides close tracking of the index, buying all index securities may lead to high transaction cost at the time of purchase and high commission at the time of reinvestment of dividends.

2. **Stratified Sampling or Representative Sampling:** Under this method, the portfolio manager buys a representative sample of securities out of many stocks comprising the benchmark index. While the weights of large stocks in the sample reflect their proportion in index, the smaller stocks are purchased on the basis of their aggregate characteristics like beta approximating the benchmark index. This approach solves the problem of acquiring numerous stocks and reduces the cost of transaction and rebalancing. However, the main disadvantage is that the returns of portfolio do not match the index as closely as portfolio made with full replication technique.

Semi-active equity investing

This approach is also called risk-controlled active portfolio management or enhanced indexing. It is designed for investors who desire superior returns vis-à-vis their benchmark index but do not want to incur much additional risk. To satisfy such investors, portfolio managers create an enhanced index portfolio which gives incremental returns that compensate for rise in tracking or active risk. Enhanced indexing strategies have been observed to have high information ratios because of their strict control on tracking risk.

The semi-active strategies can take two forms:

- Stock based semi-active strategies
- Derivative based semi-active strategies

The stock based enhanced indexing strategies try to generate alpha (α) by identifying the underperforming or outperforming stocks vis-à-vis the benchmarking index.

Derivative based enhanced indexing is also called synthetic indexing and it provides exposure to desired stocks through a derivative and the enhanced return is provided through something other than investment in stock.

Asset Allocation in Practice

As discussed above, the twin objectives of risk and return should guide asset allocation, bound by the investor's characteristics, objectives and constraints. The main aim of allocating funds across different asset classes is to undertake diversification with a view to minimizing risk for a given expected level of return. Therefore, risk-return characteristics of the various asset classes should be evaluated and assessed comprehensively as a necessary pre-condition to successful asset allocation.

It is a known fact that equities are the riskiest assets and hence offer the highest potential return. Conversely, treasury bills and other government securities have low risk and hence offer the lowest potential return. Most other assets lie between these two extremes. We have already discussed this risk-return tradeoff in the introductory chapters.

We also know that investors differ in their risk tolerance. The role of asset allocation is to match the risk of assets with the risk tolerance of the investors, keeping in mind their investment objectives and constraints. Proper asset allocation cushions the entire portfolio against the volatility of any one class of component assets. It ensures that the funds are spread across assets of varying risks so that expected returns can be generated. A part of portfolio, comprising of risky assets, chosen for their return potential, may fluctuate but the remaining part devoted to less risky assets remains stable.

We also know about the types of investors on the basis of their risk tolerance. They lie on a continuum of tolerance, varying from conservative risk averters to aggressive risk takers. Accordingly, we can identify a few generic portfolios created through conservative as well as aggressive asset allocation. It should be kept in mind that these are not universal solutions but just indicative allocations to give an idea about how asset allocation should be undertaken.

Conservative Portfolios

As the name suggests, conservative portfolios are based on asset allocation targeting minimization of risk. Conservative portfolios best suit the investors with low risk tolerance. The primary motive of such investors is preservation of principal or capital. Thus, conservative asset allocation comprises investing in low risk securities with low or no default risk. As a result, large chunk (75 to 80%) of such portfolios is invested in fixed-income and government securities. As suggested ideally, 5–10% of the portfolio is allocated to cash and cash-equivalents. The modern thought is that even the most conservative of investors should invest some part of the portfolio in equity (10–20%) to beat inflation, especially true for countries like India where rate of inflation erodes the real returns to a large extent. A possible asset allocation from conservative viewpoint is illustrated in figure 7.4.

Figure 7.4 Conservative portfolio.

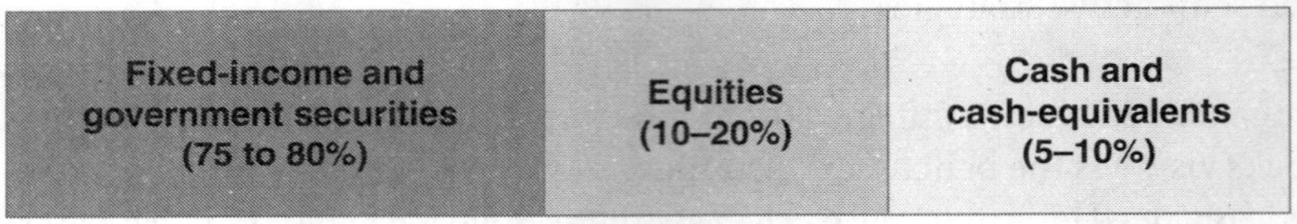

Aggressive Portfolios

As the name suggests, aggressive portfolios are based on asset allocation targeting maximization of returns. Aggressive portfolios best suit the investors with high risk tolerance. The primary motive of such investors is capital growth on long-term basis. Such investors gravitate toward equity and include fixed-income securities in their portfolio only to achieve some diversification. As a result, large chunk (75 to 80%) of aggressive portfolio is devoted to equity, 5–10% is allocated to cash and cash-equivalents and only 10–20% is invested in fixed income securities. A possible asset allocation from aggressive viewpoint is illustrated in figure 7.5.

Figure 7.5 Aggressive portfolio.

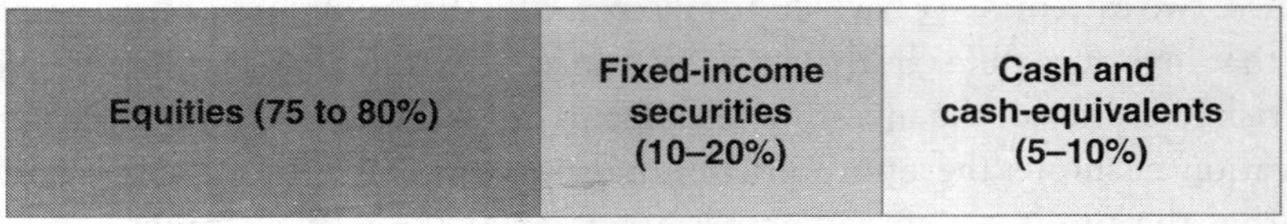

Apart from the above two basic allocations, we can identify many other intermediate portfolios such as moderate conservative, moderate, moderate aggressive and so on, by varying the percentage of the portfolio allocated to equity and fixed income securities.

Within the above broad guideline, investors can undertake asset allocation based on their specific requirements, by using any of the bond and equity investment strategies described in the preceding sections of this chapter. Many companies have developed automated asset allocators to help the investors determine their appropriate asset mix.

Behavioral Biases in Asset Allocation

Investors do not behave rationally as assumed by modern portfolio theory. There is much irrationality that influences an investor's investment decision-making. According to the supporters of behavioral finance, investors exhibit loss aversion and mental accounting. Both these behavioral tendencies have implications for asset allocation.

Loss aversion implies that investors become risk-seekers when they face the possibility of substantial loss. A portfolio manager should ascertain whether his client is loss averse because in that situation, the approach to asset allocation will have to be adjusted accordingly. There are two possible approaches to asset allocation for such clients; one is to incorporate a shortfall risk constraint in the allocation decision and the other is to use ALM approach for asset allocation. The shortfall risk constraint is suggested keeping in view the chances of the loss-averse investor facing a substantial loss.

Another behavioral bias that impacts asset allocation is regret avoidance. Regret avoidance shows sensitivity to the pain that is the outcome of a bad decision. Regret avoidance can impact asset allocation by making investors more concerned about diversification. Herd instinct can also be attributed to regret avoidance to a certain extent, especially when the concerned investor is sensitive to comparisons.

Mental accounting implies that instead of looking at his investment as a whole, the investor divides his wealth into separate accounts and buckets mentally and has different level of risk tolerance for each account, depending on the purpose of investment and source of investible surplus. For example, an investor may be saving for his daughter's wedding or just speculation and his risk tolerance will be different for the two motives. Asset the allocation, as we have discussed so far, presents the whole portfolio as one unit depending on the level of investor's risk tolerance. An investor who looks at portfolio from the point of view of mental accounting may find our asset allocation inappropriate. However, mental accounting is difficult to be addressed in asset allocation and may result in sub-optimal portfolios. The portfolio managers should discuss the advantages of using the standard asset allocation approaches with the client in such a situation.

We will discuss the influences of behavioral trendencies of the investors on portfolio management in detail in Chapter 13.

SUMMARY

☑ Portfolio management begins with the specification of investment policy and strategy. Herein the investment objectives like income, growth and/or stability are identified and investor risk tolerance/preference is mapped in terms of indifference curves.

☑ The mapping of investment objectives and constraints of individual investor leads to the next phase in the formulation of investment strategy.

- ☑ Quantification of the capital market expectations is a challenging task and it requires intensive research and use of sophisticated forecasting methods to specify the time horizon of investment, returns of the asset class under consideration and the risk assessment of the same.
- ☑ A key part of portfolio management is asset allocation. It is a major decision for all investors as selection of assets to invest in and allocating funds to them is critical to the success of investment strategy.
- ☑ Asset allocation refers to an investment strategy where one spreads one's investible surplus across different asset classes to reduce risk through diversification.
- ☑ Different types of asset allocation approaches are strategic, tactical, balanced, drifting and dynamic or insured asset allocation.
- ☑ Strategic allocation represents the execution stage of a portfolio but in the context of broad asset classes. It is actually the initiation of the portfolio construction phase of portfolio management.
- ☑ Using strategic asset allocation enables the investors to control systematic risk exposure by diversifying across distinct asset classes as opposed to homogenous set of assets.
- ☑ The main approaches to strategic asset allocation may be described as asset/liability management (ALM) approach and asset only (AO) approach.
- ☑ Tactical asset allocation involves making short-term changes/adjustment in asset-mix or asset class proportions on the basis of short-run predictions regarding an asset class performance.
- ☑ Drifting asset allocation policy advocates that no tampering may be done with the initial allocations. It is a typical 'buy and hold' strategy and recommends no rebalancing, irrespective of fluctuations in relative values.
- ☑ Balanced asset allocation policy implies periodical rebalancing of the original portfolio constructed by strategic asset allocation. This approach is also called constant mix policy.
- ☑ Dynamic or insured asset allocation is an approach that involves shifting the asset mix in response to changes in market conditions. A common dynamic asset allocation approach, called constant proportion portfolio insurance policy, is used frequently in investment.
- ☑ After asset allocation, one needs to formulate bond and equity portfolio management strategies.
- ☑ Bond portfolio managers can pursue two distinct bond management strategies: active and passive portfolio management strategy. There is also a third strategy, called immunization, which is actually a special case of passive portfolio management.
- ☑ Equity portfolio investors also have many strategies at their disposal. The main ones are active, semi-active, and passive portfolio management strategy.
- ☑ The main equity or investment styles are growth, value and market-oriented investment styles.

KEY WORDS

Buy and hold 286
Cash flow matching 279
Constant mix policy 286
Constant proportion portfolio insurance policy 287
Diversification 278
Drifting asset allocation 286
Dynamic asset allocation 287
Enhanced indexing or semi-active investment approach 284
Growth investment style 296
Immunization 295
Indexed portfolios 298
Market timing 285
Market-oriented investment style 296
Mean reversion 285
Passive investment approach 284
Portfolio optimization 278
Portfolio management 277
Portfolio selection 279
Risk tolerance 290
Shortfall risk 281
Strategic asset allocation 278
Tactical asset allocation 285
Tracking portfolio 284
Tracking risk 284
Value investment style 296

CONCEPT QUESTIONS

1. Discuss strategic asset allocation approaches in detail.
2. How does Black-Litterman model overcome the problems in implementation of mean variance criteria by institutional investors?
3. Discuss the concept of shortfall risk.
4. How do behavioral biases impact asset allocation decision? Discuss with example.
5. Has index investing taken off in India? Discuss in detail.
6. Explain the effect of changes in the market level on a portfolio constructed using drifting, balanced and dynamic asset allocation strategies with hypothetical portfolios.
7. Comparatively assess the following:
   a. Growth vs. value investing style
   b. Active vs. passive equity investment approach
8. 'Tactical asset allocation is an active strategy of investment at asset class level.' Explain the statement.
9. Explain with example how asset allocation should be adapted to the characteristics, objectives and constraints of an investor.
10. Discuss the implications of full replication and representative sampling methods of indexation.

CASELET

Investtree Advisors Ltd. is a leading investment consulting firm in India. Amit Sinha is a senior financial planner in the firm who handles star clients of the firm. He recently met Tanya Singh, daughter of a retired bureaucrat. Tanya's father has sold an ancestral property last month and promised to give her a sum of ₹70 lakh out of the total proceeds.

Tanya has been working as a very successful architect for the past five years and has bought a sprawling apartment and car. She has also saved and invested ₹40 lakh, 80% in equity mutual funds and 20% in bond mutual funds, out of her earnings.

She maintains two bank accounts, one in HSBC that she uses for day to day expenses and other in ICICI Bank, in which she maintains ₹60000 for contingency purpose. Tanya views these two accounts as separate from her investment portfolio.

Tanya is very excited about investing the money her father has promised to give her and she wants to invest this amount wisely as she is unlikely to receive such a large sum of money ever again in future from anybody. She wants to invest ₹10 lakh out of the amount received from her father in equity to earn high returns through some speculative stock picking. She plans to invest the balance ₹60 lakh in tax-free bonds of short-term maturity but with the long-term objective of saving for her retirement. She is extremely concerned about this decision as it is being taken with a view to secure her future and she has mentioned it to Amit time and again that she would be heart-broken if she were to suffer a serious loss on this amount of ₹60 lakh. She wants Amit to help her with her investments.

As an experienced financial planner, Amit wants to understand Tanya's risk tolerance and her behavioral biases before undertaking asset allocation for her. He evaluates her existing investments and her inputs during their meeting to come up with certain observations.

In your opinion, what important observations has he made?

Gauging the Portfolio Manager's Ability: Portfolio Performance Evaluation and Revision

8

CHAPTER OBJECTIVES

- ❒ Understanding the difference between time-weighted and risk-weighted measures of portfolio performance
- ❒ Evaluating portfolio performance using the key risk-weighted performance measures
- ❒ Identifying the challenges in portfolio performance measurement
- ❒ Assessing different issues in portfolio revision

Portfolio performance measurement or evaluation is the culmination of the portfolio management process. Though portfolio management is an ongoing activity with the need for revision and rebalancing to keep the portfolio aligned with the investors' objectives in response to changing market conditions, yet we call portfolio evaluation as a final step of portfolio management in the sense that it gives a measure of portfolio managers' performance during a given period.

How should a portfolio be evaluated? It has to be in terms of two key dimensions: risk and return. It has been seen that average portfolio return is not as simple a metric as it seems. Calculation of risk-adjusted returns poses a big challenge. In this chapter we will discuss the measures of portfolio performance that have evolved over a period of time. Thereafter, we will discuss portfolio revision and rebalancing.

A number of performance measures have evolved over the past few decades. We will begin our discussion with the conventional measures of performance, followed by some specific, risk-weighted measures that have found acceptance and application in the industry.

Conventional Methods of Portfolio Measurement

In the chapter on risk and return, we have discussed many measures of return on investment. Let us list those measures once again.

1. **Total Return:** Total return (holding period return) on an asset/security may be computed as

$$= \frac{\text{Cash Inflow during the Holding Period} + \text{Price Change over the Holding Period}}{\text{Purchase Price (Beginning Price) of the Asset/Security}}$$

The above equation comprises of two distinct parts:

$$\text{Current Yield} = \frac{\text{Cash Inflow received during the Holding Period}}{\text{Purchase Price (Beginning Price) of the Asset/Security}}$$

$$\text{Capital Gain/Loss} = \frac{\text{Price at the End of the Period} - \text{Purchase Price}}{\text{Purchase Price (Beginning Price) of the Asset/Security}}$$

2. **Arithmetic mean** or simply mean of a series of total returns is computed as

$$\overline{R} = \frac{\sum_{i=1}^{n} R_i}{n}$$

where
$\overline{R}$ = Arithmetic mean of total returns
R_i = i^{th} value of the total return (i = 1, 2, 3 ... n)
n = Number of total returns

3. **Geometric Average or Time – Weighted Average:**
Mathematically,

$$G = [(1 + R_1)\,(1 + R_2)\,\ldots\,(1 + R_n)]^{1/n} - 1$$

where
R = Total return
n = Number of periods
$1 + R$ = Return relative

We have already discussed the three types of returns mentioned above so we will not go into detailed calculations and discussion here.

These measures are considered inadequate for portfolio performance measurement as they do not take risk into consideration.

Risk-weighted Measures of Portfolio Performance

The returns discussed above are average returns. Average returns can be used to evaluate performance. However, evaluation of portfolio performance in terms of average returns presents an incomplete picture. To serve as a true measure of performance, returns need to be adjusted for risk. So better measures of performance would be the ones that provide a way to measure risk-adjusted outcome of a portfolio.

Before we discuss measures for risk-adjusted performance, let us recall the two main measures of risk associated with a portfolio: variance and beta. Variance is a measure of total risk and beta is a measure of systematic risk. Both are used as alternative measures of risk-adjusted portfolio performance.

The main risk-adjusted performance measures are:

1. Sharpe measure or reward-to-variability ratio
2. Treynor measure or reward-to-volatility ratio
3. Jensen alpha.
4. M^2 measure
5. Fama's net selectivity
6. Information ratio
7. Sortino ratio

Let us discuss each in detail.

Sharpe Measure

In 1966, William Forsyth Sharpe[1] developed a measure for portfolio performance that is popularly called as the Sharpe ratio. Sharpe had originally called it the 'reward-to-variability' ratio. In 1994, he revised his ratio to acknowledge that the risk-free rate varies with time. Prior to this revision, the value of risk-free rate had been assumed to be constant over time.

The Sharpe ratio or Sharpe index or Sharpe measure or reward-to-variability ratio comprises excess return (or risk premium) in the numerator and the standard deviation of the portfolio in the denominator.

Symbolically, the ratio may be represented as

$$S_t = \frac{r_p - r_f}{\sigma_p} \tag{1}$$

where

r_p = Realized return of portfolio
r_f = Risk-free rate of return
s_p = Standard deviation of portfolio return

Sharpe ratio is a measure of excess return of a portfolio per unit of total risk. Graphically, Sharpe measure may be represented as shown in Figure 8.1. In the graph, Sharpe ratio represents the slope of the line that begins at risk-free rate of return. This ratio shows how well the return on an asset compensates the investor for the risk he takes. Investors are often advised to choose securities with high Sharpe ratios. Sharpe measure is a continuation of his work on capital asset pricing model (CAPM) but it uses total risk instead of beta to compare portfolios to the capital market line. If Sharpe ratio of a portfolio or security $(S_t) > S_m$ (Sharpe ratio of market), the asset has earned more than the risk premium required by the capital market line, indicating superior performance by the portfolio manager. In this case, the portfolio will plot above CML as shown in Figure 8.2.

[1] William F. Sharpe, "Mutual Fund Performance," *Journal of Business* 39, January 1966.

Figure 8.1 Graphical representation of Sharpe measure.

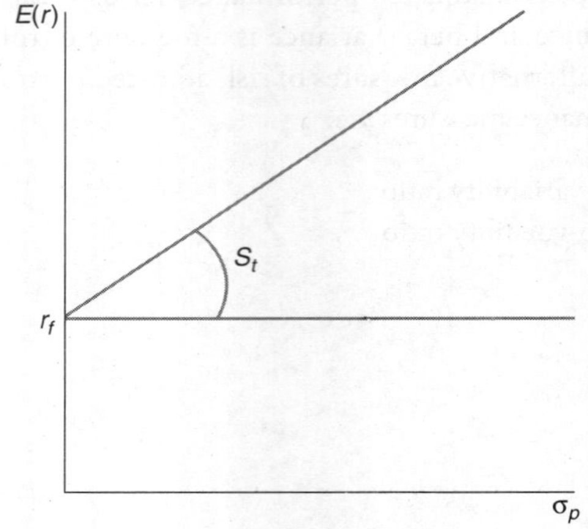

If $S_t < S_m$, the asset has earned less than the risk premium required by the capital market line, indicating poor performance by the portfolio manager. In this case, the portfolio will plot below CML, as shown in Figure 8.2.

Figure 8.2 CML and Sharpe ratio.

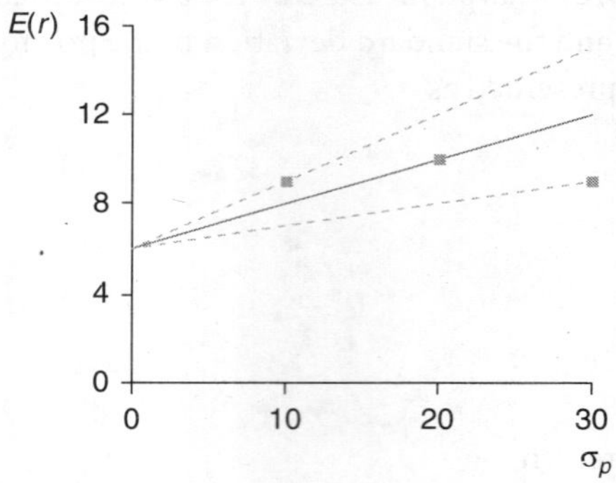

The larger the value of Sharpe ratio, the better the performance of portfolio. Let us understand the ratio and its implications with the help of a Numerical Example.

Numerical Example 1

Suppose that the 15-year annual return for the S&P BSE SENSEX (market portfolio) is 10% and its standard deviation is 18%. The average annual return on treasury bills (the risk-free rate) is 5%. You are required to evaluate the performance of three portfolio managers with the following 15-year results:

Manager	Annual return	Portfolio standard deviation
Manager A	13%	0.11
Manager B	17%	0.21
Manager C	18%	0.27

Solution:

The performance can be evaluated using Sharpe ratio.

$$\text{S ratio of market} = \frac{(0.10-0.05)}{0.18} = 0.278$$

$$\text{S ratio of manager A} = \frac{(0.13-0.05)}{0.11} = 0.727$$

$$\text{S ratio of manager B} = \frac{(0.17-.05)}{0.21} = 0.0571$$

$$\text{S ratio of manager C} = \frac{(0.18-0.05)}{0.27} = 0.481$$

All three managers have exceeded the market as shown by the Sharpe ratio. The best performance has been given by manager A as the Sharpe ratio of his portfolio is the highest, though the annual returns of the portfolio managed by manager C were highest. Thus, we find that the best portfolio is not necessarily the one with the highest return. It is the risk-adjusted return that is more important.

Treynor Measure/Ratio

Treynor[2] was the first researcher who computed a measure of the portfolio performance. He proposed a risk-adjusted performance measure in 1965 and became the first researcher to provide investors with a comprehensive measure of portfolio performance that took risk into consideration. The Treynor ratio or index or measure or reward-to-volatility ratio comprises excess return (or risk premium) in the numerator and beta of the portfolio in the denominator.

Symbolically, the ratio may be represented as

$$T_n = \frac{r_p - r_f}{\beta_p} \qquad (2)$$

[2] Jack L. Treynor, "How to Rate Management Investment Funds," *Harvard Business Review* 43, January–February 1966.

where
r_p = Realized return of portfolio
r_f = Risk-free rate of return
β_p = Beta coefficient of the portfolio

Treynor ratio represents the portfolio's return per unit of systematic risk. Graphically, Treynor ratio may be represented as shown in Figure 8.3.

Figure 8.3 Graphical representation of Treynor measure.

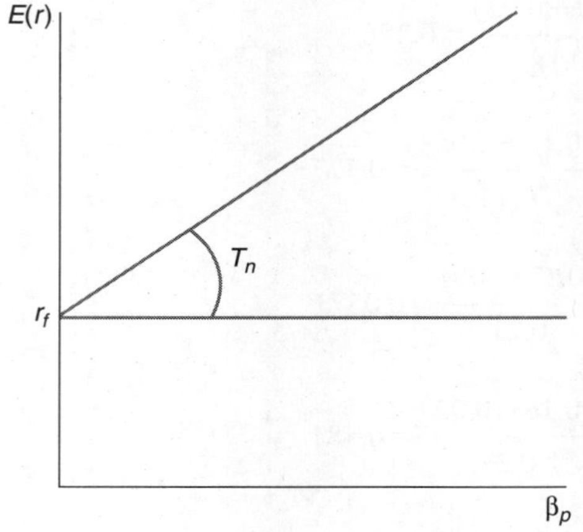

Treynor ratio represents the slope of the line that begins at risk-free rate of return. As stated above, Treynor ratio measures the excess return or risk premium per unit of risk as measured by beta. The beta coefficient is the volatility measure of a stock, portfolio or the market itself. The greater the slope of the line, the better the risk-return tradeoff.

Treynor ratio rests on the implicit assumption that the portfolio is well-diversified. This means that the firm specific risk of the component securities of the portfolio has been eliminated and only the systematic risk remains. This ratio can be understood through the concept of characteristic line discussed in Sharpe's single index model. Characteristic line is a representation of the relationship between a portfolio's return and a given market return, i.e., portfolio's performance is assessed in terms of the performance of the market. The Treynor index uses the security market line as a benchmark.

If Treynor measure (T_n) for a security or a portfolio > Treynor measure (T_m) for the market, the portfolio would plot above the security market line, indicating superior performance by the portfolio manager. If $T_n < T_m$, the portfolio would plot below the security market line, indicating poor performance by the portfolio manager as shown in Figure 8.4.

The greater the value of Treynor measure, the better the performance of portfolio. All rational investors would like to maximize Treynor ratio. However, the ratio is just a ranking criteria and does not quantify the value added, if any, by active portfolio management.

Ideal fund: Defined in the context of market's return, an ideal fund is one that rises faster than rising market and falls slower than falling market returns. Ideal fund may achieve such a performance by short selling stocks

Figure 8.4 SML and Treynor ratio.

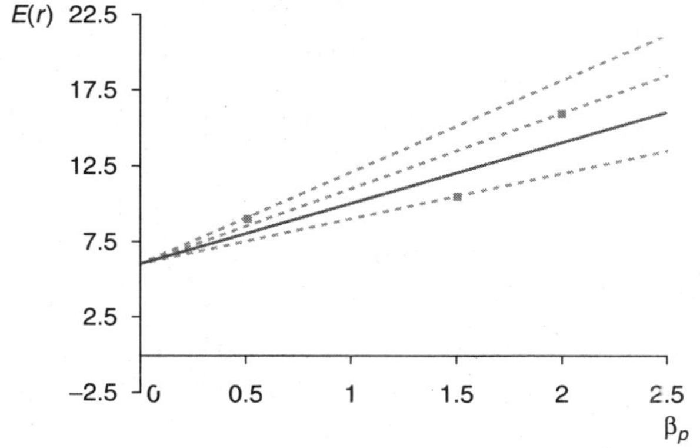

during decline or by investing in treasury bills or other risk-free return instruments. The characteristic line of an ideal fund is exhibited in Figure 8.5. It can be seen that the fund's return rises more than proportionately with increase in the market returns. When the fund return is assumed to move linearly with market, the characteristic line represents this relationship. The slope of characteristic lines represents the volatility of the fund's return. The steepness of the slope indicates the sensitivity of a fund to the market's performance.

Figure 8.5 Treynor's characteristic line of an ideal fund.

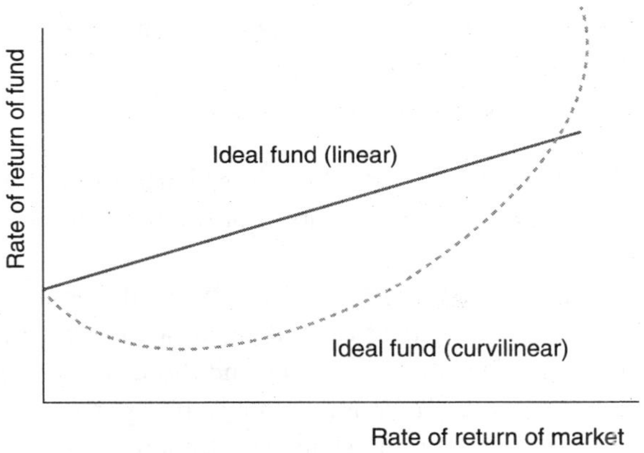

Let us understand the ratio and its implications with the help of a Numerical Example.

Numerical Example 2

Suppose that the 15-year annual return for the S&P BSE SENSEX (market portfolio) is 10% and its standard deviation is 18%. The average annual return on treasury bills (the risk-free rate) is 5%. You are required to evaluate the performance of three portfolio managers with the following 15-year results:

Managers	Average annual return	Beta
Manager A	10%	0.95
Manager B	15%	1.05
Manager C	16%	1.20

Solution:

The performance can be evaluated using Treynor ratio.

$$\text{T ratio of market} = \frac{(0.10-0.05)}{1} = 0.05$$

$$\text{T ratio of manager A} = \frac{(0.10-0.05)}{0.95} = 0.052$$

$$\text{T ratio of manager B} = \frac{(0.15-0.05)}{1.05} = 0.095$$

$$\text{T ratio of manager C} = \frac{(0.16-0.05)}{1.20} = 0.0917$$

We see that the portfolio that has performed better on a risk-adjusted basis (Treynor ratio) has not given the highest total returns. Here manager B has demonstrated the best outcome of all three, though all three managers have performed better than the market as a whole.

Comparative assessment of Sharpe and Treynor ratio The Sharpe ratio is almost identical to the Treynor ratio, except that the risk measure is the standard deviation of the portfolio instead of considering only the systematic risk, as represented by beta.

Both Sharpe and Treynor ratios express a linear relationship between the risk and return of portfolio and differ only in their measure of risk. Further, both give identical ranking in case of well-diversified portfolios because in well-diversified portfolio, total risk and systematic risk are one and the same. If a portfolio is not well-diversified, Treynor and Sharpe ratio give different results. Treynor ratio may rank a portfolio high whereas Sharps ratio may rank it low on account of poor diversification (the unsystematic risk component plays dominant role).

Jensen's Alpha

Sharpe and Treynor ratios are tools for ranking of portfolios/funds on the basis of their relative performance on a risk-adjusted basis. A third measure, named Jensen's alpha, after its developer Michael Jensen[3], provides an

[3] Michael C. Jensen, "The Performance of Mutual Funds in the Period 1945–1964," *Journal of Finance*, May 1968; and "Risk, the Pricing of Capital Assets, and the Evaluation of Investment Portfolios," *Journal of Business*, April 1969.

absolute measure of risk-adjusted returns. Michael Jensen first used Jensen's alpha to evaluate the performance of mutual fund managers in 1968.

Jensen's alpha uses CAPM as a definite standard/benchmark to measure the returns of a portfolio. Alpha is used to determine the abnormal return of a security or portfolio over the theoretical expected return given by an asset pricing model. In other words, Jensen's alpha is a measure of the predictive ability of a fund manager. For a given level of risk, superior predictive ability enables a manager to generate higher returns than an ordinary investor.

Mathematically, Jensen's alpha measures the excess of a portfolio's actual returns over the returns it was expected to earn as measured by CAPM. The CAPM return is the return that a portfolio can be expected to earn, given its beta (risk). So the excess returns above CAPM indicate the ability of a manager to generate returns higher than those commensurate with the given level of portfolio risk.

The formula is broken down as follows:

$$\text{Jensen's Alpha} = \text{Actual Portfolio Return} - \text{Expected return as per CAPM (SML)}$$

where

$$\text{CAPM Return} = \text{Risk-Free Rate of Return} + \text{Beta (Return on Market Portfolio} - \text{Risk-Free Rate of Return)}$$

Symbolically, CAPM may be expressed as:

$$E(r_i) = r_f + \beta_i (E(r_m) - r_f)$$

If, the actual return of a portfolio is represented by r_p, Jensen's alpha can be given as

$$\alpha = r_p - E(r_i)$$

or

$$\alpha = r_p - \{r_f + \beta_i [E(r_m) - r_f]\} \quad (3)$$

where

r_p = Actual return of a portfolio
r_f = Risk-free rate of return
β_i = Systematic risk of security
$E(r_m)$ = Expected return on market index

Graphically, Jensen's alpha may be represented as shown in Figure 8.6. The Jensen alpha measures how much of the portfolio's actual return is attributable to the manager's ability to generate above-average returns, adjusted for market risk. Alpha measures the degree to which managers are earning significant returns after accounting for market risk, as measured by beta. If the manager is earning a fair return for the given portfolio's systematic risk, then alpha will be zero. A portfolio with positive excess return will have a positive alpha, while a portfolio with negative excess return will have a negative alpha. The higher the ratio, the better the performance of the manager.

Portfolio and fund managers consider α as very important measure. A positive value of α is taken to signify a manager's superior skills and a negative value of α is considered bad. A negative α means that the manager has failed to perform, even as much as an unmanaged portfolio. This could sometimes be on the account of high

Figure 8.6 Graphical representation of Jensen's alpha.

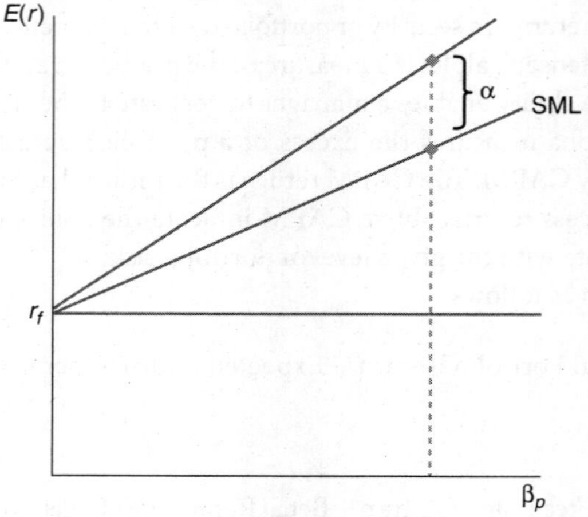

cost of analysis, selection and portfolio management process. Zero α indicates neutral performance like any unmanaged portfolio with a basic buy and hold strategy.

Many researchers have criticized α as a measure of performance on the grounds that the historical performance of an equity mutual fund cannot be taken as an accurate predictor of its future performance.

Let us understand the computation of Jensen α with the help of a Numerical Example.

Numerical Example 3

Suppose the annual return for the S&P BSE SENSEX (market portfolio) is 10% and its standard deviation is 18%. The average annual return on treasury bills (the risk-free rate) is 5%. You are required to calculate alpha for the portfolios managed by three portfolio managers with the following results:

Manager	Average annual return	Beta
Manager D	11%	0.95
Manager E	16%	1.10
Manager F	16%	1.25

Solution:

First, we calculate the portfolio's expected return:

$$ER(D) = 0.05 + 0.95\ (0.10 - 0.05) = 0.0975 \text{ or } 9.75\%$$

$$ER(E) = 0.05 + 1.10\ (0.10 - 0.05) = 0.1050 \text{ or } 10.50\%$$

$$ER(F) = 0.05 + 1.25\ (0.10 - 0.05) = 0.1125 \text{ or } 11.25\%$$

Then, we calculate the portfolio's alpha by subtracting the expected return of the portfolio from the average actual return earned by it:

$$\text{Alpha of portfolio D} = 11\% - 9.75\% = 1.25\%$$

$$\text{Alpha of portfolio E} = 16\% - 10.5\% = 5.5\%$$

$$\text{Alpha of portfolio F} = 16\% - 11.25\% = 4.75\%$$

Which manager performed best? Manager E performed best because he has generated higher alpha as compared to portfolio F, which has same level of return. Given the value of β equal to 1.1, portfolio E would have been expected to yield lower returns.

The M^2 measure of performance

Leah and Franco Modigliani[4] popularized a variant of Sharpe ratio which had initially been proposed by Graham and Harvey[5]. This measure of performance has come to be known as M^2 measure.

The reason for development of this measure is the fact that Sharpe ratio is useful in ranking portfolios but the actual value is difficult to interpret. Suppose a portfolio has Sharpe ratio of 0.79. It will be considered to have performed better in the market than a portfolio with Sharpe ratio of 0.75. This means that the first portfolio has outperformed the second portfolio by 0.04. But does this difference of 0.04 has any economic significance? Sharpe ratio cannot answer this question. Rates can be compared but these ratios are pure numbers and hence difficult to interpret.

M^2 has been developed to overcome these limitations of Sharpe ratio. It is easy to interpret numerically as compared to Sharpe ratio and has gained popularity because it is expressed as a rate of return. Like Sharpe ratio, M^2 also uses volatility as a measure of risk and can be mathematically expressed as:

$$M^2 = r_p^* - r_m \tag{4}$$

where
r_p^* = Return on an adjusted portfolio with a volatility that is matched with volatility of market index.
r_m = Return on market index.

M^2 measure is based on conceptualization of a adjusted portfolio that is mixed with a position in t-bills (risk-free rate) such that its volatility (standard deviation) is same as that of the market index, like S&P BSE SENSEX or S&P CNX NIFTY.

For example, for a managed portfolio that has 1.5 times the volatility of the market index, adjusted portfolio (P^*) will have a mix of about 34 percent investment in t-bills and 64 percent investment in the managed portfolio. This adjusted portfolio (P^*) has the same standard deviation as the market index.

---

[4] Franco Modigliani and Leah Modigliani, "Risk-Adjusted Performance," *Journal of Portfolio Management*, Winter 1997, 45–54.
[5] John R. Graham and Campbell R. Harvey, "Grading the Performance of Market Timing Newsletters," *Financial Analysts Journal* 53, November/December 1997, 54–66.

In case of a managed portfolio with a lower standard deviation than the market index, an adjusted portfolio with volatility equal to the index is created by borrowing money and investing in the portfolio. This adjustment of risk of managed portfolio brings the two portfolios (managed and market) on level playing field in terms of risk, paving way for comparison of their return.

A graphical representation of the M^2 measure is exhibited in Figure 8.7.

Figure 8.7 Graphical representation of M^2 measure.

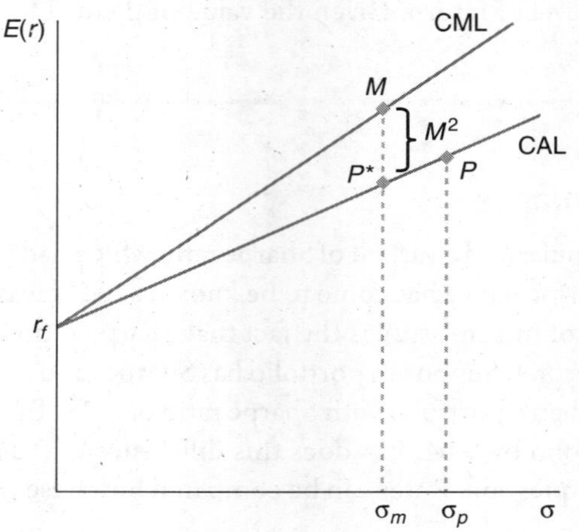

As we can see in Figure 8.7, portfolio *P* has a standard deviation higher than market portfolio. To create an adjusted portfolio, we move down the capital allocation line corresponding to portfolio *P* by adding more t-bills to the portfolio *P* until the standard deviation of the adjusted portfolio becomes same as that of the market index. The M^2 measure is the vertical distance or the difference between the expected returns of the adjusted portfolio P^* and the market portfolio *M*. We can deduce from Figure 8.7 that *P* will have a negative M^2 measure if its capital allocation line is less steep than the capital market line. In other words, M^2 measure of a portfolio will be negative when its Sharpe ratio is less than that of the market index.

M^2 measure is used to measure how well a portfolio's return has rewarded an investor for the amount of risk he has taken relative to the market index and risk-free rate. Thus, an investment that has a very high risk as compared to market index, but offers a very small advantage, might have lower risk-adjusted performance than some other portfolio that has comparatively low risk relative to the benchmark, but similar returns.

Because it is directly derived from the Sharpe ratio, any ranking of portfolios using the M^2 measure would be the same as rankings using the Sharpe ratio.

Let us illustrate the construction of an adjusted portfolio with the help of a Numerical Example.

Numerical Example 4

Consider the following information about a certain period during which the t-bill rate was 5%.

	Managed portfolio	Market index
Average returns (%)	32%	24%
Beta	1.25	1.0
Standard deviation	50%	30%

Construct an adjusted portfolio and compute M^2.

Solution:

It can be seen in the table given above that the risk (standard deviation) of the managed portfolio is higher than the market index. Therefore, its proportion in the adjusted portfolio will be $= 30/50 = 0.6$ or 60%. Therefore, 40% of the adjusted portfolio will be invested in t-bills.

The returns of the adjusted portfolio may be computed as:

$$= 0.6 \times 32 + 0.4 \times 5$$

$$= 21.2\%$$

We know,

$$M^2 = r_p^* - r_m$$

$$= 21.2 - 24$$

$$= - 2.85$$

Negative value as M^2 implies that the portfolio has a lower Sharpe ratio than the market index.

Fama's Net Selectivity: Decomposition of Performance

The portfolio evaluation measures discussed so far evaluate the overall performance of a portfolio or a fund. Eugene Fama has provided a measure of performance that breaks down the performance of a fund into various components. The framework for breaking down performance into components is called Fama's decomposition of total returns. It is based on the total risk of the portfolio.

In the first step, the total returns on a portfolio can be divided into two components: Risk-free return and Excess return.

Excess return is attributable to factors such as superior stock selection and risk bearing. Accordingly, excess return may be split into:

Risk premium + Return from Selection of Stock

Risk premium is related to the level of risk born by the investor and the return from stock selection is called return from stock selectivity.

Theoretically, unsystematic risk should disappear almost completely in a well-diversified portfolio, leaving behind only the systematic risk. But in reality, no portfolio can be diversified well enough to eliminate the unsystematic risk completely. Hence, most portfolios would have a systematic risk + small amount of unsystematic risk.

In light of the above discussion, risk premium on a portfolio can be broken into two components:

Return for bearing systematic risk + Return for bearing unsystematic risk

The preceding breakdowns can be summarized into one single equation:

$$\text{Return on Portfolio} = \text{Risk-free return } (r_f) + \text{Return from systematic risk or market risk } (r_1) + \text{Return from unsystematic risk } (r_2) + \text{Return from Pure Selection } (r_3)$$

Let's consider each component on the right hand side of the equation:

r_f = Risk-free rate (rate of return on t-bills)

r_1 = Return due to market risk which is calculated as $\beta_p(r_m - r_f)$

r_m = Return on index, β_p = beta of the portfolio

r_2 = Returns resulting from imperfect diversification calculated as $\left\{\left(\frac{\sigma_p}{\sigma_m}\right) - \beta_p\right\}(r_m - r_f)$

σ_p = Standard deviation of the portfolio

σ_m = Standard deviation of the market index

Let us discuss imperfect diversification now. A portfolio can be said to be perfectly diversified if its returns are found to be perfectly correlated with the returns of the market index, i.e., the coefficient of their correlation = $r_{pm} = 1$.

Further, we know $\beta_p = \dfrac{r_{pm}\sigma_p\sigma_m}{\sigma_m^2}$

If $r_{pm} = 1$, $\beta_p = \dfrac{\sigma_p\sigma_m}{\sigma_m^2}$

or

$$\beta_p = \frac{\sigma_p}{\sigma_m}$$

In a perfectly diversified portfolio, the impact of imperfect diversification is zero.

r_3 = Superior return from pure selectivity

It may be calculated as

$$= r_p - (r_f + r_1 + r_2)$$

The return from pure selectivity is additional return that a portfolio earns on account of the manager's superior stock selection skill. It is the return over and above the return commensurate with the total risk of portfolio as measured by standard deviation.

Mathematically, return due to selectivity may be given as the difference between the actual return earned by a portfolio and the return mandated by the level of total portfolio risk. This is called Fama's net selectivity and is measured as:

$$r_p - \left\{ r_f + \left(\frac{\sigma_p}{\sigma_m} \right) (r_m - r_f) \right\} \tag{5}$$

where

r_p = Actual return on portfolio
r_f = Risk-free return
r_m = Return on index
σ_p = Standard deviation of the portfolio
σ_m = Standard deviation of the market index

A negative net selectivity implies poor stock selection. It means that the actual return on the portfolio is less than the return it was expected to earn, given its total risk. A positive net selection is indicative of superior stock selection.

Let us understand the concept of net selectivity with the help of a Numerical Example.

Numerical Example 5

Consider a mutual fund A and a market index. Following information is available regarding the performance of the two over past several years:

	Mutual fund A	Market index
Returns (%)	19	16
Beta	1.25	1.0
Standard deviation	30%	20%

The risk-free rate of return during the period was 8%. Decompose the portfolio return.

Solution:

The portfolio return can be decomposed into four parts as per Fama's net selectivity:

$$= r_f + r_1 + r_2 + r_3$$

$$r_f = 8\%$$

r_1 = Returns due to market risk which is calculated $= \beta_p (r_m - r_f)$

$= 1.25\,(16 - 8) = 10\%$

$$r_2 = \text{Returns resulting from imperfect diversification} = \left\{\left(\frac{\sigma_p}{\sigma_m}\right) - \beta_p\right\}(r_m - r_f)$$

$$= \left\{\left(\frac{30}{20}\right) - 1.25\right\}(16 - 8)$$

$$= 0.25 \times 8$$

$$= 2\%$$

r_3 = Superior returns from pure selectivity $= r_p - (r_f + r_1 + r_2)$

$= 19 - (8 + 10 + 2)$

$= -\,1\%$

The net selectivity is negative indicating poor stock selection.

Fama's decomposition of total returns helps in identifying the skills involved in active portfolio management.

Information Ratio

Information ratio relates the excess return of a portfolio over certain benchmark to their volatility. It is calculated by dividing α of the portfolio by non-systematic risk of the portfolio. Intuitively, it is a measure of the abnormal return per unit of risk that ideally should have been diversified away (residual risk as measured by $\sigma(e)$) by holding the market index portfolio. Thus, the information ratio can be said to be a measure of active manager's performance against a passive benchmark. Mathematically,

$$\text{Information ratio} = \frac{\alpha}{\sigma(e)} \qquad (6)$$

In other words, information ratio is a measure of the extra return that a portfolio manager can generate by doing security analysis compared to the unique risk of the firm that he would incur if he were over or under-weight in securities relative to the passive market index. Further, while α represents active return, $\sigma(e)$ represents tracking error i.e the standard deviation of the active returns. The higher the ratio, the better it is as it indicates higher active return for the portfolio.

The ratio also identifies the consistency of a portfolio manager. The higher the ratio, the more the consistency. Let us understand the computation of information ratio with the help of a Numerical Example.

Numerical Example 6

Use the following information about a portfolio *X* and market index to compute its information ratio.

	Portfolio *X*	Market index
Average return	36	25
Beta	1.25	1
Standard deviation	40	30
Non-systematic risk $\sigma(e)$	19	0

The risk-free rate of return during the period was 6%.

Solution:

We know,

$$\text{Information ratio} = \frac{\alpha}{\sigma(e)}$$

Therefore, to calculate information ratio, we need α and $\sigma(e)$. The non-systematic risk $\sigma(e)$ is given. We need to calculate alpha.

α can be calculated using the formula for Jensen's α

$$\alpha = r_p - \{r_f + \beta_i\,(E(r_m) - r_f))$$

$$= 36 - \{6 + 1.25\,(25 - 6)\}$$

$$= 6.25$$

Therefore,

$$\text{Information ratio} = \frac{\alpha}{\sigma(e)} = \frac{6.25}{19} = 0.329$$

Numerical Example 7

Consider the given data to highlight the issues with the use of sharpe ratio for portfolio performance evaluation. Also discuss how information ratio can yield improved analysis of performance of portfolios.

	Manager A	Manager B	Index
Annualized returns	5.6%	5.6%	3.8
Standard derivation	7.9%	3.4%	
Standard derivation of excess return	1.95%	3.92%	

Risk-free rate is 5%.

Solution:

1. **Sharpe Ratio:** Sharpe ratio is computed as:

$$\frac{r_p - r_f}{\sigma_p}$$

$$\text{Manager A} = \frac{5.6-5}{7.9} = 0.076$$

$$\text{Manager B} = \frac{5.6-5}{3.4} = 0.176$$

According to Sharpe ratio, Manager B has performed better.

2. **Information Ratio:** Information ratio is computed as:

$$\frac{\alpha}{\sigma_e} = \frac{\text{Excess return}}{\text{Standard derivation of excess return}}$$

$$\text{Manager A} = \frac{5.6-3.8}{1.95} = 0.923$$

$$\text{Manager B} = \frac{5.6-3.8}{3.92} = 0.459$$

Higher IR shows that Manager A has performed better. Though both Manager A and B have outperformed the index by same amount, Manager A has done so with lower tracking error.

Since Manager A has been successful in generating same excess return as B but with less volatility, he has greater skill in stock selection.

Sharpe ratio relies on risk-free rate for calculating performance of active manager, relative to total risk. This may lead to erroneous conclusion.

Sortino's Ratio

Sortino's ratio is also a measure of risk-adjusted returns of a portfolio and it is named after Frank A. Sortino. Dr. Frank Sortino came up with the idea of an improved measure of risk-adjusted return in 1980 which was named as Sortino's ratio by Brian Rom at Investment Technologies. The first calculation based on the ratio was published in the *Journal of Risk Management* in September 1981. It is actually a modification of Sharpe ratio. The difference between the two is that Sharpe ratio takes both upside as well as downside volatility into account whereas Sortino's ratio takes only downside risk into account by using semi-variance in the denominator. We have discussed the concept of upside and downside risk and semi variance in Chapter 3.

Sortino's ratio is a measure of how much the return on portfolio varies from the minimal acceptable level. A large value of Sortino's ratio indicates low risk of occurrence of substantial losses.

Sortino's ratio may be calculated as:

$$\text{or} = \frac{(\bar{r} - r_r)}{\sigma_{\text{down}}} \tag{7}$$

where

$\bar{r}$ = Average return

r_r = Minimum acceptable return (MAR)

σ_{down} = Downside risk

The ratio considers only the returns that fall below MAR. For example, if MAR is 11%, the downside risk will measure the deviation for each period where the risk falls below 11%.

The denominator in equation (7) can be calculated as:

$$\sigma_{\text{down}} = \sqrt{\frac{\Sigma r_d^2}{N}} \tag{8}$$

where

$r_d = (r_i < r_r) - r_r$

r_i = Return for period *i*

r_r = Minimum acceptable returns

N = Number of periods

The downside risk can be annualized by multiplying equation (8) by $\sqrt{N}$. Downside deviation is usually calculated for 24 to 36 months.

In the context of Sortino's ratio, we can also look at upside and downside potential. Upside potential is a measure of excess of return over MAR and is calculated as:

$$\text{Upside potential} = \frac{\Sigma r_u}{N} \tag{9}$$

where

$$r_u = (r_i > r_r) - r_r$$

The upside potential ratio is given as

$$\text{Upside potential ratio} = \frac{(\sum r_u)}{\sigma_{\text{down}}} \quad (10)$$

i.e.,
$$\frac{\text{Sum of upside deviations}}{\text{Downside standard deviation or risk}}$$

Similarly,

$$\text{Downside potential} = \frac{(\sum r_d)}{N} \quad (11)$$

where

$$r_d = (r_i < r_r) - r_r$$

Let us understand Sortino's ratio with the help of a Numerical Example.

Numerical Example 8

Consider the returns given in the table below. Assuming monthly minimum acceptable rate to be 7%, compute the following:

- Monthly and annualized downside risk
- Upside and downside potential
- Upside potential ratio
- Sortino's ratio (monthly and annualized)

r_i	4.9	−4.5	7.3	2.1	5.9	−2.5	8.3	6.8	−7	3	−0.7	−1.3	5	4	−0.3

Solution:

We need to determine downside (r_d) and upside (r_u) deviations as shown in the table:

	r_i	$r_d = (r_i < 0.7) - 0.7$	r_d^2	r_u
	4.9	0	0	4.2
	−4.5	−5.2	27.04	0
	7.3	0	0	6.6

(Continued)

Continued

	r_i	$r_d = (r_i < 0.7) - 0.7$	r_d^2	r_u
	2.1	0	0	1.4
	5.9	0	0	5.2
	−2.5	−3.2	10.24	0
	8.3	0	0	7.6
	6.8	0	0	6.1
	−7	−7.7	59.29	0
	3	0	0	2.3
	−0.7	−1.4	1.96	0
	−1.3	−2	4	0
	5	0	0	4.3
	4	0	0	3.3
	−0.3	−1	1	0
Σ	31	20.5	103.53	41
$\bar{r}$	2.07			

1. **Downside Risk:** Monthly

$$\sigma_{\text{down}} = \sqrt{\frac{\Sigma r_d^2}{N}} = \sqrt{\frac{103.53}{15}} = 2.63$$

Annualized

$$\sigma_{\text{down}} = 2.63\sqrt{(12)} = 9.10$$

2. **Upside and Downside Potential:** Upside potential

$$\frac{(\Sigma r_u)}{N} = \frac{41}{15} = 2.73$$

Downside potential

$$\frac{(\Sigma r_d)}{N} = \frac{20.5}{15} = 1.37$$

3. **Upside Potential Ratio:**

$$= \frac{(\sum r_u)}{\sigma_{\text{down}}} = \frac{20.5}{9.10}$$

4. **Sortino Ratio (Monthly and Annualized):** Monthly

$$= \frac{(\bar{r} - r_r)}{\sigma_{\text{down}}} = \frac{(2.07 - 0.7)}{9.10} = 0.15$$

Annualized

$$= \frac{(\bar{r} - r_r)}{\sigma_{\text{down}}} = 0.15(\sqrt{12}) = 0.52$$

Mutual Fund Performance Analysis

We will discuss mutual funds in more detail in Chapter 17. However, as we are on the topic of portfolio performance measurement, let us discuss how the performance of mutual funds is measured.

The performance of mutual funds is measured in terms of Net asset value (NAV).

$$\text{NAV} = \frac{(\text{Market value of all securities held by fund} + \text{cash and cash equivalent holdings} - \text{fund liabilities})}{\text{Total fund units outstanding}}$$

A single holding period return on a mutual fund is computed as:

$$r_p = \frac{\{(\text{NAV}_t - \text{NAV}_{t-1}) + D_t + C_t\}}{\text{NAV}_{t-1}} \tag{12}$$

where

NAV_t = NAV at the end of the holding period
NAV_{t-1} = NAV at the beginning of the holding period
D_t = Cash disbursement per unit during the holding period
C_t = Capital gains disbursement during the holding period
r_p can be calculated for different mutual funds and compared with the market index, which can serve as a benchmark for comparative evaluation.

The risk-adjusted performance measures discussed above are also computed for mutual funds for evaluation and comparison purpose. The excel window given below exhibits the performance of ICICI Blue Chip, Religare Mid & Small, HSBC Tax Saver, UTI Equity Fund, SBI Magnum, Mirae Asset India, DSP BlackRock and Reliance Tax Saver Fund based on average parameters computed for a period from January 2009 to October 2014. 30 Stock Index of BSE has been taken to represent the market index and an average of G-sec annual yield has been used as risk-free rate.

	A	B	C	D	E	F	G	H	I	J
1 2		Average Returns	Standard Deviation	Beta Coefficient	Sharpe's Measure	Treynor's Measure	Jensen's Measure	Ranking as per Sharpe	Ranking as per Treynor	Ranking as per Jensen
3	ICICI Blue Chip	2.14%	5.52%	86.33%	27.89%	1.78%	0.21%	4	6	3
4	Religare Mid & Small	2.81%	6.24%	84.69%	35.42%	2.61%	0.34%	1	1	1
5	HSBC Tax Saver	2.04%	6.04%	90.29%	23.84%	1.59%	0.14%	8	8	5
6	UTI Equity Fund	2.08%	5.37%	81.93%	27.56%	1.81%	0.27%	5	5	2
7	SBI Magnum	2.04%	5.81%	86.42%	24.88%	1.67%	0.20%	7	7	4
8	Mirae Asset India	2.50%	6.56%	101.11%	28.97%	1.88%	-0.02%	3	4	7
9	DSP BlackRock	3.09%	8.07%	110.91%	30.86%	2.25%	-0.27%	2	2	8
10	Reliance Tax Saver Fund	2.49%	7.02%	97.98%	26.89%	1.93%	0.04%	6	3	6
11	30 Stock Index BSE	1.77%	6.27%	1	18.70%	0.011734346	0.00%			
12	T-Bill Return	0.60%								

Source: Case Study "Numbers do not Lie" authored by Dr. Shalini Talwar, Ms. Shweta Kathar and Ms. Warada Bhagwat, published in Case Studies in Management Bharti Publications, 2015.

Challenges in Performance Measurement

The essence of performance evaluation is to measure the returns generated by the portfolio management industry. Portfolio performance measures are a key aspect of the investment decision process. Though performance management is very important but its real utility lies in applying it properly. In today's highly competitive investment industry, performance is measured too frequently and judged too harshly. There are certain issues with performance measurement such as:

1. Performance measurement requires quantification of metrics that may not be completely quantifiable.
2. Availability of a variety of measures that use easily computable data has led to a 'short-termism' in portfolio performance measurement and consequently in investment decisions.
3. Coming to the specific measures, although Jensen's alpha is theoretically a very sound performance measure, it is difficult to use in practice. The reason is that even for very skillful managers, the value of alpha is likely to be small. This would make it difficult to statistically prove that the alpha is positive.
4. Managers chasing superior performance have got into the practice of trying to time the market by anticipating the market up and down movements. The attempt to time the market may result in ever-changing portfolio betas and other parameters, making evaluation difficult. The cult of market timing itself may not be so desirable.
5. True performance and its superiority can be measured correctly when the evaluation is in the context of a long period. The recent trend of measuring performance every now and then has taken away the real purpose of such an exercise.
6. Changing parameters of actively managed portfolios make accurate performance evaluation all the more elusive. Even when the portfolio mean and variance are constant, many observations are needed for significant results.

Performance Attribution

Performance attribution refers to the activity of the decomposition of overall portfolio performance into micro components reflecting various decisions taken in the portfolio selection process: asset allocation, sector allocation and security selection.

Performance attribution begins with the establishment of a benchmark portfolio called the bogey that captures the returns that a classic buy and hold or passive strategy would generate. We know that the essence of a passive strategy is neutral allocation of funds across broad asset classes in tandem with investor's risk aversion and holding an index portfolio within each asset class.

Since the passive strategy does away with both asset allocation and security selection decisions, we can explain the difference between the return on managed portfolio and the bogey portfolio in terms of deviations from the neutral allocation across asset classes and deviations from the index portfolio within asset classes.

The performance attribution study begins with asset allocation across broad asset classes and gradually narrows down to specific securities. Aggregation of the outcome/performance of the decisions taken at different stages of portfolio construction process captures the difference between the performance of the managed portfolio and that of the 'bogey' or the benchmark portfolio. The most commonly used attribution system breaks the performance of a portfolio into three components, namely:

1. Asset allocation across broad asset classes like domestic equity, foreign equity, domestic fixed income securities, etc.
2. Sector or industry chosen within each market.
3. Security choice within each sector.

The difference of returns between the managed portfolio and the bogey is explained by attribution of excess returns to each of the above listed components.

Let us understand the concept of performance attribution with the help of a Numerical Example.

Numerical Example 9

Consider a managed portfolio A that invests in equity, FIS and money market. The return of this portfolio, is 5.98% over the month. Perform attribution analysis for this portfolio assuming a hypothetical equity index, say PTC index giving 6.12% monthly returns, a FIS index, say NCB index, generating a monthly return of 1.65% and money market yielding 0.57% monthly.

Solution:

The first step of performance attribution study is the establishment of bogey, the benchmark portfolio for comparing the performance of the managed portfolio. The bogey has passive asset allocation with neutral weights being assigned to each asset class based on the risk tolerance of the investor.

In the current example, the bogey will consist of indexed portfolio of PTC index, NCB index and money market. According to the investor's risk tolerance, the portfolio weights for the bogey are 0.58 in equity, 0.27 in FIS and 0.15 in money market. Thus, the bogey is created using a completely passive strategy with no asset allocation or security selection decision. The returns on the bogey portfolio may be calculated as given below:

Component Asset	Benchmark Weight	% Return of Index during the Month
Equity (PTC Index)	0.58	6.12
FIS (NCB Index)	0.27	1.65
Money Market	0.15	0.57
Return of Bogey Portfolio	4.0806	

A portfolio manager can try to generate a return higher than the passive strategy (bogey) by either departing from neutral asset allocation or selecting securities to depart from passive index within each asset class or both. The managed portfolio being discussed in this example has a given return of 5.98% over the month. Thus, the excess return generated by the managed portfolio is:

$$5.98 - 4.08 = 1.9\%$$

Let us see what these returns can be attributed to.

Impact of asset allocation decision on excess returns generated by the managed portfolio:

Suppose the portfolio manager takes a decision to make a managed portfolio comprising PTC index, NCB index and money market by allocating 0.72 to equity, 0.10 to FIS and 0.18 to money market without allowing for effect of active portfolio management of securities selected within each class.

Component Asset	Actual Weight in each Asset Class	Benchmark Weight	Active or Excess Weight	% Return of Index during the Month	Contribution of Excess Weights to Performance (%)
Equity (PTC Index)	0.72	0.58	0.14	6.12	$0.14 \times 6.12 = 0.8568$
FIS (NCB Index)	0.1	0.27	–0.17	1.65	$(-0.17) \times 1.65 = -0.2805$
Money Market	0.18	0.15	0.03	0.57	$0.03 \times 0.57 = 0.0171$
Excess return of Managed Portfolio	1.9			Contribution of Asset Allocation	0.5934

It can be seen in the above table that shift in weights of bogey to create a managed portfolio has garnered an excess return of 0.5934 %. This has been achieved mainly by being overweight in equity, which has a return of 6.12% over the month. Thus, it can be said that a manager can achieve superior performance by being overweight in markets that perform well.

Impact of security selection decision on excess returns generated by managed portfolio:

The total excess return of our managed portfolio is 1.9%. 0.59% of this 1.9% comes from asset allocation decision. The remaining 1.31% can be attributed to security selection within each asset class.

Component Asset	% Return of Portfolio during the Month	% Return of Index during the Month	Portfolio Weight	Excess Performance	Contribution (%)
Equity (PTC Index)	7.91	6.12	0.72	1.79	1.29
FIS (NCB Index)	1.86	1.65	0.1	0.21	0.02
				Contribution of Security Selection	1.31

It can be seen in the above table that the equity part of the managed portfolio yields 7.91% returns as against 6.12% returned by the equity index over the month. Similarly, the FIS return is 1.86% as against 1.65% returned by the FIS index over the month. The total excess return due to superior security selection is 1.31%.

Impact of sector selection decision on excess returns generated by managed portfolio:

The excess return of 1.31% generated by superior security selection can be analyzed in the context for both, the equity and the FIS components, to attribute performance to sector selection. We will discuss sector allocation for equity here.

Let us assume there are seven sectors A, B, C, D, E, F and G. The active weights and the weights of these sectors are displayed in the table given below:

Sector	Weight in Managed Portfolio (%)	Weight in Index (%)	Active Weight (%)	Sector Return (%)	Contribution
A	1.79	8.1	–6.31	5.7	–0.36
B	7.86	4.6	3.26	7.2	0.23
C	38.89	22.67	16.22	11	1.78
D	1.1	11	–9.9	0.7	–0.07
E	21.67	19.12	2.55	6.1	0.16
F	13.26	14.18	–0.92	5.9	–0.05
G	8.69	9.23	–0.54	4.75	–0.03
				Contribution of Sector Selection	1.67

It can be seen in the above table that the excess return generated due to superior sector selection is 1.67%. This means that out of 1.79% of excess return of equity component of managed portfolio over equity index, 1.67% is attributable to sector selection. Therefore, the effect of security selection within sectors is 1.79–1.67 = 0.12%.

It can be also be seen that excess return is generated by overweighting sectors that are expected to perform well and underweighting the sectors that are expected to underperform.

Portfolio Revision

Investment is mainly driven by an investor's investment objectives and constraints. Over time, these may undergo a change. It could also happen that the performance of the portfolio is not in line with the investor's expectations. Even the most well constructed portfolios tend to become inefficient over time and therefore need to be revised periodically. Several things can happen with the passage of time, causing the asset allocation of a portfolio to drift away from the original plan, making the portfolio inefficient for the investor.

Whatever the reason, the key point here is that portfolio management is not a static activity. It is a dynamic activity, as the portfolios need to be changed periodically on the basis of their performance measurement and investor's goals. This change, that may be done either by changing the proportion of funds invested in the securities constituting the portfolio or by adding or removing constituent securities, is called portfolio revision. Portfolio revision is an integral part of the portfolio management process. The reasons that cause managers to revise investment portfolios may be summarized as:

1. Shift in the investment objectives of the investors from earnings to capital appreciation, change in risk tolerance, need to reduce invested funds or any other change in investor's original investment inputs.
2. Drift in asset allocation from the original plan.
3. Inability of the chosen security to fulfill the investor's expectations regarding return and growth.
4. Changes in macroeconomic situation that might make some chosen securities less attractive then before.
5. Dynamic developments in the capital markets.

Portfolio revision entails two things viz., portfolio rebalancing and portfolio upgradation.

Portfolio rebalancing implies reviewing and revising the portfolio composition, i.e., the asset mix of the portfolio. There are three basic policies for portfolio rebalancing:

1. Buy and hold policy,
2. Portfolio insurance policy and
3. Constant mix policy.

These have been discussed in detail in the chapter on asset allocation (Chapter 7).

The initial portfolio is left untouched under the buy and hold policy. Under this policy, irrespective of what happens to the values of constituents, no rebalancing is undertaken. For example, if the initial portfolio has a stock-bond mix of 60:40 and after a few months it drifts to 80:40 because the stock component has appreciated and the bond component has remained stagnant, under buy and hold strategy, the portfolio mix is allowed to drift.

Under the portfolio insurance policy, the exposure to stocks is increased when the portfolio increases in value and decreased when the portfolio decreases in value. The basic plan is to ensure that the portfolio value does not plunge below a certain base level. The constant mix policy requires maintenance of the proportions of asset classes, mainly stocks and bonds in line with their target value. For example, if the desired mix of stocks and bonds 60:40, this policy calls for rebalancing of the portfolio in response to changes in the relative values of components with a view to maintain the target proportions.

In addition to the strategies for overall portfolio, managers use many strategies for revising the proportions of individual stocks that together make the equity component of the overall portfolio. The two key strategies that managers use to revise the weights of individual securities comprising the equity portfolio are:

1. Constant proportion policy
2. Constant beta policy

The aim of constant proportion policy for asset allocation is to assign equal weights to all securities initially and restore the proportions at various intervals. Constant beta policy aims at maintaining the beta of the portfolio. These two strategies have also been discussed with examples in Chapter 7.

Portfolio upgradation implies re-assessment of the risk-return profile of component securities (both stocks and bonds) with a view to sell the over-priced ones and buy the underpriced securities. Portfolio upgradation also involves other changes that the investor may want to undertake to enhance the performance of the portfolio.

However, portfolio revision, both rebalancing and upgradation come with a cost. The main constraints in portfolio revision may be listed as:

1. Transaction costs such as commission and brokerage incurred while buying and selling of securities. Existence of transaction costs can reduce the potential gains from portfolio revision.
2. Tax is payable on the capital gains arising from sale of securities as well as on the transaction of buying and selling securities. Usually, long-term capital gains are taxed at a lower rate as compared to short-term capital gains. Frequent churning of the portfolio to rebalance or upgrade it may give rise to short-term capital gains that would be taxed at a higher rate as compared to long-term capital gains. The prevalence of higher tax on short-term capital gains may act as a constraint to frequent portfolio changes.
3. Portfolio revision is a difficult and time-consuming exercise. There are no set rules for rebalancing and upgradation. There is an intrinsic difficulty in planning and executing the two.

In view of the preceding discussion, it can be said that portfolio revision calls for an appropriate response to the constant friction between the costs and benefits of rebalancing and upgradation of portfolio.

SUMMARY

- ☑ Though portfolio management is an ongoing activity with need for revision and rebalancing to keep the portfolio aligned with investors' objectives in response to changing market conditions, yet we call portfolio evaluation as a final step of portfolio management in the sense that it gives a measure of portfolio managers' performance during a given period.
- ☑ Some of the conventional measures of performance are total returns, arithmetic average and geometric mean.
- ☑ Average returns can be used to evaluate performance. However, evaluation of portfolio performance in terms of average returns presents an incomplete picture. To serve as a true measure of performance, returns needed to be adjusted for risk.
- ☑ The main risk-adjusted performance measures are: Sharpe ratio or reward-to-variability ratio, Treynor ratio or reward-to-volatility ratio, Jensen's alpha, M^2 measure, Fama's net selectivity, Information ratio and Sortino's ratio.
- ☑ The Sharpe ratio or Sharpe index or Sharpe measure or reward-to-variability ratio comprises excess return (or risk premium) in the numerator and the standard deviation of the portfolio in the denominator.
- ☑ The Treynor ratio or index or measure, or reward-to-volatility ratio comprises excess return (or risk premium) in the numerator and beta of the portfolio in the denominator.
- ☑ Defined in the context of market's return, an ideal fund is one that rises faster than the rising market and falls slower than the falling market returns.

☑ Jensen's alpha provides an absolute measure of risk-adjusted returns. Michael Jensen first used Jensen's alpha to evaluate the performance of mutual fund managers in 1968.

☑ M^2 measure is based on conceptualization of a managed portfolio that is mixed with a position in t-bills (risk-free rate) such that its volatility (standard deviation) is the same as that of the market index.

☑ Eugene Fama has provided a measure of performance that breaks down the performance of a fund into various components. The framework for breaking down performance into components is called Fama's decomposition of total returns.

☑ Information ratio is calculated by dividing α of the portfolio by non-systematic risk of the portfolio. It is also called as tracking error in the industry.

☑ Sortino's ratio takes only downside risk into account by using semi-variance in the denominator.

☑ Changing parameters of actively managed portfolios make accurate performance evaluation all the more elusive. Even when the portfolio's mean and variance are constant, many observations are needed for significant results.

☑ Even the most well constructed portfolios tend to become inefficient over time and need to be revised periodically. Over time, several things can happen which can cause the asset allocation of a portfolio to drift away from the original plan and make the portfolio inefficient for an investor.

KEY WORDS

Arithmetic mean **306**
Asset allocation **328**
Downside risk **325**
Fama's net selectivity **317**
Geometric average **306**
Ideal fund **310**
Information ratio **320**
Jensen's alpha **312**
M^2 measure **315**
Net asset value **326**
Non-systematic risk **320**
Performance attribution **328**
Portfolio rebalancing **331**
Portfolio revision **331**
Portfolio upgrading **331**
Residual risk **320**
Risk premium **307**
Risk-weighted measures **306**
Selection of stock **317**
Sharpe measure **307**
Sortino's ratio **323**
Time-weight average **306**
Total return **306**
Treynor measure **309**
Upside potential **326**

PRACTICE PROBLEMS

1. An investor has gathered the following information about five mutual funds, namely A, B, C, D and E:

Mutual funds	Return (%)	Std. deviation (%)	Beta
A	15	5	1.5
B	10	4	0.5
C	17	7	1
D	11	6	0.7
E	19	5	1.3

Return on risk-free asset is 5% and return on market is 18%. Evaluate these mutual funds using Sharpe, Treynor and Jensen measures.

2. KKK and CPZ are two mutual funds. KKK has a beta of 1.5 and CPZ has a beta of 3.1. The standard deviations of KKK and CPZ funds are 15% and 21.43%. The mean return of market index is 12% and its standard deviation is 8%. Risk-free rate of return is 8%. Return of KKK is 15% and CPZ is 22%. Compute using Sharpe, Treynor and Jensen indices.

3. Mr. A owns units of three different mutual funds, namely R, S and T. The following particulars are available to him:

Funds	$R_p - R_F$	Beta
R	7.7	1.02
S	11.4	0.98
T	11.6	1.08
Market	$R_m - R_F = 7.8$	1.00

He wants to dispose any one mutual fund for his personal expenditure. Which fund should he dispose? Suggest using Jensen measure.

4. An investor owns a portfolio that over the last five years has produced 16.8% annual return. During that time, the portfolio produced a 1.15 beta. Further, the risk-free return and the market return were 7.4% and 15% per year, respectively. Evaluate the portfolio using Treynor index.

5. The following information is provided regarding the performance of the given funds:

	R_p	s_p	Beta
Birla advantage	25.38	4.0	.24
PICICI GP	36.35	6.88	.52
Alliance equity	46.56	4.36	.64
S&P 500 CNX	36.74	3.71	1.00
Risk-free rate	8.00		

Using the inputs, rank the funds according to the predictive ability of their fund managers.

6. There are two equity funds, A and B, the details of which are as follows:

	Fund A	Fund B
Actual return from the fund	17%	20%
Beta coefficient	1.65	0.7

The market return is 17% and the risk-free interest rate is 7%. Evaluate the portfolios on the basis of Jensen's measure.

7. Consider the following information about a certain period during which the t-bill rate was 6%.

	Managed portfolio	Market index
Average returns (%)	25%	20%
Beta	1.35	1.0
Standard deviation	45%	30%
Non-systematic risk	19%	0

Calculate:

a. Sharpe, Treynor and Jensen measures.
b. M^2 and construct an adjusted portfolio.
c. Information ratio.

Comment if the managed portfolio has outperformed the market?

8. Compare the following two portfolios on the basis of Sharpe and Treynor ratio and offer your comments. Risk-free rate of return is 7%.

Portfolio	Return from portfolio	Std. deviation	Beta
A	10%	13	0.70
B	20%	25	1.45
Market portfolio	15%	18	1.00

9. Consider the returns given in the table below. Assuming monthly minimum acceptable rate to be 8%, compute the following:

- Monthly and annualized downside risk
- Upside and downside potential
- Upside potential ratio
- Sortino ratio (monthly & annualized)

r_i	5.9	−3.8	7.8	2.6	5.8	−2.9	8.9	6.8	−7.2	2.9	−0.3	−1.5	5.8	5	−0.4

10. Consider a mutual fund named Tiger Contra fund and a market index. Following information is available regarding the performance of the two over past several years:

	Tiger Contra Fund	Market index
Returns (%)	24	19
Beta	1.5	1.0
Standard deviation	35%	23%

The risk-free rate of return during the period was 8%. Decompose the portfolio returns.

CASELET

Sam Waugh is interested in investing in mutual funds in India. He has been an active investor in the stock market and has earned handsome returns for many years now. After intensive study and discussions with his friends, he shortlists the following five mutual funds and approaches you for advice:

- ICICI Prudential US Blue chip Equity Fund
- HDFC Top 200 Fund
- SBI Magnum SFU-FMCG Fund
- Sun F & C Value Fund
- Sundaram Growth Fund

You are an investment consultant. To give Sam sound advice, you collect the following information about the above listed mutual funds:

Mutual fund	Return (%)	Std. deviation (%)	Beta
ICICI Prudential US Blue chip Equity Fund	19	6	0.8
HDFC Top 200 Fund	22	6.75	1.15
SBI Magnum SFU-FMCG Fund	17	3.85	1
Sun F & C Value Fund	11	6	0.72
Sundaram Growth Fund	18	5	1.25

Return on risk-free asset is 5% and return on market is 16%. Evaluate these mutual funds using Sharpe, Treynor and Jensen measures and comment whether Sam has made an acceptable selection based on their past performance.

Critical Component of Analytical Framework: Valuation of Equity

9

CHAPTER OBJECTIVES

- ❒ Understanding the concept of intrinsic value
- ❒ Analyzing various methods and models for valuation of equity
- ❒ Computing the value of equity using discounted cash flow and relative valuation techniques
- ❒ Critiquing the efficacy of various valuation techniques

While making investment decision, an investor/analyst likes to determine what is her/his required rate of return. Once this rate is determined, the investment avenues/alternatives can be evaluated to see whether they fit the investor's requirements. In case of certain instruments like treasury bills, savings accounts and other fixed income securities, such an evaluation is easy because they provide known cash flows. However, most investments have only expected/projected cash flows and a stated market price and the investors are required to estimate/infer the value of such instruments (for e.g., equity) to determine whether the current market price of the asset is consistent with the intrinsic value computed by them. To compute the intrinsic value, the investors need to know/generate the cash flows associated with the asset and their required rate of return. This process is called valuation and it is a question that all investors, analysts, researchers, academicians in the field, regulators and portfolio managers try to address/answer with varying degrees of success.

Valuation may be described as the process of estimation of the value of an investment alternative/asset on the basis of the variables that affect its returns in the future. Since valuation is based on projection of the future, skill and expertise are very important to its success.

Investment analysts need to understand various methods and models of valuation of equity and bond. In this chapter we will discuss equity valuation in detail and bond valuation will be discussed in Chapters 15 and 16. Let us first understand the concept of value in the context of equity shares and then we will move to the valuation process followed by specific valuation techniques.

What is Value?

Understanding the word 'value' is important for an equity analyst. There are different terms in literature in the context of value, namely intrinsic value, fair value, going-concern value and liquidation value, to name a few. Only 'intrinsic value' and 'going-concern value' are of relevance to us in the context of investment in equity.

Intrinsic Value

It is that value which reflects the true value of a share. Intrinsic value may be defined as the actual value of a security, as opposed to its book value or current market price. It is calculated as the present value of future earnings that the investors expect the company to generate for them. In other words, intrinsic value is a measure of the right value of a stock that attempts to quantify the total net assets that a company is expected to build in the future. Intrinsic value computation takes into account both, the future earnings and the future sale value of the company. Intrinsic value computation using future earnings is based on the fact that ownership of a stock entitles the holder to a share of the company's future earnings.

Though the efficient market theory (discussed in Chapter 14) suggests that a security's market price is the best estimate of its intrinsic value but in reality, shares are not usually priced at their intrinsic value. In the real market condition, mispricing exists, i.e., there is a difference between the current market price (what an investor is willing to pay for the stock) and intrinsic value (what the stock is really worth). Analysts and investors use many analytical tools and techniques to estimate the intrinsic value of shares with a view to identify investments whose true value is different from their current market value. The idea is to take advantage of mispricing till it exists because it is generally accepted that eventually all share prices converge towards their intrinsic value. To summarize, the aim of the valuation process is to determine the intrinsic value of a share and compare it with its market price to take advantage of mispricing. In other words, the aim of the valuation process is to identify the undervalued shares with a view to buy them and/or identify overvalued shares with a view to sell them. Shares are determined to be under or overvalued in the context of their market price. The idea behind buying undervalued shares or selling overvalued shares is the belief that the market is mean-reverting, i.e., it always tends towards its right value or the intrinsic value. Therefore, an undervalued or underpriced security is bought with the hope that its price will rise in future and an overvalued or overpriced security is sold, fearing a fall in its price sometime in the future.

While valuing equity, it should be kept in mind that there is always an uncertainty surrounding the computations because no model can reflect all the sources of risk in an asset's price and use of multiple models increases the dilemma further. Not only do the forecasts remain uncertain but also the time taken for convergence of market price towards its intrinsic value. Further, temporal market conditions or some corporate event may change the intrinsic value itself. Analysts and investors need to take into account the extremely dynamic nature of all the variables involved in security valuation and adjust their estimates and expectations accordingly.

Going-Concern and Liquidation Value

A company has a different value if it is expected to continue to operate in the foreseeable future as compared to the value it is calculated to have if it is dissolved immediately. The value of the firm expected to continue its business activities in relevant economic timeframe is called the going-concern value. The models that we will discuss later in this chapter are based on the going-concern value.

An alternative value, the liquidation value, is a value that applies to a company in financial distress, i.e., a company that is not expected to continue its operations in the foreseeable future. This value is generally not considered while valuing securities from the point of view of investment. The intrinsic value of a share estimated under the going-concern value is the relevant true value from the point of view of buying and selling shares.

Valuation Process

There are two general approaches to the valuation process. Bottom-up and top-down. In the top-down approach, the emphasis is on the fact that both economy and industry have a significant impact on the returns of an individual share. In the bottom-up approach, the idea is to pick a stock that is relatively undervalued vis-à-vis its market price based on the belief that such a stock can give good returns irrespective of the industry it belongs to or the economy it operates in.

We will focus on the top-down approach because it seems to be more broad-based, logical and empirically proven. It is a fact that the strongest of companies fail to perform well if the overall economy is in recession. Thus, an understanding of the broad factors characterizing the economy is a better starting point for equity analysis for it to be more sound and accurate.

Figure 9.1 The top-down 3-step valuation process.

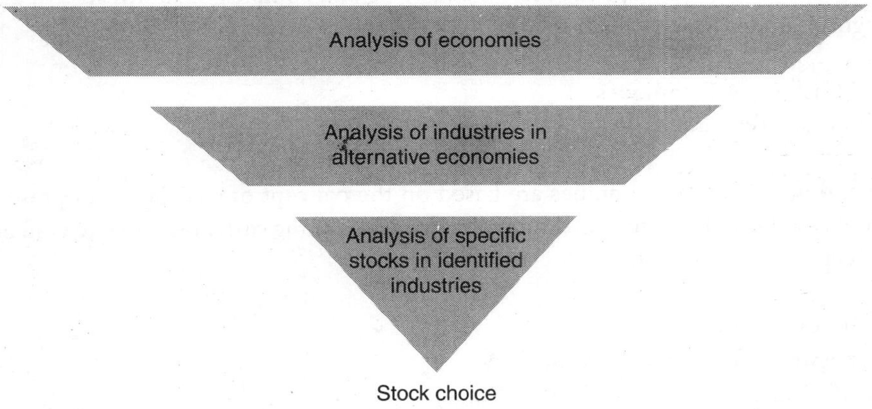

Step 1: Analysis of Economies

The economic policies of the government of the country under consideration play a big role in influencing the performance of companies and their share prices. Fiscal and monetary policies and their impact on taxes, interest rate, inflation and money supply have a bearing on the credit available to the firms, cost of raw material and labor and interest burden on leveraged firms. These factors in turn affect profit after tax (PAT) and consequently the earning per share (EPS) of the firm. The EPS, as we all know, has a direct impact on the share price of the concerned firm.

There is no denying that broad macroeconomic conditions play a large role in a firm's performance and they need to be analyzed before identifying the industries whose shares can be chosen for investment. Same logic applies in case of evaluating foreign as well as domestic equity. We will discuss the macroeconomic factors in detail in the next chapter.

Step 2: Analysis and Identification of Industries

The idea behind industry analysis is to find which industries will be impacted positively and which will be impacted negatively by the economic environment that is expected to prevail domestically and globally. Obviously, analysts would want to identify industries that are expected to perform well in the expected macroeconomic conditions. Here understanding of business cycle and industry life cycle play a big role. We will discuss industry analysis in detail in the next chapter.

Step 3: Analysis of Specific Stocks in Identified Industries

In this step, the aim is to pick winners from the industry identified in the preceding step. Here the financial statements of the company, past as well as projected, are used as a basis for computing the intrinsic value of the stock using various models discussed below. Company analysis has been discussed in detail in Chapter 11.

Valuation Models for Common Stock

Valuation of common stock is perhaps the most challenging and complex of all investment avenues. There are two broad categories under which valuation models of the equity stocks fall:

1. Discounted Cash Flow Techniques
2. Relative Valuation Techniques

Discounted cash flow valuation techniques are based on the concept of calculation of present value of some measure of future cash flow of the share including dividend, operating cash flow and free cash flow. Accordingly, there are three techniques for valuation:

1. Dividend Discount Models
2. Present Value Model for Operating Cash Flow
3. Present Value Model for Free Cash Flow to Equity

Relative valuation techniques value the stock on the basis of its current price vis-à-vis a variable significant to valuation like cash flow, book value, earnings or sales. The main techniques/models of relative valuation are:

1. Price/Earnings Ratio (P/E)
2. Price/Sales Ratio (P/S)
3. Price/Book Value Ratio (P/BV)
4. Price/Cash flow Ratio (P/CF)
5. Enterprise value/EBITDA

The above techniques have many common variables. The first is the investors' required rate of return as it impacts the discount rate. The second variable or a set of variables actually, are the estimated growth rates of dividends, sales, cash flows, etc. These estimates are a forecast of future and different analysts are more than likely to come up with different estimations despite using the same models because an element of judgment and intuition is also involved in making forecasts. Here the skills of analysts are of paramount importance.

The DCF techniques are theoretically correct and allow flexibility to accommodate changes in sales and earnings in terms of different growth rates across periods. Once you are able to make forecast of growth rates and compute each measure of cash flow, DCF techniques can be applied with ease. The potential challenges in application, rather effective application, of the DCF techniques also come from the estimation of growth rates, both in terms of quantum and duration. Inaccurate forecast of the growth rate can lead to completely wrong intrinsic value estimations. Another issue related to the effective use of DCF is the determination of the discount rate to be used. The reliability of the intrinsic value calculated using the DCF techniques depends on how well the analyst has adjusted his estimated inputs to the conditions prevailing currently in the market.

Relative valuation techniques have an advantage in the context of current market situation because they give information on how the market values stock in the prevailing conditions at various levels: individual scrips within an industry, alternative industries and the market as a whole. The problem with relative valuation techniques is that though they provide information on how market is valuing securities yet they give no indication if these valuations are appropriate, leading to wrong conclusions about valuations. This imposes certain restrictions on the use of relative valuation techniques. It is best to use relative valuation techniques when the market as a whole and the industry of the stock under consideration is not seriously overvalued or undervalued. Further, relative valuation techniques can be used effectively when there is a substantial set of comparable entities in terms of risk, size and industry.

Let us discuss both DCF and relative valuation techniques in detail now.

Discounted Cash Flow Techniques

All DCF valuation techniques are based on the following basic model:

$$V_i = \sum_{t=1}^{n} \left[\frac{CF_t}{(1+k)^t} \right] \tag{1}$$

where
V_i = Value of stock i
n = Life of the asset
k = Discount rate
t = Time
CF = Cash flow in period t

This equation asserts that the value of an asset is the present value of all future cash flows associated with it, discounted at an appropriate rate. The DCF equity valuation models differ according to the cash flow they use. Dividend Discount Model is the best known and most widely used as well. Another commonly used DCF model is free cash flow valuation model.

Dividend Discount Model

The model assumes that the value of a stock is equal to the present value of all future dividends or infinite stream of dividends. At this stage, the readers are expected to be familiar with the concept of time value of money.

Mathematically, the value of a stock for an infinite holding period may be calculated as:

$$V_i = \frac{D_1}{1+k} + \frac{D_2}{(1+k)^2} + \frac{D_3}{(1+k)^3} + \cdots + \frac{D_\infty}{(1+k)^\infty}$$

$$= \sum_{t=1}^{n} \left[\frac{D_t}{(1+k)^t} \right] \tag{2}$$

V_i = Value of stock i
n = Life of the asset
k = Required rate of return on stock i or alternatively the market capitalization rate
t = Time
D_t = Dividend in period t

The same model is valid for a finite holding period. Let us understand how. Suppose there is a stock that is held for a single holding period of one year. We know the current value V_0 of a share is given as:

$$V_0 = \left(\frac{D_1}{1+k} \right) + \left(\frac{P_1}{1+k} \right) \tag{3}$$

where P_1 is the price at which the share will be sold at the end of one year, D_1 is dividend in year 1 and V_0 is the value in the current year at $t = 0$. Here, D_1 and P_1 are the two cash flows associated with this share held for one year. Now, D_1 can be predicted from the company's dividend history but P_1 needs to be estimated by the analyst.

By definition, P_1 should be equal to present value of dividend in year 2 (D_2) and price at the end of year 2 (P_2). Hence,

$$P_1 = V_1 = \frac{(D_2 + P_2)}{(1+k)} \tag{4}$$

where

In addition to the symbols used above,

D_2 = Dividend in year 2
P_2 = Price at the end of year 2

Substituting this value of P_1 in equation 3, we get

$$V_0 = \left(\frac{D_1}{1+k} \right) + \left[\frac{D_2 + P_2}{(1+k)(1+k)} \right]$$

$$= \left(\frac{D_1}{1+k} \right) + \left[\frac{D_2}{(1+k)^2} \right] + \left[\frac{P_2}{(1+k)^2} \right] \tag{5}$$

The above equation may be described as the present value of dividends and the selling price of the share at the end of year 2. Now we need to forecast P_2 on the basis of D_3 and P_3 (dividend and price at the end of year 3) and thus the process will continue. It can be generalized for n years, giving us equation 2 that we had started our discussion of DDM with.

$$V_i = \sum_{t=1}^{n}\left[\frac{D_t}{(1+k)^t}\right]$$

The above equation has only dividend as the variable for determination of value, but this doesn't mean that capital gains or price are irrelevant to this model. Price is implicit in this formula because the price at which the equity share sells in future is determined by the dividend forecasts at the time the share is sold to realize capital gains.

The primary assertion of DDM is that the future prices of a share are determined by cash flows accruing to the shareholders and those cash flows are dividends.

We will now consider DDM in the light of different dividend scenarios like

1. Constant-growth of dividends
2. Temporary supernormal growth of dividends

1. **Constant-Growth DDM:** Equation (2) illustrated above is not of much practical use, as it requires us to forecast dividends for indefinite time in future. Certain assumptions need to be introduced to make this model practically useful and usable. One common way of doing this is by assuming that dividend grows at a rate 'g,' such that if D_0 is dividend in the current year, and dividend is growing at a stable growth rate of 'g,' then dividend in year 1 (D_1) may be computed as:

$$D_1 = D_0(1+g)$$

Similarly,

$$D_2 = D_1(1+g) \text{ or } D_0(1+g)(1+g)$$

$$D_3 = D_2(1+g) \text{ or } D_0(1+g)(1+g)(1+g)$$

.

.

$$D_{10} = D_0(1+g)^{10}$$

$$D_n = D_0(1+g)^n \qquad (6)$$

Substituting the values of D_1, D_2, D_3, etc. in equation (2), the formula for computation of intrinsic value may be written as:

$$V_0 = \left[\frac{D_0(1+g)}{(1+k)}\right] + \left[\frac{D_0(1+g)^2}{(1+k)^2}\right] + \left[\frac{D_0(1+g)^3}{(1+k)^3}\right] + \cdots \qquad (7)$$

At this stage, you may recall the present value of perpetuity concept, where present value of ₹1 of perpetuity at discount rate, k, is given by $1/k$. Therefore, equation (7) can be rewritten as present value of perpetuity of dividends as follows:

$$V_0 = \frac{D_0(1+g)}{(k-g)}$$

$$= \frac{D_1}{k-g} \qquad (8)$$

The derivation of equation (8) is given after the Numerical Examples. Let us talk about $(k-g)$ in the denominator. Had the dividends not been expected to grow at the rate 'g,' the present value of the perpetuity would have been

$$V_0 = \frac{D_1}{k}$$

Equation (8) is a generalization of the perpetuity formula to provide for growing perpetuity vis-à-vis a stagnant perpetuity. The presence of 'g' in the denominator suggests that as growth rate of dividends increases, the price of share increases.

The model illustrated in equation (8) is called the constant growth model or Gordon's Model after M.J. Gordon who popularized it.

As an extension of equation (8), we can talk about preference shares and their present value. By definition, preference shares have fixed rate of dividend, therefore $g = 0$. Thus, the intrinsic value of preference shares is given by:

$$V_0 = \frac{D_1}{k} \qquad (9)$$

Let us understand the model with the help of few Numerical Examples.

Numerical Example 1

If the growth rate of dividend is 5% and the most recent dividend is ₹3.75, calculate the value of the share. ($k = 12\%$)

Solution:

$$D_1 = D_0(1+g) = 3.75(1+0.05) = 3.94$$

Similarly,

$$D_2 = D_0(1+g)^2 = 3.75(1+0.05)^2 = 4.13 \ldots \text{ and so on.}$$

We know from above discussion $V_0 = D_1/k - g$, therefore, the current value of the given share is:

$$= \frac{3.94}{0.12 - 0.05}$$

$$= ₹56.29$$

Numerical Example 2

Calculate the value of preferred stock, given the fixed dividend is equal to ₹3 and the discount rate is 8%.

Solution:

In the case of preference shares, the dividend is fixed. Therefore, $g = 0$. Hence value of preferred stock is computed as:

$$V_0 = \frac{D_1}{k} = \frac{3}{0.08}$$

$$= ₹37.5$$

Equation (8) can be derived as follows:

We know that the intrinsic value of a share is the present value of infinite stream of dividends. Symbolically,

$$V_0 = \left[\frac{D_1}{(1+k)}\right] + \left[\frac{D_1(1+g)}{(1+k)^2}\right] + \left[\frac{D_1(1+g)^2}{(1+k)^3}\right] + \cdots \qquad \text{(a)}$$

Multiplying LHS and RHS with $(1 + k)/(1 + g)$, we get

$$V_0\left(\frac{1+k}{1+g}\right) = \frac{D_1}{1+g} + \frac{D_1}{1+k} + \frac{D_1(1+g)}{(1+k)^2} + \cdots \qquad \text{(b)}$$

In equation (b)

$\frac{D_1}{1+k} + \frac{D_1(1+g)}{(1+k)^2} + \frac{D_1(1+g)^2}{(1+k)^3}$ is nothing but V_0. Therefore, we can rewrite equation (b) as:

$$V_0\left(\frac{1+k}{1+g}\right) = \frac{D_1}{1+g} + V_0$$

or

$$V_0\left(\frac{1+k}{1+g}\right) - V_0 = \frac{D_1}{1+g}$$

or

$$V_0\left(\frac{1+k}{1+g} - 1\right) = \frac{D_1}{1+g}$$

or

$$V_0\left(\frac{1+k-1-g}{1+g}\right)=\frac{D_1}{1+g}$$

or

$$V_0=\frac{D_1}{k-g}$$

Let us solve a few more Numerical Examples to understand the model better.

Numerical Example 3

Super Cement Industries has just paid a dividend for ₹4 per share. The dividend is expected to grow at a constant rate of 7% indefinitely. The beta of the stock is 1, the risk-free rate is 6% and the market risk premium is 9%. Calculate the intrinsic value of the stock. What will be the intrinsic value of the stock if its beta is 1.3, i.e., the stock is riskier?

Solution:

The intrinsic value of the stock can be calculated using the formula: $V_0 = D_1/k - g$

$$D_1 = D_0(1+g) = 4(1+0.07) = 4.28$$

$$g = 7\%$$

k has to be calculated using CAPM

$$R_i = R_F + \beta_i(R_m - R_F)$$

$$= 0.06 + 1(0.09)$$

$$= 15\%$$

$$k = 15\%$$

Substituting the values of D_1, g and k in $V_0 = D_1/k - g$

$$V_0 = \frac{4.28}{0.15-0.07}$$

$$= \frac{4.28}{0.08}$$

$$= ₹53.5$$

If the stock is riskier as reflected in the higher beta of 1.3, its value would obviously be lower as a result of higher value of k.

The value of k, when beta is 1.3

$$= 0.06 + (1.3)(0.09)$$

$$= 17.7\%$$

$$k = 17.7\%$$

Substituting the values of D_1, g and k in $V_0 = D_1/k - g$

$$V_0 = \frac{4.28}{0.177 - 0.07}$$

$$= \frac{4.28}{0.107}$$

$$= ₹40$$

Thus riskier the stock, lower is its current value.

We can see that the price of the stock will be higher if:

1. Its discount rate or capitalization rate or the investor's required rate of return is lower (k is lower)
2. Its expected dividend is larger
3. Its g is larger.

Implication of constant growth DDM The implication of constant growth DDM is that the share prices are expected to grow at the same rate as the dividends. Let us see why.

We know all future prices of a share can be computed using the formula $P_0 = V_0 = \dfrac{D_1}{k-g}$.

If the price in next year is P_1, then

$$P_1 = \frac{D_2}{k - g}$$

$$= \frac{D_1(1+g)}{k - g}$$

$$=\left(\frac{D_1}{k-g}\right)+[1+g]$$

Since $D_1/(k-g)=P_0$, therefore the above equation can be rewritten as:

$$P_1=P_0\,(1+g) \tag{10}$$

or

$$\frac{P_1-P_0}{P_0}=g \tag{11}$$

Thus, constant growth DDM implies that the price of a share in any year will also grow at the same rate as that of dividends.

We know the expected return of the stock for single holding period can be calculated as:

$$\left[\frac{D_1+(P_1-P_0)}{P_0}\right]$$

or

$$\frac{D_1}{P_0}+\frac{(P_1-P_0)}{P_0}$$

From equation (11), $(P_1-P_0)/P_0=g$, therefore expected return of a stock as per constant growth DDM can be written as:

$$E(r)=\left(\frac{D_1}{P_0}\right)+g \tag{12}$$

For a stock selling at intrinsic value, i.e., if price is equal to the intrinsic value ($P_0=V_0$), equation 11 implies $E(r)=k$, i.e., the investor's required rate of return is equal to the discount rate.

Numerical Example 4

The prevailing price of the stock of Gordon Company Ltd. is ₹26 per share. The company is expected to pay a dividend of ₹1.2 per share at the end of the next year. It has been forecasted by many analysts that the stock will reach a price of ₹30 at the end of one year. This forecast is considered to be quite reliable.

1. Should the investor buy the share at current price, if his required rate of return is 20%?
2. What should the price of the share be at the end of the year, if the investor's required rate of return is 15%?

Solution:

1. For a single holding period, the cash flow that an investor can expect for the share is equal to the dividend for one year and the price at which he will be able to sell the share at the end of the year. Therefore, its current value or price should be equal to the present value of these two cash flows discounted at the investor's required rate of return, i.e., 20%.

$$V_0 = P_0 = \left(\frac{D_1}{1+r}\right) + \left(\frac{P_1}{1+r}\right)$$

$$= \left(\frac{1.2}{1+0.2}\right) + \left(\frac{30}{1+0.2}\right)$$

$$= ₹26$$

Since the price or the value computed using DDM is same as the price prevailing in the market, the investor can buy the share.

2. $P_1 = ?$, if $P_0 = 26$, $D_1 = ₹1.2$ per share and $r = 15\%$

$$P_0 = \left(\frac{D_1}{1+r}\right) + \left(\frac{P_1}{1+r}\right)$$

$$26 = \left(\frac{1.2}{1+0.15}\right) + \left(\frac{P_1}{1+0.15}\right)$$

$$P_1 = ₹28.70$$

Numerical Example 5

BB Brokers Ltd. have advised their client, Mr. Sharma, to buy stock of Hot Springs Ltd. and hold it for 5 years. They expect the company to pay a dividend of ₹3.5 per share for the coming 5 years and expect the share to sell for ₹60 at the end of 5 years. If the investor's expected rate of return is 10%, what is the price he should pay to buy the share now?

Solution:

Given $D_1 = D_2 = D_3 = D_4 = D_5 = 3.5; P_5 = 60; k = 10\%$

Using the formula:

$$P_0 = \left[\frac{D_1}{(1+k)}\right] + \left[\frac{D_2}{(1+k)^2}\right] + \left[\frac{D_3}{(1+k)^3}\right] + \left[\frac{D_4}{(1+k)^4}\right] + \left[\frac{D_5}{(1+k)^5}\right] + \left[\frac{P_5}{(1+k)^5}\right]$$

$$= \left[\frac{3.5}{(1+0.10)}\right] + \left[\frac{3.5}{(1+0.10)^2}\right] + \left[\frac{3.5}{(1+0.10)^3}\right] + \left[\frac{3.5}{(1+0.10)^4}\right] + \left[\frac{3.5}{(1+0.10)^5}\right] + \left[\frac{60}{(1+0.10)^5}\right]$$

$$= ₹50.52$$

Mr. Sharma should pay ₹50.52 for the share of HSL.

---

2. **Multi-Stage DDM:** You may observe that constant growth DDM is valid only when $g < k$. In case some analyst comes up with an estimate of g that is greater than k, then such a rate would be considered to be unsustainable in the long run. Further, it is also impractical to assume that the dividends would continue to grow at the same rate for infinite time in the future.

   It is more realistic to apply different growth rates to dividends in different periods. The model to be used for calculation of intrinsic value in such a situation is called multi-stage DDM.

   Multi-stage DDM implies that the dividends do not grow at a constant rate g, rather they grow at varying rates through the years. The model is, in fact, an extension of constant-growth DDM.

   We will begin our discussion of multi-stage DDM with the simplest extension of the constant growth model, a two-stage growth model. The model assumes that the extraordinary growth (good or bad) will persist for a finite number of years followed by an indefinite normal growth rate and the dividends will also grow in the proportion of the growth rate.

   For illustrating the two-stage growth model, let us consider a share with extraordinary growth rate (g_1) for n years. The current price of the share can be given by following equation:

$$P_0 = \left\{\left[\frac{D_1}{(1+k)}\right] + \left[\frac{D_1(1+g_1)}{(1+k)^2}\right] + \left[\frac{D_1(1+g_1)^2}{(1+k)^3}\right] + \cdots + \left[\frac{D_1(1+g_1)^{n-1}}{(1+k)^n}\right]\right\} + \left[\frac{P_n}{(1+k)^n}\right] \qquad (13)$$

where
P_0 = Current price per share
D_1 = Dividend a year hence
g_1 = Extraordinary (supernormal) growth rate applicable for 'n' number of years
P_n = Price of the share at the end of year 'n'
k = Required rate of return on stock or alternatively the market capitalization rate

We know from our discussion in the preceding part of this chapter that the bracketed part of equation (13) is the present value of a growing annuity and can be rewritten as:

$$D_1\left\{\frac{1-[(1+g_1)/(1+k)^n]}{(k-g_1)}\right\} \qquad (14)$$

Using equation (14), equation (13) can be rewritten as:

$$P_0 = D_1 \left\{ \frac{1-[(1+g_1)/(1+k)^n]}{k-g_1} \right\} + \frac{P_n}{(1+k)^n} \quad (15)$$

As mentioned above, we are working on a two-stage growth model where the growth rate is supernormal for n years (g_1) and constant thereafter (g_2). For dividends growing infinitely at a constant rate of g_2 after n years, we can calculate the value of P_n using constant-growth model exhibited in equation (8).

Therefore,

$$P_n = \frac{D_{n+1}}{(k-g_2)} \quad (16)$$

where

P_n = Price of the share at the end of year 'n'
D_{n+1} = Dividend in $(n+1)^{\text{th}}$ year
G_2 = Growth rate applicable after 'n' number of years

The dividend in $n + 1^{\text{th}}$ year can be computed as:

$$D_{n+1} = D_1 (1+g_1)^{n-1}(1+g_2) \quad (17)$$

Therefore the equation (16) can also be expressed as

$$P_n = \frac{D_1(1+g_1)^{n-1}(1+g_2)}{(k-g_2)} \quad (18)$$

Substituting the value of P_n from equation (18) in equation (15), we get

$$P_0 = D_1 \left\{ \frac{1-[(1+g_1)/(1+k)^n]}{k-g_1} \right\} + \left\{ \frac{D_1(1+g_1)^{n-1}(1+g_2)}{k-g_2} \right\} \left\{ \frac{1}{(1+k)^1} \right\} \quad (19)$$

Numerical Example 6

Consider a company, JJ Connect Ltd. The company is performing quite well and is expected to grow at a super-normal growth rate of 20% for coming 6 years. Thereafter it is expected to grow at a constant rate of 10%. The current dividend on the company's share is ₹2. Calculate the intrinsic value of the share of this company, if the equity investors required rate of return is 15%.

Solution:

Given:

$D_0 = 2.00$

$n = 6$ years
$g_1 = 20\%$
$g_2 = 10\%$
$k = 15\%$

It can be ascertained from the given inputs that we need to use the DD model here. Since two rates of growth are given, we need to use the two-stage DDM given below:

$$P_0 = D_1\left\{\frac{1-[(1+g_1)/(1+k)^n]}{k-g_1}\right\}+\left\{\frac{D_1(1+g_1)^{n-1}(1+g_2)}{k-g_2}\right\}\left\{\frac{1}{(1+k)^n}\right\}$$

$D_1 = D_0(1+g_1) = 2(1+.020) = 2.40$. We have rest of the inputs.

Substituting the values in the above formula, we get

$$P_0 = \left[\frac{2.4[\{1-((1+0.20)/(1+0.15))^6\}]}{(0.15-0.20)}\right]+\left[\frac{2.4(1+0.20)^5(1+0.10)/(0.15-0.10)}{[1/(1+0.15)^6]}\right]$$

$$=\left[2.4\left[\frac{(1-1.291)}{(-0.05)}\right]+\left[\frac{2.4(2.488)(1.10)}{0.05}\right](0.4323)\right]$$

$= ₹70.76.$

Spreadsheet Application 1 The above numerical can be solved in excel also. The spreadsheet is exhibited below:

	A	B	C
1	**Given variables**	**Numerical value of variables**	
2	Current dividend	2	
3	No. of years of super-normal growth	6	
4	Super-normal growth rate	0.2	
5	Constant growth rate	0.1	
6	Required rate of return	0.15	
7	**Calculated variables**		
8	Dividend expected 1 year hence	B2*(1+B4)	2.4
9	Current intrinsic value	B8*((1-((1+B4)/(1+B6))^B3))/(B6-B4)+((B8*(1+B4)^(B3-1))*(1+B5)/(B6-B5))/(1+B6)^B3	70.7649421

The two-stage model can be extended to include more phases of varying growth rates, which is more aligned with the reality. In real market conditions, it is not possible to sustain a growth rate higher than required rate of return because such high growth rates would attract other firms to enter the industry leading to a decrease in concerned firm's profits and therefore its ROE and growth rate. Thus, after what may be termed as a temporary supernormal growth period, a firm's growth rate can be realistically assumed to decline, eventually stabilizing at a constant level that is consistent with the constant-growth model explained above.

Numerical Example 7

Kingston Wires Ltd. has a current dividend of ₹2 per share. The expected rate of growth of dividends of the company is as given below:

Year	Growth rate of dividend in %
1–3	25
4–6	20
7–9	15
10 onwards	8

If the company's cost of equity (same as investors required rate of return) is 14%, compute the current value/intrinsic value of the share.

Solution:

In this numerical, multiple growth rates are given, so we need to extend the two-stage model given below to make it multi-stage DDM.

$$P_0 = D_1\left\{\frac{1-[(1+g_1)/(1+k)^n]}{k-g_1}\right\}+\left\{\frac{D_1(1+g_1)^{n-1}(1+g_2)}{k-g_2}\right\}\left\{\frac{1}{(1+k)^n}\right\}$$

For multiple growth rates, P_0 may be calculated as:

$$P_0=\left[\frac{2(1+0.25)}{(1+0.14)}\right]+\left[\frac{2(1+0.25)^2}{(1+0.14)^2}\right]+\left[\frac{2(1+0.25)^3}{(1+0.14)^3}\right]+\left[\frac{2((1+0.25)^3)(1+0.20)}{(1+0.14)^4}\right]$$

$$+\left[\frac{2((1+0.25)^3)(1+0.20)^2}{(1+0.14)^5}\right]+\left[\frac{2((1+0.25)^3)(1+0.20)^3}{(1+0.14)^6}\right]+\left[\frac{2((1+0.25)^3)((1+0.20)^3)(1+0.15)}{(1+0.14)^7}\right]$$

$$+\left[\frac{[2((1+0.25)^3)((1+0.20)^3)((1+0.15)^2)}{(1+0.14)^8}\right]+\left[\frac{2((1+0.25)^3)((1+0.20)^3)((1+0.15)^3)}{(1+0.14)^9}\right]$$

$$+\left[\frac{2((1+0.25)^{3})((1+0.20)^{3})((1+0.15)^{3})\{(1+1.08)/(0.14-0.08)\}}{(1+0.14)^{9}}\right]$$

$$= ₹56.823$$

Spreadsheet Application 2 The estimated dividend for the next year of Derek Securities Ltd. is ₹1.20 per share. The expected rate of growth of dividends of the company is as given below:

Year	Growth rate of dividend in %
2015–2018	10
2019–2029	7
2030 onwards	At terminal/constant growth rate

Beta of the stock is beta 0.8, market risk premium is 0.07, risk-free rate of return is 8.7%, retention ratio of the firm is 50% and the return on equity is 0.1. Calculate the intrinsic value of the share.

Solution:

The solution is exhibited in the spreadsheet. Given inputs have been highlighted in bold.

	A	B	C	D	E	F	G
1	Inputs		Year	Dividend	Dividend growth rate	Term value	Cash flow
2	**beta**	**0.8**	**2015**	**1.20**			D2+F2 =1.20
3	**mkt_prem**	**0.07**	**2016**	D2*(1+E3)=1.32	0.10		D3+F3 =1.32
4	**rf**	**0.087**	**2017**	D3*(1+E4)=1.45	0.10		D4+F4=1.45
5	k_equity	B4+B2*B3 = 0.1430	**2018**	D4*(1+E5)=1.60	0.10		D5+F5 = 1.60
6	**retention ratio**	**0.5**	**2019**	D5*(1+E6)=1.71	0.07		D6+F6=1.71
7	**return on equity**	**0.1**	**2020**	D6*(1+E7)=1.83	0.07		D7+F7=1.83
8	term_gwth	B6*B7 =0.050	**2021**	D7*(1+E8)=1.96	0.07		D8+F8=1.96
9			**2022**	D8*(1+E9)=2.09	0.07		D9+F9=2.09
10			**2023**	D9*(1+E10)=2.24	0.07		D10+F10=2.24
11			**2024**	D10*(1+E11)=2.40	0.07		D11+F11=2.40
12			**2025**	D11*(1+E12)=2.56	0.07		D12+F12=2.56
13			**2026**	D12*(1+E13)=2.74	0.07		D13+F13=2.74
14			**2027**	D13*(1+E14)=2.94	0.07		D14+F14=2.94
15			**2028**	D14*(1+E15)=3.14	0.07		D15+F15=3.14
16			**2029**	D15*(1+E16)=3.36	0.07		D16+F16=3.36
17			**2030**	D16*(1+E17)=3.53	0.05	D17*(1+term_g)/(k_e - term_g =39.85)	D17+F17=43.38
18							
19						**Intrinsic value**	NPV(k_eq,G2:G17)=16.16

3. **H-Model:** The H-model is an equity valuation model that assumes a two-stage model for growth, but unlike the two-stage DDM described above, the growth rate in the initial growth phase does not remain constant, rather it declines linearly overtime as it reaches the stable perpetual growth stage. The H-model was presented by Fuller and Hsia (1984)[1] and it is based on the following assumptions:
   (a) The initial earnings or the dividend growth rate (g_a) is greater than the stable, long-run growth rate (g_n) but it declines linearly over the extraordinary growth period (assumed to last for 2H years).
   (b) After 2H years, the initial high growth rate declines to the level of stable growth rate.
   (c) The rate of decline is such that at H years, the growth rate is exactly halfway between the initial high rate and the long-run stable rate.
   (d) The shifting growth rate does not affect the dividend payout and cost of equity over time and the two remain constant.

H-model is illustrated graphically in Figure 9.2.

Figure 9.2 Graphical presentation of H-model.

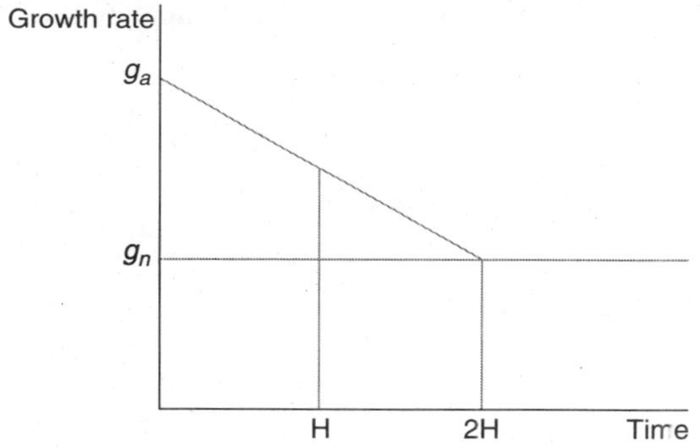

According to H-Model, the value or the price of a stock may be computed as:

$$P_0 = \left[\frac{D_0(1+g_n)}{(k-g_n)}\right] + \left[\frac{D_0 H(g_a - g_n)}{(k-g_n)}\right] \qquad (20)$$

where
P_0 = Current price per share
D_0 = Current Dividend per Share
k = Cost of equity or required rate of return on stock or alternatively the market capitalization rate
g_a = Initial growth rate
g_n = Stable growth rate at end of 2H years

[1] Russell J. Fuller and Chi-Cheng Hsia, "A Simplified Common Stock Valuation Model," *Financial Analysts Journal*, Vol. 40, No. 5, September – October, 1984, 49–56, CFA Institute, Article Stable, http://www.jstor.org/stable/4478774.

This model is useful for firms that are currently in rapid growth stage, but their growth is expected to decline gradually over time as they grow larger and start losing their differential advantage over their competitors. This model avoids the problems related with a precipitous drop in growth rate from the extraordinary level to the stable rate. However, the strict assumption laid out in the model about the drops being in linear increments each year is based upon the initial high growth rate, the stable long-run growth rate and the length of the high growth period. While small deviations from this very specific assumption do not affect the value of share significantly, large deviations can cause distortion in the outcome. Further, the assumption about the payout ratio remaining constant through both phases of growth overlooks the fact that the payout ratio usually increases as growth rate declines. Like DDM, this model can also be used only for valuing dividend-paying firms.

Let us understand H-model with the help of a Numerical Example.

Numerical Example 8

Penwood, an Indian home appliance firm, paid dividend of ₹0.75 per share on earnings per share of ₹1.25 in 2010. The payout ratio is expected to remain unchanged. The growth rate of earnings per share has been 12% over the past 5 years but it is expected to decline linearly over the next 10 years to 5%. The beta for the stock is 0.9, the market risk premium is 6% and the risk-free rate is 5%. Calculate the current value of equity using the H-model.

Solution:

The value of firm's share can be calculated using H-model

$$P_0 = \left[\frac{D_0(1+g_n)}{(k-g_n)}\right] + \left[\frac{D_0H(g_a-g_n)}{(k-g_n)}\right]$$

Given,

$D_0 = ₹0.75$

$g_n = 5\%$

$g_a = 12\%$

$H = 5$ years (10/2)

$k =$ to be calculated using CAPM

$$\text{Cost of equity} = k = 5\% + 0.9^*6\% = 10.4\%$$

Substituting all values in the equation above

$$P_0 = \left[\frac{0.75(1+0.05)}{(0.104-0.05)}\right] + \left[\frac{0.75^*5^*(0.12-0.05)}{(0.014-0.05)}\right]$$

$= 14.58 + 4.86$

$= ₹19.44$

Understanding growth rate

Let us understand the concept of '*g*' (growth rate), which is the most critical input in DDM. Since the growth rate is central to DDM, we should understand what drives it.

The two main drivers of growth are:

1. **Plough Back Ratio as Opposed to Dividend Payout Ratio:** This gives a measure of the proportion of profits that are retained or conversely, distributed as dividends.
2. **Return on Equity**, a key performance measure for any firm.

To understand how the retention ratio affects growth rate, let us suppose there are two companies, A and B. Both companies expect to earn ₹10 in the coming year at a market capitalization rate of 11%. If both have a 100% dividend payout policy, they will be valued at 8/0.11 (D_1/k as explained above). Thus, both companies will be valued at ₹72.73 per share. With all earnings getting distributed, the firms will not grow as the capital and earnings capacity will remain unchanged.

However, if firm A has a profitable project that generates a return of 16% (yielding a rate of return higher than *k*, which is 11%), it can increase its value by reducing its DPR from 100% and increasing its plough back ratio from 0%. (This plough back ratio represents the earnings retained by the firm and it is also called as earnings retention ratio, denoted by *b*). When firm A increases it retention ratio, it takes away a part of its earnings to invest them in a project to generate 15% return for its shareholders. Had it distributed all earnings, the investors would have been left with the money to be invested in other opportunities at a fair market rate of 11% only. If firm A chooses to retain a part of its earnings to reinvest them at a higher rate, such strategy will eventually lead to higher dividends and higher value of shares. The growth rate that will be generated on the basis of such retention will depend on the investment made, return generated on equity and its further reinvestment to increase the value of the firm's asset.

To take our example further, suppose firm A begins by investing ₹200 lakh in plant and machinery and it is financed using only equity. If the return on equity (ROE) is 16%, then total earnings are 200 × 16% = ₹32 lakh. If the number of outstanding shares is ₹4 lakh, then the company has generated an EPS of ₹8 per share.

Now this firm can either choose to distribute the entire earnings or retain a part of it and reinvest it. Suppose, the firm reinvests 50% of ₹32 lakh, then its assets increase by 50% × 32 = ₹16 lakh, i.e., by 8%. This percentage increase in asset is actually equal to ROE × retention ratio (ROE × *b*). These additional assets help the company generate more income proportionally and pay out higher dividends.

In fact, the growth rate of dividends may be given as = ROE × *b* (plough back rate).

Numerical Example 9

Sandbag Ltd. has an equity worth ₹100 at the beginning of the year and it has a policy of distributing 50% of its earnings as dividend to its shareholders. If the return on equity of the firm is 20%, calculate the growth rate of the company and its retained earnings and dividends for the coming 4 years.

Solution:

Given:

Equity = 100, Dividend payout = 50% of earnings

We need to compute growth rate, which can be calculated using following formula:

$$g = \text{ROE} \times \text{Ploughback ratio}$$

$$\text{ROE} = 20\%$$

Ploughback ratio = 0.50 (since 50% of the earnings are distributed as dividend)

Thus, $g = 0.20 \times 0.50$

$= 0.10$ or 10%

Computing retained earnings for coming 4 years:

Item	Year 1	Year 2	Year 3	Year 4	Year 5
Equity	100	100 + 10 = 110	110 + 11 = 121	121 + 12.1 = 133.1	133.1 + 13.31 = 146.41
ROE	20%	20%	20%	20%	20%
Earnings	100 × 0.2 = 20	110 × 0.2 = 22	121 × 0.2 = 24.2	133.1 × 0.2 = 26.62	146.51 × 0.2 = 29.28
Ploughback ratio	0.5	0.5	0.5	0.5	0.5
Dividend	**20 × 0.5 = 10**	**22 × 0.5 = 11**	**24.2 × 0.5 = 12.1**	**26.62 × 0.5 = 13.31**	**29.28 × 0.5 = 14.64**
Retained earnings	**20 − 10 = 10**	**22 − 11 = 11**	**24.2 − 12.1 = 12.1**	**26.62 − 13.31 = 13.31**	**29.28 − 14.64 = 14.64**

It can be concluded from the above discussion that a company can increase the growth rate of its dividends by investing in opportunities that yield higher returns than the firm's required rate of return or the market capitalization rate. In other words, the firms that have positive net present value of investment opportunities (also called PVGO, i.e., present value of growth opportunities) can increase their value by retaining their earnings and investing them in positive NPV projects.

Application of DDM

It is obvious that constant growth DDM is a theoretical simplification that is usually not observed in the growth patterns of firms in any industry. We know that firms pass through various phases of life cycle that impact their growth rates and dividend profile. In the introductory or the early phase of the life cycle, most firms have expansion plans and they tend to reinvest their earnings, resulting in low payout ratio and rapid growth. As the firms enter the maturity phase, scope for expansion decreases, since the installed capacity is sufficient to meet the demand in the market. In such a phase, firms tend to raise the dividend payout ratio rather than retain their earnings so the dividends increase for some time at higher rate but as the growth opportunities decrease, the dividend moves to a slower rate of growth.

The two-stage DDM illustrated above is better representative of reality than the constant growth model but it needs to be expanded further to accommodate more than two growth rates. Many security analysts assume three-stage growth model. The approach may differ from assuming initial temporary supernormal growth to making year-by-year forecasts, finally moving to stable growth, with some transition period in between. The calculations can be very tedious.

Free Cash Flow Valuation Model

The free cash flow valuation model offers an alternative to DDM. This model values a firm on the basis of free cash flow (cash flow to firm or equity shareholders net of capital expenditures). The free cash flow that is discounted in this model could either be FCFF (Free cash flow to firm) or FCFE (Free cash flow to equity). While FCFF is discounted at firm's weighted average cost of capital to obtain the value of the firm, FCFE is discounted at the firm's cost of equity to calculate the market value of equity. FCFE can also be computed by subtracting the existing value of debt from the value of the firm computed using FCFF.

The FCFF/FCFE model can be applied for valuation in the following manner:

1. In a manner similar to two-stage DDM, a finite period is identified wherein the firm is expected to grow at a higher rate followed by an indefinite period of steady/constant growth where ROIC (return on invested capital) and cost of capital become stable.
2. Forecast of yearly FCF (free cash flow) is prepared for a finite period. We know FCF is the post-tax flow that accrues from the operations of the firm, net of investment in net working capital and capital expenditure. It includes cash flow available to both equity and debt holders.

$$\text{FCFF} = \text{EBIT}\ (1-t) + \text{Depreciation} - \text{Capital Expenditure} - \text{Increase in Net Working Capital (NWC)}$$

$$\text{FCFE} = \text{FCFF} - \text{Interest Expense}\ (1-t) + \text{Increase in Net Debt}$$

where
EBIT = Earnings before interest and tax
t = Corporate tax rate

3. Thereafter the weighted average cost of capital of the firm (k_o) is determined. Remember, if FCFF is discounted, then we require k_o and if FCFE is being discounted, we require k_e as the discount rate.
4. We also need to determine the value of the firm at the end of the finite high growth period or the beginning of the stable growth period (also called the horizon value of the firm). Let it be represented by V_H. We know the value of a firm in constant growth model is given by:

$$V_H = \frac{\text{FCFF}_{H+1}}{(k_o - g)} \tag{21}$$

Therefore, the value of a firm (also called Enterprise Value), can be computed as:

$$EV = \left[\frac{\text{FCFF}_1}{(1+k_o)}\right] + \left[\frac{\text{FCFF}_2}{(1+k_o)^2}\right] \cdots \left[\frac{\text{FCFF}_n}{(1+k_o)^n}\right] + \left[\frac{V_H}{(1+k_o)^H}\right]$$

or

$$EV \text{ or firm value} = \sum_{t=1}^{H}\left[\frac{\text{FCFF}_t}{(1+k_o)^t}\right] + \left[\frac{V_H}{(1+k_o)^H}\right] \quad (22)$$

Where the first part is the PV of FCFF during the finite period of higher growth and second part is the present value of the horizon value or the terminal value.

5. To derive the market value of equity, we can either discount FCFE or subtract preference and debt value from EV as calculated in equation (21).
   Mathematically,

$$\text{Market value of equity} = \sum_{t=1}^{H}\left[\frac{\text{FCFF}_t}{(1+k_e)^t}\right] + \left[\frac{V_H}{(1+k_e)^H}\right] \quad (23)$$

or

$$\text{Market value of equity} = \text{EV (enterprise value)} - \text{PV (preference value)} - \text{DV (debt value)} \quad (24)$$

The horizon or the terminal value used in the FCF valuation model is critical for estimation of the intrinsic value of a share. Some analysts simply use the present value of a perpetuity growing at a constant rate. However, those seeking more accuracy in their computation use some multiple of book value or EBIT or FCF or earnings.

Numerical Example 10

The balance sheet of Winchem Limited at the end of the year (at present) is as follows:

₹ in Crore

Liabilities		Assets	
Shareholders' funds	250	Fixed assets (net)	400
Equity Capital (10 crore shares of ₹10 each)	100	Net Working Capital	100
Reserves & Surplus	100		
Loan funds (9 percent)	250		
	500		500

The rate of growth of revenues and assets is expected to be 18% in the first four years, 12% in the next two years and 7% thereafter. The return on invested capital is expected to be 11% and the cost of equity is 16%. The effective tax rate is 33.33 percent and the pre-tax cost of debt is 10%. The firm is expected to maintain its current debt equity ratio. Use the FCF approach to determine the intrinsic value of the firm.

Solution:

Given

1. Three growth rates: 18%, 12% and 7% (steady growth rate at the end of year 7)
2. Since return on invested capital (ROIC) = 11%, therefore NOPAT for each year will be calculated as:

   NOPAT = ROIC × invested capital

3. Net investment = Asset value at the beginning of the year × Growth rate
4. FCF = NOPAT − Net investment
5. Debt equity ratio = 1:1, Cost of Debt = 10%, Cost of Equity = 16%
6. Horizon value $= \dfrac{FCF_H\,(1+\text{steady growth rate})}{(k_o - g)}$
7. Enterprise value = PV of FCF and horizon value, discounted at k_o
8. The equity value = Enterprise value − Debt
9. Intrinsic value of the share = Enterprise value/no. of shares
10. No. of shares = 10 crore

Free Cash Flow Forecast

	1	2	3	4	5	6	7
Asset Value	500	590	696	822	969	1085	1216
NOPAT	55	65	77	90	107	119	134
Net investment	90	106	125	148	116	130	85
FCF	**−35**	**−41**	**−49**	**−58**	**−10**	**−11**	**49**
Growth rate	0.18	0.18	0.18	0.18	0.12	0.12	0.07

Weighted average cost of capital = k_o = 0.5 × 16 + 0.5 × 10 × (1 − 0.333) = 11.33%

Horizon value of Winchem:

$$V_H = 49 \times \frac{(1+0.07)}{(.1133-0.07)} = \mathbf{1201}$$

Enterprise Value of Winchem:

$$EV = \left(\frac{-35}{1+0.1133}\right) + \left(\frac{-41}{1+0.1133^2}\right) + \left(\frac{-49}{1+0.1133^3}\right) + \left(\frac{-58}{1+0.1133^4}\right)$$

$$+ \left(\frac{-10}{1+0.1133^5}\right) + \left(\frac{-11}{1+0.1133^6}\right) + \left(\frac{49}{1+0.1133^7}\right) + \left(\frac{1201}{1+0.1133^7}\right)$$

$$= \text{₹}\mathbf{440.52\ Crore}$$

Equity Value:

$$= 440.52 - 250 = 190.52$$

Intrinsic Value:

$$= \frac{190.52}{10}$$

$$= 19.05$$

The FCF models are more useful in case of firms paying no dividend (where DDM cannot be applied), however they can be applied to dividend paying firms as well.

Beyond the Basics 9.1 The Hamada Equation: Unlevered Betas

In 1969, Robert Hamada gave the Hamada Equation through his paper titled "Portfolio Analysis, Market Equilibrium, and Corporation Finance." Hamada's equation is useful in determining the cost of capital to be used for computation of intrinsic value. It relates the betas of levered and unlevered firms. The difference between the two betas represents the effect of how the business is financed, i.e., the effect of the capital structure decision of the firm.

The equation combines Modigliani-Miller theorem with Capital Asset Pricing Model and is useful in determining the effect of financial leverage on a firm. Hamada's equation separates business risk of a firm as measured by the beta of an unlevered firm from that of a levered firm (that has the financial risk of leverage as well). Financial risk due leverage can be removed by computation of unleveraged beta.

Unlevered beta is calculated using following formula:

$$B_U = \frac{B_L}{[1 + (1 - T_c) \times (D/E)]}$$

where B_U is unlevered beta, B_L is levered beta, T_c is corporate tax rate and D/E is debt equity ratio.

Relative Valuation Techniques

The DCF models discussed in the preceding section calculate the intrinsic value of a share by making forecasts of growth and discount rates, based on certain parameters. As against these, many analysts use relative valuation techniques on the basis of the belief that it is possible to estimate value of a firm by comparing it to similar firms.

Relative valuation ratios can be computed in many ways, as given below:

1. **Relative Valuation Ratios Based on Earnings Multiples:**

   P/E ratio and its variants

   Enterprise value/EBIT

   Enterprise value/EBITDA

   Enterprise value/Cash flow

2. **Relative Valuation Ratios Based on Book Multiples:**

   $$\frac{\text{Price}}{\text{Book value (of equity)}} \text{ or P/BV ratio}$$

3. **Relative Valuation Ratios Based on Revenues:**

   $$\frac{\text{Price}}{\text{Sales per share}} \text{ or P/S ratio}$$

   $$\frac{\text{Enterprise value}}{\text{Sales per share}} \text{ or EV/S ratio}$$

Most widely used comparison metrics include relative valuation ratios such as book value, sales, earnings and cash flow. Now a days, enterprise value/EBITDA has also become a key metric in relative valuation. The stock price of a firm is affected by all the variables mentioned above. The main relative valuation ratios discussed in this section are:

1. P/E ratio
2. Price to sales ratio
3. Price to book value ratio
4. Price to cash flow ratio
5. Enterprise value/EBITDA

Of all the relative valuation ratios (also called comparative valuation or comparable valuation ratios) mentioned above, the P/E ratio or the earning multiplier model is the most popularly and widely used model in real-world stock market analysis.

P/E Ratio

The P/E model is based on the underlying concept of how much money the investors are willing to pay for a rupee of expected earnings (estimated 12-month earnings). The P/E ratio is calculated as:

$$\text{P/E Ratio or Earning multiple} = \frac{\text{Current market price}}{\text{Estimated 12-month earning}}$$

Symbolically,

$$\text{P/E} = \frac{\text{MPS}}{\text{Expected EPS}} \qquad (25)$$

Equation (25) is a measure of the current attitude of the investors towards the value of the stock under consideration. The investors can decide whether the stock's P/E is too high or low by comparing it with some benchmark, which could be a similar firm or industry to which the firm belongs or even the market as a whole.

There are a number of variants of the basic P/E ratio in use, depending on how the price and earnings are defined. Price used could be the current market price or average market price for the year. Earnings could be the earnings of latest financial year or trailing 12 months (Trailing P/E) or forecasted EPS (Forward P/E). Let us understand the concept with the help of a Numerical Example.

Numerical Example 11

The equity stock of Capital Systems Ltd. is trading for ₹150 on 1 August 2005. Following EPS data is available for computation of P/E:

1. EPS of last year (1 April 2004 to 31 March 2005): ₹8
2. EPS of trailing twelve months (1 July 2004 to 30 June 2005): ₹8.7
3. EPS expected for the current year (1 April 2005 to 31 March 2006): ₹9
4. EPS expected for the following year (1 April 2006 to 31 March 2007): ₹10.2

Calculate P/E ratios using the above information and suggest which P/E ratio should ideally be used by investors.

Solution:

Depending on the four types of earnings given, we can compute following P/E ratios:

1. EPS of last year (1 April 2004 to 31 March 2005): ₹8

$$\text{P/E} = \frac{150}{8} = 18.75$$

2. EPS of trailing twelve months (1 July 2004 to 30 June 2005): ₹8.7

$$\text{P/E} = \frac{150}{8.7} = 17.24$$

3. EPS expected for the current year (1 April 2005 to 31 March 2006): ₹9

$$P/E = \frac{150}{9} = 16.67$$

4. EPS expected for the following year (1 April 2006 to 31 March 2007): ₹10.2

$$P/E = \frac{150}{10.2} = 14.71$$

P/E ratio based on current year's expected earnings should be used.

Whether to buy high P/E stocks or low P/E ones? The answer depends on the investor. Some investors buy at low P/E and sell at high P/E. Others see high P/E as a sign of future growth. The important thing to consider is what price you are paying for a company's earnings today and determine if the future growth expectations warrant such a price. It is also important to look at the P/E of a company in the context of its industry peers to see its relative valuation. If the firm's P/E is higher than the industry average or peer firms, this means that the market is positive about the prospects of the firm. If it fails to live up to the expectations raised by its high P/E ratio, it will face a situation of potential fall in its stock price.

Deriving P/E ratio through DDM

Though the P/E ratio offers an alternative to the DCF techniques for equity valuation, yet it can be derived from one of the discounted cash flow models: DDM (Dividend discount model). Let us see how.

We know single-stage DDM is given as:

$$P_0 = \frac{D_1}{(k-g)} \tag{26}$$

In case of 100% payout, $D_1 = E_1$. However, the dividend will be different from earnings if the firm decides to retain a part of its earnings to invest in positive NPV growth opportunities. Thus, in case of retention of earnings, dividends may be calculated as:

$$D_1 = E_1(1-b) \tag{27}$$

where

b is the retention ratio and represents the proportion of funds retained by the firm. E_1 is the expected earnings during the next 12 months. Further, the firm invests the retained earnings in positive NPV projects to grow at rate 'g.' Assuming the retained earnings are invested entirely by the firm to generate return on equity (ROE), the growth rate 'g' can be calculated as:

$$g = \text{ROE} \times b \tag{28}$$

Using values of D_1 and g from equation (27) and (28), equation (26) can be rewritten as:

$$P_0 = \frac{E_1(1-b)}{k-(\text{ROE}\times b)} \tag{29}$$

Equation (29) can be written as

$$\frac{P_0}{E_1} = \frac{(1-b)}{k-(\text{ROE}\times b)} \tag{30}$$

Another way of calculating P/E ratio is by dividing both sides of formula given in equation (26) by E_1 to get:

$$\frac{P_0}{E_1} = \frac{(D_1/E_1)}{(k-g)} \tag{31}$$

It can be easily deduced from equation (29) that P/E ratio of a firm would increase with its ROE and retention ratio (b). But this statement needs to be analyzed further. It has been observed that 'g' may increase with the increase in retention ratio (b) but whether P/E will also increase, depends on the level of ROE vis-à-vis 'k' (i.e., firm's capitalization rate). If the expected ROE is less than 'k,' the investors would prefer dividends to retention as the reinvestment rate is less attractive. Therefore, for ROE $< k$, the value of the firm will decline with the increase in retention ratio. Vice versa is true as well, i.e., if ROE $> k$, the value of the firm will increase with the increase in retention ratio. At ROE $= k$, investors will be indifferent to either and the value of the share will remain unaffected by b.

A rough thumb rule on the relationship between P/E and g, called PEG ratio was used by Peter Lynch in his book, "One Up on Wall Street." PEG ratio or P/E to g ratio can be summarized as 'P/E ratio ought to be roughly equal to g' or 'PEG should be approximately equal to 1.' The implication of PEG ratio is that if the value of the ratio exceeds 1, the stock market is overvalued and if PEG is less than 1, then the market is undervalued.

Another thumb rule found in the literature is that P/E for the market as a whole should be inverse of the real rate of return required by equity investors. This factors in the role of inflation in influencing equity income.

One more thumb rule is that P/E for market as a whole should be inverse of PLR (benchmark rate charged by commercial banks) for lending to prime borrowers. All these thumb rules cannot be said to be universally acceptable and/or observable and need to be taken with a pinch of salt.

Let us understand P/E ratio with the help of a Numerical Example.

Numerical Example 12

The dividends of Brian Distilleries Ltd. are expected to grow at a rate of 7%, the expected dividend payout ratio is 50%, the cost of equity is 12% and current earning (E_0) = ₹2 per share.

1. Calculate its P/E ratio
2. Calculate the intrinsic value of the stock
3. Discuss the changes in outcome if
   (a) The cost of equity is 14% and the growth rate is 7%
   (b) The cost of equity is 12% and the growth rate is 8%
   (c) The cost of equity is 11% and the growth rate is 10%.

Solution:

Using the formula $P_0/E_1 = (D_1/E_1)/(k-g)$, P/E ratio of Brian Distilleries Ltd. can be computed as:

1. Given: $g = 7\%$, $k = 12\%$ and $D/E = 50\%$

$$P/E = \frac{0.50}{0.12 - 0.07} = \frac{0.50}{0.05} = 10$$

2. From (a), $P/E = 10$, given $E_0 = ₹2$
   Therefore, value can be calculated as: $(P/E) \times E$
   Where E is expected earning for the next year and it can be calculated as $E_0\,(1+g) = 2(1.07) = ₹2.14$
   Intrinsic value of the share $= 10 \times 2.14 = ₹21.4$
3. The three scenarios given in (c) can be used to show that changes in values of k or g, have a large impact on P/E ratios computed using them as input.
   (a) The cost of equity is 14% and the growth rate is 7%

$$P/E = \frac{0.50}{0.14 - 0.07} = \frac{0.50}{0.07} = 7.14$$

   (b) The cost of equity is 12% and the growth rate is 8%

$$P/E = \frac{0.50}{0.12 - 0.08} = \frac{0.50}{0.04} = 12.5$$

   (c) The cost of equity is 11% and the growth rate is 10%.

$$P/E = \frac{0.50}{0.11 - 0.10} = \frac{0.50}{0.01} = 50$$

We can see in the above computations that values of k and g are very important and therefore accurate estimation of the two is the key to computation of correct intrinsic value.

Marketview 9.1 The PEG Ratio

Peter Lynch, famous investment expert, developed a new concept for investing. His approach is focused on a ratio developed by him: price to earnings growth (PEG) ratio. The PEG is used to identify undervalued stocks (stocks selling cheap) by dividing a stock's P/E ratio by its historic growth rate. Though analysts generally calculate the PEG ratio by using the estimated earnings, Lynch advocates the conservative approach of using historic data because he does not have much faith in the efficacy of the forecasts.

According to Lynch, the faster a firm is growing its earnings, the higher the P/E multiple an investor will accept and show his willingness to pay for the stock. Further, lower the PEG, more attractive the stock.

General thumb rules followed by the supporters of PEG are:

1. PEG > 1 indicates stock is fully valued.
2. PEG < 1 indicates stock is worth considering for investment.
3. PEG < 0.5 indicates stock offers an attractive investment opportunity.
4. PEG < 0.33 indicates stock offers an extremely attractive investment opportunity.
5. Investors adhering to another metric, GARP (Growth-at-a-reasonable price) avoid stocks having PEG ratios higher than one.

PEG removes distortions that creep into the P/E ratio on account of different growth rates of the firms in different phases of their life cycle. During the initial phase, the growth rates are higher than those at maturity.

If investors use the P/E ratio for investing, the companies growing at a slower pace would appear to be attractive due to their substantially lower PE multiples. On the other hand, the companies having high growth rate would appear quite expensive as they would have higher PE multiples. Naturally investors will not choose to invest in them. However, ideally a high-growth company is a better investment option. In other words, high P/E ratio stocks are actually better investments as long as the firm continues to grow at a reasonable rate.

Along with the PEG, Lynch also advocates that investors should focus on fundamental variables like the debt/equity ratio, free cash flow, earnings per share, growth rate and inventory turnover ratio. Interestingly, Lynch has identified different categories of stocks based on their growth rates and used different criteria for assessing each category. The three main categories of stocks are:

1. fast-growers (stocks with at least 20% EPS growth rates per year)
2. stalwarts (stocks with EPS growth rates between 10% and 20% per year and multi-billion-dollar sales)
3. slow-growers (stocks with less than 10% EPS growth rates and high dividend payouts).

Based on Lynch, Peter and John Rothchild (1989). One up on Wall Street. New York, NY: Simon & Schuster paperback.

P/E ratio and growth opportunities

We know from our discussion on retention ratio that the earnings of a firm depend upon the growth opportunities, i.e., avenues for investment and re-investment of funds at a rate of return higher than the required rate of return on the firm's capital (k_e in case of pure equity or unlevered firm). The price of a share would reflect this ability of the firm to generate earnings through positive NPV projects.

Therefore,

$$\text{Value/Price of a share} = \text{Value of share with 100\% payout} + \text{Present value of growth opportunities}$$

Symbolically,

$$P_0 = \left(\frac{D_1}{k}\right) + \text{PVGO} \tag{32}$$

Since in the case of 100% dividend payout ratio, $D_1 = E_1$(earnings), we can rewrite equation (32) as:

$$P_0 = \left(\frac{E_1}{k}\right) + \text{PVGO} \tag{33}$$

Rearranging equation (33), we get

$$\frac{P_0}{E_1} = \left(\frac{1}{k}\right)\left(\frac{1 + \text{PVGO}}{(E_1/k)}\right) \tag{34}$$

The above equation has some simple implications:

1. If PVGO = 0, the value or price of a firm is same as perpetuity with no growth and it can be calculated as E_1/k.
2. PVGO/(E_1/k) represents the ratio of value due to growth opportunities. It implies that as the positive NPV opportunities increase, the firm commands a higher price with respect to its current earnings. Thus a firm with high growth opportunities has a high P/E and vice versa. We can also say that a high P/E ratio indicates high growth opportunity for the firm under consideration.
3. Obviously, the differences in growth opportunities are the underlying cause of varying P/E ratios of various firms.
4. It can be said that high P/E ratio is an indicator of market's optimism regarding PVGO of a firm and invariably the analysts put a buy recommendation on shares they are optimistic about.

Alternative models for estimation of P/E ratio

Many researchers have attempted to estimate the P/E ratio by relating it to various economic variables. Two models standout for their contribution. They are:

1. **Whitbeck-Kisor Model:** Whitbeck-Kisor employed cross-sectional regression analysis to relate price-earnings multiple to certain variables like growth rate of earnings, dividend payment rate and variability of earnings.

   They used 135 stocks listed in US for the purpose of multiple regression to estimate the relationship between P/E and the variables mentioned above. The regression equation so generated was:

$$\text{P/E} = 8.2 + 1.5 \text{ growth rate of earnings } (g) + 0.067\frac{\text{D}}{\text{E}} - 0.2 \text{ variability of earnings } (\sigma) \tag{35}$$

The decision rule for analysts is: compare theoretical P/E computed using the model with the actual P/E value and if

Theoretical P/E > Actual P/E Sell the stock

Theoretical P/E < Actual P/E Buy the stock

It needs to be understood that the model suffers from a drawback common to all empirical models and that drawback is its sensitivity to the input data.

Let us solve a Numerical Example to understand the model.

Numerical Example 13

Quick Logistics Ltd. has a P/E ratio of 24%. Use Whitbeck-Kisor model to advice an equity investor to buy, sell or hold the stock if the growth rate is 15%, dividend payout ratio is 40% and the variability of earnings is 6%.

Solution:

Using the Whitbeck-Kisor model P/E may be computed as:

$$P/E = 8.2 + 1.5 \text{ growth rate of earnings } (g) + 0.067\frac{D}{E} - 0.2 \text{ variability of earnings } (\sigma)$$

Substituting the given values in the above formula, we get

$$P/E = 8.2 + 1.5(15) + 0.067(40) - 0.2(6)\ 6$$

$$= 8.2 + 22.5 + 2.68 - 1.2$$

$$= 32.18\%$$

Since the actual value of P/E (24%) is less than the theoretical P/E (32.18%), the investor can be adviced to short sell the stock.

2. **Graham-Dodd Model:** Benjamin Graham (Warren Buffet's mentor) and David Dodd developed the concept of value investing during the great depression in US and published it in their iconic book 'Security Analysis' in 1934. They identified earnings, dividends, assets and capital structure as intrinsic factors in determination of P/E ratio.

   They performed an empirical study on the historical data of a group of large mature companies to establish a relationship between earnings, growth and P/E ratio and deduced the following earnings multiplier equation:

$$P/E = 8.5 + 2 \times \text{Growth} \tag{36}$$

or

$$\text{Price} = \text{Earnings}\ (8.5 + 2g) \tag{37}$$

They showed empirically that average no-growth stocks sold at a price that was 8.5 times their earnings and increase in P/E ratio was twice that of the rate of earnings growth.

The decision rule for analysts here is:

If the price calculated using the above equation is more than the current price, then the stock is undervalued and should be considered a 'buy.' Again, Graham-Dodd specified that such a buy call should be taken only if the current price is 80% or less than the calculated price. This was done to avoid bias in empirical calculations. This model, developed during the great depression, has come to be of great use in evaluating cyclical stocks.

Numerical Example 14

Angel Broking has predicted that the sales of Sunshine Soya Ltd will grow by 10% till 2014. If the company has a growth rate of earnings equal to10% and earnings per share equal to ₹5 for the financial year 2011–12, calculate the estimated price of its share. Its closing price is ₹120. What should an investor do?

Solution:

Using Graham-Dodd model, price can be calculated as:

$$\text{Price} = \text{Earnings}\ (8.5 + 2g)$$

Substituting the given values in the above equation, we get:

$$\text{Price} = 5\ [8.5 + (2 \times 10)]$$

$$= ₹142.5$$

Since the actual price is approximately 84% of the estimated price, the investor should buy the share.

Critique of P/E ratio as a valuation technique

P/E ratio is a widely used metric in investment management. It is also published in financial newspapers and magazines. In general, P/E ratio seems to be preferred over DCF techniques for valuation because it offers certain obvious advantages over the DCF models like:

1. P/E ratio enables the comparison of prices of stocks having different EPS as it indicates price per rupee of earnings of a share.

2. The ease of estimation makes the technique popular, as DCF is quite complicated.
3. The Price earning multiple can be applied to both, dividend paying and non-dividend paying companies whereas some DCF techniques like DDM are usable only for dividend paying companies.

However, P/E analysis is not without pitfalls. The earnings in the denominator of the ratio are the accounting earnings reported by the company and thus fluctuate in accuracy due to all the issues related to accounting policies and window-dressing that enable the company to ignore certain expenses or under-report certain accounting information within the legal framework of accounting policies. Therefore, the earnings thus reported may not reflect true picture of a firm's profitability and may really be outcome of some 'creative accounting.' Further, arbitrary accounting rules used for inventory valuation and depreciation at historical cost lead to under-reporting of true economic values during periods of high inflation and vice-versa. Empirical studies have found that P/E ratios have tended to be lower in high inflation periods, showing that market has assessed the earnings to be of 'lower quality' during periods of high inflation. What actually happens is that the earnings become artificially distorted due to high rate of inflation. To conclude, the earnings used in P/E multiple are simply computed based on accounting principles and do not represent 'economic earnings,' therefore a major factor impacting the P/E ratio is the distortion in earnings due to business cycles.

Another important point to note is that P/E should be computed using the following formula:

$$\text{P/E ratio or earning multiple} = \frac{\text{Current market price}}{\text{Estimated 12-month earning}}$$

The above formula implies that the earnings should be computed using earnings expected in the future and not the current earnings. However, in the P/E ratio published in newspapers reporting stock market data, the denominator is equal to the latest reported accounting earnings. The P/E ratio thus computed may be misleading because the current earnings could be substantially different from the future earnings.

Other Relative Valuation Ratios

1. **Price-to-Sales Ratio**: Though P/E ratio is the most widely used relative valuation technique, at times it may simply not be possible to use it in certain cases. For instance, it cannot be used for valuation of new or start-up firms where there is no track record of earnings. Price-to-sales ratio offers a good alternative and it is being used quite extensively now for valuing new firms. It is computed as:

$$P/S = \frac{\text{Stock price at time } t}{\text{Expected annual sales per share at time } t+1} \tag{38}$$

Many known analysts use this ratio for security analysis. The reason is that consistent strong sales are key requirement for a growth company. Retained earnings, when invested, will give future earnings only through rise in sales. Profit margin is a key metric but rise in sales is the important beginning point of growth for any company. Further, sales figure can be easily assumed to be the least manipulated figure reported in financial statements. A popular thumb rule indicates that P/S ratio equal to 1 should be used as benchmark and the firms with P/S ratio less than 1 should be considered undervalued and should, thus, be bought.

Note that like in P/E ratio where E represents future earnings, the denominator of P/S ratio is also the expected sales and not current annual sales. This is where the challenge comes because like any other forecast, sales forecasts may also be difficult to derive for many stocks.

The problems in using P/S ratio mainly come from the wide variation of this ratio across industries, making it difficult to use it for comparing firms across industries. The reason is that sales per share vary diversely among different types of industries. Further, the profit margins also vary across industries.

2. **Price-to-Book Ratio**: Many analysts view book value as useful and easily available measure of value. It can be used to gauge how aggressively the market has valued the firm. The ratio is computed as:

$$\text{Price-to-book ratio} = \frac{\text{Stock price at time } t}{\text{Book value per share at } t+1} \tag{39}$$

Book value at time $t+1$ is the book value estimated at the end of the year.

Book value per share is measured as the net worth of the company divided by the number of issued equity shares. P/BV ratio is a function of the firm's return on equity (ROE) relative to k_e (cost of equity). If ROE $= k_e$, the P/BV ratio is equal to 1. If ROE $> k_e$, the investors would be willing to pay a premium for the share of the company over its book value since it is a growth company.

A high value of P/BV indicates that the stock is overvalued and a low value indicates the opposite. As in the case of P/E and PEG ratios, determination of a stock being overvalued and undervalued is done subjectively. Value investors place emphasis on stocks whose book values are more than their market price.

Identifying undervalued or overvalued securities using price-to-book value

Price-to-book value can also be expressed in terms of ROE. We know that the basic DDM for calculation of current price is:

$$P_0 = \frac{D_1}{(k-g)}$$

We also know that ROE $=$ EPS_0/Book Value of Equity (BV_0)

$$D_1 = (\text{Dividend payout ratio} \times EPS_0) \times (1+g)$$

$$EPS_0 = ROE \times BV_0$$

Using the above value of EPS_0, D_1 can be computed as:

$$D_1 = (ROE \times BV_0 \times \text{Dividend payout ratio}) \times (1+g)$$

Substituting the above value of D_1, the simple DDM equation can be rewritten as:

$$P_0 = (ROE \times BV_0 \times \text{Dividend payout ratio}) \times \frac{(1+g)}{(k-g)} \tag{40}$$

And Price-to-book value ratio can be expressed as

$$\frac{P_0}{BV_0} = (\text{ROE} \times \text{Dividend payout ratio}) \times \frac{(1+g)}{(k-g)} \tag{41}$$

If the return on equity is based upon expected earnings in the next time period, i.e., EPS_1, then the above equation can be simplified to,

$$V = \frac{P_0}{BV_0} = \frac{(\text{ROE} \times \text{Dividend payout ratio})}{(k-g)} \tag{42}$$

We can modify the above equation further by using the following relationship between ROE, *g* and Dividend payout ratio

$$g = (1 - \text{Dividend payout ratio}) \times \text{ROE}$$

or

$$\text{Dividend payout ratio} = \frac{(\text{ROE} - g)}{\text{ROE}}$$

Using the above value of Dividend Payout ratio, equation (42) can be rewritten as:

$$V = \frac{P_0}{BV_0} = \frac{(\text{ROE} - g)}{(k-g)} \tag{43}$$

Figure 9.3 PBV-ROE matrix.

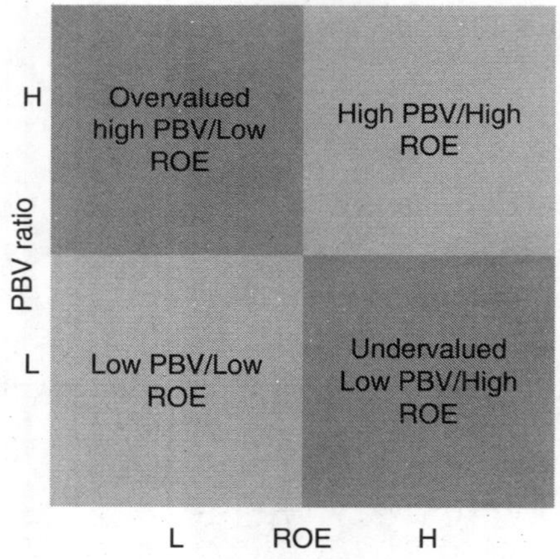

The above equation shows that the price-book value ratio of a constant growth firm is determined by the differential between its ROE and the required rate of return. This relation between price-book value ratio and ROE can be used for finding undervalued securities. On the basis of this relationship, it can be said that firms that have high ROE can be expected to sell for price well above their book value. Conversely firms that have low ROE can be expected to sell for price well below their book value.

So obviously, a mismatch of price-book value ratios and returns on equity, i.e., high P/BV ratios and low ROE (overvalued) or low P/BV ratios and high ROE (undervalued) should attract the attention of analysts. Over and undervaluation of securities using P/BV ratio can be expressed through matrix illustrated in Figure 9.3.

This ratio was more popular in the banking industry in the past but after the three-factor asset-pricing model was given by Fama-French in 1992, it has gained popularity as a relative valuation ratio across all types of firms.

Again it is important to understand that the denominator should be equal to future book value and not the current book value. This is also where the problem comes in implementing the model. Future estimated book value is generally not available. It needs to be determined if one intends to use this ratio for valuation.

3. **Price-to-Cash Flow Ratio**: Price/Cash flow is a good alternative relative valuation ratio because it is not subject to the vagaries of accounting practices as earnings are. Cash flow, a measure of actual cash flowing into and out of the firm, is not affected excessively by accounting policies. Further, cash flow generated by a firm indicates its capability to finance its own growth without having to raise funds from external sources. Another advantage of using cash flow over earnings per share for valuation is that a firm can have negative earnings per share but still report positive cash flow per share. Hence, a growing section of analysts prefer to use this ratio instead of P/E ratio in security analysis.

   Cash flow is computed by adding non-cash expenses, such as depreciation and amortization, to net income and the cash flow thus computed is divided by the total number of equity shares to calculate cash flow per share. The ratio is computed as:

$$\text{P/CF} = \frac{\text{Price per share at time } t}{\text{Cash flow per share at time } t+1} \tag{44}$$

   Again the same caution needs to be exercised. The denominator is computed using estimated and not current cash flow per share. As to which cash flow to use, some analysts tend to use free cash flows while others prefer operating cash flows.

   This ratio is affected by the same factors as the P/E ratio. These include expected growth rate of cash flow measure used and the variability of the cash flow series over time to indicate the risk of the stock. As with the P/E ratio, the lower the price–to–cash flow ratio, the more attractive is the value of the company.

4. **Enterprise Value/EBITDA:** Though most analysts rely on market capitalization to determine valuation ratios, enterprise value is actually a more effective tool. It may be calculated as:

$$\text{Enterprise value} = \text{Market cap} + \text{Debt} - \text{Cash} \tag{45}$$

   A leveraged firm with more debt relative to cash will have an EV that is significantly higher than its market capitalization. This kind of difference between market capitalization and EV is very important from the perspective of valuation. For example a firm with a market cap of ₹1,000 and a profit of ₹100 will have a P/E equal to 10. If it has ₹500 in net debt in its balance sheet, its EV will be ₹1500 and its debt-adjusted P/E, or EV/E, will be 15. We have used EV/E for the sake of simplicity. Usually, enterprise value is compared to EBITDA.

   EBITDA is an indicator of the firm's financial performance and is calculated as:

$$\text{EBITDA} = \text{Revenue} - \text{Expenses (excluding interest, tax, depreciation and amortization)} \quad (46)$$

It is gaining popularity as a valuation measure because this ratio can be computed even for firms that are reporting net losses, since EBITDA is usually positive. Further, it makes inter-firm comparison possible even in the case of firms with different financial leverage. The ratio is considered to be more appropriate than the P/E ratio for high growth firms.

Marketview 9.2 Concept of Growth and Value Investing

Growth investing may be defined as an approach to invest in which investors target firms that have higher growth rate of earnings than those of the market. Growth investors seek to maximize their capital gains.

Value investing is an approach in which investors seek stocks that are selling for less than their intrinsic values, i.e., undervalued stocks. The basic idea behind picking undervalued securities is that the value investors believe that market overreacts to news, good and bad, causing fluctuations in prices that do not correspond with long-term fundamentals of the firm and the prices can be expected to increase eventually.

Although growth and value investing are considered to be conflicting investment strategies, a more practical view is to consider them complementary. Both value and growth investors apply basic valuation principles for determination of intrinsic value and calculation of relative valuation ratios.

Choosing Between Different Relative Valuation Ratios

As discussed above, there are many relative valuation ratios for an analyst to choose from; each with its set of benefits and limitations. Faced with the dilemma of choice, an analyst/investor should ideally do one of the following things for effective valuation:

1. Use a simple average of the valuations obtained from different ratios.
2. Use a weighted average of the valuations obtained from different ratios (where the weight of each ratio can be determined on the basis of its importance).
3. Select a ratio that he thinks is the best and base all valuation on that ratio (usually the best way as choosing the best makes one delve deeply into the ratio and gain insights about it).

Critique of Relative Valuation Method

Like the DCF valuation tools, relative valuation method also suffers from many limitations. Relative valuation models cannot be applied effectively for comparing firms that differ in business models and products. So most valuation ratios are more useful for inter-firm comparison within the same industry. Relative valuation models should incorporate differences between assets, since no two assets are alike. There are also challenges in comparison of firms within an industry on account of difference in the assets. For example, relative valuation ratios may not be effective when used to compare Pizza Hut, a fast food chain and Mainland China that operates on a more formal sit-down, dining concept. You may note that both are in food business but different in concept and price points. Therefore, comparing their margins or any other ratio would be not of much relevance

Marketview 9.3 Indian Stocks and their PEG Ratios

Companies with PEG ratios of less than 0.5 are the best							
					Analyst recomm		
Company	Industry	PE	5-year EPS growth (%)	PEG	Total	BUY	1-year return (%)
Arvind	Textiles	10.55	53.96	0.20	11	10	65.25
Bajaj finance	Asset financing services	10.66	88.64	0.12	20	16	18.10
CESC	Power generation	8.49	10.50	0.81	30	19	36.91
Development credit bank	Banking services	9.17	12.55	0.73	26	25	17.14
eClerx services	ITES	14.96	15.70	0.95	19	12	79.78
Entertainment network (India)	Media (broadcasting)	19.96	33.10	0.60	12	10	56.72
Indraprastha gas	LNG storage & distribution	10.65	15.21	0.70	28	18	5.42
Jammu and kashmir bank	Banking services	5.65	23.99	0.24	19	17	0.83
Kajaria ceramics	Ceramics	23.08	46.27	0.50	20	17	54.19
Mindtree	Computer software	13.98	24.46	0.57	44	23	86.65
Torrent paharmaceuticals	Drugs & pharmaceuticals	13.22	28.57	0.46	27	18	58.55
Va tech wabag	Industrial machinery	16.31	50.46	0.32	18	14	6.27

in valuation since their business models are different. Hence, the first step in ensuring effective outcome in relative valuation is to choose as similar businesses as possible. Another problem with the use of relative valuation models is the assumption that the market has valued the business correctly. A favorable relative valuation ratio cannot be taken as an assurance that the 'cheaper' company will outperform the other firms in the industry. The limitations of valuation models may be summarized as:

1. These models are not of much use for comparing values across different asset classes.
2. These models do not give a clue about the stock market valuations, i.e., whether the market is overvalued or undervalued.

Beyond the Basics 9.2 Residual Income Method for Equity Valuation

As discussed above, a company can be valued using different methods. An analyst can choose to use relative valuation approach and compare multiples of a firm with other firms within its industry or he can opt to use an absolute valuation model such as dividend discount method to calculate the intrinsic value of the firm. Apart from DDM and other DCF variants, there is one more method of absolute valuation that is very popular amongst analysts, though not commonly known. This method is called the residual income method of equity valuation.

The residual income model calculates a more accurate value of equity by adjusting the forecasts of a firm's earnings to compensate for the cost of equity. Though the concept of residual income is old, it has received a lot of attention in the recent years, mostly under the name of Economic value added (EVA).

Residual income of a firm is calculated as: Net income – Equity charge

where

$$\text{Equity Charge} = \text{Total Equity Capital} \times \text{Cost of Equity}$$

The importance of computation of residual income can be understood with the help of following example: Suppose, Creative Media Ltd. reported earnings of ₹100000 last year. It has a total equity capital of ₹970000 and its cost of equity is 11%. Calculate its residual income.

Solution:

$$\text{Equity Charge} = 970000 \times 0.11 = 106700$$

$$\text{Net Income} = ₹100000$$

$$\text{Residual Income} = 100000 - 106700 = -₹6700$$

The above calculations show that even though the company has a positive net income, i.e., it is showing a profit on an accounting basis yet it is economically unprofitable for equity shareholders, given the level of risk.

Calculating intrinsic value using residual income

DCF technique is used to calculate intrinsic value using residual income. The value of a firm in residual income method is defined as the sum of the book value and the present values of its expected future residual incomes. The forecasted residual incomes are discounted at cost of equity or the rate of return required on equity.

$$V_0 = BV_0 + \left[\frac{RI_1}{(1+k^1)}\right] + \left[\frac{RI_2}{(1+k^2)}\right] + \left[\frac{RI_3}{(1+k^3)}\right] + \cdots$$

The residual income approach makes it possible to use DCF for computation of intrinsic value for firms that do not pay dividends and/or do not have positive free cash flow. However, like other DCF techniques, this method is also a vulnerable misrepresentation of a firm's historic financial statements.

However, a comprehensive relative valuation process definitely helps the investors by preventing them from making their investment decisions based on one or two variables. Relative valuation models can help investors answer the question about choice of stock within a sector. It is important to identify the metrics that matter most and understand their implications fully. Though relative valuation models are quite popular, it has to be understood that in the long run, analysis of fundamental factors is the correct way to value any asset.

Valuing the Stock: What is the Best Way to Proceed?

All valuation models discussed above are quite comprehensive and well researched yet no analyst has been successful in always selecting the appropriate stock to buy or sell. In other words, even the best of portfolio managers and security analysts have lost money by making wrong calls. Does this mean that all valuation models are fallacious? Actually, no. Most models are capable of providing good estimates but the estimates that seem good at one point in time may simply turn out to be sub-optimal at some other point in time. The reason is that the valuation techniques are themselves evolving with research. So the importance of variables may vary over time. Further, all firms operate in a very dynamic environment where a single event can bring about a sudden distress or turn a bad performer around.

So is security analysis useless? Not at all. It is just that analysts should realize that in addition to the measurable investment returns on security (which can be predicted with comparative accuracy), there are also certain speculative returns that cannot be forecasted with accuracy. To factor in this uncertainty, analysts should update their

Beyond the Basics 9.3 Valuing the Market

Q ratio is a popular asset-based model for estimating the fair value of the stock market as a whole. It was developed by Nobel Laureate, James Tobin and is calculated by dividing the total price or value of the market by the replacement cost of the tangible assets of all its companies.

$$Q = \text{market value} \div \text{replacement value}$$

The market value of a company is calculated as the sum of the market value of its debt and equity. Tobin had hypothesized that in a rightly priced market, the combined market values of all the listed companies should approximately equal the combined replacement cost of their tangible assets, i.e., their *Q* ratio should be 1.

A *Q* ratio of more than one indicates that the market value of assets or the share prices are greater than their replacement cost. This means that capex can be expected to create wealth for shareholders. Hence, the companies should look to increase their capex, but should not undertake acquisition. They should raise funds for capital expenditure. Issue of more capital is likely to reduce share prices and increase the prices of assets, pushing *Q* towards one.

A *Q* value of less than one implies that the market value of the assets or the share prices are less than the replacement cost of the assets. In such a situation, acquisitions will be cheaper than capex and companies would look to undertake acquisition rather than set up from the scratch. This is likely to increase share prices and reduce asset prices, taking *Q* up towards one.

The cyclically adjusted P/E (CAPE) ratio is another method used to determine whether the market as a whole is correctly valued. CAPE is a simple modification of the P/E ratio to take into account the effect of the economic cycle on profits and it is often used in conjunction with Tobin's *Q*.

valuation models periodically, choose their input variables with care to make adjustment for the dynamic corporate environment and review their return estimate for unanticipated and speculative returns.

Implementing the Valuation Models: Computation of Inputs

Having established the valuation models to help us predict the future price of equity shares and estimate their intrinsic value, now we need to understand how to compute the inputs required for applying the valuation models described in the chapter. The two key inputs that are required in most valuation models are:

1. Required rate of return
2. Expected growth rate of earnings, dividends, sales, book value, cash flow and other variables

Required rate of return is that discount rate which is used in most cash flow models. It also affects all the relative valuation techniques. The only point of difference is that for the present value of dividends and free cash flow to equity, the appropriate discount rate is cost of equity whereas free cash flow to firm is discounted at the weighted average cost of capital.

A firm's cost of equity is mainly dependent on the real risk-free rate in the economy and a risk premium for taking the risk of investing in equity. The real risk-free rate implies the minimum rate of return that an investor requires as an inducement to part with his money. It depends on the real growth rate of the economy the investor is domiciled in and the rate of inflation in that economy, as the real risk-free rate is obtained by adjusting the effect of expected inflation. Risk premium is the additional return that the investors require as an inducement to bear additional risk by putting their funds in risky assets. Risk premium depends on the exchange rate risk, liquidity risk, financial risk, business risk, country risk, interest rate risk and so on. A premium has to be computed to account for all the risks relevant to stock under consideration. Further, risk premium of a stock changes over time with changes in the underlying factors.

Expected growth rate of equity earnings per share (EPS) for a pure equity firm is given as $g =$ retention or plough back ratio $\times$ return on equity. This means that a firm can increase its growth rate by increasing its retention ratio, which is management's decision, but is actually dependent on the level of ROE. The level of ROE, in turn, is a result of the changes in the operating performance of the firm. Let us examine ROE by breaking it into its components based on Dupont analysis.

$$\text{ROE} = \frac{\text{Net income}}{\text{Sales}} \times \frac{\text{Sales}}{\text{Total assets}} \times \frac{\text{Total assets}}{\text{Equity}}$$

or

$$\text{ROE} = \text{Profit margin} \times \text{Total asset turnover} \times \text{Financial leverage}$$

The first two are an outcome of the operating performance of the firm and the third item is the outcome of the firm's financing decision. Net profit margin, an indicator of the firm's profitability on sales, changes over the time for many companies as it is highly sensitive to the business cycles. For growth companies, profit margin ratio is one of the first metric to decline because of the increase in competition that might lead to price-cutting to sustain sales. During the recessionary phases also it declines because of lower sales or price-cutting or higher percentage of fixed costs (again an outcome of lower sales).

The second component is an indicator of management's operating efficiency. The product of the first and the second component is called return on assets (ROA), which is a measure of firm's operating performance before its financing structure is factored in. The last ratio is a measure of financial leverage and it is an outcome of the financing decision of the management.

Thus, to predict ROE, one needs to estimate the above three components. This estimate of ROE when multiplied by the retention ratio, gives the value of the expected growth rate. It is important that while predicting *g*, we also predict the growth rate of *g*, i.e., how long a firm will be able to sustain the estimated value. An alternative approach to measurement of *g* is to use the historical growth rates of earnings, sales, dividend and cash flow accrued in the past. These can be measured using:

1. Arithmetic mean or geometric mean of annual percentage change
2. Linear regression of time series of annual percentage change
3. Log-linear regression models regressing natural log of EPS.

Analysis of historical growth rates and plotting them on time series graphs provide a significant insight into the trends as well as variability of growth rates over time.

Estimation of Intrinsic Value Using P/E Ratio

In practice, the intrinsic value of a share is determined using the P/E ratio. The steps involved in the computation are:

Forecasting expecting earning per share (EPS)

As a starting point of valuation exercise, analysts need to forecast the future EPS and cash flow per share of the firm on the basis of projection of costs and revenues. The idea behind estimation of cash flow is that depreciation is not an out flow, it is merely an accounting adjustment and so cash flow is a better indicator of earnings accruing to the equity holders. Determination of the level of expected earnings is based on a number of assumptions about factors affecting the performance of company and its profitability. These include factors like future sales, demand growth, interest rates, cost of raw material and other production inputs, import duties, price of product, regulatory environment, economic factors, income tax rate, asset turnover, capacity utilization, production efficiency and so on. The assumptions are based on analysts' judgment and educated guess but it is not entirely subjective. Analysts solicit information about the prospects of a company from various sources like research agencies, experts, suppliers, company officials, customers, competitors of the firm and so on. A thorough quantitative and qualitative analysis is undertaken to make the best possible estimates of earnings and the factors that drive them, as described in detail in Chapter 11.

Making right projections requires a tremendous amount of skill and expertise because any valuation is as good as the projections it is based on. Usually a single forecast is not prepared. It is always better to work with ranges and specify few scenarios: optimistic, pessimistic and most likely – and analyze how the company and its earnings are going to fare in each scenario outlined by the analysts.

Estimation of P/E ratio

A number of variants of the basic P/E ratios are in use, depending on how the price and earnings are defined. Price used could be the current market price or average market price for the year. Earnings could be the earnings of latest financial year or trailing 12 months (Trailing P/E) or forecasted EPS (Forward P/E). The method of calculation of P/E using different values of EPS has been illustrated in Numerical Example 12. P/E can also be calculated using constant growth DDM, as illustrated in Numerical Example 13. In order to use DDM for calculation of P/E ratio, the analysts need to forecast dividend payout, required rate of return of equity and the growth rate, in addition to forecasting the earnings. The computation of all these inputs has been explained in detail in the preceding sections of the chapter. An average of historical P/E can also be used to arrive at a reasonable estimate of future P/E.

Some analysts also use cross-section analysis to determine the P/E ratio of the firm under study. Such a computation may either be based on determination of P/E of the firm on the basis of P/E of comparative firms in the industry or on the basis of cross-section regression analysis by using key fundamental variables such as earnings growth rate, market share, size of the company, dividend payout ratio, variability of earnings, etc. as independent variables and estimating their coefficients.

In practice, P/E ratio is computed using two or three methods and weighted P/E is computed by assigning different or same weights to each P/E. This is done to ensure as accurate forecast of P/E as possible.

Determination of value anchor and value range

Value anchor is basically the price of the share or the intrinsic value and it is calculated by using the two key inputs computed in steps 1 and 2. Therefore, the value or the value anchor of a share is calculated as:

$$\text{Projected EPS} \times \text{Appropriate P/E}$$

However, most analysts use value range rather than value anchor for the purpose of taking a buy or sell decision based on comparison of intrinsic value with the prevailing market price per share. This is because a point estimate or a specific estimate might not be very reliable in the face of uncertainty in the operating environment of the firm.

SUMMARY

- ☑ Intrinsic value is a measure of the right value of a stock that attempts to quantify the total net assets that a company is expected to build in the future.
- ☑ The process of computation of the intrinsic value is called valuation and it is a question that all investors, analysts, researchers, academicians in the field, regulators and portfolio managers try to address/answer with varying degrees of success.
- ☑ The aim of the valuation process is to determine the intrinsic value of a share and compare it with its market price to take advantage of mispricing.
- ☑ There are two broad categories under which valuation models of the equity stocks fall: Discounted Cash Flow Techniques and Relative Valuation Techniques.
- ☑ Discounted cash flow valuation techniques are based on the concept of calculation of present value of some measure of future cash flow of the share including dividend, operating cash flow and free cash flow.
- ☑ There are three techniques for valuation under DCF method: Dividend Discount Models, Present Value Model for Operating Cash Flow and Present Value Model for Free Cash Flow to Equity.
- ☑ The primary assertion of DDM is that the future prices of a share are determined by cash flows accruing to the shareholders and those cash flows are dividends.

- ☑ The implication of constant growth DDM is that the share prices are expected to grow at the same rate as the dividends.
- ☑ Multi-stage DDM implies that the dividends do not grow at a constant rate *g*, rather they grow at varying rates through the years. The model is, in fact, an extension of constant-growth DDM.
- ☑ The free cash flow valuation model offers an alternative to DDM. This model values the firm on the basis of free cash flow (cash flow to firm or equity shareholders net of capital expenditures).
- ☑ The FCF models are more useful in case of firms paying no dividend (where DDM cannot be applied), however they can be applied to dividend paying firms as well.
- ☑ Relative valuation techniques value the stock on the basis of its current price vis-à-vis a variable significant to valuation like cash flow, book value, earnings or sales.
- ☑ The main techniques/models of relative valuation are: Price/Earnings Ratio (P/E), Price/Sales Ratio (P/S), Price/Book Value Ratio (P/BV), Price/Cash flow Ratio (P/CF) and Enterprise value/EBITDA.
- ☑ The P/E model is based on the underlying concept of how much money the investors are willing to pay for a rupee of expected earnings (estimated 12-month earnings).
- ☑ There are a number of variants of the basic P/E ratios in use, depending on how the price and earnings are defined. The price used could be the current market price or average market price for the year.
- ☑ Though most analysts rely on market capitalization to determine valuation ratios, enterprise value is actually a more effective tool. It is gaining popularity as a valuation measure because Enterprise value/EBITDA can be computed even for firms that are reporting net losses, since EBITDA is usually positive. Further, it makes inter-firm comparison possible even in the case of firms with different financial leverage. This ratio is considered to be more appropriate than the PE ratio for high growth firms.

KEY WORDS

CONCEPT QUESTIONS

1. Equity valuation is very important from an investor's point of view. Explain.
2. Can the firms in the same industry be expected to have the same P/E ratio? Discuss
3. Discuss the drivers of growth rate and their role in determination of the value of a firm.
4. Write a comparative note on the challenges in using DCF techniques for equity valuation from the point of view of an equity analyst.
5. Though relative valuation techniques are widely used in equity valuation, they suffer from some serious limitations. Comment.
6. As an equity analyst would you choose to use DDM or P/E ratio for valuing common stock? Justify your choice.
7. Why is constant growth DDM considered a theoretical simplification?
8. How can an analyst effectively use various relative valuation ratios for valuing the equity accurately?
9. Intrinsic value is a key concept in taking investment decision. Explain.
10. How can P/E ratio be used by investors for making buying and selling decisions in stock market?
11. You are reading an equity research report on Cruise Bank, and the analyst claims that the stock is undervalued on the basis of the fact that its P/E ratio is 11.38 while the average P/E ratio of the banking sector in the country is 33.65. Do you agree with the analyst's claim?

PRACTICE PROBLEMS

1. KVR Bottling Ltd. has maintained its historic growth rate of 7% and paid a dividend for ₹1.20 per share yesterday. Sam plans to purchase the share today as his investment adviser has told him that KVR is doing well and its dividend growth rate can be expected to be 8% per year for the next three years. At the end of three years the share is expected to sell at the price of ₹48.

   Use the above information to answer the following questions:

   a. What price should Sam be willing to pay for the stock if his required rate of return is 13%?
   b. What is the maximum price he should pay if he believes that KVR's dividends would continue to grow at a rate of 8% indefinitely (his required rate of return is 13%)?
   c. If KVR's dividends would continue to grow at a rate of 8% indefinitely and Sam's required rate of return is 13%, what will the price of the share be at the end of Year 3?

2. BB Bearings Ltd. is currently a favorite of many investors. Ken House is an analyst with Invest Well Ltd. BB has attracted his attention as well and he is trying to value the stock using the FCFE model. He has

estimated that BB's FCFE can be expected to grow at 26% for 2 years and 13% thereafter. Working capital, capital expenditure and depreciation are all expected to grow proportionately with FCFE. If the required rate of return on equity is 15%, calculate the following:

a. The amount of FCFE per share for the year 2013.
b. The current value per share of BB Bearings Ltd. based on the 2-stage FCFE model.

Income statement	2012	2013
Revenue	470	598
Depreciation	25	27
Other operating costs	375	455
Income before tax	70	116
Tax	21	35
Net income	49	81
Dividends	16	23
EPS	0.6125	1.015
DPS	0.2	0.2875
Outstanding shares (millions)	80	80
Current assets	201	326
Fixed assets	474	489
Total assets	675	815
Current liabilities	57	141
Long-term debt	0	0
Total liabilities	57	141
Shareholders' equity	618	674
Total liabilities and equity	675	815
Capital expenditures	34	38

3. Crater Fireworks Ltd. (CFL) paid a dividend of ₹6 last year out of an earning of ₹10 per share. Analysts expect the company to maintain its historic payout ratio and pay the dividends accordingly from an anticipated EPS of ₹11 next year. Use this information to answer the following:

   a. How much should an investor pay for it now if he expects the stock to sell for ₹130 after one year? His required rate of return is 13%.

b. If the selling price is expected to be ₹105, then what is the maximum price an investor with a required rate of return of 9% will be willing to pay for the share?
c. If the investor expects the dividends to grow at a constant rate of 8% in the foreseeable future, what is the price he would be willing to pay to acquire the share right now? His required rate of return is 11%.
d. Analysts have come to know that the company has signed a five-year contract for providing fireworks for all IPL and CLT20 matches. This is a very positive news and thus the analysts revise their growth estimate for CFL to 9%. If the required rate of return is 11%, what is the maximum P/E ratio that the analysts would apply to the company? What is the maximum price the investor with a required rate of return of 11% will be willing to pay for it?

4. KWB Transformers Ltd. (KWB) has a ROE of 9% and beta of 1.20. Analysts expect the company to maintain indefinitely its plough back ratio of 2/3. The company has just paid current dividend on an earning of ₹3 per share. Market is expected to return 13% in the coming year and t-bills yield 6% return. Use this information to answer the following:

a. What is the correct price at which KWB should sell?
b. What is it trailing and forward P/E ratio?
c. Calculate the present value of growth opportunities (PVGO).

5. Goldfish securities is a large brokerage house that uses capital asset pricing model (CAPM) and dividend discount model (DDM) to value stocks. Peter House is an equity analyst working with the firm. He has recently valued the stock of VM Airways using his company's standard approach to valuation. Now he wants to value NJ Airways using the same models using the following information:

	VM airways	NJ airways
Beta	1.35	1.10
Market price	₹80	₹96
Intrinsic value	₹110	

Risk-free rate is 4.50% and expected market return is 14%. Use the above information to answer the following:

a. Calculate the cost of equity of NJ Airways.
b. NJ Airways has recently declared dividend per share of ₹6.50. House estimates the EPS and dividend growth rates for NJ Airways as 11% p.a. for the first 3 years and constant rate of 9% p.a. thereafter. Calculate the intrinsic value of the share.
c. Which company's shares should House recommend for purchase? Why?

6. Nancy is analyzing Rock Salt Company (RSC) for her client who has a required rate of return of 12%. The company has a ROE of 15% and it has consistently paid 40% of its annual earnings as dividends. She needs answers to the following questions before her meeting with the client:

a. What is the dividend growth rate of RSC?
b. What is the P/E ratio of the company?

c. There is a strong rumor in the market that the company might increase its dividend payout ratio to 50%. What will the P/E be in case of an increase in the payout ratio?

7. Groove Furniture Ltd. (GFL) has consistently retained 50% of its earnings and invested it in projects with a rate of return of 18% per annum. It is anticipated that the company would continue to adhere to its policy of paying 50% of its earnings as dividends. If the EPS is expected to be ₹2 and the stock of GFL is currently selling at ₹15 per share, answer the following:

   a. If the current market price reflects the intrinsic value as computed using the DDM, what is the stock investors' rate of return?
   b. What will be its intrinsic value if the company moves to a zero retention policy?
   c. What is the value of PVGO?
   d. What will the value of GFL stocks be if the dividend payout ratio is decreased to 25%?

   Comment on the variation in the intrinsic value.

8. People Textile Ltd. (PTL) has a 17% growth rate of earnings and the market anticipates that the same super-normal growth rate will be sustained for another four years. After that, the growth rate is expected to fall to 11% and the same is expected to persist for another four years. Thereafter, the terminal or constant or sustainable growth rate is expected to be 6%. The investors' required rate of return on PTL's stock is 16%. If the current dividend paid by the company is ₹2.00, calculate its intrinsic value.

9. The market price of the share of Sweet Chilies Entertainment Ltd. is ₹50. A research study undertaken by Invest Tree Ltd. has found that the rate of return on the company's stock has been 20% and the same is expected to continue for the next 5 years. Thereafter, the rate of return is expected to grow indefinitely at 10%. If the dividend in the current year is ₹5 and the investor's required rate of return is 25%, use two-stage DDM to calculate the price of the stock. Should the share be bought?

10. Sicily Fashion Ltd. (SFL) has just paid a dividend of ₹16 per share. The growth rate of dividend is expected to be 24% per year for the next 3 years and then settle down to 5% per year indefinitely. The appropriate market capitalization rate for this company is 20% per year. Use the above information to calculate:

   a. The intrinsic value of a share of SFL today.
   b. The current and expected dividend yield for next year, assuming the share is selling at its intrinsic value.
   c. The expected price of SFL share a year from now, assuming the share is selling at its intrinsic value today.
   d. The expected capital gain if you acquire the share today and sell it after one year.

CASELET 1

McCain Ltd. is a well-known research company. In a recent report released by them, they have strongly contented that by 2015, India will become the leading producer and supplier of high temperature ceramic fiber products. The products have a wide range of industrial application and their demand has been rising across the globe. Two Indian companies producing high temperature ceramic fiber products, Unitfrax Ltd. (UL) and Gabetrax Ltd. (GL) are performing well and are expected to benefit from the increasing local and global demand for their products.

Patrick Keen, an analyst, wants to invest in the shares of one of the two companies. His required rate of return from his investment is 13% and he wants to invest for a holding period of one year. He researches the prospects of the two companies and comes up with following data: The two companies are listed on both, BSE and NSE. The current share price of UL on NSE is ₹50 and that of GL is ₹100. The face value of each of the two stocks is ₹5. Like most Indian companies, these two companies have also been paying dividends consistently in the past. The dividend growth rate of UL is 11% and that of GL is 10%. UL and GL are expected to pay a dividend of ₹1.5 and ₹2.3, respectively, in the next year. The EPS is expected to be ₹2.6 for UL and ₹4 for GL.

Keen has also prepared an estimate of the likely prices that could be expected to prevail after one year for the two stocks. His estimate for UL is ₹57, 60 or 65 and for GL is ₹112, 126 or 133. Which share should he buy?

CASELET 2

Aditya is an analyst with PRC Ltd. The firm specializes in equity research. As the Indian economy has grown, the movement of goods from one part of the country to another has increased considerably. The freight transportation companies have been performing well, despite the rising fuel costs. With the new government coming in, the outlook for freight transport companies has improved. Fuel price cut in the recent times is being taken as a very positive sign by the market. Aditya has been in search of a new sector to invest in and the freight transportation sector attracts his attention. After detailed analysis of the sector, he decides to analyze Deccan Freight Ltd. further. The company has a large market share, innovative and visionary top management team and a very positive image as reliable and trustworthy freight movers. Help Aditya compute the intrinsic value range for Deccan Freight Ltd. using the financial information given below (the data is hypothetical and grouped for ease of analysis) to decide the price at which he should buy the share:

Year end	2012	2013	2014	Assumptions for 2015
Net sales/income	722	780	830	Increase by 11%
Cost of goods sold	565	590	625	Increase by 12%
Gross profit	157	190	205	
Operating expenses	67	62	78	Increase by 8.5%
Operating profit	90	128	127	
Non-operating surplus/deficit	0	−8	4	No change
Profit before interest and tax	90	120	131	
Interest	21	24	25	Decrease by 4%

(Continued)

Continued

Year end		2012	2013	2014	Assumptions for 2015
Profit before tax		69	96	106	
Tax/Provision for tax		35	38	35	Increase by 5%
Profit after tax		34	58	71	
Dividend		28	30	30	
Retained earnings		6	28	41	
Share capital (₹10 par value)		160	160	160	
Reserves and Surplus		115	145	185	
Shareholders' funds		275	305	345	
Loan funds		212	229	222	
Capital employed		487	534	567	
Net fixed assets		335	395	415	
Investments		17	22	27	
Net current assets		135	117	125	
Total assets		487	534	567	
Earning per share		2.13	3.63	4.44	
Market price at the end of the year		25.5	28	31.5	
Market price at the end of 2011	20.1				
Beta	1.2				
Risk-free rate of return	8.82%				
Expected market risk premium	7.50%				

The Broader Picture: Macroeconomic and Industry Analysis

10

CHAPTER OBJECTIVES

- ❒ Understanding the key components of fundamental analysis
- ❒ Assessing key indicators related to global and domestic economy
- ❒ Evaluating industries in terms of business cycles and industry life cycle
- ❒ Discussing economic forecasting models

Any investment decision begins with an analysis to identify assets to which the investible funds can be allocated. In the case of equity shares, the first step in making investment decision regarding a particular share is the determination of its intrinsic value. To calculate the intrinsic or the right/proper/correct value of a firm's share, security analysts need to forecast the earnings and dividends of that firm. They also need to determine a discount rate at which the projected dividends should be brought to the present. This discount rate should reflect the risk of investment in equity of the firm under consideration.

We have already discussed the mechanism of computation of intrinsic value in detail in the chapter 9.

The process of determination of intrinsic value of a share to ascertain its prospects is called fundamental analysis. Analysts use fundamental analysis to study the determinants of value such as earnings and dividends. Future earnings of a firm depend on its business success and affect the amount of dividends that it can distribute to its existing shareholders. Earnings and dividends together impact the price that a share can fetch in the market.

Business success of a firm depends upon the environment of the industry to which the firm belongs. The industry is impacted by broad factors in the economy, both at domestic and global level. Therefore, fundamental analysts have to keep the bigger picture in mind and evaluate not only the firm but also the industry it belongs to and various macroeconomic variables.

Thus, fundamental analysis is termed as E-I-C analysis, i.e., economy, industry and company analysis. Some analysts use the bottom up approach, i.e., start with the analysis of the company and build up to economy analysis. However, it is advisable to use the top-down approach, i.e., begin with the analysis of broad economic environment and move down to industry before narrowing down to a single firm.

Evidence collected and analyzed by many researchers reveals that the movements in the price of a stock can be attributed to the following factors in given proportions:

1. Company-specific factors: 30–35%
2. Industry-related factors: 15–20%
3. Economy-wide factors: 30–35%
4. Unexplained/other factors: 15–25%

We will focus on macroeconomic and industry related factors in this chapter and take up company analysis in the next chapter. While discussing macroeconomic factors, we will consider both, the international and the national economy-related factors that can have an impact on the performance of a company and the price of its shares. In industry analysis, we will study the industry life cycle, sensitivity of the industry to the business cycle and other issues that have a bearing upon the industry performance.

Macroeconomic Analysis

The International Factors: Analyzing the Global Economy

The world economies are getting more and more connected and integrated. The performance of a firm in any country is likely to be affected by a number of variables in the global economy. The direct influences can be the volume of exports, the price of imported inputs or the cross-border investments a firm makes in other countries. For example, Euro zone is one of the biggest exporting partners of India.

Marketview 10.1 IMF View on World Economy

The title of World Economic Outlook, October 2014 viz., 'Legacies, Clouds, Uncertainties' says it all.

Weaker-than-expected global activity during the beginning of 2014 has led to the downward revision of global growth forecast to 3.3% for 2014 and 3.8% for 2015.

According to the outlook published in October 2014, short-term downside risks have increased on the back of geopolitical tensions, a reversal of risk spread and volatility compression in financial markets across the globe. Medium-term risk mentioned by the outlook includes lower growth in the advanced economies and a decline in growth in the emerging markets.

Given the higher level of risks, advanced economies will require continued support from monetary and fiscal policy to sustain growth. In emerging economies, the support for growth is expected to come from macroeconomic measures but due to external vulnerabilities of these countries, the scope of these policies is limited.

Further, according to the outlook, all economies, advanced, emerging as well as developing, need to introduce structural reforms to strengthen their growth potential.

Source: http://www.imf.org/external/pubs/ft/weo/2014/02/pdf/text.pdf, accessed on December 19, 2014.

When Euro zone entered the sovereign debt crisis, the earnings of many firms in India went down. Similarly, rise in price of crude oil in international markets affects the profits of firms in India as the cost of inputs increases. In yet another example, Indian firms have faced serious challenges in the recent years due to low-cost manufacturing in China. Changes in global economy like fluctuations in dollar rate, economic sanctions, bilateral agreements, trade barriers, etc. influence the performance of many firms, causing their earnings to fluctuate.

In addition to the direct economy related factors, global political environment presents broader threats like political instability, wars, etc. that also have a bearing on the performance of firms in a country.

Marketview 10.2 The Great Rupee Depreciation of 2013

Indian economy made quite a speedy recovery from the global crisis of 2008. The capital inflows increased from $7.8 bn to $51.8 bn in 2009–10 and $57 bn in 2010–11 on account of both FDI and FII. External Commercial Borrowings also picked up in 2010–11. REER (6 currency) appreciated by 13% in 2010–11 and 36 REER by 7.7%. But the tide turned once again. The year 2012 turned out to be a very volatile time for the Indian rupee. It plummeted again after the brief spell of appreciation in January and February 2012 that was triggered by inflow of foreign capital as FIIs' investment limit in government bonds neared expiry date. It slipped by 11.3% in June 2012, as compared to March and by almost 24.9% on a year-on-year basis. On June 25, 2012, rupee touched a one-year high of ₹57.88 to the USD.

The reasons for the rupee depreciation may not be India-specific, but the consequences definitely are. The fall in the value of a currency not only impairs its pride, but has many serious economic implications as well. The rupee depreciation has muted foreign capital inflow, raised external debt servicing burden and increased India's oil and fertilizers subsidy burden.

Analysts expect India Inc. to be severely impacted by the rupee's depreciation against the dollar given the large foreign currency debt on the books and only partial hedging. Moreover, the rupee's depreciation will lift input costs across many sectors amidst weak demand environment as reflected in low double-digit top line growth expected in 2013–14. Even exporters are unlikely to benefit significantly as clients may seek to renegotiate contracts.

Sources: Shalini Talwar, "Southward Bound Rupee: Dynamics of Currency Depreciation," *IRC's International Journal of Multidisciplinary Research in Social & Management Sciences*, Vol. 1/No. 3, 45–58, July–September 2013.

A fundamental analyst needs to assess the global economic and other environmental influences that are likely to affect the performance of a firm before moving on to industry and finally the company analysis.

The National Factors: Analyzing the Domestic Economy

Firms operating in any country are influenced directly by the macroeconomic policies pursued by the government of that country. The macroeconomic policies fall in two broad classes, supply-side polices and demand-side policies. Two demand-side policies that have always been the focus of attention are fiscal and monetary policies. In the recent past, supply-side policies have also been gaining a lot of attention of the regulators.

Fiscal policy: Parameters such as tax rates and tax-related incentives have a direct impact on the mood of the economy. Additional taxes on raw materials or certain products like cigarettes can decrease the spending on these products or increase their cost of production and influence their operating performance.

An increase or decrease in government spending has a direct influence on the economy; decrease deflates demand for goods and services while an increase in spending has a multiplier effect and is good for the economy. For example, the recent proposal to build no-frills airports in smaller cities would not only increase their connectivity but also provide employment to people, increase demand for construction material and equipment. This would raise the income of the concerned firms and many of them might expand their operations to meet increase in demand. Rise in income of firms would lead to increase in the income of their employees, resulting in increase in demand of consumption goods. Thus, an overall positive impact will be produced for all the stakeholders in the economy. Similarly, decrease or no change in the government spending can deflate the economy, creating a negative impact on all the stakeholders.

It also needs to be noted that though the increase in tax-rates increases the funds in the hands of the government and thereby the possibility of increase in government spending, it also reduces the disposable incomes in the hands of people, thereby reducing consumption spending. Therefore, fiscal policy measures need to be balanced.

Despite the theoretical effectiveness of fiscal policy, it is quite cumbersome to formulate and often ends up being influenced by political agenda rather than economic considerations. However, it continues to be a major demand-side tool.

The best barometer of fiscal policy is the budgetary deficit or surplus. Deficit would imply government spending is more than what it is collecting by the way of taxes. A deficit is likely to stimulate the economy. However, beyond a certain level, budgetary deficit weakens the economy. It is, therefore, important for the analysts to view fiscal policy in the right context.

Monetary policy: It is a tool used by the government to ease or tighten the money supply in the economy. The main tool of monetary policy is the interest rate.

When the government is seeking to stimulate investment and consumption, it lowers the short-term interest rates. This increases money supply or liquidity in the system. However, many economists are of

Beyond the Basics 10.1 Interest Rates and Inflation

Interest and inflation are two key economic numbers that have a direct impact on investment yield. With the result, they play a big role in the investment decisions of the investors.

Inflation erodes the purchasing power of money. To counter the impact of inflation, investors seek to invest in avenues that generate yields higher than the expected rate of inflation. A direct implication of this is that as inflation rises, companies or governments issuing debt instruments are forced to raise the rate of interest to lure the investors. Thus, changes in inflation lead to changes in the rates of interest. Investors should keep a close eye on the actual and expected rates of interest and inflation to ensure that the value of their investment appreciates over time.

Source: http://www.economywatch.com/inflation/economy/interest-rates.html, accessed on December 7, 2014.

the view that expansion in money supply often results in inflation without a long term impact on economic activity. In fact, balancing the money supply and interest rates continues to be the biggest challenge for the policy makers.

Monetary policy is less cumbersome to formulate and implement as compared to fiscal changes but it is almost as broad in its impact on the economy. A restrictive monetary policy may stunt the growth and expansion of business by reducing money supply and making credit expensive.

The main tools used by the government to regulate money supply are repo rates, open market operations, reserve requirements and direct credit control.

Marketview 10.3 Key Rates in India

Bank Rate	9.00% (w.e.f. 28/01/2014)	Increased from 8.75% which was continuing since 29/10/2013
Cash Reserve Ratio (CRR)	4.00% (w.e.f. 09/02/2013) – announced on 29/01/2013	Decreased from 4.25% which was continuing since 30/10/2012
Statutory Liquidity Ratio (SLR)	22.00% (w.e.f. 09/08/2014) (announced on 05/08/2014)	Decreased from 22.50% which was continuing since 14/06/2014
Repo Rate under LAF	8.00% (w.e.f. 28/01/2014)	Increased from 7.75% which was continuing since 29/10/2013
Reverse Repo Rate under LAF	7.00% (w.e.f 28/01/2014)	Increased from 6.75% which was continuing since 29/10/2013

Source: http://www.allbankingsolutions.com/DATA.HTM, accessed on November 16, 2014.

These tools are used by RBI to regulate money supply in the economy. Repo rate is the rate at which RBI lends to the banking sector. The current repo rate is 8%. To pursue a contractionary policy, RBI raises the repo rate, and to pursue expansionary monetary policy, it decreases the repo rates.

Open market operations are the activities of RBI to buy and sell government securities. When RBI buys government securities, it increases money supply, and when it sells securities, it decreases money supply in the economy.

Marketview 10.4 History of Repo Rates in India

(Since 2005)	%
26-Oct-05	6.25
24-Jan-06	6.5
08-Jun-06	6.75
25-Jul-06	7
30-Oct-06	7.25
31-Jan-07	7.5
30-Mar-07	7.75
12-Jun-08	8
25-Jun-08	8.5
30-Jul-08	9
20-Oct-08	8
03-Nov-08	7.5
08-Dec-08	6.5
05-Jan-09	5.5
05-Mar-09	5
21-Apr-09	4.75
19-Mar-10	5
20-Apr-10	5.25
02-Jul-10	5.5
27-Jul-10	5.75
16-Sep-10	6
02-Nov-10	6.25
25-Jan-11	6.5
17-Mar-11	6.75
03-May-11	7.25

(*Continued*)

Continued

(Since 2005)	%
16-Jun-11	7.5
26-Jun-11	8
16-Sep-11	8.25
25-Oct-11	8.5
17-Apr-12	8
29-Jan-13	7.75
19-Mar-13	7.5
03-May-13	7.25
20-Sep-13	7.5
29-Oct-13	7.75
18-Dec-13	7.75
28-Jan-14	8

Source: http://www.allbankingsolutions.com/Banking-Tutor/Chronology-Repo-Rate-India.shtml, accessed on November 16, 2014.

Reserve requirements are referred to as CRR (cash reserve ratio), and SLR (statutory liquidity ratio). CRR refers to the cash that banks are required to maintain with RBI as a percentage of their demand and time liability. SLR is the ratio of cash in hand of the bank, their balances in current account of PSU banks and RBI, gold and approved securities to their demand and time liabilities. Clearly, a decrease in CRR and SLR is an expansionary monetary policy and an increase in CRR and SLR is a contractionary monetary policy.

The RBI also resorts to direct credit control tools to regulate money supply in the economy. It can be in the form of limits on lending to certain sectors or according priority to agriculture or any other specific sector.

Both monetary and fiscal policies influence portfolio investments, though the impact of monetary policy is less immediate and direct as compared to the fiscal policy.

Supply-side policy: The fiscal and monetary policy tools operate on the basis of economic belief that the economy needs to be pushed toward full employment equilibrium. On the other hand, supply-side policy tools are more positive and aim to create an environment to increase the productive potential of the economy. The goal of supply-side oriented economic policies is to create an environment in which all stakeholders (particularly workers and owners of capital) have the incentive and the ability to produce more.

Supply-side economists look at tax policy in a considerably different manner as compared to the fiscal policy point of view. They support lower tax rates as they believe that lower tax rates will push the investments up and motivate people to work hard, thereby stimulating economic growth.

Macroeconomic Indicators

There are many key macroeconomic variables that have an impact on the operations and earnings of a firm. These include:

1. Gross domestic product (GDP)
2. Industrial growth rate
3. Exchange rate
4. Interest rates
5. Inflation
6. Balance of payments and forex reserves
7. Savings and investments
8. Government budget deficit/surplus
9. Borrowing and debt

All these factors shape the economy and the firm, being a component of the same system is also impacted by them.

GDP growth rate is the barometer of any economy and India has had a good track record of GDP growth in the new millennium. Since GDP represents the average growth rate of all sectors in the economy viz., agricultural, industrial and services sector; India's healthy GDP in recent times has positively impacted the firms and stock markets in the country.

Marketview 10.5 India's GDP

The past decade has seen India register tremendous growth in terms of GDP, industrial production, exports and other macroeconomic parameters. Its share in world GDP has also grown.

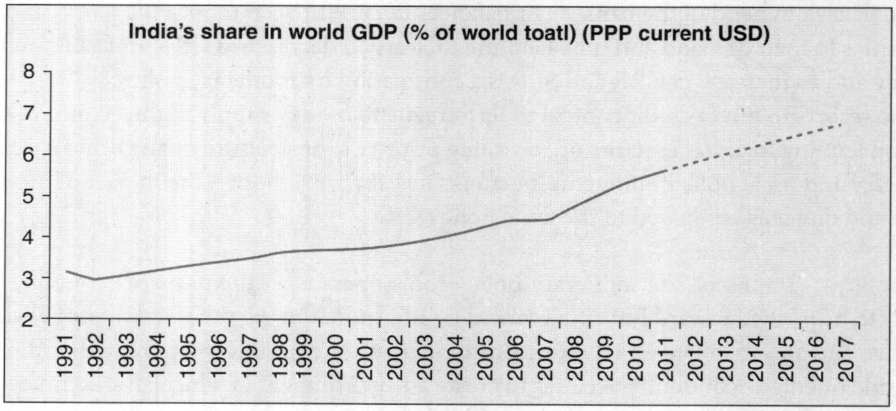

Source: IMF World Economic Outlook (April 2012), accessed on January 3, 2015.

For stock investors, listed companies are important. As the listed companies play a crucial role in the industrial sector, stock market analysts depend more on industrial growth rates to analyze stocks. They track the index of industrial production and use it to forecast prices. Stock markets in India swing quite significantly in response to the agricultural data and monsoon also. So the analysts keenly track the industrial, agricultural and monsoon related data to forecast the share prices.

Marketview 10.6 India's Macroeconomic Performance (Key Parameters)

Key parameters	2005–06	2011–12	Change
Real GDP (INR billion)[1]	32,542	52,220	60% higher
Real per capita GDP (INR)[1]	33,548	46,221	38% higher
Investment/GDP (%)[2]	35.8	37.6[**]	5% higher
Export (US $ bn)[1]	103	303	194% higher
General government gross debt (% GDP)[1]	77.4	64.9[**]	16% higher
Workers remittances (US $ bn)[2]	28.0[+]	63.7[++]	127% higher
Gross international reserves (US $ bn)[1]	151[#]	294[##]	94% higher
Foreign direct investment inflow (US $ bn)	9.1	46.8	414% higher
Foreign direct investment outflow (US $ bn)	6.1	25.8[**]	323% higher

Sources:

1. Reserve Bank of India data (as on March 2012), accessed on November 13, 2014.
2. IMF WEO Database April 2012, accessed on November 13, 2014.

[**] For FY 2010–11

[+] for calendar year 2006[++] for calendar year 2011

[#] As on March 31, 2006[##] As on March 30, 2012

Savings and investments rates in the economy are of great interest to analysts because ultimately the shares need to be bought and the money to buy shares would come from the savings only. Higher the savings and investment rates, the better it is for the markets.

Inflation is another key number that is tracked by the analysts because inflation seems to produce strong influence on industries. Some react positively while others seem to react negatively to inflation. On the whole,

Marketview 10.7 Savings and Investment Rates

As per the data published by IMF WEO in April 2012, India's savings and investment rates rank amongst the highest in the world, better than most other emerging economies.

Savings as % of GDP

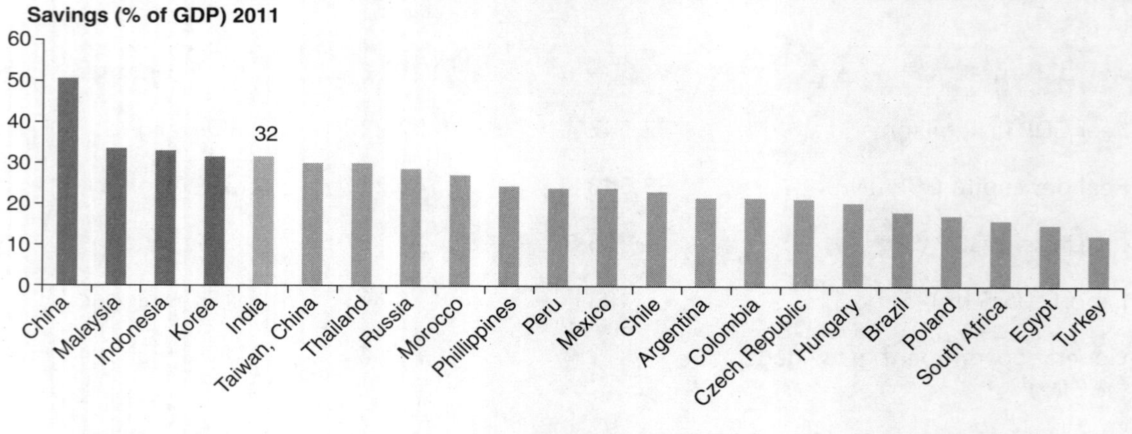

Source: IMF WEO, April 2012, accessed on January 7, 2015.

Gross Domestic Investment as % of GDP

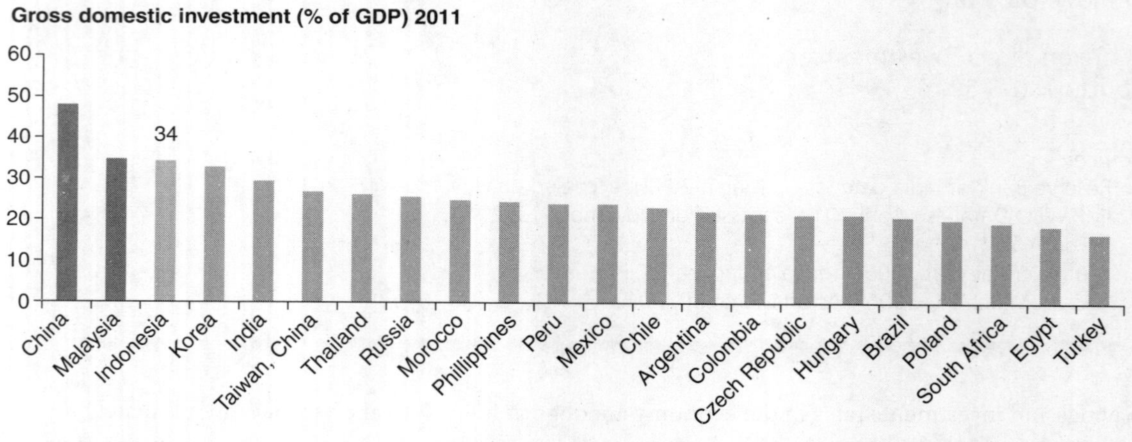

Source: IMF WEO, April 2012, accessed on January 7, 2015.

research has shown that not all inflation is bad. A mild level of inflation is actually found to be good for the stock markets. Money supply, budgetary deficit and interest rates influence the economy and firms directly as well as indirectly, as discussed above.

Exchange rate fluctuations affect imports and exports. Strengthening of the rupee vis-à-vis the dollar is good for importers and the concerned firms benefit from it. Weakening of the Rupee is good for the exporting firms. Therefore, analysts need to view the firms in the light of rupee-dollar movements as well.

With the opening up of the economy in 1991, India has experienced inflow of foreign investments, both in the form of FDI in firms and FII investments into the stock markets. Net FII inflows push the stock markets up. FDI impacts stock markets indirectly by providing capital to the domestic firms to expand their operations and increase their earnings.

Marketview 10.8 Surging FII Inflows

During the past 15 years, India has attracted a large amount of debt and equity investment from foreign institutional investors. It has emerged as one of the most favored market for FII investment over the years. Foreign institutional investors pumped in nearly $18 billion into India's $1.1 trillion stock market in 2013, an amount second only to Japan in Asia.

FII inflows in equity and debt

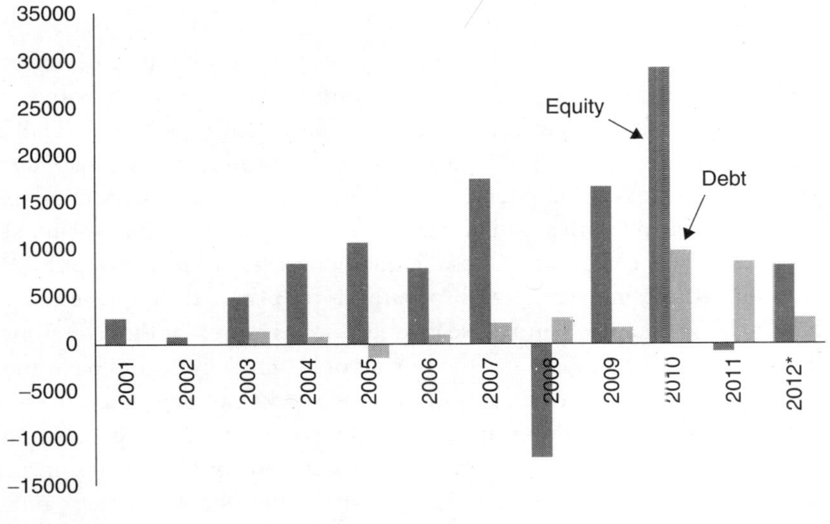

Figure in USD million* 2012 Data is up to 28 May 2012

Source: SEBI website, accessed on January 7, 2015.

Business Cycles

The key macroeconomic indicators discussed above fluctuate over a period of time, taking the economy through various good and bad spells. Despite the policy tools used by the governments, economies go through spells of high inflation, low growth, unemployment, huge deficit, etc. This happens because the economies pass through recurrent phases of contraction and expansion called business cycles (Figure 10.1).

Figure 10.1 The business cycle.

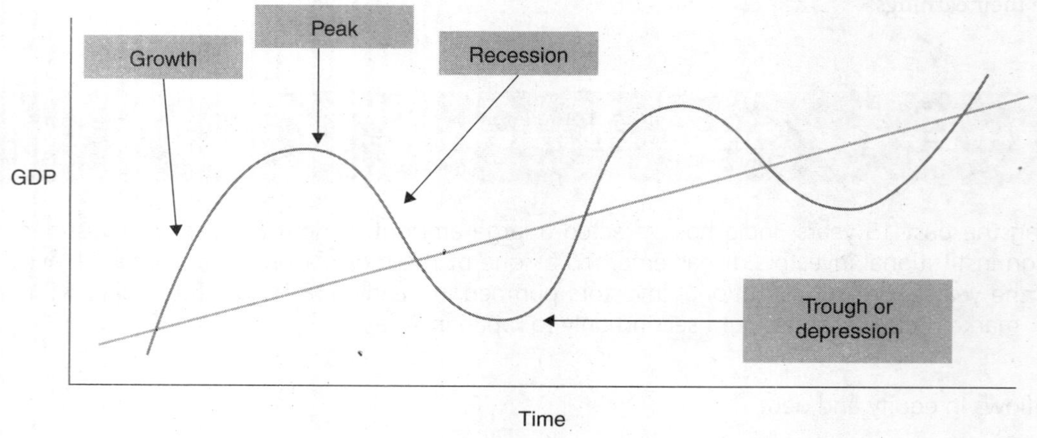

As the economy passes through subsequent peaks and troughs, performance of different industries can be expected to fluctuate. Some industries, called cyclical industries, are more sensitive to business cycles. These industries can be expected to outperform the others when recovery sets in and fall behind the others when recession sets in. Examples of cyclical industries are the producers of consumer durables such as automobiles and the producers of capital goods. Cyclical industries tend to do well in expansion but bear the brunt of slowdown. Other industries, called defensive industries, have little or no sensitivity to business cycles, i.e., to the state of the economy. These include pharmaceutical firms, public utilities and food producers and processors. These industries tend to outperform others during recession. We have already talked about systematic risk in Chapter 3 and these business cycles represent that component of the security risk. Fundamental analysts need to understand the impact of business cycle and have an ability to forecast them. Knowing whether an industry is cyclical or defensive, stocks can be chosen from the cyclical firms, when upswing is expected, because in boom time, these industries tend to outperform the others, causing their share prices to rise the most. These represent the high beta stocks. Conversely, if recession is likely to set in or prevail, analysts can choose defensive industries or low beta stocks, as these remain unaffected by economic conditions.

Obviously, as a fundamental analyst, one needs to develop skills and use tools to make accurate forecast about macroeconomic indicators and business cycles. It is not easy to forecast any of these indicators, but there are many models available at the disposal of the analyst. Let us now discuss few economic forecasting models.

Economic Forecasting Models

Analysts may look to develop forecasts of economic variables for short (up to 3 years), intermediate (up to 5 years) or long-term (beyond five years), depending on the investment horizon under consideration. However, in practice the forecasts are short-term only because the environment of investment is very dynamic and even if long-term forecasts are made, they need to be adjusted periodically to the changing situation. The fact is that a long-term is considered to comprise many short-terms. Thus, a long-term forecast is nothing but an outcome of a series of short-term estimates.

The task of forecasting is quite specialized and no analyst can be expected to undertake the exercise on his own, but an understanding of forecasting tools and techniques is essential for all fundamental analysts. Let us briefly review the main short-term (up to one year) forecasting techniques used for economic forecasting.

1. **Anticipatory Surveys:** The best place to begin forecasting is asking the experts and connected people in government and industry to express their views about the expected economic environment. Obviously, a lot of personal opinion might color the response and an analyst needs to decide whether the aggregate survey findings are accurate or do they grossly over or underestimate the likely future scenario. However, these surveys are easy to undertake and access. They provide a good beginning point in economic forecasting.
2. **Indicator or Barometric Approach:** All countries have some or the other lead indicator index that is considered to be a barometer of the economy. The indicator approach was pioneered by Wesley C. Mitchell, Arthur F. Burns and Geoffery H. Moore at national Bureau of Economic Research (NBER), USA. Nowadays many indicator based indices are published.

   Factors like Real M_2, consumer expectations, permits for new buildings, orders for plant and equipment, etc. are usually considered as key lead indicators. Similarly, lagging indicators include factors like outstanding commercial loans, duration of unemployment, changes in labor cost, ratio of inventories to sales, etc. The key coincident indicators are industrial production, sales, personal income, non-agricultural employes, etc.
3. **Econometric Model Building:** Econometrics applies mathematical solutions and statistical techniques to economic problems. It makes the user specify independent and dependent variables to spell the key relationships and is hence more precise than the techniques described above. However, econometric models, based on specification of simultaneous equations, are quite complex and most analysts may find them difficult to implement. In addition, vast amount of input data required for these models makes their use more challenging. However, these models are quite effective in giving us a blueprint of the economy on the basis of clearly spelt endogenous and exogenous variables.
4. **Opportunistic Model Building:** Opportunistic model building draws heavily upon the national accounting framework and it is perhaps the most widely used and very practical approach towards economic forecasting. To apply opportunistic model building, the forecaster has to begin with certain hypothesis regarding total demand/total income during the period for which the forecast is being made. Such hypothetical figures are based on assumptions about certain factors such as political environment, inflation, tax rates, interest rates, etc. Thereafter, he has to forecast GNP first by estimating the likely levels of the GNP components like net exports, consumption expenditures and gross private domestic investment. The forecaster is then required to independently arrive at a priori forecasts of GNP, to test the consistency of his forecast. The final estimates are arrived at on the basis of judgment and ingenuity

Marketview 10.9 India's Economic Indicators

Markets	Last	Previous	Average	Unit	Reference
Currency	61.4	61.94	33.16		10/31/14
Government bond 10Y	8.28	8.51	9.22	Percent	10/30/14
Stock market	27346.33	26630.51	6431.74	Index points	10/30/14
GDP	1876.8	1858.7	517.27	USD Billion	12/31/13
GDP annual growth rate	5.7	4.6	5.82	Percent	06/30/14
Gross fixed capital formation	5356.22	5037.1	3576.58	INR Billion	02/15/14
Unemployment rate	5.2	6.3	7.58	Percent	12/31/12
Inflation rate	6.46	7.73	9.35	Percent	09/15/14
Interest rate	8	8	6.66	Percent	09/30/14
Interbank rate	8.65	8.52	7.57	Percent	07/15/14
Money supply M1	21346.82	21474.15	4079.49	INR Billion	07/15/14
Money supply M2	21770.46	21524.56	7387.16	INR Billion	07/15/14
Money supply M3	98060.68	97538.48	15715.99	INR Billion	07/15/14
Foreign exchange reserves	313682	314118.5	178393.18	USD Million	10/17/14
Current account to GDP	−1.7	−4.7	−1.45	Percent	12/31/13
External debt	390048	345819	150725	USD Million	12/31/13
Foreign direct investment	2390	4753	997.7	USD Million	06/13/14

(Continued)

Continued

Markets	Last	Previous	Average	Unit	Reference
Business confidence	57.4	53.7	58.69		09/30/14
Industrial production	0.4	0.4	6.64	Percent	08/15/14
Bank lending rate	10.25	10.25	14.06	Percent	08/15/14

Source: http://www.tradingeconomics.com/india/indicators, accessed on December 9, 2014.

after adjusting for many circular effects. The whole process is quite complicated to be handled by a security analyst.

Despite the challenges in forecasting economic conditions, a fundamental analyst has to take into consideration economic data while making investment decision. If he is unable to develop the forecasts himself, there are a number of government publications available to help him in this regard. Economic information about India is available at the websites of Reserve Bank of India and MOSPI – Ministry of Statistics and Programme Implementation.

Industry Analysis

We discussed economy analysis in the preceding part of the chapter. Now we will discuss the 'I' of E-I-C indicators. The objective of industry analysis is to study various industries with a view to finding out their prospects. This is an important part of fundamental analysis because to identify a firm, we first need to identify the industry. Just as it is difficult for any industry to do well in troubled economy, it is impossible for a firm to do well in an ailing industry. So to pick a winner, we need to first identify a winning industry. Just as economic indicators are difficult to forecast with accuracy, it is not easy to estimate exactly the prospects of various industrial sectors but it is possible, through careful analysis, to determine the general health of each sector and direction it can be expected to take in the future.

From an analyst's viewpoint, industry analysis should enable him to:

1. Identify the relevant economic factors that have a direct bearing on different industrial sectors.
2. Estimate expected performance of various industrial sectors under a set of assumptions about important economic indicators.

While analyzing industries, analysts need to consider various key characteristics of the industry groups under the study. Few important characteristics are:

1. **Permanence:** What we mean by permanence here is whether the industry will continue to exist for a long time or just disappear in the short-term. In this era of rapidly evolving technology, replacement industry can come up at a rapid pace. Since there is no point in holding stock of an industry that is not going to be there, an analyst should assess the permanence of the industry he is studying.
2. **Historical Record of Sales and Earnings:** Sales and earnings are the two pillars that determine the success of any firm and its stock. Since an analyst needs to forecast future sales and earnings performance of the industry under the study, the best starting point is the past performance, a data which is readily available. Such analysis will also enable the analyst to determine growth rates, trends and average level of sales and earnings, which can help him in making informed forecasts about the future. The reason why many analysts are uncomfortable with new industries is the lack of sufficiently long track record of sales and earnings to help them judge the response of the industry in different economic conditions.
3. **Other Factors:** There are many inputs that go into industry analysis but three key ones may be noted here: labor conditions, competition and attitude of the government.

   Labor conditions, particularly, existence of unions, can be a serious issue in manufacturing industries. Many industries have faced fluctuating fortunes in the past due to labor issues.

Though we are studying industry as a whole, yet competition from new entrants should also be considered while assessing the fortunes of the existing players in the industry. This is important because entry of new participants can be a game changer for existing firms in terms of need to expand the operations, advertise more, lower the price and loss of advantage arising from economies of scale.

The attitude of the government can also impact the fortune of an industry. The government can boost an industry by giving tax sops, financial support, favorable legislation, restrictive legislation against foreign competitors, etc. Unfavorable attitude of the government toward an industry can create unnecessary friction and hamper the performance of the industry and ultimately impact its sales and earnings negatively.

Marketview 10.10 Labor Problems at Maruti; A Permanent Risk for Investors?

Since the turn of the new century, there have been at least four instances of labor problems at Maruti Suzuki India Ltd. which resulted in halt in production at its factories. The one in 2012 was particularly violent and was followed by a drop of 9% in the stock of Maruti.

Though Maruti's stock remained a firm favorite of the brokers as the company had performed exceedingly well in auto sales, yet the labor issues eroded its premium. For instance, the Maruti stock fell from trading at a 60% premium to the BSE Auto index earlier in 2012 to trading at a 40% premium to the sectoral index by the end of the year.

Declining premiums and increasing labor problems have dented the confidence of the investors in the stock as well.

Source: http://www.livemint.com/Money/BF1dLwJE88RbifylaYQyxM/Labour-problems-at-Maruti-a-permanent-risk-for-investors.html, accessed on December 28, 2014.

Thus, the key factors that need to be analyzed with respect to the industry are:

1. Permanence
2. Sales and earnings
3. Degree of competition
4. Labor conditions
5. Attitude of the government

Most of the above parameters can be analyzed by:

1. Analyzing industry life cycle stage of the industry under the study.
2. Studying the characteristics and structure of the industry under analysis.
3. By assessing the sensitivity of the industry under the study to business cycles.
4. Using Porter's model to evaluate the profit potential of the industry.

There are discussed in detail below.

Industry Life Cycle

Industries have been observed to go through four well-defined phases or stages as exhibited in Figure 10.2:

1. **Start up or Pioneering Phase:** During this phase, many new firms enter the industry to take advantage of high demand for product or to use new technology to their advantage. This stage is very chaotic in which

Figure 10.2 Industry life cycle stages.

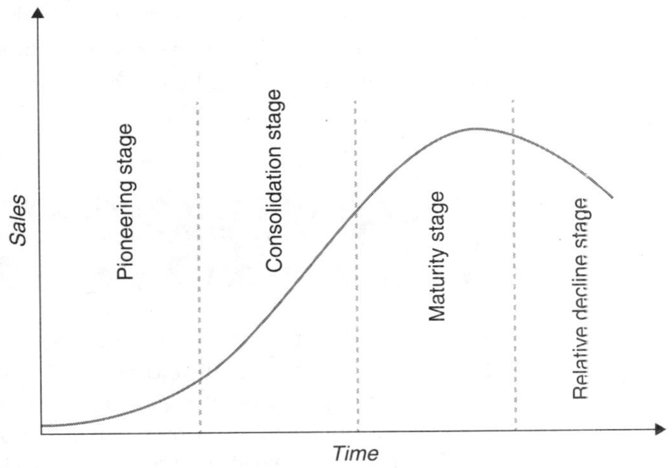

few players experience rapid growth while others fall out due to keen competition. It is difficult to predict sales and earning accurately at this stage.

2. **Consolidation Stage or Stable Growth Stage:** Once the chaotic, start-up stage is over and the product becomes established, things settle down and stabilize. Few of the surviving firms experience significant increase in sales and earnings and emerge as industry leaders. At this stage, it is easier to predict sales, earnings, market share, etc. The surviving firms stabilize and are more likely to closely follow the pattern of performance of the overall industry. At this stage, industry as a whole grows at a faster rate than the rest of the economy as product penetration and usage increase.
3. **Maturity Stage:** This stage begins as the industry is more or less fully developed and it settles down from above-average growth to a more sedate pace where it just tracks the general economy. By now, the product has reached its full potential for use and has become far more standardized. This is the phase where real price war begins as the participating firms are forced to compete on the basis of price. With the result, profit margins become narrower. The firms at this stage are sometimes characterized as cash cows, having stable cash flow but limited expansion potential.
4. **Relative Decline Stage:** This is a stage where industry might even start lagging the general economy. It can be expected to shrink due to product obsolescence, low-cost substitutes and technological innovations.

Implication of Life Cycle Stage for Investment

Most industries have been observed to go through the stages described above but they differ in the relative duration of each stage and the growth rates within each stage. As an analyst, it is difficult to define the stage at which industry is and the precise rate at which it will grow.

There is a general tendency to invest in high-growth industries but then again it is likely that the growth potential is already reflected in the price of the share, making it difficult to make money from the knowledge that the chosen industry is high-growth industry. Peter Lynch, a famous portfolio manager, has an investment strategy of investing in low-growth industries. So there really are no rules. However, the ultimate decrease in growth, as shown by the life cycle stage, has some implications for investors. Investors should pay adequate attention to the industry in stock selection process and be careful in choosing start-up stocks, which appeal speculators a lot. Once they identify the growth stage, it is smart to increase ones holdings and decrease them during the maturity stage. Signals of decline in the industry should be taken to mean that it is time to disinvest and move to some other industry.

Marketview 10.11 Concept of Sunrise and Sunset Industries

Analysts often talk about stocks/companies in the context of their belonging to sunrise or sunset industries. In terms of investment, a sunrise industry is a developing or growing industry that is believed to have the potential to become a large and dominant sector. A sunrise industry typically exhibits fast-paced growth and offers many opportunities to the constituent firms to grow. Since the firms belonging to sunrise industries show a lot of promise, investors briskly move in to take advantageous positions in their stock, mainly to benefit from rise in the price of the stock in the future. A very good example of sunrise industry is the technology industry in the 1990s. Many investors seemed to understand the huge potential of the sector and were keen to subscribe to the IPOs of the numerous new companies that had mushroomed in the sector. People who had invested in technology stock at that time have experienced tremendous growth in their stock portfolios as the industry has delivered on the promise it showed when it was new.

Sunrise industries also represent a different or a new way of approaching existing problems. For instance, group of firms that generated alternative energy by harnessing wind and solar power represented sunrise industry in the 2000s, replacing coal and other non-renewable sources of energy that were more prevalent at that time.

On the other hand, a sunset industry is an industry that is now on a decline due to changing market conditions, the appearance of new technology and change in taste and/or interest amongst the customers. The term sunset also indicates an industry that was once forceful and growing rapidly. The fact is that as newer technology and ideas come up, a sunrise industry experiences sluggish growth, goes into a decline and becomes a sunset industry.

Sources: http://www.businessdictionary.com/definition/sunset-industry.html#ixzz3Hj3D0GHq and http://www.wisegeek.com/what-is-a-sunrise-industry.htm, accessed on December 1, 2014.

Structure and Characteristics of an Industry

Each Industry is unique and before ear-marking any industry for investment, analysts should study the distinct features and characteristics of the industry under consideration in terms of the number of firms in the industry, government policies, product homogeneity or differentiation, pricing and cost challenges, competition from the entry of new firms, availability of substitutes, determinants and cyclicality of demand, labor productivity, profitability, innovation, research and development, and the ability to make transition to newer technologies. Obviously, the more nimble the industry in adapting to changes, the less cumbersome its structure and the more broad-based the demand, the better its prospects for growth.

Sensitivity of the Industry to Business Cycles

We have already discussed business cycles in the preceding section of this chapter. The sensitivity of a firm to business cycles is reflected in its earnings which in turn is determined by three factors:

1. **Sensitivity of Sales to Business Cycles:** Certain products like food, drugs, personal care items and other necessities show little sensitivity to the business cycle. So the industries selling these and similar products do not show massive fall with recession. Same is the case with products like cigarettes, where the level of income is not a determinant of demand. On the other hand, sales of firms in the industries like movies, automobiles, machine tools, steel, transportation, etc. are highly sensitive to business cycles. Thus, industries should be chosen for investment keeping in mind their sensitivities to business cycles and the forecast regarding the economic conditions expected to prevail during the investment period.
2. **Operating Leverage:** Operating leverage is a measure of changes in a firm's profits to changes in sales. It depends on the split between fixed and variable costs. We know that fixed costs remain

constant irrespective of the quantity produced and sold for a given installed capacity. Variable cost changes with the level of output within the installed capacity levels. Firms that have higher proportion of variable costs are less sensitive to business cycles because they can control costs by lowering production when sales are declining. However, firms with high proportion of fixed cost have to face swings in profit margins and sales in response to changes in economic environment because they will continue to incur the fixed costs irrespective of the level of their sales. Such firms are said to have high degree of operating leverage and smallest swings in economic condition can have large impact on their profitability.

An analyst should, thus, find out the cost composition of the firms in the industry to understand the sensitivity of the industry to business cycle.

3. **Financial Leverage:** Financial leverage is a measure of the sensitivity of a firm's profit to the level of debt in its capital structure. This is because whatever the level of sales interest has to be paid mandatorily on the borrowings, causing profits to be erratic in response to the fluctuations in sales. Thus, higher the leverage (debt), the greater the sensitivity of a firm to business cycles.

Hence, capital structure is another key factor that analysts need to understand in order to identify the right industries to invest in, given the economic condition expected to prevail during the investment period under consideration.

The relationship between business cycle and industry analysis is viewed by many analysts in terms of sector rotation. The idea is very simple but logical. Sector rotation is simply shifting the portfolio constituents in favor of industries or sectors that are expected to outperform in the forecasted economic conditions.

Here, the analysts try to identify industries that are expected to fare better during high inflation and interest rate where basic commodities are going through price pressures. In such a time, investment in industries engaged in mining or processing minerals or crude might be a good decision. Similarly, pharma companies, food processing industries and other industries such as basic necessities will be a good portfolio choice during recessionary phase as they are less sensitive to business cycles. Likewise, financial firms can be a good bet towards the end of recession. As the recovery is about to set in, capital goods and construction equipment manufactures' stock might be a good buy because at this stage where economy is on the verge of recovery, investment in these goods increase. When the economy is expanding and income is rising, the cyclical industries selling consumer durables, luxury goods, etc. are likely to emerge as winning stocks.

However, this theoretical possibility is difficult to apply in practice as making accurate forecasts about economic conditions expected to prevail at a given point in time is quite difficult.

Porter's Model to Evaluate Profit Potential of a Firm

As we have seen, competitive forces play a key role in the movement of an industry through various life cycle stages. Each life cycle stage has an investment implication; therefore, an analyst needs to understand the competitive forces that impact the life-cycle stages. Here we will look at the five-factor model given by Michael Porter ([1] and [2]).

---

[1] Michael Porter, *Competitive Advantage: Creating and Sustaining Superior Performance*, New York: Free Press, 1985.
[2] Michael E. Porter, *Competitive Strategy: Techniques for Analyzing Industries and Competition*, The Free Press, 1980.

Porter argued that the profit potential of an industry is dependent on five determinants of competition (Figure 10.3).

Figure 10.3 Porter's model.

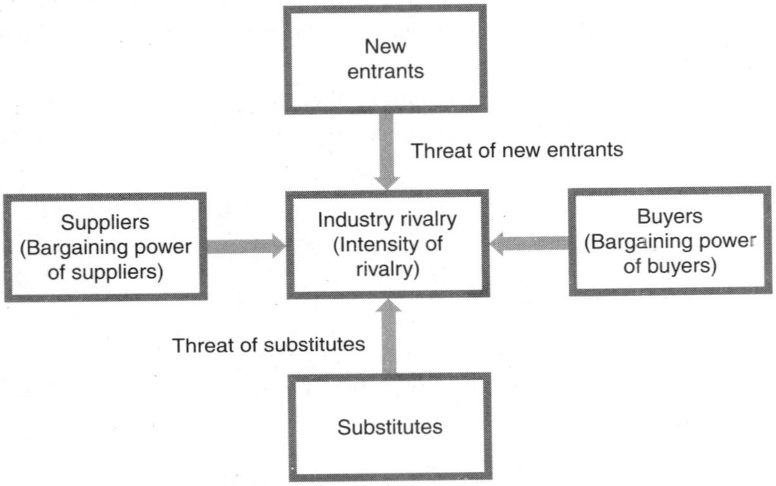

Porter's 5 forces

1. **Threat of New Entrants:** New entrants in the existing industry are likely to put pressure on sales of existing firms, push their cost and bring down prices thereby pushing the earnings and profits down. The industries that have barriers to the entry of new firms may face lower threat from new entrants and the pressure that they may put on the profitability of the existing firms. Barriers could be in the form of high initial capital investment, economies of scale for existing firms, customer loyalty, control over distribution channels, restrictive government policies, benefit of product differentiation and proprietary experience curve.
2. **Rivalry between Existing Competitors (Industry Rivalry):** Rivalry between existing firms in the industry is just as likely to erode the profit potential as the entry of new firms. Industries where there are large number of participating firms selling almost homogeneous product, face issues related to competition based on price, costs, quality, service, etc. With so many firms vying for limited market share, counter moves to competitors' strategies dampen the average profitability of the industry as a whole.
3. **Threat of Substitute Products:** Substitute products pose competitive threats from outside the industry group and corrode its average profit potential. The threat of substitutes that can be used as replacement is the greatest when the price-performance advantage offered by the substitute is attractive and consumers are not required to incur cost or effort in switching to the substitute. The availability of substitutes, thus, imposes a ceiling on the performance of the firm.

4. **Bargaining Power of the Buyers:** Buyers present a competitive force and bargain as a whole to ask for price cut, better quality, service or warranty. This can depress profitability of the industry as a whole. The bargaining power of buyers is more when they purchase large amount of a firm's product. They can switch to other suppliers easily and exploit the opportunity of backward integration.
5. **Bargaining Power of Suppliers:** Profit potential of an industry can be severely impacted by the suppliers who have strong bargaining power. Their bargaining power can stem from monopolistic control over the supply of inputs, lack of substitutes, lack of opportunity for backward integration, possibility of suppliers to go ahead with forward integration and high cost of delays or shortages. Prime example of this kind of bargaining is in the labor market where labor unions use collective bargaining power to pressurize firms into paying higher wages.

On the whole, fundamental analysis in the context of economy related and industry related analysis is a very broad, comprehensive and challenging task. It requires the analyst to possess the right skills, knowledge and attitude.

SUMMARY

☑ The process of determination of intrinsic value of a share to ascertain its prospects is called fundamental analysis.

☑ Fundamental analysis is termed as E-I-C analysis, i.e., economy, industry and company analysis.

☑ Changes in global economy like fluctuations in dollar rate, economic sanctions, bilateral agreements, trade barriers, etc. influence the performance of many firms, causing their earnings to fluctuate.

☑ Firms operating in any country are influenced directly by the macroeconomic policies pursued by the government of that country.

☑ The macroeconomic policies fall in two broad classes: supply-side polices and demand-side policies. Two demand-side policies that have always been the focus of attention are fiscal and monetary policies.

☑ There are many key macroeconomic variables that have an impact on the operations and earnings of a firm like gross domestic product, industrial growth rate, exchange rate, interest rates and inflation.

☑ Economies pass through recurrent phases of contraction and expansion called business cycles.

☑ Fundamental analysts need to understand the impact of business cycle and have an ability to forecast them.

☑ Cyclical industries are more sensitive to business cycles. These industries can be expected to outperform the others when recovery sets in and fall behind the others when recession sets in.

☑ Defensive industries have little or no sensitivity to business cycles, i.e., to the state of the economy.

- ☑ A fundamental analyst needs to develop skills and use tools to make accurate forecast about macroeconomic indicators and business cycles.
- ☑ Analysts may look to develop forecasts of economic variables for short, intermediate or long-term, depending on the investment horizon under consideration.
- ☑ The main short-term forecasting techniques used for economic forecasting are: anticipatory surveys, indicator or barometric approach, econometric model building and opportunistic model building.
- ☑ From an analyst's viewpoint, industry analysis enables him to identify the relevant economic factors that have a direct bearing on different industrial sectors and expected performance of various industrial sectors under a set of assumptions about important economic indicators.
- ☑ The key factors that need to be analyzed with respect to the industry are: permanence, sales and earnings, degree of competition, labor conditions and attitude of the government.
- ☑ According to Porter, the profit potential of an industry is dependent on five determinants of competition: threat of new entrants, rivalry between existing firms, pressure from substitute products, bargaining power of buyers and bargaining power of sellers.

KEY WORDS

CONCEPT QUESTIONS

1. Discuss in detail how the recent developments in the global economy can be expected to have an impact on the earnings performance of the healthcare sector in India.
2. Write an analytical note on the macroeconomic performance of the Indian economy since the global financial crisis of 2008.
3. Evaluate the profit potential of ICICI bank using the Porter's model.

4. Assess the impact of the political environment of a country on the performance of companies in light of the changes in the political environment of India in the year 2014.

5. Discuss the impact of business cycles on the stock prices of firms listed on the stock market.

6. Critically assess the efficacy of various forecasting models at the disposal of an analyst.

7. Fundamental analysis is a comprehensive approach to security analysis. Discuss.

8. How do industry life cycle stages impact the performance of a firm and its share price? Explain with the help of aviation industry in India.

9. Briefly enumerate the factors that an analyst needs to study to determine the characteristics of an industry.

10. What are the most critical variables one needs to track to forecast the outlook for the real estate sector in India?

CASELET

The sectoral report of Indian automobile industry available at http://www.ibef.org/ is given below. The industry as a whole seems to be doing very well. Analyze the industry using porter's model.

The Indian automobile sector is one of India's most vibrant industries. The industry accounts for 22% of the country's manufacturing gross domestic product (GDP). It comprises passenger cars, two-wheelers, three-wheelers and commercial vehicles and is currently the seventh-largest in the world with an average annual production of 17.5 million vehicles, of which 2.3 million are exported. The Indian auto market has the potential to dominate the global auto industry, provided a conducive environment is created for potential innovators to come up with new pilot projects.

The next few years are projected to show solid but cautious growth due to improved affordability, rising incomes and untapped markets. All these open up an opportunity for the automobile manufactures in India. In addition, with the government's backing and a special focus on exports of small cars, multi-utility vehicles (MUVs), two and three-wheelers and auto components, the automotive sector's contribution to the GDP is expected to double, reaching a turnover of US$ 145 billion in 2016, according to the Automotive Mission Plan (AMP) 2006–2016.

The Indian government encourages foreign investment in the automobile sector and allows 100% FDI under the automatic route. It is a fully delicensed industry and free imports of automotive components are allowed. Moreover, the government has not laid down any minimum investment criteria for the automobile industry and has formulated the Automotive Mission Plan for the period 2006–2016 which aims to accelerate and sustain growth in this sector. The plan also aims to double the contribution of the automotive sector to the country's GDP by taking its turnover to US$ 145 billion and providing additional employment to 25 million people by 2016.

Faster economic growth coupled with the government's policies is likely to drive volumes and revive the Indian automobile sector. A fall in interest rates and stable fuel prices are expected to create an environment conducive for growth in this industry. Many foreign companies have also started to show their presence in India leading to a very competitive automobile market in the country, which augurs well for the sector's growth.

It has been predicted by IHS Automotive, a global market information provider that India will become the third largest automotive market in the world by 2016, ahead of Japan, Germany and Brazil, riding on its domestic automotive sales.

Source: http://www.ibef.org/industry/india-automobiles.aspx, accessed on December 16, 2014.

Micro Analysis of a Stock: Company Analysis

11

CHAPTER OBJECTIVES

- ❒ Understanding the importance of company analysis as a part of fundamental analysis
- ❒ Distinguishing between the qualitative and quantitative factors impacting the performance of a company
- ❒ Studying the tools for analysis of financial statements
- ❒ Analyzing key equity-related metrics like ROE, EPS and DPS
- ❒ Applying analytical tools to assess the performance of the firms

The ultimate aim of fundamental analysis is to identify a particular stock or a few stocks to invest in. The decision could also be expanded to decide whether to continue to hold certain stocks or sell them, depending on their future prospects.

We have already discussed the *E* and *I* or *E-I-C* framework for fundamental analysis and we now need to understand, the real action, i.e., the company analysis. The aim of company analysis is to determine the intrinsic value of shares, based on the forecast of the future earnings of the equity shares and comparing the same with the current market price to decide whether the security is rightly or under or overpriced (intrinsic value being the right price). Estimation of intrinsic value requires forecast of future stream of earnings based on the future performance. Forecasting future performance requires a deep understanding of the strategy of the firm, signals from the past performance, quality of earnings, information contained in financial statements, quality of management, corporate governance and other quantitative and qualitative aspects that can have bearing on the future performance of the firm. We have already discussed various valuation techniques in detail in Chapter 9.

In our subsequent discussion, we will focus on analysis of information available from the internal and external sources that can enable analysts to form correct expectations about the future prospects of a firm and take a buy, hold or sell call on its equity.

Analysis of available information goes beyond plain number crunching and requires superior judgment and intuition to assess the underlying relationships more clearly and identify more complex, less apparent interplay of various types of information and inputs available in the environment.

Fundamental analysis at this stage refers to the task of subjecting the available data to microscopic scrutiny by rearranging, sifting and sorting it. The internal and external information referred to above comes from various sources. Internal information is the accounting data published by the company, press releases by the company, the statements of the authorized personnel and at times, private statements made by the company officials.

External information is the information generated independently outside the company. It plays the role of supplementing the internal information by overcoming any bias in the company-generated data.

Qualitative and Quantitative Factors for Company Analysis

The ultimate objective of the economy and industry analysis is to buy shares of a particular company in the industry identified for investment. By doing so an investor is actually buying a stake in the company he chooses. Hence, the future of the company and its business health is important for the investors. To understand the strength and the health of a company, investors need to undertake company analysis, which basically means analyzing the business of the company. The plethora of data and information available about companies, particularly in the modern era of World Wide Web, is mind-boggling and unmanageable. The first task while undertaking company analysis is to develop a sense of proportion and identify the key factors for the study out of the unlimited degree of detail that is available. Study of nonessentials should be avoided. Analysts need to focus only on certain key parameters. In many places in the financial literature, the key factors to be analyzed have been classified into two broad groups, the quantitative and the qualitative factors.

Qualitative factors are related to the matters that may require subjective judgment of investors like the relative position of the company in the industry, nature of the business, the business model, company's research and development; its physical, geographical and operating characteristics, labor-management relations, corporate governance, the quality, expertise and character of the management and the outlook of the analysts for the firm, industry and for the business as a whole.

On the other hand, quantitative analysis focuses on measurable rubrics like earnings, sales, assets, liabilities, capitalization, dividends, operating statistics, production efficiency, price-to-earnings ratios and other numerical factors that are more easily obtainable, quantifiable and more amenable for reaching unambiguous and explicit conclusions.

Thus, company analysis is a study of the quantitative and the qualitative aspects of a firm with a view to ascertaining its well being in terms of its products, future projects, strategy, financial performance, the effectiveness of its management and a host of other factors as exhibited in Figure 11.1. Thus, company analysis goes far beyond the exercise of analysis of financial statements.

Qualitative analysis, in conjunction with the time-tested traditional quantitative appraisal of a company, enables the analysts and investors to develop a more comprehensive understanding of the prospects of a company. We will analyze both quantitative and qualitative factors that have a bearing on the profitability and performance of a firm.

Qualitative Analysis of Firms

Qualitative factors, while not measurable in terms of numbers, are just as important as the quantifiable statistics in assessing the value of a company from the point of view of investing in its shares. Therefore, though factors like bank recognition, reputation of management, quality of personnel and so on may not necessarily be measureable in money terms but are still tremendously significant in evaluating whether one is making a right investment decision by investing in the shares of that company. A deep knowledge of the less tangible and measurable characteristics of a company can prevent potential loss by investing in a firm that may have been performing well

Figure 11.1 Qualitative and quantitative factors in company analysis.

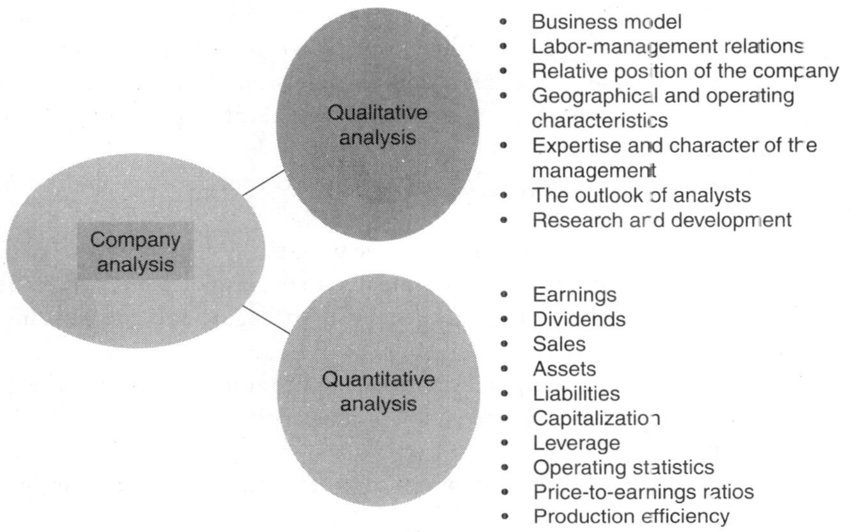

in the recent past but has a directionless and ineffective management or a questionable business model. Information for analyzing qualitative aspects of a company can be obtained from sources such as company websites, annual reports, shareholder conference calls, media reports and business publications.

Let us discuss some of the important qualitative factors that have vital impact on the value of a firm.

Strategy analysis

The aim of strategy analysis is to identify the drivers of profit potential of a firm. Since fundamental analysis is all about determining the value of a share based on its expected earnings, strategy of a firm plays a key role in assessing the investment attractiveness of a firm. Strategy of a firm determines its direction and profit potential. The profit potential of a firm is directly linked with its industry choice, i.e., the industry it is a part of. Further, the profitability of a firm is directly linked with its competitive strategy, a blueprint of how it deals with the competing firms and its corporate strategy, a plan of how it aligns its diverse business portfolios to make a synergistic whole. Both, competitive and corporate strategies have significant impact on a firm's ability to grow and sustain the growth momentum. An analyst should make a careful study of the corporate and competitive strategy of a firm to determine whether the conclusions of financial analysis actually reflect sustainable business realities. In this context, both corporate and competitive strategies, discussed below, should be evaluated.

1. **Corporate Strategy:** It is concerned with value creation through management of diverse businesses and challenges. Here the capability of the management is a key factor. While analyzing an individual business in a multi-business conglomerate, it is essential to assess not only the profit potential of that business but also the economic perils and advantages of managing different businesses under one umbrella. There are examples of some very successful companies that have managed diverse businesses effectively to create value like Reliance Industries, Wadia Group, Larsen and Toubro, Mahindra and Mahindra, Tata Sons and

so on. At the same time, there is the case of UB group that was taken to unprecedented heights by Vijay Mallya before the entire group became unstable due to Mallya's ill-fated entry into aviation in 2005 and its subsequent debacle.

Multi-business firms can create corporate value through savings in business interaction of its individual business with interrelated activities. Whether a multi-business unit offers more value as a whole than a simple collection of focused firms depends on certain factors that can impact value creation in this context. The key factors may be enumerated as:

(a) The divison of its decision-making rights between the corporate office and business units and its impact on the economies of scope.
(b) Impact of performance measurement and incentive payment system on agency cost.
(c) Savings in transaction costs inside a firm as compared to the cost of using market mechanism.
(d) Capability and proficiency of the top management in managing and coordinating diverse business synergistically.
(e) Existence of factors that have the potential to create economies of scope. These factors could be organizational processes, structures, brand equity, proprietary know-how or product, limited distribution channels and so on.
(f) Imperfections in the labor, product or financial markets in the operating environment that can offer scope for creating value.
(g) The extent of fit between the resources and the profile of the diverse businesses of the firm.
(h) Goal congruence, specialist managers and the right degree of decentralization that fosters realization of economies of scope.

2. **Competitive Strategy:** A firm's relative position within its industry is the key determinant of a firm's profitability vis-à-vis the industry average. A firm can ensure above average profitability in the long run through sustainable competitive advantage. Competitive strategy of a firm plays a key role in helping a firm take up a leadership role in its industry. According to Michael Porter, a firm can gain and sustain competitive advantage through cost leadership and product differentiation which may be described as:
(a) Cost leadership is about using economies of scale, R&D, etc. to reduce costs to gain competitive advantage. For example, Reliance Industries pursues a cost-leadership strategy in petro-chemicals industry. To gain cost leadership, a firm has to try to become the lowest cost producer of the product in its industry. Cost leadership depends on a variety of factors and is related to the structure of the industry. The factors that need to be considered by a firm to gain cost advantage include the pursuit of economies of scale, proprietary know-how, privileged access to raw materials, better access to distribution channels and other factors. A firm that has been successful in achieving and sustaining overall cost leadership can be an above average performer in its industry, provided it is able to command prices for its products at or near the industry average.
(b) A firm pursuing differentiation strategy for competitive advantage needs to create a product or identify an attribute that is unique in its industry and has some dimensions that would be valued by the buyers, increasing their willingness to pay more for it. For example, during the first decade of the new century, Jet Airways was able to create a differentiation strategy for itself and was successful in creating a large group of loyal fliers who preferred to travel with Jet only, despite its premium pricing.

The two basic types of competitive strategies described above, when combined with the scope of activities for which a firm seeks to achieve either of these advantages, lead to three generic leadership strategies: cost leadership, differentiation, and focus. The two variants of the focus strategy are cost focus and differentiation focus. A firm choosing to pursue a focus strategy identifies a segment or group of segments in the industry and customizes its strategy to serve that group only. If it chooses cost focus, then the firm seeks a cost advantage in its chosen segment and if it chooses differentiation focus, then the firm seeks differentiation in its selected segment. Porter's generic strategies are exhibited in Figure 11.2[1].

Figure 11.2 Porter's generic strategies.

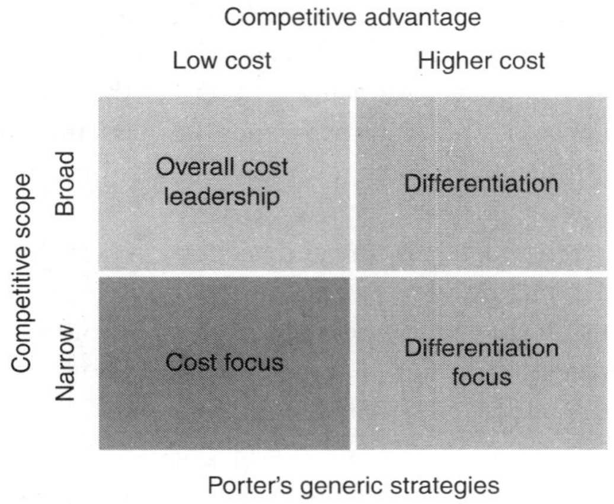

Business model of the firm

Business model refers to the way a firm operates, i.e., its mode of revenue generation, level of expenses, the leanness of the organizational structure, the strength of its sales and marketing efforts, etc. Understanding the business model of a firm can enable the analyst to predict, with fair accuracy, the future prospects of that firm.

Analysis of business model answers the most fundamental question: what exactly does the company do or how does it make money? Business models may be simple or complex. Whether simple or complicated, a business model basically describes the company's operations, expenses, structures, revenue generation methods and sales and marketing efforts. These details are available in the public domain and can be found on company website and annual reports. For example, knowing that Godrej group is doing well is not enough for an investor. He has to know more about the specific units and their business models. If he is interested in Godrej Properties, the real estate arm of the Godrej group, then he has to know that in 2010 it tweaked its business model of developing properties for outright sale to developing projects that it will own, manage and lease. This can have long-run impact on the performance of the company. Similarly, Reliance group is doing well as a whole but Reliance Retail, with its business model which created a large base of stores, is struggling.

Unless they understand a company's business model, the analysts should not contemplate investing in it because failure to understand business models implies failure to identify drivers of the future growth and revenue generation. Investing on such shaky grounds can make them vulnerable to potential losses.

---

[1] Michael E. Porter, *Competitive Advantage*, The Free Press, New York, 1985, 11–15.

Corporate governance

Corporate governance has come to occupy a central place in the assessment of a firm by equity analysts, investors and regulators. In simple terms, corporate governance refers to the set of rules, processes or laws that guide how businesses are operated, regulated, monitored and controlled. It is a broad term and includes both the internal parameters defined by the company charter and its bylaws, and the external parameters laid down by the regulators, consumer groups and other public forums.

In formal terms, corporate governance refers to a framework of policies within an organization that describes and prescribes the relationships and responsibilities between management, directors and stakeholders.

Whether the parameters are internal or external or both, the basic idea of corporate governance is to define a structure that ensures that the profit-seeking firm adheres to certain accepted ethical standards and best practices.

Corporate governance or good corporate governance determines the effectiveness of systems and practices put in place by a firm to ensure accountability, transparency, fairness and protection of all stakeholders. In general, good corporate governance can help an organization achieve objectives like:

1. creating organizational culture that fosters secure and healthy operating environment
2. motivating performance and attracting talent
3. developing effective strategies for the achievement of stakeholders' objectives
4. enhancing the company's reputation
5. protecting company from being exploited by self-serving personnel

Marketview 11.1 Corporate Governance Issues at Maruti Suzuki

Suzuki Motor Corporation (SMC) had come up with a proposal to set up a wholly owned subsidiary in India that seemed to adversely affect the interests of the minority shareholders of its existing partly owned subsidiary, Maruti Suzuki India Ltd. Markets and all classes of investors reacted quite adversely to the proposal, causing SMC to water it down and seek the consent of the minority shareholders of Maruti in accordance with the provisions of Section 188 of the new Companies Act. It also issued several clarifications regarding the funding and transfer of the plant to Maruti.

This entire drama at SMC has raised certain corporate governance issues for the company, namely:

1. What is the need for a wholly owned subsidiary in India when there is a successfully running partly owned subsidiary in the country? In fact, Maruti's royalty payment to SMC last year was more than SMC's net profit from its business in Japan. Further, creation of a separate wholly owned subsidiary when a partly owned one already exists can lead to a conflict of interest.
2. Maruti has about ₹7,500 crore of free cash lying unused in its balance-sheet, earning approximately half of what the firm earns as return on its capital employed (ROCE). SMC has not talked about these funds at all.
3. Many transfer pricing issues in transactions between the wholly owned subsidiary and the parent are expected to come up because Maruti will be procuring the cars produced by the new plant at a certain cost. Maruti's minority shareholders are worried that in due course of time, their company's role will become limited to being a marketing unit for selling cars produced by the new subsidiary.

Source: http://www.thehindu.com/opinion/editorial/issues-of-corporate-governance/article5806315.ece, accessed on December 29, 2014.

The corporate governance initiatives in India have been undertaken by the Ministry of Corporate Affairs (MCA) and the Securities and Exchange Board of India (SEBI). The first regulatory framework related to corporate governance, enshrined as Clause 49 of the Listing Agreement for listed companies in India, was put in place by the SEBI in February 2000 on the basis of the recommendations of Kumarmangalam Birla Committee Report. SEBI maintains the standards of corporate governance in companies in India through the Securities Contracts (Regulation) Act, 1956; Securities and Exchange Board of India Act, 1992; and Depositories Act, 1996. In the recent past, many high profile scams involving abuse of corporate power like the Satyam scam, NSEL scam, DLF issues and so on have brought corporate governance framework in India under intense scrutiny. Recently, SEBI has finalized stricter corporate governance norms for listed companies including stringent disclosures and protection of investor rights, particularly equitable treatment for minority and foreign shareholders.

Good corporate governance is ensured through inducting independent directors on the board of directors, making sure that the accounting information going out of the firm is accurate and prepared on the basis of consistent accounting standards. The role of independent board of directors is so important that SEBI has made it compulsory for the listed companies to have 50% independent directors on the board if the chairman is an executive member or at least one-third independent directors if the chairman is a non-executive member. All listed companies are required to give information about independent directors in their annual reports.

Analysts and investors looking to study the corporate governance structure of a firm should look at a few key areas including stakeholder rights, structure of the board of directors, takeover defenses, financial and information transparency.

Quality of management

Analysts are divided in their view on evaluation of management in a qualitative way to assess a firm. Some say that the quality of management is already reflected in the sales and earnings performance of the company. However, many management experts believe that year on year performance is one thing but the vision of management and its quality are key in preparing the company for future and shaping its profitability. It has been proven, time and again that quality of management is important in ensuring continued success of a firm. The case of Infosys is a prime example of how management quality and leadership troubles have taken a revered company to a place where it is in news for all the wrong reasons.

Marketview 11.2 Management Issues at Infosys

Since its foundation in 1981, Infosys and its founder Nagavara Ramarao Narayana Murthy (there were six other engineers as well on the founding team) have been applauded for everything that has been achieved by the company. The company's business model to deliver excellence, its leadership and its commitment to ensure better corporate governance have been widely appreciated and cited as an example to follow for upcoming businesses.

Infosys is credited with many firsts in Indian corporate history:

1. First Indian company to offer stock options to employees.
2. First Indian company to list on the Nasdaq.
3. First in India to report quarterly financials, issue guidance against insider trading, introduce the concept of a lead independent director and have directors assessed by peers.

But times have changed now. India's once iconic company has run into deep trouble, mostly internal to it. It has lost key leaders, as many senior executives have quit. This has created a crisis of leadership and client relationship for the company. The biggest issue is that of leadership succession.

Two most important stakeholders in Infosys – clients and employees—have responded adversely to the evolving management crisis at the company. The number of active clients and customers has increased at a very slow pace and at the same time, the attrition rate has risen to 18.7%, the highest among large software companies.

Since his return, N R Narayana Murthy has appeared to focus on operational issues only and the long term vision seems to be missing.

Sources: http://businesstoday.intoday.in/story/infosys-woes-profit-revenue-growth/1/191782.html. http://articles.economictimes.indiatimes.com/2014-04-15/news/49155640_1_n-r-narayana-murthy-clients-revenue-growth-guidance, accessed on November 25, 2014.

Analysts and investors should evaluate the management of a company because even the best business models can fail if the top management is unable to execute the plan properly. The challenge is to find relevant information. Most publicly available information, particular on the company website, does not reveal much. The few ways in which investors and analysts can try to evaluate the quality of management are:

1. **Annual Reports:** Annual reports usually begin with a section titled Management discussion and analysis. It is essentially a detailed commentary about management's outlook in terms of business model, strategic alliances, financial performance, regulatory challenges and key disputes and their settlement. Though it is usually a fancy presentation or a very routine one, some worthwhile information can emerge if one sits down to study the annual reports of the past few years.

   For example, the management discussion and analysis section of Jet Airways (India) Limited Annual Report 2013 covers the following information:
   - Industry Structure and Development
   - Analysis of Operational Performance Fiscal 2013 compared to Fiscal 2012
   - Initiatives
   - Outlook/Restructuring Measures
   - Internal Control Systems
   - Opportunities, Risks, Concerns and Threats

   The contents given under the heads, Outlook/Restructuring Measures and Opportunities, Risks, Concerns and Threats are reproduced in the exhibit 1.

   As stated above, the information has little analytical value as far as evaluation of quality of management is concerned.
2. **Management Ownership of Company's Stock:** If the members of top management are also the company's shareholders, it should be taken as a positive sign. Investors can confidently assume that if a majority of management's wealth is in the company's stock, they will do the right thing.

   Keeping a track of the changes in management's stockholding is also important for analysts. If the management has been selling its stock (information is available with the stock exchange on which the company is listed), then it could be an indication of troubled times for the company in the future. In such a situation, the investors would be wise not to invest in the company or pull out their stake, if already invested.

In evaluating the quality of management, analysts should try to determine the ability of the management to integrate Strategic Business Units (SBUs), implement and execute projects and plans, plan for training and development of employees, invest in R&D and their commitment to organizational missions and goals.

Analysis of other variables to size up the position of the firm

In addition to the factors discussed above, the future prospects of a firm can be sized up through an assessment of the following variables:

1. **Market Share:** The size of a company's market share is the best indicator of its success. Higher the market share, stronger the position of the company vis-à-vis its competitors in the industry. Large market share is an indicator of comparatively secure current and future earnings. Further, large market share also makes the company more competitive as it can take advantage of economies of scale and absorb the fixed costs better, especially beneficial in case of a capital-intensive industry.
2. **Raw Material and Other Inputs:** A company's profits can be affected adversely if the cost of raw material, fuel, power and other production inputs rises on account of either scarcity or the bargaining power of supplier. Erratic supply of raw material can also disrupt production schedules and cause supply of finished goods to fluctuate. Moreover, if a company is forced to pay more for its inputs as compared to its competitors, its profit margins also shrink and its earnings get impacted. An analyst should always ascertain this aspect of a company's performance.
3. **Customer Base:** A company might be very profitable but if it is serving a small group of customers, then it is always risky to invest in such a company. The reason is that even if it losses one customer, its revenues get dramatically affected. For example, if a company is making a product solely for government, then it will always be susceptible to change in either the policies of the government or a change in the government itself.
4. **Regulatory Environment:** The regulatory environment of the firm is also important from the point of view of an analyst. If a company is selling a product whose price is controlled by the government or a license is required to manufacture or sell the product, then such a company's earnings can fluctuate due to changes in policy or sudden reduction in price by the government. Heavy regulation, however necessary, can seriously impair the attractiveness of a firm from investment point of view. For example, in 2013 the Indian government raised the number of drugs that are subject to price controls to 348 from 74, affecting up to 30% of the total sales in the country and there is a proposal to bring more drugs under control. The move has adversely affected the sales of global and local companies like Pfizer, GlaxoSmithKline and Abbott Laboratories and Wockhardt Ltd. Analysts should keep these regulatory impositions in mind while assessing the potential risks and rewards of buying equity of any company.
5. **Order Book Position:** Order book position clearly shows the future performance of the company. Deterioration in order position or having an order position representing a short duration in future is an indication of trouble in times to come. Thus, analysts should also try to find out the order book position of a company in their effort to size up the worthiness of a company for investment purpose.
6. **Other Factors:** In addition to the factors listed above, capacity utilization, expansion plans, production capabilities, technological upgradation plans, marketing capabilities, access to distribution channels, effectiveness of finance policies, fairness of accounting policies, personnel management policies and organizational culture also provide important cues for sizing up the position of a company.

The information for analyzing the above-mentioned factors has to be collected from multiple sources. Some of it can be found in the annual reports of the company, some from its website or officials and the rest from the media releases and research reports.

Quantitative Analysis of Firms

Quantitative analysis of a firm is an assessment of its earnings, dividends, sales, costs, capital structure, assets and liabilities, operating statistics, price earning ratio and other quantifiable parameters of performance. The main approach to quantitative analysis of a firm is the analysis of the information contained in its financial statements. Analysis of financial statements can enable the analysts to assess a company's credit worthiness, corporate excellence, value its equity shares, forecast bankruptcy, assess its market risk, evaluate its financial soundness and confirm its comparative standing vis-à-vis its competitors.

Exhibit 11.1 Management's Discussion and Analysis, Jet Airways (India) Limited Annual Report 2013

Outlook / Restructuring Measures

Starting Fiscal 2014, capacity increases are expected to be moderate in the industry. The demand growth is expected to climb up to double digits in the second half of the current fiscal. Airlines are regaining pricing power and industry load factors are starting to move northward.

Operating cost environment continues to be difficult with rupee depreciation, high crude prices and significant increase in landing and navigation costs. Airlines will have no choice but to pass on these increases to the passenger. This may affect the passenger growth in the short term as it will become unaffordable for the customer.

Crude oil prices, over the last few weeks, have been hovering over USD 100 per barrel, if this gets stable, it should help us to keep costs lower since fuel costs represent close to 40% of our costs. But the recent weakening of the Indian Rupee vis-à-vis the US Dollar will pose cost challenges since our outflows in foreign currency are higher than foreign inflows.

We continue in our endeavor on cost cutting measures, explore various avenues of ancillary revenues and process improvements across all segments of the business. We believe that this will help the Company in maximizing profitability in the medium to long term. The proposed Jet-Etihad deal will bring immediate revenue growth and cost synergy opportunities for both the airlines and will help strengthen Jet Airways balance sheet. Key cost benefits and synergies in fleet acquisition, maintenance, joint purchasing opportunities for fuel, spare parts, equipment and catering supplies, as well as external services such as insurance and technology support will come through. Other areas of co-operation will include joint training of pilots, cabin crew and engineers, as well as maintenance of common aircraft types and consolidation of guest loyalty programs. The alliance will bring significant guest benefits with expanded code sharing, creating a combined network of 140 destinations, these benefits will result in accelerated return of the Company to sustainable profitability.

Opportunities, Risks, Concerns and Threats

Indian economy continues to grow at a healthy pace as compared to other economies across the world and is expected to post growth rates of 5% to 6% per annum for the next few years.

After a year of slump in demand, the growth is expected to touch double digit in the current fiscal. But, there is expected to be short-term challenges like pressure on the Indian rupee vis-à-vis dollar, high crude oil prices as well as significant increase in landing and navigation charges which is likely to put pressure on the profitability.

The Jet-Etihad deal presents us with a big opportunity to expand our footprints in international market, improving our balance sheet, enhancing revenues and bringing synergies in costs. This should help us to be more competitive in domestic and international market.

Company's fleet strategy will be that of moderate growth in this difficult environment wherein, we will look to consolidate our position on existing routes, discontinue non strategic routes which are loss making and selectively add new capacity in markets which will increase and improve our network revenues and performance.

Source: Quoted from the Annual Report of Jet Airways, accessed on November 30, 2014.

Financial statements published periodically by the firms as per the statutory requirements are considered very important source of company information by the investors and analysts. Financial statements are audited by independent auditors and are trusted by people to be factual. However, as seen in various cases, the information could be manipulated. The case of Indian IT major, Satyam, is a case in point where the financial statements were manipulated by the company officials. Even the role of auditors of the firm, Pricewaterhouse Coopers (PwC), has come under scanner for failing to detect the irregularities in the financial statements of Satyam.

Marketview 11.3 The Satyam Scam Case, 2009 (As filed by CBI)

"This was perhaps India's biggest corporate fraud case where M/s Satyam Computer Services Limited (M/s SCSL) caused loss to the investors to the tune of ₹14,162 crore. The company head, Ramalinga Raju and members of his family secured illegal gains to the tune of about ₹2,743 crore by various tricks. The fraud was perpetrated by inflating the revenue of the company through false sales invoices and showing corresponding gains by forging the bank statements with the connivance of the Statutory and Internal Auditors of the company. The annual financial statements of the company with inflated revenue were published for several years and this lead to higher price of the scrip in the market. In the process, innocent investors were lured to invest in the company. Attempts were made to conceal the fraud by acquiring the companies of kith and kin."

Source: Quoted from http://cbi.nic.in/fromarchives/satyam/satyam.php, accessed on November 25, 2014.

Marketview 11.4 The Story of the Satyam Scam

According to the findings of SEBI probe, the Satyam scam that rocked our country few years back was a case of financial mis-statements to the tune of nearly ₹12,320 crore.

At the core of the misdeeds of the founder of Satyam, Ramalinga Raju, were the unlawful gains that he and his family members and other accomplices made by selling or pledging Satyam's shares at inflated prices achieved by over-statement of bank balances, creating fake customers, over-stating revenues and under-reporting liabilities.

The company books were cooked up by excluding certain receipts and payments, resulting in thousands of crores of misreporting. Through fake invoices, the company's revenue was over-stated by ₹4,783 crore over a period of 5–6 years. Fictitious invoices were also created to show fake debtors on the books to the tune of ₹500 crore. Bank balances were inflated by about ₹1,732 crore and fixed deposits by ₹3,308 crore to create an aura of highly successful company. Fake interest receipts worth ₹376 crore were also shown on the books.

Most shockingly, there were large mismatches between the TDS (tax deducted at source) amounts shown in the audited balance sheets and that in the income tax returns.

Source: http://www.rediff.com/business/slide-show/slide-show-1-satyam-scam-sebi-pegs-biggest-corporate-fraud-at-rs-12320-cr/20140715.htm#4, accessed on November 2, 2014.

An analyst, therefore, needs to have an ability to judge the efficacy of these statements as a reflection of the business reality of the firm under consideration.

Let us try to understand the regulatory framework for the preparation of these statements and the biases or misreporting that can creep into their preparation.

Financial Reporting: Framework and Biases

Financial statement have to be prepared by companies in India according to the specified accounting standards which give a detailed description of the rules and procedures to be followed in reporting of accounting information. All financial statements like statement of profit and loss, balance sheet and cash flow statement prepared by the companies according to the accounting standards are verified by the external auditors. All statements are prepared on accrual basis of accounting, i.e., revenues are recognized when sale is made or service is provided and not when cash actually comes in. Similarly, expense is recognized when goods are used or service is received and not when cash is paid for them. A lot of discretion and complex judgment goes into preparation of financial statements and the company can manipulate the information to mislead the regulators and the investors.

Though accounting standards and conventions are quite comprehensive, yet they contain in themselves many loopholes and introduce bias in reporting financial information. The accounting rules provide scope for treating costs, revenues and profits under different set of rules and this reduces the comparability of the statements. It also provides leeway to managers to use their discretion to disguise reality. The fact, however, remains that accounting information is used by outsiders, particularly investors, as a window to look into the company and know about its processes and operations. An analyst should understand the way these statements are prepared and the information contained therein as analysis of financial statements has always been a key part of investment analysis and decision-making. Not only do the financial statements give information about the past but also help analysts in making projections about the future. The tool of financial analysis that is most popular with analysts is ratio analysis. Various financial ratios are used to judge the economic prospects of the firm and assess the quality of its earnings. Let us now briefly examine the main financial statements and ratios that can help analysts in judging a company's financial performance.

Key Financial Statements

1. **Statement of Profit and Loss:** It is a summary of revenues and expenses, i.e., profitability of a company over a period of time, usually a year. As can be seen from the sample statement given in Table 11.1, the main classes of expenses are cost of goods sold, direct costs, general selling and administrative expenses (overhead costs), salaries and other costs of operating the company that are not directly attributable to production operations of the firm, interest cost of borrowed funds and taxes on earnings.

   Analysts also prepare a common size statement in which all the contents of the statement of profit and loss are expressed as a percentage of the total revenue of the firm. This enables comparison of financial performance across firms of different sizes. The statement of profit and loss of ITC Ltd. for the financial year ending on March 31, 2014 is exhibited in Table 11.1.

TABLE 11.1 Statement of Profit and Loss of ITC Ltd. for the financial year ending on March 31, 2014

	₹ in Crore	
Parameter	**MAR'14**	**MAR'13**
Gross sales	47,068.66	42,105.51
Less: Inter divisional transfers	0	0
Less: Sales returns	0	0
Less: Excise	13,830.06	12,204.24
Net sales	33,238.60	29,901.27
EXPENDITURE:		
Increase/Decrease in stock	−128.41	−246.35
Raw materials consumed	13,284.75	12,312.13
Power & fuel cost	613.19	550.11
Employee cost	1,608.37	1,387.01
Other manufacturing expenses	1,330.48	1,157.02
General & administration expenses	1,089.35	1,234.39
Selling & distribution expenses	1,982.31	2,088.32
Miscellaneous expenses	983.04	800.09

(Continued)

TABLE 11.1 Continued

	₹ in Crore	
Parameter	**MAR'14**	**MAR'13**
Expenses capitalized	0	0
Total expenditure	20,763.08	19,282.72
PBIDT (Excl OI)	**12,475.52**	**10,618.55**
Other income	1,107.14	967.1
Operating profit	**13,582.66**	**11,585.65**
Interest	23.63	105.91
PBDT	13,559.03	11,479.74
Depreciation	899.92	795.56
Profit before taxation & exceptional items	12,659.11	10,684.18
Exceptional income/Expenses	0	0
Profit before tax	**12,659.11**	**10,684.18**
Provision for tax	3,873.90	3,265.79
PAT	**8,785.21**	**7,418.39**
Extraordinary items	0	0
Adj. to profit after tax	0	0
Profit balance B/F	3,788.10	1,972.59
Appropriations	12,573.31	9,390.98
Equity dividend	600	525
Earnings per share (in ₹)	11.05	9.39
Book value (in ₹)	32.95	28.14

Source: http://profit.ndtv.com/stock/itc-ltd_itc/financials-profit-loss, accessed on November 25, 2014.

2. **Balance Sheet:** Balance sheet contains the information about the financial condition of a firm in terms of its assets and liabilities on any given date. Current assets of a firm include cash, accounts receivable and inventories. Fixed assets include plant, machinery, land, building and other properties owned by the company, expected to exist for a long period. The liabilities side includes short-term liabilities or current liabilities like account payable that become due within a year. Long-term debt and shareholders' equity constitute the rest of the liabilities side. Since in our current discussion we are concerned with the analysis of the company from the point of view of equity investment, let us understand the equity-related components of the balance sheet.

The Balance sheet of ITC Ltd. for the financial year ending on March 31, 2014 is exhibited in Table 11.2.

TABLE 11.2 Balance Sheet of ITC Ltd. for the financial year ending on March 31, 2014

	₹ in Crore	
Parameter	**MAR'14**	**MAR'13**
EQUITY AND LIABILITIES		
Share capital	795.32	790.18
Share warrants & outstandings		
Total reserves	25,466.70	21,497.67
Shareholder's funds	26,262.02	22,287.85
Long-term borrowings	**0**	**0**
Secured loans	0	0
Unsecured loans	51	66.4
Deferred tax assets/liabilities	1,296.96	1,203.72
Other long term Liabilities	5.09	1.79
Long term trade payables	0	1.32
Long term provisions	110	125.62
Total non-current liabilities	**1,463.05**	**1,398.85**
Current liabilities		
Trade payables	1,987.59	1,668.98
Other current liabilities	3,631.88	3,528.62
Short term borrowings	0.14	0
Short term provisions	5,884.71	5,133.13
Total current liabilities	**11,504.32**	**10,330.73**
Total liabilities	**39,229.39**	**34,017.43**
ASSETS		
Non-current Assets	**0**	**0**
Gross block	18,544.87	16,944.38
Less: accumulated depreciation	6,532.13	5,735.04
Less: impairment of assets	0	0
Net block	12,012.74	11,209.34

(Continued)

TABLE 11.2 Continued

Parameter	₹ in Crore	
	MAR'14	MAR'13
Lease adjustment A/c	0	0
Capital work in progress	2,272.94	1,472.80
Intangible assets under development	22.79	14.99
Pre-operative expenses pending	0	0
Assets in transit	0	0
Non-current investments	2,512.17	2,000.86
Long term loans & advances	1,480.02	1,727.97
Other non-current assets	0	0
Total non-current assets	**18,300.66**	**16,425.96**
Current assets loans & advances		
Currents investments	6,311.26	5,059.43
Inventories	7,359.54	6,600.20
Sundry debtors	2,165.36	1,163.34
Cash & bank	3,289.37	3,615.00
Other current assets	269.69	216.36
Short term loans & advances	1,533.51	937.14
Total current assets	**20,928.73**	**17,591.47**
Net current assets (Including current investments)	9,424.41	7,260.74
Total current assets (Excluding current investments)	14,617.47	12,532.04
Miscellaneous expenses not written off	0	0
Total assets	**39,229.39**	**34,017.43**
Contingent liabilities	361.5	466.54
Total debt	66.54	77.67
Book value	32.95	28.14
Adjusted book value	32.95	28.14

Source: http://profit.ndtv.com/stock/itc-ltd_itc/financials, accessed on November 25, 2014.

The difference between total assets and total liabilities is equal to the shareholders' equity. This difference is also called as book value or net worth of the firm. Equity capital comprises par value of issued equity, additional paid-up capital and retained earnings. Par value and additional paid-up capital represent the amount of equity realized from the sale of equity shares to public and retained earnings represent the accumulation of undistributed profits. Like statement of P&L, analysts generate common-size balance sheets, where all items are expressed as percentage of total assets to enable inter-firm comparison.

3. **Statement of Cash Flow:** As stated in the introduction, statement of profit and loss and balance sheet are prepared on the basis of accrual method of accounting and they do not give a true picture of the actual cash flowing in and out of the firm. Hence, a statement of cash flow is prepared to represent the cash position of the firm, i.e., the cash implication of all the transactions undertaken by it.

   In the statement of cash flow, cash inflows and outflows are reported under three activities: operating, investing and financing activities. The cash flow statement gives a true picture of the health of a firm. If a firm is showing profits but has no cash and needs to borrow to pay dividends, then it is an indicator of illiquidity and the fact that dividends may dry up in the future.

   The cash flow statement of ITC Ltd. for the financial year ending on March 31, 2014 is exhibited in Table 11.3.

TABLE 11.3 Cash flow statement of ITC Ltd. for the financial year ending on March 31, 2014

		₹ in Crore
Parameter	**MAR'14**	**MAR'13**
Net profit before taxes	12,659.11	10,684.18
Adjustments for expenses & provisions	−167.46	−38.51
Adjustments for liabilities & assets	−1,732.15	−1,049.43
Cash flow from operating activities	6,962.30	6,709.89
Cash flow from investing activities	−2,823.29	−3,580.78
Cash flow from financing activities	−4,173.85	−3,232.55
Effect of exchange fluctuation on translation reserve	0	0
Net increase/(decrease) in cash & cash equivalents	−34.84	−103.44
Opening cash & cash equivalents	155.9	259.34
Cash & cash equivalent on amalgamation/take over/merger	0	0
Cash & cash equivalent of subsidiaries under liquidations	0	0
Translation adjustment on reserves/op cash balances from subsidiaries	0	0
Effect of foreign exchange fluctuations	0	0
Closing cash & cash equivalent	121.06	155.9

Source: http://profit.ndtv.com/stock/itc-ltd_itc/financials-cash-flow, accessed on November 25, 2014.

Analyzing Financial Statements and Information

We have already discussed equity valuation methods. To apply these methods, we need to forecast earnings of the firm under study. The beginning point of any such future estimation is a historical analysis of key accounting information contained in the financial statements of the company. Financial analysis is the process of identifying the financial strengths and weaknesses of the firm by properly establishing relationships between the item on the balance sheet and the statement of profit and loss.

The analysis of financial statements is mainly undertaken using the following tools:

1. **Ratio Analysis**: Ratio analysis is used to evaluate relationship among items of financial statement. The ratios are used to identify trends over time for one company or to compare two or more companies at one point in time. Financial statement ratio analysis focuses on three key aspects of a business: liquidity, profitability and solvency. To summarize, ratio analysis is a tool to ascertain a firm's:
   (a) Liquidity position
   (b) Profitability
   (c) Solvency
   (d) Financial stability
   (e) Quality of the management
   (f) Safety and security of the loans and advances

   A ratio can be expressed as a percentage, proportion or pure number. The main types of financial ratios calculated for financial analysis of a firm are:

   (a) *Liquidity ratios*: Liquidity ratios measure a firm's ability to meet its current obligations. They show the ability of a firm to meet its short-term obligations.
   Following are the key liquidity ratios that are computed by analysts:

$$\text{Current ratio} = \frac{\text{Current asets}}{\text{Current liabilities}}$$

$$\text{Quick ratio} = \frac{\text{Current assets} - \text{Inventories}}{\text{Current liabilities}}$$

$$\text{Cash ratio} = \frac{\text{Cash} + \text{Marketable securities}}{\text{Current liabilities}}$$

   Higher the liquidity ratio, the greater the margin of safety of the creditors. Though high liquidity ratios indicate better liquidity/short term solvency position of a firm, but very high liquidity ratios indicate slack management practices. Thus, firms should aim for a reasonable liquidity ratio. Though there is no hard and fast rule, a current ratio of 2:1 and acid-test ratio of 1:1 is considered satisfactory. The quick or acid test ratio takes into consideration the differences in the liquidity of the components of current assests. It is a rigorous measure and superior to the current ratio.

   (b) *Solvency or leverage ratios*: Solvency ratios measure the dependence of a firm on borrowed funds. Following are the key leverage ratios that are computed by the analysts:

$$\text{Debt equity ratio} = \frac{\text{Debt}}{\text{Owner's equity}}$$

$$\text{Interest coverage ratio} = \frac{\text{EBIT}}{\text{Interest expense}}$$

$$\text{Interest burden} = \frac{\text{EBIT} - \text{Interest expense}}{\text{EBIT}}$$

$$\text{Debt service coverage ratio (DSCR)} = \frac{[\text{PAT} + \text{Interest} + \text{Depreciation} + \text{Other non-cash expenses}]}{\text{Installment}}$$

$$\text{Leverage} = \left[\frac{\text{Asset}}{\text{Equity}}\right] - 1 + \left[\frac{\text{Debt}}{\text{Equity}}\right]$$

The capital structure or leverage ratios throw light on the long-term solvency of a firm. There are two types of such ratios: (a) structural and (b) coverage. These show the companies' ability to pay interest and repay debt. D/E indicates the margin of safety to the creditors. D/E of 2:1 is usually acceptable. High debt equity ratio indicates that owners are putting in relatively less money of their own. Coverage ratios measure the firm's ability to pay certain fixed charges. DSCR of 2:1 is considered as satisfactory ratio by lending financial institutions

(c) *Turnover ratios:* Turnover or activity ratios measure the firm's efficiency in utilizing its assets. Following are the key turnover ratios that are computed by the analysts:

$$\text{Inventory turnover ratio} = \frac{\text{Cost of goods sold}}{\text{Average inventory}}$$

$$\text{Debtors turnover ratio} = \frac{\text{Net credit sales}}{\text{Average debtors}}$$

$$\text{Creditors turnover ratio} = \frac{\text{Net credit purchases}}{\text{Average creditors}}$$

$$\text{Days receivables} = \left[\frac{\text{Average accounts receivable}}{\text{Annual sales}}\right] \times 365$$

$$\text{Total asset turnover} = \frac{\text{Sales}}{\text{Average total assets}}$$

$$\text{Fixed asset turnover} = \frac{\text{Sales}}{\text{Average fixed assets}}$$

High inventory turnover ratio is desirable from liquidity point of view. A high debtors, turnover ratio indicates a shorter time-lag between credit sales and cash collection. A low creditors, turnover ratio reflects liberal credit terms granted by the suppliers.

(d) *Profitability ratios:* Profitability ratios measure a firm's overall efficiency and effectiveness in generating profit. Following are the key profitability ratios that are computed by the analysts:

$$\text{Gross profit margin} = \frac{\text{Gross profit}}{\text{Net sales}}$$

$$\text{Net profit margin} = \frac{\text{EAT or net profit}}{\text{Net sales}}$$

$$\text{Return on assets} = \frac{\text{EBIT}}{\text{Average total assets}}$$

[Net income/Average total assets] is also used as a measure of ROA, many a times interest is added back to net income.

$$\text{Return on equity} = \frac{\text{Net income}}{\text{Average shareholders' equity}}$$

A high gross profit ratio is a sign of good management. A high net profit ratio would ensure adequate return to the owners as well as enable a firm to withstand adverse economic conditions. ROA is an indicator of how profitable a company is relative to its total assets. It gives an idea as to how efficient the management is in using its assets, both debt and equity, to generate earnings. In other words, ROA indicates how effectively the firm is employing its debt and equity investment to generate its net income. The higher the ROA, the better it is.

ROA tells us what earnings were generated from invested capital (assets). It is also called return on investment (ROI). It is often used as a comparative measure to compare a firm's year-on-year performance or to compare it with other firms in the industry. Two firms in the same industry earning same profit may not be same from investment point of view. ROA is the metric that can be used to decide which firm to choose for investment. Suppose, TCL Ltd. and KBL Ltd., both firms in same industry, have a net income of ₹10 million. However, the total assets of TCL are ₹50 million and those of KBL are ₹100 million. Therefore, ROA of TCL at 20% is higher than ROA of KBL at 10%. Obviously, TCL is employing its assets or funds more efficiently.

ROE is a key metric of financial analysis from equity point of view. It is also known as return on net worth (RONW). It measures a firm's profitability by revealing how much profit a company generates with the money the shareholders have invested. The ROE is useful for comparing the profitability of a company to that of other firms in the same industry.

(e) *Equity-related ratios*: Equity-related ratios measure the shareholders' return and value. Following are the key profitability ratios that are computed by the analysts:

$$\text{Price earning ratio} = \frac{\text{Market price per share}}{\text{Earnings per share}}$$

$$\text{Earnings yield} = \frac{\text{Earnings per share}}{\text{Market price per share}}$$

$$\text{Dividend per share} = \frac{\text{Dividends}}{\text{Number of ordinary shares}}$$

$$\text{Market-to-book} = \frac{\text{Market price per share}}{\text{Book value per share}}$$

$$\text{Dividend payout ratio} = \frac{\text{Dividend per share}}{\text{Earnings per share}}$$

$$\text{Dividend yield} = \frac{\text{Dividend per share}}{\text{Market price per share}}$$

Equity-related ratios measure the shareholders' return and value. Earnings per share serves as an indicator of a company's profitability. It is generally considered to be the single most important variable in determining a share's price. It is also a major component used to calculate the price-to-earnings valuation ratio. A high P/E suggests that investors are expecting higher earnings growth in the future compared to companies with a lower P/E. It reflects growth prospects, corporate image, etc. The earnings yield (which is the inverse of the P/E ratio) shows the percentage of each rupee invested in the stock that was earned by the company. The earnings yield is used by many investment managers to determine optimal asset allocations.

A summary of all the ratios discussed above is compiled in Table 11.4. Most of these ratios are very important from equity analysis point of view.

TABLE 11.4 Key Financial Ratios

Liquidity Ratios
$\text{Current ratio} = \frac{\text{Current asets}}{\text{Current liabilities}}$
$\text{Quick ratio} = \frac{\text{Current assets} - \text{Inventories}}{\text{Current liabilities}}$
$\text{Quick ratio} = \frac{\text{Current assets} - \text{Inventories}}{\text{Current liabilities}}$

(Continued)

TABLE 11.4 Continued

Solvency or Leverage Ratios

$$\text{Debt equity ratio} = \frac{\text{Debt}}{\text{Owner's equity}}$$

$$\text{Interest coverage ratio} = \frac{\text{EBIT}}{\text{Interest expense}}$$

$$\text{Interest burden} = \frac{\text{EBIT} - \text{Interest expense}}{\text{EBIT}}$$

$$\text{Debt service coverage ratio} = \frac{[\text{PAT} + \text{Interest} + \text{Depreciation} + \text{Other non-cash expenses}]}{\text{Installment}}$$

$$\text{Leverage} = \left[\frac{\text{Asset}}{\text{Equity}}\right] - 1 + \left[\frac{\text{Debt}}{\text{Equity}}\right]$$

Profitability Ratios

$$\text{Gross profit margin} = \frac{\text{Gross profit}}{\text{Net sales}}$$

$$\text{Net profit margin} = \frac{\text{EAT or net profit}}{\text{Net sales}}$$

$$\text{Return on assets} = \frac{\text{EBIT}}{\text{Average total assets}}$$

$$\text{Return on equity} = \frac{\text{Net income}}{\text{Average shareholders' equity}}$$

Turnover Ratios

$$\text{Inventory turnover ratio} = \frac{\text{Cost of goods sold}}{\text{Average inventory}}$$

$$\text{Debtors turnover ratio} = \frac{\text{Net credit sales}}{\text{Average debtors}}$$

$$\text{Creditors turnover ratio} = \frac{\text{Net credit purchases}}{\text{Average creditors}}$$

(*Continued*)

TABLE 11.4 Continued

Turnover Ratios
$$\text{Days receivables} = \left[\frac{\text{Average accounts receivable}}{\text{Annual sales}}\right] \times 365$$
$$\text{Total asset turnover} = \frac{\text{Sales}}{\text{Average total assets}}$$
$$\text{Fixed asset turnover} = \frac{\text{Sales}}{\text{Average fixed assets}}$$
Equity-related Ratios
$$\text{Price earning ratio} = \frac{\text{Market price per share}}{\text{Earnings per share}}$$
$$\text{Earnings yield} = \frac{\text{Earnings per share}}{\text{Market price per share}}$$
$$\text{Dividend per share} = \frac{\text{Dividends}}{\text{Number of ordinary shares}}$$
$$\text{Market-to-book} = \frac{\text{Market price per share}}{\text{Book value per share}}$$
$$\text{Dividend payout ratio} = \frac{\text{Dividend per share}}{\text{Earnings per share}}$$
$$\text{Dividend yield} = \frac{\text{Dividend per share}}{\text{Market price per share}}$$

Numerical Example 1

Use the information given in the balance sheet and statement of profit and loss of PC Agro to compute key ratios on the basis of following assumptions:

1. All sales are credit sales
2. Tax rate is 30%
3. Cost of goods sold is ₹560 million
4. ₹100 million of long-term borrowing is payable within 1 year
5. Par value of share ₹10

Balance Sheet of PC Agro Ltd. as on March 31, 2012		
		₹ in million
	2012	2011
EQUITY AND LIABILITIES		
Shareholders' funds	850	790
Share capital	300	300
Reserves and surplus	550	490
Non-current liabilities	555	523
Long-term borrowings	420	400
Deferred tax liabilities (net)	70	64
Long-term provisions	65	59
Current liabilities	315	307
Short-term borrowings	180	190
Trade payables	95	85
Other current liabilities	27	21
Short-term provisions	13	11
Total	1720	1620
ASSETS		
Non-current assets	648	602
Fixed assets	525	490
Non-current investments	100	92
Long-term loans and advances	23	20
Current assets	1072	1018
Current investments	45	75
Inventories	490	470
Trade receivables	480	425
Cash and cash equivalents	12	10
Short-term loans and advances	45	38
Total	1720	1620

Statement of Profit and Loss for PC Agro Ltd. for the year ended March 31, 2012	
	₹ in million
Revenue from operations	1010
Other income	35
Total revenues	1045
Expenses	
Material expenses	410
Employee benefits expenses	290
Finance costs	70
Depreciation and amortization expenses	47
Other expenses	25
Total expenses	842
Profit before exceptional and extraordinary items and tax	203
Exceptional items	0
Profit before extraordinary items and tax	203
Extraordinary items	0
Profit before tax	203
Tax expenses	60.9
Profit (loss for the period)	142.1
Dividends	60

Solution:

The key ratios may be calculated as:

$$\text{Current ratio} = \frac{\text{Current assets}}{\text{Current liabilities*}}$$

$$= \frac{1072}{(315+100)} = 2.6$$

$$\text{Acid-test ratio} = \frac{\text{Current assets} - \text{Inventories}}{\text{Current liabilities}}$$

$$= \frac{(1072-490)}{(315+100)} = 1.4$$

$$\text{Cash ratio} = \frac{\text{Cash} + \text{Marketable securities}}{\text{Current liabilities}}$$

$$= \frac{(12+45)}{(315+100)} = 0.14$$

$$\text{Debt-equity ratio} = \frac{\text{Debt(total liabilities)}}{\text{Owner's equity}}$$

$$= \frac{(555+315)}{850} = 1.02$$

$$\text{Interest coverage ratio} = \frac{\text{EBIT or PBIT}}{\text{Interest expense}}$$

$$= \frac{(70+203)}{70} = 3.9$$

$$\text{Fixed charges coverage ratio} = \frac{(\text{PBIT} + \text{Depreciation and Amortization})}{(\text{Interest} + (\text{Repayment of loan}/(\text{1-tax rate}))}$$

$$= \frac{(203+70+47)}{(70+(100/(1-0.30))} = 1.50$$

$$\text{Inventory turnover ratio} = \frac{\text{Cost of goods sold}}{\text{Average inventory}}$$

$$= \frac{560}{(490+470)/2} = 1.17$$

$$\text{Debtors turnover} = \frac{\text{Net credit sales}}{\text{Average debtors}}$$

$$= \frac{1010}{(480+425)/2} = 2.23$$

$$\text{Average collection period} = \frac{365}{\text{Debtors turnover}}$$

$$= \frac{365}{2.23} = 163\ \text{days}$$

$$\text{Total assets turnover ratio} = \frac{\text{Sales}}{\text{Average total assets}}$$

$$= \frac{1010}{(1720+1620)/2} = 0.60$$

$$\text{Gross profit margin} = \frac{\text{Gross profit}}{\text{Net sales or revenues from operation}}$$

$$= \left(\frac{(1010 - 560)}{1010}\right) \times 100 = 44.55$$

$$\text{Net profit margin} = \frac{\text{EAT or net profit}}{\text{Net sales}}$$

$$= \left(\frac{142.1}{1010}\right) \times 100 = 14.07\%$$

$$\text{Return on assets} = \frac{\text{EBIT}}{\text{Average total assets}}$$

$$= \left(\frac{(70 + 203)}{(1720 + 1620)/2}\right) \times 100 = 16.35\%$$

$$\text{Return on equity} = \frac{\text{Net income or equity earnings}}{\text{Average shareholders' equity}}$$

$$= \left(\frac{142.1}{(850 + 790)/2}\right) \times 100 = 17.33\%$$

2. **Comparative Financial Statements**: Comparative financial statement is a statement that compares information contained in the financial statements of a company across different time periods. The comparison is done with a view to identify the trends in the financial data contained in the statement of P&L, balance sheet or cash flow statement of different time periods.

Analysts use comparative statements to examine the effect of business decisions on the profits of a firm. Trends identified through the use of comparative financial statements can be used to evaluate the performance of the managers, the business units and the new products at a glance without having to waste time on going through mountains of papers.

Comparative financial statements are also used for making comparisons between different firms in an industry.

3. **Common Size Statements**: A common size statement is a financial statement that displays all items of financial performance contained in various financial statements as percentages of a common base figure such as revenue. Such conversion makes it easy to analyze performance of a firm across multiple periods or compare it with other firms. This kind of analysis is also called vertical analysis.

   Formatting financial statements to convert them into common size statements reduces the bias that can creep in while analyzing companies of differing sizes. Analysts prefer to use common size statements because these statements help them spot trends that raw financial statements may not reveal.

   The common figure used for creating a common size balance sheet is total assets but at times total liabilities are also used when analysts want to focus on the obligations of the firm and judge whether the firm is conservative or aggressive in managing its debts burden. A common size balance sheet gives deep insight into a firm's capital structure and its relative funding position as compared to its rival firms. In this context, analysts often seek to determine the optimal capital structure for the industry as a whole. By comparing the firm's capital structure with the optimal structure determined for the industry, analysts can decide whether the firm is over-leveraged or under-leveraged. Further, excess retention, inventory build-up, liquidity position in terms of cash component of current assets, goodwill, debt repayment capacity and so on can also be easily examined through the use of common size statement.

   Usually sales are used for making common size statement of profit and loss. The results are same as the margins computed to determine the profitability of a company. For example, a net profit margin is calculated by dividing net income by sales. Common size cash flow statement is also computed as a percent of total sales. It is useful for understanding capital expenditures in the context of the revenues. Expressing cash flow items like debt issuance as percentage of sales helps in studying the extent to which these items are being utilized to generate overall revenue.

   The biggest advantage of a common-size analysis is that it helps analysts identify radical swings in a firm's financial metrics. Rapid increases or decreases can be spotted very easily using these statements.

Numerical Example 2

Use the information given in the balance sheet and statement of profit and loss of MSD Sports Interactive Ltd. to prepare a common size statement.

Statement of Profit and Loss for MSD Sports Interactive Ltd for the year ended on March 31, 20X0 and 20X1		
		₹ in million
	20X1	**20X0**
Total revenues	820	710
Expenses excluding financing cost and tax	580	530
Profit before financing cost and tax	240	180
Financing cost	60	50

(Continued)

Continued

Statement of Profit and Loss for MSD Sports Interactive Ltd for the year ended on March 31, 20X0 and 20X1		
		₹ in million
	20X1	20X0
Profit before tax	180	130
Tax	54	39
Profit (loss) for the period	126	91

Balance Sheet of MSD Sports Interactive Ltd. as on March 31, 20X0 and 20X1		
		₹ in million
	20X1	20X0
Shareholders' funds	480	430
Non-current liabilities: Long-term borrowings	130	100
Other non-current liabilities	60	50
Current liabilities	300	230
Total	970	810
Non-current assets: Fixed assets	380	330
Other non-current assets	90	140
Current assets	500	340
Total	970	810

Solution:

The common size statement has been prepared by restating every amount on the balance sheet as a percentage of total assets and restating every amount on the statement of profit and loss as a percentage of total revenues.

Statement of Profit and Loss for MSD Sports Interactive Ltd. for the year ended on March 31, 20X0 and 20X1				
	Regular (₹ in million)		Common Size (%)	
	20X0	20X1	20X0	20X1
Total revenues	710	820	100	100
Expenses excluding financing cost and tax	530	580	75	71

(Continued)

Continued

Statement of Profit and Loss for MSD Sports Interactive Ltd. for the year ended on March 31, 20X0 and 20X1				
	Regular (₹ in million)		Common Size (%)	
	20X0	20X1	20X0	20X1
Profit before financing cost and tax	180	240	25	29
Financing cost	50	60	7	7
Profit before tax	130	180	18	22
Tax	39	54	5	7
Profit (loss) for the period	91	126	13	15
Balance sheet of MSD Sports Interactive Ltd. as on March 31, 20X0 and 20X1				
	Regular (₹ in million)		Common Size (%)	
	20X0	20X1	20X0	20X1
Shareholders' funds	430	480	53	49
Non-current liabilities: Long-term borrowings	100	130	12	13
Other non-current liabilities	50	60	6	6
Current liabilities	230	300	28	31
Total	810	970	100	100
Non-current assets: Fixed assets	330	380	41	39
Other non-current assets	140	90	17	9
Current assets	340	500	42	53
Total	810	970	100	100

4. **Common Base Statements:** A common base statement is obtained by expressing the financial data in balance sheet and statement of profit and loss as a percentage of a base year. For example, the current assets reported on the balance sheet as on March 31, of 2014, 2013, 2012, 2011 and 2010 will be expressed as a percentage of the March 31, 2010 amount. So if the value in 2012 is 148, it shows that the level of current assets at the end of financial year 2012 is 148% of the level it was at the end of the financial year 2010. The same analysis is done for each item contained in balance sheet and statement of profit and loss. This type of financial statement analysis is also called horizontal analysis and it allows the analysts to see how each item on the balance sheet and statement of profit and loss has changed in relationship to the changes in other items.

Numerical Example 3

Use the information given in the balance sheet and statement of profit and loss of MSD Sports Interactive Ltd. to prepare a common base statement.

Statement of Profit and Loss for MSD Sports Interactive Ltd. for the year ended on March 31, 20X0 and 20X1		
		₹ in million
	20X1	**20X0**
Total revenues	820	710
Expenses excluding financing cost and tax	580	530
Profit before financing cost and tax	240	180
Financing cost	60	50
Profit before tax	180	130
Tax	54	39
Profit (loss) for the period	126	91

Balance sheet of MSD Sports Interactive Ltd. as at March 31, 20X0 and 20X1		
		₹ in million
	20X1	**20X0**
Shareholders' funds	480	430
Non-current liabilities: Long-term borrowings	130	100
Other non-current liabilities	60	50
Current liabilities	300	230
Total	970	810
Non-current assets: Fixed assets	380	330
Other non-current assets	90	140
Current assets	500	340
Total	970	810

Solution:

The common base statement has been prepared by restating every amount on the balance sheet and the statement of profit and loss with values of year ended on March 31, 20X0 as the base year with each item equal to 100.

Statement of profit and Loss for MSD Sports Interactive Ltd. for the year ended on March 31, 20X0 and 20X1				
	Regular (₹in million)		Common Base (%)	
	20X0	20X1	20X0	20X1
Total revenues	710	820	100	115
Expenses excluding financing cost and tax	530	580	100	109
Profit before financing cost and tax	180	240	100	133
Financing cost	50	60	100	120
Profit before tax	130	180	100	138
Tax	39	54	100	138
Profit (loss) for the period	91	126	100	138

Balance sheet of MSD Sports Interactive Ltd. as on March 31, 20X0 and 20X1				
	Regular (₹in million)		Common Base (%)	
	20X0	20X1	20X0	20X1
Shareholders' funds	430	480	100	112
Non-current liabilities: Long-term borrowings	100	130	100	130
Other non-current liabilities	50	60	100	120
Current liabilities	230	300	100	130
Total	810	970	100	120
Non-current assets: Fixed assets	330	380	100	115
Other non-current assets	140	90	100	64
Current assets	340	500	100	147
Total	810	970	100	120

A Summary of Key Indicators of Financial Performance from the Point of View of Equity Analysis

Some of the key indicators of financial performance that need to be examined thoroughly by analysts are discussed below:

1. **Profitability Measures: Level of Earnings:** Profitability measures focus on earnings generated by a firm. The main measure of profitability from the equity point of view is ROE (Return on equity). It is a key indicator of a firm's financial performance and is measured as:

$$\frac{(\text{Profit after tax/equity earnings})}{\text{Book value of equity}}$$

Fluctuations in ROE are a major concern of the analysts, so they need to identify and understand the factors that have an effect of ROE. The factors affecting ROE can be isolated by decomposing it using the Dupont analysis.

$$\text{ROE} = \left(\frac{\text{Profit after tax}}{\text{Sales}}\right) \times \left(\frac{\text{Sales}}{\text{Assets}}\right) \times \left(\frac{\text{Assets}}{\text{Equity}}\right)$$

Profit after tax / Sales	Sales / Assets	Assets / Equity
↓	↓	↓
Net profit margin	Asset turnover	Equity multiplier

Another way of decomposing ROE is:

$$\text{ROE} = \left(\frac{\text{PBIT}}{\text{Sales}}\right) \times \left(\frac{\text{Sales}}{\text{Assets}}\right) \times \left(\frac{\text{PBT}}{\text{PBIT}}\right) \times \left(\frac{\text{PAT}}{\text{PBT}}\right) \times \left(\frac{\text{Asset}}{\text{Equity}}\right)$$

PBIT / Sales	Sales / Assets	PBT / PBIT	PAT / PBT	Asset / Equity
↓	↓	↓	↓	↓
PBIT efficiency (Return on Sales or operating profit margin)	Asset turnover	Interest burden ratio	Tax burden ratio	Financial leverage

Return on equity (ROE) and return on assets (ROA) are two key ratios for assessing the effectiveness of a firm's top management in managing the capital invested. These two are interrelated.

We have seen above that ROE may be expressed as:

$$\left(\frac{\text{Profit after tax or NI}}{\text{Sales}}\right) \times \left(\frac{\text{Sales}}{\text{Assets}}\right) \times \left(\frac{\text{Assets}}{\text{Equity}}\right)$$

The first two ratios represent ROA. $\left(\text{We know ROA} = \frac{\text{NI or PAT}}{\text{Assets}}\right)$

$$\text{Therefore, ROE} = \left(\frac{\text{Net income or PAT}}{\text{Total assets}}\right) \times \left(\frac{\text{Total assets}}{\text{Shareholders' equity}}\right)$$

$$\text{or} \quad \text{ROE} = \text{ROA} \times \left(\frac{\text{Total assets}}{\text{Shareholders' equity}}\right)$$

Numerical Example 4

Calculate return on equity for OSS Travels Ltd. using the following information:

1. Debt to total assets ratio = 0.7
2. Net profit margin = 9%
3. Total assets turnover ratio = 2.7 times

Solution:

$$\text{ROE} = \frac{\text{PAT or Net profit}}{\text{Equity}}$$

From the given information it can be calculated using Dupont analysis:

$$\text{ROE} = \underbrace{\left(\frac{\text{Profit after tax}}{\text{Sales}}\right)}_{\text{Net profit margin}} \times \underbrace{\left(\frac{\text{Sales}}{\text{Assets}}\right)}_{\text{Asset turnover}} \times \underbrace{\left(\frac{\text{Assets}}{\text{Equity}}\right)}_{\text{Equity multiplier}}$$

Given: Net profit margin = 9%

Total assets turnover ratio = 2.7 times

$$\frac{\text{Assets}}{\text{Equity}} = ?$$

Assets/Equity can be calculated using the given debt to total assets ratio (0.7).

$$\frac{\text{Equity}}{\text{Assets}} = 1 - \frac{\text{Debt}}{\text{Assets}} = 1 - 0.7 = 0.3$$

Hence, $\frac{\text{Assets}}{\text{Equity}} = \frac{1}{0.3}$

ROE may be calculated as:

$$0.09 \times 2.7 \times \left(\frac{1}{0.3}\right) = 0.81 \text{ or } 81\%$$

Profit margin and asset turnover are the most useful ways of evaluating firms in the same industry but they can lead to misleading results for inter-industry firms. Further, a high ROE does not mean stock is a good pick. However, analysts can consider shares of troubled firms with low ROE if their price is low enough.

From earnings point of view, an analyst should examine book value per share.

HIGH BOOK VALUE PER SHARE	Favorable indicator
LOW BOOK VALUE PER SHARE	Unfavorable indicator

Beyond the Basics 11.1 Value of ROE

Value of ROE or VRE is a metric used by some value investors and it is calculated by dividing the value of ROE in percentage by the P/E ratio. It is a tool for deciding whether a share is overvalued or undervalued.

General thumb rule is:

A stock is considered to be overvalued if VRE <1
A stock can be considered for investment if VRE >1
A stock is considered to be very attractive for investment if VRE >2
A stock can be considered to be extremely attractive for investment if VRE >3

2. **Liquidity Ratios:** The liquidity position of a company is very useful in evaluating the riskiness of a firm's stock as it provides a measure of the financial strength of the firm. The main liquidity ratios that are calculated are current ratio, quick ratio and cash ratio. These are measured as a proportion of current assets to current liabilities. Declining liquidity ratios are a signal of financial ill health.
3. **Turnover Ratios:** A firm's efficiency in resource utilization is measured through turnover ratios like fixed asset turnover ratio, inventory turnover ratio and average collection period. We have discussed these ratios in the preceding sections of this chapter. Lower fixed asset and inventory turnover ratios indicate excess plant capacity and/or poor inventory management. Higher average collection period indicates issues in receivables management procedures. Usually turnover ratios are compared with industry average to decide the relative performance of a firm.
4. **Measures of Growth Performance:** Since one of the main objectives of financial analysis is to measure historical or ex-post growth rate, analysts calculate CAGR (Compound annual growth rate) of variables like dividend per share, earning per share, sales, net profit, etc. Sustainable growth rate can be computed to ascertain the kind of growth that can be maintained by a firm over a period of time.

   CAGR is calculated as:

$$\left(\frac{\text{End period value of the variable}}{\text{Beginning period value of the variable}}\right)^{1/n} - 1$$

where n is the duration under consideration.

The sustainable growth rate of a firm can be computed as follows:

$$g = ROE \times b$$

where b is the retention ratio.

The growth in earnings may also be calculated using Dupont analysis by substituting the value of ROE as:

$$\left(\frac{\text{Profit after tax}}{\text{Sales}}\right) \times \left(\frac{\text{Sales}}{\text{Assets}}\right) \times \left(\frac{\text{Assets}}{\text{Equity}}\right)$$

and retention ratio may be rewritten as: $\dfrac{\text{Retained earnings (RE)}}{\text{PAT}}$

Substituting the above values in $g = ROE \times b$ and rearranging, we get

$$g = \frac{\text{RE}}{\text{Equity}}$$

You may recall that we have already talked about this growth rate in our chapter on equity valuation.

From growth point of view, an analyst should examine ROE, CAGR and sustainable growth rate.

HIGH RETURN ON EQUITY	Favorable indicator
LOW RETURN ON EQUITY	Unfavorable indicator
HIGH CAGR IN SALES AND EPS	Favorable indicator
LOW CAGR IN SALES AND EPS	Unfavorable indicator
HIGH SUSTAINABLE GROWTH RATE	Favorable indicator
LOW SUSTAINABLE GROWTH RATE	Unfavorable indicator

5. **Economic Value Added:** Though financial ratios give a key insight into the profitability of a firm, these measures of performance may not be adequate in making the correct estimation of a firm's value. In real terms, a firm is considered to be operationally successful its performance only if it is able to generate a risk-adjusted return on its project that is higher than the return the investors could have earned by investing money on their own in the capital market. Merely retaining the earnings would not be sufficient to increase the stock price. The undistributed profits will increase the price of the firm's stock in the market only if the firm is able to earn a higher rate of return on the reinvested funds than the opportunity cost of capital (the market capitalization rate). We can account for this opportunity cost by calculating economic value added (EVA). Conceptually, EVA measures the excess returns of a firm (over and above its opportunity cost of capital) in monetary terms. In EVA analysis, opportunity cost of capital is treated like a real cost that needs to be deducted from the revenues to compute profit of the firm. EVA can be used to assess the

efficiency in deployment of capital because if a firm is earning profit but it fails to cover its opportunity cost, it is an indication of the need to redeploy capital to more effective uses. EVA may be calculated as:

EVA = Net operating profit after taxes (NOPAT) – (Capital invested × Overall cost of capital of the firm)

6. **Equity Related Ratios:** Book value per share, earning per share, dividend per share, price to book value ratio, earnings yield, price earnings ratio and dividend payout ratios are some of the key ratios that interest equity analysts a lot. Let us go into these ratios in a little detail as they are significant in equity analysis.

   (a) Book value per share

   $$\frac{\text{(Paid up equity + Reserves and surplus)}}{\text{Number of outstanding equity shares}}$$

   (b) Earnings per share

   $$\frac{\text{(PAT-Preference dividend) or Equity earnings}}{\text{Number of outstanding equity shares}}$$

Beyond the Basics 11.2 Quality of EPS

EPS is a key number for investors but it is susceptible to manipulation. EPS, as reported in financial statements in line with the accounting standards, may suffer from manipulation and misreporting. To protect investors' interests, analysts should always consider EPS quality. A high-quality EPS is a metric that is a relatively true reflection of what the company has actually earned, i.e., the cash it has generated.

To judge whether the reported EPS is low or high quality, operating cash flow per share should be computed and compared with reported EPS. If operating cash flow per share (calculated by dividing operating cash flow by the number of shares) is greater than the reported EPS, earnings are of a high quality because the company has been able to generate more cash than is reported in the statement of profit and loss.

Since the number of equity shares may change for any accounting period, weighted average number of outstanding shares should be used for EPS computation in any period for accuracy. The number of outstanding shares may change in any period on account of:

(i) *Exercise of stock options and conversion of warrants*: Stock options and warrants give their holders a right to purchase stock from the company. Whenever one of these instruments is converted into shares, the float and the number of outstanding shares increase. For example, suppose Quest Publishers Ltd. issues 200 warrants to be converted into one equity share each. When all these warrants are converted into shares, then the number of outstanding shares of Quest Publishers Ltd. will increase by 200. This will result in what is known as dilution of control.

(ii) Conversion of Convertible Preferential shares also has the same effect as above.

(iii) Follow on public offer (FPO), i.e., issue of additional equity shares.

(iv) Share split, causing the number of shares to increase or reverse split, causing the number of shares to decrease.

(v) Share buyback, causing the number of shares to decrease.

(vi) Right or bonus issue to the existing shareholders.

The change of number of outstanding equity shares requires additional calculation for the purpose of EPS.

Suppose, Quest Publishers Ltd. has 15 lakh shares at the beginning of the financial year 2013. After 7 months, it comes with a FPO and issues 5 lakh shares, taking the total number of shares to 20 lakh. In such a situation, total number of outstanding equity shares for calculating EPS for that year will be:

$$\text{Weight of 15 lakh shares} = \frac{7}{12} = .58$$

$$\text{Weight of 20 lakh shares} = \frac{5}{12} = .42$$

Therefore, the weighted average number of outstanding shares of Quest Publishers Ltd. is: $0.58 \times 15 + 0.42 \times 20 = 8.7 + 8.4 = 17.1$ Lakh

Similarly, the number of outstanding equity shares also increases when a firm comes out with a bonus issue. When a company issues bonus shares, the liquidity in the stock increases but the effective EPS, book value and other per share values reduce. However, the performance of company has not gone down. So to get a true picture of company's performance, the basic EPS is adjusted to reflect the effect of capitalization of free reserves, i.e., issue of bonus shares. Bonus issues are received positively by the market because declaration of bonus issue is a sign of improving profitability, though the price usually gets adjusted to the increase in the number of shares. Analysts should keep an eye on the bonus history of firms as it may turn out to be a good indicator of a healthy firm.

The effect of bonus issue on the EPS in the post bonus period is reflected in the adjusted EPS.

$$\text{Adjusted EPS} = \text{EPS} \times \text{Bonus adjustment factor}$$

where

$$\text{Bonus adjustment factor} = \frac{\text{Capital after bonus issue}}{\text{Capital before bonus issue}}$$

Diluted EPS: Equity investors should take into consideration all the convertible securities while analyzing a company for investing in its shares. The reason is that when the convertibles get activated, the number of outstanding shares increases, resulting in lower EPS for existing shareholders. An EPS computed taking all convertible securities into consideration is called diluted EPS.

Beyond the Basics 11.3 Lerner and Carlton Model for EPS calculation

Lerner and Carlton have given a model for calculation of EPS. It is illustrated below:

$$\text{EPS} = \frac{(I - T)\,[R + (R - I)L/E]E}{\text{Number of common shares outstanding}}$$

where
EPS = Earnings per share
T = Effective tax rate (Tax exposure/EBT)
R = Before tax return on assets (EBIT/A)
I = Effective interest rate (Interest expense/liabilities)
L = Total liabilities
E = Equity

The model gives a more comprehensive assessment of EPS. According to this model the factors that affect earnings per share are:

- Equity base of the company
- Debt-equity ratio
- Utilization of assets in the company
- Effective cost of the borrowed funds
- Effective tax rate paid by the company
- Margin on sales

(c) Earnings yield

$$\frac{\text{Earnings per share}}{\text{Market price per share}}$$

or

$$\frac{\text{ROE}}{(\text{Market price per share/Book value per share})}$$

Thus a company with high ROE can actually have low earnings yield if its P/B is higher.

(d) Dividend per share

$$\frac{\text{Dividend declared or paid}}{\text{Number of outstanding equity shares}}$$

or

$$\text{Dividend Per Share} = \text{Earnings per share} \times \text{DPR (Dividend payout ratio)}$$

In India, dividend is declared in terms of percentage of the paid-up value of the share under consideration.

(e) Dividend payout ratio

$$\frac{\text{Distributed equity earnings}}{\text{Total equity earnings}}$$

i.e., portion of equity earning that is declared to be distributed to the shareholders. The remaining part is called retained earnings.

(f) *Price earnings ratio:* We have discussed this ratio in detail in the chapter on equity valuation. Here it needs to be pointed out that P/E can also be computed as MPS/EPS. The period for which the value of MPS and EPS is taken, determine whether the P/E computed is retrospective (backward looking) or prospective (forward looking).

$$\text{Retrospective P/E} = \frac{\text{MPS at the end of year } n}{\text{EPS at the end of year } n}$$

$$\text{Prospective P/E} = \frac{\text{MPS at the beginning of year } n}{\text{EPS at the beginning of year } n}$$

Prospective P/E is more popular in investment analysis. The analysts use P/E as an indicator of stocks to choose. They believe that a low P/E stock is more attractive than a high P/E stock. But we need to understand that though a low P/E stock allows one to pay less for current earnings, but a high P/E stock can be a good bargain if earnings are expected to grow at a good rate. A high P/E indicates that the market believes that the firm has attractive growth opportunities.

(g) *Market-book-value ratio:* It is another important valuation ratio which is measured as MPS of the equity share/book value. It reflects how much the investors are ready to pay for a rupee of shareholders' equity per share. Again, like P/E, it might be retrospective or prospective. Retrospective measure of P/B is more widely used in investment management.

Many analysts tend to see the book value as the floor or the base supporting the market price and consider a low market-book-value share a safer investment. They tend to rule out high P/B shares in stock selection. P/B can also be seen as a good measure of growth opportunities.

(h) *Risk of equity investment:* In the context of equity share, risk exposure can be measured in terms of:
   (i) Volatility of ROE
   (ii) Beta

Volatility of ROE is a measure of deviation of ROE from the forecasted value over a period of time. It is measured as:

$$\text{Volatility of ROE} = \frac{\text{Range of ROE over } n \text{ years}}{\text{Average ROE over } n \text{ years}}$$

Beta is a measure of the sensitivity of a security's return to the return of the market (as measured by some index of market performance).

From risk exposure point of view, an analyst should examine beta and volatility of return on equity.

LOW VOLATILITY OF RETURN ON EQUITY	Favorable indicator
HIGH VOLATILITY OF RETURN ON EQUITY	Unfavorable indicator
LOW BETA	Favorable indicator
HIGH BETA	Unfavorable indicator

In equity analysis, the financial ratios are compared with a specified benchmark (past performance or industry performance). On the whole, while analyzing financial information quantitatively, analysts tend to favor stocks with low beta, low ROE volatility, high book value per share, high ROE, high CAGR of EPS and sales and high sustainable growth rate.

7. **Leverage Ratios:** Leverage ratios, also known as capital structure ratios, are used to assess the risk of a firm arising from the use of debt in the capital. Leverage ratios may be structural or coverage ratios. The structural ratios provide a measure of the proportion of debt and equity and the coverage ratios measure the ability to service the debt burden. We have already discussed leverage ratios in detail.
8. **Assessment of Risk:** In addition to the assessment of future earnings, the variability of these expected earnings also needs to be evaluated. In other words, the risk that the future earnings might not turn out to be as expected or anticipated should also be measured and analyzed by the investors. Since a firm's earnings are driven mainly by sales, the best measure of risk of variability of earnings is one that captures the impact of variability of sales on profit. Such measure is called degree of total leverage (DTL) and it is computed as:

$$DTL = \frac{\text{Contribution}}{\text{Profit before tax}}$$

where Contribution = Sales – Variable Costs

Degree of total leverage determines the total risk of a firm and is equal to the product of DFL and DOL. It is a measure of percentage change in PBT in response to 1% change in sales.

Thus, DTL is further sub-divided into two constituents, Degree of operating leverage (DOL) and Degree of financial leverage (DFL).

DOL arises from the cost structure of the firm and it determines the business risk of the firm. DFL arises from the capital structure of the firm and determines the financial risk of the firm.

DOL is a measure of percentage change in EBIT in response to 1% change in sales. It is computed as:

$$DOL = \frac{\text{Contribution}}{\text{EBIT}}$$

DFL is a measure of percentage change in PBT in response to 1% change in EBIT. It is computed as:

$$DFL = \frac{\text{EBIT}}{\text{PBT}}$$

Numerical Example 5

Calculate the following using the summary information of the financial performance of MCH Ltd. given below:

1. Bonus adjustment factor
2. EPS and adjusted EPS
3. Prospective P/E
4. Retrospective Price-to-Book ratio
5. Volatility of ROE

					₹ in million
Year	**2009**	**2010**	**2011**	**2012**	**2013**
PAT	160	145	170	165	185
Equity (₹10 par value)	300	300	300	350	350
Shareholder's funds	700	760	835	890	995
Market price per share (end of the year)	70	56	69	59	81

The company came out with a bonus issue in the year 2012.

Solution:

1. **Bonus Adjustment Factor:** The company came with bonus issue in 2012. The adjustment factor may be calculated as:

$$= \frac{\text{Capital after bonus issue}}{\text{Capital before bonus issue}}$$

$$= \frac{350}{300}$$

$$= 1.17$$

This factor will apply to the EPS of 2012 and 2013.

2. **EPS and Adjusted EPS**

Year	**2009**	**2010**	**2011**	**2012**	**2013**
EPS	160/30 = 5.33	145/30 = 4.83	170/30 = 5.67	165/35 = 4.71	185/35 = 5.29
Adjusted EPS	5.33	4.83	5.67	4.71 × 1.17 = 5.51	5.29 × 1.17 = 6.19

3. **Prospective P/E**

Year	2009	2010	2011	2012
Prospective P/E = Price at the end of Year/ EPS forecast for the current year	70/4.83 = 14.92	56/5.67 = 9.88	69/4.71 = 14.65	59/5.29 = 11.15

4. **Retrospective Price-to-Book Ratio:** Since Retrospective P/B = Price at the end of the year/Book value per share, we need to calculate book value per share.

Year	2009	2010	2011	2012	2013
Book Value per share	700/30 = 23.33	760/30 = 25.33	835/30 = 27.83	890/35 = 25.43	995/35 = 28.43
Retrospective P/B	70/23.33 = 3	56/25.33 = 2.21	69/27.83 = 2.48	59/25.43 = 2.32	81/28.43 = 2.85

5. **Volatility of ROE**

Year	2009	2010	2011	2012	2013
ROE = PAT/Shareholders' funds	(160/700) × 100 = 23%	(145/760) × 100 = 19%	(170/835) × 100 = 20%	(165/890) × 100 = 19%	(185/995) × 100 = 19%

$$\text{Volatility of ROE} = \frac{\text{Range of ROE over } n \text{ years}}{\text{Average ROE over } n \text{ years}}$$

$$\text{Range of ROE} = \frac{(23-19)}{(23+19+20+19+19)/5} = 0.20$$

In conclusion, it can be said that an analyst should use a multi-dimensional approach in analyzing firms for investing with a view to ascertaining and confirming its present situation and further prospects. For this purpose, a qualitative as well as a quantitative analysis needs to be undertaken. The key reference points are quality of management and employees, production and research capabilities, availability and cost of inputs, attitude of government, regulatory requirements, order position of finished goods, markets and distribution channels, accounting policies and information contained in financial statements.

Numerical Example 6

MLA Industries Ltd. has a long history of growth and profitability. It has a very strong position in retail sector. Analyze the financial information of the firm by calculating the following and suggest whether the share is undervalued or overvalued:

1. Decompose the ROE of the last two years in terms of five factors.
2. Calculate the CAGR of sales and EPS for the given period.
3. Calculate the sustainable growth rate based on the average retention ratio and the average return on equity for the past 2 years.
4. Calculate the following for the 20X4 and 20X5: return on equity, book value per share, EPS and Prospective P/E ratio.
5. Estimate the EPS for the next year (20X6) using the following assumptions:
   (a) Net sales are projected to grow at 13%. (b) Interest will increase by 9% over its 20X5 value. (c) PBIT/Net sales ratio is expected to improve by 2% over its 20X5 value.
6. Calculate the P/E ratio of the firm using the constant growth model based on the following information:
   (a) The dividend payout ratio for 20X6 is expected to be equal to the average dividend payout ratio for the two preceding periods. (b) The required rate of return is estimated with the help of the CAPM (Risk-free return = 7%, Market risk premium = 9%, Beta of MLA's stock is 0.8). (c) The dividend is expected to grow at the average sustainable growth rate of the previous two periods.

The current market price of the share of MLA is ₹105. The effective tax rate is 30%.
The Financial statements of the firm are given below:

					₹ in crore
Summary of statement of profit and loss	**20X1**	**20X2**	**20X3**	**20X4**	**20X5**
Net sales	550	600	620	675	735
Profit before interest and tax	65	81	90	108	112
Interest	20	22	23	25	27
Profit before tax	45	59	67	83	85
Tax	13.5	17.7	20.1	24.9	25.5
Profit after tax	31.5	41.3	46.9	58.1	59.5
Dividends	8	10	12	14	14

					₹ in crore
Summary of balance sheet	**20X1**	**20X2**	**20X3**	**20X4**	**20X5**
Equity capital (₹10 par)	60	60	60	60	60
Reserves and surplus	180	213	250	300	350
Loan funds	120	130	135	140	143
Capital employed	360	403	445	500	553

(Continued)

Continued

					₹ in crore
Summary of balance sheet	**20X1**	**20X2**	**20X3**	**20X4**	**20X5**
Net fixed assets	248	268	300	340	369
Investments	18	19	23	28	25
Net current assets	94	116	122	132	159
Total assets	360	403	445	500	553
Market price per share (year-end)	49	63	87	98	105

Solution:

1. **Decomposition of the ROE of the Last Two Years in Terms of Five Factors:**

$$\text{ROE} = \left(\frac{\text{PBIT}}{\text{Sales}}\right) \times \left(\frac{\text{Sales}}{\text{Assets}}\right) \times \left(\frac{\text{PBT}}{\text{PBIT}}\right) \times \left(\frac{\text{PAT}}{\text{PBT}}\right) \times \left(\frac{\text{Asset}}{\text{Equity}}\right)$$

Year	**20X4**	**20X5**
PBIT/Sales	$= (108/675) \times 100 = 16.0$	$= (112/735) \times 100 = 15.238$
Sales/Assets	$= 675/500 = 1.350$	$= 735/553 = 1.329$
PBT/PBIT	$= 83/108 = 0.769$	$= 85/112 = 0.759$
PAT/PBT	$= 58.1/83 = 0.700$	$= 59.5/85 = 0.700$
Asset/Equity	$= 500/(60 + 300) = 1.389$	$= 553/(60 + 350) = 1.349$
ROE	$= 16 \times 1.35 \times 0.769 \times 0.70 \times 1.389$ $= 16.1\%$	$= 15.238 \times 1.329 \times 0.759 \times 0.700 \times 1.349$ $= 14.5\%$

2. **Calculate the CAGR of Sales and EPS for the Given Period:**

$$\text{CAGR in Sales} = \left(\frac{\text{End period value of the variable}}{\text{Beginning period value of the variable}}\right)^{1/n} - 1 = \left(\left(\frac{735}{550}\right)^{0.25} - 1\right) \times 100 = 7.52\%$$

$$\text{CAGR in EPS} = \left(\frac{\text{end period value of the variable}}{\text{beginning period value of the variable}}\right)^{1/n} - 1 = \left(\left(\frac{9.9}{5.25}\right)^{0.25} - 1\right) \times 100 = 17.23\%$$

3. **Calculate the Sustainable Growth Rate Based on the Average Retention Ratio and the Average Return on Equity for the Past 2 Years.**

Year	20X4	20X5	Average
Retention ratio = Retained earnings/PAT	= (58.1 – 14)/58.1 = 0.76	= (59.5 – 14)/59.5 = 0.76	= 0.762
Return on equity = PAT/ Shareholders funds	= (58.1/(300 + 60)) × 100 = 16.1%	= (59.5/(350 + 60)) × 100 = 14.5	15.326%
Sustainable growth = Avg. ROE × Avg. b	= 0.762 × 15.326 = 11.7%		

4. **Calculate the Following for 20X4 and 20X5: Return on Equity, Book Value Per Share, EPS and prospective PE Ratio.**

Year	20X4	20X5
Return on equity = PAT/Equity	= 58.1/(300 + 60) = 16.1%	= 59.5/(350 + 60) = 14.5%
Book value per share = (Paid up equity + Reserves and surplus)/ No. of outstanding equity shares	= (300 + 60)/6 = ₹60.0	= (350 + 60)/6 = ₹68.3
EPS = (PAT-Preference dividend) or Equity earnings/No. of outstanding equity shares	= 58.1/6 = ₹9.7	= 59.5/6 = ₹9.9
Price per share (Beginning of the year)	₹87.0	₹98.0
Prospective P/E = Price at the beginning of the year/EPS	= 87/9.7 = 9.0	= 98/9.9 = 9.9

5. **Estimate of EPS for the Next Year (20X6) Using the Following Assumptions:**
   (a) Net sales are projected to grow at 13%.

   Therefore, the estimated net sales for 20X6 is = 735 + 735 × 0.13 = ₹830.6

   (b) Interest will increase by 9% over its 20X5 value.

   Interest = 27 + 27 × 0.09 = ₹29.43

   (c) PBIT/Net sales ratio is expected to improve by 1% over its 20X5 value.
   PBIT/Sales for 20X5 has been calculated above as 15.238%

Therefore, $\frac{\text{PBIT}}{\text{Sales}}$ for 20X6 = 15.238 + 2 = 17.24%

Hence, PBIT for 20X6 = $\left(\frac{17.24}{100}\right) \times 830.6 =$ ₹143.17

Thus, the summary of key numbers for 20X6 is:

	₹ in crore
Net Sales	830.6
PBIT	143.17
Interest	29.43
PBT	113.74
Tax	34.12
PAT	79.62

$$\text{EPS} = \frac{\text{Equity earnings}}{\text{Number of outstanding equity shares}}$$

$$= \frac{79.62}{6} = 13.27$$

6. **PE ratio of the Firm Using the Constant Growth Model:**
   (a) The dividend payout ratio for 20X6 is expected to be equal to the average dividend payout ratio for the two preceding periods.

Year	20X4	20X5	Average
Dividend payout ratio = Distributed equity earnings/ Total equity earnings	= 14/58.1 = 0.2410	= 14/59.5 = 0.2353	0.238

   (b) The required rate of return is estimated with the help of

   CAPM (Risk-free return = 7%, Market risk premium = 9%, Beta of MLA Industries stock is 0.8).

   Required rate of return = 0.07 + 0.8 × 0.09 = 0.142

   (c) The dividend is expected to grow at average sustainable growth rate of the previous two periods. Sustainable growth rate has been calculated above

   Sustainable growth = Avg. ROE × Avg. b = 0.762 × 15.326 = 11.7%

$$\text{P/E ratio} = \frac{\text{Payout ratio}}{(\text{Required rate of return} - g)}$$

Substituting the values,

$$\text{P/E ratio} = \frac{0.238}{(0.142 - 0.117)}$$

$$= 9.43$$

$$\text{Intrinsic value of share or value anchor} = \text{P/E} \times \text{EPS}$$

$$= 9.43 \times 13.27$$

$$= ₹125.20$$

The share is currently selling at ₹105. Thus, it is undervalued and can be considered for buying.

Numerical Example 7

Kevin wants to buy shares of Share Resorts Ltd because he has come to know that the company pays 50% of its earnings as dividend. Help him analyze the performance of the company, using the key financial information given below and answer the following questions:

1. What has caused the EBIT to decrease?
2. What is the sustainable growth rate of the company?

Assume that the rate of interest on the loan is 10% and the tax rate is 30%.

Statement of Profit and Loss of Share Resorts Ltd for the year ended on March 31, 2013		
		₹ in million
Year	**2013**	**2012**
Sales	1890	1710
Less: Cost of goods sold	1170	970
Gross Profit	720	740
Less: Operating expenses	610	570
EBIT	110	170

Balance Sheet of Share Resorts Ltd as on March 31, 2013	
	₹in million
Current assets	410
Fixed assets	970
Total assets	1380
Current liabilities	330
Long term loan	500
Net worth	550
Total liabilities	1380

Solution:

1. To analyze year-on-year change in the items of statement of profit and loss, we need to measure the percentage change in the items and make common size statement.

Year	2012	2013	% change
Sales	1710	1890	10.53
Less: Cost of goods sold	970	1170	20.62
Gross profit	740	720	–2.70
Less: Operating expenses	570	610	7.02
EBIT	170	110	–35.29

Year-on-year percentage change computations show that despite increase in sales by 10.53%, EBIT has decreased by 35.29%, mainly on account of the increase in cost of goods sold by 20.62% and increase in operating expense by 7.02%.

Common size statement can be made to understand why EBIT has fallen the way it has.

Year	2013	2013	2012	2012
Sales	1890	100%	1710	100%
Less: Cost of goods sold	1170	61.90%	970	56.73%
Gross profit	720	38.10%	740	43.27%
Less: Operating expenses	610	32.28%	570	33.33%
EBIT	110	5.82%	170	9.94%

The above statement shows that operating expenses as percentage of sales have come down by nearly 1%. This is possibly the reason why EBIT has fallen less than it could have. As percentage of sales, EBIT has come down from 9.94% to 5.82% whereas cost of goods sold has risen by approximately 5% from 2012 to 2013, as percentage of sales. In absolute terms the cost of goods sold has increased by nearly 21%.

2. Computation of sustainable growth rate, g

We know, $g = br$

b = retention ratio = 1-payout ratio

Given, payout ratio = 50%, therefore $b = 1 - 0.50 = 50\%$

$$r = \text{ROE} = \frac{\text{PAT or Net income}}{\text{Equity}}$$

Equity = shareholders' funds = net worth is given. It is ₹550 million

We need to calculate PAT.

EBIT	110
Less: Interest (10% on 500)	50
Taxable income	60
Less: Tax (30%)	18
Net income or PAT	42

Therefore,

$$\text{ROE} = \left(\frac{42}{550}\right) \times 100 = 7.37$$

Hence, $g = 0.50 \times 7.37 = 3.685\%$

Fundamental Analysis in Action

The fundamental analysts undertake the study of E-I-C indicators to identify firms in whose shares money can be invested. The ultimate choice of stocks depends on the computation of their intrinsic value and comparing it with the current market price to judge whether the share is undervalued or overvalued. Investment practitioners and portfolio managers have developed many tools for determining whether the stock is undervalued or overvalued. The basic idea behind the determination of value is to detect mispricing and try to earn profits from such knowledge.

Marketview 11.5 Types of Companies and Stocks

Types of Companies

1. **Speculative Companies:** Speculative companies are companies that invest in business enterprises with an uncertain and indefinite outcome in terms of performance. For example, a mining company is an example of a speculative company. Nobody has real idea about the amount and usefulness of the deposits that will be mined.
2. **Cyclical Companies:** Cyclical companies are companies whose earnings tend to fluctuate or move with the business cycle.
3. **Defensive Companies:** Defensive companies are companies whose earnings are comparatively unaffected by the swings in business cycle.
4. **Growth Companies:** Growth companies are companies that are consistently able to identify and invest in projects that generate growth in earnings.

Types of Stocks

1. **Speculative Stock:** A speculative stock is a stock that has extreme volatility, i.e., potential for a large return, as well as a possibility of sizeable loss.
2. **Cyclical Stock:** A cyclical stock is a stock that moves with the market in the context of business cycle. The stocks of sectors like capital goods, banking and real estate are cyclical stocks.
3. **Defensive Stock:** A defensive stock is a stock that does not usually lose its value relative to the business cycle downturns. The stocks of sectors like pharmaceuticals, fast moving consumer goods and information technology are defensive stocks.
4. **Growth Stock:** A growth stock is a stock that generates a higher rate of return as compared to other stocks with the same volatility.

Marketview 11.6 Buy/Sell Recommendations

The basic idea behind equity research is to give investment recommendation. On the basis of investment style, objectives and research output, an equity research analyst can provide a buy, sell or hold recommendation for the share he is analyzing.

The same share may end up getting a buy recommendation from one analyst and a sell from another if the investment styles are different.

A value investor buys a security that is trading at a discount to its intrinsic value and sells it when it is trading above it fair value. On the other hand, a growth investor buys shares in companies with above average future growth prospects. The two type of investors may end up getting different investment advice due to the difference in their investment styles. Let us see how:

Suppose, based on his research, an analyst concludes the following:

Current stock price:	₹2435
Valuation (based on DCF):	₹2435

Outlook: The near to mid-term outlook for the company is very positive. It is expected that the revenue and earnings of the company will grow at a higher rate than the rate of economic growth. The firm's revenue and earnings growth is expected to outpace the industry growth as well.

In such situation, a value manager will recommend a sell because according to him, the share has reached its intrinsic value. So if an investor has been holding the share, he should sell it now. Conversely, growth manger will recommend a buy on account of the excellent projections about the company's future revenues and earnings growth.

Fundamental analysis and the dissemination of information about mispriced shares play a vital role in the market. When security analysts determine that a share is mispriced, they percolate this information to their clients. Some of those clients might choose to act on the information, i.e., buy the share if it is undervalued and sell the share if it is overvalued. Their buying/selling affects the prevailing price in the market. As the news of mispricing reaches is more and more people, the share prices react further till the analysts' information is fully reflected in the stock price. If the recommendation/views of the analysts' are based on accurate projection, no subsequent counter-reaction in the price of the stock would be expected. If the projections are inaccurate, then the prices are likely to return to their previous levels after some time.

Given the impact of the recommendations of the analysts, due caution should be exercised by them while analyzing a company for the purpose of equity investment. The main sources of errors or inaccuracy in making precise forecasts about a company's future performance come from the following sources:

1. Inadequacy, incompleteness and incorrectness of the data available for analysis. Fundamental analysis depends to a large extent on financial statements. The veracity of these statements is doubtful in many cases, as discussed in the preceding part of the chapter.
2. The future is uncertain and it is not possible to predict it with certainty.
3. Market is driven by a number of irrational factors. Rational forecasts made by analysts on the basis of available data may be proven incorrect due to irrational behavioral influences in the market.

   In addition to external factors causing errors in forecast, there are certain sources of errors in forecasting that are internal to an analyst. These are:
   (a) Misjudgments about the economy.
   (b) Misjudgments about the industry.
   (c) Misjudgments about the firm.

Fundamental Analysis and Efficient Market Hypothesis

We know that fundamental analysts believe that each stock has an intrinsic value that reflects its underlying economic factors. Fundamental analysis also asserts that the current market prices of shares may deviate from their intrinsic value but ultimately converge to it due to behavior of the investors. If the prevailing price of a scrip in the market is below its intrinsic value, then the investors move in to buy such an undervalued share (provided transaction costs are covered) because it can be expected to move up toward its intrinsic value. This buying behavior of the investors pushes up the demand for the share and its price begins to rise. Opposite happens in case of overvalued shares where investors move in to sell it, increasing its supply and pushing its price down.

Thus, fundamental analysts believe that through a superior job of estimating an accurate intrinsic value, the investors can make superior market timing decisions consistently and generate above-average returns through acquiring undervalued securities. Efficient market hypothesis (EMH) contends that all available information is already reflected in the price of a security. So fundamental analysts who examine the historical E-I-C data cannot consistently beat the buy and hold strategy proposed by EMH. To make superior profits consistently, analysts need to make accurate forecasts about relevant variables causing long-run price movements. In reality, estimation of relevant variables is not just about using the right valuation model or formula. It is as much an art as it is a science. Superior analysis requires ability, skill and intuition to interpret the impact of available information on intrinsic value better than all others, and the acumen to estimate the future values of relevant variables more accurately than others. We will discuss EMH is detail in Chapter 14.

SUMMARY

- ☑ The aim of company analysis is to determine the intrinsic value of its shares based on the forecast of the future earnings of the equity shares and comparing the same with the current market price to decide whether the security in rightly or under or overpriced.
- ☑ Company analysis is an analysis of information available from the internal and external sources that can enable analysts to form correct expectations about the future prospects of a firm and take a buy, hold or sell call on its equity.
- ☑ Internal information is the accounting data published by the company, press releases and the statements of the authorized personnel and at times, private statements made by the company officials.
- ☑ External information is the information generated independently outside the company. It plays the role of supplementing the internal information by overcoming any bias in company-generated data.
- ☑ The key factors to be analyzed while undertaking company analysis can be classified into two broad groups, the quantitative and the qualitative factors.
- ☑ These two factors are related to matters that may require subjective judgment of investors like the relative position of the company in the industry, the nature of the business, the business model, company's research and development efforts and so on.
- ☑ Quantitative analysis focuses on measurable rubrics like earnings, sales, assets, liabilities, capitalization, dividends, operating statistics and so on. The main approach to quantitative analysis of a firm is the analysis of the information contained in its financial statements.
- ☑ Financial statements published periodically by the firms as per the statutory requirements are considered very important source of company information by the investors and the analysts.
- ☑ Financial statements are audited by independent auditors and are trusted by people to be factual. However, as seen in various cases, the information could be manipulated.

☑ The analysis of financial statements is mainly undertaken using ratio analysis, and preparing common size and common base statements.

☑ Return on equity (ROE) and return on assets (ROA) are two key ratios for assessing the effectiveness of a firm's top management in managing the capital invested. These two are interrelated.

☑ Book value per share, earning per share, dividend per share, price to book value ratio, earnings yield, price earnings ratio and dividend payout ratios are some of the key ratios that interest equity analysts a lot.

☑ On the whole, while analyzing the financial information quantitatively, analysts tend to favor stocks with low beta, low ROE volatility, high book value per share, high ROE, high CAGR of EPS and sales and high sustainable growth rate.

KEY WORDS

CONCEPT QUESTIONS

1. How can an analyst judge the ability of a firm's competitive strategy to create value?
2. Though company analysis for equity investment is largely driven by analysis of financial statements, an analyst must never forget to question the efficacy of the published financial statements. Discuss.
3. "Fundamental analysis at its microscopic best should go beyond the financial data available for analysis." Bring out the criticality of qualitative analysis while undertaking security analysis for equity investment.
4. Various tools of analysis of financial statements tell a story that remains hidden when one looks at published financial statements. Explain with example.
5. Explain the impact of changes in capital structure and dividend policy on the performance of a stock in the share market. Use hypothetical data to illustrate your answer.
6. As a security analyst you will be responsible for analyzing various stocks and making buy, sell and hold recommendations for your clients. Briefly discuss the factors that you will take into account to determine the investment worthiness of a scrip.

7. Discuss the impact of corporate action to increase or decrease the number of outstanding shares on EPS. Why should an analyst be concerned about these events and what should he do to improve the quality of his analysis in the light of such events.

8. Value and growth investment styles have impact on equity analyst's recommendations. Do you agree or disagree? Present all aspects of the debate to clarify your position.

9. "Return on equity (ROE) and return on assets (ROA) are two key ratios for assessing the effectiveness of a firm's top management in managing the capital invested." Elucidate.

10. Now-a-days, media reports often discuss the performance of companies in terms of rise in their EVA. Critique the efficacy of EVA vis-à-vis other traditional metrics of performance like ROE and EPS in the context of listed Indian companies.

PRACTICE PROBLEMS

1. The statement of profit and loss of Hero MotoCorp is given below for the financial year ended on March 31, 2014. Compare the financial performance in 2014 as compared to 2013. Calculate the year-on-year change in the items of the income statement and comment on the possible causes of increase/decrease.

Statement of profit and loss of Hero MotoCorp for the financial year ended on March 31, 2014

		₹ in crore
Parameter	**MAR'14**	**MAR'13**
Gross sales	27,155.82	25,659.91
Less: Inter divisional transfers	0	0
Less: Sales returns	0	0
Less: Excise	1,880.35	1,891.80
Net sales	25,275.47	23,768.11
EXPENDITURE:		
Increase/Decrease in stock	8.36	32.8
Raw materials consumed	18,314.38	17,458.31
Power & Fuel cost	137.46	129.18
Employee cost	930.04	820.92
Other manufacturing expenses	371.03	282.67
General & administration expenses	959.96	854.7

(Continued)

Continued

		₹ in crore
Parameter	**MAR'14**	**MAR'13**
Selling & distribution expenses	493.47	468.71
Miscellaneous expenses	613.56	529.79
Expenses capitalized	0	0
Total expenditure	21,828.26	20,577.08
PBIDT (Excl OI)	**3,447.21**	**3,191.03**
Other income	539.23	491.83
Operating profit	**3,986.44**	**3,682.86**
Interest	11.82	11.91
PBDT	3,974.62	3,670.95
Depreciation	1,107.37	1,141.75
Profit before taxation & Exceptional items	2,867.25	2,529.20
Exceptional income/Expenses	0	0
Profit before tax	**2,867.25**	**2,529.20**
Provision for tax	758.17	411.04
PAT	**2,109.08**	**2,118.16**
Extraordinary items	0	0
Adj. to profit after tax	0	0
Profit balance B/F	3,039.98	2,538.57
Appropriations	5,149.06	4,656.73
Equity dividend	3,250.00	3,000.00
Earnings per share (in ₹)	105.61	106.07
Book value (in ₹)	280.41	250.69

2. Calculate the key financial ratios using past five years' financial information of Sun Pharmaceutical Industries Ltd. given below. Comment on the key ratios and the changes in them.

   Statement of profit and loss Sun Pharmaceutical Industries Ltd. for the financial year ended on March 31, 2014.

(₹ in crore)					
	Mar'14	Mar'13	Mar'12	Mar'11	Mar'10
Income					
Operating income	2,828.79	2,432.14	4,015.56	3,107.57	1,845.09
Expenses					
Material consumed	1,250.06	1,067.34	1,176.06	995.26	847.55
Manufacturing expenses	115.8	93.4	68.76	46.59	100.28
Personnel expenses	279.63	234.87	316.56	261.09	174.71
Selling expenses	–	–	–	–	196.89
Administrative expenses	1,166.23	523.85	695.56	480.55	274.14
Expenses capitalized	–	–	–	–	–
Cost of sales	2,811.72	1,919.46	2,256.94	1,783.49	1,593.57
Operating profit	17.07	512.68	1,758.62	1,324.08	251.52
Other recurring income	159.38	236.17	342.85	194.13	798.35
Adjusted PBDIT	176.45	748.85	2,101.47	1,518.21	1,049.87
Financial expenses	–	–	–	–	0.44
Depreciation	101.94	85.82	75.72	64.23	69.47
Other write offs	–	–	–	–	–
Adjusted PBT	74.51	663.03	2,025.75	1,453.98	979.96
Tax charges	27.43	146.48	28.34	70.18	50.51
Adjusted PAT	47.08	516.55	1,997.41	1,383.80	929.45
Non recurring items	–2,875.60	–	–299.92	–	–32.37
Other non cash adjustments	–	–	–	–	1.57
Reported net profit	–2,828.52	516.55	1,697.49	1,383.80	898.65
Earnings before appropriation	379.53	3,865.84	4,049.19	3,272.95	2,521.24
Equity dividend	257.87	429.79	440.12	362.45	284.79
Preference dividend	–	–	–	–	–
Dividend tax	52.8	88	71.4	58.8	47.3
Retained earnings	68.86	3,348.05	3,537.67	2,851.70	2,189.15

Balance Sheet of Sun Pharmaceutical Industries Ltd. for the financial year ended on March 31, 2014.

					(₹ in crore)
	Mar'14	**Mar'13**	**Mar'12**	**Mar'11**	**Mar'10**
Sources of funds					
Owner's fund					
Equity share capital	207.12	103.56	103.56	103.56	103.56
Share application money	–	–	–	–	–
Preference share capital	–	–	–	–	–
Reserves & surplus	7,200.76	7,685.32	7,774.56	6,576.97	5,614.42
Loan funds					
Secured loans	8.81	43.13	40.3	50.53	29.49
Unsecured loans	2,400.20	–	–	–	–
Total	9,816.89	7,832.01	7,918.42	6,731.06	5,747.47
Uses of funds					
Fixed assets					
Gross block	1,947.47	1,720.70	1,478.93	1,235.51	1,159.76
Less: revaluation reserve	–	–	–	–	–
Less: accumulated depreciation	680.3	584.91	501.63	441.12	419.24
Net block	1,267.17	1,135.79	977.3	794.39	740.52
Capital work-in-progress	480.46	348.04	248.87	195.65	92.15
Investments	7,015.73	4,317.54	4,437.78	3,601.42	3,951.69
Net current assets					
Current assets, loans & advances	5,073.64	3,445.12	3,467.25	3,015.14	1,694.04
Less: current liabilities & provisions	4,020.11	1,414.48	1,212.78	875.54	730.93
Total net current assets	1,053.53	2,030.64	2,254.47	2,139.60	963.11
Miscellaneous expenses not written	–	–	–	–	–
Total	9,816.89	7,832.01	7,918.42	6,731.06	5,747.47

(Continued)

Continued

(₹ in crore)					
	Mar'14	Mar'13	Mar'12	Mar'11	Mar'10
Notes:					
Book value of unquoted investments	6,954.00	4,255.81	4,363.80	3,528.67	3,580.97
Market value of quoted investments	63.97	66.6	75.36	72.91	571.22
Contingent liabilities	1,816.58	1,103.37	783.65	477.83	184.22
Number of equity shares outstanding (Lacs)	20711.64	10355.82	10355.82	10355.82	2071.16

3. Use the information given in the balance sheet and statement of profit and loss of RC Fashions Ltd. to compute key ratios on the basis of following assumptions:

   a. All sales are credit sales
   b. Tax rate is 30%
   c. Cost of goods sold is ₹450 million
   d. ₹100 million of long-term borrowing is payable within 1 year
   e. Par value of share ₹10

Balance sheet of RC Fashions Ltd. as on March 31, 2014		
		₹ in million
	2014	2013
EQUITY AND LIABILITIES		
Shareholders' funds	600	540
Share capital	250	250
Reserves and surplus	350	290
Non-current liabilities	496	431
Long-term borrowings	390	340
Deferred tax liabilities (net)	55	49
Long-term provisions	51	42

(Continued)

Continued

Balance sheet of RC Fashions Ltd. as on March 31, 2014		
		₹ in million
	2014	**2013**
Current Liabilities	272	244
Short-term borrowings	160	150
Trade payables	80	70
Other current liabilities	21	15
Short-term provisions	11	9
Total	1368	1215
ASSETS		
Non-current assets	520	442
Fixed assets	410	355
Non-current investments	90	72
Long-term loans and advances	20	15
Current assets	848	773
Current investments	37	56
Inventories	385	355
Trade receivables	380	325
Cash and cash equivalents	11	9
Short-term loans and advances	35	28
Total	1368	1215

Statement of Profit and Loss for RC Fashions Ltd. for the year ended on March 31, 2014	
	₹ in million
Revenue from operations	910
Other income	28
Total revenues	938

(*Continued*)

Continued

Statement of Profit and Loss for RC Fashions Ltd. for the year ended on March 31, 2014	
	₹ in million
Expenses	
Material expenses	375
Employee benefits expenses	245
Finance costs	60
Depreciation and amortization expenses	38
Other expenses	22
Total expenses	740
Profit before exceptional and extraordinary items and tax	198
Exceptional items	0

4. Use the information given in the balance sheet and statement of profit and loss of ILM Ltd. to prepare a common size and common base statement, assuming a tax rate of 40%.

Statement of Profit and Loss for ILM Ltd. for the year ended on March 31, 2011		
		₹ in million
	2011	**2010**
Total revenues	1190	980
Expenses excluding financing cost and tax	870	710
Profit before financing cost and tax	320	270
Financing cost	120	100
Profit before tax	200	170
Tax	80	68
Profit (loss) for the period	120	102
Balance Sheet of ILM Ltd. as at Year ended on March 31, 2011		
		₹ in Million
	2011	**2010**
Shareholders' funds	550	500
Non-current liabilities: Long-term borrowings	260	200

(Continued)

Continued

Statement of Profit and Loss for ILM Ltd. for the year ended on March 31, 2011		
		₹ in million
	2011	2010
Other non-current liabilities	110	85
Current liabilities	450	330
Total	1370	1115
Non-current assets: Fixed assets	570	490
Other non-current assets	170	195
Current assets	630	430
Total	1370	1115

5. During the last financial year, Creek Machineries Ltd. reported following ratios based on their financial performance:

Ratio	Value
Sales/Assets	2.4
Net Income/EBIT	0.75
EBIT/Sales	0.20
Assets/Equity	3.5

Calculate ROA and ROE.

6. Mohan Manufacturers Ltd. reported the following information about its financial performance at the end of the financial year March 31, 2013.

	₹ in Crore
Assets	2000
Liabilities	1400
Shareholders' equity	1100
Net income	400
Dividend per share	0.4
Share price	40
Average shares outstanding	160

Calculate its key equity related ratios.

7. **Case:** Bestyear Tyres Ltd. has a long history of growth and profitability. It has a very strong presence in its sector. Analyze the financial information of the firm by calculating the following to suggest whether the share is undervalued or overvalued:

   a. Decompose the ROE for the last two years in terms of five factors.
   b. Calculate the CAGR of sales and EPS for the given period.
   c. Calculate the sustainable growth rate based on the average retention ratio and the average return on equity for the past 2 years.
   d. Calculate the following for the year 2013 and 2014: return on equity, book value per share, EPS and Prospective PE ratio
   e. Estimate the EPS for the next year (2015) using the following assumptions: (i) Net sales are projected to grow at 11%. (ii) Interest will increase by 7% over its 2014 value (iii) PBIT/Net sales ratio is expected to improve by 1% over its 2014 value.
   f. Calculate the P/E ratio of the firm using the constant growth model based on following information: (i) The dividend payout ratio for 2015 is expected to be equal to the average dividend payout ratio for the two preceding periods. (ii) The required rate of return is estimated with the help of the CAPM (Risk-free return = 6%, Market risk premium = 7%, Beta of Bestyear stock is 1.1). (iii) The dividend is expected to grow at average sustainable growth rate of the previous two periods.

The current market price of the share of Bestyear is ₹41. The effective tax rate is 30%.

The Financial statements of the firm are given below:

					₹ in Crore
Summary of statement of profit and loss	**2010**	**2011**	**2012**	**2013**	**2014**
Net sales	650	700	720	775	835
Profit before interest and tax	70	93	101	121	132
Interest	40	44	50	60	77
Profit before tax	30	49	51	61	55
Tax	9	14.7	15.3	18.3	16.5
Profit after tax	21	34.3	35.7	42.7	38.5
Dividends	9	11	13	16	16

					₹ in Crore
Summary of balance sheet	**2010**	**2011**	**2012**	**2013**	**2014**
Equity capital (₹10 par)	70	70	70	70	70
Reserves and surplus	186	214	245	267	312

(Continued)

Continued

					₹ in Crore
Summary of balance sheet	**2010**	**2011**	**2012**	**2013**	**2014**
Loan funds	200	220	240	260	275
Capital employed	456	504	555	597	657
Net fixed assets	310	345	376	396	454
Investments	25	31	37	45	34
Net current assets	121	128	142	156	169
Total assets	456	504	555	597	657
Market price per share (year end)	25	29	34	38	41

8. **Case:** Rohan Kaul is a young professional with very good income. He wants to invest some of his savings in the share market. Though he is not a market professional, he has undertaken some research and knows that the capital structure of a firm and its dividend policy have an impact on its share price. Rohan's friend, Krish has recently bought shares of TXG Ltd. Krish has bought this share on the basis of the fact that the economy is on an upswing and TXG Ltd. can be expected to do well as it belongs to a cyclical industry. The share has risen from ₹435 when Krish bought it to ₹440 now. Rohan also wants to buy the shares of the company but wants to tread carefully and therefore, study the capital structure before taking the decision to buy its shares. Use the information given below to help Rohan analyze TXG Ltd. further and decide whether he should buy the share at ₹440.

			₹ in million
Item	**2004**	**2009**	**2014**
Equity (Par value ₹10)	0.02	0.16	15.6
Retained earnings	36	65	130
Reserves and surplus	7	9	8
Long-term debt (12%)	14	11	13
Total assets			
Dividends	3.5	5.2	12.5
P/E multiple of the industry			12.45

9. Calculate the following using the summary information of the financial performance of MFM Ltd. given below:

   a. Bonus adjustment factor

b. EPS and adjusted EPS
c. Prospective P/E
d. Retrospective Price-to-Book ratio
e. Volatility of ROE

					₹ in million
Year	**2004**	**2005**	**2007**	**2008**	**2009**
PAT	1109	1210	1450	1680	1940
Equity (₹10 par value)	1600	1600	1600	1650	1650
Shareholder's funds	3070	3660	4760	5890	6010
Market price per share (end of the year)	125	146	167	142	168

The company came out with a bonus issue in the year 2008.

10. **Case:** Mr. Kishore has been investing in the stock market for the last 20 years. His returns have been largely mixed. So far his approach to investment has been to buy the shares that his morning walk cronies recommend. Recently, he came across an interesting MOOC in Westward University. The MOOC was about using ratio analysis for the purpose of equity investment decision. The key learning that Kishore got from the MOOC was that cash is the king and the current assets are key to deciding a company's liquidity position. Having completed the MOOC, Kishore sits down with the financial statements of three firms (KCC Cement, JCL Motors and TTT Ltd.) his friends have been talking about and prepares a summary of the information he considers important for equity investment. He confines his analysis to the current financial statement. He has mainly listed all the items of current assets in percentage terms and calculated the liquidity ratios. The information summarized by Kishore is given below:

Item	**KCC Cement**		**JCL Motors**		**TTT Ltd.**	
Year	**2013**	**2014**	**2013**	**2014**	**2013**	**2014**
Cash in hand	14	14	35	28	33	33
Inventory	44	48	34	36	30	30
Receivables	39	37	25	28	34	33
Other current assets	5	5	10	11	3	4
Net sales to inventory	4.1	3.91	4.62	4.31	5.78	5.32
Net sales to working capital	3.32	2.99	3.12	2.87	2.93	2.82
Current ratio	2.2	2.6	2.05	2.28	2.80	2.59
Acid test ratio	1.29	1.45	1.37	1.51	1.94	1.79

Which company should Kishore choose and why?

CASELET

Divya is a young equity analyst who has joined QFM Investment Advisors recently. In her first assignment, her supervisor asks her to analyze the financial performance of IHS Industries Ltd. and suggest whether QFM should recommend a buy on this share. Divya decides to use only ratio analysis to study the firm and calculates the following ratios:

Year	2011	2012	2013	2014
Gross profit margin (%)	51.8	54.1	56.7	58.05
Profit margin (EBIT/Sales %)	11.1	9.6	8.1	7.2
Return on assets (%)	19.2	16.9	15.1	13.1
Return on equity (%)	20.8	19.9	13.9	15.7
Total asset turnover	1.76	1.72	1.80	1.71
Debt equity ratio	1.41	1.49	1.57	1.62
Book value per share	15.78	17.97	17.59	19.27
Dividend per share (DPS)	1.30	1.45	1.57	1.61
Earnings per share (EPS)	3.4	3.71	2.55	3.25
Dividend payout ratio (%)	38.24	39.1	61.57	49.54
Market price of the share at the end of the year (₹)	37	49	49	50

On the basis of the above ratios, She recommends a buy on this share. Her justification is that all the equity-related parameters: earnings per share, dividend per share, market price per share and book value per share have increased over the previous year's level. Her supervisor says that she cannot recommend a buy on the basis of analysis undertaken by her and assigns the work of analyzing the share again to a more experienced member of his team. Do you agree with the supervisor? If yes, why?

APPENDIX

Fundamental Analysis Report

Comprehensive fundamental analysis report for Ashok Leyland Limited, prepared by ACK Capital Management Private Limited is illustrated below.[1]

ACK Capital Management

ACK Capital Management Pvt. Ltd.

9th May, 2014

Ashok Leyland Ltd.:

Rating Analysis	
Rating	ACCUMULATE
CMP	Rs 23.85
Target	Rs 25.23
Target Period	12 months
Potential Upside	5.78%

Stock Info	
Sector	Commercial Vehicles
Market Cap (Rs Cr)	6,864.55
52 Week High/Low	Rs 26.4/11.82
Face Value	Rs 1
Bloomberg Code	AL:IN
Reuters Code	ASOK.NS
BSE Code	500477
NSE Code	ASHOKLEY

Share Holding pattern %	
Promoters	41.52
FII	12.72
DII	13.30
Others	32.46

Price Movement with Sensex

Investment Rational:

Expansion of product portfolio - Increased market share in LCV and M&HCV segments

The introduction of various products across the LCV and ICV segments would help Ashok Leyland diversify its offerings and also reduce its dependency on the cyclical M&HCV segment. Above all, the persistence displayed by Ashok Leyland in increasing its market share (from 1% to 7% in LCVs and 24% to 27% in M&HCVs) across all the segments in a shrinking domestic market would give it a strong base to recover once the sales turn around.

Improving Working Capital and Debt Levels situation

Ashok Leyland is focusing on becoming operationally efficient so that the working capital investment and hence the loans in its books can be kept under control. It succeeded at reducing the working capital requirement by over Rs. 800 crores and the debt by about Rs. 760 crores as compared to the H1 '14 levels.

Aim to increase its exports in terms of market share and percentage of total company revenue

With fresh order wins from the Zimbabwe government and an expected new order from the Sri Lankan government for over Rs. 300 crores and Rs. 237 crores respectively, Ashok Leyland seems to move ahead in its plan to increase the export revenues as a part of its total revenue. This is supplemented by the fact that Ashok Leyland gained the export market share in all the segments while the total industry exports shrunk.

Capital Expenditures and new product launches will benefit Ashok Leyland as industry picks up

With majority of its Capex spending in manufacturing capacity and joint ventures done, Ashok Leyland is set to reap the benefits once the manufacturing and mining sectors revive.

[1] The author acknowledges the help extended by Mr Sunil Kamdar (Director, ACK Capital) and Mr. Dattatraya Bhandarkar (PGDM-FS, Batch 2013–15 SIMSR, Mumbai) in making the report available for publishing in this book.

ACK Capital Management

ACK Capital Management Pvt. Ltd.

Industry Overview:

The Indian Commercial Vehicle industry has experienced a consistent volume growth in the past decade with the CAGR being over 15.7% from FY'06 to FY'12. However, the industry has been experiencing a slowdown and hence a contraction in sales volumes starting with FY'12, mainly owing to factors like **slowdown in the economy**, stalled infrastructure projects and **fall in the industrial activity** in terms of **manufacturing and mining activities**. The issue was further compounded by **deregulation of diesel prices** and **sluggish growth in freight transport rates**, which put a downward pressure on the profitability of road transportation industry and hence on the demand for commercial vehicles.

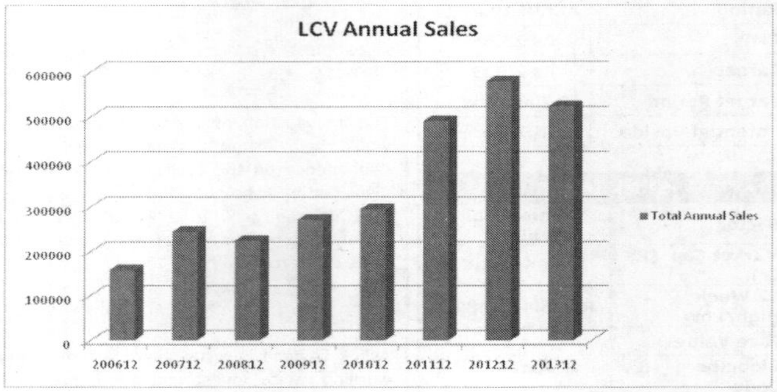

Fig 1: Domestic LCV Sales

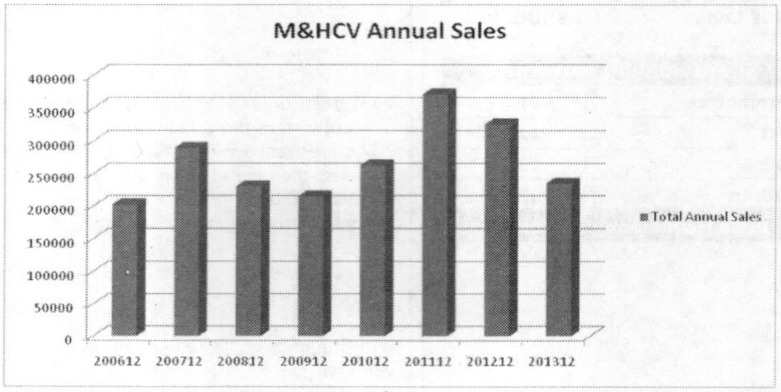

Fig 2: Domestic M&HCV Sales

Capital Management

ACK Capital Management Pvt. Ltd.

The sales of the **Medium & Heavy Commercial Vehicles** displays a high correlation with the manufacturing and mining activity as explained from FY'08 to FY'14. There is a **correlation of 0.61 between the M&HCV sales and the Mining IIP** figures and of **0.62 between the M&HCV sales and Manufacturing IIP** figures. However, there exists a lag in the improvement of the Commercial Vehicles sales over the improvement in the mining and manufacturing activity in the country. This indicates that the current trend of improving activity in the Mining sector in the states of Karnataka and Goa will benefit the M&HCV sales correspondingly.

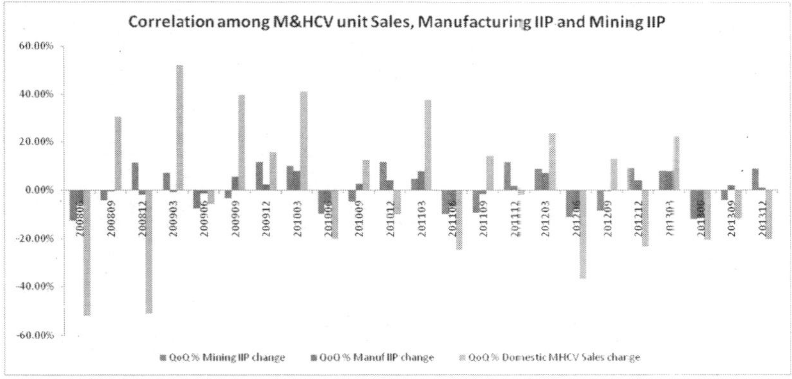

Fig 3: Correlation of Domestic M&HCV Sales with Manufacturing IIP and Mining IIP

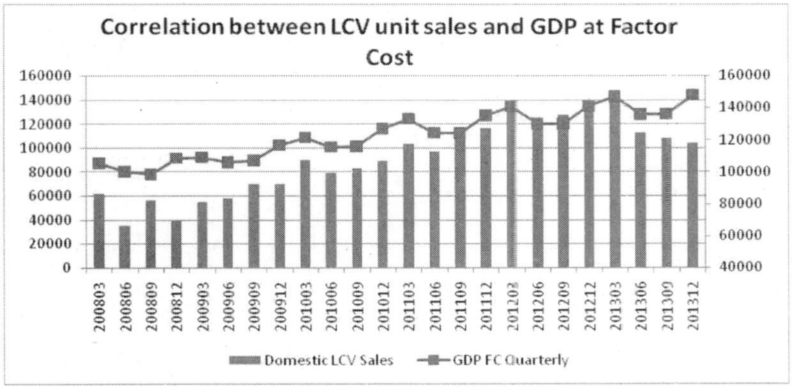

Fig 4: Correlation of Domestic Light Commercial Vehicle Sales with GDP at Factor Cost

ACK Capital Management Pvt. Ltd.

Further, the LCV sales, apart from being influenced by the manufacturing activity(**strong correlation of 0.9 between LCV sales and Manufacturing IIP**), are also influenced by GDP figures owing to the driving factor of consumption spending which is accounted for in the GDP figures(**strong correlation of 0.91 between LCV Sales and GDP FC**). Moreover, they display lesser cyclicality than their M&HCV counterparts, thus helping companies to weather downtrends in the economic conditions.

ACK Capital Management

ACK Capital Management Pvt. Ltd.

Company Overview:

Ashok Leyland has been a long standing name in the Commercial Vehicles industry of India. It is the **3rd largest industry player by sales volume(12.95%)**. The company has been **primarily known for its presence in the Medium and Heavy Commercial Vehicles segment**, where it is the 2nd largest market share holder(**26.7%**). It is dominant in the **M&HCV Bus segment** where it is the **market leader in the domestic market** with a **market share of 41.2%** and also in the export market with a market share of 63.6%. Ashok Leyland has **joint ventures with four companies** : With Nissan for Light Commercial Vehicles, with John Deere for construction equipment, with Continental AG for infotronics products and services and with Alteams Group for manufacturing aluminum components for automotive sectors. Ashok Leyland has also done a few acquisitions to augment its export market business. It has acquired Czech Republic based truck manufacturing company, Avia, to expand in the European markets and has a 75% stake in the UK-based bus manufacturing company, Optare, to have presence in the bus segment in the developed countries. In terms of Business segments, majority of Ashok Leyland's business revenues come from its Vehicles business followed by the Spare parts and Trading operations business.

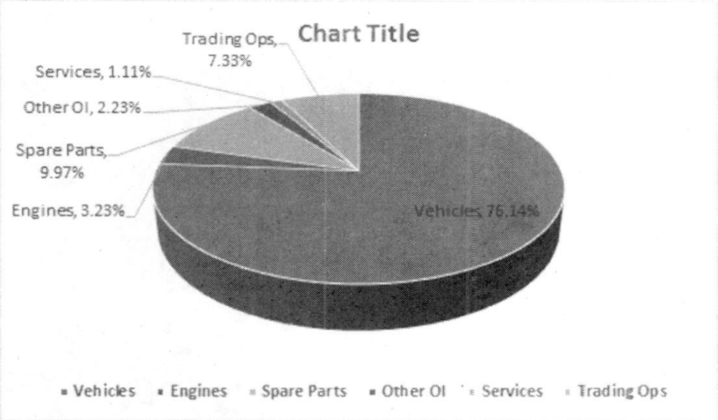

Fig 5: Ashok Leyland revenue contribution from all the businesses

ACK Capital Management

ACK Capital Management Pvt. Ltd.

Investment Rational:

Expansion of product portfolio - Increased market share in LCV and M&HCV segments

While the commercial vehicle industry started experiencing a slow-down right since 2011, Ashok Leyland has managed to slice out some market share from the competition in both, LCV and M&HCV segments. Since FY 2011, Ashok Leyland has been foraying into new segments. It has consistently **gained market share in the LCV segment** from 1% in the year ending Dec'11 to 7% in the year ending Dec'13 This increase has been attributed to the launch of new products, primarily Dost.

The **LCV sales revenue as a percentage of the total revenue increased** from 2% in the year ending Dec'11 to 16.35% inyear ending Dec'12 to 22.5%inyearending Dec'13. This move has been **aimed at reducing its dependency on the cyclical M&HCV sales** and developing a product portfolio of LCVs and ICVs which are increasingly gaining focus because of the reduced capacity utilization of transportation company vehicle fleet and also because of rising prominence of the hub and spoke model.

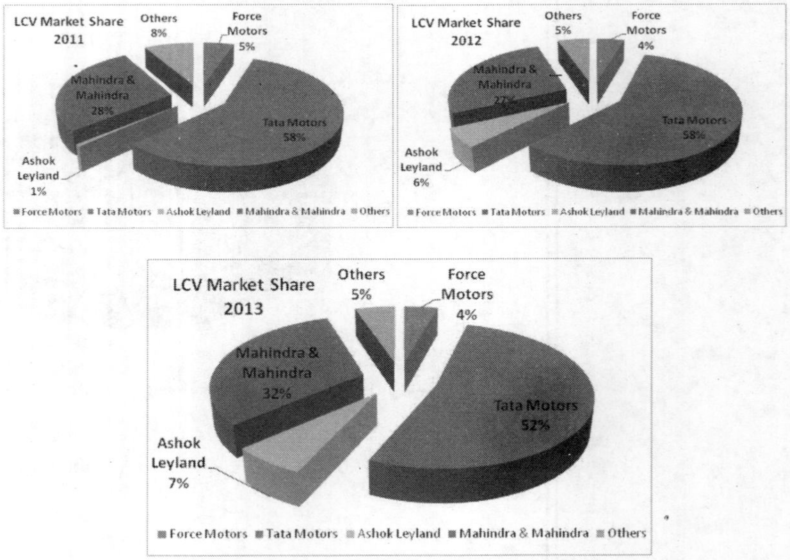

Fig 6: Shift in market share of companies in the LCV segment from FY'12 to FY'14

ACK Capital Management

ACK Capital Management Pvt. Ltd.

On similar lines, Ashok Leyland has also **managed to gain the market share in M&HCV segment** from 24% in year ending Dec'11 to 27% in year ending Dec'13 **while the M&HCV market segment experienced a yearly compression of about 21%**. The Current trend of improving activity in Mining sector in the states of Karnataka and Goa will benefit **Ashok Leyland,** as it is the **2nd largest market share holder** in the M&HCV segment.

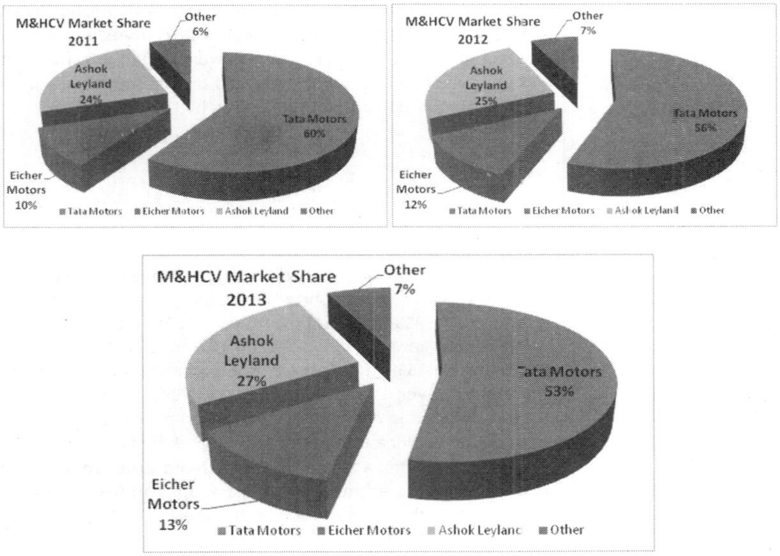

Fig 7: Shift in the market share of companies in the M&HCV segment from FY'12 to FY'14

The recently **launched ICV named Boss**, which was launched in 4 southern states of the country, has **gained market share in all those states**. As Ashok Leyland completes its all India launch of this vehicle, it is expected to gain more market share in the emerging ICV market as well.

ACK Capital Management

ACK Capital Management Pvt. Ltd.

Improving Working Capital and Debt Levels situation

Ashok Leyland has been focusing on becoming operationally efficient by **reducing its working capital requirements**, which it plans to achieve by controlling its inventory levels through Manufacturing Resource Planning and also by selling some of its non-core assets. The company has managed to **reduce its working capital requirement by Rs. 800 Crores** by the end of Q3 as compared to the H1 levels, primarily by managing the inventory levels well (a **reduction in Finished Goods inventory from 7,500 to 4,200**). The **sale of non-core assets and investments** has further generated a profit of Rs. 134 Crores. These two things were aimed at reducing the debt in the books of Ashok Leyland, which stands reduced by an amount of Rs. 760 crores (from a peak of Rs. 6160 Crores in H1 to Rs. 5400 Crores by the end of Q3).

Aim to increase its exports in terms of market share and percentage of total company revenue

Ashok Leyland has also **gained market share in the export LCV and M&HCV markets**, both of which shrunk over the years(M&HCV shrunk by 13.9% and LCV shrunk by 21.2% annually) from year ending Dec'11 to year ending Dec'13. It gained a marginal market share in LCV exports from 1% to 2% over the horizon and it had gained from 40% to 45% in export M&HCV exports from year ending Dec'11 to year ending Dec'12. However its share declined to 38% primarily owing to a significant fall in exports to Sri Lanka, which is Ashok Leyland's primary export market(40% of its total exports), because of significant increase in import duties and high levy charges. However, Ashok Leyland has gained a **sizeable order from Zimbabwe government for over Rs. 300 Crores and also expects an order from the Sri Lankan government for Rs. 237 Crores**. Both these orders will be honored in FY'14.

Capital Expenditures and new product launches will benefit Ashok Leyland as industry picks up

Ashok Leyland is **done with the majority of its Capital Expenditures and investments**, both in the manufacturing capacities and technology for new product launches and also in their joint ventures. **As the manufacturing and mining industry is expected to pick up** with an improvement in economic and political conditions in FY'15, these **investments will start to pay off in favor of Ashok Leyland**, primarily **due to a consistent gain in market share** that it has achieved from FY'12 till date.

ACK Capital Management Pvt. Ltd.

Valuation:

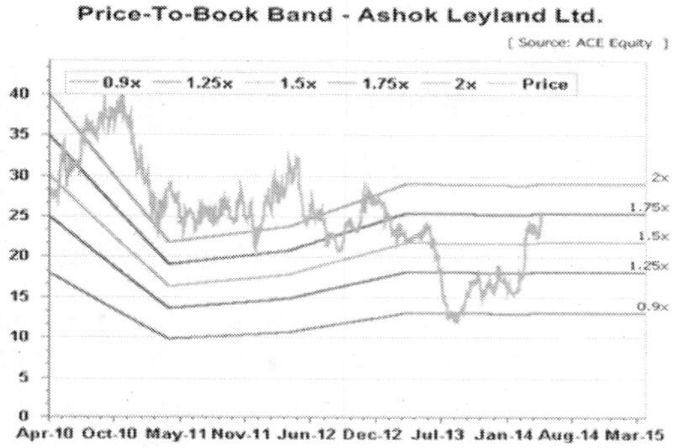

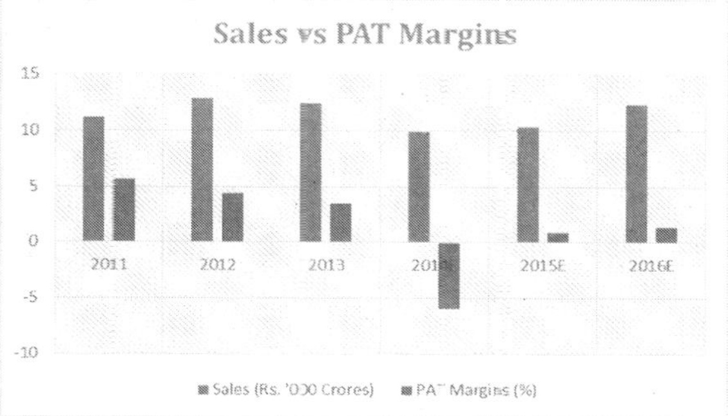

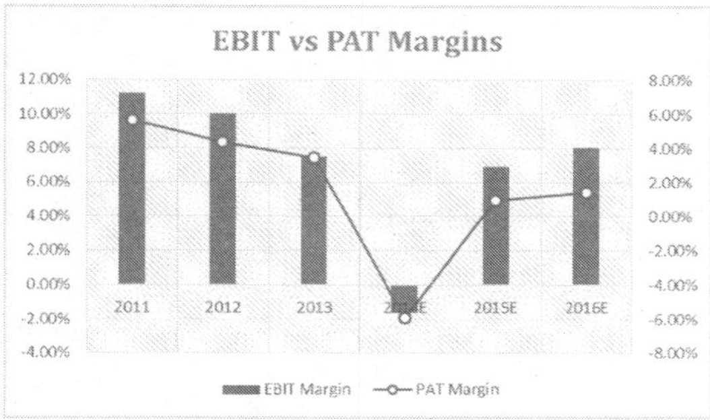

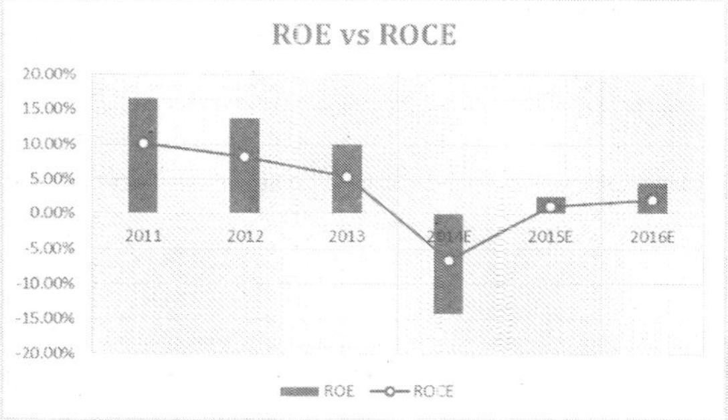

As can be seen from the Price to Book Forward band, the share price has been consolidating in the forward Price to Book band of 1.5x and 1.75x. It is recommended to accumulate Ashok Leyland in the price range of Rs. 21.8 to Rs. 25.42. We value Ashok Leyland at FY'15E Price to Book of 1.75x. As per our understanding, the fair value for Ashok Leyland is Rs. 25.23.

ACK Capital Management

ACK Capital Management Pvt. Ltd.

Forecasts:

Income Statement

DESCRIPTION	Mar-16 E	Mar-15 E	Mar-14	Mar-13
No of Months	12.00	12.00	12.00	12.00
INCOME :				
Gross Sales	13692.70	11410.58	10970.18	13947.98
Less: Inter divisional transfers				
Less: Sales Returns	486.09	405.08	394.93	649.42
Less: Excise Duty	796.40	662.38	641.76	817.36
Net Sales	12410.21	10343.12	9933.50	12481.20
EXPENDITURE :				
Increase/Decrease in Stock	18.21	124.60	526.57	271.98
Raw Material Consumed	9105.65	7580.30	7380.74	8851.16
Power & Fuel Cost	79.99	64.66	65.82	86.00
Employee Cost	1054.34	895.50	1031.20	1075.51
Other Manufacturing Expenses	251.64	205.77	213.92	260.92
General and Administration Expenses	733.24	611.04	680.15	845.48
Selling and Distribution Expenses	204.51	179.40	208.43	213.69
Miscellaneous Expenses	2.74	3.42	1.10	
Less: Expenses Capitalised				
Total Expenditure	11450.32	9664.69	10107.92	11604.73
Operating Profit (Excl OI)	959.89	678.43	-174.43	876.47
Other Income	40.74	41.08	10.97	62.35
Operating Profit	1000.62	719.51	-163.46	938.82
Interest	333.19	319.50	427.84	376.89
PBDT	667.43	400.01	-591.29	561.93
Depreciation	356.69	282.98	329.11	380.78
Profit Before Taxation & Exceptional Items	310.74	117.03	-920.40	181.15
Exceptional Income / Expenses	29.58	11.20	178.81	289.56
Profit Before Tax	340.32	128.23	-741.58	470.71
Provision for Tax	164.31	30.81	-151.39	37.00
Profit After Tax	176.00	97.43	-590.20	433.71
Equity Dividend %	70.00	40.00		60.00
Earnings Per Share	0.66	0.37	-2.11	1.63
Adjusted EPS	0.66	0.37	-2.11	1.63

ACK Capital Management

ACK Capital Management Pvt. Ltd.

Balance Sheet

DESCRIPTION	Mar-16	Mar-15	Mar-14	Mar-13
EQUITY AND LIABILITIES				
Share Capital	266.07	266.07	266.07	266.07
Share Warrants & Outstandings	0.00	0.00	0.00	0.00
Total Reserves	3603.59	3571.75	3598.84	4189.04
Shareholder's Funds	3869.66	3837.82	3864.91	4455.10
Long-Term Borrowings				
Secured Loans	1317.71	1265.80	1539.55	1223.33
Unsecured Loans	1677.08	1611.02	1924.45	1514.51
Deferred Tax Assets / Liabilities	483.37	458.01	505.97	527.37
Other Long Term Liabilities	26.45	30.15	40.05	1.78
Long Term Provisions	80.43	77.27	78.85	78.51
Total Non-Current Liabilities	3585.04	3442.25	4088.87	3345.50
Current Liabilities				
Trade Payables	2496.97	2171.28	1973.89	2485.37
Other Current Liabilities	1696.11	1730.73	1648.31	1735.06
Short Term Borrowings	1063.04	966.40	1073.78	766.98
Short Term Provisions	393.18	323.01	269.18	308.68
Total Current Liabilities	5649.29	5191.41	4965.15	5296.10
Total Liabilities	13103.99	12471.48	12918.93	13096.70
ASSETS				
Non-Current Assets				
Fixed Assets	6363.70	6332.04	6269.35	5970.81
Non Current Investments	2564.97	2331.79	2454.51	2337.63
Long Term Loans & Advances	425.62	472.91	497.80	452.54
Other Non Current Assets	38.83	37.03	41.15	39.19
Total Non-Current Assets	9393.17	9173.77	9262.81	8800.17
Current Assets Loans & Advances				
Currents Investments				
Inventories	1569.91	1365.13	1515.82	1896.02
Sundry Debtors	1264.70	1149.72	1277.47	1419.41
Cash and Bank	18.28	18.28	16.62	13.94
Other Current Assets	376.17	341.97	379.97	444.41
Short Term Loans and Advances	481.77	422.60	465.25	522.75
Total Current Assets	3710.82	3297.71	3656.12	4296.53
Miscellaneous Expenses not written off				
Total Assets	13103.99	12471.48	12918.93	13096.70
Book Value	14.54	14.42	14.53	11.87

ACK Capital Management Pvt. Ltd.

Disclaimer:

This report is for the personal information of the authorized recipient and does not construe to be any investment, legal or taxation advice to you. ACK Capital Management Ltd (ACK) is not soliciting any action based upon it. This report is not for public distribution and has been furnished to you solely for your information and should not be reproduced or redistributed to any other person in any form.

The report is based upon information that we consider reliable, but we do not represent that it is accurate or complete, and it should not be relied upon such. ACK or any of its affiliates or employees shall not be in any way responsible for any loss or damage that may arise to any person from any inadvertent error in the information contained in this report. ACK or any of its affiliates or employees do not provide, at any time, any express or implied warranty of any kind, regarding any matter pertaining to this report, including without limitation the implied warranties of merchantability, fitness for a particular purpose, and non-infringement. The recipients of this report should rely on their own investigations.

ACK and/or its affiliates and/or employees may have interests/positions, financial or otherwise in the securities mentioned in this report. This information is subject to change without any prior notice. ACK reserves the right to make modifications and alternations to this statement as may be required from time to time. Nevertheless, ACK is committed to providing independent and transparent recommendations to its clients, and would be happy to provide information in response to specific client queries.

Tracing Price Trends and Patterns: Technical Analysis

12

CHAPTER OBJECTIVES

- ❒ Understanding the basic premises of technical analysis
- ❒ Assessing the Dow theory and the Elliott Wave Principle
- ❒ Evaluating continuation and reversal patterns in detail
- ❒ Appreciating the worth of technical analysis in making trading decisions
- ❒ Elucidating the limitations in use of technical analysis for investment decision

In the preceding chapters, we discussed fundamental analysis, an approach to security analysis that estimates intrinsic value of a share on the basis of the earnings and dividend of the company. It is based on the belief that the market is 90% psychological and 10% logical. The view of fundamental analysts is to buy a share if its market price is less than its intrinsic value and sell the share if its price is more than its intrinsic value. This is based on the general view of fundamentalists that the price of a share always tends towards its intrinsic value over a period of time.

There is another group of analysts that uses an alternative approach to predict the behavior of stock prices, this approach is called technical analysis. It is based on the assumption that the market is 90% psychological and 10% logical. This means that technical analysts believe that the price fluctuations in the market are caused not only by logical, value-driven factors but many emotional and irrational factors as well. Technical analysts analyze the price data to generate superior returns in the stock market. They use charts and graphs to plot past price data and predict the direction of the future price movement.

Technical analysts do not deny the usefulness of fundamental information but believe that it is possible to exploit the time taken by prices to adjust to a new equilibrium, i.e., move towards their intrinsic value. Technical analysis is based on the belief that patterns in volume and prices of shares reflect the forces of demand and supply in the market. Technicians believe that such patterns, whatever their underlying causes, continue to persist for some period of time and can be used to predict whether the prices can be expected to move upwards or downwards and at times even by how much.

Technical analysis is actually used as a supplement to fundamental analysis rather than as its substitute. Fundamental analysis can be used to detect buy/sell signal and technical analysis will then be effective in deciding the timing of sell or buy order. For example, suppose fundamental analysis indicates a buy but technical analysis indicates prices are likely to fall. In such situations, postponement of purchase decision can yield higher holding period returns. Similarly, a sell indicated by fundamental analysis can be executed a little later if technical analysts expects prices to rise.

On the basis of the above discussion, technical analysis may be described as an approach to decision making based on identification of trends in price movements and recognizing the onset of the reversal of prevailing trend. This is where the real challenge lies in technical analysis. Price of shares moves in patterns within the trend and it is difficult to identify a reversal within the trend or the reversal in the trend itself. Technical analysis is based on the basic premise that the prices of shares are determined by the interaction of the market forces of demand and supply. Demand and supply of shares are, in turn, influenced by a number of rational and irrational factors driven by emotions and behavioral biases. Given the impact of fundamental and psychological factors, the prices of shares move in persistent, detectable trends, minor deviations notwithstanding. These trends persist over observable periods of time and get reversed due to the shifts in the forces of demand and supply. Technical analysts believe that charting the movement in prices to analyze past price data can help them predict future price movement.

The basic premises of technical analysis may be summarized as:

1. The price of a security in the stock market is dependent on the forces of demand and supply operating in the market.
2. The supply and demand of a security in the market is affected by a number of rational and irrational influences.
3. The direction of price movement of a security persists over observable periods of time, i.e., prices move in distinct trends.
4. The trends in stock price movement are reversed in response to changes in the forces of demand and supply operating in the market.
5. Trends and trend reversals can be detected through charts plotted using stock price data.
6. The past price data can be plotted to form certain distinct patterns to forecast future direction of the price movement because technicians believe that history tends to repeat itself.
7. Technical analysts primarily use price data for analysis because they believe that all the information is reflected in prices, i.e., market discounts everything.

Though technical analysts work only with price and volume data, the tools that they can use are varied and large in numbers. Technical analysis, being the oldest approach of security analysis, has witnessed development of a variety of indicators over the time that help analysts in predicting future direction of the price movement. Technical analysis can be applied to any asset including currency, bond, equity and commodity but we will focus on equity stock.

Tools and Techniques of Technical Analysis

Just as there are multiple ways of valuing equity using fundamental analysis, there are also many tools and techniques used by technical analysts. Guided by their belief that the market discounts everything, including fundamental factors, the technical analysts believe that the prices move in trends that tend to repeat themselves time and again. To detect these trends, some analysts rely on chart patterns whereas others tend to use tools called indicators and oscillators or a combination of different tools. We will begin our discussion with a study of the Dow's theory, Elliot's Wave theory and Fibonacci retracement before moving to the charting techniques, oscillators and indicators.

The Dow Theory

The Dow theory is the foundation of technical analysis; therefore, a discussion on technical analysis should rightly begin with an introduction to the theory. The Dow theory is more than a century old, having been formulated through a series of Wall Street Journal editorials written by Charles H. Dow. Actually, what is now called as the Dow theory is a compilation of the collective market wisdom of Charles Dow and William Peter Hamilton.

The theory essentially represents how Dow thought the stock market behaved and how the market behavior was a reflection of the prevailing business environment. He believed that the stock market was a dependable barometer of the business conditions and a thorough analysis of the market as a whole could be used to assess the business performance and predict the future movements in the market and the individual stocks. Dow applied his theory to construct the Dow Jones Industrial Index and the Dow Jones Rail Index.

Since technical analysis has its roots in the Dow's theory, security analysts using technical analysis should understand the basics of this theory clearly. Let us now discuss the basic tenets/propositions of the Dow theory.

The key propositions of the Dow theory are:

1. **The Market Discounts Everything:** This implies that the market takes into account all the known information – past, present and even future and the same gets reflected in the prices of stocks and market index levels. The information could be just about anything from cash reserve ratio data to inflation and GDP numbers to anticipated earnings and dividend announcements by companies to even the emotions of the investors. The only information that is not reflected in the prices is the totally unanticipated or unknowable event like a natural calamity or a sudden assassination of a political leader. However, even such events find an expression in current price levels, the risks of their occurrence is priced into the market. The changes in price levels occur as the market responds and adjusts to reflect any new information that comes in. It is important to note that this adjustment in prices is for the short-run, without affecting the medium or the long-run trend.
2. **Closing Price is the Key Input:** The Dow theory is focused on price or market data only rather than the fundamental statistics like macroeconomic indicators or the company performance. Further, the price data that the Dow's theory is concerned with is the closing price and not the intra-day movements. It should be mentioned here that this theory is concerned mainly with the movements of the overall markets, rather than individual scrips. The Dow theory states that the pattern of price movements in the market can be identified with the help of line charts. These charts are plotted using the closing price data of the market against the corresponding trading day.
3. **Trend Analysis can be Used to Determine the Direction of the Movement of the Market:** The Dow theory mentions the existence of three distinct cyclical trends that can be observed in the movement of the market: primary, secondary and minor. These trends are simultaneous in nature. The theory uses peak-and-trough analysis to identify the three trends. A primary trend is the long-range cycle that can last for more than a year and it could be upward, indicating a bull run or downward, indicating a bear market. The secondary trend is a restraining force on the primary trend and is always in the opposite direction of the primary movement. In fact, it is called correction and lasts for an intermediate period from few weeks to a few months. To explain further, in a bull market, the secondary trend would move downwards for some short duration and in a bear market, secondary trend would move upwards for some short duration. A correction in upward direction is called rally and a correction in downward direction is called reaction. The third trend in the market is the minor movement that represents day-to-day fluctuations and has no analytical value. We will discuss these trends in detail a little later in the chapter.

4. **A Trend Persists Until a Comprehensible Reversal Takes Place:** According to the Dow theory, a market moving upwards would continue to do so until a major reversal occurs. This implies that the market continues to move in the same direction for a considerable period of time, as represented by the primary trend discussed above. In other words, market displays inertia and moves in the same direction until strong disruption like changed economic or business conditions cause it to move conclusively in the reverse direction. The reversal of trend is explained in terms of peaks and troughs discussed in detail a little later in this chapter.
5. **Reversals can Occur when All the Indices of Market Performance are in Agreement:** The theory states that the markets would continue to move in the same direction for a long period of time until a significant reversal (from bear to bull market or vice-versa) is signaled by all major stock market indices. This implies that the rise in any one index in a falling market cannot be taken to be a signal of reversal in bear trend or a fall in one or few indices in a rising market cannot be treated as an indicator of reversal in the primary bull trend. The reason behind this is the basic belief of the theory that the stock market is a reflection of the prevalent business conditions; it moves up when these conditions are good and down when the conditions are bad. This implies that if all the indices are not moving in the same direction, there is confusion about the prevailing market conditions and no clear primary trend can develop in such a situation.
6. **Trend should be Supported and Confirmed by Volumes:** Volumes are also important to reinforce the direction of movement of markets indicated by the price data. Volume data acts as the secondary but confirmatory indicator of the direction of movement signaled by market indices. This implies that a movement of price in the direction of the trend should be supported by an underlying rise in the volume and a movement of price in the opposite direction of the trend should have an underlying decrease in the volume, i.e., in a downtrend, the volume should fall when the price moves upwards and rise when the price falls. The reasoning behind this is simple. Increased volume when price falls during a downtrend indicates that the traders believe in the strength of the bear trend and are more willing to sell a scrip in apprehension of further fall in the price. Correction periods are usually marked by low volume because most traders stick to their positions, as they believe that the momentum of the primary movement will continue. Similarly, if the volume behaves contrary to the existing trend, it signals a weakness in the trend. For instance, a fall in volume in a bull market when the price is rising, is an indicator of upcoming dissipation in buying. Obviously, the chances of continuation of uptrend are low if most buyers turn sellers.
7. **The Idea of Line Ranges or Trading Ranges:** The Dow theory has also put forth the idea of line ranges, called trading ranges nowadays. The line ranges represent the periods of consolidation where prices move sideways. This is the time when traders should follow a wait and watch strategy before concluding the direction of the market. They should ideally hold back, until the trend line is breached, to decide the direction of the trend. For example, if the price falls below the line, it is more than likely that the market is going to move downwards.

Marketview 12.1 The Story of the Dow Theory

In 1882, Charles Dow and Edward Jones, two newspaper reporters, decided to publish their own newspaper to report accurate financial news. In 1899, the *Wall Street Journal* (WSJ) was started.

Even before the *Wall Street Journal* came into existence, Charles Dow had started computing stock market averages and compiled an index from 14 companies comprising 12 railroad and 2 industrial companies on February 20, 1885. He didn't give any formal expression to his theory. It was only expressed through his editorials written during 1900–1902. Dow passed away in 1902

Hamilton, who had joined WSJ in 1899, published the implications of the Dow's theory in a series of editorials titled "The Price Movement." He also published a book titled "The Stock Market Barometer" in 1922.

Hamilton successfully applied the theory between 1900 and 1921 to forecast the Panic of 1907, the sluggish market preceding World War I and a bear market in 1917.

Robert Rhea, another well-known Dowist, published a book called "The Dow theory" in 1932. The book forms the main basis of what we know about the Dow theory today.

Source: Based on excerpt drawn from http://www.scribd.com/doc/, accessed on November 16, 2014.

A closer look at the three trends identified by the Dow theory

As mentioned above, according to the Dow theory, the market moves in three distinct trends: primary trends that are the major movements and can be in upward or downward direction; secondary or intermedia trends are corrections of the primary movement and they last for short duration; and the minor trends, representing day-to-day fluctuations which are not significant from analysis point of view. Further, it should be noted that the secondary movements are often more volatile than the primary movements. An upward primary trend may typically have a number of downward secondary movements.

The minor trend is usually a corrective movement within a secondary trend. It might go against the direction of the intermediate trend. Though the Dow theorists are primarily concerned with the primary and secondary trends, however, it would be wrong to completely ignore the minor movements. These short-run fluctuations should also be considered, though always in the context of the larger picture, as they are also a part of the other two trends. Over-emphasis on minor fluctuation is not advised as the short-term volatility can distort the long-term implications and cause the traders to take irrational decisions. Figure 12.1 exhibits the primary, secondary and minor trends.

Figure 12.1 The primary, secondary and minor trends in BSE SENSEX.

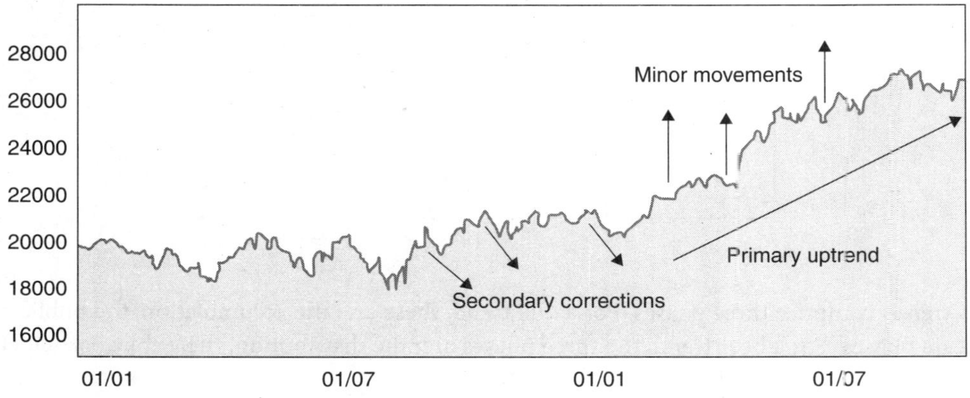

Source: www.bseindia.com, accessed on November 19, 2014.

Let us discuss the primary trend in detail now.

In the Dow theory, the primary trend is the most important movement that needs to be determined by the analysts. This is because the primary trend affects the movement of the prices of the scrips as well as the secondary and the minor trends. It is a long-term trend that, according to Dow, persists and it could last between one to three years. The primary trend changes only after there is a confirmed reversal. (Explained further while discussing peaks and trough). Figure 12.2 exhibits a bull primary trend and Figure 12.3 exhibits a bear primary trend.

Figure 12.2 Primary uptrend.

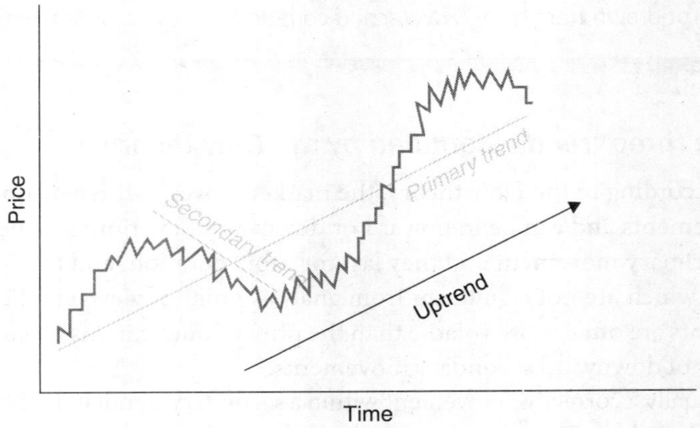

Figure 12.3 Primary downtrend.

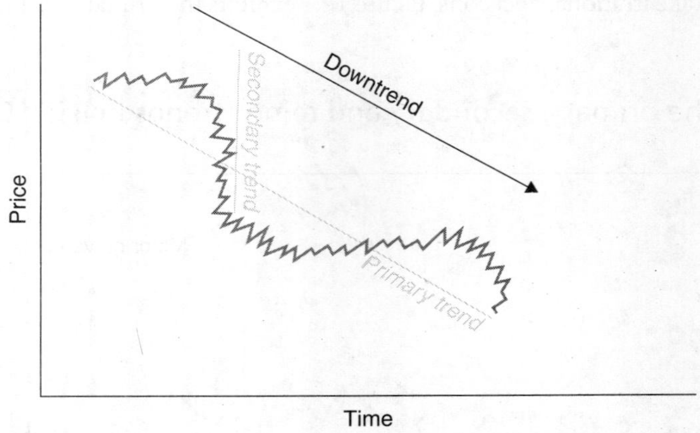

Primary trends comprise three phases. For a bull trend, these are: the accumulation, the public participation and the excess phases. For a bear trend, the three phases are: the distribution, the public participation and the panic phases.

Let us now discuss the three phases both in bull and bear markets.

1. **Primary Upward Trend (Bull Market):**
   (a) *The accumulation phase:* This phase occurs at the beginning of an uptrend, where the informed investors enter the market as it is priced at a very attractive level. The reason behind attractive pricing is that the accumulation phase typically occurs at the end of a bear run with market having discounted all bad news and offering limited downside risk. However, this phase is difficult to spot as it occurs at the end of a downtrend and one never knows if it is a reversal or just a secondary correction. The sentiment in the market continues to be pessimistic as people fear that the further fall in prices is just round the corner.

   What actually happens in accumulation phase is that the selling pressure wanes off and the downtrend flattens out. The start of accumulation phase marks a period of price consolidation and the later stages of this phase are marked by further rise in the prices. The uptrend is confirmed when the market does not fall back to the previous lows.

   (b) *Public participation phase:* As the recovery, anticipated by informed investors, begins to set in, the new uptrend enters this phase. The public participation phase is marked by more positive sentiment riding on the back of strong economic growth and earnings performance by the companies. The generally improved sentiment pulls the investors back into the market, increasing the demand and the prices thereof. This phase not only lasts for the longest time but also witnesses largest price movement, causing the traders to take long positions. This is a reaffirmation of the setting in of the upward trend.

   (c) *The excess phase:* This is the last phase of the uptrend marked by a selling by the informed investors to the new entrants. The market is characterized by 'irrational exuberance' where people feel that everything will continue to be great and good. The late entrants get into a buying spree without realizing that they are entering the market near the top. The market falls soon; causing a selling spree that pulls the market down further. During this phase, the analysts watch for signals to indicate weakening of the uptrend or strengthening of the downward movement.

2. **Primary Downward Trend (Bear Market):**
   (a) *The distribution phase:* The first phase of the bear market is marked by the selling off or distribution of their positions by the informed investors; hence the name distribution phase. It is opposite of the accumulation phase of the bull run and it sets in near the end of the uptrend where the market is distinctly overbought. Despite the selling by these investors, the market sentiment remains positive. Continued buying is witnessed as the late entrants buy into the market in anticipation of further rise in it. This phase is difficult to spot as it might be mistaken for a downward secondary correction within the primary up trend.

   The beginning of the distribution phase is characterized by a peaking of the market wherein the price starts to flatten out and selling pressure rises. In the latter part of this phase, more and more investors start selling, causing the prices to fail further. The downtrend is confirmed when the market does not exceed the previous highs.

   (b) *Public participation phase:* As in the case of public participation phase of the bull market, this phase of bear market is the longest and witnesses the largest price movement, though in the downward direction. It becomes quite obvious that the business conditions are deteriorating and the sentiment becomes more negative with time. The market goes on discounting the depressed conditions and the selling spree rises. Most traders take short positions as the downtrend becomes more persistent.

   (c) *The panic phase:* The panic phase is the last phase of the bear market. As the name suggests, during this phase, the market is in a frenzy, with everyone trying to dump their holdings quickly. These sellers are usually the investors who had entered the bull market during the excess phase. The general sentiment is negative, spurred by the dismal economic indicators and corporate earnings. When it seems that there is nowhere to go but down, things start changing and the accumulation phase of the bull market inches its way in. Thus, the cycle continues.

The Dow theory in practice: interpreting signals and identifying trends

One of the most challenging tasks faced by the technical analysts is the determination of the duration of a price movement within the prevailing primary trend before it reverses. The key to technical analysis is to identify the direction of the primary trend and to trade with it, until there is significant evidence suggesting a reversal in it. This also represents the toughest task in using technical analysis for trading. Accurate identification of trend reversal is a skill that needs to be honed with practice.

The technique offered by the Dow theory for identification of trend reversals is called peak-and-trough analysis. The Dow theory postulates that the movement of market consists of a series of peaks and troughs, though over the long run it moves in a distinct upward or downward direction. A peak represents the highest price of a market movement, conversely a trough is the point of lowest price of a market at a given time.

The bull market comprises successively higher peaks and troughs as exhibited in Figure 12.4.

Figure 12.4 Upward trend.

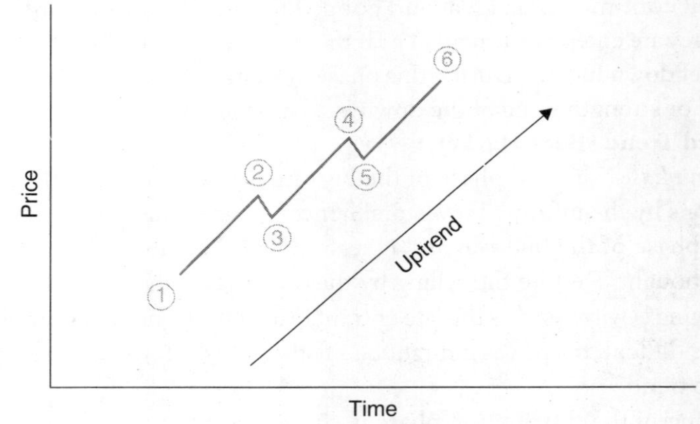

In Figure 12.4, points 2 and 4 represent the peaks, where 4 is higher than 2. Similarly, 3 and 5 represent the troughs, where 5 is higher than 3. A reversal in upward trend will come when the subsequent peak is unable to reach a new high and the subsequent trough is not able to remain above the previous trough as shown in Figure 12.5. It is clear that the peak represented by 6 is lower than the peaks represented by 2 and 4. Similarly, the trough represented by 5 is lower than the troughs represented by 1 and 3. When this happens, the bull market moves in the downward direction, signaling trend reversal and setting in of the bear market.

The bear market comprises successively lower peaks and troughs as exhibited in Figure 12.6.

In Figure 12.6, points 2 and 4 represent the peaks, where 4 is lower than 2. Similarly, 1 and 3 represent the troughs, where 3 is lower than 1. A reversal in downward trend will come when the subsequent peak is higher than the previous peak and the subsequent trough is higher than the previous trough as shown in Figure 12.7.

Figure 12.5 Reversal in upward trend.

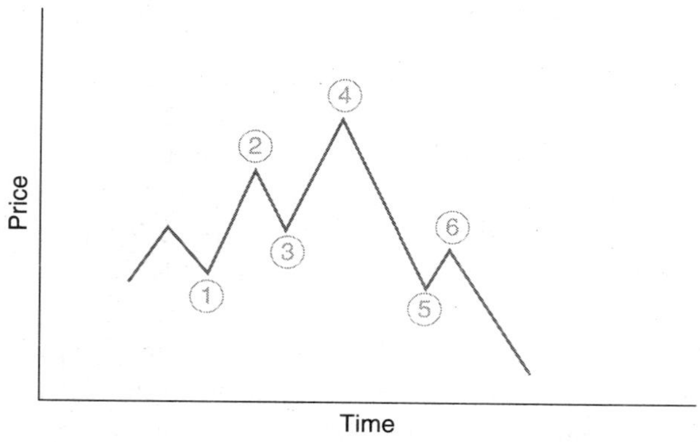

Figure 12.6 Downward trend.

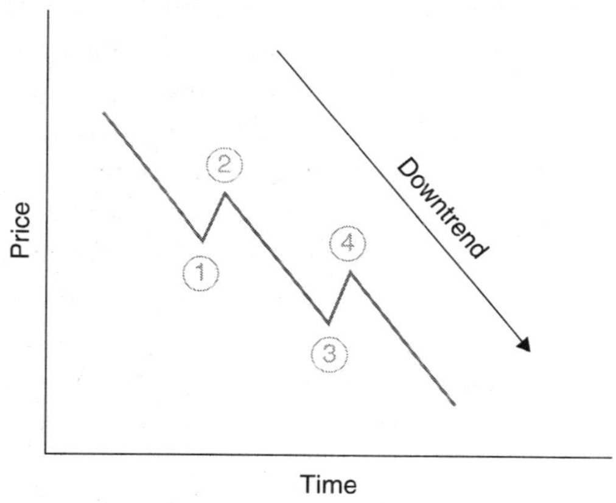

Figure 12.7 Reversal in downward trend.

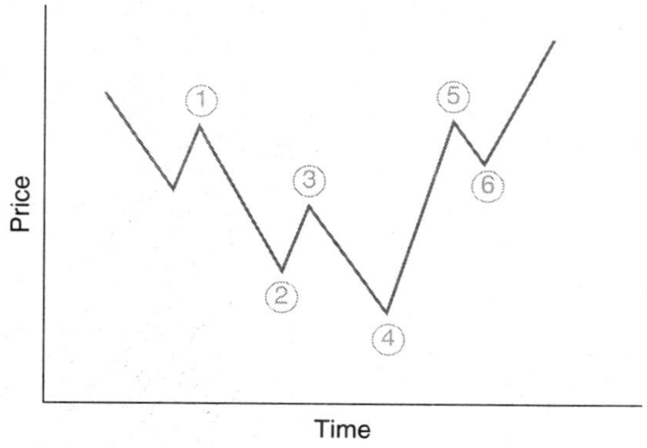

It is clear that the trough, represented by 6, is higher than the troughs represented by 2 and 4. Similarly, the peak represented by 5 is higher than the peak represented by 3. When this happens, the bear market moves in the upward direction, signaling trend reversal and setting in of the bull market.

The Elliott Wave Theory

The Elliott Wave theory was developed by Ralph Nelson the Elliott in the early twentieth century. It is based on the basic principle that every action has an opposite reaction. The Elliott used the stock market data from the Dow Jones Industrial Average to show that the stock market price movement followed a structural design that reflected a basic harmony existing in the nature. He used this discovery to develop a rational system for analyzing the stock market.

The basic premise of the theory is that stock markets move in repetitive upward and downward cycles and make distinct patterns. The Elliott called these patterns waves. Since these patterns are repetitive, the Elliott concluded that they have predictive value. The Elliott's theory also draws upon the Dow theory.

A wave may be described as the movement of price from one change in the direction of its movement to another. The Elliott's wave principle implies that every market decision represents both cause and effect, i.e., on one hand, each market decision is an outcome of some meaningful information and on the other hand, it generates some meaningful information as well. Each market transaction begins by being effect of some information and once completed, it becomes a cause by generating transactional data for investors.

The Elliott attributed these wave like movements to the crowd behavior, psychology of people and their response to various influences in the investing environment. According to the theory, demand and supply pressures, manifested through buying and selling impulses in the market, generate waves in the price movements.

The fractal nature of the market allowed it to be broken down and studied in detail by the Elliott, who found that stock trading patterns were structured in the same way as the fractals in the mathematical structures. Elliott identified a total of eight waves comprising a cycle. He further divided these eight waves into two distinct groups of 5-3.

The theory states that the waves 1 to 5, exhibited in Figure 12.8, represent the main trend. These five waves comprise two sets of sub-waves. Waves 1, 3 and 5 move in the direction of the trend and are termed as impulse

Figure 12.8 The Elliott's 5-3 wave pattern.

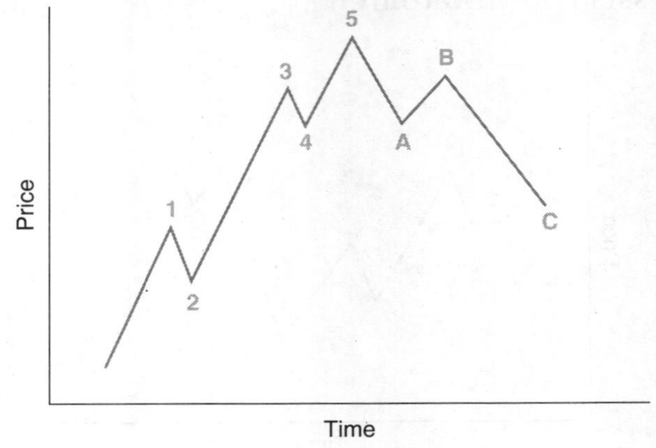

waves as they propel the market. Waves 2 and 4 move in the opposite direction of the trend and are called corrective waves or reaction waves, as they are countertrends that cause partial retracement of the markets. Wave 2 corrects wave 1 and wave 4 corrects wave 3. At any given time, the market can be identified as being somewhere in 5-wave pattern, which represents the overriding form of market progress.

After completion of wave 5, the set of three waves, represented by A, B and C, begins as another group of corrective waves. Waves A and C move against the trend and wave B moves in the direction of the trend. This 5–3 set of waves completes one cycle in the market and thereafter represents two subdivisions of the next higher 5–3 set of waves. In other words, each completed cycle of eight waves becomes a building block to form much larger version of the same wave patterns. According to the theory, the basic 5–3 pattern always persists in the market though the duration and amplitude may vary each time it is repeated. A small part of such continuous wave movement is exhibited in Figure 12.9.

Figure 12.9 A closer look at the Elliott Wave pattern.

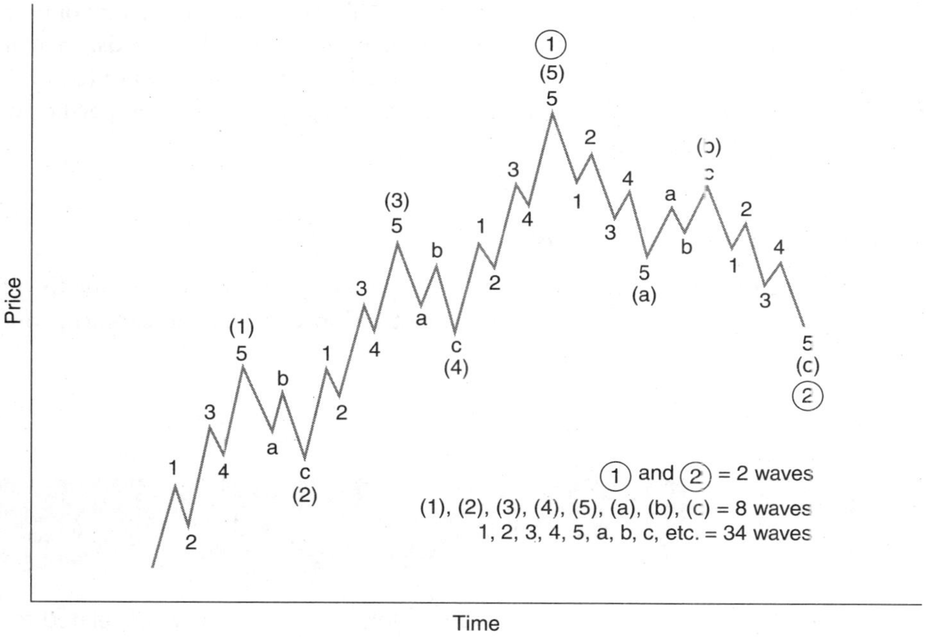

Figure 12.9 illustrates impulse waves as well as full cycle components. It is critical to note here that Figure 12.9 not only exhibits a larger version of Figure 12.8, but it also presents a microscopic view, i.e., a detailed view of the cycle exhibited in Figure 12.8. Figure 12.9 exhibits two major waves represented by encircled 1 and 2 or eight waves represented by 1, 2, 3, 4, 5, a, b and c within brackets or thirty-four waves represented by 1, 2, 3, 4, 5, a, b and c, repeated many times.

Thus, the wave theory implies that waves of any degree in any series always subdivide and re-subdivide into waves of lesser degree and simultaneously become components of the waves of a higher degree.

Further, the Elliott Wave theory has assigned a series of categories to the waves based on the relative size or degree. The Elliott identified nine degrees of waves, from the smallest wriggle on an hourly price chart to the biggest wave that could be assumed to exist from the available data. He chose some interesting names for these degrees of waves that have been listed below, from the largest to the smallest:

1. Grand Supercycle
2. Supercycle
3. Cycle
4. Primary
5. Intermediate
6. Minor
7. Minute
8. Minuette
9. Subminuette

It is important for analysts to understand that these labels/names refer to distinctly identifiable degrees of waves. The Cycle waves are subdivided into Primary waves that are further subdivided into Intermediate waves that in turn get subdivided into Minor and sub-Minor waves. Analysts can use this system of nomenclature to exactly identify the position of a wave in the overall market progression. In other words, an analyst can state the following 'CNX NIFTY is in Minute wave v of Minor wave 1 of Intermediate wave (3) of Primary wave of Cycle wave I of Supercycle wave (V) of the current Grand Supercycle' to identify a specific point along the history of Indian stock market progression.

Using the Elliott Wave theory for trading

A trader interested in using the Elliott's theory for day-to-day trading needs to determine the main wave go long as the pattern persists and then sell or go short as the pattern looses steam, indicating upcoming reversal. Figure 12.10 exhibits the Elliott Waves in CNX NIFTY.

Marketview 12.2 Refined the Elliott Trader (RET)

RET is a software that enables the technical traders to apply research discoveries related to the Elliot wave theory to make their trading strategies more effective and increase their profits. It uses patterns to tell traders what the markets can be expected to do. The software forecasts financial markets by identifying when common the Elliott Wave patterns have started and then calculating where the patterns are most likely to complete.

Although RET is a quite complex software package that uses sophisticated techniques for pattern recognition and probability algorithms, yet it is easy to use as it is designed to be as automated as possible. Users require only basic skills to derive accurate market forecasts with explicit entry/exit signals.

Source: http://refined-elliott-trader.software.informer.com/, accessed on December 16, 2014.

Figure 12.10 The Elliott Waves in S&P CNX NIFTY.

Source: http://elliottwaveindia.blogspot.in/, a blog by Ashish Kyal, accessed on August 20, 2015.

The Wave Principle is theoretically simple to apply if its basic theme is assumed to give complete description of the market behavior. However, in the real world dynamics, applying the Elliott's theory is rather challenging and subjective. Nonetheless advances in information technology have helped reduce subjectivity in the use of the Elliott Wave theory. Advanced statistical analysis has proven mathematically that the wave theory is indeed reliable as it is based on universally proven principles of market behavior.

Using Fibonacci Sequence and the Golden Ratio in Technical Analysis

Leonardo Fibonacci, an Italian mathematician, gave a sequence of numbers that is named Fibonacci sequence after him. The series runs as: 0, 1, 1, 2, 3, 5, 8, 13, 21, 34, 55, 89, 144, 233, 377, 610... here each subsequent term is simply the sum of the two preceding terms. The golden ratio, which is used to describe the proportion of all things in nature from an atom to celestial bodies, has been derived from Fibonacci Sequence. The golden ratio is equal to 1.618 and it is nothing else but the quotient of the adjacent terms of the Fibonacci series. The financial markets have also been observed to conform to this 'golden ratio.' Technical analysts use this ratio and the Fibonacci sequence for the purpose of generating patterns to provide cues for trading decisions.

For using the Fibonacci series in technical analysis, the golden ratio is transformed into three key percentages: 38.2%, 50% and 61.8%, all derived from the series. For example, the 38.2% ratio is computed by dividing any number in the Fibonacci sequence by the number two places ahead. For example: $89/233 = 0.3819$.

Some analysts use many more percentages like 23.6%, 161.8%, 423% and so on. However, 38.2%, 50% and 61.8% are used more frequently in technical analysis.

Beyond the Basics 12.1 The Magic of Golden ratio

An Italian mathematician from Pisa, Leonardo Pisano Bogollo (1170–1250), introduced the Fibonacci series to the West. The series starts from 0 and extends to infinity. It runs as follows:

0, 1, 1, 2, 3, 5, 8, 13, 21, 34, 55, 89, 144, 233, 377, 610...

Some of the unique mathematical properties of the series are:

1. Apart from the first two numbers of the series, 0 and 1, each number is the sum of the two preceding numbers in the series. For example, 1 + 2 = 3, 2 + 3 = 5, 5 + 8 = 13 8 + 13 = 21 and so on.
2. Any number in the series when divided by the preceding number approximates 1.618. For example, 34/21 = 1.6190, 55/34 = 1.6176, 89/55 = 1.6181 and so on. 1.618 is called the Golden Ratio or Golden Mean, or Phi. Its inverse is 0.618. These ratios can be observed all around us, be it nature, architecture, art or biology.
3. Any number in the series when divided by the subsequent number approximates 0.6180. For example, 13/21 = 0.6190, 21/34 = .6176 and so on. This is the basis for the 61.8% retracement explained in this chapter.
4. Any number in the series when divided by a number two places higher approximates .3820. For example 13/34 = .382, 21/55 = .3818 34/89 = .3820 and so on. This forms a basis for the 38.2% retracement explained in this chapter. An interesting observation is that 1 – .618 = .382.
5. Similarly, 23.6% retracement comes from the outcome of dividing a number in Fibonacci series by another number from the series, three places higher. For example, 13/55 = .2363, 21/89 = .2359, and 34/144 = .2361.

Source: Stockcharts.com/school/doku.pha?id=chart-school:chartanalysis:fibonacciarcs, accessed on August 20, 2015.

Fibonacci sequence and its inherent ratio is applied for technical analysis through three primary tools:

- Fibonacci retracement patterns
- Fibonacci arcs
- Fibonacci fans

Let us discuss each in detail.

1. **Fibonacci Retracement Patterns:** Fibonacci retracement patterns are very popular among technical traders and the analysts for identifying reversals on a stock price chart. Fibonacci retracement patterns are based on the observation that the stocks often pull back a certain percentage of the previous move before changing direction or reversing. These retracement percentages are often found to occur at three levels: 38.2%, 50%, and 61.8%. Of these, 38.2% and 61.8% come from the Fibonacci sequence. Though 50% is not

a part of the sequence, it is used because traders agree universally that stocks have a tendency to reverse after retracing half (50%) of the previous move. Fibonacci retracement may be explained clearly with the help of Figure 12.11.

Figure 12.11 Fibonacci retracement.

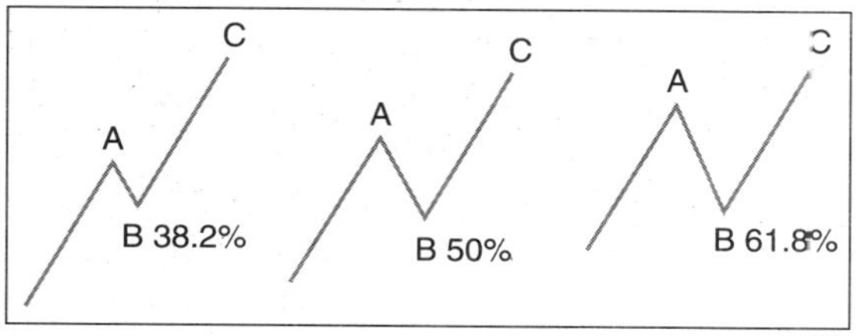

Figure 12.11 exhibits the reversal points at all three percentages: 38.2%, 50% and 61.8% for a stock that is in upward trend. Once the stock, say TCS, reaches point A during its bull run, it shows reversal and retraces its gains to fall back to point B (pull back could be 38.2%, 50% and 61.8%) before continuing its uptrend to move towards point C. These retracements or pullbacks are watched keenly by traders to initiate long or short positions.

Having understood Fibonacci retracement, let us see how it can be used in technical analysis. In practice, analysts use Fibonacci retracements to indicate areas of support or resistance. To calculate the support and resistance level, two extreme points (usually a major peak and trough) on a stock price chart are identified.

Figure 12.12 Fibonacci retracement for ICICI Bank Limited.

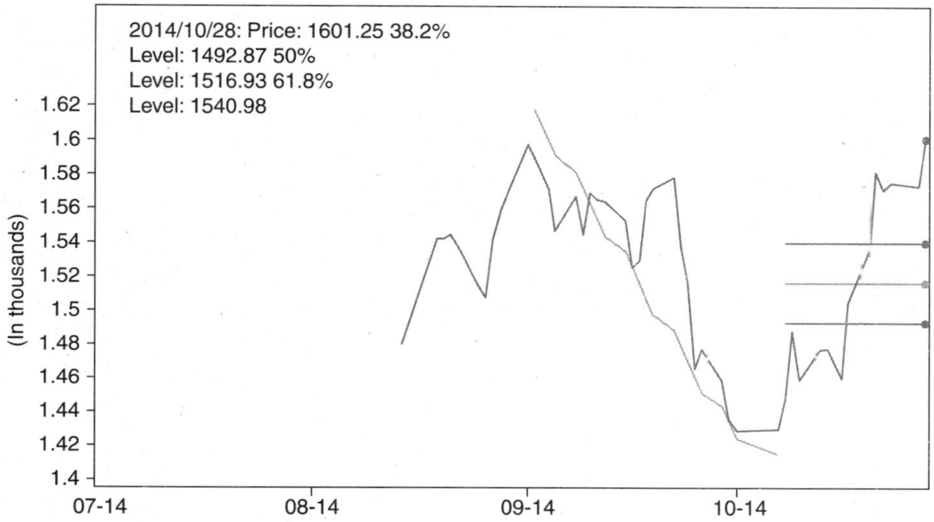

Thereafter, five horizontal lines are drawn by keeping the vertical distance between them from 0% (at the chosen trough on the price) to 100% (at the chosen peak on the price chart). The other three lines are drawn at the levels indicated by 61.8%, 50% and 38.2%. After any significant price fluctuation, the new support and resistance levels are typically observed at or near these lines. Fibonacci retracement for ICICI Bank Limited is exhibited in Figure 12.12.

As a trader, to identify signs for reversal, you can plot these retracements once the stock starts to pull back. However, a stock should not be bought just because it has entered the retracement area. Traders should wait for the pattern to emerge around 38.2% area. If the reversal does not take place at this level, the price chart is likely to drop to the 50% level, enabling them to buy cheaper and so on and so forth. Basic idea is that the activity around these percentages give cues to go long or short and profit from the positions taken. Many software are available for plotting Fibonacci retracements.

2. **Fibonacci Arcs**: Fibonacci arcs consist of three curved lines or percentage arcs or half circles drawn with a view to anticipate key support and resistance levels and areas of ranging for a stock. Of the three arcs, the first and third are based on the Fibonacci sequence and are drawn at 38.2% and 61.8%, respectively. The second or the middle arc is drawn at 50%.

Like Fibonacci retracement, Fibonacci arcs are also based on the distance between major price peak and trough. The distance between peak and trough is 100. Therefore, a 31.8% Fibonacci Arc would be a 31.8 unit semi-circle.

After an upward movement, Fibonacci arcs are calculated using a base line extending from chosen trough to peak. The arcs are drawn with a radii of .382, .50 and .618 to the base line. The main idea behind the use of arcs is identification of probable support or reversal areas to keep an eye on price retracement after an uptrend or resistance on price retracement after a downtrend. Figure 12.13 exhibits the Fibonacci arcs.

Figure 12.13 Fibonacci arcs.

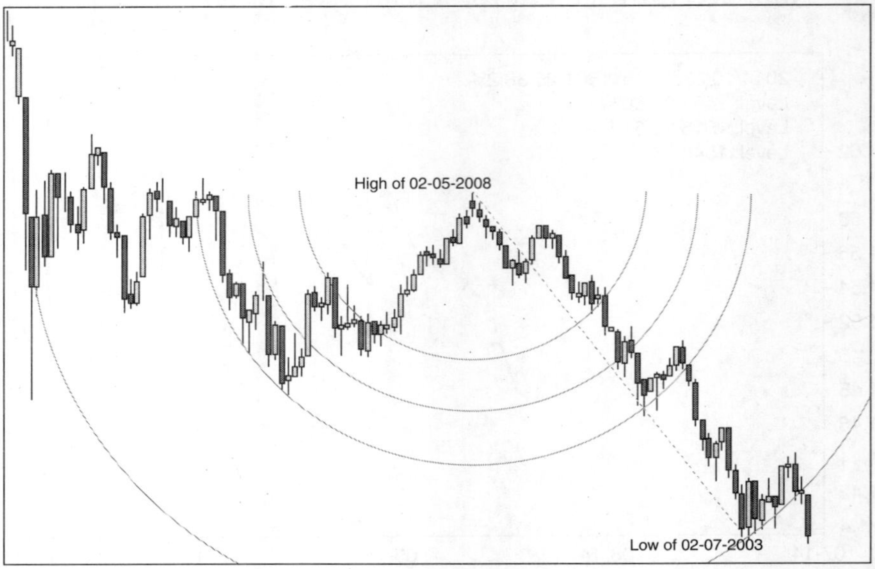

Fibonacci arcs use levels similar to the Fibonacci retracement but they add a time element to the Fibonacci retracement, which is concerned with the change in price only. However, in the case of Fibonacci arcs, the angle of a baseline that extends from trough to peak after a rise in price depends on the time elapsed. It has a positive slope. At the same time, the angle of baseline that extends from peak to trough after a fall in the price also depends on the time elapsed but the slope is negative. The slope as well as the length of the baseline change with both price and time. Obviously, a bigger price movement over a longer period of time would result in a longer baseline with wider Fibonacci arcs.

Trading with Fibonacci arcs is done by identifying breakouts. Once the arc levels have been traced, the next step is to observe the performance of the stock price at these key levels. If the stock price breaks above both a recent high and an arc resistance level, as denoted by 38.2%, 50% or 61.8%, the tracer should go long in the stock and wait for the next higher Fibonacci arc level to sell the stock outright.

Usually, Fibonacci arcs are plotted with Fibonacci fans (discussed below) and the support and resistance levels are given by the points of intersection of these lines.

3. **Fibonacci Fans:** Fibonacci fans consist of three diagonal lines that are drawn using the Fibonacci ratios (38.2%, 50% and 61.8%) to identify support and resistance levels or reversal points. Like the above two tools, Fibonacci fans are also drawn by first identifying the peak and trough level of stock price. Thereafter a trend line or a baseline is drawn, suppose, from a trough to the opposing peak between two extreme points. This is followed by drawing an invisible vertical line through the second extreme point or the rightmost point and dividing it into three Fibonacci levels: 38.2%, 50% and 61.8%. Finally the diagonal lines representing the Fibonacci fans are drawn from the first extreme point or the leftmost point through each of these points. These diagonal lines are the indicators of support and resistance levels. After that, the three trend lines intersecting this invisible vertical line at Fibonacci levels of 38.2, 50, and 61.8% are drawn from the first extreme point. These lines can be rising or falling.

Rising Fibonacci fan lines extend from trough to peak and pass through the retracement levels based on the upward price movement and can be used to identify potential support levels. Conversely, the falling fan

Figure 12.14 Fibonacci fans.

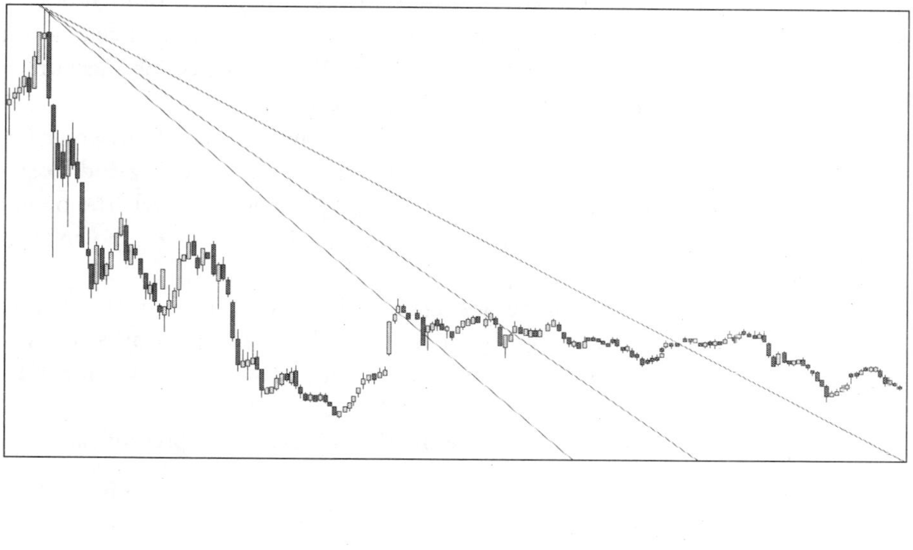

lines extend from a peak to trough and pass through the retracements levels based on the downward price movement and can be used to identify potential resistance levels.

Fibonacci Fans are mainly used to measure the speed of the movement of a trend in upward or downward direction. General rule is that if the price moves below the fan trend line, then it is likely to fall further to the level of next fan trend line. Thus, the fan trend lines act as support in a bull run or uptrend.

In case of a bear run or downtrend, the fan trend lines act as resistance. General rule is that if the price moves above the fan trend line, then it is likely to rise further to the level of next fan trend line, which will then act as resistance. Figure 12.14 exhibits the Fibonacci fans.

It should be kept in mind that no tool is perfect in itself. The chartists and traders should confirm the support and resistance levels and other signals using more than one tool.

We have comprehensively discussed the three main stays of technical analysis: The Dow theory, the Elliott Wave theory and the Fibonacci tools. Let us now move to the study technical analysis in practice. We will first discuss the charting techniques.

Charting Techniques

Consistent with the Dow's theory, technicians use a number of charting techniques to generate charts to identify patterns and trends. In fact, a chart of price movement is used as a beginning point of security analysis, even by severest critics of technical analysis because they provide a wealth of information at a glance. The four main types of charts are:

1. Line Chart
2. Bar Charts
3. Candlestick Charts
4. Point and Figure Charts

Let us try to understand each type of chart or charting technique used in technical analysis.

1. **Line Chart:** It is the most basic chart that is drawn using the closing price data over a given period of time. Such charts give no information about intra-day price movements or day's low or high price or opening or closing prices. Line chart gives a visual picture of the movement of the closing price of a stock because analysts often consider closing price to be a key indicator. Figure 12.15 exhibits line chart drawn for stock price of Infosys for a period of three months, from July 28, 2014 to October 28, 2014.
2. **Bar Chart:** A bar chart gives more information than a line chart. The bar chart is drawn using a series of vertical lines that represent the high and low for the trading period. The opening and closing lines are represented on the vertical line by marking a horizontal dash at the relevant level. The opening price is shown by a horizontal dash on the left side of the vertical bar and the closing price is shown by a horizontal dash on the right of the vertical bar.

   In general, if the opening price is lower than the closing price, then the vertical bar is shaded black or blue to indicate a price gain. Conversely, if the opening price is higher than the closing price, the vertical bar is colored red, indicating a price drop. Figure 12.16 exhibits bar chart drawn for stock price of Infosys for a period of three months, from July 28, 2014 to October 28, 2014.

   In Figure 12.16, the dark sticks represent fall in price and the lighter sticks represent gain in price.

Figure 12.15 Line chart of Infosys (July 28, 2014 to October 28, 2014).

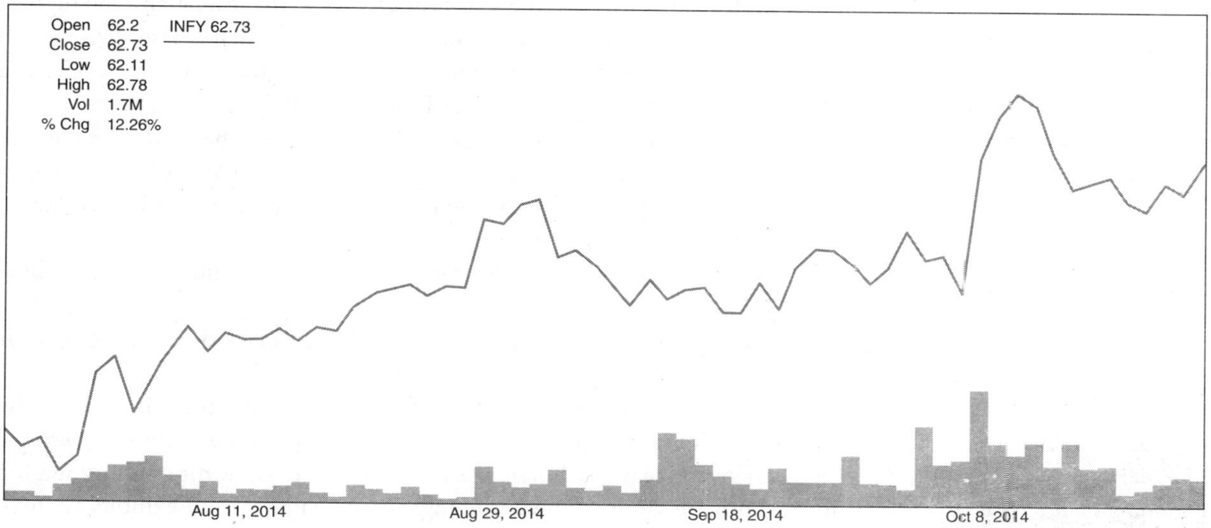

Source: http://finance.yahoo.com/echarts, accessed on December 31, 2014.

Figure 12.16 Bar chart of Infosys (July 28, 2014 to October 28, 2014).

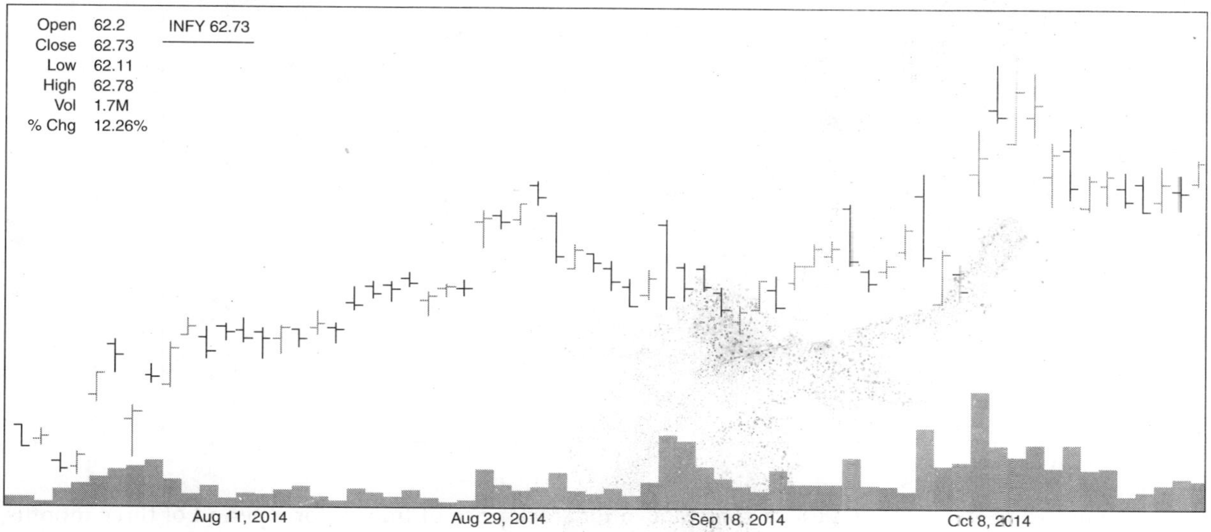

Source: http://finance.yahoo.com/echarts, accessed on December 4, 2014.

3. **Candlestick:** The candlestick chart resembles a bar chart in information content, but it is constructed differently. It is one of the most popular charts used by technical analysts. It is plotted on a day-to-day basis using the highest, lowest, opening and closing prices of the stock for each day. The lowest and the highest prices are joined by forming a bar that is a vertical line, as in the case of the bar chart. The opening and closing prices of the day fall between the lowest and the highest prices and are illustrated by a rectangle. The formation of rectangle makes the bar look like a Japanese candlestick and hence the name, candlestick chart. Each day's price movement is represented by an individual candlestick. Like the bar charts, the candlestick charts are also plotted using different colors. Unfortunately, the colors to be used are not standardized, so we need to decode the color depending on the site we are using for analysis. However, the basic concept remains the same and different colors are used for indicating:
   (a) A gain in price, i.e., when the stock closes above the opening trade (usually white or green or blue candlestick is used in this case) and
   (b) A fall in price, i.e., when the stock closes below the opening trade (usually black or red candlestick is used in this case)

   A third type of candlestick, called a Doji, is used on the days where the opening price is same as the closing price, i.e., there is no gain or loss. It is also called a neutral candlestick and is represented by a single vertical line joining the day's high and low price with a horizontal hash across it to show the opening and the closing price (as mentioned above, both are same, so there is a single hash). Figure 12.17 exhibits all three types of candlesticks.

Figure 12.17 Three types of candlesticks.

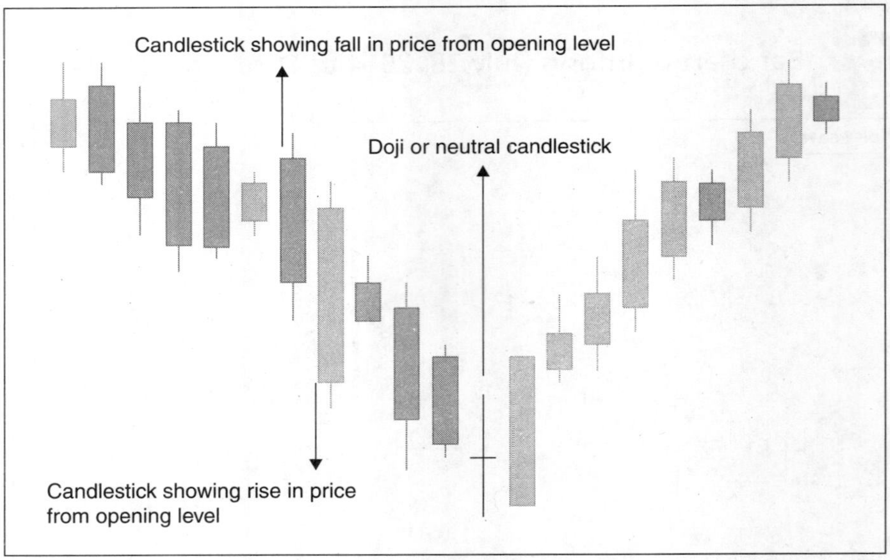

Figure 12.18 exhibits candlestick chart drawn for stock price of Infosys for a period of three months, from July 28, 2014 to October 28, 2014.

In Figure 12.18, the dark candlesticks represent fall in price and the lighter candlesticks represent gain in price.

Figure 12.18 Candlestick chart of Infosys (July 28, 2014 to October 28, 2014).

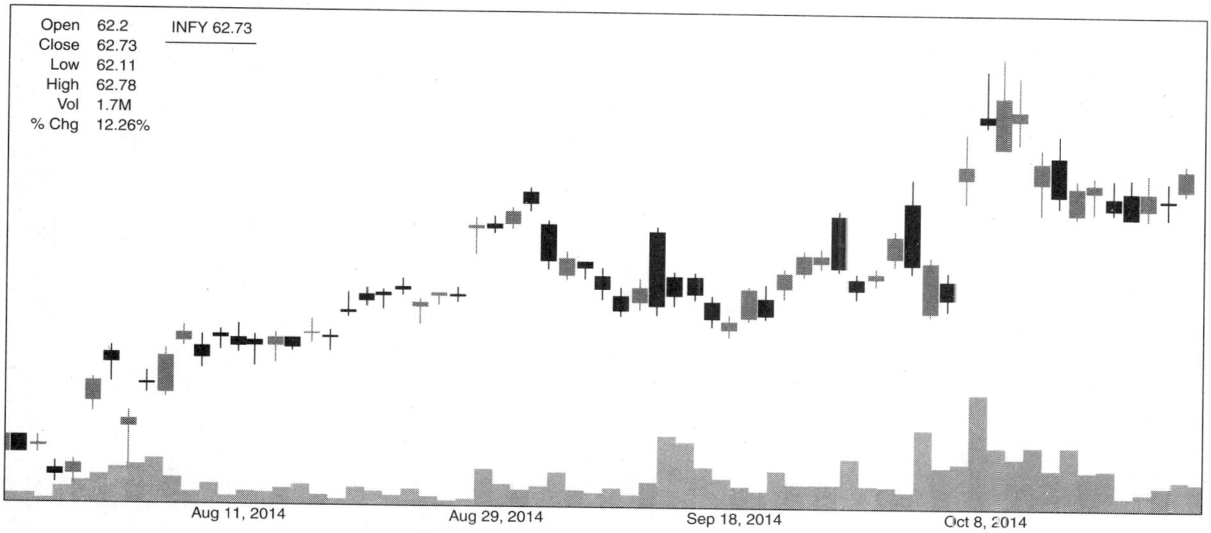

Source: http://finance.yahoo.com/echarts, accessed on December 4, 2014.

4. **Point and Figure Charts:** The point and figure chart is the oldest type of chart used by the technical traders. This chart plots the price movement in a stock using a series of Xs and Os. The Xs represent the rising price trends and the Os represent the falling price trends. As long as the price changes in the same direction, it is recorded in the same column. When the price moves from one trend to another, the chart shifts to the right, showing a change in trend. The vertical scale of the chart represents price change but the horizontal scale does not indicate time.

   The point and figure chart records only significant price changes and it is not concerned with time and volume. For example, for a stock in the price range of ₹100 to ₹120, price changes of ₹2 or more only may be plotted. Here ₹2 becomes the reversal criterion, i.e., an indicator of how much the price has to move in order for a column of Os to become a column of Xs, or vice versa. The extent of change to be recorded can be set according to the chartist's discretion. Figure 12.19 exhibits point and figure chart drawn for CNX NIFTY for a period from October 2011 to October 2014.

   The advantage of using point and figure chart is that it removes the insignificant price movement and reduces distortions in traders' views of the price trends.

   In technical analysis, the charts described above are plotted with an express purpose of analyzing the trend to generate trading cues. We will now discuss trends and trend lines in detail.

Trends

The charts are used to study trends. We have already talked about uptrend and downtrend during our discussion on the Dow theory. Let us revisit the concept in a more formal manner now.

In simple words, a trend may be defined as the general direction of the movement of the price of an asset or market as a whole. Trends vary in length and can be short-term, intermediate-term or long term. Technical

Figure 12.19 Point and Figure for S&P CNX NIFTY (October 2011 to October 2014).

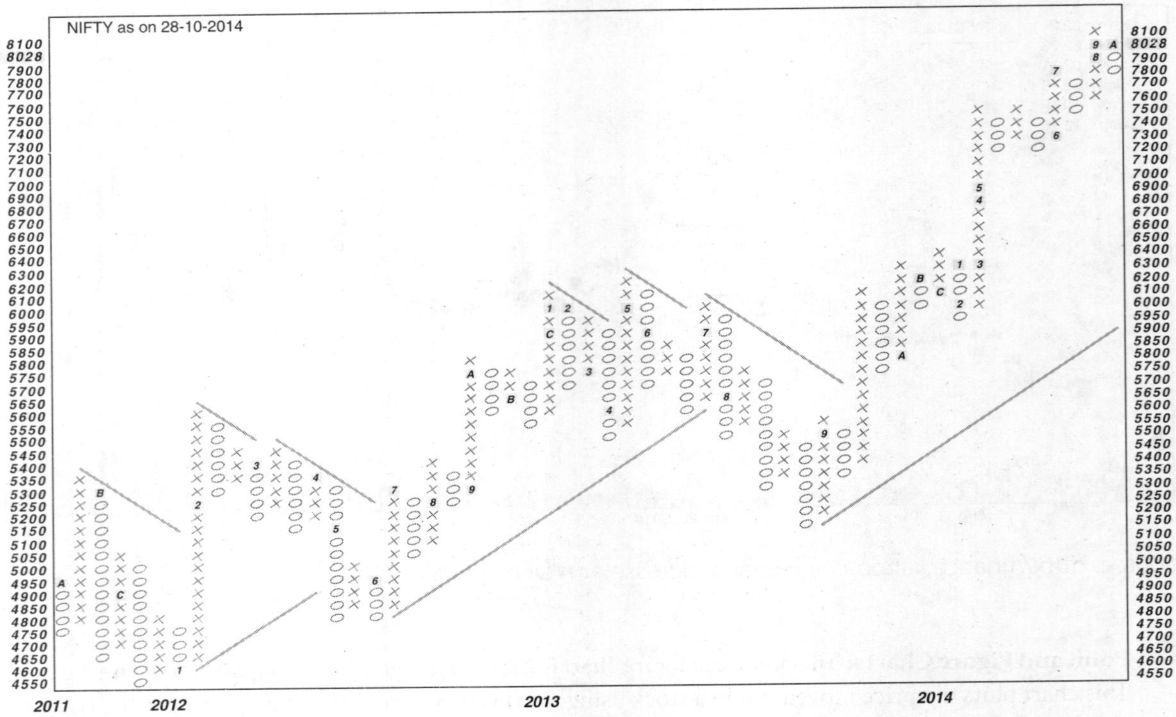

Marketview 12.3 Point and Figure Charts

Point and figure charts are the oldest charts used by technical analysts.

It is a charting technique that plots price against changes in direction of price movement by plotting a column of Xs as the price rises and a column of Os as the price falls.

It is used to predict financial market prices. From the perspective of long-term investment, P&F charts have been described by many analysts as one of the simplest ways of determining accurate entry and exit points in stock market trading.

Though the technique is over 100 years old, yet it has never been popular amongst technical analysts. However, there seems to be a growing interest in it in the charting community in the recent past. In India, a company named Chartink has launched these charts recently.

Source: http://nseguide.com/announcements/chartink-lauches-point-and-figure-charts/, accessed on January 7, 2015.

analysts believe that if a trend can be identified, then it can be used for trading profitably. The study of trend in the past data to try to predict future direction of movement is based on the belief of technical analysts that the history repeats itself.

In case of stock price movement, the following types of trends can be identified:

1. Uptrend indicating a period of bull run
2. Downtrend indicating a period of bear run
3. Sideways/Horizontal trend indicating a lack of a well-defined trend in upward or downward direction

As discussed in the Dow theory, the stock prices do not follow a smooth path, rather the movement of prices comprises of a series of highs and lows that together constitute a trend. Therefore, an uptrend actually comprises of a series of highs and lows. The uptrend would continue as long as there are higher highs and higher lows. A downtrend also comprises of a series of highs and lows, but it has lower lows and lower highs. We have discussed this in detail while talking about peaks and troughs analysis in the Dow theory.

Trend lines are drawn in the direction of the long-term trend. They are smooth lines that follow the upward direction of price movement in the case of uptrend and the downward direction of price movement in the case of downtrend.

The lengths of trends are also important. As mentioned above, trends may be short-term, intermediate-term or long-term. These can be interpreted in terms of the primary, secondary and minor movements in stock prices postulated by Dow. A long-term trend is a major trend in stock market that lasts longer than a year. An intermediate trend is of shorter duration and usually lasts between one and three months. A short-term trend refers to fluctuations in prices occurring for less than a month to even a day.

As shown by the Elliott wave theory, a long-term trend is composed of several intermediate trends, often moving against the direction of the major trend. For example if the long-term trend is in downward direction, an intermediate trend will move in upward direction. The short-term trends are actually the components of both the long-term and the intermediate trends.

The choice of input data to be used for charting for the purpose of analyzing trends is very important. If long-term trend is to be identified, it is best to use weekly price data or a daily price data spanning long periods like 5 years. Daily price data charts spanning a short period are best for analyzing both intermediate and short-term trends.

Trends provide important trading cues. Identification of trend reversals at early stages can enable traders to take positions that may help them earn profit. For example, if a trader identifies a reversing downtrend early on, he can go long in the stock and sell it when the price rises with the consolidation of the reversal. Similarly, a trader can go short in a stock that is starting to reverse from an uptrend.

Chart Patterns

A chart pattern may be described as a distinct formation on a stock price chart that indicates a trading signal, or signifies the future direction of price movements. These patterns are used by chartists to identify prevailing trends and trend reversals and use them as inputs to generate buy and sell signals.

The use of chart patterns in technical analysis rests on one of its basic premise; history tends to repeat itself in the stock market. The idea behind the use of patterns is that repetitive patterns can be used to predict future price movements to identify profitable trading opportunities.

There are two distinct types of chart patterns used in technical analysis viz., reversal patterns and continuation patterns. In addition, there are two patterns; support and resistance and channels that are discussed by some authors with trend lines. However, we will discuss these patterns in this section only because these two patterns are also indicators of trends and reversals. Therefore our discussion in this section will focus on:

1. Support and resistance
2. Channels
3. Continuation patterns
4. Reversal patterns

1. **Support and Resistance:** Support indicates the price level through which a stock or market seldom falls, while resistance indicates the upper limit that a stock or a market seldom surpasses or breaches. Support is actually an upward trend line that connects the lows of an upward trend. It is a line that props the price of a stock when it falls from an uptrend. Similarly, resistance is a downward trend line that connects the highs of the downward trend. It is a line that prevents the price of a stock from rising further away from a downtrend.

   Most stocks have a distinct support and resistance level and tend to trade between this range for long periods of time. Such a movement becomes more observable when a stock is trading in a sideways or horizontal manner.

   Support and resistance levels are typical outcomes of the forces of demand and supply operating in the market and the psychology of the market as a whole. Support represents the level at which the traders are willing to buy the stock, pushing the price up in the process. Resistance represents the level at which the traders sell the stock, pushing the prices down in the process.

   While the stock prices tend to move between their support and resistance levels, it is possible that these levels are broken. Once a support or resistance level is broken, its role gets reversed. Thus, if the price falls below the support level, then this breached support level becomes the new resistance level for the stock price. Similarly, if the price rises above the resistance level, the breached resistance becomes the new support. For such a reversal to occur in the true sense, the price movement breaching the support or resistance should be very strong. Figure 12.20 illustrates support and resistance formation and the role reversal after breakout.

   As long as the price moves between support and resistance, the trend can be expected to persist. However, every break beyond either support or resistance cannot be taken as a confirmation of trend reversal. For example, if the price falls below the support in a downward trending support and the resistance channel, it indicates the acceleration of downtrend, not its reversal.

   Further, the support and resistance levels of a share do not remain fixed. They shift in response to the changes in the market forces of demand and supply and a change in the psychology of the investors, creating new support and resistance for the stock.

   Figure 12.21, 12.22 and 12.23 illustrate the support and resistance levels of CNX NIFTY, Bharti Airtel and Reliance Industries for a period extending from July 2010 to April 2012.

   Since support and resistance levels test as well as confirm trends, they can be analyzed by traders to trigger trading decisions. For example, if a trader has been successful in identifying some important level of support that has been tested by the price line several times but has not been breached, then he or she can decide to buy shares at this level as the share prices can be expected to rise after reaching this level. It is also important to keep in mind that the volatility in prices is usually high around the support and resistance

Figure 12.20 Support and resistance formation and role reversal after breakout.

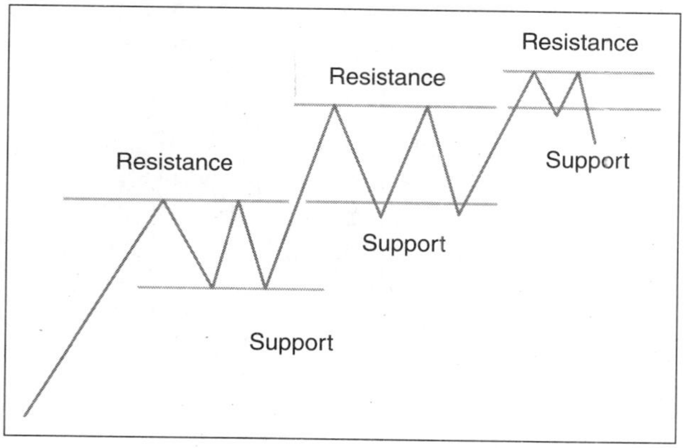

Figure 12.21 The support and resistance levels of S&P CNX NIFTY (July 2010 to April 2012).

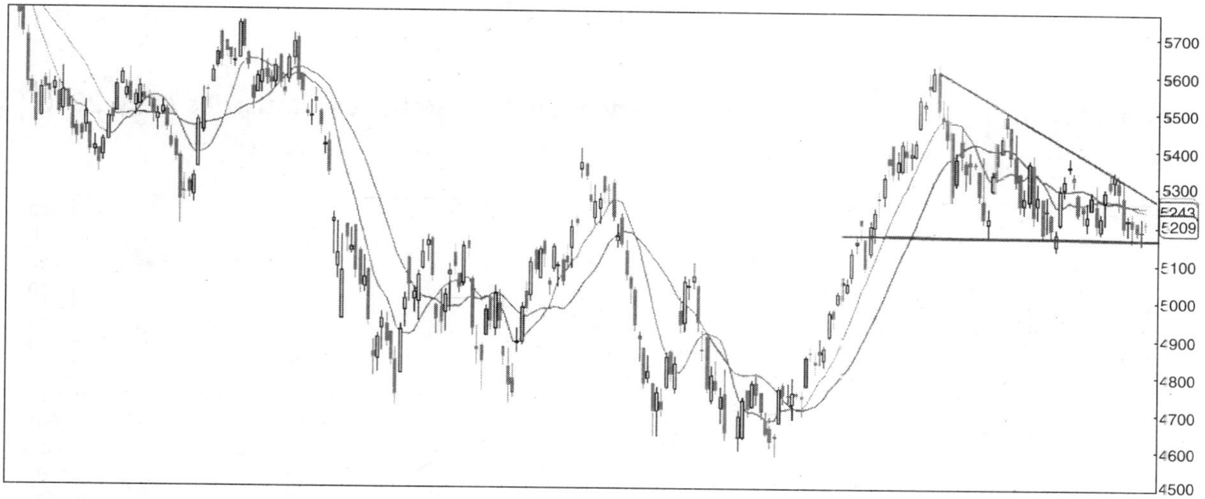

levels, so the traders should avoid trading around these areas. Ideally, a buy order should be placed a few points above the support level if one is bullish about the stock.

2. **Channels:** Strong support and resistance levels create channels, in which the upper trend line is formed by connecting a series of highs whereas lower trend line is created by connecting a series of lows. A channel can have upward, downward or sideways slope. Price of stock remains range-bound within the channel and breaks away from the trend line of the channel which is a strong indicator of a sharp movement in price in the direction of the break. Channels are extremely useful in distinctly displaying the trend and illustrating important areas of support and resistance in the stock price movement. Figure 12.24 exhibits an upward sloping channel.

Figure 12.22 The support and resistance levels of Bharti Airtel (July 2010 to April 2012).

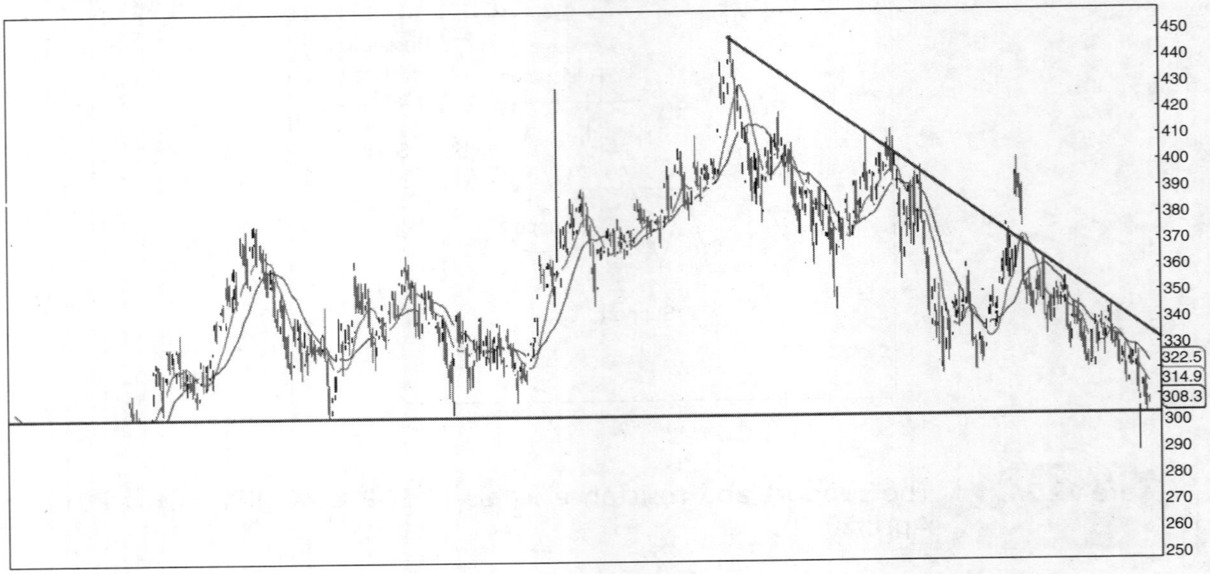

Figure 12.23 The support and resistance levels of Reliance Industries (July 2010 to April 2012).

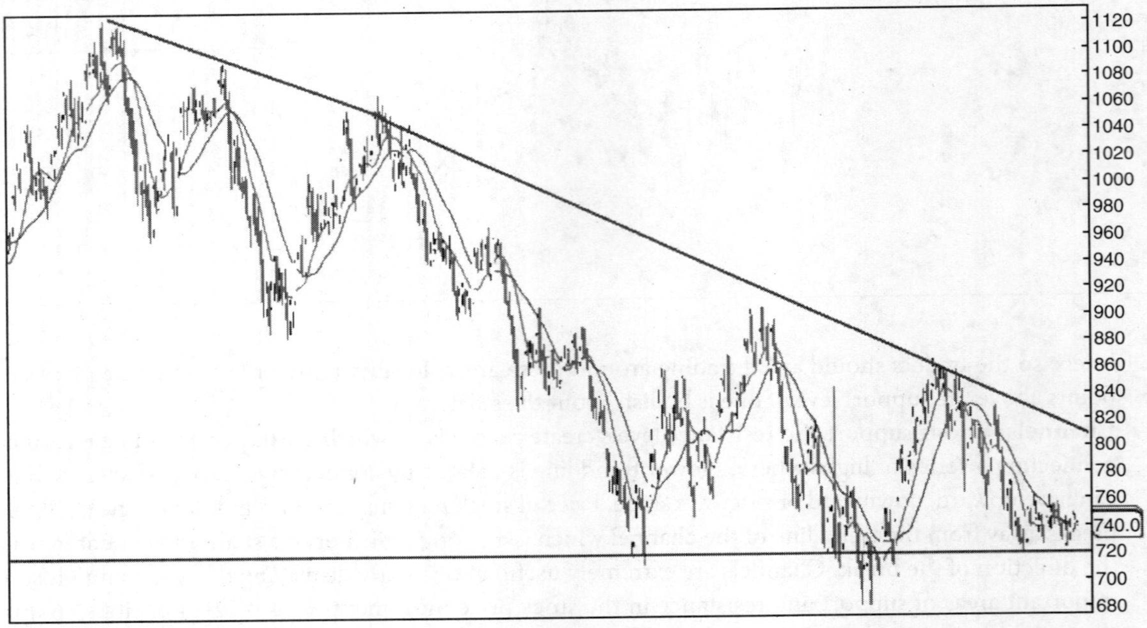

Figure 12.24 Upward sloping channel.

Source: http://elliottwaveindia.blogspot.in/2013/12/elliott-wave-channeling-rsi-applied-cn.html, a blog by Ashish Kyal, accessed on August 20,2015.

3. **Continuation Patterns:** Continuation patterns are distinct chart formations that indicate continuation of the existing trend. They typically occur in the middle of a trend and provide breathing space or a pause to earlier sharp rise or fall. The continuation patterns can have varying durations, but the outcome is the same. Once the pattern is complete, the price moves in the direction of the original trend. Most commonly identified continuation patterns are: triangles, flags, pennants and cup and handle.
   (a) *Triangles:* Triangles are the most popular continuation patterns that occur due to the convergence of price range. Triangles are formed when the movement of price leads to the formation of two or more consecutive ascending bottoms or descending tops. In other words, triangles are formed when price movement displays higher lows and lower highs. The formation of a triangle becomes apparent when an upper trend line is drawn to connect the consecutive tops and a lower trend line is drawn to connect the consecutive bottoms. Triangles can be formed during both, an uptrend and a downtrend. In either case, a drop in volume is observed while the price moves within the triangle and a breakout from this continuation pattern is more often than not accompanied by rise in trading volume. Figure 12.25 illustrates the triangle formation for Gitanjali Gems.

   Three basic types of triangles are used in technical analysis are symmetric, ascending and descending triangles (exhibited in Figure 12.26). Trading implications of all three are same. Triangle formation and breakout is exhibited in Figure 12.27 for Idea cellular.

Figure 12.25 Triangle formation for Gitanjali Gems.

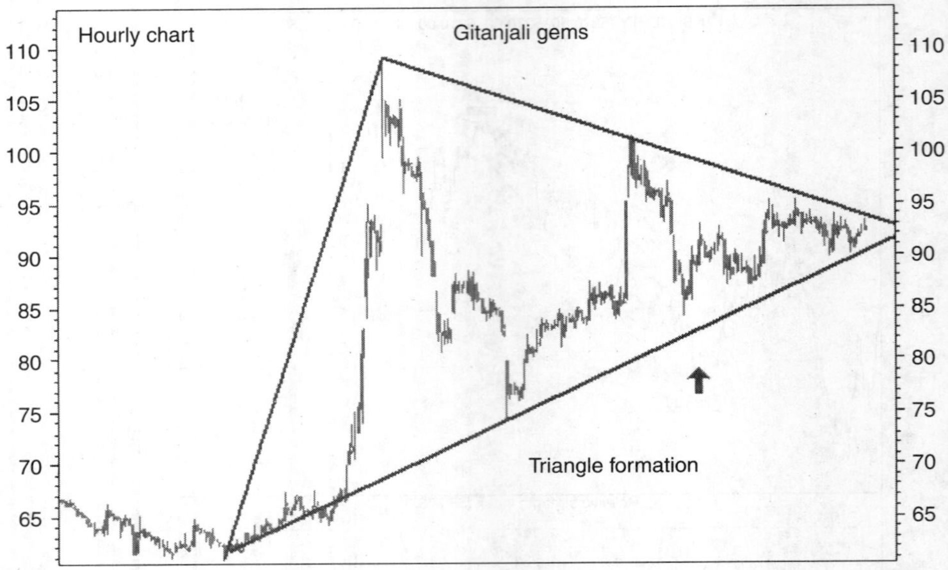

Figure 12.26 Ascending and descending triangles.

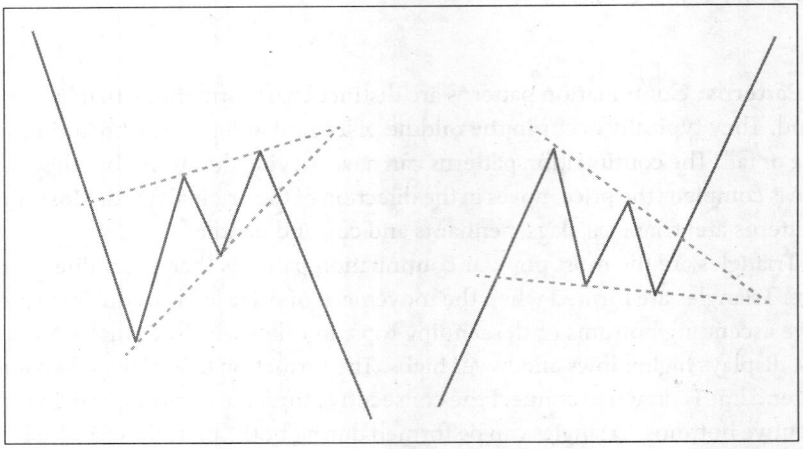

(b) *Flags and pennants*: Flags are considered to be reliable continuation patterns and they represent a brief pause in the trend, often in a fast moving market. Flags are formed when the price of a stock becomes confined to a small range between trend lines that are parallel, upward sloping or downward sloping. Flag looks like a parallelogram. As in the case of triangle formation, the volume drops during the flag formation and picks up on break out. The duration of flags is generally short.

Figure 12.27 Idea triangle pattern breakout.

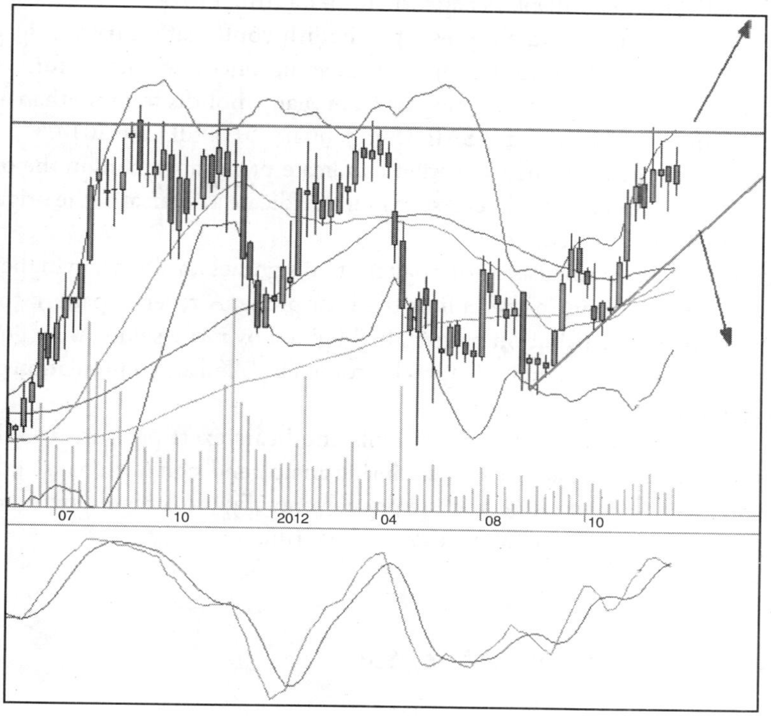

Figure 12.28 Flag and pennant formation.

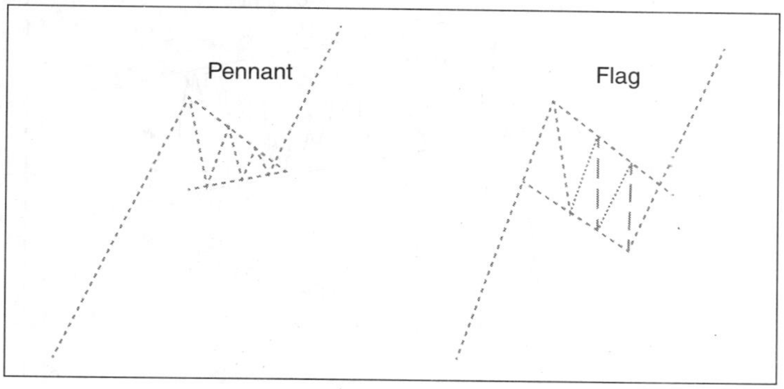

Pennant formation resembles a symmetrical triangle but it is smaller as compared to triangle formation. The upper trend line connecting the tops slopes downwards and the lower trend line connecting the bottoms slopes upwards. The pennant pattern is formed in the middle of a trend on convergence of the prices for a small range and it signals continuation of the original trend. Here also a break out from the pennant is marked by an increase in volume. Flag and pennant formation is illustrated in Figure 12.28. Figure 12.29 displays flag formation for SBI.

(c) *Cup and handle:* A cup and handle represents a bullish continuation pattern in which the uptrend has halted but can be expected to continue to move up once the pattern formation is completed. This pattern takes a long time to form, ranging from many months to more than a year. Figure 12.30 exhibits cup and handle formation for SAIL from January 2014 till June 2014.

4. **Reversal Patterns:** Just as the continuation patterns indicate price movement in the original direction of the trend after the patterns are completed, reversal patterns indicate a reversal of the original direction of the trend after the patterns are completed.

A reversal pattern may be described as a price pattern that signifies an alteration in the prevailing uptrend or downtrend. Reversals can occur in the bull or the bear phase. A reversal pattern that forms when the market has peaked is called a distribution pattern, highlighted by more selling than buying. On the other hand, reversal pattern that forms when market has bottomed is called an accumulation pattern, highlighted by more buying than selling.

Reversal patterns present periods where both bulls and bears exert pressure and the prevailing trend gives in. In other words, a reversal pattern formed during an uptrend signifies a pause in the bull run, where both bulls and bears exert equal pressure and the price eventually breaks out downwards, giving in to the bears. Exactly opposite happens in case of a prevailing bear run.

Figure 12.29 Bullish flag formation for SBI.

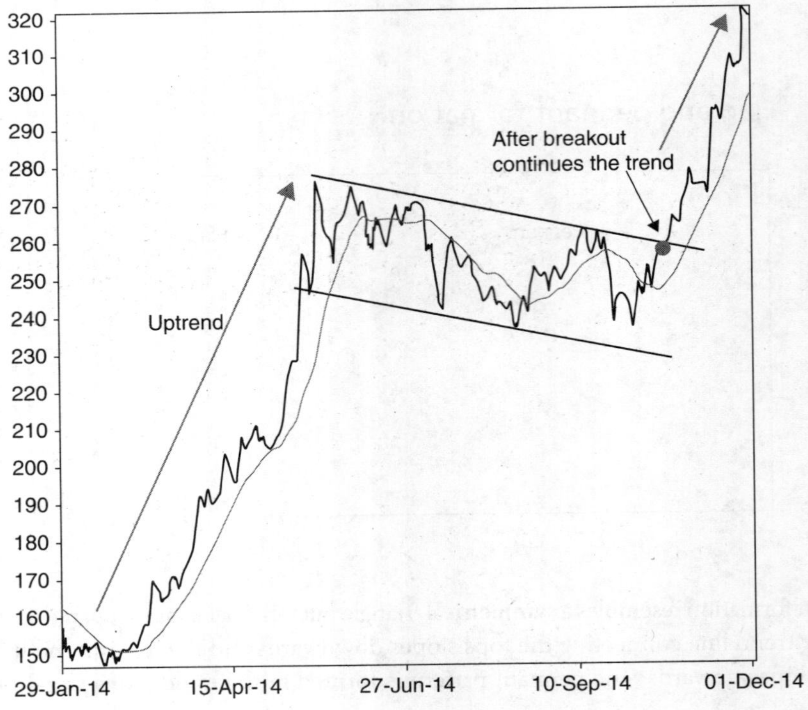

Figure 12.30 Cup and handle formation for IFB India.

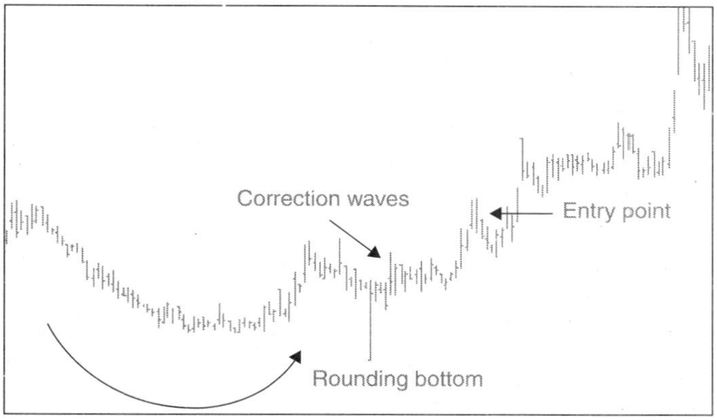

Source: http://www.traderstrainingzone.com/chart-pattern/cup-with-handle, accessed on August 21, 2015.

As with the continuation patterns, the magnitude of price break out is expected to be larger if the preceding reversal pattern has taken longer time to develop.

Common reversal patterns used in technical analysis include:

(a) *Head-and-shoulders:* The head-and-shoulders pattern is one of the most reliable chart patterns in technical analysis. It is a reversal pattern which signals that the price can be expected to move against the original trend.

There are two forms of the head-and-shoulders pattern. One is the head-and-shoulders top that is usually formed at the peak of a bull run and it is a signal that the stock price is likely to fall, once the pattern formation is completed. The second version of this pattern, the head-and-shoulders bottom or inverse head-and-shoulders, is usually formed at the bottom of a bear run and it is a signal that the stock price is likely to rise, once the pattern formation is completed. Both versions of the head-and-shoulder pattern are displayed in Figure 12.31.

This pattern comprises of four parts, two shoulders, one head and a neckline. Obviously, the shoulders are lower than the head. Neckline is actually a horizontal trend line that connects the peaks (in case of inverse head-and-shoulder formation) and troughs (in case of top head-and-shoulder formation) that exist between the head and the two shoulders. The patterns get confirmed when the neckline is breached, after the completion of the formation of the second shoulder of the pattern.

The first or the left shoulder, in case of top head-and-shoulder formation, is formed when prices peak due to strong buying in an ongoing bull trend. A drop in volume and a short downward swing follows this. However, buying momentum picks up again when the price drops and the shoulder formation is completed. Buying pressure takes the price and volume up, leading to the formation of the head. As prices peak, demand is exhausted and volumes drop, taking the price down, nearly to the level of previous downswing. This completes the head formation. The remaining buyers in the market move in to buy the stock at this price, causing another rally. This rally takes the price to a peak, nearly to the level of the right shoulder. Thereafter, the price line moves down, penetrating the neckline of

Figure 12.31 Head-and-shoulders and Inverse head-and-shoulders formation.

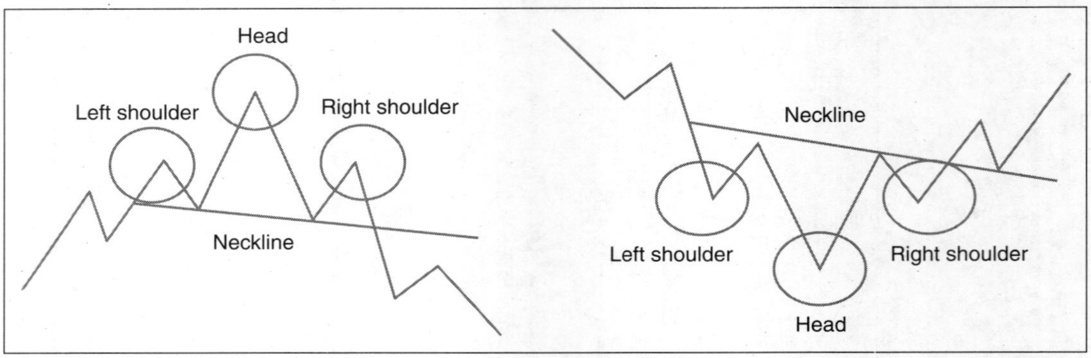

the formation. This marks the onset of bear run. Exactly opposite happens in case of inverse head-and-shoulder formation.

As in case of all other patterns, volumes drop during the formation of the pattern and pick up as the break out occurs. Figure 12.32 exhibits head-and-shoulder formation for Castrol India.

(b) *Double tops and bottoms:* Double tops and bottoms are an indication of the failed attempts of the price line to penetrate a support or resistance level. In the case of a double top, resistance is the barrier. After two successive attempts to breach the resistance, the price line often reverses its original trend. In the case of a double bottom, support is the barrier. After two successive attempts to breach the support, the price line often reverses its original trend. Both formations are illustrated in Figure 12.33.

There are many other reversal patterns such as rounding bottom or saucer bottom, triple bottom, triple top and wedge that can also be analyzed for triggering trading decisions. It is important to mention that wedges are both continuation as well as reversal patterns. Therefore, they should be used with caution.

Figure 12.32 Head-and-shoulder formation for Castrol India.

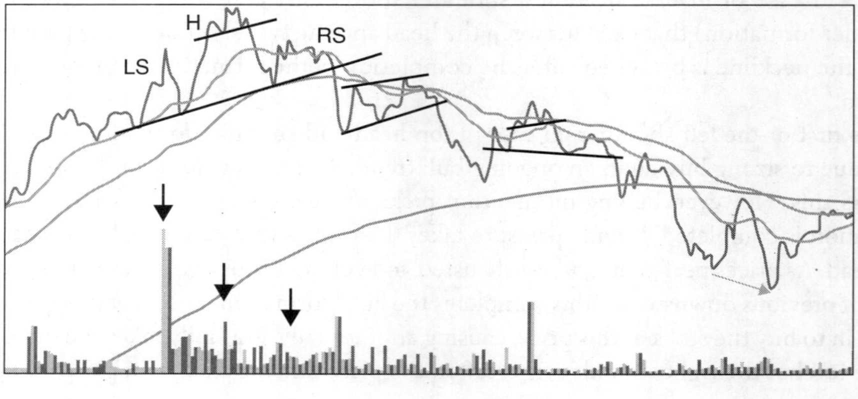

Figure 12.33 Double tops and bottoms formation.

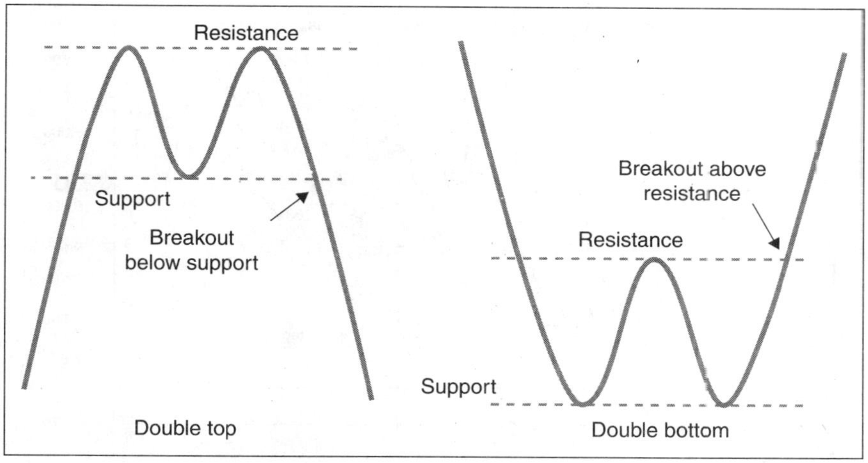

Gaps

A discussion about chart patterns is incomplete without talking about a formation called gap. A gap in a price chart is an empty space between two consecutive trading periods and this occurs due to a large difference in prices between two periods, as exhibited in Figure 12.34. For example, if a stock was trading between ₹95 and ₹100 on the 11th day of a month and it opens at ₹120 on the 12th day of the month then there will be a huge gap on the price chart. Gaps are important as they generally indicate the occurrence of some significant event in the concerned company such as an unanticipated positive announcement.

There are four types of gaps namely, breakaway, runaway, common and exhaustion gaps. A breakaway gap occurs at the initiation of a trend, a runaway or continuation gap is formed mid-trend and an exhaustion gap occurs near the end of a trend. A common gap cannot be placed in pattern of price movement.

Figure 12.34 Gap formation.

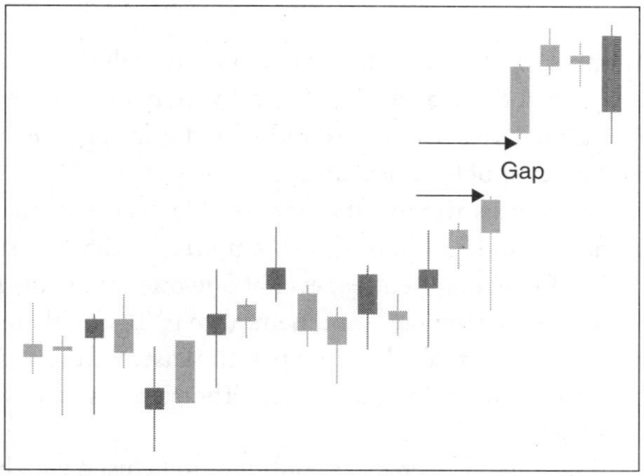

Figure 12.35 Gap formation in NIFTY.

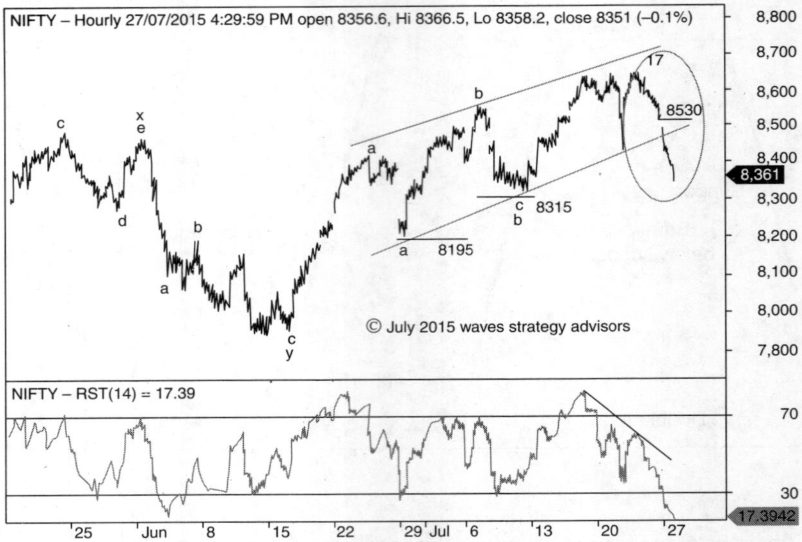

Source: http://elliottwaveindia.blogspot.in/2015/07/nifty-reversed-and-broke-wedge-shaped.html a blog by Ashish Kyal, accessed on August 21, 2015.

Traders can use these gaps for making profit. For example, they can buy a share in after-hours of trading when a positive earnings announcement comes in because the stock can be expected to trade at a gap the next day.

As discussed above, the charts plotted using stock price data are a mine of information. Various patterns that emerge on historical price charts provide important clues and triggers for trading decisions. However, caution needs to be exercised in using chart patterns for taking trading positions since there is no single chart pattern that can tell you with 100% accuracy where the stock price is headed. There is scope for multiple perspectives and interpretation while using chart patterns in technical analysis and this makes charting more of an art than science.

Technical analysis offers a number of advantages to the traders and analysts. It is simple and easy to apply. The main appeal of technical analysis lies in the availability of a vast variety of tools and software that are relatively easy to use. The chart patterns and their visual appeal is undoubtedly strong. The 'when to buy signal' given by the chart formation is a big point in favor of technical analysis.

However, the critics of technical analysis aver that it is not possible to best the market by using technical tools. The proponents of efficient market hypothesis have shown empirically that the stock prices follow a random walk and do not exhibit trends. It is further argued that even if one trader benefits from technical trading rules, others would move in to take advantage of the same and neutralize it. The market place is dynamic and the old technical trading rules, known to all, may actually be of no practical use. Further, a lot of subjective judgment is required in actually acting on the cues thrown by the patterns. The patterns seem to be clearer in hindsight but are difficult to discern while they are being formed.

All the criticism notwithstanding, technical analysis continues to be used widely across the globe.

SUMMARY

☑ Technical analysis is based on the assumption that the market is 90% psychological and 10% logical.

☑ Technical analysts analyze the price data to generate superior returns in the stock market. They use charts and graphs to plot the past price data and predict the direction of future price movement.

☑ The Dow theory is the foundation of technical analysis.

☑ Dow held that the stock market being a dependable barometer of the business conditions; a thorough analysis of the market as a whole could be used to assess the business performance and predict the future movements in the market and individual stocks.

☑ According to the Dow theory, the market moves in three distinct trends: primary trends that are the major movements and can be in upward or downward direction; secondary trends that are corrections of the primary movement and last for a short duration; and the minor trends, representing day-to-day fluctuations which are not significant from analysis point of view.

☑ The basic premise of the Elliott wave theory is that stock markets move in repetitive upward and downward cycles and make distinct patterns.

☑ Technical analysts use golden ratio and the Fibonacci sequence for the purpose of generating patterns to provide cues for trading decisions.

☑ Consistent with the Dow's theory, technicians use a number of charting techniques to generate charts to identify patterns and trends. The four main types of charts are:
- Line Chart
- Bar Charts
- Candlestick Charts
- Point and Figure Charts

☑ Study of trend in past data to try to predict future direction of movement is based on the belief of technical analysts that the history repeats itself.

☑ In case of stock price movement, following types of trends can be identified:
- Uptrend indicating a period of bull run
- Downtrend indicating a period of bear run
- Sideways/Horizontal trend indicating a lack of a well-defined trend in upward or downward direction

☑ A chart pattern may be described as a distinct formation on a stock price chart that indicates a trading signal, or signifies the future direction of price movements.

☑ There are two distinct types of chart patterns used in technical analysis viz., reversal patterns and continuation patterns. In addition, there are two more patterns: support and resistance and channels.

☑ These patterns are used by chartists to identify prevailing trends and trend reversals and use them as inputs to generate buy and sell signals.

☑ Gaps in a price chart are empty spaces between two consecutive trading periods and this occurs due to a large difference in prices between the two periods.

KEY WORDS

CONCEPT QUESTIONS

1. Suppose you are an ace analyst in your firm and you are appearing for an interview for the post of chief analyst at a globally acclaimed asset management company. The interview panel asks you to answer the following in concise terms:
   a. Why use technical analysis for security research?
   b. Which is the best and the most reliable chart pattern and why?
   c. Is closing price the best input for charting?
2. What do technical analysts mean when they say that the market is 90% psychological and 10% logical?
3. A researcher in equity market should always keep an eye on the price-volume relationship. Comment.
4. How can a trader use Fibonacci sequence to take profitable long or short positions in the market?
5. The Elliott Wave theory is subjective and more than a little challenging to apply. Do you agree?
6. Plot one-year closing price data of Cipla Ltd, Hero MotoCorp Ltd, ITC Ltd, Larsen & Toubro Ltd and NTPC Ltd and comment on the performance of the stock of these companies. (Download data from www.bseindia.com)
7. Fundamental and technical analysis are complementary approaches in taking trading positions or making investment decision. Explain the statement with an example of how you will use the two to buy a scrip.
8. It is said that the Dow theory is the foundation of technical analysis. Is the statement true in the context of the modern investment environment? Has the Dow theory lost its relevance with time?
9. Do you believe that technical analysis is a sound approach to be used in making investment decisions? If yes, why? If no, why?
10. While the chart patterns are glamorous and mystical in appeal, they might prove to be misleading and difficult to interpret. Discuss.

11. What are the types of price movements postulated in the Dow theory, and how are they used by a technician?

12. Why is the volume of trading important and how do technicians use it in their analysis?

13. What are support and resistance levels, when do they occur, and how are they used by technicians?

CASELET

Cairn India is one of the largest independent oil and gas exploration and production companies in India with a market capitalization of ~ US$ 10 billion. It was rated as the fastest-growing energy company in the world, as per 2012 and 2013 Platts Top 250 Global Energy Company Rankings.

Cairn India operates ~ 30% of India's domestic crude oil production. Through its affiliates, Cairn India has been operating for close to 20 years, playing an active role in developing India's oil and gas resources. To date, it has opened 4 frontier basins with over 40 discoveries, 31 in Rajasthan alone.

The Mangala field in Rajasthan, discovered in January 2004, is the largest onshore oil discovery in India in more than two decades. Mangala, Bhagyam and Aishwariya fields – major discoveries in the Rajasthan block have gross ultimate oil recovery of over 1 billion barrels.

Cairn India has a portfolio of 9 blocks – one block in Rajasthan, which contains multiple assets, two on the west coast and four on the east coast of India and one each in Sri Lanka and South Africa. Oil and gas are currently being produced from Rajasthan, Ravva and Cambay. (https://www.cairnindia.com/about-us)

The price chart of the company is given below.

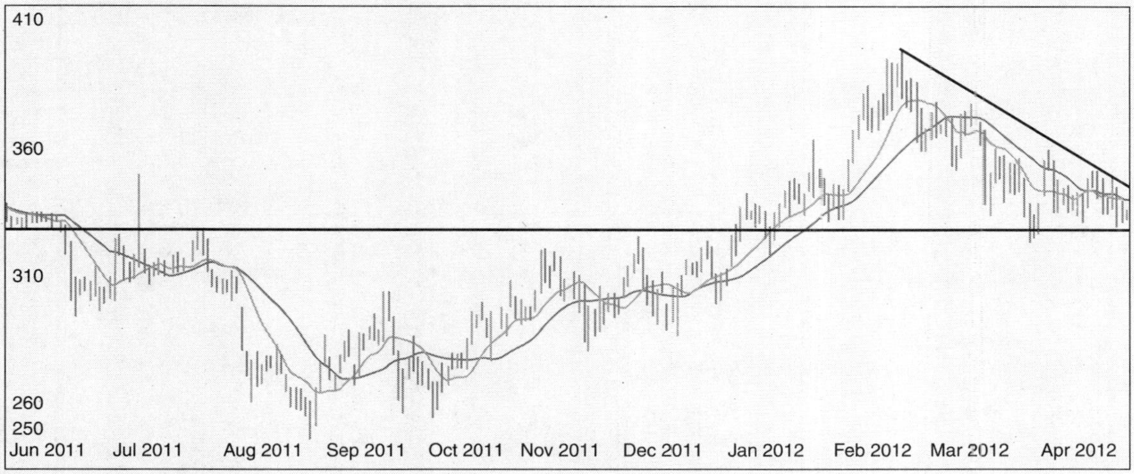

Mr. Singh, wants to buy share of Cairn India. Use the information and the price chart given above to advise him on whether he should buy the share and also when?

Decoding the Esoteric Aura: Technical Analysis and Behavioral Finance

13

CHAPTER OBJECTIVES

- ❒ Understanding the usefulness of indicators in technical analysis
- ❒ Learning to use different indicators to formulate trading strategies
- ❒ Evaluating the efficacy of different indicators through case studies
- ❒ Assessing the basic arguments of supporters of behavioral finance
- ❒ Critiquing the contentions of behaviorists and supporters of standard financial theory.

In the preceding chapter, we discussed various charting techniques and chart formations that are used by technical analysts for taking buy and sell decisions by predicting the future direction of the movement of the market. The chart formations are often difficult to detect, as the markets do not move in a straight line rather, the rise or the fall in the market is erratic. Over the years certain mathematical tools have been developed that can be used to smoothen the erratic movement, identify overbought or oversold conditions and the possibility of a trend reversal. These tools are called indicators and oscillators. Indicators are used as a supplementary measures to generate additional information for analysis of the securities under consideration. Indicators are a very useful source of additional information in technical analysis as they help detect momentum, trends and volatility in price movements of securities. In this chapter, we will discuss the key indicators, oscillators and trading strategies used by the traders to take buy and sell decisions.

The computation of the indicators is based on the price and volume of a security. Indicators are used to measure volatility, trends and momentum. The main benefit of indicators is that they can be used to confirm trends in price movement emerging in the chart patterns and to generate buy and sell signals.

The indicators may be leading or lagging indicators. An indicator that precedes the price movements is called the leading indicator. Obviously a leading indicator would have a predictive quality and is useful during periods of non-trending trading ranges or horizontal movements in the prices. An indicator that follows price movement is called a lagging indicator. It is used as a confirmation tool, mainly during trending periods.

Indicators may be constructed within bounded ranges or outside them. The range bound indicators are called oscillators. Oscillators have a range, for example, between 0 and 100. When the value is near 100, it indicates signal periods where the security is overbought, similarly, when the value is near 0, it indicates signal periods where the security is oversold.

Non-bounded indicators also form buy and sell signals and display strength or weakness. Further, indicators are used to form the buy and sell signals through crossovers and divergence. Crossovers are observed when either the price line moves through the moving average line or when two different moving averages cross over each other. Divergence is observed when the price trend and indicator trend are moving in the opposite direction and it indicates that the direction of the price trend is weakening.

Marketview 13.1 Top-down Approach to Technical Analysis

The top-down approach begins with broad-based macro analysis which involves an analysis of the overall market through the major indices such as the S&P BSE SENSEX and CNX NIFTY followed by sector analysis to identify the strongest and weakest set of stocks within the aggregate market. The broad market and sector analysis is followed by the analysis of individual stock to identify the potential winners and losers among the sectors selected.

Though many traders tend to use a single indicator for buy and sell signals, ideally they should be used as supplementary tools, in conjunction with other indicators, charts and price movement.

Let us discuss few key indicators like moving averages, relative strength index, rate of change indicator and stochastic oscillator.

Moving Averages

Moving average (MA) is used to smoothen the price movement of a security. It is a measure of the average price of a security over a specified period of time. Technical analysts compute daily moving average (DMA) or a 5-day moving average or for any number of days, '*n*.' The average price thus computed is plotted to identify the true trends by removing fluctuations or noise. It is one of the most popular indicators used to gauge the direction of the prevailing trend.

Moving averages are of different types on the basis of the way they are calculated, but the interpretation remains the same. The types of MA vary according to the difference in weights placed on the price levels. The three most common types of moving averages are simple, linear and exponential.

Simple Moving Average (SMA)

SMA is calculated by taking a sum of all the past closing price levels over the period under consideration and dividing the result by the number of prices used in the calculation, i.e., arithmetic mean is calculated. For example, in a 15-day moving average, the last 15 closing prices are summed up and divided by 15. If a trader wishes to see a 55-day average instead, the same calculations would be made, but the prices of past 55 days have to be considered. SMA is a duration-based tool. Let us understand the calculations with the help of a Numerical Example.

Numerical Example 1

Use the daily closing prices of S&P BSE SENSEX for a period from November 3, 2014 through November 28, 2014 to calculate the 5-day moving average.

Solution:

To calculate 5-day moving average, sum of 5 most recent prices is taken, leaving out each past price as we move ahead. The sum for each day, beginning from the 5th day onward is divided by 5 to get 5-day moving average from 5th day onward.

The first value in column 3 is obtained by adding the prices of first five trading days i.e., November 3, 2014 to November 11, 2014. Each subsequent value in column 3 is obtained by deleting the first closing price and adding the sixth closing price. For instance, to calculate the second value in column 3, closing price of November 3, 2014 is dropped and closing price of November 12, 2014 is added and the process continues. To compute SMA, each value in column 3 is divided by 5 and recorded in the adjacent cell in column 4.

Trading day	Closing price	Sum of 5 most recent prices	Simple moving average
03-Nov-14	27860.38		
05-Nov-14	27914.88		
07-Nov-14	27868.63		
10-Nov-14	27874.73		
11-Nov-14	27910.06	139429.68	27885.935
12-Nov-14	28008.9	139578.2	27915.64
13-Nov-14	27940.64	139602.96	27920.592
14-Nov-14	28046.66	139780.99	27956.198
17-Nov-14	28177.88	140084.14	28016.828
18-Nov-14	28163.29	140337.37	28067.474
19-Nov-14	28032.85	140361.32	28072.264
20-Nov-14	28067.56	140488.24	28097.648
21-Nov-14	28334.63	140776.21	28155.242
24-Nov-14	28499.54	141097.87	28219.574
25-Nov-14	28338.05	141272.63	28254.526
26-Nov-14	28386.19	141625.97	28325.194
27-Nov-14	28438.91	141997.32	28399.464
28-Nov-14	28693.99	142356.68	28471.336

Moving averages can be used to identify prevailing trends and trend reversals. They can also be used to set up support and resistance levels. Analysts frequently use 30 week or 200 day moving average to identify long-term trends, 55-day MA to identify intermediate trend and 10-day MA to identify short-term trend. The buy-sell signals are generated by plotting security's closing price levels and the SMA. The signal given by the MA analysis are:

1. **Buy Signal:** Buy if,
   (a) The stock price line falls below rising MA line.
   (b) The stock price line rises up through a flattening MA line.
   (c) The stock price line that is above the MA line falls but reverses the fall before it reaches the MA line.
2. **Sell Signal:** Sell if,
   (a) The stock price line rises above falling MA line.
   (b) The stock price line falls through a flattening MA line.
   (c) The stock price line that is below the MA line rises but reverses the rise before it reaches the MA line.

Traders also determine the momentum by comparing a pair of moving averages. If a short-term MA lies above a long-term MA, it indicates uptrend. Conversely, if a long-term MA lies above a shorter-term MA, it signals a downward movement in the trend.

Momentum compares the current price to the price *n* periods ago. It is calculated as:

Current price – the price *n* periods ago

(*n* is the number of periods chosen by the technical analyst)

If the current price is higher than the price *n* periods ago, then the momentum indicator is said to be positive. In contrast, if the current price is lower than the price *n* periods ago, then the momentum indicator is negative. Let us analyze the case of HCLTECH to understanding how SMA can be used as a trading strategy.

Spreadsheet Application 1[1] Use MS Excel to calculate SMA of different duration for HCLTECH for a period starting from September 26, 2012. Assume the amount of exposure in the stock to be ₹1000000 to calculate net profit/loss for SMA computed for 9, 12 and 20 days.

Soultion:

The SMA values computed using MS Excel can help as know whether to buy or sell the HCLTECH stock or a daily basis.

The SMA forms an average trendline for the actual stock price for all days in the period under consideration. When SMA is considered for longer duration, it is more smooth and gives a more accurate indication of the trend. Figure 13.1 shows how the actual stock price and the SMA lines are formed over period.

The spreadsheet shows how SMA works. On changing the number of days used to calculate SMA, the net profit/loss also varies depending on the trends. If the number of days are 9, the net profit/loss is ₹3,306,795 for the given exposure amount. On the same lines, if the number of days for SMA is taken as 12, net profit/loss = ₹2,799,059 and similarly taking no. of days = 20, net profit/loss becomes ₹2,317,532.

[1] This application has been prepared by Zameer Shah, MMS Finance 2013–15, K.J Somaiya Institute of Management Studies and Research, Mumbai.

A	B	C	D	E	F	G	H	I	J	K	L	M	N	O	P	Q	R	S	T
Symbol	Date	Close Price	DMA	Signal	Buy Price	Sell Price	Lots	Lots	Qty	Total Exposure	PnL Calc	PnL Calc	PnL	Brokerage	STT	Total Cost	Net PnL	Net PnL	No. of Days
HCLTECH	26-Sep-12	568.85						0	0	0	0	0	0	0	0	0	0	3,306,795	9
HCLTECH	27-Sep-12	583.45								0	15	0	0	0	0	0	0		
HCLTECH	28-Sep-12	577.45								0	-6	0	0	0	0	0	0		
HCLTECH	01-Oct-12	581.15								0	4	0	0	0	0	0	0		
HCLTECH	03-Oct-12	591.35								0	10	0	0	0	0	0	0		
HCLTECH	04-Oct-12	589.05								0	-2	0	0	0	0	0	0		
HCLTECH	05-Oct-12	573.55								0	-16	0	0	0	0	0	0		
HCLTECH	08-Oct-12	558.75								0	-15	0	0	0	0	0	0		
HCLTECH	09-Oct-12	560.75	576.04	SHORT		560.75	35	35	-1,750	981,313	2	3,500	-3,500	294	98	393	-3,893		
HCLTECH	10-Oct-12	565.3	575.64	SHORT		565.30	35			989,275	5	7,962	-7,962	0	0	0	-7,962		
HCLTECH	11-Oct-12	576.85	574.91	LONG	576.85		34	34	1,700	980,645	12	19,635	19,635	294	0	294	19,341		
HCLTECH	12-Oct-12	581.65	575.38	LONG	581.65		34			988,805	5	8,160	8,160	0	0	0	8,160		
HCLTECH	15-Oct-12	583.7	575.66	LONG	583.70		34			992,290	2	3,485	3,485	0	0	0	3,485		
HCLTECH	16-Oct-12	584.5	574.90	LONG	584.50		34			993,650	1	1,360	1,360	0	0	0	1,360		
HCLTECH	17-Oct-12	580.55	573.96	LONG	580.55		34			986,935	-4	-6,715	-6,715	0	0	0	-6,715		

Source: Model developed by Zameer Shah.

Figure 13.1 Actual closing price of HCLTECH and the 9-day SMA lines.

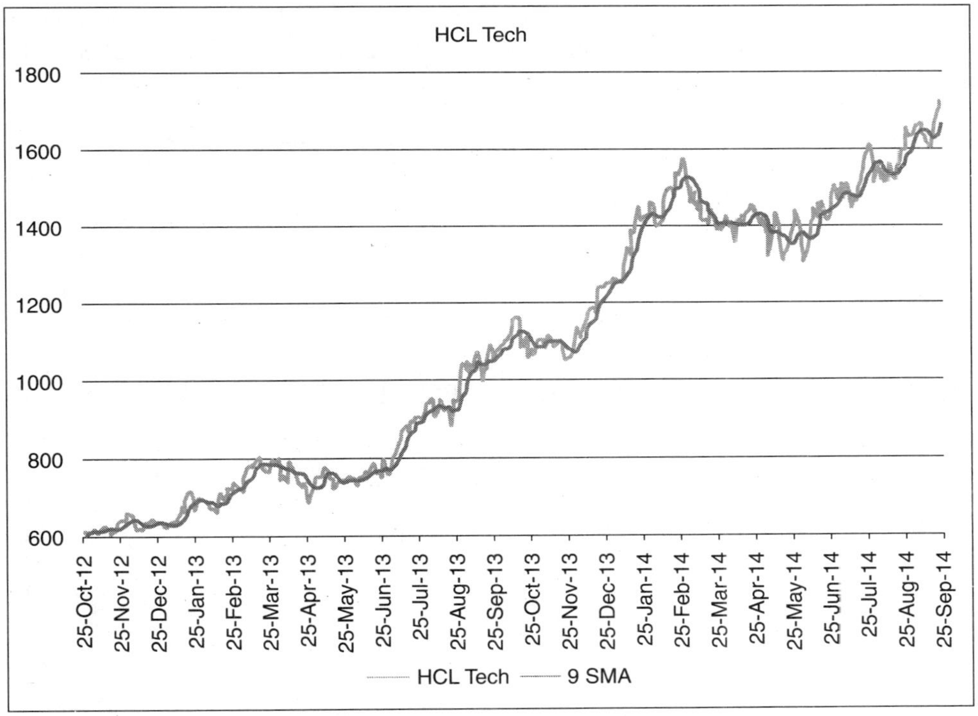

As can be seen in Figure 13.1, the SMA line is smooth whereas the daily closing price line is showing fluctuating movement. The point at which the SMA cuts the actual price line, is the point where the stock must be bought or sold. When the actual price is trending down, stock should be sold and when the two intersect in uptrend, the stock must be bought. For larger time periods, the SMA is flatter and thus less risky but on the other hand the returns are also lower. Thus, the length of MA must be decided on the basis of the amount of risk one is ready to take.

SMA is considered by many analysts to have limited usefulness because each data point in the series has the same impact on the result, irrespective of where it occurs. Critics feel that most recent data is more important and should be given higher weightage. This kind of criticism has led to the development of other types of moving averages.

Linear Weighted Moving Average

The linear weighted moving average (LWMA) is computed by first multiplying the closing prices with their respective positions in the sequence and then dividing the sum of weighted values by the sum of the number of periods. For example, in a six-day linear weighted average, today's closing price is multiplied by six, yesterday's by five and so on, until the first day in the period under consideration is reached. The weighted numbers so obtained are added together and divided by the sum of the multipliers. It is not very popular and is used only to address the problem of equal weighting.

Exponential Moving Average

Exponential moving average (EMA) uses a smoothing factor to place a higher weight on more recent data points as compared to older ones. Figure 13.2 illustrate the SMA and EMA lines for S&P BSE SENSEX. It is calculated by using the following formula:

$$\text{EMA} = (\text{Current Closing Price} - \text{Previous EMA}) \times \text{Factor} + \text{Previous EMA}$$

where

$$\text{Factor} = \frac{2}{(n+1)}$$

Figure 13.2 SMA and EMA lines for S&P BSE SENSEX.

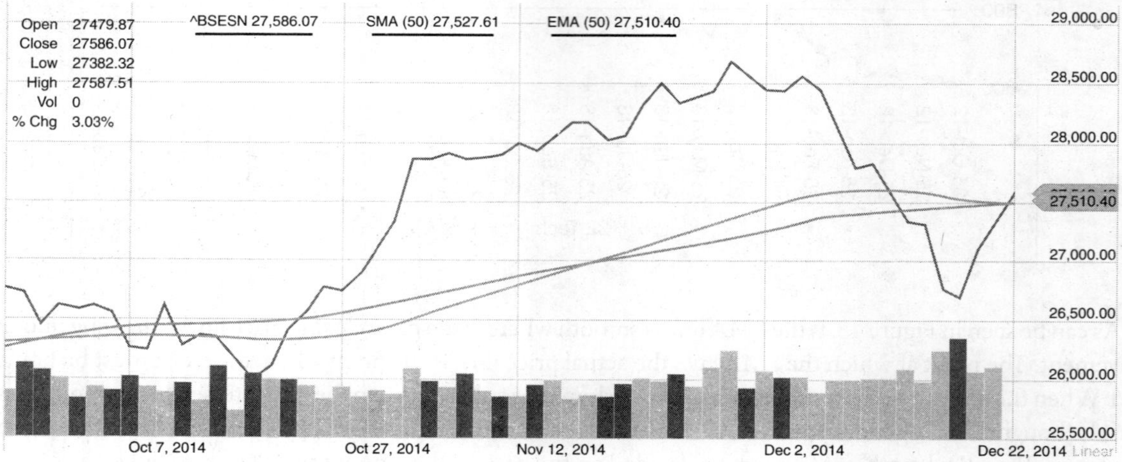

Source: http://finance.yahoo.com/echarts, accessed on January 2, 2015.

where

n = The number of days for which the average is calculated.

Let us understand the calculation of EMA with the help of a Numerical Example.

Figure 13.2 illustrates the SMA and EMA lines for S&P BSE SENSEX.

Numerical Example 2

Assume closing price for ten-day period for a hypothetical stock D and calculate 5–day EMA.

Solution:

The closing price of first day is taken as the EMA of the first day. The EMA for second day onwards is calculated using the formula:

$$\text{EMA} = (\text{Current Closing Price} - \text{Previous EMA}) \times \text{Factor} + \text{Previous EMA}$$

and

$$\text{Factor} = \frac{2}{(n+1)}$$

Since we are calculating 5 day EMA, $n = 5$

Therefore,

$$\text{Factor} = \frac{2}{(5+1)} = 0.33.$$

The second day EMA is calculated as: $(36 - 34) \times 0.33 + 34 = 34.66$

EMA for each day is calculated in the same manner.

Days	Closing price	EMA
1	34	34
2	36	34.66
3	37.5	35.60
4	40	37.05
5	42.5	38.85
6	43	40.22
7	44	41.47
8	42.5	41.81
9	43	42.20
10	44	42.79

The correct 5-day EMA is available from 6th day onwards.

EMA is more efficient than the linear weighted average and more responsive to new information as compared to SMA.

Moving Average Convergence Divergence

The moving average convergence divergence (MACD) is an oscillator that is one of the most popular indicators in technical analysis. It can be used as a trend or momentum indicator. It measures short-term momentum compared to long-term momentum to help signal the current direction of momentum.

$$\text{MACD} = \text{Shorter term moving average} - \text{Longer term moving average}$$

It provides a measurement of the momentum and intensity of the trading of a stock. It can give early signals of trend continuation or reversal. However, traders use it more frequently to gauge the strength of the price movement rather than to determine the direction of a trend.

The MACD indicator uses two exponential moving averages: a short or fast EMA and a long or slow EMA. It represents the difference between the above two moving averages plotted against a centerline. The two moving averages are equal at the centerline. In the chart, an exponential moving average of the MACD itself is also plotted.

MACD measures short-term momentum as compared to longer-term momentum to confirm the current direction of momentum. A positive MACD indicates that the shorter term moving average is above the longer-term moving average, thereby signaling upward momentum. On the other hand, a negative MACD indicates that the shorter term moving average is below the longer-term moving average, thereby signaling downward momentum.

There are three ways to interpret the MACD:

1. Moving Average Crossovers
2. MACD Histogram
3. MACD Divergences

A MACD line crossing over the centerline signals a moving average crossover. The most common EMAs used for MACD calculations are: the 26-day and 12-day EMAs. When the 12-day EMA crosses over 26 day EMA, a buy signal in generated and when it crosses below the 26-day EMA, sell signed is generated. A signal line is usually created by using a nine-day EMA of the MACD values. The signal line is used to determine buy and sell signals. A buy signal is generated when the MACD line crosses above the signal line. Conversely, when the MACD line crosses below the signal line, a sell signal is generated. There are no hard and fast rules regarding the EMA durations to be used. These can be adjusted to meet the needs of the analysts and the security under consideration. Typically, for more volatile securities, shorter term averages should be used while for less volatile securities longer-term averages should be used.

The MACD histogram is a visual representation of the difference between the MACD and its nine-day EMA (signal line). When the MACD is above its nine-day EMA, the histogram is positive and when the MACD is below its nine-day EMA, the histogram is negative. In case of prices in uptrend, the histogram becomes larger as the speed of the price movement increases, and contracts as price movement decreases. The same thing works in reverse when the prices are in downtrend. The changes in the MACD histogram precede the changes that occur in MACD. It indicates the changes in trends earlier than the MACD signal line. However, it may also cause more false signals at times.

The histogram helps in identification of the centre line crossovers and divergences without difficulty. In fact, the MACD histogram is the reason behind the popularity of this indicator to measure momentum as it responds to the speed of price change.

$$\text{MACD histogram} = \text{MACD line} - \text{Signal line}$$

Figure 13.3 shows the MACD, MACD signal line and MACD histogram for SENSEX.

Figure 13.3 The MACD, MACD signal line and MACD histogram for SENSEX.

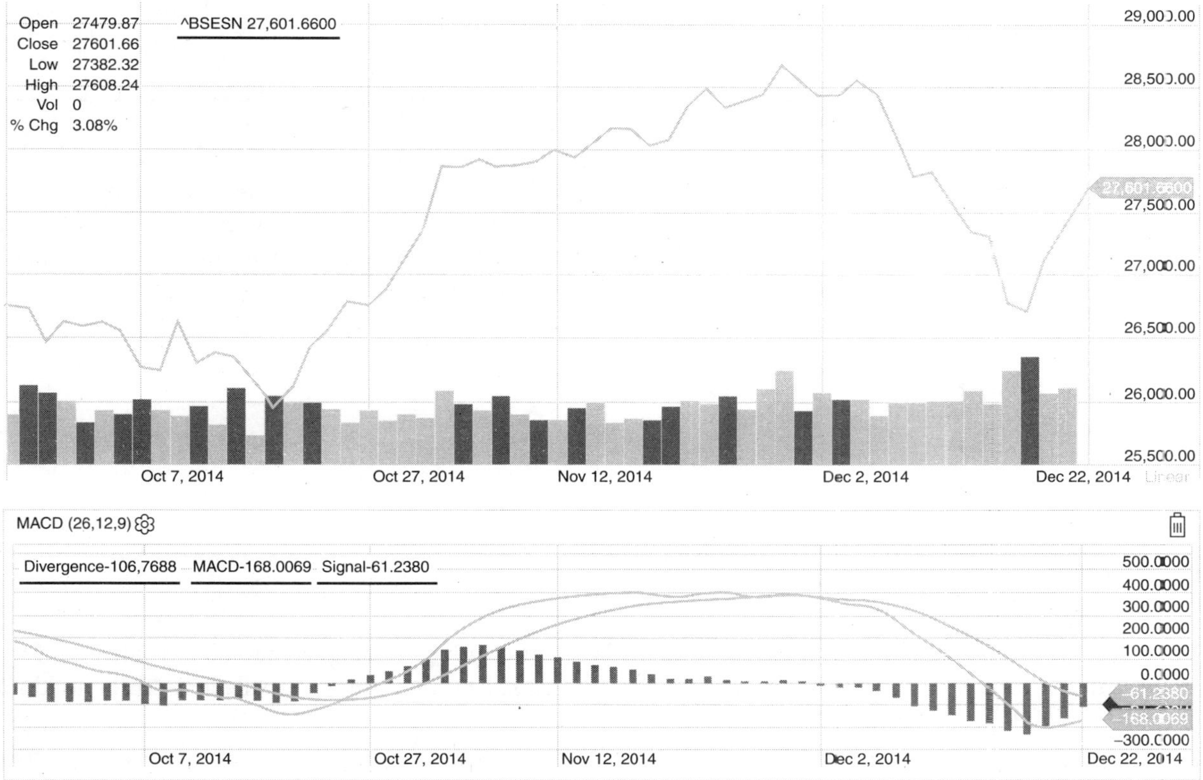

Source: http://finance.yahoo.com/echarts, accessed on January 2, 2015.

There are some observations with respect to MACD histogram that should be kept in mind:

1. The histogram crosses the zero line when MACD crosses the signal line.

2. The value on the histogram is positive when the value of MACD is greater than the value of the signal line.
3. The value on the histogram is negative if the value of MACD is less than the value of the signal line.
4. When the histogram is above the zero line, it is a buy signal.
5. When MACD histogram intersects the zero line downwards with negative values, it is a sell signal.

Trading divergence is one of the ways in which the MACD histogram is used. Traders find chart points at which price displays a new swing high or a new swing low, but the MACD histogram does not, indicating a divergence between price and momentum. Bearish divergence is said to occur if the indicator suggests that a price should be going down but the price continues to maintain its current uptrend.

Bullish divergence occurs if the indicator suggests that price should be bottoming and heading higher but the actual price continues to be in downtrend. These divergences can be used as a signal to get out of a long or short position before profits get eroded. However, trading divergences should be used with caution. They have failed more than they have succeeded as a trading strategy.

Relative Strength Index

The relative strength index (RSI) is also a well-known momentum indicator. It is based on the assumption that in case of few securities, prices rise rapidly during uptrend but fall slowly during downtrend as compared to the market as a whole. Such securities are said to have greater relative strength and they tend to outperform the market. RSI compares the magnitude of recent gains to recent losses with a view to determine overbought and oversold conditions of a security. It is calculated using the following formula:

$$\text{RSI} = 100 - \left(\frac{100}{(1+\text{RS})}\right)$$

where

$$\text{RS} = \frac{\text{Average gains per day}}{\text{Average loss per day}}$$

Though standard calculation for RSI uses 14 trading days, however it can be adjusted to meet the needs of the trader and the market. If shorter trading period is used, the RSI becomes more volatile and can be used for shorter term trades.

RSI is plotted between a range of zero to 100. A reading above 70 suggests that a security is overbought, while a reading below 30 suggests that it is oversold as shown in Figure 13.4. When RSI crosses the 30 line from below and is rising, a buy signal is indicated. When the RSI crosses the 70 line from above and is falling, sell signal is indicated. This indicator can identify whether a security's price has been unfairly pushed to the prevailing levels and whether a reversal can be anticipated. Figure 13.5 exhibits RSI for SENSEX.

Let us try to understand RSI calculations with the help of a Numerical Example.

Figure 13.4 RSI chart.

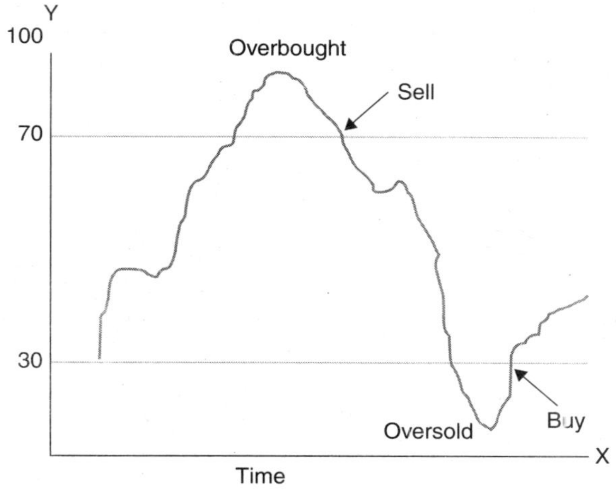

Figure 13.5 RSI for SENSEX.

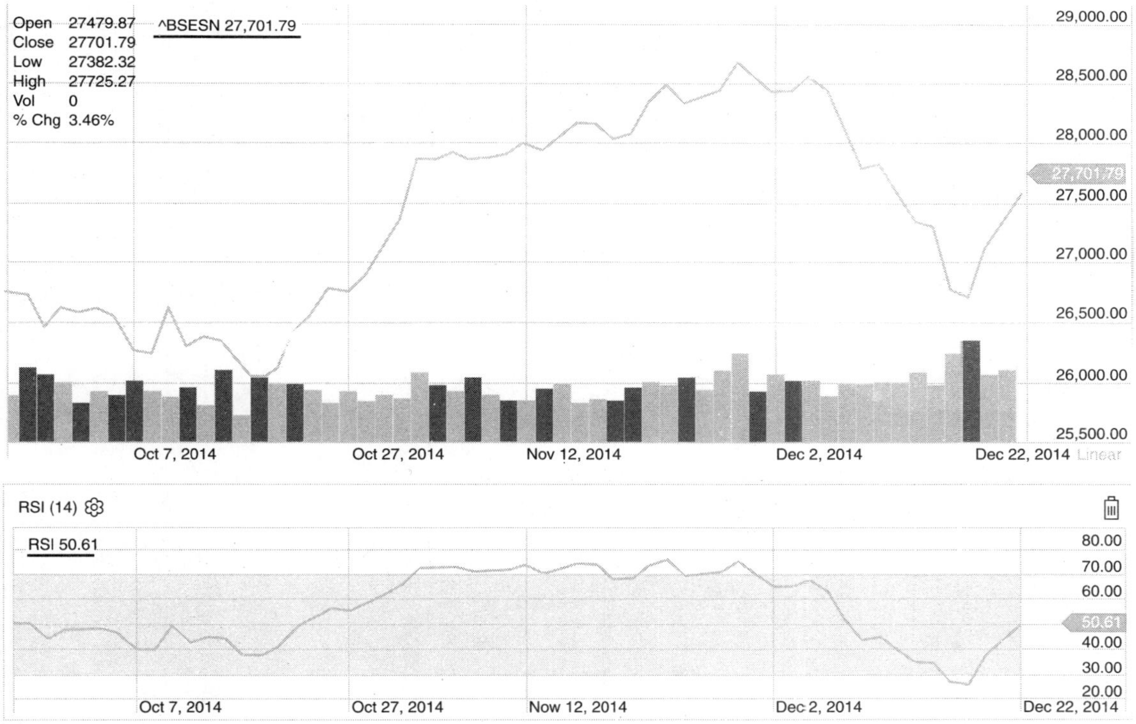

Source: http://finance.yahoo.com/echarts, accessed on January 2, 2015.

Numerical Example 3

Calculate 14-day RSI using the given closing price levels.

Solution:

RSI can be calculated using the formula:

$$RSI = 100 - \left(\frac{100}{(1+RS)}\right)$$

where

$$RS = \frac{\text{Average gains per day}}{\text{Average loss per day}}$$

First we need to calculate 14-day average gain and loss. As shown in the table below, total 14-day gain is 25. Therefore, 14-day average gain = 25/14 = 1.786.

Similarly, 14-day average loss $= \frac{10}{14} = 0.714$.

Days	Closing price	Gain	Loss
1	230	–	–
2	232	2	–
3	230	–	2
4	235	5	–
5	237	2	–
6	234	–	3
7	236	2	–
8	240	4	–
9	240	–	–
10	242	2	–
11	239	–	3
12	241	2	–

(Continued)

Continued

Days	Closing price	Gain	Loss
13	245	4	–
14	243	–	2
15	245	2	
Total		**25**	**10**

RS may be computed as 1.786/0.714 = 2.50

$$RSI = 100 - \left[\frac{100}{(1+250)}\right] = 71.42$$

This is the RSI for the 15th day.

RSI calculations can be made in models generated in MS Excel. A screenshot of the model is displayed in Spreadsheet application 2.

Spreadsheet Application 2 MS Excel-based Model for RSI Calculation for HDIL

1																								
2																								
3																								
4																								
5																								
6	487	Available weeks																						
7	498	Last data row																						
8										10	Period Slow RSI Calculations				5	Period Quick RSI Calculations								
9													Thresholds					Thresholds						
10							50	10					50	20				50	20	Slow RSI crossing above buy line and price above Slow MA	Slow RSI crossing below sell line or price below Slow MA	Slow RSI in Up Trend	Slow RSI in Down Trend	
11	Date	Open	High	Low	Close	Volume	Slow MA (50)	Quick MA (10)	Delta Close	Slow UP(10) Smoothed	Slow DN(10) Smoothed	Slow RSI (10)	Buy: 50	Sell: 20	Quick UP(5) Smoothed	Quick DN(5) Smoothed	Quick RSI (5)	Buy: 50	Sell: 20	B01	B02	B03	B04	B
12	1-Jan-13	112.2	115.4	112.2	114.9	7844024	85.96	117.31	-0.80	1.62	1.06	60.41	50	20	0.79	1.05	43.13	50	20	FALSE	FALSE	TRUE	FALSE	F
13	2-Jan-13	115.45	116.85	115.25	115.7	7836819	85.01	117.68	-0.80	1.80	1.09	62.27	50	20	0.99	1.11	47.24	50	20	FALSE	FALSE	TRUE	FALSE	F
14	3-Jan-13	116	116.9	114.55	116.5	8448862	84.01	118.12	-1.90	2.00	1.12	64.04	50	20	1.24	1.18	51.13	50	20	FALSE	FALSE	TRUE	FALSE	F
15	4-Jan-13	116	118.9	115.05	118.4	11927390	83.04	118.43	1.05	2.22	1.04	68.19	50	20	1.55	1.01	60.64	50	20	FALSE	FALSE	TRUE	FALSE	F
16	7-Jan-13	119.1	119.1	116.8	117.35	8811923	81.98	118.73	-0.85	2.35	1.15	67.13	50	20	1.67	1.26	57.11	50	20	FALSE	FALSE	TRUE	FALSE	F
17	8-Jan-13	117	118.7	115.5	118.2	8303839	80.91	119.09	-1.95	2.61	1.18	68.81	50	20	2.09	1.36	60.63	50	20	FALSE	FALSE	TRUE	FALSE	F
18	9-Jan-13	118.7	122.75	118.35	120.15	17027630	79.77	118.52	2.15	2.90	1.10	72.53	50	20	2.62	1.21	68.35	50	20	FALSE	FALSE	TRUE	FALSE	F
19	10-Jan-13	121.15	121.9	116.65	118	16925302	78.34	116.13	4.30	2.98	1.22	70.97	50	20	2.73	1.51	64.34	50	20	FALSE	FALSE	TRUE	FALSE	F
20	11-Jan-13	118.1	118.7	113.15	113.7	11868154	76.93	111.77	-6.50	2.84	1.36	67.67	50	20	2.34	1.89	55.29	50	20	FALSE	FALSE	TRUE	FALSE	F
21	14-Jan-13	114.1	120.8	112.7	120.2	13381825	75.58	108.69	1.60	3.15	0.78	80.07	50	20	2.93	0.74	79.78	50	20	FALSE	FALSE	TRUE	FALSE	F
22	15-Jan-13	120.2	120.9	117.95	118.6	11188768	74.11	105.04	-1.45	3.33	0.87	79.23	50	20	3.26	0.93	77.84	50	20	FALSE	FALSE	TRUE	FALSE	F
23	16-Jan-13	118.4	123.9	118.35	120.05	30605048	72.65	101.22	0.40	3.70	0.81	82.06	50	20	4.07	0.80	83.64	50	20	FALSE	FALSE	TRUE	FALSE	F
24	17-Jan-13	120.85	122.1	118	119.65	15181926	71.17	96.81	-1.70	4.06	0.90	81.90	50	20	4.99	1.00	83.37	50	20	FALSE	FALSE	TRUE	FALSE	F
25	18-Jan-13	120.3	123	120	121.35	13116493	69.78	92.51	0.35	4.51	0.81	84.81	50	20	6.24	0.82	88.38	50	20	FALSE	FALSE	TRUE	FALSE	F
26	21-Jan-13	121.1	122.35	119.4	121	7604650	68.37	88.18	8.55	4.98	0.90	84.71	50	20	7.71	1.03	88.27	50	20	FALSE	FALSE	TRUE	FALSE	F
27	22-Jan-13	120.5	121.45	111.4	112.45	16841241	66.97	83.65	16.20	4.58	1.00	82.11	50	20	7.50	1.28	85.41	50	20	FALSE	FALSE	TRUE	FALSE	F
28	23-Jan-13	113.75	114.4	93.65	96.25	81041361	65.68	79.86	21.80	3.29	1.11	74.78	50	20	5.33	1.60	76.89	50	20	TRUE	FALSE	TRUE	FALSE	
29	24-Jan-13	96.5	97.6	72.3	74.45	1.57E+08	64.74	77.66	-8.45	1.23	1.23	49.98	50	20	1.21	2.00	37.70	50	20	FALSE	FALSE	TRUE	FALSE	F
30	25-Jan-13	73.4	84.9	68	82.9	1.05E+08	64.19	77.45	-0.75	1.37	0.43	76.08	50	20	1.51	0.39	79.50	50	20	FALSE	FALSE	TRUE	FALSE	F
31	28-Jan-13	83.9	84.85	79.75	83.65	42760006	63.46	76.28	3.25	1.52	0.39	79.39	50	20	1.89	0.30	86.30	50	20	FALSE	FALSE	TRUE	FALSE	F
32	29-Jan-13	84	85.8	77.6	80.4	42324368	62.73	75.13	4.45	1.33	0.44	75.17	50	20	1.55	0.38	80.52	50	20	FALSE	FALSE	TRUE	FALSE	F
33	30-Jan-13	81	81.75	75.5	75.95	29514258	62.07	74.10	-0.75	0.98	0.49	66.81	50	20	0.83	0.47	63.85	50	20	FALSE	FALSE	TRUE	FALSE	F
34	31-Jan-13	75.9	78.45	74.45	76.7	25681764	61.49	73.34	-1.30	1.09	0.46	70.41	50	20	1.04	0.40	72.18	50	20	FALSE	FALSE	TRUE	FALSE	F
35	1-Feb-13	76.8	79.5	76.8	78	24050334	60.89	72.41	2.30	1.21	0.36	76.87	50	20	1.30	0.17	88.13	50	20	FALSE	FALSE	TRUE	FALSE	F

Generated by Zameer Shah, MMS Finance, 2013–15, KJ Sowmiya Institutes of Management Studies and Reseacher, Mumbai.

Rate of Change Indicator

The Rate-of-Change (ROC) indicator, often referred to as simply Momentum, is a pure momentum oscillator that is used to measure the percent change in price from one period to the next. ROC is also called velocity indicator because it measures the rate of change in price or the strength of momentum of change.

The ROC calculations compare the most recent price with the price "*n*" periods in the past. It is calculated by using the following formula:

$$\frac{(\text{Closing price today} - \text{Closing price "}n\text{" periods ago})}{\text{Closing price "}n\text{" periods ago}}$$

or

$$\text{ROC} = \text{Price Ratio} - 1$$

where

$$\text{Price ratio} = \frac{\text{Closing price today}}{\text{Closing price "}n\text{" periods ago}}$$

The ROC values can be positive, negative or zero.

Let us try to understand the ROC calculations with the help of a Numerical Example.

Numerical Example 4

Calculate 7 day ROC using the given closing price data.

Solution:

We can calculate ROC using the following formula:

$$\text{ROC} = \text{Price Ratio} - 1$$

where

$$\text{Price ratio} = \frac{\text{Closing price today}}{\text{Closing price "}n\text{" periods ago}}$$

The ROC values thus calculated are given in the table below.

Days	Closing price	Closing price 7 days ago	Price ratio	ROC = Ratio − 1
1	230			
2	232			

(Continued)

Continued

Days	Closing price	Closing price 7 days ago	Price ratio	ROC = Ratio − 1
3	232			
4	239			
5	238			
6	234			
7	236			
8	240	230	1.043	0.043
9	240	232	1.034	0.034
10	242	232	1.043	0.043
11	239	239	1.000	0.000
12	236	238	0.992	−0.008
13	239	234	1.021	0.021
14	242	236	1.025	0.025
15	241	240	1.004	0.004
16	241	240	1.004	0.004
17	243	242	1.004	0.004
18	243	239	1.017	0.017
19	242	236	1.025	0.025
20	243	239	1.017	0.017

ROC signals include centerline crossovers, divergences and overbought or oversold indicators. The plot of ROC forms an oscillator that tends to fluctuate above and below the zero line as shown in Figure 13.6. When the ROC line lies above zero line, the price is rising and when it lies below the zero line, the price is falling.

Traders use crossovers across the zero line in ROC plot to identify buy and sell signal. When the ROC line crosses upwards from below the zero line, it indicates buying opportunity whereas a downside crossing from above the zero line indicates selling opportunity. ROC should be used along with the price levels to confirm the buy and sell signals.

Further, the overbought zone lies above the zero line and ideally, shares in this zone should be sold. The oversold zone lies below the zero line and ideally, shares in this zone should be bought.

Traders generally use values greater than zero to indicate an increase in upward momentum and a value less than zero to indicate an increase in selling pressure. However, some of the most important signals are generated when the price of the security and the ROC show divergence, i.e., move in opposite directions.

Figure 13.7 exhibits the ROC plot for CNX NIFTY.

Figure 13.6 ROC chart.

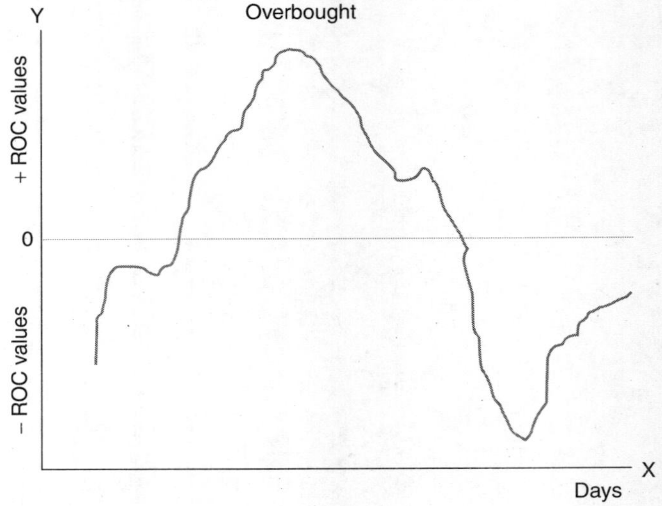

Figure 13.7 The ROC plot for CNX NIFTY.

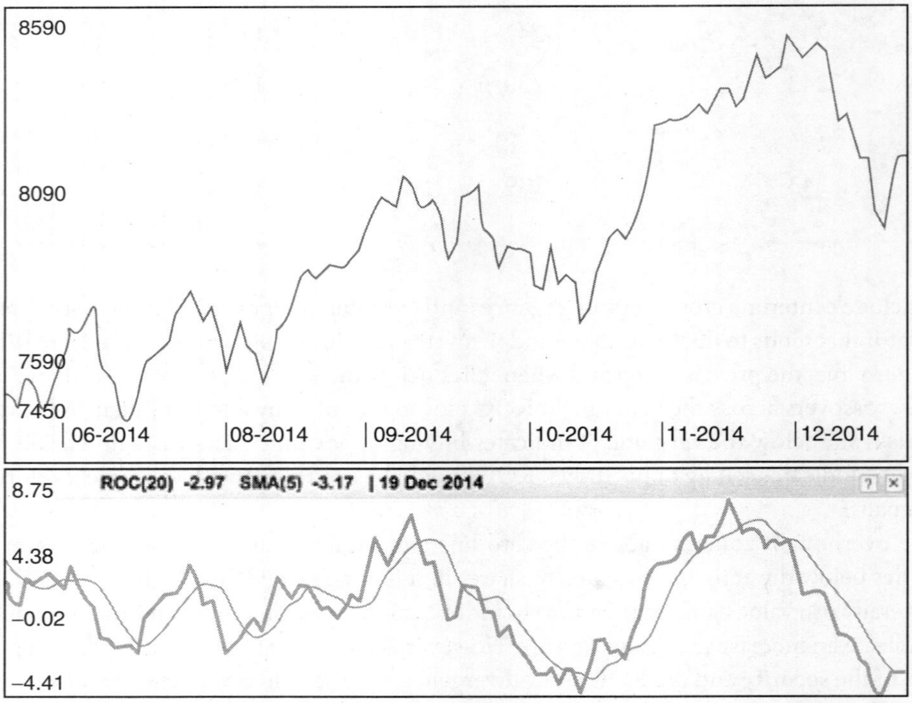

Stochastic Oscillator

The stochastic oscillator is another very popular momentum indicator. This indicator rests on the idea that in an uptrend, the stock price should be closing near the highs of the trading range, thereby signaling upward momentum. In a downtrend, the stock price should be closing near the lows of the trading range, thereby signaling downward momentum. It compares where the price has closed relative to its price range over the time period under consideration.

The Stochastic indicator is exhibited as two lines – '%K' and '%D.' The main line is called '%K' and it is faster than '%D' line. '%D' is a moving average of '%K.' Typically, the %K line is shown as a solid line and the %D line is shown as a dotted line. The %D line is considered to be the more important of the two lines as it is seen to indicate better signals.

The two lines oscillate between 0 and 100. The indicator signals overbought conditions above 80 and oversold conditions below 20.

Though the stochastic indicator is usually constructed for 5 days, weeks or months, yet sometimes traders use different periods. The formula used for the construction of %K line is:

$$\%K = 100\left\{\frac{(C - L_5)}{(H_5 - L_5)}\right\}$$

where
C = Most recent closing price
L_5 = Lowest price touched by the scrip during the last 5 days
H_5 = Highest price touched by the scrip during the last 5 days

The formula used for the construction of %D line is:

$$\%D = 100\left(\frac{H_3}{L_3}\right)$$

where
H_3 = Three day sum of $(C - L_5)$
L_3 = Three day sum of $(H_5 - L_5)$

The formula given above calculates the fast stochastic, which is too fast to be used for intra-day trading. This problem is overcome by calculating slow stochastic, where the %D line of the fast stochastic becomes the %K line of slow stochastic. The %D line of slow stochastic is the three-day SMA of slow %K line. Thus, fast stochastic needs to be calculated to arrive at slow stochastic. Figure 13.8 displays the fast and slow stochastics for Bank NIFTY.

A stochastic oscillator may be interpreted as:

1. Buy the scrip if its %K or %D falls below a specific level (say 20) and then rises above that level.
2. Sell the scrip if the oscillator rises above a specific level (say 80) and then falls below that level.
3. Buy if the %K line rises above the %D line and sell if the %K line falls below the %D line.

Figure 13.8 The fast and slow stochastic for bank NIFTY.

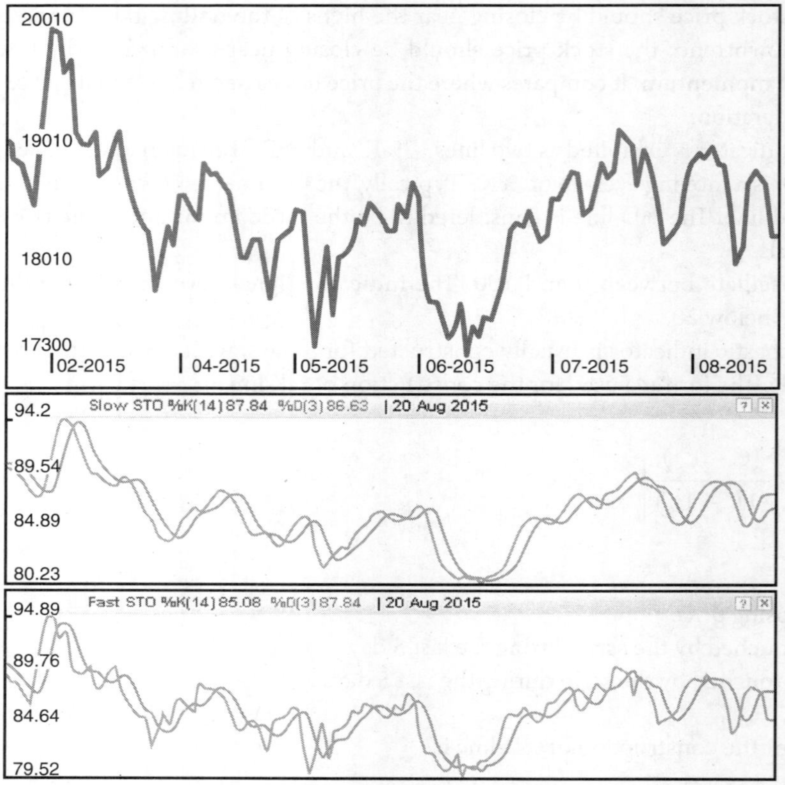

4. Look for diverging signals. For example, a divergent signal may emerge if prices are making a series of new highs but the stochastic is failing to surpass its previous highs.

Let us understand the working of stochastic indicator with the help of a Numerical Example.

Numerical Example 5

Calculate 5-day stochastic using the high, low and closing price data for stock X.

Solution:

The formula used for the construction of %K line is:

$$\%K = 100\left\{\frac{(C - L_5)}{(H_5 - L_5)}\right\}$$

The formula used for the construction of %D line is:

$$\%D = 100\left(\frac{H_3}{L_3}\right)$$

where
H_3 = Three day sum of $(C - L_5)$
L_3 = Three day sum of $(H_5 - L_5)$
$L_3 = H_5 - L_5$

For November 11, 2014, %K = 100 {(93 − 90)/(99 − 90)} = 33.33. Similarly the values for November 12 and 13 can be calculated as given in the table below.

$$\%D = 100\left(\frac{H_3}{L_3}\right) = 100\left\{\frac{(3+2+1)}{(9+9+7)}\right\} = 24$$

Trading day	High	Low	Closing	$H_3 = (C - L_5)$	$L_3 = H_5 - L_5$	%K	%D
03-Nov-14	98	96	97				
05-Nov-14	99	97	98				
07-Nov-14	97	95.5	96				
10-Nov-14	93	90	92.5				
11-Nov-14	95	91	93	3	9	33.33	
12-Nov-14	93	91	92	2	9	22.22	
13-Nov-14	93	90.5	91	1	7	14.29	24

Marketview 13.2 Millisecond Frequency Trading or MFT

A new concept in modern trading, Millisecond Frequency Trading or MFT has come up recently as opposed to High Frequency Trading (HFT). MFT takes place at a mind boggling microsecond frequency Some of the MFT strategies used in equities, forex and futures trading are ratio trade, stop hunting flipping, order flow, impact of size imbalances and ticking.

Beyond the Basics 13.1 Average Directional Index

It is a well-known fact that risk can be reduced and profit potential increased by trading in the direction of a strong trend. The average directional index (ADX) is a tool used by traders to quantify trend strength.

ADX is calculated on the basis of a moving average of price range expansion over a specified time frame. It is non-directional and is plotted in a single line with values ranging from 0 to 100. ADX values are used by traders to identify the strongest and most profitable trends in price movement (upward or downward).

Technical Indicators

In addition to the tools described above and the charts discussed in the previous chapter, technicians also use certain indicators like breadth indicators and market sentiment indicators to assess the overall market situation.

Breadth Indicators

1. **Breadth of Market Analysis:** Breadth of market is a measure of the difference between the number of shares that have advanced and the number of shares that have declined in the market during a period. It helps to explain the cause of changes in the direction of the market, as a whole, as represented by indices of market activity. The breadth of market is calculated by finding the daily net difference between the number of shares that have risen in price or advanced and the number of shares that have fallen in price or declined. A continuous cumulative index is formed by adding each day's difference to next day's difference as shown in Table 13.1.

TABLE 13.1 Calculation of breadth of market

Day	Advances	Declines	Daily difference	Breadth (cumulative difference)
1	710	340	370	370
2	480	520	–40	330
3	340	730	–390	–60
4	590	370	220	160
5	720	290	430	590

The index of advance-decline is plotted as a line graph. It is also known as advance-decline line. This line is compared with one or two market averages. Normally, the two lines move together. But if the two lines move in the opposite direction, i.e., they show divergence, an important signal occurs. For instance, if in a bull market, the market average is in uptrend but the breadth of market is moving downwards, then this divergence can be interpreted to signal an upcoming bear trend in the market.

On the other hand, if the market average is moving downwards but the advance-decline line is rising, it can be interpreted to signal an upcoming bull trend in the market.

2. **Volume:** Change in volume is tracked by analysts along with the price changes as an indicator of changes in demand and supply in the market. Typically with other things remaining equal, a high trading volume is taken as a bullish sign and a low trading volume is taken as a bearish sign. If low volumes occur in conjunction with falling prices, it is considered to give a strong bear signal.

Sentiment Indicators

1. **TRIN Statistics:** The TRIN (TRading INdex), also known as Arms index, was given by Richard W. Arms, Jr. in 1967[2]. It is calculated as follows:

$$\frac{(\text{Advancing issues}/\text{Declining issues})}{(\text{Advancing volume}/\text{Declining volume})}$$

As explained above, any rise/advance is considered more bullish if it is accompanied with increase in trading volume.

A TRIN statistics of 1.0 typically indicates that buying and selling pressure is balanced. TRIN rises in response to increase in selling pressure and falls in response to increase in buying pressure. Therefore, high TRIN values are observed near market lows and low TRIN values are observed near market peaks.

2. **Short-Interest:** The short interest in a stock is described as the number of shares that have been sold short but have not been bought back yet. The short interest ratio is calculated as:

$$\frac{\text{Number of shares sold short}}{\text{Average daily trading volume}}.$$

Investors do short selling when they fear a fall in prices. Thus, a high short interest ratio indicates that most investors are expecting a fall in price.

However, a high short interest is interpreted by analysts as a sign of increase in buying activity in near future as the short sellers would have to eventually buy the shares they have sold short to close their positions. This buying activity will increase the demand and have positive effect on prices.

Marketview 13.3 Theory of Contrary Opinion

Theory of contrary opinion is a theory that suggests that an investor should analyze and understand popular opinion and then invest contrary to it. It is reflected in the statement – "When everybody thinks alike, everyone is likely to be wrong," written by Humphrey B. Neill[3] in his seminal contrary opinion book, The Art of Contrary Thinking (1954). Many indicators have been developed on the basis of this theory including mutual fund liquidity and put/call ratio.

---

[2] Richard Arms, *The Arms Index (TRIN Index): An Introduction to Volume Analysis*, Marketplace Books, 1996.

[3] Humphrey B. Neill, *The Art of Contrary Thinking*, Caxton Press, 1954.

3. **Mutual Fund Liquidity Ratio:** It is a ratio that compares the amount of cash held by a mutual fund relative to its total assets. The mutual fund liquidity ratio can be used to gauge the demand for shares and the bullishness or bearishness of fund managers. For instance, if mutual fund liquidity is high, i.e., the funds are sitting on a large amount of cash, theoretically it is interpreted to indicate that they have a bearish sentiment towards the market. Conversely, low mutual fund liquidity can be interpreted to indicate that the mutual funds have found lucrative investing opportunities in the market and are bullish towards it.
4. **Put/Call Ratio:** The put/call ratio is another sentiment indicator that can be used to gauge the overall sentiment (bullish or bearish) of the market. The ratio is calculated by dividing the number of put options purchased by the number of call options purchased. A rise in this ratio can be interpreted to indicate that the investors are purchasing more put options than call options, indicating that they are either speculating that the market will turn bearish, or they are trying to hedge their investments in the event of a sell-off.

   A high put/call ratio can be interpreted to indicate that the investors are investing in instruments that can be expected to gain when prices decrease rather than when they show an uptrend. Further, the ratio can also rise on account of decrease in the number of calls purchased, indicating that the market is starting to dampen its bullish stance.

   The put-call ratio is used by traders as a contrarian indicator. Analysts use extreme values of this ratio as a key indicator. This means that many analysts treat a large put/call ratio as a sign of a buying opportunity because they believe that the market is holding an unreasonably bearish outlook and it can be expected to adjust when those with short positions move to cover them. Conversely, a low ratio is interpreted by traders to be a sign of selling opportunity.
5. **Open Interest in the Futures and Options Segment:** Open interest is a measure of the total number of futures contracts that are not closed or delivered at the end of a particular trading day. It is a key number that is used by the analysts to confirm trends and trend reversals in the market. Increasing open interest implies that the money is flowing into the marketplace, indicating that the prevailing trend (up, down or horizontal) can be expected to continue. Decreasing or declining open interest gives a clear signal that the market is liquidating, thereby indicating that the prevailing price trend can be expected to end soon.

Technical Analysis and Behavioral Finance

Technical analysis involves analyzing the price and volume data generated by market activity. The main aim of technical analysis is to use historical data to establish certain trading rules for buying and selling securities profitably. As explained in the preceding discussion, technical analysts do not measure a security's intrinsic

Marketview 13.4 Top-down Approach to Technical Analysis

The top-down approach begins with broad-based macro analysis which involves an analysis of the overall market through the major indices such as the S&P BSE SENSEX and CNX NIFTY followed by sector analysis to identify the strongest and weakest set of stocks within the aggregate market. The broad market and sector analysis is followed by the analysis of an individual stock to identify the potential winners and losers among the sectors selected.

Marketview 13.5 Problems with Technical Analysis

Technical analysts are more concerned with what rather than why. Tony Plummer[4] has very effectively paraphrased Oscar Wilde in his book 'The Psychology of Technical Analysis' by stating "A technical analyst knows the price of everything, but the value of nothing."

By focusing only on the current and the historical prices, technicians use a direct approach that does not give any thought to why the price is at a particular level. On the other hand, fundamental analysts are concerned with why the price is what it is.

value. Instead they use price charts, indicators and oscillators to identify trends and patterns that can indicate future activity. Understanding the emotions in the market is also an important part of this kind of analysis. Latest research has also shown that emotions and psychology play a very important role in influencing the actions of stock market participants. This role of psychology in the stock markets is studied under a new but rapidly evolving field called Behavioral Finance.

Researchers have found many links between the technical trading and behavioral finance over the years. Kyle and Wang (1997)[5] found that overconfident investors underestimate the risks associated with investments and believe they can earn large returns. Odean (1998a)[6] found that investors were more willing to recognize paper gains than paper losses. Barber and Odean (2000)[7] found that individual investors expose themselves to a high level of risk by trading excessively. Coval and Shumway(2002)[8] found that Chicago Board of Trade proprietary traders suffered from a loss-aversion bias.

Clearly, there exists enough evidence to indicate that there are many common elements between technical and behavioral theory. So far, we have discussed the elements of technical analysis. Let us now try to understand the key aspects of behavioral finance.

Behavioral Finance

The preceding discussions have focused upon the well-defined standard financial theory with its rational assumptions and assertions about the functioning and the informational efficiency/inefficiency of the capital market. For a long time, traditionalists using quantitative models to guide investment decisions dominated investment management theories. However, owing to a lot of discrepancy in theories and the observed results, a new field of study emerged in 1990s, this time influenced by the psychologists. This new field is known 'Behavioral Finance' and it deals with the psychological traits that influence investment decisions taken by

---

[4] Tony Plummer, *The Psychology of Technical Analysis: Profiting from Crowd Behavior and the Dynamics of Price*, Probus Publishing company, 1993.

[5] A. Kyle and F.A. Wang, "Speculation Duopoly with Agreement to Disagree: Can Overconfidence Survive the Market Test?" *Journal of Finance*, 1997, 52, 2073–2090.

[6] Terrance Odean, "Are Investors Reluctant to Realize their Losses?", *Journal of Finance*, 1998a, 53, 1775–1798.

[7] Brad M. Barber and Terrance Odean, "Trading is Hazardous to your Wealth: The Common Stock Investment Performance of Individual Investors", *Journal of Finance*, 55, 773–806.

[8] Joshua D. Coval and Tyler Shumway, "Do behavioral biases affect prices?" Harvard University working paper, September 2002.

individual investors, portfolio managers and analysts. The beginning point for behavioral finance is that investors do not behave rationally as required for the success of the standard financial theory models.

Behavioral finance and the thought formulated by it were initially not accepted by the financial theorists, but now it has gained acceptance and emerged as an important field of study in investment theory. The award of Nobel Prize in Economics in 2002 to psychologist Daniel Kahneman and experimental economist Vernon Smith has helped behavioral finance theorists strengthen their position.

Before venturing into deeper discussion on behavioral finance, let's understand how it differs from the tenets of the traditional finance. Traditional finance assumes that people analyze all investment decisions objectively, logically and rationally on the basis of risk and return characteristics of the asset classes under consideration. Further, the markets are assumed to be efficient where security prices are unbiased estimates of their correct or intrinsic values.

On the other hand, behavioral finance is built on the assumption that people tend to behave irrationally and subjectively in processing relevant investment information. They employ heuristics (imperfect rules of thumb) in evaluating asset classes such that many biases come in, causing them to commit errors in investment decisions. Further, behavioral finance accepts that investment decision-making is not always independent; rather emotions, biases and herd instincts play an important role in investment choice. Proponents of behavioral finance assert that heuristic-driven biases, emotions, presuppositions and social factors cause the securities to be priced at a level different from their intrinsic value as computed by the fundamental analysts, causing the markets to be inefficient.

Behavioral finance rests on the premise that real people make decisions in a way that cannot be explained by the standard theories. Individuals make complicated decisions due to certain irrationalities that can be classified into two categories:

1. Inability of the investors to always process information correctly and infer correct probability distribution.
2. The tendency to make incorrect, inconsistent or suboptimal decisions even when they are given a probability distribution of returns.

It is further contended that irrationality of investors alone does not make the markets inefficient. Theoretically it is expected that even if irrationality of investors causes the prices to deviate from their intrinsic value, the arbitrageurs would step in to make profits from mispricing and push the prices back to their intrinsic levels. However, this does not always happen in real market conditions due to the limited action of the arbitrageurs. In practice, the actions of arbitrageurs to take advantage of mispricing are not able to push the prices to their intrinsic value. What the above argument of behaviorists implies is that even when mispricing is there, easy profit opportunities may not exist but that would not mean that the market is efficient. The arguments offered by behavioral finance seem to explain a lot of anomalies in the market. With the result, despite the lack of a unified theory, behavioral finance has become an important part of explaining investment behavior of individuals, portfolio managers and analysts. The behavioral school argues that inability of investors to generate abnormal risk-adjusted profits should not be taken as a conclusive proof of the efficiency of markets. There seems enough weight in the arguments of the supporters of behavioral finance to take the debate further. Let us now examine the biases, errors and irrationalities that can affect investment behavior of investors.

1. **Errors in Information Processing:** As stated above, investors tend to infer incorrect probability distributions about future returns due to errors in processing relevant information. Behaviorists have uncovered many biases that lead to errors in information processing. These include:
   (a) *Overconfidence*: People tend to place too much confidence in their ability to make precise forecasts about the future rate of return. Such over-confidence leads investors to have a more active portfolio

management strategy despite empirical evidence that such strategy may not give higher returns vis-à-vis a passive strategy. Overconfidence in investment decisions has been attributed to many well-researched factors such as illusion of knowledge, illusion of control and self-attribution bias.

Illusion of knowledge implies that though human mind is designed to extract wide range of information from the available data, it is usually not able to judge the adequacy of the information for decision-making under uncertainty. Investors tend to over-estimate the importance of the information they possess and trade actively but fail to outperform the market.

Illusion of control often results from chance positive outcomes that may be totally fortuitous but make investors believe that they are in control of the decision. As a result they grow in confidence and trade more actively, believing they have control over future in an uncertain environment.

It can be argued that failure would correct such an illusion but behaviorists explain that people tend to remain confident by remembering their successes and attributing their failures to chance. This is called self-attribution bias wherein investors believe that all positive outcomes are due to their skills and the negative outcomes are due to ill luck. Further, overconfidence persists because it is a human tendency to view future optimistically rather than getting depressed about the past.

(b) *Confirmation bias*: People tend to overlook or discard the information that is contrary to their way of thinking and seek information that conforms to their view. It has been observed that investors spend more time looking for information to validate their views rather than searching for information that might give them reason/s to oppose their current stand. For example, many investors and analysts hold the view that stocks of all growth companies are good stocks. They try to reinforce this belief by looking for more information to support their opinion. As a result, they end up incorrectly valuing stocks of growth companies that are generally popular.

(c) *Conservatism*: The conservatism bias implies that investors exhibit inertia in updating their views in the light of new information about investments. This means that they react slowly or under-react to the news about stocks, causing the prices to adjust gradually to new information. This goes against the assertions of efficient market hypothesis and gives rise to momentum in the market. This tendency is also referred to as anchoring. Let us understand the concept of anchoring with the help of the example of a company with very good long-term earning forecast. Suddenly, the company reports lower then expected profits. Despite this negative news, the share price might not fall immediately as people will persist in their belief that the company is good. However, over time the price will come down, as people will adjust gradually to the new announcement. Empirically, the effect of anchoring is well documented and it is called post-earnings announcement drift.

(d) *Representativeness and sample size neglect:* This bias indicates the tendency of people to assume that even a small sample is a good representative of a large population. This lack of concern for sample size may lead them to infer a pattern too quickly and extrapolate it too far in the future, obviously incorrectly. If the sample used by them is indicative of good earnings, investors may revise their assessment of the stock and buy it, pushing the price up. Eventually the market will correct the gap between the price and the intrinsic value.

Thus, the investors exhibit a tendency to form judgment based on stereotypes which could be healthy past returns, good track record of performance, good company image, very good performance of the stock in the recent past, etc. Such a tendency can lead to mispricing which eventually gets corrected.

(e) *Familiarity or aversion for ambiguity:* Familiarity almost always makes people comfortable. The same concept is manifested in investments where people tend to invest more in domestic companies (home country bias), local companies (local company bias) or the companies they work for (own company bias). In other words, the investors are suspicious of the stocks they do not know much about.

2. **Behavioral Biases:** Even if people do not exhibit errors in information processing, they tend to make sub-optimal and subjective investment decisions. Several behavioral biases affect how investors make risk return trade-off and take investment decisions. Some of them are explained below:
   (a) *Prospects theory:* Research has shown that investors fear losses more than they value gains. They tend to hold on to losers for too long and sell the winners too soon, i.e., they exhibit what is known as loss aversion. This behavior is explained by behaviorists on the basis of 'prospect theory' which asserts that utility does not depend on absolute wealth or level of wealth (as postulated by traditional finance) but on changes in wealth from the prevailing level. You may recall that according to standard financial theory, for a typical rational risk averse individual, higher absolute wealth provides higher utility, but at a diminishing rate (as shown in the Figure 13.9).

   However, according to the prospects theory, an investor showing loss aversion would have utility depending on the changes in wealth, resulting in a curve that is more convex than concaven below zero, as shown in the Figure 13.10.

   Such a utility curve implies that the risk aversion of investors does not decrease with the increase in wealth. This probably explains the higher average equity risk premiums observed historically. The convex curvature to the left of zero also implies that when it comes to losses, investors are more risk seeking instead of being risk averse.
   (b) *Affect heuristics*: People almost always act on their intuition or gut feeling. This behavior of people to do what feels emotionally right has been called 'affect heuristics' by psychologists. It involves various mental short-cuts that can lead to biased decisions.
   (c) *Framing*: At times, decisions are affected by how choices or options are framed. The same investment choice may be rejected when defined in terms of risk surrounding possible gains but accepted when it is described in terms of risk surrounding potential losses. This is consistent with prospects theory explained above wherein investors tend to be risk seeking in terms of losses. This tendency to choose on the basis of how a problem is described is called frame dependence and it is an outcome of many emotional and cognitive factors.
   (d) *Narrow framing*: A rational investor, as described by standard theory, looks at all investments (stocks, bonds, real estate and other alternative investments) in totality over the investment horizon. However,

Figure 13.9 Conventional utility curve.

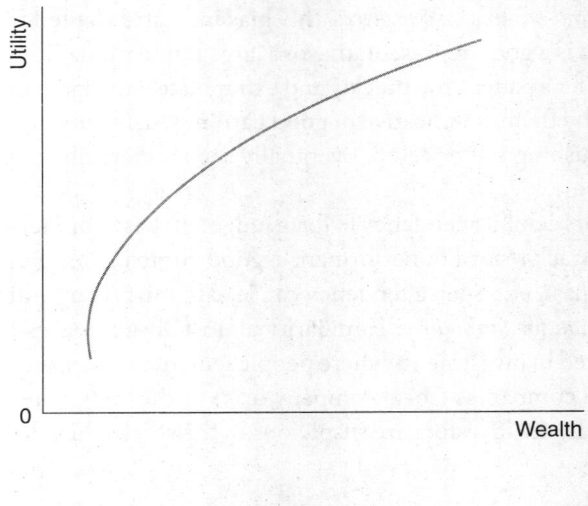

Figure 13.10 Utility curve under prospects theory.

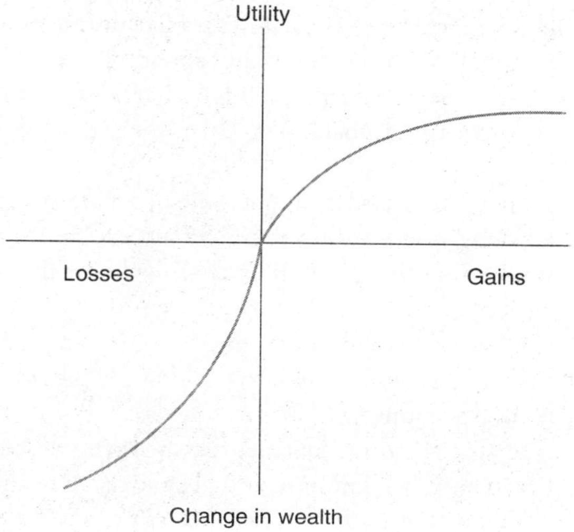

in reality, the investors look at each investment separately and focus on their individual price movements and short-term gains and losses even when the investment horizon is long. Such narrow framing causes them to overestimate risk and losses. It leads to myopic risk aversion where they fail to see that even though the returns of individual securities in the portfolio are negative, the returns of the total portfolio are likely to be positive. They also fail to see the fact that although stock market has been observed to produce negative returns in the short run, it has almost always generated positive returns in the long run.

Due to narrow framing, the loss averse people display bias by allocating too little of their funds to stock. They also tend to sell the stocks that have appreciated and hold on to the stocks that have depreciated in price.

(e) *Regret aversion or avoidance*: Psychologists have observed that people feel emotional pain when their decisions turn sour. The more unconventional the decision, the greater is the regret. For example, an investor whose blue chip securities portfolio gives negative returns may just attribute it to bad luck and do not feel much regret. But if he has actively decided to put money in startup companies and the portfolio gives negative returns, the regret is more. Behaviorists also talk of regret in terms of omission (not taking an action) and regret in terms of commission (taking an action). Regret of commission is typically more emotionally painful than regret of omission.

(f) *Escalation bias*: Escalation bias is a behavioral tendency of people to put more money into a failure/loss rather than into a success, as they feel responsible for it. This leads to a popular practice of 'averaging down,' i.e., buying more of the stock as it declines in value since it was purchased. Most investors do not seem inclined to reassess the initial valuation that could have missed some negative news. They are not willing to sell the stock, rather they seem more inclined to reaffirm their initial valuation and consider the fallen stock a bargain buy and accumulate more of it.

(g) *Mental accounting:* According to traditional finance, all financial decisions should be based on an assessment of their overall impact on wealth in the long run. In reality, people do not have the vision and emotional ability to evaluate each decision in such rational terms. Mental accounting is an expression of this constraint of people. It refers to a form of framing in which people separate certain investment decisions from others. For example, an investor may be ready to take more risk with his general investment account but remain very conservative about an investment he has made for his daughter's wedding. Mental accounting gets manifested in a number of ways:

(i) Buying stocks paying high cash dividends and spending the dividend without any misgivings. They would, however, not be willing to sell few shares of another company that is giving the same rate of return. The reason is that the investors think that sale of shares would mean dipping into their capital.

(ii) Loss aversion described above is also an outcome of mental accounting wherein investors tend to hold on to loss making stocks as they mentally separate unrealized paper loss from the actual loss that would come from selling the said stock. We know that from economic viewpoint the two are one and the same.

(iii) Tendency to sell off losers together to confine loss to a single period and tendency to realize gains from winners over a period of time to prolong the pleasure of positive outcome is also a manifestation of mental accounting.

(h) *Other biases*: Buying winners, i.e., buying securities that are rising, status quo bias, i.e., not being confident enough to act, herd's instinct and innumeracy, i.e., blocks in dealing with numbers comfortably are some of the other behavioral biases that investors tend to exhibit.

3. **Limits to Arbitrage:** As discussed above, the behavioral biases would not matter in stock prices if the actions of rational arbitrageurs acting to fully exploit mispricing were effective enough to correct the misalignment between the prevailing price and the intrinsic value of the stock. Behaviorists argue that in practice several influences limit the ability of the arbitrageurs to take advantage of mispricing. These may be listed as:

(a) *Model risk*: As we saw in our detailed discussions on equity valuation, there is always a risk that the model used to determine intrinsic value is faulty and that the prevailing price is the right price. In light of this, acting upon mispricing could be risky and not that profitable. This realization limits the efforts to pursue the perceived deviation of prices from the intrinsic value.

(b) *Fundamental risk*: Underpriced shares appear to be a good buy but they are not risk-free because it is difficult to predict how long the under-pricing will persist. Even though it is a given that prices will eventually converge to the right value, it is quite difficult to predict the time that will be taken for

Marketview 13.6 Noise Trading

The term, noise trading, refers to compulsive or hyperactive trading activity in markets that is done on the basis of market noises. Market noises are erratic minor price moves driven by flow of irrelevant information without real changes in security's fundamentals or economic situations and prospects.

Traders who trade irrationally, frantically and erratically on misunderstood news or unverifiable rumors are called noise traders. They reflect the investor sentiment. It is a term introduced by Albert Kyle (1985)[9] and Fischer Black (1986)[10].

[9] Albert Kyle, "Continuous Auctions and Insider Trading", *Econometrics*, November 1985, 53, 1315–36.

[10] Ficher Black, "Noise", *Journal of Finance*, 1986, 41, 529–43.

such a convergence. The time taken for convergence may be well beyond the arbitrageur's investment horizon. There is a fundamental risk that a fund manager may lose clients on the basis of short-run losses. He may also face the risk of running out of capital while waiting for the prices to converge to their intrinsic values. This risk constraints the traders from taking decisive steps to exploit mispricing.

(c) *Transaction costs*: Acting on mispricing involves costs and it is difficult to forecast if the gains from trading mispriced securities would offset these costs. This is particularly true in case of overpricing. Short selling a security means incurring certain costs as the short sellers might have to return the borrowed security on short notice, causing them to compromise their gains. Thus, transaction costs also act as a constraint and limit the extent to which traders would be willing to pursue mispricing.

Takeaway from Behaviorists' Arguments

Traditional finance has been around for the longest time and behavioral finance is a relatively new field. The proponents of efficient market hypothesis have tried to explain away the irrationalities and inefficiencies proposed by behaviorists on the basis of risk premiums and data mining. However, anomalies and mispricing have been observed to persist, giving proof of inefficiency in the market.

Persistence of anomalies in non-sample data and the tendency of certain portfolios to outperform others have helped behaviorists gain sufficient ground to make the traditional theorists consider their irrationality argument. However, the extent of impact of irrationality in investment decision-making in financial markets is something that continues to remain debatable. The supporters of standard financial theory and efficient market hypothesis contend that behaviorists have not put forth any theory with underlying principles and that they argue only on the basis of some conveniently chosen observations.

Considering both sides of the debate, it can be said that despite all criticism that has been heaped on the behaviorists' view, it is difficult to outrightly reject the impact of human nature and psychology on financial decisions. Financial economists need to make room for the behavioral argument, particularly in the context of explaining many market related observations that cannot be explained on the basis of the standard financial theory.

We have to accept that behavioral biases do exist and they impair the quality of financial decisions in the market. Traders and investors need to be aware of the potential pitfalls of falling prey to these biases.

Marketview 13.7 Fusion Investing

Charles M.C. Lee[11] has forged an innovative approach to investment decision-making known as "fusion investing." The main implication of this approach is that value investors need to take investor sentiments into account while determining a trading strategy.

Fusion investing is the integration of fundamental analysis and behavioral finance. The thought has its beginning in the formal model given by Robert Shiller[12] in 1984, in which he has incorporated a term to represent the demand from noise traders (who reflect investor sentiments) along with the fundamental values derived from discounting expected dividends to determine the market price of securities.

---

[11] Charles Lee, "Fusion Investing" in Equity Valuation *in a Global* Context, Charlotteuille, 2003, VA: AIMR.

[12] R. Shiller, "Stock Prices and Social Dynamics", Brooking papers on Economic activity, 1984, 457–510.

SUMMARY

- ☑ Technical analysis involves analyzing the price and volume data generated by market activity. The main aim of technical analysis is to use historical data to establish certain trading rules for buying and selling securities profitably.
- ☑ Over the years, certain mathematical tools have been developed that can be used to smoothen the erratic price movement, identify overbought or oversold conditions and the possibility of a trend reversal. These tools are called indicators and oscillators.
- ☑ Indicators are a very useful source of additional information in technical analysis as they help detect the momentum, trends and volatility in price movements of securities.
- ☑ The indicators may be leading or lagging indicators.
- ☑ Indicators are used to form buy and sell signals through crossovers and divergence.
- ☑ Though many traders tend to use a single indicator for buy and sell signals, ideally they should be used as supplementary tools, in conjunction with other indicators, charts and price movement.
- ☑ Many indicators like RSI, MACD, ROC, stochastic and ADX are used by traders for formulating technical trading strategies.
- ☑ In addition to the tools named above and the charts discussed in the previous chapter, technicians also use certain indicators like breadth indicators and market sentiment indicators to assess the overall market situation.
- ☑ Latest research has shown that emotions and psychology play a very important role in influencing the actions of stock market participants. This role of psychology in the stock markets is studied under a new but rapidly evolving field called behavioral finance.
- ☑ Many investors and analysts hold the view that stocks of all growth companies are good stocks. They try to reinforce this belief by looking for more information to support their opinion. As a result, they end up incorrectly valuing stocks of growth companies that are generally popular.
- ☑ Investors exhibit a tendency to form judgment based on stereotypes which could be healthy past returns, good track record of performance, good company image, very good performance of the stock in the recent past, etc. Such a tendency can lead to mispricing which eventually gets corrected.
- ☑ Research has shown that investors fear losses more than they value gains. They tend to hold on to losses for too long and sell the winners too soon, i.e., they exhibit what is known as loss aversion.
- ☑ Escalation bias is a behavioral tendency of people to put more money into a failure/loss rather than into a success, as they feel responsible for it.
- ☑ According to traditional finance, all financial decisions should be based on an assessment of their overall impact on wealth in the long run. In reality, people do not have the vision and emotional ability to evaluate each decision in such rational terms.
- ☑ Behaviorists argue that in practice several influences limit the ability of the arbitrageurs to take advantage of mispricing.

- ☑ Persistence of anomalies in non-sample data and the tendency of certain portfolios to outperform others have helped behaviorists gain sufficient ground to make the traditional theorists consider their irrationality argument.
- ☑ The extent of impact of irrationality in investment decision-making on asset pricing in financial markets is something that continues to remain debatable.
- ☑ The supporters of standard financial theory and EMH contend that behaviorists have not put forth any theory with underlying principles and that they argue only on the basis of some conveniently chosen observations.
- ☑ Considering both sides of the debate, it can be said that despite all criticism that has been heaped on the behaviorists' view, it is difficult to outrightly reject the impact of human nature and psychology on financial decisions.
- ☑ Financial economists need to make room for the behavioral argument, particularly in the context of explaining many market related observations that cannot be explained on the basis of the standard financial theory.

KEY WORDS

Advance-decline line 552
Average directional index 552
Bear signal 553
Behavioral finance 554
Breadth of market 552
Bull signal 553
Confirmation Bias 557
Conservatism bias 557
Contrary opinion 553
Crossovers 534
Divergence 540
Exponential moving average 538
Framing 558
Fusion investing 561
Heuristics 558
Indicators 552
Loss-aversion bias 555
MACD histogram 540
Mental accounting 559
Moving average convergence divergence 540
Mutual fund liquidity ratio 554
Noise trading 560
Prospects theory 558
Put-call ratio 554
Rate of change indicator 546
Regret aversion 559
Relative strength index 542
Representativeness 557
Short interest 553
Simple moving average 534
Stochastic oscillator 549
Trading volume 553
TRIN statistics 553

CONCEPT QUESTIONS

1. Explain with example how change in the duration of moving average can change potential profits generated by a trader.
2. Behavioral finance has challenged the very core of efficient market hypothesis. Discuss.
3. Theoretically arbitrage sounds like a very effective way of responding to mispricing in the market but practically there are many limits to arbitrage. Explain.

4. How do behavioral biases impact the risk-return trade-off made by investors in financial markets?
5. Indicators are a very useful source of additional information in technical analysis as they help detect momentum, trends and volatility in price movements of securities. Explain.
6. What is trading divergence? How do the traders use it?
7. Calculate the breadth of market using the following data:

Day	Advances	Declines
1	1580	740
2	860	920
3	940	1330
4	1690	680
5	1480	1000

8. Use the daily closing prices of HCC for a period from October 1, 2014 through November 28, 2014 to calculate the 10-day moving average.

01-Oct-14	32.2
07-Oct-14	31.2
08-Oct-14	31.1
09-Oct-14	32.2
10-Oct-14	31.05
13-Oct-14	30.85
14-Oct-14	28.75
16-Oct-14	27.85
17-Oct-14	26.75
20-Oct-14	28.05
21-Oct-14	28.4
22-Oct-14	28.45
23-Oct-14	29.55
27-Oct-14	28.9
28-Oct-14	30.3

(Continued)

Continued

29-Oct-14	30.05
30-Oct-14	29.65
31-Oct-14	33.1
03-Nov-14	34.95
05-Nov-14	34.75
07-Nov-14	33.25
10-Nov-14	34.1
11-Nov-14	36.75
12-Nov-14	35.1
13-Nov-14	34.2
14-Nov-14	34.7
17-Nov-14	34.8
18-Nov-14	35.15
19-Nov-14	33.45
20-Nov-14	33.1
21-Nov-14	32.7
24-Nov-14	32.35
25-Nov-14	29.95
26-Nov-14	31.6
27-Nov-14	30.75
28-Nov-14	30.85

9. Calculate 5-day stochastic using the high, low and closing price data for the given stock.

Trading day	High	Low	Closing
1	295	290	293
2	300	293	295
3	298	291	293
4	293	289	291
5	295	292	296
6	293	291	292
7	294	290	293

10. Assume closing price for a 15-day period of a hypothetical stock to calculate 5 – day EMA.

Days	Closing price
1	335
2	338
3	340
4	342
5	345
6	342
7	344
8	346
9	344
10	346
11	348
12	349
13	347
14	346
15	348

CASELET 1[1]

Changing Betas

Beta indicates the relationship of the stock with its market and is the measure of the stock's volatility. This case study is intended to show how beta of a stock can change over time. The case considers two examples one of Dr Reddy's stock with CNX NIFTY and another of Tata Steel, again with CNX NIFTY.

[1] Contributed by Zameer Shah

CASELET 2[2]

This case exhibits how the profit/loss changes with the indicator used. It further shows that applying an indicator alone is not always sufficient. Sometimes use of a combination of indicators to determine the trend and indicate a signal is required. Stock price of HDIL is used for the purpose of analysis.

---

[2] Contributed by Zameer Shah

Efficient Market Hypothesis: Does the Market Remain Unbeaten?

14

CHAPTER OBJECTIVES

- ❐ Understanding the concept of random walk and efficient markets
- ❐ Testing different forms of efficiency
- ❐ Discussing the implication of EMH for investors, fundamental analysts and chartists
- ❐ Critiquing the role of EMH in modern finance

So far, we have analyzed securities from the point of view of risk and return associated with investment in those securities. Once the risk and return profile is available, the investor becomes better equipped to buy/sell a given security. But what price to buy or to sell a security at, is a question that needs to be answered before the investment decision is actually executed. For this purpose, 'security analysis' is undertaken to study the stock price behavior. There are three approaches to security analysis that are discussed in finance literature:

- Fundamental Analysis
- Technical Analysis
- Efficient Market Hypothesis (EMH)

The fundamental analysts believe that by analyzing the key economic and financial variables related to economy, industry and company, they can estimate the intrinsic or the right value of a security and then determine what investment action to take. The technical analysts or chartists maintain that fundamental analysis is really not required; all that needs to be done is to study historical/past price patterns of securities and then decide how current price behavior fits into the past behavior. Since the technicians believe that history tends to repeat itself, they study past price patterns to forecast future movements in price.

The random-walk school or the efficient market hypothesis contradicts both the fundamentalists and the chartists by proposing that the stock price changes are random and cannot be predicted on the basis of analysis of any kind. We have already discussed fundamental and technical analysis in detail in the preceeding chapters. In this chapter, we will discuss efficient market hypothesis (EMH).

Till the late 1940s and early 1950s, it was generally believed that fundamental and/or technical analysis can 'beat the market,' i.e., help investors in generating superior risk-adjusted return. Evidences started emerging to the contrary during the 1950s and 1960s, when some studies revealed that stock price changes (not prices themselves) followed a random walk pattern that could not be predicted in advance.

Study of stock price data was as favorite an exercise of the researches in the past as it is today. During 1950s, time series analysis of stock price data by an analyst threw up some surprising results. It was observed that the stock prices did not follow any predictable pattern, i.e., price of a share was as likely to go up from a level as it was to go down. This discovery was in direct contradiction with the existing view at that time when it was believed that share prices followed certain patterns or trends (Dow's theory).

Such a random behavior may seem to imply erratically psychological and irrationally functioning market, but it actually underlines the fact that stock markets are well-functioning entities where prices of securities are at their fair levels due to intense competition and behavior of the participants.

The idea of stock prices exhibiting no pattern or trend was formalized into a theory by Engene Fama[1] in 1960s. He introduced the term efficient capital market to explain the random behavior of the stock price movement. This theory, known as 'Efficient Market Hypothesis'(EMH) or 'Random Walk Hypothesis' has come to occupy an important place in the investment theory. It has been subjected to a lot of critical analysis and has found both detractors and supporters amongst the researchers. One important contribution of the theory has been the furthering of the active versus passive portfolio management debate and the conception of index funds.

The central idea of EMH is that analysts cannot beat the market for a sustained period of time. Many investment managers like Warren Buffet have questioned the idea that stocks are fairly priced in the markets. However, EMH has profound implications for analysts and investors alike and it needs to be studied in depth to appreciate its significance.

Random Movement of Stock Price and Market Efficiency

Maurice Kendall is believed to have initiated the random walk debate. As a statistician looking for patterns in stock price time series, he was surprised to discover a total absence of any regular cycle. This surprise discovery of Kendall was supported by the researchers at that time. Another study that deserves a mention in this context is that of Osborne, a physicist, who compared the stock price movement to 'Brownian motion' (movement of very small particles suspended in a liquid medium). Many other researchers have also produced interesting work supporting the 'Random Walk Hypothesis.' Random walk is a term that is used in the financial literature to describe a time series of price where all subsequent changes in the prices are due to chance and unpredictable departures from previous price levels.

How did the term "Efficient Market" emerge? As random walk hypothesis came to find more empirical support, the next obvious question was what would lead to such a random walk of stock prices? Numerous studies and deliberations led to the conclusion that the random walk exhibited by the stock prices was an indicator and outcome of the efficiency of the capital markets.

The term efficient market implies a market where the prices of securities are driven by information and keen competition amongst the participants. An efficient capital market may be best described as a market that is efficient in processing information available from different sources. The implication of this statement is that the measure for efficiency of market in this context is not 'transactional efficiency.' Rather, it is informational efficiency, i.e., the ability to adjust to new information. In other words, in an efficient market, prices are almost immediately and fully reflected in the available information.

---

[1] Engene Fama, "Random walk in stock Market Prices," *Financial Analysts Journal*, 1965.

In an efficient market, all the information impacting security prices is available freely and instantaneously to all the participants and the current prices reflect all the available information. With the result, the share price changes only in response to new information, which is unrelated to all existing information. Since the new information cannot be forecasted in advance, the future direction of price change cannot be predicted as well. To conclude, an efficient capital market is a market that is informationally efficient since in this market the prices of securities adjust rapidly to the dissemination of new information.

Why are Capital Markets Efficient and What are the Implications of Efficiency?

The idea of an efficient capital market was introduced by Eugene Fama in 1965, who said that in an efficient market, on an average, the competition will cause the full effects of new information on intrinsic values to be reflected 'instantaneously' in actual prices.

As mentioned above, the concept of efficiency rests on the belief that markets are quite quick in reflecting information about individual scrips as well as the stock market as a whole. This implies that as soon as some information comes up, the news spreads very quickly and gets incorporated into the prices of concerned stock without much delay. Thus, neither technical analysis nor fundamental analysis can help the investors identify undervalued or mispriced stocks that would enable them to achieve returns greater than those that could be generated by holding a randomly selected portfolio of individual securities with comparable risk.

The concept of efficient markets has attracted a lot of interest from the financial theorists since it was introduced by Fama in 1965. Fama himself put forth many varied descriptions/definitions of the term.

Professor Eugene Fama, who gave the phrase 'efficient markets,' has described an efficient market as a market in which competition among intelligent participants creates a situation where security prices reflect all the past information and the effect of the events that the market expects to occur in the future. It can be said that in an efficient market the price of a security represents a good estimate of its intrinsic value at any given point in time.

According to Dyckman and Morse (1986)[2] an efficient market is one in which the prices of securities behave as though they reflect all available information fully and that they react almost instantaneously and in an unbiased manner to any new information that come in.

Malkiel (1992)[3] has also emphasized the fact that a capital market that fully and correctly reflects all related information can be called an efficient market.

A recent example of quick response of market to new news is the fall in the share price of Financial Technologies on August 1, 2013 by 60% in reaction to the news of NSEL scam. Figure 14.1 exhibits the movement in the price of FT share vis-à-vis SENSEX over a period ranging from July 15, 2013 to October 15, 2013.

The concept of market efficiency being discussed here rests on few assumptions/premises:

1. There are a large number of investors seeking to maxmize profit. They analyze securities and value them, independent of all other participants.

---

[2] Thomas R. Dyckman and Dale Morse, *Efficient Capital Markets and Accounting: A Critical Analysis*, Prentice-Hall, 1986.

[3] B. Malkiel, *Efficient market hypothesis. New Palgrave Dictionary of Money and Finance*, London: Macmillan, 1992.

Figure 14.1 Fall in the share price of financial technologies on August 1, 2013.

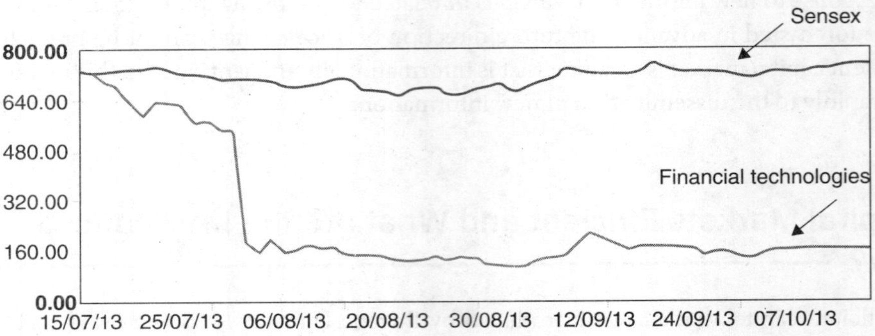

2. Prices of securities are driven by information. All existing information is already reflected in the current price level. The new information that comes in is random in content and timing and cannot be predicted.
3. Intense competition amongst a large number of participants ensures that the security prices adjust rapidly to reflect the new information that has come in. This adjustment is just unbiased, not always perfect. It means that there might be under-adjustment or over-adjustment but the key lies in the fact that it cannot be predicted.

Figure 14.2 Efficient market hypothesis.

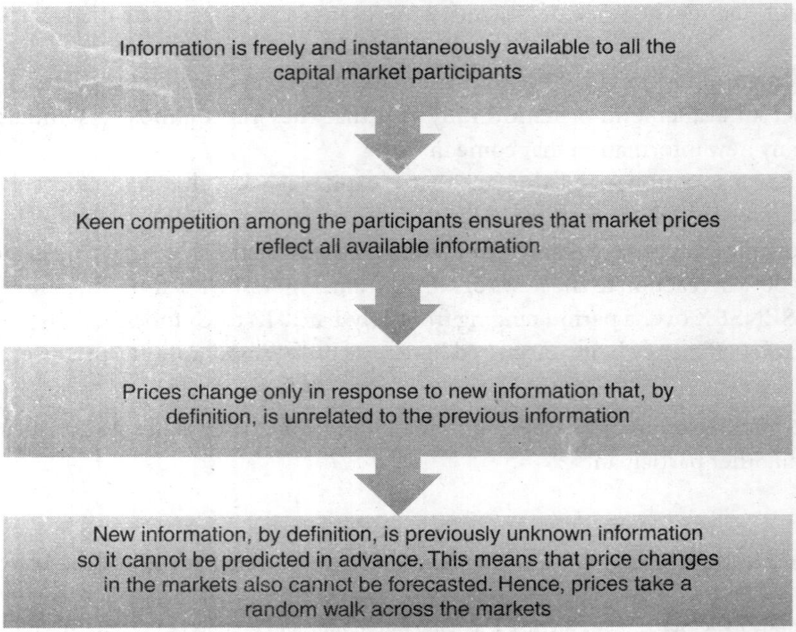

Since market efficiency is the outcome of competition amongst participants reacting to new information, some minimum amount of trading is essential for price adjustment and the more the trading by a large number of participants, the farther will be the price adjustment.

The main implication of informationally efficient market is that security prices prevailing at any time are an unbiased reflection of all the currently available information including the risk of holding a particular security. Therefore, the expected returns implicit in the prevailing market price also take the risk into consideration. In other words, in an efficient market the price of a security is an unprejudiced presentation of its intrinsic value. Thus, when investors buy a security in an informationally efficient market, the rate of return that they receive is consistent with the level of perceived risk of the stock. In terms of the asset pricing models discussed in the preceding chapters, in an efficient market all securities should lie on the security market line (SML).

It should be noted that efficient markets and random walk do not imply irrationality. On the contrary, they imply that the price changes cannot be predicted because intelligent investors always strive to collect relevant information before the rest of the market becomes aware of it. Efficiency results from all such attempts.

A Closer Look at the Efficient Market Hypothesis

The fact that security prices take a random walk across time and that the capital markets are efficient is largely based on the empirical evidence where not only financial economists but also physicists and statisticians contributed to prove that price did move in a manner that could be predicted. However, all the empirical work went on for some time without much theoretical framework. Fama tried to formalize the notion of random walk of prices by presenting efficient market theory in terms of fair game model, where investors believe that the current prices completely reflect all the available information about the security and the expected returns based upon the prevailing price, are commensurate with the perceived risk. Fama's formal presentation of random walk is called 'Efficient Market Hypothesis.' To provide an extensive theoretical framework for this theory, Fama divided EMH into three levels of efficiency:

1. Weak Form
2. Semi-strong Form
3. Strong Form

The three forms differ on the basis of levels of information available. Fama also divided the empirical results into three categories of evidence supporting the category. In Figure 14.3, the concentric circles represent two things:

1. The amount of information that each form of the EMH reflects. It is obvious that the weak form covers the least amount of information and the strong form covers maximum amount of information.
2. Each successive form of EMH includes the previous ones.

Weak-form efficient market hypothesis

The weak-form efficient market hypothesis asserts that the security prices prevailing in the market fully reflect all the relevant security market information that is contained in the past prices of the security. This form of efficiency assumes that all the market information that can be derived from studying historical price movement, trading volume, stock trades, rates of return, odd lot transactions, short interest, insider transactions, transactions

Figure 14.3 Forms of market efficiency.

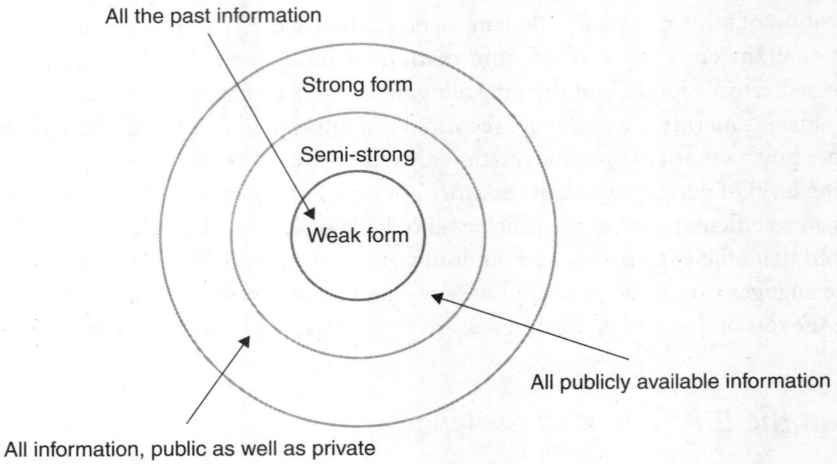

by exchange specialists and other market statistics is already reflected in the current price, implying that trend analysis is a redundant exercise.

All the historical stock market information is already easily available in the public domain and if such data could be used to generate lucrative buy/sell signals, all analysts would have learned how to exploit these signals. When all participants would act on the same signal, it would lose its value to give extra gain to anybody. By stating that the market statistics provide no information that can be used to forecast future prices, weak-form efficiency directly repudiates technical analysis. The stock price changes are random as the information that drives these changes also arrives randomly. Most research provides evidence in the support of the notion that the markets exhibit weak-form efficiency.

Semi-strong form of efficiency

Semi-strong form of EMH asserts that the current market price of a security not only fully reflects all the security market information but also all the other publicly available information about the security. This includes non-market information on company's performance like earnings, quality of management, product line, P/E ratio, dividend announcements, price-book value ratio, divided-yield ratio, stock splits, buybacks, accounting practices, pending lawsuits, patents, macroeconomic data, industry reports, corporate announcements and the impact of political environment are also reflected in the current price.

This form of EMH implies that as soon as the above-stated items of news become public, security prices get adjusted to reflect them. Even if the adjustment is not a correct one, the market populated by large number of participants would take a very short time to analyze the information and adjust the price to the correct level. Thus no analyst would be able to earn extra profit through fundamental analysis. Even when the adjustments in price to reflect new information are not correct, analysts cannot earn superior returns because there is no way to predict whether there will be under-adjustment or over-adjustment. Thus a trading strategy based on incorrect absorption of price information also cannot be formulated. Obviously, investors who take a decision on security after the new information becomes public will not be able to derive extra risk-adjusted returns by trading due to the element of transaction costs and quick adjustment of price to the new information. Since semi-strong form says that prices of securities fully reflect all publicly available information and expectations about the future, old information cannot be used to earn superior risk-adjusted returns.

Therefore this form of EMH repudiates fundamental analysis.

The research evidence in support of this form of efficiency is somewhat mixed. Most studies have found that the markets are reasonably efficient in the semi-strong sense, but some studies have also come up with evidence against it.

Strong-form of efficiency

This form of EMH takes the theory to a completely different level by asserting that the current prices reflect all the information: market related, non-market related and private information, i.e., information available to the company insiders. The implication of this form of EMH is that no group of investors can have monopolistic access to any information impacting prices that can help them earn superior risk-adjusted returns. This means even the knowledge of relevant, non-public information cannot be used to beat the market.

Marketview 14.1 SEBI and Insider Trading in India

Insider trading is quite rampant in India and needs to be controlled. The first step towards curbing insider trading in India was the issue of SEBI (Prohibition of Insider Trading) Regulations in 1992. These regulations were recently reviewed by a high level committee constituted under the chairmanship of Justice (Shri.) N.K. Sodhi. The committee has made many recommendations to strengthen the legal framework for prohibition of insider trading in India. It has proposed a combination of principles-based regulations and rules that are backed by principles with a view to discourage and control insider trading in India.

Strong-form EMH contains within it the weak and semi-strong form and further assumes the existence of perfect markets where all information is available to everyone at no cost. The research evidence in favor of this extreme form of efficiency is very thin. Most studies have found that the markets are not strongly efficient. It can be argued that corporate insiders might have access to relevant pricing information, long enough for them to make profit from trading before the information comes in public domain. In fact, insider trading has been under scanner since a long time in India as it is a matter of great concern for the regulators as well as the investors.

Marketview 14.2 Few Prominent Insider Trading Cases in India

In 1998, the purchase of a sizeable chunk of Brooke Bond Lipton shares by HLL before its public announcement about the merger of the two outfits came under the SEBI scanner as alleged case of misuse of price sensitive information. SEBI pulled up Hindustan Lever (now Hindustan Unilever) and its then five directors for alleged insider trading. It was the first case in India where SEBI passed an order related to insider trading.

A former company secretary and CFO of Wockhardt was accused by SEBI in 2006 of trading in Wockhardt shares on the basis of his knowledge about the price-sensitive information related to the unpublished financial results of the company.

In 2006, SEBI alleged that a former MD of Tata Finance was guilty of insider trading as he had helped the former director of Nishkalp Investment and Trading, a subsidiary of Tata Finance, to offload a large chunk of Nishkalp's shares at a premium, prior to the public announcement of huge losses incurred by the NBFC.

Empirical Evidence of EMH

In the preceding paragraphs, we have discussed the three forms of market efficiency. Now we will review the empirical evidence in the support of these three forms. Like most hypothesis in economics and finance, the evidence supporting EMH or refuting it is not conclusive. Different tests have been used by the researchers to test all the three forms. There are many direct tests for weak-form efficiency but most tests for semi-strong form are indirect. They are based on announcements pertaining to non-market factors such as stock-split, etc. EMH, in its strongest form has also been tested only indirectly through measuring mutual-fund performance.

As mentioned above, some of the direct and indirect tests and studies have supported EMH while others have revealed certain anomalies that refute the hypothesis. Let us first discuss the tests used to support or refute the weak form of EMH in detail, followed by the tests for other two forms.

Marketview 14.3 Indian Capital Markets and Weak-Form Efficiency

A number of researchers have found the evidence of weak-form efficiency in Indian Market.

Mohanty (2001) used Sensex, BSE 100 and BSE 200 for a period of five years from 1996 through 2001 to produce evidence in favor of random walk model in the Indian markets. Samantha (2004) studied BSE 100 for a period spanning form January 1993 to December 2001. The study found that for a part of the period under consideration (January 1993 to July 1996), the market displayed considerable inefficiency and for the remaining period (August 1996 to December 1999), high level of efficiency could be seen in the market. Verma and Rao (2007) studied the companies included in BSE 100 by applying the serial correlation and unit root tests for a period from 1998 to 2001. The study did not yield conclusive evidence in the favor of efficiency or inefficiency in the Indian stock markets, i.e., the results of the study were mixed. Gupta and Basu (2007) tested NSE and BSE for a period from 1991 to 2006 and discovered the evidence of autocorrelation in both markets, thereby rejecting the existence of the weak form of efficiency in the Indian markets.

Renuka Sharma and Ramesh Chander (2011) studied the market proxies of BSE such as Sensex, BSE 100 and BSE 500 to examine whether the Indian markets, as represented by the proxies used for the study, followed random walk model. Again, the results differed during the different phases under the study.

Source: http://administrator.asiapacific.edu/. Asia-Pacific Finance and Accounting Review, Vol. 1, No. 3, April – June 2013 pp. 25–36, ISSN: 2278–1838 www.asiapacific.edu/far, accessed on January 1, 2015.

Empirical Test of Weak Form

The tests for weak form of EMH are mainly related to the study of the pattern of stock returns to test whether it is possible to find if analyzing trends in past prices (technical analysis) can enable investors to earn superior returns. The tests for weak form can be looked at as two major groups of tests, one group involving statistical tests for independence of returns and the second group including comparison of risk-return outcome of trading rules based on technical analysis versus a simple buy and hold strategy.

Tests of independence of returns

As stated in the preceding part of the chapter, weak-form EMH contends that the security prices reflect all the past information and they move randomly to only new information that comes in. This independence or randomness can be tested through three main types of tests:

1. **Serial Correlation Test:** One way to test for randomness in stock price changes is to check whether they have any serial or auto-correlations. Since the basis of EMH is the independence of price changes over time, serial correlation or autocorrelation tests are of particular significance. The test measures the existence and significance of any kind of correlation (+ or −) between the return in a period say t and $t-1$ or $t-2$. Insignificant correlations would support EMH. This means that if the price changes in one period are not correlated with the price changes in some other period, then such price changes are considered to be serially independent, as proposed by the weak-form efficiency.

   Correlation tests try to determine if price changes in subsequent periods are correlated with the preceding changes in prices. This means that the correlation tests check if the price changes in the subsequent period $t+1$ are correlated to price changes in the preceding period, t. If price changes happen to be correlated, then a plot of price change will be a straight line indicating that on an average, a price rise in period t is followed by a price rise in period $t+1$, if there is a positive correlation. Similarly, if there is a negative correlation between the price changes, then a decline in price in period $t+1$ would follow, on an average, a rise in price in period t.

   If the plot of price change is scattered, i.e., the points plot in such a way that there does not appear any linear relationship in the scatter diagram, then no or zero correlation can be said to exist across periods. Figure 14.4 exhibits the scatter plot of price changes in the daily price of ICICI stock at t and $t+1$ for the month of April 2014. The scatter shows no correlation in price change in t and $t+1$.

   Over the years, numerous studies employing different stocks across different markets in different countries using different time lags have been conducted. Most studies have confirmed the randomness of the stock price change. Several researchers have examined autocorrelations amongst stock returns over a short period with varying lag of 1, 2, 4 or more days and found the serial correlation to be insignificant, thereby supporting weak form EMH.

   However, in more recent studies focusing on portfolio rather than individual securities, strong auto-correlation has been found in returns of portfolios particularly those of small market size stocks. Studies conducted to test weak-form market efficiency in Indian markets have found that the auto-correlations exist, thereby indicating that the markets are weak-form inefficient to a certain extent.
2. **Run Tests:** The researchers testing EMH prefer another measure, called the run test over serial correlations because correlation coefficients being statistical measures, can be susceptible to extreme values of the series.

   To explain it further, use of correlation coefficient to evaluate the possibility of independence in a particular series can be problematic at times because correlation coefficients can be dominated by extreme

Figure 14.4 Scatter plot of price changes in the price of ICICI stock at t and $t + 1$.

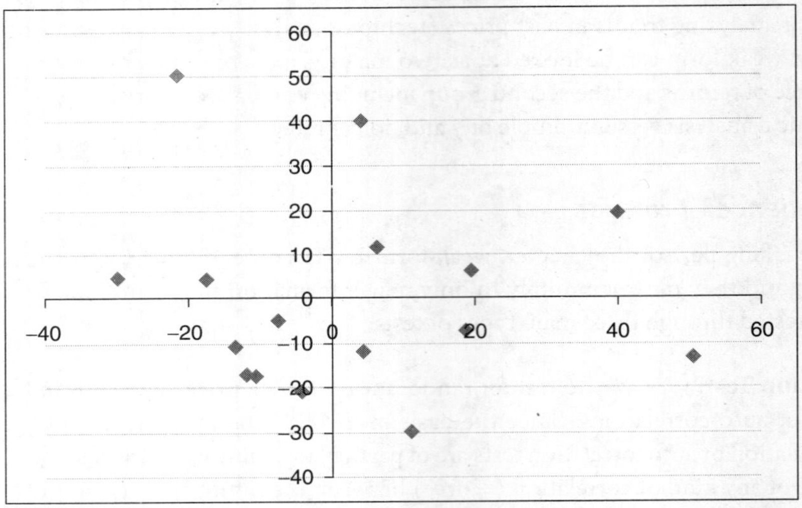

values. An extremely large and/or extremely low value in the series can unduly influence the value of the correlation coefficient thus computed. To overcome this possible issue, some researchers use run tests. Run tests observe only the signs of the series and not their absolute values.

The researchers then merely count the number of runs-consecutive sequences of signs in the same direction.

To conduct a run test, each increase in stock price is shown by (+) and each decrease is shown by (−). Given a series of stock price changes, each price change is designated as a plus (+) if it represents an increase or a minus (−) if it represents a decrease.

The resultant series of price change may look something like:

+ + − + − − + + + − −

A run is said to have occurred when there is no difference in two consecutive signs. Each run ends with the change in sign and subsequently a new run begins.

For example, in the given series of pluses and minuses, there are six runs:

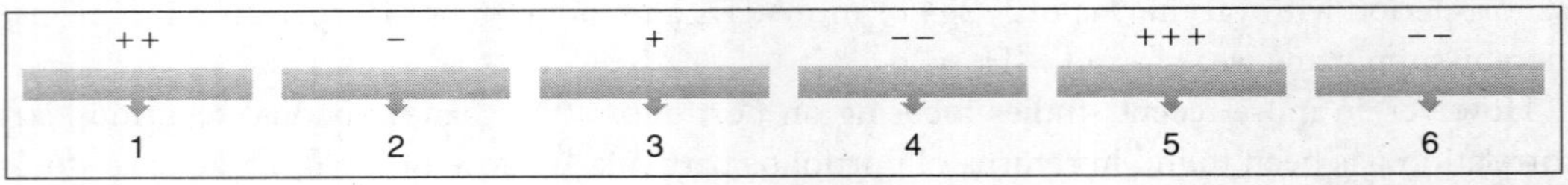

The researchers count the runs and compare them with the number that can be expected from a randomly generated series of price change.

If we perform a run test on the daily price data of ICICI Bank for April 2014, we get a series as given below:

+ − − − + − − + + + + + − + − −

TABLE 14.1 Daily price data for ICICI Bank (April 2014)

Date	Close price	Price change
31-Mar-10	1223.8	
1-Apr-10	1242.55	18.75
2-Apr-10	1235.2	–7.35
3-Apr-10	1230.35	–4.85
6-Apr-10	1209.05	–21.3
8-Apr-10	1259.55	50.5
9-Apr-10	1246.15	–13.4
10-Apr-10	1235.5	–10.65
14-Apr-10	1218.05	–17.45
15-Apr-10	1222.3	4.25
16-Apr-10	1262	39.7
20-Apr-10	1281.55	19.55
21-Apr-10	1287.9	6.35
22-Apr-10	1299.05	11.15
24-Apr-10	1269.3	–29.75
27-Apr-10	1273.85	4.55
28-Apr-10	1262.05	–11.8
29-Apr-10	1244.8	–17.25

There are 8 runs.

Many studies have been carried out, employing the 'run test' of independence. By and large, the results of these tests seem to strongly support the random walk model.

3. **Filter Rules Test:** The empirical tests of random walk that we have studied so far have been aimed at testing whether successive price changes are in fact independent or in statistical terms, the coefficients of serial-correlations are not statistically significantly different from zero. If independence is proved, then we can conclude that stock price changes appear to be random, and therefore developing successful mechanical trading systems to generate superior returns would be extremely difficult.

Now we will discuss another set of tests that investigate the random-walk hypothesis using a different and a more direct approach. These tests are called filter tests and these have been developed as direct tests of specific mechanical trading strategies.

Technical analysts use many trading strategies based on historical prices to earn returns. One such strategy is '*x*' percent filter rule which implies that an investor would trade in a stock when the change in price will exceed the filter value (x%) set for it. Thus, if the price of the stock was to increase by x% from a base, the investor would buy it as he envisions a positive breakout. On the other hand, if the price falls from a peak by x%, the investor would sell the stock, expecting the downfall to continue. He may even consider short selling. Different traders assign different values of x varying from 0.5% to 50%. If EMH or random walk were to hold true, returns of traders using filter rules should not outperform a simple buy and hold strategy.

Many studies have been conducted to test the filter rule outcome against simple buy and hold, and in most cases the filter rule strategy has not outperformed the buy and hold strategy, specially after taking the transaction costs into consideration.

Long horizon returns and weak form EMH It has been observed that though the returns over short horizon (single holding period) show only minor autocorrelation (supporting EMH); the returns over long term (multiple holding periods) tend to have strong negative correlation (refuting EMH). In other words, returns over short horizons are characterized by minor positive serial correlation or no correlation and the returns over long horizons have been found to have pronounced negative serial correlation. This strong negative correlation has been explained in the literature through what is known as 'fads hypothesis' which states that the stock prices have a tendency to overreact to news or new information. Such overreaction results in positive correlation over short horizons and negative correlation over long horizons. In other words, prices show a tendency to overshoot in the short run but correct themselves in the long run. This observation reflects EMH and states that market prices display excessive volatility around intrinsic values. Researchers have argued that markets are inefficient as witnessed from their mean reversion tendencies and excessive volatility. The supporters of EMH have defended that changing market risk premium causes volatility and not market inefficiency.

Other tests of random walk

1. **Distribution Patterns:** It is a well-known statistical rule that a plot of random occurrences would follow a normal distribution. If the price changes are random as postulated by EMH, then when plotted they should take the shape of a bell curve. Thus, if security price changes are randomly generated events, then their distribution should also be approximately normal. When such a test was conducted by researchers, only very slight deviations from normality were seen, confirming the weak form random walk theory.
2. **Reversal Effect:** Several recent studies have reported that there is a tendency of poorly performing stocks of one time period (a week or month) to perform better in the subsequent time periods. Conversely, some studies have also found the tendency of the best-performing stocks of one period to perform very poorly in the next period. If this indicates a pattern and if it holds true, then it should lead to a simple technical-based trading strategy. The strategy would be to buy shares of the stocks that have recently done poorly and sell shares that have done well. This is called as the reversal effect. If such an effect continues to persist even after many investors have tried to exploit it, then it would contradict the weak form efficient-market theory.

Empirical Test of Semi-Strong Form

Semi-strong form of EMH assumes that the security prices adjust almost instantaneously to all new public information and thus at any point in time, the current prices reflect all the already publicly available information. This implies that by using the publicly available information the investors, the will not be able to earn superior risk-adjusted returns.

The semi-strong form of the EMH has attracted a lot of attention of the researchers. This form of EMH is tested by checking/observing whether announcements such as earnings reports, dividends, changes in accounting information, stock splits and so on are quickly and adequately reflected in the stock prices. Further, the tests also check to see if analysts can use this data when it becomes available to them to earn superior returns.

The semi-strong form of EMH has been tested through numerous empirical studies. Researchers have tested this form of EMH indirectly by examining the efficacy of specific investment strategies to generate superior risk-adjusted returns for the investors. If any strategy is successful in generating excess return, it would repudiate EMH in its semi-strong form.

The strategies could be related to:

1. Trading on information events like earnings announcements which are usually tested with an event study.
2. Trading on an observable characteristic of a firm like price-earnings ratio which are usually tested using a portfolio study.

The three main types of studies used to test semi-strong form of EMH are:

1. **Event Study:** These tests basically examine if it is possible to trade on information like bonus issues, earnings, dividends, etc. to earn superior risk-adjusted returns on a security.
2. **Portfolio Study:** These tests examine if any observable characteristic of a firm like price-book value ratio, P/E ratio or dividend yield can be used as information to trade on to generate superior returns.
3. **Time Series Analysis:** These studies examine if it is possible to use publicly available information to gain superior returns over short or long horizons.

Let us examine each of the above mentioned studies in detail.

1. **Event Study:** An event study investigates the reactions of the market to specific information events like earning reports. It also examines the existence of excess market returns around these events. These studies examine abnormal return rates during the period immediately following a specific announcement such as earnings, follow-on issue of equity, dividend, etc. to see whether an investor can earn above normal profit by investing after the release of the information under study.

   The main steps in event study are:

   (a) Identify the event to be examined and specify the date on which the event was announced.

   (b) Determine a return window and calculate market returns before, on and after the announcement date. Here the researchers need to determine the period for calculating returns – weekly, daily or some other interval. They also need to decide how many periods are to be considered before and after the announcement.

   (c) Calculate the excess returns for the period specified above by making adjustment for market performance and risk. The difference between actual returns and expected returns will indicate if abnormal returns have been generated.

   $$\text{Abnormal Return} = \text{Actual Return} - \text{Expected Return}$$

   The expected return is usually computed using capital asset pricing model (CAPM) discussed in Chapters 6.

(d) Compute average abnormal or excess returns and their standard error across all firms. Average abnormal returns are computed as:

$$A_b R_t = \frac{\sum_{t=1}^{n} A_b R_{it}}{n}$$

$A_b R_t$ is the average abnormal return for the period and $A_b R_{it}$ is the abnormal return for the ith firm for period t and n is the number of firms. Standard deviation of sample average gives us the measure of standard error (SE).

(e) In the end, examine if the abnormal/excess returns are non-zero around the announcement date. For this purpose, *t*-statistic should be estimated for each day.

$$t\text{-statistic for return on day } t = \frac{A_b R_t}{\text{SE}}$$

Statistically significant t-statistic implies that the information event has had an impact on returns. Positive excess returns indicate positive effect of the news and negative sign of the excess return indicates negative or adverse effect of the news.

Several event studies have been conducted by the researchers to examine the market response to a broad spectrum of events like corporate restructuring announcements, announcements regarding changes in accounting policies, stock splits and unanticipated global events and macroeconomic news.

The results of event studies are mixed. Many event studies support the semi-strong form efficient market hypothesis. A study undertaken by Fama, Fisher, Jensen, and Roll[4] has provided evidence in the favor of semi-strong form. They tested the speed of the reaction of the market to a firm's announcement of a stock split and the accompanying information with respect to a change in its dividend policy using returns data for 940 stock splits on the New York Stock Exchange for the period 1927–1959. They found that during the period preceding the split, the stocks earned returns higher than those predicted by the market model. However, after the split, the returns were more or less in line with the predictions of the market model. It was concluded that the market was efficient in its response to the information event.

Ball and Brown[5] conducted a study to analyze the market's ability to absorb the informational content of reported annual earnings per share by dividing firms under the study into two groups. The first group comprised of firms whose earnings increased in relation to the average corporate earnings and the second group comprised of firms whose earnings decreased in relation to the average corporate earnings.

They found that companies with 'good' earnings reports (better than forecast) experienced price increases in their stock and those with 'bad' earnings reports (lower than forecast) experienced stock price declines. Interestingly, it was observed that nearly 85% of the informational content of the

[4] E. Fama, L. Fisher, M. Jensen and R. Roll, "The Adjustment of stock Prices to New Information," *International Economic* Review 10, 1969, 1–21.

[5] Ray J. Ball and P. Brown, "An empirical evaluation of accounting income numbers," *Journal of Accounting Research*, Autumn 1968, 159–178.

announcement of annual earnings was reflected in price movements of the stock prior to the actual release of annual earnings figure. To summarize, Ball and Brown found evidence in favor of semi-strong form of EMH by showing that the group with good earnings report, earned positive excess returns. To put it differently, Ball and Brown found that before the actual announcement of earnings the group with bad earnings report generated negative excess returns. However, after the announcements, both groups earned normal returns.

There are enough number of event studies that have detracted the validity of the semi-strong form of efficiency. For example, a study undertaken by Bernard and Thomas[6] found that the adjustment of stock prices was gradual, not quick, to the announcements containing information about unanticipated changes in quarterly earnings.

2. **Portfolio Study:** Researchers using portfolio study to test EMH create a portfolio of stocks based on some common characteristic like low P/E, or PBV and track it over a certain period of time to see whether it generates abnormal returns or superior risk-adjusted returns. Average abnormal returns (actual-expected returns) are calculated across various portfolios and many parametric and non-parametric statistical tests are used to test if such returns differ for the portfolio under the study or not.

The results of portfolio studies are also mixed. Many portfolio studies suggest that it is not possible to earn superior risk-adjusted returns by trading on some observable characteristics, thereby supporting EMH. However, most recent studies have strongly repudiated semi-strong form of EMH as some studies have discovered that P/E ratio, the size of the firm, its market capitalization, etc. can be used to predict superior risk- adjusted returns.

Basu[7] tested for the informational content of the P/E ratios by analyzing the performance of equity shares with respect to their P/E ratios. The study examined whether low P/E stocks outperformed stocks with high P/E ratios on an average. If the values of past P/E ratios helped investors in generating superior returns, it would be a repudiation of the semi-strong form EMH. In other words, if publicly available information about past P/E ratios has enabled an investor to buy a particular type of stock and generate abnormal returns, then this would be a direct contradiction of the semi-strong form of efficient market hypothesis. The results of Basu's study indicated that the portfolios comprising of low P/E stocks earned superior returns relative to the markets and the portfolios of high P/E stocks turned out a much lower performance relative to the overall market. To summarize, the study found that low P/E stocks tend to outperform the high P/E stocks, even after adjustments for risk.

Similarly some researchers have hypothesized that stocks having low PEG ratios (discussed in chapter 9) (less than 1) would experience superior rates of return while stocks with PEG in the range of 3 or 4, would generate below-average return. If this held true, it would refute semi-strong form of EMH. However, subsequent studies have yielded mixed results and not supported the hypothesis of inverse relationship between PEG and future returns.

In yet another study, researchers found that shares of small firms (measured by market capitalization) tended to outperform the stocks of large firms in terms of risk-adjusted rate of return. This difference in returns on account of the difference in market capitalization is called the *size effect*. This empirical observation also finds mixed support in research.

---

[6] V.L. Bernard and J.K. Thomas, "Post-earning-announcement drift: Delayed Price response or Risk Premium?" *Journal of Accounting Research*, 1989, 27, 1–36.

[7] S. Basu, "Investment Performance of Commonstock in relation to their Price-Earning Ratios: A Test of Efficient Market Hypothesis," *Journal of Finance*, 1977, 32(3), 663–682.

Yet another characteristic, book-to-market value ratio (BV/MV) along with the size effect was found to be a dominant influence on a cross-section of average return by Fama and French[8] in their seminal work where they evaluated the combined effect of P/E ratio, market beta, BV/MV and size on cross-section of returns (average).

Several other portfolio studies have also documented inefficiencies and anomalies. For instance, Rolf Banz[9] found that stocks of small firms listed on NYSE, on an average, outperformed the stocks of large firms listed on NYSE, in terms of risk-adjusted returns.

In conclusion, portfolio studies comprising the study of the portfolios formed on the basis of P/E, size or BV/MV provide strong evidence against semi-strong EMH. These have been called anomalies and are discussed in detail later on in the chapter.

3. **Time Series Analysis:** In time series analysis, it is assumed that long-run historical returns are the best predictors of future returns in an efficient market. The studies testing EMH based on time series analysis try to determine whether superior returns can be generated using publicly available information over short-run (one to six months) or long-run (one to five years) The results of these studies have indicated that analysis of long-run returns to make forecasts has been quite successful but prediction of short-run returns has not been so successful.

   Few important studies may be cited as follows:

   (a) *Quarterly earnings report:* Many studies have examined whether future returns can be estimated on the basis of quarterly earnings report released publicly. Some tests have focussed on 'earnings surprise,' i.e., examining firms that have reported larger than anticipated earnings. If the semi-strong form of EMH were to hold true, then prices should have adjusted rapidly to these surprises. But the test results show that such an announcement was followed by a few weeks of abnormal returns, thereby repudiating semi-strong EMH.

   (b) *Dividend yield studies:* Researchers have found a positive relationship between dividend yield and the future long-run returns on securities. A similar relationship is found to exist between long-run returns on stocks and bonds and bond default spread (difference between yields on highly rated long-term corporate bonds and low grade bonds). The positive relationship implies that high dividend yield and bond default spread cause investors to expect high return on bond and stocks (on account of high risk aversion).

   (c) *Calendar anomalies:* The tests based on calendar studies examine whether there are certain patterns/trends in rates of returns during the calendar year that would enable the investors to predict future returns. The studies include the January effect, the day-of-the-week effect, Monday effect, etc. These have been called anomalies because persistent mispricing has been observed on certain days/weeks/months. The main anomalies found by researches over the years have been discussed below:

      (i) *January effect*: Researchers have observed that stock prices tend to rise in the first month of every calendar year more than any other month. Various explanations have been offered to analyze this rise. One explanation is that the investors sell loss making shares in December to avail tax benefits from capital loss and buy same or other stock in January, pushing up the prices. Such pattern, which would put downward pressure on stock prices in November-December and cause them to rise in January, is inconsistent with semi-strong form of EMH. In an efficient market, the mispricing would be eliminated by arbitrageurs who would buy when others are selling in

---

[8] E.F. Fama and K.R. French, "The cross-section of Expected Stock Returns," *The Journal of Finance*, 1992, 47(2), 427.

[9] Rolf W. Banz, "The relationship between Return and Market Value of common stocks," *Journal of Finance*, 1981, 9, 3–18.

December and sell when others are buying in January. Researchers have also claimed that the buying in January is spiked due to lots of new information about firms at the beginning of the year and on account of increased inflows into portfolios in the New Year. However, all these explain the January effect to some extent only and it has to be accepted as an anomaly.

The study of January effect was extended by some researchers to include the size-effect in it to study what may be called small-firm in January effect. The studies in relation to the size and January effect found that portfolios comprising small firms enabled investors to earn abnormal returns throughout the month of January, giving us the small-firm-in-January anomaly.

In yet another twist to the January effect, researchers came up with a neglected-firm-in-January effect. Neglected firms here imply small firms that are less researched, making less information available about them. This lack of information makes neglected small firms riskier, resulting in higher returns. It was found that January effect was most pronounced for the neglected firms.

Moving on to other calendar anomalies, a group of studies have found significant monthly effect as observed in market's cumulative advancement during the first half of the trading months.

(ii) *Weekend effect*: Another anomaly is the weekend effect wherein it was found that average returns on Mondays were significantly negative for quite a long period whereas the average returns for other days of the week were positive. This anomaly has also been called day-of-the-week effect. In connection to the large firms, it is termed as weekend effect as the negative returns on Monday were found to occur before the markets opened. For smaller firms, most of the negative returns under this effect came during trading on Monday and hence the effect was called Monday trading day effect.

Obviously these predictable trends observed on a continuous basis can possible be only in a market that is not efficient.

Clearly semi-strong form finds mixed empirical support. On one hand it has received strong support from a range of event studies and on the other hand it has been repudiated rather strongly by many studies focusing on prediction of rates of return over time and for a specific cross-section of securities. These studies include time series analysis of calendar patterns, quarterly earnings surprises, risk premium, etc. As stated above, specific firm characteristics also tend to counter the assertions of semi-strong EMH and indicate inefficiencies. Further, the recurrent stock market crashes reported from around the world without any substantial new information also cast a shadow on semi-strong EMH.

Empirical Test of Strong form EMH

In its strongest form, EMH states that all the available information, public and private, is reflected in security prices and it is not possible to generate superior returns on the basis of private information or through specialized analysis of information in public domain. For this purpose, researchers have analyzed the performance of corporate insiders, specialists in stock exchange, seasoned security analysts and professional fund/money managers. Let us examine the findings under each category.

1. **Corporate Insiders:** Corporate insiders include directors and senior officials of the firm who are privy to a lot of information about the company before the information becomes public. They can potentially use such information to earn abnormal returns.

A study of the reports (to be filed mandatorily) of corporate insiders on their sale and purchase of the share of the firm in which they are insiders, shows that they have enjoyed abnormal returns continuously by selling prior to low return and holding prior to high returns. This shows that they had access to some private information that enabled them to formulate a strategy to earn superior profits. This refutes the claims of strong form of EMH.

2. **Specialist in Stock Exchange:** India does not have these functionaries at present but stock exchange specialists (market makers who ensure liquidity in secondary markets) in US have been observed to earn above-average returns as they have a monopolistic access to information about unfilled limit orders. This again repudiates strong-form EMH.
3. **Security Analysts:** These are seasoned professionals with the ability and skill to identify undervalued stocks to generate superior risk-adjusted returns. Though they do not have the informational edge like the stock market specialists and corporate insiders, they do have the expertise and skill to be able to identify undervalued stocks. Empirical evidence shows that though some analysts do exhibit superior skills, most of them have not been able to make excess returns over a sustained period of time.
4. **Professional Money/Fund Managers:** Most researchers use the mutual fund performance data to study the performance of professional fund managers. It has generally been found that most mutual funds have not been able to match or exceed the performance of a simple buy and hold strategy advocated by EMH.

As with semi-strong form, the tests of strong form EMH have yielded mixed result so far. The ability of corporate insiders and stock exchange specialists to earn superior risk-adjusted return does not support EMH but the findings pertaining to the performance of security analysts and professional money managers seem to support EMH in most empirical studies.

So are the Markets Efficient or Not?

Despite the anomalies and mixed outcome of empirical tests, EMH continues to find support, particularly in the academic community. However, the practitioners do not have much faith in its tenets. There are two interesting observations that keep the EMH debate alive: one is the role of selection bias and the other is the role of chance.

1. **Selection Bias:** It implies a situation in which we observe the outcomes that have failed to produce superior return, i.e., outcomes biased significantly towards failed techniques. This happens because managers tend to keep schemes that give superior returns a secret to protect themselves from competition. At the same time they publicize the schemes that fail to earn superior returns. This selection bias prevents the true data on portfolio managers' performance from reaching the researchers.
2. **Role of Chance:** Many researchers claim that superior returns earned by portfolios could be the outcome of pure chance and have nothing to do with the skills of their managers. Successful investors think that they have superior analytical skills but others will almost always attribute their success to plain luck.

So it cannot be conclusively said that markets are efficient or inefficient. In this context a new thought has been gaining ground, that of *semi-efficient market hypothesis* which holds that few stocks are priced more efficiently than the other stocks trading in the market. It usually happens that certain stocks are traded and analyzed more actively than the other stocks in the market. These stocks are more likely to be fairly priced. As against this, there are many stocks that are not traded or followed much and they are likely to be mispriced.

This kind of observation in the markets indicates a pecking order of efficiency, where few stocks tend to be efficiently priced whereas others tend to be mispriced.

The reality is that even if inefficiencies exist, it is quite difficult to take advantage of them. According to Richard Roll[10], it is quite difficult to find trading strategies to exploit inefficiencies in market that would beat a buy and hold strategy net of the cost of applying the trading strategy.

Implication of EMH

We have explored EMH extensively through various empirical tests conducted by researchers from time to time. Now we need to understand the significance of EMH in terms of investment management. Can EMH help individual investors, analysts, institutions and portfolio managers make better investment decisions? Understanding the implications of EMH becomes more important in the light of the mixed results of empirical tests related to EMH. Some tests strongly support market efficiency while others reject it completely. The key implications of EMH are:

1. **Trust Market Prices:** The most vital implication of the EMH for investors and analysts is, 'trust market prices.' From the above discussion, we know that efficient market prices of securities reflect all known information and they are fairly priced, i.e., on an average investors get exactly what they pay for. This fair price of each security reflects the present value of its expected future cash flows. These cash flows are dependent on factors such as volatility and liquidity. The EMH contends that though prices are rationally based, changes in prices are expected to be random and unpredictable. The randomness of prices come from the fact that they change in response to new information, which by its very nature, is unpredictable
2. **EMH and Technical & Fundamental Analysis:** Technical analysts base their investment decisions on past results. EMH, however, believes that past results cannot be used to beat the market. As a result, EMH negates the use of technical analysis as a means to generate investment returns. With respect to fundamental analysis, the EMH also states that all publicly available information is already reflected in security prices and as such, abnormal returns cannot be generated through the use of this information. This negates the use of fundamental analysis as a means to generate investment returns.

   Thus, if the tests of EMH are to be believed then technical analysis would not be effective in helping analysts earn superior returns. All said and done, in practice, technical analysis and its fancy tools continue to be widely used and written about. Fundamental analysis is also a popular tool used by analysts to compute intrinsic value of a share by forecasting the earnings of a company. However, it is quite challenging to analyse macroeconomic variables, industry related factors and company specific metrics to make accurate forecasts and earn superior returns.

   EMH states that due to difficulties in superior analysis, it is not possible to beat the market and investors should invest in index funds or exchange traded fund (ETF). However, if one is able to undertake superior analysis then one should choose stocks actively but concentrate on neglected firms and firms with low or moderate market capitalization, where the chances of mispricing are more (as seen in tests for semi-strong form of EMH).

---

[10] Richard Roll, "What every CFO should know about scientific progress in financial Economics: What is known and what remains to be resolved." *Financial Management*, 1994, 69–75.

3. **EMH and the Portfolio Management Process:** The portfolio management process begins with an investment policy statement, including an investor's objectives and constraints. Given EMH, the portfolio management process should thus, not focus on achieving above-average returns for the investor. Rather, it should focus purely on risks, given that above average returns are not achievable.

   A portfolio manager's goal is to outperform a specific benchmark with specific investment ideas. The EMH implies that this goal is unachievable. A portfolio manager would not be able to achieve above average returns.

4. **EMH and Investing in Index Funds:** Given the discussion on the EMH, the overall assumption is that no investor is able to generate an abnormal return in the market. If that is the case, an investor can only expect to make a return equal to the market return. An investor should thus focus on minimizing his costs to invest. To achieve a market rate of return, diversification across numerous stocks is required, which may not be an option for a smaller investor. As such, an index fund would be the most appropriate investment vehicle, allowing the investor to achieve the market rate of return in a cost effective manner.

   Index fund is a type of mutual fund that matches or tracks the components of a market index, such as the Standard & Poor's 500 Index (S&P 500), CNX Nifty Index and S&P BSE SENSEX. An index mutual fund provides broader market exposure, lower operating expenses and lower portfolio turnover. Investing in index funds or indexing is a passive form of investment that has been successful in beating the most actively managed mutual funds.

Beating The Market Debate: Active Versus Passive Portfolio Management

The efficient market debate plays an important role in influencing investment decision in terms of active and passive investing. Active investment strategy seeks to churn the portfolio, i.e., change assets and/or funds invested in them to generate superior returns. Active strategy is based on the argument that less efficient markets provide the opportunity for making profit through superior analysis. Conversely, a passive strategy is a buy and hold strategy. Passive managers tend to make very few changes over the time in their initially chosen mix of assets and the funds invested in them. They follow a predetermined investment strategy that remains unchanged under varying market conditions. As discussed above, EMH advocates a passive or simple buy and hold strategy.

A Critique of Efficient Market Theory

EMH deals with one of the most basic and exciting issues in investment management – why and how the prices of the securities change in the markets. According to the basic tenets of EMH, the main cause of price changes is the arrival of new information. Markets adjust to this information and this is why the price changes. Further, if a market adjusts quickly and, on an average, without bias, to new information then it is said to be 'efficient.' As a result of this quick adjustment, the current prices of securities reflect all available information at any given point in time. The adjustment in price happens before an investor has time to trade on and profit from a new piece of information. Therefore, there is no reason to believe that prices are too high or too low.

Thus the basic idea behind EMH is that expert stock selection or timing the market cannot help investors generate superior returns as the prices always reflect all the relevant information. Thus, efficient markets do not give opportunity to investors to beat the market through superior selection. Purchasing riskier securities is the only way to generate potential higher returns.

It can be said that according to the efficient market hypothesis, any time an investor buys and sells securities, he is engaging in a game of chance, not skill. The believers of EMH argue that it is pointless to search for mispriced stocks or to try to predict trends in the market through either fundamental or technical analysis.

Although this theory is a cornerstone of modern financial theory, it is highly controversial and has been met with a lot of opposition, especially from the technical analysts. The chartists contend that stock prices are largely based on investors' expectations; therefore it makes sense to believe that past prices influence future prices. Example of Warren Buffett is often cited by the detractors of EMH. Buffet has consistently beaten the market over long periods of time, which should have been impossible, according to the EMH.

It is also contended that the assumption of EMH that all investors perceive all available information in precisely the same manner is incorrect. Availability of numerous methods for analysing and valuing stocks pose many problems for the validity of the EMH. One investor could be a value investor, looking for undervalued stocks while another investor could be looking for stocks with better growth potential. In all likelihood both these investors would already have arrived at a different assessment of the stock's fair value. Therefore, opponents of EMH point out that, since investors value stocks differently, it is not possible to ascertain the fair worth of a stock under an efficient market.

Further, according to the efficient market hypothesis, if one investor has generated profit, it means that the entire universe of investors has generated profit for the same amount of investment. We know that in reality, this is not necessarily the case. Investors do not earn identical returns for the same amount of investment. If no investor had any advantage over another and stock picking was not profitable, then what explains the range of annual returns in the mutual fund industry from significant losses to high profits?

It has to be accepted that the efficient market hypothesis, like all theories, is not a perfect description of market and market behavior. However, it is too substantial to be rejected off-hand.

SUMMARY

- ☑ Random walk is a term used in the financial literature to describe a time series of price where all subsequent changes in the prices are chance and unpredictable departures from previous price levels.
- ☑ The idea of stock prices exhibiting no pattern or trend was formalized into a theory by Engene Fama in 1960s. He introduced the term efficient capital market to explain the random behavior of the stock price movement. This theory, known as 'Efficient Market Hypothesis'(EMH) or 'Random Walk Hypothesis' has come to occupy an important place in the investment theory.
- ☑ EMH deals with one of the most basic and exciting issues in investment management – why and how the prices of securities change in the markets. The central idea of EMH is that analysts cannot beat the market for a sustained period of time.
- ☑ The term efficient market implies a market where the prices of securities are driven by information and keen competition amongst the participants. An efficient capital market may be best described as a market that is efficient in processing information available from different sources.
- ☑ Fama's formal presentation of random walk is called "Efficient Market Hypothesis". To provide an extensive theoretical framework for Efficient Market Hypothesis, Fama has divided it into three levels of efficiency:

weak form, semi-strong form and strong form. The three forms differ on the basis of levels of information available.

☑ The weak-form efficient market hypothesis asserts that the security prices prevailing in the market fully reflect all the relevant security market information that is contained in the past prices of the security.

☑ Semi-strong form of EMH asserts that the current market price of a security not only fully reflects all the security market information but also all other publicly available information about the security.

☑ Strong form of EMH takes the theory to a completely different level by asserting that the current prices reflect all the information: market related, non-market related and private information, i.e., information available to company insiders.

☑ Different tests have been used by researchers to test all three forms of efficiency. There are many direct tests for weak-form efficiency but most tests for semi-strong form are indirect. EMH, in its strongest form has also been tested only indirectly through measuring mutual-fund performance.

☑ The results of the empirical tests for the three levels of efficiency have been mixed. Researchers have found some anomalies like size effect, January effect, neglected firm effect, day-of-the-week effect and so on which provide evidence that market is not completely efficient.

☑ It cannot be conclusively said that markets are efficient or inefficient. In this context, a new thought has been gaining ground, that of the *semi-efficient market hypothesis*, which holds that few stocks are priced more efficiently than the other stocks trading in the market.

☑ The most vital implication of the EMH for investors and analysts is: 'trust market prices.'

☑ The random-walk school or the efficient market hypothesis contradicts both the fundamentalists and the chartists by proposing that the stock price changes are random and cannot be predicted on the basis of analysis of any kind.

☑ Technical analysts base their investment decisions on the past prices. EMH, however, believes that past results cannot be used to best the market. As a result, EMH negates the use of technical analysis as a means to generate investment returns.

☑ With respect to fundamental analysis, the EMH also states that all publicly available information is already reflected in security prices and as such, abnormal returns cannot be generated through the use of this information. This negates the use of fundamental analysis as a means to generate investment returns.

☑ The efficient market debate plays an important role in influencing investment decision in terms of active and passive investing. EMH advocates a passive or simple buy and hold strategy.

KEY WORDS

Abnormal return 581
Active portfolio management 588
Book-to-market value ratio 584
Indexing 588
Informational efficiency 570
Insider trading 575
Selection bias 586
Semi-efficient market hypothesis 586
Semi-strong form efficiency 574

Corporate insiders 585
Day-of-the-week effect 584
Distribution patterns 580
Earnings surprises 585
Efficient market 570
Efficient market hypothesis 569
Event study 581
Filter rules test 579
Index fund 588
January effect 584
Monday effect 584
P/E ratio 581
Passive portfolio management 588
Portfolio study 581
Random-walk 569
Reversal effect 580
Role of chance 586
Run test 577
Serial correlation test 577
Size effect 583
Specialist in stock exchange 586
Standard error 582
Strong form efficiency 575
Time series analysis 581
Transactional efficiency 570
t-statistics 582
Weak-form efficiency 574

CONCEPT QUESTIONS

1. Does the fact that a capital market exhibits weak form efficiency automatically imply that it is also strong-form efficient? Conversely, is a strong-form efficient market automatically weak-form efficient as well? Discuss.

2. Do chartists and fundamental analysts make the market efficient or inefficient? Explain.

3. Do Indian stocks exhibit the neglected firm effect? Elaborate with examples.

4. Bring out the differences between the transactionally efficient markets and the informationally efficient markets.

5. Mutual fund performance is considered to be a proof of the fact that market cannot be beaten by superior analysis or stock picking. Does this hold true in India? Compare the performance of top-ranked mutual funds with CNX Nifty to assess the statement.

6. If the different types of information given below get reflected quickly and fully in security prices, what form of market efficiency is indicated by each?
   a. Limit orders in the books of stock exchange specialist.
   b. An investment company's published report on the prospects of a company.
   c. The fluctuations in the price of Bajaj Auto Limited over the past few months.
   d. A firm's recent quarterly earnings announcement.
   e. A confidential board meeting to discuss the upcoming stock split.
   f. Historical t-bill rates.

7. a. Is it not human to act on the information you have access to? Can insider trading be justified as a behavioral tendency? Can insider trading benefit the markets?
   b. Express your views on the high profile Rajat Gupta case on insider trading.

8. Discuss the implication of serial correlation and filter tests for the supporters of:
   a. Technical analysis
   b. Fundamental analysis
   c. Efficient market hypothesis

9. a. The active versus passive portfolio management debate hinges on the ability of the investor to undertake superior analysis. Discuss.
   b. Do index funds really return as much as the index they track or are there differences between the return of the index funds and the index they replicate? Discuss.

10. Based on your understanding of market efficiency or, for that matter, inefficiency, what is the investment advice that you would like to give to an average investor?

Overview of Fixed Income Securities: Unveiling Debt Securities[1]

15

CHAPTER OBJECTIVES

- ❒ Understanding various types of fixed income security issued
- ❒ Estimating the price of a bond
- ❒ Calculating various measures of bond yield
- ❒ Analyzing the impact of change in tenure and interest rate on bond prices
- ❒ Identifying the risks in bond investment
- ❒ Discussing the concept of warrants and convertibles attached to bonds

This chapter aims at introducing various types of fixed income securities, concepts of yield and basic bond valuation theorems. It further discusses the risks associated with the investment in Debt instruments.

Owing to the allure of the potential rewards normally associated with stock investing, investors often lack interest in understanding fixed income securities, often referred as bond investment. After all, bonds are assumed to be quite simplistic investment vehicles with their returns explicitly elucidated by a fixed mathematical formulation. Due to a bond's fixed interest income, one expects that their price will not be subject to wide range of vacillation. Bonds as an asset class serve as an anchor to an adverse future happening which a portfolio of varied asset classes would be subject to. For those investors for whom modest and promised returns are more acceptable than an all equity portfolio (over the long term), fixed income securities bring that much needed balance in their portfolios.

This chapter starts with an outline of the cosmos of fixed income markets, including treasury, corporate and bonds popular in the international arena. It discusses both the short term, called as money market bonds as well as long term bonds with a special focus on the Indian fixed income markets. In the next section, different risks associated with bond investments are categorized and explained. Thereafter bond pricing is conferred with myriad measures of bond returns such as current yield, yield to maturity, yield to call and realized compound rate of return. Finally, the impact of various bond features namely, coupon, yield and time on the prices of bond is discussed under bond value theorems.

---

[1] This chapter has been written by Ms. Nupur Gupta-Bhattacharya, MBA, CFA (India), working as Assistant Professor in the Department of Finance at K.J. Somaiya Institute of Management Studies and Research, Mumbai, India.

Meaning of Debt

Debt securities are often called fixed income securities as they assure a fixed stream of income that is determined according to a specified formula. A bond is a security that is issued in relation with a borrowing arrangement. The borrower (corporation selling) issues a bond to the lender (investor) for some amount of cash, the bond is the "IOU" of the borrower. This agreement necessitates the issuer (Corporate Entity or Government) to make specified payments to the bond holder (investor) on specified dates. A classic coupon bond obligates the issuer to make annual or semiannual payments of interest to the bondholder for the life of the bond. These interim cash flows are called coupon payments, generally paid at a fixed rate of interest on the face value of the bond (hence the name fixed income securities). When the bond matures, the issuer pays back the debt by paying the bondholder the bond's par value (equivalently, its face value or can be at a premium to the par value). The coupon rate, maturity date and the par value of the bond are part of the bond indenture, which is the agreement between the issuer and the bondholder.

To illustrate, a bond with a par value of ₹1,000 and a coupon rate of 9.5% might be sold to an investor for ₹970. The bond holder is then entitled to a payment of 9.5% of ₹1,000 (par value), or ₹95 per year, for the stated life of the bond, say 15 years. The ₹95 payment typically comes in two semiannual installments of ₹47.5 each. At the end of the 15 year life of the bond, the issuer also pays ₹1,000 par value to the bondholder.

Classification of Debt Instruments

Debt instruments (or fixed income securities or bond instruments) can be classified under two headings on the basis of tenure of maturity:

1. **Money Market Instruments:** These are short term bond instruments with generally a period of maturity of up to one year.
2. **Long Term Instruments:** These are all the other bond instruments (except money market instruments) with maturity of more than one year.

Types of money market instruments

The term money market refers to the market for short term requirement and deployment of funds. Instruments having a maturity period of less than one year are known as ***money market instruments***. In Indian fixed income markets, the most active transactions of the money market are in the market for overnight and term money between banks and financial institutions (called call money) and the market for Repo (short form of Re-purchase Transactions). Call money markets, where the day-to-day imbalances in the funds position of scheduled commercial banks are eased out and Repo transactions dealing with sale and buy back agreements of government securities are examples of very short-term money market products. There is an extensive range of participants in the money markets of India. The list includes banks, primary dealers, financial institutions, mutual funds, trusts, provident funds, etc. dealing in these instruments. Money market instruments and the participants of money market are regulated by the Reserve Bank of India.[2]

[2] The Fixed Income Money Market and Derivatives Association of India (FIMMDA), an association of commercial banks, financial institutions and primary dealers is a voluntary market body for the bond, money and derivatives market in India.

Types of debt of more than a year

Many a times one finds the words bonds and debentures being used interchangeably. There exists a difference between bonds and debentures. Bond is secured over a charge of some asset of the issuer. Debentures, on the other hand, are unsecured and carry a higher rate of interest. In case of financial difficulties and bankruptcy faced by the issuer, debenture holders are considered as general creditors. Hence they are paid later than bond holders. Nevertheless both refer to debt or fixed income securities.

Bonds may be ***registered*** or ***bearer*** bonds. With bearer bonds, investors can cut off the coupons and send them to the obligor for receiving payments. In case of registered bonds, investor receives the payment automatically at the appropriate time. All new bond issues in Indian market (example bonds issued by Rural Electrification Corporation, National Highways Authority of India in 2014) are compulsorily in the registered form. Few corporate bonds are called ***income bonds***, as they contain a provision permitting the firm to omit or delay the payment of interest if the earnings are too low. Such bonds are called deferrable bonds (Banks in India can issue bonds with interest payments deferrable, as part of their Tier II capital under Basel accord), as they give opportunity to the issuer to defer the bond payments up to certain number of years in case of financial distress.

Zero coupon bonds are a special category of bonds. As the name suggests, they do not provide coupon payments to the investors. They sell at a discount to their face values, frequently at deep discount owing to their long maturity (hence also called as deep discount bonds). However they redeem at par. (All money market instruments in India can be regarded as zero coupon bonds in the sense that they are issued at discount and redeemed at par value.) ***Non Money Market*** **Zero-coupon bonds** purchased at a large **discount** are known as **deep discount Bonds**. National Bank for Agriculture and Rural Development (NABARD) issued zero coupon bonds with a maturity of 6.13 years (qualifying it as a deep discount bond) in 2012, for redemption on January 1, 2009 at a price of ₹12,340 per bond. On maturity, the investors would receive ₹20,000 per bond. Similarly Jyothy Laboratories Limited infused ₹4,000 millions through the issuance of 3 year, zero coupon bond in December 2013. Tax-free bonds differ from tax saving bonds. The interest income from the instrument is not taxed in tax-free bonds while investible amount does not form part of the total income in tax saving bonds. In tax-free bonds there is no upper limit. Every financial year, infrastructure companies such as NHAI, NHB, REC, HUDCO, issued bonds. These are popularly known as Infrastructure bonds in India.

In 2006, the Government Securities Act was passed by Parliament to facilitate wider participation in the Government securities market and to create provisions for the issue of Separately Traded Registered Interest and Principal Securities (STRIPS)[3]. The RBI had released the draft guidelines on ***Separate Trading of Registered Principle and Security*** (STRIPS) on May 14, 2009. RBI had said in the draft norms that bonds with maturity dates of January 2 and July 2, irrespective of the year of maturity, will be eligible for stripping. Primary dealers and treasury heads of banks welcomed the move to issue more floating bonds as well as the STRIPS norms. Stripping is the process of separating a standard coupon-bearing bond into its individual coupon and principal components. For example, a 5 year coupon bearing bond can be stripped into 10 interests (called coupons in bond investment parlance) and one principal instrument, all of which thenceforth would become zero coupon bonds.

The Indian Union Budget of 2013–14 had announced the introduction of instruments that will protect retail savings from inflation. These are internationally known as inflation-linked securities or simply, linkers. These securities are designed to protect bond holders from the erosion of purchasing power of fixed nominal coupon payments due to inflation. The Reserve Bank of India (RBI)'s Inflation Indexed National Savings Securities-Cumulative (IINSS-C) issued in 2013 with maturity period of ten years is one such example. Interest

---

[3] RBI Publications. bi.org.in/scripts/PublicationsView.aspx?id=15725, accessed on December 10, 2014.

rate on these securities is linked to final combined consumer price index [CPI (Base: 2010 = 100)]. Interest rate is comprised of two parts, fixed rate (1.5%) and inflation rate, based on three-month lag CPI which will be compounded with the principal on a half-yearly basis and paid only at the time of maturity. The tenor is fixed at 10 years.

In contrast to a bond which has a fixed coupon that is fixed to its whole life, bonds can be issued with floating rates of coupons. Such bonds are called ***floating rate bonds***. In this the coupon varies over the instrument's life and gets reset at designated dates, based on the value of some reference rate adjusted for a spread. A floater may have restriction on the maximum (minimum) coupon rate that will be paid at any reset date called a cap (floor). A major risk involved in floaters has to do with changes in the firm's financial strength. The yield spread is fixed over the life of the security, which may be many years. If the financial health of the firm weakens, then investors may demand a greater yield premium than is offered by the security. Hence although the coupon rate on floaters adjusts to changes in the general level of market interest rates, it does not adjust to changes in the financial condition of the firm.

If a bond's agreement contains a call provision, the issuer holds the right to retire the debt, partially or wholly before the date of redemption. In falling interest set-up, it benefits the corporation issuing the bond to replace a high cost bond issue (high coupons) with a lower cost one. Such a transaction is called ***refunding option***. A call feature benefits the corporates holding high cash reserves, to restructure their balance sheets by retiring debt early. On the other hand, it's detrimental for the investors, who run the risk of losing a high coupon paying bond, when market interest rates fall in the economy. As the call feature benefits the issuer and places the bond holders at a disadvantageous position, callable bonds carry higher yields in comparison to non-callable bonds. In addition, callable bonds typically may come with a period of call protection, an initial time during which the bonds are not callable. Such bonds are referred to as ***deferred callable bonds***. Bonds which are non-callable for life, are called ***bullet bonds***. If a bond does not have any protection against an early call, then it is said to be currently callable.

Opposite to the call option which is invoked from the issuer's side is the put option on a bond. It is an option given to the bond holder to sell the bond back to the issuer, in case of rising interest rates in the economy. If the bond's coupon is too low, it will be optimum for the investors not to retain the bond, instead reclaim principal, which can be invested at current yields. Similarly, if the bond's coupon rate exceeds the current market yields, the bond holder may choose to extend the bond's life. Such options are called ***extendable options***.

Bonds require a payment of par value to be made at the end of their life. Since this payment entails a huge cash flow for the issuer, a ***sinking fund provision*** contained in the bond's indenture helps the issuers to spread the payments over a number of years. This provision contained in the bond's agreement requires the issuer to retire a certain amount of outstanding debt each year. Generally a sinking fund functions in two ways. Firstly the issuing firm may purchase the amount of bonds to be retired in the open market, if their prices are below par. This enables them to check underpricing of bonds in the secondary market. Alternatively, the firm may make payments to the trustee who is authorized to monitor the agreement, and who will call certain number of bonds to be redeemed by a draw at a prearranged call price, usually at a par value.

A ***convertible bond*** is one that can be exchanged for a specified amount of common stock of the issuing firm. The conversion cannot be reversed and the terms of the conversion are set by the company in the bond's indenture. The conversion ratio is the number of shares for which each bond may be exchanged. In September 1993, Reliance Petroleum Ltd. (RPL), a part of the Reliance Group made an initial public offering (IPO) to partly finance its ₹51.42 billion refinery project. RPL planned to establish a 9-million-tonne refinery at Jamnagar, Gujarat. They provided an option to investors to opt for equity shares at the time of Triple Option Convertible Debenture (TOCD) conversion in September 1997 in case the listed price of RPL stocks was higher. The TOCDs were made more attractive by allowing the payment to be made in installments of the sum of ₹60 spread over a period of three years. The instrument included two equity shares allotted to the investors at the face value, of ₹10 each. These two equity shares were allotted as soon as the first installment of ₹20 was paid. The remaining amount of ₹40 comprised a non-convertible portion accompanied by two detachable warrants, each of which could be converted into an equity share by paying ₹20 per share, i.e., at a premium of ₹10.

The conversion privilege may be permitted for all or some portion of the bond's life. The conversion ratio may decline overtime. It is always adjusted for stock splits and bonus issues. Convertible bonds are typically ***callable*** by the issuer. This enables the issuer to force conversion of the issue. This means that when the issuer calls the bond, the investor is forced to convert the bond or allow it to be redeemed at the call price. Convertible bondholders benefit from price appreciation of the company's stock. Again, this benefit comes at a price. Generally convertible bonds offer coupon rates and stated yields to maturity which is lower than the non-convertible bonds. However, the actual return on the convertible bond may exceed the stated yield to maturity if the option to convert becomes profitable.

Bond Pricing

In this section the pricing of fixed income securities will be explained and illustrated. The section is organized as follows: first the present-value analysis is applied to explain how a bond's price is determined. As a bond's coupon and principal repayments all occur months or years in the future, the price an investor would be willing to pay for a claim to those payments depends on the value of rupees to be received in the future compared to rupees in hand today. This present value calculations depend on market rates. As seen in previous chapter on "Risk and Return Analysis," the nominal risk-free interest rate equals the sum of (1) a real risk–free rate of return and (2) a premium above the real rate to compensate for expected inflation. In addition, because most bonds are not riskless, the discount rate will embody an additional premium that reflects bond specific characteristics such as default risk, liquidity, tax attributes, call risks and so on. Before going into the valuation of bonds, it is necessary to familiarize with certain bond related terms:

1. **Face Value/Par Value**: This is the value stated on the face of the bond and is also known as par value. It represents the amount of borrowing by the firm which it specifies to repay after a specific period of time, i.e., the time of maturity. A bond is generally issued at face value or par value which is usually ₹100 and may sometimes be ₹1,000.
2. **Coupon Rate or Interest:** A bond carries a specific rate of interest which is also called the coupon rate. The interest rate payable is simply the par value × coupon rate. Interest paid on a bond is a tax deductible expense for the issuing body.
3. **Maturity:** A bond is issued for a specific period of time. It is repaid on maturity. Typically corporate bonds have a maturity period of 7–10 years whereas government bonds have maturity period up to 20–25 years.
4. **Redemption Value:** The value which a bond holder gets on maturity is called redemption value. A bond may be redeemed at par, at premium (more than par) or at discount (less than par value).
5. **Market Value or Price:** A bond may be traded in a stock exchange. Market value is the price at which the bond is usually bought or sold. Market value may be different from par value or redemption value.

Determining the cash flow

The first step in determining the price of a bond is to determine its cash flow. In practice, determining the cash flow of a bond is not simple, even if we ignore the possibility of default. The only case in which the cash flow is known with certainty is for fixed rate, option-free bonds. For callable bonds, the cash flow depends on whether the issuer elects to call the issue. In the case of a putable bond, it depends on whether the bondholder elects to put the issue. In either case, the date that the option will be exercised is not known. Thus the cash flow is uncertain. The cash flow of an option-free bond (i.e., noncallable/nonputable bond), also called straight or simple vanilla bonds consists of, (1) periodic coupon interest payments to the maturity date and (2) the par (or maturity) value at maturity. The periodic coupon payments are made over any time interval. Most bonds issued in India pay coupon interest either annually or semiannually. We shall discuss the pricing of bonds for both annual coupon paying as well as semiannual coupon paying bonds. In this chapter, the basic elements of bond pricing where the cash flow is assumed to be known are presented. The cash flow for an option-free bond consists of an annuity (i.e., the fixed coupon interest paid every 6 months) and the par or maturity value.

Determining the required yield

The interest rate that an investor wants from investing in a bond is called the required yield from the point of view of the investor. It is similar to the cost of issuance of debentures (or bonds) incurred by the issuing agency (corporate or government). The required yield is determined by investigating the yields offered on similar bonds in the market in terms of the same credit quality and the same maturity. The required yield typically is specified as an annual interest rate. When the cash flows are semiannual, the convention is to use one-half the annual interest rate as the periodic interest rate with which to discount the cash flows.

Although one yield is used to calculate the present value of all cash flows, there are academic arguments for using a different yield to discount the cash flow for each period. Essentially, these theoretical arguments posit that each cash flow can be viewed as a zero-coupon bond, and therefore, the cash flow of a bond can be viewed as a package of zero-coupon bonds. The appropriate yield for each cash flow then would be based on the theoretical rate on a zero-coupon bond with a maturity equal to the time that the cash flow will be received. However, for the purpose of this chapter only one yield to discount all cash flows is being discussed.

With the above background, it is quite clear that the holder of a bond receives a fixed annual interest payment for a certain number of years and a fixed principal repayment (equal to par value) at the time of maturity. Therefore, the intrinsic value (or the present value) of a bond can now be written as:

$$V_0\ (\text{Or } P_0) = \sum_{t=1}^{n} \frac{1}{(1+k_d)^t} + \frac{F}{(1+k_d)^n}$$

or (in terms of present value interest factor and annuity tables)

$$V_0 = I \times PVIFA\ (k_d, n) + F \times PVIF\ (k_d, n)$$

where

V_0 = Intrinsic value of the bond
P_0 = Present value of the bond
I = Annual interest payable on bond
F = Principal amount (par value) repayable at the maturity time
N = Maturity period of the bond
K_d = Cost of capital (the prevailing interest factor also called as yield or YTM or required rate of return)

Numerical Example 1

Consider a bond whose par value is ₹1, 000, bears a coupon rate of 12% and has maturity period of 3 years. The required rate of return on the bond is 10%. What is the value of the bond?

$$\text{Value of Bond} = \text{₹}120 \times \text{PVIFA}\,(10\%, 3\text{yrs}) + \text{₹}1000 \times \text{PVIF}\,(10\%, 3\text{ yrs})$$

$$= \text{₹}120 \times (2.487) + 1{,}000 \times (0.751)$$

$$= \text{₹}298.44 + \text{₹}751$$

$$= \text{₹}1{,}049.44$$

Spreadsheet Application 1

Excel Function to calculate bond price is the present value function

Bond price = PV (rate, nper, pmt, fv, type)

In **Numerical Example 1**, Value of Bond = (0.10,3,120,1000,0), which works out to be equal to ₹1,049.74. (There is a minor difference in the MS Excel and Interest factor tables as Interest factor approximates the results.)

Spreadsheet output is produced as under

	A	B	C
1			
2	Value of Bond	(₹1,049.74)	
3			

	A	B	C
1			
2	Value of Bond	=PV(0.1,3,120,1000,0)	
3			

Bond values with semi-annual interest

Most bonds carry interest payment semi–annually. As half-yearly interest amounts can be reinvested the value of such bonds would be more than the bonds with annual interest payments. Hence the annual coupon based bond valuation model gets modified to account for the dual compounding in a year.

- Annual interest payment, i.e., I, must be divided by two to obtain interest payment semi-annually
- Number of years to maturity will have to be multiplied by two to get the number of half yearly periods
- Discount rate is divided by two to get the discount rate for half yearly period

Thus the annual coupon based bond valuation model becomes as follows:

$$V_0 = \sum_{t=1}^{2n} \frac{I/2}{(1+K_d/2)^t} + \frac{F}{(1+K_d/2)^{2n}}$$

or (in terms of present value interest factor and annuity tables)

$$V_0 = \frac{I}{2} \times PVIFA\left(\frac{k_d}{2}, 2n\right) + F \times PVIF\left(\frac{k_d}{2}, 2n\right)$$

where
V_0 = Intrinsic value of the bond
$I/2$ = Semi-annual interest payment
F = Principal amount (Par Value) repayable at the maturity time
$K_d/2$ = Cost of capital (the prevailing interest factor also called as yield or YTM or required rate of return) for half–year period
$2n$ = Maturity period expressed in half-yearly periods

Numerical Example 2

A bond of ₹1,000 value carries a coupon rate of 10% and a maturity period of 6 years. Interest is payable semi–annually. If the required rate of return is 12%, calculate the value of the bond.

$$V_0 = \sum_{t=1}^{12} \frac{100/2}{(1+0.12/2)^{12}} + \frac{1000}{(1+0.12/2)^{12}}$$

Value = ₹50 × (PVIFA 6%, 12 yrs) + 1,000 × (PVIF 6%, 12 yrs)

= ₹50 × (8.384) + 1,000 × (0.497)

= ₹419.2 + ₹497

= ₹916.20

In **Numerical Example 2**, Value of Bond = (0.06, 12, 50, 1000, 0), which works out to be equal to ₹1,049.74. (There is minor difference in The MS Excel and Interest factor tables as Interest factor approximates the results.)

Day Count Convention Used in Debt Market

Day count convention refers to the method used for arriving at the holding period (number of days) of a bond to calculate the accrued interest. As the use of different day count conventions can result in different accrued interest amounts, it is appropriate that all the participants in the market follow a uniform day count convention.

For example, the conventions followed in Indian market are given below:

1. **Bond Market:** The day count convention followed is *30/360*, which means that irrespective of the actual number of days in a month, the number of days in a month is taken as 30 and the number of days in a year is taken as 360. In Ms-Excel to count the number of days for bond market, option 4 is chosen.
2. **Money Market:** The day count convention followed is *actual/365*, which means that the actual number of days in a month is taken for number of days (numerator) whereas the number of days in a year is taken as 365 days. Hence, in the case of Treasury bills, which are essentially money market instruments, money market convention is followed. In Microsoft-Excel to count the number of days for bond market, option 3 is chosen.

Accrued interest: The bond prices that one observes being quoted in the financial pages are not actually the prices that investors pay for the bond. These quoted prices do not include the interest that accrues between coupon payments. If a bond is purchased between coupon payments, the buyer must pay the seller for accrued interest, which is the prorated share of the upcoming semiannual coupon. Accrued interest is the interest calculated for the broken period from the *last coupon day till a day prior to the settlement date of the trade.* Since the seller of the security is holding the security for the period up to the day prior to the settlement date of the trade, he is entitled to receive the coupon for the period held. During settlement of the trade, the buyer of security pays the accrued interest in addition to the agreed price and thus pays the 'consideration amount.'

Numerical Example 3

For example, for a trade of ₹5 crore (face value) of security 6.49% due for redemption in 2015 for settlement date August 26, 2009 at a price of ₹96.95, the consideration amount payable to the seller of the security is worked out as follows:

Here the price quoted is called '**clean price**' as the 'accrued interest' component is not added to it. The last coupon date being June 8, 2009, the number of days in broken period till August 25, 2009 (one day prior to settlement date) are 78.

Spreadsheet Application 2

Using Excel Option to get number of days:

Here, Start date: 6/8/2009

End date: 8/26/2009

Number of days = days 360 (start date, end date, method)
In this example, we get number of days = 78 = (6/8/2009, 8/26/2009, 4)

Spreadsheet output is produced as under

The accrued interest on ₹100 face value for 78 days

$$= 6.49 \times \left(\frac{78}{360}\right)$$

$$= ₹1.4062$$

	A	B	C
1			
2			
3	No. of days	78	
4			

	A	B	C	D	E	F
1						
2						
3	No. of days	=DAYS360(DATE(2009,6,8),DATE(2009,8,26),4)				
4						

When we add the accrued interest component to the 'clean price,' the resultant price is called the '***dirty price.***' In the given case, it is 96.95 + 1.4062 = ₹98.3562

The total consideration amount

$$= \text{Face value of trade} \times \text{dirty price}$$

$$= 5{,}00{,}00{,}000 \times \left(\frac{98.3562}{100}\right)$$

$$= ₹4{,}91{,}78{,}083.33$$

Bond-Yield Measures

In the above section we explained how to compute the price of a bond given the required yield. In this section we will demonstrate how various yield measures for a bond are calculated given its price. First let's recall the sources of potential return from holding a bond.

An investor who purchases a bond can expect to receive a *rupee* return from one or more of the following sources:

1. The coupon interest payments made by the issuer.
2. Any capital gain (or capital loss—negative rupee returns) when the bond matures, is called or is sold.
3. Income from reinvestment of the coupon interest payments.

This last source of dollar return is referred to as *interest-on-interest.*

Five yield measures are commonly cited by market participants to measure the potential return from investing in a bond—one period rate of return, current yield, yield-to-maturity, yield-to-call and realized yield to maturity. These yield measures are expressed as a *percent* return rather than as a rupee return. However, any yield measure should consider each of the three potential sources of return just cited. Below we discuss these five yield measures and assess whether they consider the three sources of potential return.

1. **One Period Rate of Return:** If a bond is purchased and then sold within one year, its rate of return (or yield) over this single holding period as given in the chapter on "Risk and Return analysis" is defined as follows:

$$\frac{[\text{Price gain or loss during holding period}] + [\text{Coupon interest rate (if paid)}]}{[\text{Purchase price at the beginning of the holding period}]}$$

The holding period can be calculated by using the count function of Days 360 (as discussed in the section on Accrued Interest Calculation)

If the bond price falls by an amount exceeding the payment received from coupon interest, the one period rate of return turns out to be negative.

Numerical Example 4

Mr. Jaswani purchased a ₹1,000 par value bond for ₹880. The coupon payment on his bond is ₹80 i.e., 8%. One year later the bond is quoting at ₹920. Mr. Jaswani sells the bond at the quoted price. The rate of return of Mr. X for this one year period is:

$$\text{One period holding period return} = \frac{(920-880)+80}{880} = 13.63\%$$

2. **Current Yield:** Current yield measures the rate of return earned on a bond if it is purchased at its current market price and if the coupon interest is received.

$$\text{Current yield} = \frac{\text{Coupon interest}}{\text{Current market price}}$$

In the example cited above (Numerical Example 4), the current yield works out to be

$$\text{Current yield} = \frac{80}{920} = 8.69\%$$

The current yield considers only the coupon interest and no other source of return that will affect an investor's return. For example, in **Numerical Example 4** no consideration is given to the capital gain that the investor will realize when the bond matures. No recognition is given to the capital loss that the investor will realize when a bond sells at discount to its purchase price. The interest-on-interest from reinvesting coupon payments is ignored. One important thing to be noted here is that coupon rate and current yield are two different measures. Coupon rate and current yield will be equal if the bond's market price equals its face value (We will discuss this point in details in the next section under Bond Value Theorems).

3. **Yield to Maturity:** Before we move on to the discussion on yield to maturity, we need to understand that bonds are compared on the basis of yield and not on the basis of prices at which they are being quoted. Another point to be noted here is that yields are not same as coupon rates of bonds. ***Yield to Maturity*** is the rate of return earned by an investor who purchases a bond and holds it till maturity. The YTM is the discount rate which equals the present value of promised cash flows to the current market price (purchase price). It is similar to the internal rate of return on any investment, as IRR is the interest rate that will make the present value of the cash flows equal to the price (or initial investment). YTM is same as Cost of Debenture (K_d), when looked at from the issuer's point of view. The yield-to-maturity is computed in the same way as the yield; the cash flows are those which the investor would realize by holding the bond to maturity. For a semiannual-pay bond, doubling the interest rate or discount rate gives the yield-to-maturity.

Numerical Example 5

Consider a ₹1,000 par value bond whose current market price is ₹950. The bond carries a coupon rate of 8% and has a maturity period of 6 years. What would be the rate of return that an investor earns if he purchases the bond and holds it till maturity?

The rate of return earned also referred to as yield to maturity, is the value of K_d in the following equation.

$$P_0 = \sum_{t=1}^{n} \frac{I}{(1+K_d)^t} + \frac{F}{(1+K_d)^n}$$

$$₹950 = \sum_{t=1}^{6} \frac{80}{(1+K_d)^t} + \frac{1000}{(1+K_d)^6}$$

or by using interest factor tables

$$₹950 = 80 \times PVIFA\ (k_d, 6\text{ years}) + 1000 \times PVIF\ (k_d, 6\text{ years})$$

To find the value of K_d in the above equation, several values of K_d will have to be tried out in order to reach the input value. Hit and trial method is used in order to obtain the right value of K_d.

Let's us take K_d as 10% and solve the equation.

On solving, the above expression becomes as follows:

$$950 = 80 \times PVIFA\,(10\%, 6) + 1000 \times PVIF\,(10\%, 6)$$

$$= 80 \times 4.3553 + 1000 \times 0.5645$$

$$\neq 912.924$$

Now lets us put K_d as 9% and solve the equation.

On solving, the above expression becomes as follows:

$$950 = 80 \times PVIFA\,(9\%, 6) + 1000 \times PVIF\,(9\%, 6)$$

$$= 80 \times 4.4859 + 1000 \times 0.5963$$

$$\neq 955.172$$

From the above it is clear that K_d lies between 9% and 10%. Now we have to use linear interpolation in the range of 9% and 10%. Using it we find that K_d is equal to the following:

$$9\% + (10\% - 9\%) \times \frac{(950 - 912.924)}{(955.172 - 912.924)}$$

$$= 9\% + 1\% \times \frac{(37.076)}{(42.248)}$$

$$= 9\% + 1\% \times 0.877$$

$$= 9.0087\%$$

On rounding off up to two decimals, the yield to maturity works out to be 9.01%.

An approximation formula is suggested by Gabriel A. Hawawini and Ashok Vora[4], as trial and error method calculations are too tedious and time consuming. The following is an approximation formula to find out the approximate YTM on a bond.

Approximate Formulae:

$$\text{YTM} \approx \frac{\left[1 + \dfrac{(F - P)}{n}\right]}{0.4\,F + 0.6\,P}$$

[4] G.A. Hawawini and A. Vora, "Yield Approximation: A historical perspective," *The Journal of Finance*, 1982, Vol. XXXVII, No. 1, 145–156.

where
YTM = Yield to maturity
I = Annual interest payment
F = Par value or redemption value of the bond
P = Current market price of the bond
N = Years to maturity

Numerical Example 6

Abhineetya Industries Ltd. has issued its bond at a par value of ₹500. The same bond is trading at BSE at ₹435. The coupon rate is 12% and it has a maturity period of 7 years. What is the YTM? (Use approximate formulae).

$$\text{YTM} \approx \frac{\left[60 + \dfrac{(500-435)}{7}\right]}{[(0.4\times 500)+(0.6\times 435)]}$$

$$\approx 15\%$$

Spreadsheet Application 3 Using Excel to calculate Yield to Maturity.

Bond particulars	Semi – Annual coupon	Annual coupon
Settlement date	1/1/2012	1/1/2012
Maturity date	1/1/2032	1/1/2032
Annual coupon rate	0.09	0.09
Bond price (clean)	972	972
Redemption value	1000	1000
No. of coupons in a year	2	1
Basis	4	4
Yield to maturity (in decimals)	0.010557	0.010560

'Yield to maturity = YIELD (Settlement date, Maturity date, Annual coupon rate, Bond price, Redemption value, No. of coupons, Basis)"

Spreadsheet output is produced as under

	A	B
1	Data	Description
2	1ST JAN, 2012	Settlement date
3	1ST JAN, 2032	Maturity date
4	9.00%	Percent coupon
5	972	Price
6	1,000	Redemption value
7	2	Frequency is semiannual
8	4	30/360 basis
9	YIELD =	0.0105567

	A	B	C	D	E
1	Data	Description			
2	1ST JAN, 2012	Settlement date			
3	1ST JAN, 2032	Maturity date			
4	9.00%	Percent coupon			
5	972	Price			
6	1,000	Redemption value			
7	2	Frequency is semiannual			
8	4	30/360 basis			
9	YIELD =	=YIELD(DATE(2012,1,1),DATE(2032,1,1),A4,A5,A6,A7,A8)			

4. **Yield to Call:** For a callable bond, investors also compute another yield (or internal rate of return) measure, the *yield-to-call*. The cash flows for computing the yield-to-call are those which would result if the issue were called on some assumed call date. The yield to call is the interest rate that will make the present value of the cash flows if the bond is held to the assumed call date equal to the price of the bond (generally the full price). Normally when market interest rates fall, the present value of the bond's scheduled payment rises (due to a lower denominator now). The call provision allows the issuer to repurchase the bond at the call price. If the call price is less than the present value of the scheduled payments, the issuing agency may call back the bond from the investors. This is a loss for the investors and is called call risk. This type of risk is discussed later in this chapter under the subsection "Unsystematic Risks in Debt Investments." **Numerical Example** 7 depicts the concept of yield to call.

Numerical Example 7

A bond which has a coupon of 13% and a par value of ₹100 is callable at the end of three years at a premium of 10%. It matures in six years and pays coupon semi–annually. The market price is ₹107. Given this data, compute the yield to call (YTC).

Solution:

Here Price = 107, Maturity value = 110, Number of half years after which the bond is called is = 6 and half yearly coupon rate = 13 ÷ 2 = 6.5%.

While computing the YTC of the bond, the total life span of the bond (6 yrs) is of no significance.

$$107 = 6.50 \times (PVIFA_{Kd/2,6}) + 110 \times (PVIF_{Kd/2,6})$$

Through linear interpolation we find the value of K_d (here YTC) as 12. 95 %

Or by using the approximate formulae

$$\text{YTM} \approx \frac{\left[1 + \frac{(F-P)}{n}\right]}{0.4\,F + 0.6\,P}$$

So,

$$YTC \approx \frac{\left[6.5 + \frac{(110-107)}{6}\right]}{[(0.4 \times 110) + (0.6 \times 107)]}$$

$$YTC \approx 6.46\%$$

Since this is half yearly YTC,

$$\text{The annual YTC} \approx 6.46\% \times 2$$

$$\approx 12.939\%$$

5. **Realized Yield to Maturity (Realized Compound Return):** Let's recall the basic bond pricing formulae

$$P_0 = \sum_{t=1}^{n} \frac{I}{(1+K_d)^t} + \frac{F}{(1+K_d)^n}$$

or

$$P_0 = I \times PVIFA\,(K_d, n) + F \times PVIF\,(K_d, n)$$

Here K_d (also the YTM) is that interest rate which equalizes the price of the bond to the present value of its scheduled payments. There is basic assumption in YTM calculation: "*that the cash flows are reinvested at the rate of the existing YTM.*" Now, since future is uncertain, the reinvestment rate applicable to future cash flow may vary, i.e., coupons may not be invested at the same rate as the YTM, hence we have this concept of realized YTM (RYTM), also called realized compound return. RYTM can be calculated as follows:

$$\text{Present Market Price of Bond} \times (1 + \text{RYTM})^n = \text{Terminal Value of Bond}$$

where n = the full term of the bond, till it is held by the investor

Hence RYTM can be worked out as:

$$\text{RYTM} = \sqrt[n]{\frac{\text{Terminal value of bond}}{\text{Present market price of bond}}} - 1$$

Numerical Example 8 will make the concept of RYTM clearer.

Numerical Example 8

Luna Systems Ltd. has issued 14% NCDs with a face value of ₹100. The market price of these NCDs as on the date of issue was ₹87. Interest is payable semi-annually and the NCDs will be redeemed after three years from the date of issue.

1. If an investor reinvests the coupon payments at 12% p.a. compounded half-yearly, compute the RYTM.
2. If the interest payments are not reinvested, what would be the RYTM?

Solution:

1. Computation of RYTM when coupon payments are reinvested at 12% compounded half yearly:

Recall: Present Market Price of Bond $\times (1 + \text{RYTM})^n =$ Terminal Value of Bond

On redemption date the investor will receive an amount which equals the future value of interest payments received during the three years and the principal of ₹100. This is expressed as:

$$= (7) \times (FVIF_{6\%,5}) + (7) \times (FVIF_{6\%,4}) + (7) \times (FVIF_{6\%,3}) + (7) \times (FVIF_{6\%,2}) + (7) \times (FVIF_{6\%,1}) + 107$$

$$= (41.83) + 107$$

$$= 148.83$$

Since the investor purchases the bond at ₹87 and receives ₹148.83 at the end of three years, the realized YTM is obtained from solving the equation:

$$87 \times (1 + \text{RYTM})^3 = 148.83$$

$$(1 + \text{RYTM})^3 = 1.710$$

Hence RYTM = 19.59%

2. Computation of RYTM when coupon payments are not reinvested. In that case the intermediate interest payments received during the three year period comprising a part of the terminal value of the bond, received by the investor would be:

₹42 + ₹100 = ₹142

The realized YTM is calculated as:

$$87 \times (1 + \text{RYTM})^3 = 142$$

$$(1 + \text{RYTM})^3 = 1.632$$

Hence RYTM = 17.74%

However in an economy the future interest rate estimation pose great deal of ambiguity, as the rates at which intervening coupons will be reinvested cannot be known for sure. Hence, realized compound return can be computed only after the investment period ends. It cannot be computed in advance without a lucid forecast of future reinvestment rates. This condenses much of the appeal of the realized YTM or realized compound return concept. We will see the impact of changes in market interest rates on the terminal value of the bond in the next chapter *Investing Lucratively in Fixed Income Securities: Yield Curve and Bond Portfolio Management* under the sub section of Semi Active Strategy of Bond Management.

Bond Value Theorems

Based on the bond valuation model, several bond value theorems have been derived which states the effect of these bond variables—coupons, time and yield to maturity on bond values (prices):

1. **Relationship Between the Required Rate of Return, Coupon Rate and Current Yield:** For a bond issue at a given point in time, the coupon rate and the term-to-maturity are fixed. Consequently, as yields in the market place change, the only variable that an investor faces a change in, are the bond prices. Bond prices change to compensate for the new yield required in the market.

   The first theorem states the relationship between coupon rates and yield to maturity.

   "When the required rate of return is equal to the coupon rate, the value of the bond is equal to its par value."

   i.e., if K_d (YTM) = Coupon rate, then value of a bond = Par value

   Let us understand this principle with the help of an example:

Numerical Example 9

Consider a bond of Periyar Telecommunications Ltd. having the following features:

Par Value: ₹100
Coupon rate: 12%
Years to maturity: 5 years

Find out the issue price of the bond, if the required rate of return is 12%.

Solution:

If the required rate of return is 12% (same as the coupon rate) the value of the bond is worked out as follows:

$$V_0 = I \times (PVIFA_{x,n}) + F \times (PVIFA_{x,n})$$

$$= 12 \times (\text{PVIFA}_{12\%,5}) + 100 \times (\text{PVIF}_{12\%,5})$$

$$= 12 \times (3.605) + 100 \times (0.567)$$

$$= 43.26 + 56.7$$

$$= 99.96 \approx 100$$

In this case the current yield of the bond works out to be: $12 \div 100 = 12\%$

*"When the required rate of return '**x**' is greater than the coupon rate, the value of the bond is less than its par value."*

i.e., YTM > coupon rate, then the value of bond < par value

Consider the same bond of **Numerical Example 9**, except that its required rate of return is now 14%. Find out the value of the bond.

If the required rate of return is 14% (greater than the coupon rate), then the value of the bond is

$$V_0 = I \times (PVIFA_{x,n}) + F \times (PVIFA_{x,n})$$

$$= 12 \times (\text{PVIFA}_{14\%,5}) + 100 \times (\text{PVIF}_{14\%,5})$$

$$= 12 \times (3.433) + 100 \times (0.519)$$

$$= 41.196 + 51.9$$

$$= 93.1$$

In this case the current yield of the bond works out to be: $12 \div 93.1 = 12.89\ \%$

*"When the required rate of return '**x**' is less than the coupon rate, the value of the bond is greater than its par value."*

When the required yield in the market is below the coupon rate, the price of the bond must be above its par value. This occurs because investors who could purchase the bond at par are getting a coupon rate in excess of what the market requires. As a result, investors would bid up the price of the bond because its yield is attractive. It will bid up to a price that offers the required yield in the market. A bond whose price is above its par value is said to be selling at a *premium*.

i.e., If Ytm < coupon rate, then the value of bond > par value

Consider the same bond of **Numerical Example 9**, except that its required rate of return is now 10%. Find out the value of the bond.

If the required rate of return is 10% (lesser than the coupon rate), then the value of the bond is

$$V_0 = I \times (PVIFA_{x,n}) + F \times (PVIFA_{x,n})$$

$$= 12 \times (\text{PVIFA}_{10\%,5}) + 100 \times (\text{PVIF}_{10\%,5})$$

$$= 12 \times (3.791) + 100 \times (0.621)$$

$$= 45.492 + 62.1$$

$$= 107.59$$

In this case, the current yield of the bond works out to be: $12 \div 107.59 = 11.15\%$

The above relationship among the coupon rate, current yield and yield-to-maturity is summarized as follows:

Bond selling at	Relationship
Par	Coupon rate = current yield = yield-to-maturity
Discount	Coupon rate < current yield < yield-to-maturity
Premium	Coupon rate > current yield > yield-to-maturity

2. **Impact of Time Path of a Bond on its Prices:** This theorem establishes the impact of time on the prices of bonds, if the required yield is unchanged between the time of the bond's purchase and its maturity date. We saw from the previous bond value theorem that for a bond selling at par value, the coupon rate is equivalent to its required yield. As the bond moves closer to maturity, the bond will maintain its price at par levels. Thus, for a bond selling at par, its price will remain at par as the bond moves toward the maturity date. However, prices of bonds will not remain constant for a bond selling at a premium or at a discount. The price of a bond will change because of one or more of the following reasons:
   (a) If interest rates in the economy increases (or decreases) because of Government's monetary policy, the price of a bond will decrease (or increase).
   (b) For corporate bonds, a change in the required yield due to changes in the spread to government bonds changes (narrows or widens), corporate bond prices will change.
   (c) A change in the perceived credit quality of the issuer impacts prices of bonds. Assuming that interest rates in the economy and yield spreads between Corporate bonds and Government Bonds do not change, the price of a Corporate bond will increase (or decrease) if it's perceived credit quality has improved (deteriorated).
   (d) For bonds with embedded options (e.g., callable bonds, putable bonds and convertible bonds), the price of the bond will change as the factors that affect the value of the embedded options change.

This bond value theorem demonstrates the effect of the number of years to maturity on bond values.

"When the required rate of return (ytm) is greater than the coupon rate, the discount on the bond declines as maturity approaches."

Numerical Example 10

Consider a bond of Phyron Ltd. with the following features:

Par value: ₹1,000
Coupon rate: 11%
Years to maturity: 7

If the required rate of return is 13%, then the value of the bond is:

$$V_0 = I \times (PVIFA_{x,n}) + F \times (PVIFA_{x,n})$$

$$= 110 \times (\text{PVIFA}_{13\%,7}) + 1000 \times (\text{PVIF}_{13\%,5})$$

$$= 110 \times (4.423) + 1000 \times (0.425)$$

$$= 486.53 + 425$$

$$= 911.53$$

One year from now, when the maturity period will be 6 years, the value of the bond will be:

$$V_0 = I \times (PVIFA_{x,n}) + F \times (PVIFA_{x,n})$$

$$= 110 \times (\text{PVIFA}_{13\%,6}) + 1000 \times (\text{PVIF}_{13\%,6})$$

$$= 110 \times (3.998) + 1000 \times (0.480)$$

$$= 439.78 + 480$$

$$= 919.78$$

TABLE 15.1 Impact of time path on prices of a bond Issued at a discount

Years to maturity	Bond value
5	929.87
4	940.14
3	952.71
2	966.48
1	982.35
0	1,000.00

For a required rate of return of 13%, the value of the bond will increase with passage of time, i.e., until its maturity. This is depicted in Table 15.1.

*"When the required rate of return '**x**' is less than the coupon rate, the premium on the bond declines as maturity approaches."*

If the required rate of return on the bond of Phyron Ltd. discussed in **Numerical Example 10** is 9%, it will have a value of:

$$V_0 = I \times (PVIFA_{x,n}) + F \times (PVIFA_{x,n})$$

$$= 110 \times (\text{PVIFA}_{9\%,7}) + 1000 \times (\text{PVIF}_{9\%,7})$$

$$= 110 \times (5.033) + 1000 \times (0.447)$$

$$= 553.63 + 447$$

$$= 1000.63$$

One year hence, when the maturity period will be 6 years the value of the bond will become as follows:

$$V_0 = I \times (PVIFA_{x,n}) + F \times (PVIFA_{x,n})$$

$$= 110 \times (\text{PVIFA}_{9\%,6}) + 1000 \times (\text{PVIF}_{9\%,6})$$

$$= 110 \times (4.486) + 1000 \times (0.596)$$

$$= 493.46 + 596$$

$$= 1089.46$$

For a required rate of return of 9%, the value of the bond decreases with the passage of time, i.e., until maturity. This is depicted in Table 15.2.

TABLE 15.2 Impact of time path on prices of a bond Issued at a premium

Years to maturity	Bond value
5	1077.90
4	1064.40
3	1050.41
2	1035.49
1	1017.87
0	1,000.00

3. **Impact of Yield to Maturity on Bond Prices:** As YTM determines a bond's market price and vice–versa, we can say that the bond's price will fluctuate in response to the change in market interest rates in the following ways.

   "A bond's price moves inversely proportional to its yield to maturity."

   The present value principle states that the present value of a cash flow varies in inverse proportion to the interest rate used as a discount rate. As such if the YTM of the bond rises, the bond's market price drops and if the YTM falls, the bond's market price rises.

Numerical Example 11

The YTM of a ₹1,000 par value bond bearing a coupon rate of 10% and maturing in 9 years is 12%. Thus, the market value of the bond works out to be ₹878 (calculated using bond pricing formulae). Now, if the YTM increases to 14%, the market value of the bond will drop to ₹803 as calculated below:

$$100 \times (PVIFA_{14\%,9}) + 1000 \times (PVIF_{14\%,9})$$

$$= 100 \times 4.946 + 1000 \times 0.308$$

$$\approx ₹803$$

If the YTM of the same bond comes down to 8%, then the market value of the bond rises to ₹1,125.

Now we will investigate the impact of YTM on bond prices with respect to bonds with difference in term to maturity, difference in coupons and differences in YTM, one by one.

1. For a given difference between YTM and coupon rate of the bonds, the longer the term to maturity, the greater will be the change in price with change in YTM. It is so because, in case of long maturity bonds, a change in YTM is cumulatively applied to the entire series of the coupon payments and the principal payment is discounted at the new rate for the entire number of years to maturity. While in case of short–term maturity bonds, the new YTM is applied to relatively few coupon payments. Moreover principal payment are also discounted for only a short period of time, thus long-term bonds are more variable to changes in interest rates than short–term bonds. **Numerical Example 11** depicts this nature of two similar bonds differing only in term to maturity.

   Let us take two hypothetical bonds differing only in term to maturity.

   It can be observed that the market value of the bonds when the YTM was equal to coupon rate was equal to the face value of the bonds, i.e., ₹1,000. When however the YTM increased to 11%, the market value of the bond with shorter maturity dropped by only 2.5% to ₹975 whereas the market value of the bond with longer maturity period of 7 years dropped by 4.9% to ₹953.2. Thus, the long-term bonds are by nature more sensitive to interest rate changes than short-term bonds.

	Bond A	Bond B
Face value	₹1000	₹1000
Coupon rate	10%	10%
YTM	11%	11%
Years to maturity	3	7
Market value at YTM of 10%	₹1000	₹1000
Market value at YTM of 11%	$100 \times PVIFA_{11\%,3} + 1000 \times PVIF_{11\%,3}$ = ₹975	$100 \times PVIFA_{11\%,7} + 1000 \times PVIF_{11\%,7}$ = ₹953.2
Change in price	2.5%	4.9%

- Given the maturity, the change in bond price will be greater with a decrease in the bond's YTM in comparison to the change in bond price with an equal increase in the bond's YTM. That is, for equal sized increases and decreases in the YTM, price movements are not symmetrical. The same can be understood with the help of **Numerical Example 12**.

Numerical Example 12

Let us consider a ₹1,000 par value bond with a coupon of 12% and maturity period of 5 years. Let the YTM be 12%. Since the coupon rate and YTM are the same, the bond would sell in the market at a price equal to its par value, i.e., ₹1000. A 1% increase in YTM to 13% changes the price of the bond as follows:

$$120 \times PVIFA_{13\%,\,5} + 1000 \times PVIF_{13\%,\,5} = ₹965.04$$

which is a decrease of 3.49% from the original bond price of ₹1000.

Similarly, let us consider a decrease of 1% in YTM to 11%. This changes the price of the bond as follows:

$$120 \times PVIFA_{11\%,\,5} + 1000 \times PVIF_{11\%,\,5} = ₹1{,}036.52$$

which is an increase of 3.65% from the original price of the bond of ₹1000.

Thus we conclude that an increase in bond's yield caused a decrease in bond prices. However this decrease in bond prices was smaller in magnitude (3.49%) than the price increase caused by an equal–size decrease in yield to maturity (3.65%). This property is due to the inherent convexity (or curvature) of the bond, which is discussed in detail in Chapter 16 on *Investing Lucratively in Fixed Income Securities: Yield Curve and Bond Portfolio Management.*

2. For any given change in YTM, the percentage price change in case of bonds of high coupon rate will be smaller than in case of bonds of low coupon rate, other things remaining the same. The same can be understood with the help of **Numerical Example 13**.

Numerical Example 13

Consider two bonds X and Y with the par value of ₹1,000, maturing in 4 years and YTM of 10%. Bond X bears coupon rate of 10% whereas Bond Y bears coupon rate of 12%.

	Bond X	Bond Y
Market price at YTM of 10%	₹1000	₹1063.40
Market price at the changed YTM of 12%	₹939.70	₹1000.44
Change in price	6.03%	5.92%

Change in price with the change in YTM in case of Bond Y carrying a higher coupon rate of 12% is only 5.925, whereas in case of Bond X with a coupon rate of 10% the change in the price is 6.03%.

3. A change in the YTM affects the bonds with a higher YTM more than a bond with lower YTM. Let us examine this property with the help of **Numerical Example 14**.

Numerical Example 14

Consider a ₹1,000 par value ABC bond with a coupon rate of 12%, maturity period of 6 years and YTM of 10%. The market value of the bond is worked out using bond pricing model and found to be ₹1,087.

Consider another identical bond EFG having a different YTM of 15%. The market value of the bond is worked out using bond pricing model and found to be ₹886.08.

Suppose there is an increase in YTM by 20%, i.e., YTM of bond ABC rises to 12% (10*1.2) and bond EFG rises to 18% (i.e., 20*1.2). Then the market value of both the bonds will change to:

Bond ABC : $120 \times PVIFA_{12\%, 6} + 1000 \times PVIF_{12\%, 6}$

$= ₹1,000$

Bond EFG : $120 \times PVIFA_{18\%, 6} + 1000 \times PVIF_{18\%, 6}$

$= ₹789.76$

Market value of ABC bond with a lower YTM decreased by 8% whereas in case of XYZ bond with a higher YTM the decrease is 10.87%.

Risks in Fixed Income Security Investment

The risk which a fixed income is exposed to, from the day of its purchase to the day of its sale can be divided into three parts: (1) the loss in the market value of the security if it is sold before maturity, (2) default in the receipt of cash flows (coupons) in the interim, and any additional income from the reinvestment of these cash flows, and (3) receipts of final redemption value on maturity of the bond. The different types of risks which a fixed income security investor is exposed to can be broadly categorized as follows:

1. **Systematic Risks:** Under this type of risk, the most important risks are *interest rate risks* and *purchasing power risk*. Interest rate risk refers to the possibility that income and/or capital loss would occur because of an increase in the level of interest rates; this is the major risk element for most high-quality, investment-grade debt securities. As interest rates are defined in nominal terms, it represents a rate of exchange between the present and the future value of rupees. Though financial contracts are stated in nominal terms, i.e., they contain the real interest rates and the expected inflation in an economy. However, when inflation is higher than expected, the borrower (corporate issuing the bond) gains at the expense of the lender (bond investor) and vice versa.
   (a) *Interest rate risk or market risk:* For an investor, who plans to hold the fixed income security up till its maturity, the change in the bond's price before the maturity is not a concern. However, for an investor who may have to sell the fixed income before its maturity, an increase in interest rate would result in a capital loss. This risk is referred to as ***market risk*** or ***interest rate risk***, which is the major risk faced by a fixed income security investor. To control interest-rate risk, it is necessary to quantify it. The most universally used measure of interest-rate risk is *duration*. Duration is the approximate percentage change in the price of a bond or bond portfolio due to a 100 basis point change in yields. A detailed discussion on application of duration is covered in Chapter 16. There are two components on interest rate risk, namely, the price risk and reinvestment risk.
      (i) *Price risk:* Let us understand price risk with the help of a simple example. Let us say, the general level of interest rates in the economy stands at 6%. A bond with a coupon rate of 6% and face value of ₹1000 is likely to sell at par value. This is because a buyer of this bond will be indifferent to buying this bond and saving directly with a bank. We have also seen under bond value theorem that a bond having coupon rate same as the yield would sell at par value.

      Now, if the interest rate increases by 100 basis points to 7%, then bondholders with a 6% coupon rate are more likely to sell the bond and keep the money in a bank account instead. This selling pressure will adjust bond prices downward. Hence, at higher interest rates, bond prices will generally be lower. Similarly, if interest rates drop to 5%, the 6% bond coupon rate will become more attractive and buyers will start purchasing this bond instead. The buying pressures will adjust the bond prices upward. Hence, at lower interest rates, bond prices will generally be higher. We have seen under bond value theorems that prices of bonds are inversely proportional to the rates of interest prevailing in the economy or bond yields. The reaction of high investment grade bonds to the change in interest rates (yields), vary with respect to the maturity, coupon rate and the general level of yields from which the change has occurred. This volatility of the price of the bond increases as maturity increases, coupon rate declines and yield fluctuations are large.

      (ii) *Reinvestment rate risk:* The cash flows received from the security are (or assumed to be) reinvested. The additional income from such reinvestment (called as *interest-on-interest)* depends on the prevailing interest rate levels at the time of reinvestment, as well as on the reinvestment strategy. The variability in the returns from reinvestment, as a part of a given strategy, due to changes in market rates is called *reinvestment risk*. The risk here is that the rate at which interim cash flows can be reinvested will fall, thereby reducing the interest on interest income (which is a potential loss). Reinvestment risk is greater for longer holding periods. It is also greater for securities with large, early cash flows such as high-coupon bonds. It should be noted that price risk and reinvestment risk opposes each other. For example, interest-rate risk is the risk that interest rates will rise, thereby reducing the price of a fixed income security. In contrast, reinvestment risk is the risk that interest rates will fall. A strategy based to counter the effects of these two offsetting risks is called "immunization" and is discussed in details in Chapter 16.

(b) *Inflation or purchasing power risk:* ***Inflation or purchasing power risk*** arises because of the variation in the value of cash flows from a security due to inflation, as measured in terms of purchasing power. For example, if an investor purchases a five year bond in which he or she can realize a coupon rate of 7%, but the rate of inflation is 8%, then the purchasing power of the cash flow gets eroded. For all but inflation-adjusted securities, and adjustable or floating rate bonds, an investor is exposed to inflation risk because the interest rate the issuer promises to make is fixed for the life of the security. To the extent that interest rates reflect the expected inflation rate; floating-rate bonds have a lower level of inflation risk.

2. **Unsystematic Risk:** In forecasting purchasing power and interest rate risk, what one talks about are expectations concerning the outlook for economy. These major sources of risk in fixed-income securities impact the prices of bond across sectors and credit rating of the issuer. Impairment in the quality of a high grade investment bond may cause a loss in its market value, which may become permanent in case of default. Secondary quality bonds may improve in quality over time due to increased earnings and asset protection, or they may be paid at maturity despite underlying uncertainties. Such bonds will provide an extra return as capital appreciation in addition to interest. These types of risks are examples of unsystematic risks in fixed income security investment. They are discussed below.

(a) *Liquidity risk:* ***Liquidity risk*** is the risk that the investor will have to sell a bond below its intrinsic value. The primary measure of liquidity is the size of the spread between the bid price and the ask price quoted by a dealer. The wider the bid-ask spread, the greater is the liquidity risk A liquid market generally can be characterized by small bid-ask spreads which do not materially increase for large transactions.

(b) *Credit risk:* ***Credit risk*** of a bond includes the risk that the issuer will fail to pay on its obligation (also called the default risk). The risk that the bond's value will decline and/or the bond's price performance will be worse as compared to another bond held by the investor. This could be because either (a) the market requires a higher spread due to a perceived augmentation in the risk owing to the chances of the issuer defaulting on his payment, or (b) companies that assign ratings to bonds may lower a bond's rating. The first risk is referred to as ***default risk***. The second risk is based on the reason for the adverse or inferior performance. The risk attributable to an increase in the spread or, more specifically, the credit spread demanded by the market is referred to as ***credit spread risk***; the risk attributable to a lowering of the credit rating (i.e., a downgrading) is referred to as ***downgrade risk***.

Once a credit rating is assigned to a debt obligation, a rating agency monitors the credit quality of the issuer and may reassign a different credit rating to its bonds in future. An "upgrade" occurs when there is an improvement in the credit quality of an issue; a "downgrade" occurs when there is deterioration in the credit quality of an issue. As noted earlier, downgrade risk is the risk that an issue will be downgraded. Typically, before an issue's rating is changed, the rating agency will announce in advance that it is reviewing the issue with the potential for upgrade or downgrade. The issue in such cases is said to be on "rating watch" or "credit watch." In the announcement, the rating agency will state the direction of the potential change in rating—upgrade or downgrade. Credit rating assigned by CRISIL has been explained in Chapter 2.

(c) *Event and sector risk:* Sporadically, the ability of an issuer to make interest and principal payments may change unexpectedly by (1) a natural or industrial accident or (2) a takeover or corporate restructuring. These risks are referred to as *event risk.* Bonds in different sectors of the market respond differently to environmental and taxation changes announced by the Central Government. This so happens because of a combination of some or all of the preceding risks, as well as others. Examples include discount versus premium coupon bonds, industrial versus utility bonds and corporate versus mortgage-backed bonds. The possibility of adverse differential movement of specific sectors of the market is called *sector risk.*

(d) *Timing or call risk:* As explained in the previous section under '*Types of Debt of more than a year,*' bonds may contain a provision that allows the issuer to retire, or 'call,' all or part of the issue before the maturity date (known as callable bonds). The issuer usually holds this right to refinance the bond in the future if market interest rates decline below the coupon rate. An investor may face three inconveniences from call provision present in a bond. Firstly, the cash flow pattern of a callable bond is not known with certainty. Secondly, because the issuer may call the bonds when interest rates have dropped, the investor is thus exposed to reinvestment risk. This is because, the investor will now have to reinvest the proceeds received when the bond is called at lower interest rates. Finally, the capital appreciation potential of a bond will be restricted. This so happens because, the price of a callable bond may not rise much above the price at which the issuer may call the bond.

(e) *Sinking fund provision risk:* The presence of a sinking fund in a bond issue may prove to be a mixed blessing for fixed income investor. Though, such provision offers the bondholder some assurance that a regular redemption of the bond by the issuer may take place. This may also provide some price support for the bond in a period of high interest rate. The sinking fund, however, can work to the disadvantage of an investor. Suppose that an investor is having an investment in one of the early bonds to be called for a sinking fund. All the time and effort put by the investor in cherry picking and analyzing the bond now goes futile, and the investor will have to choose new instruments for purchase. At the time when market interest rates or yields begin to fall, an investor who is holding a bond with a high coupon is still obligated to surrender the issue in case of a sinking fund provision invoked by the issuer.

Warrants and Convertibles

Warrants

Warrants and convertibles are frequently used instruments of financing, all over the world. They have also gained popularity in India. The wide issuance of these instruments is explained with different concepts focusing on cheaper debt, matching cash flows, financial synergy and low agency costs. A *warrant* is an option in which an issuer permits a fixed income investor to buy from the former a certain number of shares of common stock at a specified price. An equity warrant is a call option from the point of view of a fixed income instrument investor. Here the investor has an option to buy a stated number of equity shares of the issuing company. They are like calls to the extent that they entitle the holder of the bond to buy a fixed number of equity shares at a predetermined price during some specified period of time. It gives the holder of the bond the right to subscribe to the equity shares of the company, generally at a discount to the market price. Like call options, warrants may expire on a certain date. They may also be perpetual warrants which may never expire. Most warrants are detachable from the bond or preferred stock to which they are attached at the time of issue. If detached, warrants can be traded as independent securities, like call options. The chief benefit to the investor is the financial leverage the warrant provides. However, warrants lead to dilution of equity, when exercised. Warrants are distributed to stock holders in lieu of a stock or cash dividend or sold directly as a new security issue. Sometimes, the companies issue preference shares or debentures with less favorable terms (lower coupons). Hence to compensate, it issues warrants to "sweeten the offering." Few Indian Companies have issued warrants since early 1990s. For example, a debenture or bond may be sold by the company with warrants. In 1991 Reliance Industries issued under Series – 'J' 76,00,000 – 14% secured redeemable non-convertible debentures of ₹150 aggregating to ₹114 crore attached with a detachable warrant, to the equity shareholders on rights basis in the proportion of one debenture for every 20 equity shares held.[5]

Marketview 15.1

The Ministry of Finance has decided to allow the issue of partly paid shares and warrants by the Indian companies to foreign investors. In this view, RBI has notified the Foreign Exchange Management (Transfer or Issue of Security by a Person Resident outside India) (Ninth Amendment) Regulations, 2014 on June 30, 2014. The said amendment basically permits foreign investment in partly paid-up shares and warrants issued by Indian companies.

Source: SEBI. http://www.sebi.gov.in/cms/sebi_data/attachdocs/1417511914375.pdf, accessed on December 14, 2014.

Convertible debentures

A financial instrument that can be converted into a different security of the same company under specific conditions is referred to as a convertible security. A convertible debenture, as the name suggests, is a debenture which is convertible partly or fully, into equity shares. If it is partially converted, it is referred to as "partly convertible debentures" and if the debentures are convertible into equity shares at the end of maturity fully, it is referred to as "fully convertible debentures." The option of conversion is either at the discretion of the investors, i.e., (optional) or compulsory (if it is specified). Convertible bond or preferred stock is converted into specified number of shares. Usually, in this conversion, no cash in involved; simply, the old security is traded and appropriate number of new securities are issued in turn.

Conversion Ratio and Conversion Value

The ***conversion ratio*** gives the number of shares of stock received for each convertible security. If only the conversion ratio is given, the par conversion price can be obtained by dividing the conversion ratio multiplied by the face or par value of the convertible security. The conversion value represents the market value of the

[5] http://www.moneycontrol.com/company-facts/relianceindustries/history/RI, accessed on December 14, 2014.

convertible if it were converted into stock; this is the minimum value of the convertible based on the current price of the issuer's stock. The ***conversion value*** is obtained by multiplying the conversion ratio by the stock's current market price.

For example, consider a convertible bond with ₹1000 (par value) converted into 25 equity shares. If the market price of the share is, say ₹50, then the conversion value of the bond is ₹1250 (25 × 50). If the conversion price of the bond is, say, ₹1300, then the conversion premium of the bond is ₹1300 – ₹1250, i.e., ₹50.

As the converted stock is affected by tax, corporate investors are less keen to invest, whereas the individual investors are attracted toward converted securities as they need not have to pay tax.

Convertible securities have great complexity in their maturities. Some may be converted only after an initial period. Some may be converted up to the bond's maturity date; others only for a stated, shorter periods. Some securities may have different conversion ratios for different years. **Numerical Example 15** discusses the pricing of a fully convertible bond.

Numerical Example 15

M/S. Geetha Tyres Ltd. has issued fully convertible debentures at a face value of ₹100 with coupon rate of 15% p.a. which is converted into 4 equity shares (at a price of ₹25 each) at the end of 3 years.

An investor wanted to buy debentures in secondary market after a year of its issue. Let us find out the value of convertible if his required rate of return is 18% and price of share is expected to be ₹45 at the end of 3 years.

The value of convertible is determined as follows:

$$\sum_{t=1}^{n}\frac{C}{(1+r)^t}+\frac{(P_n)\times\text{Conversion ratio}}{(1+r)^n}$$

where

C = Coupon rate

R = Required rate of return

P_n = Expected price of equity share on conversion

n = No. of years to maturity

$$=\frac{15}{(1.18)^1}+\frac{15}{(1.18)^2}+\frac{45\times 4}{(1.18)^2}$$

$$=12.71+10.77+\frac{180}{(1.18)^2}$$

$$=12.71+10.77+129.27$$

$$=152.75$$

Thus value of a convertible is approximately ₹152.75.

The investors preferring to minimize the risk can opt for warrants, as it acts like a call option and convertible preferred stocks of bonds as they combine the benefits of fixed income investing with the option of sharing in the price appreciation benefits normally reserved for the common stock holders.

SUMMARY

☑ Debt securities are often called fixed income securities as they assure a fixed stream of income that is determined according to a specified formula.

☑ Instruments having a maturity period of less than one year are known as *money market instruments*. In Indian fixed income markets, the most active transactions of the money market are in the market for overnight and term money between banks and financial institutions (called call money) and the market for Repo transactions.

☑ *Zero coupon bonds* are a special category of bonds. As the name suggests, they do not provide coupon payments to the investors. They sell at a discount to their face values, frequently at deep discount owing to their long maturity (hence also called deep discount bonds).

☑ Accrued interest is the interest calculated for the broken period from the *last coupon day till a day prior to the settlement date of the trade*. Prices of bonds quoted on stock exchanges is quoted as per 'clean price' as the 'accrued interest' component is not added to it.

☑ Interest rate risk refers to the possibility that income and/or capital loss would occur because of an increase in the level of interest rates; this is the major risk element for most high-quality investment-grade debt securities.

☑ *Liquidity risk* is the risk that the investor will have to sell a bond below its true value where the true value is indicated by a recent transaction. The primary measure of liquidity is the size of the spread between the bid price and the ask price quoted by a dealer.

☑ Credit risks can be decomposed into credit spread risk and downgrade risk. The risk attributable to an increase in the credit spread demanded by the market is referred to as credit spread risk; the risk attributable to a lowering of the credit rating (i.e., a downgrading) is referred to as downgrade risk.

☑ Bonds may contain a provision that allows the issuer to retire, or "call," all or part of the issue before the maturity date (known as callable bonds). The issuer usually retains this right to refinance the bond in the future if market interest rates decline below the coupon rate.

☑ The cash flow of an option-free bond (i.e., noncallable/nonputable bond) consists of (1) periodic coupon interest payments to the maturity date and (2) the par (or maturity) value at maturity. Although the periodic coupon payments can be made over any time interval (weekly, monthly, quarterly, semiannually or annually), most bonds issued in India pay coupon interest semiannually.

☑ The interest rate that an investor wants from investing in a bond is called the *required yield*. The required yield is determined by investigating the yields offered on comparable bonds in the market. By comparable, we mean option-free bonds of the same credit quality and the same maturity.

☑ Current yield measures the rate of return earned on a bond if it is purchased at its current market price and if the coupon interest is received. Coupon rate and current yield are two different measures. Coupon rate and current yield will be equal if the bond's market price equals its face value.

☑ Yield to maturity is the rate of return earned by an investor who purchases a bond and holds it till maturity. The YTM is the discount rate which equals the present value of promised cash flows to the current market price (purchase price).

☑ The cash flows for computing the yield-to-call are those which would result if the issue were called on some assumed call date. The yield-to-call is the interest rate that will make the present value of the cash flows if the bond is held to the assumed call date, equal to the price of the bond (i.e., the full price).

☑ The realized yield to maturity return is the compound rate of growth of invested funds, assuming that all coupon payments are reinvested.

☑ When the coupon rate is greater than the required yield, the price is greater than the par value. When the price is greater than the par value, the coupon rate is greater than the required yield.

☑ An equity warrant is a call option from the point of view of a fixed income instrument investor. They are like calls to the extent that they entitle the holder of the bond to buy a fixed number of equity shares at a predetermined price during some specified period of time. A convertible debenture, as the name suggests, is a debenture which is convertible partly or fully, into equity shares.

KEY WORDS

CONCEPT QUESTIONS

1. Discuss the transformation which has taken place in the Indian debt market, post liberalization, since 1991.
2. Find out about retail debt market and wholesale debt market segment in India. Discuss the various fixed income instruments traded in the wholesale debt market of India.
3. Why do some bonds have embedded options? Would a put privilege in a bond be more beneficial to an investor than holding a bond with floating interest rate?

4. Explain with the help of an illustration, the differences in the various yield measures of a bond-current yield, yield to maturity, yield to call and realized yield to maturity.

5. How are bonds rated in India? What is the methodology adopted by credit rating agencies in India to rate long term instruments?

6. A security analyst is responsible for making recommendations to clients about buying and selling bonds and making other investment decisions. What are the risks in bond investments that should be taken into account while evaluating investment in bonds? Discuss them briefly.

7. Enlist some advantages and disadvantages to an issuer of bonds of periodic repayments of principal via a sinking fund.

8. What are the different bond valuation theorems? Do they also hold good for Zero Coupon Bonds?

9. Explain the concept of clean price and dirty price in the realm of fixed income investments. In the Indian secondary market at what prices do the bonds trade?

10. Why are some bonds convertible? How can such bonds be valued? Is the convertible clause attached to bonds optional or compulsory from the point of view of investors?

PRACTICE PROBLEMS

1. The market price of a ₹1,000 par value bond carrying a coupon rate of 14% and maturing after 5 years is ₹1,050. What is the yield to maturity (YTM) on this bond? What is the approximate YTM? What will be the realized yield to maturity if the reinvestment rate is a) 14%, b) 12%?

2. A 20-year maturity, 8% coupon bond paying bond on semiannual basis is callable in 5 years. The call price is ₹1,050. The bond is currently selling at a yield to maturity of 7% p.a.
   Compute:

   a. Yield to call of the bond.
   b. Yield to maturity of the bond.
   c. Yield to call, if the call price is ₹1,050 but now the bond can be called in 2 years instead of 5 years.

3. Identify the major risks associated with the following investment alternatives. Explain with reasons in a couple of lines.

   a. For an investor who plans to hold a security for one year, purchasing a treasury security that matures in one year versus purchasing a treasury security that matures in 30 years.
   b. For an investor who plans to hold an investment for 10 years, purchasing a treasury security that matures in 10 years versus purchasing an AAA corporate security that matures in 10 years.
   c. For an investor who plans to hold an investment for two years, purchasing a zero-coupon treasury security that matures in one year versus purchasing a zero coupon treasury security that matures in two years.
   d. For an investor who plans to hold an investment for five years, purchasing an AA sovereign bond (with dollar denominated cash flow payments) versus purchasing a US corporate bond with a B rating.

e. For a U.S. investor who plans to hold an investment for six years, purchasing a treasury security that matures in six years versus purchasing an Italian government security that matures in six years and is denominated in *lira*.

4. Calculate the missing values for each of the following ₹2000 par value zero coupon bonds, assuming semi-annual compounding.

Bond	Maturity (in years)	Yield to maturity	Price
A	25	12%	?
B	?	8%	₹1200
C	10	?	₹700

5. A floating rate issue has the following coupon formula:

Yield of one year Government of India Bond + 30 basis points with a cap of 7% and a floor of 4.5%.

The coupon rate is reset every year. Suppose that at the reset date the yield of one year Government of India Bond is as shown below. Compute the coupon rate for the next year:

	Yield of one year Government of India bond	Coupon rate
First reset date	5.8%	?
Second rest date	6.5%	?
Third reset date	6.9%	?
Fourth reset date	6.8%	?
Fifth reset date	5.75	?
Sixth reset date	5.0%	?
Seventh reset date	4.15	?
Eight reset date	3.9%	?
Ninth reset date	3.25	?
Tenth reset date	4.4%	?

6. A 7.5 % bond with 2016 as its maturity year, has a settlement date of December 15, 2014 at a price of ₹193.95. The face value of the bond is ₹200. Calculate the dirty price of the bond if the last coupon date was August 20, 2014.

7. M/s Shreeradhe System's 16% NCD is being quoted in the market as on June 30, 2014 at ₹80. Face value of the NCD is ₹100. The NCD would be redeemed on June 30, 2016. The interest is payable semi-annually on June 30, and December 31, of every year.

a. Calculate the Current Yield and YTM as on June 30, 2014.
b. Mr. Trivedi holding about 300 debentures of M/S Shree Radhe Systems can reinvest the interest payments at 10% p.a. compounded half yearly. Calculate the realized yield on the investment assuming Mr. Trivedi will hold the investment till date of maturity.
c. Calculate the realized yield to maturity on the assumption that the intermediate coupon payments are not available for reinvestment.

8. You are considering investing in one of the following bonds:

Bonds	Coupon rate	Maturity	Price/₹100 par value
Bond A	13%	10 years	₹75
Bond B	9%	6 years	₹60

Your income tax is 30% and your capital gains are effectively taxed at 10%. The capital gains tax are paid at the time of maturity of the bonds. Coupons received are taxed at the marginal income tax rate. Calculate the post-tax yield to maturity of the two bonds.

9. Suppose a client observes the following two benchmark spreads for two bonds:

Bond issue U rated A: 150 basis points

Bond issue V rated BBB: 135 basis points

Your client is confused because he thought the lower-rated bond (bond V) should offer a higher benchmark spread than the higher-rated bond (bond U). Explain why the benchmark spread may be lower for bond V.

10. Assume that market rates of interest in the economy are expected to increase in the near future. Under this circumstance, which is a better measure of return, current yield, yield to call or yield to maturity on a fixed income security? Explain.

CASELET

Consider two bonds X and Y. They have the following features:

Features	Bond X	Bond Y
Face value	₹500	₹500
Coupon rate	9%	12%
YTM	9%	12%
Term to maturity	4 years	4 years
Coupon payment frequency	Semi annually	Semi annually

1. What are the current prices of the bonds X and Y?
2. If the market interest rates increase by 1 percentage point, what will be the new price of each bond? What is your observation regarding the price changes in case of bonds X and Y?
3. If the YTMS of bonds X and Y are 10% and 15% respectively, what will be their market prices?
4. In case of part (c), if the YTM now increases by 15% in case of the two bonds, what will be the new market prices of the two bonds? What is your observation in this case on prices of bonds when the YTM changes by same rate?
5. However you forecast that market interest rates in the economy will become 8% across all bonds. If your forecast is correct, which bond would you purchase today? (Justify your choice by determining the percentage changes in each bond in comparison to the original data given in the caselet).

REFERENCES

B. Tuckman, Fixed Income Securities, "Tools for today's Markets," 2nd Edition, Wiley Finance, New Jersey, 2002.

D.E. Fischer and R.J. Jordon, *Security Analysis and Portfolio Management*, Dorling Kindersley (India) Pvt. Ltd: Pearson Education Inc., 1995.

FIMMDA-NSE Debt Market Basic Module, National Stock Exchange of India Limited, 2009.

Fixed Income Securities, Dun and Bradstreet-McGraw Hill Professional: Finance essential Series, India, 2008.

F.J. Fabozzi, *Bond markets, Analysis and Strategies*. Englewood Cliffs, N.J.: Prentice Hall, 1993.

G.A. Hawawini and A. Vora, (1982): "Yield Approximation: A historical perspective." *The Journal of Finance*, Vol. XXXVII, No. 1, 145–156. DOI: 10.1111/j.1540-6261.1982.tb01100.x

"The Handbook of Fixed Income Securities," in ed. by F.J. Fabozzi, 7th Edition, McGraw Hill Companies, 2005.

Z. Bodie, A. Kane, A. Marcus and P. Mohanty, *Investments*, 8th Edition, Mc Graw Hill Education, 2009.

Investing Lucratively in Fixed Income Securities: Yield Curve and Bond Portfolio Management[1]

16

CHAPTER OBJECTIVES

- Understanding how interest rates are determined for various bonds
- Explaining theories of term structure of interest rates
- Understanding the concept of Yield Curve and factors which determine it
- Evaluating the concept and properties of Duration
- Learning to immunize a bond portfolio against interest rate risks
- Discussing the passive and active strategies of bond portfolio management

There is no distinct interest rate for any economy; rather, there is a mutually supporting structure of interest rates. In Chapter 15, for the sake of ease it was assumed that the interest rates, being used to discount cash flows of any maturity, were constant. However in the real world this is rarely the case. The interest rate that a borrower has to pay depends on a myriad of factors. In this chapter we will describe those factors. We will begin with a discussion on the determinants of the general level of interest rates in the economy. Next, we would focus on one particular factor that affects the interest rate demanded in an economy for a particular security, maturity. The relationship between yield and maturity (or term) is called the *term structure of interest rates*, graphically depicted in a curve called as the yield curve. This relationship is vital in the valuation of securities and shows how yield to maturity is related to term to maturity for bonds.

Interest rate risk is critical in formulating both active and passive bond management strategies. At first an analysis of the sensitivity of bond prices to interest rate fluctuations is discussed. This sensitivity is measured by the duration of the bond; hence a considerable emphasis is given to the concept of duration, its calculation and its application in immunizing a bond portfolio against interest rate risk. Finally in the chapter, we turn to various strategies that bond portfolio managers practice, making a conspicuous distinction between passive and active strategies. In a passive investment strategy, fund managers try to maintain an appropriate risk-return balance in the given market situation, rather than attempting to beat the market by exploiting superior market information. However in active fund management strategy, a fund manager attempts to achieve returns greater than those commensurate with the risk undertaken.

[1] This chapter has been written by Ms. Nupur Gupta-Bhattacharya, MBA, CFA (India), working as Assistant Professor in the Department of Finance at K.J. Somaiya Institute of Management Studies and Research, Mumbai, India.

Determinants of Interest Rates of Bonds

We have spent a lot of time discussing the required yield (interest rate) on a bond in Chapter 15. However there is an important point to remember; there is no single market yield. Every bond has its own yield. Other things being equal, the price of a bond falls when the required rate of return rises and the price of a bond rises when the required rate of return falls. Since this required rate of return has a significant impact on bond prices, one should know what drives the required rate of return, synonymously referred in this chapter as *yield* or interest rates. The interest rate on a bond is determined by basically two factors: short-term risk-free interest or the base rate and the risk premium.

Short-Term Risk-Free Interest Rate

The securities issued by the Government of India's (GOI) treasury are backed by the full faith and credit worthiness of the sovereign. Consequently, market participants throughout the economy view them as having no credit risk. Therefore, interest rates on these GOI Treasury securities are the benchmark interest rates throughout the Indian economy. The minimum interest rate or base interest rate that investors will demand for investing in a non-treasury (or non–government) security is the yield offered on a comparable maturity for an ongoing[2] treasury security (example, yield of 364 days Treasury bill will be taken as a benchmark for a corporate bond issued for one year). The base interest rate is also referred to as the benchmark interest rate. This short term risk free rate can be decomposed into two parts: The expected real rate of return and the expected inflation. The expected real rate of return represents the rate at which consumers (who are also investors) are willing to sacrifice their current consumption for future consumption. For example, if a consumer is willing to give up 100 units of real goods in return for 105 units a year from now, the expected real rate of return is five percent. As there is a preference for current consumption over future consumption, the expected real rate is positive, but it is likely to be inclined to vary widely across time and across economies.

Risk Premium

Market participants describe interest rates on non-Treasury securities as trading at a spread to a particular ongoing Treasury security. For example, if the yield on a 10-year non-Treasury security is 8.68% and the yield on a 10-year Treasury security is 7.68%, the spread is 100 basis points. This spread reflects the additional risks an investor faces by acquiring a security that is not issued by the Indian government and therefore can be called a *risk premium*. Thus we can express the interest rate offered on a non-Treasury security as:

Base interest rate + Risk premium

The factors that affect this spread or premium include (1) the type of issuer, (2) the issuer's perceived creditworthiness, (3) the term or maturity of the instrument, (4) provisions that grant either the issuer or the investor the option to do something, (5) the taxability of the interest received by investors, and (6) the expected liquidity of the issue.

---

[2] Called as on the run treasury (These are the most recently issued Treasury bond or note of a particular maturity).

1. **Types of Issuers:** A key feature of a debt obligation is the nature of the issuer. In addition to the Government of India, there are public sector undertakings, local bodies and corporations (domestic and foreign) that issue bonds. These classes of issuers are referred to as market sectors. The spread between the interest rate offered in two sectors of the bond market with the same maturity is referred to as an *intermarket-sector spread.* The spread between two issues within a single market sector is called an *intramarket-sector spread.*
2. **Perceived Creditworthiness of Issuer:** *Default risk* or *credit risk (already discussed in Chapter 15)* refers to the risk that the issuer of a bond may be unable to make timely payment of principal and/or interest. Most market participants rely primarily on commercial rating companies (like CRISIL Ltd., ICRA Ltd., Care Ltd etc.), to assess the default risk of an issuer. The spread between government securities and non-government securities that are identical in all respects except for quality is referred to as a *credit spread* or *quality spread.*
3. **Term-to-Maturity:** The spread between any two maturity sectors of the same market segment (or sector, e.g., within government sector or within corporate entities) is *maturity spread.* The relationship between the yields on comparable securities with different maturities, as mentioned earlier, is called the *term structure of interest rates* discussed later in this chapter. The term-to-maturity topic is very important, and we have devoted more time to this topic later in this chapter.
4. **Inclusion of Options:** It is not rare for a bond issue to include a provision that gives the bond-holder or the issuer an option to exercise to one's benefit. An option that is included in a bond issue is referred to as an *embedded option.* We discussed types of embedded options in Chapter 15. The most common type of option in a bond issue is the call provision, which grants the issuer the right to retire the debt, fully or partially, before the scheduled maturity date. The inclusion of a call feature benefits the issuer by allowing them to swap an old bond issue with a lower-interest-cost issue when interest rates in the market decline. In effect, a call provision allows the issuer to modify the maturity of a bond. The exercise of a call provision is detrimental to the interest of the bondholder because the bond-holder must now reinvest the proceeds received at a lower interest rate.

   The presence of an embedded option affects both the spread of an issue relative to a government security and the spread relative to otherwise comparable issues that do not have an embedded option. In general, investors will demand a larger spread to a comparable government security for an issue with an embedded option that is to the benefit of the issuer (such as a call option) than for an issue without such an option. In contrast, investors will require a smaller spread to a comparable to government security for an issue with an embedded option that is to the benefit of the investor (such as a put option or a conversion option). In fact, the interest rate on a bond with an option that is favorable to an investor may be less than that on a comparable Treasury security.
5. **Taxability of Interest:** Taxable bonds need to pay a higher yield to lure investors than non-taxable bonds. In 2003, the Government of India came out with two issues for long-term government bonds. The two issues were the 6.5% non-taxable (with maturity of five years) and the 8% taxable (with maturity of six years) bonds. Unless exempted under the Indian income tax code, interest income of bonds and debentures is taxable at the hands of the investor. The difference in yield between tax-exempt securities and government securities is typically measured not in basis points but in percentage terms. The yield on a taxable bond issue after income taxes are paid is equal to:

$$\text{After-tax yield} = \text{Pretax yield} \times (1 - \text{Income tax rate})$$

Numrical Example 1 depicts the impact of taxes on the yield of a taxable bond.

Numerical Example 1

Suppose that a taxable bond issue offers a yield of 8% and is acquired by an investor facing an income tax rate of 30%. The after-tax yield would be:

$$\text{After-tax yield} = 0.08 \times (1 - 0.30) = 0.056 = 5.60\%$$

Notice that the lower the income tax rate, the lower is the equivalent taxable yield. For example, in Illustration 16.1, if the income tax rate for another investor is 20% rather than 30%, the equivalent taxable yield would be 6.4% rather than 5.6%.

6. **Expected Liquidity of an Issue:** If one does not wish to hold a bond until its maturity, one can always sell it in the secondary bonds market (NSE and/or BSE) and book profits. The liquidity of a bond depends on its trade volumes after listing. However, to be on the safe side, one should give preference to companies that are planning to list on both the BSE and the NSE. Bonds trade with different degrees of liquidity. The greater the expected liquidity at which an issue will trade, the lower is the yield that investors get. As noted earlier, treasury or government securities are the most liquid securities in the world. The lower yield offered on Treasury securities relative to non-Treasury securities reflects the difference in liquidity as well as seeming credit risk. Even within the Treasury market, on-the-run issues have greater liquidity than off-the-run issues[3].

The Term Structure of Interest Rates: The Yield Curve

The term structure of interest rates plays an important role in the valuation of bonds. For a given bond issuer, such as the Government of India, the structure of yields that is observed for bonds with different terms to maturity (but no other difference) is called the *term structure of interest rates.* In financial parlance, a diagram of the rates prevailing on a class of securities that are alike in every respect, except term to maturity provides us with a *yield curve.* The most common portrait of yields plotted against time, or yield curve is for marketable Government securities issued by the Indian Government. Table 16.1 presents a comparative table of yield of 10 year Government (Treasury) Bond across various countries.

The record of interest rates, when viewed according to term to maturity, suggests that at times short term rates are above long term rates, and vice versa. We want to explain the possible determinants of such changes in the term structure of interest rates. Figure 16.1 shows the yields of the Government of India 10 year Bonds for the period ranging from 2000 to 2014.

As can be seen in the above Figure 16.1 the yields fell from 2000-2004, thereafter increased from 2004 to 2008 and remained range bound (or flat) from 2008 to 2012. Financial Theory states that any long term interest rate is the expected value of future short–term interest rates (this is called the *Expectations Theory*[4]). An investor

[3] Off the run are all Treasury bonds and notes issued before the most recently issued bond or note of a particular maturity. These are the opposite of on-the-run treasuries.

[4] The expectations theory was first propounded in 1896 by Yale University Economists, Irving Fischer and later developed by Hicks (1946) and popularized by Shiller (1990).

TABLE 16.1 Comparative table of yield of 10 year government (Treasury) bond across countries

Country	Government Bond 10Y	Reference	Previous	Highest	Lowest	Unit	Gain/Loss from Previous day
Australia	2.93	14-Dec	3.1	16.4	2.69	percent	[+]
Brazil	12.63	14-Dec	11.82	17.91	9.11	percent	[+]
Canada	1.76	14-Dec	1.84	12.45	1.58	percent	[+]
China	3.8	14-Dec	3.55	4.85	2.52	percent	[+]
Euro Area	0.17	14-Dec	0.18	2.57	0.17	percent	[+]
France	0.89	14-Dec	0.97	11.84	0.89	percent	[+]
Germany	0.62	14-Dec	0.7	10.8	0.62	percent	[+]
India	7.83	14-Dec	8.08	14.76	4.96	percent	[+]
Indonesia	8.08	14-Dec	7.69	20.76	4.99	percent	[+]
Italy	2.06	14-Dec	2.02	15.29	1.94	percent	[+]
Japan	0.4	14-Dec	0.42	7.92	0.39	percent	[+]
Mexico	6.11	14-Dec	5.77	12.07	4.42	percent	[+]
Netherlands	0.75	14-Dec	0.82	9.31	0.75	percent	[+]
Russia	12.99	14-Dec	10.61	16.33	6.26	percent	[+]
South Korea	2.69	14-Dec	2.58	7.91	2.58	percent	[+]
Spain	1.88	14-Dec	1.9	14.03	1.79	percent	[+]
Switzerland	0.26	14-Dec	0.3	5.63	0.26	percent	[+]
Turkey	8.23	14-Dec	7.6	11.29	6.02	percent	[+]
United Kingdom	1.8	14-Dec	1.92	16.09	1.38	percent	[+]
United States	2.17	14-Dec	2.19	15.82	1.4	percent	[+]

Source: Trading Economics. http://www.tradingeconomics.com/india/government-bond-yield, accessed on December 15, 2014.

makes a choice between buying a long-term instrument and buying a short-term instrument, and rolling it over based on what he thinks rates will be at the time of reinvestment. For example, the yield on a 30-year bond should thus be the expected average yield of the next 120 three-month treasury bills. Our next section explains the reasons for different types of yield curves.

Figure 16.1 Shape of Yield Curve of Government of India 10 year bond for the period between 2000 and 2014.

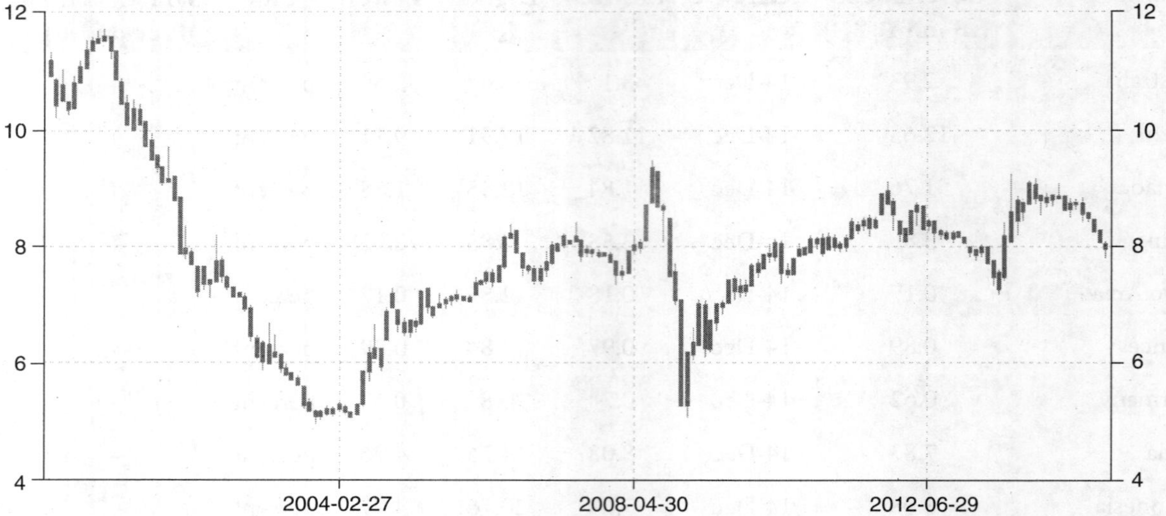

Source: http://www.tradingeconomics.com/india/government-bond-yield, accessed on December 17, 2014.

Marketview 16.1 NSE Zero Coupon Yield Curve (ZCYC)

In its ongoing endeavor to innovate in the Indian debt market segment, National stock exchange of India Limited (NSEIL) has modeled a 'Zero Coupon Yield Curve' (ZCYC) which enables valuation of sovereign securities of varying maturities to create uniform valuation standards in the market. The ZCYC was developed to suit the requirements of the banking industry, financial institutions, mutual funds and insurance companies, who have considerable investment in sovereign papers. NSE ZCYC facilitates in improving Asset Liability Management of Institutions with realistic valuations of portfolio of sovereign papers.

The 'zero coupon yield curve' (ZCYC in short) is based on the basic premise of 'time value of money' – that a given amount of money due today has a value different from the same amount due at a future point of time. An individual ready to part with his money today has to be compensated in terms of a higher amount due in future. This compensation is the interest component. The rate of interest to be paid would vary with the time period that elapses between when the principal amount is being foregone and the time at which the amount is repaid. Hence, at any point one finds different spot rates of interest associated with different terms to maturity. The term structure of interest rates, or ZCYC, is the set of such spot interest rates. Thus the ZCYC involves estimation of the appropriate set of interest rates that goes into deriving the present value relation. This is done by specifying a functional form of the interest rate-maturity relation/discount function/forward rate function. The present form of the ZCYC uses the 'Nelson-Siegel' (NS) functional form [Nelson & Siegel (1987)] using data on secondary market trades in Government securities reported on the Wholesale Debt Market segment of the National Stock Exchange (NSE-WDM).

The ZCYC represents the relationship between interest rate and maturity for a set of 'similar' securities, as on a given date. To derive the 'true' term structure, one needs to have a data of bonds that are identical in every respect excluding term to maturity. Government securities do, in practice, differ in coupon rates; nevertheless, these come closest to satisfying the requirement, and hence most empirical studies have concentrated on this segment of the securities market.

Once an estimate of the term structure based on default-free government securities is acquired, it can be used to price all non-sovereign fixed income instruments after adjusting them for a suitable credit spread. The ZCYC are used to value government securities that do not trade on a given day, or to provide default-free valuations for corporate bonds. An estimate of the ZCYC at regular intervals over a period of time provides us with a time-series of the interest rate structure in the economy, which can be used to analyze the extent of impact of monetary policy. This also forms an input for Value at Risk systems for fixed income systems and portfolios.

Source: http://www.nseindia.com/products/content/debt/wdm/nse_zcyc.htm, accessed on December 17, 2014.

Determinants of the Shape of the Term Structure

If we plot the term structure and the yield-to-maturity, at successive maturities against time—what will it look like? Figure 16.2 depicts the four shapes that have appeared with some frequency over time. *Panel A* depicts an "***Upward sloping yield curve***," i.e., yield rises steadily as maturity increases. Generally most yield curves follow this "***normal shape***." *Panel B* depicts a "***Downward-sloping or inverted yield curve***," where yields decline as maturity increases. *Panel C* depicts a "***Flat yield curve***," in which there is little difference between short-term and long-term rates for bonds of the same credit quality. This type of yield curve is often seen during transitions between normal and inverted curves. *Panel D* depicts a unique shape of the yield curve, *called the* "***Humped shaped yield curve***." This curve is often referred to as a bell-shaped curve because of its shape. This curve indicates that mid-term rates of bonds exceed both long and short term rates. Generally, a humped yield curve cannot be explained by market theories and is a transitional state.

Nevertheless, the real shape of the yield curve depends on the economic situation, government's fiscal and monetary policies, expectation about future rates, inflation, foreign exchange rates, foreign capital inflows and outflows. The term structure of interest rates has three characteristics: Firstly, the change in yields of different term bonds tends to move in the same direction. Secondly, the yields on short-term bonds are more volatile than long-term bonds and lastly, the yields on long-term bonds tend to be higher than short-term bonds. What determines the term structure of interest rates? This question has long puzzled academicians and practitioners. Four principal explanations have been offered: the expectations theory, the liquidity preference theory, the preferred habitat theory and the market segmentation theory.

The expectations theory

According to the pure form of expectations theory, the forward rates exclusively represent expectation about future rates. Thus the entire term structure at a given time reflects the market's current expectations of future short-term rates. Given this theory, a rising term structure, as shown in Panel *A* of Figure 16.2, must indicate that

Figure 16.2 Yield curve shapes.

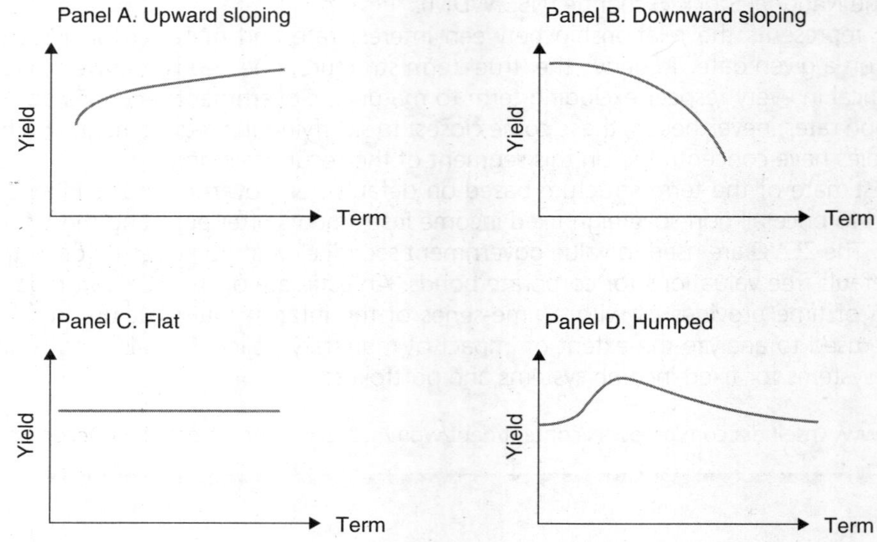

the market anticipates short-term rates to rise throughout the future. Similarly, a flat yield curve anticipates that future short-term rates will be mostly constant, and a downward sloping yield curve must reflect an expectation that future short-term rates will decline gradually.

Let us analyze the nature of an upward sloping yield curve by investigating the behavior of various market participants, when there is an expectation of a rising short-term future rate. Initially let us assume flat term structure. Now there is favorable economic news which leads market participants to expect interest rates to rise.

1. **Investors** interested in a long-term bond investment would not want to buy long-term bonds as they would expect the yield structure to rise in the future. This would result in a price decline for the bonds and a capital loss on the long-term bonds purchased (due to lack of demand in the market). Instead, these investors would want to invest in short-term debt obligations until the rise in yield has actually taken place, thereby enabling them to reinvest their funds at the higher yield.
2. **Speculators** would anticipate a decline in the price of long-term bonds with future rising rates. Therefore would want to sell any long-term bonds they currently own and possibly "short sell" some they do not own. As interest rates rise as expected, the price of longer-term bonds will fall. Because the speculator sold these bonds short and can purchase them at a lower price to cover the short sale, a profit can be earned by them. The proceeds received from the selling of long-term debt issues or the shorting of longer-term bonds may be invested in short-term debt obligations.
3. **Borrowers** wishing to acquire long-term funds would be dragged toward borrowing now, as they expect that borrowing at a later time would be more expensive.

All these responses would tend either to lower the net demand for or to increase the supply of long-maturity bonds, and these two responses would increase demand for short-term debt obligations. This would require a rise in long-term yields in relation to short-term yields; that is, these actions by investors, speculators, and borrowers would tilt the term structure upward until it is consistent with expectations of higher future interest rates, vice versa, an unexpected event leading to the expectation of lower future rates will result in a downward-sloping yield curve. According to this theory, the current term structure of interest rates is determined by the consensus forecast of future interest rates. To understand this hypothesis, let us consider Figure 16.3.

Figure 16.3 Representation of forward rates and short future rates.

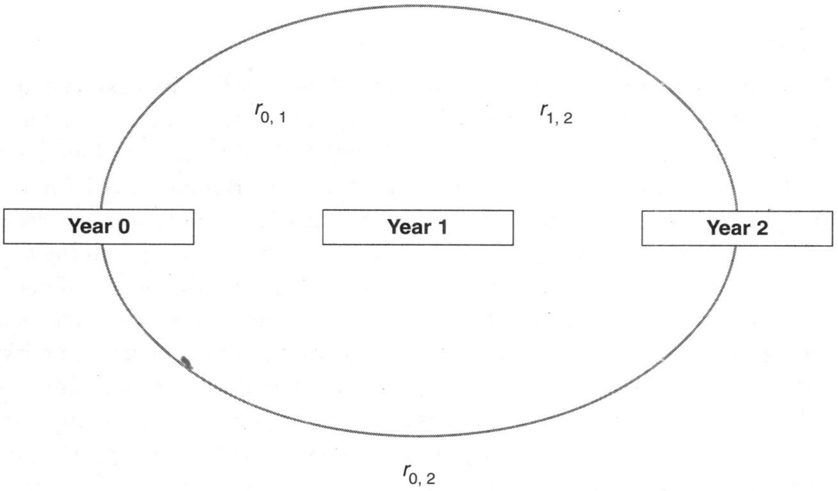

As represented in Figure 16.3, at time 0 there is short-term interest rate $r_{0,1}$ for money borrowed in year 0 and repayable in year 1. There is also a long-term interest rate $r_{0,2}$ for money borrowed in year 0 for repayment in year 2. Linking these two rates is an unobservable "***forward rate***" rate $r_{1,2}$ that is expected to prevail in year 1 for money to be borrowed then for repayment in year 2. In terms of this forward rate, one can write the arbitrage condition as:

$$(1+r_{0,2})^2=(1+r_{0,1})\times(1+r_{1,2})$$

This equation states that the total money (i.e., principal plus interest) repaid in year 2 should be the same even when the money is borrowed long-term at $r_{0,1}$ and then "rolled-over" in year 1 at the then prevailing short-term rate $r_{1,2}$. This equation assumes that the investor must be indifferent between these two alternatives.

For example, if the one year interest rate is 15% ($r_{0,1}=15\%$) but it is expected to go up to 20% at the end of one year ($r_{1,2}=20\%$), then the identity states that:

$$(1+r_{0,2})^2=(1+0.15)\times(1+0.20)=1.38$$

So deriving the two–year rate ..... $r_{0,2}$ will be 17.5%

On the other hand, if the short term rate had been expected to go down to 10%, then we would have had:

$$(1+r_{0,2})^2=(1+0.15)\times(1+0.10)=1.265$$

So the two-year rate $r_{0,2}$ in this case would have been 12.47%.

That is, an investor will opt for one year security now only when he is certain that the interest rate after one year is greater than the interest rate on two year security. In case the investor feels that the interest rate on one year security is going to decline after one year, he will opt for a two year instrument. An upward sloping yield curve, according to this theory indicates that the investors expect the interest rates to rise, a flat yield curve indicates that the investor expects the rates to remain at the same level and downward sloping curve indicates that the investor expects a fall in the interest rates.

The liquidity preference theory

The drawback of the expectations theory is that it does not account for the risks associated with investing in bonds. The return over any investment period would be dependent on the maturity of the instrument initially acquired and also on the time at which the investor need to liquidate the instrument. Nonetheless, we know that there is indeed risk in holding a long-term bond for one period, and that risk increases with the bond's maturity because maturity and price volatility are directly related. Given this uncertainty, and the reasonable consideration that investors typically do not like uncertainty, some economists have suggested the Liquidity Premium Theory. This theory states that investors will hold longer-term maturities if they are offered a long-term rate higher than the average of expected future rates by a risk premium and this risk premium related to the term to maturity positively (***Keynes 1930, 1936; Hicks 1939***). According to this theory, the forward rates should reflect both future interest-rate expectations and a liquidity premium (called as the liquidity risk premium), and the premium should be higher for longer maturities. Thus an upward-sloping yield curve may reflect expectations that future interest rates either will rise or will be flat (or even fall) but with a liquidity premium increasing fast enough with maturity so as to produce an upward-sloping yield curve. According to this theory:

$$\text{Forward Interest Rates} = \text{Expected future short} - \text{Term interest rates} + \text{Liquidity Premium}$$

The preferred habitat theory

Another theory, known as the *preferred-habitat theory,* adopts that the term structure reflects the expectation of the future path of interest rates and liquidity risk premium. However, this theory rejects the claim that the risk premium must rise uniformly with maturity[5]. Advocates of the preferred-habitat theory say that the latter conclusion could be accepted if all investors intend to liquidate their investment at the shortest possible date and all borrowers are anxious to borrow long. However, institutions have holding periods dictated by the nature of their liabilities.

If the demand and supply of funds in a given maturity range do not match, some lenders and borrowers would be persuaded to shift to maturities showing the opposite imbalances. However, they will need to be compensated by an appropriate risk premium that reflects the extent of aversion to either price or reinvestment risk.

Thus this theory proposes that the shape of the yield curve is determined by both expectations of future interest rates and a risk premium, positive or negative, to induce market participants to shift out of their preferred habitat. Clearly, according to this theory, yield curves sloping up, down, flat or humped are all possible.

---

[5] This theory was proposed by John Culbertson (1957) and Franco Modigliani and Richard Sutch (1966). According to the preferred-habitat view, there are investor clienteles with preferences for specific maturities, and the interest rate for a given maturity is influenced by the demand of the corresponding clientele and the supply of bonds with that maturity.

The market-segmentation theory

The *market-segmentation theory* identifies that investors may have their preferred habitats dictated by the nature of their liabilities. This theory also suggests that the major reason for the shape of the yield curve lies in asset-liability management constraints regulated or self-imposed upon government and corporate agencies issuing bonds and by creditors in case of individual investors. This restricts the lending (and financing) ability of individuals and corporates to specific maturity sectors[6]. However, the market-segmentation theory differs from the preferred-habitat theory in that it assumes that neither investors nor borrowers are willing to shift from one maturity sector to another to take advantage of opportunities arising from differences between expectations and forward rates. Thus, for the segmentation theory, the shape of the yield curve is determined by the supply of and demand for securities within each maturity sector.

Interest Rate Risk

In the previous chapter, we have seen an inverse relationship that exists between bond prices and yields. As interest rates rise (and fall), bond holders experience capital losses (and gains). These fluctuations in bond prices at the time of sale (in case of bond trading; not if bonds are kept till maturity), makes fixed income investments risky. This interest rate risk arises in spite of the fact that even the coupon and principal payments are guaranteed, as in the case of government securities.

Interest Rate sensitivity of Coupon Bonds

The sensitivity of bond prices to changes in market interest rates (yields) is obviously a great concern to investors. The same is being explained with the help of Numerical Example 2:

Numerical Example 2

Let us consider four bonds exhibiting the following properties:

Bond	Coupon	Maturity	Initial YTM
A	12%	5 years	10%
B	12%	25 years	10%
C	6%	25 years	10%
D	6%	25 years	8%

[6] This theory was suggested in J.M. Culbertson, "The Term Structure of Interest Rates," *Quarterly Journal of Economics*, November 1957, 489–504.

The four bonds A, B, C and D are different in terms of coupon rates, initial yield to maturity and time to maturity. The four bonds depict that bond prices decrease when yields rise and this relationship of bond prices with yield is convex, meaning that decrease in yields has bigger impacts on price than increase in yields of equal magnitude. This relationship which can also be viewed graphically, as in Figure 16.4, can be summarized as follows:

Figure 16.4 Interest rate sensitivity of bonds.

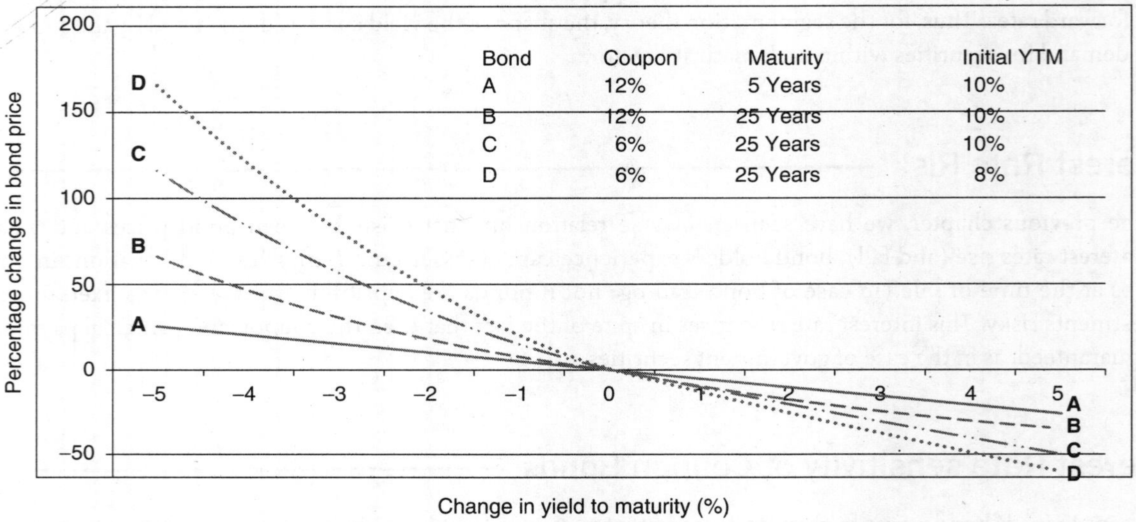

1. Bond prices and yields are inversely related as yields increase, bond prices fall; as yields fall, bond prices rise. However this relationship is not linear. We will discuss about this in further section of this chapter under the section "***Convexity.***"

   When we compare the interest rate sensitivity of bonds A and B, which are identical except for maturity, it can be seen from Figure 16.4 that bond B, which has a longer maturity than bond A, exhibits greater sensitivity to interest rate changes.
2. Prices of long-term bonds tend to be more sensitive to interest rate changes than prices of short-term bonds.

   This property is not astounding. For example, if rates increase, the bond is less valuable as its cash flows are discounted at a new higher rate now. The impact of the higher discount rate will be greater as the rate is applied to more distant cash flows.

   We observe that while bond B has five times the maturity of bond A, it has less than five times the interest rate sensitivity. Although interest rate sensitivity seems to increase with maturity, but its increase is less proportionate as bond maturity increases.
3. The sensitivity of bond prices to changes in yield increases at a decreasing rate as maturity increases. In other words, interest rate risk is asymmetrically proportional to bond maturity.

   Consider bonds B and C, which are identical in all respects except for coupon rate. The lower coupon bond exhibits greater sensitivity to changes in interest rates. This is a general property of bond prices.
4. Interest rate risk is inversely related to the bond's coupon rate. Prices of low coupon bonds are more sensitive to changes in interest rates than prices of high coupon bonds.

Finally, bonds C and D are identical except for the yield to maturity at which the bonds currently sell. Yet bond C, with a higher yield to maturity, is less sensitive to changes in yields.

5. The sensitivity of a bond's price to a change in its yield is inversely related to the yield to maturity at which the bond is currently selling.

These properties exhibiting the impact of interest rate on bond prices were described by ***Malkiel*** in his seminal paper in 1962[7]. The last property was popularized by ***Homer and Liebowitz*** in their popular book "***Inside The Yield Book,***" published first in 1972[8].

Interest Rate Sensitivity of Zero Coupon Bonds

Let us now look at a zero-coupon bonds. The results are shown in Numerical Example 3. Notice that for each maturity, the price of the zero-coupon bond cascades by a greater amount relatively than the price of the 9% coupon bond. As we know that the long term bonds are more susceptible to interest rate movements than short term bonds, this observation implies that a zero-coupon bond represents a longer term bond than an equal time to maturity in comparison to a coupon bond (of the same maturity).

Numerical Example 3

Consider two bonds A (coupon paying bond) and B (zero coupon bond). Let us find the prices of these two bonds at varying maturity across two YTMs.

Prices of Bond A – 9% coupon bond paying coupons annually

Yield to Maturity	Time =1 year	Time = 5 years	Time = 10 years
9%	1000	1000	1000
10%	990.90	962.09	938.55
Fall in Price (%)	0.91	3.79	6.14

Prices of Bond B – zero – coupon bond using annual compounding

Yield to Maturity	Time = 1 year	Time = 5 years	Time = 10 years
9%	917.43	649.93	422.41
10%	909.09	620.92	385.54
Fall in Price (%)	0.91	4.46	8.73

[7] B.G. Malkiel, "Expectations, Bond prices, and the Term Structure of Interest rates," *Quarterly Journal of Economics*, 1962, Vol. 76, 197–218.

[8] S. Homer and M.L. Liebowitz, "Inside the Yield book: New Tools for Bond Market Strategy," Englewood Cliffs, NJ: Prentice Hall, 1972.

It can be seen from Numerical Example 3, that for each maturity, the price of the zero-coupon bond falls by a greater proportional percentage than the coupon paying bond. This point puts forward the concept of the effective maturity of a bond. We can make this concept of effective maturity mathematically accurate. To start, note that the times to maturity of the two bonds in this example are not perfect measures of the long- or short-term nature of the bonds. The 10-year 9% bond in this example is not a perfect measure of the long- or short-term nature of the bonds. The coupon paying bond makes regular payments, each having its own maturity. Hence a coupon bond can be viewed as a portfolio of coupon payments. The effective maturity of the bond is therefore some sort of average of the maturities of all the cash flows paid out by the bond. The zero coupon bond, by contrast, makes only one payment at maturity. Its time to maturity is, therefore, a well-defined concept.

A bond with higher coupon carries a higher portion of value tied to its coupons rather than the ultimate payment of the par value. Hence this "portfolio of coupons" is more heavily weighted towards the earlier maturity payment, which gives it a lower "effective maturity." Similarly, the price sensitivity of a bond falls with yield to maturity. A higher yield reduces the present value of all the bond's payments, but more so for distant payments. Therefore, at a higher yield, a higher portion of the bond's value is due to its earlier payments, which contains a lower effective maturity and interest rate sensitivity. Hence the overall sensitivity of the bond price to changes in yield is lesser than that of coupon paying bonds.

Duration

We saw in the previous section that, maturity is a major determinant of interest rate risk. However, maturity alone is not sufficient to measure interest rate sensitivity. For example, bonds B and C in Figure 16.4, although they have the same maturity, the higher-coupon bond is less price sensitive to interest rate changes. Obviously, we need to know more than a bond's maturity to quantify its interest rate risk. To deal with the vagueness in the concept of the "maturity" of a coupon bond, as it makes many payments; one needs an exact measure of the average maturity of the bond's promised cash flows. This would serve as a valuable estimate of the effective maturity of the bond. Bond portfolio managers across the globe use this estimate as a guide to the sensitivity of a bond to interest rate changes. This estimate is called the ***Duration*** of the bond. Frederick Macaulay termed this effective maturity concept as the duration of the bond[9]. Macaulay's Duration equals weighted average of the times to each coupon or principal payment made by the bond. The weight linked with each payment time is clearly related to the "importance" or weightage of that payment to the value (price) of the bond at issuance. The weight applied to each payment time is the proportion of the total value of the bond accounted for by that payment, which is nothing but the present value of each bond payment divided by the bond price.

The weight W_t, associated with each cash flow (denoted as CF_t) arising at the tth period is defined as:

$$W_t = \frac{CF_t \div (1+y)^t}{\text{Bond price}}$$

[9] F. Macaulay, "Some theoretical Problems suggested by the movements of Interest Rates, Bond yields, and Stock Prices in the United States since 1856," New York: National Bureau of Economic Research, 1938, 24–53.

where y is the bond's yield to maturity and t is time period when the cash flow is due from the bond. The numerator on the right hand side of the equation is the present value of the cash flow occurring at time t, while the denominator is the value of all the payments forthcoming from the bond. These weights should sum to 1.0 as the sum of the present value of the cash flows discounted at yield to maturity equals bond price.

Using this value to calculate the weighted average of the times until the receipt of each of the bond's payments, we obtain Macaulay's duration formula:

$$D=\sum_{t=1}^{T} t\times W_t$$

or

$$D=\frac{\Sigma[(t\times CF_t)\div(1+y)^t]}{\Sigma[(CF_t)]\div(1+y)^t}$$

or

in terms of interest factor notations

$$\text{Duration}=\frac{[\{(PVIF_{y,1})\times(CF_1)\times 1\}+\{(PVIF_{y,2})\times(CF_2)\times 2\}+\cdots\{(PVIF_{y,t})\times(CF_t)\times t\}]}{\text{Bond price}}$$

For calculating the PV of the cash flow, the YTM of the bond is used as the discount rate. The duration of a bond can also be interpreted as in effect, it represents the weighted average life of a bond, consider the size and timing of each cash flow.

What do you think would be the duration of a zero coupon bond?

Numerical Example 4

Calculate the duration for the following bond:

Face Value:	₹200
Coupon Rate:	15% annually
Yrs. to maturity:	6
Redemption Value (same as Par Value):	₹100
Current Market Price:	₹179
YTM	18%

What do you infer from the answer?

Solution:

Calculation of Duration

(1) Year	(2) Cash flow	(3) PV at 18%	(4) Proportion of bond's value (value at col 3 ÷ $\sum$ of col 3)	(5) Proportion of bond's value × time (col 4 × col 1)
1	30	25.42	0.1420	0.1420
2	30	21.55	0.1204	0.2407
3	30	18.26	0.1020	0.3060
4	30	15.47	0.0864	0.3457
5	30	13.11	0.0733	0.3662
6	230	85.19	0.4756	2.856
Summation		179.01		**4.256**

Duration = 4.256 years

This is the point in years, where the weighted cash flow payments before this point exactly balances all the weighted cash flows after this point. This point can be understood where the fulcrum gets balanced.

Spreadsheet Application 1 Calculation of duration using Microsoft Excel spreadsheets has been illustrated in case of a 30-year coupon paying bond with annual coupons being paid at 10% and an initial yield to maturity of 10%.

Steps	Particulars	Value	Excel syntax used
Step 1	Face Value	1000	
	Coupon payable per annum	10%	
	Years to maturity	30	
	Redemption value	1000	
	Current market price	1000	
	Settlement date (can be any date, if the date of purchase is not certain)	1/1/2000	
	Maturity	1/1/2030	
	Frequency of coupon payment in a year	1	
	Basis (bond market instrument has day count convention of 4- Recall: discussed in Chapter 15)	4	

(Continued)

Continued

Steps	Particulars	Value	Excel syntax used
Step 2	Yield	0.10000	**"= YIELD(Settlement date, Maturity date, coupon rate, price of bond, redemption value, frequency of coupon payment, basis)"**
Step 3	Duration	9.177	**"= Duration(Settlement date, maturity date, coupon amount, yield, frequency of coupon payment, basis)"**

Spreadsheet Output is as under:

	A	B
1	**Particulars**	**Value**
2	Face Value	1000
3	Coupon payable per annum	10%
4	Coupon amount	100
5	Years to Maturity	30
6	Redemption Value	1000
7	Current market price	1000
8	Settlement Date (can be any date, if the date of purchase is not certain)	1/1/2000
9	Maturity	1/1/2030
10	Frequency of coupon payment in a year	1
11	Basis	4
12	Yield	0.1
13	Duration	9.177

	A	B
1	**Particulars**	**Value**
2	Face Value	1000
3	Coupon payable per annum	10%
4	Coupon amount	100
5	Years to Maturity	30
6	Redemption Value	1000
7	Current market price	1000
8	Settlement Date (can be any date, if the date of purchase is not certain)	1/1/2000
9	Maturity	1/1/2030
10	Frequency of coupon payment in a year	1
11	Basis	4
12	Yield	0.1
13	Duration	=DURATION(B8,B9,B4,B12,B10,4)

Duration is a key concept in fixed-income portfolio management for at least three reasons: First, as we have noted, it is a simple guide of the effective average maturity of the portfolio. Secondly, it turns out to be an essential tool in insulating bond portfolios from interest rate risk (This is called as immunization, discussed later in this chapter). The application is further seen in Numerical Example 3, under the sub topic of immunization. Thirdly, duration is a measure of the interest rate sensitivity of a portfolio, which is discussed below.

Recall that interest rate risk has two components:

1. Price risk (that portion of interest rate risk which has a negative impact on the price of a bond).
2. Reinvestment risk (that portion of interest rate risk which has a positive impact on the price of a bond).

Since they are of opposite signs, eliminating this risk is a must. Eliminating these two types of risks from a bond portfolio is referred to as ***immunization***.

We have seen that long-term bonds are more sensitive to interest rate movements than short-term bonds. The duration measure enables us to quantify this relationship. Specifically, it can be shown that when interest rates change, the proportional change in a bond's price can be related to the change in its yield to maturity, y, according to the rule.

$$\frac{\Delta P}{P} = -D \times \left[\frac{\Delta(1+y)}{1+y}\right]$$

The proportional price change equals the proportional change in 1 plus the bond's yield times the bond's duration. This is nothing but the first derivative of the change in the price of the bond with respect to its yield to maturity. Practitioners commonly use the above equation in a slightly different form. They define it as the ***Modified Duration*** (*MD*) of the bond:

$$MD = \frac{D}{(1+y)}$$

Note that $\Delta(1+y) = \Delta y$ hence,

$$\frac{\Delta P}{P} = -D \times \Delta y$$

The percentage change in bond price is just the product of modified duration and the change in the bond's yield to maturity. Because the percentage change in the bond price is proportional to modified duration, this modified duration is a natural measure of the bond's exposure to changes in interest rates. Let us look at Numerical Example 5, which calculates the change in bond prices due to changes in yields as explained by the Modified Duration of the bond.

Numerical Example 5

A bond issued at ₹500 matures in six years and pays a coupon of 10% annually. Its market price is ₹422.23. The YTM on this bond is 14%. If the YTM increases by 2%; calculate the percentage change in price of the bond.

Hint to Solution:

First we will calculate the duration, then the modified duration and finally find the % change in the price of a bond if YTM increases by 2%.

Solution:

The calculation of the duration and the MD is shown:

Period	Cash flow	PVIF at 14%	PV of cash flow	Weighted PV of cash flow
Col. No. (1)	Col. No. (2)	Col. No. (3)	Col. No. (4) = Col. No. (2) × Col. No. (3)	Col. No. (5) = Col. No. (4) × Col. No. (1)
1	50	0.877193	43.85965	43.85965
2	50	0.769468	38.47338	76.94675
3	50	0.674972	33.74858	101.2457
4	50	0.59208	29.60401	118.4161

(*Continued*)

Continued

Period	Cash flow	PVIF at 14%	PV of cash flow	Weighted PV of cash flow
5	50	0.519369	25.96843	129.8422
6	550	0.455587	250.5726	1503.436
Sum			422.23	1973.75

$$\textit{Duration}\ (D) = 1973.75 \div 422.23$$

$$= 4.67 \text{ years.}$$

$$\textit{Modified Duration}\,(MD) = \frac{D}{1+\dfrac{r}{p}}$$

$$= \frac{4.67}{1+\dfrac{0.14}{1}}$$

$$= 4.1 \text{ years}$$

Given change in YTM = 2%

Price change in bond = – MD × change in YTM × Price of bond

= −4.1 × 2% × 422.23

= – ₹34.62

That is, the price of the bond falls by ₹34.62 to ₹387.61 from ₹422.23.

Determinants of Duration

Malkiel's bond pricing relationships, which were discussed earlier in the chapter, reveals the determinants of interest rate sensitivity. Duration allows bond portfolio managers to compute that sensitivity, which enhances their ability to devise investment strategies. For example, if a bond portfolio manager wishes to speculate on interest rates, duration confirms the strength of his estimation. Conversely, if the manager wishes to remain on the fence on future market interest rates, he can simply match the interest rate sensitivity of a chosen bond market-index. Hence duration allows portfolio managers to measure that sensitivity and replicate it in the portfolio under his management. For these reasons, it happens to be crucial to understand the determinants of duration. In this section the rules pertaining to duration are presented. Figure 16.4 graphically supports the set of laws pertaining to duration.

Rule I: *The duration of a zero coupon bond equals it's time to maturity*

It has been experienced that a coupon paying bond will always have a lower duration than a no coupon or zero or deep discount bond, with equal maturity. This is so because coupons paid early in the life of the bond lowers the bond's weighted average time until its maturity.

Rule II: *Holding maturity constant, a bond's duration is lower when the coupon rate is higher*

This property is a simple extension of the previous property. It can be attributed to the impact of early coupon payments on the weighted average maturity of a bond's payment. The higher the coupon, the higher is the weight of the early payments and the lower is the weighted average maturity of the payments. In case of higher coupon paying bonds, a higher fraction of the total value of the bond is tied up in its earlier coupon payments, whose values are relatively insensitive to yields. Whereas, the later coupon payments and the repayment of par value are more sensitive to yield change sensitivity.

Let us compare the bonds plotted in Figure 16.4.

Rule III: *Holding the coupon rate constant, a bond's duration generally increases with its time to maturity*

This property is reasonably instinctive as time period is involved while calculating duration of a bond. It can be observed from Figure 16.4 that for a zero-coupon bond, maturity and duration are equal. However, for coupon bonds, duration increases at a lesser pace with a year's increase in maturity. We further see in Figure 16.4 that the two 12% coupon bonds have different durations when they sell at different yields to maturity. The lower yield bond has a longer duration. This so happens, because at lower yields the more distant payments made by the bond have relatively greater present values (due to a higher denominator effect) which account for a greater share of the bond's total value. Thus in the weighted average calculation of duration, these distant payments receive greater weights, thereby resulting in a higher duration measure.

Rule IV: *Holding all other factors constant, duration of a coupon paying bond varies inversely with its bond's yield to maturity.*

A higher *YTM* reduces the present value of the entire bond's payments (due to a lower denominator effect), thereby reducing the value of more distant payments by a greater proportional amount. As a result, at higher yields, a higher fraction of the total value of the bond lies in its earlier payments, thereby reducing effective maturity.

Rule V: *The duration of level (equal sized cash flows) perpetuity is approximately equal to:*

$$\frac{1+\text{yield}}{\text{yield}}$$

Perpetuity is an annuity of cash flows from a fixed income security, which begins on a fixed date and continues indefinitely. Fixed coupon payments received on irredeemable bonds and debentures are examples of perpetuity. Although, the series of cash flows is indefinite but its duration is finite. The formula for the duration of perpetuity is especially simple as there is no principal repayment. For example, at an eight percent yield, the duration of a perpetuity that pays a fixed coupon, say ₹100 per year forever will be equal to:

$$\frac{1.08}{.08}=13.5$$

Hence we see from this rule that maturity and duration can be very different. While the maturity of perpetuity is infinite, the duration of the bond at an 8 percent yield is only 13.5 years.

Rule VI: *The duration of a level annuity approximately is:*

$$\text{Duration of level annuity} = \frac{1+y}{y} - \frac{\text{Number of payments}}{[(1+\text{yield})^{\text{Number of payments}}]-1}$$

The second type of cash flow stream that lends itself to a quick formula is an annuity. Annuity provides a stream of equal cash flows for a given number of periods. But unlike perpetuity, payments stop after T periods.

For example, a 20-year annual annuity with a yield of 10 percent will have duration of:

$$\frac{1.10}{0.10} - \frac{20}{[1.10^{20}]-1} = 7.51 \text{ years}$$

Rule VII: *The duration of a coupon bond approximately is:*

$$\frac{1+y}{y} - \frac{(1+y)+T(c-y)}{c[(1+y)^{T}-1]+y}$$

Where y is the bond's yield per payment period, T is the number of payment periods and c is the coupon rate per payment period.

Rule VIII: *The duration for a bond portfolio is equal to the weighted average of the duration for each type of bond in the portfolio:*

$$\textbf{Portfolio Duration} = W_1 \times D_1 + W_2 \times D_2 + \ldots + W_K \times D_K$$

where

w_i = Market value of bond i/market value of portfolio
D_i = Duration of bond i
K = Number of bonds in portfolio

To better measure the interest rate exposure of a portfolio, it is better to measure the contribution of the issue or sector duration to the portfolio duration rather than just measuring the market value of that issue or sector to the value of the portfolio:

$$\textbf{Portfolio Duration Contribution} = \textbf{Weight of Issue in Portfolio} \times \textbf{Duration of Issue}$$

Convexity

Duration is a key instrument to assess the interest rate sensitivity in fixed income portfolio management. The formula of modified duration states that the percentage change in prices of bonds is directly and linearly proportional to the change in yield. However, this is only an approximation. The actual bond pricing relationships discussed earlier as displayed in Figure 16.5 shows that the actual relationship is curvilinear. The duration rule provides an approximation which is fairly close, for small changes in the yield. However, as the yield change becomes bigger, the approximation becomes poorer. Figure 16.4 demonstrates this point. It presents the percentage change in bond price in response to a change in the bond's yield to maturity in a linear fashion.

To illustrate this point consider a 30-year maturity, 10 percentage coupon paying bond, selling at an initial yield to maturity of 10 percent. The straight line is the percentage price change predicted by the duration rule. The slope of the straight line is calculated by taking its derivative with respect to its initial yield to maturity. It is nothing but the modified duration of the bond. The modified duration of this bond is 9.42 years. Figure 16.5 shows that the straight line plot of $-D \times \Delta y = -9.42 \times \Delta y$ as well as the curved line reflecting the actual relationship between yield change and the price change. It can be seen in Figure 16.5 that the straight line (the duration approximation) always understates the value of the bond and; it undervalues the increase in bond prices when the yield falls and it overrates the decline in price when the yield rises. This is due to the curvature of the true price–yield relationship. Curves with shapes such as that of the price-yield relationship are said to be convex, and the curvature of the price-yield curve is called the ***CONVEXITY*** of the bond.

Figure 16.5 Bond price convexity for 8% bond with 30 Yrs. Maturity at initial YTM of 8%.

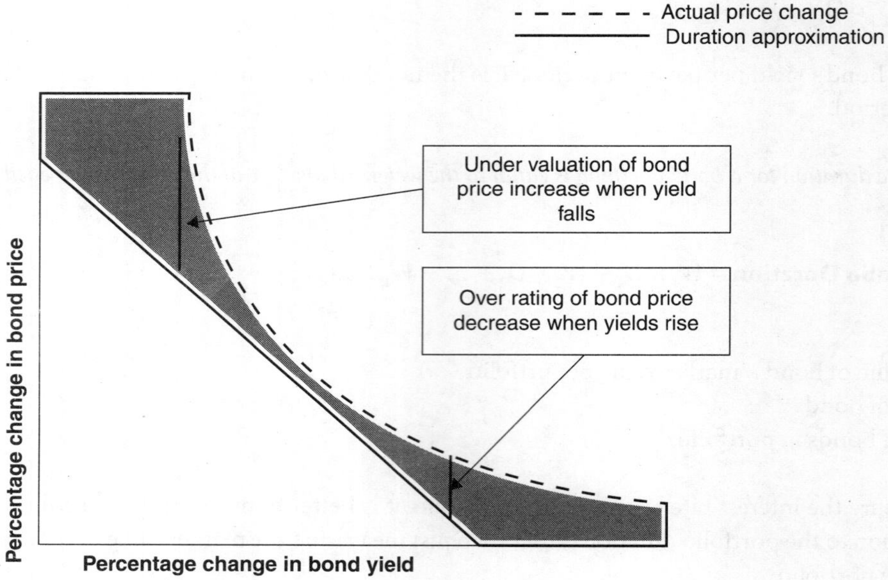

Convexity can be quantified as the rate of change of the slope of the price-yield curve, as a fraction of the bond price. Bonds with higher convexity, exhibit higher curvature in their price yield relationship.

The formula for computing convexity is given as follows:

$$\text{Convexity} = \sum_{t=1}^{n} \frac{\dfrac{(t^2 + t) \times c_t}{(1+y)^t}}{P \times (1+y)^2}$$

Where c_t is the cash flow at the end of year t, y is the yield to maturity and P is the price of the bond.

By using both duration and convexity we can estimate more accurately the effect of interest rate change on bond price changes. Adding the effect of convexity to the formulae of change in bond price estimation:

$$\% \text{ change in bond price} = -\text{Modified Duration} \times \% \text{ yield change} + \frac{1}{2} \times \text{convexity} \times (\text{yield change})^2$$

Numerical Example 6

Consider the same bond as depicted in Figure 16.5 and discussed in Spreadsheet application 1. Its term to maturity is 30 years, coupon is paid at 10% and Yield to maturity of the bond is also 10%. As modified duration of the bond works out to be 9.42 years, a change in yield from 10% to 11% would result in price decline of the bond as calculated below:

$$\% \text{ change in bond price} = -\text{Modified Duration} \times \% \text{ yield change}$$

$$\% \text{ change in bond price} = -9.42 \times .01$$

$$\% \text{ change in bond price} = 9.42\%$$

New price of bond = ₹905.8

Now let us adjust this bond for its convexity, to assess the real change in the price of the bond.

Period (t)	Coupons	PV of cash flow @10%	PV of cash flows $\times t(t+1)$
1	100	90.90909	181.8182
2	100	82.64463	495.8678
3	100	75.13148	901.5778
4	100	68.30135	1366.027
5	100	62.09213	1862.764
6	100	56.44739	2370.791
7	100	51.31581	2873.685
8	100	46.65074	3358.853
9	100	42.40976	3816.879
10	100	38.55433	4240.976
11	100	35.04939	4626.519
12	100	31.86308	4970.641

(*Continued*)

Continued

Period (t)	Coupons	PV of cash flow @10%	PV of cash flows $\times t(t+1)$
13	100	28.96644	5271.892
14	100	26.33313	5529.956
15	100	23.9392	5745.409
16	100	21.76291	5919.512
17	100	19.78447	6054.047
18	100	17.98588	6151.171
19	100	16.3508	6213.304
20	100	14.86436	6243.032
21	100	13.51306	6243.032
22	100	12.2846	6216.006
23	100	11.16782	6164.634
24	100	10.15256	6091.536
25	100	9.2296	5999.24
26	100	8.390545	5890.163
27	100	7.627768	5766.593
28	100	6.934335	5630.68
29	100	6.303941	5484.429
30	1100	63.03941	58626.65
Total		1000	190307.7

$$\text{Convexity} = [(1 \div (1.1)^2] \times (1 \div 1000) \times 190307.7 = 157.28$$

$$\%\text{ change in bond price} = -\text{ Modified Duration} \times \%\text{ yield change} + \frac{1}{2} \times \text{convexity} \times (\text{yield change})^2$$

$$\%\text{ change in bond price} = -9.42 \times 0.1 + \frac{1}{2} \times 157.28 \times (.01)^2 \times 157.28 \times (.01)^2$$

$$\%\text{ change in bond price} = 8.63\%$$

New price of bond after adjusting for convexity = ₹913.7

We see that after adjusting the convexity measure, the drop in the price of the bond is lesser as compared to applying only modified duration rule to estimate price change. Nevertheless, duration rule is a popular interest risk sensitivity measure and is fairly effective, in case of small changes in yields.

Convexity is generally considered as a desirable trait in a bond. Bonds with greater curvature gain more in price when yields fall than they lose when yields rise. As interest rate falls, a bond with a higher curvature (and thus convexity) enjoys a higher price increase. As interest rates increase, the decrease in the price of the bond is lesser. This makes convexity desirable. But it does not come for free to investors. Investors will have to pay higher prices and accept lower yields to maturity on bonds with greater convexity.

Passive bond management strategies

Bonds have obtained incredible significance and hence managing a portfolio of bonds has become fairly complex. Bond investors may follow a variety of strategies ranging from passive to active. When investors believe that securities are fairly priced, i.e., the expected returns from bonds are justified by the risk undertaken, such beliefs are called as ***Passive Bond Management Strategies***. Here investor does not actively tries to outperform the market. Though, it does not mean that the investor does nothing. Even under a passive strategy, an investor will have to (a) determine whether bonds are suitable investment avenues for him, (b) asses various risks in bond selection – default risk, liquidity risk, call risk, etc. and reasonably diversify his holdings across bonds of varying maturity, and (c) periodically monitor his bond portfolio to ensure that his holdings match his risk preferences and objectives.

Two of the commonly followed passive bond portfolio management strategies are discussed below:

1. **Buy and Hold Strategy:** As the name suggests, under this strategy an investor purchases and holds a security to maturity or redemption (in case of call provision invoked by the issuer) and then he reinvests the cash proceeds in similar securities. Here the investor stays with his bond investment and does not churn (sell before maturity) his bond investments in order to improve returns or minimize risks. The bond investment is so chosen such that it meets the investment objectives of the investor. Hence considerable time is spent by the investor in the initial selection of the bond.

   This strategy is used primarily by income maximization investors who are interested in the largest coupon income over a desired horizon. Such classes of investors include retired persons, endowment funds, bond mutual funds and insurance companies that are seeking the regular yield over an extended period of time. Another technique for a passive strategy is an index fund. Index funds basically provide diversification along with minimum transaction costs. In addition a portfolio can be built that mirrors a well–known bond index. I – Bex is a popular bond index in India[10].
2. **Bond Laddering Strategy:** A bond laddering strategy entails buying bonds scheduled to come at several different dates in the future, rather than all in the same year. For example, an investor might buy similar amounts of bonds due in one year, two years, three years, and so on up to ten years. This process is known as bond laddering strategy, as each bucket of bonds with varying maturity represents a step on the investment maturity ladder. In India, it may be observed that fixed income investors invest in National

---

[10] http://articles.economictimes.indiatimes.com/2008-05-09/news/28414933_1_bse-bond-index-icici-securities-primary-dealership, accessed on December 15, 2014.

Saving Certificates (NSC) issued by Post Offices. They have a maturity of six years. Investors generally buy these papers for six years and fund the purchases from the seventh year from the proceeds of the first NSC. This way a chain of bonds of varying maturity helps investors to finance their needs arising at various stages of their life cycle.

When short term rates are lower than longer term rates, a well-built bond ladder is likely to produce significantly higher returns than money market mutual funds or short term bank deposits. This strategy is especially useful for those investors who need amounts of money available on certain future dates, for example to pay for one's marriage expenses, child birth and child's education and so on. Laddering has a lot of investment worth because the investor is not making a consolidated big investment which would mature at one time. A rise in interest rate scenario would drive down the prices of long term bonds, resulting in capital losses for investors who need to sell bonds before the redemption date. In case of fall in interest rates, this strategy would give protection to investors who have locked up their investments in high yield bonds (of course, if the bond issuer does not exercise his call option).

Semi-Active and Active Bond Management Strategy

1. **Immunization:** A major problem encountered in managing bond portfolios is locking a given yield which meets the objective of ending wealth (also called terminal value of the bond) requirement at a future date. In the event of flat term structure of interest rates , there will be no change in the level of market rates between the time of purchase of the bond and the date of sale of the bond in future (owing to fund requirement by the investor). In such a case, an investor can buy a bond with a maturity equal to a desired investment horizon and his ending wealth from the bond investment would be equal to the promised yield to maturity. Unfortunately, in the real world, term structures of interest rates are not flat and keep changing over time. Hence bond holders are exposed to interest rate risk. This interest rate risk may be divided into two parts: 1) the price risk – which arises from the inverse relationship between bond prices and yields and 2) the reinvestment risk – which arises from the reinvestment of future coupons at a new interest rate. The price risk and the reinvestment risk move in opposite directions. In the event of fall in interest rates, there is a twofold consequence for the investor: (a) the price of the bond rises and (b) the return on reinvestment of future coupons falls. Vice-versa in the event of a rise in interest rate, (a) the price of the bond falls and (b) the reinvestment of future coupons happen at a higher rate of interest.

   These two sub components of interest rate risks have two opposite effect on the ending wealth desired by a bond holder. If the magnitude impact of both these risks is equal, i.e., they cancel each other, we say that the bond portfolio is insulated or ***IMMUNIZED*** against the interest rate risk. If a bond holder chooses a bond whose duration is equal to his investment horizon, we say the bond portfolio is immunized from interest rate fluctuations. Numerical Example 7 will make the concept of Immunization more explicit.

Numerical Example 7

Consider a 13.3% bond redeemable on 01/07/2019 at a premium of 10%. If the interest rate prevailing in the market on 01/07/2014 is 15%, at what price was this bond trading in the market on 01/07/2014? Assuming the face value of the bond as ₹100, let us see the cash inflows and outflows arising out of this bond investment from investor's point of view:

Year	0	1	2	3	4	5
Cash flow	?	13.3	13.3	13.3	13.3	123.3*
Present values @15%		11.67	10.23	8.98	7.87	64.04
Sum of present values	= 102.79 which is the price of the Bond					

* In the last year the cash inflow for the investor would be ₹13.3 + ₹110 = ₹123.3

1. Now consider what would happen to Praveen, an investor who needs money only after five years, if he decides to hold the above mentioned bond till maturity, and reinvests the annual interest payments. How much money will he have at the end of 5 years?

   Let us calculate the ending wealth for Praveen assuming, he holds the bond till maturity and reinvests all the coupons at the prevailing market interest rates of 15%.

Year	1	2	3	4	5
Cash flow	13.3	13.3	13.3	13.3	123.3
Future values @15% at end of fifth year	23.26	20.23	17.59	15.30	123.3*
Sum of future values or ending wealth at end of fifth year	**= 199.67**				

* In the fifth year the future value of the cash flow of ₹123.3 would not be compounded, hence would remain the same.

What would happen if immediately after Praveen buys the bond, the market interest rate drops to 14%?

Let us calculate the ending wealth for Praveen assuming, he holds the bond till maturity and reinvests all the coupons at the prevailing market interest rates of 14%.

Year	1	2	3	4	5
Cash flow	13.3	13.3	13.3	13.3	123.3
Future values @14% at end of fifth year	22.46	19.70	17.28	15.16	123.3
Sum of future values or ending wealth at end of fifth year	**= 197.91**				

We observe that the ending wealth has gone down in comparison to the original interest rate scenario of 15%. Here a fall in interest rate has resulted in the rise in price of bond being overpowered by the reinvestment risk, as the future coupons are now getting reinvested at a lower rate.

We say in terms of magnitude:

Reinvestment Risk > Price Risk

What would happen to Praveen, if immediately after buying the bond, the interest rate rises to 16% instead of 14%?

Let us calculate the ending wealth for Praveen assuming, he holds the bond till maturity and reinvests all the coupons at the prevailing market interest rates of 16%.

Year	1	2	3	4	5
Cash flow	13.3	13.3	13.3	13.3	123.3
Future values @16% at end of fifth year	24.08	20.76	17.90	15.43	123.3
Sum of future values or ending wealth at end of fifth year	= **201.47**				

We observe that the ending wealth has gone up in comparison to the original interest rate scenario of 15%. Here a rise in interest rate has resulted in the fall in price of bond being overpowered by the reinvestment risk, as the future coupons are now getting reinvested at a higher rate.

Again we see that in terms of magnitude:

Reinvestment Risk > Price Risk

2. Now let us consider another investor Dinesh, who has a holding period of only 3 years. He buys the above-mentioned bond on July 1, 2014, reinvests all interest for three years and plans to sell the bond on July 1, 2017. How much money will he have at the end of 3 years?

   Let us calculate the ending wealth for Dinesh assuming, he holds the bond till maturity and reinvests all the coupons at the prevailing market interest rates of 15%.

   Before we work out the ending wealth for Dinesh at the end of third year, we first calculate the market price of the bond at the end of the third year.

Year	4	5
Cash flow	13.3	123.3
Present values @15% at end of third year	11.57	93.23
Sum of present values at the end of the third year	= **104.80**	

Let us calculate the ending wealth for Dinesh assuming, he holds the bond till third year, and reinvests all the coupons at the prevailing market interest rates of 15%.

Year	1	2	3
Cash flow	13.3	13.3	13.3
Future values @15% at end of third year	17.59	15.30	13.3 + 104.80*
Sum of future values or ending wealth at end of third year	= **150.99**		

* Market price of the bond prevailing in the third year calculated using present value technique

What would happen to the ending wealth of Dinesh if immediately after he buying the bond, the interest rate drops to 14%?

Let us calculate the ending wealth for Dinesh assuming, he holds the bond till third year and reinvests all the coupons at the prevailing market interest rates of 14%.

Before we work out the ending wealth for Dinesh at the end of third year, we first calculate the market price of the bond at the end of the third year (at new interest rate of 14%).

Year	**4**	**5**
Cash flow	13.3	123.3
Present values @14% at end of third year	11.67	94.88
Sum of present values at the end of the third year	= **106.54**	

Let us calculate the ending wealth for Dinesh assuming, he holds the bond till third year and reinvests all the coupons at the prevailing market interest rates of 14 %.

Year	**1**	**2**	**3**
Cash flow	13.3	13.3	13.3
Future values @14% at end of third year	17.28	15.16	13.3 + 106.54*
Sum of future values or ending wealth at end of third year	= **152.28**		

* Market price of the bond prevailing in the third year calculated using present value technique

We observe that the ending wealth has gone up in comparison to the original interest rate scenario of 15%. Here a fall in interest rate has resulted in the rise in price of bond overpowering the reinvestment risk, as the future coupons are now getting reinvested at a lower rate.

We say in terms of magnitude:

Price Risk > Reinvestment Risk

What would happen if immediately after he buys the bond, the interest rate rises to 16% instead of 14%?

Before we work out the ending wealth for Dinesh at the end of third year, we first calculate the market price of the bond at the end of the third year (at new interest rate of 16%).

Year	**4**	**5**
Cash flow	13.3	123.3
Present values @16% at end of third year	11.47	91.63
Sum of present values at the end of the third year	= **103.10**	

Let us calculate the ending wealth for Dinesh assuming, he holds the bond till third year and reinvests all the coupons at the prevailing market interest rates of 16 %.

Year	1	2	3
Cash flow	13.3	13.3	13.3
Future values @16% at end of third year	17.90	15.43	13.3 + 103.10*
Sum of future values or ending wealth at end of third year	= **149.73**		

* Market price of the bond prevailing in the third year calculated using present value technique

We observe that the ending wealth has gone down in comparison to the original interest rate scenario of 15%. Here a rise in interest rate has resulted in the fall in price of bond which overpowers the reinvestment risk, as the future coupons are now getting reinvested at a higher rate.

Again we see that in terms of magnitude:

Price Risk > Reinvestment Risk

3. Now let us consider another investor Rina, who has a holding period of only 4 years. She bought the above bond on July 1, 2014, reinvests all interest for three years and plans to sell the bond on July 1, 2018. How much money will she have at the end of 4 years?

   Let us calculate the ending wealth for Rina assuming, she holds the bond till maturity and reinvests all the coupons at the prevailing market interest rates of 15%.

   Before we work out the ending wealth for Rina at the end of fourth year, we first calculate the market price of the bond at the end of the fourth year.

Year	5
Cash flow	123.3
Present values @15% at end of fourth year	107.22

Let us calculate the ending wealth for Rina assuming, she holds the bond till fourth year and reinvests all the coupons at the prevailing market interest rates of 15%.

Year	1	2	3	4
Cash flow	13.3	13.3	13.3	13.3
Future values @15% at end of fourth year	20.23	17.59	15.30	13.3 + 107.22*
Sum of future values or ending wealth at end of fourth year	= **173.64**			

* Market price of the bond prevailing in the fourth year calculated using present value technique

What would happen to the ending wealth of Rina if immediately after buying the bond, the interest rate drops to 14%?

Let us calculate the ending wealth for Rina assuming, she holds the bond till fourth year and reinvests all the coupons at the prevailing market interest rates of 14%.

Before we work out the ending wealth for Rina at the end of fourth year, we first calculate the market price of the bond at the end of the fourth year.

Year	5
Cash flow	123.3
Present values @14% at end of fourth year	108.16

Let us calculate the ending wealth for Rina assuming, she holds the bond till fourth year and reinvests all the coupons at the prevailing market interest rates of 14%.

Year	1	2	3	4
Cash flow	13.3	13.3	13.3	13.3
Future values @14% at end of fourth year	19.70	17.28	15.16	13.3 + 108.16*
Sum of future values or ending wealth at end of fourth year	= **173.6**			

* Market price of the bond prevailing in the fourth year calculated using present value technique

We observe that the ending wealth has remained almost the same (minor difference due to rounding off of decimal values) in comparison to the original interest rate scenario of 15%. Here a fall in interest rate has resulted in the rise in price of bond being equalized in magnitude by the reinvestment risk, as the future coupons are now getting reinvested at a lower rate.

We say in terms of magnitude:

Reinvestment Risk = Price Risk

What would happen if immediately after Rina buys the bond, the interest rate rises to 16% instead of 14%?

Before we work out the ending wealth for Rina at the end of fourth year, we first calculate the market price of the bond at the end of the fourth year.

Year	5
Cash flow	123.3
Present values @16% at end of fourth year	106.29

Let us calculate the ending wealth for Rina assuming, she holds the bond till fourth year and reinvests all the coupons at the prevailing market interest rates of 16%.

Year	1	2	3	4
Cash flow	13.3	13.3	13.3	13.3
Future values @16% at end of fourth year	20.76	17.90	15.43	13.3 + 106.29*
Sum of future values or ending wealth at end of fourth year	= **173.68**			

* Market price of the bond prevailing in the fourth year calculated using present value technique

We observe that the ending wealth has remained almost the same (minor difference due to rounding off of decimal values) in comparison to the original interest rate scenario of 15% (as well as 14%). Here a rise in interest rate has resulted in the fall in price of bond being equalized in magnitude by the reinvestment risk, as the future coupons are now getting reinvested at a higher rate.

We say in terms of magnitude:

Reinvestment Risk = Price Risk

Hence we say that four years is the effective maturity or "***Duration***" of the bond. Holding the bond equal to its duration, immunizes the bond against any upward or downward movement of interest rates.

Hence it can be concluded that on holding the bond to its duration:

Reinvestment Risk = Price Risk

Cash Flow Matching

There appears to be a simple solution to the problem associated with coupon paying bonds, in the event of interest rate fluctuations: simple buy a zero coupon bond which exactly matches the projected cash requirement at maturity. This bond management strategy is called ***cash flow matching***. This strategy automatically immunizes a portfolio from interest rate risk because the cash flow from the bond offsets the future obligation.

Cash flow matching entails four steps. First, the liability payments stream is determined. Next, from the bond universe, few bonds are selected according to quality criteria. Third, investor objectives and constraints are identified. Finally, the optimal portfolio is chosen. If structured properly, the portfolio would cash itself out in the sense that between every two successive liability payments, the cash flow from principal payments and coupon receipts, plus any accrued interest from a prior balance, would be sufficient to cover the next liability payment.

This cash flow matching strategy is a single period strategy. A series of cash flow matching strategy involves matching cash flows on a multi-period basis. Such a strategy is called ***dedication strategy***. In dedication strategy, the purpose to fund a sequence of liability payments as they come due, with no interest rate risk is met. As the bond portfolio manager buys a series of zero coupon bonds that match the stream of future obligations, this eliminates interest rate risk and thus the need for periodic rebalancing.

The main drawback of cash flow matching strategy is that it imposes constraints on bond selection. It may not be feasible when fund obligations of the future may simply not get zero coupon bonds of matching maturity.

As bonds cannot typically be selected to accurately match the cash flow of liabilities, a certain amount of cash must be kept with oneself to pay liabilities as they come. Thus, a downside of cash flow matching strategy over immunization is that the cash is not fully invested. In such a case, immunization strategy would be appropriate.

Active Bond Management Strategy

The growing interest in active bond management was launched by the increased volatility of interest rates. This increased volatility brings both greater opportunities as well as risks in managing fixed-income portfolios. When the objective of investing fixed income securities is to enhance the total return from the portfolio, given investor's risk appetite, active bond management strategies generally become imperative to be used. The total return from bond investment includes price appreciation, coupon income and reinvestment returns, accomplishing this objective may necessitate the investor to trade off one form of return for another in anticipation that the total return will be increased.

Two types of strategies that seem well suited for this objective are (1) portfolio shifts in anticipation of changes in the overall structure of interest rates, and (2) bond swaps, which attempt to exploit transitory deviations in the price/yield structure of the bond. As both these strategies entail a great deal of time, investors seeking to increase total return are expected to be actively involved in the management of their bond portfolios.

1. **Interest rate Anticipation:** Switching bonds based upon interest rate forecasting can be the most dynamic bond portfolio action. It is the riskiest strategy for managing bonds. With interest rate anticipation, an investor makes a forecast of the direction and quantum of change. The risk is twofold – Firstly, since one is making an estimate, one's expectation might be wrong and it could be detrimental to one's overall return position. Secondly, if one currently owns a portfolio, rebalancing one's portfolio will change its duration, which in turn can alter one's risk and expected return's position. The types of portfolio decisions required can be categorized into four categories: maturity, quality, sector and coupon. Of these, maturity is probably the most important strategy in active bond portfolio management.
   (a) *Decision with respect to maturity:* The general rule for interest rate anticipation is to increase one's investment in long duration bonds when interest rates are expected to decline. Long duration bonds generally have long maturity and low coupon rates. As interest rates in the economy fall, prices of bonds increase. This enhances the opportunity to increase total return in the short run through price appreciation. However, such a move also produces a low level of income through coupons and reinvestment (as rates have fallen in the economy). The decision about the type of long duration bonds to invest in, must consider the need for current income. One should have a reasonable estimate about how low and how soon one thinks interest rates will fall. If interest rates decline only slightly, long duration will not produce as much price appreciation, as the low coupon reinvestment will discount the overall gain. Nevertheless the additional income when combined with some price appreciation may provide better overall return.

       Expectations of an increase in interest rates will provide for altogether different portfolio considerations. When interest rates are expected to rise, a primary concern for fixed income investors is the preservation of their capital, i.e., the need to avoid a large price decline due to increased interest rates. Investors would instinctively move into very short term, highly liquid investments, such as money market instruments. The short duration of these money market instruments makes their values relatively insensitive to change in market yields. As changes in interest rates usually affects short-term yields more than long-term yields, these short-term securities' yields will swiftly reflect the rate increase in terms of price fall.

(b) *Decision with respect to sector:* By forecasting the changes in yield spreads between different sectors of bonds, i.e., government securities, corporate debentures, mortgage backed securities, etc. the bond manager can add incremental returns to the portfolio. The factors which determine the yield spread between the bonds of various sectors can be – supply and demand positions of issues, earnings position of the sector, influence of economic factors, etc. If a bond portfolio manager can anticipate the factors which causes these yields spreads, he can formulate appropriate strategies to profit from any expected differentials.

Assuming that the yield spread is 100 basis points between government securities and AAA rated corporate debentures. If one expects the spread to widen, the investor should sell his investments in AAA rated corporate dentures and buy government securities. On actual widening of the spread, the relative prices of government securities will increase thereby offering scope for incremental returns to the investor, who can now sell the government security and buy back the corporate debenture, which would be quoting at a lower price now.

(c) *Decision with respect to quality:* Quality spreads of bonds change because of expected changes in economic prospects. Usually credit or quality spreads between government securities and non–government bonds widen during economic downturn or recession, because of the increase in risk premium during recession. In a declining economy, corporate houses experience declining revenues and cash flows; this increases the uncertainty around the corporate bonds to make coupons payments and principal repayment. This necessitates the corporate to increase the yield of their bonds to induce investors. Hence the yield spread increases between government securities and non-government bonds. A complete opposite situation arises in case of economic upturn or boom, where the yield spread between government and non-government securities narrows. A bond fund manager should buy high quality bonds (government securities) in case of economic downturn and lower quality bonds in case of economic upturn.

(d) *Decision with respect to coupon:* In case of rise in interest rates, if the increase is not large, by shifting from long-term securities to short-term securities, an investor may be sacrificing too much income in order to avoid price declines. In such a case, investor's total return can be enhanced even more by moving into higher-coupon, intermediate–term bonds, whose values are not affected greatly by rising yields. Such high coupon bonds trading at above their redemption price are often called Cushion bonds. Although their potential for further price appreciation is restricted regardless of further declines in long-term interest rates, in a subsequent period of rising interest rates the high coupon provides a cushion against significant price declines. Such a bond generally comes with a call feature and sells at a premium (due to its high-coupon). Moderately rising interest rates do not affect its price as much as for long-term, low coupon bonds with longer maturity. Thus by investing in a cushion bond, one enjoys a higher coupon and reinvestment income, while potentially incurring only moderate price decline in the event of rise in interest rates.

2. **Bond Swaps:** Another approach, the investor may take, in increasing the total return to the portfolio, is the use of bond swapping techniques. A bond swap occurs whenever an investor sells a bond and exchanges it with another. Bond swapping also called as ***bond substitution***, is done to take advantage of temporary aberrations in the bond market due to supply and demand factors, such as long or short dealer positions and purchases to satisfy sinking fund requirement. Such swaps may result in exchanging bonds of similar quality, sector, coupon and maturity at relatively favorable levels. These changes may be

independent of interest rate forecasts and depend upon opportunities ordinarily available only for a brief period of time.

3. **Substitution Swap:** A substitution swap is a swap in which securities are similar in all respects except that the bond purchased has a higher promised yield to maturity than the existing bond. In the strictest sense, two bond's coupon, default risk and maturity are the same. Hence if these two bonds are perfect substitutes, then the market forces should bring the yields of these two bonds together at some point of time in the future. Thus the investor, by selling the lower–yield bond and purchasing the higher yield bond, has the opportunity to increase the overall return. If the market is fairly efficient, the gain should be realized in a short period of time.

   An example of a substitution swap would be the sale of a 20–year maturity, 8 percent AAA corporate bond, priced at ₹100 with yield of 4 percent semi-annually and buying of a 20-year, 8 percent AAA corporate bond, priced at ₹97.696 yielding 4.15 percent semi-annually. The logic is that if both the bonds have about the same credit rating, then there is no apparent reason for the first bond to give a lower yield. Therefore, the higher yield provided by the second bond makes it an attractive option to purchase.

4. **Pure Yield Pick-up Swap:** With a pure yield pick–up swap, the investor seeks to increase the portfolio's yield to maturity by swapping out of a lower–yield bond into a higher–yield bond. Because this swap usually involves switching from a lower coupon bond to a higher coupon bond, the current yield is also increased. However, because higher–coupon bonds typically have call features, the swap may increase the call risk of the portfolio. In addition, for yield swaps across different rating classifications, the default risk of the portfolio may also be altered.

   An example of a substitution swap would be the sale of a 20-year, 9 percent AAA corporate bond, priced at ₹95.560 to yield 4.75 percent semi-annually and buying a 20-year, 10 percent AA Corporate bond, priced at ₹100 to yield 5.00 percent semi-annually.

   The pure yield pick–up swap, is not without its risks. An investor may have to accept a callable bond as well as securities with a lower credit rating.

SUMMARY

☑ The interest rate on a bond is determined by: short-term risk free interest and the risk premium. The factors that affect premium depend upon the type of issuer, the issuer's perceived creditworthiness, the term or maturity of the instrument, provisions that grant either the issuer or the investor the option to do something, the taxability of the interest received by investors and the expected liquidity of the issue.

☑ The structure of yields that is observed for bonds with different terms to maturity but with no other difference is called the *term structure of interest rates*. In everyday financial dialect, a diagram of the rates prevailing on a class of securities that are alike in every respect, except term to maturity provides us with a *yield curve*.

☑ Yield curves are generally upward sloping, however, they can be downward sloping, flat as well as humped shaped.

☑ There are four theories which explain the reason behind the shape of the yield curve. The expectations theory states that the entire term structure at a given time reflects the market's current expectations of future short-term rates. The Liquidity Premium Theory states that investors will hold longer-term maturities if they are offered a long-term rate higher than the average of expected future rates by a risk premium and this risk premium related to the term to maturity positively. The preferred Habitat theory proposes that the shape of the yield curve is determined by both expectations of future interest rates and a risk premium, positive or negative, to induce market participants to shift out of their preferred habitat. The fourth theory, the market-segmentation theory differs from the preferred-habitat theory in that it assumes that neither investors nor borrowers are willing to shift from one maturity sector to another to take advantage of opportunities arising from differences between expectations and forward rates.

☑ Bond prices and yields are inversely related as prices of long-term bonds tend to be more sensitive to interest rate changes than prices of short-term bonds. Interest rate risk is asymmetrically proportional to bond maturity. Interest rate risk is inversely related to the bond's coupon rate.

☑ Macaulay's Duration equals weighted average of the times to each coupon or principal payment made by the bond. Bond Portfolio Managers across the globe use this estimate as a guide to the sensitivity of a bond to interest rate changes. Modified duration is the first derivative of the change in the price of the bond with respect to its yield to maturity.

☑ Coupon paying bonds have duration less than their maturity. Duration of a zero coupon bond is always equal to its maturity.

☑ Interest rate risk has two components—price risk and reinvestment risk. Since these two types of interest rate risks are of opposite signs, eliminating this risk is a must. Eliminating these two types of risks from a bond portfolio is referred to as ***immunization.***

☑ Convexity can be quantified as the rate of change of the slope of the price-yield curve, as a fraction of the bond price. Bonds with higher convexity exhibit higher curvature in their price–yield relationship.

☑ Under passive bond management strategies, investor does not actively try to outperform the market. There are two types of passive bond management strategies – Buy and Hold strategy and Bond Laddering Strategy. Under buy and hold strategy, an investor purchases and holds a security to maturity or redemption and reinvests the maturity proceeds. A bond laddering strategy entails buying bonds scheduled to come at several different dates in the future, rather than all in the same year.

☑ Semi-active strategies involve duration matching of the bond with the timing of investor's requirement of maturity proceeds. Immunization and cash flow matching are two semi-active bond management strategies.

☑ Under Active Bond Management Strategy, there are two types of strategies (1) portfolio shifts in anticipation of changes in the overall structure of interest rates, and (2) bond swaps, which attempt to exploit transitory deviations in the price/yield structure of the bond.

KEY WORDS

Active bond management strategy **661**
Bond laddering strategy **653**
Bond swaps **662**
Buy and hold strategy **653**
Cash flow matching **660**
Convexity **649**
Expectations theory **635**
Immunization **654**
Macaulay's duration **642**
Interest rate anticipation **661**
Liquidity preference theory **638**
Market-segmentation theory **639**
Modified duration **646**
Passive bond management strategies **653**

CONCEPT QUESTIONS

1. Interest rates is a powerful weapon in the hands of the RBI. The level of existing interest rates in an economy assumes crucial importance in a host of scenarios. From cost of liquidity in the system to keeping speculators in the forex market at bay, interest rates are employed to influence the overall economic activity in the economy. Explain the chief determinants of interest rates in an economy.
2. What is a yield curve? How is the slope of the yield curve defined and measured?
3. Assume the following average yields on GOI bonds:

Term to maturity	Yield
1 year	11%
5 years	10.5%
10 years	9.75%
15 years	9%
20 years	8%

   Given, the term structure of Interest rates implied by the above-mentioned data, comment on the shape of the yield curve. Discuss how each of the theories of term structure of interest rates would explain this shape of the yield curve.
4. How is a bond's price volatility related to its duration?
5. Rank the following bonds in descending order of their durations with the help of bond duration properties. Do not use calculations.
   a. 20% coupon 20 – year, ytm at 15%
   b. 20% coupon 15 – year, ytm at 15%
   c. Zero coupon 20 – year, ytm at 15%
   d. 10% coupon 20 – year, ytm at 15%
   e. 20% coupon 15 – year, ytm at 20%
6. What is bond convexity? Is it a desirable feature while cherry picking bonds in one's portfolio? Why or why not?
7. a. What is meant by the term "Reinvestment Risk?" Is reinvestment risk greater when the current market rate is 8% or 12%? Why?

b. What are the differences in the reinvestment risk between a 6% annual coupon paying bond currently selling at ₹83 to yield 8.6% YTM and a 10 percent semi-annual coupon paying bond selling at ₹108 to yield 8.6% YTM?
c. Will reinvestment risk be different between two 9% bonds, one due in 2016 and the other due in 2021? Why so?

8. You are a bond portfolio manager. Your client is concerned about the apparent discrepancy between the following two statements:

   a. Short-term interest rates are more volatile than long-term rates.
   b. The rates of return of long-term bonds are more volatile than returns on short-term securities.

   Discuss why these two statements are not necessarily incoherent.

9. What are the various passive, semi-active and active strategies of bond portfolio management? Which ones are popularly practiced by Indian bond portfolio managers?

10. How does a fixed income securities trader profit from falling yield spreads between GOI bonds and bonds issued by the private sector corporate bodies?

PRACTICE PROBLEMS

1. Quick soft systems has issued bonds with a face value of ₹500. The coupon rate is 12% and is payable semi–annually. The market price is ₹475. The principle amount will be redeemed in two equal installments at the end of third and fourth years. You are required to calculate:

   a. Duration and modified duration of the bond.
   b. Interest rate risk for a 1% increase in the interest rates.

2. Answer the following questions:

   a. Consider two bonds, one with 5 years to maturity and the other with 20 years to maturity. Both have face value of ₹1000 and 8% coupon rates (with annual interest payments), and both sell at par. Assume that the yields of both bonds fall to 6%. Calculate the increase in the bond prices. What percentage of this increase in each case comes from a change in the present t value of the bond's principals and what percentage comes from a change in the present value of the bond's interest payments?
   b. Consider a bond selling at its par value of ₹1000 with 6 years to maturity and a 7% coupon rate (with annual interest payments). Calculate the bond's duration.
   c. If the YTM of the bond in part (b) above increases to 10%, what would happen to the bond's duration? Why does this change occur?

3. An investor wants to realize a target rate of return (yield) of 12% on his bond portfolio investment over a 6 year investment horizon. He has two options:

   a. Buy a 12% bond maturing after 9 years which is selling at the par value of ₹1000.
   b. Buy a 12% bond maturing after 6 years which is also selling at par value of ₹1000.

Both the bonds pay interest annually:

a. What will be the terminal value and realized yield under each option if:
   (i) Interest rate declines by 1 percentage point after purchase of the bond, assuming that the change in interest rate occurs before the first coupon payment.
   (ii) There is no change in market interest rates.
   (iii) Interest rate increases by 1 percentage point after the purchase of the bond, assuming that the change in interest rate occurs before the first coupon payment?

b. Which bond should the investor choose?

4. Raghu Jetley has a liability maturing in 5 years from now. To be able to meet the liability, he wants to invest in fixed income securities. He is considering two bonds. Bond A carries a coupon of 12% on a face value of ₹1000 and matures in 5 years from now. Bond B is of face value ₹1000 and carries a coupon of 10% payable annually and matures at the end of 7 years from now. While bond A is trading at par, bond B is trading at ₹750. If Mr. Jetley does not want to face any interest rate risk, in which of the two bonds should he invest? Explain with calculations.

5. Shravan is considering investment in one of the following bonds:

   Bond A: It is a ₹1,000 par value bond carrying a coupon rate of 13% and maturing after 5 years. YTM of the bond is 14%.
   Bond B: It is a ₹1000 par value bond carrying a coupon rate of 14% and maturing after 7 years. The bond is selling at its par value.
   Bond C: It is a ₹1000 par value zero-coupon bond with YTM of 14% and maturing after 6 years. Answer the following sub questions:

   a. Calculate the duration of the three bonds.
   b. Estimate and comment upon the interest rate risks associated with the bonds if the interest rate declines by 1%.
   c. If you want to realize a return of 14% over a holding period of 5 years, which bond would you prefer? Why?

6. Xen Engineering Ltd. has raised ₹650 crore through an issue of non–convertible debentures to finance its expansion and diversification plan at Kopri. These debentures have been assigned an AAA rating by CRISIL, meaning the highest safety with respect to repayment of interest and principal.

   Each NCD has a face value of ₹100 with a coupon of 12 percent payable semi-annually. These semi-annual payments will be made on the last working day of September and March each year. The NCD's will be redeemed in 3 installments viz., 20 percent at the end of the third year, 30 percent at the end of the fourth year and balance 50 percent at the end of the fifth year.

   An investor wants to analyze the worth of the bond from an investment perspective. The NCDs have just begun trading on the wholesale debt segment of the National Stock Exchange and are trading at ₹95.75. Calculate the duration of the NCD.

7. AMB Ltd. has made the first of its kind triple bond issue. The term of issue of the first type, the Deep discount bond is as follows:

   The bond has a face value of ₹1,00,000 which is issued at a deep discounted price of ₹2,700 with a maturity of 25 years. The investor has been given an option (put option) to seek redemption at the end of every 5 years. The redemption prices are as follows:

End of year	5	10	15	20	25
Price (₹)	5,700	12,000	25,000	50,000	1,00,000

AMB Ltd. has an option (call option) to redeem at the end of every five years provided IDBI notifies the bondholders of its intention at least 6 months in advance.

Answer the following questions:

a. Comment on the yield curve of the Deep Discount Bond.
b. When is an investor better off exercising the option of redemption?
c. Under what circumstances will IDBI exercise its call option? If it does, what is the effect on the returns to an investor?

8. A recently issued bond has a maturity of 11 years and pays an 8% coupon rate (with annual coupon payments). The bond is currently selling at par value.

a. What are the duration and convexity of the bond?
b. Find the actual price of the bond assuming that its yield to maturity immediately increases from 8% to 9% (this change in interest rate happens before the first coupon payment of the bond).
c. What are the predicted price of the bond using duration rule and convexity rule?
d. Why do the price estimates differ as calculated under part (c)?

9. Mr. Premchandani estimates that there will be annual cash outflows of ₹40,000 for four years from the end of three years from now. Mr. Premchandani wants to immunize the payments by investing in the following two bonds:

Bond A	A zero coupon bond of face value of ₹1,000 maturing after 6 years and currently traded at ₹455.60
Bond B	12% coupon bearing bond of face value of ₹1,000 maturing after 5 years redeemable at par value and currently traded at ₹930.90

Assume the interest rate remains at 14%.

As Mr. Premchandani's portfolio manager, you are required to determine the proportion of funds to be invested in bonds A and B such that Mr. Premchandani's payments are immunized.

10. The following yields currently exists for the bonds given below:

Bonds	Yield to maturity (%)
Long-term GOI bonds	12.5
Long-term AAA corporate bonds	13.5
Long-term BBB corporate bonds	14.0

Assume the following to be normal yield spreads:

a. The spread between long-term AAA bonds and long-term GOI bonds is 150 bps.
b. The spread between long-term BBB bonds and long-term AAA bonds is 150bps.

You are required to suggest a strategy to profit from this abnormal scenario.

CASELET

A bond portfolio manager of Sherwood Deals is building a portfolio of bonds from three companies: Alpha, Beta and Gamma. These bonds will be used to fund a pension fund outflow scheduled in six years. The current yield in the economy is 8%. All bonds have a ₹1000 par value.

Bond	Coupon	Maturity	Maturity	Duration
Alpha	8%	Annual	10 years	7.35 years
Beta	9%	Annual	8 years	6.15 years
Gamma	7%	Semi-annual	5 years	4.30 years

1. Assuming the bond portfolio manager of Sherwood Deals has been instructed to keep 40 percent of the portfolio's money in alpha bonds, calculate the percentage amounts of beta and gamma bonds that need to be purchased to immunize the portfolio.
2. Now that the portfolio has been constructed, an interest–rate change occurs, increasing the current yield to 10 percent. The new durations for those bonds are:

   Alpha = 7.15 years

   Beta = 6.03 years

   Gamma = 4.27 years

   Is the bond portfolio still immunized? Why or why not?
3. Determine the new percentage amounts of Beta and Gamma bonds that are needed to re-immunize the portfolio (alpha remains at 40% of the portfolio).

REFERENCES

B.G. Malkiel, "Expectations, Bond prices, and the Term Structure of Interest rates," *Quarterly Journal of Economics*, 1962, Vol. 76, 197–218.

F. Modigliani and R. Sutch, "Innovations in Interest Rate Policy," *American Economic Review*, May 1966, 178–197.

J.M. Culbertson, "The Term Structure of Interest Rates," *Quarterly Journal of Economics*, November 1957, 489–504.

J.M. Keynes, *A Treatise on Money*. Volume 2, 1st Edn. London: Macmillan, 1930.

J.M. Keynes, *The General Theory of Employment, Interest and Money*, 1st Edn. London: Macmillan, 1936.

J.R. Hicks, "Mr. Hawtrey on Bank Rate and the Long-Term Rate of Interest," *The Manchester School of Economics and Social Studies*, 1939, Vol. 10, Issue 1, 21–37.

J.R. Hicks, *Value and Capital*, 2nd Edn. London: Oxford University Press, 1946.

R.J. Shiller, "The Term Structure of Interest Rates," in B. Friedman and F. Hahn, (eds.), *The Handbook of Monetary Economics*, 1990, (Amsterdam: North Holland).

S. Homer and M.L. Liebowitz, *Inside the Yield book: New Tools for Bond Market Strategy*, Englewood Cliffs, NJ: Prentice Hall, 1972.

S.K. Barua, J.R. Varma and V. Raghunathan, *Portfolio Management*, First Revised Edition, New Delhi: Tata McGraw Hill, 1992.

Z. Bodie, A. Kane, A. Marcus and P. Mohanty, *Investments*, 8th Edn. New Delhi: Mc Graw Hill Education, 2009.

Pooled Investments: Mutual Funds

17

CHAPTER OBJECTIVES

- ❐ Understanding the role of different entities in mutual fund operations
- ❐ Evaluating different mutual fund schemes available in India
- ❐ Assessing the advantages and disadvantages of investing in mutual funds
- ❐ Measuring the costs and returns associated with mutual funds and their impact on investors returns
- ❐ Gaining insight into the regulatory and tax aspects of mutual fund investment

A collection of instruments across which an investor has spread his funds is referred to as investment portfolio. Investment theory recommends that investors should try to make sure that their investment portfolio is a balanced portfolio, i.e., they have a mix of instruments varying from highly risky investments with higher expected rates of return to low volatility instruments with lower rates of return. The basic principle of diversification requires that an investor should spread his money across multiple investment vehicles. The main aim of investing ones' funds in different asset classes is to maximize returns or minimize risk of losing the funds invested.

The word investment vehicle refers to any asset in which investors can put their savings with the aim to multiply their wealth. A wide variety of investment vehicles are available at the disposal of the investors to construct their portfolio. In other words, an investment vehicle is an asset/product used by investors to try to generate positive returns. Stocks and bonds are the two most commonly known and used investment vehicles. As we know, stocks represent the ownership capital. Equity shareholders actually hold an interest or stake in a company listed and publicly traded on stock market like Bombay Stock Exchange (BSE) and National Stock Exchange (NSE). The price of the shares on the stock exchange keeps on changing on the basis of a number of factors such as company's earnings, the quality of its management, its future prospects and projects, relative strength of competitors, performance of the industry and economy-wide factors. The investors can buy any share they want from the stock market at the prevailing market price. The decision to buy a share should be taken after a detailed analysis of various factors and the past price movement of the stock under consideration.

On the other hand, bonds refer to debt and investment in bonds is actually the purchase of debt. The return on bonds is called interest and it is paid at a fixed or floating rate. Private entities or sovereign government may issue bonds. Treasury bills are bonds issued by the government and they are considered to be very safe investments. Municipal bonds are another type of government bonds, issued by the local government. Bonds issued by government bodies are the worst performing by way of returns but they are traditionally popular with investors primarily concerned with preserving their principal. Bonds issued by private entities are called corporate bonds. Corporate bonds usually offer a better rate of return than bonds issued by government entities, but they are a bit more risky. Some corporate bonds are also listed and traded on stock exchanges, though in India the corporate bond market is not as deep as the equity market. Compared to bonds, stocks provide relatively higher potential returns but at the same time, stocks come with a higher risk of losing some or all of your investment.

So far our discussion has been focused primarily on equity and to some extent bonds. But, in the real world, investment portfolios would not comprise of equity alone or a mix of debt and equity. There are many other investment avenues and asset classes available for investors to construct their portfolios. A portfolio can comprise of a mix of domestic and foreign equities, domestic and foreign fixed income securities, cash and cash equivalents, commodities, real estate, derivatives, mutual funds and other alternative investments. Different investment vehicles are exhibited in Figure 17.1.

Figure 17.1 Different investment vehicles.

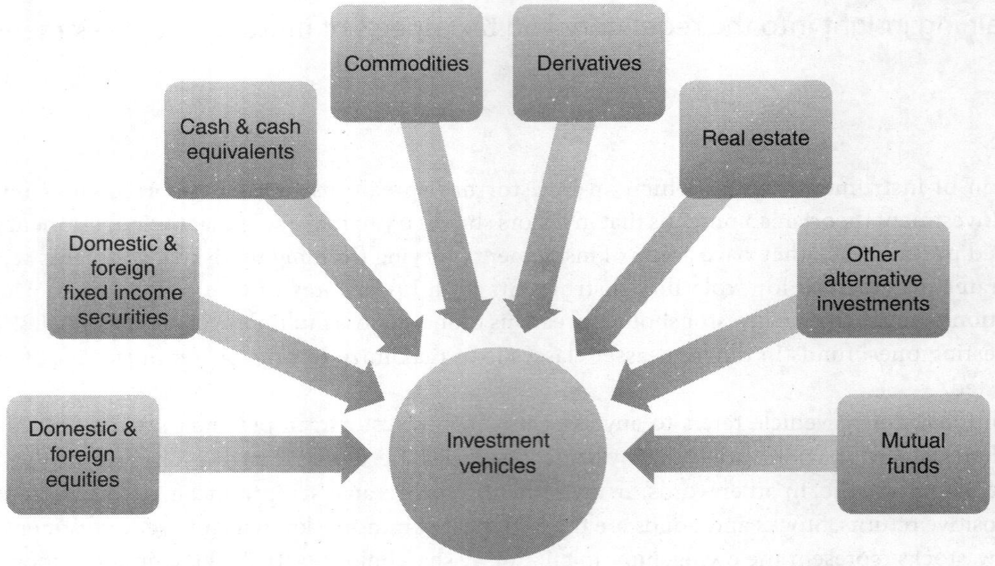

The types of investments listed above can be grouped into four different groups on the basis of their risk. The four types are:

1. **No Risk or Very Low Risk Investment Vehicles: Cash and Cash Equivalents**
   Cash and cash equivalents are low risk investment vehicles that typically provide very low return on investment and have literally no inflation protection. They are short-term and can be easily liquidated and converted into cash, within a period of one year or less. The assets that are usually called cash equivalents are savings accounts, certificates of deposit, treasury bills and money market funds.

2. **The Low Risk Investments Group: High-Quality Bonds (Fixed-Income Securities)**
   Most pension and retirement money falls into this category of investment vehicles globally as they provide a very good balance between risk and returns for long-term investments. This group mainly comprises zero coupon bonds, high quality corporate bonds, bond-based mutual funds and ETFs.
3. **Moderate Risk Investments Group: High Quality Stocks and Stock-Based Mutual Funds**
   This class of investment vehicles mainly includes equity shares of the companies that are performing well and ensuring that their shares trade at a good price in the market. This group mainly comprises blue chip stocks, stock-based mutual funds and ETFs and moderate risk bonds.
4. **High Risk or Speculative Investments Group: Hedge Funds, Junk Bonds and Equity**
   This group comprises investment vehicles that can be expected to turn in very high returns but this possibility comes with a high probability of extreme variability of these returns. This group mainly comprises derivatives, junk bonds, high risk mutual funds and ETFs, equity stocks (other than blue chips and high quality stocks), antiques, precious metals, hedge funds and currency.

Though traditionally the focus of investments has been domestic equity and bonds, of late, more and more investors are becoming interested in other investment avenues like derivatives, mutual funds, commodities, real estate and foreign investment avenues. As mutual funds represent a fast growing class of assets, we will discuss their features and other dimensions in detail in this chapter.

Mutual Funds

In simple terms, a mutual fund may be described as a collective investment vehicle. It is a collection of stocks and bonds. When an investor invests in a mutual fund, he actually pools his money together with a number of other investors, which enables him to invest in specific securities through a professional manager. Mutual funds are established with a specific strategy in mind, and they can be of different types according to their distinct focus on large stocks, small stocks, stocks in certain countries, bonds from governments, bonds from companies, stocks and bonds, stocks in certain industries, fund of funds and so on.

The primary advantage of a mutual fund is that investors can invest their money in assets of varying risks without undertaking extensive research and analysis that are often needed to choose a sound investment. Theoretically, a mutual fund should generate a better return than any investment the investor selects himself. A mutual fund is a trust constituted as per the provisions of the Indian Trust Act, 1881 and registered with SEBI. By participating in a mutual fund scheme, an investor becomes the owner of investments made under the scheme in the proportion to his contribution.

Indian mutual fund industry was stagnant for quite some time. In fact, till 1986, Unit Trust of India was the only mutual fund in India. After 1986 also, the mutual fund industry continued to be in the domain of public sector. It was only in 1992 (after the economic liberalization in 1991) that the regulators allowed private sector companies to sell mutual fund schemes to public in India.

The mutual fund industry in India that started in 1963 with the establishment of Unit Trust of India (UTI), has grown from strength to strength. The first scheme launched by UTI was Unit Scheme 1964. At the end of the year 1988, UTI had ₹6,700 crore of assets under management. After 1987, public sector mutual funds set up by public sector banks and Life Insurance Corporation of India (LIC) and General Insurance Corporation of India (GIC) entered the mutual fund market in India. SBI Mutual Fund was the first non-UTI public sector mutual fund established in 1987, followed by the establishment of Canbank Mutual Fund, Punjab National Bank Mutual Fund, Indian Bank Mutual Fund, Bank of India Mutual Fund and Bank of Baroda Mutual Fund.

LIC and GIC also established their mutual funds around the same time. At the end of 1993, the assets under management of the Indian mutual fund industry were ₹47,004 crore.

Post liberalization era saw the entry of private sector mutual funds in 1993 when the erstwhile Kothari Pioneer became the first private sector mutual fund to be registered in India. Since then the number of mutual funds has increased exponentially. By the end of January 2003, there were 33 mutual funds with total assets of ₹1,21,805 crore. However, Unit Trust of India continued to dominate the sector with ₹44,541 crore of assets under management. Post February 2003, after the bifurcation of UTI, the Indian Mutual fund industry entered a phase of growth and consolidation, with private sector players taking the centre-stage. The assets under management of mutual funds in India increased by 6.85 % from June 2014 to September 2014. In fact, during one month (July to August 2014), assets under management (AUM) of the country's 45 fund houses increased from ₹10,06,452 crore to ₹10,12,824 crore – up by ₹6,372 crore. The equity mutual funds witnessed an inflow of ₹5,217 crore during this period, taking the assets base to ₹2.35 lakh crore, balanced fund had an inflow of ₹448 crore taking the AUM to ₹17,293 crore and liquid funds' AUM grew from ₹2.44 lakh crore to ₹2.45 lakh crore. However, income funds' asset base fell to ₹4.61 lakh crore in August 2014 from ₹4.71 lakh crore in the preceding month, led by the outflows of ₹12,696 crore. Sector wise resource mobilization by mutual funds during 2013–14 is exhibit in Table 17.1.

Mutual funds have continued to gain immense popularity as an investment vehicle in India and their assets under management have grown at a fast pace. However, in comparison to global growth levels, Indian mutual funds are at quite a low level of penetration. Despite the tremendous growth in assets under management, the size of mutual fund industry assets in India is less than 5% of GDP as compared to 70% in the US, 61% in France and 37% in Brazil.

The Indian mutual fund industry is in a state of flux, with many consolidations and exit of some foreign mutual funds.

Marketview 17.1 Recent Developments in Indian Mutual Fund Industry

Indian mutual fund industry is witnessing a string of exits by foreign fund houses. Sometime back US-based Fidelity and Morgan Stanley had exited the domestic market after selling assets to L&T MF and HDFC MF, respectively. Latest in the line is ING Investment Management India. Birla Sun Life Mutual Fund, a part of Aditya Birla Financial Services Group is rumored to have acquired the assets of the company for a yet undisclosed amount. According to AMFI reports, ING Investment Management had average assets under management of ₹563.82 crore by the end of last financial year.

Source: Based on story published at http://articles.economictimes.indiatimes.com/2014-05-15/news/49873510_1_mumbai-ing-investment-management-india-assets, accessed on November 25, 2014.

Though Indian mutual fund sector has registered healthy growth, it continues to be very small compared to insurance and other financial services in the country.

Mutual Fund Operations

In India, the main parties involved in mutual fund operations are:

TABLE 17.1 Sector-wise resource mobilization by mutual funds during 2013–14 (₹ in crore)

Month/ year	Private sector MFs				Private sector MFs				UTI MF				
	Open-ended	Close-ended	Interval	Total	Open-ended	Close-ended	Interval	Total	Open-ended	Close-ended	Interval	Total	Grand total
1	2	3	4	5	6	7	8	9	10	11	12	13	14
Mobilisation of funds													
2012–13	58,62,749	58,175	7,022	59,27,947	6,98,358	8,230	NA	7,06,589	6,26,821	5,641	888	6,33,350	72,67,885
2013–14	79,12,853	1,21,634	14,909	80,49,397	9,01,807	14,377	166	9,16,351	7,92,865	8,356	1,130	8,02,352	97,68,100
Repurchases/Redemption													
2012–13	57,76,161	80,387	6,297	58,62,845	6,86,483	13,131	166	6,99,781	6,21,562	5,067	2,092	6,28,750	71,91,346
2013–14	79,19,832	70,564	10,161	80,00,559	9,02,818	8,925	64	9,11,808	7,95,328	5,136	1,486	8,01,950	97,14,318
Net inflow/Outflow of funds													
2012–13	86,588	−22,212	725	65,102	11,875	−4,901	−166	6,808	5,259	574	−1,204	4,629	76,539
2013–14	−6,979	51,069	4,748	48,838	−1,011	5,452	101	4,542	−2,463	3,220	−355	401	53,782

Source: www.sebi.gov.in, accessed on November 18, 2014.

1. **Sponsors:** Sponsors are the initiators/promoters of a mutual fund. A sponsor can be a bank or a financial services company or a financial institution who needs to obtain license from SEBI to sponsor a mutual fund. For example, Reliance Capital sponsoring Reliance mutual funds. Sponsors are the settlers of mutual fund trust and they delegate functions to the trustees.
2. **Trustees:** The trustees of mutual fund are appointed by the sponsors from amongst individuals or a body corporate. To ensure fairness, SEBI has stipulated that at least 2/3 of the trustees are independent. Trustees hold the properties of various schemes in trust for the benefit of investors. They appoint asset management companies and monitor their functioning.
3. **Asset Management Company (AMC):** AMC is appointed by the trustees of mutual fund to manage the operational aspects of mutual fund like new schemes, designing of schemes, managing investments, investor service and interaction, etc. They are the face of mutual fund and are required to be registered with SEBI under Portfolio Managers Rules and Regulations, 1993.

   The income of AMC comes from the investment management and advisory fees based on the size of the schemes managed by it. In India, there are certain caps on this fee. The fee allowed is 1.25% of weekly average net asset up to first ₹100 crore and 1% of weekly average net assets thereafter. Fund managers are the key functionaries in AMCs. They are assisted by a team of analysts to study industries, sectors, companies and markets.
4. **Custodians:** The custodians are separate entities who handle the assets of a mutual fund. They look after back office operations like receipt and delivery of securities, distribution of dividends and collection of income.
5. **Registrars and Transfer Agents:** Registrars and transfer agents are approved by SEBI. Sponsors have the freedom to decide whether they want to handle functions like issue of units, release of fact sheets, etc. in-house or outsource them to the SEBI approved functionaries.

Mutual Fund Schemes

1. **On the Basis of Structure, Mutual Fund Schemes are Broadly Classified as Open-Ended, Close-Ended and Interval Schemes:** Close ended mutual funds are also termed as traded mutual funds as they can be bought and sold like a normal share on the stock exchanges where they are listed. Usually close-ended mutual funds focus on a specific industry or sector.

   A close-end mutual fund raises a fixed amount of capital only once through a new fund offer (NFO) by issuing a fixed number of units to be purchased by the investors. Close-ended schemes do not issue new units on an ongoing basis. Once the issue closes, the close-ended fund is listed and traded like a stock on a stock exchange. A unit of close-end mutual fund represents a proportion of a specialized portfolio of securities that is actively managed by professional investment advisors. In a close-ended mutual fund, the number of shares/units always remains fixed. These funds have a stipulated maturity period like 5–7 years. Some close-ended funds have an option of selling back the units to the mutual fund company through periodic repurchase at NAV related prices.

   The market price of a close-end mutual fund varies from NAV of the scheme in response to changes in market forces of supply and demand as well as on the account of the changes in values of the securities comprising the portfolio of the fund. The prices are also influenced by the expectations of the unit-holders and other market factors. Typically the prices of close-ended mutual funds converge towards NAV of the scheme as it reaches its maturity. In other words, close-ended mutual funds generally trade at a discount to NAV but the discount decreases as maturity approaches.

Open-ended mutual funds are the conventional type of mutual funds and they are more common compared to the close-ended mutual funds. Unlike the close-ended mutual funds, in open-ended mutual funds, the fund house continuously buys and sells units from/to the investors. They are always open for subscription. There is no restriction on the amount of units the fund will issue. The fund size keeps on changing as new units are created and issued if there is demand for the same and the old units are eliminated if there is redemption pressure or increased supply. It should, however, be noted that if the fund manager determines that the fund's total assets have become too large to be effectively managed to achieve its stated objective, the fund can be closed to new investors and at times even be closed to new investment by existing fund investors.

Open-ended mutual funds have no fixed date of maturity on which the units would be permanently redeemed or terminated. The sale and purchase of units of open-ended schemes takes place directly between the investor on one hand and the fund house on the other. By selling and buying back fund shares on tap, these schemes provide investors with a very liquid investing vehicle.

Open-ended vs. close-ended mutual funds

Open-ended funds limit a fund managers' ability to take long-term bets on good stocks as they have to sell a part of fund's holdings every time there is a redemption request. The lock-in feature of the close-ended funds gives fund managers the freedom to continue to hold a stock trading low for a long period, to try and generate better returns. Further, in case of less liquid, small and mid cap stocks, the lock-in period of close-ended mutual funds minimizes excessive redemptions. In an open-ended mutual fund, the fund house has to sell certain stocks at a loss if it gets redemption request.

Further, fund managers of close-ended funds churn portfolios less frequently, hold stocks and have a low turnover ratio. A low turnover ratio implies a lower expense ratio (annual fee charged by the fund house from investors) because every time the portfolio is churned, the fund house incurs the cost of transaction by way of brokerage fee and securities transaction tax.

However, close-ended funds suffer from many limitations as well. The investment in these funds can only be in lump-sum and SIP (systematic investment plan) is not possible as it can be subscribed only during a limited period. This can prevent small investors from investing in close-ended funds. Further investing a lump-sum effectively requires the investors to get the timing of the investment right, which is quite difficult in case of retail investors. If investors enter the fund at the wrong time, they can end up losing most of their capital, especially in case of schemes investing in small-cap stocks.

The lock-in period, eulogized above as a virtue, is itself a source of limitation for close-ended funds. Lock-in period, usually three years, not only deprives the investors from exiting a badly performing fund but also results in increased expense for them because it allows the AMCs to pay their agents the full commission upfront for the duration of the lock-in period.

In addition to the above woes, most close-ended funds are illiquid despite being listed on exchanges because of the low trading volume. This makes post lock-in period exit difficult as well. On top of it all, the close-ended mutual funds are subject to secondary market volatility and usually trade at a discount from the scheme's NAV. This affects the investor's returns when he sells his close-ended units in the secondary market.

The limitations of the close-end mutual funds far outweigh the advantages they offer to the investors. Thus, investors, especially retail investors, are better off investing in open-ended schemes that have recorded consistent performance and have achieved their stated investment objectives year after year. The returns of open-ended funds in India have also been superior to the best performing close-ended funds over a span of last five years.

Interval schemes are the schemes that combine the features of both, the open-ended and the close-ended schemes. The units of interval schemes may be listed and traded on a stock exchange or they may be open for subscription or redemption during pre-specified intervals at prices related to the scheme NAVs.

2. **On the Basis of Investment Objectives, the Mutual Fund Schemes are of Following Types:**
   (a) *Equity (Growth) schemes*
   (b) *Income schemes*
   (c) *Balanced schemes*
   (d) *Money market/liquid schemes*
   (e) *Tax saving schemes*
   (f) *Offshore funds*
   (g) *Gilt funds*
   (h) *Special schemes like index schemes, etc.*

   Let us understand the features of each of the above listed schemes.

   (a) *Growth schemes,* also known as equity schemes, aim to provide capital appreciation to the investors over medium to long term. A large proportion of the funds of these schemes is invested in equities. The fund managers of these schemes are willing to bear short-term decline in value in expectation of future appreciation. Such schemes are best suited to the investors in their prime earning years and seeking long-term growth. Investors desirous of generating regular income or investing their money for short-term should not invest in growth or equity schemes. The variety of equity mutual funds schemes offered ranges from diversified (across sectors) to large cap to mid cap to index scheme to equity linked saving schemes for tax savings. Some of the top ranked equity mutual funds in India are Birla Sun Life Top 100 Fund, BNP Paribas Equity Fund, SBI Blue Chip Fund and UTI Equity Fund.

   (b) *Income schemes,* also known as debt schemes, aim to provide limited capital appreciation but regular and steady income to the unitholders. The fund managers of these schemes generally invest in debt instruments viz., cash and bonds. These range from liquid schemes to gilt schemes to fixed maturity plans to floating rate debt schemes.

   These schemes usually make regular payments to their investors, although dividends can also be reinvested to buy more units of the scheme. Such schemes are best suited to retired people who require regular income and capital protection.

   The downside of these schemes comes from fluctuations in interest rates of the debt instruments or from the default in payment by the bond issuer. Rise in interest rates can cause the NAV to fall and vice versa. Risk of default is non-existent or very low in the income funds that invest in government securities. Some of the top ranked income funds in India are HDFC High Interest Fund – Dynamic Plan, Reliance Dynamic Bond Fund, UTI-Dynamic Bond Fund, BNP Paribas Flexi Debt Fund, Canara Robeco Dynamic Bond Fund, DSP BlackRock Strategic Bond Fund, ICICI Prudential Income Opportunities Fund, L&T Flexi Bond Fund, Tata Income Fund and UTI Bond Fund.

   (c) *Balanced funds* try to offer the best of both worlds to their investors by aiming for a balanced mix of equities and debt instruments. They invest in both stocks and fixed income securities in the proportion indicated in their offer documents, usually 50:50. The objective of these schemes is to provide both income and growth by distributing a part of the income and capital gains they generate, from time to time. The mix of debt and equity enables these schemes to retain a relatively low risk. The debt element of the fund earns a regular income and acts as the safety net during market fluctuations, while equities provide the potential for higher capital appreciation. Balanced schemes are best suited to investors seeking regular income and moderate capital appreciation. Some of the top ranked balanced funds in India are ICICI Prudential Balanced Fund, HDFC Balanced Fund, HDFC Prudence Fund, Tata Balanced Fund, Birla Sun Life 95 Fund, Canara Robeco Balance, Franklin India Balanced Fund, Reliance Regular Savings Fund – Balanced and SBI Magnum Balanced Fund.

(d) *Money market funds*, also called liquid schemes, aim to provide stability, liquidity, preservation of capital, slightly higher interest rates than bank deposits and moderate income. Since safety and liquidity is their important criteria, the fund managers of such schemes prefer to invest in short-term instruments with comparatively higher safety such as treasury bills, commercial paper, interbank call money market and certificates of deposit. Returns on these schemes fluctuate with changes in the interest rates prevailing in the call money market. These schemes are best suited for corporates and high net worth individual investors seeking to invest their considerable surplus funds for short periods. Some of the top ranked liquid funds in India are Canara Robeco Liquid, DSP BlackRock Liquidity Fund, Pramerica Liquid Fund, SBI Premier Liquid Fund, Axis Liquid Fund, DWS Insta Cash Plus Fund and HSBC Cash Fund.

(e) *Tax saving schemes*, also called equity linked saving schemes aim to offer tax incentives to the investors under income tax laws prescribed from time to time. The latest provision notified vide Union Budget 2014 has made contribution to mutual fund schemes notified under Section 10(23D) of the Income Tax Act (normally referred to as ELSS Mutual Fund Schemes or Tax Saving Mutual Fund Schemes) eligible for investment for tax saving purpose with a mandatory lock-in period of 3 years. The funds are best suited to investors seeking tax incentives and rebates. They have the added advantage of offering long-term growth opportunities because they invest in equities. ELSS also make the stock market more buoyant by promoting long-term investments in equities. Some of the top ranked ELSS in India are Axis Long Term Equity Fund, Reliance Tax Saver Fund, BNP Paribas Long Term Equity Fund, ICICI Prudential Tax Plan, Principal Tax Saving Fund and Religare Invesco Tax Plan.

Marketview 17.2 Categories of Mutual Funds in India

1. Balanced Funds
2. Credit Opportunities Funds
3. Diversified Equity Funds
4. Equity Linked Savings Scheme (ELSS)
5. Index Funds
6. Large Cap-oriented Equity Funds
7. Liquid Funds
8. Long Term Gilt Funds
9. Long Term Income Funds
10. Monthly Income Plan – Aggressive
11. Short Term Income Funds
12. Small and Mid-cap Equity Funds
13. Thematic – Infrastructure Funds
14. Ultra Short-term Debt Funds

(f) *Offshore funds* specialize in investing in assets of foreign companies or corporations. They aim to offer investors access to international markets and major exchanges. Offshore funds may be thematic, country-specific or a mix of asset-specific and country-specific. They are structured in a manner similar to the traditional mutual funds. The main advantage of the offshore mutual funds is that they provide country and sector diversification and enable the investors to generate better returns by investing in global brands and business. Offshore funds come with significant risks as well. The main risks involved in investing in offshore funds are volatility in the global capital markets, fluctuation in interest rates, currency exchange rates swings, changes in government policies, diverse taxation laws and other political and economic developments. These funds are regulated by the RBI directives. Some of the notable Indian offshore funds are ICICI Prudential US Bluechip Equity Fund, DWS Gold and Precious Metal Offshore fund, HSBC Brazil Equity Fund, Franklin US Opportunities Fund, Reliance US Dollar Fund and DSP BlackRock US Flexible Equity Fund. Recently a Mumbai-based financial advisory firm, Jain Investment, has launched an offshore fund called India Exception Equity Fund, with a portfolio of 10–20 Indian companies. The fund, planned to be a dollar fund, has the objective of raising at least $5 million or ₹30 crore by March 2015 from foreign nationals. The minimum subscription amount is $10,00,00 (₹61 lakh).

(g) *Gilt funds* are income/debt funds that invest exclusively in securities issued by the government. These schemes are low risk as government securities have no default risk. Theoretically, NAVs of these schemes fluctuate in response to changes in interest rates and other economic factors.

(h) *Special schemes*

(i) *Index funds* represent passive investment strategy and replicate the movements of benchmark indices. Index funds are constructed to replicate the performance of a particular index of market performance such as the S&P CNX Nifty or SENSEX. This means that the portfolio of these schemes will consist of only those stocks that constitute the index that they replicate. Even the proportionate holding of each stock in fund is identical to weightage of the stocks in the index. With the result, the returns from such schemes can be expected to be more or less equivalent to those of the benchmark index. Index funds is a very popular concept in the west. Some of the top rated index funds in India are Goldman Sachs Nifty Exchange Traded Scheme (GS Nifty BeES), IDBI Nifty Index Fund, HDFC Index Fund – Nifty Plan, HDFC Index Fund – Sensex Plan, Reliance Index Fund – Nifty Plan, SBI Nifty Index Fund, UTI Nifty Index Fund, Franklin India Index Fund – NSE Nifty Plan and ICICI Prudential Index Fund – Nifty Plan.

(ii) *Sector specific funds* are the funds that invest in the securities of only those sectors or industries or capital market segments such as large caps, mid caps or small caps that have been specified in the offer documents of the schemes. Accordingly there can be technology fund, pharmaceuticals fund, infrastructure fund, fast moving consumer goods (FMCG) fund, mid-cap fund and so on. The returns of these funds depend on the performance of the sectors/industries/segment they invest in. These funds usually give higher returns but they are more risky than diversified funds. The reason is that the risk is not spread, rather it remains limited to a specific sector/segment. If something goes wrong with the entire sector/segment, the returns plunge. Therefore, investors of these funds need to be more watchful and ready to exit at an appropriate time. The main aim of these schemes is to provide a relatively high return opportunity within the equity space, of course at a higher risk.

(iii) *Other mutual fund products:*

- Hedge funds

- Exchange traded funds (ETF)
- Structured products
- Fund of funds schemes
- Arbitrage funds
- International funds
- Real estate investment trusts (REIT)

Hedge funds are the variants of mutual funds that enjoy lighter regulations as compared to mutual funds. They are open to high net worth individuals only and engage in activities like short sales, use of leverage and derivatives. Such activities are a complete no-no for mutual funds. Hedge funds contribute to market efficiency and enhance liquidity in the capital markets. They serve as a risk management tool for investors and provide valuable portfolio diversification opportunities. Hedge funds aim to generate positive annual returns, keep volatility low and preserve capital by trading a range of strategies across different asset classes – equities, commodities, currencies, debt and a range of derivatives like – futures, options, swaps and forwards. Their strategies revolve around constructing a conservative investment portfolio with the principal aim to preserve wealth and increase risk adjusted absolute returns rather than to beat a benchmark.

Both mutual funds and hedge funds are managed portfolios but hedge funds are managed much more aggressively. Since hedge funds are allowed to take speculate positions in derivatives and engage in short selling, they are able to make money even in falling market. Mutual fund managers or long only managers, are not on allowed to short sell and are typically considered safer.

Exchange traded funds have caught investors' fancy in India in the recent times. They are a hybrid of open and close-ended index funds. They are listed like a close-ended fund and they create and redeem units according to changes in demand like any open-ended fund.

Exchange traded funds are investment vehicles that are listed and traded like stocks on stock exchanges. Since ETFs track certain indices of market performance (e.g., S&P BSE SENSEX or the BANKEX), their returns depend on the movement of the chosen index. They are similar to index funds and/or sectoral funds in that they track an index, a commodity or a sector but they differ from index funds and/or sectoral funds in that they are traded on stock exchanges. Because the ETFS are traded like stocks, their price changes throughout the day as they are bought and sold and their NAV is not calculated every day as it is done for mutual funds. ETFs give the advantages of diversification of an index fund along with the ability to sell short, buy on margin and purchase even one share. Further, the expense ratios for ETFs are generally lower than those of the most open-ended index mutual funds. They also have a lower tracking error as compared to most open-ended index mutual funds. ETFs are considered to be better than close-ended index funds because they trade near their NAV or fair value whereas close-ended index funds trade at a discount from their NAV. Some of the top ranked ETFs in India are GS Bank BeES, GS PSU Bank BeES, Motilal MOSt Shares Midcap 100 ETF, Kotak PSU Bank ETF and IIFL Nifty ETF.

Structured products are a kind of funds that draw upon derivatives in combination with debt. Their attraction lies in high upside potential and protection against downside risk.

(iv) *Fund of Funds (FoF) schemes* are schemes that invest in a portfolio of mutual funds, i.e., they invest either in other schemes of the same AMC or mutual funds of other companies. The main aim of fund of funds scheme is that it spreads risks across a larger set of securities. A fund of funds invests in various mutual fund schemes to provide a high degree of diversification and tax advantage.

International funds are the mutual funds that invest in cross-border instruments listed on foreign exchanges or debt issued by foreign entities.

Arbitrage funds are mutual funds that leverage the price differential between the cash and derivatives market to try and generate superior returns. These funds are hybrid in nature as they can invest in both debt and equity. These funds are suitable for low risk taking investors. The main aim of the fund managers of these funds is to take advantage of market inefficiencies to generate profits. Most Arbitrage funds aim to provide returns superior to liquid funds without taking any market risk at all. As these funds invest mostly in equities, their tax treatment is the same as that of equity funds.

Real estate investment trusts are companies that own or fund income-producing real estate. REITs, modeled like mutual funds, are quasi debt-equity instruments. They allow the investors to invest in portfolios of large-scale properties by buying their units or shares. REITs aim to provide the investors benefit of both stable income streams and long-term capital appreciation. Globally, REITS pay out all of their taxable income as dividends to their shareholders. The property developers also benefit from REITs as they improve property market transparency, smoothen volatility in the sector and increase the possibility of lowering the cost of capital on funds raised for development of real estate.

Marketview 17.3 Real Estate Investment Trusts in India

The stock market regulator in India, the Securities and Exchange Board of India (SEBI) had announced guidelines for the creation of real estate investment trusts (REITs) in India sometime back. On the same lines as mutual funds that pool funds for investment in equity and debt, REITs would pool funds from investors to invest in income-generating (rental assets) properties. Thus, REITs offer investors a way to diversify their portfolios by including investment in real estate without actually buying a property. Like mutual funds, REITs will also issue units to investors, which will be listed and traded on exchanges. They are expected to establish a new asset class, which would be like a quasi debt-equity instrument, offering risk-averse investors the benefits of both, yield as well as capital appreciation. Further, REITs are expected to improve transparency in property market, smoothen volatility in property prices and lower the cost of capital for developers.

Source: Based on story published at: http://www.moneycontrol.com/news/business/how-reits-will-begame-changer-for-indian-real-estate_1170812.html, accessed on January 15, 2015.

3. **On the Basis of the Assets they Invest in, Mutual Funds are of Following Types:**
   (a) *Equity schemes*
   (b) *Debt schemes*
   (c) *Hybrid schemes.*

   Equity schemes invest a bulk of their portfolio in equities. Different types of equity schemes in India include diversified equity schemes, index schemes, ELSS, thematic equity schemes, sectoral equity schemes and market segment equity schemes.

Debt schemes mainly invest in debt instruments and cash. Different types of debt schemes in India include capital protection funds, gilt schemes, floating rate debt schemes, mixed debt schemes and fixed maturity plans.

Hybrid schemes invest in both debt and equity. The different types of hybrid schemes in India include equity-oriented schemes, debt-oriented schemes and variable asset allocation schemes.

Key Measures/Parameters in Mutual Fund Investment

The following are some of the key costs and performance measures important from the point of view of mutual fund investment:

1. **Entry and Exit Loads:** Entry and exit loads refer to the cost of investing in mutual funds. Entry load is imposed on an investor when he buys the units. All schemes do not impose entry load, accordingly, there are load schemes (imposing entry load) and no load schemes. Now, no entry load is imposed on the mutual fund applications received directly by the company. Exit load is a charge imposed by the company when the investor sells off the units held by him. It usually varies between no-load to 3%.
2. **Net Asset Value (NAV):** It is the actual value of a unit of any mutual fund scheme on any given trading day.
   It is computed as:

$$\text{NAV} = \frac{(\text{Market value of fund's Investments} + \text{Receivables} + \text{Accrued income} - \text{Liabilities} - \text{Accrued expenses})}{\text{Number of outstanding units}}$$

3. **Rate of Return:** Like for any other investment, the rate of return can be calculated for mutual funds for a month-long, quarter-long, year-long or any other duration or holding period.
   It is computed as:

$$\text{Rate of return} = \frac{\{(\text{NAV at the end of the period} - \text{NAV at the beginning of the period}) + \text{Dividend}\}}{\text{NAV at the beginning of the period}}$$

   The return of scheme from the date of issue is called compounded annual total return (CATR) and it can be calculated on NAV basis or price basis. It makes adjustments for dividends, bonus and rights and includes reinvestment of dividends, wherever applicable.

   On price basis, CATR reflects the return to investors in terms of repurchase or market price. It is based on the assumption that the dividend earned by the unit is reinvested at the prevailing market price or reissue price. On NAV basis, CATR measures the return generated by the fund or NAV and it assumes that the dividend earned is reinvested in the scheme at the NAV prevailing on the day it is announced.
4. **Ex-Mark:** Ex-mark is actually R^2 (coefficient of determination) that we have discussed in the preceding chapters. It is a term coined by John C. Bogle to indicate the extent to which the returns of a mutual fund are explained by financial markets.
5. **Portfolio Turnover Ratio:** Mutual fund schemes have varied asset mix and investments across broad asset classes like cash, stocks and bonds. In order to ensure good returns, fund managers may churn the portfolio of the scheme from time to time. Portfolio turnover ratio is related to the churning of the portfolio. It is measured as:

$$= \frac{\text{Lower of sales or purchase during a given period}}{\text{Average daily net assets}}$$

Marketview 17.4 Benchmarking Mutual Funds in India

The Securities and Exchange Board of India (SEBI) has made it mandatory since 2010 for mutual funds in India to declare a benchmark, usually an index of market performance that would serve as a standard to evaluate the performance of the mutual fund in terms of its returns. SENSEX and Nifty are the most widely followed benchmarks for mutual funds in India.

SEBI guidelines require mutual funds to disclose their performance during the past 1, 3 and 10 years as well as since launch vis-à-vis the benchmark index chosen by the fund house.

Benchmarking helps investors compare the performance of their funds with that of the broader market. Benchmarks also help fund houses set target returns and endeavor to perform better than the chosen index. The concept of benchmarking is simple. The NAV of funds fluctuates with the market. The volatility of NAV is also measured in terms of beta. If a fund does better than its rising benchmark index, say Nifty, then it is said to have out-performed the index. Conversely, if a fund rises less than its rising benchmark index, then it is said to have under-performed the index.

Investing in Mutual Funds: Investors' Perspective

The advantages offered by mutual funds in terms of diversification and professional management of investible surplus are offset by the risks involved in investing in them. The fees and taxes chargeable on mutual funds erode their returns. Mutual funds sound very attractive but before investing in them, investors should gain adequate insight into the pros and cons of inve sting in mutual funds.

The Upsides of Mutual Fund Investments

1. **Benefit of Diversification and Professional Management of Funds:** Highly qualified and experienced money managers are employed by fund houses to analyze, select and monitor the performance of the assets held by the mutual funds. Mutual funds, through their assortment of assets, provide diversification opportunities far more easily than individual security selections to create a diversified portfolio.
2. **Liquidity:** Mutual fund can be sold easily at the prevailing NAV at any time. This makes them very liquid instruments.
3. **Regulatory Control and Transparency:** Mutual funds in India are subject to stringent regulatory control by SEBI and they are required to act within the ambit of the restrictions imposed by SEBI. A slew of regulations has ensured that the mutual funds offer transparency and protect investor interests.
4. **Availability of Ratings:** Many agencies in India furnish extensive information on mutual funds' performance. Value Research, Economic Times and CRISIL publish relevant information to judge the performance of various mutual funds in India. Availability of such extensive data makes it easier for investors to choose mutual funds that best suit their investment objectives and risk tolerance.

Value Research publishes Mutual Fund Performance Report to help investors track the progress of fund within the relevant fund category and benchmarks. The expanded edition of the Mutual Fund Performance Report includes: the risk-adjusted ratings, trailing return averages for each fund category, leaders and laggards in each fund category, trailing total returns for nine time periods – from one month to seven years, trailing total returns for corresponding periods of 10 leading debt and equity benchmarks, each fund's ranking in its category, fund's complete modern portfolio theory statistics based on trailing three-year period, standard deviation, Sharpe's Ratio, Treynor Ratio, Alpha, Beta and R-squared.

CRISIL publishes mutual fund rankings within a peer group and for open-ended schemes only. Ranking is based on the parameters like superior return score, mean return and volatility, downside risk probability, portfolio concentration analysis, liquidity analysis, asset quality, modified duration/average maturity asset size and tracking error.

5. **Multiple Options:** There are a variety of mutual funds available for investors. Within the broad categories described above, many options are available for investors like systematic investment plan, dividend plan, dividend reinvestment plan, systematic withdrawal plan and systematic transfer plan.

   Within a scheme chosen by them, investors can opt for (i) dividend payout option and receive dividend as and when declared by scheme, (ii) dividend reinvestment option and receive more units of the scheme by getting the dividend declared by the scheme reinvested at the applicable NAV or (iii) growth option where there is no dividend and the gains of the scheme are reflected in the NAV.

   An additional advantage of investing in many mutual funds is that lump-sum investment is not required. Even small amounts can be invested at regular intervals (usually monthly) to buy more and more units. Such scheme is called systematic investment plan (SIP) and it offers two main advantages, namely enabling even small investors to invest their savings and helping investors in rupee cost averaging (rupee cost averaging implies that investor buys fewer units at higher price and more units at low price as the amount of SIP remains unchanged every month).

   On the same lines as SIP is another scheme that gives investors tremendous flexibility. It is systematic transfer plan (STP). STP is a scheme that enables the investors to transfer funds from one scheme to another gradually. This can be beneficial for investors who want to invest their money in stages in equity market. They can invest their entire surplus in a liquid fund and opt for STP rather than the equity fund. This way they can continue to earn a return on funds yet not invested in equity and have the convenience of automatic transfer of pre-specified amount to equity.

   Systematic withdrawal plan (SWP) is like SIP in reverse direction, i.e., instead of putting funds in a scheme at regular intervals, investors withdraw already invested funds from a scheme at regular intervals.

6. **Ease of Transaction:** Mutual funds are easy to invest in and there are many value-added services that are also available for the investors such as multiple distribution channels, cheque book facility, redemption over phone, mobile alerts, emails and so on.

   To make purchase of mutual funds easier, since January 1, 2013, the choice of investing in the Direct Plan option of any of the existing schemes of mutual funds has been opened for investors. Under this option, investors deal directly with a mutual fund house without any intermediary or third party like a distributor, agent, financial planner, bank, online broker or a portal.

7. **Tax Advantage:** There are two key aspects of mutual funds from the income tax point of view. One is the schemes that allow for savings in tax payable and second is the extent of income tax payable on income generated through investment in various mutual funds schemes. The Income Tax Act, 1961 offers deductions from the taxable income on investment made in ELSS plans under Section 80C up to ₹1,50,000, making them attractive for investors.

Under the provisions of Section 10 (23D) of the Income Tax Act, any income received by the mutual fund is exempt from tax, i.e., funds do not have to pay any tax on the gains obtained from selling securities that they buy on behalf of their investors. Further, equity mutual fund schemes do not have to pay dividend distribution tax (DDT) while companies paying dividend have to pay 15% plus surcharge as DDT and the dividend income on mutual funds is tax exempt in the hands of the investors.

The Disadvantages of Investing in Mutual Funds

The major source of disadvantage of investing in mutual funds comes from the costs associated with investing in them. Fund houses levy certain charges as expenses to be incurred by the investors who hold mutual fund units. The costs/expenses associated with investing in mutual fund are:

1. **Initial Issue Expenses of Mutual Funds:** Initial issue expenses are expenses incurred on the launch of the scheme (NFO) such as marketing and advertising expenses, publicity material and so on. Prior to 2006, SEBI regulations had allowed all funds to charge up to 6% of the assets as initial issue expenses to each newly launched scheme. Thus, if a mutual fund scheme had collected ₹300 crore by incurring initial expense of ₹18 Crore, AMC was allowed to take that ₹18 crore from the investors' pooled money, bringing the NAV immediately down to ₹9.4 (after deducting the 6% towards expenses on ₹10 as initial NAV offered in the NFO).

   To prevent the NAV from coming down, SEBI banned the fund houses from charging the investors for initial issue expenses for open-ended mutual funds in 2006. This amount is now to be borne by the AMC (fund house).
2. **Annual Charge on Assets Under Management (AUM):** Asset management companies (AMCs) manage the assets of various mutual funds schemes and they charge investors for professional fund management and certain operational costs. The costs include advisory fees, fund administration expenses, sales/agent commissions, registrar and transfer agent fees, legal and audit fees and marketing and selling expenses. All these expenses are grouped together under an umbrella term called 'total expense ratio' (TER). Since the net asset value of a mutual fund scheme is calculated using net of all liabilities including TER, therefore a higher TER results in lower returns and vice versa. As per SEBI guidelines, TER should be lower as AUM increases.

   TER is an annual charge on AUM in percentage terms and it represents the cost incurred to operate a fund. It is calculated as:

$$\text{TER} = \frac{(\text{Total expenses during an accounting period}) \times 100}{\text{Total net assets of the fund}}$$

   Different funds can have different expense ratios subjected to the cap specified by SEBI based on the type of fund. Equity funds can charge a maximum of 2.5% whereas a debt fund can charge 2.25% of the average weekly net assets. Expense ratio is not of much concern for equity funds. Expense ratios for equity funds vary between 2.2% and 2.5%. Since on an average, for equity funds that have delivered approximately 20% in the past decade, expense ratio is a secondary consideration while investing in them. The top funds such as HDFC Equity or Franklin India Prima Plus have had the lowest expense ratios of 2.2–2.3% in the past few years. On the other hand, Birla Sun Life Top 100, has had an expense ratio of 2.8%.

Thus, investment in equity funds should not be affected upfront by the consideration of expense ratio, however, while comparing different equity funds with similar strategy and performance, the expense ratio can be used as a differentiator.

Expense ratio matters much more in case of debt funds as they do not generate the high returns that equity funds do. Lower expense ratio for debt funds spells better performance. For example top performing gilt funds like L&T Gilt Fund, IDFC G-Sec and Tata Gilt Mid Term have returned 7–8% annually in the last five years with expense ratios varying from 1.3% to 1.8%. One of the under-performing funds in the past few years, LIC Nomura G-Sec has one of the highest expense ratios of 2.3%.

Other funds following a passive strategy such as index funds should also keep a track of their expense ratio to perform better.

Recently, SEBI has asked mutual funds to launch schemes under a single plan so that all investors are subject to a single expense structure. Currently, TER is linked to the investment amount, which, in turn, depends on the type of plan – retail, institutional and super-institutional. Mutual funds have also been asked by SEBI to provide a separate plan for direct investments in new as well as existing schemes by excluding distribution expenses and commission.

3. **Mutual Fund Loads:** Loads are one time charges that are levied, over and above the TER, either at the time of entering or exiting a mutual fund scheme. Accordingly, there is an entry load and an exit load. Entry load is a front-end charged on the basis of NAV at the time of investing in a mutual fund scheme. Before entry load was abolished by SEBI in August 2009, this charge was about 2.25% of the value of investment.

   Exit load is charged by fund house at the time of redemption or transfer of an investment between schemes. It is deducted from the NAV and the amount realized goes to the Asset Management Company and not into the pool of funds of the scheme. High exit load is used by funds as a strategy to prevent the investors from quitting the scheme. In the recent past there has been a trend in fund houses to increase the exit load of their schemes. Investors quitting a scheme have to pay the asset management company. HDFC Prudence fund has increased the duration of exit from 12 to 18 months for the purpose of levying an exit load of 1%. DSP Blackrock Focused 25 Fund has increased the duration from 1 year to 2 years to charge an exit load of 1%. Franklin India Income Fund that had an exit load of 0.5% if redeemed before completion of three months from allotment, now levies an exit load of 0.5% if redeemed before 48 months are completed. In fact, the exit load it charges is as high as 3% for withdrawal within the first 12 months of allotment.

4. **Other Costs Borne by Mutual Fund Investors:** There are also some indirect costs that mutual fund investors have to bear throughout the investment tenure. One such cost is the cost of executing the transactions for mutual fund portfolios. These costs include the commissions for buying and selling securities, security transaction tax and market impact costs. The greater the frequency of churning of the fund portfolio, the higher the transaction cost incidental on the investors. In addition to transaction costs, the investor who opens a demat account for mutual fund investment, has to pay for opening the account, for maintenance of the account and the brokerage charges.

   All the costs discussed above, both direct and indirect, drag the returns down significantly and investors should give them due consideration before investing in mutual funds.

Choosing the Right Mutual Fund Scheme

Mutual funds are lauded by all and sundry as good investment option to generate returns. But for an individual wanting to invest in mutual funds, choice of the right mutual fund scheme becomes a daunting task. Large variety of products, multiple options within each product category and mind-boggling amount of analysis – all come together to make the landscape of mutual fund investment rather overwhelming for the investors. A few simple things described below can help investors narrow down on the scheme best suited for them out of the plethora of options:

1. **Investment Goals:** An investor should always begin his investment planning with a clearly spelled out outcome he expects from the investment. An investor could have a goal of earning a certain rate of return on his investment. Once this required rate of return is determined, an investor can determine the risk he is willing to take. With the risk-return profile in place, it becomes simpler for an investor to undertake mutual fund selection.
2. **Time Horizon:** Investment goal also determines the time horizon of investments and the mutual funds one should choose. For example, if an investor wants to invest money for long-term, say 10 years, he has the flexibility to take more risks and choose an equity fund. However, if the investor wants regular income and investment horizon up to 2–3 years, he can opt for a low-risk debt fund. Similarly, if an investor has a very low risk appetite, he can opt for gilt funds. Clear statement of investment goal, risk tolerance and time horizon help determine the exact scheme to be chosen.
3. **Existing Investments:** Existing investments should also be considered while making additional investment to expand one's portfolio. Diversification is the key principle of investment. So new investments should be chosen in a way that they diversify the portfolio and reduce overall risk exposure. For example, a person already holding bonds in his portfolio, might want to invest in some equity mutual fund to bring more balance in his overall investment portfolio.
4. **Portfolio of the Fund Being Considered:** Mutual funds pool investors' funds and invest them in different securities according to their stated investment objectives. An investor should not only stop at deciding whether to invest in equity or debt or balanced fund, but also look at the micro picture within each category to check the composition of the portfolio of schemes therein. Schemes investing in securities one already holds in existing portfolio should be avoided. Further, risk profile of the component securities and the investment style of the fund scheme should also match with the investors' requirements.
5. **Performance Record, Ranking and Ratings:** Mutual funds industry is a very transparent industry. Regulations require that mutual fund factsheet is made public at regular intervals. Easy availability of information about fund's track record can help investors choose mutual fund schemes that may be expected to perform well in the future. While a good performance in the past is not an assurance that the fund will continue to perform well in the future, it does help in establishing the skills of the fund manager and ensuring a level of comfort about the fund's scope of performance.
6. **Choosing Equity or Debt Fund:** While a large variety of mutual fund schemes are available, equity and debt can be clearly identified as the two broad types of funds.

   Investors desirous of investing in equity funds should consider the following factors while choosing a scheme:

   (a) Expense ratio, entry and exit load
   (b) Beta, dividend yield and NAV
   (c) Track record of performance
   (d) Component securities and extent of diversification
   (e) Performance of fund vis-à-vis the benchmark index

Investors desirous of investing in debt funds should consider following factors while choosing a scheme:

1. Credit risk is the risk which is related to the rating of the component debt securities. Credit rating agencies like CRISIL and ICRA rate the debt instruments to indicate the credit risk. The highest rating is 'AAA' and lowest is 'D.' An investor should verify the credit ratings of the component schemes of a debt fund to determine its overall credit risk.
2. Interest rate risk is a risk to which debt schemes with long duration are exposed. Most gilt and mixed debt schemes have an average duration of approximately five years and they are vulnerable to interest rate risk. Conversely, debt schemes like cash schemes, fixed maturity plans and floating rate schemes are relatively immune to the fluctuations in the interest rates.
3. Expense ratio represents a cost to investors. Obviously the higher the expense ratio, the higher the cost to the investor. Debt schemes have varying expense ratios depending on the type of scheme. For instance, expense ratio is usually quite high for mixed debt schemes, moderate for gilt schemes and low for floating rate schemes, cash schemes and fixed maturity plans.

In conclusion, mutual funds offer an attractive investment avenue, provided they are chosen with care and deep deliberation.

SUMMARY

- ☑ The basic principle of diversification requires that an investor should spread his money across multiple investment vehicles. The main aim behind investing ones funds in different asset classes is to maximize returns or minimize risk of losing the funds invested.
- ☑ There are many investment avenues and asset classes available for investors to construct their portfolios. A portfolio can comprise a mix of domestic and foreign equities, domestic and foreign fixed income securities, cash and cash equivalents, commodities, real estate, derivatives, mutual funds and other alternative investments.
- ☑ In simple terms, a mutual fund may be described as a collective investment vehicle. When an investor invests in a mutual fund, he actually pools his money together with a number of other investors.
- ☑ The primary advantage of a mutual fund is that investors can invest their money in assets of varying risks without undertaking extensive research and analysis that are often needed to choose a sound investment.
- ☑ Mutual fund industry in India is growing at a rapid pace. According to the latest data available, the assets under management of mutual funds in India increased by 6.85 % from June 2014 to September 2014.
- ☑ Mutual funds have continued to gain immense popularity as an investment vehicle in India and their assets under management have grown at a fast pace. However, in comparison to global growth levels, Indian mutual funds are at quite a low level of penetration.
- ☑ In India, the main parties involved in mutual fund operation are sponsors, trustees, asset management companies, custodians and registrar and transfer agents.
- ☑ On the basis of structure, mutual fund schemes are broadly classified as open-ended, close-ended and interval schemes.

☑ Close-ended mutual funds are also termed as traded mutual funds as they can be bought and sold like a normal share on the stock exchanges where they are listed.

☑ Open-ended mutual funds are the conventional type of mutual funds and they are more common compared to the close-ended mutual funds. They are always open for subscription. Open-ended mutual funds have no fixed date of maturity on which the units would be permanently redeemed or terminated.

☑ Interval schemes are the schemes that combine the features of both, the open-ended and the close-ended schemes.

☑ On the basis of investment objectives, the mutual fund schemes may be classified as: equity (growth) schemes, income schemes, balanced schemes, money market/liquid schemes, tax saving schemes, offshore funds, gilt funds, index schemes and so on.

☑ Growth schemes, also known as equity schemes, aim to provide capital appreciation to investors over medium to long term.

☑ Income schemes, also known as debt schemes, aim to provide limited capital appreciation but regular and steady income to the unit holders.

☑ Balanced funds invest in both stocks and fixed income securities in the proportion indicated in their offer documents, usually 50:50.

☑ Money market funds, also called liquid schemes, aim to provide stability, liquidity, preservation of capital, slightly higher interest rates than bank deposits and moderate income.

☑ Tax saving schemes, also called equity linked savings schemes, aim to offer tax incentives to the investors under income tax laws prescribed from time to time.

☑ Index funds represent passive investment strategy and replicate the movements of benchmark indices.

☑ Sector specific funds are the funds that invest in the securities of only those sectors or industries or capital market segments such as large caps, mid caps or small caps that have been specified in the offer documents of the schemes.

☑ Fund of funds (FoF) schemes are schemes that invest in a portfolio of mutual funds, i.e., they invest either in other schemes of the same AMC or mutual funds of other companies.

☑ Other mutual fund products include exchange traded funds (ETF), structured products, arbitrage funds, international funds and real estate investment trusts (REITs).

☑ The key costs and performance measures important from the point of view of mutual fund investment are entry and exit loads, net asset value (NAV), compounded annual total return (CATR), ex-mark, portfolio turnover ratio, initial issue expenses of mutual funds, annual charge on assets under management and total expense ratio.

☑ The upsides of mutual fund investments are benefit of diversification and professional management of funds, liquidity, regulatory control, transparency, availability of ratings, multiple options, ease of transaction and tax advantage.

☑ The major source of disadvantage of investing in mutual funds comes from the costs associated with investing in them.

☑ While choosing their mutual funds, investors should take into consideration their investment goals, time horizon, existing investments, portfolio of the fund being considered and performance record, ranking and rating of the schemes and component securities.

KEY WORDS

Arbitrage funds 681
Assets under management 673
Balanced schemes 680
Close-ended schemes 678
Compounded annual total return 683
Diversification 671
Dividend distribution tax 686
Dividend plan 685
Dividend reinvestment plan 685
Entry and exit load 683
Equity (growth) schemes 678
Ex-mark 683
Exchange traded funds 681
Fund of funds schemes 681
Gilt funds 678
Hedge funds 673
Income schemes 678
Index schemes 678
International funds 681
Interval schemes 676
Money market/liquid schemes 678
Mutual fund 671
Net asset value 683
New fund offer 676
Offshore funds 678
Open-ended schemes 677
Portfolio turnover ratio 683
Real estate investment trusts 681
Structured products 681
Systematic investment plan 677
Systematic transfer plan 685
Systematic withdrawal plan 685
Tax saving schemes 678
Total expense ratio 686

CONCEPT QUESTIONS

1. "Mutual fund industry in India is in a state of flux." Discuss the statement in light of the recent events in the mutual fund industry
2. "One of the key advantages of investing in mutual funds in India is proactive regulatory control, transparency and investor protection measures." Discuss the role of SEBI in transforming the regulatory environment for mutual fund investing in India.
3. Critique the features of close- and open-ended funds from investors' point of view.
4. Hedge funds and mutual funds are same yet different. Elaborate upon the statement.
5. Comment on the implications of the latest tax provisions on the performance of mutual funds in India.
6. What are the parameters that an investor should consider while investing in equity or debt schemes.
7. Can exchange traded funds be called a hybrid of both close-ended and open-ended funds? Why?
8. Which mutual fund scheme, debt or equity, is more popular in India in terms of asset under management? Why?
9. Discuss the multiple investment options offered by various mutual fund schemes and their implications for investors.
10. Describe CRISIL's mutual fund ranking methodology in detail and comment on its efficacy.

Hedging and Trading Strategies using Derivatives: The Futures Contracts 18

CHAPTER OBJECTIVES

- ❒ Understanding the concept of derivatives with special reference to futures
- ❒ Evaluating the pricing mechanism of futures
- ❒ Analyzing the key terms related to futures trading
- ❒ Assessing different trading strategies using futures contracts

Individuals and institutional investors invest their funds in various financial assets such as bonds and stocks. The price of these assets fluctuates in the market, exposing the investors to volatility in returns. Prices of stocks, bonds, foreign currencies, petroleum and other commodities fluctuate all the time, and pose significant risk to corporations whose businesses are linked to such instruments and commodities in one way or the other. Risk is indeed a key characteristic of all commodity and capital markets where prices of traded assets vary in the response to market forces of demand-supply and numerous other factors that are beyond the control of the investors.

As the volume of trade in financial markets has grown in the past few decades, the variability of asset prices, interest rates and exchange rates has become a more significant factor in eroding the value of investments and exposing the corporate world to rising financial risk. The increased volume of transactions in the recent times has made it essential for the investment community to seek better ways to protect investments against such variability or risk. In times characterized by high volume and higher volatility, risk management becomes critically important to preserve and grow the wealth of the entire financial sector.

To reduce this extreme volatility, modern finance has provided a method called hedging. Hedging is nothing but taking positions to offset risks and it is undertaken through instruments called derivatives. Derivatives are typically used to hedge risk, but investors can also use them for speculative investments.

Derivatives have emerged as the key instruments to counter the risk management challenges faced by investors in the current era. Financial engineering, a branch of finance that applies mathematical techniques to solve financial problems, has led to immense growth of derivatives trading in the modern times.

Derivatives are instruments that can help investors make additional profits by correctly forecasting the future price or they can act as safety nets against losses in the spot market, where the value of the underlying assets changes as it is traded.

Though the origin of derivatives can be traced to ancient Greece, the beginning of derivatives trading in its present form can be attributed to the establishment the Chicago Board Options Exchange in 1973 and the publication of option pricing model by the pioneer financial engineers, Fischer Black and Myron Scholes.

The engineering of various derivative instruments has provided the investment community an ingenious and cost effective solution to the problem of managing the unpredictability in the asset price behavior. In the increasingly integrated world financial markets, derivatives are playing a key role of enhancing market liquidity and efficiency, enabling price discovery and facilitating the flow of trade and finance. The fact is that financial derivatives have transformed and re-energized the world of finance by offering innovative and inventive ways of comprehending, estimating, measuring and managing risks in financial and commercial interactions.

What is a Financial Derivative?

The word financial derivative refers to a security that derives its value from the underlying assets that could be stocks or indices. Financial derivatives are instruments for hedging the risk involved in selling, buying and holding bonds, stocks and currencies. Derivatives derive their payoffs from financial variables like stock price, interest rate, commodity price, index level and exchange rate. They facilitate the exchange of their underlying financial asset on some date in future at prices determined in the present, thereby cushioning the investors against adverse movement in the prices of underlying asset in future. A financial derivative may be looked at as a contract that indicates the rights and obligations of the parties to the contract: the issuer of the derivative and the holder of the derivative.

With Securities Laws (Second Amendment) Act 1999, derivatives have been included in the definition of securities. The term derivative has been defined in Securities Contracts (Regulations) Act as:

1. A security derived from a debt instrument, share, loan, whether secured or unsecured, risk instrument or contract for differences or any other form of security;
2. A contract which derives its value from the prices, or index of prices, of underlying securities.

   Derivatives can have financial or real assets as their underlying instruments. Accordingly, there can be derivatives based on commodities including grain, cotton or oil, precious metals like gold and silver, foreign exchange rates or currencies, bonds of varying maturities, equity shares in different segments and over-the-counter (OTC) money market products such as loans or deposits. Since derivatives are contracts, they can have any kind of underlying asset. There are even derivatives based on weather data, such as the amount of snowfall or the number of cloudy days in a particular region.

Use of Derivatives

Investors can use derivatives mainly to enhance their returns and to transfer the risk associated with investments. The most important use to which derivatives are put is the transfer of market risk from risk-averse investors to those with a higher risk tolerance. Thus, derivatives enhance safety for risk-averse investors on one hand and enable the risk seeking speculators to generate additional profits through risky, contrarian trades on the other hand.

Use of derivatives allows investors to protect their existing as well as future holdings of securities against fluctuations in prices. In other words, derivatives enable the investors to offset the risk associated with a currently held position in the market and the position that an investor is planning to take in the market on some future date. This is called hedging. Thus, derivatives help investors hedge both the risk of fall in prices of the currently held assets and the risk of rise in prices of the assets an investor is planning to acquire.

Derivatives are used as leveraged investments because they enable investors to capture profits arising from movement in prices of the underlying assets. In other words, derivatives can be used by investors to earn money on their long-term investments that are lying idle. Derivatives market allows investors to conduct transactions to take advantage of price fluctuations in their existing assets in the short-term without actually selling them. The element of leverage magnifies both gains and losses from derivatives. Despite the risks, derivatives are popular among investors because they trade at a price lower than the price of the underlying asset and enable the investors to have control over more assets for lesser money.

Main Participants in the Derivatives Markets

The main participants in the derivative markets are hedgers, speculators and arbitrageurs. Hedgers participate in the market to offset the risk associated with the price of an asset. Speculators transact in derivatives to make profits by taking speculative positions. In the Indian markets, there are two types of speculators—day traders and the position traders. The day traders try to take advantage of the intra-day fluctuations in prices of assets and they settle all their trades by undertaking an opposite trade by the end of the day, i.e., they net their positions on the same day and do not keep any overnight exposure to the markets. On the other hand, position traders take a much longer view, varying from a week to about a month, to generate superior returns. They rely heavily on news and tips and are more likely to use formal tools like technical analysis to predict trends and prices.

There is another set of speculators in Indian markets, called margin traders. They trade using the unique payment mechanism of the derivative markets. To trade in derivatives, traders are not required to pay the total value of their position upfront. Instead, they have to deposit only a fraction of the total sum called margin. This is called margin trading and it results in a high leverage factor in derivative trading. Speculators maintain large outstanding positions (typically three to five times the quantity that their capital investment would have allowed them to buy in the cash market) with a small deposit. At the time of settlement they either pay on the basis of their outstanding position or conduct an opposing trade that would net off this amount.

Arbitrageurs participate in the derivatives market to take advantage of the discrepancy between the spot and future prices of assets. They exploit the imperfections and inefficiencies in the market that result in discrepancy between the price of an asset in the cash market (it can be lower or higher than it should be) and its price in the derivatives market.

Derivatives have emerged as the key instruments in managing risk. Their trading across the world is quite substantial now. Their usage over the last two decades has expanded rapidly in advanced economies and emerging markets in both exchange-traded and OTC contracts across all underlying asset classes including equity, indices, interest-rate, currency and credit.

Derivative Market in India

The derivatives market in India is relatively new, having established in June 2000 when both the NSE and the BSE commenced trading in equity derivatives. Index futures were the first type of derivate instruments to be launched in India, followed by index options, options in individual stocks and futures in single stock derivatives within a span of one year. Since then, the landscape of equity derivatives trading in India has altered immensely with the introduction of new products, higher volumes, newer contracts and advanced risk management framework for exchange-traded derivatives.

Despite its nascence in India, the derivatives market has registered exponential growth both in terms of volume and number of traded contracts. Table 18.1 displays the product-wise derivatives turnover at NSE, BSE and MCX-SX (*Percent*).

TABLE 18.1 Product-wise derivatives turnover at NSE, BSE and MCX-SX (*Percent*)

Year/Month	Index futures	Index options	Single stock options	Single stock futures
1	2	3	4	5
2008–09	**32.4**	**33.9**	**2.1**	**31.6**
2009–10	**22.3**	**45.5**	**2.9**	**29.4**
2010–11	**14.9**	**62.8**	**3.5**	**18.8**
2011–12	**11.7**	**72.6**	**3.0**	**12.7**
2012–13	**6.8**	**77.0**	**5.2**	**10.9**
2013–14	**6.7**	**77.5**	**5.2**	**10.6**
Apr-13	6.5	74.8	7.3	11.3
May-13	6.2	78.1	5.5	10.2
Jun-13	6.8	79.9	4.2	9.1
Jul-13	6.0	79.2	5.3	9.5
Aug-13	7.4	79.9	3.8	8.9
Sep-13	8.6	77.0	4.0	10.4
Oct-13	7.8	75.9	5.4	10.8
Nov-13	7.3	76.7	4.7	11.3
Dec-13	7.0	75.4	4.9	12.7
Jan-14	6.0	77.3	5.8	10.9
Feb-14	5.5	78.5	5.1	10.8
Mar-14	5.9	76.3	6.0	11.8

Source: BSE, NSE, MCX-SX, accessed on December 31, 2014.

The derivatives turnover on the NSE has exceeded its equity market turnover, having risen from ₹23,654 million in 2000–2001 to ₹292,482,211 million in 2010–2011. The business growth in futures and option segment on NSE in exhibited in Table 18.2.

OTC as well as exchange traded derivatives have grown in India in terms of both volume and the role in financial development and contribution to economic growth.

TABLE 18.2 Business growth in futures and option segment on NSE

Year	Index futures		Vol futures		Stock futures		Index options		Stock options		Total		Average daily turnover (₹ cr.)
	No. of contracts	Turnover (₹ cr.)	No. of contracts	Turnover (₹ cr.)	No. of contracts	Turnover (₹ cr.)	No. of contracts	Notional turnover (₹ cr.)	No. of contracts	Notional turnover (₹ cr.)	No. of contracts	Turnover (₹ cr.)	
2014–15	61642870	2286485.73	10643	2179.69	134352806	5063937.64	571784779	21201473.18	52311691	2003171.67	820102789	30557247.83	206467.89
2013–14	105252983	3083103.23	17546	2193.24	170414186	4949281.72	928565175	27767341.25	80174431	2409488.61	1284424321	38211408.05	152236.69
2012–13	96100385	2527130.76	–	–	147711691	4223872.02	820877149	22781574.14	66778193	2000427.29	1131467418	31533003.96	126638.57
2011–12	146188740	3577998.41	–	–	158344617	4074670.73	864017736	22720031.64	36494371	977031.13	1205045464	31349731.74	125902.54
2010–11	165023653	4356754.53	–	–	186041459	5495756.70	650638557	18365365.76	32508393	1030344.21	1034212062	29248221.09	115150.48
2009–10	178306889	3934388.67	–	–	145591240	5195246.64	341379523	8027964.20	14016270	506065.18	679293922	17663664.57	72392.07
2008–09	210428103	3570111.40	–	–	221577980	3479642.12	212088444	3731501.84	13295970	229226.81	657390497	11010482.20	45310.63
2007–08	156598579	3820667.27	–	–	203587952	7548563.23	55366038	1362110.88	9460631	359136.55	425013200	13090477.75	52153.30
2006–07	81487424	2539574	–	–	104955401	3830967	25157438	791906	5283310	193795	216883573	7356242	29543
2005–06	58537886	1513755	–	–	80905493	2791697	12935116	338469	5240776	180253	157619271	4824174	19220
2004–05	21635449	772147	–	–	47043066	1484056	3293558	121943	5045112	168836	77017185	2546982	10107
2003–04	17191668	554446	–	–	32368842	1305939	1732414	52816	5583071	217207	56886776	2130610	8388
2002–03	2126763	43952	–	–	10676843	286533	442241	9246	3523062	100131	16768909	439862	1752
2001–02	1025588	21483	–	–	1957856	51515	175900	3765	1037529	25163	4196873	101926	410
2000–01	90580	2365	–	–	–	–	–	–	–	–	90580	2365	11

Source: http://www.nse-india.com/, accessed on December 31, 2014.

Classification of Derivatives

Derivatives can be classified on the basis of the way they are transacted, on the basis of their underlying assets or on the basis of the types of contracts.

1. **Derivatives may be Classified into the Following Two Types on the Basis of where they are Transacted:**
   (a) Privately traded over-the-counter (OTC) derivatives.
   (b) Exchange-traded derivatives (ETD).

   OTC derivatives are derivatives that are contracted through transactions negotiated between two parties directly rather than through an exchange. Some financial derivatives, such as a swap, a forward rate agreement or an exotic option, are usually transacted between the contracting parties directly over the counter. OTC derivatives are also called unlisted derivatives. Since OTC derivatives are not listed or regulated by exchanges, they require customization of the terms of the derivative contract by the parties involved. The terms of OTC derivatives are generally highly flexible. ETD derivatives are contracts traded on regulated exchanges where the contracts are standardized by the exchange in terms of underlying asset, quantity, expiration date and strike price. Exchange-traded derivatives are also known as listed derivatives. Futures and options are examples of ETD.

   OTC derivatives are not regulated and there are no formal rules for risk and burden-sharing. The fact that OTC derivatives have no mechanisms for ensuring market stability and protecting the collective interests of market participants from the counter-party risk, the use of OTC derivatives presents a very real threat of systemic financial meltdown. In view of the inherent and largely uncontrollable risks associated with OTC derivatives, there have been debates across the globe to regulate this segment more.
2. **Derivatives can be Classified into Two Broad Categories Based on their Underlying Assets:**
   (a) Commodity derivatives
   (b) Financial derivatives

   In case of commodity derivatives, the underlying assets can be commodities like cotton, rice, wheat, gold, silver, etc. whereas in case of financial derivatives, the underlying assets can be currencies, stocks, bonds and other interest rates bearing securities.
3. **Derivatives may be Classified into the Following Four Types on the Basis of the Nature of the Contract:**
   (a) Forwards
   (b) Futures
   (c) Options
   (d) Swaps

   Of the above four derivative instruments, futures and options are exchange-traded derivatives and they are in the form of standard contracts. A forward is an over-the-counter derivative. It is a tailor-made contract between two parties. A swap is a derivative in which two counterparties exchange cash flows of their financial instruments. Most swaps are OTC contracts.

Derivatives Based on the Nature of Contract

As mentioned above, there are four types of derivatives based on the nature of contract, namely forwards, futures, options and swaps.

We will discuss futures in detail in the next few sections of the chapter but first let us define forwards and swaps briefly. Options will be discussed in the next chapter.

Forwards

A commitment between two parties to trade an asset on a pre-specified future date is a forward contract. A forward is a non-standardized agreement between two parties to exchange a certain, pre-specified amount of money for a pre-determined quantity of a good or service on a pre-specified date in future. The pre-specified price is called delivery price and the future date is called delivery date. In this contract, the seller agrees to sell a certain good or service to the buyer in the future and it is settled at maturity. In this contract generally no money changes hands between the counterparties before the delivery date.

Key features of forward contracts are:

1. Forwards are over-the-counter (OTC) derivative instruments.
2. Forwards are settled/delivered at the forward price agreed on at the trade date or initial agreement.
3. Completely customized terms of contract: Forwards provide scope for the contract between the counter-parties to be highly flexible. The two parties can work out mutually agreeable terms of contract to fit their specific needs, including exact delivery time and precise specifications regarding the underlying asset.
4. Counterparty default risk: Since forwards are agreements between two parties coming together on their own, the risk of counterparty default, i.e., the risk that the other party may not keep its side of agreement to make the required delivery or payment, is very high.
5. Forwards are held till maturity and have no market liquidity.
6. The initial value of a forward contract is zero as no money exchanges hands at the time of contract negotiation.
7. Forward contracts entail market risk and the payoffs from the contract depend on the quantum of difference between the market or actual price and contract price.
8. The profit or loss on a forward contract is realized on time only, i.e., at the time of settlement.

Let us try to understand forwards with the following example:

Mr. A agrees on July 1 to buy 100 liters of mustard oil on October 1 in the same year at a price of ₹145 per liter from an oil supplier; Mr. A has bought forward oil. In other words, he has gone long in mustard oil.

At the same time the counterparty, the oil supplier, has sold forward or he has gone short in mustard oil. No money or goods changed hands on July 1, the date when the deal was signed, only the terms of transaction that will take place on October 1 have been specified.

Mr. A is obliged to buy at the contract price and similarly, the oil seller is obligated to sell oil to Mr. A at the pre-specified price. So what are the payoffs in a forward contract? If the spot price of oil on October 1 is more than the contract price, it is Mr. A's gain. To generalize, the payoff or gain of forward buyer is spot price on maturity date minus contract price.

Obviously, the payoff of forward seller would be the mirror image of the payoff of the counterparty. The gain of forward seller is loss of forward buyer and vice-versa. Figure 18.1 exhibits the payoffs to the forward buyer and forward seller.

Swaps

Swaps are contracts where two counterparties exchange cash flows related to their financial assets. The cash flows are usually referred to as legs of the swap. All swaps have a notional principal, a specified tenor and predetermined payment intervals. Swaps are cash-settled contracts between two parties to exchange cash flow streams and they can entail any type of future cash flow as long as the present value of the cash flow streams exchanged is equal. The series of cash flow streams in swaps are so structured that the payments are synchronized and occur on the same dates. Synchronization of payments allows for netting of cash flows against each

Figure 18.1 Payoffs to the forward buyer and forward seller.

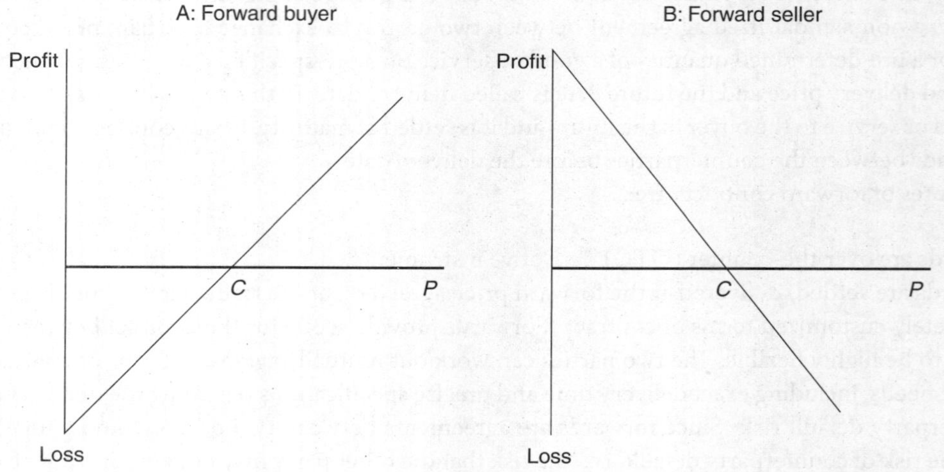

C = Contract price, *P* = Actual price

other, provided they are in the same currency. Typically, the principal amounts of the loans are netted to zero and the periodic interest payments are matched so as to net them against one another.

An exchange of cash flows between the two parties in swaps allows them to diversify their income, while continuing to hold their original assets. For example, an investor owning equity shares can exchange the volatile returns from his more risky equity investment with fixed income from an instrument with lower risk—without actually liquidating his equity position. In other words, swaps enable the investors to change the character of an asset or liability without liquidating it.

Swaps are used by institutions and investors to hedge certain risks such as interest rate risk, currency risk or to speculate on expected changes in underlying prices.

Swaps were first introduced in 1981 when IBM and the World Bank entered into a swap agreement. Over the years, swaps have become the most heavily traded financial contracts in the world and gained a lot of notoriety as well (you may recall credit default swaps or CDS that had become a household name after the global financial meltdown of 2008). Derivatives trading survey, 2013 conducted by BIS revealed that FX swaps were the most actively traded instruments in April 2013, at $2.2 trillion per day, followed by spot trading at $2.0 trillion.

Most swaps are traded over-the-counter (OTC) and are tailor-made for the counterparties. However, some types of swaps are also traded on futures markets such as the Chicago Mercantile Exchange, the Chicago Board Options Exchange, Intercontinental Exchange and Frankfurt-based Eurex AG.

Main types of swaps transacted in the derivative market include equity swaps, currency swaps, interest rate swaps and commodity swaps.

1. Typically, in **Equity Swaps**, an equity-based cash flow from a stock is traded for a fixed-income cash flow (such as a benchmark rate). Equity swaps are swaps in which one of the legs (the cash flow), called the floating leg, is usually pegged to a floating rate such as LIBOR. The other leg, called the equity leg, is pegged to the performance of either an equity share or a stock market index. Though most equity swaps have a

floating leg vs. an equity leg, it is possible to have equity swaps with two equity legs. For example, the counterparties to an equity swap with two equity legs may agree to exchange the dividends from two stocks of approximately the same value.

Equity swaps may take different forms, but the purpose remains the same, i.e., diversification of the cash flows of the parties without requiring them to buy new assets and hedging specific positions in investment portfolios. Equity swaps can also be used to avoid taxation legally.

2. **Interest Rate Swaps** are OTC derivative contracts that involve the exchange of one stream of future interest payments for another in the same currency, based on a specified principal amount. Interest rate swaps are typically used to manage exposure to interest rate fluctuations or to get a marginally lower interest rate. Interest rate swaps are also used for speculation and arbitrage. These may be fixed-for-floating rate, fixed-for-fixed rate or floating-for-floating rate swaps.
3. **Currency Swaps** are swaps that involve an exchange of principal and interest in one currency for principal and interest in another currency; followed by the exchange of principal amounts again at maturity. In currency swaps, both the principal and interest are exchanged in full, unlike interest rate swaps. Typically, in a currency swap, one party pays a fixed interest rate, while another pays a floating rate. However, other options such as fixed-fixed and floating-floating interest rates may also be used. Currency swaps are often used by investors to profit from the inefficiencies of international debt markets.
4. **Commodity Swaps** are swaps in which cash flows dependent on the price of an underlying commodity are exchanged with the aim to hedge against the fluctuations in the price of a commodity. No commodities are exchanged during the transaction.

The difference between a swap and a forward contract is that a swap implies a series of payments in the future, whereas a forward involves only one future payment.

Futures

Futures contracts are an important innovation in the field of finance. Futures are standardized form of forward contract. A futures contract, like a forward contract, is also an agreement between two parties—a buyer and a seller—to buy or sell something at a pre-specified future date for a pre-specified price. The difference between the two contracts is that while forwards are tailor-made agreements between two parties, futures are standardized contracts normally traded on organized stock exchanges. Further, forwards usually end in delivery, whereas futures are traded on futures exchanges on the basis of daily settlement procedure.

The key features of futures contracts are:

1. Futures are best described as exchange-traded forward contracts.
2. Exchange's clearinghouse is always the counterparty to a futures contract, so the buyers of futures contract assume exposure to the risk of default by the exchange's clearinghouse which actually means that there is no default risk. In other words, futures contracts have low or no default risk because the exchange acts as a counterparty and guarantees delivery and payment through its clearinghouse.
3. The clearing house protects itself from default by requiring its counterparties to settle gains and losses or mark-to-market their positions on a daily basis.
4. Futures are contracts that are transacted through brokerage firms that hold seats on the futures exchanges that trade in the contracts the investors are interested in. Thus, futures are also transacted through brokers like common stock.

5. The terms of a futures contract such as delivery places and dates, volume or quantity, technical specifications like quality, trading and credit procedures are standardized for each type of contract by the exchange they are traded on.
6. Futures are protected against credit risk through mitigation measures such as mark-to-market, daily settlement and margin requirement.
7. In the daily settlement procedure, investors incurring losses pay every day to investors who have made profit.
8. The market value of futures contracts is reset to zero at the end of each trading day.
9. The marking-to-market feature resulting in daily cash flows can skew the futures prices and cause them to diverge from corresponding forward prices.
10. Futures are settled at the settlement price that is fixed on the last trading date of the futures contract and the counterparty on a futures contract is randomly chosen by the exchange.
11. An investor investing in futures contracts has the freedom to offset his future position by engaging in an opposite transaction before the maturity of the futures contract.
12. In futures contracts, cash flows before the maturity of the contract take the form of margin requirements and periodic margin calls.
13. The futures market is considered to be highly leveraged due to its margins. In this market, investors get control over large cash amounts of assets by depositing relatively small amount of cash into their margin account.
14. The leveraged nature of futures implies that a small change in futures price can translate into huge gain or loss.
15. Going long, going short and spreads are the most common strategies used by traders in the futures market.
16. Since futures are traded on organized exchanges on highly standardized terms, they have deep liquidity during the entire tenure of their currency.
17. Typically the transactions in the futures market are settled in cash and the actual physical asset is bought or sold in the cash market at the prevailing price.
18. The spot and futures prices normally converge at the expiration of a futures contract.

In this chapter, we will discuss futures contracts in detail.

Types of Futures Contracts and their Trading Mechanism

As mention above, futures are exchange traded forward contracts. Futures contracts are available on different kinds of assets—shares, indices, commodities, currency pairs and so on.

There are two broad categories of futures, (1) commodity futures and (2) financial futures.

Commodity Futures

1. **Commodity Futures** where the underlying asset is a commodity like oil or jute. Commodity futures are not a new product. Researchers have found evidence to indicate that some form of futures trading in commodities existed in China 6000 years ago. Modern trade in commodities futures can also be traced many centuries earlier to 17th century in Osaka, Japan. The establishment of the Chicago Board of Trade (CBOT) in 1848 marked the beginning of the organized trading of commodities futures on an exchange. India also has a rich history of vibrant commodities market that has its origin in the constitution of the Bombay Cotton Trade Association during the year 1875. Prior to its discontinuation in the mid 1960s, Indian commodities market was quite well entrenched. The revival of the commodities market came with the initiation of a spate of reforms for economic liberalization.

In 2002, there were 20 commodity exchanges in India trading 42 commodities. In 2002, commodity futures were re-introduced in India. The government also allowed three screen-based, nation-wide multi-commodity exchanges to be set up with the approval of the Forward Markets Commission, the regulatory authority for commodity exchanges in India. National Commodity & Derivative Exchange (NCDEX), Multi Commodity Exchange (MCX) and National Multi Commodity Exchange of India (NMCE) are the main exchanges where commodity futures are traded in India. In terms of market share, MCX has a market share of close to 70%, NCDEX has a market share of around 25% and balance 5% is with NMCE.

Commodities futures contracts and the exchanges they trade on are governed by the provisions of Forward Contracts (Regulation) Act, 1952 in India. Commodity futures are globally considered to be an important component of a well-diversified investment portfolio. In fact, returns from most of the commodities have been higher than the global inflation rate for a period of more than fifty years from 1951 to 2006, making investments in commodity an effective hedge against inflation.

In modern times, commodity futures have become an important way of investing in commodities. Commodity futures are an attractive investment avenue as they are traded on margins. Trading on margins gives the investors greater leverage and thus the ability to generate higher returns as they need to deposit only a fraction of the value of the futures contract with the broker to meet the margin requirements. Further, commodity futures are extremely liquid and an investor can liquidate his position quite easily whenever he wants. Extra returns can also be generated by investing the profits from a trade elsewhere, without closing the position in the contract. As with any commodity related product, commodity futures provide investors excellent hedge against inflation and an effective means of portfolio diversification. For example, it is well-known that gold prices have historically had a low correlation with most other financial asset prices such as stocks and thus gold offers a good option for creating a well-diversified portfolio.

Marketview 18.1 Commodities traded in Commodity Exchanges

A large variety of commodities are traded on commodity exchanges around the world. Some of the commodities traded on various futures exchanges are:

Foodstuff	Industrial metals	Precious metal	Energy
Coffee	Copper	Gold	Crude oil
Suger	Lead	Platinum	Natural gas
Cocoa	Zinc	Palladium	
Maize	Tin	Silver	
Rough rice	Aluminum		
Soybean	Nickel		
Wheat	Recycled		
Sunflower oil			
Barley			
Orange juice			

TABLE 18.3 NCDEX futures contracts Friday, November 14, 2014

Product Name	Exp Dt	Open	High	Low	Close	LTP	Chg	(%) Chg	AV TP.	Spot P.	Best B.	Best S.
29 mm Cotton	19-Dec-14	15690	15760	15690	15780	15750	–30	–0.19	15756	15632.8	15310	16250
Barley	20-Nov-14	1650.5	1651	1646	1636	1650	14	0.86	1649.2	1601.8	1642	1653.5
Barley	19-Dec-14	1653.5	1665	1652	1654	1661	7	0.42	1660.2	1601.8	1660	1665
Barley	20-Jan-15	1658	1670	1658	1652	1668	16	0.97	1666.6	1601.8	1661	1675
Castor Seed	20-Nov-14	4748	4790	4738	4757	4758	1	0.02	4763.9	4742.85	4729	4795
Castor Seed	19-Dec-14	4814	4857	4784	4820	4818	–2	–0.04	4827	4742.85	4817	4818
Castor Seed	20-Jan-15	4879	4922	4850	4882	4885	3	0.06	4892.9	4742.85	4881	4886
Castor Seed	20-Feb-15	4905	4950	4884	4906	4920	14	0.29	4923.9	4742.85	4904	5053
Castor Seed	20-Mar-15	4925	4966	4925	4928	4966	38	0.77	4945	4742.85	4880	5008
Castor Seed 1 MT	11-Dec-14	4816	4852	4796	4824	4820	–4	–0.08	4825.2	4742.85	4800	4868
Castor Seed 2 MT	12-Jan-15	4900	4900	4900	4882	4900	18	0.37	4900	0	4762	4950
Chana	20-Nov-15	3181	3217	3181	3206	3210	4	0.12	3208.6	3114.75	3207	3216
Chana	19-Dec-14	3181	3207	3171	3183	3195	12	0.38	3190.5	3114.75	3192	3195
Chana	20-Jan-15	3220	3247	3211	3223	3233	10	0.31	3229.2	3114.75	3232	3239

Source: www.ncdex.com, accessed on December 31, 2014.

The contract specifications, trading parameters, delivery and settlement procedure of the futures contracts in different commodities are specified by the concerned exchange through circulars. For example, NCDEX launched its cotton seed futures contract on January 2, 2014 as per the following contract specifications: "Industrial grade cotton seed, with basis centre at Akola in Maharashtra and additional delivery centers at Yavatmal, Aurangabad and Rajkot at a tick size of Re. 1 and lot size of 10 MT." Table 18.3 exhibits the NCDEX futures contracts on Friday, November 14, 2014.

Types of commodity futures markets

The futures market for a commodity can be *normal* or *inverted*. A normal futures market may be defined as the market where the price of the nearby contract is less than the price of the distant futures contract. Conversely, an inverted futures market may be defined as the market where the price of the nearby contract is greater than the price of the distant contract. An inverted futures market is observed when there are shortages in underlying commodities on account of short-term supply disruptions.

Let us understand the commodity futures contract with the help of the following example:

Suppose that in September, the spot or current price of sugarcane is ₹2,500 per tonne and the futures price is ₹2,700 per tonne. Consider a sugarcane farmer who is trying to secure a selling price for his next crop and a sugar mill that is trying to secure a buying price for its raw material in order to determine how much to charge the wholesalers for its final product, refined sugar, next year.

The farmer and the mill can enter into a futures contract requiring the delivery of 500 tonnes of sugarcane to the mill in December at a price of ₹2700 per tonne. The contract fixes and locks in a price for both parties. Now this contract, not the sugarcane physically, can be traded in the futures market.

Of the two counterparties, the farmer holds the short position as he has agreed to sell the underlying asset and the sugar mill holds the long position as it has agreed to buy the underlying asset.

The price of the contract is 50000 tonnes of sugarcane at the price of ₹2700 per tonne. Since this contract is being traded on futures exchange, its profits and losses will be calculated on a daily basis. Suppose, the price on futures contracts for sugarcane increases to ₹2800 per tonne a day after the initial contract.

The farmer, as the holder of the short position, has lost ₹100 per tonne because the selling price has increased from the future price at which he is obliged to sell his sugarcane as per the terms of the contract. The sugar mill has profited by ₹100 per tonne.

On the day the price change occurs, the farmer's account is debited by ₹5000000 (₹100 per tonne × 50000 tonnes) and the sugar mill's account is credited with the same amount.

To understand what will happen at the expiration of this contract, let us assume that the spot price of the sugarcane rises to ₹3000 due to increase in the support price by the government. The sugar mill benefits from this rise and gains ₹300 per tonne on its futures contract but it still has to buy sugarcane.

Thus its gain of ₹1.5 crore (₹300 per tonne × 50000 tonnes) on its futures contract will be offset against the higher cost of sugarcane in the spot market. Similarly, the farmer's loss of ₹1.5 crore is offset against the higher price for which he can sell his sugarcane in the spot market.

Financial Futures

Financial futures where the underlying asset is a financial instrument like currency, stock, stock index, bond, government security, etc. There are four main classes of financial futures:

1. Forex futures based on currencies
2. Interest rate futures based on interest rates
3. Stock index futures based on stock indices
4. Single stock futures based on any one share

   Stock futures and index futures are the two most common futures contracts used in India. Let us discuss them in detail.

Stock futures

1. **Stock Futures** are the derivative contracts that help an investor to buy or sell a set of equity shares at a fixed price by a certain date. Since futures are standardized contracts, they can be traded only according to the specifications laid down by the exchange on which they are traded. Some key characteristics/specifications of stock futures contracts in India are:
   (a) *Lot/Contract size*: In the derivatives market, each equity/stock futures contract consists of a fixed lot of the underlying share specified by the exchange and it can vary from stock to stock. Contracts cannot be traded for a single share. For instance, Infosys futures contract has a lot size of 125 shares whereas Reliance Industries Ltd. (RIL) has a contract size of 250 shares. This implies that when an investor buys one futures contract of Infosys, he actually buys its 125 shares.
   (b) *Duration*: Futures contracts may have durations of 1 month, 2 months and 3 months. These are called near month, middle month and far month, respectively. The month of expiry of the contract is called the contract month. New contracts are issued for all three durations on the day after the expiry of the existing contracts.
   (c) *Expiry*: All three maturities are traded simultaneously and they expire on the last Thursday of their respective contract months. If the last Thursday of the month is a holiday, they expire on the preceding business day. As a near-month contract expires, the middle-month contract becomes near-month contract and the far-month contract becomes middle-month contract and so on.

   For example, suppose Kevin buys a single November futures contract of ACC Ltd. that is trading at ₹1,700 per share. Its lot size is 250 shares. This means, Kevin is willing to buy/sell ACC stock at a fixed price of ₹1700 per share on the last Thursday in November.

   At that time, the price of ACC stock in the cash market could be above or below ₹1700 depending on the prevailing market conditions. Kevin can take advantage of this difference in prices to make profits.

   If the price on the last Thursday of November is ₹1800 in the cash market, Kevin's futures position will be settled at that price. He will receive a profit of ₹100 per share (the settlement price of ₹1800 less his cost price of ₹1700 multiplied by lot size = 100×250).

   If the price on the last Thursday of November is ₹1600 in the cash market, Kevin's futures position will be settled at that price. He will incur a loss of ₹25000 on the contract (difference between the settlement price of ₹1600 and his cost price of ₹1700 multiplied by lot size = 100×250).

   This amount is adjusted with the margins maintained by Kevin. If he receives profits, they will be added to the margins and if he makes a loss, the amount will be deducted from the margins. Table 18.4 exhibits the details of futures of ACC Ltd.

Kevin need not hold the future till expiry. He can also come out of the futures contract on ACC before its expiry date. In case he exits the contract before expiry, any gains or losses that he has made are settled by adjusting them against his margins.

TABLE 18.4 Futures of ACC Ltd.

Futures of ACC Ltd.			
Near Expiry date	27/11/2014	Lot Size	250
Futures Summary			
Closing Price	1517.6	Premium/Discount	6.75
Previous Close	1506.75	Change %	0.72
Futures OI	1342.00 K	Change %	2.52
Futures Contracts	1581	Change %	–20.71

Index futures

1. **Index Futures** are futures contracts available on indices of market performance like S&P BSE SENSEX, CNX NIFTY and S&P 500. Such contracts help investors make money on the basis of movement of the underlying indices. Index futures also have standardized specifications laid down by the exchanges they are traded on. Some key characteristics/specifications of index futures contracts in India are:
   (a) *Contract size*: Just like stock futures, index futures contracts are also traded in lots. The difference is that there are no underlying shares whose price is specified. This means that if investors buy index futures on S&P BSE SENSEX, they do not purchase futures of the stocks belonging to the index. Instead, they buy level of the stock index, i.e., its value converted into rupees. To illustrate the concept of lot in the context of index futures, let us consider the example of NSE's main index CNX NIFTY at a level of 8300. Assuming that NSE stipulates that each point of index is equivalent to ₹1 and the lot size of this contract is 50, then to buy one contract of index futures on NIFTY, an investor would be required to pay ₹4,15,000 ($8300 \times 1 \times 50$). Table 18.5 exhibits the lot size of some NSE indices.
   (b) *Duration*: Index futures too have three contract series open for trading at any point in time—the near-month (1 month), middle-month (2 months) and far-month (3 months) index futures contracts.

TABLE 18.5 Lot size of few NSE indices

Underlying	Symbol	Market Lot
BANK NIFTY	BANKNIFTY	50
CNX 100	CNX100	100
CNX IT	CNXIT	100
CNX NIFTY Junior	JUNIOR	100
NIFTY Midcap 50	NIFTYMCAP50	300
S&P CNX NIFTY	NIFTY	50

(c) *Expiry*: In case of index futures, physical settlement is not possible. Therefore, an open position in index futures is settled by entering into an opposing transaction on or before the day of expiry.

Let us understand the working of index futures with a simple example. Suppose NIFTY stands at 8300 points in the cash market today and Kevin buys one NIFTY November future at the price prevailing in the futures market.

This price of one November futures contract could be anywhere above, below or at ₹4.15 lakhs (8300 × 50), depending on the prevailing market conditions.

In our example, let us assume that Kevin decides to hold his NIFTY future that he bought at 8300. This contract expires on the last Thursday of November. On that day, the exchange will settle his contract at the closing price of the NIFTY prevailing on that day. So, if on that day, the NIFTY stands at 8260, he has made a loss of ₹2,000 (difference in index levels 40 × lot size of 50 units).

His broker will deduct the amount from the margins Kevin has deposited with him and forward it to the stock exchange. The exchange, in turn, will forward it to the seller, who has made that profit. However, if NIFTY closes at 8340, Kevin would have made a profit of ₹2,000, which would be added to his account.

Kevin can also choose to exit his index futures contract before the date of expiry if he believes that the market will rise before the expiry of his contract period and that he can get a better price for it on an earlier date. In case of such an exit, the exchange will settle the contract by comparing the index levels when he bought and when he exits the contract. Depending on the profit or loss, his margin account will be credited or debited.

Participants in the Futures Markets

Futures contracts are mainly used by hedgers, arbitrageurs and speculators. Let up discuss their role in futures market:

1. **Hedgers:** Hedgers are market participants who trade in futures to offset the anticipated risky position they hold in the spot market. Hedgers are parties who face risk due to a prior position they hold in a financial asset or commodity and they take positions in futures of these commodities or financial assets to protect themselves against the risk they are exposed to. For example, consider a farmer who is expecting to produce 'n' tonnes of rice from his farm in 2 months from now. He is exposed to the risk of fall in price of rice two months from now. He can hedge this risk by selling rice futures now to protect himself against future price fluctuations.
2. **Arbitrageurs:** Arbitrage is the opportunity to make profit from price differential between markets. Arbitrageurs are the participants who exploit the price difference between different markets. In futures market, arbitrage can take two forms:
   (a) Cash-futures arbitrage where arbitrageur takes advantage of the difference in prices between cash and futures market. For example, suppose the spot SENSEX is 26900, one-month SENSEX future is 27250 and the risk-free interest rate is 1% per month. This means that SENSEX futures are trading above their theoretical value of 27169. The theoretical value of 27169 is arrived at by assuming the growth in SENSEX at risk-free rate. The pricing error is equal to 27250 − 27169 = 81. Arbitrageur can exploit this difference by buying spot SENSEX and selling SENSEX futures.
   (b) Index arbitrage which is quite complicated. To enable investors to take advantage of index arbitrage without worrying about the complexities, a new mechanism has evolved called 'program trading.'

Marketview 18.2 Program Trading

The term program trading refers to the trades based on signals from computer programs. The New York Stock Exchange defines program trading as any trade by a member firm involving fifteen or more stocks simultaneously with an aggregate value in excess of $1 million. Primarily institutional investors use it for large-volume trades. In these trades, orders from the trader's computer are entered directly into the market's computer system and executed automatically. The use of program trading has increased in recent years due to reduced trading costs on account of technological advances, increased investments in equity by institutional investors and extensive portfolio diversification undertaken by high net worth investors. Further, these large trades undertaken in program trading are also hedged at times by an offsetting position in index futures. Program trading has been associated with many trading strategies like duration averaging, portfolio insurance and index arbitrage.

The downside of program trading is that program trades are usually triggered if index price rises or falls to a certain pre-specified level. This has the potential of creating very volatile situations. Thus, restrictions are always placed by exchanges on times when program trading can be used.

Source: Based on www.programtrading.com, accessed on January 7, 2015.

3. **Speculators:** We know that the speculators are market participants who engage in trading with the sole motive of earning profit from short-term price fluctuations in asset prices. In future market also, the speculators buy or sell contracts to earn profits from price fluctuations. Role of speculators is very important in the functioning of futures market. They impact the liquidity in the market and absorb the excess supply/demand generated by hedgers trading to protect themselves against the anticipated risks associated with their existing positions. The speculators act as counterparty to hedgers and assume the risk of fluctuations that the hedgers are looking to avoid. Actually, the actions of speculators tend to stabilize the markets by dampening the volatility of prices over time.

Key Terms in Futures Trading

Futures trading is more complicated than stock trading. There are certain typical aspects of futures trading that we need to understand. Key terms related to futures trading are discussed below:

1. **Marking-to-Market:** A typical feature of a futures contract is that it is not settled at maturity like a forwards contract. A futures contract is marked-to-market on a periodic basis, i.e., the payoffs on futures contracts are settled periodically. For example, suppose Mr. X takes long position in a futures contract on Monday morning. The contract is going to mature on Friday afternoon. Assuming the agreed upon price of the contract is ₹100 and that at the close of trading on Monday, the price of the contract is ₹106, three things will occur due to marking-to-market feature of futures. First Mr. X will receive ₹6 as a positive payoff from buying the future. Second, the existing futures contract for ₹100 will be cancelled and third, Mr. X will be issued new futures contract priced at ₹106. To summarize, the entire working in one statement, we can say that the value of a futures contract is set to zero at the end of the trading day.

2. **Margins:** There are different kinds of margins prescribed by the exchange as a percentage of the total value of the futures contracts. Without margins, investors cannot trade in the futures market. To trade in future on Indian exchanges, investors have to pay certain amount upfront. This is called initial margin and it is to be deposited with the broker as a security deposit. Initial margin is defined as a percentage of an investor's open position and is set for different positions by the exchange on the basis of the average volatility of the concerned asset over a specified period of time and the interest cost. Initial margin amounts fluctuate daily depending on the market value of open positions of an investor in futures contract. Initial margin is usually around 5–10%. The idea behind the margin is to ensure that obligations arising out of futures contracts are honored. Both parties of futures contract have to meet the margin requirement.

   Another margin, called the exposure margin, is also set by the exchange to control volatility and excessive speculation in the futures markets. It is levied on the value of the contract bought or sold. Another margin, mark-to-market margin, covers the difference between the cost of the contract and its closing price on the day the contract is purchased. This margin covers the daily differences in closing prices of the futures contract. Since futures contracts trade on a marking-to-market basis, the margins deposited by investors keep on changing with payoffs every day. Therefore, there is another concept called maintenance or variation margin, which refers to the level below which the margin money is not allowed to deplete. This is also fixed by the exchange. If an investor sustains loss and the margins deplete below the critical level, he gets a margin call to replenish the margin amount.
3. **Closing Out Contracts and Settlement:** Selling futures can close out a long position and buying futures can close out a short position in futures. The net difference is settled in cash without any delivery of the underlying asset. The contracts held till expiration date may be settled for cash or physical delivery, but most contracts are not held till expiry. The futures are marked-to-market, so daily closing price is the settlement price for a given day. The final settlement price is the closing price of the underlying asset on the last day of trading.
4. **Basis Risk:** The difference between the spot price (cash price) and the relevant futures price of a futures contract is called basis. The basis can be positive or negative.

$$\text{Basis} = \text{Spot price} - \text{Futures price}$$

   For example, when NIFTY futures are trading at 6800 and the spot NIFTY is 6700, the basis is said to be 100. On maturity date of the contract, the basis must be zero.

   The difference between future and spot, i.e., basis should ideally reflect changes in interest rate only. However, in reality the basis oscillates around its ideal value within an almost perceptible band. These fluctuations in basis from its ideal value lead to what is known as basis risk. Existence of basis risk reduces the effectiveness of futures as a useful tool for speculators and hedgers.

   Basis is usually a negative number because of carrying charges. In a normal market situation, spot prices are lower than the nearby futures prices. As the delivery on the futures approaches, carrying charges diminish and the price difference between cash and futures decreases.
5. **Price Limits:** Prices on futures contracts can move only in ticks, which indicate the minimum amount that they can move by. Ticks are established by the futures exchanges. Futures exchanges also pose limits on the maximum gain or loss on a futures contract that is allowed in a trading session. The price limits are imposed by the exchanges in order to protect the futures contracts against extreme volatility, panic buying or selling, overreaction to some news item and manipulations within the market. If anytime during the day, daily trading limit is reached, trading is halted for any trades that break the threshold or even suspended for that particular contract. It can be resumed later at the discretion of the exchange.

6. **Reverse Trade:** The clearinghouse of exchange plays a key role in futures trading on any exchange. It becomes the seller to holders of long position (buyers) and buyer to the holders of short position (sellers). Clearing house is obligated to fulfill its side of the contract, so it is the only party that can be hurt in case the counterparty defaults in its obligation. To protect its clearinghouses against unfulfilled obligations, the exchange imposes margins on investors trading in futures.

   Due to participation of clearinghouse, it becomes very easy for brokers to liquidate their positions. Long positions are unwound by doing short side of the contract and short positions can be undone simply by doing long side of the contract. Such trades, undertaken to close out a position, are called reverse trades in futures trading.

7. **Open Interest:** Open interest indicates the total number of futures contracts that are not closed or delivered at the end of a particular trading day. In other words, open interest in futures contracts is the total number of contracts that have not been squared off, expired or settled with delivery. Since each contract has a buyer and a seller, total open interest for a given market is a total of only buyers or only sellers, not a total of both buyers and sellers. Further, open interest is a number that changes each day. It is a key number that is used by analysts to confirm trends and trend reversals for futures contracts.

   Open interest measures the in flow of money into the futures market. Increasing open interest implies that money is flowing into the marketplace, indicating that the prevailing trend can be expected to continue.

   Decreasing or declining open interest gives a clear signal that the market is liquidating, thereby indicating that the prevailing price trend can be expected to end soon. Thus, tracking open interest data can be useful in trading toward the end of major market moves. For example, a leveling off of an open interest subsequent to a sustained price rise is taken as an early warning signal of the approaching end of uptrend or bull market.

   Open interest is also used for trend confirmation. For instance, a rising open interest along with a rise in price is taken to be a confirmation of an upward trend. A flat or falling open interest accompanied with increasing or falling prices may be taken to indicate a possible reversal of trend.

   The relationship between open interest and price trend in the market is illustrated in Table 18.6.

TABLE 18.6 The relationship between open interest and price trend in the market

Prevailing price trend	Level of open interest	Indication
Rising	Rising	Market is Strong
Rising	Falling	Market is Weakening
Falling	Rising	Market is Weak
Falling	Falling	Market is Strengthening

Beyond the Basics 18.1 Statistical Characteristics of Futures Prices

First order autocorrelation

Futures prices exhibit a statistically significant first-order autocorrelation. However, autocorrelation is not strong enough to allow profitable trading strategies.

Volatility
There is enough evidence to conclude that futures trading does not increase the volatility of the cash market.

Time to Expiration and Futures Price Volatility
Futures price volatility is higher, i.e., the price changes are large when there is more information about the future spot price.

Pricing of Futures Contracts

Futures are derivative products that draw their value from the price of the underlying stocks or indices. However, the pricing is not so direct or simple. A difference between the prices of the underlying asset in the cash segment and in the derivatives segment always prevails. This difference can be understood through two pricing models used for the pricing of futures contracts. These are:

1. The Cost of Carry Model
2. The Expectancy Model

The Cost of Carry Model

Most futures contracts can be priced on the basis of arbitrage, i.e., a price or range of prices at which investors will not be able to create long or short positions in futures contracts and their underlying asset to make riskless profits with no initial investment. *Cash-and-carry* and *reverse cash and carry* arbitrage form the basis of the cost of carry pricing model for futures contracts.

The model is based on certain assumptions:

1. The investors can go long or short in an asset at the same price at which they can go long or short in its futures contracts.
2. Investors can borrow and lend at the same interest rate (risk-free rate). Further there is no limit on the amount of funds that can be borrowed.
3. There are no restrictions on short selling.
4. There is no margin requirement for trades.

National Stock Exchange (NSE), India uses fair value calculation of futures to determine the no-arbitrage limits on the price of a futures contract. This is the basis for the cost-of-carry model. According to the cost-of-carry model, the futures price should depend upon two things:

1. The current spot price (the price at which the asset trades in the spot or the cash market).
2. The cost of carrying or storing the underlying goods from now until the futures contract matures.

Symbolically, $F = S + C$

where
F = Futures price

S = Spot price
C = Holding costs or carry cost.

The above equation can also be expressed as:

$$F = S\,(1 + r)^T$$

where
r = Cost of financing
T = Time till expiration

If $F < S\,(1 + r)^T$ or $F > S\,(1 + r)^T$, then arbitrage opportunities would exist.

Carry cost refers to the cost of holding the asset till the futures contract matures. The components of holding cost vary with the underlying assets. In certain cases, the holding cost may even be negative. In the case of commodity futures, the holding cost or the carry cost includes interest paid to acquire and hold the asset, cost of financing plus cost of storage and insurance, etc. In the case of equity futures, the holding cost is the cost of financing minus the dividends.

There is also a concept of carry return that is defined as a monetary benefit from actually owning the underlying asset. Other things being equal, a carry return will lower the futures price relative to the spot price. Conversely, other things being equal, a carry cost increases the futures price relative to the spot price. Carry returns include dividends, interest, etc.

We are using the concept of discrete compounding, where interest rates are compounded at discrete intervals, i.e., annually or semiannually, as it is more intuitive and simpler to work with. If we use the concept of continuous compounding, the above equation would be expressed as:

$$F = Se^{rT}$$

where
r = Cost of financing (using continuously compounded interest rate)
T = Time till expiration
e = 2.71828

Pricing of futures contracts on commodities

Commodities may be further classified as storable and perishable commodities. The perishable nature of certain commodities makes it difficult to price their futures contracts on the basis of arbitrage (cost of carry model), as the commodity has to be storable for this pricing model to be applicable. Let us discuss the pricing of the futures contracts of both types of commodities.

1. **Storable Commodities:** As mentioned above, the carrying costs relevant for commodities are costs of storing and insuring the commodity. Further, we also know that other things being equal, these carrying costs increase the futures prices. In case of applying the cost of carry model to commodities, we need to understand a concept called '*convenience yield.*' In reverse cash-and-carry arbitrage trades, the underlying asset needs to be sold short or out of inventory held by the investor. It works out to be a simple transaction in case of financial assets, but is more complicated in case of commodities. The reason is that commodities

are often held because the owners need them as part of their businesses. For example, oil refineries hold or own crude oil, but they will not sell it to engage in reverse cash-and-carry arbitrage even if they get an opportunity to earn riskless profits. The refineries will not lend their stock of crude oil to a short seller either. This reluctance or inability of commodity market participants to part with their inventory of commodities despite risk-free profit making opportunities can be understood through the concept of convenience yield.

The convenience yield may be best explained as an unobservable or hidden variable that is a measure of the marginal benefit derived from owning the underlying asset. The impact of convenience yield is reflected in terms of the lowering of the futures prices.

Let us understand the pricing of futures contract on commodities with the help of an example. Suppose the spot price of copper is ₹450/kg. If the cost of financing is 10% annually, the futures price of 100 gms of copper at the expiry of the contract at the end of the month (assuming we are at the first day of the month) can be calculated as:

$$F = S\,(1 + r)^T$$

$S =$ ₹450/kg, therefore for 100 grams it will be ₹45
$r =$ Financing cost $= 10\%$

$$T = \frac{30}{365}$$

Storage cost is assumed to be zero since the quantity is very small.

The fair value of the contract

$$= 45\,(1 + 0.10)^{(30/365)}$$

$$= 45.354$$

If the contract is of a longer duration, say three-months, then the cost of financing will increase the fair value or futures price. Therefore, the futures price would be $F = 45\,(1 + 0.10)^{(90/365)} =$ ₹46.07

Similarly, if the contract is for 20,000 kg. of copper instead of 100 gms, then the element of storage cost will come in and the price of the futures contract will also include cost of storage (c).

Symbolically,

$$F = S\,(1 + r + c)^T$$

The effect of convenience yield (say *cy*) on futures price can be understood through the following equation.

$$F = S\,(1 + r - cy)^T$$

2. **Perishable Commodities:** The pricing of a futures contract on an underlying perishable commodity is influenced by:
   (a) *The expected spot price ($E(S_0)$) of the underlying commodity*: If the market expects the spot price of the underlying commodity to increase before the expiry date of the futures contract, then the futures prices will be more than the current spot price of the commodity.

Conversely, if the market expects a decline in the spot price, the futures price will be less than the current spot price.

(b) *Risk premium associated with taking a position in futures contract*: Risk premium associated with a position in futures contract is dependent on whether the buyer is seen as providing a service to the seller or vice versa. Let us consider the following cases to understand the pricing of futures contracts in the context of the perishable commodities:

Case 1: When buyer of the contract is seen as the provider of service

In the case of futures contract on agricultural produce, farmers (producer) are the main sellers of futures contracts and investors who buy the contract can be seen as providing the farmers a service and they will expect a risk premium. In such cases, the futures price will be lower than the expected spot price. Therefore,

$$\text{Futures price} = \text{Expected Spot Price} - \text{Expected Risk Premium}$$

When futures prices are less than the spot prices, then this type of relationship between futures and spot prices is called normal backwardation, as exhibited in Figure 18.2.

Figure 18.2 Normal backwardation.

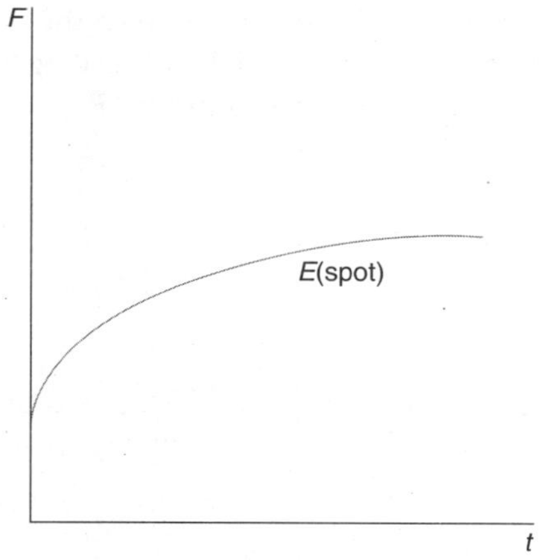

Case 2: When seller of the contract is seen as the provider of service

In case of futures contract on inputs/raw material for industrial users, the firm (user) buying the futures contract is in need of the commodity, so investors who sell the contract can be seen as the providers of service. Therefore, they will expect a risk premium for selling the contract. Therefore,

$$\text{Futures price} = \text{Expected Spot Price} + \text{Expected Risk Premium}$$

When futures prices are more than the spot prices, then this type of relationship between futures and spot prices is called normal contango, as exhibited in Figure 18.3.

Figure 18.3 Normal contango.

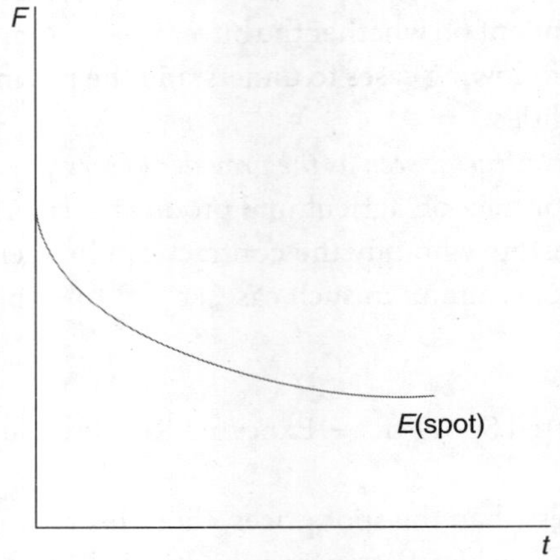

Case 3: When neither buyer nor seller of the futures contract is seen as the provider of service

The reality of the commodity markets in the present times is that the market is not dominated by users or producers (hedgers), rather it is dominated by speculators. Thus, both the buyers and the sellers speculate on the price and the distinction between the providers and the receivers of service is not there. With the result, the net benefit can be zero, leading to a zero risk premium. In such cases, the futures price will be equal to expected spot price (Expectations hypothesis), as exhibited in Figure 18.4. Therefore,

Futures price = Expected spot price

Figure 18.4 Expectations hypothesis.

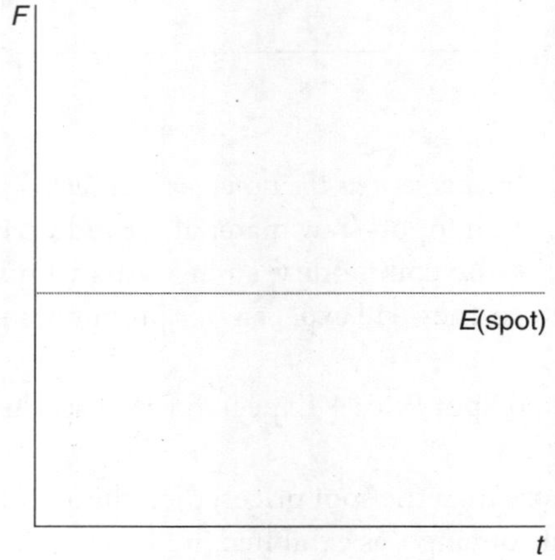

Pricing of equity index futures

The equity index futures differ from the commodity futures by way of having no costs of storage. Instead, there is a stream of dividends, which is a negative cost if one is long in the stock and a positive cost if one is short in the stock. Therefore, for equity index futures, cost of carry is calculated as:

Cost of carry = Financing cost − Dividends.

It can be seen that an accurate forecasting of dividends is crucial for a more accurate estimate of the futures price. Let us understand the pricing of index futures using expected dividend amount and expected dividend yield.

1. **Pricing of Index Futures Using the Expected Dividend Amount:** The price of index futures is also determined by using the cost-of-carry model. Here, the carrying cost is equal to the difference between the cost of financing the acquisition price of the portfolio underlying the index and the present value of future stream of dividends expected from the stocks in the index portfolio.

   Let us understand the pricing of the index futures using the expected dividend amount with the help of an example. Suppose Rita buys a new two-month futures contract on NIFTY traded on NSE by borrowing money at the rate of 10% per annum. Following additional information is also available:

   (a) HDFC Bank Ltd. will be declaring a dividend of ₹10 per share, 15 days after the purchase of the contract.

   (b) Current value of NIFTY is 8300 and NIFTY trades with a multiplier of 50. Therefore, the value of the contract is $50 \times 8300 =$ ₹415,000.

   (c) The weight of HDFC Bank Ltd. in NIFTY is 6%. Therefore, its value in NIFTY is ₹24900 ($415{,}000 \times 0.06$).

   (d) If the market price of HDFC Bank Ltd. is ₹930, then a traded unit of NIFTY involves 27 (24900/930) shares (approximately) of HDFC Bank Ltd.

   Given the above information, the price of the futures contract of NIFTY may be calculated as explained below:

   Cost of carry needs to be reduced by the extent of dividend received.

   The amount of dividend received is ₹270 (27×10). Since the dividend is received 15 days later, it will be compounded for the remaining 45 days of the contract. We also need the amount of dividend received per unit of NIFTY. Hence, we divide the compounded dividend by 50.

$$F = 8300\,(0.10)^{(60/365)} - \frac{(27\times 10)(1+0.10)^{(45/365)}}{50} = ₹8425.60$$

2. **Pricing of Index Futures Using the Expected Dividend Yield:** If the dividend flow throughout the year is generally uniform, then annual dividend yield should be calculated. The cost-of-carry model needs to be modified to accommodate the dividend yield in the following manner:

$$F = S\,(1 + r - q)^T$$

   where

   F = Futures price

   S = Spot index value

   r = Cost of financing

q = Expected dividend yield
T = Holding period

Let us understand the pricing of the index futures using the expected dividend yield with the help of an example. Suppose Rita buys a new two-month futures contract on NIFTY traded on NSE by borrowing money at the rate of 10% per annum and the dividend yield on NIFTY is 2% annualized. The spot value of NIFTY is 8300. The fair value of the futures contract can be calculated as:

$$F = 8300\,(1 + 0.10 - 0.02)^{(60/365)} = ₹8400.20$$

Pricing of equity/stock futures

The same approach is applicable to individual stocks as well as stock indices. Like index futures, stock futures are also cash settled; there is no delivery of the underlying stocks. The equity futures also differ from the commodity futures by way of having no costs of storage. Instead, there is a stream of dividends, which is a negative cost if one is long in the stock and a positive cost if one is short in the stock.

Therefore, for equity futures, Cost of carry = Financing cost – Dividends.

Thus, an accurate forecasting of dividends is crucial for a more accurate estimate of the futures price. Let us understand the pricing of futures using dividends.

1. **Pricing of Stock Futures When no Dividend is Expected:** The price of equity futures is also determined using the cost-of-carry model. Here, the carrying cost is equal to the difference between the cost of financing the acquisition price of stock and the present value of future stream of dividends expected from it. If no dividends are expected during the life of the contract, pricing the futures on that stock is very simple. It can be calculated by multiplying the spot price by the cost of carry.

   Let us understand the pricing of the stock futures in case of no dividends are paid during the contract duration, with the help of an example. Suppose Oscar buys two-month futures contract on L&T that trade on NSE by borrowing money at the rate of 10% per annum. No dividends are expected during the two-month period and the spot price of L&T is ₹1620. The price of the futures contract may be calculated as:

   $$F = 1620\,(1 + 0.10)^{(60/365)} = ₹1645.58$$

2. **Pricing of Stock Futures When Dividend are Expected:** In case of pricing of stock futures when dividend is expected, cost by carry is equal to the difference between the financing cost and dividends as explained above.

   Let us understand the pricing of the stock futures using the expected dividend amount with the help of an example. Suppose Rita buys a new two-month futures contract on HDFC Bank Ltd. traded on NSE by borrowing money at the rate of 10% per annum. Following additional information is also available:

   (a) HDFC Bank Ltd. will be declaring a dividend of ₹10 per share 15 days after the purchase of the contract.

   (b) The market price of HDFC Bank Ltd. is ₹930.

   The price of the futures contract on HDFC Bank Ltd. may be calculated using the above information as:

The amount of dividend received is ₹10. Since the dividend is received 15 days later, it will be compounded for the remaining 45 days of the contract.

$$F = 930\,(1 + 0.10)^{(60/365)} - 10\,(1 + 0.10)^{(45/365)}) = ₹934.56$$

The cost of carry model describes an arbitrage relation between the futures price, spot price and the cost of carrying the asset. The simple yet rational implication of this model is that if it is cheaper to buy and store an asset than to get into a futures contract then, an arbitrageur will find it profitable to take a short position in the futures contract, borrow funds equal to the present value of the futures price and buy and store the asset. At contract maturity, the stored asset will be delivered and the proceeds will be used to repay the loan. Conversely, if the futures price is less than the cost of acquiring and storing the underlying asset, the arbitrageur will profit from taking a long position in the futures contract and short selling the commodity (with the short sale proceeds net of storage cost invested at the risk-free rate). At contract maturity, delivery received from the long position in futures contract will be used to meet short sale commitments. The payment for delivery from the long position in futures contract will be made by using the invested short sale net proceeds.

The basic idea behind cost-of-carry pricing model is that keeping a position open in the cash market has many benefits and costs. The price of a futures contract reflects these costs and benefits. Further, this model gives an approximate idea about the true futures contract price. However, the price observed in the market is driven by the forces of demand and supply that act as price–discovery mechanism. With the result, the price observed in the market may differ from the so-called true price, calculated by the model.

The Expectancy Model of Futures Pricing

According to the expectancy model of futures pricing, the futures price of any asset, be it commodity, index or equity, is basically what the spot price of that asset is expected to be in the future. In other words, the model says that the futures price is equal to the expected spot price on some future date. The expectancy theory can also be taken to infer that if the futures contracts are priced appropriately, the prevailing prices of the futures contracts should give some indication about the level of spot prices at some point in the future.

Symbolically,

$$F_{0,t} = E\,(S_0)$$

where

$E\,(S_0)$ = The expected spot price on some future date

The main implication of this statement is that if the overall market sentiment shows a bullish inclination or tilt toward a higher price for an asset in the future, the futures price of the asset can be expected to be positive. Conversely, a rise in bearish sentiment in the market can be expected to lead to a fall in the futures price of the concerned asset.

Thus, this model does not believe that there is any relationship between the present spot price of the asset and its futures price, and this is where it differs from the cost-of-carry model.

In expectancy model, what matters is only what the future spot price of the asset is expected to be. This explains why many stock market participants take trends in futures prices into consideration to forecast the price fluctuations that can be expected in the cash segment.

Futures Trading Strategies

Trading strategies in any asset class depend on the views of the trading community about the market movements. There are four typical views that investors can have about the market: Bullish indicating a rising trend, bearish indicating a falling trend, volatile indicating rapid fluctuations but clear direction and neutral or stable indicating a period of stability or low fluctuations in levels. These expectations about market movement have implications for formulation of futures trading strategies.

The main trading strategies or approaches in futures contract are:

1. Speculative trading strategies
2. Hedging strategies
3. Arbitrage strategies

The above trading strategies or approaches in futures contract are discussed below in detail.

Speculative Trading Strategies

The most common strategies used in the futures markets are: going long, going short and spreads.

1. **Going Long:** When a speculator is trying to profit from an anticipated rise in future price he goes long in the futures contract, i.e., he enters a contract to buy and take delivery of the underlying asset at the price specified in the contract.
   Payoffs of long position in futures: Since in a futures contract, the future price is decided in present, the gain of the investor comes from the rise in price of the underlying asset over and above the price specified in the contract. For example, suppose Mr. Y buys a March 2013 contract (underlying stock: MFM Ltd.) at ₹745. Then the rise in price of share beyond ₹745 or fall below ₹745 will result in a gain on loss to the investor. Figure 18.5 exhibits payoffs in long position in futures.

Figure 18.5 Payoffs in long position in futures.

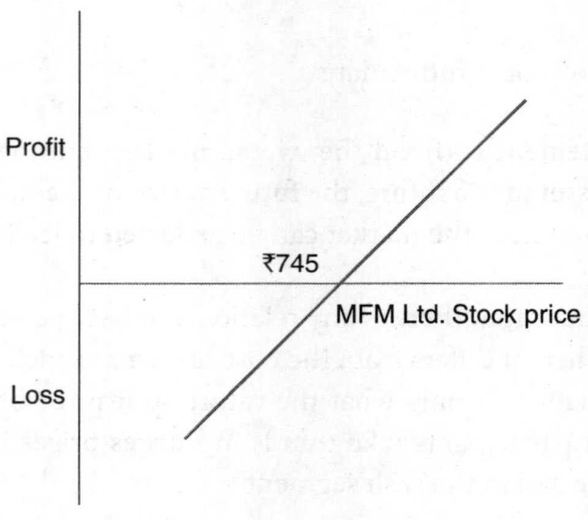

2. **Going Short:** When a speculator is trying to profit from an anticipated fall in future price he goes short in the futures contract, i.e., he enters a contract to sell and give delivery of the underlying asset at the price specified in the contract.

Figure 18.6 Payoffs in short position in futures.

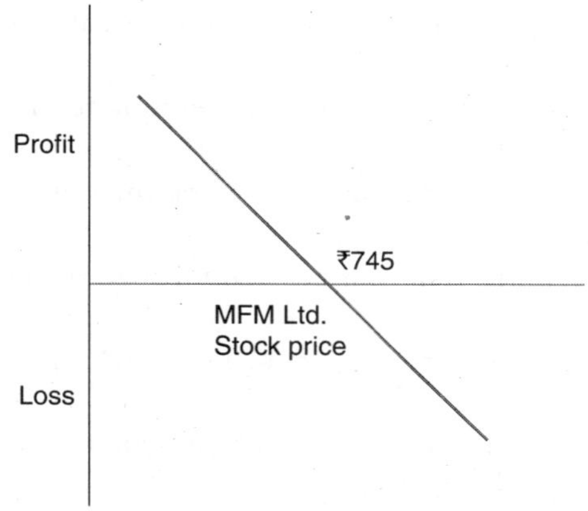

Payoffs of short position in futures: Here the payoffs are reverse of what happens in the long position. The investor loses if the price rises and gains if the price falls on the expiration date. Figure 18.6 exhibits payoffs in short position in futures.

3. **Spreads:** A spread is a measure of the difference in price between two futures contracts on the same commodity for two different maturity dates.

$$\text{Spread} = F_{0,t+k} - F_{0,t}$$

where
$F_{0,t}$ = The current futures price for delivery of the underlying asset at time t.
$F_{0,t+k}$ = The current futures price for delivery of the same underlying asset at time $t+k$.

Spreads are a way of benefiting from the price difference between two different contracts of the same commodity. Spreading is one of the most conservative and moderate forms of trading in the futures market because it is much safer than taking naked long/short positions in futures contracts.

There are many different types of spreads, including:

(a) *Calendar spread*: Calendar spread involves the simultaneous purchase and sale of two futures of the same type, having the same price but different delivery dates. Thus, a calendar spread requires a trader to take a long position, in a futures series expiring in any one calendar month and an offsetting, i.e., a short position in the same futures but for a series expiring in any month other than the expiry month of the series in which long position has been taken.

The spread tracks the difference between the prices of long and short positions. Therefore, the risk of trading changes from that of fluctuation in price to that of the difference between the two positions of the spread. It results in less volatile positions than the outright futures positions.

(b) *Bull and bear spreads:* Calendar spreads that are long in near term futures contracts and short in longer term futures contracts are known as 'bull spreads' while futures calendar spreads that are short in near term and long in longer term futures contracts are known as 'bear spreads.' To summarize,

Bull spread: A futures bull spread is formed when following positions are taken:

Long current month Futures + Short mid or far month futures

Bear spread: A futures bear spread is formed when following positions are taken:

Short current month futures + Long mid or far month futures

Bull spreads are useful in lowering the margin requirement and risk. It is best to use bull calendar spreads if:

(i) The price spread between near term and further term futures contracts are expected to narrow down in a normal market.

(ii) The price spread between near term and further term futures contracts are expected to widen in an inverted market.

Bear spreads are also useful in lowering the margin requirement and risk. It is best to use bear calendar spreads if:

(i) The price spread between near term and further term futures contracts are expected to widen in a normal market.

(ii) The price spread between near term and further term futures contracts are expected to narrow down in an inverted market.

(c) *Inter-market spread*: Inter-market spread involves going long in one contract, say Long July Iron ore and going short in another contract of the same month, say Short July Silver.

(d) *Inter-exchange spread*: This is a type of spread in which positions are created in different futures exchanges. For example, the investor may create positions in the futures exchanges of NSE and BSE simultaneously.

Arbitrage Strategies

As explained earlier, if $F < S(1+r)^T$ or $F > S(1+r)^T$, then arbitrage opportunities would exist. This means there will be arbitrage opportunities whenever the futures prices move away from their fair value. Such deviations will trigger cash and carry or reverse cash and carry arbitrage, depending on the level of futures price and bring the prices back to the convergence level as exhibited in Figure 18.7.

Cash and carry arbitrage represents a strategy of holding a combination of a long position in an asset such as a stock or commodity and a short position in the futures contract of the same asset. The set of trades that make up the cash and carry arbitrage are borrow, buy the underlying asset and go short in its futures contract.

The borrowed funds will have to be repaid with interest on the delivery day of the futures contract. Selling the futures contract locks in the selling price of the underlying asset. Cash-and-carry arbitrage establishes a maximum futures price. If the futures price is too high, then this set of trades will lead to an arbitrage profit.

This arbitrage strategy tries to exploit pricing inefficiencies for an asset in the spot and futures markets in order to make riskless profits and it is viable only if the cash inflow from the short position in futures exceeds the purchase and carrying costs of the long position in the asset under consideration.

Let us try to understand the concept of cash and carry arbitrage with the help of an example.

Figure 18.7 Convergence of futures and spot prices in future.

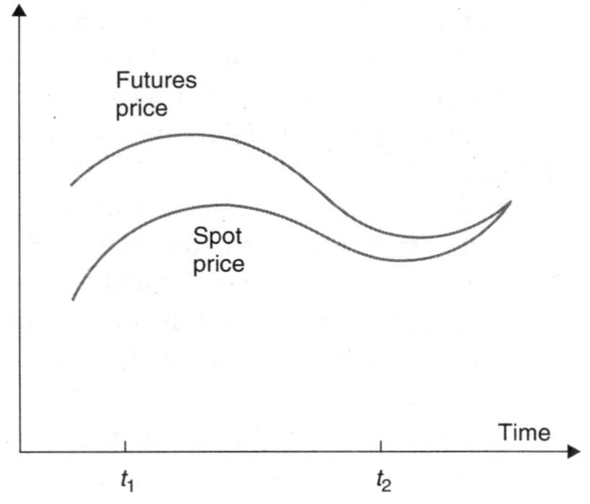

Suppose, the share of MMM Ltd. is currently trading at ₹200, while its one-month futures contract is priced at ₹208. In addition, the monthly carrying cost for the share of MMM Ltd. amounts to ₹6. A trader can buy the share of MMM Ltd. at ₹200 and simultaneously go short in its futures contract at ₹208. By carrying the contract till expiration and delivering against it, he can make an arbitrage or riskless profit of ₹2.

Reverse cash and carry arbitrage represents the strategy of holding a combination of a short position in an asset such as a stock or commodity and a long position in the futures contract of the same asset. The set of trades that make up the reverse cash and carry arbitrage are sell the underlying asset (short or out of existing holdings), go long in its futures contract and lend the proceeds from the sale of asset. Reverse cash-and-carry arbitrage establishes a minimum futures price. If the futures price is too low, then this set of trades will lead to an arbitrage profit.

This arbitrage strategy tries to exploit pricing inefficiencies for an asset in the spot and futures markets in order to make riskless profits and it is viable only if the futures price is low in relation to the spot price of the asset. In other words, the inflow from the short sale of the asset should exceed the price of the futures contract and the carrying costs associated with the short position in the asset.

Let us try to understand the concept of reverse cash and carry arbitrage with the help of an example.

Suppose, the share of MMM Ltd. is currently trading at ₹208, while its one-month futures contract is priced at ₹200. In addition, the monthly carrying cost (for example, dividends that are payable by the short seller) for the short position in share of MMM Ltd. amount to ₹4. A trader can initiate a short position in the share of MMM Ltd at ₹208 and simultaneously go long in its futures contract at ₹200. By carrying the contract till expiration and accepting delivery against it to cover his short position in the asset, he can make an arbitrage or riskless profit of ₹4.

To summarize the above discussion, the cash and carry arbitrage trades require that investors borrow money to buy the underlying asset in cash (spot) and go short in the overpriced futures contract and hold it till expiration. Here, traders or arbitrageurs realize a profit without any initial cash flow. On the other hand, reverse cash-and-carry arbitrage trades require that investors to sell the underlying asset, lend the proceeds and go long in the cheap futures contract of the same asset. Again, traders or arbitrageurs realize a profit without any initial cash flow.

Hedging Strategies

Hedging may be defined as the act of counterbalancing the risk of fluctuation of price of an asset by taking an offsetting position. Futures contracts are one of the most popular derivatives used to hedge risk. As the futures contracts remove the uncertainty about the future price of an asset, they are very useful in controlling the risk exposure that an investor has in a trade. By locking in a price for which a particular asset can be bought or sold, companies are able to eliminate the uncertainty surrounding some assets that they have to deal in on some future date. There are two types of hedges, long and short.

A long futures hedge is used to lock in the price of an asset one needs to buy in the future. For example, New Era Jewelers Ltd. knows that in six months it will have to buy 600 kilogram of silver to fulfill an order for the wedding of a rich NRI's daughter. The spot price of silver is ₹35800 per kilogram and the six-month futures price is ₹35600 per kilogram. By buying the futures contract, New Era Jewelers Ltd. can lock in a price of ₹35600 per kilogram. This reduces their risk because they will be able to buy 600 kilogram of silver for ₹35600 per kilogram in six months.

Similarly, if a company is required to sell an asset in the future, then it can hedge its risk by taking short position in the future contract of that asset.

Thus, companies can use futures to hedge risks arising from interest rates, exchange rates and other market variables during the course of their main business.

Understanding the dynamics of hedging using futures

1. **Long Hedge for Purchase of an Asset**
   F_0: Futures price at the time hedging position is taken
   F_t: Futures price at the time asset is purchased
   S_t: Price of asset at the time of purchase
   b_t: Basis at the time of purchase $= S_t - F_t$

Gain on futures	$F_t - F_0$
Net amount paid to buy the asset	$S_t - (F_t - F_0) = F_0 + b_t$

2. **Short Hedge for Sale of an Asset**
   F_0: Futures price at the time hedging position is taken
   F_t: Futures price at the time asset is sold
   S_t: Price of asset at the time of sale
   b_t: Basis at the time of sale $= S_t - F_t$

Gain on futures	$F_0 - F_t$
Net amount received from sale of the asset	$S_t + (F_0 - F_t) = F_0 + b_t$

3. **Cross Hedging:** An investor wanting to hedge his risk in the asset for which no futures contract is available, has to choose a contract whose futures price is most highly positively correlated with his asset's price. This is known as cross hedging.

To apply any of the hedging strategies discussed above, the investors/traders need to compute the optimal hedge ratio or the minimum variance hedge ratio.

4. **Optimal Hedge Ratio or Minimum Variance Hedge Ratio:** To undertake hedging effectively, an investor should determine the proportion of the exposure that should optimally be hedged. This is known as optimal hedge ratio (h) and it is calculated as:

$$h = r\left(\frac{\sigma_s}{\sigma_F}\right)$$

where
σ_s = The standard deviation of ΔS, the change in the spot price during the hedging period
σ_F = The standard deviation of ΔF, the change in the futures price during the hedging period
r = The coefficient of correlation between ΔS and ΔF

Using hedging to offset risk associated with equity and commodity trading

1. **Hedging with Stock Index Futures:**
Case 1: Hedging of inventory risk, i.e., when the stock is held by the investor

An investor holding a portfolio of stocks is exposed to the risk of decline in the market value of his holdings, particular in times of high volatility. The investor can hedge this risk by selling equity index futures and lock-in the prevailing equity prices. Such hedge can be effective in eliminating the price risk faced by the investor, provided the portfolio held by the investor is at least broadly similar to the composition of the equity index underlying the futures contract chosen for hedging.

For example, consider an investor who holds a portfolio of equity shares and sells a futures contract on an index that is broadly similar to his portfolio. If equity prices of the component securities of his portfolio decline by 25% over the next one month, the investor will lose this much on his holdings. However, he will make a profit of 25% on the futures contract which had locked-in the higher earlier price. Thus, loss on the equity portfolio will be offset by profit on the equity index futures contract.

To hedge the risk in a portfolio, the number of index contracts that should be shorted can be calculated as:

$$= \beta\left(\frac{V_A}{V_F}\right)$$

where
β = Beta (measure of systematic risk)
V_A = The current value of the portfolio
V_F = The current value of one futures contract (futures price × contract size)

For example, if the value of SENSEX contract is ₹3 lakh, the value of the portfolio is ₹5 lakh and its beta is 1.2, then the number of contracts to be bought or sold may be calculated as:

$$1.2\left(\frac{500000}{300000}\right) = 2$$

Thus, to completely hedge the portfolio risk, 2 SENSEX futures are required.

The portfolio beta can also be increased or decreased by using hedging. In such cases, optimal number of contracts is calculated as:

$$(\beta^* - \beta)\left(\frac{V_A}{V_F}\right)$$

where
β^* = Expected beta of the portfolio
β = Present beta of the portfolio

Case 2: Hedging of risk of price rise of the stock the investor is anticipating to purchase on some future date
Consider an investor who is expecting to receive certain amount of money that he plans to invest in equity. The risk that he faces is that by the time the funds become available for purchasing equities, the equity prices might rise. This kind of risk can be hedged by buying equity index futures.

In the event of rise in equity prices, the index and the contract's value will also rise. So in a rising market, the contract's settlement price on its expiry date will be higher than the purchase price paid for it. The investor will thus earn a profit on the futures contract that will compensate for the increase in the cost of the investments that the investor had planned to purchase with the funds he is expecting to receive.

2. **Hedging in Commodities:** Commodity traders take hedging decisions on the basis of this variation in '*basis*.' The basis can either increase or decrease. An increasing basis means that it is becoming less negative or more positive. This is called a strong or strengthening or narrowing basis. This happens when cash price is increasing faster in comparison to futures price. A decreasing basis means that it is becoming more negative or less positive. This is called a weakening or widening basis. This happens when the cash price decreases faster in comparison to futures price.

   As explained earlier, basis is the difference between the spot price and the futures price. Basis serves as the key to various hedging strategies in futures. Typically, as the date of expiration comes closer, the basis reduces, indicating the convergence of the futures price toward the spot price and on the date of expiration, it becomes zero. However, in market conditions, the actual difference between the spot and the futures price may not be the same as theoretical cost-of-carry calculations. It can vary on account of the movements in demand and supply of the underlying commodity at current and expected levels in the future. The relationship between spot price, futures price, basis and market conditions may be summarized as follows:

Spot price vs. futures price	Basis	Market condition
Spot price < futures price	Negative	Contango or normal
Spot price > futures price	Positive	Backwardation or abnormal

   Hedging strategy using basis may be presented as:

Long hedge	High cash price	Low cash price
Strong basis	Delay cash purchase, no hedging required	Delay cash purchase Hedge – long futures
Weak basis	Purchase immediate requirements only	Purchase as much as possible and store or hedge using futures
Short hedge	**High cash price**	**Low cash price**
Strong basis	Sell product in cash	Sell product Re-own by going long on futures
Weak basis	Delay cash sales/store product Hedge – short futures	Store for selling later

The long hedger or the buyer of the commodity prefers a weakening basis where the cash price is lower than futures price. In this situation, the hedger's procurement price in the spot market will be less than in the futures market.

The short hedger or the seller of the commodity prefers the strengthening basis where the cash price is higher than the futures and the hedger gets a higher selling price in the spot market than the futures market.

The preceding discussion highlights the fact that futures contract can be used effectively for hedging and speculating, provided the investor understands their mechanics clearly.

SUMMARY

☑ Financial engineering, a branch of finance that applies mathematical techniques to solve financial problems, has led to immense growth of derivatives trading in the modern times.

☑ The word financial derivative refers to a security that derives its value from the underlying assets that could be stocks, indices or other assets.

☑ Derivatives have emerged as the key instruments to counter the risk management challenges faced by investors in the current era.

☑ The main participants in the derivatives markets are hedgers, speculators and arbitrageurs.

☑ The derivatives market in India is relatively new, having been established in June 2000 when both the NSE and the BSE commenced trading in equity derivatives. Since then, the landscape of equity derivatives trading in India has altered immensely with the introduction of new products, higher volumes, newer contracts and advanced risk management framework for exchange-traded derivatives.

☑ Derivatives may also be classified into following two types on the basis of where they are transacted: privately traded over-the-counter (OTC) derivatives and exchange-traded derivatives (ETD).

☑ Derivatives can be classified into two broad categories based on their underlying assets: Commodity derivatives and Financial derivatives.

- ☑ Derivatives may also be classified into the following four types on the basis of the nature of the contract: Forwards, Futures, Options and Swaps.
- ☑ A forward is a non-standardized agreement between two parties to exchange a certain, pre-specified amount of money for a pre-determined quantity of a good or service on a pre-specified date in future.
- ☑ Swaps are contracts where two counterparties exchange cash flows related to their financial assets.
- ☑ Futures are standardized form of forward contract.
- ☑ A futures contract, like a forward contract, is also an agreement between two parties – a buyer and a seller – to buy or sell something at a pre-specified future date for a pre-specified price.
- ☑ Futures contracts are available on different kinds of assets – shares, indices, commodities, currency pairs and so on. The main types of futures are commodity futures, index futures and stock futures.
- ☑ Going long, going short and spreads are the most common strategies used by traders in the futures market.
- ☑ The spot and futures prices normally converge at the expiration of a futures contract.
- ☑ In modern times, commodity futures have become an important way of investing in commodities. Commodity futures are an attractive investment avenue as they are traded on margins.
- ☑ Stock futures and index futures are the two most common futures contracts used in India.
- ☑ Stock futures are the derivative contracts that help an investor to buy or sell a set of equity shares at a fixed price by a certain date.
- ☑ Index futures are futures contracts available on indices of market performance like S&P BSE Sensex, CNX NIFTY and S&P 500.
- ☑ A typical feature of a futures contract is that it is not settled on maturity like a forward contract. A futures contract is marked-to-market on a periodic basis, i.e., the payoffs on futures contracts are settled periodically.
- ☑ There are different kinds of margins prescribed by the exchange as a percentage of the total value of the futures contracts. Without margins, investors cannot trade in the futures market.
- ☑ The futures are marked-to-market, so daily closing price is the settlement price for a given day. The final settlement price is the closing price of the underlying asset on the last day of trading.
- ☑ The difference between the spot price (cash price) and the relevant futures price of a futures contract is called basis. The basis can be positive or negative.
- ☑ Prices on futures contracts can move only in ticks, which indicate the minimum amount that they can move by. Ticks are established by the futures exchanges.
- ☑ Open interest in futures contracts is the total number of contracts that have not been squared off, expired or settled with delivery.
- ☑ Pricing of futures is done through two pricing models: The Cost of Carry Model and The Expectancy Model.
- ☑ The main trading strategies or approaches in futures contract are: Speculative trading strategies, Hedging strategies and Arbitrage strategies

KEY WORDS

CONCEPT QUESTIONS

1. An exporter with a receivable of USD 100,000 in three months' time and worried about depreciation of the USD over that period should hedge using which of the following positions in USDINR futures: (a) long position or (b) short position.

2. Ajay has a short position in NIFTY futures at 8168. What will be the mark-to-market cash flow for this position if NIFTY futures settle at (i) 8134 or (ii) 8215 at the end of the day?

3. What is the effect of strengthening of the basis on a short hedge?

4. An airline company has hedged its imports of Aviation Turbine Fuel (ATF) by going long in heating oil futures. The correlation between the price changes of heating oil and ATF is 0.92. The standard deviation of daily price changes of heating oil futures and spot ATF are 0.80% and 1.2% respectively. Compute the minimum variance hedge ratio that the company should adopt.

5. An equity trader with a large short position in NIFTY futures and worried about a sharp rise in the index over the next one month should hedge by taking which of the following positions in the Index futures (a) long position or (b) short position.

6. The stock of ITC Ltd is trading at ₹368.70. Assuming a risk-free rate of 8% p.a. what should be the 'fair' price of a one-month futures contract on ITC stock?

7. Continuing Q.6, if one-month ITC futures are traded at ₹374.85, is there any arbitrage opportunity involved? How can it be exploited?

8. The dividend yield on the NIFTY stock index is estimated to be 5.2% p.a. If the continuously compounded risk-free rate is 8% and the current value of NIFTY is 8100, what should be the fair value of a 3-month NIFTY futures contract?

9. Explain why a commodity futures contract may trade at a lower price than the spot price. Why is reverse cash-carry arbitrage not always possible in case of commodities?

10. Today is 20 May 2015. A farmer who wants to hedge the price risk on cotton which will be harvested in September 2015 should take a short position in cotton futures for which delivery month – (i) May 2015 (ii) June 2015 (iii) July 2015 (iv) August 2015 (v) September 2015.

Hedging Risk with Derivatives: Options[1]

19

CHAPTER OBJECTIVES

- ❒ Understanding the basic properties of options and the basic option positions
- ❒ Learning to determine minimum and maximum prices for options under no-arbitrage conditions
- ❒ Applying the Black-Scholes Option Pricing Model for pricing options
- ❒ Analyzing how options can be used for trading, hedging and arbitrage in different situations

In this chapter we learn about another important derivative security known as the '**option contract.**' Options are considered to be 'younger' than forwards and futures contracts. The trading volume in options has exploded over the last few decades particularly after the publication of the celebrated option-pricing formula by Fisher Black and Myron Scholes. However, research shows that option trading existed several hundred years ago in ancient Greece. The 'tulip mania' in Holland during the 17th century also involved options.

Benefits of Options Vis-à-Vis Forwards

Why options? The answer to this lies in the 'binding' nature of the forwards or futures contract. The main disadvantage of using forwards or futures contracts is that they are binding upon both parties of the contract. For instance, an exporter who has entered into a contract to sell USD 100,000 to his bank three months forward at ₹61 is locked into a contract to deliver the dollars at ₹61. The bank too is bound to buy the dollars at ₹61. Thus neither party can avail the benefit of a favorable exchange rate.

How are options an improvement over the forward contract? Let us continue the earlier example of the exporter wishing to hedge his receivable of USD 100,000. The exporter would welcome a contract which can (i) compel the bank to buy his dollars at ₹61 if the dollar has depreciated to ₹58 in 3 months' time (ii) but at the same time allow the exporter himself the freedom to offload his dollars at a higher rate in the market should the

[1] This chapter has been written by Ms. Aparna Bhat, FCA, FRM, working as Assistant Professor in Department of Finance at K.J. Somaiya Institute of Management Studies and Research, Mumbai, India.

dollar appreciate beyond ₹61. Buying a suitable option would help the exporter to achieve this objective. This '**asymmetric**' nature of pay-offs is what distinguishes an option from a forward contract. Let us first get down to the nitty-gritty of understanding the terminology of the options world.

Definitions and Terminology

An option is a contract between a buyer and a seller which allows the **buyer** the **right but not the obligation** to buy or sell a specified quantity of the underlying asset at or before a specified date at a specified price agreed upon today.

A **call option** gives its buyer or holder the **right** but not the obligation to **buy** a specified quantity of the underlying asset at a specified price at or before a specified date.

A **put option** gives its buyer or holder the **right** but not the obligation to **sell** a specified quantity of the underlying asset at a specified price at or before a specified date.

The person selling an option is known as the **option writer.**

The **exercise price** or **strike price** is the specified price at which the underlying may be bought or sold.

The **expiration date** or **maturity date** is the specified date at or before which the option may be exercised.

An **American style** option can be exercised at any time before the expiry date. A **European style** option can be exercised only on the expiry date.

Option **premium** is the price paid by the buyer for buying the option. The premium is required to compensate the seller for a potential loss because the obligation of the seller is unlimited.

An option contract may be **settled** either in **cash** or by **physical delivery** of the underlying asset.

Options are traded in the over-the-counter (OTC) market as well as on organized stock or futures exchanges. The terms and features of OTC options are decided by the counterparties to the option contract. OTC options are typically settled by actual delivery of the underlying.

Numerical Example 1

Physical settlement of currency option in the OTC market On November 21 Engineers Ltd. contracts to import machinery parts costing EUR 750,000 from a German supplier. Spot EURINR exchange rate is ₹77.62 on November 21. The consignment is due after three months. To hedge against the risk of rupee depreciation against the euro, Engineers Ltd. buys a 3-month call option with a strike price of 78 from its bank. This option can be exercised only on the due date which is February 21. On February 21 if the euro is trading below ₹78, say at ₹75.85, Engineers Ltd. will not exercise the call option rather buy the euro at the market rate since it is lower than the strike price. On the other hand, if the euro has appreciated to say ₹80.95, Engineers Ltd. will exercise the call option. The option contract will be physically settled. The bank will deliver EUR 750,000 to Engineers Ltd. The amount to be paid to the bank by Engineers Ltd. will be the strike price of the option, i.e., ₹58,500,000 (₹78 × 750,000 euro).

Exchange-traded options have standardized features known as 'contract specifications.' These are decided by the exchange launching the contract and may be changed by the exchange from time to time.

Exchange-traded options are settled either in cash or by physical delivery. In India options on stocks, stock indices and the dollar-rupee exchange rate are traded on stock exchanges. These options are settled in cash and not by actual delivery of the underlying asset.

Numerical Example 2

Cash settlement of call options on underlying stock On November 28, Ajay purchases one call option for ₹12.50 on the stock of Godrej Industries Ltd. The option has a strike price of 280 and will expire on December 24. The lot size of Godrej Industries is 1000 which means that one call option gives the holder exposure to 1000 shares of the company.

TABLE 19.1 Contract specifications for stock options traded on the NSE

Parameter	Specification	Explanation
Underlying	145 securities	There are currently 145 stocks on which option contracts can be traded.
Instrument type	OPTSTK	This nomenclature indicates that the instrument is an option on a security.
Underlying	Symbol of underlying security	
Option type	CE/PE (European call or put)	Exercise is possible only on expiry date.
Expiry day	Last Thursday of expiry month; if that is a trading holiday, then previous trading day	The near-month option contract ceases to exist on the expiry date.
Strike price	Strike Price	The price at which the option can be exercised. SEBI stipulates that at least 3 strike prices must be offered—one at-the-money and one each in-the-money and out-of-the-money.
Trading cycle	3 month trading cycle – the near month (one), the next month (two) and the far month (three)	On a given date stock option contracts are available for trading for three different expiry dates.
Strike price intervals	Depending on underlying volatility	The difference between two consecutive strike prices. It is different for each security.
Permitted lot size	Underlying specific	Determines the exposure of the buyer and seller. It is different for each security.
Price steps	₹0.05	The minimum amount by which the option price will move.
Price bands	A contract specific price range based on its delta value is computed and updated on a daily basis	

On December 24, if the stock of Godrej Industries is trading above the strike price, say at ₹310, then exercising the call option is profitable for Ajay. This is because the call option gives Ajay the right to buy shares in Godrej Industries at the strike price of ₹280 while the market price is higher. However, exchange-traded stock options in India are settled in cash and not by physical delivery. Hence on exercising the option Ajay will receive the difference between the stock price on expiry and the strike price of the option. The pay-off from the call option will be:

Stock price at expiry:	₹310
Less: Strike price of call option:	₹280
Pay-off:	₹ 30

The total pay-off to Ajay will be ₹30000 (₹30 per lot × lot size). However, the profit realized by Ajay will be smaller because of the premium paid to buy the option.

Pay-off:	₹30000
Premium paid:	₹12500 (₹12.50 per lot × lot size)
Profit:	₹17500

Numerical Example 3

Cash settlement of put options on underlying index On November 28, Neeta buys for ₹71.60 a put option on the NIFTY with a strike price of 8550. The lot size of NIFTY options is 25 implying that the put gives Neeta the exposure to 25 units of the NIFTY. The option will expire on December 24. If on December 24 the NIFTY is at 7820, exercising the put will be profitable for Neeta because the put gives her the right to deliver 25 units of NIFTY for ₹8550 when the spot price is 7820. However because of obvious difficulties involved in physical delivery of shares underlying a stock index, index options are generally settled in cash. Hence on exercising the put Neeta will receive the difference between the strike price of her put option and the spot price of the NIFTY on expiry. The pay-off will thus be:

Strike price of put option:	8550
Less: NIFTY value at expiry	7820
Pay-off:	₹730

The total pay-off will be ₹18250 (₹730 × lot size). The actual profit realized by Neeta will be lower because of the premium paid to buy the put.

Pay-off:	₹18250
Premium paid:	₹ 1790 (₹71.60 per lot × lot size)
Profit:	₹16460

We can thus summarize the rules regarding pay-off of options on the expiry date as under:

> Pay-off for call options = Price of underlying asset on expiry date less strike price of call
>
> Pay-off for put options = Strike price of put less price of underlying asset on expiry date

Can an option have a negative pay-off? To understand this let us revisit Numerical Example 2 regarding Ajay and his call option on Godrej Industries. If on the expiry date, Godrej Industries stock is trading at ₹256, the pay-off of the call, (the difference between the stock price and the strike price) would be negative, thus implying that it is not profitable for Ajay to exercise the option. Ajay would therefore not exercise the option but let it lapse. In such a case, the pay-off from the call option would be zero.

This highlights an important distinction between options and forwards/futures. While a forward/futures contract may have a negative value for one of the holders because of its 'binding' nature, an option can *never* have a negative pay-off for its holder/buyer because the holder/buyer would *not* choose to exercise the option if such an exercise would result in loss. The option can, however, result in a negative pay-off for its seller/writer because the seller/writer would be compelled to fulfill his part of the bargain if the buyer requires him to do so.

This brings us to an interesting feature of options viz., 'option moneyness.' 'Moneyness' denotes the profitability of an option. An **'in-the-money'** option is an option the exercise of which is profitable for the holder. An **'out-of-the-money'** option is one which, if exercised, would result in a loss to the holder. Options are **'at-the-money'** if the result of exercise would be neither profit nor loss. This would happen when the strike price of the option is close to the market price of the underlying.

A **call** option is:
In-the-money when: Price of underlying asset > Strike price
Out-of-the-money when: Price of underlying asset < Strike price

A **put** option is:
In-the-money when: Strike price > Price of underlying asset
Out-of-the-money when: Strike price < Price of underlying asset

Both options would be at-the-money when: Price of underlying = Strike price

Components of the Option Premium

As explained earlier the option premium is the price paid by the buyer for buying the option. It can be broken down into two parts – **intrinsic value** and **time value.**

- Intrinsic value of call option = Max (Spot price-Strike price, 0)
- Intrinsic value of put option = Max (Strike price-Spot price, 0)

The intrinsic value is simply the amount of positive pay-off resulting to an option holder by an immediate exercise of the option. If exercising the option would result in a negative pay-off, the intrinsic value is taken to be zero. An option can never have a negative intrinsic value for the option holder.

The time value of an option is simply the difference between the option price and its intrinsic value. Consider a stock which is trading at ₹100. A one-month American call option on this stock with a strike price of ₹90 trades at ₹15. If the option is exercised immediately the pay-off to the holder will be ₹10. So why should this option trade at ₹15 when its intrinsic value is only ₹10? It is because the option buyer feels that there is a distinct possibility that the stock price may rise further till expiry thereby increasing the intrinsic value. Time value reflects the excess amount which the option buyer is willing to pay for this possibility.

The intrinsic value is determined only by the price of the underlying asset. Higher the underlying price, higher is the intrinsic value for a call and lower the intrinsic value for a put. Time value depends mainly on the remaining time to maturity and is generally higher for options with longer time to maturity. This is because the longer time to maturity increases the possibility of the option becoming more in-the-money. Time value declines as the option approaches expiry. This property is known as '**time decay**' of an option.

Some other terms associated with exchange-traded option contracts are given below:

1. **Open Interest:** This is simply the total number of option contracts that are outstanding as on a given date. For instance, on November 28 the open interest of the NIFTY December 2014 call option contract with a strike price of 8550 was 99975 contracts. This means that positions to the tune of 99975 contracts have been opened by market participants in this contract and these positions have not yet been closed. Open interest in a contract is very small when the contract is newly opened and grows as the contract approaches expiry. As the expiry date of the near-month contract draws closer, participants 'roll over' their positions from the near month to the next month and open interest in the near month contract starts declining. On the expiry date, the open interest in the near-month contract will become zero as all open positions would have been shifted to the next month contract. Why is knowledge of open interest important to a market participant? The amount of open interest at each strike price indicates the possible areas of technical 'support' and 'resistance.'
2. **Put-Call Ratio:** This is the ratio of number of puts traded to number of calls traded. A high ratio indicates that a larger number of puts have been traded than calls, thus, implying that the market sentiment is bearish. A low ratio would imply that the sentiment is bullish. This ratio is often perceived as a contrarian indicator. Whenever the ratio becomes too high as compared to its historical average, it suggests that the market may have bottomed out and a recovery may be around the corner. Again when the ratio falls well below its historical average it may be an indicator that the market has peaked and is ripe for a fall.

Basic Positions Using Options

Let us now understand the **four basic positions** that can be taken using options.

Long Call	Long Put
Short Call	Short Put

These basic positions form the building blocks of all trading and hedging strategies involving options. The following section deals with the pay-offs from each of these positions at expiry.

Long Call

Suppose that on December 23, 2014, a trader called Ajay buys a call option on the NIFTY with a strike price of 8200 and expiring on January 29, 2015. The premium paid by him for buying the option is ₹225. Let us look at some possible values that NIFTY can take on the expiry date and the resulting payoffs to Ajay.

TABLE 19.2 Pay-off table for long call position

NIFTY value on expiry	Premium paid	Exercise pay-off	Net pay-off
8120	−225	0	−225
8175	−225	0	−225
8260	−225	60	−165
8400	−225	200	−25
8425	−225	225	0
8450	−225	250	25
8510	−225	310	85

Table 19.2 depicts the exercise pay-off (gross) and net pay-off from the long call position. The net pay-off is obtained by deducting the premium paid from the exercise pay-off. It is clear from the above table that as long as NIFTY stays below 8200 the call option is out-of-the-money for Ajay and hence the exercise pay-off would be zero in such cases. The exercise would yield a positive payoff only when NIFTY rises above 8200. The call would be in-the-money for Ajay at all prices above 8200. He will of course start making a net profit only after NIFTY rises above 8425 which is the break-even point.

Break-even point for long call = Strike price + Premium paid

The pay-off profile at expiry for a long call position can be described as follows:

1. Exercise pay-off is positive and increasing for successive values of the underlying higher than the strike price of the call.
2. Exercise pay-off is zero at all values of the underlying lower than or equal to the strike price.

If we draw a graph representing the exercise pay-off of a long call, the graph will not be a straight line. It will look more like a hockey stick. Hence options are said to have **non-linear** pay-offs.

In Figure 19.1 the x-axis represents the different values of NIFTY at expiry while the y-axis depicts the pay-off at expiry. The upward sloping part of the 'hockey stick' above the x-axis represents the possible gains on the position should the underlying expire at a price higher than the strike price of the call. The flat straight line below the x-axis represents the loss on the position should the option expire at-the-money or out-of-the-money. The loss is equal to the premium paid for buying the call.

Short Call

What about the person who has sold this call to Ajay? Let us call him Vijay. Vijay has received a premium of ₹225 for selling the call to Ajay. Obviously, Vijay's short call position is safe as long as NIFTY remains below the call strike price of 8200. If NIFTY expires below 8200 Vijay gets to keep the entire premium already received by him. But if the expiry price of NIFTY is higher than 8200, Ajay will exercise the call and Vijay will have to part

Figure 19.1 Pay-off profile of long call.

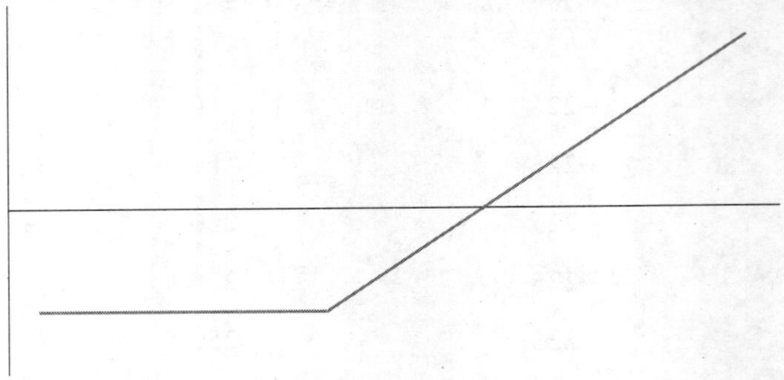

with an amount equal to the difference between the NIFTY spot price at expiry and the strike price of 8200. Vijay's short call position will start losing money after NIFTY rises above 8425.

Table 19.3 depicts the exercise pay-off (gross) and net pay-off from the short call position. The net pay-off is obtained by adding the premium received to the exercise pay-off. The pay-off profile at expiry for Vijay's short call position can be described as follows:

TABLE 19.3 Pay-off table for short call position

NIFTY value on expiry	Premium received	Exercise pay-off	Net pay-off
8120	225	0	225
8175	225	0	225
8260	225	−60	165
8400	225	−200	25
8425	225	−225	0
8450	225	−250	−25
8510	225	−310	−85

1. Exercise pay-off is negative and increasing for successive values of the underlying higher than the strike price of the call.
2. Exercise pay-off is zero at all values of the underlying lower than or equal to the strike price.

Hence the pay-off profile of the short call position is also non-linear.

We can see that the pay-off profile of the short call position is a mirror image of the long call position. In this case the flat, straight part of the graph above the x-axis shows the fixed amount earned by the position when the option expires out-of-the-money or at-the-money. This is equal to the premium received for selling the call. The downward sloping part of the graph shows the possible losses on the position when the underlying expires at a price higher than the strike price of the call.

Figure 19.2 Pay-off profile of short call.

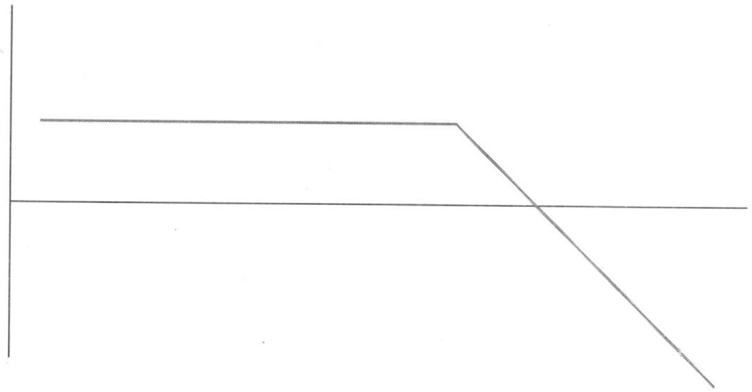

Long Put

Suppose that on December 24, 2014. Nirmala buys a put option on the NIFTY with a strike price of 8200 and expiring on January 29, 2015. She pays a premium of ₹99 for buying the put. The pay-off table for Nirmala's long put position for possible values of NIFTY at expiry is depicted in Table 19.4.

TABLE 19.4 Pay-off table for long put position

NIFTY value on expiry	Premium paid	Exercise pay-off	Net pay-off
7925	–99	275	176
8005	–99	195	96
8050	–99	150	51
8101	–99	99	0
8178	–99	22	–77
8200	–99	0	–99
8290	–99	0	–99

It is evident from the table that Nirmala's long put position will lose a fixed amount of ₹99 if NIFTY expires at any price higher than 8200. The position will be in-the-money and yield a positive gross pay-off if NIFTY expires below 8200. However, the net pay-off after accounting for the premium paid by her will be positive only when NIFTY expires below 8101, i.e., 8200-99.

> Break-even point for long put = Strike price – Premium paid

The pay-off profile at expiry for Nirmala's long put position can be described as follows:

1. Exercise pay-off is positive and increasing for successive values of the underlying lower than the strike price of the put.
2. Exercise pay-off is zero at all values of the underlying higher than or equal to the strike price of the put.

The upward sloping part of the graph above the *x*-axis in Figure 19.3 shows the possible gains to be made when the underlying expires at any price below the strike price of the put. The flat part of the graph below the *x*-axis shows the fixed amount of loss when the underlying expires at or above the strike price. This loss is equal to the premium paid for buying the put.

Figure 19.3 Pay-off profile of long put.

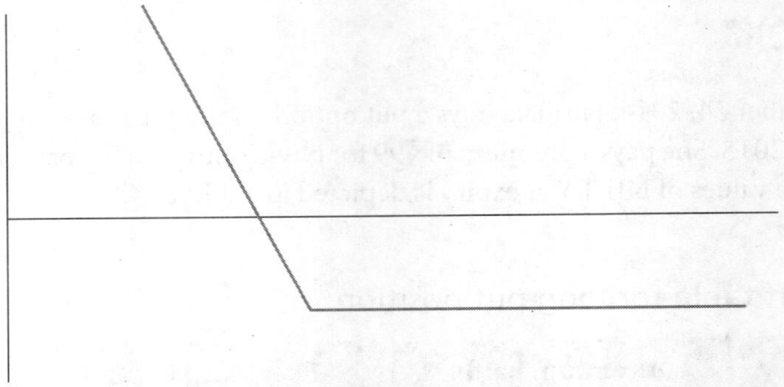

Short Put

From the preceding discussion you may be able to guess the pay-off profile of a short put position. Yes, it will be the mirror image of the long put position.

TABLE 19.5 Pay-off table for shortput position

NIFTY value on expiry	Premium received	Exercise pay-off	Net pay-off
7925	99	−275	−176
8005	99	−195	−96
8050	99	−150	−51
8101	99	99	0
8178	99	−22	77
8200	99	0	99
8290	99	0	99

The person selling a put will receive a premium for the same. He will be able to keep the entire premium if the underlying expires at or above the strike price of the put. The pay-off for the short put position will be negative if the underlying expires below the strike price of the put.

Figure 19.4 Pay-off profile of a short put.

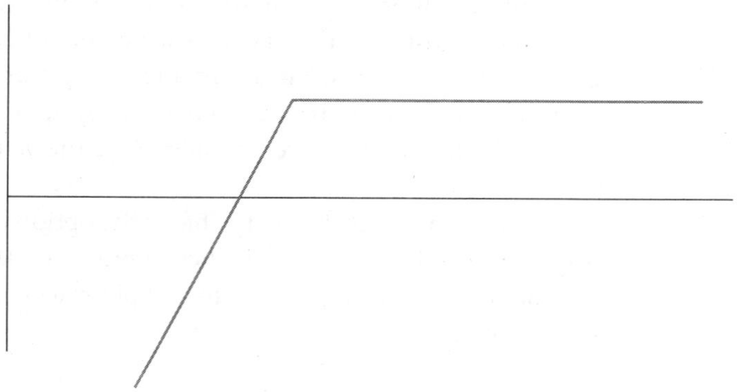

Determinants of Option Price

What determines the price of an option? We know that the price of a forward or futures contract is determined by the spot price, the rate of interest and the time to maturity. Options are more complex instruments and their price depends upon a larger number of factors which are explained here:

1. **The Spot Price:** The price of the underlying asset keeps changing over the life of the option. Given a particular strike price, any change in the price of the underlying asset will lead to a change in the price of the call or put on the underlying asset. There is a direct relationship between the underlying price and price of a call option on the underlying. This is because higher the spot price of the underlying asset, higher is the intrinsic value of the call and vice versa. The price of the put is inversely related to the underlying price because higher the spot price, lower is the intrinsic value of the put and vice versa.
2. **Strike Price:** The exercise price or strike price of an option remains constant throughout its life. The price of a call option is inversely related to its strike price. Consider a stock trading at ₹100 and two call options on this stock each maturing after a month, one with a strike price of 110 and the other with a strike price of 120. While both calls are currently out-of-the-money, if the stock price starts rising the call with strike price of 110 will become in-the-money sooner than the call with the strike price of 120. As the probability of the option becoming profitable is higher for the call with a lower strike price, such a call will command a higher premium than a call with a higher strike price. The price of put options, however, is directly related to the strike price. Thus a put with a higher strike price is more valuable than one with a lower strike price.
3. **Time to Maturity:** Options with a higher time to maturity have a higher possibility of becoming in-the-money by the expiry date. Hence both call and put options with longer time to maturity are more valuable than those with shorter time to maturity. However this principle may not hold when a large dividend is expected during the life of the option.

4. **Volatility of the Underlying:** As the price of the underlying asset becomes more volatile, the chances of the asset price rising or falling sharply increase. If the asset price goes up sharply, the intrinsic value of call options increases thereby benefitting holders of call options. If the asset price drops sharply call option holders only lose their premium. Similarly, with any sharp drop in asset price put options become more valuable while put holders will suffer only a loss of premium incase of any sudden increase in asset price. Thus we can see that an increase in volatility benefits the holders of both call and put options.
5. **Risk-Free Interest Rate:** The relationship between the interest rate and option price is more complex than the earlier factors. To put it simply, a call option is an indirect way of buying the underlying stock. Holding a call option allows the holder to postpone the payment which he otherwise would have made for an outright purchase of the stock. When interest rates start increasing this deferment of payment becomes more valuable and hence call options gain in value. Since put options lead to deferred receipt of money unlike an outright asset sale, higher interest rates would reduce the value of put options, other things remaining constant.
6. **Amount of Dividends:** Any dividend paid on the stock over the life of the option has the effect of reducing the ex-dividend stock price. This leads to decline in the value of call options on the stock and increase in the value of put options. Hence call prices are inversely related to and put prices are directly related to the amount of dividend expected over the option life.

No-Arbitrage Conditions for Option Prices

The pricing of options requires the application of a model based on assumptions regarding the movement of the underlying price, the volatility over the life of the option and absence of market friction. However, even without the application of any particular model it is possible to arrive at certain minimum and maximum prices within which an option price should lie so that there are no arbitrage opportunities. These minimum and maximum prices are known as the 'upper' and 'lower' bounds or the 'model-free' prices that fulfill the no-arbitrage condition.

Bounds for Options

1. **Upper Bound:** Since a call option represents simply an alternative route for buying the stock, the option itself can never be worth more than the stock. Hence the upper bound for a call option is the current stock price. The upper bound for calls is therefore $c \leq S_0$.

   The maximum pay-off for a put option would occur when the stock price falls to zero and in that case the pay-off would be equal to the strike price of the put. Hence the price of a put option can never exceed its strike price. The upper bound for American puts is therefore $P \leq K$ while that for European puts is $p \leq K \times e^{-rt}$.
2. **Lower Bounds for European Options on a Stock Which is Not Expected to Pay Any Dividend:**

   Let us consider a hypothetical example to understand the **lower bound for a European call option.** Consider two alternative portfolios X and Y whose composition is as under:

   Portfolio X: One call option on underlying stock maturing at time t and a risk-free investment equal to present value of the call strike price, $K \times e^{-rt}$

   Portfolio Y: One unit of the underlying stock, S_0.

   There are two possible scenarios on expiry: the stock price at expiry, S_t can be lower or higher than the strike price of the call.

Scenario 1: If $S_t < K$,
Portfolio X: the call option will be worth zero as it is out-of-the-money while the risk-free investment will grow to an amount equal to K.
Portfolio Y: The stock will be valued at S_t.
In this case since $S_t < K$, portfolio X is worth more than portfolio Y.

Scenario 2: If $S_t > K$,
Portfolio X: the call option will now be in-the-money and yield a pay-off $S_t - K$ while the risk-free investment will grow to an amount equal to K. Hence net value of portfolio X will be S_t.
Portfolio Y: The stock will be valued at S_t as before.
Portfolio X is worth the same as portfolio Y in this case.
As we can see the value of portfolio X is either the same as or greater than that of portfolio Y under any scenario. Hence

$$c + K \times e^{-rt} \geq S_0 \quad \text{or}$$

$$c \geq S_0 - K \times e^{-rt} \tag{1}$$

Also we know that any option can never have a negative value for its holder because of the feature of optionality.

Hence $c \geq 0$ (2)

Putting together equations (1) and (2) we can derive the lower bound for a European call on a non-dividend paying stock as under:

$$c \geq \max\,(S_0 - K \times e^{-rt}, 0) \tag{3}$$

Consider another example to derive the **lower bound of a European put**. Two alternative portfolios A and B are as given:

Portfolio A: One European put and one unit of underlying stock, S_0.
Portfolio B: A risk-free investment equal to present value of the put strike price, $K \times e^{-rt}$.
On expiry, if $S_t < K$, the put will be exercised and result in a pay-off equal to $K - S_t$ while the stock will be worth S_t. Hence the net value of portfolio A will be K. The risk-free investment in Portfolio B will be worth K. Hence both portfolios will be worth the same.

If $S_t > K$ on expiry, the put will expire worthless and the stock in portfolio A will be worth S_t. Portfolio B will once again be worth K. Since $S_t > K$, portfolio A is worth more than portfolio B.

Thus portfolio A is always worth more than portfolio B. Hence $p + S_0 \geq K \times e^{-rt}$

or $$p \geq K \times e^{-rt} - S_0 \tag{4}$$

Since we know that $p \geq 0$ (5)

Combining (4) and (5) leads us to the lower bound for a European put on a non-dividend paying stock:

$$p \geq \max\,(K \times e^{-rt} - S_0, 0) \tag{6}$$

Numerical Example 4

Shares of Maruti Ltd. trade at ₹3330. What should be the minimum price for a European call on Maruti shares with a strike price of 3300 and maturing in three months? Assume a risk-free rate of 8% p.a. and the stock is not expected to pay any dividend over the next three months.

Solution:

Here S_0 = ₹3330, $K = 3300$, $r = 0.08$ and $t = 3/12$ or 0.25. Applying equation (3), the present value of the strike = ₹3234.66. The difference between the spot price and the present value of strike is ₹95.34, which is the minimum value for the call option.

Numerical Example 5

Shares of Wipro Ltd. are traded at ₹547. Find the minimum value for a put option on Wipro shares with a strike price of 540 and maturing in one month. Assume a risk-free rate of 8% p.a. and the stock is not expected to pay any dividend over the next one month.

Solution:

Here S_0 = ₹547, $K = 540$, $r = 0.08$ and $t = 1/12$ or 0.0833. Applying equation (6) we get $p >= \max(536.412 - 547, 0)$. Hence the minimum value of the put will be zero as its value cannot be negative.

Put-Call Parity

Besides the no-arbitrage conditions which must be fulfilled while pricing options there is a further condition which should be fulfilled by prices of calls and puts with the same strike price and maturing on the same date. This condition is known as the **'Put-call parity.'** It simply states the relationship between calls and puts with the same strike price and time to maturity. It can be stated as below:

$$c + K \times e^{-rt} = p + S_0 \tag{7}$$

The above equation implies that we can arrive at the fair price of a European put option on an underlying stock given the value of a European call on the same stock with the same strike price and time to maturity as that of the put. Arbitrage opportunities arise if put-call parity does not hold. Such a situation is explained in further sections.

Another interesting outcome of the put-call parity condition is that it enables the construction of 'synthetic' positions by combining positions in different options and the underlying. These are tabulated in Table 19.6.

TABLE 19.6 Synthetic strategies

Combination	Resulting position	Risk and reward
Long call and short put	Synthetic long position in underlying	Unlimited gain if underlying price rises and unlimited loss if underlying price falls
Long stock/futures and long put	Synthetic call	Unlimited gain if underlying price rises and limited loss if underlying price falls
Long call and short stock/futures	Synthetic put	Unlimited gain if underlying price falls and limited loss if underlying price rises
Long put and short call	Synthetic short position in underlying	Unlimited gain if underlying price falls and unlimited loss if underlying price rises

Why should we bother learning about synthetic strategies? Such strategies make sense if the 'synthetic' position is cheaper to construct than the 'direct' position. In such a case one can arbitrage between the synthetic and direct position.

Pricing of Options

Having examined the bounds on option prices which ensure that there are no opportunities for risk-free arbitrage we now look at a formal model for pricing options. Pricing options is not as straightforward as pricing forwards/futures because the cost-of-carry model cannot be applied to options. This is because while both parties under a forward contract are under an obligation to perform their part of the bargain, there is no certainty that the buyer of the option will exercise the option. Hence the option writer cannot simply buy the underlying and hold it till expiry. What the option writer needs to know is the probability that the option will be exercised on the expiry date, i.e., the probability that the stock price on expiry will exceed the strike price in case of a call and probability that strike price will exceed the spot price on expiry in case of a put. Also, he needs to estimate the potential pay-off that would result if the option ends in-the-money. The difference between the present value of the probability-weighted pay-off on expiry and the present value of the strike price to be paid on expiry is the value of a European call option.

Fisher Black and Myron Scholes were the first to develop a closed-form solution, i.e., a formula, for valuing European call and put options in 1973. According to the Black-Scholes Option Pricing Model (BSOPM) the value of a European call option on underlying stock can be derived as follows:

$$c = S_0 N(d_1) - K.\exp^{-rt} N(d_2) \qquad (8)$$

where S_0 = current stock price, K = strike price of call, r = risk-free rate of interest, t = time till expiry, σ is the volatility of the underlying asset and $N(.)$ is the cumulative standard normal distribution function with d_1 and d_2 defined as given here:

$$d_1 = \frac{\ln\left(\frac{S_0}{K}\right) + (r + 0.5 \times \sigma^2)t}{\sigma\sqrt{t}}$$

and $d_2 = d_1 - \sigma\sqrt{t}$

In this model, $S_0N(d_1)$ represents the present value of the expected pay-off resulting from exercising the call when it is in-the-money while $K.\exp^{-rt}N(d_2)$ is simply the present value of the expected payment of strike price to be made on exercising the call. The value of the call is the difference between these two values. Value of a put can be derived using put-call parity.

The BSOPM is based upon a number of simplifying assumptions such as:

1. The stock price follows a continuous path with no jumps.
2. The volatility of the underlying stock price remains constant over the life of the option.
3. The stock is not expected to pay any dividends over the life of the option.
4. There are no transaction costs and no restrictions on short-selling of stock.
5. Borrowing and lending can be done at the same risk-free rate of return.

Most of these assumptions such as absence of dividend and transaction costs have been relaxed in later versions of the model. The assumption of constant volatility too has been done away with by later scholars who developed models based on stochastic or time-varying volatility.

Spreadsheet Application 1 Using BSOPM to value a European call option.

Shares of TCS Ltd. trade at ₹2510. Volatility of the stock price is estimated at 20% p.a. Assuming a risk-free rate of 8% p.a. find the value of a call option on TCS shares with a strike price of 2500 and maturity of 1 month.

Solution:

Here $S_0 = 2510$, $K = 2500$, $r = 0.08$, $t = 1/12$ or 0.0833, $\sigma = 0.20$

$$d_1 = \frac{(\ln(2510/2500) + (0.08 + 0.5 \times 0.2^2) \times (1/12))}{(0.2 \times \sqrt{(1/12)})} = 0.213481$$

$$d_2 = 0.213481 - 0.2 \times \sqrt{\left(\frac{1}{12}\right)}$$

$N(d_1)$ and $N(d_2)$ represent the cumulative probability distribution for standardized normal variables d_1 and d_2 and can be calculated using the NORMSDIST function in Excel.

$$N(d_1) = \text{NORMSDIST}(0.213481) = 0.584524 \text{ and } N(d_2) = 0.561884$$

Plugging these values in the BSOPM we get the value of a 1-month call on TCS shares as:

$$C = 2510 \times 0.584524 - 2500 \times \exp\left(-0.08 \times \frac{1}{12}\right) \times 0.561884 = 71.78.$$

	A	B	C
1	Cells marked yellow for data entry		
2	Do not enter anything into cells marked blue		
3			
4	Input data		
5	Spot	2510	
6	Strike	2500	
7	Volatility	0.2	* Annualized volatility
8	Risk-free Interest	0.08	
9	Time to maturity	0.083333	** Should be a fraction of a year
10			
11	Computation		
12	d1	0.2135	
13	d2	0.1557	
14	N(d1)	0.5845	
15	N(d2)	0.5619	
16			
17	Call price	71.78	

	A	B	C	D
1	Cells marked yellow for data entry			
2	Do not enter anything into cells marked blue			
3				
4	Input data			
5	Spot	2510		
6	Strike	2500		
7	Volatility	0.2	* Annualized volatility	
8	Risk-free Interest	0.08		
9	Time to maturity	0.083333	** Should be a fraction of a year	
10				
11	Computation			
12	d1	0.2135		
13	d2	0.1557		
14	N(d1)	0.5845		
15	N(d2)	0.5619		
16				
17	Call price	=B5*B14-(B6*EXP(-B8*B9)*B15)		

Applications of Options

We have thus far examined the basic positions that can be formed using options and also the issue of pricing options. It is now time to understand the applications of options. Options have three main applications in finance in line with other derivative contracts:

1. Trading
2. Hedging
3. Arbitrage

Options can be combined with the underlying or positions in different options may be combined in order to execute a trading view or to hedge an exposure or simply to gain from a mispricing by the market. These combinations are referred to as 'strategies.' We will look at option strategies for trading, hedging and arbitrage. In order to keep things simple, we will examine all these strategies assuming that the positions are held till the expiry date of the options.

But before we do this let us first understand the dual function of options. Options are unique because they permit a market participant to express a view (i) about the direction of the underlying price or (ii) about the future volatility of the underlying or (iii) about both. This is an important feature which distinguishes options from forward and future contracts that allow the market participant to speculate only about the direction of the underlying price.

Using Options for a Directional View of the Underlying

A market participant may have a directional view of the underlying, i.e., he may expect the underlying price to rise (a bullish view) or fall (a bearish view). There are two ways of expressing a 'bullish' view on the underlying as explained here:

Investor *A*	Investor B
View: Strongly believes that price of underlying asset is likely to rise	View: Strongly believes that price of underlying asset is not likely to fall
Action: Buy a call option on the underlying	Action: Short a put option on the underlying

Although the view underlying both positions is essentially the same the consequences are very different should the view turn out to be wrong. The long call position will result in a limited loss to its buyer while the short put position has the potential to trigger an unlimited loss for the writer.

Continuing the same line of thought we can see that there are also two ways of expressing a 'bearish' view on the underlying.

Investor *X*	Investor *Y*
View: Strongly believes that price of underlying asset is likely to fall	View: Strongly believes that price of underlying asset is not likely to rise
Action: Buy a put option on the underlying	Action: Short a call option on the underlying

Again the underlying view is basically the same but consequences of a wrong view are different.

We can sum up this discussion about the use of options for a directional view as follows:

Bullish view of underlying	Bearish view of underlying
Long call	Long put
Short put	Short call

Using Options for a View of the Underlying Volatility

How does higher volatility affect the option price?

Suppose a stock trading at ₹2500 has a daily average price movement of 1%. Any unexpected good news about the stock or about the broader economy on a given day may cause the stock price to jump by 4 to 5%. This will naturally lead to a higher pay-off on call options on the stock. Call options will be much in demand and therefore the price of calls will rise. Similarly, unanticipated bad news may lead to the stock price falling by 4–5% and in this case put option holders will reap large benefits. There will be a spurt in the price of puts. Thus unexpected good or bad news drives the stock price volatility higher and leads to increase in price of calls or puts.

It stands to reason then that a person who expects underlying volatility to go up should buy options while one who expects a decline in volatility would be better off selling options.

Trading Strategies Using Options

Any strategy for trading in options would first require a market participant to determine his view on (a) volatility of the underlying price and (b) direction of the underlying price. As explained in the earlier section options can be used to express a view about both direction and volatility. The following table shows how this can be implemented.

View: Bullish about volatility		View: Bearish about volatility	
Action: Buy options		Action: Sell options	
View: Bullish about direction	View: Bearish about direction	View: Bullish about direction	View: Bearish about direction
Buy calls	Buy puts	Sell puts	Sell calls

Trading options involve three main types of strategies—outright positions, spreads and combinations.

Outright Trading

This involves buying or selling naked calls or puts according to the view about direction and volatility of the underlying. These are the four basic positions which have been discussed above.

Spreads

These involve a buy and sell position in two options of the same class but having different strike price or time to maturity. Spreads can be classified into 'vertical' or 'horizontal' spreads. Vertical spreads involve calls or puts maturing at the same time but differing in terms of strike prices. Horizontal spreads also known as calendar spreads involve the same class of options with the same strike price but with different time to maturity. Spreads can be used to execute a bearish or bullish view about the direction of the underlying.

Let us first consider bullish spreads constructed with call options.

Bullish call spread

Numerical Example 6

A currency trader feels that the spot USDINR which is currently at 63.46 may rise to ₹65 in the near term. However, past trends indicate that any rise of the USD above ₹65 will be capped because of intervention by the RBI to prevent any sharp depreciation of the rupee. What strategy should be used in such a situation?

Solution:

The trader should buy one-month at-the-money (ATM) calls on USDINR at a strike price of 63.50 and sell one-month out-of-the-money (OTM) calls at a strike of 65.

Rationale for the strategy: The ATM call is bought because the trader is certain that the dollar will appreciate from the current level till 65. The OTM call at 65 strike price is sold because the trader feels that there is a remote possibility of any further rise of the dollar above 65. The premium received for writing the OTM call partially offsets the cost of buying the ATM call.

Cost of the strategy: There is a cash outflow for buying the ATM call and a cash inflow for selling the OTM call. Assume that the ATM call option costs ₹0.32 and the OTM call ₹0.0025. The net cost of the strategy would be ₹0.3175.

Gain/Loss from the strategy: The strategy will lose a fixed amount of ₹0.3175 if the USDINR expires at any level lower than 63.50. If USDINR closes at any point between 63.50 and 65, the strategy will result in partial recovery of the cost. For instance, suppose the exchange rate on expiry is ₹63.95. In this case, the long call with strike price of 63.50 will be ITM and result in a pay-off of ₹0.45. The short call at strike price 65 will remain OTM for its buyer and will not result in any cash outflow. Hence gross pay-off will be ₹0.45 and net pay-off after accounting for the premium paid would be ₹0.1375. If the USDINR closes above 65 on the expiry date, say at 65.75, then the long call as well as short call would be ITM for the respective buyers. The long call will yield a positive pay-off of ₹2.25 while the short call will result in a negative pay-off of ₹0.75. The gross pay-off hence will be ₹1.50 and net pay-off ₹1.1825. The net pay-off will be capped at ₹1.1825 for all exchange rates above 65.

TABLE 19.7 Pay-off table for a bullish call spread

USDINR rate on expiry	Premium paid	Exercise pay-off on long call	Exercise pay-off on short call	Net pay-off
62.10	−0.3175	0	0	−0.3175
62.95	−0.3175	0	0	−0.3175
63.50	−0.3175	0	0	−0.3175
63.8175	−0.3175	0.3175	0	0
64.85	−0.3175	1.35	0	1.0325
65.00	−0.3175	1.50	0	1.1825
65.55	−0.3175	2.05	−0.55	1.1825

Figure 19.5 Pay-off profile for bullish call spread.

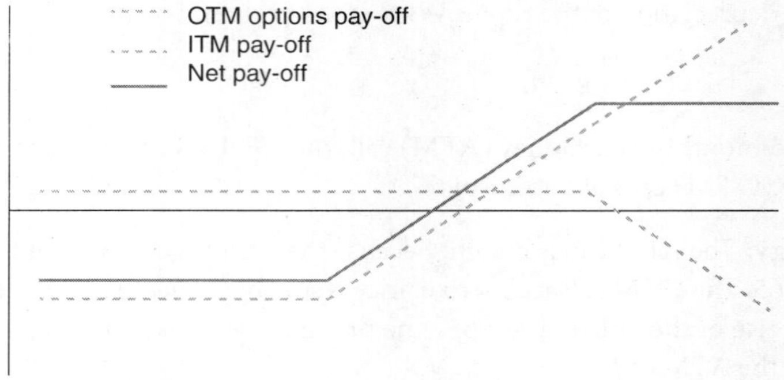

The bullish call spread is thus a limited gain and limited loss strategy to be adopted when an investor is moderately bullish about the underlying.

Bullish put spread

This is again a strategy for an investor who has a bullish view about the underlying. This time the strategy is executed using put options and involves selling an ATM put and buying an OTM put at a lower strike. The ATM put is sold because the option writer is convinced that the underlying will not fall. Buying the OTM put protects the option writer from unlimited loss in case his view turns out to be wrong. Since the ATM put is costlier than the OTM put, this strategy results in an initial net cash inflow for the option writer. It is again a limited gain and limited loss strategy.

Bearish spread: This strategy is useful when the investor has a bearish view of the underlying. Again the strategy can be constructed either by buying puts or selling calls. As usual this decision will depend upon whether underlying volatility is expected to rise or fall. A bearish put spread would be used by an investor who expects a sharp, immediate decline in the share price but expects the share price to be supported at a lower level. Such an investor would buy an ATM put to gain from the immediate price fall. He would also sell an OTM put at a lower strike price where the technical support is expected to hold. The premium received for selling the OTM put reduces the cost of the strategy.

Bearish put spread

Numerical Example 7

An investor expects Infosys Technologies to report lower-than expected profits for the current quarter. He fears that unfavorable results next week may cause the stock price to decline by as much as 5% from the current level of ₹1932. However, technical charts show strong support at ₹1830. This support has not been breached in recent times. What kind of strategy will be beneficial in this situation?

Solution:

The investor should buy an ATM put at strike price of 1925 and sell an OTM put at a strike price of 1825.

Rationale for the strategy: This investor is bearish on the stock price direction but bullish on volatility as he expects a substantial price movement in the near term. He should therefore buy ATM puts on the stock. However as he is convinced that the price fall is likely to halt at the support of ₹1830, the investor may choose to sell a put at a strike price of 1825. The premium received for shorting the put can reduce the expenses of buying the ATM put.

Cost of the strategy: Assuming that the ATM put trades at ₹69 and the OTM put at ₹23, the strategy entails an initial cash outflow of ₹46.

Gain/loss from the strategy: Table 19.8 explains the gain/loss on the strategy.

TABLE 19.8 Pay-off table for a bearish put spread

Infy spot price on expiry	Premium paid	Exercise pay-off on long put	Exercise pay-off on short put	Net pay-off
1940	−46	0	0	−46
1900	−46	25	0	−21
1879	−46	46	0	0
1855	−46	80	0	34
1825	−46	100	0	54
1800	−46	125	−25	54

This strategy makes a limited loss of ₹46 when the stock closes at or above the upper strike price of 1925. Break-even point is at 1879. The strategy returns a small gain if the stock closes below the break-even point but above the lower strike price of 1825. Maximum gain is capped at ₹54 and occurs if the stock closes at or below the strike price of 1825.

Bearish call spread

This strategy aims to execute a bearish view on direction as well as volatility of the underlying. This would involve selling an ATM call and simultaneously buying protection by going long in an OTM call. The construction of the pay-off table and pay-off profile for this strategy is left as an exercise for the reader.

Calendar spread

This strategy involves buying and selling the same type of option with the same strike price on the same underlying asset but maturing in different months. It is known as a 'horizontal spread' because the strategy is spread across different months rather than different strike prices. A **long calendar spread** involves selling an option with a short maturity and buying the same option with the same strike but having a longer maturity. The aim is to profit from a difference in the expected volatility of the underlying over the short term and long term as well as gain from the 'time decay' of the short maturity option.

Rationale for the strategy: When an 'event' such as declaration of corporate earnings is just around the corner the stock price is expected to be volatile in the near term. Since option prices are directly related to the level of underlying volatility expected over the option's life, the prices of options maturing in the short term are driven higher because of the event. However underlying volatility is expected to subside once the event is over or the news is known to the market and hence options with longer term to maturity are priced lower. The trader putting on a long calendar spread shorts the short-maturity option which has a higher level of expected volatility built into it. At the same time he buys the longer maturity option which has a lower level of volatility priced in. The trader expects the price of the short maturity option to decline quickly because of (a) decline in the volatility after the event and (b) decline in remaining time to maturity as the option approaches its expiry date. At the same time the trader expects the price of the long term option to either remain at the same level or rise slightly. This is because the long term option is not as sensitive to the impact of the event or news as the short term option.

Butterfly spread

This strategy is constructed using calls or puts at three different strike prices.

A **long butterfly spread** using calls involves the following transactions:

1. Buying an ITM call at strike price K1
2. Buying an OTM call at strike price K3
3. Selling 2 calls at a strike price K2 which is mid-way between K1 and K3. K2 is generally the ATM strike.

This spread will result in a limited gain if the underlying expires at a price close to the ATM strike K2. The spread results in a small loss if the underlying volatility increases and the price on expiry is far away from K2. Hence a **long butterfly spread is bearish on volatility**. The trader buying a butterfly spread expects minimal volatility in the underlying price.

Numerical Example 8

Using a long butterfly call spread The spot dollar-rupee rate is 63.6725 on December 29. A currency trader feels that the currency pair will remain range-bound over the next one month with low volatility. The traded prices of calls at different strike prices are as given here:

63.50 strike price (ITM): ₹0.18
63.75 strike price (ATM): ₹0.0025
64.00 strike (OTM): ₹0.0025

Show how a butterfly spread will result in a limited gain or loss in this situation assuming different closing rates on expiry.

Solution:

Since the trader is bearish on volatility he should buy the butterfly spread. The following positions will be taken:

Buy ITM call for ₹0.18 and OTM call for ₹0.0025
Sell 2 ATM calls for total premium of ₹0.0050
Net cash outflow for the strategy: ₹0.1775

Table 19.9 shows that the strategy has two break-even points, the lower one at 63.6775 and the upper one at 63.8225. Maximum gain occurs when the USDINR is exactly at the ATM strike price of ₹63.75 on expiry and is limited to ₹72.50. The gain reduces and loss increases for all price levels away from the ATM strike. Maximum loss is equal to the net premium paid for the strategy, i.e., ₹177.50.

TABLE 19.9 Pay-off table for a long butterfly call spread

USD/INR on expiry	Pay-off from 1long ITM call	Pay-off from 2 short ATM calls	Pay-off from 1long OTM call	Net premium paid	Net pay-off from strategy
63.50	0	0	0	−177.50	−177.50
63.65	150	0	0	−177.50	−27.50
63.6775	177.50	0	0	−177.50	0
63.70	200	0	0	−177.50	22.50
63.75	250	0	0	−177.50	72.50
63.80	300	−100	0	−177.50	22.50
63.8225	322.50	−145	0	−177.50	0
63.90	400	−300	0	−177.50	−77.50
64.00	500	−500	0	−177.50	−177.50
64.10	600	−700	100	−177.50	−177.50

Figure 19.6 Pay-off profile of long butterfly call spread.

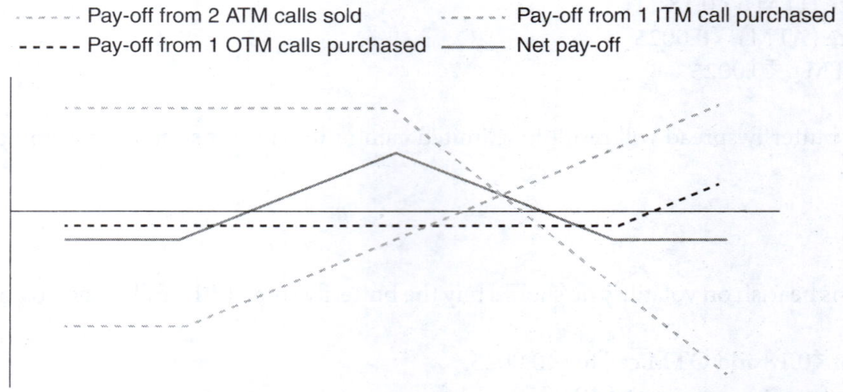

Box spread

This strategy is a combination of bullish spread and bearish spread and is constructed using calls and puts on the same underlying and same strike prices. The strategy results in a fixed return. The cost of constructing the strategy is compared with the inflow on expiry to decide whether the box spread should be bought or sold. A long box spread is constructed if the expected inflow on expiry is greater than the premium paid for constructing the box spread and vice versa. For instance, a long box spread involves the following transactions:

1. Buy ITM call at strike price K1 and short OTM call with strike K2 (bullish call spread).
2. Buy ITM put with strike price K2 and short OTM put with strike price K1 (bearish put spread).

The above transactions would result in net outflow of premium. There is a risk-free arbitrage opportunity if the net premium paid is less than the combined pay-off on expiry and in such a case the box spread is bought in order to lock in the arbitrage gain. The box spread is sold if the net premium involved is greater than the pay-off at expiry.

We can sum up the discussion on spread strategies as follows:

1. Spreads involve opposite trades (buy and sell) in options on the same underlying but differing in strike price or time to maturity. These can be bullish or bearish in nature.
2. Vertical spreads involve options on the same underlying and same expiry dates but with different strike prices. Horizontal spreads or calendar spreads are constructed using options of the same underlying and same strike prices but with different expiry dates.
3. Spreads result in a limited gain or limited loss and hence are a conservative type of strategy. Because of this feature exchanges usually charge lower margins for spread trades.

Combinations

This is a type of trading strategy that involves options of different types on the same underlying. The most popular combinations are straddles and strangles.

Straddle

This involves buying or selling both call and put options on the same underlying and with the same strike price and time to maturity. A long straddle strategy is adopted by an investor who expects the price of the underlying to move by a large amount but is not certain about the direction of the price move. A trader who expects the underlying asset to remain range-bound may earn premium by selling a straddle. The straddle is therefore a volatility-based strategy and is neutral as regards the direction of the underlying asset price.

Numerical Example 9

Using a long straddle The verdict of a US court regarding a patent infringement case involving a large pharmaceutical MNC is expected next week. An unfavorable verdict is expected to cost USD 500 million to the company in the form of penalties and loss of future revenue from the US markets and hence would most likely lead to a sharp fall in the stock price. A favorable verdict is expected to trigger a relief rally in the stock price. The stock is currently trading at ₹820 and the ATM call and put expiring within one month are traded at ₹23 and ₹18, respectively. What strategy is advisable in this situation?

Solution:

As the investor expects the stock to move by a large amount after the declaration of the verdict but is not sure of the direction of the move he should buy a straddle. Thus the investor should buy the one-month ATM call and put involving an initial outflow of ₹23 + 18 = ₹41.

TABLE 19.10 Pay-off table for a long straddle

Stock price on expiry	Pay-off from long call	Pay-off from long put	Premium paid	Net pay-off from strategy
705	0	115	–41	74
770	0	50	–41	9
820	0	0	–41	–41
865	45	0	–41	4
905	85	0	–41	44

The pay-off table shows that the maximum loss for the strategy occurs when the stock closes exactly at the ATM strike price on expiry. Gains increase as the stock at expiry moves farther away from the ATM strike price. Thus the strategy benefits from an increase in the underlying volatility and loses when the underlying remains range-bound.

Figure 19.7 Pay-off profile of long straddle.

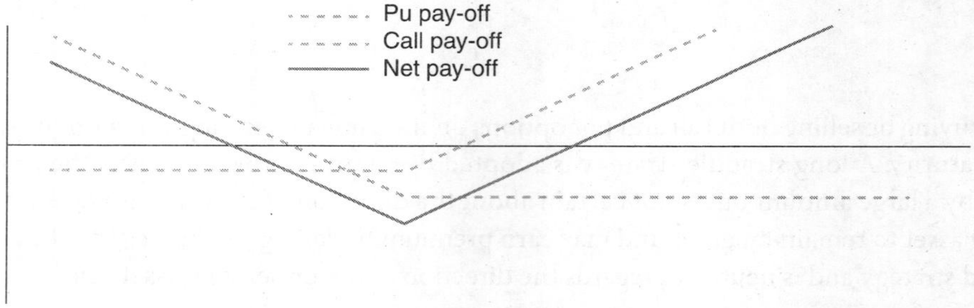

The short straddle strategy involves shorting both call and put at the same strike price and time to maturity. The trader executing a short straddle expects the underlying price to move in a range-bound manner. The maximum gain is the amount of premium received while the potential loss is unlimited.

Strangle

This involves buying or selling both call and put options on the same underlying and time to maturity but with different strike prices. The long strangle entails buying an out-of-the-money call and an out-of-the-money put.

Again the strategy is suitable when the underlying is expected to be very volatile and the direction of the movement cannot be anticipated. The gain is unlimited and loss is limited to the premium paid. The short strangle anticipates a low level of volatility and is a limited gain but unlimited loss strategy.

Hedging Strategies Using Options

Options can be used for hedging a long or short position in the underlying asset. These strategies are summarized below:

1. **Protective Call:** In this case a short position in the underlying asset is hedged by a long call position. The trader has a bearish view on the underlying and therefore shorts the underlying asset or futures. At the same time he buys a call on the underlying so as to protect himself from any unexpected rise in the underlying. The strategy results in a large gain if the underlying asset declines in value but makes a limited loss should the underlying rise in value.
2. **Protective Put:** This is a case of a long position in the underlying being hedged by a long put position. It makes a large gain with a rise in the underlying price but a limited loss with a fall in the underlying price.
3. **Covered Call:** A trader who is bearish about the direction of the underlying price as well as underlying volatility would prefer to short a call on the underlying. When the short call position is hedged by taking a long position in the underlying the result is a covered call strategy. The strategy makes a limited gain when the underlying gains in value but unlimited loss when the underlying declines in value.
4. **Covered Put:** A trader who expects the underlying to gain in value but anticipates a low level of volatility would prefer to short a put on the underlying. When the short put position is hedged by a short position in the underlying the resulting strategy is known as a 'covered put' strategy. Here the gain is limited when the underlying declines in value but there is unlimited loss when the underlying rises.

Arbitrage Using Options

Opportunities for arbitrage arise when (a) traded prices of options differ from their 'fair' or theoretical prices, i.e., violation of lower bounds or (b) there is violation of put-call parity condition.

Numerical Example 10

Violation of lower bound condition for call option Shares of Tata Steel Ltd. are trading at ₹405. Risk-free interest rate is 8% p.a. A call option on Tata Steel shares with a strike price of 400 and maturing in one month is trading at ₹6. Is there any arbitrage opportunity?

Solution:

The lower bound for the price of a call option is $c \geq \max(S_0 - K \times e^{-rt}, 0)$. Here $S_0 = 405$, $K = 400$, $r = 0.08$ and $t = 1/12$. Hence minimum price for the call should be higher of zero or 405 − 397.34 = ₹7.66. Since the call is being traded at ₹6 it is underpriced. To capture the arbitrage gain the following transactions should be executed:

1. Buy the call at ₹6 and short the stock at ₹405
2. Invest the net amount 405 − 6 = ₹399 at the risk-free rate of 8% for 1 month.

On expiry assume two different scenarios for the closing price.

Tata steel closes at ₹485	Tata steel closes at ₹325
Pay-off on long call: ₹85, i.e., 485 − 400	Pay-off on long call: 0
Buy back the short stock at ₹485	Buy back the short stock at ₹325
Proceeds from investment: ₹401.66	Proceeds from investment: ₹401.66
Net inflow on expiry: 401.66 + 85 − 485 = ₹1.66	Net inflow on expiry: 401.66 − 325 = ₹76.66

Check that the gain from this strategy is: (a) capped at ₹1.66 for all closing prices of the stock which are higher than the strike price of 400 and (b) unbounded and goes on increasing for progressively lower closing prices below 400. Why is this so?

This is because the long call and short stock strategy is effectively a 'synthetic' put. Hence the potential gain is unlimited as the stock price falls. As the stock price increases the loss on the short stock position is compensated by the long call and the net gain is capped at ₹1.66.

Numerical Example 11

Arbitrage resulting from violation of put-call parity Mahindra and Mahindra shares are trading at ₹1251. Call option with a strike price of ₹1240 and expiring after 1 month is quoting at ₹47.50. Assume that risk-free interest rate is 8% and M&M will not pay any dividend over the next 1 month. You are required to compute the following:

1. Using put-call parity find out the fair price of a put option with the strike of ₹1240 and expiring after 1 month.
2. If the put is actually trading at ₹23.15, what strategy should be adopted to lock in the arbitrage gain? Compute the arbitrage gain assuming that M&M shares close at ₹1275 on the expiry date.

Solution:

Here $S_0 = 1251$, $K = 1240$, $r = 0.08$, $t = 1/12$ or 0.0833 and $c =$ ₹47.50. Using equation (7) we derive the value of the put as ₹28.26. Since the traded price is lower than the fair value, the put is underpriced by the market. The difference between the fair price and traded price is ₹5.11 which represents the arbitrage opportunity. To exploit this opportunity the following trades need to be executed: (a) Buy the put at the market price of ₹23.15 and buy the underlying stock at ₹1251. (b) Short the call at the market price of ₹47.50 (c) Borrow the net amount ₹1226.65 (1251 + 23.15 − 47.50) at the risk-free rate of 8% for 1 month. M&M shares are worth ₹1275 on expiry date. The trader will now sell the shares held by him for ₹1275. The put bought by him will expire worthless. The short call position will be in-the-money and entail a pay-out of ₹35. The borrowing will grow to ₹1234.86 ($1226.65 \times \exp(0.08 \times 1/12)$) and will have to be repaid. The net cash inflow will thus be 1275 − 35 − 1234.86 = ₹5.14, which is equal to the difference between the fair price and traded price of the put.

Option Trading in India

Option trading in India is permitted for stocks, stock index and currencies. Commodity options are not currently allowed to be traded in India. Options on stocks and stock index are traded on the stock exchanges, NSE and Bombay Stock Exchange (BSE). Bulk of the trading in options is concentrated in index options and options on stocks are not as liquid. Currency options were till recently traded in the over-the-counter market between banks and corporate entities. Exchange-based trading in currency options was permitted by the RBI and SEBI with effect from October 2010. At present currency options on the USDINR pair are traded on the stock exchanges and are very heavily traded.

SUMMARY

- ☑ Options are instruments with an asymmetrical pay-off.
- ☑ A call option gives its buyer or holder the right but not the obligation to buy a specified quantity of the underlying asset at a specified price at or before a specified date.
- ☑ A put option gives its buyer or holder the right but not the obligation to sell a specified quantity of the underlying asset at a specified price at or before a specified date.
- ☑ Option premium comprises an intrinsic value and a time value. Options exhibit time decay.
- ☑ Minimum and maximum prices for an option can be determined under conditions which ensure that there is no arbitrage opportunity.
- ☑ The Black-Scholes Option Pricing Model is the most popular model for pricing European options.
- ☑ Options can be used to execute a view on the direction as well as volatility of underlying.
- ☑ Options can be used for trading, hedging and arbitrage.
- ☑ Trading strategies include vertical and horizontal spreads and volatility-based strategies.
- ☑ Hedging strategies include protective calls and puts and covered calls and puts.
- ☑ Arbitrage opportunities arise when option prices violate the lower bound or the put-call parity.

KEY WORDS

Black-scholes option pricing model 745
Covered call 757
Covered put 757
Exercise style 732
Intrinsic value 735
Protective call 757
Protective put 757
Put-call parity 744
Spread strategies 755
Straddle 755
Strangle 756
Strike price 741
Time value 735

CONCEPT QUESTIONS

1. A currency trader buys a put on the USDINR rate with a strike price of 63.50 and a maturity of one month. What is the intrinsic value of this option if the USDINR is ₹62.98?
2. Continuing the above example in which of the following cases will the time value of the put be higher? (i) When the USDINR is at ₹63.49 or (ii) when USDINR is 62.75.
3. Consider two call options on Tata Steel, both with a strike price of ₹480. The first call matures after 2 weeks while the second call has six weeks till expiry. Which call will have a higher time value?
4. The USDINR is currently at ₹58.20. A currency trader is of the opinion that the dollar will not depreciate below ₹58 but will remain range-bound between 58.05 and 58.20. Which position should he prefer in this situation – long USDINR calls or short USDINR puts with suitable strike price?
5. Shares of HDFC Ltd. are being traded at ₹1122. If the risk-free interest rate is 8% p.a., find the lower bound for a call option on HDFC Ltd. with a strike price of ₹1120 and maturity of one month.
6. If the stock of IFCI Ltd. is trading at ₹37.75 and a one-month call option on IFCI with a strike price of 37.50 and maturing in one month is trading at ₹1.85, what should be the minimum price for a one-month put option on IFCI with a strike price of 37.50? Assume a risk-free rate of 8% p.a. continuously compounded.
7. If the stock of Infosys is expected to be very volatile following its quarterly earnings report, which strategy can be expected to be more profitable – (a) long butterfly call spread or (b) short butterfly call spread?
8. A protective call involves which of the following positions – (a) long position in underlying stock and long position in put (b) short position in call and long position in stock (c) short position in stock and long position in call.
9. An investor who anticipates a high volatility in the stock of Sun Pharma Ltd. following the announcement of the Court verdict in a patent infringement case buys an ATM straddle composed of one call option and one put option with strike price of 820 and maturity of one month. The premium for the call and put is ₹22 and ₹17, respectively. Calculate the break-even points for this position.
10. Which spread strategy is appropriate in a situation where the stock is expected to fall sharply from the current price of ₹500 to ₹462 but is expected to stabilize around ₹460? (a) Sell put with strike price of 500 and buy put with strike price of 460 (b) sell call with strike price of 500 and buy call with strike price 460 (c) buy put with strike price of 500 and sell put with strike price of 460 (d) buy call with strike price of 500 and sell call with strike price of 460.

Choices Galore: Investing in India and Abroad

20

CHAPTER OBJECTIVES

- ❐ Evaluating developments in Indian capital markets
- ❐ Understanding the concept of beta based and dividend-based portfolios
- ❐ Discussing about the common mistakes made by investors in India
- ❐ Elaborating upon the concept of international investment from the perspective of Indian investors
- ❐ Measuring international portfolio performance

Investing in India[1]

To invest in capital markets in India, investors need to understand the nature of Indian economy and certain aspects of portfolio management. Both are discussed in detail in the following sections.

Indian Economy from an Investor's Perspectives

Indian economy has been witnessing one of the worst times with the macroeconomic data giving jitters to the policy makers. The last 10 years saw Indian economy growing at 7.5 to 8% GDP while the world economy registered a growth rate of 2.5% to 3% GDP. Currently, the Indian economy has registered GDP growth of 4.7% in March 2014 which was below the forecasted 5% mark and also the lowest in preceding ten years. This has raised several questions about the potential of world's largest democracy. However, not all economic indicators are bad.

Indian economy is witnessing a mixed bag of economic data with the Current Account deficit standing at $35 billion as against the earlier estimates of $88 billion. In terms of percentage, the current account deficit came to 2.3% of the GDP which gave the government much comfort on the macroeconomic front. The fiscal deficit which was another area of concern has also reduced to 4.6% of GDP as against the earlier target of 4.8% of the GDP. The exports have picked up and reached $312 billion as against the target of $325 which has ensured

[1] Contributed by Mr. Vispi Rusi Bhathena, CEO, BSE Broker's Forum, Mumbai and Dr. V. Aditya Srinivas, COO & Chief Economist, BSE Broker's Forum, Mumbai.

that slowly and gradually the economy would come back on track. Let us understand some key parts of Indian economy from an investor's perspective, namely, currency and capital markets.

Currency Front

On the currency front, which is the lead indicator of the economy, the Indian rupee depreciated to 68 level in 2013 from 42 level in 2011. This clearly reflects the lack of confidence of the foreign investors in our economy.

The prevailing economic scenario was marked by high inflation, high interest rates, low investments, shrinking IIP and controversial tax aspects like retrospective tax. All of this culminated into the rupee touching its all time low. The steps taken by RBI like reduction in the foreign investment by an individual from 2,00,000 dollars to 75000 dollars actually did more damage since the foreign investors saw this as a capital control method which could lead to further out flow of capital. From June to August 2013, the FII were net sellers to the tune of ₹23000 crore which lead to the sudden and drastic fall in the value of the rupee. This was then curtailed by the NRI remittances where the Indians working outside India sent $34 billion since there is huge interest rate arbitrage opportunity in India.

Sectoral Performance

The key sectors of Indian economy are going through challenging times. The infrastructure sector is under huge pressure as there are a lot of projects which have been stuck due to clearance of environmental issues by the government. As per one estimate, around 341 mega projects worth ₹10 lakh crore are stuck up due to some or the other hurdles in the approval process.

The banking sector which was considered as one of the best sectors in 2008 and 2011, when the world was crippled by the global financial crisis and the Eurozone crisis, is now facing the problem of rising NPAs and eroding bottom-line.

The AIBEA (All India Bank Employees Association) has recently published data about the rising NPAs in the banking sector which is a real threat to the entire financial system. NPAs levels in Indian banks are listed in Table 20.1.

TABLE 20.1 NPAs, in the banking sector

Particulars	Date	₹ crore
Bad loans in public sector banks	March 2008	₹39000 crore
Bad loans in public sector banks	March 2013	₹1,64,000 crore
Bad loans in public sector banks	Sept 2013	₹2,36,000 crore
Bad loans restructured and shown as good loans		₹3,25,000 crore
Fresh bad loans in last 7 years		₹4,95,000 crore
Profits transferred and adjusted for provisions towards bad loans	2008 to 2013	₹1,40,000 crore
Bad loans in 172 corporate accounts (₹100 crore and above)		₹37000 crore

The banking sector, which emerged as a winner during 2008 and 2011 crisis, has lost its luster now, and is giving sleepless nights to the government. With the rising NPAs and no signs of recovery, any significant default by the corporate group would lead to financial distress. This would create huge stress in the system as a whole.

Capital Market Perspective

The Indian stock market which is often called the "Barometer of the Economy" has seen the market rise to an all-time high in 2014. Though the markets continue to be high, the retail participation is at the lowest level as the brokers are finding it difficult to get retail investors back to the markets.

The Indian capital market has the distinct feature of being heavily dependent on the foreign flows. The Foreign Institutional Investors have invested around ₹30,000 crore in the Indian stock market from January to March 2014.

Indian debt instruments have also attracted the attention of international investors. The reason is that the globally the interest rates are near 1 to 2%, while in India they are still at 9 to 10%. This attracts huge FII interest in the debt segment. From January to March 2014, FIIs have invested ₹30,000 crore into the Indian Debt market as well.

Foreign Institutional Investors are holding stocks worth $200 billion of the Indian companies' shares. If they sell even 10% that is $20 billion, then the markets would go for a tailspin kind of a situation. Table 20.2 shows the power of FII in Indian markets.

TABLE 20.2 Flow of FII investment in Indian markets

Year	Net FII flows (₹in crore)	Index level
2007	+70,000	21206
2008	52,000	7697
2009	+83,000	18000
2010	+1,30,000	20000
2011	−2700	15500
2012	+1,10,000	20,000
2013	+1,20,000	21000 .

Table 20.2 clearly shows that there is a huge influence of the FIIs on the Indian markets. The year 2007 saw tremendous inflows of the FIIs funds which took the index to an all-time high of 21000 and the rupee also reached a high of 38 vis-à-vis the dollar. The year 2008 saw the world go through the Global Financial Crisis during which FIIs pulled out ₹52000 crore from the Indian stock markets. With the result, the Indian markets gave a negative return of 52%. The market plunged to an all-time low of 7697 on October 24, 2008.

However, during the same year, the world economy grew at 1% GDP while the Indian GDP grew at 6.2%. This showed the world that Indian Economy was resilient enough to withstand the pressure of global slowdown due to its inherent domestic consumption. Assured by this resilience, FII invested ₹2,15,000 crore in 2009 and 2010 in India. This clearly proves that FII follows good GDP numbers.

The year 2011 brought the Euro Zone crisis with it. The result was global pessimism that also triggered FII selling in India. The index gave negative return of 24.65% which made Indian stock market the worst performer of the year. The year 2012 and 2013 were relatively better since once again the Foreign Institutional Investors pumped money into the Indian market. They invested huge amounts which took the index back to 20,000 levels.

In the last 4 years, FIIs have invested ₹3,71,000 crore. This is more than the total investments that came in the last 9 years starting from 2001. In the last 4 years, barring 2011, average net investment buying by FII has been $20 billion.

Despite the interest of international investors, the situation at the grass root level in Indian markets is worrying as proved by the fact that 600 brokers have shut their business since April 2013. The number of people who have become unemployed has crossed 18000. The absence of the retail investors can also be judged from the fact that Bombay Stock Exchange (BSE) cash market turnover reduced by 70%, from ₹11 lakh crore in 2011 to ₹3 lakh crore in December 2013. Similarly on the National Stock Exchange (NSE) cash market turnover reduced by 48% from ₹35 lakh crore to ₹18 lakh crore. Clearly, we need to attract more retail participation.

A Look at Portfolio Management from Retail Investor's Perspective

The retail investors are often caught on the wrong side of the market since they have the tendency to sell when the market falls and buy when the market rises. They tend to have too many stocks in their portfolio which reduces the benefits of diversification. Many a times, the stocks are not fundamentally picked, rather they are bought just because of some tip or rumour floating in the market.

Since retail investors also have a psychology of being comfortable when the markets are rising, they end up buying the stocks without understanding the long-term fundamentals of the company. This leaves them with stocks with poor fundamentals. With the result, when euphoria around the stock ends, the stock crashes suddenly. This causes the price to come down heavily with the retail investors being trapped with the stocks. Investors can use the approaches discussed here to make a sound portfolio.

Beta Based Portfolio

An investor should make his portfolio keeping in mind the kind of risk appetite he has for the market-related risks. If the risk appetite is high, then he can go for stocks with beta greater than 1, if he has moderate risk appetite then he can go for stocks having beta equal to 1 and if the risk appetite is less, then he should go with stocks having beta less than 1.

Thus to begin with, the investors need to undertake their own risk analysis and evaluate their risk taking capacity in terms of volatility which they can absorb. They also need to understand the difference between trading and investment and which mode is more suitable for them as per their risk taking ability.

Dividend Based Portfolio

In this approach to construct a portfolio, the stocks which give dividends on a regular basis should also be considered as worthy candidates for a portfolio as they would give regular income which is tax free in the hands of the investors. An important aspect is that dividend based portfolio ensures that the companies are fundamentally sound since dividend involves cash outflow which is paid out of profit.

Further, investors need to avoid the following common mistakes:

1. **Timing the Market:** Investors try to time the market, i.e., try to catch the top and bottom, which is next to impossible. No one can actually predict the level of top and bottom. The retail investor, in his attempts to catch the top and bottom, always misses the opportunity to remain invested.
2. **Averaging the Best Tool:** Investors rush to buy a stock when its price goes down without analyzing the fundamentals of the company. Many a times, more buying results in further blocking of capital and ultimately the investor loses all the money he has invested.
3. **Price Cannot Fall More:** When the share price of a company falls severely, the retail investor buys the share thinking that it cannot fall further. But if the fundamentals of the company are weak, then share price can fall further and thus the new money invested by the investor also gets blocked. One needs to check whether the fall in the price of the share is due to sentimental reasons or due to poor fundamentals.
4. **Price Cannot Rise Further:** The price of the share goes up when there is positive change in the fundamentals of the company. This does not mean that the price cannot rise further once it has reached a particular level.
5. **Blindly Following Others:** One should understand one's own risk and return expectations and should never copy others' style of investments. The risk taking capacity of every individual is different and hence one should judge one's own holding capacity.
6. **Buying Cheaper or Penny Stocks:** Generally, investors are interested in buying the stocks which are very low priced since they feel that they would be able to buy more number of shares with less money. But this psychology is wrong as this would lead to accumulation of stocks with poor or no fundamentals. The risk in such shares is that they may get delisted voluntarily or may be suspended by the stock exchange for non-compliance.

Stock market is the reflection of the economy. Indian stock market offers good opportunities to create wealth. But this wealth is created in the long term only. Since 1979 till 2013, the CAGR return of the SENSEX has been 16.25% which is more than any other financial instrument. One needs to understand that equity is a long-term product and stocks should be selected based on fundamentals. One should also regularly update one's portfolio through portfolio revision and evaluation. The stocks that are showing the fundamental problems should be removed and good quality stocks should be added. Investors can also go for systematic investment options whereby small fixed amounts should be invested every month on a regular basis. This would help to create good wealth in the long term since the average cost of buying would get reduced.

Investing Beyond Borders (International Investment)[2]

The liberalization in India in 1991 has lowered the barriers to cross-border flow of investment. Riding the wave of globalization and liberalization, Indians now have access to a host of investment products offered by international players globally. Many factors have contributed to the increase in the quantum of international investment. Globalization, liberalization and increased integration of the financial markets have definitely stimulated flow

[2] The section on international investment is written by Dr. Shalini Talwar.

of funds across international borders. Growth of multinational corporations, financial innovations, changes in regulations, reduction in exchange control and the advances in communication technology are some of the factors that have contributed to the increase in international investments.

The opening up of international investment opportunities has opened up gateways to heaven as well as hell. While the gains are manifold, the downside of international investing is sufficiently high for all investors to tread with caution. In this section, we will discuss the pains and gains of international investment from the perspective of Indian investors.

Meaning of International Portfolio Investment

International portfolio investment refers to investment in foreign equity, mutual funds, bonds and other cross-border securities. The rules of portfolio management remain the same whether the assets are domestic or foreign, but the analysis becomes more complicated in case of foreign assets. This is due to the additional risk imposed by currency movements, political and regulatory environment and availability of information.

Key Decisions in Investing Overseas

It took India twelve years after liberalization to allow its citizens to invest in cross-border financial markets. In early 2003, RBI permitted Indians to invest in mutual funds in international markets with an upper limit of USD 25000 in a calendar year. Thereafter the limit was enhanced to USD 200,000 in a calendar year. Now Indians can invest in a large array of financial products like equity, mutual funds, foreign currencies, derivatives, hedge funds, insurance policies and a host of other instruments in global financial markets.

Equity transactions in foreign stocks can take place through a domestic broker who has tie up with international broker/s or directly through an online broker abroad. Indian investors can also take exposure of international equity by buying the exchange-traded funds[3] of foreign countries that are listed on domestic stock exchanges like BSE and NSE. There are certain important decisions that Indian investors interested investing abroad need to take. These are:

Selection of markets

The basic rationale underlying portfolio investment is diversification. It becomes even more important in case of international investment. Simply choosing any foreign country for the purpose of identifying investment assets is a bad idea because it exposes investors to undue risk. Therefore, investors looking to diversify internationally should begin with the identification of a mix of countries including advanced economies, emerging market economies and to some extent, less developed markets. This would enable them to spread their portfolio risk across economies and help them to identify markets with less correlation.

Choice of asset/asset classes

After identifying the countries, an investor investing internationally needs to filter the asset choices available to him. Like domestic asset classes, inter nationally also, an investor has to choose from government securities,

[3] Goldman Sachs Hang Seng Exchange Traded Scheme (Hang Seng BeES) is India's first international ETF that opened for trading in 2010.

bonds, stocks, mutual funds, etc. The choice of assets is guided by the same principles of risk and return as in case of domestic investment.

Measurement of risk and return on foreign investments

Since exchange rate movements come into play in international investments, the calculation of risk and return is more complicated in international portfolio investment as compared to domestic portfolio investment. The rupee return earned by an Indian investor investing globally depends on the return he generates in the currency of the market he is investing in and the exchange rate between that currency and INR.

Return: Mathematically, rate of return from investing in i^{th} foreign market in rupee terms may be given as:

$$R_{INR} = (1 + R_i)(1 + e_i) - 1 \quad (1)$$

where
R_{INR} = Return in INR
R_i = Return in currency of foreign country
e_i = Exchange rate between INR and currency of that country

Value of e_i depends on the appreciation or depreciation of INR. e_i is positive, if the foreign currency appreciates vis-a-vis INR and e_i is negative if the foreign currency depreciates vis-à-vis INR. For example, suppose Mr. Mohan, a resident of India, has just sold the APPLE shares he bought a year ago and his rate of return in dollar terms (R_i) is 15%. During his holding period, US dollar depreciates 5% against INR. $e_i = -0.05$. Therefore, according to equation (1), return of Mr. Mohan in rupee terms is $= (1 + 0.15)(1 + (-0.05)) - 1 = 0.0925$.

As in domestic portfolio investment, models have been developed to forecast expected return of international investment. Ex-post analysis of past standard deviation is one of the ways of trying to predict future variability of returns. A model taking macroeconomic indicators into consideration has also been proposed for the purpose of forecasting expected return on international investment. It is symbolically expressed as:

$$E(R) = 4 + 2\ (\text{growth in GNP}) - \text{Change in inflation} \quad (2)$$

To forecast expected return, one needs to forecast the two economic variables.

As in the case of domestic investment, asset-pricing models can be applied for calculating returns in international investment, but they need to be adapted to adjust for international factors. Let us see how capital asset pricing model (CAPM) and arbitrage pricing theory (APT) can be used in international portfolio investment return calculation.

1. **CAPM:** As a simple adjustment, the beta of a security should be calculated vis-à-vis its sensitivity to variation in an index representative of world market portfolio. However, the challenge comes from the fact that world market portfolio may not be accessible to Indian investors on account of barriers to flow of capital, magnitude of transaction costs, tax regulations and political considerations.

   Further, investors in different countries are faced with different efficient frontiers because exchange rate risk and its assessment vary for investors living in different countries. So CAPM might indicate lower premium than actually carried by foreign investors in the context of less accessible assets.

2. **APT:** APT, with its multi-factor based broad approach seems to be more useful in computation of expected returns on international investment. The various factors that can be used in applying APT in international context may be listed as:
   (a) Broad-based global index like GDOW (Global DOW)
   (b) Domestic index representing home country of investor (Say, S&P BSE SENSEX)
   (c) Industrial sector index
   (d) Exchange rate measure
   (e) Lead indicator of economic performance.

Risk: The risks associated with investing across border may be explained as:

1. **Currency Risk:** Due to the movement in exchange rate.
2. **Political Risk:** Different countries in the world have different levels of governance and stability. Many emerging and less developed economies are vulnerable to political unrest.
3. **Investor Protection and Regulatory Risk:** Different countries have different rules and regulations regarding transparency and investor protection. Some countries have very stringent norms while others are very lax in protecting the rights of the investors.
4. **Liquidity Risk:** Many markets do not have enough depth and have a very small percentage of listed and actively traded securities. Such markets tend to be illiquid.
5. **Level of Market Efficiency:** Markets of advanced economies are more deep and efficient, leading to better price discovery as compared to less developed economies where markets may tend to be mispriced.
6. **Economic Stability:** After the sovereign debt crisis, economic stability of the governments in different countries has also come into question.

All these factors make risk assessment more contorted in the contest of international investing.

The risk of international investing is also measured in terms of variance or standard deviation as in the case of domestic investment. Mathematically,

Variance of returns in INR or Var (R_{INR})

$$= \text{Var}\ (R_i) + \text{Var}(e_i) + 2\ \text{Cov}\ (R_i\ e_i) + \Delta\ \text{Var} \quad (3)$$

where

Var (R_i) is the variability of returns in foreign currency
Var(e_i) is the variability of exchange rate change
Cov $(R_i\ e_i)$ measures the degree of co-movement between foreign currency returns and exchange rate fluctuations
Δ Var is a measure of the contribution of $R_i\ e_i$ (cross-product term) to the risk in international investment

Clearly, exchange rate contributes to the risk of international investment to a large extent.

Measurement of international portfolio performance

Research has found that risk predictions have been generally more accurate than return predictions. In terms of measures of portfolio performance discussed early on in the text book, an international investor should continue to hold his foreign security provided:

$$\frac{(E(R_f)-r_f)}{\sigma_f} > \left(\frac{(E(R_d)-r_f)}{\sigma_d}\right)(r_{f,d}) \qquad (4)$$

where
$E(R_f)$ = Expected return on foreign security
$E(R_d)$ = Expected return on domestic security
σ_f = Standard deviation of return of foreign security
σ_d = Standard deviation of return of domestic security
r_f = Risk-free rate
$r_{f,d}$ = Correlation between returns of foreign security and domestic security

Equation (4) can also be written as:

$$(E(R_f)-r_f) > (E(R_d)-r_f)\left\{\left(\frac{\sigma_f}{\sigma_d}\right) r_{f,d}\right\} \qquad (5)$$

An investor would benefit from holding foreign security as long as $\{(\sigma_f/\sigma_d)\ r_{f,d}\}$ is less than 1.
Thus, the decision to invest in international markets depends on:

1. Correlation between the two securities across countries.
2. Variance of returns of domestic and foreign securities.
3. Expected return from each country.

Benefits of International Investment

Investing in opportunities across the globe provides following advantages to the investors:

1. **Availability of Wider Range of Investment Assets**: When an investor ventures to invest outside India, he gets access to a wider variety of instruments. Many overseas financial markets are more developed and deeper than the markets in India. They are way ahead in innovations as well. With the result, the financial products available in those markets are more flexible and tend to fit the investment objectives of the investors better.

   Further, the valuations in Indian markets are being seen by many as stretched and little unrealistic. Investors may benefit more by investing in markets that are more realistically priced.
2. **Better Diversification Opportunities:** By investing across markets with low correlations and business cycles that are not synchronized, investors can hope to get better risk-return trade-off. The economies across the globe represent a wide diversity of profile. Table 20.3 exhibits the correlation coefficients of daily returns of S&P BSE SENSEX and international stock indices (2009–2013). To benefit from diversification opportunities internationally, investors need to understand the nature and types of economies globally.

TABLE 20.3 Correlation coefficients of daily returns of S&P BSE SENSEX and International Stock Indices (2009–2013)

A	B	C	D	E	F	G	H	I	J	K	L	M	N	O	P	Q	R
	SENSEX	CNX NIFTY	S&P 500	S&P/TSX Composite index	FTSE 100	DAX	CAC 40	EURONEXT BEL-20	NZX 50 INDEX GROSS	STI	NIKKEI	JCI	Merval	Ibovespa	MEXBOL	XU100	NGSEINDX
SENSEX	1																
CNX NIFTY	0.981	1															
S&P 500	0.736	0.744	1														
S&P/TSX Composite index	0.831	0.831	0.697	1													
FTSE 100	0.812	0.815	0.910	0.848	1												
DAX	0.800	0.801	0.928	0.806	0.935	1											
CAC 40	0.633	0.614	0.412	0.677	0.615	0.632	1										
EURONEXT BEL-20	0.790	0.777	0.547	0.779	0.738	0.734	0.955	1									
NZX 50 INDEX GROSS	0.634	0.635	0.921	0.515	0.802	0.871	0.395	0.502	1								
STI	0.874	0.877	0.727	0.714	0.755	0.763	0.491	0.659	0.659	1							
NiKKEI	0.072	0.053	0.025	0.109	0.164	0.112	0.315	0.312	0.025	-0.077	1						
JCI	0.783	0.793	0.927	0.750	0.861	0.876	0.294	0.474	0.820	0.777	-0.038	1					
Merval	0.768	0.747	0.818	0.762	0.846	0.858	0.599	0.699	0.782	0.716	0.240	0.763	1				
Ibovespa	0.497	0.482	-0.035	0.433	0.168	0.056	0.399	0.456	-0.194	0.448	0.087	0.062	0.168	1			
MEXBOL	0.822	0.834	0.930	0.767	0.878	0.879	0.370	0.541	0.816	0.820	-0.055	0.958	0.758	0.180	1		
XU100	0.877	0.894	0.898	0.782	0.896	0.908	0.533	0.700	0.843	0.859	0.025	0.911	0.800	0.177	0.925	1	
NGSEINDX	0.432	0.420	0.643	0.239	0.531	0.655	0.422	0.457	0.809	0.456	0.084	0.484	0.604	-0.325	0.478	0.617	1

Economies have been classified by IMF (International Monetary Fund)[4] into following groups on the basis of their stage of development:

1. Advanced Economies or Markets
2. Emerging Economies or Markets
3. Frontier Markets or Pre-emerging Economies

1. **Developed or Advanced Economies:** 'Advanced Economy' is a term used by IMF to represent the developed countries. IMF has not specified any particular level of GDP or growth rate for identifying any economy as advanced economy. However, all economies with a high gross domestic product per capita and high degree of industrialization are classified as advanced economies. IMF also uses Human Development Index (exhibited in Table 20.4) to identify advanced economies. Advanced economies include the United States, countries in Euro zone, Canada, Japan, Australia and New Zealand.

   These countries have been popular among international investors for a long time. They are preferred because of the safety and stability they offer but investors seeking high returns have started moving away from these markets.
2. **Emerging Economies or Markets:** Emerging Economy is a term used to represent a group of economies that is showing signs of remarkable growth and moving progressively towards becoming more developed and advanced. Their financial markets also exhibit advancing degrees of liquidity and regulatory oversight. India, Brazil, Russia, China, Thailand and South Africa are some of the emerging economies that have been under spotlight in recent times. Current trends have shown that the financial markets of these economies have become quite popular with investors looking for diversification and high returns. These economies have been reporting substantially high growth rate as compared to advanced economies as illustrated in Figure 20.1.

   The higher returns from investments in emerging markets come with a higher degree of risk due to political instability, volatility of exchange rate, infrastructure issues, poor corporate governance, limited liquidity in equity and debt markets and lack of depth, penetration and efficiency in capital markets.

   Multitude of risks notwithstanding, emerging markets are attracting excessive attention of global investors. So much so that Morgan Stanley Capital International (MSCI) has designed an index to measure the equity market performance in emerging markets. It is a float-adjusted market capitalization index. It comprises 21 emerging economies: Brazil, Chile, China, Colombia, Czech Republic, Egypt, Hungary, India, Indonesia, Korea, Malaysia, Mexico, Morocco, Peru, Philippines, Poland, Russia, South Africa, Taiwan, Thailand and Turkey.
3. **Frontier Countries:** Frontier country/market is a term used to separate less developed capital markets from the developing countries. The equity markets of these countries are small and less accessible, but have become "investable" for international investors on account of their fast-growing economies and huge return potential. The stock markets of these countries are less established and developed than those of the emerging markets. At times, frontier markets/countries are also called "pre-emerging markets."

   Frontier markets are sought after by investors who are chasing high returns and are willing to accept the higher risks these markets are exposed to. Most of the risks faced by these countries are the same as those faced by the emerging countries or economies but the magnitude is much higher. Some of the risks investors face when they invest in frontier markets are political instability, exchange rate volatility, lack of liquidity, inadequate regulatory oversight and substandard and inconsistent financial reporting.

[4] www.imf.org/external/pubs/ft/wp/2011/wp1131. pdf, accessed on December 31, 2014.

TABLE 20.4 Human development index for advanced economies

Table 1: Human Development Index and its components

HDI rank		Human Development Index (HDI) Value	Life expectancy at birth (years)	Mean years of schooling (years)	Expected years of schooling (years)	Gross national income (GNI) per capita (2011 PPP $)	Human Development Index (HDI) Value	Change in rank
		2013	2013	2012 [a]	2012 [a]	2013	2012	2012-2013
Very high human development								
1	Norway	0.944	81.5	12.6	17.6	63,909	0.943	0
2	Australia	0.933	82.5	12.8	19.9	41,524	0.931	0
3	Switzerland	0.917	82.6	12.2	15.7	53,762	0.916	0
4	Netherlands	0.915	81.0	11.9	17.9	42,397	0.915	0
5	United States	0.914	78.9	12.9	16.5	52,308	0.912	0
6	Germany	0.911	80.7	12.9	16.3	43,049	0.911	0
7	New Zealand	0.910	81.1	12.5	19.4	32,569	0.908	0
8	Canada	0.902	81.5	12.3	15.9	41,887	0.901	0
9	Singapore	0.901	82.3	10.2 [b]	15.4 [c]	72,371	0.899	3
10	Denmark	0.900	79.4	12.1	16.9	42,880	0.900	0
11	Ireland	0.899	80.7	11.6	18.6	33,414	0.901	-3
12	Sweden	0.898	81.8	11.7 [b]	15.8	43,201	0.897	-1
13	Iceland	0.895	82.1	10.4	18.7	35,116	0.893	0
14	United Kingdom	0.892	80.5	12.3	16.2	35,002	0.890	0
15	Hong Kong, China (SAR)	0.891	83.4	10.0	15.6	52,383	0.889	0
15	Korea (Republic of)	0.891	81.5	11.8	17.0	30,345	0.888	1
17	Japan	0.890	83.6	11.5	15.3	36,747	0.888	-1

Source: http://hdr.undp.org/en/content/table-1-human-development-index-and-its-components, accessed on January 3, 2015.

Figure 20.1 Global GDP growth.

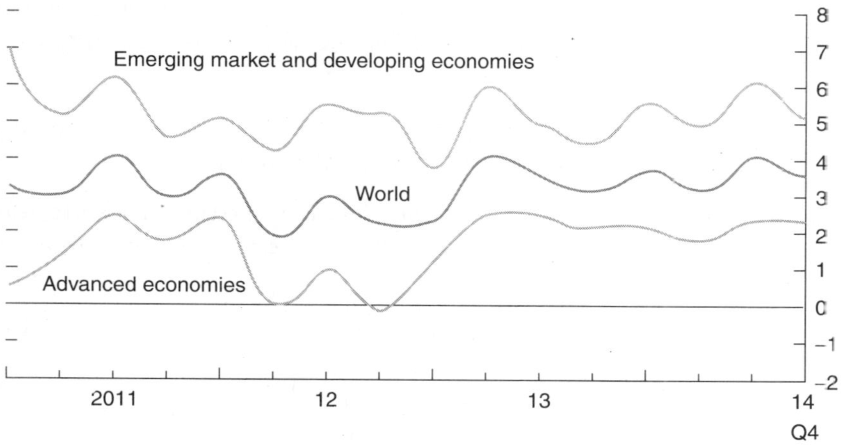

The advantage of investing in frontier markets is that they have low correlation with developed markets and can provide the benefits of a diversified portfolio to international investors. The countries classified as frontier countries are Bangladesh, Kenya, Nigeria, Mozambique, Vietnam, Bolivia, Ghana, Honduras, Mongolia, Senegal, Tanzania and Zambia.

SUMMARY

- ☑ Indian economy registered a GDP growth of 4.7% in March 2014 which was below the 5% mark and also a ten year low.
- ☑ The Current Account deficit stands at $35 billion as against the earlier estimates of $88 billion.
- ☑ On the currency front, which is the lead indicator of the economy, the Indian rupee had depreciated to 68 in 2013 from 42 in 2011 vis-à-vis US dollar.
- ☑ The current economic scenario is marked by high inflation, high interest rates, low investments, shrinking IIP and controversial tax aspects like retrospective tax.
- ☑ The Indian capital market depends heavily on the foreign flows.
- ☑ The Foreign Institutional Investors have invested around ₹30,000 crore into the Indian stock market from January to March 2014.
- ☑ Foreign Institutional Investors are holding stocks worth $200 billion of the Indian companies' shares. If they sell even 10% that is $20 billion then the markets would go into a tailspin.
- ☑ There is very low retail participation in equity markets in India.
- ☑ Retail investors have a psychology of being comfortable when the markets are rising. They end up buying the stocks without understanding the long-term fundamentals of the company.

☑ Other common mistakes made by investors while investing in capital markets are timing the markets, averaging the best tool, assuming price cannot fall more or rise further and blindly following others.

☑ Indian stock market offers good opportunities to create wealth. But this wealth is created in the long term only. Since 1979 till 2013, the CAGR return of the SENSEX has been 16.25% which is more than any other financial instrument.

☑ Globalization, liberalization and increased integration of the financial markets have lowered the barriers between the countries and stimulated flow of funds across the border.

☑ The opening up of international investment opportunities has opened up gateways to heaven as well as hell. While the gains are manifold, the downside of international investing is sufficiently high for all investors to tread with caution.

☑ It took India twelve years after liberalization to allow its citizens to invest in cross-border financial markets.
The decision to invest in international markets depends on:
(a) Correlation between the two securities across countries.
(b) Variance of returns of domestic and foreign securities.
(c) Expected return from each country.

☑ Key decisions in investing overseas are almost same as those that are required to be taken for investing in domestic market.

☑ However due to exchange rate movements, the calculation of risk and return is more complicated in international portfolio investment as compared to domestic portfolio investment.

☑ The rupee return earned by an Indian investor investing globally depends on the return he generates in the currency of the market he is investing in and the exchange rate between that currency and INR.

☑ As in the case of domestic investment, asset-pricing models can be applied for calculating returns in international investment, but they need to be adapted to adjust for international factors.

☑ The risks associated with investing across border are currency risk, political risk, investor protection and regulatory risk, liquidity risk, level of market efficiency, and economic stability.

☑ The risk of international investing is also measured in terms of variance of standard deviation as in the case of domestic investment.

☑ Investing in opportunities across the globe provides the advantage of availability of wider range of investment assets and better diversification opportunities to the investors.

KEY WORDS

Exchange-traded funds 766
Frontier markets 771
International portfolio investment 766
Regulatory risk 768
Variance 768

CONCEPT QUESTIONS

1. "Stock Market is the barometer of the economy." Explain the statement and cite various instances in the history of stock markets in India when the signals emerging from the markets and the key macroeconomic numbers have been divergent.

2. Write a commentary on the statement of Indian economy since the global financial meltdown in 2008 with special reference to the increased sensitivity of the economy to global cues.

3. Over the years, FIIs have become the key drivers of growth in the stock market of India. Some analysts call FII investment in India a ticking time bomb. There is a fear that the Indian markets are extremely susceptible to the FIIs' buying behavior, so much so that the regulators are forced to give in to their demands at times. Should the FIIs be given so much importance in our economy? If yes, why? If no, why?

4. In the context of the FII investment, there was a massive FII pull out following certain regulatory changes pertaining to Participatory Notes in India few years back. Critically analyze the events that unfolded at that point in time.

5. What are the common mistakes that investors commit in making portfolio investment decisions? What is the likely outcome of these mistakes on the risk-return outcome of the investment decision?

6. Mr. Gautam, a resident of India, has just sold the AT&T Inc. shares he had bought a year ago and his rate of return in dollar terms (R_i) is 18%%. During his holding period, US dollar appreciated 7% against INR. Calculate his return in rupee terms.

7. "Emerging markets are attracting increasing attention of international investors." Examine the veracity of the information by examining the data pertaining to international investment in BRICS countries.

8. Calculate the correlation between the stock markets of G-7 countries on one hand and the stock markets of G-20 countries on the other hand. Comment on the degree of correlations that exist between pairs of markets under each group.

9. Economies across the globe have been classified into advanced economies, emerging economies and frontier economies in response to the changing growth dynamics in the world markets. Comment on the differences in the risk-return profile of the equity markets in the countries categorized under the above stated classes.

10. Construct an international portfolio of funds comprising 5 to 7 index funds with international indices having low positive or negative correlations.

Case Study 1

Numbers Do Not Lie*

Dr. Shalini Talwar[1], Shweta Kathar[2] & Warada Bhagwat[3]

On November 1, 2014, Swati Sharma was thinking about her future. She was focused, determined and believed in planning before executing. She made certain plans for her future and wanted to make sure that she was able to execute them to her satisfaction. Her plans included foreign travels, buying an apartment in New Delhi and a small holiday home in Shimla. She knew that all her plans required substantial amount of funds. The thought of funds diverted her attention to her savings.

Swati had been working for some time now. She had always been a careful spender and had saved a substantial amount of money. Most of her money was invested in traditional instruments like bank fixed deposits. On the advice of her friends and relatives, Swati had put some of her savings in equity but she had always been anxious about the safety of the funds invested in equity.

As she continued to be in a ponderous mood, her apprehensions about her future financial security increased. She had gone through many articles that had been published in newspapers related to investments, wealth maximization and financial planning. She had read enough to know that she had to do something to make her investments more lucrative and well-planned.

She was not convinced with the way she had been investing her savings so far and was worried about losing time.

She had little knowledge about investments and wanted to know more about investing effectively to meet her future plans. After a couple of days, Swati met her bank manager who had been helping her take her investment decisions for a number of years now. She shared her concerns with him. The bank manager advised her to meet a financial planner to help her in her investments.

Swati had apprehensions about meeting a professional manager as she felt that the amount of her savings was too small and may not get the attention of a professional. However her apprehensions were not justified. Financial planning is never restricted by the size of one's income or savings. Her concerns were definitely ill-founded.

The bank manager convinced Swati that the level of income and savings may act as a base for deciding how much to consume and how much to save (invest), but it was not to be taken as a deterrent in seeking professional advice. The manager further explained to Swati that she should undertake appropriate planning to invest as soon as possible if she did not want to lose out on the power of compounding.

He gave her an assurance that a financial planner would help her earn reasonable returns at a low level of risk. This could be made possible by "not putting all eggs in one basket" i.e. diversifying investments. Diversification implies spreading one's savings across different assets so that one is not exposed to excessive risk. The basic

---

* Reprinted with permission from Bharti Publications.

[1] Associate Professor, Finance, KJ Somaiya Institute of Management Studies and Research, Mumbai.

[2] PGDM, Financial Services (2013–15), KJ Somaniya Institute of Management Studies and Research, Mumbai.

[3] PGDM, Financial Services (2013–15, KJ Somaniya Institute of Management Studies and Research, Mumbai.

principle of diversification requires the investors to spread their funds across multiple investment vehicles. The main aim behind investing one's funds in different asset classes is to maximize returns from investments and minimize the risk of losing the corpus.

A collection of assets across which an investor spreads his/her investible funds is referred to as investment portfolio. Investment theory postulates that the investors should aim to have a balanced portfolio i.e. have a mix of securities varying from high risk instruments with higher expected rates of return and low risk assets with lower rates of return.

Financial planners are investment professionals who help their clients meet their long-term financial objective by preparing a financial plan that is aligned with the client's status and goals. They prepare the financial plan on the basis of their client's investment objectives and constraints.

Financial planners undertake financial planning for their clients in terms of retirement planning, investment planning, asset allocation, tax planning, etc. Financial planning begins with the identification of investment objectives like income, growth, stability and mapping of investor risk tolerance. Investment objectives basically spell out the return requirement and risk characteristics of an investor. The flip side of investment objectives is represented by investment constraints of an investor that relate to taxation, regulatory requirements, investment horizon, liquidity and the different circumstances which the investors come across. To summarize, investible amount, expected rate of return and duration of investment are the key factors that are taken into consideration to prepare financial plans. Along with these main factors, the client's age, health, background, spending patterns etc. are also taken into consideration. After analyzing requirements of the individuals, the financial planners try to factor most of the needs and prepare the financial plans accordingly.

Maxim, Swati's financial planner, had a series of meetings with her. On the basis of these meetings, he realized that she was a fairly conservative person who was unwilling to take high level of risk. She was wary of investing directly in equity markets because of the volatility attached to it and expertise required for stock picking.

Maxim pointed out that the equity markets have been recording returns of about 14 to 15 % over the years and the past one year had been very good for the markets. However, Swati was not ready to invest in equity as she had read many stories about sudden plunges in stock markets and the losses that people had incurred on account of such crashes. Maxim was surprised to learn that though Swati was afraid of the volatility in the equity markets, she had a fair idea of how the stock market functioned.

After he analyzed her investments, Maxim created a profile of her existing investments. Swati had a portfolio that was concentrated in debt products (70%), equity (15%) and gold (15%). The real-estate was for personal use and there were some other small investments in Public Provident Fund. On the whole, it was a portfolio that was skewed toward safety and conservatism. At the same time, he realized that Swati was ready to come out of her comfort zone and invest in more lucrative avenues.

Understanding Swati's lack of comfort with direct investment in equity, Maxim decided to prepare a financial plan for her that was largely based on investing in top mutual funds with proven track record of profits.

In simple terms, a mutual fund is a collective investment vehicle. It is an assortment of stocks and bonds. When an investor invests in a mutual fund, he/she pools his/her money together with a number of other investors. The pooled funds are invested in specific securities through professional managers. Mutual funds are established with a specific strategy in mind and they can be of different types on the basis of their distinct focus. Accordingly, there can be large stock mutual funds, small cap mutual funds, country-specific mutual funds, g-sec mutual funds, sectoral funds, fund of funds and so on.

The main advantage of a mutual fund is that investors can invest their money in assets of varying risks without undertaking extensive research and analysis that is often necessary to choose assets for investment. A mutual fund can be expected to generate a better return than a portfolio constructed by an investor by selecting the securities on his own. Thus, mutual funds give benefit of diversification and professional management. The variety of mutual funds available is very large and investors have option of investing in equity (growth) schemes, income schemes, balanced schemes, money market/liquid schemes, tax saving schemes, offshore funds, gilt funds and index schemes to name a few.

In a marathon meeting, Maxim explained the concept of mutual funds and their operations to Swati in detail. She liked the idea and gave him a go ahead. He then moved to the task of identifying the suitable funds for Swati. The major aspects that he analyzed were expense ratio, entry and exit load, beta, dividend yield, NAV, rating, track record of performance, component securities & extent of diversification, performance of fund vis-à-vis the benchmark index, number of years of existence and the specific purpose of the fund.

Many agencies in India furnish extensive information on mutual funds' performance and assign ratings to them. *Value Research*, *Economic Times* and *CRISIL* publish relevant information to judge performance of various mutual funds in India. Availability of ratings makes it easier for investors to choose mutual funds that best suit their investment objectives and risk tolerance.

Benchmark index is usually an index of market performance that serves as a standard to evaluate the performance of a mutual fund in terms of its returns. For example, the SENSEX and Nifty are the most widely followed benchmarks for mutual funds in India. Benchmarking helps investors compare the performance of their funds with that of the broader market. The NAV of funds fluctuates with the market. The volatility of NAV is measured in terms of beta. If a fund does better than its rising benchmark index, say Nifty, then it is said to have outperformed the index. Conversely, if a fund rises less than its rising benchmark index, then it is said to have under-performed the index.

Maxim analyzed the performance of indices representing different sectors to help him better understand the performance of the mutual funds he had identified. The indices that he analyzed were S&P BSE SENSEX, BSE Durables, BSE FMCG, Tech BSE and BSE Oil & Gas (Refer Exhibit 1). He decided to use S&P BSE SENSEX for benchmarking the funds he had earmarked for Swati's portfolio.

The S&P BSE Sensex is the benchmark equity index that reflects the performance of Indian stock markets and the health of the Indian economy. It consists of 30 well-established companies listed on the exchange.

Maxim finally came up with a list of mutual funds that he felt would suit Swati's risk-return profile. He short-listed only the funds that were top-rated and top performing funds in their respective segments. They were: Religare Mid and Small, HSBC Tax Saver, SBI Magnum, UTI Equity fund, ICICI Blue Chip, Mirae Asset India, DSP Blackrock and Reliance Tax Saver fund. He analyzed the risk and return profile of the selected mutual funds. His calculations are illustrated in Exhibit 2 through 5.

Religare Mid and Small Cap Fund was launched in 2008 and since then has performed really well. Its annualized returns are 21.8% and 28.3% in the last 3 and 5 years respectively. This fund has impressed investors with its unconventional stock choices and consistent performance over last 6 years.

HSBC tax saver fund seeks to achieve capital appreciation in long term by making investments in a diversified portfolio. The portfolio consists of equity and equity related instruments of companies across myriad industries and sectors without any capitalization bias.

SBI Magnum Multiplier Plus Scheme was converted into an open-ended plan in April 1998. It aims to achieve capital appreciation through equity investments. Its portfolio comprises equity related instruments, debt instruments, securitized debt and money market instruments.

UTI Equity fund has a history of 22 years and is one of the oldest Indian mutual funds. It is one of the most consistent large cap funds in the past 7 years. It has returns of 20%, 16.7% and 18.7% over last 10, 5 and 3 years respectively. This fund is extremely diversified with holdings of about 70 stocks.

ICICI Blue Chip fund was launched in mid-2008 when the markets were not in a great condition. This fund currently has a portfolio with 60% of Nifty Stocks. Its annualized 5 years returns and category average is 23.18% and 16.62%, respectively.

Mirae Asset India is the only fund with South Korean parentage. It was launched in March 2008 and consists of few equities. This fund has outperformed the benchmark for last 5 years. It was down by 19% when the markets were down by 27% which shows a considerable performance.

DSP Blackrock aims to achieve appreciation of capital in long term by making investments in portfolio that comprises stocks of companies other than top 300 companies by market capitalization.

Reliance Tax Saver fund is one of the largest and oldest fund in ELSS category. This fund lagged its benchmark in 2010 and trailed in 2013. But in recent times it has been performing extremely well. Even with these ups and downs, the fund has considerable returns of 21.8% over past 5 years. The fund is top performer for periods of 1 and 3 years.

Explain Maxim's choice of mutual funds and the underlying calculations to Swati.

Exhibit 1 Average Monthly Returns of Key BSE Indices (2009–2014)

	Consumer Durable Index	FMCG Index	Tech BSE Index	Sensex	Oil & Gas Index
2009	8.19%	3.15%	5.83%	6.20%	5.36%
2010	4.53%	2.42%	1.87%	1.45%	0.24%
2011	−1.31%	0.86%	−1.32%	−2.16%	−2.66%
2012	3.43%	3.31%	0.20%	2.03%	1.17%
2013	−2.00%	1.00%	3.50%	0.79%	0.44%
2014	5.46%	1.30%	1.34%	2.83%	2.20%

Exhibit 2 Average Monthly Returns of Selected Mutual Fund (2009–2014)

	ICICI Blue Chip	Religare Mid Small	HSBC Tax Server	UTI Equity Fund	SBI Magnum	Mirae Asset India	DSP Blackrock	Reliance Tax Server FUnd
2009	6.36%	7.71%	6.21%	6.22%	6.63%	8.17%	8.95%	6.38%
2010	2.03%	2.60%	1.45%	1.63%	1.53%	1.82%	3.21%	1.79%
2011	−1.29%	−1.55%	−2.14%	−1.63%	−2.30%	−1.68%	−2.41%	−2.12%
2012	2.10%	3.14%	2.86%	2.43%	2.45%	2.52%	2.96%	3.34%
2013	0.89%	1.04%	0.41%	0.70%	0.94%	0.81%	0.49%	0.47%
2014	3.29%	4.62%	4.12%	3.72%	3.65%	4.09%	6.36%	5.95%

Exhibit 3 Average Monthly Returns of Selected Mutual Funds (2009–2014)

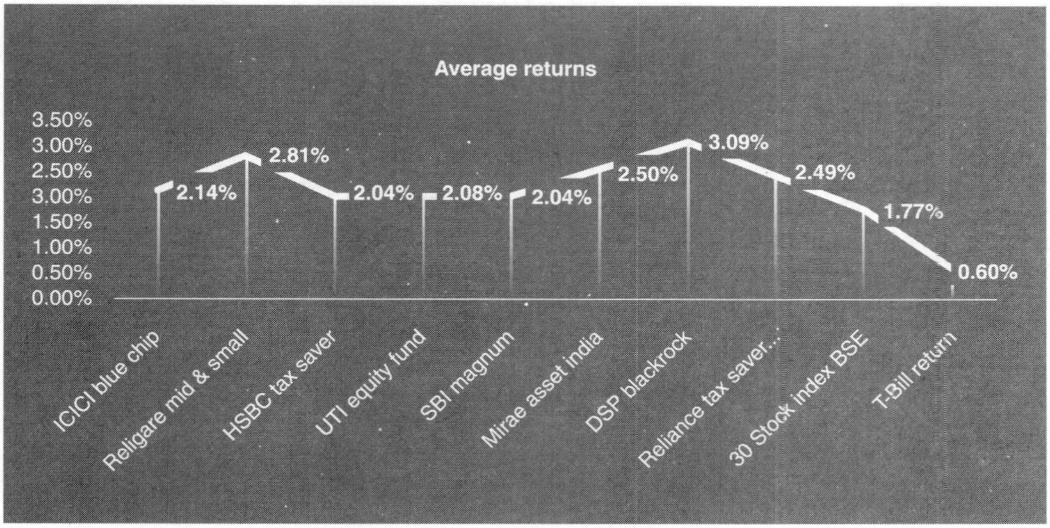

Exhibit 4 Performance of Selected Mutual Funds (2009–2014)

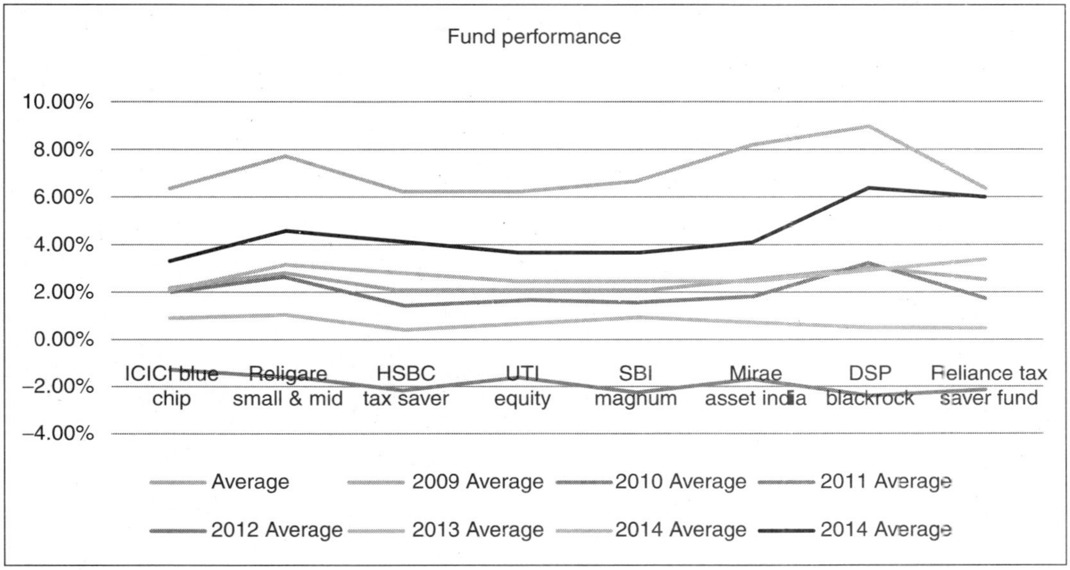

Exhibit 5 Performance of Selected Indices and Funds over the Years (2009–2014)

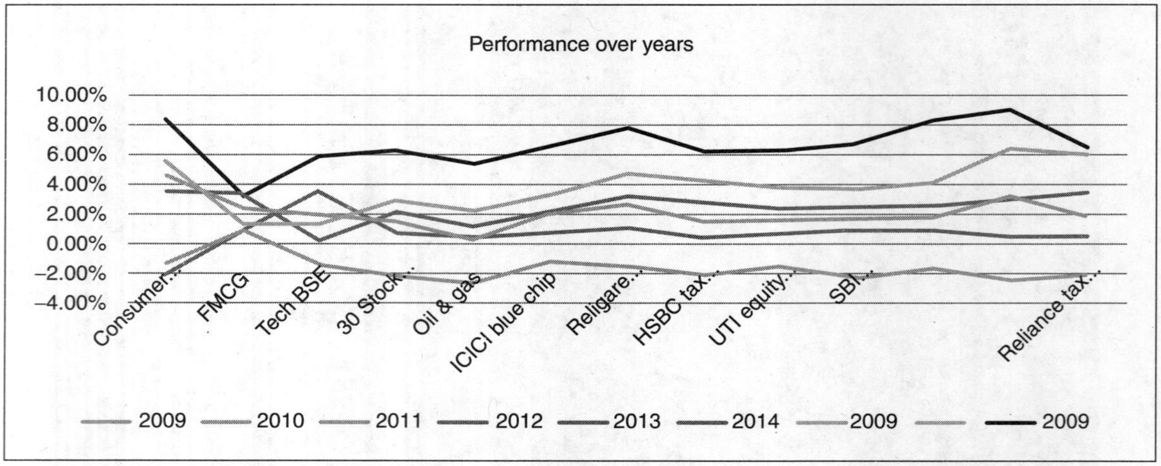

Case Study 2

Bird's Eye-view of S&P BSE SENSEX*

Dr. Shalini Talwar[1], Mansi Gorasia[2] & Prachiti Naiksatam[3]

Raghu Iyer had been investing in equity since past five years. His investments in the equity market had been made without undertaking any research or analysis or seeking any professional advice. As a result, he had not earned remarkable returns so far. In fact, he had lost a part of his corpus on more than one occasion. But he was not ready to give up investing in equity as he had heard from many people that the equity markets in India had consistently returned good profits over past so many years. Not willing to quit equity investment, he decided to find out where he was going wrong. Why was he losing money in a market where others seemed to be generating superior returns?

He discussed the issue with a number of his friends who also invested in the equity markets. Through the discussions, he got to know enough to realize that investment in equity was not as simple a decision as he had thought it to be. His discussions with his friends made him realize that the approach that he had been using so far for choosing stocks had been incorrect and adhoc. His approach to equity investment had been driven by randomly picking stocks of companies that were in news for some reason. Obviously, such an approach would land him in trouble again. Instead of meeting a professional financial planner for advice, Raghu decided to take the bull by the horn and enrolled for an e-learning programme to learn more about investing in equity to generate superior returns.

During the course of the three-month programme, he came to know about the modern portfolio theory (MPT) and its main tenet that the investment in equity should be done in a way that shares having lowest possible correlation are put together in portfolio.

A portfolio is nothing but a collection of securities that are brought together to spread the risk of investment. Each investment faces the downside risk that the returns realized may be less than the returns expected by the investors. There is an upside risk as well, which can be described as the possibility that the realized returns or actual returns are more than the expected or the estimated returns.

According to MPT, the problem of choice of securities/assets is not limited to choosing each security in isolation; rather it is a process of selecting a group of them out of numerous feasible combinations that make up possible portfolios. MPT hypothesizes that a rational investor will always seek to maximize returns for a given level of risk or minimize risk for a given level of return. It is well known that all investment decisions rest on a trade-off between risk and return. Higher returns are associated with higher risk. MPT has quantified diversification by providing formula to measure portfolio risk and expected return. It uses standard deviation

---

* Reprinted with permission from Bharti Publications.

[1] Associate Professor, Finance, KJ Somaiya Institute of Management Studies and Research, Mumbai.

[2] MMS Finance (2013–15), KJ Somaniya Institute of Management Studies and Research, Mumbai.

[3] MMS Finance (2013–15), KJ Somaniya Institute of Management Studies and Research, Mumbai.

or variance as a proxy for measurement of portfolio risk. Further, it uses expected return of individual securities for the calculation of portfolio returns.

After reading about MPT in detail, Raghu realized that the choice of securities for a portfolio depended on how each security or share behaved vis-à-vis another comprising the portfolio. This risk is formally called interactive risk and is measured by correlation or covariance. The lower the correlation, the better its effect on diversification. A negative correlation is better still.

He also came to know that he could distribute his funds across securities in such a way that the portfolio so formed can have a risk that is less than the risk of any of the component securities taken individually.

As the programme progressed, Raghu also came to know about capital asset pricing model (CAPM). CAPM is an asset pricing model that gives an equation through which the expected rate of return for a share can be computed. The rate so calculated can be compared with the investor's estimated rate of return to determine whether the asset is under-valued, fairly-valued or over-valued. Accordingly, a share can be bought, sold or held.

The CAPM is based on the fact that a security's returns vary with the market and the degree of sensitivity of a security's return to the movement in the market, represented by an index like S&P BSE SENSEX, is measured by beta. Beta is a measure of the systematic risk of a security and it can be positive or negative. The market has beta of one. A company with beta greater than 1 is said to move in the direction of the market but more than proportionately.

At the end of the section about CAPM, Raghu was able to summarize that the risk of a security can be split into two parts: systematic and unsystematic risk. He also realized that high beta stock could be expected to give good returns in a bull market. Armed with the knowledge about portfolio risk and return characteristics, Raghu was ready to construct his portfolio. But as he thought about getting down to making the equity investment, he became more and more daunted by the task. He realized that the execution of portfolio decision was not a simple thing. The biggest question was how to choose shares out of the 5000 plus equities listed on the leading stock exchanges in the country. If he followed MPT, he would have to compute unimaginable number of correlations. But he also knew that MPT gave a sound approach to diversification.

Finally, Raghu overcame the challenge of identifying the scrips to be analyzed for inclusion in the portfolio by deciding to invest only in the stocks that constituted the S&P BSE SENSEX. The reason is that SENSEX is leading stock index of the country and it comprises scrips that are blue-chips and have high volume of trading. SENSEX reflects the performance of the Bombay Stock Exchange Ltd. (BSE Ltd.), which is the oldest stock exchange in the country. BSE is has been used efficient and effectively by the corporate sector for raising capital for more than a century now. BSE has more than 500 listed members and it is the world's No. 1 exchange in terms of listed members. The companies listed on BSE Ltd commanded a total market capitalization of USD 1.6 Trillion as of June 2014.

S&P BSE SENSEX is India's most widely tracked stock market benchmark index. It is traded internationally on the EUREX as well as leading exchanges of the BRICS nations other than India (Brazil, Russia, China and South Africa). First compiled in 1986, S&P BSE SENSEX comprises 30 stocks representing financially sound, blue-chip companies that represent key sectors of Indian economy. It is widely reported in domestic as well as international markets through print and electronic media. It is scientifically designed and is based on globally accepted methodology for construction and review of indices. The base year of S&P BSE SENSEX is 1978–79 and it is calculated on a free-float market capitalization methodology which is a widely followed across the globe and used by many major index providers like MSCI, FTSE, STOXX and Dow Jones.

Since Raghu had decided to make his equity portfolio using some of the stocks that constituted SENSEX, he downloaded the names of all the securities that constitute SENSEX. (Refer Exhibit 1)

The list of shares increased Raghu's apprehension again. Each share listed above represented a company that was well-known and well-established. Choosing a select few out of such an elite club seemed impossible to Raghu.

His dilemma was further increased when he read about indexing. Indexing is a part of passive portfolio management strategy that involves investing in an index fund that replicates a leading index of market activity like CNX NIFTY or BSE SENSEX. Indexing is a form of passive fund management that gives the investors an advantage of low management expense ratio and has been historically observed to outperform most actively managed mutual funds. If he used indexing or passive investing strategy, he would be saved from choosing individual stocks.

Raghu decided to explore the option of passive investing a little more. He found some SENSEX based index funds like HDFC Index Fund – Sensex Plan, SBI Sensex ETF, Tata Index Fund Sensex Plan, LIC NOMURA Index Sensex and LIC NOMURA Index – Sensex Plan. According to various websites ranking and reporting mutual fund performance, most of these funds had done reasonably well in the recent past. Raghu was tempted to invest in index funds replicating SENSEX.

But something was stopping him from investing his money in one or more of the above listed index funds. That something was the thrill of active portfolio management that he had been experiencing for the past five years. He felt confident that after his e-learning programme, he was equipped with sufficient knowledge to '*seek alpha*'. Seeking alpha is a term that refers to generation of superior portfolio returns through better stock selection. His e-learning programme had broadened his horizons for sure as far as knowledge about equity investing was concerned.

So Raghu once again mentally prepared himself to actively manage his equity portfolio. He felt that he could generate higher returns by picking certain high beta stocks as the markets were currently in a bull phase with SENSEX having raced to 25000 points and beyond in a short span of time. In such a time, active management of portfolio can be expected to yield superior returns than an indexing strategy. But stock selection and entering and exiting the market at the right time was the key to generating superior returns in such a market.

While downloading the names of the securities from the BSE website: *www.bseindia.com*, Raghu had seen that the opening and closing price data related to each stock was available freely on the website. He recalled a part of his course that explained regression and computation of standard deviation, correlation etc. using MS Excel. Excited as he was about that part of his learning, he felt he would not be able to undertake such calculations on his own. At the same time, he did not want to hire a portfolio manager.

Krish was an analyst working for PCW Securities Limited. Raghu's office was located in the same building as his and Krish had travelled with Raghu to work on a couple of occasions in the past. One day, while driving to work, Raghu spotted Krish waiting for a cab and offered to give him a ride. While driving, he shared his dilemma and problems in investing with Krish. Knowing that Raghu did not want to seek professional advice, Krish offered to help him in his individual capacity to analyze the BSE component securities using the theories that Raghu had learnt about in his e-learning programme viz. modern portfolio theory and capital asset pricing model.

Krish decided to focus on the S&P BSE SENSEX securities only as Raghu was really keen to invest in some of them. After analysis, Krish suggested two alternative portfolios to Raghu:

Portfolio1: BHEL, CIPLA, Dr. Reddy's Labs , Hero Motocorp, HUL, Infosys

Portfolio 2: HUL, Tata Motors, Tata Power, Tata Steel, TCS, Wipro

Explain Krish's choice and the underlying calculations to Raghu.

Exhibit 1 Component Securities of S&P BSE SENSEX

AXIS BANK	HEROMOTOCORP	ONGC
BAJAJ AUTO	HINDALCO	RELAINCE
BHARTI AIRTEL	HUL	SBI
BHEL	ICICI BANK	SSLT
CIPLA	INFOSYS	SUNPHARMA
COAL INDIA	ITC	TATA MOTORS
DR. REDDYS LABS	L&T	TATA POWER
GAIL	MARUTI	TATA STEEL
HDFC	M&M	TCS
HDFC BANK	NTPC	WIPRO

Index

O

P

Q

R